Footprint Peru

Ben Box
5th edition

*"We need the tonic of wildness... At the same time that we are
earnest to explore and learn all things, we require that all things
be mysterious and unexplorable, that land and sea be infinitely wild,
unsurveyed and unfathomed by us because unfathomable.
We can never have enough of Nature."*

Henry David Thoreau, Walden

Peru Highlights

See colour maps at back of book

ECUADOR

LORETO

Río Marañó

TUMBES

Tumbes

AMAZONAS

Río Huallaga

Río Ucuy

Sullana

Piura

PIURA

Jaén

Chachapoyas

Moyobamba

CAJAMARCA

Tarapoto

LAMBAYEQUE

SAN-MARTIN

Chiclayo

Cajamarca

LA LIBERTAD

Púcallp

Trujillo

Cordillera Blanca

HUANUCO

Chimbote

ANCASH

Huaraz

Huánuco

PASCO

Cerro De Pasco

JUNIN

La Oroya

Huancayo

LIMA

LIMA

Huancavelica

HUAN
CAVELC

Pacific Ocean

Pisco

Ica

ICA

Nasc

---

① Cabo Blanco
Inspiration for Hemingway's *Old Man and the Sea* and one of the country's major surfing spots

② Tucumé
Massive 1,000-year-old complex of 26 pyramids, inhabited by terrible demons

③ Kuélap
A pre-Columbian fortress, buried high in jungle-clad mountains

④ Huaca del la Luna
Startling new murals inside a Moche pyramid

⑤ Cañón del Pato
Thrill-a-minute bus ride through a spectacular, narrow pass

⑥ Cordillera Blanca
Beautiful and terrifying, these mountains are the highest in Peru

⑦ Chavín de Huantar
2,500-year-old fortress temple; one of Peru's most important pre-Columbian sites

⑧ Lima
Bold, brash and buzzing, with the best food and nightlife in the country

⑨ Nasca Lines
Whales, spiders and humming birds, etched in the desert sand over 2,500 years ago

N

| 0 km | 100 |
| 0 miles | 100 |

COLOMBIA

Iquitos
⑪

Río Amazonas

BRAZIL

UCAYALI

MADRE DE DIOS

CUSCO

⑫

Puerto
Maldonado

Ayacucho
⑩

⑬ Machu Picchu
⑭ ⑮ Cusco

Abancay

APURIMAC

⑯

BOLIVIA

AYACUCHO

PUNO

AREQUIPA

Juliaca

⑰

⑱ Lake
Titicaca

Arequipa
⑲

Puno

MOQUEGUA

Moquegua

TACNA

Ilo

Tacna

CHILE

⑩ Ayacucho
The Holy Week celebrations in this colonial city are a sight to behold

⑪ Iquitos
An isolated city on the banks of the Amazon

⑫ Manu National Park
One of the largest protected areas of rainforest; home to jaguars and giant otters

⑬ Machu Picchu
Peru's number one attraction remains a special place

⑭ Choquequirao
A 'lost city' only reachable by some tough trekking

⑮ Cusco
Gringo capital of South America and a fascinating place

⑯ Río Apurimac
The true source of the Amazon, offers amazing whitewater rafting

⑰ Colca Canyon
Come face-to-face with the condor, the largest bird of prey in the world

⑱ Lake Titicaca
Birthplace of the Inca Empire and home to communities unaffected by modern civilization

⑲ Santa Catalina Convent
This city within a city is the most enchanting colonial structure on the entire continent

4

Contents

A trip to a local market is a great way to gain an insight into day-to-day Peruvian life.

Inside front cover
Sleeping and eating
price codes

Inside back cover
Author biography

A lake with a view
Massive walls of rock and snow surround the turquoise, glacial waters of Laguna Parón, a popular two-day trek from the likeable town of Caraz in the Cordillera Blanca.

A foot in the door

Ever since the intrepid explorer Hiram Bingham first described Machu Picchu as a "wonderland", the fabled Inca city has become one of the most recognized images in the world. So much so that it virtually represents Peru, acting as a magnet for every visitor. But it's not even half the story. Peru has more ancient archaeological sites than any other country in South America, and more are being found all the time. One recent discovery, Caral, in the coastal desert, has turned the world of archaeology on its head and challenged accepted thinking on the entire theory of urban development.

There is much more to Peru than old stones, however. Of the 117 recognized life zones on the planet, Peru has 84, from mangroves to cloud forest, mist-fuelled oases in the desert to glacial lakes. It also has 28 out of 32 climate types. Amazingly, 60 percent of the country is jungle, even though less than six percent of its population lives there. The physical barrier of the Andes has prevented Peru from integrating the tropical lowlands, so much of its jungle remains intact and this vast green carpet is home to the greatest diversity of plants and wildlife on the planet. Not a year goes by without the recording of plants and animals previously unknown to science.

Peru is also a country of fiestas, and it would be an unusual visit to Peru that did not encounter at least one. Masks and costumes tell centuries-old stories and reveal an intense spirituality which enriches daily life. Christian saints are carried through the streets as if they were the Inca emperors' sacred remains. Pachamama – Mother Earth – is offered a drop of every drink and animal spirits and old combats come alive in masquerades. Peru is a wonderland, indeed, with the uncanny knack of springing new surprises at every turn.

Riches and rags

When the Spanish *conquistadores* arrived in Peru, they found immense displays of gold and silver, which they plundered with abandon. Such an experience could have made Peru secretive about its riches, but today there are many treasures for all to see. Lima and Cusco house much of the wealth: Cusco with its elegant Plaza de Armas and hotels and restaurants befitting a world-class tourist destination; Lima with its size, modernity and the gulf between rich and poor. But each is a world apart from the rest of the country. Elsewhere things are more intimate: general stores selling everything, unnamed restaurants offering *almuerzos*, every other house a speedy internet, dentist or optician. There are odd juxta- positions, too. The TV, which is never off, advertises goods that are out of the reach of many. In a busy street lined with smart shops a girl implores you to buy toilet paper. The top of the range bus you travel on passes an old woman prodding a mixed herd of pigs, donkeys and goats along the road.

Nice and icy
Cornices and ice fields on Huascarán, at 6,768 m the highest of Peru's Andean giants, provide a spectacular challenge for climbers.

A land of sacrifice

It is easy to appreciate the pride that Peruvians take in their natural surroundings, the country's past achievements, its precolonial heritage and lasting traditions. You'll have no reluctance in sharing the reverence for snow-capped mountains, or marvelling at the grace of river dolphins. But the obvious attractions conceal a more ambiguous reality. The mountains and the jungle hold mineral reserves, which may bring financial prosperity but with an inevitable environmental cost. Moreover, at the other end of the economic scale, when a pittance is paid for produce sweated from precipitous hillsides, it's not surprising that inequality breeds disillusion. During autocratic ex-president Fujimori's term of office, political institutions were neglected. Now, people suspect that the government and major investors will not advance the benefits to all and it is not uncommon to hear unfavourable comparisons between the present administration's public works and those of Fujimori.

City in the sky
No longer a lost city, Machu Picchu is one of the premier tourist destinations in the world, but it still manages to be one of the most magical.

1 *At clay licks in the Manu Biosphere Reserve and Tambopata National Reserve, scarlet macaws gather to peck essential minerals from the clay.* ▶▶ *See page 548.*

2 *The universal appeal of surfing: signs point to beaches around the world, but Peru remains one of the favourites.* ▶▶ *See page 75.*

3 *Guinea pig is one of the delicacies of Andean cuisine, prepared in many ways, but most famous as* cuy chactado, *seared guinea pig.* ▶▶ *See page 63.*

4 *At Sacsayhuaman, dancers reenact one of the rituals of the Inca sun festival, Inti Raymi, held at the winter solstice.* ▶▶ *See page 155.*

5 *Domesticated for thousands of years, llamas are beasts of burden and providers of wool, food and fuel.* ▶▶ *See page 609.*

6 *Startling masks and bright costumes are at the heart of any festival, as here at Easter in Cusco.* ▶▶ *See page 66.*

7 *Great efforts have been made to spruce up Lima's colonial centre, now a UNESCO World Heritage Site.* ▶▶ *See page 95.*

8 *Giant river otters, monkeys and macaws are just some of the wildlife attractions at Lago Sandoval.* ▶▶ *See page 550.*

9 *If kayaking is your thing, Peru is your country.* ▶▶ *See page 71.*

10 *Discoveries continue to be unearthed throughout Peru; here, around Nasca, archaeologists continue their work.* ▶▶ *See page 302.*

11 *Sealions and marine birds take to the Pacific waters around the arches and caves of the Ballestas Islands, near the city of Pisco.* ▶▶ *See page 291.*

12 *The Santa Catalina convent was closed to the outside world for centuries. If in Arequipa, a wander around the complex is sure to be a highlight.* ▶▶ *See page 256.*

Tales of the unexpected

At the end of the Inca Trail is the Intipinku, the Gate of the Sun. Through it you not only see Machu Picchu for the first time, but you are lead back through history to the cultures out of which the Inca civilization grew. The 2,500-year-old fortress temple of Chavín de Huantar, in the lee of the snow-covered peaks of the Cordillera Blanca, represents one of the most influential societies of pre-Columbian times. The Nasca Lines, huge figures of animals and geometric patterns etched into the southern coastal desert between 200 BC and AD 600, are still puzzling scientists. Near the elegant colonial city of Trujillo, on Peru's northern coast, are Chan Chán, the largest adobe city in the world, and the massive adobe pyramids of Huaca del Sol and Huaca de la Luna. Further north still, the twin pyramid complex of Sipán has revealed some of the finest examples of pre-Columbian jewellery, pottery and textiles yet found on the continent. Also here are the mysterious and evocative ruins of Tucumé, a huge city of 26 pyramids, and Sicán, whose pyramids rise out of a forest of algorrob trees. In the northeast, where the Andean mountains drop to meet the vast Amazonian lowlands, the cities and cliffside tombs of the cloud people lie hidden in the forest. The most visited of these, Kuélap, is the greatest pre-Columbian fortress in the Americas.

Thrills, hills and Pacific breaks

Machu Picchu's near neighbour, Cusco, is the gateway to living and natural history. Its festivals are a microcosm of 3,000 others. It gives access to the

Constant maintenance is needed to keep the floating islands of Lake Titicaca watertight: a centuries-old way of life based around the totora reed.

Vivid textiles have a deep significance in the Andes, not just in their symbolism, but also as a memory of the time when fine cloth was the most highly-prized possession.

jungle reserves of Manu and Tambopata, where the tally of birds, mammals, reptiles, butterflies and plants has yet to be fully catalogued. Without doubt, Peru is the best place on earth for seeing jungle wildlife, but Cusco is not the sole entry point. From the Amazon city of Iquitos you can go to Pacaya-Samiria on whose tracks and waterways you can watch Peru's wild heart to your own heart's content. In northern Peru, just as in Cusco, the sporting possibilities are endless: hiking to ruined cities, whitewater rafting or biking down the highest mountains. Huaraz in the Cordillera Blanca is a mecca for climbers and there are fabulous treks in the Chachapoyas area. And, as everyone surely knows, Peru was the birthplace of surfing (in 2004 the women's world champion was a Peruvian).

Frozen in time

Look south beyond Cusco, too, to the islands in the sparkling waters of Lake Titicaca, where communities preserve traditions untouched by modernity. In the magnificent city of Arequipa, watched over by volcanoes, the high walls of Santa Catalina convent hide a perfectly preserved miniature colonial town which was, until recently, closed to the outside world. Nearby are the Colca and Cotahuasi Canyons, remarkable chasms twice as deep as the Grand Canyon, where you can trek along prehispanic agricultural terraces which are still in use, and look for mighty condors rising on the thermals.

The light fantastic

Peru is a deeply spiritual country, where the observance of Catholic holy days and beliefs is infused with respect for indigenous traditions and for the natural world.

Essentials

∗ Footprint features

Planning your trip

Where to go

The variety which Peru can offer the visitor is enormous. The problem is, if you're on a tight schedule, how to fit it all in. Obviously people's tastes differ, but the suggested itineraries below should give an idea of what you can cover comfortably in the time available. Above all, don't attempt too much. Just take it easy and give yourself time to appreciate one of the most beautiful and fascinating countries on Earth. There are four main areas: the southern circuit, the northern circuit, the central highlands and the jungle. From them you can select the elements which suit you best and, providing the transport links are OK, you can tailor your own itinerary. If short of time, flying gives the greatest flexibility, but almost all flights depart from Lima.

One to two weeks

While a one-week visit on its own to Peru would be very restrictive, there are certain places that fit neatly into seven days of travelling. **Southern Peru** offers a very rewarding short circuit covering the most important and popular sites in this part of the country. **Cusco** and **Machu Picchu**, the crown jewels of the Inca Empire, frequently comprise a week (or less), but if you plan to hike the **Inca Trail** or any of the challenging alternatives, you need to consider two weeks in the region. Beautiful **Titicaca**, the highest navigable lake in the world, and the white city of **Arequipa** can be combined with Cusco into a fortnight, using air, rail and road travel.

As an alternative to the highlands, try a week on the **southern coast**, taking in the **Paracas peninsula** (near Pisco), with its marine birdlife, and the incredible **Nasca and Palpa Lines**.

Huaraz, in the **Cordillera Blanca**, is only seven hours by road from Lima and one of the world's premier high altitude recreation areas, with unparalleled ease of access. A week's hiking or climbing in the Cordillera and neighbouring areas is a practical option. It can also easily be linked with the coastal archaeological sites near the colonial city of **Trujillo** (eg Chan Chán, the Huacas del Sol and de la Luna) and further north, around **Chiclayo** (eg Lambayeque with the Brüning and Sipán Museums, Sipán itself, Túcume and Sicán), to fill two weeks. Alternatively, the **Cajamarca** area includes the pleasant city itself, plus thermal baths, archaeological and more recent historical sites and beautiful countryside. To get there quickly from Huaraz, you have to return to the coast for flights from Lima or bus services from Lima, Trujillo or Chiclayo.

Peru's **eastern jungle** includes zones with some of the highest levels of biodiversity in the world. There are two distinct areas with tourism development, north and southeast, with a central zone which has little infrastructure. The southeastern jungle contains the **Manu National Park** and the **Tambopata National Reserve**. These provide wonderful opportunities for watchers of birds, butterflies and animals and for plant lovers. A trip to the southeastern jungle is usually done as part of a visit to Cusco, but can be an item on its own. Flying both ways to **Puerto Maldonado** is the only viable option if short of time. Going overland to the Amazon Basin is also possible. The adventurous way is from Cusco to Puerto Maldonado (the most popular tours involve going one way by road, the other by air), but from Lima to the **central jungle**, via Tarma, is easy enough for people to do on a holiday weekend (and is therefore crowded at such times). The Amazonian city of **Iquitos** is the jumping off point for the northern jungle, where there is a good network of jungle lodges on the river or its tributaries. Flying to Iquitos is one option, either from Lima, or from **Tarapoto**, which can be reached by a beautiful road which descends from the mountains just north of Chachapoyas. Alternatively, you can go overland to Pucallpa and then take a river boat downstream to Iquitos.

A trip to the **Central Andes** from Lima can be done fairly quickly, calling at **Huancayo**, **Huancavelica** and **Ayacucho** in a week to 10 days. Alternatively, the route from Cusco to the Central Highlands is rewarding, but since there are no flights between Cusco and Ayacucho, the only, if rather demanding option is by bus. Obviously the more time you allow, the greater the variety of sights to see, especially in the **Mantaro Valley** near Huancayo, and the places of historical interest around Ayacucho. These are also two of the best places for handicrafts.

At any time, a few extra days in **Lima** visiting its fascinating museums will give you an overview of what you'll be seeing later. And in the meanwhile, you can experience the capital's great nightlife.

Three to four weeks

Adding an extra week or two to the basic southern itinerary would allow you to see much more of Cusco, especially the **Sacred Valley of the Incas**. You can also explore the **Colca** or **Cotahuasi Canyons** from Arequipa, or, from **Puno**, the shores and islands of Lake Titicaca.

Cajamarca gives access to the more remote **Chachapoyas** region, which contains a bewildering number of prehispanic archaeological sites. A week minimum here would be a good idea. Access by road is from the southwest through **Celendín**. There is also a more northerly road route to Chachapoyas from Chiclayo, where you should stop to see the nearby archaeological sites. You can break up a tour of archaeology and mountains with some surfing at **Puerto Chicama** (north of Trujillo) and there are many more beaches in the far north near **Piura** and Tumbes. **Tumbes** also has some wildlife parks, such as coastal mangroves, unlike those in other parts of the country.

If planning on spending more time in the Central Highlands, one variation is to travel overland from **Cerro de Pasco** via Oyón and Churín to **Huacho**, on the coast north of Lima. You would then be close to the recently discovered, intriguing city of **Caral**. Another good option is to combine the Central Highlands with the Cordillera Blanca, taking a series of buses between Huaraz and **Huánuco**, via La Unión and Huallanca. Finally, the **Cordillera Huayhuash** offers some rewarding long-distance, high-altitude trekking. It is most easily reached from Huaraz, via Chiquián, but should not be attempted unless you have a week to spare.

Essentials Planning your trip

When to go

Climate

Peru's high season in the highlands is from May to September, when the weather is most stable for hiking and climbing. At this time the days are generally clear and sunny, though nights can be very cold at high altitude. During the wettest months in the highlands, November to April, some roads become impassable and hiking trails can be very muddy. April and May, at the tail end of the highland rainy season, is a beautiful time to see the Peruvian Andes, but the rain may linger, so be prepared. For a more detailed description of conditions in the Cordillera Blanca, see page 76.

On the coast, high seasons are September and Christmas to February. The summer months are from December to April, but from approximately May to October much of this area is covered with *la garúa*, a blanket of cloud and mist. At this time only the northern beaches near Tumbes are warm enough for pleasant swimming.

The best time to visit the jungle is during the dry season, from April to October. During the wet season, November to April, it is oppressively hot (40º C and above) and while it only rains for a few hours at a time, which is not enough to spoil your trip, it is enough to make some roads virtually impassable.

Festivals

Every bit as important as knowing where to go and what the weather will be like, is Peru's festival calendar. At any given time of the year there'll be a festival somewhere in the country, drawing people from miles around.

Major *fiestas* such as **Carnaval** (throughout February) and **Semana Santa** (March/April) take place during the wet season. June and July are also big months for *fiestas*, particularly in Cusco, which spends the whole of June in celebration.

Check the websites of **PromPerú** and **South American Explorers**, see Finding out more page 29. For a list of the major national holidays and festivals, see page 66. For a detailed list of local festival dates, see under each town in the travelling text. For a description of some of the main festivals and their historic roots, see under Culture, on page 595.

Tour operators

Many tour operators handle more than one type of adventure tourism. Look under all types of sport for those with more than one activity on offer.

UK and Ireland

Andean Trails, The Clockhouse, Bonnington Mill Business Centre, 72 Newhaven Rd, Edinburgh, EH6 5QG, T0131-467 7086, www.andeantrails.co.uk. For mountain biking, trekking and other adventure tours.
Andes, 37a St Andrews St, Castle Douglas, Kirkcudbrightshire, DG7 1EN, Scotland, T01556-503929, www.andes. org.uk. For climbing trips in Peru and throughout South America.
Audley Latin America, 6 Willows Gate, Stratton Audley, Oxfordshire, OX27 9AU, T01869-276210, www.audleytravel.com.

Austral Tours, 20 Upper Tachbrook St, London SW1V 1SH, T020-7233 5384, www.latinamerica.co.uk.
Condor Journeys and Adventures, 2 Ferry Bank, Colintraive, Argyll PA22 3AR, T01700-841318, www. condorjourneys-adventures.com. Eco and adventure tourism with specially designed tours to suit your requirements.
Dragoman, Camp Green, Debenham, Stowmarket, Suffolk IP14 6LA, T0870-499 4475, www.dragoman.co.uk. Contact this outfit for overland camping and/or hotel journeys throughout both South and Central America.

Exodus Travels, Grange Mills, 9 Weir Rd, London SW12 0NE, T020-8675 5550, www.exodus.co.uk Experienced in adventure travel, including cultural tours and trekking and biking holidays. **Explore**, 1 Frederick St, Aldershot, Hants GU11 1LQ, T0870-333 4002, www.explore. co.uk. Highly respected operator with offices in Ireland, Australia, New Zealand, USA, Canada, Hong Kong, Belgium, Netherlands, Denmark, Norway and South Africa. They offer 2- to 5-week tours in more than 90 countries worldwide including Peru. Small groups. Well executed.

Essentials Planning your trip

Galapagos Cruises, 6 Keyes Rd, London, NW2 3XA, T020 8933 0613. This outfit offers good tailor-made tours.

Guerba Expeditions, Wessex House, 40 Station Rd, Westbury, Wiltshire BA13 3JN, T01373-826611, www.guerba.com. Specializes in adventure holidays, from trekking safaris to wilderness camping.

High Places, Globe Centre, Penistone Rd, Sheffield, S6 3AE, T0114-2757500, www.highplaces.co.uk. Trekking and mountaineering trips.

Journey Latin America, 12-13 Heathfield Terr, Chiswick, London, W4 4JE, T020-8747 8315, and 12 St Ann's Sq, 2nd floor, Manchester, M2 7HW, T0161-832 1441, www.journeyarlatinamerica.co.uk. The world's leading tailor-made specialist for Latin America, running escorted tours throughout the region, they also offer a wide range of flight options.

KE Adventure Travel, 32 Lake Rd, Keswick, Cumbria, CA12 5DQ, T017687-73966, www.keadventure.com. Specialist in adventure tours, including 3-week cycling trips in and around Cusco.

Kumuka Expeditions, 40 Earls Court Rd, London W8 6EJ, T0806-068 8855, and Level 4, 46-48 York St, Sydney, NSW 2000, Australia, T1306-667277, www.kumuka.com. Overland tour operator for small groups, escorted or truck-based.

Last Frontiers, Fleet Marston Farm, Aylesbury, Buckinghamshire HP18 0QT, T01296-653000, www.lastfrontiers.com. South American specialists offering tailor-made itineraries as well as discounted air fares and air passes.

Llama Travel, Oxford House, 49A Oxford Rd, London, N4 3EY, T020 7263 3000, mail@llamatravel.com. Tours throughout Peru.

Naturetrek, Cheriton Mill, Cheriton, Alresford, Hants, SO24 0NG, T01962-733051, www.naturetrek.co.uk. Bird-watching tours throughout the continent, also botany, natural history tours, treks and cruises.

Select Latin America (incorporating **Galapagos Adventure Tours**), 79 Maltings Pl, 169 Tower Bridge Rd, London SE1 3LJ, UK, T0207 407 1478, www.selectlatinamerica.com. Quality tailor-made holidays and small group tours.

South American Experience, 47 Causton St, Pimlico, London, SW1P 4AT, T020-7976 5511, www.southamericanexperience.com. Apart from booking flights and accommodation, also offer tailor-made trips.

Steppes Latin America, 51 Castle St, Cirencester, Gloucestershire, GL7 1QD, T01285-885333, www.stepeslatinamerica.co.uk.

Sunvil Latin America, Sunvil House, Upper Sq, Old Isleworth, Middlesex, TW7 7BJ, T020 8758 4774, www.sunvil.co.uk. Small groups or individual tours.
The Adventure Company, 15 Turk St, Alton, GU34 1AG, T0870-794 1009, www.adventurecompany.co.uk.
Trailbreak, Unit 1, Bridge Farm, Reading Rd, Arborfield, Berkshire, RG2 9HT, T0118-976 2491, www.trailbreak.co.uk. For mountain biking adventures.
Tribes Travel, 12 The Business Centre, Earl Soham, Woodbridge, Suffolk, IP13 7SA, T01728-695971, www.tribes.co.uk. Tour company with an associated charitable foundation which aims to relieve poverty in indigenous communities.
Trips Worldwide, 14 Frederick Pl, Clifton, Bristol, BS8 1AS, T0117-311 4400, www.tripsworldwide.co.uk.
Tucan Travel, 316 Uxbridge Rd, London, W3 9RE, T020 8896 1600, www.tucantravel.com.
Veloso Tours, ground floor, 34 Warple Way, London W3 0RG, T020-8762 0616, www.veloso.com.

Continental Europe

South American Tours, Stephanstrasse 13, D-60313, Frankfurt/M, Germany, T+49-69-405 8970, and rue Nothomb 18, B-1040 Bruxelles, T0032-2-640 6963, www.southamericantours.de. For holidays, business travel, or special packages. Has own office at Av Miguel Dasso 117, piso 14, San Isidro, Lima, T01-422 7254, satperu@terra.com.pe, and in New York, Miami, Mexico, Quito, Rio de Janeiro, Santiago de Chile and Buenos Aires.

North America

4starSouthAmerica, in USA and Canada T1-800-747 4540, Europe T+49-(700)-4444 7827, UK, T0871-711 5370, www.4starsouth america.com. Online tour operator. For flights in US T1-800-887 5686, www.4starflights.com.

Discover Latinamerica, 6205 Blue Lagoon Drive, suite 310, Miami, FL 33126, T305-266 5827, http://r5.cocha.com/produccion/start. nsf/inicio?OpenForm&param=discoverchile &login.

eXito, 108 Rutgers St, Fort Collins, CO 80525, T1-800-655 4053, T970-482 3019 (worldwide), www.exito-travel.com.

GAP Adventures, 355 Eglinton Av East, Toronto, Ontario, M4P 1M5, T1-800-465 5600, www.gap.ca.

Ladatco Tours, 2200 S Dixie Highway, suite 704, Coconut Grove, FL 33133, T1-800-327 6162, www.ladatco.com. Based in Miami, run 'themed' explorer tours based around the Incas, mysticism etc.

Lost World Adventures, 337 Shadowmoor Drive, Decatur, GA 30030, T800-999 0558, www.lostworldadventures.com.

Myths and Mountains, 976 Tee Court, Incline Village, NV 89451, T775-832 5454, www.mythsandmountains.com.

Pedal Peru, PO Box 1921, Fraser, CO 80442, T1-800- 708-8604, www.pedal peru.com. Multi-sport adventures.

Peru For Less, 420 Throckmorton, suite 1110, Fort Worth, TX76102, 877-269 0309, and Av Los Corregidor 1450, casa 13, p 3, La Molina, Lima 12, T01-365 4142. Tours to Peru at prices which aim to be the lowest outside Peru.

Peru Mountain Bike, in US T1-866 865 bike, in UK T0871-871 6759, in Peru, Av Arequipa 5241-504, Miraflores, Lima 18, T01-447 2057, www.perumountainbike.com. Organizes mountain bike trips, working in conjunction with Peruvian companies in Huaraz, Caraz, Cusco and Huancayo.

Puchka Peru, www.puchkaperu.com. Specializes in textiles, folk art and market tours.

South American Journeys, 9921 Cabanas Avenue, Tujunga, CA 91042, T1-800-884 7474, and Av La Marina 592, Iquitos, T065-251078, www.southamericaexp.com. Small

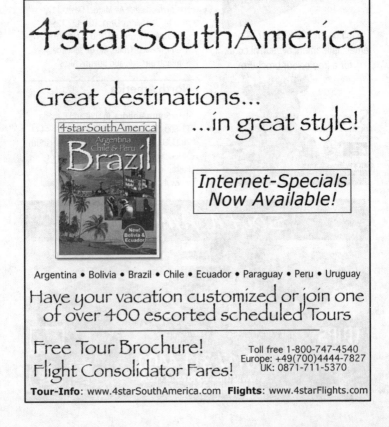

group tours off the beaten track, Peruvian guides, involvement in ecological projects.
Tambo Tours, 20919 Coral Bridge Lane, Suite 225-A, Spring, TX, 77388, USA, T1-888-2-GO-PERU (246-7378) T001-281 528 9448, www.2GOPERU. com. Long-established adventure and tour specialist with offices in Peru and USA . Customized trips to the Amazon and archaeological sites of Peru and Ecuador. Daily departures for groups and Individuals.
Wildland Adventures, 3516 NE 155 St, Seattle, WA 98155-7412, USA, T206-365 0686, T800-345 4453, www.wildland.com. Specializes in cultural and natural history tours to the Andes and Amazon.

South America

Kolibri Expeditions, contact Gunnar Engblom, Lima, T01-476 5016, T9900 7886 (mob), www.kolibriexpeditions.com. Trip reports, recent sightings, travel tips, travel partners, range extensions, identification help, www.birding-peru.com. Birding Peru e-group: birdingperu-subscribe@yahoo groups.com.
Victor Travel Service, Manuel Mattos 325, Lima 31, T01-567 5083, www.overlandperu. com. This outfit offers cheap, overland tours throughout Peru.

Australia

Adventure World, 73 Walker St, North Sydney, NSW 2060, T02-8913 0755, F9956 7707, and 4th floor, 197 St Georges Terrace, Perth 6000, T08-9226 4524, F9281 3299, www.adventureworld.com.au. Escorted group tours, locally escorted tours and packages to Peru and all of Latin America.
Tucan, see above, under UK and Ireland.

Essentials Planning your trip

Finding out more

Outside Peru, tourist information can be obtained from Peruvian embassies and consulates, see page 36. For tourist organisations within Peru, see page 47. For newspapers, radio and TV websites, see Keeping in touch page 84.

With regard to security, it is better to seek advice before you leave from your own consulate than from travel agencies. Before you travel you can contact the **British Foreign and Commonwealth Office**, Travel Advice Unit, T0870 606 0290. Footprint is a partner in the Foreign and Commonwealth Office's 'Know before you go' campaign www.fco.gov.uk/knowbeforeyougo. **US State Department's Bureau of Consular Affairs**, Overseas Citizens Services, T202-647 4000 (travellers' hotline 647 5225), http://travel.state.gov/travel_warnings.html, is useful, as is Australian Department of Foreign Affairs, T61-2-6261 3305, www.dfat.gov.au/consular/advice/advices_mnu.html.

Essentials Planning your trip

Websites

www.aboutcusco.com, www.cuscoon line.com, www.cuscoperu.com and www.cusco.net Among many pages for Cusco, in Spanish, English and other languages.
www.machupicchu.com For Machu Picchu, the site of Machu Picchu Inc, of Key Biscayne, Florida.
www.machupicchu.org More than just Macchu Picchu, a library of all things related to the Inca region and Peru.
www.arequipa-tourism.com Site about Arequipa in Spanish and English.
www.yachay.com.pe/especiales/nasca Nasca lines (in Spanish).
www.andeanexplorer.com and http://huaylas.com For Huaraz and the Callejón de Huaylas, both available in English.
www.perunorte.com Northern Peru (La Libertad, Cajamarca and Lambayeque, in Spanish, English and German).
www.xanga.com/TrujilloPeru Mainly for the north of the country.
www.piuranet.com For Piura.
www.adonde.com and www.perulinks.com/ Two portals, latter in Spanish and English. General information.
www.andeantravelweb.com/peru Andean adventure travel, with advice, links

and more (English and Spanish).
www.conam.gob.pe National Environmental Commission (Spanish).
http://gci275.com/peru/ Peruvian Graffiti, a site with politics, culture, economics, recent history and good links.
Www.geocities.com/perutraveller/ English tourist information aimed at independent travellers.
http://gibbons.best.vwh.net Andean culture and Quechua (English).
www.perucultural.org.pe For information on cultural activities, museums and Peruvian pre-Columbian textiles (Spanish).
www.perurail.com Peru Rail.
www.planeta.com Ron Mader's web-sitewhich contains masses of useful inform-ation on ecotourism, conservation, travel, news, links, language schools and articles.
www.rree.gob.pe Ministry of Foreign Affairs for consular information etc.
www.terra.com.pe Click on Turismo to get to the travel page (in Spanish).
www.traficoperu.com On-line travel agent with lots of information (Spanish and English).
Http://travel.peru.com/travel/english/ Peru.Com's travel page in English, or http://travel.peru.com/travel/spanish for the Spanish version).
www.yachay.com.pe Red Científica Peruana, click on Turismo to get to the travel page.

Language

The official language is **Spanish. Quechua,** an Andean language which predates the Incas, has been given some official status and there is much pride in its use, but

despite the fact that it is spoken by millions of people in the Sierra who have little or no knowledge of Spanish, it is not used in schools. Another important indigenous language is **Aymara,** used in the area around Lake Titicaca. The jungle is home to a plethora of languages but Spanish is spoken in all but the remotest areas. **English** is not spoken widely, except by those employed in the tourism industry (eg hotel, tour agency and airline staff). See page 616 for some basic Spanish for travellers.

Language courses are listed in the directories of cities and towns. **AmeriSpan** ① *T1-800-879 6640, T215-751 1100 (worldwide), www.amerispan.com,* organizes programmes throughout Latin America from its North American and Guatemalan bases. They also have lots of information about travelling in the region. **LanguagesAbroad.com** ① *317 Adelaide St West, Suite 900, Toronto, Ontario, Canada, M5V 1P9, T416-925 2112, toll free 1-800-219 9924, www.languagesabroad.com,* offers Spanish and Portuguese programmes in every South American country except Colombia and Paraguay. They also have language immersion courses throughout the world. Similarly, **Cactus** ① *4 Clarence House, 30-31 North St, Brighton BN1 1EB, T0845-130 4775, www.cactuslanguage.com.* **Spanish Abroad** ① *5112N, 4th St, suite 103, Phoenix, A285018, T602-778 6791, www.spanishabroad.com.* For a list of Spanish schools, see www.planeta.com/ecotravel/schools/schoolist.html.

Disabled travellers

As with most underdeveloped countries, facilities for the disabled traveller are sadly lacking. Wheelchair ramps are a rare luxury and getting a wheelchair into a bathroom or toilet is well nigh impossible, except for some of the more upmarket hotels. The entrance to many cheap hotels is up a narrow flight of stairs. Pavements are often in a poor state of repair (even fully able people need to look out for uncovered manholes and other unexpected traps). Visually and hearing-impaired travellers are similarly poorly catered for as a rule, but experienced guides can often provide tours with individual attention. Disabled Peruvians obviously have to cope with these problems and mainly rely on the help of others to get on and off public transport and generally move around.

The Ministerio de la Mujer y Desarrollo Social (Ministry for Women and Social Development) incorporates a Consejo Nacional de Integración de la Persona con Discapacidad, CONADIS (National Council for the Integration of Disabled People, www.conadisperu.gob.pe – in Spanish). **CONADIS,** together with **PromPerú,** private business, **SATH** (see next paragraph) and **Kéroul** of Québec, has been involved in a project called *Peru: Towards an Accessible Tourism* and the *First Report on Accessibility*

in Peru for Tourists with Disabilities was published in 2001. The report identifies many challenges in a number of major tourist sites. For instance, archaeological sites such as Machu Picchu and Chan Chán, being World Heritage Sites, may not be altered for accessibility although the latter, apart from soft sand in places, is almost entirely accessible. Specially trained personnel, however, can provide assistance to those with disabilities in these cases. The project can be accessed through the PromPerú website; click on Turismo acesible/Accessible tourism.

Some travel companies are beginning to specialize in exciting holidays, tailor-made for individuals depending on their level of disability. For those with access to the internet, a **Global Access Disabled Travel Network Site** is www.geo cities.com/Paris/1502. It is dedicated to providing information for 'disabled adventurers' and includes a number of reviews and tips from members of the public. Another informative site, with lots of advice on how to travel with specific disabilities, plus listings and links belongs to the **Society for Accessible Travel and Hospitality**, www.sath.org. One company in Cusco which offers tours for disabled people is **Apumayo**, see Cusco Tours and activities page 173.

Gay and lesbian travellers

Movemiento Homosexual de Lima (MHOL) ① *C Mariscal Miller 828, Jesús María, T01-433 5519 (English from 1630 on), mhol@terra.com.pe.* Great contact about the gay community in Lima. On-line resources for gay travellers in Peru are http://gaylimape.tripod.com (a good site, in English, with lots of links and information), www.deambiente.com and www.gayperu.com (both in Spanish). In the Lima section we include the names of gay-friendly establishments. There are also gay-friendly places in Cusco, but the scene is not very active there (perhaps the best place to enquire is the *Café Macondo*). This does not imply, however, that there is hostility towards gay and lesbian travellers. As a major tourist centre which welcomes a huge variety of visitors, Cusco is probably more open than anywhere in Peru.

Student travellers

If you are in full-time education you will be entitled to an **International Student Identity Card**, which gives you special prices on all forms of transport (air, sea, rail etc), and access to a variety of other concessions and services. If you need to find the location of your nearest ISIC office contact: **The ISIC Association** ① *Herengracht 479, 1017 BS Amsterdam, Holland, T+31-20-421 2800, F+31-20-421 2810, www.istc.org.*

Students can obtain very few reductions in Peru with an international student's card, except in and around Cusco, at museums and Instituto Nacinal de Cultura sites. To be any use in Peru, it must bear the owner's photograph. An ISIC card can be obtained in Lima from **Intej** ① *Av San Martín 240, Barranco, T01-247 3230,* or ① *Portal Comercio 141, p 2, T084-621351, Cusco, www.intej.org.*

Travelling with children

Travel with children can bring you into closer contact with local families and, generally, presents no special problems – in fact the path is often smoother for family groups. Officials tend to be more amenable where children are concerned and they are pleased if your child knows a little Spanish. **South American Explorers** in Lima, page 91, and Cusco, page 147, can provide lots of useful information on travelling with children in Peru.

Getting from A to B involves a lot of time waiting for buses, trains, and especially for aeroplanes. You should take reading material with you. Train travel is limited to Cusco–Machu Picchu, Cusco–Puno and Huancayo–Huancavelica. The Peru Rail services in the Cusco region are comfortable, with tables between seats, so that games can be played. Elsewhere, you must be prepared for bus or more cramped *colectivo* travel.

Food can be a problem if the children are not adaptable. A small immersion heater and jug for making hot drinks is invaluable, but remember that electric current varies. In restaurants, you can normally buy children's helpings, or divide one full-size helping between two children.

On all long-distance buses you pay a **fare** for each seat, and there are no half-fares if the children occupy a seat each. For shorter trips it is cheaper, if less comfortable, to seat small children on your knee. On sightseeing tours you should *always* bargain for a family rate – often children can go free.

In all **hotels**, try to negotiate family rates. If charges are per person, always insist that two children will occupy one bed only, therefore counting as one tariff You can almost always get a reduced rate at cheaper hotels.

Women travellers

Generally women travellers should find visiting Peru an enjoyable experience. However, machismo is alive and well here and you should be prepared for this and try not to over-react. When you set out, err on the side of caution until your instincts have adjusted to the customs of a new culture.

It is easier for men to take the friendliness of locals at face value; women may be subject to much unwanted attention. To help minimize this, do not wear suggestive clothing and do not flirt. By wearing a wedding ring, carrying a photograph of your 'husband' and 'children', and saying that your 'husband' is close at hand, you may dissuade an aspiring suitor. If politeness fails, do not feel bad about showing offence and departing. When accepting a social invitation, make sure that someone knows the address and the time you left. Ask if you can bring a friend (even if you do not intend to do so).

If, as a single woman, you can befriend a local woman, you will learn much more about the country you are visiting as well as finding out how best to deal with the barrage of suggestive comments, whistles and hisses that will invariably come your way. Travelling with another *gringa* may not exempt you from this attention, but at least should give you moral support.

Unless actively avoiding foreigners like yourself, don't go too far from the beaten track. There is a very definite 'gringo trail' which you can join, or follow, if seeking company. This can be helpful when looking for safe accommodation, especially if arriving after dark (which is best avoided). Remember that for a single woman a taxi at night can be as dangerous as wandering around on her own. A good rule is always to act with confidence, as though you know where you are going, even if you do not. Someone who looks lost is more likely to attract unwanted attention.

Working in Peru

There are many opportunities for volunteer work in Peru (South American Explorers have a full-time staffer and an extensive database). Volunteers do not need a visa for Peru, but you must check with a Peruvian consulate that this applies to you. On **www.trabajovoluntario.org**, a site which offers volunteers and organizations to get in touch, you can browse for opportunities in Peru (in Spanish and English). In Cusco,

Hope Foundation (at Marani Hotel – address given under Cusco, Sleeping page 156) and **Amauta Spanish School** (address under Cusco page 183) accept volunteers. **Socio Adventures** ⓘ *Casilla 431, Cajamarca, T076-831118, www.socioadventures.com,* incorporates building a cooking stove into a 5-day trekking programme. For information outside Peru on voluntary work and working abroad, try **www.idealist.org** for non-profit and community organizations, volunteer opportunities and non-profit careers. There is some overlap between volunteering and gap year or career break tourism as many people who make this type of trip are going to do some form of work. There is an increasing amount of help for students on a gap year and the career-break market is growing fast. Here is a list of ideas: **www.gapyear.com, www.gap.org.uk** and **www.yearoutgroup.org** for that year away. For range of options, try **www.gvi.co.uk** (Global Vision International), or **www.i-to- i.com**. More specific (but not limited to South America) are **www.raleigh.org.uk** (Raleigh International), **www.madventurer.com** and **www.thepodsite.co.uk** (Personal Overseas Development), with projects only in Peru and **www.teaching-abroad.co.uk** (Teaching and Projects Abroad), for more than teaching, including in Peru. The website **www.amerispan.com**, which is principally concerned with language learning and teaching, also has a comprehensive list of volunteer opportunities.

Before you travel

Getting in

Visas

No visa is necessary for countries of Western Europe, Asia, North or South America, the Caribbean or citizens of Australia, New Zealand or South Africa. Travellers from Fiji and India do need Visas. Tourist cards are obtained on flights arriving in Peru or at border crossings. The tourist card allows you up to a maximum of 90 days in Peru. The form is in duplicate and you give up the original on arrival and the copy on departure. This means you need to keep the copy as you will need to give it to the officials when you leave. A new tourist card is issued on re-entry to Peru but extensions are obtained with your current tourist card so you just take it and your passport to immigration when asking for extensions. If your tourist card is lost or stolen, apply to get a new one at **Migraciones** ⓘ *Avenida España 700 y Avenida Huaraz, Breña, Lima,* between 0900 to 1330, Monday to Friday. It shouldn't cost anything to replace your tourist card if you do it in Lima.

Tourist visas Tourist visas for citizens of countries not listed above cost £21.60 (approximately US$36), for which you require a valid passport, a departure ticket from Peru (or a letter of guarantee from a travel agency), two colour passport photos, one application form and proof of economic solvency.

All foreigners should be able to produce on demand some recognizable means of identification, preferably a passport. You must present your passport when reserving tickets for internal, as well as, international travel. An alternative is to photocopy the important pages of your passport – including the immigration stamp, and have it legalized by a 'Notario público', which costs US$1.50. This way you can avoid showing your passport.

An onward ticket is not usually asked for at the land frontiers at Tacna, Aguas Verdes, La Tina, Yunguyo or Desaguadero. Travellers arriving by air are not asked for an onward flight ticket at Lima airport, but it is quite possible that you will not be allowed to board a plane in your home country without showing an onward ticket.

Remember that it is your responsibility to ensure that your passport is stamped in and out when you cross frontiers. The absence of entry and exit stamps can cause serious difficulties: seek out the proper migration offices if the stamping process is not carried out as you cross.

You should always carry your passport in a safe place about your person, or if not leaving the city or town you're in, deposit it in the hotel safe. If staying in Peru for several weeks, it is worth while registering at your Consulate. Then, if your passport is stolen, the process of replacing it is simplified and speeded up.

The extension process in Lima Immigration is as follows: go to the third floor and enter the long narrow hall with many 'teller' windows. Go to window number 5 and present your passport and tourist card. The official will give you a receipt for US$20 (the cost of a one-month extension) which you will pay at the Banco de la Nación on the same floor. Then go down to the first floor and buy form F007 for S/.24 (US$6.75 November 2004 price). Fill out the form and return to window 5 on the third floor. Give the official the paid receipt, the filled-out form, your passport and tourist card. You have now finished your part of the process. Next, you will wait 2 minutes for your passport to be stamped and signed. You have just completed a not-so-painful Peruvian bureaucratic process. Note Three extensions like this are permitted; you are only allowed to buy extensions for one month at a time. Peruvian law states that a tourist can remain in the country for a maximum of six months, after which time you must leave. Crossing the border out of Peru and returning immediately is acceptable. You will then receive another 90 days and the process begins all over again.

To summarize, you are given 90 days upon entering the country. You can buy 90 more for US$20 each (not at the same time) for a total of six months (180 days). Once your six months is completed, you must leave Peru (no exceptions). This simply means crossing into a bordering country for the day (depending on where, you can come back immediately) and returning with a fresh 90 days stamped in your passport.

If you let your tourist visa expire you will be subject to a fine of US$20 on departure or extension of your visa. The fine is at the discretion of the immigration official (he could ask for more) so it's recommended that you are super-friendly. If you extend an expired visa, the extension will start from the day the visa expired. You can extend your visa in Lima, Cusco, Puno, Puerto Maldonado, and Iquitos, but in the provinces it can take more time than in Lima.

Business visas Visitors who are going to receive money from Peruvian sources must have a business visa: requirements are a valid passport, two colour passport photos, return ticket and a letter from an employer or Chamber of Commerce stating the nature of business, length of stay and guarantee that any Peruvian taxes will be paid. The visa costs £21.60 (or equivalent). On arrival business visitors must register with the Dirección General de Contribuciones for tax purposes.

Student visas To obtain a one year student visa you must have: proof of adequate funds, affiliation to a Peruvian body, a letter of recommendation from your own and a Peruvian Consul, a letter of moral and economic guarantee from a Peruvian citizen and four photographs (frontal and profile). You must also have a health check certificate which takes four weeks to get and costs US$10. Also, to obtain a student visa, if applying within Peru, you have to leave the country and collect it in La Paz, Arica or Guayaquil from Peruvian immigration (it costs US$20).

Embassies and consulates

Austria, Gottfried Keller-Gasse 2/35, 1030 Vienna, T715 7486, embperu.austria@peru.jet2web.at.
Australia, 40 Brisbane Avenue Suite 8, Ground Floor, Barton ACT 2600, Canberra, PO Box 106 Red Hill, T61-2-6273 8752, www.embaperu.org.au Consulate in Sydney.
Belgium, Consulate General, Rue de Praetere 2-4, 2nd floor, 1000 Brussels, T641 8760, consulate.peru@conperbruselas.be.
Canada, 130 Albert Street, Suite 1901, Ottawa, Ontario K1P 5G4, T1-613-238 1777, emperuca@bellnet.ca Consulates in Montréal, Toronto and Vancouver.
France, 50 Avenue Kleber, 75116 Paris, T33-1-5370 4200, www.amb-perou.fr/.
Germany, Mohrenstrasse 42, 10117 Berlin, T49-30-206 4103, www.embajada-peru.de Consulates in Frankfurt and Hamburg.
Israel, 37 Revov Ha-Marganit Shikun Vatikim, 52 584 Ramat Gan, Israel, T972-3-613 5591, emperu@021.net.il
Italy, Via Francesco Siacci N 4, 00197 Roma, T39-06-8069 1510, amb.peru@agora.stm.it.

Consulates in Genoa and Milan.
Japan, 4-4-27 Higashi Shibuya-ku, Tokyo 150-0011, T81-3-3406 4243, embperutokio@embperujapan.org. Consulate General www.cpetokio.org/.
Netherlands, Nassauplein 4, 2585 EA, The Hague, T31-70-365 3500, embperu@bart.nl.
New Zealand, Level 8, 40 Mercer Street, Cigna House, Wellington, T64-4-499 8087, embassy.peru@xtra.co.nz.
Norway, Consulate General, Munkendansveien 35, 0119 Oslo, T2323 7688, peru@via.no.
South Africa, Infotech Building, Suite 201, Arcadia Street, 1090 Hatfield, 0083 Pretoria, T27-12- 342 2390, emperu@iafrica.co.
Spain, C Príncipe de Vergara 36, 5to Derecha, 28001 Madrid, T34-91-431 4242, lepru@embajadaperu.es. Consulate in Barcelona.
Sweden, Brunnsgatan 21 B, 111 38 Stockholm, T46-8-440 8740, www.webmakers/peru.
Switzerland, Thunstrasse No 36, CH-3005 Berne, T41-31-351 8555, lepruberna02@bluewin.ch. Consulates in

Geneva and Zurich.
UK, 52 Sloane St, London SW1X 9SP,
T020-7235 1917, F7235 4463,
www.peruembassy-uk.com.
USA, 1700 Massachusetts Avenue NW,

Washington DC 20036, T1-202-833 9860,
F1-202-659 8124, www.peruemb.org.
Consulates in Los Angeles, Miami, New York,
Chicago, Houston, Boston, Denver, San
Francisco.

Customs

When travelling into Peru you can bring 20 pack of cigarettes (400 cigarettes), 50 cigars or 500 g of tobacco, three litres of alcohol and new articles for personal use of gifts valued at up to US$300. There are certain items that cannot be brought in duty-free: these include computers (but laptops are OK). The value added tax for items that are not considered duty-free but are still intended for personal use is generally 20%. Personal items such as laptops, cameras, bicycles, hiking and climbing equipment and anything else necessary for adventure sports are exempt from taxes and should be regarded as personal effects that will not be sold or left in Peru. All customs agents should be satisfied by this and allow you to pass. Anything that looks like it's being brought in for resale, however, could give you trouble.

It is illegal to take items of archaeological interest out of Peru. This means that any pre-Columbian pottery or Inca artefacts cannot leave Peru. If you are purchasing extremely good replicas make sure the pieces have the artist's name on them or that they have a tag which shows that they are not originals. It is very important to realize that no matter how simple it seems, there is no point in trying to take anything illegal out of the country – this includes drugs. The security personnel and customs officials are experts at their job, so save yourself the wasted time, money and energy of 10 years in jail.

Vaccinations

For more a detailed description of necessary vaccinations, a checklist of useful medicines to take with you and other matters relating to health, see Health section on page 77. Before you travel, have a check up with your doctor and arrange your immunizations well in advance. Iif your own doctor is unfamiliar with health in South America, ring a specialist travel clinic. You should be protected by immunisation against typhoid, polio, tetanus and hepatitis A. A yellow fever vaccination certificate is required if you are coming from infected areas of the world. If you are going to the Peruvian jungle, especially if you will be living rough, you should be vaccinated against yellow fever. Moreover, tours to Manu and Tambopata booked outside Peru state that a yellow fever vaccination certificate is required to be allowed to enter either region. Check malaria prophylaxis for all lowland rural areas to be visited and particularly if you will be on the borders of Bolivia, Brazil, Colombia or Ecuador. Vaccination against cholera is not necessary.

What to take

Everybody has their own preferences, but listed here are the most often mentioned. These include an inflatable **travel pillow** for neck support; **hiking boots; waterproof clothing; wax earplugs** (vital for noisy hotels); **rubber sandals** (to wear in showers to avoid athlete's foot);a **sheet sleeping-bag** to avoid sleeping on filthy sheets in cheap hotels; a **clothes line**; a **water bottle**; a universal bath- and basin-**plug** of the flanged type that will fit any waste-pipe; a **Swiss Army knife** (do not carry it in your hand luggage on an airoplane); an **alarm clock** for early morning departures; **candles** or a **torch/flashlight**; an **adaptor; padlocks** (for the doors of the cheapest hotels, tent zips, and backpacks as a deterrent to thieves); a small **first aid kit**; and a **sun hat**.

Useful medicines include **lip salve** with sun protection, and pre-moistened **wipes**. Always carry **toilet paper,** which is especially important on long bus trips. **Contact lens solution** is readily available in pharmacies and *boticas* in all major towns.

Insurance

We strongly recommend that you invest in a good insurance policy which covers you for theft or loss of possessions and money, the cost of medical and dental treatment, cancellation of flights, delays in travel arrangements, accidents, missed departures, lost baggage, lost passport and personal liability and legal expenses. Also check on inclusion of 'dangerous activities' if you plan on doing any. These generally include climbing, diving, skiing, horse riding, parachuting, even trekking. You should always read the small print carefully. Not all policies cover ambulance, helicopter rescue or emergency flights home.

There are a variety of policies to choose from, so it's best to shop around. Your travel agent can advise on the best deals available. Reputable student travel organizations often offer good value policies. Travellers from North America can try the **International Student Insurance Service (ISIS),** which is available through STA, T800 7814040, www.sta-travel.com. Companies worth trying in Britain include **Direct Line Insurance,** T0845-246 8704, http://uk.directline.com/travelling/index.htm and the **Flexicover Group,** T0870 9909292, www.flexicover.net. Some companies will not cover those over 65. The best policies for older travellers are through **Age Concern,** T0800 009966, www.ageconcern.org.uk.

Money

Currency

The **nuevo sol** (new sol, S/.) is the official currency of Peru. It is divided in 100 *céntimos* (cents) with coins valued at S/.5, S/.2, S/.1 and 50, 20, 10 and 5 *céntimo* pieces although the latter is being phased out as it is virtually worthless. A 1-céntimo coin also exists, but seems only to be given out in change when paying airport tax. Notes in circulation are S/.200, S/.100, S/.50, S/.20 and S/.10.

Try to break down notes whenever you can as there is a country-wide shortage of change (or so it seems) and it will make life simpler if you get change whenever you can. It is difficult to get change in shops and museums and sometimes impossible from street vendors or cab drivers. In November 2004, the exchange rate was US$1 = S/. 3.31, 1 euro = S/.4.26. Prices of airline tickets, tour agency services, non-backpacker hotels and hostels, among others, are almost always quoted in dollars. You can pay in soles or dollars but it is generally easiest to pay dollars when the price is in dollars and in soles when the price is in soles. This will save you from losing on exchange rates. In major tourist centres such as Lima, Cusco and Arequipa dollars are frequently accepted.

Almost no one, certainly not banks, will accept dollar bills that are ripped, taped, stapled or torn. Do not accept damaged dollars from anyone; simply tell them you would like another bill. Likewise, ask your bank at home to give you only nice, crisp, clean dollars and keep your dollars neat in your money belt or wallet so they don't accidentally tear.

Forgeries of dollars and soles are not uncommon. Always check the sol notes you have received, even at the bank. Money changers, especially at borders, mix fake notes with genuine bills when giving wads of soles for other currencies. Hold the bills up to the light to check the watermark and that the colours change

Money matters

Low-value US dollar bills should be carried for changing into soles if arriving in the country when banks or *casas de cambio* are closed. They are also useful for shopping. In larger establishments in cities which receive many tourists, dollars are accepted instead of soles. If you are travelling on the cheap it is essential to keep in funds; watch weekends and public holidays carefully and never run out of local currency. Take plenty of local currency, in small denominations, when making trips in the provinces.

There is a nationwide shortage of small change.

It's best to stick to well-known and well-accepted brands of travellers' cheques. These include American Express, Visa and MasterCard. Thomas Cook cheques are reasonably well-known as well (but note that Thomas Cook does not have a representation in Peru). This will avoid suspicious looks or flat out "no's" from storeowners who believe you may have forged your travellers' cheques.

according to the angle of the light. The line down the side of the bill in which the amount of the money is written should appear green, blue and pink at different angles; fake bills are only pink and have no hologram properties. There should be tiny pieces of thread in the paper (not glued on). Check to see that the faces are clear. Also, the paper should not feel smooth like a photocopy but rougher and fibrous. Try not to accept brand new notes, especially if changing on the street, slightly used notes are less likely to be forgeries. There are posters in public places explaining what to look for in forged sol notes. In parts of the country, forged one- and five-sol coins are in circulation. The fakes are slightly off-colour, the surface copper can be scratched off and they tend to bear a recent date.

Credit cards

Visa (by far the most widely accepted card in Peru), **MasterCard, American Express** and **Diners Club** are all valid. There is often an 8-12 per cent commission for all credit card charges. Often, it is cheaper to use your credit card to get money (dollars or soles) out of an ATM rather than to pay for your purchases. Of course, this depends on your interest rate for cash advances on your credit cards – ask your bank or card provider about this. Another option is to put extra money on your credit cards and use them as a bank card. Most banks are affiliated with Visa /Plus system; those that you will find in almost every town and city are **BCP** and **BBVA Continental**. **Interbank** ATMs accept Visa, Plus, Mastercard, Maestro, Cirrus and American Express. **Banco Weise Sudameris** ATMs accept Visa, Plus, Mastercard, Maestro and Cirrus. There are also *Red Unicard* ATMs which accept Visa, Plus, Mastercard, Maestro and Cirrus. Note that not every branch of each bank offers the same ATM services (even branches within the same city). Some ATMs incur a fee of US$1 per use. In comparison with widespread ATM use, businesses displaying credit card symbols may not accept foreign cards. Credit cards are not commonly accepted in smaller towns so go prepared with cash. Make sure you carry the phone numbers that you need in order to report your card lost or stolen. In addition, some travellers have reported problems with their credit cards being 'frozen' by their bank as soon as a charge from a foreign country occurs. To avoid this problem, notify your bank that you will be making charges in Peru (and other countries).

American Express ① *Travex SA, Avenida Santa Cruz 621, Miraflores, Lima, T01-690 0900, info@travex.com.pe.* **Diners Club** ① *Canaval y Moreyra 535, San*

Isidro, To1-221 2050 (24-hour emergency number To1-442 6572). **Mastercard**
① *Porta 111, p 6, Miraflores, To1-311 6000.* **Visa Travel Assistance**① *T108 and ask the operator for a collect call (por cobrar) to T410-581 9754/0120.*

Exchange

There are no restrictions on foreign exchange. Banks are the most discreet places to change travellers' cheques into soles. Some charge commission from 1-3 per cent, some don't, and practice seems to vary from branch to branch, month to month. The services of the **BCP** have been repeatedly recommended. Changing dollars at a bank always gives a lower rate than with *cambistas* (street changers) or *casas de cambio* (exchange houses). Always count your money in the presence of the cashier.

In Lima and many other cities, euros are as acceptable as US dollars for changing into soles (2004). Some street changers in Lima will exchange pounds sterling, but rates are poor. Other currencies carry high commission fees. For changing into or out of small amounts of dollars or euros cash, the street changers give the best rates, avoiding paperwork and queuing, but you should take care: check your soles before handing over your dollars, check their calculators, etc, and don't change money in crowded areas. If using their services think about taking a taxi after changing, to avoid being followed. Many street changers congregate near an office where the exchange 'wholesaler' operates; these will probably be offering better rates than elsewhere on the street.

Soles can be exchanged into dollars at the banks and exchange houses at Lima airport, and you can change soles for dollars with street changers and at any border. Dollars can also be bought at the various frontiers.

American Express will sell travellers' cheques to cardholders only, but will not exchange cheques into cash. Amex will hold mail for cardholders at the Lima branch only. They are also very efficient in replacing stolen cheques, though a police report is needed. Most of the main banks accept American Express travellers' cheques and **BCP** and **BSCH** accept Visa travellers' cheques. **Citibank** in Lima and some BSCH branches handle Citicorp cheques. Travellers have reported great difficulty in cashing travellers' cheques in the jungle area, even Iquitos, and other remote areas. Always sign travellers' cheques in blue or black ink or ballpen.

Money transfer

To transfer money from one bank to another you must first find out which Peruvian bank works with your bank at home. If in fact one does, you will have to go that bank in Lima (or wherever you are) and ask them what the process is to make a transfer. Depending on the bank, transfers can be completed immediately or will take up to five working days. Another option is to use **Western Union**, which has widespread representation throughout the country. **Moneygram** also has offices throughout the capital and the provinces. It exchanges most world currencies and travellers' cheques.

Cost of living

Living costs in the provinces are from 20-50 per cent below those in Lima, although Cusco is a little more expensive than other, less touristy provincial cities. For a lot of low-income Peruvians, many items are simply beyond their reach.

Cost of travelling

The approximate budget for travelling is US$25-35 per person per day for living comfortably, including transport, or US$12-15 a day for low-budget travel. Your budget will be higher the longer you stay in Lima and depending on how many flights you take between destinations. Accommodation rates range from US$3-4 per person for the most basic *alojamiento* to over US$150 for luxurious hotels in Lima and Cusco. For the price of eating out, see page 64.

Getting there

Air

From UK and Ireland

There are no direct flights to **Lima** from London. Various options are available: with **Iberia** or **Air Madrid** via Madrid (or continue with **Avianca** via Bogotá), **KLM** via Amsterdam, or **Varig** via São Paulo. Alternatively, you can fly to Miami, then fly the airlines shown below. A little more expensive are connections via Atlanta with **Delta**, or Houston with **Continental**. From Dublin, either fly to Paris and then on to Bogotá for connections, or use the above options via other European capitals or US hubs.

‡ *If you foresee returning home at a busy time (eg Christmas or Easter), a booking is advisable on any type of open-return ticket.*

From North America

Miami is the main gateway to Peru, together with Atlanta, Dallas, Houston, Los Angeles and New York. Direct flights are available from Miami with **American** and **Lan**, or with **Copa** via Panama City; through New York with **Continental**, which also flies from Houston, and **Lan**; from Atlanta with **Delta**; from Dallas with **American**; and from Los Angeles with **Lan**, **Continental**, **Copa** and **Aeromexico**. Daily connections can be made from almost all major North American cities. From Toronto **Air Canada** flies to Lima three times a week, but from Vancouver, there are no direct flights or connections; fly via one of the above gateways.

From Australia and New Zealand

There are no obvious connecting flights from either Australia or New Zealand to **Lima**. One option would be to go to Buenos Aires from Sydney or Auckland (flights twice a week with **Aerolíneas Argentinas**) and fly on from there (several daily flights). Alternatively, fly to Los Angeles and travel down from there.

From Europe and Israel

There are direct flights to **Lima** only from Amsterdam (**KLM** via Bonaire) and Barcelona and Madrid (**Iberia**). From Frankfurt, Rome or Milan, Lisbon or other European cities, connections must be made in Madrid, Caracas, Brazilian or US gateways.

The alternatives from Tel Aviv to **Lima** are with **El Al** to Miami, then on to **Lima**, or **El Al** to Madrid, then **Avianca** to **Lima** via Bogotá.

From South Africa

From Johannesburg, make connections in Buenos Aires or São Paulo.

From Latin America

There are regular flights, in many cases daily, to Peru from most South American countries: Bogotá, **Avianca**, **Aero Continente/Santa Bárbara**, **Taca** and **Lan**; Buenos Aires, **Aerolíneas Argentinas**, **Taca/Lacsa** and **Lan**; Caracas, **Aeropostal**, **Aero Continente/Santa Bárbara**, **Avianca**, **Lan** and **Taca**; Guayaquil and Quito, **Avianca**, **Taca**, **Lan Perú** and **Aeropostal**; La Paz, **Lloyd Aéreo Boliviano** (**LAB**, also to Cochabamba and Santa Cruz) and **Taca** (also to Santa Cruz); **Varig** to Rio de Janeiro and São Paulo (also **Taca**); Santiago de Chile, **Lan Perú/Lan Chile** and **Lacsa/Taca**. From Central America: Mexico City, **Taca** and **Aeromexico**; Panama, **Copa**; San José, **Taca/Lacsa**.

From Hong Kong, Seoul and Singapore, connections have to be made in Los Angeles. Make connections in Los Angeles or Miami if flying from Tokyo.

Baggage allowance

There is always a weight limit for your baggage, but there is no standard baggage allowance to Peru. If you fly via the USA you are allowed two pieces of luggage up to 32 kg per case. The American airlines are usually a bit more expensive but if you are travelling with a 40-kg bag of climbing gear, it may be worth looking into. On flights from Europe there is a weight allowance of 20 or 23 kg, although some carriers out of Europe use the two-piece system, but may not apply it in both directions. The two-piece system is gaining wider acceptance, but it is always best to check in advance. At busy times of the year it can be very difficult and expensive to bring items such as bikes and surf boards along. Many airlines will let you pay a penalty for overweight baggage – often this is US$5 per kilo – but this usually depends on how full the flight is. Check first before you assume you can bring extra luggage. The weight limit for internal flights is often 20 kg per person, or less, so keep this in mind if you plan to take any internal flights.

Discount flight agents

Using the web for booking flights, hotels and other services directly is becoming an increasingly popular way of making holiday reservations. You can make some good deals this way. Be aware, though, that cutting out the travel agents is denying yourself the experience that they can give, not just in terms of the best flights to suit your itinerary, but also advice on documents, insurance and other matters before you set out, safety, routes, lodging and times of year to travel. A reputable agent will also be bonded to give you some protection if arrangements collapse while you are travelling.

UK and Ireland

STA Travel, 86 Old Brompton Rd, London, SW7 3LQ, T0870 160 0599, www.statravel.co.uk. They have 65 other branches in the UK, including many University campuses. Specialists in low-cost student/youth flights and tours, also good for student IDs and insurance.
Trailfinders, 194 Kensington High St, London, W8 7RG, T020-7938 3939. They also have other branches in London, as well as in Birmingham, Bristol, Cambridge, Glasgow, Manchester, Newcastle, Dublin and Belfast.

North America

Air Brokers International, 685 Market Street, Suite 400, San Francisco, CA94105, T01-800-883 3273, www.airbrokers.com. Consolidator and specialist on RTW and Circle Pacific tickets.

Discount Airfares Worldwide On-Line, www.etn.nl/discount.htm. A hub of consolidator and discount agent links.
STA Travel, 5900 Wiltshire Blvd, Suite 2110, Los Angeles, CA 90036, 1-800-781-4040, www.sta-travel.com. Also branches in New York, San Francisco, Boston, Miami, Chicago, Seattle and Washington DC.
Travel CUTS, in all major Canadian cities and on university and college campuses, T1-866-246-9762, www.travelcuts.com. Specialist in student discount fares, IDs and other travel services. Branches in other Canadian cities as well as California, USA.
Travelocity, www.travelocity.com. Online consolidator.

Australia and New Zealand

Flight Centre, with offices throughout Australia and other countries. In Australia call T133 133 or log on to www.flightcentre.com.au.

STA Travel, T1300-360960, www.sta travel.com.au; 208 Swanston St, Melbourne, VIC 3000, T03-9639 0599. In NZ: 130 Cuba Street, PO Box 6604, Wellington, T04-385 0561, cuba@statravel.co.nz. Also in major towns and university campuses. **Travel.com.au**, T02 9249 6000, outside Sydney: T1300 130 482, www.travel.com.au.

Prices and discounts

Most airlines offer discounted fares on scheduled flights through agencies who specialize in this type of fare. For a list of these agencies see above. The very busy seasons are 7 December-15 January and 10 July-10 September. If you intend travelling during those times, book as far ahead as possible. Between February-May and September-November special offers may be available. Examples of fares on scheduled airlines are: from the UK a return with flexible dates will cost about US$1,065, but travelling over the Christmas/New Year period can see prices rise to over US$1,895. The picture is the same from the USA: a low season return costs from US$480 from Miami, but high season is US$675. From Los Angeles low season is US$695, high season US$905. From Sydney, Australia, a low season return is US$2,380, whereas a Christmas/New Year return will cost US$2,685.

Other fares on scheduled services fall into three groups. A) **Excursion (return) fares** with restricted validity. Some carriers permit a change of dates on payment of a fee. B) **Yearly fares** These may be bought on a one-way or return basis. Some airlines require a specified return date, changeable upon payment of a fee. To leave the return completely open is possible for an extra fee. C) **Student (or under 26) fares** Do not assume that student tickets are the cheapest; though they are often very flexible, they are usually more expensive than A) or B) above. Some airlines are flexible on the age limit, others strict. One way and returns are available. For people intending to travel a linear route and return from a different point from that at which they entered, there are 'Open Jaws' fares, which are available on student, yearly, or excursion fares.

If you buy discounted air tickets always check the reservation with the airline concerned to make sure the flight still exists. Also remember the IATA airlines' schedules change in March and October each year, so if you're going to be away a long time it's best to leave return flight coupons open. In addition, check whether you are entitled to any refund or re-issued ticket if you lose, or have stolen, a discounted air ticket. Some airlines require the repurchase of a ticket before you can apply for a refund, which will not be given until after the validity of the original ticket has expired. The Iberia group and Air France, for example, operate this costly system. Travel insurance in some cases covers lost tickets.

Airline websites

Aerolíneas Argentinas, www.aerolineas.com.ar.
Aeromexico, www.aeromexico.com.
Air France, www.airfrance.com.
Air Madrid, www.airmadrid.com.
American Airlines, www.aa.com.
Avianca, www.avianca.com.co.
British Airways, www.ba.com.
Continental, www.continental.com.
Copa, www.copaair.com.
Delta, www.delta-air.com.

El Al, www.elal.co.il.
Iberia, www.iberia.com.
KLM, www.klm.com.
LAB, www.labairlines.com.
Lacsa, www.grupotaca.com.
Lan, www18.lan.com.
Lufthansa, www.lufthansa.com.
Qantas, www.qantas.com.
Taca, www.grupotaca.com.
Varig, www.varig.com.br.

Boat

There are passenger berths on cargo ships from European and US ports to the west coast of South America. Many of these call at **Callao**, the sea port for Lima. In the main, passage is round trip only and this is a much more expensive form of transport than flying. If you have the time and want a bit of luxury, it is a great alternative.

You can also enter Peru by **river**, on the fast launches and slower passenger boats which go upstream on the Amazon from the Peru/Colombia/Brazil border to Iquitos. A final water-borne route is across Lake Titicaca: see page 252 for Crillon Tours' hydrofoils and Transturin's catamarans between Peru and Bolivia.

Useful contacts for advice and tickets

Strand Voyages (Andy Whitehouse), 1 Adam St, London WC2N 6AB, T020-7766 8220, www.strandtravel.co.uk.
Cargo Ship Voyages Ltd, Hemley, Woodbridge, Suffolk IP12 4QF, T/F01473-736265, www.cargoshipvoyages.co.uk.
The Cruise People, 88 York St, London W1H 1QT, T020-7723 2450 (reservations 0800-526313), www.members.aol.com/CruiseAZ/freighters.htm.

SGV Reisezentrum Weggis (Mr Urs Steiner), Seestrasse 7, CH-6353, Weggis, Switzerland, T041-390 1133, www.frachtschiffreisen.ch.
Travltips Cruise and Freighter Travel Association, PO Box 580188, Flushing, NY 11358, T800-8728584, www.travltips.com.
Internet Guide to Freighter Travel, www.geocities.com/freighterman.geo/main menu.html.

Rail

There are no functioning rail entry points to Peru. The last one in operation was from Arica in Chile to Tacna, see page 317.

Road

Bus

There are bus services from neighbouring countries to Peru. If coming from Bolivia, there are direct buses to Puno, Cusco and Arequipa from La Paz (see page 249). From Chile there is direct service from Arica to Tacna and Arequipa, where you can change for Lima. If travelling south from Ecuador, there are frequent services from Quito and Guayaquil to Lima and the major cities on the north coast. There are also services crossing from Ecuador to Peru which do not involve a change of bus at the

border, eg Loja-Piura. On rare occasions, customs officials at international borders **45**
may ask for a forward ticket out of the country. This means you'll have to buy the
cheapest bus ticket out of Peru before they let you in. Note that these tickets are not
transferable or refundable.

Car

The main paved entry points for vehicles are as follows. From **Bolivia**: at
Desaguadero and Yunguyo on the southeastern side of Lake Titicaca (there is also
an unpaved crossing on the north shore between Moho and Puerto Acosta). From
Chile: between Arica and Tacna. From **Ecuador**: at Aguas Verdes between
Huaquillas and Zarumilla, between Macará and La Tina and at Balsas, between Jaén
and Vilcabamba (another crossing, Alamor/Lalamor, is only possible by rowing
boat). From **Brazil**: the crossing from Assis Brasil to Iñapari is unpaved and is only
passable with ease in the dry season.

To enter Peru by private vehicle, you must have an **international driving licence**.
You also need the **registration document** in the name of the driver, or, in the case of a
car registered in someone else's name, a notarized letter of authorization. If renting a
car, your home driving licence will be accepted for up to 6 months. To drive in Peru you
must be over 21 and to rent a car over 25.

There are two recognized documents for taking a vehicle into South America: a
carnet de passages issued jointly by the **Fedération Internationale de l'Automobile**
(FIA – Paris) and the **Alliance Internationale de Tourisme** (AIT-Geneva), and the
Libreta de Pasos por Aduana issued by the **Federación Interamericana de Touring y
Automóvil Clubs** (FITAC). Officially, Peru requires either the *carnet*, or the *libreta*
and, for caravans and trailers, an inventory. The consulate in London says that a
libreta is necessary, but if you cannot obtain one a written declaration that the car
will leave Peru, authorized at a Peruvian consulate before leaving your home
country, will do instead.

The **Peruvian touring and automobile club**, Avenida César Vallejo 699, Lince,
T01-221 2432, www.touringperu.com.pe, may be able to give advice on entry
procedures. In general, motorists in South America seem to fare better with a *carnet
de passages* than without it.

Essentials Touching down

Touching down

Airport information

All international flights arrive at **Jorge Chávez Airport**, located deep in the Lima
district of Callao, 16 km from the centre of the city. The *aduana* (customs) process is
relatively painless and efficient (a push-button, red light/ green light system
operates for customs baggage checks – see also Customs page 37). Once outside
and past the gate separating arriving passengers from the general public, you're
subject to the mob of taxi drivers all vying to offer you their services. Fares depend
on where you pick up the taxi and your bargaining skills. For full details, see Lima
page 135.

While Jorge Chávez airport has all the facilities one would expect at an
international airport, it was undergoing complete remodelling in 2004. There are
exchange facilities for cash in the international arrivals hall. ATMs accept American
Express, Visa, Mastercard and the Plus, Cirrus and Maestro systems. There are also
casas de cambio (money changing desks). Public telephones are everywhere in and
around the airport. Internet facilities at US$3 per hour must be among the most

🔅 Touching down

Tourist Protection Bureau (Indecopi) 24-hour hotline for travellers' complaints T/F01-224 7888, outside Lima T0800-42579 (not from pay phones), tour@indecopi.gob.pe. This body will help with complaints regarding customs, airlines, travel agencies, accommodation, restaurants, public authorities or if you have lost, or had stolen, documents. There is an office in every town as well as kiosks and information stands.

Tourist Police, Jr Moore 268, Magdalena, at the 38th block of Av Brasil, T01-460 1060, daily 24 hrs; for public enquiries etc, Jr Pachitea at the corner of Belén, Lima, T01-424 2053. Come here if you have had property stolen. They are friendly, helpful and speak English and some German.

Police (PNP, Policía Nacional del Perú) T01-475 2995 in Lima. They have stations in every town.

Ambulance T01-225 4040 in Lima.

Emergency medical attention (SAMU) T117.

Fire service T116.

IDD code 51.

Directory enquiries National T108; International T108.

Official time 5 hrs behind GMT.

Official languages Spanish and Quechua.

Business hours Shops 0900 or 1000-1230 and 1500 or 1600-2000, or 1000-1900. In the main cities, supermarkets do not close for lunch, some in Lima open 24 hours. Some are closed on Saturday and most on Sun- day. Banks in Lima are open 0945 to 1700. Outside Lima they generally close 1200 to 1500, lunch hour closing varies. Many banks in Lima and Cusco have Saturday morning hours from 0945 to 1200. Offices have continuous hours 0900-1700. Most close on Saturday. Government offices Monday-Friday 0830-1130, January to March. The rest of year Monday-Friday 0900-1230, 1500-1700, but this changes frequently.

General sales tax 19%, automatically added to the bill.

Voltage 220 volts AC, 60 cycles throughout the country, except Arequipa (50 cycles). Most 4- and 5-star hotels have 110 volts AC. Plugs are either American flat-pin or twin flat and round pin combined.

Weights and measures The metric system is compulsory.

expensive in the country. There are post offices, too. Branches of **City Café** have fast computers for internet access at US$1.75 per hour. The **Zeta** bookstalls have a good selection of English language guidebooks. Information desks can be found in the national foyer and in the international foyer. There is also a helpful desk in the international arrivals hall. It can make hotel and transport reservations. They often say that cheaper hotels are full or unsafe and, if you allow them to make a choice for you, it will probably be more expensive than you want (they may get commission). Hotels in the immediate airport area are generally for short-stay couples and are not appealing, especially after a long-haul flight. The larger, more expensive hotels in Miraflores and San Isidro have their own buses at the airport, and charge for transfer. Several *hostales* also provide transport to and from the airport. See Lima listings for hotels near Jorge Chávez.

Departure information

Airlines recommend that you arrive at the airport three hours before international flights and two hours before domestic flights. Check-in for international flights closes one hour before departure, 30 minutes for domestic flights, after which you may not be permitted to board. Drivers of the cars entering the car park are subject to a document check.

Tax

There is a US$28 departure tax for international flights which is never included in the price of your ticket. It may be paid in dollars or soles. For national flights the airport tax is approxiamtely US$5, payable only in soles. Tickets purchased in Peru will also have the 19 per cent state tax, but this will be included in the price of the ticket. It is very important to reconfirm your flights when flying internally in Peru or leaving the country. This is generally done 48-72 hours in advance and can be done by phoning or visiting the airline office directly or, sometimes, by going to a travel agent for which you may have to pay a service charge. If you do not reconfirm your internal or international flight, you may not get on the plane. See also Customs page 37.

Tourist information

Tourism promotion and information is handled by **PromPerú** ① *Edificio Mincetur, Calle Uno Oeste 50, piso 13, urb Córpac, San Isidro, T01-224 3131, www.peru.org.pe, or www.peru.info*. They produce promotional material but offer no direct information service to individual tourists. The website does carry plenty of background and other information and they produce a monthly travel news magazine, *Kilca*, available by email: go to www.peru.info/kilca/boletinkilca.htm. PromPerú runs an information and assistance service, **i perú**, T01-574 8000 (24 hours). Its main office in Lima ① *Jorge Basadre 610, San Isidro, T01-421 1227, iperulima@promperu.gob.pe*, opens Monday-Friday 0900-1830 and there is a 24-hour office at Jorge Chávez airport. There are also offices around the country; addresses are given in the text. Other offices in most towns, either run by the municipality, or independently, provide tourist information. The number of places with their own website is growing; these are given in the relevant part of the text. Further information can obtained online from **Canatur**, Cámara Nacional de Turismo, at www.go2peru.com, the official travel planning website, with background details, bookings and practical information. **Indecopi** is the government-run consumer protection and tourist complaint bureau; see page 46. In overall charge of tourism is the Ministerio de Comercio Exterior y Turismo ① *Calle Uno 50, Urb Córpac, San Isidro, Lima, T01-224 3347, www.mincetur.gob.pe*.

South American Explorers

This non-profit, educational organization functions primarily as an information network for Peru and South America and is the most useful organization for travellers in the continent. They have offices in Lima, Cusco, Quito and the USA. Full details are given in the Lima and Cusco sections, see pages 92 and 147.

Useful tourism organizations

Apavit (Asociación Peruana de Agencias de Viaje y Turismo), Antonio Roca 121, Santa Beatriz, Lima, T01-433 7610, www.apavit.com.
Apotur (Asociación Peruana de Operadores

de Turismo), Bajada Balta 169, p 2, Miraflores, Lima 18, T01-445 0382, apotur@amauta.rcp.net.pe.
Aptae (Asociación Peruana de Operadores de Turismo de Aventura y

Ecoturismo), San Fernando 287, Miraflores, Lima 18, T01-241 4765, www.aptaeperu.com.pe. **Agotur** (Asociación de Guías Oficiales de Turismo), Baltazar La Torre 165, depto 101-D, San Isidro, Lima, T01-422 8937, agoturlima@yahoo.com.

Local customs and laws

Clothing

Most Latin Americans, if they can afford it, devote great care to their clothes and appearance. It is appreciated if visitors do likewise. How you dress is mostly how people will judge you. This is particularly important when dealing with officials. Buying clothing locally can help you to look less like a tourist. Women should pack at least one medium- to long-length skirt and men might want to consider bringing a smart sweater or jacket. Nice sweaters and wool shawls can be easily purchased in Peru and make good additions to your wardrobe.

In general, clothing is less formal in the tropical lowlands, where men and women do wear shorts. In the highlands, people are more conservative, though wearing shorts is acceptable on hiking trails. Men should not be seen bare-chested in populated areas.

Courtesy

Politeness – even a little ceremoniousness – is much appreciated in Peruvian society. So much so, in fact, that business cards can prove useful. Men should always remove any headgear and say *con permiso* when entering offices, and shake hands with other men. Women or men meeting women usually greet each other with one kiss on the cheek. When introduced, Peruvians will probably expect to greet visitors in the same way. Always say *Buenos días* (until midday) or *Buenas tardes* and wait for a reply before proceeding further.

When dealing with officials, always remember to be friendly and courteous no matter how trying the circumstances. Never be impatient and do not criticize situations in public (the officials may know more English than you think and they can certainly interpret gestures and facial expressions). In some situations, however, politeness can be a liability. Most Peruvians are disorderly queuers. In commercial transactions (buying a meal, goods in a shop, etc) politeness should be accompanied by firmness, and always ask the price first.

Politeness should also be extended to street traders. Saying *no, gracias* with a smile is better than an arrogant dismissal. Whether you give money to beggars is a personal matter, but your decision should be influenced by whether a person is begging out of need or trying to cash in on the tourist trail. In the former case, local people giving may provide an indication. Giving money to children is a separate issue, upon which most agree: don't do it. There are occasions where giving food in a restaurant may be appropriate, but first inform yourself of local practice.

In Peru it is common for locals to throw their rubbish, paper, wrappers and bottles into the street. Sometimes when asking a local where the rubbish bin is, they will indicate to you that it is the street. This does not give you the right to apply the 'when in Rome' theory. There are rubbish bins in public areas in many centres and tourists should use them.

Time-keeping

Peruvians, as with most Latin Americans, have a fairly relaxed attitude towards time. They will think nothing of arriving an hour or so late on social occasions. If you expect to meet someone more or less at an exact time, you can tell them that you want to meet *en punto* or specify *la hora inglesa* (English time).

Tipping

In most of the better restaurants a 10 per cent service charge is included in the bill, but you can give an extra 5 per cent as a tip if the service is good. The most basic restaurants do not include a tip in the bill, and tips are not expected. Taxi drivers are not tipped – bargain the price down, then pay extra for good service if you get it. Tip cloakroom attendants and hairdressers (very high class only), US$0.50-$1; railway or airport porters, US$0.50; car wash boys, US$0.30; car 'watch' boys, US$0.20. If going on a trek or tour it is customary to tip the guide, as well as the cook and porters.

Toilets

Most Peruvian toilets are adequate but the further you go from main population and tourist centres, the poorer the facilities, so you may require a strong stomach and the ability to hold your breath for a long time. Almost without exception used toilet paper or feminine hygiene products should not be flushed down the pan, but placed in the receptacle provided. This applies even in quite expensive hotels. Not doing so will block the pan or drain, which can be a considerable health risk. It is quite common for people to stand on the toilet seat, as they do in Asia.

Responsible tourism

Travel to the furthest corners of the globe is now commonplace and the mass movement of people for leisure and business is a major source of foreign exchange and economic development in many parts of South America. In some regions (eg Machu Picchu) it is probably the most significant economic activity.

The benefits of international travel are self-evident for both hosts and travellers – employment, increased understanding of different cultures, business and leisure opportunities. At the same time there is clearly a downside to the industry. Where visitor pressure is high and/or poorly regulated, adverse impacts to society and the natural environment may be apparent. Paradoxically, this is as true in undeveloped and pristine areas (where culture and the natural environment are less 'prepared' for even small numbers of visitors) as in major resort destinations.

The travel industry is growing rapidly and increasingly the impacts of this supposedly 'smokeless' industry are becoming apparent. These impacts can seem remote and unrelated to an individual trip or holiday (eg air travel is clearly implicated in global warming and damage to the ozone layer, resort location and construction can destroy natural habitats and restrict traditional rights and activities), but individual choice and awareness can make a difference in many instances (see box) and collectively, travellers can have a significant effect in shaping a more responsible and sustainable industry.

Of course travel can have beneficial impacts and this is something to which every traveller can contribute – many national parks are part funded by receipts from visitors. Similarly, travellers can promote patronage and protection of important archaeological sites and heritage through their interest and contributions via entrance and performance fees. They can also support small-scale enterprises by staying in locally run hotels and hostels, eating in local restaurants and by purchasing local goods, supplies and arts and crafts.

In the last decade, there has been a phenomenal growth in tourism that promotes and supports the conservation of natural environments and is also fair and equitable to local communities. This 'ecotourism' segment is probably the fastest growing sector of the travel industry and provides a vast and growing range of destinations and activities in South America. While the authenticity of some ecotourism operators' claims need to be interpreted with care, there is clearly both a huge demand for this type of activity and also significant opportunities to support worthwhile conservation and social

⁝ How big is your footprint?

1 Where possible choose a destination, tour operator or hotel with a proven ethical and environmental commitment – if in doubt ask.
2 Spend money on locally produced (rather than imported) goods and services and use common sense when bargaining – your few dollars saved may be a week's salary to others.
3 Use water and electricity carefully – travellers may receive preferential supply while the needs of local communities are overlooked.
4 Learn about local etiquette and culture – consider local norms and behaviour and dress appropriately for local cultures and situations.
5 Protect wildlife and other natural resources – don't buy souvenirs or goods made from wildlife unless they are clearly sustainably produced and are not protected under CITES legislation.
6 Don't give money or sweets to children – it encourages begging – instead give to a recognized project, charity or school.
7 Always ask before taking photographs or videos of people.
8 Consider staying in local accommodation rather than foreign owned hotels – the economic benefits for host communities are far greater – and there are more opportunities to learn about local culture.
9 Make a voluntary contribution to Climate Care, www.co2.org, to counteract the pollution caused by tax-free fuel on your flight.

development initiatives. If you are concerned about the application of the principles of ecotourism, in Peru as elsewhere, you need to make an informed choice by finding out in advance how establishments such as jungle lodges cope with waste and effluent disposal, whether they create the equivalent of 'monkey islands' by obtaining animals in the wild and putting them in the lodge's property, what their policy is towards employing and training local staff, and so on.

Organizations such as **Conservation International** ① *T001-202-912 1000, www.ecotour.org*, the **International Ecotourism Society** ① *T001-802-651 9818, http://ecotourism.org*, **Planeta** ① *www.planeta.com* and **Tourism Concern** ① *T+44-20-7133 3330, www.tourismconcern.org.uk*, have begun to develop and/or promote ecotourism projects and destinations and their web sites are an excellent source of information and details for sites and initiatives throughout South America. Additionally, organizations such as **Earthwatch** ① *T+44-1865-318838 or T978-461 0081 (in US), www.earthwatch.org*, and **Discovery Initiatives** ① *T+44-1285-643333, www.discoveryinitiatives.com*, offer opportunities to participate directly in scientific research and development projects throughout the region.

South America offers unique and unforgettable experiences – often based on the natural environment, cultural heritage and local society. These are the reasons many of us choose to travel and why many more will want to do so in the future. Shouldn't we provide an opportunity for future travellers and hosts to enjoy the quality of experience and interaction that we take for granted?

Safety

The following notes on personal safety should not hide the fact that most Peruvians are hospitable and helpful. Peru is not a highly dangerous country to travel in, but it is and by using a mixture of common sense and vigilance you can minimize the risks.

You need to take care everywhere but particularly in poor areas of cities, as this is where most theft takes place. While you should take local advice about being out at night, do not assume that daytime is safer than nighttime. If walking after dark, walk in the road, not on the pavement. You should also be on your guard during festivals, at markets and when streets are crowded. Care should be taken at all times and in most parts of Lima. Over the past couple of years there has been an alarming increase in aggressive assaults in centres along the Gringo Trail. Places like Arequipa, Puno and in particular Cusco have, at times, been plagued by waves of strangle muggings. Check with **South American Explorers** for a current summary of the situation and how to keep safe. A friendly attitude on your part, smiling even when you've thwarted a thief's attempt, can help you out of trouble. Be especially careful arriving at or leaving from bus and train stations. Stations are obvious places to catch people with a lot of important belongings. Do not set your bag down without putting your foot on it, even just to double check your tickets. Be wary of accepting food, drink, sweets or cigarettes from unknown people on buses or trains; they may be drugged. Try to find a travel companion if alone, as this will reduce the strain of watching your belongings.

Keep all documents secure and hide your main cash supply in different places or under your clothes. Some ideas: sew extra pockets inside shirts and trousers; close pockets with a zip or safety pin; moneybelts (best worn below the waist rather than around the neck); neck or leg pouches; and elasticated support bandages. Keep cameras in bags, take spare spectacles and don't wear wrist-watches (even cheap ones have been ripped off arms!) or jewellery. If you wear a shoulder-bag, carry it in front of you. Small personal alarms are a good idea. Backpacks are vulnerable to slashers: a good idea is to cover the pack with a sack (a plastic one will also keep out rain and dust) with maybe a layer of wire netting between. Make photocopies of important documents and give them to family or friends. Alternatively send yourself an email containing all important details, addresses, etc which you can access in an emergency. It is best to leave any valuables you don't need in your hotel's safe-deposit box. But keep a record of what you have deposited. If you don't trust the hotel, lock everything in your pack and secure that in your room (some people take eyelet-screws for padlocking cupboards or drawers). If you lose your valuables, always report it to the police and note details of the report for insurance purposes.

If someone smears mustard, or sprays paint or shampoo on to your clothes, walk on to a safe, private place to clean yourself up. Similarly, ignore strangers' remarks like 'what's that on your shoulder?' or 'have you seen that dirt on your shoe?'. Furthermore, don't bend over to pick up money or other items in the street. These are all ruses intended to distract your attention and make it easy for an accomplice to rob you. If someone follows you when you're in the street, let him catch up with you and 'give him the eye'. Ruses involving 'plainclothes policemen' are infrequent, but it is worth knowing that the real police only have the right to see your passport (not your money, tickets or hotel room).

Although some illegal drugs are readily available, anyone found carrying even the smallest amount is automatically assumed to be a drug trafficker. If arrested on any charge the wait for trial in prison can take up to a year and is particularly unpleasant. Unfortunately, we have received reports of drug-planting, or mere accusation of drug-trafficking by the PNP (Policía Nacional de Perú) on foreigners in Lima, with US$1,000 demanded for release. If you are asked by the narcotics police to go to the toilets to have your bags searched, insist on taking a witness. Tricks employed to get foreigners into trouble over drugs include slipping a packet of cocaine into the money you are exchanging, being invited to a party or somewhere involving a taxi ride, or simply being asked on the street if you want to buy cocaine. In all cases, a plain clothes 'policeman' will discover the planted cocaine – in your money or at your feet in the taxi – and will ask to see your passport and money. He will then return them, minus a large part of your cash. Beware also of thieves dressed as policemen asking for your passport and wanting to search for drugs; searching is only permitted if prior paperwork is done.

The activities of Sendero Luminoso and MRTA (Movimiento Revolucionario Túpac Amaru) appear to be a thing of the past, although it would be wrong to suggest that either organization is completely dead. In 2004 it was safe to travel to all parts of Peru, with the exception of the **Huallaga Valley**. This includes areas **near Tingo María**, as well as jungle areas **east of Ayacucho**. This is an important region for cocaine growing and trafficking, in which there remains some terrorist involvement. Keep yourself informed and always ask locals and other travellers about the conditions up ahead, especially if you are going off the beaten track. While in Lima or Cusco, you can check in at **South American Explorers**, for latest travel updates (Lima T01-445 3306, Cusco T084-245484).

Whereas in North America and Europe, we are accustomed to law enforcement on a systematic basis; in general law enforcement in Latin America is achieved by periodic campaigns. Be aware that you are required to carry some identification even if it is just a photocopy of your passport. The tourist police in Lima are excellent and you should report any incidents to them. In Lima the office for public enquiries etc is on Jr de la Unión 10th block, Lima, T01-424 2053. Double check that all reports written by the police, especially in Cusco, actually state your complaint. There have been some mix-ups, and insurance companies seldom honour claims for 'lost' baggage. In the event of a vehicle accident in which anyone is injured, all drivers involved are automatically detained until blame has been established, and this does not usually take less than two weeks.

Never offer a bribe unless you are fully conversant with local customs. Wait until the official makes the suggestion, or offer money in some form which is apparently not bribery, eg 'In our country we have a system of on-the-spot fines (*multas de inmediato*). Is there a similar system here?' Do not assume that an official who accepts a bribe is prepared to do anything else that is illegal. You bribe him to persuade him to do his job, or to persuade him not to do it, or to do it more quickly, or more slowly. You do not bribe him to do something which is against the law. If an official suggests that a bribe must be paid before you can proceed on your way, be patient and he may relent.

Getting around

Although Peru's geography is dominated by the Andes, one of the world's major mountain ranges, great steps have been taken to improve major roads and enlarge the paved network linking the Pacific coast with the Highlands. This also means that there are various options, albeit on rougher roads, for the traveller wishing to go to, or from northern Peru from the centre of the country, avoiding Lima. But it is worth taking some time to plan an overland journey in advance, checking which roads are finished, which have roadworks and which will be affected by the weather. The highland and jungle wet season, from mid-October to late March, can seriously hamper travel, so allow extra time if planning to go overland at this time. Peru also, unfortunately, suffers more than its fair share of natural disasters, such as the El Niño weather phenomenon. This can have dramatic effects on overland travel. See page 20.

If you only have a couple of weeks, travelling by air is the sensible option. It allows access to most major regions and means you can spend more time at your destination and less getting there. On the downside, though, air travel

Air

The main national carrier serving the most travelled routes – Arequipa, Chiclayo, Cusco, Iquitos, Juliaca, Piura, Puerto Maldonado, Pucallpa, Tacna, Tarapoto, Trujillo and Tumbes – is **Tans**. **Lan**, part of the group formerly called **Lan Chile**, flies to many major cities and **Grupo Taca** (the Central American airline) offers service on the Lima-Cusco route. They are generally reckoned to have the better service. These airlines generally cost the same, between US$69-99 one-way anywhere in the country from Lima. For shorter flights it may cost a bit less. On the other hand, it is not unusual for the prices to go up at holiday times (Semana Santa, May Day, Inti Raymi, 28-29 July, Christmas and New Year), and for elections. During these times and the northern hemisphere summer seats can be hard to come by, especially on the Lima–Cusco–Lima route, so book early. Often it is best to wait to purchase internal flights until your arrival. There are no deals for round trip tickets and prices can rise within four days of the flight. For destinations in the highlands such as Andahuaylas, Ayacucho and Cajamarca flights are offered by **Aero Cóndor** and **LC Busre**. Huánuco and jungle airports such as Atalaya, Satipo, Tingo María and Tocache are served by **Star-Up**. Ticketing for these airlines is not possible at many travel agencies, so it is better to contact the airline direct for information and reservations (see below).

In 2004 the domestic airline industry was in choas, with airlines being grounded for short periods for political and/or financial reasons. At the time of going to press, one of the main domestic carriers, **Nuevo Continente**, ceased to exist. Outstanding issues still have not been resolved.

It is common for flight times to change, earlier or later, or be cancelled because of weather delays especially in the wet season. Do not be surprised or perturbed by this, often there is nothing the airline can do. Always give yourself an extra day between national and international flights to allow for any schedule changes. Flights are often overbooked so it is **very important** to reconfirm your tickets at least 24 hours of your flight and be at the airport well in advance. By law, the clerk can start to sell reserved seats to stand-by travellers 30 minutes before the flight.

Internal flight prices are given in US dollars but can be paid in soles and the price should include the 19 per cent general sales tax. Tickets are not interchangeable between companies but sometimes exceptions will be made in the case of

(side margin) Essentials Getting around

cancellations. Do check with companies as to whether there are specials happening. If the price sounds too good to be true double check your ticket to make sure you are not being sold a ticket for Peruvian nationals; these tickets are often half price but you need to show Peruvian ID to get on the plane.

To save time and hassle, travel with carry-on luggage only (48cm x 24cm x 37cm). This will guarantee that your luggage arrives at the airport when you do.

Domestic airlines

Aero Cóndor, C Juan de Arona 781, San Isidro, T01-614 6000, www.aerocondor.com.pe. Flights to Andahuaylas, Ayacucho, Cajamarca and over the Nazca Lines.

Lan, Av José Pardo 513, Miraflores, T01-213 8200, www18.lan.com. Flights to Arequipa, Chiclayo, Cusco, Iquitos, Juliaca, Piura, Puerto Maldonado and Trujillo.

LC Busre, Los Tulipanes 218, Lince, T01-619 1313, www.lcbusre.com.pe. Flights to Ayacucho and Cajamarca.

Star Up, Av José Pardo 269, Miraflores, T01-447 7573. To Huánuco and jungle airports.

Taca Perú, Av Comandante Espinar 331, Miraflores, T01-213 7000, www.grupotaca.com. Flights between Lima nd Cusco.

Tans, Jr Belén 1015, Lima centre, and Av Arequipa 5200, Miraflores, T01-213 6000, www.tans.com.pe. Flights to most major destinations in Peru.

Rail

Peru's national rail service was privatized in 1999. The lines of major interest to the traveller are Puno-Juliaca-Cusco and Cusco or Urubamba-Machu Picchu. They are operated by **PerúRail SA**, which provides luxury services and a backpacker train. For information, To84-221992, www.perurail.com. The other railway which carries passengers is the line from Lima to Huancayo, with a continuation to Huancavelica in the Central Highlands. The service from the capital to Huancayo runs on some holiday weekends through the year; check www.incasdelperu.com for the latest schedule. Huancayo-Huancavelica has daily passenger services. Train schedules may be cut in the rainy season.

River

On almost any trip to the Amazon Basin, a boat journey will be required at some point, either to get you to a jungle lodge, or to go between river ports. Motorized canoes with canopies usually take passengers to jungle lodges. They normally provide life jackets and have seats which are not very comfortable on long journeys, so a cushion may come in handy. Being open to the elements, the breeze can be a welcome relief from the heat and humidity in the daytime, but they can also be cold in the early morning and if there is any rain about it will blow into your face. Take a waterproof to keep you dry and warm. You sit very close to the water and you soon learn to respect the driver's mate's knowledge of the river.

Public river transport cannot be regarded as luxurious by any stretch of the imagination, although on the route from Iquitos to Brazil, some posh boats do run. Boats can be extremely uncomfortable, but with patience, perseverance and a strong stomach it is still far from impossible to travel this way. Accommodation is either in a cabin, frequently tiny and dirty, which will be more expensive than slinging your hammock in the general hammock area. If you choose to sleep in a hammock, hang it away from lightbulbs (they aren't switched off at night and attract all sorts of strange insects) and away from the engines, which usually emit noxious fumes and, of course, noise. Another useful tip is not to sling your hammock near the bottom of the stairwell on double decked river boats, as this is where the cook slaughters the livestock every morning. Do try to find somewhere sheltered from the cold, damp night breeze. Take rope for hanging your hammock, plus string and sarongs for privacy. Use a double hammock of material (not string) for warmth; you may need a blanket as well. Boats have irregular schedules. Keep an eye on the departure notices (usually chalk boards) and look for a boat that other passengers have started to board. The captain will often let you embark a couple of days before departure. The captain, and only the captain, will take payment. You need to take: plenty of drinking water (the silt in the rivers will clog filters; purifying tablets may not kill giardia); decent food to relieve the appalling meals; eating utensils; plenty of prophylactic enteritis tablets; a bag to put your rubbish in (rather than doing as the other passengers do, ie chucking it all overboard); mosquito repellent and long-sleeved shirts and long trousers for after dusk. DEET is the best mosquito repellent but it will be washed directly into the river and it is lethal to most fish. Being able to speak Spanish is essential. Thieves are unscrupulous: do not leave anything out of sight, not even your shoes under your hammock at night. Women travellers can expect the usual unwanted attention, but it becomes more uncomfortable when confined to the small boat.

Road

Peru's road network is being upgraded and better roads mean better bus services and improved conditions for drivers. Peru, however, is no different from other Latin American countries in that travelling by road at night or in bad weather should be treated with great care. It is also true that there are many more unpaved than paved roads, so extended overland travel is not really an option if you only have a few weeks' holiday. Detailed accounts of major and minor road conditions are given in the travelling text.

Improving the road system is one of the Peruvian government's top priorities. More and more major routes are being paved. The Pan-American Highway runs north-south through the coastal desert and is mostly in good condition. Also paved and well-maintained is the direct road which branches off the Pan-American at Pativilca and runs up to Huaraz and on to Caraz. The Northern route from Chiclayo through to Tarapoto is almost entirely paved. It is complete to Moyobamba, plus the spur to Jaén, and is being heavily worked on to Tarapoto. Cajamarca has a smart new road connection to the coast to serve the Yanacocha mining operation. The Central Highway from Lima to Huancayo is mostly paved. It continues (mostly paved) to Pucallpa in the Amazon basin. There is also a paved road from La Oroya to Tarma and Satipo. South of Lima, there's the paved 'Liberatores' highway from Pisco to Ayacucho. From Nasca to Abancay and on to Cusco is paved. This is now the main route from Lima to Cusco. The main roads in and to the Sacred Valley from Cusco are also paved. The Cusco-Puno highway is fully paved and is a fast, comfortable journey to rival the train. The paved road continues along the south shore of Lake Titicaca to Desaguadero on the Bolivian border. In the south, the road which runs into the Sierra to Arequipa is in good condition. From Arequipa the road to Puno is newly paved. The new route to Desaguadero from the coast via Moquegua is one of the nicest highways in the country. Roads from Arequipa to Mollendo and Matarani are also excellent.

All other roads in the mountains are of dirt, some good, some very bad. Each year they are affected by heavy rain and mud slides, especially those on the eastern slopes of the mountains. Repairs can be delayed because of a shortage of funds. This makes for slow travel and frequent breakdowns. Note that some of these roads can be dangerous or impassable in the rainy season. Check beforehand with locals (not with bus companies, who only want to sell tickets) as accidents are common at these times.

Bus

Services along the coast to the north and south as well as inland to Huancayo, Ayacucho and Huaraz are very good. There are direct (*ejecutivo*) service buses to major centres (different companies use different titles for their top class or executive services, eg **Imperial, Ideal, Royal**). As well as *ejecutivo*, many bus companies have regular (local) service and the difference between the two is often great. Many buses have bathrooms, movies and reclining seats (*bus cama*); if any or all of these services are important to you, ask before you buy your ticket. **Ormeño** and **Cruz del Sur** are the two bus lines generally thought to have the best service with the most routes. *Cruz del Sur* accepts Visa cards and gives 10 per cent discount to ISIC and Under26 cardholders (you may have to insist). **Civa** also offer extensive coverage throughout the nation, but are not in the same class as **Ormeño** and **Cruz del Sur**. There are many smaller but still excellent bus lines that run only to specific areas.

With the nicer companies or *ejecutivo* service you will get a receipt for your luggage, it will be locked under the bus and you shouldn't have to worry about it at stops because the storage is not usually opened. On local buses there will be lots of people getting on and off the buses, loading and unloading bags, so it's best to watch your luggage. It will provide you with a good excuse to get off the bus and stretch anyway. Do not put your day bag above your head inside the bus; keep it at your feet or beside you. It is too easy for someone to grab your bag and get off without your realizing. If you decide to get off the bus at a stop, take all your carry-on items with you. Tickets for *ejecutivo* service buses can cost up to double those of the local service buses. If you want to buy a return ticket from Lima, it is quite often cheaper to wait and buy the return portion when you arrive at your destination. This isn't the case always, but on the major lines things seem to cost more from the capital.

For long journeys be sure to take water and possibly a bit of food, although it is always possible to buy food at the stops along the way. See the warning under Safety, about not accepting food or drinks from fellow passengers. For mountain routes, have a blanket or at least a jacket handy as the temperature at night can drop quite low. Night buses along the coast and into main highland areas are generally fine. Once you get off the beaten track, the quality of buses and roads deteriorates and you may want to stick to the day buses. If your bus breaks down and you have to get on another bus, you will probably have to pay for the ticket, but keep your old ticket as some bus companies will give refunds. The back seats tend to be the most bumpy and the exhaust pipe is almost always on the left-hand side of the bus.

It is best to try to arrive at your destination during the day; it is safer and easier to find accommodation. Prices of tickets are raised 60-100 per cent during Semana Santa (Easter), Fiestas Patrias (Independence Day – July 28 and 29), Navidad (Christmas) and special local events. Prices will usually go up a few days before the holiday and possibly remain higher a few days after. Tickets also sell out during these times so if travelling then, buy your ticket as soon as you know what day you want to travel.

Car

Toll roads in Peru include: Aguas Verdes-Tumbes, many on the Pan- American Highway between Tumbes and Lima, Pativilca-Huaraz, Lima-Pucusana, Ica-Nasca, Lima (highway around city), and Variante-Pacasmayo; these vary from US$1.50 to US$0.50. Ecuador to Chile/Bolivia on main roads comes to about US$20.

Motorcycles are exempt from road tolls: use the extreme righthand lane at
toll gates.

The **Touring and Automobile Club of Peru** has offices in most provincial cities offering help to tourists and particularly to members of the leading motoring associations. They give news about the roads and hotels along the way, although for the most up to date information try the bus and *colectivo* offices. Touring y Automovil Club ① *Avenida César Vallejo 699, Lince, Lima, T01-221 2432, www.touringperu.com.pe*.

Gasoline is sold by its equivalent octane rating. Leaded, 84 octane (ochenta y cuatro); and unleaded 90 octane (noventa); 95 (noventa y cinco); and 97 (noventa y siete). Unleaded is widely available along the Panamericana and in cities with over 250,000 people. In the Central Highlands, however, unleaded fuel is rarely on sale. Diesel is referred to as 'petróleo' and is marked on the price signs as D2. Prices are between US$3.55-4.55 for gasoline and around US$2.90 for diesel. The cost along the coast outside urban areas is slightly lower; and slightly higher in the highlands. Since the introduction in 1998 of the 'Law of Amazonia' prices for fuel in the jungle are the cheapest in the country. Filling stations are called *grifos*. Always make sure that your tank is full before branching off a major highway, fill up whenever possible and make sure you put in the correct fuel for your vehicle. Gasoline, diesel and kerosene are often sold at the same filling station.

Peruvian drivers tend to regard traffic lanes and traffic lights as recommendations, at most. In Lima never trust the green light. No-parking signs are painted at the roadside and illegally parked cars are towed away. Do not leave your vehicle on the street in Lima, always put it in a car park (called *playa*), where the usual charge is US$0.75-1 per hour. If you want to sleep in your car, check with the local tourist police first. They may allow you to park near their office. Transit police in silver Landcruisers park beside the road everywhere. They check on vehicles frequently, including to see that seatbelts are being worn, so be prepared to pull over. Usually the police are friendly and helpful with directions.

Roads go to very high **altitudes** in Peru – make sure that the spark is properly adjusted and consider use of smaller carburettor jets if driving much at altitude. Avoid mountain travel between November and April. Take two planks of wood in case your car gets stuck in soft soil when allowing other vehicles to pass. Never travel off the main roads without being self-sufficient. If you need mechanical assistance in the mountains ask for the nearest mining or road construction camp. Four-wheel drive is not necessary, but it does give you greater flexibility in mountain and jungle territory, although you may not get far in Amazonas, where roads are frequently impassable.

Wherever you travel you should expect from time to time to find roads that are badly maintained, damaged or closed during the wet season, and delays because of floods, landslides and huge potholes. Don't plan your schedules too tightly. If you have to drive at night, do not go fast; many local vehicles have poor lights and street lighting is bad. The disadvantages of travelling in your own vehicle include the difficulties of getting insurance, theft, finding guarded parking places, maintenance on appalling roads and nervous exhaustion. These may outweigh the advantages of mobility and independence.

Apart from the mechanical aspects, spare no ingenuity in making your car secure. Use a heavy chain and padlocks to chain doors shut, fit security catches on windows, and remove interior window winders (so that a hand reaching in from a forced vent cannot open the window). All these will help, but none is foolproof. Anything on the outside – wing mirrors, spot lamps, motifs etc – is likely to be stolen. So are wheels if not secured by locking nuts.

Try never to leave the car unattended except in a locked garage or guarded parking space. Remove all belongings and leave the empty glove compartment open when the car is unattended. Also lock the clutch or accelerator to the steering wheel with a heavy, obvious chain or lock. Street children will generally protect your car fiercely in exchange for a tip. Be sure to note down key numbers and carry spares of the most important ones (but don't keep all spares inside the vehicle).

Insurance for the vehicle against accident, damage or theft is best arranged in the country of origin, but it is getting increasingly difficult to find agencies who offer this service. It is very expensive to insure against accident and theft, especially as you should take into account the value of the car increased by duties calculated in real (ie non-devaluing) terms. If the car is stolen or written off you will be required to pay very high import duty on its value. Get the legally required minimum cover, which is not expensive, as soon as you can, because if you should be involved in an accident and are uninsured, your car could be confiscated. If anyone is hurt, do not pick them up (you may become liable). Seek assistance from the nearest police station or hospital if you are able to do so.

The minimum age for renting a car is 25. Car hire companies are given in the text. They do tend to be very expensive, reflecting the high costs and accident rates. Hotels and tourist agencies will tell you where to find cheaper rates, but you will need to check that you have such basics as spare wheel, toolkit and functioning lights etc. Check exactly what the hirer's insurance policy covers. In many cases it will only protect you against minor bumps and scrapes, not major accidents, nor 'natural' damage (eg flooding). Ask if extra cover is available. Also find out, if using a credit card, whether the card automatically includes insurance.

Combis, colectivos and trucks

Combis operate between most small towns in the Andes on 1-3-hour journeys. This makes it possible, in many cases, just to turn up and travel within an hour or two. On rougher roads, combis are minibuses (invariably Japanese), while on better roads there are also slightly more expensive and much faster car colectivos. Colectivos usually charge twice the bus fare and leave only when full. They go almost anywhere in Peru. Most firms have offices. If you book one day in advance, they will pick you up at your hotel or in the main plaza. Trucks are not always much cheaper than buses. They charge 75 per cent of the bus fare, but are wholly unpredictable. They are not recommended for long trips, and comfort depends on the load.

Taxi

Taxi prices are fixed in the highland towns and cost around US$1-1.20 for anywhere in the urban areas. In Lima prices range from US$1.50-3, but fares are not fixed. Some drivers work for companies that do have standard fares. Ask locals what the price should be and always set the price beforehand.

Taxis at airports are often a bit more expensive, but ask locals what the price should be as taxi drivers may try to charge you three times the correct price. Many taxi drivers work for commission from hotels and will try to convince you to go to that hotel. Feel free to choose your own hotel and go there. If you walk away from the Arrivals gate a bit, the fares should go down to a price that is reasonable.

Another common form of public transport is the *mototaxi*, or *motocarro*. This is a three-wheel motorcycle with an awning covering the double-seat behind the driver. In some places, like Iquitos and Tarapoto, they are ubiquitous and the only way to get around. Fares are about US$1.

Motorcycling

The motorcycle should be off-road capable. A road bike can go most places an off-road bike can go. Get to know the bike before you go, ask the dealers in your country what goes wrong with it and arrange a link whereby you can get parts flown out to you. Get the book for international dealer coverage from your manufacturer, but

don't rely on it. They frequently have few or no parts for modern, large machinery. An 59
Abus D or chain will keep the bike secure. A cheap alarm gives you peace of mind if you
leave the bike outside a hotel at night. Most hotels will allow you
to bring the bike inside (see accommodation listings in the
travelling text for details). Look for hotels that have a courtyard or
more secure parking and never leave luggage on the bike
overnight or whilst unattended. Passport, International Driving
Licence, bike registration document are necessary. Riders fare
much better with a *carnet de passages* than without it.

People are generally very amicable to motorcyclists and you can make many friends by returning friendship to those who show an interest in you.

Cycling

Unless you are planning a journey almost exclusively on paved roads a mountain bike
is strongly recommended. The good quality ones (and the cast iron rule is never to
skimp on quality), are incredibly tough and rugged, with low gear ratios for difficult
terrain, wide tyres with plenty of tread for good road-holding, cantilever brakes, and a
low centre of gravity for improved stability. Choose a chrome-alloy frame over
aluminium as it can be welded if necessary. Once an aluminium frame breaks, it's
broke. End of story and trip. Although touring bikes, and to a lesser extent mountain
bikes and spares are available in the larger cities, remember that in the developing
world most indigenous manufactured goods are shoddy. Buy everything you possibly
can before you leave home.

Take a small but comprehensive tool kit (to include chain rivet and crank
removers, a spoke key and possibly a block remover), a spare tyre and inner tubes, a
puncture repair kit with plenty of extra patches and glue, a set of brake blocks, brake
and gear cables and all types of nuts and bolts, at least 12 spokes (best taped to the
chain stay), a light oil for the chain (eg Finish-Line Teflon Dry-Lube), tube of waterproof
grease, a pump secured by a pump lock, a Blackburn parking block (a most
invaluable accessory, cheap and virtually weightless), a cyclometer, a loud bell, and a
secure lock and chain.

Many cycle tourists opt for rugged trailers as opposed to the old rack and
pannier system. The biggest advantage is the fact that you still have a bike,
instantly, not an over laden tank on two wheels. It would be a shame to ride the
length of Peru and miss out on the amazing trail riding at your fingertips. BOB's
(Beast of Burden) Yak Plus trailer is a great rugged choice that comes with a 90-litre
bomber dry sac for your gear. The dry sac is similar to a lighter weigh climbing haul
bag so it's rugged and watertight. Trailers are also much more rugged than racks
and are much easier to weld.

If you prefer, strong and waterproof front and back panniers are a must and
should be carried on the strongest racks available. A top bag-cum-rucksack makes a
good addition for use on and off the bike. A front bag is good for maps, camera,
compass, etc. Waterproof and wind resistant goretex jacket and overtrousers are
invaluable. All equipment and clothes should be packed in plastic bags to give extra
protection against dust and rain. Also protect all documents, etc carried close to the
body from sweat.

Wind, not hills is the enemy of the cyclist. Try to make the best use of the times of
day when there is little; mornings tend to be best but there is no steadfast rule. Take
care to avoid dehydration by drinking regularly. In hot, dry areas with limited supplies
of **water,** be sure to carry an ample supply. Give your bicycle a thorough **daily check**
for loose nuts or bolts or bearings. See that all parts run smoothly. A good chain
should last 5,000 miles, 8,000 km or more, but be sure to keep it as clean as possible
– an old toothbrush is good for this – and to oil it lightly from time to time. Most towns
have a bicycle shop of some description, but it is best to do your own repairs and
adjustments whenever possible. Carry zap-straps to fasten components together
quickly and securely when disassembled for bus or plane transport. Always see that

your bicycle is secure when sightseeing or overnighting (most hotels will allow bikes to be kept in rooms). Most cyclists agree that the main danger comes from other traffic. A rearview mirror has been frequently recommended to forewarn you of vehicles which are too close behind. You also need to watch out for hazards such as oncoming, overtaking vehicles, unstable loads on trucks and protruding loads. Make yourself conspicuous by wearing bright clothing and a helmet.

South American Explorers have valuable cycling information that is continuously updated. The Expedition Advisory Centre, administered by the **Royal Geographical Society** ① *1 Kensington Gore, London SW7 2AR*, has published a useful monograph entitled *Bicycle Expeditions*, by Paul Vickers. Published in March 1990, it can be downloaded from the RGS's website (www.rgs.org). Useful websites are *Bike South America*, www.e-ddws.com/bsa/ and www.cci.asso.fr/cac.htm. This is the site of Cyclo Accueil Cyclo ① *3 rue Limouzin, 42160 Andrézieux, France*, an organization of long-haul tourers who open their homes for free to passing cyclists.

Hitchhiking

Hitchhiking in Peru is neither easy, owing to the lack of private vehicles, nor entirely risk-free. For obvious reasons, a lone female should not hitch by herself. Besides, you are more likely to get a lift if you are with a partner, be they male or female. The best combination is a male and female together. Positioning is also key. Freight traffic in Peru has to stop at the police *garitas* outside each town and these are the best places to try (also toll points, but these are further from towns).

Drivers usually ask for money but don't always expect to get it. In mountain and jungle areas you usually have to pay drivers of lorries, vans and even private cars; ask the driver first how much he is going to charge, and then recheck with the locals.

Maps

It is a good idea to get as many as possible in your home country before leaving, especially if travelling by land. A recommended series of general maps is that published by **International Travel Map Productions** (ITM) ① *345 West Broadway, Vancouver BC, V5Y 1P8, Canada, T604-879 3621, www.itmb.com*, compiled with historical notes by the late Kevin Healey. Relevant to this handbook are South America North West (1:4M) and Amazon Basin (1:4M). Another map series that has been mentioned is that of New World Edition, Bertelsmann, Neumarkter Strasse 18, 81673 München, Germany, *Südamerika Nord, Südamerika Sud* (both 1:4M).

Good maps are available from street sellers in the centre of Lima, or in better bookshops (published by Lima 2000, T01-440 3486, www.lima2000.com.pe, costing US$10, or US$14 in booklet form). Lima 2000's *Mapa Vial del Perú* (1:2,200,000) is probably the best and most correct road map available for the country. 'Westermanns Monatshefte; folio Ecuador, Peru, Bolivien has excellent maps of Peru, especially the archaeological sites. A cheaper, less accurate, and less discreet map is published by **Cartográfica Nacional** for US$3-4. The **Instituto Geográfico Nacional** in Lima sells a selection of good, accurate country and regional maps (see page 130). **South American Explorers**, who will give good advice on road conditions (see page 47), stock an excellent collection of country, regional and topographical maps. In the UK, **Stanfords** ① *12-14 Longacre, London, WC2E 9LP, T020-78361321, www.stanfords.co.uk*, also branches in Manchester and Bristol, stocks an excellent range.

The **Touring and Automobile Club of Peru**, see page 57, sells a road map at US$5 (Mapa Vial del Perú, 1:3,000,000, Ed 1980) and route maps covering most of Peru (Hojas de Ruta, North, Centre and South, US$1.65 each), which have no information on road conditions. The *Guía Toyota* (Spanish), which is published annually, is one of the best guides for venturing off the beaten track.

Sleeping

Accommodation is plentiful throughout the price ranges and finding a hotel room to suit your budget should not present any problems, especially in the main tourist areas and larger towns and cities. The exception to this is during the Christmas and Easter holiday periods, Carnival, Cusco in June and Independence celebrations at the end of July, when all hotels seem to be crowded. It's advisable to book in advance at these times and during school holidays and local festivals, see page 66.

Hotels, hostals, pensiones, etc

There are many top class hotels in Lima and the main tourist centres, such as Cusco, Arequipa, Iquitos and Trujillo. In less visited places the choice of better class hotels is more limited. Accommodation is more expensive in Lima, where good budget hotels tend to be busy. The best value accommodation can be found in the busiest tourist centres, especially Cusco, which is full of excellent value hotels throughout the range. Accommodation also tends to be more expensive in jungle towns such as Iquitos and Puerto Maldonado and in the north compared with the south, especially on the coast. If you want a room with air conditioning expect to pay around 30 per cent extra.

All hotels in the upper price brackets charge 19 per cent general sales tax (IGV) and 10 per cent service on top of prices (foreigners should not have to pay the sales tax on hotel rooms; neither is included in prices given in the accommodation listings, unless specified). The more expensive hotels also charge in dollars according to the parallel rate of exchange at midnight.

By law all places that offer accommodation now have a plaque outside bearing the letters **H** (Hotel), **Hs** (Hostal), **HR** (Hotel Residencial) or **P** (Pensión) according to type. A hotel has 51 rooms or more, a hostal 50 or fewer, but the categories do not describe quality or facilities. Generally speaking, though, a *pensión* or *hospedaje* will be cheaper than a hotel or *hostal*. Most mid-range hotels have their own restaurants serving lunch and dinner, as well as breakfast. Many budget places serve breakfast – almost invariably mean continental breakfast. Most places are friendly and helpful, irrespective of the price, particularly smaller *pensiones* and *hospedajes*, which are often family-run and will treat you as another member of the family.

The cheapest (and often the nastiest) hotels can be found around bus and train stations. If you're just passing through and need a bed for the night, then they may be okay. The better value accommodation is generally found on and around the main plaza (though not always).

Reception areas in hotels may be misleading, so it is a good idea to see the room before booking. Many hoteliers try to offload their least desirable rooms first. If you're shown a dark box without any furniture, ask if there's another room with a window or a desk. The difference is often surprising. The electric showers used in many hotels (basic up to mid-range) are a health and safety nightmare. Avoid touching any part of the shower while it is producing hot water and always get out before you switch it off.

At airports, bus or train stations, hotel representatives meet new arrivals and show them brochures of their properties. If not using their services when booking a hotel from an airport, or station by phone, always talk to the hotel yourself; do not let anyone do it for you (except an accredited hotel booking service). You will be told the hotel of your choice is full and be directed to a more expensive one.

Youth hostels

The office of the Youth Hostel Association of Peru (**Asociación Peruana de Albergues Turísticos Juveniles** and **Administradora Peruana Hostelling International**) ① *Av Casimiro Ulloa 328, Miraflores, Lima T01-446-5488, www.limahostell.com.pe/aphi/.*

A bed for the night

Prices given are for two people sharing a double room with bathroom (shower and toilet), unless the establishment charges per person. If travelling alone, it's usually cheaper to share with others in a room with three or four beds. Prices are for the busy seasons (May-September, Christmas-February and Holy Week). During the low season, when many places may be half empty, it's often possible to bargain the room rate down.

LL (over US$150), **L** (US$100-149) and **AL** (US$66-99) Hotels in these categories are usually only found in Lima and the main tourist centres. They should offer pool, sauna, gym, jacuzzi, all business facilities (including email), several restaurants, bars and often a casino. Most will provide a safe box in each room.

A (US$46-65) and **B** (US$31-45) The better value hotels in these categories provide more than the standard facilities and a fair degree of comfort. Most will include breakfast and many offer 'extras' such as cable TV, minibar, and tea and coffee making facilities. They may also provide tourist information and their own transport. Service is generally better and most accept credit cards. At the top end of the range, some may have a swimming pool, sauna and jacuzzi.

C (US$21-30) and **D** (US$12-20) Hotels in these categories range from very comfortable to functional, but there are some real bargains to be had. At these prices you should expect a reasonably sized, comfortable room with a/c (in tropical regions), your own bathroom, constant hot water, a towel, soap and toilet paper, TV, and a restaurant.

E (US$7-11) and **F** (US$4-6) Usually in these ranges you can expect some degree of comfort and cleanliness, a private bathroom with hot water (certainly in **E**) and perhaps continental breakfast thrown in. Again, the best value hotels will be listed in the travelling text. Many of those catering for foreign tourists in the more popular regions offer excellent value for money and many have their own restaurant and offer services such as laundry, safe deposit box, money exchange and luggage store. Rooms in **F** hotels may have a private bathroom, though this tends to be the exception rather than the rule. Any **F** establishment that provides these facilities, as well as being clean and providing hot water, will be recommended in our hotel listings. Breakfast is rarely included in the price.

G (up to US$4) A room in this price range usually consists of little more than a bed and four walls, with barely enough room to swing a cat. If you're lucky you may have a window, a table and chair. Cheap places don't always supply soap, towels and toilet paper. In colder (higher) regions they may not supply enough blankets, so take your own or a sleeping bag.

It has information about Youth Hostels all around the world. For information about International Student Identity Cards (ISIC) and lists of discounts available to cardholders contact **Intej**, see Student travellers, page 32.

Camping

This normally presents no problems in Peru. There can, however, be problems with robbery when camping close to a small village. Avoid such a location, or ask permission to camp in a backyard or *chacra* (farmland). Most Peruvians are used to campers, but in some remote places, people have never seen a tent. Be casual about leave a tent unattended.

Obey the following rules for 'wild' camping: arrive in daylight and pitch your tent as it gets dark; ask permission to camp from the parish priest, or the fire chief, or the police, or a farmer regarding his own property; never ask a group of people – especially young people; never camp on a beach (because of sandflies and thieves). Also avoid camping at sea level, river beds or on or below bluffs when El Niño rains are forecast as flash floods can occur; tidal waves may also follow earth tremors. If you can't get information from anyone, camp in a spot where you can't be seen from the nearest inhabited place, or road, and make sure no one saw you go there.

Camping gas in little blue bottles is available in the main cities. Those with stoves designed for lead-free gasoline should use *ron de quemar*, available from hardware shops (*ferreterías*). White gas is called *bencina*, also available from hardware stores. If you use a stove system that requires canisters make sure you dispose of the empty canisters properly. It is very sad and unsightly to go on a hike and find blue gas canisters and toilet paper strewn about. Keep in mind as well that you are responsible for the trash that your group, guide or muledriver may drop and it is up to you to say something and pick up the rubbish. Often the rubbish that is on the trails is blamed on locals and this is not usually the case – low-impact travelling is everyone's responsibility and while you are picking up your own trash, pick up other people's too.

Eating

Food

Not surprisingly for a country with such a diversity of geography and climates, Peru boasts the continent's most extensive menu. Its cuisine varies from region to region, but basically can be divided into coastal, highland and tropical.

Coastal cuisine

The best coastal dishes are those with seafood bases, with the most popular being the jewel in the culinary crown, *ceviche*. This delicious dish of raw white fish marinated in lemon juice, onion and hot peppers can be found in neighbouring countries, but Peruvian is best. Traditionally, *ceviche* is served with corn-on-the-cob, *cancha* (toasted corn), yucca and sweet potatoes. Another mouth-watering fish dish is *escabeche* – fish with onions, hot green pepper, red peppers, prawns (*langostinos*), cumin, hard-boiled eggs, olives, and sprinkled with cheese. For fish on its own, don't miss the excellent *corvina*, or white sea bass. You should also try *chupe de camarones*, which is a shrimp stew made with varying and somewhat surprising ingredients. Other fish dishes include *parihuela*, a popular bouillabaisse which includes *yuyo de mar*, a tangy seaweed, and *aguadito*, a thick rice and fish soup said to have rejuvenating powers.

Fish isn't just eaten on the coast. A favourite northern coastal dish is *seco de cabrito*, roasted kid (baby goat) served with beans and rice, or *seco de cordero* which uses lamb instead. Also good is a*ji de gallina*, a rich and spicy creamed chicken, and duck is excellent. People on the coast are referred to as *criollos* (see page 583) and *criollo* cooking can be found throughout the country. Two popular examples are *cau cau*, made with tripe, potatoes, peppers and parsley, served with rice, and *anticuchos*, which are shish kebabs of beef heart with garlic, peppers, cumin seeds and vinegar.

Restaurant prices

The prices that are given for restaurants and other eateries throughout the guide refer to the cost of a two-course meal for one person, excluding tips or drinks.
¶¶¶ US$12 and over.
¶¶ US$6-12.
¶ Under US$6.

Highland cuisine

The staples of highland cooking, corn and potatoes, date back to Inca times and are found in a remarkable variety of shapes, sizes and colours. Two good potato dishes are *causa* and *carapulca*. *Causa* is made with yellow potatoes, lemons, pepper, hard-boiled eggs, olives, lettuce, sweet cooked corn, sweet cooked potato, fresh cheese, and served with onion sauce. You will also find *causa* on coastal menus: the mashed potato is wrapped around the filling, which often contains crabmeat. Another potato dish is *papa a la huancaína*, which is topped with a spicy sauce made with milk and cheese. The most commonly eaten corn dishes are *choclo con queso*, corn on the cob with cheese, and *tamales*, boiled corn dumplings filled with meat and wrapped in a banana leaf.

Meat dishes are many and varied. *Ollucos con charqui* is a kind of potato with dried meat, *sancochado* is meat and all kinds of vegetables stewed together and seasoned with ground garlic and *lomo a la huancaína* is beef with egg and cheese sauce. A dish almost guaranteed to appear on every restaurant menu is *lomo saltado*, a kind of stir-fried beef with onions, vinegar, ginger, chilli, tomatoes and fried potatoes, served with rice. *Rocoto relleno* is spicy bell pepper stuffed with beef and vegetables, *palta rellena* is avocado filled with chicken or Russian salad, *estofado de carne* is a stew which often contains wine and *carne en adobo* is a cut and seasoned steak. Others include *fritos*, fried pork, usually eaten in the morning, *chicharrones*, deep fried chunks of pork ribs and chicken, and *lechón*, suckling pig. And not forgetting that popular childhood pet, *cuy* (guinea pig), which is considered a real delicacy.

Very filling and good value are the many soups on offer, such as *yacu-chupe*, a green soup which has a basis of potato, with cheese, garlic, coriander leaves, parsley, peppers, eggs, onions, and mint, and *sopa a la criolla* containing thin noodles, beef heart, bits of egg and vegetables and pleasantly spiced. And not to be outdone in the fish department, *trucha* (trout) is delicious, particularly from Lake Titicaca.

Tropical cuisine

The main ingredient in much jungle cuisine is fish, especially the succulent, dolphin-sized *paiche*, which comes with the delicious *palmito*, or palm-hearts, and the ever-present yucca and fried bananas. Other popular dishes include *sopa de motelo* (turtle soup), *sajino* (roast wild boar) and *lagarto* (caiman). *Juanes* are a jungle version of *tamales*, stuffed with chicken and rice.

Desserts and fruits

The Peruvian sweet tooth is evident in the huge number of desserts and confections from which to choose. These include: *cocada al horno* – coconut, with yolk of egg, sesame seed, wine and butter; *picarones* – frittered cassava flour and eggs fried in fat and served with honey; *mazamorra morada* – purple maize, sweet potato starch, lemons, various dried fruits, sticks of ground cinnamon and cloves and perfumed pepper; *manjar blanco* – milk, sugar and eggs; *maná* – an almond paste with eggs, vanilla and milk; *alfajores* – shortbread biscuit with *manjar blanco*, pineapple, peanuts, etc; *pastelillos* – yuccas with sweet potato, sugar and anise fried in fat and powdered with sugar and served hot; and *zango de pasas*, made with maize, syrup, raisins and sugar. *Turrón*, the Lima nougat, is worth trying. *Tejas* are pieces of fruit or nut enveloped in *manjar blanco* and covered in chocolate or icing sugar – delicious.

The various Peruvian fruits are wonderful. They include bananas, the citrus fruits, pineapples, dates, avocados (*paltas*), eggfruit (*lúcuma*), the custard apple (*chirimoya*) which can be as big as your head, quince, *papaya*, mango, guava, the passion-fruit (*maracuyá*) and the soursop (*guanábana*). These should be tried as juices or ice cream – an unforgettable experience. For a glossary of food and drink terms, see page 623.

Eating out

The high-class hotels and restaurants serve international food and, on demand, some native dishes, but the best places to find native food at its best are the taverns (*chicherías*) and the local restaurants (*picanterías*).

Lunch is the main meal, and apart from the most exclusive places, most restaurants have one or two set lunch menus, called *menú ejecutivo* or *menú económico*. The set menu has the advantage of being served almost immediately and also usually **cheap**. The *menú ejecutivo* costs US$2 or more for a three-course meal with a soft drink and it offers greater choice and more interesting dishes than the *menú económico*, which costs US$1.50-2.50. Don't leave it too late, though, most Peruvians eat lunch around 1230-1400. There are many Chinese restaurants (*chifas*) in Peru which serve good food at reasonable prices. For really economically minded people the *Comedores populares* found in the markets of most cities offer a standard three course meal for as little as US$1 (see Health, page 77).

For those who wish to eschew such good value, the menu is called *la carta*. An *à la carte* lunch or dinner costs US$5-8, but can go up to an **expensive** US$80 in a first-class restaurant, with drinks and wine included. Middle and high-class restaurants may add 10% service, but do include the 19% sales tax to the bill (which foreigners do have to pay). This is not shown on the price list or menu, so check in advance. Lower class restaurants charge only tax, while cheap, local restaurants charge no taxes. Dinner in restaurants is normally about 1900 onwards, but choice may be more limited than lunchtime. Peruvians tend to ask guests for dinner at 2000.

The situation for **vegetarians** is improving, but slowly. In tourist centres you should have no problem finding a vegetarian restaurant (or a restaurant that has vegetarian options), especially Cusco and Arequipa and, of course, Lima. Elsewhere, choice is limited and you may find that, as a non-meat eater, you are not understood. Vegetarians and people with allergies should be able to list (in Spanish) all the foods they cannot eat. By saying *no como carne* (I don't eat meat), people may assume that you eat chicken and eggs. If you do eat eggs, make sure they are cooked thoroughly. Restaurant staff will often bend over backwards to get you exactly what you want but you need to request it.

Drink

Peru's most famous drink is **pisco**, a grape brandy used in the wonderful pisco sour, a deceptively potent cocktail which also includes egg whites and lemon juice. The most renowned brands come from the Ica Valley. Other favourites are *chilcano*, a longer refreshing drink made with *guinda*, a local cherry brandy, and *algarrobina*, a sweet cocktail made with the syrup from the fruit of the carob tree, egg whites, evaporated milk, pisco and cinnamon.

Some Peruvian **wines** are good, others are acidic and poor. The best are the Ica wines Tacama and Ocucaje, and both come in red, white and rosé, sweet and dry varieties. They cost around US$5 a bottle, or more. Tacama Blancs de Blancs and brut

Champagne have been recommended, also Gran Tinto Reserva Especial. Viña Santo Tomás, from Chincha, is reasonable and cheap, but Casapalca is not for the discerning palate.

Peruvian **beer** is good, but became pretty much the same the country after many individual brewers were swallowed up by the multinational Backus and Johnson (now owned by Bavaria of Colombia). This has happened to the *Cusqueña*, *Arequipeña*, *Callao* and *Trujillo* brands. Peruvians who had their favourites are lamenting this change. In Lima, the *Cristal* and *Pilsner* are both pretty good and served everywhere. Those who fancy a change from the ubiquitous pilsner type beers should look out for the sweetish *maltina* brown ale. A good dark beer is Trujillo Malta.

Chicha de jora is a strong but refreshing **maize beer**, usually homemade and not easy to come by, and *chicha morada* is a soft drink made with purple maize. **Coffee** in Peru is usually brought to the table in a small jug accompanied by a mug of hot water to which you add the coffee essence. If you want coffee with milk, a mug of milk is brought. The number of cafés serving good, fresh coffee is growing. There are many different kinds of herb **tea**: the commonest are *manzanilla* (camomile), *mate de coca* (frequently served in the highlands to stave off the discomforts of altitude sickness) and *hierbaluisa* (lemon grass).

Entertainment

Bars and clubs

Bars as we understand them in Europe or North America are not prevalent in Peru, except in the main tourist centres. Other than in the poorer working class districts, most people seem to do their drinking in restaurants, *peñas*, discos or at *fiestas*.

If you want to party in Peru, head for Barranco in Lima, or Cusco. Other places like Arequipa, Puno and Huaraz have bars and discos, but with nothing like the variety or vibrancy. Barranco, an attractive seaside suburb of Lima, boasts perhaps the best nightlife in the country, see page 125. At weekends it throbs with young *limeños* out for a good time. It is also a great place for a romantic early evening drink while you watch the sun slip into the Pacific Ocean. Barranco is a short taxi ride from Miraflores suburb, which has its own fair share of trendy bars and nightclubs.

As befits its nickname of 'Gringo Capital of South America', Cusco has a staggering selection of bars and nightclubs, all within a few streets on and around the Plaza de Armas. There are British and Irish pubs, American and couch bars. Discos play Latin, techno, rock and golden oldies; some have live bands. For a less energetic evening, *peñas* offer floorshows of traditional music. Many also serve dinner. Look out for the flyers which give free entry plus a complimentary drink.

Take it easy on the booze when you first arrive in Cusco or Puno. Having a hangover and altitude sickness at the same time is no joke. Also be aware of the dangers of trying to score drugs in nightclubs, see Safety page 50.

Festivals and events

Festivals

Two of the major festival dates are **Carnaval**, which is held over the weekend before **Ash Wednesday**, and **Semana Santa** (Holy Week), which ends on **Easter Sunday**. Carnival is celebrated in most of the Andes and Semana Santa throughout Peru. Accommodation and transport is heavily booked at these times and prices rise considerably. Book tickets and make hotel bookings early.

Another important festival is **Fiesta de la Cruz**, held on the first of **May** in much of the central and southern highlands and on the coast. In Cusco, the entire month of **June** is one huge *fiesta*, culminating in **Inti Raymi**, on **24 June**, one of Peru's prime tourist attractions. This date is also celebrated for **San Juan** in the jungle lowlands. Many places on the coast celebrate **San Pedro y San Pablo** on the **29 June**, and Huaraz celebrates a week-long festival of Andinismo at the beginning of the month.

The two main festivals in Lima are **Santa Rosa de Lima**, on **30 August**, and **Señor de los Milagros**, held on several dates throughout **October**.

Another national festival is **Todos los Santos** (All Saints) on **1 November**, and on **8 December** is **Festividad de la Inmaculada Concepción**. See individual towns for local festival listings.

National holidays

Apart from the festivals listed above, the main holidays are: **1 January**, New Year; **6 January**, *Bajada de Reyes*; **1 May**, Labour Day; **28-29 July**, Independence (Fiestas Patrias); **7 October**, Battle of Angamos; **24-25 December**, *Navidad*.

Most businesses such as banks, airline offices and tourist agencies close for the official holidays while supermarkets and street markets may be open. This depends a lot on where you are so ask around before the holiday. Sometimes holidays that fall during mid-week will be moved to the following Monday to make a long weekend. If you are going to spend a holiday in a certain area, find out what the local customs and events are. Often there are parades, processions, special types of food or certain traditions (like yellow underwear on New Year's Eve) that characterize the event. This will allow you to delve into the customs of the region you are travelling in. The high season for foreign tourism in Peru is June to September while national tourism peaks on certain holidays, Navidad, Semana Santa and Fiestas Patrias. Prices rise and accommodation and bus tickets are harder to come by. If you know when you will be travelling buy your ticket in advance.

Shopping

Almost everyone who visits Peru will end up buying a souvenir of some sort from the vast array of arts and crafts (*artesanía*) on offer. The best, and cheapest, place to shop for souvenirs, and pretty much anything else in Peru, is in the street markets which can be found absolutely everywhere. The country also has its share of shiny, modern shopping centres, especially in the capital, but remember that the high overheads are reflected in the prices.

What to buy

It is possible to find any kind of **handicraft** in the capital. The prices are often the same as in the highlands, and the quality is high. Good buys are: silver and gold handicrafts; Indian hand-spun and hand-woven textiles; manufactured textiles in Indian designs; llama and alpaca wool products such as ponchos, rugs, hats, blankets, slippers, coats and sweaters; **arpilleras** (appliqué pictures of Peruvian life), which are made with great skill and originality by women in the shanty towns; and fine leather products which are mostly hand made. Another good buy is **clothing** made from high quality Pima cotton, grown in Peru.

The **mate burilado**, or engraved gourd found in every tourist shop, is cheap and one of the most genuine expressions of folk art in Peru. These are cheaper if bought in the villages of Cochas Grande or Cochas Chico near Huancayo in the Central Highlands. The Mantaro Valley is generally renowned for its folk culture, including all manner of *artesanía*, see Huancayo page 489.

⁞ Snap happy

Pre-paid Kodak slide **film** cannot be developed in Peru and is also very hard to find. Kodachrome is almost impossible to buy. If worried about posting exposed films home, either take them with you, or have them developed, but not printed, once you have checked the laboratory's quality. Postal authorities may use less sensitive equipment for X-ray screening than airports. Developing black and white film is a problem. Often it is shoddily machine-processed and the negatives are ruined. Ask the lab if you can see an example of their work and if they hand-develop. Exposed film can be protected in humid areas by putting it in a balloon and tying a knot. Similarly keeping your camera in a plastic bag may reduce the effects of humidity. In major tourist centres such as Cusco, there is no shortage of shops selling cards for digital cameras, but they are not cheap, and you can find places which will transfer photos to CD.

Alpaca clothing, such as sweaters, hats and gloves, is cheaper in the Sierra, especially in Puno. Another good source is Arequipa, where alpaca cloth for suits, coats, etc (mixed with 40 per cent sheep's wool) can be bought cheaply from factories. However, although Lima is more expensive, it is often impossible to find the same quality of goods elsewhere. Genuine alpaca is odourless wet or dry, wet llama 'stinks'.

One of the best places in Peru to look for *artesanía* is Ayacucho in the Central Highlands. Here you'll find excellent woven textiles, as well as the beautifully intricate **retablos**, or Saint Mark's boxes, see page 591. Cusco is one of the main weaving centres and a good place to shop for textiles, as well as excellent woodcarvings, see page 170. Also recommended for textiles is Cajamarca. The island of Taquile on Lake Titicaca is a good place to buy **ch'uspas** (bags for coca leaves), **chumpis** (belts) and **chullos** (knitted hats). For a more detailed look at Peruvian arts and crafts, see page 588.

Bargaining

Sooner or later almost everyone has to bargain in Peru. Only the rich and famous can afford to pay the prices quoted by taxi drivers, receptionists and self-proclaimed guides. The great majority of Peruvians are honest and extremely hard working, but their country is poor and often in turmoil, the future is uncertain and the overwhelming majority of people live below the poverty line. Foreigners are seen as rich, even if they are backpackers or students. In order to bring prices down, it is extremely helpful to speak at least some Spanish and/or to convince locals that you live, work or study in Peru and therefore know the real price. See page 135 for the box on bargaining in the capital's taxis.

You will not have to bargain in restaurants, department stores, expensive hotels or airline offices. However, almost all the rest is negotiable. Almost all better-class hotels have 'corporate' rates. Just say that you work for some company, that you are a journalist (they never check ID), or you are a researcher. This way you can usually get a reduction. If you think a lower price is appropriate in a cheaper hotel, ask for "una rebaja" or "una rebajita, por favor". You can negotiate the price of a tour booked through a travel agency, but not an aeroplane, bus or train ticket. In fact, you will probably get a better price directly from the airline ticket office.

Bargaining is expected when you are shopping for artwork, handicrafts, souvenirs, or even food in the market. Remember, though, that most of handicrafts, including alpaca and woollen goods, are made by hand. Ask yourself if it is worth taking advantage of the piteous state of the people you are buying from. Keep in mind, these people are making a living not playing a game and the 50 centavos you save by bargaining may buy the seller two loaves of bread. You want the fair price not the lowest one, so bargain only when you feel you are being ripped off. Remember that some Peruvians are so desperate that they will have to sell you their goods at any price, in order to survive. Please, don't take advantage of it.

Sport and activities

Activities

The website www.ohperu.com/diversion/aventura.htm has a list of adventure sports specialists and associations.

Birdwatching

Peru is the number one country in the world for birds. Its varied geography and topography, and its wildernesses of so many different life zones have endowed Peru with the greatest biodiversity and variety of birds on earth. Some 18.5 per cent of all the bird species in the world and 45 per cent of all neotropical birds occur in Peru. This is why Peru is the best destination for birds on the continent dubbed 'the bird continent' by professional birders.

A birding trip to Peru is possible during any month of the year, as birds breed all year round. There is, however, a definite peak in breeding activity – and consequently birdsong – just before the rains come in October, and this makes it rather easier to locate many birds between September and Christmas.

Rainwear is recommended for the mountains, especially during the rainy season between December and April. But in the tropical lowlands an umbrella is the way to go. Lightweight hiking boots are probably the best general footwear, but wellingtons (rubber boots) are preferred by many neotropical birders for the lowland rainforests.

Apart from the usual binoculars, a telescope is helpful in many areas, whilst a tape recorder and shotgun microphone can be very useful for calling out skulking forest birds, although experience in using this type of equipment is recommended, particularly to limit disturbance to the birds.

If your experience of Neotropical birding is limited, the potential number of species which may be seen on a three or four week trip can be daunting. A four-week trip can produce over 750 species, and some of the identifications can be tricky! You may want to take an experienced bird guide with you who can introduce you to, for example, the mysteries of foliage-gleaner and woodcreeper identification, or you may want to 'do it yourself' and identify the birds on your own. Books that cover the birds of Peru are listed on page 606.

Details of the following key sites are given in the main travelling text: **Paracas National Reserve** (page 289); **Lomas de Lachay** (page 370); **Huascarán Biosphere Reserve** (page 328); **Tambopata National Reserve** (page 551); **Iquitos** (page 528); **Manu Biosphere Reserve** (page 545). Some of the other birding hot-spots of Peru are listed below, but there are many more. A great three-to four-week combination is about 16 days in Manu, then two to three days in the highlands at Abra Málaga and two to three days in the Huascarán Biosphere Reserve. A trip into the Marañón Valley (Chiclayo-Cajamarca) can be substituted for Manu; this allows access to some of the most sought-after endemics, but would produce far fewer species. More information on the birds of Peru is given in the Flora and fauna section on page 608. In 2004

PromPerú started a promotion on birdwatching, *Peru, a true paradise of birds*, with useful accompanying literature and lists of contacts. Special focus is being given to northern Peru, with its Tumbesian dry forest and Pacific slopes of the Andes, see for instance the Chaparrí Private Conservation Area, page 404, and the protected areas around Tumbes, page 70.

Cave diving

Diving in underground lakes is not yet widely known in Peru, but there is an organization which can provide information; **Centre of Subterranean Explorations of Peru** (Centro de Exploraciones Subterráneas del Perú, CEESPE), Av Brasil 1815, Jesús María, Lima 11, T01-463 4722, www.geocities.com/cespeleo/CEESPE.html. Sr Carlos Morales is very helpful.

A cave which has attracted international expeditions is the **Gruta de Huagapo** or 'The Cave that Weeps', located in the Valle de Palcamayo 30 km northwest of Tarma in the Department of Junín, at 3,572 m, see page 506.

Climbing and rock climbing

The attractions are obvious. The **Cordillera Blanca** is an ice climber's paradise. It takes just one or two days to reach the snowline on most mountains in this, the most intensive grouping of glaciated peaks in South America. The statistics are impressive: more than 50 summits between 5,000 and 6,000 m; over 20 surpassing 6,000 m; 663 glaciers; and there are no peak fees. It is not unusual for climbers to reach three or more 6,000-m summits, climbed Alpine style, over a three-week trip. The degree of difficulty ranges between **Pisco** (5,752 m), an excellent acclimatizer or novice's mountain, **Copa** (6,173 m), of moderate difficulty, and the tremendous challenges such as **Alpamayo** (5,957 m), **Artesonraju** (6,025 m), **Quitaraju** (6,036 m) and **Ranrapalca** (6,162 m). Huaraz, the main climbing centre of the Cordillera Blanca (see page 329), has a growing infrastructure and is home to the **Peruvian Mountain Guide Association** (see below).

The **Huayhuash** (see page 363) is a little more remote and Chiquián, northwest of the range, and Cajatambo to the south, have few facilities for climbers. It is possible to contact guides, *arrieros*, porters and cooks in Chiquián, although it is best to enquire in Huaraz first. Mules may need to be brought down from villages higher up. The Huayhuash has some of the most spectacular ice walls in Peru. The **Jirishancas** and **Yerupajas** (Grande and Chico) are the most popular and demanding.

The **Cordilleras Vilcabamba and Vilcanota** (see page 219) have the enticing peaks of **Salkantay** (6,271 m) and **Ausangate** (6,398 m), but Cusco is not developed for climbing. This is one of the genuine attractions of Peruvian Andinismo – there is always another mountain slightly more remote to feed the appetite. **Huagurunchu** (5,730 m), for instance in the central Andes, is barely known and **Coropuna**, Peru's third highest at 6,425 m, is hardly ever climbed.

In the *quebradas*, where the rock is most solid (frost-shattered higher up) this is becoming more popular, particularly in the **Quebrada de Llaca**, near Huaraz, and for beginners at **Monterrey** (see page 328). To get to Quebrada de Llaca, take a camioneta from Jirón Caraz (one block behind Raimondi) for Marian and Monterrey, US$1. At Marian, take a path leading off from the football pitch to Quebrada de Llaca. Other rock climbs in the Huaraz area are the boulders of Huanchac, the 'Sphinx', or Torre de Parón and routes in the Rurec Valley.

Technical equipment such as rope, harness, double boots, ice hammers, helmets, crampons, carabiners, pitons, chocks and ice screws can all be hired in Huaraz quite cheaply, but they can be of poor quality.

Founded in 1980, **Peruvian Mountain Guide Association (AGMP)** is housed in the Casa de Guías and is a member of the International Federation of Mountain Guides Association (IFMGA). It regulates and trains guides and the three classes of porter, which are: 1) those with some ice climbing experience, who are most useful; 2) those who carry loads only on paths, who are less useful; and 3) *arrieros* (mule drivers), cooks and camp guardians. The AGMP also sets prices and organizes rescues, though don't rely on this. One criticism of the organization is that some of the guides only have experience on the most popular mountains such as Alpamayo and Huascarán and that its influence does not extend much beyond the Cordillera Blanca and Huayhuash. However, its continued development is a positive step.

Diving

Diving off the **Paracas peninsula** is rewarding, as is the warmer tropical ocean, with larger fish, off **Tumbes**. It is also practised in the **Bahía de Pucusana**. The best season for visibility is March to November because the rivers from the mountains don't deposit silt in the sea. See Lima page 131.

> ‡ The chill of the Humboldt current puts many people off diving in the Peruvian waters.

Essentials Sport & activities

Kayaking

Peru offers outstanding whitewater kayaking for all standards of paddlers from novice to expert. Many first descents remain unattempted owing to logistical difficulties, though they are slowly being ticked off by a dedicated crew of local and internationally renowned kayakers. For the holiday paddler, you are probably best joining up with a raft company who will gladly carry all your gear (plus any non paddling companions) and provide you with superb food whilst you enjoy the river from an unladen kayak. There is a surprising selection of latest model kayaks available in Peru for hire from about US$10-20 a day.

For complete novices, some companies offer two- to three-day kayak courses on the **Urubamba** and **Apurímac** that can be booked locally. For expedition paddlers, bringing your own canoe is the best option though it is getting increasingly more expensive to fly with your boats around Peru. A knowledge of Spanish is indispensable.

Mountain biking

With its amazing diversity of trails, tracks and rough roads, Peru is surely one of the last great mountain bike destinations yet to be fully discovered. Whether you are interested in a two-day downhill blast from the Andes to the Amazon Jungle or an extended off-road journey, then Peru has some of the world's best biking opportunities. The problem is finding the routes as trail maps are virtually non-existent and the few main roads are often congested with traffic and far from fun to travel along. A few specialist agencies run by dedicated mountain bikers are now exploring the intricate web of paths, single tracks and dirt roads that criss-crosses the Andes, putting together exciting routes to suit everyone from the weekend warrior to the long-distance touring cyclist, the extreme downhiller to the casual day tripper.

If you are considering a dedicated cycling holiday, then it is best to bring your bike from home. It's pretty easy, just get a bike box from your local shop, deflate the tyres, take the pedals off and turn the handlebars. It is worth checking first that your airline is happy to take your bike: some are, some will want to charge. Make sure your bike is in good condition before you depart as spares and repairs are hard to come by, especially if your bike is very complicated (eg: XT V-brake blocks are virtually impossible to find and rear suspension/disc brakes parts are totally unavailable). A tip from a Peruvian mountain bike guide: take plenty of inner tubes, brake blocks,

 Extreme Mule Biking is not quite yet taking off but is in its planning stages. This radical sport involves trekking with your bike on a mule to the top of some really high passes and descending to inaccessible places on outrageous single tracks you probably wouldn't dream of doing at home. Experts only.

chain lube and a quick release seat. Leave all panniers at home and rely on the support vehicle whenever you get tired as there will be plenty more riding later.

If you are hiring a bike, be it for one-day or longer, the basic rule is you get what you pay for. For as little as US$5-10 a day you can get a cheap imitation of a mountain bike that will be fine on a paved road, but will almost certainly not stand up to the rigors of off-roading. For US$20-25 you should be able to find something half-decent with front shocks, v-brakes, helmet and gloves. Bear in mind that there are not many high-quality, well-maintained bikes available in Peru so you should check any hire bike thoroughly before riding it.

When signing up for a mountain bike trip, remember that you are in the Andes so if you are worried about your fitness and the altitude, make sure you get a predominantly downhill trip. Check there is a support vehicle available throughout the entire trip, not just dropping you off and meeting you at the end. Check the guide is carrying a first aid kit, at the very least a puncture repair kit (preferably a comprehensive tool kit) and is knowledgeable about bike mechanics. Bikes regularly go wrong, punctures are frequent and people do fall off, so it is essential that your guide/company provides this minimum cover.

On longer trips ask for detailed trip dossiers, describing the ups and downs and total distances of the routes, check how much is just dirt-road (suitable for just about anyone of reasonable fitness) and how much is single-track (often demanding considerable experience and fitness). Also it is good to know what support will be provided in the way of experienced bike guides, trained bike mechanics on hand, radio communications, spare bikes provided, cooking and dining facilities, toilet facilities etc.

Parapenting and hang gliding

Vuelo Libre is just taking off in Peru. Flying from the coastal cliffs is easy and the thermals are good. The **Callejón de Huaylas** is more risky owing to variable thermals, crosswinds and a lack of good landing sites, but there is a strong allure to flying at 6,000 m in front of the glaciers of Huascarán. The area with the greatest potential is the **Sacred Valley** of Cusco which has excellent launch sites, thermals and reasonable landing sites. The season in the Sierra is May to October, with the best months being August and September. Some flights in Peru have exceeded 6,500 m.

Rafting

Peru is rapidly becoming one of the world's premier destinations for whitewater rafting. Several of its rivers are rated in the world's top ten and a rafting trip, be it for one or ten days, is now high on any adventurer's "must-do" list of activities while travelling in Peru. It is not just the adrenaline rush of big rapids that attract, it is the whole experience of accessing areas beyond the reach of motor vehicles, whether tackling sheer-sided, mile-deep canyons, travelling silently through pristine rainforest, or canoeing across the stark Altiplano, high in the Andes.

Before you leap in the first raft that floats by, a word of warning and a bit of advice will help you ensure that your rafting 'trip of a lifetime' really is as safe, as environmentally friendly and as fun as you want it to be.

Basically, the very remoteness and amazing locations that make Peruvian whitewater rivers so attractive mean that dealing with an emergency (should it occur) can be difficult, if nigh on impossible. As the sport of rafting has increased in popularity over the last few years, so too have the number of accidents (including fatalities), yet the rafting industry remains virtually unchecked. How then, do you ensure your safety on what are undoubtedly some of the best whitewater runs anywhere in South America if not the whole world?

If you are keen on your rafting and are looking to join a rafting expedition of some length, then it is definitely worth signing up in advance before you set foot in Peru.

Some long expeditions have fewer than two or three scheduled departures a year and the companies that offer them only accept bookings well in advance as they are logistically extremely difficult to organize. For the popular day trips and expeditions on the Apurímac there are regular departures (the latter in the dry season only – see below). If you can spare a couple of days to wait for a departure then it is fine to book in Cusco. It also gives you the chance to talk to the company who will be operating your tour and to meet the guides. There are day trip departures all year and frequent multi-day departures in the high season. Note that the difficulty of the sections changes between the dry and rainy season. Some become extremely difficult or un-runable in the rainy season. The dry season is April/May to September (but can be as late as November), the rainy season December to March.

New legislation, yet to be fully implemented, demands that Class 4+ guides hold the internationally recognized qualifications of Swift Water Rescue Technician and hold current first aid certificates. All rafting equipment will be checked regularly to ensure it meets basic safety standards, eg life jackets that actually float etc. At present there are a number of guides with the relevant qualifications, but you will only find them at companies who operate the longer, multi-day trips. Moreover, equipment standards in some of the companies are woefully low and it may prove difficult to enforce the new rules, should they be put in place, but at least it will be a step in the right direction.

At present (and probably in the foreseeable future), as with many of Peru's adventure options, it simply boils down to 'You get what you pay for'. Rafting is an inherently dangerous sport and doing it in Peru with the wrong operator can quite seriously be endangering your life. If price is all that matters bear in mind the following comments: the cheaper the price, the less you get, be it with safety cover, experience of guides, quality of equipment, quantity of food, emergency back up and environmental awareness.

Often on trips you will be required to show proof that your travel insurance will cover you for whitewater rafting (occasionally you may be asked to sign an insurance disclaimer). If you are unsure about it, and are planning to go rafting, it is worth checking with your insurance company before you leave, as some policies have an additional charge. Very few policies cover Grade 5 rafting – read the small print. When signing up you should ask about the experience of the guides or even, if possible, meet them. At present there is no exam or qualification required to become a river guide, but certain things are essential of your guide. Firstly find out his command of English (or whatever language – there are a few German speaking guides available), essential if you are going to understand his commands. Find out his experience. How many times has he done this particular stretch of river? Many Peruvian guides have worked overseas in the off-season, from Chile to Costa Rica, Europe and New Zealand. The more international experience your guide has, the more aware he will be of international safety practices. All guides should have some experience in rescue techniques. All guides must have knowledge of First Aid. Ask when they last took a course and what level they are at.

Good equipment is essential for your safe enjoyment of your trip. If possible ask to see some of the gear provided. Basic essentials include self-bailing rafts for all but the calmest of rivers. Check how old your raft is and where it was made. Satellite phones are an essential piece of safety equipment on long trips in remote areas: does the company use them (they are not yet standard on the Apurímac)? Paddles should be of plastic and metal construction. Wooden paddles can snap, but a few companies use locally-made ones which can be excellent, but expensive (in either case, losing a paddle should be of less importance to the company than the safety of the rafter). Helmets should always be provided and fit correctly (again, home-made fibreglass copies are an accident waiting to happen). Life jackets must be of a lifeguard-recognized quality and be replaced regularly as they have a tendency to

66 99 The desert meets the ocean via hundreds of beaches ideal for lovers of watersports and fine seafood, as well as those who simply want to lie on the beach with a good book...

loose their flotation. Locally made jackets look the business, but in fact are very poor floaters. Does your company provide wetsuits (some of the rivers are surprisingly cold), or, at the very least, quality Splash jackets, as the wind can cause you to chill rapidly? On the longer trips, dry bags are provided - what state are these in? How old are they? Do they leak? There is nothing worse than a soggy sleeping bag at the end of a day's rafting. Are tents provided? And most importantly (for the jungle) do the zips on the mosquito net work and is it rain proof? Does the company provide mosquito netting dining tents? Tables? Chairs? These apparent excesses are very nice when camping for some time at the bottom of a sandfly-infested canyon!

Back onto First Aid: ask to see the First Aid kit and find out what is in there and, most importantly, do they know how to use it? When was it last checked? Updated? Pretty basic stuff, but if someone used all the lomotil you could come unstuck.

After a tough day on the river, the last thing you want to do is get sick from the food. Good, wholesome food is relatively cheap in Peru and can make all the difference on a long trip. Once again, you pay for what you get. Ask if there's a vegetarian option. On the food preparation, simple precautions will help you stay healthy. Are all vegetables soaked in iodine before serving? Do the cooks wash their hands and is there soap available for the clients? Are the plates, pots and cutlery washed in iodine or simply swilled in the river? (Stop and think how many villages up stream use that river as their main sewage outlet.) All are simple ways to avoid getting sick. On the Apurímac, the operator should provide a chemical toilet and remove all toilet paper and other rubbish. In the past, certain beaches have been subject to a completely uncaring attitude over toilet paper and human excrement. At the very least your company should provide a lighter for burning the paper and a trowel to go dig a hole. Simple rules to follow are always shit below the high-water mark so at least in the rainy season it will wash clean, always bury it good and deep and watch out when burning the paper so as not to start a fire. It is normal practice for guides to check the campsite on arrival to ensure it is clean and then again before leaving. If your company does not, make it your responsibility to encourage other members of the group to keep the campsites clean. When cooking bottled gas is used. Neither drift wood nor cut trees should be burnt.

Above all it is your safety on the river that is important. Some companies are now offering safety kayaks as standard as well as safety catarafts on certain rivers. This is definitely a step in the right direction but one that is open to misuse. Sometimes safety kayakers have little or no experience of what they are required to do and are merely along for the ride, sometimes they are asked to shoot video (rendering the safety cover useless). A safety cataraft is a powerful tool in the right hands, but weigh it down with equipment and it is of little use. All companies should carry at the very least a 'Wrap kit' consisting of static ropes, carabiners, slings and pulleys should a raft unfortunately get stuck. But more importantly, do the guides know how to use it?

So if all this doom and gloom has not put you off, you are now equipped to go out there and find the company that offers what you are looking for at a price you think is reasonable. Bear in mind a day's rafting in the USA can cost between US$75

-120 for a basic one-day. In Peru you might get the same for just US$25 but ask 75 yourself "What am I getting for so little?". After all, rafts and equipment cost the same, in fact more, in Peru.

Skiing

Without the aid of lifts, skiing in Peru is largely for the high altitude enthusiast. **Pastoruri**, at 5,000 m, has the only piste and holds a championship during *Semana del Andinismo* at the end of the November to June season. **Pisco, Vallunaraju** and **Caullaraju** are also used for skiing. **Huascarán** and **Copa** have been tackled by experienced ski-mountaineers and the eastern flank of **Coropuna** also has potential. There is, however, a high possibility of crevasses on Copa and Huascarán from November to March. Those thinking of skiing the more difficult peaks should have some technical climbing experience and a guide is recommended. The *Casa de Guías* has the names of at least eight people with skiing experience; they are not instructors but have taken groups to most peaks.

The extreme ski descent craze has hit the **Cordillera Blanca** and **Huayhuash** in a big way. Since *North Face Extreme* skied and snowboarded Artesonraju in the late 1990s, the flood gates have opened. There is practically no peak that is considered out of the question.

Surfing

Peru is a top internationally renowned surfing destination. Its main draws are the variety of wave and the year-round action. Point Break, Left and Right Reef Break and waves up to 6 m can all be found during the seasons; September to February in the north and March to December in the south, though May is often ideal south of Lima.

Ocean swells are affected by two currents; the warm El Niño in the north and the cold Humboldt current in the south arriving from Antartica. **Pimentel**, near Chiclayo, is the dividing point between these two effects but a wet suit is normally required anywhere south of Piura.

The biggest wave is at **Pico Alto** (sometimes 6 m in May), south of Lima, and the largest break is 800 m at **Chicama**, near Trujillo. There are more than 30 top surfing beaches. North of Lima these include: Chicama, Pacasmayo, Punta Tur, Punta Nonura, El Golf, Cabo Blanco, Los Organos and Máncora (all left break). **South of Lima** the best beaches are: Punta Hermosa, Punta Rocas (right break) and Pico Alto (right break, best in May), the pick of the bunch; Huaico/Santa Rosa (left break), Cabo Negro (left break), Sangallán (right break); El Olón, Piedras Negras and Caleta La Cruz, all near Ilo (the first two left, La Cruz right break).

International competitions are held at Pico Alto (Balin Open in May) and Punta Rocas (during the summer months). A surfing magazine *Tablista* is published bimonthly. Also lookout for the free *X3Mag*. Useful websites are www.peruazul. com.pe, www.bodyboardperu.com and www.wannasurf.com (enter Peru in Search box for north, south, Lima and central coast). See Lima page 131.

Swimming

Peru's Pacific coastline is more than 3,000 km long. This desert shore is crossed by 52 rivers, which rush down from the Andes to create scores of fertile oases. The desert meets the ocean via hundreds of beaches ideal for lovers of water sports and fine seafood, as well as those who simply want to lie on the beach with a good book and soak up the sun after their adventures in Peru's highlands and rainforests. There are pristine stretches of fine white sand with palm tree backdrops, while other beaches are covered with round pebbles or surrounded by exotic mangroves. Not all beaches draw surfers to the powerful waves generated by the immense Pacific. Others offer calm waters ideal for swimming. The warmest water is to be found in northern Peru, southward from **Tumbes** on the **Ecuadorean border**. There are many bathing resorts near **Lima** (do not swim at, or even visit, these beaches alone), but they are pretty quiet when the winter fog descends. In the main, though, sunny skies are guaranteed throughout the year right the way down to **Tacna** on the Chilean frontier. Note that the current off the coast can be very strong, making it too dangerous to swim in places; enquire locally.

Trekking

Peru has some outstanding circuits around the Nevados. The best known are the **Llanganuco to Santa Cruz** loop, see page 346, the **Ausangate circuit** and a strenuous trek around the Huayhuash, see page 363. For treks from Caraz, see page 346, for treks from Carhuaz, see page 342, and for information on trekking in the Cordillera Blanca and Huayhuash in general, see page 325.

The other type of trekking for which Peru is justifiably renowned is walking among ruins, and, above all, for the **Inca Trail** (see page 202 and the comments on new regulations on this most popular of routes). However, there are many other walks of this type in a country rich in archaeological heritage. Some of the best are: the **valley of the Río Atuen** near Leimebamba and the entire **Chachapoyas region** (see page 451); the **Tantamayo** ruins above the Marañón; the **Cotahuasi canyon** (see page 277); and beyond Machu Picchu to **Vilcabamba** (see page 210) and **Choquequirao**. People tend to think of the Inca Trail to Machu Picchu as the only stretch of Inca roadway that can be walked. It is, however, a tiny fraction of the Incas' road network and vestiges of the Capaq Ñan (the Royal Road) can be found the length of the country. In places it is well-preserved, still in use and makes for excellent trekking. In other parts it has been lost, but new interest in the road will, it is hoped, lead to its recognition as having supreme architectural and cultural value and make it accessible for walkers and Inca enthusiasts.

Most walking is on clear trails well-trodden by *campesinos* who populate most parts of the Peruvian Andes. If you camp on their land, ask permission first and, of course, do not leave any litter. Tents, sleeping bags, mats and stoves can easily be hired in Huaraz and Cusco but check carefully for quality.

Conditions for trekking and climbing May to September is the dry season in the Cordilleras. October, November and April can be fine, particularly for trekking. Most bad weather comes from the east and temperatures plummet around twilight. The optimum months for extreme ice climbing are from late May to mid July. In early May there is a risk of avalanche from sheered neve ice layers. It is best to climb early in the day as the snow becomes slushy later on.

After July successive hot sunny days will have melted some of the main support (compacted ice) particularly on north facing slopes. On the other hand, high altitude rock climbs are less troubled by ice after July. On south facing slopes the ice and snow never consolidates quite as well.

Spectator sports

Without a doubt, the most popular sport to watch is **football** (soccer). In Lima the rivalry between the two main clubs, **Alianza** and **La U** (Universitario) is legendary, but in 2004 the Cusco side, **Ciencianos**, carried all before them. Every village, it seems, has a football pitch, even if it means comandeering the only piece of flat land for the purpose.

Most spectator sports are represented in Lima, but nothing matches the attraction of football. There is, for instance, **horse racing** (information at www.peruhipico.com) and, throughout the country, great interest in the Peruvian participatory, such as riding in the Sierra. **Bullfighting** is popular in Lima and there are two seasons, July and October to the first week in December.

Other sports that have a minority interest (in Peruvian terms) include cycling, tennis (www.tenisperu.com.pe), golf and rugby union (http://rugby7.com/peru.asp).

Cultural tourism

This covers more esoteric pursuits such as archaeology and mystical tourism. Several of the tour operators listed on page 20 offer customized packages for special interest groups. Local operators offering these more specialized tours are listed in the travelling text under the relevant location. Cultural tourism is a rapidly growing niche market. Under the umbrella heading Al-Tur, **PromPerú** has 31 interesting community-based tourism projects in archaeology, agro-tourism, education, jungle trips, llama trekking, nature tourism and traditional medicine. A CD-ROM (*Turismo Vivencial – Experiential Tourism*) and information are available from PromPeru; for details see Tourist information, page 47.

For information on specialized shamanic healing and mystical tourism, see Cusco Tour operators page 173.

The **Instituto Nacional de Cultura**, in the Museo de la Nación, see page 103, should be contacted by archaeologists for permits and information. The **Museo Nacional de Antropología y Arqueología** in Pueblo Libre, see page 103, is the centre for archaeological investigation and the Museo de la Nación holds exhibitions.

Health

It should be no surprise that the health care in the region is varied: there are some decent private and government clinics/hospitals, which more often than not follow the more aggressive American style of medicine (where you will be referred straight to a specialist) but as with all medical care, first impressions count. If a facility is grubby and staff wear grey coats instead of white ones, then be wary of the general standard of medicine and hygiene. Its worth contacting your embassy or consulate on arrival and asking where the recommended (ie those used by diplomats) clinics are. Providing embassies with information of your whereabouts can be also useful if a friend/relative gets ill at home and there is a desperate search for you around the globe. You can also ask them about locally recommended medical do's and don'ts. If you do get ill, and you have the opportunity, you should also ask your medical insurer whether they are satisfied that the medical centre or hospital that you have been referred to is of a suitable standard.

However, before discussing the disease-related health risks involved in travel within Peru remember to try to avoid road accidents. You can reduce the likelihood of accidents by not drinking and driving, wearing a seatbelt in cars and a helmet on motorbikes, but you should be aware that others on the road may think that they rea in the remake of Death Race 2000.

Ideally, you should see your GP or travel clinic at least six weeks before your departure for general advice on travel risks, malaria and vaccinations. Make sure you have travel insurance, get a dental check (especially if you are going to be away for more than a month), know your own blood group and if you suffer a long-term condition such as diabetes or epilepsy make sure someone knows or that you have a Medic Alert bracelet/necklace with this information on it.

Polio Obligatory if nil in last 10 years

Tetanus Obligatory if nil in last 10 years (but after 5 doses you have had enough for life)

Typhoid Obligatoryif nil in last 3 years

Yellow fever It is best and easiest to get vaccinated. Vaccination is recommended for travelers going outside of urban areas, most notably jungle areas below 8,200 feet (2,500 m). However, it is true that the disease risk is negligible for travel to coastal areas or to Cuzco city, Machu Picchu, any intermediate tourist points in the Urubamba Valley (the only route between Cuzco and Machu Picchu), and other Andean highland destinations such as Puno, Lake Titicaca, Arequipa, and Colca Canyon. but few travelers will have a trip that does not include risk areas.

Rabies Recommended if travelling to jungle and/or remote areas

Hepatitis A Recommended as the disease can be caught easily from food/water

Malaria

If you only visit the city of Lima or the highland tourist areas (Cuzco, Machu Picchu, Lake Titicaca) there is no known risk. However, all other areas except the following departments carry a risk: Arequipa, Moquegua, Puno, and Tacna.

The choice of malaria drug depends on where you will travel, which type of malaria you may be exposed to, and your medical/ psychological history. Always check with your doctor or travel clinic for the most up to date advice.

items to take with you

Mosquito repellents Remember that DEET (Di-ethyltoluamide) is the gold standard. Apply the repellent every four to six hours but more often if you are sweating heavily. If a non-DEET product is used check who tested it. Validated products (tested at the London School of Hygiene and Tropical Medicine) include Mosiguard, Non-DEET Jungle formula and non-DEET Autan. If you want to use citronella remember that it must be applied very frequently (ie hourly) to be effective. If you are popular target for insect bites or develop lumps quite soon after being bitten, carry an Aspivenin kit. This syringe suction device is available from many chemists and draws out some of the allergic materials and provides quick relief.

Sun Block The Australians have a great campaign, which has reduced skin cancer. It is called Slip, Slap, Slop. Slip on a shirt, Slap on a hat, Slop on sun screen.

Pain killers Paracetomol or a suitable painkiller can have multiple uses for symptoms but remember that more than eight paracetomol a day can lead to liver failure.

Ciproxin (Ciprofloaxcin) A useful antibiotic for some forms of travellers diarrhoea (see below).

Anti-malarials Important to take for the key areas. Specialist advice is required as to which type to take. General principles are that all except Malarone should be continued for four weeks after leaving the malarial area. Malarone needs to be continued for only seven days afterwards (if a tablet is missed or vomited seek specialist advice). The start times for the anti-malarials vary in that if you have never taken Lariam (Mefloquine) before it is advised to start it at least two to three weeks before the entry to a malarial zone (this is to help identify serious side-effects early). Chloroquine and Paludrine are often started a week before the trip to establish a pattern but Doxycycline and Malarone can be started only one to two days before entry to the malarial area. NB It is risky to buy medicinal tablets abroad because the doses may differ and there may be a trade in false drugs.

Immodium A great standby for those diarrhoeas that occur at awkward times (ie before a long coach/train journey or on a trek). It helps stop the flow of diarrhoea and in my view is of more benefit than harm. (It was believed that letting the bacteria or viruses flow out had to be more beneficial. However, with Immodium they still come out, just in a more solid form.)

Pepto-Bismol Used a lot by Americans for diarrhoea. It certainly relieves symptoms but like Immodium it is not a cure for underlying disease. Be aware that it turns the stool black as well as making it more solid.

MedicAlert These simple bracelets, or an equivalent, should be carried or worn by anyone with a significant medical condition.

For longer trips involving jungle treks taking a clean needle pack, clean dental pack and water filtration devices are common-sense measures.

Further information

Websites

Foreign and Commonwealth Office (FCO) (UK), www.fco.gov.uk This is a key travel advice site, with useful information on the country, people, climate and lists the UK embassies/consulates. The site also promotes the concept of 'Know Before You Go'. And encourages travel insurance and appropriate travel health advice. It has links to the Department of Health travel advice site, see below.

Department of Health Travel Advice (UK), www.doh.gov.uk/traveladvice This excellent site is also available as a free booklet, the T6, from Post Offices. It lists the vaccine advice requirements for each country.

Medic Alert (UK), www.medicalalert.co.uk This is the website of the foundation that produces bracelets and necklaces for those with existing medical problems. Once you have ordered your bracelet/necklace you write your key medical details on paper inside it, so that if you collapse, a medical person can identify you as someone with epilepsy or allergy to peanuts etc.

Blood Care Foundation (UK), www.bloodcare.org.uk The Blood Care Foundation is a Kent-based charity "dedicated to the provision of screened blood and resuscitation fluids in countries where these are not readily available." They will dispatch certified non-infected blood of the right type to your hospital/clinic. The blood is flown in from various centres around the world.

Public Health Laboratory Service (UK), www.phls.org.uk This site has up to date malaria advice guidelines for travel around the world. It gives specific advice about the right drugs for each location. It also has useful information for those who are pregnant, suffering from epilepsy or planning to travel with children.

Centers for Disease Control and Prevention (USA), www.cdc.gov This site from the US Government gives excellent advice on travel health, has useful disease maps and details of disease outbreaks.

World Health Organisation, www.who.int The WHO site has links to the WHO Blue Book (it was Yellow up to last year) on travel advice. This lists the diseases in different regions of the world. It describes vaccination schedules and makes clear which countries have Yellow Fever Vaccination certificate requirements and malarial risk.

Tropical Medicine Bureau (Ireland), www.tmb.ie This Irish based site has a good collection of general travel health information and disease risks.

Fit for Travel (UK), www.fitfortravel.scot.nhs.uk This site from Scotland provides a quick A-Z of vaccine and travel health advice requirements for each country.

British Travel Health Association (UK), www.btha.org This is the official website of an organization of travel health professionals.

NetDoctor (UK), www.Netdoctor.co.uk This general health advice site has a useful section on travel and has an "ask the expert", interactive chat forum.

Travel Screening Services (UK), www.travelscreening.co.uk This is the website of the doctor who wrote this section. A private clinic dedicated to integrated travel health. The clinic gives vaccine, travel health advice, email and SMS text vaccine reminders and screens returned travellers for tropical diseases.

Books

The Travellers Good Health Guide by Dr Ted Lankester, ISBN 0-85969-827-0. Expedition Medicine (The Royal Geographic Society) Editors David Warrell and Sarah Anderson, ISBN 1 86197 040-4. International Travel and Health World Health Organisation Geneva, ISBN 92 4 158026 7. The World's Most Dangerous Places by Robert Young Pelton, Coskun Aral and Wink Dulles, ISBN 1-566952-140-9.

Leaflets

The Travellers Guide to Health (T6) can be obtained by calling the Health Literature Line on 0800 555 777. Advice for travellers on avoiding the risks of HIV and AIDS (Travel Safe) available from Department of Health, PO Box 777, London SE1 6XH. The Blood Care Foundation order form PO Box 7, Sevenoaks, Kent TN13 2SZ T44- (0)1732-742427.

On the road

The greater disease risk in Peru is caused by the greater volume of disease carriers in the shape of mosquitoes and sandflies. The key viral disease is Dengue fever, which is transmitted by a mosquito that bites during the day. The disease is like a very nasty form of the 'flu with two to three days of illness, followed by a short period of recovery, then a second attack of illness. Westerners very rarely get the worst haemorrhagic form of the disease. Bacterial diseases include tuberculosis (TB) and some causes of the more common traveller's diarrhoea. The parasitic diseases are many but the two key ones are malaria and South American trypanosomiasis (known as Chagas Disease). The latter kills fit, young South American footballers and was recently reported to affect 3 donors who had received organs from a South American women in the USA.

Diarrhoea and intestinal upset

This is almost inevitable. One study showed that up to 70 per cent of all travellers may suffer during their trip.

Symptoms Diarrhoea can refer either to loose stools or an increased frequency; both of these can be a nuisance. It should be short lasting but persistence beyond

Cures Ciproxin (Ciprofloaxcin) is a useful antibiotic for bacterial traveller's diarrhoea. It can be obtained by private prescription in the UK which is expensive, or bought over the counter in South American pharmacies. You need to take one 500mg tablet when the diarrhoea starts and if you do not feel better in 24 hours, the diarrhoea is likely to have a non-bacterial cause and may be viral (in which case there is little you can do apart from keep yourself rehydrated and wait for it to settle on its own). The key treatment with all diarrhoeas is rehydration. Try to keep hydrated by taking the right mixture of salt and water. This is available as Oral Rehydration Salts (ORS) in ready-made sachets or can be made up by adding a teaspoon of sugar and a half teaspoon of salt to a litre of clean water. Drink at least one large cup of this drink for each loose stool. You can also use flat carbonated drinks as an alternative. Immodium and Pepto- Bismol provide symptomatic relief.

Prevention The standard advice is to be careful with water and ice for drinking. Ask yourself where the water came from. If you have any doubts then boil it or filter and treat it. There are many filter/treatment devices now available on the market. Food can also transmit disease. Be wary of salads (what were they washed in, who handled them), re-heated foods or food that has been left out in the sun having been cooked earlier in the day. There is a simple adage that says wash it, peel it, boil it or forget it. Also be wary of unpasteurized dairy products, these can transmit a range of diseases from brucellosis (fevers and constipation), to listeria (meningitis) and tuberculosis of the gut (obstruction, constipation, fevers and weight loss).

Malaria and insect bite prevention

Symptoms Malaria can cause death within 24 hours. It can start as something just resembling an attack of flu. You may feel tired, lethargic, headachy; or worse, develop fits, followed by coma and then death. Have a low index of suspicion because it is very easy to write off vague symptoms, which may actually be malaria. Whilst abroad and on return get tested as soon as possible, the test could save your life.

Cures Treatment is with drugs and may be oral or into a vein depending on the seriousness of the infection. Remember ABCD: Awareness (of whether the disease is present in the area you are travelling in), Bite avoidance, Chemoprohylaxis, Diagnosis.

Prevention This is best summarized by the B and C of the ABCD, bite avoidance and chemoprophylaxis. Wear clothes that cover arms and legs and use effective insect repellents in areas with known risks of insect-spread disease. Use a mosquito net dipped in permethrin as both a physical and chemical barrier at night in the same areas. Guard against the contraction of malaria with the correct anti-malarials (see above). Some would prefer to take test kits for malaria with them and have standby treatment available. However, the field tests of the blood kits have had poor results: when you have malaria you are usually too ill to be able to do the tests correctly enough to make the right diagnosis. Standby treatment (treatment that you carry and take yourself for malaria) should still ideally be supervised by a doctor since the drugs themselves can be toxic if taken incorrectly. The Royal Homeopathic Hospital in the UK does not advocate homeopathic options for malaria prevention or treatment.

Altitude Sickness

Symptoms This can creep up on you as just a mild headache with nausea or lethargy. The more serious disease is caused by fluid collecting in the brain in the enclosed space of the skull and can lead to coma and death. There is also a lung disease version with breathlessness and fluid infiltration of the lungs.

Cures The best cure is to descend as soon as possible.

Prevention Get acclimatized. Do not try to reach the highest levels on your first few days of arrival. Climbers like to take treatment drugs as protective measures but this can lead to macho idiocy and death. The peaks are still there and so are the trails, whether it takes you a bit longer than someone else does not matter as long as you come back down alive.

Underwater health

Symptoms If you go diving make sure that you are fit do so. The British Scuba Association (BSAC), Telford's Quay, South Pier Road, Ellesmere Port, Cheshire CH65 4FL, United Kingdom, T01513-506200, F01513-506215, www.bsac.com, can put you in touch with doctors who do medical examinations. Protect your feet from cuts, beach dog parasites (larva migrans) and sea urchins. The latter are almost impossible to remove but can be dissolved with lime or vinegar. Keep an eye out for secondary infection.

Cures Antibiotics for secondary infections. Serious diving injuries may need time in a decompression chamber.

Prevention Check that the dive company know what they are doing, have appropriate certification from BSAC or Professional Association of Diving Instructors (PADI) ① *Unit 7, St Philips Central, Albert Rd, St Philips, Bristol, BS2 0TD, T0117-3007234, www.padi.com*, and that the equipment is well maintained.

Sun protection

Symptoms White Britons are notorious for becoming red in hot countries because they like to stay out longer than everyone else and do not use adequate sun protection. This can lead to sunburn, which is painful and followed by flaking of skin. Aloe vera gel is a good pain reliever for sunburn. Long-term sun damage leads to a loss of elasticity of skin and the development of pre-cancerous lesions. Many years later a mild or a very malignant form of cancer may develop. The milder basal cell carcinoma, if detected early, can be treated by cutting it out or freezing it. The much nastier malignant melanoma may have already spread to bone and brain at the time that it is first noticed.

Prevention Sun screen. SPF stands for Sun Protection Factor. It is measured by determining how long a given person takes to "burn" with and without the sunscreen product on. So, if it takes 10 times longer to burn with the sunscreen product applied, then that product has an SPF of 10. If it only takes twice as long then the SPF is 2. The higher the SPF the greater the protection. However, do not just use higher factors just to stay out in the sun longer. 'Flash frying' (desperate bursts of excessive exposure), as it is called, is known to increase the risks of skin cancer. Follow the Australians' with their Slip, Slap, Slop campaign.

Dengue fever

Symptoms This disease can be contracted throughout South America. In travellers this can cause a severe 'flu-like illness which includes symptoms of fever, lethargy, enlarged lymph glands and muscle pains. It starts suddenly, lasts for 2-3 days, seems to get better for 2-3 days and then kicks in again for another 2-3 days. It is usually all over in an unpleasant week. The local children are prone to the much nastier haemorrhagic form of the disease, which causes them to bleed from internal organs, mucous membranes and often leads to their death.

Cures The traveller's version of the disease is self limiting and forces rest and recuperation on the sufferer.

Prevention The mosquitoes that carry the Dengue virus bite during the day unlike the malaria mosquitoes. Which sadly means that repellent application and covered limbs are a 24 hour issue. Check your accommodation for flower pots and shallow pools of water since these are where the dengue-carrying mosquitoes breed.

Hepatitis

Symptoms Hepatitis means inflammation of the liver. Viral causes of the disease can be acquired anywhere in South America. The most obvious symptom is a yellowing of your skin or the whites of your eyes. However, prior to this all that you may notice is itching and tiredness.

Cures Early on, depending on the type of hepatitis, a vaccine or immunoglobulin may reduce the duration of the illness.

Prevention Pre-travel hepatitis A vaccine is the best bet. Hepatitis B (for which there is a vaccine) is spread through blood and unprotected sexual intercourse, both of these can be avoided. Unfortunately there is no vaccine for hepatitis C or the increasing alphabetical list of other Hepatitis viruses.

Leishmaniasis

Symptoms A skin form of this disease occurs in Peru. If infected, you may notice a raised lump, which leads to a purplish discoloration on white skin and a possible ulcer. The parasite is transmitted by the bite of a sandfly. Sandflies do not fly very far and the greatest risk is at ground levels, so if you can avoid sleeping on the jungle floor, do so. There is another rarer form which is caused by a sub species of the parasite, this affects the musocal tissues such as lips and nose. Treatment and mode of transmission are the same.

Cures Several weeks treatment is required under specialist supervision. The drugs are toxic but if not taken in sufficient amounts, recurrence of the disease is more likely.

Prevention Sleep above ground, under a permethrin treated net, use insect repellent and get a specialist opinion on any unusual skin lesions as soon as you can.

Schistosomiasis

A fluke is a sort of flattened worm. Schistosomiasis can be acquired through wading through stagnant water and swimming in such waters.

Symptoms The liver fluke may cause jaundice, gall stone symptoms, right-sided abdominal pain, liver test abnormalities and changes in the white cell pattern of the blood. Schistosomiasis can cause a local skin itch at first exposure, fever after a few weeks and much later diarrhoea, abdominal pain and spleen or liver enlargement.

Cures A single drug cures Schistosomiasis. The same dug can be used for the liver fluke but this infestation is much more difficult to treat.

Prevention Avoid infected waters, be careful with unwashed vegetables check the CDC, WHO websites and a travel clinic specialist for up-to-date information on the whereabouts of the disease.

Chagas Disease

Symptoms The disease occurs throughout South America, affects locals more than travellers, but travellers can be exposed by sleeping in mud-constructed huts where the bug that carries the parasite bites and defaecates on an exposed part of skin. You may notice nothing at all or a local swelling, with fever, tiredness and enlargement of lymph glands, spleen and liver. The seriousness of the parasite infection is caused by the long-term effects which include gross enlargement of the heart and/or guts.

Cures Early treatment is required with toxic drugs.

Prevention Sleep under a permethrin treated bed net and use insect repellents.

Sexual Health

The range of visible and invisible diseases is awesome. Unprotected sex can spread HIV, Hepatitis B and C, Gonorrhea (green discharge), chlamydia (nothing to see but may cause painful urination and later female infertility), painful recurrent herpes, syphilis and warts, just to name a few. You can cut down the risk by using condoms, a femidom or avoiding sex altogether. Consider getting a sexual health check on your return home.

Keeping in touch

Details of organizations which can help you sort out any problems or give advice, such as **South American Explorers**, **British Council** and **Alliance Française**, or addresses of embassies and consulates, can be found in the Lima and Cusco 'Ins and outs' and 'Directories'.

Internet and email

You can find internet access everywhere. Centres with high tourism have internet cafés on every corner; many of them have net2phone. Internet cafés are listed in the travelling text under each town, except where there are too many to mention, like Lima. Internet cafés are incredibly cheap to use, normally about US$0.50 per hour. When they first open in the morning is often a good time to use cyber cafés, as they are less busy then. Access is generally quick. Internet access is more expensive in hotel business centres and in out of the way places.

Post

The name of the postal system is **Serpost**. Sending parcels and mail can be done at any post office but Correo Central on the Plaza de Armas in Lima is the best place. The office is open Monday to Friday from 0800 to 1800. Stamps, envelopes and cloth sacks (to send bigger parcels in) can all be bought there. It costs US$1 to mail a letter up to 20 g anywhere in the Americas, US$1.50 to Europe and US$1.70 to Australia. You can also mail letters *expreso* for about US$0.55, extra to the Americas, US$0.90 to the rest of the world, and they will arrive a little more quickly. Don't put tape on envelopes or packages, wait until you get to the post office and use the glue they have. It is very expensive to mail large packages out of Peru so it is best not to plan to send things home from here. For emergency or important documents, DHL and Federal Express are also options in Lima (check in city of Lima section for addresses).

To receive mail, letters can be sent to Poste Restante/General Delivery (*lista de correos*), your embassy, or, for cardholders, American Express offices. Members of the **South American Explorers** can have post and packages sent to them at either of the Peruvian offices. Remember that there is no W in Spanish; look under V, or ask. For the smallest risk of misunderstanding, use title, initial and surname only. If having items sent to you by courier (eg DHL), do not use poste restante, but an address such as a hotel: a signature is required on receipt. Try not to have articles sent by post to Peru – taxes can be 200 per cent of the value.

Telephone

The main service provider is **Telefónica**, www.telefonica.com.pe, (or **Telser** in Cusco) which has offices in all large and medium-sized towns. **Telefónica** offices are usually administrative and phones are provided on the street outside. Local, national and international calls can be made from public phone boxes with prepaid phone cards. Remove the card from its plastic covering (which should not be broken) and, on the back, scratch off the dark grey strip to reveal the card's number. You have to dial this number when told to do so by the operator. Cards can be bought at **Telefónica** offices or the many private phone offices. Also on sale in larger towns are cards for a number of other carriers for long distance calls, such as **Americatel, InkaNet, Peru Golbal** and **Tel Mex**. Their rates are very competitive and there are usually special offers. Each carrier has a prefix code which you must dial, as well as the card's secret code. Not every phone takes cards; **Telefónica**, for instance, has its own phones for its 147 service (national and international). The SuperPlus 147 card for one long-distance call is very good value at S/.20 (US$5.70) for 48 minutes. You can also use coins to make calls: from public phones it costs US$1 per minute to North America, US$1.40 to Europe and US$1.50 to Australia and New Zealand. Collect calls are possible to almost anywhere by ringing the international operator (108). This service also has the numbers for international direct options and they speak English. Your home telephone company can give you the number to call as well. Net Phones are popular; costs and service vary but can be as cheap as US$5 per hour to the USA. Calls to everywhere else are usually at least 50 per cent more. Faxes cost about US$1.50 per page to North America, US$2 to most of Western Europe and US$2.50 to Israel. The cost to receive is about US$1 per page. In smaller towns, you may have to hunt around for a phone booth that will permit international calls.

There are three mobile networks in Peru, **Telefónica Movistar**, **TIM** and **Bellsouth**. *Telefónica* has the most extensive network. Mobile phones brought into Peru which operate at 800 mhz may be activated at a *Telefónica* technical services office. *TIM* phones from Europe will operate in Peru, but calls cannot be diverted to another line if the phone number dialled is unanswered. *Bellsouth* uses TDMA technology and their technical staff would have to see a foreign phone to verify its compatibility. European mobiles are not compatible with *Bellsouth*. If you need to have a mobile phone, it's best to buy one locally. All three companies sell phones, which take prepaid cards, special offers start as low as US$45. All mobile phone numbers are prefixed by 9.

Media

Newspapers Lima has several daily papers. The most informative are *El Comercio* and *La República*. *El Comercio* is good for international news and has a near monopoly on classified ads. It also has a good weekly tourism section. *La República* takes a more liberal-left approach and contains the *Crónica Judicial*. Its weekly tourism section, *Andares*, is recommended. Among the others are *Expreso* and *Ojo*. *Gestión* is a business daily. Very popular are the sensationalist papers, written in raunchy slang and featuring acres of bare female flesh on their pages. The main provincial cities have at least one newspaper each. There are a number of websites which provide regular news updates: **El Comercio** www.elcomercioperu.com.pe/; **Expreso**, www.expreso.com.pe; **Gestión** www.gestion.com.pe/; **La República**, www.larepublica.com.pe. The following also have access to the daily news: www.limapost.com, www.terra.com.pe, www.peru.com

Magazines The most widely read magazine is the weekly news magazine *Caretas*, which gives a very considered angle on current affairs and is often critical of government policy, www.caretas.com.pe A bi-monthly magazine called *Rumbos* (English and Spanish together) is a good all-round 'what's happening in Peru' magazine, Monthlies include *Business*, *Proceso Económico*, *Debate* and *Idede*. There is a weekly economic and political magazine in English, the *Andean Report*, with useful information and articles.

Radio Radio is far more important in imparting news to Peruvians than newspapers, partly due to the fact that limited plane routes make it difficult to get papers to much of the population on the same day. There are countless local and community radio stations which cover even the most far-flung places. The most popular stations are *Radioprogramas del Perú* (www.rpp.com.pe), which features round-the-clock news, and *Cadena Peruana de Noticias* (www.cpnradio.com.pe).

A shortwave (world band) radio offers a practical means to brush up on the language, keep abreast of current events, sample popular culture and absorb some of the richly varied regional music. International broadcasters such as the **BBC World Service**, the **Voice of America**, Boston (Mass)-based **Monitor Radio International** (operated by *Christian Science Monitor*) and the Quito-based Evangelical station, **HCJB**, keep the traveller informed in both English and Spanish.

Essentials Keeping in touch

Compact or miniature portables are recommended, with digital tuning and a full range of shortwave bands, as well as FM, long and medium wave. Advice on models (£150 for a decent one) and wavelengths can be found in the *Passport to World Band Radio* (Box 300, Penn's Park, PA 18943, USA, £12.25). Details of local stations are listed in *World Radio TV Handbook*, PO Box 9027, 1006 AA Amsterdam, The Netherlands, £15.50 (www.amazon.co.uk prices). Both of these, free wavelength guides and selected radio sets are available from the BBC World Service Bookshop, Bush House Arcade, Bush House, Strand, London WC2B 4PH, UK, T020-7557 2576.

TV Many hotels include televisions in rooms, the more expensive the hotel, the more cable channels there will be on the set. There will almost certainly be US channels, often the BBC, Italian and occasionally German channels. You can find movies, sports, music, nature/discovery and news (CNN in both English and Spanish). Local channels include América Televisión (www.americatv.com.pe), Cable Mágico (www.cablemagico.com.pe), Frecuencia Latina (www.frecuencialatina.com.pe) and 24 Horas (www.24horas.com.pe).

● Footprint features

Introduction

The well-established cliché is to call Lima a city of contradictions, but it's difficult to get beyond that description. Here you'll encounter grinding poverty and conspicuous wealth in abundance. The hardships of the poor in this sprawling metropolis of 8,000,000 inhabitants are all too evident in the lives of those struggling to get by in the crowded streets and frantic bus lanes. The rubbish-strewn districts between airport and city and, even more so, the shantytowns on the outskirts emphasize the vast divisions within society. Most visitors, though, have the option of heading for Miraflores, San Isidro or Barranco, where smart restaurants and elegant hotels rub shoulders with pre-Inca pyramids, and neat parks and the cliff-top Larcomar shopping centre overlook the ocean. Lima's image as a place to avoid or quickly pass through is enhanced by the thick grey blanket of cloud that descends in May and hangs around for the next seven months. Wait until the blanket is pulled aside in November to reveal bright blue skies and suddenly all Limeños descend on the city's popular coastal resorts. Weekends then become a raucous mix of sun, sea, salsa and ceviche. Lima can also entertain, excite and inform. It boasts some of the finest historical monuments and museums in the country. The colonial centre, with its grand Plaza de Armas, fine churches and beautiful wooden balconies, is one of Peru's ten UNESCO World Heritage sites and strenuous efforts are being made to refurbish the historical districts. The city's cuisine has earned it the title 'Gastronomic Capital of the Americas' and the bars, discos and peñas of Barranco and Miraflores ring to the sounds of everything from techno to traditional music. Scratch beneath that coating of grime and decay and you'll find one of the most vibrant and hospitable cities anywhere.

★ Don't miss...

1 **Plaza de Armas** Step into the main square and try to imagine the days when it was the headquarters of Spain's South American empire, page 95.
2 **San Francisco** One of the city's original churches, with some beautiful decorations and a set of ghoulish catacombs, page 98.
3 **Barranco** Another side of Lima and a must to visit for its nightlife and its fashionable modern art galleries, page 109.
4 **Larcomar** Looking for something contemporary? Here are shops, entertainment and watering holes carved out of the cliffs, page 108.
5 **Parque del Amor** One of Lima's most romantic places with its giant statue of lovers kissing and its view of the sea. If inspired to fly you can go parapenting nearby, page 108.
6 **Pachacámac** Escape from the rush of the traffic at this vast pre-Columbian ceremonial centre, rescued from the desert sands. In the museum look for the statue that was the heart of the cult, page 113.
7 **Rosa Náutica** For the ultimate, nostalgic dining experience, come to this restaurant on an old pier jutting into the Pacific, page 123.
8 **Petit Thouars market** Overload yourself with handicrafts in the largest concentration of typical goods in the country, page 130.

Lima

Ins and outs → *Phone code: 01. Colour map 5, grid A1. Population: 8,000,000.*

Getting there

All **international flights** land at Jorge Chávez Airport, some 16 km west of the centre of the city. It is a little further to Miraflores and Barranco. Transport into town is easy if a bit expensive. Remise taxis (Mitsui or CMV) have representatives at desks outside International Arrivals and National Arrivals, US$7.25 to San Miguel, US$11.75 to the city centre, US$14.50 to San Isidro and Miraflores, US$17.50 to Barranco. This is the safest option, but also the most expensive. There are many taxi drivers offering their services outside Arrivals. Regular taxis do not use meters, so make sure you fix the price before getting in and insist on being taken to the hotel of your choice, not the driver's. An illuminated sign outside the airport shows official taxi charges and there is usually a policeman monitoring the taxis. It helps to have exact change in soles to avoid having to break a large bill along the way. If you are feeling confident and not too jet-lagged, go to the car park exit and find a taxi outside the perimeter, by the roundabout. They charge US$3 to the city centre. The security guards may help you find a taxi. All vehicles can enter the airport for 10 minutes at no charge. After that, it's S/.3.50 (US$1) every 30 minutes. Taxis that have been waiting for more than the allotted free time will try to make the passenger pay the toll upon leaving the airport. Always establish who will pay before getting in.

There is a bus service, Urbanito, from the airport to the centre, Breña and San Miguel US$3, Pueblo Libre, San Isidro and Miraflores US$5 (slow, calling at all hotels), T01-424 3650, T9957 3238 (mob), urbanito@terra.com.pe. Local buses (US$0.35) and *colectivos* run between the airport perimeter and the city centre and suburbs. Their routes are given on the front window: 'Tacna' for the centre, 'Miraflores' for Miraflores. Outside the pedestrian exit are the bus, *colectivo* and taxi stops, but there is more choice for buses at the roundabout by the car entrance. At busy times (which is anytime other than very late at night or early morning) luggage may not be allowed on buses. Do not take the cheapest, stopping buses which go to the city centre along Avenida Faucett. They are frequently robbed. Pay a little more for a non-stopping bus.

All hire companies have offices at the airport. The larger international chains, **Avis, Budget, Dollar, Hertz**, are usually cheaper and have better-maintained vehicles than local firms. The airport in Lima is the best, most cost-effective place to arrange car hire.

If you arrive in Lima by **bus**, it is likely you'll pull into the main terminal at Jr Carlos Zavala, just south of the historical centre of Lima. Take a taxi to your hotel even if it's close, as this area is not safe day or night. Some of the high-class bus companies have terminals in safer areas. ▸▸ *For further details, see Transport page 134.*

Arriving at night

Barring delays, there are usually no flight arrivals between 0100 and 0530. (There are money-changing facilities and information services to meet all flights.) However, as check-in time is supposed to be three hours before an international flight, and many flights depart from 0600 onwards, the airport starts to wake up between 0300 and 0400. No matter what time of night or day, though, there are people offering taxi rides into town and, as there are no hotels in the immediate vicinity of the airport, you must take some form of transport to get a bed and somewhere to stow your bags. Your best bet is to decide on a hotel before you even get to Lima. Most will arrange to pick you up from the airport, either free as part of the room rate, or for a fee of between US$12 and US$20 (depending on the category of hotel and how many people are in the vehicle). If you haven't arranged a room, don't leave the airport perimeter to find a public taxi or bus in the dark. The expensive remises services or the official taxis are the safest option. If you wish to stay in the airport until first light, the airport has seating areas, but you will have to leave the international arrivals zone and either take the stairs between international and national concourses, or ask if you can enter the national zone to find the seating there. The airport is safe.

Getting around

Downtown Lima can be explored on foot in the daytime, but take all the usual precautions. The central hotels are fairly close to the many of the tourist sites. At night taxis are a safer option. Miraflores is about 15 km south of the centre. Many of the better hotels and restaurants are located here and in neighbouring San Isidro.

The Lima public transportation system, at first glance very intimidating, is actually quite good. There are three different types of vehicles that will stop whenever flagged down: buses, combis, and *colectivos*. They can be distinguished by size; big and long, mid-size and mini-vans or cars, respectively. The flat-rate fare for the first two types of vehicle is US$0.35, the third cost a little more. On public holidays, Sunday and from 2400 to 0500 every night, a small charge is added to the fare. Always try to pay with change to avoid hassles, delays and dirty looks from the *cobrador* (driver's assistant). Routes on any public transportation vehicle are posted on windscreens with coloured stickers. Destinations written on the side of any vehicle should be ignored. ▸▸ For further details, see Transport page 134.

Best time to visit

Only 12° south of the equator, you would expect a tropical climate, but Lima has two distinct seasons. The winter is from May-November, when a damp *garúa* (sea mist) hangs over the city, making everything look greyer than it is already. It is damp and cold, 8° to 15°C. The sun breaks through around November and temperatures rise as high as 30°C. Note that the temperature in the coastal suburbs is lower than the centre because of the sea's influence. You should protect yourself against the sun's rays when visiting the beaches around Lima, or elsewhere in Peru.

Tourist information

i perú has offices at ① *Jorge Chávez International Airport, T01-574 8000, open 24 hrs a day; Casa Basadre, Av Jorge Basadre 610, San Isidro, T01-421 1627, Mon-Fri 0830-1830; Larcomar shopping centre, Módulo 14, Plaza Gourmet, Miraflores, T01-445 9400, Mon-Fri 1200-2000.* **Info Perú** ① *Jr de la Unión (Belén) 1066, of 102,*

Impressions of Lima

Ever since the earthquake of 1746 all but razed the city to the ground, descriptions of Lima have tended towards the unfavourable.

Take the German naturalist and traveller, Alexander Von Humboldt, for instance, who considered life in the city to be tedious with its lack of diversions, and described touring round the capital in 1802 thus: "the filthyness of the streets, strewn with dead dogs and donkeys, and the unevenness of the ground make it impossible to enjoy." Charles Darwin, who made a short visit in 1839 during his historic research trip on the Beagle, was no less graphic in his appraisal. He found it "in a wretched state of decay; the streets are nearly unpaved and heaps of filth are piled up in all directions where black vultures pick up bits of carrion."

Rather more complimentary was Jean Jacques Tschudi, the Swiss naturalist who made extensive explorations in Peru. He wrote: "The impression produced at first sight of Lima is by no means favourable, for the periphery, the quarter which the stranger first enters, contains none but old, dilapidated and dirty homes; but on approaching the vicinity of the principal square, the place improves so greatly that the miserable appearance it presents at first sight is easily forgotten."

The French feminist, Flora Tristan, who was Paul Gauguin's grandmother, came to Peru in 1834. She travelled extensively in the country and wrote a fascinating account of her experience, Peregrinaciones de una Paria, in which she painted Lima in a most favourable light: "The city has many beautiful monuments", she wrote, "The homes are neatly constructed, the streets well marked out, are long and wide." Paul Gauguin himself spent his early formative years in Lima, where he was brought by his parents who were fleeing Napoleon Bonaparte's France. Towards the end of his life Gauguin wrote a collection of memoirs in which he included his impressions of Lima.

T01-424 7963, infoperu@qnet.com.pe, Mon-Fri 0930-1800, Sat 0930-1400, is a very helpful office with lots of good advice, English, French spoken. Ask for the helpful, free, Peru Guide published in English by Lima Editora ① T01-444 0815, available at travel agencies or other tourist organizations.

As much an agency as tourist office, but highly recommended nonetheless is Siduith Ferrer Herrera, CEO of Fertur Perú ① Jr Junín 211, Plaza de Armas, T01-427 1958; Schell 485, Miraflores, T01-445 1974, http://ferturperu.tripod.com, 0900-1900. Her agency not only offers up to date, correct tourist information on a national level, but also great prices on national and international flights, discounts for those with ISIC and Youth cards and South American Explorers members (of which she is one). Other services include flight reconfirmations, hotel reservations, transfers to and from the airport or bus stations and book exchange at the Junín branch.

South American Explorers ① Piura 135, Miraflores (Casilla 3714, Lima 100), T/F01-445 3306, T800 274 0568 (USA), www.SAexplorers.org, Mon-Fri 0930-1700 (till 2000 on Wed) and Sat 0930-1300. SAE is a non-profit educational organization which functions as a travel resource centre for South America and is widely recognized as the best place to get the most up to date information regarding everything from travel advisories to volunteer opportunities. A yearly membership is currently US$50 per person and US$80 per couple. Services include access to member-written trip reports, a full map room for reference, an extensive library in English and a book exchange. Members are welcome to use the SAE's PO Box for receiving post and can store luggage

66 99 There were few cities in the Old World that could rival Lima's wealth and luxury, until the terrible earthquake of 1746. The city's notable elegance was instantly reduced to dust...

as well as valuables in their very secure deposit space. SAE sells official maps from the Instituto Geografico Nacional, SAE-produced trekking maps, used equipment and a large variety of Peruvian crafts. Note that all imported merchandise sold at SAE is reserved for members only, no exceptions. They host regular presentations on various topics ranging from jungle trips to freedom of the press. SAE also offers a discount in membership fees to researchers, archaeologists and scientists in exchange for information and/or presentations. If you're looking to study Spanish in Peru, hoping to travel down the Amazon or in search of a quality Inca Trail tour company, they have the information you'll need to make it happen. South American Explorers, apart from the services mentioned above, is simply a great place to step out of the hustle and bustle of Lima and delight in the serenity of a cup of tea, a magazine and good conversation with a fellow traveller. SAE has other clubhouses in Cusco, Quito (Ecuador) and Ithaca, New York. Headquarters are located in the USA ① *126 Indian Creek Rd, Ithaca, NY, 14850, T607 277 0488, www.SAexplorers.org*. Official representatives in UK: **Bradt Publications** ① *19 High St, Chalfont St Peters, Bucks, SL9 9QE, T01753-893444, info@bradtguides.com*. If signing up in UK allow four to six weeks for receipt of membership card.

Background

Lima, originally named *La Ciudad de Los Reyes*, The City of Kings, in honour of the Magi, was founded on Epiphany in 1535 by Francisco Pizarro. From then until the independence of the South American republics in the early 19th century, it was the chief city of Spanish South America. The name Lima, a corruption of the Quechua name *Rimac* (speaker), was not adopted until the end of the 16th century.

At the time of the Conquest, Lima was already an important commercial centre. It continued to grow throughout the colonial years and by 1610, the population was 26,000, of whom 10,000 were Spaniards. This was the time of greatest prosperity. The commercial centre of the city was just off the Plaza de Armas in the Calle de Mercaderes (first block of Jr de la Unión) and was full of merchandise imported from Spain, Mexico and China. All the goods from the mother country arrived at the port of Callao, from where they were distributed all over Peru and as far away as Argentina.

At this time South American trade with Spain was controlled by a monopoly of Sevillian merchants and their Limeño counterparts who profited considerably. It wasn't until the end of the 18th century that free trade was established between Spain and her colonies, allowing Peru to enjoy a period of relative wealth. Much of this wealth was reinvested in the country, particularly in Lima where educational establishments benefitted most of all.

Ever since **Francis Drake** made a surprise attack on Callao on the night of 13 February 1579, plans were made to strengthen the city's defences against the threat from English pirates. However, an argument raged over the following century between Spain and Lima as to what form the defences should take and who should pay. Finally, it was agreed to encircle the city with a wall, which was completed by 1687.

Life for the white descendants of the Spaniards was good, although *criollos* (Spaniards born in the colonies) were not allowed to hold public office in Peru. The Indians and those of mixed blood were treated as lesser citizens. Their movements were strictly controlled. They weren't allowed to live in the city centre; only in areas allocated to them, referred to as *reducciones*.

There were few cities in the Old World that could rival Lima's wealth and luxury, until the terrible earthquake of 1746. The city's notable elegance was instantly reduced to dust. Only 20 of the 3,000 houses were left standing and an estimated 4,000 people were killed. Despite the efforts of the Viceroy, José Manso de Velasco, to rebuild the city, Lima never recovered her former glory. During the 19th century man-made disasters rather than natural ones wreaked havoc on the capital and its people. The population dropped from 87,000 in 1810 to 53,000 in 1842, after the wars of Independence, and the city suffered considerable material damage during the Chilean occupation which followed the War of the Pacific.

Lima was built on both banks of the Rímac river. The walls erected at the end of the 17th century surrounded three sides while the Rímac bordered the fourth. By the time the North American railway engineer, Henry Meiggs, was contracted to demolish the city walls in 1870, Lima had already begun to spread outside the original limits. Meiggs reneged on his contract by leaving much of the wall intact in the poor area around Cercado, where the ruins can still be seen.

By the beginning of the 20th century the population had risen to 140,000 and the movement of people to the coastal areas meant that unskilled cheap labour was available to man the increasing numbers of factories. Around this time, major improvements were made to the city's infrastructure in the shape of modern sanitation, paved streets, new markets and plazas. For the entertainment of the

Lima

Related maps
A Lima centre, page 96
B San Isidro, page 104
C Miraflores, page 107
D Barranco, page 110

0 km 2	**Sleeping**	Hostal Bait Sababa **4**	Mami Panchita **3**
0 miles 2	Guest House Marfil **5**	Hostal Residencial Víctor **2**	

middle classes, a modern race track was opened in what is now the Campo de Marte, as well as the municipal theatre, the Teatro Segura. At the same time, the incumbent president, José Pardo, dramatically increased government expenditure on education, particularly in Lima.

Large-scale municipal improvements continued under the dictatorship of Augusto Leguía and the presidency of Oscar Benavides, who focussed on education for the masses, housing facilities for workers and low cost restaurants in the slum areas which were now growing up around Lima.

Lima, a city of over 8,000,000 people, continues to struggle to live up to its former reputation as the City of Kings. This has involved drastic changes in the last few years. The commercial heart has moved away from the centre of town and has taken root in more upmarket districts such as Miraflores and San Isidro. After suffering serious decline, the old centre is benefitting from great efforts to clean it up and is reestablishing itself as a place to visit. The city can, however, be seriously affected by smog at certain times of the year. It is also surrounded by *Pueblos Jóvenes*, or shanty settlements of squatters who have migrated from all parts of Peru looking for work and education (see box, page 112).

Sights

When Alberto Andrade Carmona became Mayor of Lima in 1995, he began a campaign to return the historical centre to its original beauty. This meant ejecting the ambulantes (street sellers), cleaning of the streets and sidewalks, and rehabilitation of the Plaza de Armas and Plaza San Martín. He also mounted a security force called Serenazgo to enforce public safety and order. These men are recognizable by their dark jump-suits, long night sticks, and riot gear. The municipality of Lima has also begun a time-consuming balcony restoration project, soliciting businesses and citizens to take on the financial responsibility of a balcony in need. Although many buildings in the centre are not maintained, their architectural beauty and importance is still visible and worth seeing. ▸▸ *For Sleeping, Eating and other listings, see pages 114-142.*

Central Lima

Plaza de Armas

One block south of the Río Rímac lies the Plaza de Armas, which has been declared a World Heritage site by UNESCO. The plaza used to be the city's most popular meeting point and main market. Before the building of the Acho bullring in the 1760s, bullfights were traditionally held here.

Around the great Plaza de Armas stand the **Palacio de Gobierno**, the **Cathedral**, the **Archbishop's Palace**, the **Municipalidad** and the **Club Unión**. In the centre of the plaza is a bronze fountain dating from 1650. The flower beds are planted with blooms whose colours reflect the city's celebrations, eg red and white at Independence in July, purple at El Señor de los Milagros in October.

Lima centre

Related maps
Lima, page 94
San Isidro, page 104
Miraflores, page 107
Barranco, page 110

Sleeping	Hostal Roma	Eating	Manhatten 10
El Balcón Dorado 1	& Café Carrara 9	Accllahuasy 1	Natur 11
Europa 2	Hostal San Francisco 10	Chifa Wa Lok 3	Salon Capon 12
Familia Rodríguez 3	Kamana 11	Cordano 4	San Martín 14
Granada 6	La Posada del Parque 12	El Maurito 5	
Gran Hotel Continental 4	Lima Sheraton 13	Govinda 6	
Gran Hotel Savoy 5	Maury 14	Heydi 7	
Hostal Belén 7	Pensión Ibarra 15	L'Eau Vive & Antaño 8	
Hostal España 8	Plaza Francia Inn 16	Machu Picchu 9	

⁝ The streets

Several blocks, with their own names, make up a long street, and is called a jirón (often abbreviated to Jr). You will be greatly helped by the corner signs which bear both names, of the jirón and the name of the block. The new and old names of streets are used interchangeably: remember that Colmena is also Nicolás de Piérola, Wilson is Inca Garcilaso de la Vega, and Carabaya is also Augusto N Wiese.

Palacio de Gobierno

ⓘ *To take a tour register a day in advance on T01-311 3908, or at the office of public relations, Edificio Palacio 269, oficina 201 (ask guard for directions), tours are in Spanish and English Mon-Fri, 0845 and 0945, Sat 0900, 1000, 1100, 45 mins, free.*

The Government Palace stands on the site of the original palace built by Pizarro. When the Viceroyalty was founded it became the official residence of the representative of the crown. Despite the opulent furnishings inside, the exterior remained a poor sight throughout colonial times, with shops lining the front facing the plaza. The façade was remodelled in the second half of the 19th century, then transformed in 1921, following a terrible fire. In 1937, the palace was totally rebuilt. The changing of the guard is at 1200.

The Cathedral

ⓘ *T01-427 9647, Mon-Sat 0900-1630, all-inclusive entrance ticket is US$1.50.*

The Cathedral stands on the site of two previous buildings. The first, finished in 1555, was partly paid for by Francisca Pizarro on the condition that her father, the *Conquistador*, was buried there. A larger church, however, was soon required to complement the city's status as an Archbishopric. In 1625, the three naves of the main building were completed while work continued on the towers and main door. The new building was reduced to rubble in the earthquake of 1746 and the existing church, completed in 1755, is a reconstruction on the lines of the original.

The interior is immediately impressive, with its massive columns and high nave. Also of note are the splendidly carved stalls (mid-17th century), the silver-covered altars surrounded by fine woodwork, mosaic-covered walls bearing the coats of arms of Lima and Pizarro and an allegory of Pizarro's commanders, the 'Thirteen Men of Isla del Gallo'. The assumed remains of Francisco Pizarro lie in a small chapel, the first on the right of the entrance, in a glass coffin, though later research indicates that they reside in the crypt. There is a **Museo de Arte Religioso** in the cathedral, with free guided tours (English available, give tip), ask to see the picture restoration room.

Next to the cathedral is the **Archbishop's Palace**, rebuilt in 1924, with a superb wooden balcony.

Around the Municipalidad

Just behind the Municipalidad de Lima is **Pasaje Ribera el Viejo**, which has been restored and now is a pleasant place to hang out with several good cafés with outdoor seating. **Museo Filatélico** ⓘ *off Plaza de Armas, Mon-Sun 0815-1300, 1400-1800, free*, in the central post office (correo) contains an incomplete collection of Peruvian stamps and information on the Inca postal system. There is a stamp exchange in front of the museum every Saturday and Sunday, 0900-1300. You can buy stamps here as well, particularly commemorative issues.

Casa Aliaga ⓘ *Unión 224, T01-424 5110, tours only through Lima Tours*, is still occupied by the Aliaga family but has been opened to the public. It contains what is said to be the oldest ceiling in Lima and is furnished entirely in the colonial style. Don

Lima Central Lima

Jerónimo de Aliaga was one of the 13 commanders to arrive with Francisco Pizarro and all 13 were given land around the main square to build their own houses when Lima was founded in 1535.

Santo Domingo

① *Church and monastery on the first block of Jr Camaná, T01-427 6793, Mon-Sat 0900-1230, 1500-1800, Sun and holidays, mornings only, US$0.75.*

Built in 1549, the church is still as originally planned with a nave and two aisles covered by a vaulted ceiling, though the present ceiling dates from the 17th century. The cloister is one of the most attractive in the city and dates from 1603. The second cloister is much less elaborate. A chapel, dedicated to San Martín de Porres, one of Peru's most revered saints, leads off from a side corridor. Between the two cloisters is the Chapter House (1730), which was once the premises of the Universidad de San Marcos. Beneath the sacristy are the tombs of San Martín de Porres and Santa Rosa de Lima (see below). In 1669, Pope Clement presented the alabaster statue of Santa Rosa in front of the altar. The Basílica de La Veracruz is open lunchtimes. The main hall has some interesting relics.

Behind Santo Domingo is **Alameda Chabuca Granda**, named after one of Peru's greatest singers and composers. In the evening there are free art and music shows and you can sample food and sweets from all over Peru.

A couple of blocks beyond Santo Domingo is **Casa de Oquendo** or **Osambela** ① *Conde de Superunda 298*. It is said that José de San Martín stayed after proclaiming independence from Spain. The house is typical of Lima secular architecture with two patios and a broad staircase leading from the first to the upper floor.

San Francisco and around

① *Church and monastery stand on the first block of Jr Lampa, corner of Ancash, T01-4271381, daily 0930-1730, US$1.50, US$0.50 children, guided tours only.*

The baroque church, which was finished in 1674, was one of the few edifices to withstand the 1746 earthquake. The nave and aisles are lavishly decorated in the Moorish, or Mudéjar, style. The choir, which dates from 1673, is notable for its beautifully-carved seats in Nicaraguan hardwood and its Mudéjar ceiling. There is a valuable collection of paintings by the Spanish artist, Francisco de Zuburán (1598-1664), which depict the apostles and various saints.

The monastery is famous for the Sevillian tilework and panelled ceiling in the cloisters (1620). The 17th-century *retablos* in the main cloister are carved from cedar and represent scenes from the life of San Francisco, as do the paintings. A broad staircase leading down to a smaller cloister is covered by a remarkable carved wooden dome (nicknamed *la media naranja* – the half orange) dating from 1625. Next to this smaller cloister is the Capilla de la Soledad where a café is open to the public. The library contains 25,000 volumes. In the refectory, see the painting of the Last Supper in which Christ and his disciples are seated at a round table. Look for the devil at Judas Iscariot's shoulder. The Catacombs under the church and part of the monastery are well worth seeing. This is where an estimated 25,000 Limeños were buried before the main cemetery was opened in 1808.

Opposite the San Francisco church is a historic mansion worth visiting, the late 16th-century **Casa de Jarava** or **Pilatos** ① *Jr Ancash 390*. Two blocks beyond is **Casa de las Trece Monedas** ① *Jr Ancash 536*, built in 1787 by Counts from Genoa. It still has the original doors and window grills.

Plaza Bolívar

Wedged between Avenida Abancay and Jr Ayacucho is Plaza Bolívar, from where General José de San Martín proclaimed Peru's independence. The plaza is dominated by the equestrian statue of the Liberator. Behind lies the Congress

A fashion for passion

A unique form of women's dress worn by Lima's upper class *mestizas* – women born in the colonies of Spanish origin – in the 18th century was the saya and *manto*. Both were of Moorish origin. The *saya* was an overskirt of dark silk, worn tight at the waist with either a narrow or wide bottom. The *manto* was like a thick, black veil fastened by a band at the back of the waist where it joined the *saya*. It was brought over the shoulders and head and drawn over the face so closely that only a small, triangular space was left uncovered, sufficient for one eye to peep through. This earned them the title *Las Tapadas*, or "covered ones".

The fashion was created by Lima's mestizas in order to compete in the flirting stakes with their Spanish-born counterparts, whose tiny waists and coquettish fan-waving was turning men's heads. The *tapadas*, though veiled, were by no means modest. Their skirts were daringly short, revealing their appealingly tiny feet, and necklines plunged to scandalously low levels. The French feminist, Flora Tristan, was much taken with this brazen show. She commented: "I am sure it needs little imagination to appreciate the consequences of this time-honoured practice."

One consequence of this fashion, which ensured anonymity, was that Lima's *mestizas* could freely indulge in romantic trysts with their lovers. Often, however, they were content with some playful flirting – sometimes with their unwitting husbands. Another consequence of their anonymity was political. Many tapadas used their afternoon strolls to pass notes and messages to the organizers of the independence movement. This romantic and political intrigue usually took place on the Paseo de Aguas, a popular walkway of pools and gardens built by the Viceroy.

building which occupies the former site of the **Universidad de San Marcos**, the first University in the Americas. Founded by the Dominicans in 1551, students first began to use this building in 1574. The University now occupies other premises away from the city centre.

Museo del Tribunal de la Santa Inquisición ① *C Junín 548, near the corner of Av Abancay, Mon-Sun 0900-1700, free, students offer to show you round for a tip; good explanations in English*, has a main hall with a splendidly carved mahogany ceiling which remains untouched. The Court of Inquisition was first held here in 1584, after being moved from its first home opposite the church of La Merced. From 1829 until 1938 the building was used by the Senate. In the basement there is an accurate recreation *in situ* of the gruesome tortures. The whole tour is fascinating, if a little morbid. A description in English is available at the desk.

Jirón Ucayali

Museo Banco Central de Reserva ① *Jr Ucayali at Jr Lampa, T01-427 6250, ext 2660, Tue-Fri 1000-1630, Sat-Sun 1000-1300, free, photography prohibited.* This has a large collection of pottery from the Vicus or Piura culture (AD 500-600) and gold objects from Lambayeque, as well as 19th- and 20th-century paintings. Both modern and ancient exhibitions are highly recommended.

Palacio Torre Tagle ① *Jr Ucayali 363, during working hours, Mon-Fri, visitors may enter the patio only.* The city's best surviving specimen of secular colonial architecture, it was built in 1735 for Don José Bernardo de Tagle y Bracho, to whom

Guilt by inquisition

Established by Royal Decree in 1569, the Court of Inquisition was soon to prove a particularly cruel form of justice, even in the context of Spanish rule.

During its existence, the Church meted out many horrific tortures on innocent people. Among the most fashionable methods of making the accused confess their 'sins' were burning, dismemberment and asphyxiation, to name but a few. The most common form of punishment was public flogging, followed by exile and the not so appealing death by burning. Up until 1776, 86 people are recorded to have been burned alive and 458 excommunicated.

Given that no witnesses were called except the informer and that the accused were not allowed to know the identity of their accusers, this may have been less a test of religious conviction than a means of settling old scores. This Kafkaesque nightmare was then carried into the realms of surreal absurdity during the process of judgement. A statue of Christ was the final arbiter of guilt or innocence but had to express its belief in the prisoner's innocence with a shake of the head. Needless to say, not too many walked free.

The Inquisition was abolished by the Viceroy in 1813 but later reinstated before finally being proscribed in 1820.

King Philip V gave the title of First Marquis of Torre Tagle. The house remained in the family until it was acquired by the government in 1918. Today, it is still used by the Foreign Ministry, but visitors are allowed to enter courtyards to inspect the fine, Moorish-influenced wood-carving in the balconies, wrought iron work, and a 16th-century coach complete with commode.

Opposite, **Casa de la Rada**, or **Goyoneche** ① *Jr Ucayali 358,* is an extremely fine mid-18th-century town house in the French manner which now belongs to a bank. The patio and first reception room are open occasionally to the public.

San Pedro ① *on the third block of Jr Ucayali, Mon-Sat 0930-1145, 1700-1800.* The church, finished by Jesuits in 1638, has an unadorned façade, different from any other in the city. In one of the massive towers hangs a five tonne bell called *La Abuelita* (the grandmother), first rung in 1590, which sounded the Declaration of Independence in 1821. The contrast between the sober exterior and sumptuous interior couldn't be more striking. The altars are marvellous, in particular the high altar, attributed to the skilled craftsman, Matías Maestro. The church also boasts Moorish-style balconies and rich, gilded wood carvings in the choir and vestry, all tiled throughout. The most important paintings in the church are hung near the main entrance. In the monastery, the sacristy is a beautiful example of 17th-century architecture. Also of note are La Capilla de Nuestra Señora de la O and the penitentiary. Several Viceroys are buried below.

Jirón de la Unión

The Jirón de la Unión, the main shopping street, runs from the Plaza de Armas. It has been converted into a pedestrian precinct which teems with life in the evening. In the two blocks south of Jirón de la Unión, known as Calle Belén, several shops sell souvenirs and curios.

La Merced ① *Plazuela de la Merced, Unión y Miró Quesada, T01-427 8199, Mon-Sat 0800-1245, 1600-2000, Sun 0700-1300, 1600-2000; monastery 0800-1200 and 1500-1730 daily*, was the first church to be built in Lima, and it is said that it was the site where the first Mass took place. At independence the Virgin of La Merced was made a Marshal of the Peruvian army. The restored colonial façade is a fine example of Baroque architecture. Inside are some magnificent altars and the tilework on some of the walls is noteworthy. A door from the right of the nave leads into the monastery where you can see some 18th-century religious paintings in the sacristy. The cloister dates from 1546.

A couple of blocks further on, the 18th-century **Jesús María** ① *on the corner of Jr Moquegua and Jr Camaná, T01-427 6809, Mon-Sat 0900-1200, 1500-1700*, contains some of the finest paintings and gilded Baroque altars in all of Lima.

South of Jr de la Unión, the **Plaza San Martín** has a statue of San Martín in the centre. It has been restored and is now a nice place to sit and relax.

San Agustín and around
① *Corner of Jr Ica and Jr Camaná, west of the Plaza de Armas, T01-427 7548, 0830-1130, 1630-1900 (ring for entry).* San Agustín's façade (1720) is a splendid example of churrigueresque architecture. There are carved choir stalls and effigies, and a sculpture of Death, said to have frightened its maker into an early grave. Since being damaged in the last earthquake the church has been sensitively restored, but the sculpture of Death is in storage (to protect tourists of a more nervous disposition).

Museo Teatral ① *Teatro Segura, Jr Huancavelica 251, T01-426 7206, 0900-1300, 1400-1700*, contains a collection of mementoes and photographs of people who have appeared on the Lima stage.

AAA Theatre (Amateur Artists' Association) ① *Jr Ica 323*, is in a lovely 18th-century house with an *azaguán*, a covered area between the door and patio, a common feature in houses of this period. Further along Ica is **Casa La Riva** ① *Jr Ica 426*, which has an 18th-century porch and balconies, a small gallery with some 20th-century paintings. It is run by the Entre Nous Society.

Las Nazarenas Church
① *On Av Tacna, fourth block, T01-423 5718, 0700-1200 and 1600-2000.* This 18th-century church was built around an image of Christ Crucified painted by a liberated slave in the mid-16th century. In the earthquake of 1655, the church collapsed but the painting on the wall remained intact. This was deemed a miracle and the painting became the most venerated image in Lima. Together with an oil copy of *El Señor de los Milagros* (Lord of Miracles), the image is encased in a gold frame and carried on a silver litter – the whole weighing nearly a ton – through the streets on 18, 19, and 28 October and again on 1 November (All Saints' Day). The whole city is decked out in purple. *El Comercio* newspaper and local pamphlets give details of times and routes.

Santuario de Santa Rosa
① *Av Tacna, first block, T01-425 1279, 0930-1300, 1500-1800, free.*
Santa Rosa is the first Saint of the Americas and Patron Saint of Lima. Born on 20 April 1586, Rosa of Lima became a member of the third Order of St Dominic and established an infirmary for destitute children and old people in her family home. She died at the age of 31 on 23 August 1617 and was beatified on 16 December 1668. Her day is 30 August. The small but graceful church was built in 1728 and contains the 'Little Doctor' image of Jesus who helped Rosa cure the sick. Beyond the church is a sanctuary where she was born and lived. There is a tiny room where she would allow herself only two hours' sleep each night on a bed of two tree trunks with stones as pillows. A chapel was later built on the site.

The hermitage in the garden was built by Rosa herself and she would retire there to pray alone. The well, into which she threw the key to the padlocked chain around her waist, now receives petitions from the faithful for forgiveness and thanksgivings.

Plaza Dos de Mayo is just over a kilometre west of the Plaza de Armas. About 1 km due south of this again is the circular **Plaza Bolognesi**, from which many major *avenidas* radiate.

San Marcelo ① *Av de la Emancipación, fourth block*, is another church worth seeing for its two beautiful colonial doors is San Marcelo. The interior is also remarkable, particularly the 18th-century gold leaf high altar and pulpit and the religious paintings sited above attractive Sevillian tiles.

Museo Nacional de la Cultura Peruana ① *Av Alfonso Ugarte 650, T01-423 5892, Tue-Sun 1000-1700, US$1, free guide in Spanish*, has an extraordinary mock Tiahuanaco façade houses a rather disjointed collection of pre-Columbian and modern artefacts, including *mate burilado* (carved gourds), *retablos*, textiles, *keros* and *huacos*. There are examples of ceramics and cloth from some Amazonian tribes and a set of watercolours by Pancho Fierro, the 19th-century *costumbrista* artist.

South of the centre

Museo de Arte Italiano ① *Paseo de la República 250, T01-423 9932, Mon-Fri 1000-1700, US$1*. South of the Plaza San Martín, the Museo de Arte Italiano is in a wonderful neo-classical building, given by the Italian colony to Peru on the centenary of its independence. Note the remarkable mosaic murals on the outside. It consists of a large collection of Italian and other European works of art, including sculpture, lithographs and etchings. The museum now also houses the Instituto de Arte Contemporáneo, which has many exhibitions.

Museo de Arte ① *9 de Diciembre (Paseo Colón) 125, T01-423 6332, Thu-Tue 1000-1700, US$3.65. Free guide, signs in English*. The Museo de Arte in the Palacio de la Exposición, was built in 1868 in Parque de la Exposición. There are more than 7,000 exhibits, giving a chronological history of Peruvian cultures and art from the Paracas civilization up to today. It includes excellent examples of 17th- and 18th-century Cusco paintings, a beautiful display of carved furniture, heavy silver and jewelled stirrups and also pre-Columbian pottery. The *Filmoteca* (movie club) is on the premises and shows films just about every night. See the local paper for details, or look in the museum itself.

Gran Parque Cultural de Lima ① *at the Museo de Arte, 0800-2030*. This large park was inaugurated in January 2000 by both the mayor of Lima, Alberto Andrade, and the then President Alberto Fujimori. It has a middle-sized outdoor amphitheatre, Japanese garden, food court and children's activities. Relaxing strolls through this green, peaceful and safe oasis in the centre of Lima are recommended.

Museo de Historia Natural ① *Av Arenales 1256, Jesús María, T01-471 0117, Mon-Fri 0900-1500, Sat 0900-1700, Sun 0900-1300, US$1 (students US$0.50)*. The museum belongs to Universidad de San Marcos. Its exhibits comprise Peruvian flora, birds, mammals, butterflies, insects, minerals and shells.

Northeast of the Plaza de Armas

From the Plaza de Armas, passing the Government Palace on the left, straight ahead is the **Desamparados Station** of the Central Railway. The name, meaning "the helpless ones", comes from the orphanage and church that used to be nearby.

Puente de Piedra, behind the Palacio de Gobierno is a Roman-style stone bridge built in 1610. Until about 1870 it was the only bridge strong enough to take carriages across the river Rímac to the district of the same name. Though this part of the city enjoyed considerable popularity in Colonial times, it could no longer be considered fashionable.

Alameda de los Descalzos was designed in the early 17th century as a restful place to stroll and soon became one of the most popular meeting places. People of all social classes would gather here for their Sunday walk, some up to the cross at the top of **Cerro San Cristóbal**. Today, however, you would be ill-advised to follow in their footsteps, as this can be a dangerous area to wander around alone. Robberies are common on Cerro San Cristóbal, so do not walk up; take a taxi (US$4.50). Worth visiting on the Alameda de los Descalzos, though, is the **Convento de los Descalzos** ① *T01-481 0441, 1000-1300, 1500-1800 except Tue, US$1, by guided tour only, 45 mins in Spanish, worth it.* Founded in 1592, it now contains over 300 paintings of the Cusco, Quito and Lima schools, which line the four main cloisters and two ornate chapels. The chapel of El Carmen was constructed in 1730 and is notable for its baroque gold leaf altar. A small chapel dedicated to Nuestra Señora de la Rosa Mística has some fine Cusqueña paintings. Opposite, in the chapel dedicated to Señora de los Angeles, Admiral Grau made his last confession before the battle of Angamos. The museum shows the life of the Franciscan friars during colonial and early republican periods. The cellar, infirmary, pharmacy and a typical cell have been restored. The library has not yet been incorporated into the tour (researchers may be permitted to see specific books on request). Near the Alameda is the **Paseo de Aguas**, which was also popular for a Sunday stroll in days gone by. Tours can be taken by *Ofistur* combis (from in front of Santo Domingo church, every 15 minutes at the weekend, lasting about an hour, US$1.50). The tour goes through the old *barrio* of Rímac and an improved shanty town area (but still a rough area) up to the top of Cerro San Cristóbal for spectacular views over much of Lima. You pass the Inka Cola factory, too. Check the cloud level first, otherwise you will see very little.

Plaza de Acho ① *on Jr Hualgayoc*, is the bullring, famous for once being the largest in the world and the first in Spanish America, inaugurated on 20 January 1766. Limeños have always been great enthusiasts of bullfighting and in 1798 a royal decree had to be passed forbidding fights on Sundays as people were failing to attend mass. Next to the bullring is the **Museo Taurino** ① *Hualgayoc 332, T01-482 3360, Mon-Sat 0800-1800, US$1; students US$0.50, photography US$2.* Apart from matador's relics, the museum contains good collections of paintings and engravings, some of the latter by Goya.

Barrio Chino

East of the historical centre of Lima, next to the *Mercado Central* or Central Market, is Lima's Chinatown, or *barrio chino*, located within the district of Barrios Altos. Peru is home to the largest population of first-generation Chinese in all of Latin America. Chinese people born in Peru (referred to as 'Tu-San') number more than 1,000,000. Some of the first immigrants arrived at the port of Callao in 1849 from the Chinese provinces of Canton and Fukien to work the coastal fields, replacing the black slaves given their freedom by then-president Ramón Castilla in 1851. More Chinese began to arrive, settling in the north: Chiclayo, Trujillo and the jungle town of Iquitos.

On the seventh block of Jr Ucayali is the locally famous **Portada China**, the arch that stretches across the street and is the gateway to Chinatown. It was a gift from the Chinese government officially inaugurated by Lima mayor Alberto Andrade in July 1997. For authentic Chinese cuisine, see page 121.

Museo de la Nación

① *Javier Prado Este 2465, San Borja, T01-476 9878, Tue-Sun 0900-1700, closed major public holidays. US$1.80, 50% discount with ISIC card.*

 July is the month when the most famous fighters come from Spain for the Fiestas Patrias.
● The season is also from October to the first week of December. Famous toreros practise in the Lima ring and fighting bulls are of Spanish stock.

Lima Central Lima

This is the anthropological and archaeological museum for the exhibition and study of the art and history of the aboriginal races of Peru. There are good explanations in Spanish and English on Peruvian history, with ceramics, textiles and displays of many ruins in Peru. It is arranged so that you can follow the development of Peruvian precolonial history through to the time of the Incas. A visit is recommended before you go to see the archaeological sites themselves. There are displays of the tomb of the Señor de Sipán, artefacts from Batán Grande near Chiclayo (Sicán culture), reconstructions of the friezes found at Huaca La Luna and Huaca El Brujo, near

San Isidro

To 13

Av Javier Prado Oeste

i peru

Related maps
Lima, page 94
Lima centre, page 96
Miraflores, page 107
Barranco, page 110

Av Basadre

Granda

Rivera

Choquehuanca

Huaca
Huallamarca

Centro Empresarial
Camino Real

Andes

Av Mira Quesada

Lima Golf Course

Alzmora

Placencia

Av Pezet

Cervantes

Roosevelt

Cavero

Monclova

Esquilache

El
Olivar

Alvarez Calderón

Yerovi

Parque
Roosevelt

CCPUCP
(Cultural
Centre)

M Roaud

Salazar

Santa Margarita

Parque
La Redonda

F Salas

Pardo y Aliaga

Maurtua

Av Angamos Oste

Clínica Anglo
Americana

E Wong
Supermarket

Av Santa Cruz

Poli Museum

Librería Crisol
& Cine Planet

Ovalo
Gutiérrez

Meiggs

To Museo Amano

N

0 metres 200
0 yards 200

Sleeping
Albergue Juvenil Malka 1
Country Club &
  Le Perroquet 2
Garden 10
Home Perú 5

Libertador 4
Lima Tamba 11
Sans Souci 6
Sofitel Royal Park 7
Sonesta Posada del Inca
  El Olivar 3

Swissôtel Lima 8
Villa Molina 9

Eating
Alfresco 1
Antica Pizzería 13

To José Antonio (9 blocks)

To Mini Market Kosher & Qubba (7 blocks)

Trujillo, and of Sechín and other sites. Also included is the **Museo Peruano de** **Ciencias de la Salud**, which has a collection of ceramics and mummies, plus an explanation of pre-Columbian lifestyle, divided into five sections: *micuy* (Quechua for food), *hampi* (medicine), *onccoy* (disease), *hampini* (healing) and *causay* (life). Temporary exhibitions are held in the basement, where there is also an Instituto de Cultura bookshop. The museum also has a cafetería. From Av Garcilaso de la Vega in downtown Lima take a combi with a window sticker that says 'Javier Prado/Aviación'. Get off at the 21st block of Javier Prado at Avenida Aviación. From Miraflores take a

Antica Taberna 7
Asia de Cuba 5
Bohemia 2
Café Olé & Pastelería
    Montserrat 10
chilis 3

Delicass & Café
    Positano 4
Matsuei 6
News Café 8
Segundo Muelle 9
Valentino 12

bus down Avenida Arequipa to Avenida Javier Prado (27th block), then take a bus with a window sticker saying 'Todo Javier Prado' or 'Aviación'. A taxi from downtown Lima or from the centre of Miraflores costs US$2.

Museo de Oro del Perú y Armas del Mundo

ⓘ *Alonso de Molina 1100, Monterrico, T345 1292, 1130-1900, US$9.*

This museum used to be on the main tourist circuit in Lima, with visitors flocking to see the huge, if chaotic collection of gold and silver pieces, as well as the collections of textiles, weaponry and military uniforms. That was until it was declared by a Congressional committee, the INC (National Institute of Culture) and Indecopi (the Tourist Protection Bureau) in 2001 that many of the objects, perhaps 98 percent, were fakes. If correct, that represents fraud on a massive scale. In 2004 the museum was being rehabilitated.

Lima suburbs

Pueblo Libre

Museo Nacional de Antropología, Arqueología e Historia ⓘ *Plaza Bolívar, not to be confused with Plaza Bolívar in the centre, T01-463 5070, Tue-Sat 0900-1700, Sun 0900-1600, US$3, photo permit US$5, guides are available*, is the original museum of archaeology and anthropology. On display are ceramics of the Chimú, Nasca, Mochica and Ichma (Pachacámac) cultures, various Inca curiosities and works of art, and interesting textiles. The museum houses the Raimondi Stela and the Tello obelisk from Chavín, and a reconstruction of one of the galleries at Chavín. It also has a model of Machu Picchu.

Museo Nacional de Historia ① *Plaza Bolívar, T01-463 2009,* is in a mansion built by Viceroy Pezuela and occupied by San Martín (1821-1822) and Bolívar (1823-1826). It is next to the Museo de Antropología y Arqueología. The exhibits comprise colonial and early republican paintings, manuscripts, portraits, uniforms, etc. The paintings are mainly of historical episodes.

To get to both museums from the centre, take any public transportation vehicle on Av Brasil with a window sticker saying 'Todo Brasil.' Get off at the 21st block called Av Vivanco. Walk about five blocks down Vivanco. The museum will be on your left. From Miraflores, take bus SM 18 Carabayllo-Chorrillos, marked 'Bolívar, Arequipa, Larcomar', get out at block 8 of Bolívar, by the Hospital Santa Rosa, and walk down Av San Martín 5 blocks till you see the 'blue line'; turn left. The 'blue line' marked on the pavement, a bit faded in places, links the Museo Nacional de Antropología, Arqueología e Historia to the Museo Arqueológico Rafael Larco Herrera (see next paragraph), 10 minutes' walk. Taxi from downtown Lima US$2; from Miraflores US$2.

Museo Arqueológico Rafael Larco Herrera ① *Av Bolívar 1515, T01-461 1312, http://museolarco.perucultural.org.pe, 0900-1800; texts in Spanish, English and French, US$6.35 (half price for students), disabled access, guides, no photography,* is located in an 18th-century mansion. Built on a seventh-century pre-Columbian pyramid, this museum has a collection which gives an excellent overview on the development of Peruvian cultures through their pottery. It has the world's largest collection of Moche, Sicán and Chimú pieces. There is a Gold and Silver of Ancient Peru exhibition, a magnificent textile collection and a fascinating erotica section. It is surrounded by beautiful gardens. Take any bus to the 15th block of Avenida Brasil. Then take a bus down Avenida Bolívar. Or, from Miraflores, take the SM 18 Carabayllo-Chorrillos, see above, to block 15 of Bolívar. Taxi from downtown, Miraflores or San Isidro, 15 minutes, US$2.50. Follow the 'blue line' marked on the pavement to the Museo Nacional de Antropología, Arqueología e Historia (see above), 10 minutes' walk.

Around Pueblo Libre

The plain exterior of the church of **Santa María Magdalena**, on Jr San Martín, conceals some fine ornamentation and art inside. **Parque de las Leyendas** ① *La Mar, T01-464 4282, 0900-1730, US$2,* is arranged to represent the three regions of Peru: the coast, the mountainous sierra, and the tropical jungles of the Selva, with appropriate houses, animals and plants and children's playground. It contins a *huaca* from the Maranga culture, AD 500, and gets very crowded at weekends. To get there from 24th block of Avenida de La Marina in San Miguel, take Avenida Parque Las Leyendas. Bus 23 will get you there or take a *colectivo* from Avenida Abancay, or bus 135A or *colectivo* from Avendia La Vega. Just to the east of the park is the Universidad Católica del Perú.

San Isidro

The district of San Isidro combines some upscale residential areas, many of Lima's fanciest hotels and restaurants and important commercial zones with a huge golf course smack in the middle. Along Avenida La República is **El Olivar**, an old olive grove planted by the first Spaniards which has been turned into a beautiful park. It's definitely worth a stroll either by day or night.

Between San Isidro and Miraflores, is **Huallamarca** ① *C Nicolás de Rivera 201 and Av Rosario, 0900-1700, closed Mon, US$1.75, take bus 1 from Av Tacna, or minibus 13 or 73 to Choquechaca, then walk,* also called the Pan de Azúcar, an adobe pyramid of the Maranga culture, it dates from about AD 100-500. There is a small site museum.

Miraflores

Miraflores, apart from being a nice residential part of Lima, is also home to a busy mercantile district full of fashionable shops, cafés, discotheques, fine restaurants

Miraflores

Related maps
Lima, page 94
Lima centre, page 96
San Isidro, page 104
Barranco, page 110

0 metres 50
0 yards 50

Sleeping
Albergue Turístico
    Juvenil Internacional 1 *D3*
Alemán 32 *A3*
Antigua Miraflores 2 *B1*
Apart Hotel Las
    Américas 3 *A2*
Ariosto 4 *D2*
Casa Andina 43 *D2*
Casa de la Sra Jordan 5 *C1*
Colonial Inn 6 *B2*
El Carmelo 7 *B1*
El Zaguán Lodging 40 *D3*
Eurobackpackers 39 *C1*
Explorer's House 37 *A1*
Flying Dog Backpackers 9 *C2*
Friend's House 10 *C1*
Friend's House 2 8 *C1*
Hogar del Mochilero 36 *A1*
Holiday Inn 11 *C2*
Home Perú 38 *A3*
Hospedaje Atahualpa 12 *A3*

Hospedaje José Luis 34 *D3*
Hostal Bellavista de
    Miraflores 13 *B2*
Hostal El Patio 14 *C2*
Hostal Esperanza 15 *C3*
Hostal Huaychulo 16 *A2*
Hostal La Castellana 17 *C2*
Hostal Lucerna 18 *D1*
Hostal Señorial 19 *D1*
Hostal Torreblanca 31 *A1*
Imperial Inn 20 *B1*
José Antonio 21 *C1*
La Hacienda 22 *C1*
La Paz Apart Hotel 23 *C2*
Las Américas 24 *C2*
Lex Luthor's House 25 *C1*
Madre Natura 41 *A3*
Marriott 26 *D1*
Miraflores Park 42 *D1*
Pensión Yolanda 33 *B3*
Residencial El
    Castillo Inn 27 *C3*
San Antonio Abad 28 *D3*
Sipán 35 *D2*
Sol de Oro 29 *C1*
Sonesta Posada
    del Inca 30 *C2*

Eating
Astrid y Gaston 2 *C3*
C'est Si Bon 35 *A2*
Café Café 5 *B2*
Café de la Paz 6 *B2*
Café Voltaire 7 *B3*
Café Z 27 *B2*
Chef's Café 8 *C2*
Chifa Kun Fa 9 *C2*
Chifa Wa Lok 42 *A3*
Confitería La Biela 24 *B2*
Cuarto y Mitad 41 *A2*
Dalmacia 38 *D1*
Dino's Pizza 34 *A2*
Dove Vai 10 *B2*
El Beduino 36 *D2*
El Kapallaq 43 *B3*
El Parquetito 12 *B2*
El Rincón Gaucho 37 *D1*
Haiti 13 *B3*
Heladeria 4D 14 *A3*
Il Postino 15 *C3*
La Gloria 16 *B3*
La Palachinke 17 *B2*
Las Brujas de Cachiche 4 *B1*
La Tiendecita
    Blanca 18 *B3*

La Tranquera 19 *B2*
La Trattoria 20 *B3*
Las Tejas 21 *C2*
Mama Lola 44 *C2*
Pardo's Chicken 22 *D2*
Pizza Street 23 *B2*
Ricota & Café
    Tarata 25 *C2*
Rincón Alemán 39 *A3*
San Antonio Café 33 *A3*
Sandwich.com 3 *B2*
Señorío de Sulco 40 *A1*
Sí Señor 28 & 39 *B1 & A3*
Super Rueda 26 *B2*
Tapas Bar 46 *B3*
Vivaldi 29 *B3*
Zugatti 30 *C2*

Bars & clubs
Media Naranja 31 *B2*
Murphys 32 *C2*
The Old Pub 45 *B2*

and good hotels and guesthouses. As in the centre, there is a security force patrolling the streets, in trucks, on motorbikes or on foot.

Parque Central de Miraflores and around In the centre of all this is the beautiful Parque Central de Miraflores – **Parque Kennedy** – located between Avenida Larco and Avenida Oscar Benavides (locally known as Avenida Diagonal). This extremely well-kept park has a small open-air theatre with performances Thursday-Sunday, ranging from Afro-Peruvian music to rock'n'roll. Towards the bottom of the park is a nightly crafts market open from 1700 to 2300.

At the end of Avenida Larco and running along the promenade is the renovated **Parque Salazar** and the very modern shopping centre called **Centro Comercial Larcomar**. Here the shopping centre's terraces, which have been carved out of the cliff, contain expensive shops, hip cafés and restaurants, an open-air internet café and discos. The balustrades have a beautiful view of the ocean and the sunset. The 12-screen cinema is one of the best in Lima and even has a 'cine-bar' in the twelfth theatre. Don't forget to check out the Cosmic Bowling Alley with its black lights and fluorescent balls. A few hundred metres to the north is the renovated Parque Champagnat and then, across the bridge over the gorge, the famous **Parque del Amor** where on just about any night you'll see at least one wedding party taking photos of the newly married couple. Peruvians are nothing if not romantic.

The beach has a great view of the whole Lima coastline from Chorrillos to La Punta. **Rosa Náutica**, a very expensive restaurant/discotheque, see page 123, occupies a pier that juts out from the beach. A Lima dining institution for those willing to part with a nice chunk of change.

Museo Ricardo Palma ① *C General Suárez 189, T01-445 5836, Mon-Fri 0915-1245 and 1430-1700, small entrance fee; photography fee US$3.* The house of the author, poet and historian is now a museum. He is one of Peru's most famous literary figures, best known for his work *Tradiciones Peruanas*, which covers the country's colonial period, see Literature page 597.

Huaca Pucllana ① *at the intersection of C Borgoña y Tarapacá, near the 45th block of Av Arequipa, free, 0900-1700, closed Tue.* This is a fifth- to eighth-century AD ceremonial and administrative centre of the pre-Inca, Lima culture. The pyramid, of small adobe bricks, is 23 m high. Guided tours only in Spanish are available. It has a site museum. See also Eating page 121.

Museo Arqueológico Amano ① *C Retiro 160 near the 11th block of Av Angamos Oeste, T01-441 2909, open by appointment Mon-Fri in the afternoons only, free, photography prohibited.* This very fine private collection of artefacts from the Chancay, Chimú and Nasca periods, owned by the late Mr Yoshitaro Amano, boasts one of the most complete exhibits of Chancay weaving. It is particularly interesting for pottery and pre-Columbian textiles, all superbly displayed and lit. Take a bus or *colectivo* to the corner of Avenida Arequipa y Avenida Angamos and another one to the 11th block of Avenida Angamos Oeste. Alternatively a taxi from downtown costs US$2 or from Parque Kennedy US$1.

Poli Museum ① *Almte Cochrane 466, T01-422 2437, tours cost US$10 per person irrespective of the size of the group, allow 2 hrs, call in advance to arrange tours.* This is one of the best private collections of colonial paintings, silver, cloth and furniture in Peru. It also has a fine collection of pre-Columbian ceramics and gold, including material from Sipán. Guided tours are given in Spanish only and delivered rapidly by Sr Poli or his son, whose views are often contrary to long-held opinions about the symbolism of Peruvian cultures.

Barranco

South of Miraflores is Barranco, which was already a seaside resort by the end of the 17th century. During Spanish rule, it was a getaway for the rich who lived in or near the centre. Nowadays, Barranco is something of an intellectual haven, with artists' workshops and chic galleries.

> ✷ No visit to Lima would be complete without a tour of Barranco's 'sights'.

The attractive public library, formerly the town hall, stands on the delightful plaza. Nearby is the interesting *bajada*, a steep path leading down to the beach, where many of Lima's artists live. The **Puente de los Suspiros** (Bridge of Sighs), leads towards the Malecón, with fine views of the bay.

Barranco is a quiet, sleepy suburb during the day but comes alive at night when the city's young flock here to party at weekends. Squeezed together into a few streets are dozens of good bars and restaurants.

An antique train wagon that discontinued its Barranco-Lima service in 1965 now offers a pleasant, albeit very short, ride (six blocks) down Avenida Pedro de Osma to the door of the museum of the same name. There is a video on board describing the train's history. The train runs Tuesday-Sunday from 1000 to 1700, depending on the number of passengers. Tickets can be bought at the **Electricity Museum** ① *Av Pedro de Osma 105, T01-477 6577, US$0.70.*

Museo de Arte Colonial Pedro de Osma ① *Av Pedro de Osma 421, T01-467 0141, Tue-Sun 1000-1330, 1430-1800, US$3, bus 2, 54 or colectivo from Av Tacna*, has a private collection of colonial art of the Cusco, Ayacucho and Arequipa schools. The number of visitors is limited to 10 at any one time.

Chorrillos

This disctrict, beyond Barranco, has a redesigned, fashionable beachfront with mosaics and parks. It has always been popular resort and it is a good place to go to find fish restaurants. Playa Herradura is a little further on and is well-known for surfing. From Chorrillos you can get to some of the sites, like Pachacámac and Pántanos de Villa, which are south of the city.

Callao → *Phone code: 01. Colour map 3, grid C3.*

There is no separation between Lima and Callao, the two cities run into each other and the road between the two is lined with factories. But Callao is a city in its own right, the second largest in Peru with over one million inhabitants (much more if you include shantytown dwellers). Shipyards, far from sea, load the fishing vessels they build on huge lorries and launch them into the ocean at Callao. Jorge Chávez International Airport is located here (not in Lima) and it is the most important Peruvian port, handling 75 per cent of the nation's imports and some 25 per cent of its exports. Most parts of the city are ugly, unkempt, poor and dangerous. However, if you are willing to use some imagination and if you like ports, Callao is worth visiting. Some attempts are being made to restore the historical centre and port area.

Callao, founded in 1537, used to be one of the most important cities in South America, the only seaport on the continent authorized to trade with Spain during the 16th and 17th centuries. During much of the 16th century Spanish merchants were plagued by threats from English pirates such as Sir Francis Drake and Richard Hawkins who were all too willing to relieve the Spanish armada of its colonial spoils. The harbour was fortified in 1639 in order to prevent such attacks. In 1746, the port was completely destroyed by a massive wave, triggered by the terrible earthquake of that year. According to some sources, all 6,000 of Callao's inhabitants were drowned. The watermark is still visible on the outside of the 18th-century church of **Nuestra Señora del Carmen de la Legua** which stands near the corner of Avenida Oscar Benavides and the airport road, Avenida Elmer Faucett. In 1850, the first railway in South America was opened between Lima and Callao. It was used not only as a passenger service but, more importantly, for the growing import-export trade, transporting ore from the mines in the Central Highlands and manufactured goods from the disembarking ships.

Barranco

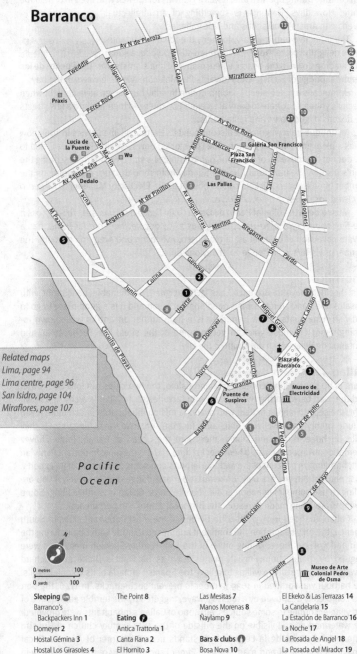

Related maps
Lima, page 94
Lima centre, page 96
San Isidro, page 104
Miraflores, page 107

Pacific
Ocean

0 metres   100
0 yards   100

Sleeping
Barranco's
  Backpackers Inn **1**
Domeyer **2**
Hostal Gémina **3**
Hostal Los Girasoles **4**
La Quinta de Alison **5**
Mochileros Hostal **6**
Suites California **7**

The Point **8**

Eating
Antica Trattoria **1**
Canta Rana **2**
El Hornito **3**
Festín **4**
La Costa Verde **5**
La Ermita **6**

Las Mesitas **7**
Manos Morenas **8**
Ñaylamp **9**

Bars & clubs
Bosa Nova **10**
De Rompe y Raja **11**
Del Carajo **12**
El Dragón **13**

El Ekeko & Las Terrazas **14**
La Candelaria **15**
La Estación de Barranco **16**
La Noche **17**
La Posada de Angel **18**
La Posada del Mirador **19**
Peña Poggi **20**
Sargento Pimienta **21**

The most elegant area of Callao proper is **Plaza Grau**. It is well-maintained and from here you can see a large part of the port and the **Palomino Islands** (inhabited by birds, seals and other marine species), including **Isla San Lorenzo**. This island has an underwater military bunker, with two famous prisoners, Abimael Guzmán, founder of Sendero Luminoso, and Víctor Polay, leader of MRTA. Trips to the islands can be arranged from the pier next to Plaza Grau. One of the agencies is called **Vientosur**. Ask around, departures are mostly unscheduled. Several houses around the **Iglesia Matriz** have been restored, but generally the centre is in a state of permanent decay. **Museo Naval del Perú** ① *Av Jorge Chávez 121, Plaza Grau, T01-429 4793, Tue-Sat 0900-1600, Sun 0900-1700, US$0.85*, has models of Peruvian and foreign ships, weapons, uniforms, torpedoes and other relics. There are also interesting photographs. Recommended if you are in the area. **La Fortaleza Real Felipe** ① *T01-429 0532, Tue-Sun 0900-1500, US$2 including guide, no cameras allowed*, is an enormous Spanish castle standing in the heart of the city. It is still used by the Peruvian armed forces so you will have to negotiate entry with a lethargic guard. If you succeed, you will be provided with a military guide and the tour may take anything up to two hours. There are some interesting uniforms, arms and artefacts inside the castle, also plenty of cannons.

La Punta

La Punta is a green, nostalgic peninsula next to Callao. It has the relaxed atmosphere of a beach resort, good local seafood restaurants, pleasant walks, friendly people and great views. It's an interesting place to come for lunch, but the ride back to Lima, even in a taxi, can be dangerous at night (you would have to drive through Callao proper). La Punta has only 6,800 permanent residents. Its main artery is Avenida Coronel Bolognesi, lined with impressive old villas. There is a well-maintained Malecón parallel to Bolognesi, a lovely walk and great views of the islands, sailing boats and Callao port. On the corner of El Malecón and Jr García y García is the **Club de Regatas Lima**, with a nice café and view from the second floor (open sporadically). Nearby is the **Club de Regatas Unión**. Along El Malecón is a pebble beach, but the water is not very clean, due to the proximity of Callao port. **Plaza Grau** is nicely restored, with a library inside the municipality building. It has no pamphlets, but you can get information about the past (La Punta was founded in 1555) and the present of La Punta there. At Plaza Grau bright pleasure boats, complete with life jackets, take trippers out to the end of La Punta beach and back. The journey is about 25 minutes and costs US$1.

Lima beaches

Lima sits next to an open bay, with its two points at La Punta (Callao) and Punta La Chira (Chorrillos). During the summer (December-March), beaches get very crowded on weekdays as much as weekends even though all the beaches lining the Lima coast have been declared unsuitable for swimming. A stroll on the beach is pleasant during daylight hours, but when the sun goes down, the thieves come out and it becomes very dangerous. Needless to say, camping is a very bad idea. Most beaches have very strong currents and extreme caution should be exercised. Lifeguards are not always present.

The **Circuito de Playas**, which begins with Playa Arica, 30 km from Lima, and ends with San Bartolo, 45 km from Lima, has many great beaches for all tastes. If you want a beach that always is packed with people, there's **El Silencio** or **Punta Rocas**. Quieter options are **Señoritas** or **Los Pulpos**. **Punta Hermosa** has frequent surfing and volleyball tournaments.

 Under a shanty town called Túpac Amaru, over 2,000 mummy bundles have been uncovered in an Inca cemetery known as Puruchuco-Huaquerones.

Shantytowns

Known as *asentamientos humanos* or *pueblos jóvenes*, the shantytowns of Lima are monumental reminders of racial division and social inequality, and of the poverty in which more than half of the capital's population lives. Millions of people have no access to clean drinking water. Most of the Peruvians living in these settlements came from the provinces, escaping misery and the civil war of the 1980-1990s. They simply took the land on the hills surrounding Lima, only trying later to legalize their property.

There are old, 'established' shantytowns like **Villa El Salvador** with almost one million inhabitants, as well as new, rapidly expanding ones like **Mi Perú** in Ventanilla, 20 km behind the Jorge Chávez airport. Some shantytowns, like **Lurigancho** and **Canto Grande**, were controlled by Shining Path during the civil war. Others (around the Central Highway that leads towards the Andes) became famous for sheltering delinquents and drug addicts. There is even one shantytown housing Cuban exiles who escaped from the island looking for 'free dom' and better life (now they wish they had stayed home). Some consist of bamboo shacks without roofs, others already have sound infrastructure including markets, shops, even small restaurants and cafés.

Social division in Peruvian society is very deep. Most of the shantytown dwellers don't even know of the existence of posh neighbourhoods like San Isidro and Miraflores. Needless to say, most inhabitants of the rich parts of Lima never visit shantytowns.

Many more voyeuristic visitors feel a fascination for Lima's poorest districts. Villa El Salvador, one of the oldest and biggest shantytowns, is the only such place that can be visited without much danger. The only safe way to travel is by hiring a taxi (roundtrip from Miraflores including an hour wait can be arranged for US$11.50). If you must go, travel only by day, wear modest clothes and, if you walk, stick to the main street. It is not recommended that you visit any other of these towns. Almost without exception, shantytowns are dangerous, especially after dark. Every week, there are countless cases of robbery, stabbing, burglary and rape. Murder is not uncommon. Under no circumstances should you travel by public transport.

If you are planning to take a bus out of Lima, you will see many shantytowns along the highway.

Excursions

Pántanos de Villa

ⓘ *0900-1700, US$1.50, guides available for groups of 15 (free).*

In the district of Chorrillos is the 396-ha wildlife sanctuary, Pántanos de Villa, an ecological wetland reserve with brackish water and abundant emergent vegetation. It provides the habitat for waterfowl typical of coastal Peru, including 17 species of migratory shorebirds. There are several species of fish, four types of reptile and over 50 species of water plants.

The visitors' centre has lots of information on the walls, in Spanish. Allow about 1½ to two hours for a visit. Take binoculars. Access is by the road which goes to the seaside district of La Villa; nearest public transport stops about 1 km away. It's best to take a taxi from Barranco, US$3.

Pachacámac

ⓘ To1-430 0168, 0900-1700, closed 1 May, US$1.50 including the small site museum, guide US$6, in English or Spanish.

Pachacámac is in the Lurín Valley, 31 km from Lima. When the Spaniards arrived, Pachacámac was the largest city and ceremonial centre. It was a vast complex of palaces and temple-pyramids, to which pilgrims went to pay homage to, and obtain divinations from the oracle Pachacámac. A wooden statue of the god (a two-faced staff) is in the site museum. Hernando Pizarro came to Pachacámac in 1533, having been sent by his brother to speed the delivery of gold from the coast for Atahualpa's ransom. However, great disappointment awaited Pizarro as there was no store of riches. In their desperate search for the promised gold the Spaniards destroyed images, killed the priests and looted the temples. The ruins encircle the top of a low hill, whose crest was crowned with a **Temple of the Sun**, a large pyramid built in 1350 of sun-baked bricks, now partially restored. Slightly apart from the main group of buildings and hidden from view is the reconstructed **House of the Mamaconas**, where the 'chosen women' were taught to weave and spin fine cloth for the Inca and his court. Various other temples and palaces can be seen. Further to the north the Temple of Urpi-Huachac, who was reputed to be the wife of Pachacámac, is in a state of total ruin. The museum has a model of the city and there is a café and toilets.

Cieneguilla

Cieneguilla, 20 km east of the centre of Lima, is a town in the country on the Lurín River, an easy escape from the city and cloud cover of Lima. It is a popular place on Sunday, with restaurants with gardens and swimming, all of which open daily for lunch, recreation centres and cabins for longer stays. Take a combi running east on Avenida Prado Este. It takes around 30-45 minutes and costs US$0.50.

Puruchuco

ⓘ End of Av Javier Prado Este, museopuruchuco.perucultural.org.pe, 0900-1600 (closed 1 May and 28 Jul), US$3.65.

In the eastern outskirts of Lima, near the stadium of La U football club, is Puruchuco, the reconstructed palace of a pre-Inca Huacho noble. There is a very good site museum, Jiménez Borja, with ceramics and textiles from the lower Rímac or Lima valley (texts in Spanish and English). The palace is labyrinthine. This is also the site of a major archaeological find, announced in 2002. Under a shanty town called Túpac Amaru, over 2,000 mummy bundles have been uncovered in an Inca cemetery known as **Puruchuco-Huaquerones**. The cemetery itself is not a new discovery, but the quantity and completeness of the mummies, plus the tens of thousands of accompanying objects, should reveal a wealth of information about the last century of Inca society before the Spanish conquest. It is clear that some of the mummies are of the Inca élite and all are well-preserved. Archaeologists estimate that only 40 per cent of the burials at the site have come to light. To see the tombs, ask the guards on Saturday morning if you can visit the archaeologists at work.

Cajamarquilla

ⓘ 0900-1700, US$1.75.

This large adobe pre-Inca city can also be visited. The turnoff (left, at Huachipa) is about 6 km on from the Puruchuco turn. The site cannot be seen from the road; look for a sign 'Zona Arqueológica' in the middle of a brickyard. Keep on driving through the yard, and Cajamarquilla is at the end of an ill-kept dirt road.

Ancón

Ancón, 30 km northwest of Lima, is reached by a double-lane asphalted highway. In the 19th and early 20th centuries, this was the smart seaside resort in Peru, but has now been deserted by the wealthy and in summer is crowded with daytrippers. It has a mix of elegant 19th-century houses with wooden balconies and modern apartment blocks. There are tennis courts and a yacht club. The beaches are very small and crowded during January-March holidays, but bathing is safe with no currents.

Beyond Ancón is a **Chancay cemetery**, from which has come much Chancay weaving and pottery, as seen in the **Museo Amano.**

Canta → *Colour map 3, grid B4. Altitude: 2,837 m.*

Canta is a popular small town on the fringes of the high Andes less than three hours from Lima by paved road. After 1½ hours, by which time the *garúa* has been left behind, you pass through **Santa Rosa de Quives**, the birthplace of the patron Saint of Lima. Her house and the adjoining Sanctuary can be visited. After two hours the petroglyphs of **Checta** are reached. Numerous, small, complex drawings cover the surface of boulders spread across a hillside 15-minutes' steep walk from the road. The path is marked.

Canta itself was founded by the Spanish in 1535. It lies on one of the initial main routes down from the mines of the sierra to Lima. It is not especially attractive, but there are good day walks and significant ruins nearby. The tourist office is on the main street, T01-244 7013, 1000-1600 Saturday and Sunday only.

The pre-Inca ruins of **Cantamarca** (3,600 m) were probably built by the Chancay culture. They consist of large *chullpas* (burial towers) made from finely cut stone, many with roofs still supported by stone pillars. Take a steep trail from 5 km up the La Viuda road. Allow two to three hours for the climb and carry water.

A few kilometres beyond Canta is Huaros (3,587 m) from which a long day walk can be made to the **Parque Arqueológico de Huischo** and the **Bosque de Puyos Raimondis** (4,050m). Beyond Huaros the road continues to the beautiful Lake Chuchun below the fourteen snow-capped peaks of the La Viuda cordillera.

Obrajillo

At weekends Limeños flock to this village set in beautiful countryside criss-crossed by fast flowing streams. Eat in the main plaza or try the trout *chicharrones* and *pachamanca* at riverside restaurants. You can visit the waterfall (US$0.30), or go riding (US$4 per hour). A one-hour walk runs up the south side of the valley, on the opposite side to the waterfall, to **Santa Rosa de Acochaca** where there is a restaurant and shop. Returning on the opposite side of the valley a detour can be made to **San Miguel** (one hour), giving a bird's eye view of Obrajillo, before descending a steep path to Obrajillo (15 minutes).

⊜ Sleeping

All hotels in the upper price brackets charge 19% state tax (IVA) and a service charge on top of prices. In hotels foreigners pay no IVA and the amount of service charged is up to the hotel. Neither is included in prices below, unless indicated otherwise.

The central colonial heart of Lima is not as safe at night as the more upmarket areas of San Isidro, Miraflores or Barranco. If you are only staying a short time in the city and want to see the main sights, the centre is convenient, but do take care. San Isidro is the poshest district, while Miraflores has a good

mix of places to stay, great ocean views, bookstores, restaurants and cinemas. From here you can commute to the centre by bus (30-45 mins) or by taxi (20-30 mins). Barranco, which is more bohemian, is a little further out.

Near the airport

There are lots of other places to stay on Av Tomás Valle, but they are almost without exception short stay and unsafe.

B Hostal Residencial Victor, Manuel Mattos

325, Urb San Amadeo de Garagay, Lima 31, T01-567 5083, hostalvictor@terra.com.pe. 5 mins from the airport by taxi, or phone or email in advance for free pick-up, clean, large comfortable rooms, with bath, hot water, cable TV, free luggage store, free internet and 10 per cent discount for Footprint Handbook owners. American breakfast, evening meals can be ordered locally, new mall with restaurants, fast food and gym nearby, very helpful, owner Víctor Melgar has a free reservation service for Peru and Bolivia. Recommended.

Central Lima *p95, map p96*

LL Lima Sheraton, Paseo de la República 170, T01-315 5022, reservas@sheraton.com. pe. All you'd expect of a 5-star hotel in this large building near the Museo de Arte Italiano. **Las Palmeras** coffee shop is good, there is a daily buffet breakfast and a good Italian restaurant, also a casino.
A Maury, Jr Ucayali 201, T01-428 8188, hotmaury@amauta.rcp.net.pe. Breakfast included. The most luxurious hotel in the historical centre, fancy, secure and very clean.
A-B Kamana, Jr Camana 547, T01-426 7204, www.hotelkamana.com. A comfortable, safe hotel with very friendly staff, TV, French and some English spoken, restaurant attached.
B El Balcón Dorado, Jr Ucayali 199, T01-427 6028, balcondorado@hotmail.com. Price includes service and continental breakfast. Centrally located, comfortable and very friendly. It has a café. Airport transfer costs US$10.
B Gran Hotel Continental, Jr Puno 196, T01-427 5890, F426 1633. Price includes

breakfast and is for remodelled rooms (*ejecutivo*), also basic, *económico* rooms, **C** 24-hr room service, clean, safe.
B Gran Hotel Savoy, Jr Cailloma 224, T01-428 3520. 210 rooms, price includes service and breakfast. It has been refurbished. Facilities include restaurant, cafeteria, bar, laundry and airport transfer.
B Hostal La Posada del Parque, Parque Hernán Velarde 60, near 2nd block of Av Petit Thouars, Santa Beatriz, T01-433 2412, www.incacountry.com. Run by Sra Mónica Moreno and her husband Leo Rovayo who both speak good English, a charmingly refurbished old house in a safe area, excellent bathrooms, cable TV, breakfast US$3 extra, airport transfer 24 hrs for US$14 for up to 3 passengers. Recommended as excellent value.
C Granada, Huancavelica 323, T/F01-427 9033. Includes breakfast and service, clean, hot water, English spoken, safe, friendly, safety deposit, clothes-washing facilities.
C Hostal Roma, Jr Ica 326, T/F01-427 7572, www.hostalroma.8m.com. With bathroom, **D** without bath, hot water all day, safe to leave luggage, basic but clean, often full, internet extra but good, motorcycle parking (**Roma Tours**, helpful for trips, reservations, flight confirmations, Dante Reyes speaks English). Highly recommended.
D Plaza Francia Inn, Jr Rufino Torrico 1117 (blue house, no sign, look for 'Ecología es vida' mural opposite), near 9th block of Av Garcilaso de la Vega (aka Wilson), T01-330 6080, T9945 4260 (mob), franciasquareinn@ yahoo.com. Dormitory **E**, very clean and cosy, hot water 24 hrs, safety box in each

Lima Sleeping

room for each bed, kitchen and laundry facilities, airport pick up for up to 4 people US$12 (send flight details in advance), discounts for ISIC cardholders, SAE members and readers of this Handbook, same owners as **Posada del Parque**. Highly recommended.
D-E Hostal de las Artes, Jr Chota 1460, Breña, T01-433 0031, artes@terra.com.pe. A nice colonial building with a small garden in one patio. Price is for room with bath; **F** without bath (no singles with bath), **G** per person in dormitory, Dutch-owned, English spoken, clean, safes in rooms and safe luggage store, gay-friendly, solar hot water system, welcoming, book exchange, airport transfer US$12. Recommended.
D-E Hostal Iquique, Jr Iquique 758, Breña, T01-433 4724, http://barrioperu.terra.com. pe/hiquique. With bathroom, **E** without bath, clean but noisy and draughty, friendly, use of kitchen, warm water, storage facilities, rooms on the top floor at the back are best. Repeated recommendations.
E Hostal San Francisco, Jr Azángaro 125-127, T01-426 2735, hostalsf@lanpro. com.pe. Dormitories with and without bathrooms, new, safe, Italian/Peruvian owners, good service, internet and cafeteria.
F Europa, Jr Ancash 376, T01-427 3351, opposite San Francisco church. Good, clean rooms with shared bathrooms, excellent hot showers, also dormitory accommodation for **G** per person, great value, friendly, popular with backpackers. Keep valuables secure.
F per person **Familia Rodríguez**, Av Nicolás de Piérola 730, 2nd floor, T01-423 6465, jotajot@terra.com.pe. With breakfast, clean, friendly, popular, some rooms noisy, will store luggage, also has dormitory accommodation with only one bathroom (same price), transport to airport US$10 per person for 2 people, US$4 per person for 3 or more, good information, secure. Recommended.
F Hostal Belén, Belén 1049, just off San Martín, T01-427 8995. Discount for groups of 3 or more but give prior notice, Italian spoken, basic breakfast extra, hot water, basic, noisy, clean, friendly.
F Hostal España, Jr Azángaro 105, T01-427 9196, www.hotelespanaperu.com. **E** with private bath (3 rooms), **G** in the dorm. A fine

old building, hot showers, friendly, English and French spoken, internet service, motorcycle parking, luggage store (free), laundry service, don't leave valuables in rooms, roof garden, good café, can be very busy.
F Pensión Ibarra, Av Tacna 359, 14th-16th floor, T/F01-427 8603 (no sign), pension ibarra@ekno.com. Breakfast US$2, discount for longer stay. Use of kitchen, balcony with views of the city, clean, friendly, very helpful owner, hot water, full board available (good small café next door).
G per person **Hostal Machu Picchu**, Av Juan Pablo Fernandini 1015 (block 10 of Av Brasil), Breña, T01-9794 4257. Family run, rooms with shared bathroom only, hot water, cheap, kitchen facilities, cable TV, laundry service, excellent value.

Lima suburbs

Pueblo Libre *p105*
E Guest House Marfil, Parque Ayacucho 126, at the 3rd block of Bolívar, T01-463 3161, cosycoyllor@yahoo.com. Clean and friendly, English spoken, breakfast, kitchen facilities and laundry free of charge, internet service, Spanish classes can be arranged, family atmosphere. Recommended.
F Hostal Bait Sababa, Av San Martín 743, near the hospital, T01-261 4990, baitsababa @hotmail.com. In the home of a Jewish family who speak Spanish, English and Hebrew, very helpful, Fri evening meal provided, restaurants, laundry, internet and phone offices nearby.

San Isidro *p106, map p104*
LL Country Club, Los Eucaliptos 590, T01-611 9000, www.accesoperu.com/ countryclub. An excellent hotel offering fine service and luxurious rooms with individual designs, thoroughly classically stylish. Safes in rooms, cable TV, free internet for guests, good bar and restaurant.
LL Sonesta Posada del Inca El Olivar, Pancho Fierro 194, T01-221 2121, www.son esta.com/peru_lima/. A luxurious hotel in a modern olive-green building, with a lawn in front and a park opposite, one of the top 5-star hotels in Lima. It has many eating

options, bar, garden, swimming pool, gym, quiet, popular with business visitors.

LL Swissôtel Lima, Vía Central, Centro Empresarial Real, T01-421 4400, reservations. lima@swissotel.com. Beautiful hotel with excellent 5-star service, 3 superb restaurants including Le Café, swimming pool.

L Libertador, Los Eucaliptos 550, T01-421 6666, www.libertador.com.pe. Member of the Golden Tulip chain, overlooking the golf course, full facilities for business travellers, comfortable rooms, bar, gym, sauna, jacuzzi, fine service, good restaurant. Recommended.

L Sofitel Royal Park, Av Camino Real 1050, T01-215 1618, www.sofitel.com. Another excellent hotel with charming rooms, part of the French group, prices can be negotiated. Highly recommended.

AL Garden Hotel, Rivera Navarrete 450, T01-442 1771, reservas@ gardenhotel.com.pe. Includes breakfast and internet access. Good, large beds, shower, small restaurant, ideal for business visitors, travel agency, close to Ormeño bus terminal. Recommended.

AL LimaTambo, Av Aramburú 1025, T01-441 9615, F440 9584. Breakfast included in the price. Italian-owned, friendly, secure, laundry service, cafetería, caters to business travellers.

B Sans Souci, Av Arequipa 2670, T01-422 6035, F441 7824. Breakfast included in the price. Clean, safe, friendly, good services and restaurant, garden, garage.

F Albergue Juvenil Malka, Los Lirios 165 (near 4th block of Av Javier Prado Este), T01-442 0162, hostelmalka@terra.com.pe. Youth hostel, 20% discount with ISIC card, dormitory style, 4-8 beds per room, English spoken, cable TV, laundry, kitchen, nice café, climbing wall. Highly recommended.

Miraflores p106, map p107

LL Las Américas, Av Benavides 415, T01-444 7272, www.hoteleslasamericas.com. A tall, silvery, glass-fronted building, 5-star, with a commercial centre, pool, gym and restaurant. Buffet breakfast is included in the price.

LL Miraflores Park, Av Malecón de la Reserva 1035, T01-242 3000, mirapark@ peruorientexpress.com.pe. At the top of the range in Lima, an Orient Express hotel with excellent service and facilities, beautiful ocean views from the luxurious rooms. Check with the hotel for monthly offers. Highly recommended.

LL-L Apart Hotel Las Américas, C General Borgoño 116, T01-241 3350, F447 9953. Suites equipped with kitchenette, good café (Café 21), conveniently located at the corner of Av José Pardo.

LL-L Marriott, Malecón de la Reserva 615, T01-217 7000, www.marriott.com. Prices are 10% higher for foreigners, but buffet breakfast is included. Across from Larcomar shopping centre, wonderful views from its towers, pool, gym, two restaurants, tennis court, also has Stellaris Casino.

LL-L Sol de Oro, Jr San Martín 305, T01-446 9876, reservas@soldeoro.com.pe. Price includes buffet breakfast. Secluded but convenient for the centre of Miraflores, very pleasant, with jacuzzi, sauna, room service, and laundry.

L Holiday Inn, Av Alfredo Benavides 300, T01-242 3200, www.holidayinnperu.com. Price includes breakfast. A very fancy Latin version of this American chain. Some rooms have kitchenette. There is a gym, bar, restaurant and laundry.

L La Hacienda, 28 de Julio 511 y Av Larco, T01-444 4346, reservas@bwlahacienda.com. Breakfast included in the price. English spoken, excellent service, has casino.

AL Antigua Miraflores, Av Grau 350 at C Francia, T01-241 6116, www.peru-hotels -inns.com. A beautiful, small and elegant hotel in a quiet but central location, very friendly service, tastefully furnished and decorated, 35 rooms, gym, cable TV, good restaurant. Recommended.

AL Ariosto, Av La Paz 769, T01-444 1414, ariosto@chavin.rcp.net.pe. Price includes buffet breakfast. A large, modern block of glass and concrete, with friendly staff, 24-hr medical assistance and all other services, travel agency and airport transfer. Recommended.

AL Colonial Inn, Comandante Espinar 310, T01-241 7471, coloinn@terra.com.pe. Price includes breakfast. A colonial style hotel with excellent service, but it can be noisy from traffic, parking.

AL José Antonio, 28 de Julio 398, T01-445 7743, www.hotelesjoseantonio.com. This clean, friendly hotel is good in all respects, including the restaurant. Price includes buffet breakfast, some suites with jacuzzi, internet, swimming pool, business facilties. Recommended.

AL La Paz Apart Hotel, Av La Paz 679, T01-242 9350, www.lapaz.com.pe. Apartments with bath, kitchen, lounge, cable TV, convenient, very clean and comfortable, helpful staff. Recommended.

AL Sonesta Posada del Inca, Alcanfores 329, T01-241 7688, www.sonesta.com/peru_miraflores. A member of this recommended chain of hotels, 28 rooms in a mustard-coloured building, conveniently located, cable TV, a/c, restaurant.

A Alemán, Arequipa 4704, T01-446 4045, haleman@terra.com.pe. No sign for this comfortable hotel, which is clean, friendly and quiet. It has a garden, breakfast is included in the price, inquire about laundry service.

A Casa Andina, Av 28 de Julio 1088, T01-241 4050, www.casa-andina.com. One of another recommended chain of hotels. All have similar facilities and décor (others in the Cusco area, Puno, Arequipa and Nasca). Very neat, with many useful touches, such as smoke detectors, emergency lighting and local maps given to all guests. Friendly service, comfortable beds, 10 minutes free internet, a/c, fridge, safe, laundry service, delivery arrangement with KFC, Burger King and Pizza Hut, buffet breakfast, other meals available.

A Hostal Esperanza, Esperanza 350, T01-444 2411, htlesperanza@ terra.com.pe. A 3-star hotel close to the Paseo de la República, modern, pleasant and secure. Breakfast included in the price, and there is a café and bar.

A Hostal La Castellana, Grimaldo del Solar 222, T01-444 4662, lacastellan@terra.com.pe.

Pleasant, with a nice garden, safe, good value, but the restaurant is expensive, laundry, English spoken, special price for South American Explorers (SAE) members. Recommended.

A Hostal Lucerna, Las Dalias 276 (parallel with 12th block of Larco), T01-445 7321, hostallucerna@terra.com.pe. Friendly, safe, clean, quiet, cosy, excellent value, but breakfast, drinks and restaurant are expensive. Recommended.

A Hostal Señorial, José González 567, T01-445 9724, senorial@viabcp.com Includes buffet breakfast, comfortable, friendly, nice garden. Recommended.

A Hostal Torreblanca, Av José Pardo 1453, 1 block from the seafront, T01-447 0142, www.torreblancaperu.com. Includes breakfast and airport pick-up. A caramel-coloured building on Plaza Centro América, at the quiet end of Miraflores. Bilingual receptionists, nice lounge, laundry, restaurant (*A Fuego Lento*) and bar, cosy rooms, will help with travel arrangements.

A San Antonio Abad, Ramón Ribeyro 301, T01-447 6766, www.hotelsanantonioabad.com. Clean, secure, quiet, good service, welcoming, tasty breakfasts, one free airport transfer with reservation. Frequently recommended.

B El Carmelo, Bolognesi 749, T01-446 0575, carmelo@amauta.rcp.net.pe. With bath and TV, in a great location a couple of blocks from the Parque del Amor, small restaurant downstairs serving *criolla* food and *ceviche*, price includes breakfast, good value and comfortable.

B Hostal Bellavista de Miraflores, Jr Bellavista 215, T/F01-445 7834, www.hostal bellavista.com. Price includes breakfast and internet, but only one machine. Convenient location, quiet, but can be noisy from outside at weekends, all rooms with cable TV, pleasant, helpful staff, a bit overpriced.

B Hostal El Patio, Diez Canseco 341, T01-444 2107, www.hostalelpatio.net. Includes continental breakfast, reductions for long stays. The patio has a fountain, lots of flowers and bird cages; there are terraces for sitting outside. Very nice suites with big bathroom and kitchen, clean, comfortable standard rooms, gay-friendly, English and French spoken, convenient, *comedor* with wood fire.

B Hostal Huaychulo, Av Dos de Mayo 494, T01-241 3130. Secure, helpful, German owner-manager also speaks English.

B Sipán, Paseo de la República 6171, T01-447 0884, www.hotelsipan.com.pe. Breakfast is included in price. Very pleasant, a blue hotel in a residential area overlooking the Paseo, rooms with bath, cable TV, fridge, security box, internet and room service. Meals in the restaurant available if booked in advance. Free airport transfers available.

B Villa Molina, B Teruel 341, T01-440 4018, villamolina@terra.com.pe. Breakfast is included, discount offered for long-stay and groups. A beautiful, quiet and friendly house.

C El Zaguán Lodging, Av Diez Canseco 736, T01-446 9356, www.elzaguanlodging.com. Price includes breakfast. No sign to this hotel that looks like a private residence near Parque Las Tradiciones, small, quiet and comfortable.

C Home Perú, Av Arequipa 4501 (no sign), T01-241 9898, www.homeperu.com. In a 1920s mansion with huge rooms, antiques in the public areas, with breakfast, rooms with and without bath, **E** per person with shared bath, group discounts. You'll be made to feel most welcome here. Use of kitchen, luggage store, English spoken, laundry service, internet, very helpful staff, safe, near Plaza Vea hypermarket. Can help with bus and plane tickets, connected to other *hostales* in the country.

C Hospedaje Atahualpa, Atahualpa 646c, T01-447 6601. Cheaper without bath, including breakfast, long-stay rates available, parking, hot water, cooking and laundry facilities, luggage stored, taxi service.

C Hostal Mami Panchita, Av Federico Callese 198, T01-263 7203, San Miguel, raymi_travels @perusat.net.pe. Dutch-Peruvian owned, English, French, Dutch, Spanish and German spoken, includes breakfast and welcome drink, comfortable rooms with bath, hot water, living room and bar, patio, recently extended, email service, book exchange, have their own **Raymi Travel agency** (good service), 15 mins from Miraflores, 20 mins from historical centre. Recommended. Several chicken places and *chifas* nearby around Mercado Magdalena.

C Pensión Yolanda, Domingo Elias 230, T01-445 7565, pensionyolanda@hotmail. com or erwinpension@yahoo.com. Price includes breakfast. English and French spoken, family house, quiet, safe, laundry, book exchange, internet and luggage store. They have travel information, can reserve flights and hotels.

C-D Imperial Inn, Bolognesi 641, T01-445 2504, imperialinn@viabcp.com. With shower, hot water, most expensive rooms have cable TV, orthopaedic beds, price includes coffee and a roll, close to Parque del Amor, good value, very friendly. Recommended.

D per person **Casa de La Sra Jordan**, Porta 724, near Parque del Amor, T01-445 9840. 8 rooms with bath or bathroom next door, all with hot water, breakfast US$1, reservations required. In the family home of 83-year-old Sra Jordan (a German woman from Chanch-amayo), friendly, quiet, discounts for long stay.

D Hospedaje José Luis, Francisco de Paula Ugarriza 727, San Antonio, T01-444 1015, www.hoteljoseluis.com.pe. Price includes breakfast. Rooms with bath, hot water, safe, quiet, clean, internet, kitchen facilities, friendly, English spoken.

D per person **Residencial El Castillo Inn**, Diez Canseco 580, T01-446 9501. All rooms with private bath and hot water, in a family home where you can use the lounge, negotiate for longer stay.

E per person **Albergue Turístico Juvenil Internacional**, Av Casimiro Ulloa 328, San Antonio between San Isidro and Miraflores, T01-446 5488, www.limahostell.com.pe. Youth hostel, dormitory accommodation, **C** in a double private room, US$2.50 discount for IHA card holders. Basic cafeteria for breakfasts, travel information, lounge with cable TV, cooking (minimal) and laundry facilities, swimming pool often empty, extra charge for kitchen facilities, clean and safe, situated in a nice villa. Recommended.

E per person **Flying Dog Backpackers**, Diez Canseco 117, T01-445 6745, www.flyingdog. esmartweb.com. Price includes breakfast in **El Parquetito** café, dormitories or private rooms, shared bath (**C** in en suite room). This is a popular place so it's best to reserve through the web. Very central, comfortable, hot water, secure, friendly, free internet and local calls, lounge with DVD and videos, book exchange, kitchen facilities. Full transport information and tickets can be arranged. A new branch is due open in early 2005.

F per person **Eurobackpackers**, Manco Cápac 471 (no sign, look for the cat with the world on his stick), www.eurobackpackers. com. New in 2003, dormitory, also double rooms, breakfast included in price, family atmosphere, comfortable, safe, internet. Already gaining a good reputation.

F per person **Explorer's House**, Av Alfredo León 158, by 10th block of Av José Pardo, T01-241 5002, explorers_house@yahoo.es. No sign, but plenty of indications of the house number, like a family home in a residential street. With breakfast, dormitory accommodation with shared bath, or double rooms with bath, hot water, use of kitchen, laundry service, Spanish classes, English spoken, TV lounge with DVD and video, very welcoming.

HOSTEL
CITY TOURS
TRAVEL AGENCY
Enrique Barron 440
BARRANCO – LIMA - PERU
(51)(1) 2474085 / (51) (1) 97282105
E-mail: info@safeinlima.com
www.safeinlima.com

F Friend's House, Jr Manco Cápac 368, T01-446 6248, friendshouse_peru@yahoo. com.mx, in dormitory. Hot water, cable TV, use of kitchen at no cost, includes breakfast, very popular with backpackers, near Larcomar shopping centre, plenty of good information and help. Highly recommended. They have another branch at José Gonzales 427, T01-446 3521. **E** per person with bath, same facilities, except private rooms only and more like a family home. Neither branch is signed.

F per person **Hogar del Mochilero** (Backpacker's Home), Jr Cesareo Chacaltana 162, T01-446 3268, maurosilva@hotmail. com. Rooms for 5-6 people, with bath and hot water, internet access a little extra, pleasant, quiet, a short walk from all main facilities, airport transfer, use of kitchen, Mauro speaks English, he and his wife, Mila, are very helpful. Recommended.

F per person **Lex Luthor's House**, Porta 550 (look for the green lights), T01-242 7059, luthorshouse@hotmail.com Breakfast included. Pleasant house, small and basic but clean, very friendly, use of kitchen, good value.

Barranco *p109, map p110*

B Hostal Gémina, Av Grau 620 in Galerías Gémina, T01-477 0712, hostalgemina @yahoo.com. A modern building whose exterior belies the interior with its old radios and sewing machines and its comfortable rooms. Price includes breakfast, with bath, hot wter, TV, café, internet place on ground floor of gallery.

B per person **Suites California**, or Villa Barranquina, Martínez Pinillos 129, corner with San Martín, T01-477 0772, hcalifor@ viabcp.com. If you are looking for a flat, this would be a good choice. Fully-equipped flatlets can sleep up to 4 (**D** per person), in a fascinating 1906 mansion, kitchen, lounge with sofa beds, bathroom, good bedrooms. Also has good restaurant and laundry services for guests.

C Domeyer, C Domeyer 296, T01-247 1413, domeyerhostel@peru.com. Friendly, clean, hot water 24 hrs, laundry service, secure, welcomes gay and lesbia travellers.

C-D La Quinta de Alison, Av 28 de Julio 281, T01-247 1515, www.hotel-laquinta.com.pe.

Breakfast extra. A modern building with lovely rooms, TV and bath, hot water, some rooms with jacuzzi (extra), excellent value, parking.

D-E Safe in Lima, Enrique Barron 440, T01-247 4085, www.safeinlima.com. A quiet, Belgian-run *hostal*, with a family atmosphere, very helpful, airport pick-up, good value.

E-F per person The Point, Malecón Junín 300, T01-247 7997, www.thepointhostel. com. Rooms in this 80-year-old house range from doubles to large dorms, all with shared bath. Becoming very popular with backpackers (book in advance at weekends), breakfast included, internet, cable TV, laundry, kitchen facilties, welcomes gay travellers, party atmosphere most of the time, The Pointless Pub open 2000 till whenever, weekly BBQ, therapeutic massage, can arrange bungee jumping, flight tickets and volunteering.

E per person Barranco's Backpackers Inn, Malecón Castilla 260, T01-247 3709, www.trekinnperu.com. All rooms shared, with lockers, hot water in bathrooms, breakfast included. If you want a room as a double the price is **C**. Kitchen, laundry service, internet access, modern.

E Hostal Los Girasoles, Av Saenz Peña 210, T01-477 2843, losgirasoles@hotmail.com. On a pleasant street near art galleries, simple rooms off a long corridor, some have TV, with bath and hot water, no breakfast.

E per person Mochileros Hostal, Av Pedro de Osma 135, 1 block from main plaza, T01-247 8643, fenallo@hotmail.com. Beautiful house, friendly English-speaking owner, huge shared rooms with lockers, gay friendly, use of kitchen, good pub on the premises, a stone's throw from Barranco nightlife.

Callao *p109*
It is not recommended that you sleep in the centre of Callao as it becomes a dangerous red-light district after sunset. There is, however, a safe place in La Punta:

AL-D La Punta, Jr Saenz Peña 486-490, La Punta, T/F01-429 1553, info@bed-and-breakfast-la-punta.com. Price includes breakfast, a variety of rooms in a recently-restored 1930s mansion, with and witout bath, spacious common rooms, patio, cable TV.

Excursions

Canta *p114*
Arrive by lunchtime at weekends because all hotels fill up.

D Cancay Vento, T01-441 5733. Friendly, clean, hot water, big bathrooms, cable TV, swimming pool. Changes US$.

D Hostal Cabaña, Obrajillo, T01-244 7135, posadaobrajillo@hotmail.com. On the Canta side of the village. The best in town.

E Alborada, is he best of several more basic hotels here, hot water and TV.

E Hospedaje Casa Blanca, Arica 402, T01-526 0282. With bath, hot water, TV, clean.

E Hostal Dodero, T01-244 7190, is the best of the *hostales* in Obrajillo.

Camping
A few km up the valley from Canta at **Huaichaullany The Hoo**. Camping in Obrajillo is possible at the waterfall (US$3 per tent) and above Santa Rosa de Acochaca.

🍴 Eating

In restaurants, both foreigners and Peruvians have to pay 19 per cent state tax (IVA) and the service charge.

Central Lima *p95, map p96*

Pasaje Olaya, on the Plaza de Armas between Jr de la Unión and Jr Carabaya, is a small pedestrian walkway with many nice restaurants frequented during lunch hours by executives. A bit on the pricey side but good. Other good places, if a little touristy, can be found in the passage behind the Municipalidad. On Sat and Sun, 1100-1700, traditional dishes from all over Peru are served in Plaza Italia, plenty of seating, music, well-organized. Highly recommended.

🍴 Antaño, Ucayali 332, opposite the Torre Tagle Palace. Good, typical Peruvian food, nice patio. Recommended.

🍴 La Choza Náutica, Jr Breña 204, close to

Plaza Bolognesi, Breña. Good *ceviches* and friendly service in this old favourite.

L'Eau Vive, Ucayali 370, also opposite the Torre Tagle Palace, T01-427 5612. Run by nuns, open Mon-Sat, 1230-1500 and 1930-2130, fixed-price lunch menu, Peruvian-style in interior dining room, or à la carte in either of the dining rooms that open onto the patio, excellent, profits go to the poor, Ave Maria is sung nightly at 2100.

Manhatten, Jr Miró Quesada 259. Open Mon-Fri 0700-1900, low end executive-type restaurant serving local and international food from US$5-10, good.

Wa Lok, Jr Paruro 864, Barrio Chino, T01-427 2656. Owner Liliana Com speaks fluent English and very friendly. Highly recommended *chifa*.

El Maurito, Jr Ucayali 212, T01-426 2538. Also serves Peruvian anbd international, good *pisco sours*.

San Martín, Av Nicolás de Piérola 890, off Plaza San Martín. Typical Peruvian food from both coast and highlands, good value, reasonably cheap.

Azato, Av Arica 298, 3 blocks from Plaza Bolognesi, Breña, T01-423 4369. Excellent and cheap Peruvian dishes.

Centro de Medicina Natural, Jr Chota 1462. Next door to Hostal de las Artes, serving very good vegetarian.

Cordano, Jr Ancash 202. Typical old Lima restaurant/watering hole, slow service and a bit grimy but full of character. Definitely worth the time it takes to drink a few beers.

Govinda, Av Garcilaso de la Vega 1670, opposite Gran Parque de Lima. A good vegetarian restaurant which also sells natural products.

Hipermercado Metro, Cusco 255, near Plaza San Martín. Has a good restaurant upstairs serving food by weight, good selection at the buffet, popular.

Kin Ten, Ucayali y Paruro, Barrio Chino. Excellent vegetarian options at this *chifa*.

Machu Picchu, near Hostal Europa at Jr Ancash 312. Huge portions, grimy bathrooms (to say the least), yet very popular, closed for breakfast.

Natur, Moquegua 132, 1 block from Jr de la Unión, T427 8281. Vegetarian, the owner, Humberto Valdivia, is one of the South American Explorers' advisers, good for food and casual conversation.

Neydi, Puno 367. Good, cheap seafood, open daily 1100-2000, popular.

Salon Capon, Jr Paruro 819, Barrio Chino, is a highly recommended *chifa*. Has another branch in Larcomar shopping centre, Miraflores, which is ¶¶¶, elegant, equally recommended.

Cafés

Café Carrara, Jr Ica 330, attached to Hostal Roma. Open daily until 2300, multiple breakfast combinations, pancakes, sandwiches, nice ambience, good.

Café-Restaurant Accllahuasy, Jr Ancash 400. Around the corner from Hostal España, open 0700-2300, good.

Lima suburbs

Pueblo Libre *p105*

Antigua Taberna Quierolo, Av San Martín 1090, 1 block from the plaza with the Museo Nacional de Antropología y Arqueología. An atmospheric old bar with glass-fronted shelves of bottles, marble bar and old photos. Has its own *bodega* next door. Serves simple lunches, sandwiches and snacks, good for wine, not open for dinner.

San Isidro *p106, map p104*

Alfresco, Santa Lucía 295 (no sign), T01-422 8915. Best known for its tempting seafood and *ceviche*, also pastas and rice dishes, expensive wines. Has two dining areas, an unfussy area at the front with white plastic furniture and a smarter area at the back.

Antica Pizzería, Av Dos de Mayo 728, T01-222 8437. Very popular, great ambience, excellent food, Italian owner. Also Antica Trattoria in Barranco at Alfonso Ugarte 242, and an excellent bar, Antica Taberna, with a limited range of food at Conquistadores 605, San Isidro, very good value, fashionable, get there early for a seat.

Asia de Cuba, Conquistadores 780, T01-222 4940. A popular place serving a mix of Asian, Cuban and Peruvian dishes. It also has a reputation for its bar and nightclub; try the martinis.

Matsuei, C Manuel Bañon 260, T01-422 4323. Sushi bar and Japanese dishes, very popular, regarded as amnog the best Japanese food in Lima.

Valentino, Manuel Bañon 215, T01-441
6174. One of Lima's best international
restaurants, formal, so well known that it
only needs a tiny brass sign.
Chilis, Ovalo Gutiérrez. A branch of the
American chain with a Peruvian twist,
popular, like most of the places on the Ovalo.
Delicass, Miguel Dasso 131. Great deli
with imported meats and cheeses, good
coffee, open late, slow service.
Segundo Muelle, Av Conquistadores 490,
T01-421 1206, and Av Canaval y Moreyra (aka
Corpac) 605. Worth a visit for its excellent
ceviche and other very good seafood dishes,
popular with the younger crowd.
MiniMarket Kasher, Av Pexet 1472. Kosher
products, excellent, cheap *chala* bread.

Cafés

Café Olé, Pancho Fierro 115 (1 block from
Hotel El Olívar). Huge selection of entrées
and desserts, also serves breakfasts and
sandwiches, very smart with prices to match.
Café Positano/Café Luna, Miguel Dasso
147. Popular with politicians, café and bistro.
News Café, Av Santa Luisa 110. Another
elegant café serving great salads and
desserts, popular, in the upper price bracket.
Pasterlería Montserrat, Av Santa Lucía 100
block, 2 doors from **Café Olé**. A much more
simple place than its neighbour, for hot
breads, cakes, pastries and coffee, smells
very appetising.

Miraflores *p106, map p107*

There are various small restaurants good for a
cheap set meal along C Los Pinos with C
Schell, at the bottom of Parque Kennedy.
C San Ramón, more commonly known as
Pizza St (across from Parque Kennedy), is a
pedestrian walkway lined with outdoor
restaurants/bars/discotheques open until the
wee small hours of the morning. It's a very
popular place with good-natured touts trying
to entice diners and drinkers with free offers.
Astrid y Gaston, Cantuarias 175, T01-444
1496. Excellent local and international cuisine,
one of the best in Lima, also has a bar.
Café Voltaire, Av Dos de Mayo 220.
International cuisine with emphasis on
French dishes, beautifully cooked food,

pleasant ambience, good service, closed Sun. **123**
Cuarto y Mitad, Av Espinar 798, T01-446
2988. This Popular grill is close to the Ovalo
Gutiérrez, it's one of places to go if you're
looking for meat (beef or ostrich); they also
serve seafood.
El Kapallaq, Av Petit Thouars 4844, T01-
444 4149. Prize-winning Peruvian restaurant
specializing in seafood and fish, excellent
ceviches. Open Mon-Fri 1200-1700 only.
El Rincón Gaucho, Av Armendáriz
580, T01-447 4778. Good grill, renowned
for its steaks.
El Señorío de Sulco, Malecón Cisneros
1470, T01-441 0183, http://senoriodesulco.
com. Overlooking a clifftop park, with ocean
views from upstairs. Forget the Footprint
grading, this is a 'five-fork' restaurant which
some believe is the best in Lima, all Peruvian
food, à la carte and buffet, *piscos*, wines, piano
music at night.
Huaca Pucllana, Gral Borgoña cuadra
8 s/n, alt cuadra 45 Av Arequipa, T01-445
4042. Open 1230-0030. Facing the
archaeological site of the same name,
contemporary Peruvian and fusion cooking,
very good food in an unusual setting.
La Gloria, Atahualpa 201, T01-446 6504.
Very smart, excellent international food and
service.
La Tranquera, Av Pardo 285. Argentine-
owned steak house, ranch-style, set back off
the street, very good.
La Trattoria, Manuel Bonilla 106, 1 block
from Parque Kennedy (no sign), T01-446
7002. The Italian cuisine is of a consistently
high quality, very popular. It also serves a
good cheesecake.
Las Brujas de Cachiche, Av Bolognesi
460, T447 1883. An old mansion converted
into bars and dining rooms, almost Alpine in
appearance. It specializes in traditional food
(menu in Spanish and English), best *lomo
saltado* in town, live *criollo* music.
Las Tejas, Diez Canseco 340. Open
1100-2300 daily, good, typical Peruvian food.
Rosa Náutica, T01-445 0149. Built on old
British-style pier, Lima Bay. Delightful opulence, finest fish cuisine, experience the
atmosphere by buying an expensive beer in
the bar at sunset. 1230-2200.

*For an explanation of sleeping and eating price codes used in this guide, see inside the
front cover. Other relevant information is found in Essentials, see pages 61-66.*

††† ††† Wa Lok, Av Angamos Oeste 703, T01-447 1280. A branch of the famous Barrio Chino *chifa*, also serving good food in a tasteful, modern setting.

††† Bohemia, Av Santa Cruz 805, Ovalo Gutiérrez. Large menu of international food, great salads and sandwiches. Also at Av El Polo 706, p 2, Surco, and at Pasaje Nicolás de Rivera 142, opposite the main post office near the Plaza de Armas, centre, T427 5537.

††† Café Tarata, Pasaje Tarata 260. Good atmosphere, family-run, good varied menu.

††† Chifa Kun Fa, San Martin 459 at Av Larco. Great Peruvian style Chinese food, excellent wan-tan soup.

††† Dalmacia, San Fernando 401. Spanish-owned, casual gourmet restaurant serving tapas and main meals, excellent, seating on the terrace.

††† El Beduino, Av 28 de Julio 1301, T01-242 6642. Good, authentic Arabic food.

††† Il Postino, Colina 401, T446 8381. This is another restaurant serving great Italian food.

††† La Palachinke, Av Schell 120 at the bottom of Parque Kennedy. At the corner of the Diagonal, so very convenient, this place is recommended for its speciality pancakes.

††† Makoto Sushi Bar, Larcomar shopping centre, also Las Begonias 522, San Isidro. Very good for Japanese food, as the name implies.

††† Mamma Lola, Diez Canseco 119, T01-241 6335. Cosy restaurant serving good, tasty Italian food, efficient service.

††† Ricota, Pasaje Tarata 248. Charming café on a walkway, huge menu, big portions.

††† Sí Señor, Av Angamos Oeste 598. Mexican food, fun, loud. Also at Bolognesi 706, cheerful, lots of low-slung lights over the tables.

† Dino's Pizza, Av Cdte Espinar 374 and many other branches. Great pizza at a good price, delivery service.

† El Parquetito, Diez Canseco 150. Sitting outside by the park, or inside, serves breakfasts and a good cheap menu.

† Madre Natura, Chiclayo 815. Natural foods shop and eating place, highly recommended, closes at 2100.

† Naturaleza, Av Larco 870. Good value vegetarian restaurant, with good fixed menu, side dishes and fabulous desserts.

† Pardo's Chicken, Av Benavides 730. Chicken and chips, very good and popular (branches throughout Lima).

† Sandwich.com, Av Diagonal 234. Good, cheap sandwiches with interesting combinations of fillings, both hot and cold, also fruits, puddings and drinks.

† Super Rueda, Porta 133, also Av José Pardo 1224. Mexican food a-la Peru, fast food style, clean, open from 0800 till midnight (0600 on Sat), Sun 1100-2300.

Cafés

Café Café, Martin Olaya 250, near the Parque Kennedy roundabout. Very popular, good atmosphere, over 100 different blends of coffee, good salads and sandwiches, very popular with 'well-to-do' Limeños. Also in Larcomar, level 3, shop 2.

Café de la Paz, Lima 351, middle of Parque Kennedy. Good café right on the park, a nice place for an outdoor drink, the meals are on the expensive side.

Café Z, Mcal Oscar R Benavides 598 y José Gálvez, past Parque Kennedy. American owned, excellent Peruvian coffee, teas, hot chocolate, and the best homemade cakes away from home, cheap too. There is an interesting variety of seating, too.

C'est si bon, Av Cdte Espinar 663. Excellent cakes by the slice or whole, best in Lima.

Chef's Café, Av Larco 763. Nice place for a sandwich or coffee. Also has a little cart in Parque Kennedy until 2200 with good hot coffee to go.

Confitería La Biela, Diagonal 200 block, next to **Dove Vai**. A shiny café with glass and metal tables indoors and out.

Dove Vai, Diagonal 228. A bright *heladería* in this block of eating places; try the *encanto* with lumps of chocolate brownie.

Haiti, Av Diagonal 160, Parque Kennedy. Open almost round the clock daily, great for people watching, good ice cream.

Heladería 4D, Angamos Oeste 408. Open 1000-0100 daily, Italian ice cream, at other locations throughout Lima.

La Tiendecita Blanca, Av Larco 111 on Parque Kennedy. One of Miraflores' oldest, expensive, good people-watching, very good cakes, European-style food and delicatessen under the Café Suisse brand.

Pin Poini, small kiosk on Parque del Amor. Good place to watch the ocean and sip real Italian coffee.

San Antonio Café, Av Angamos Oeste 1494, also Vasco Núñez de Balboa 770, Rocca de Vergallo 201, Magdalena del Mar and Av

Primavera 373, San Borja. A fashionable *pastelería* chain, serving good coffee, cakes and snacks, not too expensive.

Tapas Bar, Manuel Bonilla 103, T01-242 7922. Expensive but very good tapas bar behind huge wooden doors, the tapas are a meal in themselves, extensive wine list, reserve a table at weekends.

Vivaldi, Av Ricardo Palma 260, 1 block from Parque Kennedy. A good café remiscent of a gentleman's club, with dark wood much newspaper reading, expensive though. Also at Conquistadores 212, San Isidro, is **Vivaldi Gourmet**, the group's international restaurant.

Zugatti, Av Larco 361, across from Parque Kennedy. Good Italian gelato.

Barranco *p109, map p110*

Try the various small restaurants under the Bridge of Sighs and down towards the cliff tops, open late, great cheap Peruvian food (eg *anticuchos*). **La Ermita**, with the glass roof, has been recommended.

ŸŸŸ **Canta Rana**, Génova 101, T01-477 8934. Open daily 1200-1700, good *ceviche* expensive, small portions.

ŸŸŸ **La Costa Verde**, on Barranquito beach, T01-441 3086. Excellent fish and wine, expensive but recommended as the best by Limeños, open 1200-2400 daily, Sun buffet.

ŸŸŸ **Manos Morenas**, Av Pedro de Osma 409, T01-467 0421. Open 1230-1630, 1900-2300. A popular Barranco establishment, serving pricey creole cuisine with excellent shows some evenings (cover charge for shows).

ŸŸŸ **Ñaylamp**, Av 2 de Mayo 239, T01-467 5011. Good seafood and ceviche, fashionable and expensive. The restaurant has a garden.

ŸŸ **Antica Trattoria**, Ugarte 242, T01-247 3443. In the same group as the Antica Pizzería in San Isidro, serving Italian and

seafood dishes, wooden tables, stone floors and wooden barrels in the ceiling.

ŸŸŸ **El Hornito**, Av Grau 209, T01-477 2465. A pizzería which also serves creole food, in the heart of Barranco on corner of the main plaza.

ŸŸ **Festín**, Av Grau 323, T247 7218. Huge menu, typical and international food in a café-style environment.

ŸŸ **Las Mesitas**, Av Grau 341. Open 1200-0200. Traditional tea rooms-cum-restaurant serving creole food and old sweet dishes which you won't find anywhere else in Lima.

Chorrillos *p109*

ŸŸŸ **Costa Sur**, Av Chorrillos 180, T251 2497. Typical Peruvian dishes, good value, try the *causa* with crab. Recommended.

ŸŸŸ **El Hawaiano**, Av Guardia Civil 323, T467 0317, also at Rep de Panamá 258, Barranco. Two related seafood restaurants with an excellent daily buffet (US$16), lunch only, expensive but well worth it.

ŸŸ **Punta Arenas**, Santa Teresa 455, 1 block from the 1st block of Av Huaylas, T467 0053. Tasty seafood, popular, good value.

Callao *p109*

Ÿ **Cebichería Mateo**, C Constitución 280. Worth trying as a good place for seafood.

Ÿ **Leo**, Jr Adolfo King 182. A local place serving good food.

Excursions

Canta *p114*

Ÿ **La Casona**, just off the main street. This is the best restaurant, serving local trout in an interesting old building.

Ÿ **Restaurant Cancay Vento**, in the hotel of the same name. It has an extensive menu.

❶ Bars and clubs

Lima has an excellent nightlife, with many places to choose from, all with different styles and themes. Often there is a cover charge ranging from US$3-10 per person. Unfortunately, there are some nightclubs and bars that deny entrance to people solely on the basis of skin colour and assumed economic status. We only include here the

names of the establishments that do not practise this policy.

Central Lima *p95, map p96*

The centre of town, specifically **Jr de la Unión** has many discotheques. It's best to avoid the nightlife spots on and around the intersection of Av Tacna, Av Piérola and Av de la Vega. These places are on the rough side and the foreigner will most likely receive much unwanted attention.

720 Downtown, Av Uruguay 183, Lima centre. Exclusively gay, best in the centre, this is a rough neighbourhood so take a taxi to and from the club.

El Rincón Cervecero, Jr de la Unión (Belén) 1045. German pub without the beer, fun. Recommended.

Estadio Futbol Sports Bar, Av Nicolás de Piérola 926 on the Plaza San Martín, T01-428 8866. Beautiful bar with a discotheque on the bottom floor, international football theme, good international and creole food. Recommended.

Imperio, Jr Camaná 9th block, Lima centre. Exclusively gay, one of the older gay clubs in Lima, taxi recommended.

Piano Bar Munich, Jr de la Unión 1044 (basement). Small and fun.

Queirolo Bar, Jr Camaná 900 at Jr Quilca. Excellent for local colour, "a must". Opposite is the Centre's version of **La Noche** (see Barranco, below).

Lima suburbs

San Isidro p106, map p104
Palos de Moguer, Av Emilio Cavenecia 129, T01-221 8363. Brews 4 different kinds of beer, typical bar food.

Punto G, Av Conquistadores 512. Very popular, really small. Recommended.

Miraflores p106, map p107
Bars
Barcelona, Larcomar shopping centre, T01-445 4823. One of the best pubs in the city.

Barra Brava, Av Grau 192, T01-241 5840. Lot's of fun, sports bar(ish).

Dionygreeks Pub, Av Dos de Mayo 385, T01-447 7958. Nice pub with Greek decor.

Media Naranja, C Schell 130, at the bottom of Parque Kennedy. Brazilian bar with typical drinks and food.

Murphys, C Schell 627, T01-242 1212, www.murphysperu.com. Great Irish pub, "a must", now doing food such as fish and chips, lookout for special events and happy hours.

The Old Pub, San Ramón 295 (Pizza Street), T01-242 8155, n_ella@yahoo.com. Cosy, with live music most days, English spoken, darts.

The Clash pub and gallery, Psje Tello 269, Miraflores, T01-444 3376. Excellent drinks, friendly barstaff, and great decor, exclusively gay with shows and events.

Clubs
There are many discotheques on Pizza St by Parque Kennedy.

Cocodrilo Verde, Francisco de Paula 226 near corner with Bellavista, Miraflores. Relaxed, stylish bar, slightly pricey but worth it for the Wed night jazz, and live music at weekends, occasionally charges cover for music at weekends.

Ministry, Altos de D'Onofrio, opposite Parque Kennedy, T01-9938 9231. Good music, performances and demonstrations of dance, exhibitions, tatooing, entry US$3. Recommended.

Santa Sede, Av 28 de Julio 441. Very popular, great music, fun crowd, gay friendly. Recommended.

Satchmo, Av La Paz 538, T01-442 8425. Live jazz, creole and blues shows.

Teatriz, Larcomar shopping centre, T01-242 3084. Modern, expensive entrance fee, very popular.

Barranco p109, map p110
Barranco is the capital of Lima nightlife. The following is a short list of some of the better bars and clubs. Pasaje Sánchez Carrión, right off the main plaza, used to be the heart of it all. Watering holes and discos line both sides of this pedestrian walkway, but crowds and noise are driving people elsewhere. Av Grau, just across the street from the plaza, is also lined with bars, eg El Ekeko, Av Grau 266, and Las Terrazas, Av Grau 290. Many of the bars in this area turn into discotheques as the evening goes on.

Bars
Bosa Nova, Bolognesi 660. Chilled student-style bar with good music.

El Dragón, N de Piérola 168, t01-797 1033, dragoncultural@hotmail.com. Popular bar and venue for music, theatre and painting.

El Grill de Costa Verde, part of the **Costa Verde** restaurant on Barranco beach. Young crowd, packed at weekends.

Juanitos, Av Grau, opposite the park. Barranco's oldest bar, a perfect place to start the evening.

La Noche, Bolognesi 307, at Pasaje Sánchez Carrión. A Lima institution and high standard, live music, Mon is jazz night, kicks off around 2200 (also in Central Lima).
La Posada del Angel, three branches on Pedro de Osma between 164 and 222. These are popular bars serving snacks and meals.

La Posada del Mirador, near the *Puente de los Suspiros* (Bridge of Sighs). Beautiful view of the ocean, but you pay for the privilege. Sargento Pimienta, Bolognesi 755. Live music, always a favourite with Limeños. Opposite is the relaxed Trinidad.

🎵 Entertainment

Cinemas

The newspaper *El Comercio* lists cinema information in the section called 'Luces'. Most cinemas have reduced prices on Tue. There are many good cinemas throughout the city. Most films are in English with subtitles and cost US$2 in the centre and around US$4-5 in Miraflores. Cinemas in the centre tend to have poor sound quality. The best chains are Cinemark, Cineplanet and UVK Multicines. Others include: Cine Roma, C Teniente Fernández 242, 9th block of Av Arequipa, Santa Beatriz, T01-433 8618. Multicine Starvision El Pacífico, on the Ovalo by Parque Kennedy, T01-445 6990, in Miraflores. Cine Clubs include: Cine Club Miraflores, Av Larco 770, in the Miraflores Cultural Centre building, T01-446 2649. Filmoteca de Lima, Av 9 de Diciembre 125 (better known as Colón), T01-331 0126.

Peñas

De Cajón, C Merino 2nd block, near 6th block of Av Del Ejército, Miraflores. Good *música negra*.
De Rompe y Raja, Manuel Segura 127, Barranco, T01-247 3271. One of several *peñas* in Barranco.

Del Carajo, San Ambrosio 328, Barranco T01-247 7977. All types of traditional music, Thu-Sat from 2200.
La Candelaria, Av Bolognesi 292, Barranco, T01-247 1314. This is a good Barranco peña, Fri-Sat 2130 onwards.
La Estación de Barranco, Pedro de Osma 112, Barranco, T01-477 5030. Good, family atmosphere, varied shows.
Las Brisas de Titicaca, Pasaje Wakuski 168, at the 1st block of Av Brasil near Plaza Bolognesi, Central Lima, T01-332 1881, www.brisasdeltiticaca.com. A Lima institution for folkloric music and dance, workshops, restaurant and bar.
Peña Poggi, Av Luna Pizarro 578, Barranco, T01-247 5790. Over 30 years old, traditional. Recommended.
Sachun, Av Del Ejército 657, Miraflores, T01-441 0123. Great shows on Tue to Sat.

Theatre

There are many theatres in the city, some of which are related to Cultural centres (see p138). The press gives details of performances. Theatre and concert tickets can be booked through Teleticket, T01-242 2823.
Teatro Segura, Jr Huancavelica 265, T01-427 9491. Most professional plays are staged here.

✵ Festivals and events

On 18 Jan is the anniversary of the founding of Lima. It is preceded, on the evening of the 17th, by the Gran Serenata in the Plaza de Armas with some of Peru's best musicians. Semana Santa, or Holy Week, is a colourful spectacle with processions. The end of May sees a beer festival which attracts many famous singers from Peru and some from abroad. 28-29 Jul is Independence, with music and fireworks in the Plaza de Armas on the evening before. 30 Aug is the day of Santa Rosa de Lima. Oct is the month of Our Lord of the Miracles with impressive processions (see Las Nazarenas church, above). On 3 Nov is San Martín de Porres.

O Shopping

Art galleries

See also Cultural centres p138, many of which have art galleries, cinemas and theatres.
Artco, Rouad y Paz Soldán 325, San Isidro, T01-221 3579, www.artcogaleria.com. Mon-Fri 1100-2000, Sat 1030-1330, 1530-1950.
Galería San Francisco, Plaza San Francisco 208, Barranco, T01-477 0537. A gallery in a pleasant building on a small plaza a little way from the centre of Barranco.
La Casa Azul, Alfonso Ugarte 150, Miraflores, T01-446 6380, T9807 1661 (mob). Marcia Moreno and Jorge Rengifo, for advice on and sales of contemporary art and antique objects, handicrafts and furniture.
Lucia de la Puente, Paseo Sáenz Peña 206, Barranco, T01-477 9740, www.gluciadela puente.com. Open Mon-Sat 1100-2000. A gallery exhibiting modern Peruvian art (non-Andean), also artwork for sale and a good small café.
Praxis, C San Martin 689, Barranco, T01-477 2822. Mon-Fri 0930-1330, 1700-2100, Sat 1700-2100. Art exhibitions and sales.
Wu, Paseo Sáenz Peña 129, Barranco, T01-247 4685. Mon-Fri 1000-1300, 1400-2000, Sat 1100-1300, 1630-2000. Artist Frances Wu's studio is also a gallery of engravings, etchings and other graphics, with an emphasis on Peruvian artists, including designs taken from engraved gourds.

Bookshops

Books
Crisol, Ovalo Gutiérrez, Av Santa Cruz 816, San Isidro, T01-221 1010, Below Cine Planet. Large bookshop with café, titles in English, French and Spanish. Also in Jockey Plaza Shopping Center, Av Javier Prado Este 4200, Surco, T01-436 004.
Ibero Librerías, Av Diagonal 500, T01-242 2798, and Larco 199, T01-445 5520, Miraflores. Stocks Footprint Handbooks as well as a wide range of other titles. Outlet for **Special Book Services**, Av Angamos Oeste 301, Miraflores, T01-242 4497.
La Familia, Av Diagonal 382, T01-447 8353, and Schell 279, T01-444 3993, Miraflores. Has

a good selection of books on a wide variety of topics, helpful staff. Other branches at *La Tertulia*, CCPUCP, Av Camino Real 1075, San Isidro, and in the Jockey Plaza and El Polo commercial centres in Surco.
Librería Cultura Peruana, José Gálvez 124, Miraflores. A wide selection of books on Peruvian culture, from art and archaeology to cooking.
Virrey chain has a great selection, but few in English: Larcomar shopping centre (local 210), Miraflores, Pasaje Nicolás de Rivera, Lima centre behind the Municipalidad, T01-427 5080, and Miguel Dasso 141, San Isidro (next door is **Librería Sur**, No 143).
Zeta, Av Cdte Espinar 219, T01-446 5139 and at the airport. Stocks Footprint and other guide books.

Magazines
Whether in downtown Lima or Miraflores, almost all street kiosks sell up to date magazines in English such as *Time*, *Newsweek*, *People* etc. For the most recently published magazines and newspapers, try **Mallcco's**, Av Larco 175, on the Parque Kennedy roundabout, open daily 0800-2100. It has a wide variety of magazines (expensive but the latest releases) and newspapers from England. In front of **Café Haiti** by Parque Kennedy, you'll often see the men with stacks of newspapers for sale. These are taken from arriving international flights so tend to be only a day or two old; bargain hard. Hotel Sheraton sells the *New York Times* and the *Wall Street Journal*. Many cafés have foreign newspapers to browse through while enjoying a cup of coffee or a sandwich.

Camping equipment

Camping gas (in small blue bottles) is available from any large hardware store or bigger supermarket, about US$3.
Alpamayo, Av Larco 345, Miraflores at Parque Kennedy, T01-445 1671. Sleeping mats, boots, rock shoes, climbing gear, water filters, tents, backpacks etc, very expensive but top quality equipment. The owner speaks fluent English and offers good information.

Camping Center, Av Benavides 1620, Miraflores, T01-242 1779. Selection of tents, backpacks, stoves, camping and climbing gear.
Huantzan, Jr Tarapacá 384, Magdalena, T01-460 6101. Equipment sales and rentals, MSR stoves, backpacks, boots.
Mountain Worker, Centro Comercial Camino Real, level A, store 17, San Isidro, T01-813 8367. Quality camping gear for all types of weather, made to order products as well. Recommended.
Outdoor Peru, Centro Comercial Chacarilla, store 211, on Av Caminos del Inca 257, Surco, T01-372 0428. Decent selection.
Todo Camping, Av Angamos Oeste 350, Miraflores, near Av Arequipa, T01-447 6279. Sells 100% deet, bluet gas canisters, lots of accessories, tents, crampons and backpacks.

Handicrafts

Since so many artesans have come from the Sierra to Lima, it is possible to find any kind of handicraft in the capital. The quality is high. Among the many items which can be bought here are silver and gold handicrafts, Indian hand-spun and hand-woven textiles and manufactured textiles in Indian designs. Although Lima is more expensive, it is often impossible to find the same quality of goods elsewhere. You can find llama and alpaca wool products such as ponchos, rugs, hats, blankets, slippers, coats, sweaters, etc. Note that genuine alpaca is odourless wet or dry, but wet llama stinks.

Lima is a good place to buy *arpilleras*, appliqué pictures of Peruvian life (originated in Chile with political designs). These are made with great skill and originality by women in the shanty towns. The fine leather products on sale are mostly hand made. The *mate burilado*, or engraved gourd found in every tourist shop, is cheap and a genuine expression of folk art. These are cheaper in the villages near Huancayo (see p486).

Crafts
Agua y Tierra, Diez Canseco 298 y Alcanfores, Miraflores, T01-444 6980. Good for fine crafts and indigenous art.
Artesanía Santo Domingo, Plaza Santo Domingo, by the church of that name, in Lima centre, T01-428 9860. Good Peruvian crafts.

Centro Comercial El Alamo, corner of La Paz y Diez Canseco, Miraflores. Artesanía shops with good choice.
Kuntur Wasi, Ocharan 182, Miraflores, T01-444 0557. English-speaking owner, very knowledgeable about Peruvian textiles, frequently has exhibitions of fine folk art and crafts.
La Casa de la Mujer Artesana, Juan Pablo Ferandini 1550, Av Brasil, cuadra 15, Pueblo Libre, T01-423 8840, F423 4031. A co-operative run by the Movimiento Manuela Ramos, excellent quality work mostly from *pueblos jóvenes*, open Mon-Fri 0900-1300, 1400-1700.
Las Pallas, Cajamarca 212, 5th block of Av Grau, Barranco, T01-477 4629, Mon-Sat 0900-1900. Very high quality handicrafts (textiles, ceramics, masks, etc), English, French and German spoken. The owner is Mari Solari.

Alpaca and cotton
There are bargains in clothing made from high quality Pima cotton.
Alpaca 111, Av Larco 671, Miraflores, T01-447 1623, www.alpaca111.com. High quality alpaca, baby alpaca and vicuña items.
Alpaca 859, Av Larco 859, Miraflores. Excellent quality alpaca and baby alpaca products.
Da Capo, Aramburú 920, dpto 402, San Isidro, T01-441 0714. Beautiful alpaca scarves and shawls in new designs.
La Casa de la Alpaca, Av La Paz 665, Miraflores, T01-447 6271. Open Mon-Fri 0930-2030.
Silvania Prints, Diéz Canseco 337A, Miraflores. Sells modern silk-screen prints on Pima cotton with pre-Columbian designs.

Fine art
Dédalo, Paseo Sáenz Peña 295, Barranco, T01-477 0562. This is a labyrinthine shop selling modern designer crafts, furniture, jewellery and other items, but it is as good as a gallery. It also has a nice coffee shop and has cinema shows.

Jewellery
Ilaria, Av 2 de Mayo 308, San Isidro, T01-221 8575. Jewellery and silverware with interesting designs. There are other branches in Lima, Cusco and Arequipa. Recommended.

Lima Shopping

Maps

Dress soberly and take your passport when going to these places (except Lima 2000).
Instituto Geográfico Nacional, Av Aramburú 1190, Surquillo, T01-475 9960, F475 3085. Mon-Fri 0830-1730. They have topographical maps of the whole country, mostly at 1:100,000, political and physical maps of all departments and satellite and aerial photographs. They also have a new series of tourist maps for trekking, eg of the Cordillera Blanca, the Cusco area, at 1:250,000.
Instituto Geológico Minero Y Metalúrgico (Ingemmet), Av Canadá 1470, San Borja, T01-225 3128. Mon-Fri 0800-1300, 1400-1600. Sells a huge selection of geographic maps ranging from US$12 to US$112. Also satellite, aeromagnetic, geochemical and departmental mining maps. Enquire about new digital products.
Lima 2000, Av Arequipa 2625, Lince (near the intersection with Av Javier Prado), T01-440 3486, www.lima2000.com.pe. Mon-Fri 0900-1300 and 1400-1800. Have an excellent street map of Lima (the only one worth buying), US$10, or US$14 in booklet form. Provincial maps and a country road map as well. Good for road conditions and distances, perfect for driving or cycling.
Ministerio de Agricultura, Av Salaverry y Húsares de Junín, Jesús María, T01-433 3034. Mon-Fri 0830-1300, 1400-1700. Complete set of 1:25,000 blueline maps, good service.
Ministerio de Transporte, Av 28 de Julio 800, Lima centre, T01-433 7800. Mon-Fri 0800-1230, 1400-1600. Maps and plans of land communication routes, slow and bureaucratic.
Servicio Aerofotográfico Nacional, Las Palmas Airforce Base. Mon-Fri 0800-1400. Aerial photographs: photos from mid-1950's aerial survey available, but they are expensive. Expect a waiting period as short as one day or as long as two weeks.

Markets

Av Petit Thouars cuadras 51 a 54 (parallel to Av Arequipa, a few blocks from Parque Kennedy). Here you'll find an unnamed crafts market area with a large courtyard and lots of small flags. This is the largest crafts arcade in Miraflores. From here to Av Ricardo Palma the street is lined with crafts markets.
La Portada del Sol, on cuadra 54 of Petit Thouars, has a small café with reasonable prices and good coffee. All are open 7 days a week until late(ish).
Feria Artesanal, Av La Marina y Av Sucre, in Pueblo Libre, is smaller than it used to be but is cheaper than Av Petit Thouars. It is no longer regarded as a safe area.
Parque Kennedy, the main park of Miraflores, hosts a daily crafts market from 1700-2300.
Polvos Azules, C García Naranjo, La Victoria, just off Av Grau in the centre of town. This is the official black market of Lima. The normal connotations of a 'black market' do not apply here as this establishment is an accepted part of Lima society, condoned by the government and frequented by people of all economic backgrounds. It's good for cameras, hiking boots, music and walkmans. This is not a safe area, so be alert and put your money in your front pockets.

Music

Music City, Av José Larco 459, Miraflores. Probably the best, but not the cheapest, place to buy CDs and music tapes, all original, no pirated material.

Photography

El Ojo Ajeno, 28 de Julio 547, T01-444 6999, http://centrofotografia.perucultural.org.pe Mon-Fri 0900-2100, Sat 0900-1800. A recommended photographic gallery.
Foto Magnum, Ocoña 190, Lima Centre, T01-427 1599. Mon-Fri 0900-2000. For camera film and camera accessories.
Laboratorio Color Profesional, Av Benavides 1171, Miraflores T01-446 7421. Mon-Fri 0900-1900, Sat 0930-1300. Professional quality developing, fairly priced, touch-ups, repair services, excellent for slide developing, sells top quality equipment, film and accessories, the best you'll find in Lima. Highly recommended.
Miranda's Photography, Jr Cusco 592, 445A, centre, T01-426 7920, T9706 9097 (mob), mirandas_photography@hotmail.com. Mon-Fri 1100-1800. Good for repairs.

Supermarkets

Lima has 4 main supermarket chains: **E Wong**, **Metro**, **Plaza Vea** and **Santa Isabel** (which are usually smaller than the others).

They all are well- stocked and carry a decent supply of imported goods (Marmite, Tesco products etc). **Santa Isabel** at Av Benavides 487 y Av Alcanfores in Miraflores is open 24 hrs.

▲ Activities and tours

Cycling

Best Internacional, Av Comandante Espinar 2320, Miraflores, T01-446 4044, Mon-Sat 1000-1400, 1600-2000. Sells leisure and racing bikes, also repairs, parts and accessories.
Biclas, Av Conquistadores 641, San Isidro, T01-440 0890, Mon-Fri 1000-1300, 1600-2000, Sat 1000-1300. Knowledgeable staff, tours possible, good selection of bikes, repairs and accessories, cheap airline boxes for sale. Highly recommended.
BikeMavil, Av Aviación 4023, Surco, T01-449 8435, www.bikemavil.com. Mon-Sat 0930-2100. Rental service, repairs, excursions, selection of mountain and racing bicycles.
Casa Okuyama, Manco Cápac 590, La Victoria, T01-330 9131, www.biciperu.com. Mon-Fri 0900-1300, 1415-1800, Sat 0900-1300. Repairs, parts, try here for 28 inch tyres, excellent service.
Neuquén, Jr Paruro 875, El Cercado, T01-427 2379. For Shimano parts.
Peru Bike, 28 de Julio 1381, Miraflores, T01-241 6367, www.perubike.com. Experienced agency leading tours, specializing in the Andes, professional guiding. Also has a mountain bike school and a workshop.
Willy-Pro (Williams Arce), Av Javier Prado Este 3339, San Borja, T01-346 4082, Mon-Sat 0800-2000. Has a selection of specialized bikes and helpful staff.

Mountaineering and trekking clubs

Alpamayo, Av Larco 345, Miraflores at Parque Kennedy, T01-445 1671. Good climbing and hiking equipment shop.
Asociación de Andinismo de la Universidad de Lima, Universidad de Lima, Javier Prado Este s/n, T01-437 6767. Meetings on Wed 1800-2000, offers climbing courses.

Club de Montañeros Américo Tordoya, Jr Tarapacá 384, Magdalena, T01-460 6101. Meetings Thu 2000, contact Gonzalo Menacho. Climbing excursions ranging from easy to difficult.
Grupo Cordillera, T01-481 6649, T9917 3832 (mob). Adventure tourism, weekly excursions.
Trekking and Backpacking Club, Jr Huáscar 1152, Jesús María, Lima 11, T01-423 2515, 9987 4193 (mob), www.angelfire.com/mi2/tebac. Señor Miguel Chiri Valle, treks arranged, including in the Cordillera Blanca.

Parapenting

From Lima, Pasamayo (430 m) is a good launch zone, as are the 80-m high cliffs of the Costa Verde, which are suitable for beginners.
Fly Adventure, Jorge Chávez 658, Miraflores, T01-9816 5461 (Luis Munarriz), T9900 9150 (Eduardo Gómez). US$25 for 15-min tandem flight over the cliffs, 4 to 6-day courses US$250-350. Recommended.

Scuba diving

AquaSport, Av Conquistadores 645, San Isidro, T01-221 7270, www.aquasportperu.com. Owner is a CMAS instructor, gear for rent, tours and courses offered and quality equipment for sale.
Peru Divers, Av Huaylas 205, Chorrillos, T01-251 6231, www.perudivers.com. Open Mon-Fri 0900-1900, Sat 0900-1700. Owner Lucho Rodríguez is a certified PADI instructor who offers certification courses, tours and a wealth of good information.

Surfing

Focus, Leonardo Da Vinci 208, San Borja, T01-475 8459. Shaping factory and surf boards, some decent boards, knowledgeable about local spots and conditions, one of the better surf shops in Peru, rents boards.

Klimax, José González 488, Miraflores, T01-447 1685. Sells new and secondhand boards, knowledgeable.

Wayo Whiler, Av 28 de Julio 287, Barranco, T01-247 6343, www.wayowhilar.com.pe. Makes all kinds of boards, sells clothing and materials, rentals and repairs, email in advance to have a board ready for when you arrive, can also organize excursions and runs a surf school with his brother (US$100 per month).

Spectator sports

Matches and various athletic events take place at the National Stadium, in the centre of the city on ground given by the British community on the 100th anniversary of Peru's Declaration of Independence. The local soccer derby is *La U (Universitario)* against *Alianza Lima* (tickets US$2.50-25). Matches are also played at Alianza's stadium in the district of La Victoria and Universitario's new stadium in the La Molina district. **The Jockey Club of Peru** (Hipódromo de Monterrico) has horse races every Tue and Thu at 1900 more-or-less, Sat and Sun at 1400. Bets start at US$0.75. For information about Peruvian Paso horses contact the **Asociación Nacional de Caballos de Paso** at T01-447 6331.

Tour operators

Lima is busting at the seams with tour and travel agencies. Some are good and reliable, many are not. If possible, use agencies in or close to the area you wish to visit and always shop around. Bargaining ability is a plus. See also **Fertur Peru** p92. We have received comp- laints about agencies, or their representatives at bus offices or the airport arranging tours and collecting money for companies that either do not exist or which fall far short of what is paid for. Do not conduct business anywhere other than in the agency's office and insist on a written contract.

Class Adventure Travel, Av Grimaldo del Solar 463, Miraflores, T5411 5238 0991/92, www.cat-travel.com. Dutch-owned and run, one of the best. Highly recommended.

Coltur, Av José Pardo 138, Miraflores, T01-241 5551, www.coltur.com.pe. With offices in Cusco and Arequipa, very helpful, well-organized.

Cóndor Travel, Mayor Armando Blondet 249, San Isidro, T01-442 7305, www. condortravel.com.pe. Also has a branch in Cusco and another in Quito, Ecuador, for tours throughout the Andes.

Dasatariq, Jr Francisco Bolognesi 510, Miraflores, T01-447 7772, www.dasatariq.com. Also in Cusco. A well-organized company with a good reputation and helpful staff.

Domiruth Travel Services, Jr Rio de Janeiro 216-218, Miraflores, T01-610 6022, www.domiruth.com. pe. Tours throughout Peru, from the mystical to adventure travel.

Explorandes, C San Fernando 320, T01-445 8683, www.explorandes.com.pe. Award-winning company with a wide range of adventure and cultural tours throughout Peru. Offices in Cusco p175 and Huaraz p339.

Hada Tours, 2 de Mayo 529, Miraflores, T01-446 8157, www.hada tours.com.pe. 20 years of experience.
Highland Peru Tours, Atahualpa 197, Miraflores, T01-242 6292, www.highland peru.com.
Ideas, Ampay 036, San Miguel, T01-451 3603, ideas-mz@amauta.rcp.net.pe. Alternative tours of Lima, putting Inca and pre-Inca culture in its present context.
InkaNatura Travel, Manuel Banón 461, San Isidro, Lima 27, T01-440 0022, www.inka natura.com. Also in Cusco, offers good tours with knowledgeable guides, emphasis on sustainable tourism and conservation.
Kinjyo Travel, Las Camelias 290, San Isidro, T01-442 4000, also office in Cusco, postmast@kinj yo.com.pe.
Lima Tours, Jr Belén 1040, Lima centre, T01-424 5110, and Av Pardo y Alliaga 698, San Isidro, T01-222 2525, www.limatours. com.pe. Recommended for tours in the capital and around the country.

Marilí Tours, Diez Canseco 392, p 2, T01-242 9567, www.marilitours.com.pe. Tours of all types, including adventure and ecological, within Peru and outside.
Peru Expeditions, Av Arequipa 5241-504, Lima 18, T01-447 2057, www.Peru-exped itions.com. Specializing in expeditions in 4x4 vehicles and Andes crossings.
Peru Travel Bureau, Sebastián Tellería 45, San Isidro, T01-222 1909, postmast@ptb. com.pe. Recommended.
Roma Tours, Jr Ica 330, next to **Hostal Roma**, T/F427 7572, dantereyes@hotmail. com. Good, reliable. Administrator Dante Reyes is very friendly and speaks English.
Rutas del Peru SAC, Av Enrique Palacios 1110, Miraflores, www.rutasdelperu.com. Tailor-made trips and overland expeditions in trucks.
Servicios Aéreos AQP SA, Los Castaños 347, San Isidro, T01-222 3312, www. saaqp.com.pe. Comprehensive service, tours offered throughout the country.
Victor's Travel Service, Jr de la Unión (Belén) 1068, T01-431 4195, victortravel @terra.com.pe. Hotel reservations (no commission, free pick-up), free maps of Lima and Peru, Mon-Sat 0900-1800, very helpful.
Viracocha, Av Vasco Núñez de Balboa 191, Miraflores, T01-445 3986, F447 2429. Very helpful, especially with flights, cultural and mystical tours, also hiking, rafting and birdwatching.

Private guides
The Ministry of Industry Tourism, Integration and International Business certifies guides and can provide a list. Most are members of AGOTUR (Asociación de Guías Oficiales de Turismo), Baltazar La Torre 165, depto 101-D, San Isidro, T01-422 8937, agoturlima@yahoo.com. Always book well in advance. Most guides speak English or a language other than Spanish.
Escorted Economic Overland Peru, T/F01-567 5107, victormelgar777@ yahoo.com, is run by an experienced tour guide, Víctor Melgar. He'll escort individuals, families and groups through-out Peru and Bolivia, safely and economically. He also runs **Hostal Víctor**, see Sleeping.

🚌 Transport

Air

Domestic flight schedules are given under the relevant destinations. To enquire about arrivals or departures, T01-595 0666, www.lap.com.pe. For all other information see Ins and outs p91.

Airline offices
Domestic Aero Cóndor, C Juan de Arona 781, San Isidro, T01-614 6000. **Lan**, Av José Pardo 513, Miraflores, T01-213 8200, open 0900-1900, Sat 0900-1300. **LC Busre**, Los Tulipanes 218, Lince, T01-619 1313. **Star Up**, Av José Pardo 269, Miraflores, T01-447 7573. **Tans**, Jr Belén 1015, Lima centre, and Av Arequipa 5200, Miraflores, T01-213 6000.
International Aeroflot, Av Comandante Espinar 233, Miraflores, T01-444 8717. **Aerolíneas Argentinas**, Av José Pardo 805, p 3, Miraflores, T01-444 0810. **Air France**, Av José Pardo 601, Miraflores, T01-444 9285. **Air Madrid**, Martín Olaya 401, oficina 201, or **Tika Tours**, Pasaje Champagnat 139, Miraflores, T01-446 3644, for reservations. **Alitalia**, Mártir Olaya 129, oficina 1702, Miraflores, T01-447 3899. **American Airlines**, Av Canaval y Moreyra 390, San Isidro, and in Hotel Las Américas, Av Benavides y Av Larco, Miraflores, T01-211 7000. **Avianca**, Av Paz Soldán 225, oficina C5, San Isidro, T01-445 0506. **British Airways**, C Andalucía 174, Miraflores, T01-411 7800. **Continental**, C Victor Belaúnde 147, oficina 101, San Isidro, and in the Hotel Marriott, 13th block of Av Larco, Miraflores, T01-221 4340. **Copa**, Av Dos de Mayo 741, Miraflores, T01-610 0810. **Delta**, C Victor Belaúnde 147, San Isidro, T01-211 9211. **Iberia**, Av Camino Real 390, p 9, San Isidro, T01-411 7800. **KLM**, Av José Pardo 805, p6, Miraflores, T01-421 9500. **Lacsa**, Av Comandante Espinar 331, Miraflores, T01-446 0758. **Lan Chile**, see Domestic airlines, above. **Lloyd Aéreo Boliviano**, Av José Pardo 231, Miraflores, T01-241 5510. **Lufthansa**, Av Jorge Basadre

1330, San Isidro, T01-442 4455. **Taca Perú**, Av Comandante Espinar 331, Miraflores, T01-213 7000. **Tame**, C Andalucía 174, Miraflores, T01-422 6600. **Varig**, Av Camino Real 456, p 8, San Isidro, T01-221 0628.

Bus

Although Lima is home to a seemingly never-ending list of bus companies, only a small percentage can actually be recommended.

Local
Lima centre to Miraflores Av Arequipa runs 52 blocks between the downtown Lima area and Parque Kennedy in Miraflores. There is no shortage of public transport on this avenue; they have 'Todo Arequipa' on the windscreen. When heading towards downtown from Miraflores the window sticker should say 'Wilson/Tacna'. To get to Parque Kennedy from downtown look on the windshield for 'Larco/Schell/Miraflores', 'Chorrillos/ Huaylas' or 'Barranco/Ayacucho'.
Vía Expresa Lima's only urban freeway – Vía Expresa – runs from Plaza Grau in the centre of town, to the northern tip of the district of Barranco. This six-lane thorough-fare, locally known as *El Zanjón* (The Ditch), with a separate bus lane in the middle, is the fastest way to cross the city. In order from Plaza Grau the eight stops are: 1 Av México; 2 Av Canadá; 3 Av Javier Prado; 4 Corpac; 5 Av Aramburú; 6 Av Angamos; 7 Av Ricardo Palma, for Parque Kennedy; 8 Av Benavides. Buses downtown for the Vía Expresa can be caught on Av Tacna, Av Wilson (also called Garcilaso de la Vega), Av Bolivia and Av Alfonso Ugarte. These buses are a target of pickpockets who sometimes work in groups. If you're standing in the aisle, be extra careful.
Callao Lima is at least 20 mins away by *colectivos*, US$0.30, bus US$0.25, taxi US$3-4 to the centre or Miraflores. Do not take a bus back to Lima after dark.

● *If arriving in Lima by bus from the north and heading for the airport, you do not need to go into the centre: ask to be let out at 'Fiori' (look for the sign on top of a building on the left hand side of the highway). This is by the junction of the Panamericana and Av Tomás Valle, which leads almost to Jorge Chávez. Take a taxi from Fiori.*

⁝ How not to be taken for a ride

When the city of Lima tried to introduce meters in taxis, it failed. Almost anyone who puts a small sticker behind the windscreen can pass as a cabbie. 'Official taxis' were simply too expensive and despised by the locals and by now they have almost disappeared. If you flag down a taxi in Miraflores, you will be asked (depending on your language skills) to pay up to S/.25 (almost US$7) to go to the city centre. Some locals and ex-pats pay only S/.7 (about US$2). A reasonable price is between S/.8 and S/.12 (US$2.25-3.35), depending on the destination. Bargaining is done in a friendly, almost joking fashion and always before you enter the taxi. If you don't speak Spanish, use your fingers (one for each sol) and smile. Despite the hardship, Peruvians have a great sense of humour. When you have some cash to spare and if you like the driver – some of them are professional people just trying to make extra money – contract him by the hour for the current rate of S/.15 (US$4.15).

Pachacámac If you plan to take public transport, go to the Pan-American Highway (south-bound) and take a combi with a sticker in the window reading 'Pachacámac/Lurín' (US$0.85). Let the driver know you want to get off at the ruins. A taxi will cost approximately US$4.30, but if you don't ask the driver to wait for you (an extra cost), finding another to take you back to Lima may be a bit tricky. For organized tours contact a tour operator, listed above.

Canta Bus from/to Lima, 100 km, 3 hrs, US$2, **Trans El Chaparito** (Av G Unger 601, San Martin de Porres, Lima) and **Trans Cueva Santa** (Av G Unger 369) offer an hourly service between them at weekends and every 2 hrs on weekdays. **Cueva Santa** buses from Lima continue to **Huaros**, **Laguna Chuchun** and **La Viuda**. A few **combis** run to La Viuda daily from Canta, 3 hrs, US$2. To **Obrajillo** from Canta, 5 km, 10 mins, US$0.50. Combis leave when full. To **Huallay and Cerro de Pasco** from Canta, only occasional vehicles cross the La Viuda pass (4,500m).

Taxi colectivos
Regular private cars acting as taxis (*colectivos*) charge US$0.50. They are a faster, more comfortable option than municipal public transportation, but they are no safer. There are three routes: 1 between Av Arequipa and Av Tacna which runs from Miraflores to the centre of Lima; 2 between Plaza San Martín and Callao; 3 between the Vía Expresa and the district of Chorrillos. Look for the coloured sticker posted on the windscreen. These cars will stop at any time to pick people up. When full (usually five or six people) they will only stop to let someone off, then the process begins again to fill the empty space.

Taxis
Conventional taxis operate without meters so agree the fare before you get in. Tips are not expected. As driving a taxi in Lima (or anywhere in Peru) simply requires a windshield sticker saying 'Taxi', they come in all colours and sizes. By law, though, all must have the vehicle's registration number painted on the side. If it does not, don't take it. Yellow taxis are usually the safest since they have a number, the driver's name and radio contact. A large number of taxis are also white. The South Korean company Daewoo's Tico is most common, but they are now regarded as unsuitable for the rigours of Lima traffic (they crumple too easily), so take something more substantial. Whatever you choose, always use the seatbelt. The following are taxi fares for some of the more common routes, give or take a sol. From downtown Lima to: Parque Kennedy (Miraflores), US$2. Museo de la Nación, US$2. South American Explorers, US$2. Archaeology Museum, US$2. Immigration,

US$1.15. Barranco, US$3. From Miraflores (Parque Kennedy) to: Museo de la Nación, US$2. Archaeology Museum, US$3. Immigration, US$2. Official taxi companies, registered with the Municipality of Lima are without a doubt the safest option but cost much more than just picking one up in the street. Hourly rates possible. Some are **Taxi América**, T01-265 1960; **Moli Taxi**, T01-479 0030; **Taxi Real**, T01-470 6263; **Taxi Seguro**, T01-241 9292; **Taxi Tata**, T01-274 5151; **TCAM**, run by Carlos Astacio, T01-983 9305, safe, reliable. Recommended, knowledgeable drivers: **César A Canales N**, T01-436 6184, T9687 3310 (mob), or through **Home Perú**, only speaks Spanish, reliable. **Hugo Casanova Morella**, T01-485 7708 (he lives in La Victoria), for city tours, travel to airport, etc. **Mónica Velásquez Carlich**, T01-425 5087, T01-943 0796 (mob), vc_monica@hotmail.com, airport pick-ups, tours, speaks English.

Long distance

The area around the terminals on Av Carlos Zavala is very unsafe at any time of day but much more so at night. You are strongly advised to take a taxi to and from these terminals. Make sure you see your gear being stored on the correct bus as the place is always very busy. 'Mistakes', intentional or innocent, are not uncommon.

The following is a concise, user-friendly list of the companies repeatedly recommended for either their service or professionalism. Note that some less reputable companies are included simply because they're the only ones with buses to certain destinations. It's best to buy tickets the day before travelling. Most offer daily service. Confirm that the bus leaves from same place that the ticket was purchased. For prices and approximate duration of trip, refer to the destination. **Cruz del Sur**, Jr Quilca 531, Lima centre, T01-424 6158, www.cruzdelsur.com.pe. The website accepts Visa bookings without surcharge. This terminal has routes to many destinations in Peru with **Ideal** ('ee-de-al') service, meaning quite comfortable buses and periodic stops for food and bathroom breaks, a cheap option with a quality company. They go to: **Ica**, **Arequipa**, **Cusco**, **Puno**, **Chiclayo**, **Trujillo**, **Chincha**, **Cañete**, **Camaná**, **Ilo**, **Moquegua**, **Pisco** and **Juliaca**.

The other terminal is at Av Javier Prado Este 1109, San Isidro, T01-225 6163. This terminal offers the *Imperial* service (luxury buses), more expensive and direct, with no chance of passengers in the aisle, and *Cruzero* service (super luxury buses). They go to: **Tumbes**, **Sullana**, **Huancayo**, **Piura**, **Chiclayo**, **Trujillo**, **Huaraz**, **Jauja**, **Camaná**, **Arequipa**, **Moquegua**, **Ilo**, **Tacna**, **Cusco** and **La Paz** (this service is *Imperial* only to Arequipa, where you must transfer to an Ideal bus for the remaining leg of the trip). *Imperial* buses stop at the central terminal when going north and Ideal buses stop at the Javier Prado terminal when going south. **Ormeño**, depart from and arrive at Av Carlos Zavala 177, Lima centre, T01-427 5679; also Av Javier Prado Este 1059, 310alina, T01-472 1710, www.grupo-ormeno.com. The following buses are all owned and operated by Ormeño: *Expreso Ancash* (routes to the **Huaraz** area), *Expreso Continental* (routes to the **north**), *Expreso San Cristóbal* (to the **southeast**), *Expreso Chinchano* (to the **south coast** and **Arequipa**) and *Expreso Internacional* (despite the name, to destinations throughout Peru). Ormeño also offers *Royal Class* and *Business Class* service to certain destinations. These buses are very comfortable with bathrooms. They arrive and depart from the Javier Prado terminal, but *Business* buses stop at both terminals. Javier Prado is the best place to buy any Ormeño ticket.

Other companies include: **Transportes Atahualpa**, Jr Sandia 266, Lima Centre, T01-428 7732. Direct to Cajamarca continuing on to Celendín. **Transportes Chanchamayo**, Av Manco Cápac 1052, La Victoria, T01-265 6850. To Tarma, San Ramón and La Merced. **CIVA**, Paseo de La República 569-571, La Victoria, T01-330 4080, terminal at Av 28 de Julio y Paseo de La República, T01-332 5236, www.civa.com.pe. To all parts of the country. Has various levels of service, but mixed reports about this company. **Ettsa**, Paseo de la República cuadra 7. Good service to the **north**, **Chiclayo**, **Piura**, **Tumbes**. **Flores**, Paseo de la República cuadra 6. Good buses to the **south**. **Transportes León de Huánuco**, Av 28 de Julio 1520, La Victoria, T01-424 3893. Daily to **Huánuco**, **Tingo María** and **Pucallpa**. **Línea**, José Gálvez 999, Lima centre, T01-424 0836, www.transportes

linea.com.pe. To destinations in the **north**: Molina, Av Nicolás de Arriola 2090-92 y Av San Luis 750, San Luis, T01-324 2137/21317. Good service to **Ayacucho** via **Pisco**. **Móvil Tours**, Av Paseo de La República 749, Lima Centre near the national stadium, T01-332 0024. Recommended service to **Huaraz** (double-decker buses at 2300 and 0100, lots of leg room, comfortable), **Chiclayo** and **Chachapoyas** (should you want to go straight through). **PerúBus/Soyuz**, Av México 333, T01-266 1515, www.soyuz.com.pe. To **Ica** every 8 mins, well-organized, but the buses stop frequently so don't put luggage on the overhead racks as it's easy for bags to 'walk'. **Rodríguez**, Av Roosevelt 393, Lima Centre, T01-428 0506, terminal at Av Paseo de La República 749, opposite national stadium. To **Huaraz**, **Caraz**, **Yungay**, **Carhuaz**. Recommended to arrive in Huaraz and then use local transportation to points beyond. Good. Various levels of bus service. **Royal Tours**, Av Paseo de la República 3630, San Isidro, T01-440 6624. To **Huánuco**, **Tingo María** and **Pucallpa**.

International
Ormeño, Av Javier Prado 1059, Santa Catalina, T01-472 1710. To **Guayaquil** (29 hrs, with a change of bus at the border, US$50), **Quito** (38 hrs), **Cali** (56 hrs), **Bogotá** (70 hrs), **Caracas** (100 hrs), **Santiago** (54 hrs), **Mendoza** (78 hrs), **Buenos Aires** (90 hrs). A maximum of 20 kilos is allowed per person. Depending on the destination, extra weight penalties range from US$1-3 per kilo. **El Rápido**, Av Rivera Navarrete 2650, Lince, T01-447 6101. Service to Argentina and Uruguay only.

For international service, it's cheaper to take a bus to the border, cross and then another to your final destination. The week before and after 28 Jul (Peruvian independence day) and Semana Santa (Holy Week) are the most travelled times of the year. Bus tickets out of Lima are extremely hard to come by unless purchased in advance. Expect prices to double during these dates and check in earlier than you normally would to avoid possible problems.

Car

Most rental companies have an office at the airport, where you can arrange everything and pick up and leave the car. It's recommended to test-drive car before signing contract as quality varies. **Alkila**, Av La Paz 745, Miraflores, T01-242 3939, www.alkilarenatcar.com. **Avis Rent A Car**, Av Javier Prado Este 5233, T01-434 1111, www.avis.com. **Budget Car Rental**, Canaval y Moreyra 569, San Isidro, T01-442 8703, www.budget.com. **Hertz**, Av Cantuarias 160, Mlraflores, T01-445 5716, www.hertz.com.pe. **National**, Av España 543, Lima, T01-433 3750, www.nationalcar.com. **Paz Rent A Car**, Av Diez Canseco 319, oficina 15, Miraflores, T01-446 4395, T9993 9853 (mob).

Train

At the time of going to press, service on the Central Railway to Huancayo was running only on special occasions, such as Bank Holiday weekends. Details on p484.

● Directory

Banks
BCP (formerly Banco de Crédito), Jr Lampa 499, Lima Centre, Av Pardo 425 and Av Larco at Pasaje Tarata, Miraflores, Av Pardo y Aliaga at Av Camino Real, San Isidro. Mon-Fri 0900-1800, Sat 0930-1230. Accepts and sells American Express TCs only, accepts Visa card and branches have Visa/Plus ATM.
Banco de Comercio, Av Pardo 272 and Av Larco 265, Miraflores, Jr Lampa 560, Lima Centre (main branch). Mon-Fri 0900-1800, Sat 0930-1200. Changes and sells American Express TCs only, ATM accepts Visa/Plus.
BBVA Continental, corner of Av Larco and Av Benavides and corner of Av Larco and Pasaje Tarata, Miraflores, Jr Cusco 286, Lima Centre near Plaza San Martín. Mon-Fri 0900-1800, Sat 0930-1230. TCs (American Express). Visa/Plus ATM.
Banco Financiero, Av Ricardo Palma 278, near Parque Kennedy (main branch). Mon-Fri 0900-1800, Sat 0930-1230. TCs (American Express), ATM for Visa/Plus.
Banco Santander Central Hispano (BSCH),

Av Pardo 482 and Av Larco 479, Miraflores, Av Augusto Tamayo 120, San Isidro (main branch). Mon-Fri 0900-1800, Sat 0930-1230. TCs (Visa and Citicorp). ATM for Visa/Plus.
Banco Wiese Sudameris, Av Diagonal 176 on Parque Kennedy, Av José Pardo 697, Miraflores, Av Alfonso Ugarte 1292, Breña, Miguel Dasso 286, San Isidro. Mon-Fri 0915-1800, Sat 0930-1230. TCs (American Express only), ATM for Mastercard, Maestro and Cirrus.
Citibank, in all **Blockbuster** stores, and at Av 28 de Julio 886, Av Benavides 23rd block and Av Emilio Cavenecia 175, Miraflores, Av Las Flores 205 and in Centro Comercial Camino Real, Av Camino Real 348, San Isidro. **Blockbuster** open Sat and Sun 1000-1900. Changes and sells Citicorp cheques.
Interbank, Jr de la Union 600, Lima Centre (main branch). Mon-Fri 0900-1800. Also Av Pardo 413, Av Larco 690 and in Larcomar, Miraflores, Av Grau 300, Barranco, Av Pezet 1405 and Av Pardo y Aliaga 634, San Isidro, and supermarkets **Wong** and **Metro**. Accepts and sells American Express TCs only, ATM for Visa/Plus, Mastercard, Maestro, Cirrus and AmEx. You can also get good rates of exchange at supermarkets such as **Wong** and **Santa Isabel**.
Cajero GlobalNet ATM, Diez Canseco y Av La Paz, Miraflores. Claims to take all cards; also has phones for international calls.

Casas de cambio
There are many *casas de cambio* on and around Jr Ocoña off the Plaza San Martín. On the corner of Ocoña and Jr Camaná you'll no doubt see the large concentration of *cambistas* (street changers) with huge wads of dollars, euros and soles in one hand and a calculator in the other. They should be avoided. Changing money on the street should only be done with official street changers wearing an identity card with a photo. Keep in mind that this card doesn't *automatically* mean that they are legitimate but most likely you won't have a problem. Around Parque Kennedy and down Av Larco in Miraflores are dozens of official *cambistas* with ID photo cards attached to their usually blue, sometimes green vest. There are also those who are independent and are dressed in street clothes, but it's safer to do business with an official money changer. There are a few places on Jr de la Unión at Plaza San

Martín that will accept worn, ripped and old bills, but the exchange will be terrible. There are also several *cambios* and *cambistas* on Av José Pardo, Miraflores. A repeatedly recommended *casa de cambio* is **LAC Dolar**, Jr Camaná 779, 1 block from Plaza San Martín, p 2, T01-428 8127, also at Av La Paz 211, Miraflores, T01-242 4069. Mon-Sat 0930-1800, good rates, very helpful, safe, fast, reliable, 2% commission on cash and TCs (Amex, Citicorp, Thomas Cook, Visa), will come to your hotel if you're in a group. Another recommended *casa de cambio* is **Virgen P Socorro**, Jr Ocoña 184, T01-428 7748. Daily 0830-2000, safe, reliable and friendly.
American Express, *Travex SA*, Av Santa Cruz 621, Miraflores, T01-690 0900, info@travex. com.pe, Mon-Fri 0830-1800, Sat 0900-1300. Replaces lost or stolen Amex cheques of any currency in the world. Can purchase Amex cheques with Amex card only. Or branches of **Viajes Falabella**, eg Jr Belén 630, T01-428 9779, or Av Larco 747-753, Miraflores, T01-444 4239, lgutierrez@viajesfalabella.com.pe.
Mastercard, Porta 111, p 6, Miraflores, T01-242 2700.
Moneygram, C Ocharan 260, Miraflores, T01-447 4044. Safe and reliable agency for sending and receiving money. Locations throughout Lima and the provinces. Exchanges most world currencies and Tcs.
Western Union, Av Petit Thouars 3595, San Isidro, T01-422 0036, the main branch. Av Larco 826, Miraflores, T01-241 1220 (also **TNT** office). Jr Carabaya 693, Lima centre, T01-428 7624.

Cultural centres
Alianza Francesa, Av Arequipa 4595, Miraflores, T01-241 7014. Various cultural activities, also has a library.
CCPUCP (cultural centre of the Universidad Católica), Camino Real 1075, San Isidro, T01-222 6899. One of the best in Lima, with an excellent theatre (tickets US$7.15), European art films (US$1.45 Mon-Wed), galleries, good café and a bookshop selling art and literature titles. Recommended.
Centro Cultural de España, Natalio Sánchez 181-85, Santa Beatriz, T01-330 0412. Has an art gallery and a cinema.
Centro Cultural Peruano Japonés, Av Gregorio Escobedo 803, Jesús María, T01-463

0606. Has a concert hall, cinema, galleries, museum of Japanese immigration, cheap and excellent restaurant, lots of activities. Recommended.
Goethe Institute, Jr Nasca 722, Jesús María, T01-433 3180. 0800-2000 Mon-Fri, library, German papers.
Instituto Cultural Peruano-Norte-americano, Jr Cusco 446, Lima Centre, T01-428 3530, with library. Main branch at Av Arequipa 4798 y Angamos, Miraflores, T01-241 1940. Theatre productions and modern dance performances are just a couple of the activities the ICPNA offers. See also Language schools below.
Peruvian-British Cultural Association, Av Arequipa 3495, T01-221 7550. English library and British newspapers. Mon-Fri 0800-1300 and 1530-1930.

Doctors
For hospitals, doctors and dentists, contact your consulate for recommendations.
Backpackers Medical Care, Dr Jorge Bazan, T01-9735 2668, backpackersmc@yahoo.com. About US$13 per consultation, speaks English, frequently recommended.

Embassies and consulates
Australia, Av Víctor Belaúnde 147, Vía Principal 155, ed 3, of 1301, T01-222 8281.
Austria, Av Central 643, p 5, San Isidro, T01-442 0503.
Belgian Consulate, Angamos Oeste 392, Miraflores, T01-241 7566.
Bolivian Consulate, Los Castaños 235, San Isidro, T01-422 8231, postmast@emboli.org. pe. (0900-1330), 24 hrs for visas (except those requiring clearance from La Paz).
Brazilian Consulate, José Pardo 850, Mira-flores, T01-421 5650, Mon-Fri 0930-1300.
Canada, Libertad 130, Miraflores, T01-444 4015, lima@dfait-maeci.gc.ca.
Chilean Consulate, Javier Prado Oeste 790, San Isidro, T01-611 2211, embchile@mail. cosapidata.com.pe. Open 0900-1300, need appointment.
Colombian Consulate, Av Jorge Basadre 1580, San Isidro, T01-441 0530. Mon-Fri 0800-1400.
Ecuadorean Consulate, Las Palmeras 356, San Isidro (6th block of Av Javier Prado Oeste), T01-461 8217, embjecua@amauta. rcp.net.pe.

French Embassy, Arequipa 3415, San Isidro, T01-215 8400, FRANCE.EMBAJADA@com putextos.com.pe.
Germany, Av Arequipa 4202, Miraflores, T01-212 5016, F422 6475; emergency number T9927 8338.
Israel, Natalio Sánchez 125, p 6, Santa Beatriz, T01-433 4431.
Italy, Av G Escobedo 298, Jesús María, T01-463 2727.
Japan, Av San Felipe 356, Jesús María, T01-218 1462.
Netherlands Consulate, Av Principal 190, Santa Catalina, La Victoria, T01-476 1069, open Mon-Fri 0900-1200.
New Zealand Consulate, Av Camino Real 390, Torre Central, p 17 (Casilla 3553), San Isidro, T01-221 2833, reya@nzlatam.com. Open Mon-Fri 0830-1300, 1400-1700.
Spain, Jorge Basadre 498, San Isidro, T01-212 5155, F422 0347, open 0900-1300.
Sweden, C La Santa María 130, San Isidro, T01-442 8905, konslima@terra.com.pe.
Switzerland, Av Salaverry 3240, Magdalena, Lima 17, T01-264 0305, embsuiza@correo. tnet.com.pe.
UK, Torre Parque Mar, Av Larco 1301, p 22, T01-617 3000, www.britemb.org.pe Open 1300-2130 (Dec-Apr to 1830 Mon and Fri, and Apr-Nov to 1830 Fri), good for security information and newspapers.
USA, Av Encalada block 17, Surco, T01-434 3000, for emergencies after hours T434 3032, http://peru.usembassy.com. The Consulate is in the same building.

Hospitals and clinics
Clínica Anglo Americano, Av Salazar 3rd block, San Isidro, a few blocks from Ovalo Gutiérrez, T01-221 3656. Stocks Yellow Fever for US$18 and Tetanus for US$3. Dr Luis Manuel Valdez recommended.
Clínica Internacional, Jr Washington 1471 y Paseo Colón (9 de Diciembre), downtown Lima, T01-433 4306. Good, clean and professional, consultations up to US$35, no inoculations.
Instituto Médico Lince, León Velarde 221, near 17th and 18th blocks of Av Arenales, Lince, T01-471 2238. Dr Alejandro Bussalleu Rivera speaks English, good for stomach problems, about US$28 for initial consultation. Repeatedly recommended.
Instituto de Ginecología y Reproducción,

part of Clínica Montesur, Av Monterrico 1045, Monterrico parallel to Av Polo, T01-434 2130. Recommended gynaecologists are **Dra Alicia García** and **Dr Ladislao Prasak**.
Instituto de Medicina Tropical, Av Honorio Delgado near the Pan American Highway in the Cayetano Heredia Hospital, San Martín de Porres, T01-482 3903.
Clínica del Niño, Av Brasil 600 at 1st block of Av 28 de Julio, Breña, T01-330 0066.
Centro Anti-Rabia de Lima, Jr Austria 1300, Breña, T01-425 6313. Mon-Sat 0830-1830. Consultation is about US$2.50.
Clínica Padre Luis Tezza, Av El Polo 570, Monterrico, T01-435 6990, emergency 24 hrs T01-437 1310. Clinic specializing in a wide variety of illnesses/disorders etc, expensive; for stomach or intestinal problems, ask for Dr Raul Morales (speaks some English, US$28 for first consultation).
Clínica Santa Teresa, Av Los Halcones 410, Surquillo, T01-221 2027. Dr José Luis Calderón, general practitioner. Good.
International Chiropractors Center, Av Santa Cruz 555, Miraflores, T01-221 4764.
International Health Department, at Jorge Chávez airport, T01-517 1845. Open 24 hrs a day for vaccinations.
International Vaccination Centre, Av del Ejército 1756, San Isidro, T01-264 6889. Mon-Fri 0800-1500, Sat 0800-1400.

Internet

Lima is completely inundated with internet cafés, so you will have absolutely no problem finding one regardless of where you are. An hour will cost you approximately S/3-5 (US$0.85-1.50).

Language schools

Instituto Cultural Peruano-Norte-americano, see Cultural centres. Classes are on Mon-Fri from 0900 to 1100, US$80 per month, no private classes.
Instituto de Idiomas (Pontífica Universidad Católica del Perú), Av Camino Real 1037, San Isidro, T01-442 8761. Classes Mon-Fri 1100-1300, private lessons possible.
ESIT Idiomas de Lima, Av Javier Prado Este 4457, Surco, Lima 33, T01-434 1060, www.esit-peru.com.
Lima School of Languages, Grimaldo del Solar 469, Miraflores, T01-242 7763,

www.idiomasperu.com. US$15 per hr for private tuition, also small groups US$11 per hr. Family homestays and volunteer programmes available.
Independent teachers (enquire about rates):
Sra Lourdes Gálvez, T01-435 3910. Also Quechua.
Sra Georgelina Sadastizágal, T01-275 6460. Also Sr Mariano Herrera and Sr Dante Herrera: all these can be contacted through peruidiomas@LatinMail.com.
Srta Susy Arteaga, T01-534 9289, T9989 7271 (mob), susyarteaga@ hotmail.com or susyarteaga@ yahoo.com.
Srta Patty Félix, T01-521 2559, patty_fel24@yahoo.com.
Luis Villanueva, T01-247 7054, www.ac spanishclasses.com. Flexible, reliable, helpful.

Laundry

There are *lavanderías* (laundromats) all over Lima. Some charge by piece (expensive) while others by weight. Many have a self-service option. Next day service is the norm if you've left laundry for them to wash. Most of the hotels in the higher price range offer laundry but tend to be very expensive.
Laverap, Schell 601, Miraflores, T01-241 0759; Av Pardo y Aliaga 590, T01-422 1618, San Isidro. You can wash your own clothes or leave them to be picked up (more expensive).
Martinizing Dry Cleaning, Av Espinar 270, T01-446 2406, and Av Benavides 1763, T01-447 5547 in Miraflores, Av Dos de Mayo 1225, T01-440 2911, San Isidro. Probably the best, but very expensive.
Presto, Av Benavides 433, Miraflores, T01-242 9910. Good, reliable.
Cisne Blanco, Av Santa Cruz 1318, Miraflores, T01-221 5234.
Lavva Queen, Av Larco 1158, Miraflores, T01-444 8520.

Pharmacies

When possible it is recommended to use pharmacy chains as they are modern, well-stocked, safe and very professional. They can be found in or next to supermarkets, sometimes attached to gas station mini-marts and pretty much everywhere else. Some offer 24-hr delivery service. **Boticas Fasa**, T01-475 7070; **Boticas Torres de Limatambo**, T01-444 3022; **Farmacentro Tassara**, T01-251 0600;

Superfarma, T01-440 9000. **Pharmax**, Av Salaverry 3100, San Isidro, Centro Comercial El Polo, Monterrico (near the US embassy). Pharmacy/hypermarket, with imported goods (Jewish food products sometimes available at Av Salaverry branch, which is open 24 hrs). **Farmacia Deza**, Av Conquistadores 1140, San Isidro. The same as Pharmax, also open 24 hrs.

Post

The central post office is on Jr Camaná 195 in the centre of Lima near the Plaza de Armas. Hours are Mon-Fri 0730-1900 and Sat 0730-1600. Poste Restante is in the same building but is considered unreliable. In Miraflores the main post office is on Av Petit Thouars 5201 in Miraflores (same hrs). There are many more small branches scattered around Lima, but they are less reliable. For express service, there are a few companies to choose from: **DHL**, Los Castaños 225, San Isidro, T01-215 7500. **UPS**, Av del Ejército 2107, San Isidro, T01-264 0105. **Federal Express**, Av Jorge Chávez 475, T01-242 2280, Miraflores, C José Olaya 260, Miraflores. When receiving parcels from other countries that weigh in over 1 kg, they will be automatically sent to one of Lima's two customs post offices. Bring your passport and a lot of patience as the process can take a long time: C Teodoro Cárdenas 267, Santa Beatriz (12th block of Av Arequipa); and Av Tomás Valle, Los Olivos (near the Panamerican Highway). Long trousers must be worn when going to these offices.

Prison visits

Visits to the women's prison in the district of Chorrillos are easy and much appreciated by the inmates, both Peruvian and foreign. You must bring your passport and give the name of someone you're visiting (for the current list, check with your embassy for prisoners from your own country, or ask at South American Explorers, who have full details). You are permitted to bring food (up to 1 kg of fruit, but none that ferments), toiletries, magazines, books etc. **Establecimiento Penitenciario de Mujeres Chorrillos Santa Mónica**, has its visitors day on Sat for men and Wed and Sun for women. 0900-1300 and 1400-1600; you must leave either at

1300, or 1600. Shoes that have any kind of heel are not permitted (also no boots) and women must wear skirts below the knee which, if you don't have one, can be rented across the street from the prison. Men must wear long trousers. Visits are also possible to the men's prisons of **Callao** and **Lurigancho**.

Telephone

Easiest to use are the many independent phone offices, *locutorios*, all over the city, which take phone cards. Phone cards can be purchased in the *locutorios*, or in the street nearby. There are payphones all over the city. Some accept coins, some only phone cards and some both.

Useful addresses

Immigration, Av España 700 y Jr Huaraz, Breña , open 0900-1330. Visa extensions on 3rd floor given the same day, usually within 30 mins (expensive). Provides new entry stamps if passport is lost or stolen.

Intej, Av San Martín 240, Barranco, T01-247 3230. They can extend student cards, change flight itineraries bought with student cards.

National library, Av Abancay 4th block, with Jr Miró Quesada, T01-428 7690. Mon-Sat 0800-2000, Sun 0830-1330.

Peruvian Touring and Automobile Club: Av César Vallejo 699 (Casilla 2219), Lince, T01-221 2432, www.touringperu.com.pe Offers help to tourists and particularly to members of the leading motoring associations. Good maps available of whole country; regional routes and the South American sections of the Pan-American Highway available (US$3.50).

Tourist Police, administrative office at Jr Moore 268, Magdalena at the 38th block of Av Brasil, T01-460 1060, open daily 24 hrs; for public enquiries etc, Jr Pachitea at the corner of Belén (Jr de la Unión), Lima, T01-424 2053. They are friendly and very helpful, English spoken. It is recommended to visit when you have had property stolen.

Voluntary organizations in and around Lima often welcome volunteers. Some ask the volunteer to show up when they can, other more structured projects might ask for a commitment of at least 3 months. **South American Explorers** is the best place to find out about volunteer opportunities.

Cusco & the Sacred Valley

⁝ Footprint features

Introduction

Cusco stands at the head of the Sacred Valley of the Incas and is the jumping off point for the Inca Trail and famous Inca city of Machu Picchu. It's not surprising, therefore, that this is the prime destination for the vast majority of Peru's visitors. In fact, what was once an ancient Inca capital is now the 'gringo' capital of the entire continent. And it's easy to see why. There are Inca ruins aplenty, as well as fabulous colonial architecture, stunning scenery, great trekking, river rafting and mountain biking, beautiful textiles and other traditional handicrafts – all within easy reach of the nearest cappuccino or comfy hotel room.

The Spaniards transformed the centre of a magnificent Inca civilization into a jewel of colonial achievement. Yet the city today is not some dead monument, its history breathes through the stones. The Quechua people bring the city to life with a combination of prehispanic and Christian beliefs and every visitor is made welcome.

Starting your visit to the Cusco region outside the city has many advantages. Staying a day or two in the valley of the Urubamba river will give you time to acclimatize to the shortage of oxygen at these altitudes. And as nowhere is very far from the city, you can easily nip into town for any necessities. At Ollantaytambo and Pisac you will see Inca ruins and terraced hillsides without the overlay of the Spanish conquest. Then, when you are fit and ready, you can make your own assault on Cusco, with all the energy you need for the churches, museums, pubs, clubs, shops and many festivals which are held throughout the year. If the city life is not for you, there is no shortage of adventure, and the huge influx of visitors has encouraged the opening of new trails, some for walking, some for biking, the latest hot spot being the `lost city' of Choquequirao.

★ Don't miss...

1 **Church of San Blas** The carved pulpit is remarkable and you can get your fill of traditional crafts in the surrounding streets, page 153.

2 **Inca stonework** The Stone of 12 Angles on Calle Hatun Rumiyoc is the best example, page 153.

3 **Pisac** Walk up to the ruins above the town. It's a stiff climb, but not only are the Inca ruins worth the effort, as you go higher the views of the Urubamba valley just get better and better, page 186.

4 **Moray** In the hills above the Urubamba, three large depressions, converted into terraced crop laboratories show to perfection the Incas' thorough understanding of their environment, page 190.

5 **Machu Picchu** Find the time to peer into corners, investigate angles of stones, the weight of lintels, the outlook of windows. See how rocks and openings align themselves with peaks across the valley, page 199.

6 **Andahuayillas** Visit the Sistine Chapel of the Andes and, nearby, the equally remarkable church at Huaro. For the best view, take a strong torch as they are poorly lit, page 219.

7 **Choquequirao** The newest addition to the 'lost cities trail', only reached by adventurous trekking, including a descent to the floor of the Apurímac canyon, page 223.

Cusco city

→ *Colour map 5, grid A5. Population 275,000. Altitude 3,310 m.*

Cusco stands at the head of the Sacred Valley of the Incas and is the jumping-off point for the Inca Trail and famous Inca city of Machu Picchu. Not surprising, then, that this is the prime destination for the vast majority of Peru's visitors. In fact, the ancient Inca capital is now the 'gringo' capital of the entire continent. And it's easy to see why. There are Inca ruins aplenty, as well as fabulous colonial architecture, stunning scenery, great adventure tourism opportunities, beautiful textiles and other traditional handicrafts – all within easy reach of the nearest cappuccino or comfy hotel room.

Since there are so many sights to see in Cusco city, not even the most ardent tourist would be able to visit them all. For those with limited time, or for those who want a whistle-stop tour, a list of must-sees would comprise: the combination of Inca and colonial architecture at Qoricancha; the huge Inca ceremonial centre of Sacsayhuaman; the paintings of the Last Supper and the 1650 earthquake in the cathedral; the main altar of La Compañía de Jesús; the pulpit of San Blas; the high choir at San Francisco; the monstrance at La Merced; and the view from San Cristóbal. If you have the energy catch a taxi up to the White Christ and watch the sunset as you look out upon one of the most fascinating cities in the world. If you visit one museum make it the Museo Inka; it has the most comprehensive collection. ▶▶ *For Sleeping, Eating and other listings, see pages 156-185.*

Ins and outs

Getting there

Most travellers arriving from Lima will do so by air. No flights arrive in Cusco at night. The airport is at Quispiquilla, near the bus terminal, 1.6 km southeast of the centre. A taxi to and from the airport costs US$1-2 (US$3.50 by radio taxi). *Colectivos* to the centre cost US$0.20 from outside the airport car park to the centre.

All long-distance buses arrive and leave from the bus terminal near the Pachacútec statue in Ttio district. Transport to your hotel is not a problem as bus company representatives are often on hand.

There are two train stations in Cusco. To Juliaca and Puno, trains leave from the Estación Wanchac ① *C Pachacútec, To84-221992*. The office here offers direct information and ticket sales for all **PerúRail** services. Look out for special promotional offers. When arriving in Cusco, a tourist bus meets the train to take visitors to hotels whose touts offer rooms on the train. Machu Picchu trains leave from Estación San Pedro ① *To84-221313, opposite the Santa Ana market*. ▶▶ *For further details, see Transport page 134. For trains to Juliaca and Puno, see page 183; to Machu Picchu, see page 198.*

Getting around

The centre of Cusco is small and is easily explored on foot. Bear in mind, however, that at this altitude walking up some of the city's steep cobbled streets may leave you out of breath, so you'll need to take your time. It is even possible to walk up to Sacsayhuaman, but a better idea is to take a Combi to Tambo Machay and walk back downhill to town via Qenqo and Sacsayhuaman. Combis (minivans) are the main form of public transportation in the city: well-organized, cheap and safe. Taxis in Cusco are also cheap and recommended when arriving by air, train or bus. If you wish to explore this area on your own, Road Map(*Hoja de ruta*) No 10 is an excellent guide. You can get it from the Automóvil y Touring Club del Perú, see

❣ *Motorists beware; many streets end in flights of steps not marked as such.*

Permission to enter

A combined entry ticket to most of the sites of main historical and cultural interest in and around Cusco, called the Boleto Turístico Unificado (BTU), costs US$10 (S/.35) and is valid for five to 10 days. It permits entrance to: Santa Catalina Convent and Art Museum, Museo de Sitio Qorikancha, Museo Histórico Regional (Casa Inca Garcilazo de la Vega), Museo Palacio Municipal de Arte Contemporáneo, Museo de Arte Popular, Centro Qosqo de Arte Nativo, Monumento Pachacútec; the archaeological sites of Sacsayhuaman, Qenqo, Puka Pukara, Tambo Machay, Pisac, Ollantaytambo, Chinchero, Tipón and Piquillacta. There is also a US$6 ticket for Sacsayhuaman, Qenqo, Puka Pukara and Tambo Machay.

The BTUs can be bought at the OFEC office (Casa Garcilazo), *Plaza Regocijo, esquina C Garcilazo, T084-226919, Mon-Sat 0800-1600, Sun 0800-1200, or Av Sol 103, T227037, Mon-Fri 0800-1800, Sat 0830-1230*, or at any of the sites included in the ticket. There is a 50 per cent discount for students with a green ISIC card, which is only available at the OFEC office (Casa Garcilazo) upon presentation of the student card.

Take your ISIC card when visiting the sites, as some may ask to see it. There is no student reduction for the one-day card.

All sites are very crowded on Sundays but many churches are closed to visitors on Sundays. Be aware too that 'official' opening times are unreliable. Photography is not allowed in the Cathedral, churches, and museums.

On the back of the BTU is a map of the centre of Cusco with the main sites of interest clearly marked. It also includes a map of the tourist routes from Cusco to the Sacred Valley following the Río Urubamba towards Machu Picchu, as well as the southeastern area of Cusco on the road to Puno. The ticket includes days and hours of attention.

Entrance tickets for the Cathedral, Museo de Arte Religioso del Arzobispado, Museo Inka (El Palacio del Almirante), Santo Domingo/Qorikancha and La Merced are sold separately. Machu Picchu ruins and Inca trail entrance tickets are sold at the Instituto Nacional de Cultura (INC), *San Bernardo s/n between Mantas y Almagro, T084-236061, Mon-Fri 0900-1300, 1600-1800, Sat 0900-1100*.

page 182. They have other maps. There are very few good maps of Cusco available.
▸▸ *For further details, see Transport page 134.*

Tourist information
Official tourist information ① *Portal Mantas 117-A, next to La Merced church, T084-263176, Mon-Fri 0800-1900, Sat 0800-1400.* There is also an i perú tourist information desk ① *T084-237364, 0600-1300, at the airport, and Portal de Carrizos 250, Plaza de Armas, T084-252974, 0830-1930.* Dirección Regional de Turismo ① *Av de la Cultura 734, 3rd floor, T084-223701, Mon-Fri 0800-1300.* See box for OFEC offices and INC office for Machu Picchu. South American Explorers ① *Choquechaca 188, No 4, T084-245484, cuscoclub@saexploresrs.org, 0930-1700, Sat 0930-1300, closed Sun*, is an excellent resource for the traveller, and only a couple of minutes' walk from the Plaza de Armas. Great information on the Cusco area, along with an extensive English-language library, expedition reports, maps, weekly events, flight confirmations, phone and mail service, equipment storage and, of course, free coffee and hot chocolate for members. They are also in Lima, see page 90.

Tourist police ① *C Saphi 511, T084-249654*. If you need a *denuncia* (a report for insurance purposes), available from the Banco de la Nación, they will type it out.

Cusco

Cusco city

Sleeping 🛏

Albergue Municipal 1 *B2*
Casa Andina Koricancha 7 *C4*
Casa Elena 53 *B4*
Chaska Wasi 3 *B1*
Cusco Plaza 2 32 *B1*
El Arcano 5 *A4*
El Arqueólogo 19 *A3*
El Balcón Colonial 6 *A3*
El Grial 4 *A4*
El Monasterio 38 *B3*
Estrellita 9 *C5*

Hospedaje El Artesano de
San Blas 51 *A5*
Hospedaje Familiar
Inti Quilla 10 *A4*
Hospedaje Inka 52 *A5*
Hospedaje Jhuno 11 *A3*
Hospedaje Plaza de
San Blas 50 *A4*
Hospedaje Turístico
San Blas 13 *B4*
Hostal Amaru 15 *B4*
Hostal Andenes
de Saphi 33 *B1*
Hostal Cahuide 47 *A1*
Hostal Casa de Campo 16 *A3*
Hostal Cusco Plaza 18 *B3*
Hostal El Balcón 20 *B1*
Hostal Familiar 21 *B1*

Hostal Familiar
Carmen Alto 22 *A4*
Hostal Familiar Mirador
del Inka 23 *A4*
Hostal Kuntur Wasi 57 *A3*
Hostal Luzerna 17 *D1*
Hostal María Esther 25 *A3*
Hostal Mirador de la
Ñusta 54 *A5*
Hostal Pakcha Real 26 *A4*
Hostal Pumacurco 49 *A3*
Hostal Qorichaska 27 *C1*
Hostal Rickch'airy 28 *B1*
Hostal Rumi Punku 29 *A3*
Hostal Sambleño 30 *A4*
Hostal San Isidro
Labrador 31 *B2*
Inka's Inn 2 *B1*

Libertador 34 *C4*
Los Apus Hostal y
Mirador 35 *A3*
Los Portales 36 *D3*
Maison de la
Jeunesse 56 *D4*
Marani 37 *A4*
Niños 39 *C1*
Niños 2 12 *D1*
Novotel 40 *C4*
Pensión Alemana 41 *A3*
Posada del Sol 42 *A4*
Ruinas 55 *B4*
San Augustín
Internacional 43 *C4*
San Augustín Plaza 44 *D4*
Savoy Internacional 45 *E5*
Suecia II 46 *B2*

0 metres 100
0 yards 100

Protection Bureau (Indecopi) ① *at the tourist office at Portal Carrizos, Plaza de Armas (see above), toll free T0800-42579 (24-hour hotline, not available from pay-phones).* This organization protects the consumer rights of all tourists and helps with any problems or complaints and can be helpful in dealing with tour agencies, hotels or restaurants.

Background

The ancient Inca capital is said to have been founded around AD 1100. According to the central Inca creation myth, the Sun sent his son, Manco Cápac and the Moon sent her daughter, Mama Ocllo, to spread culture and enlightenment throughout the dark, barbaric lands. They emerged from the icy depths of Lake Titicaca and began their journey in search of the place where they would found their kingdom. They were ordered to head north from the lake until a golden staff they carried could be plunged into the ground for its entire length. The soil of the altiplano was so thin that they had to travel as far as the valley of Cusco where, on the mountain of Huanacauri, the staff fully disappeared and the soil was found to be suitably fertile. This was the sign they were looking for. They named this place Cusco, meaning 'navel of the earth'.

Today, the city's beauty cannot be overstated. It is a fascinating mix of Inca and colonial Spanish architecture: colonial churches, monasteries and convents and pre-Columbian ruins are interspersed with hotels, bars and restaurants that have sprung up to cater for the hundreds of thousands of tourists. Almost every central street has remains of Inca walls, arches and doorways. Many streets are lined with Inca stonework, now serving as the foundations for more modern dwellings.

Cusco has developed into a major commercial centre of 275,000 inhabitants, most of whom are Quechua. The city council has designated the Quechua, Qosqo, as the official spelling. Despite its growth, however,

Eating ⓐ
A Mi Manera **1** *B3*
Café Cultural
  Ritual **15** *B4 & A4*
Café Manu **2** *E6*
Casa Noble **22** *D4*
Chifa Sipan **3** *D3*
Chocolate **16** *B4*
Granja Heidi **6** *B4*
Greens **5** *A4*
Gypsy Pub & Planet
  Cusco **18** *A4*
Hatunrumiyoc **4** *B4*
Inkanato **7** *C4*
Jack's Café **14** *B4*
La Bodega **8** *A4*
Los Toldos **9** *D3*
Macondo **10** *A4*

Manzana Azul
  & Inca...fe **13** *B4*
Moni **21** *C4*
Muse **17** *A4*
Pacha-Papa **11** *B4*
Panadería El Buen
  Pastor **20** *A4*
Parrilla Andina **23** *C4*
Witches Garden **12** *A4*

Bars & clubs ⓐ
Km 0 (Arte y Tapas)
  19 *A4*
Mandela's Bar **22** *B3*

the city is still laid out much as it was in Inca times. The Incas conceived their capital in the shape of a puma and this can be seen from above, with the Río Tullumayo forming the spine, Sacsayhuaman the head and the main city centre the body. The best place for an overall view of the Cusco Valley is from the puma's head – the top of the hill of Sacsayhuaman.

Sights

Plaza de Armas and around

The heart of the city in Inca days was *Huacaypata* (the place of tears) and *Cusipata* (the place of happiness), divided by a channel of the Río Saphi. Today, Huacaypata is the Plaza de Armas and Cusipata is Plaza Regocijo. This was the great civic square of the Incas, flanked by their palaces, and was a place of solemn parades and great assemblies. Each territory conquered by the Incas had some of its soil taken to Cusco to be mingled symbolically with the soil of the Huacaypata, as a token of its incorporation into the empire. As well as the many great ceremonies, the plaza has also seen its share of executions, among them the last Inca Túpac Amaru, the rebel *conquistador* Diego de Almagro the Younger, and the 18th-century indigenous leader Túpac Amaru II.

On the northeast side of the square, the early 17th-century baroque **Cathedral** ① *Mon, Tue, Wed, Fri and Sat 1000-1130, 1400-1730, until 1000 for worshippers, Quechua Mass at 0500-0600, US$3*, forms part of a three-church complex: the cathedral itself, **Iglesia Jesús y María** (1733) on the left as you look at it and **El Triunfo** (1533) on the right. There are two entrances; the cathedral doors are used during Mass but the tourist entrance is on the left-hand side through Iglesia Jesús y María. The cathedral itself was built on the site of the Palace of Inca Wiracocha (*Kiswarcancha*) using stones from Sacsayhuaman.

The gleaming, newly renovated gilded main altar of the **Iglesia Jesús y María** draws the eyes to the end of the church. However, take the time to look up at the colourful murals which have been partially restored. The two gaudy, mirror-encrusted altars towards the front of the church are also hard to miss. Walking through into the cathedral's transept, the oldest surviving painting in Cusco can be seen. It depicts the 1650 earthquake. It also shows how within only one century the Spaniards had already divided the main plaza in two. *El Señor de los Temblores* (The Lord of the Earthquakes) can be seen being paraded around the Plaza de Armas while fire rages through the colonial buildings with their typical red-tiled roofs. Much of modern-day

Around Plaza de Armas

Plateros detail

0 metres   50
0 yards   50

Sleeping

Casa Andina
  Catedral **15** *C3*
Casa Andina Plaza **10** *C2*
El Procurador del
  Cusco **1** *A2*
Emperador Plaza **2** *C3*
Del Prado Inn **5** *B3*
Hostal Casa Grande **4** *C3*
Hostal Corihuasi **6** *A3*
Hostal Q'Awarina **11** *A2*
Hostal Qosqo **12** *C2*
Hostal Resbalosa **13** *A3*
Hostal Royal
  Frankenstein & Tangible
  Myth **14** *B1*
Hostal Turístico Plateros **7**
  Plateros detail
Munay Wasi **17** *A3*
Pensión Loreto **18** *C2*
Picoaga **19** *A1*
Posada del Viajero **20** *C3*
Royal Inka I **21** *B1*
Royal Inka II **22** *A1*
Sonesta Posada
  del Inca **8** *B2*
Tumi I **24** *A1*

Eating

Al Grano **1** *C3*
Ama Lur **2** *Plateros detail*

Auliya **22** *B1*
Ayllu **3** *B3*
Babieca **29** *A2*
Café Halliy **5** *Plateros detail*
Chez Maggy Clave
  de Do **6** *A2*
Chez Maggy El
  Corsario **7** *B2*
Chez Maggy La Antigua
  8 *A2*
Deli, El Patio & Blueberry
  Lounge **12** *B3*
Due Mondi **10** *C3*
El Cuate **11** *A2*
El Encuentro **34** *C3*
El Fogón **47** *Plateros detail*
El Truco & Taberna
  del Truco **13** *B1*
Fallen Angel **9** *B3*
Inka Grill **16** *B2*
Kintaro **17** *B1*
Kusikuy **18** *Plateros detail*
La Retama **19** *B2*
La Tertulia **20** *B2*
La Yunta **21** *B3*
Los Candiles & Café Amaru
  49 *Plateros detail*
Mía Pizza **4** *A2*
Paccha **15** *B2*
Pachacútec Grill &
  Bar **23** *B2*

Paititi **24** *C3*
Paloma Imbil **25** *A2*
Pizzería Marengo **27** *B2*
Pucará **28**
  Plateros detail
Trotamundos **30** *B2*
Tunupa & Cross
  Keys Pub **31** *B2*
Varayoc **14** *B2*
Víctor Victoria **33** *A2*
Yaku Mama **51** *A2*

Bars & clubs

El Garabato Video
  Music Club **41** *B2*
Excess **46** *B3*
Kamikaze **36** *B2*
Los Perros **37** *A2*
Magtas **45** *B3*
Mama Africa **26** *B2*
Mama América **38** *C3*
Norton Rat's
  Tavern **39** *C2*
Paddy Flaherty's **40** *C3*
Rosie O'Grady's &
  Sky Travel **42** *C3*
Spoon **35** *Plateros detail*
Sunset Video
  Café **43** *A2*
Ukuku's **44** *Plateros
  detail*

Cusco was built after this event. The choir stalls, by a 17th-century Spanish priest, are a magnificent example of colonial baroque art (80 saints and virgins are exquisitely represented), as is the elaborate pulpit. On the left is the solid-silver high altar. At the far right-hand end of the cathedral is an interesting local painting of the Last Supper. But this is the Last Supper with a difference, for Jesus is about to tuck into a plate of *cuy*, washed down with a glass of *chicha*!

Entering El Triunfo there is a stark contrast between the dark, heavy atmosphere of the cathedral and the light, simple structure of this serene church. Built on the site of *Suntur Huasi* (The Roundhouse), **El Triunfo** was the first Christian church in Cusco. The name *El Triunfo* (The Triumph) came from the Spanish victory over an indigenous rebellion in 1536. It was here that the Spaniards congregated, hiding from Manco Inca who had besieged the city, almost taking it from the invaders. The Spaniards claim to have witnessed two miracles here in their hour of need. First, they were visited by the Virgin of the Descent, who helped put out the flames devouring the thatched roofs, then came the equestrian saint, James the Greater, who helped kill many indigenous people. The two divinities are said to have led to the Spanish victory; not only was it the triumph of the Spaniards over the Incas, but also of the Catholic faith over the indigenous religion. The fine granite altar of El Triunfo is a welcome relief from the usual gilding. Here the statue of the Virgin of the Descent resides and, above her, is a wooden cross known as the Cross of Conquest, said to be the first Christian cross on Inca land brought from Spain.

On the southeast side of the plaza is the beautiful church of **La Compañía de Jesús**, built on the site of the Palace of the Serpents (*Amarucancha*, residence of the Inca Huayna Cápac). The original church was destroyed in the earthquake of 1650 and the present-day building took 17 years to construct. It was inaugurated in 1668. The altarpiece is resplendent in gold leaf: it stands 21 m high and 12 m wide. It is carved in the baroque style, but the indigenous artists felt that this was too simple to please the gods and added their own intricacies. Gold leaf abounds in the many *retablos* and on the carved pulpit.

North and northeast of the Plaza de Armas

Palacio del Almirante, just north of the Plaza de Armas, is one of Cusco's most impressive colonial buildings and houses the interesting **Museo Inka** ⓘ *C Ataud, T084-237380, Mon-Fri 0800-1700, Sat 0900-1600, US$3*, which exhibits the development of culture in the region from pre-Inca, through Inca times to the present day. The museum has a good combination of textiles, ceramics, metalwork, jewellery, architecture, technology, photographs and 3-D displays. They have an excellent collection of miniature turquoise figures and other objects made as offerings to the gods. The display of deliberately deformed skulls with trepanning is fascinating, as is the full-size tomb complete with mummies stuck in urns. Note the pillar on the balcony over the door, showing a bearded man from inside and a naked woman from the outside. During the high season local Quechuan weavers can be seen working, and selling, in the courtyard. The weavings are for sale, expensive but of very good quality.

Two blocks northeast of Plaza de Armas, the **Palacio Arzobispal** was built on the site of the palace occupied in 1400 by the Inca Roca and was formerly the home of the Marqueses de Buena Vista. It contains the **Museo de Arte Religioso** ⓘ *Hatun Rumiyoc y Herrajes, Mon-Sat, 0830-1130, 1500-1730, US$3, US$1.50 for students*, which has a fine collection of colonial paintings, furniture and mirrors. The Spanish tiles are said to be over 100 years old and each carved wooden door has a different design. The collection includes the paintings by the indigenous master, **Diego Quispe Tito**, of a 17th-century Corpus Christi procession that used to hang in the church of Santa Ana. They now hang in the two rooms at the back of the second smaller courtyard (see Fine art and sculpture, page 601). The throne in the old dining room is

In the Casa Cabrera, on the northwest side of the plaza, this beautiful **Museo de Arte Precolombino** ① *Plaza de las Nazarenas 231, T084-233210, 0900-2200, US$4.60, US$2.30 with student card.* Set around a spacious courtyard, it is dedicated to the work of the great artists of pre-Colombian Peru. Within the expertly lit and well-organized galleries are many superb examples of pottery, metalwork (largely in gold and silver) and wood carvings. There are some vividly rendered animistic designs, giving an insight into the way Peru's ancient peoples viewed their world and the creatures that inhabited it. Most of the pieces originate from the Moche, Chimú, Paracas, Nasca and Inca empires, with explanations in English and Spanish. The museum has stores such as **Alpaca 111** and **H Stern** and the **MAP Café**, see Eating, below.

Convento de las Nazarenas, on Plaza de las Nazarenas, is now an annex of **El Monasterio hotel**, see page 158. You can see the Inca-colonial doorway with a mermaid motif, but ask permission to view the lovely 18th-century frescos inside. **El Monasterio** itself is well worth a visit – ask at reception if you can have a wander. Built in 1595 on the site of an Inca palace, it was originally the **Seminary of San Antonio Abad** (a Peruvian National Historical Landmark). One of its most remarkable features is the baroque chapel, constructed after the 1650 earthquake. If you are not disturbing mealtimes, check out the dining room. This is where the monks used to sing.

San Blas

The San Blas district, called Tococache in Inca times, has been put on the tourist map by the large number of shops and galleries which sell local carvings, ceramics and paintings. See page 171. Even though it's a bit of climb from the Plaza de Armas, it has also become a popular place to stay and eat, with lots of choice and nothing too expensive. The **church of San Blas** ① *Carmen Bajo, 1800-1130, 1400-1730, closed Thu mornings, US$3, US$1.50 for students*, is a simple rectangular adobe building whose walls were reinforced with stone after the 1650 and 1950 earthquakes. It houses one of the most famous pieces of wood carving found in the Americas, a beautiful mestizo pulpit carved from a single cedar trunk.

East and southeast of the Plaza de Armas

The magnificent church, convent and museum of **Santa Catalina** ① *Arequipa at Santa Catalina Angosta, Sat-Thu 0900-1730, Fri 0900-1500, entrance with BTU visitors' ticket, guided tours by English-speaking students (tip is expected), church daily 0700-0800* , is is built upon the foundations of the *Acllahuasi* (House of the Chosen Women), whose nobility, virtue and beauty permitted them to be prepared for ceremonial and domestic duties – some were chosen to bear the Inca king's children. Today the convent is a closed order where the nuns have no contact with the outside world. The church has an ornate, gilded altarpiece and a beautifully carved pulpit. The museum has a wonderful collection of Cuzqueño school paintings spanning the decades of Spanish rule – a good guide can point out how the style changes from the heavy European influence to the more indigenous style.

Much original Inca stonework can be seen in the streets and most particularly in the Callejón Loreto, running southeast past La Compañía de Jesús from the main plaza. The walls of the *Acllahuasi* (House of the Chosen Women) are on one side, and of the *Amarucancha* on the other. There are also Inca remains in Calle San Agustín, to the east of the plaza. The famous **Stone of 12 Angles** is in Calle Hatun Rumiyoc half-way along its second block, on the right-hand side going away from the plaza. The finest stonework is in the celebrated curved wall beneath the west end of Santo Domingo. This was rebuilt after the 1950 earthquake, at which time a niche that once contained a shrine was found at the inner top of the wall. Excavations have revealed Inca baths below here, and more Inca retaining walls. Another superb stretch of late-Inca stonework is in Calle Ahuacpinta, outside Qoricancha, to the east or left as you enter. True Inca stonework is wider at the base than at the top and features ever-smaller stones as the walls rise. Doorways and niches are trapezoidal. The Incas clearly learnt that the combination of these four techniques helped their structures to withstand earthquakes. This explains why, in two huge earthquakes (1650 and 1950), Inca walls stayed standing while colonial buildings tumbled down.

Qoricancha at Santo Domingo

ⓘ *Mon-Sat 0800-1700, Sun 1400-1600 (except holidays), US$1.80 (not on the BTU Visitor Ticket). There are guides outside who charge around US$2-3.*

This is one of the most fascinating sights in Cusco. Behind the walls of the Catholic church are remains of what was once the centre of the vast Inca society. The Golden Palace and Temple of the Sun was a complex filled with such fabulous treasures of gold and silver it took the Spanish three months to melt it all down. The Solar Garden contained life-sized gold sculptures of men, women, children, animals, insects and flowers were placed in homage to the Sun God. On the walls were more than 700 gold sheets weighing about 2 kg each. The *conquistadores* sent these back intact to prove to the King of Spain how rich their discovery was. There would also have been a large solar disc in the shape of a round face with rays and flames. This disc has never been found.

The first Inca, Manco Cápac, is said to have built the temple when he left Lake Titicaca and founded Cusco with Mama Ocllo. However, it was the ninth Inca, Pachacútec, who transformed it. When the Spaniards arrived, the complex was awarded to Juan Pizarro, the younger brother of Francisco. He in turn willed it to the Dominicans who ripped much of it down to build their church.

Walk first into the courtyard then turn around to face the door you just passed through. Behind and to the left of the paintings (representing the life of Santo Domingo Guzmán) is Santo Domingo. This was where the *Temple of the Sun* stood, a massive structure 80 m wide, 20 m deep and 7 m in height. Only the curved wall of the western end still exists and will be seen (complete with a large crack from the 1950 earthquake), when you later walk left through to the lookout over the Solar Garden. Still in the baroque cloister, close by and facing the way you came in, turn left and cross to the remains of the *Temple of the Moon*, identifiable by a series of niches. Beyond this is the so-called *Temple of Venus and the Stars*. Stars were special deities used to predict weather, wealth and crops. In the *Temple of Lightning* on the other side of the courtyard is a stone. Stand on this and you will appreciate how good the Incas were as stonemasons: all three windows are in perfect alignment.

Museo de Sitio Qoricancha ⓘ *Mon-Fri 0800-1730, Sat 0900-1700, entrance by the BTU Visitor Ticket, or US$2, guided tour in Spanish, but please give a tip*, formerly the Museo Arqueológico, is now housed in an underground site on Avenida Sol, in the gardens below Santo Domingo. It contains a limited collection of pre-Columbian artefacts, a few Spanish paintings of imitation Inca royalty dating from the 18th century and photos of the excavation of Qoricancha.

South and southwest of the Plaza de Armas

Originally built in 1534, the church of **La Merced** ⓘ *C Márquez, monastery and museum 1430-1700, church Mon-Sat 0830-1200, 1530-1730, except Sun, US$0.85* was razed in the 1650 earthquake and rebuilt by indigenous stonemasons in the late 17th century. The high altar is neoclassical with six gilded columns. There are a further 12 altars. Inside the church are buried Gonzalo Pizarro, half-brother of Francisco, and the two Almagros, father and son. Attached is a very fine monastery. The first cloister is the most beautiful with its two floors, archways and pillars. The pictures on the first floor depict the Saints of the Order (those of the second floor have been removed for restoration).

Museo de Historia Regional ① *Casa Garcilaso, C Garcilaso y Heladeros, 0730-1700, entrance with BTU tourist ticket, guide recommended,* shows the evolution of the Cuzqueño school of painting. It also contains Inca agricultural implements, a mummy from Nasca complete with 1 m-long hair, colonial furniture and paintings, a small photographic exhibition of the 1950 earthquake and mementos of more recent times.

Three blocks southwest of the Plaza de Armas, the austere church of **San Francisco** ① *Plaza San Francisco, 0600-0800, 1800-2000,* reflects many indigenous influences, but it has a wonderful monastery, cloister and choir. Although at the time of writing the monastery was not officially open to the public, it is possible to visit. Approach the door to the left of the church and knock on it. The cloister is the oldest in the city, built in the Renaissance style, but with diverse influences. The ground floor has several crypts containing human bones. The fabulous high choir contains 92 detailed carvings of martyrs and saints.

West and northwest of the Plaza de Armas

Above Cusco, on the road up to Sacsayhuaman, is **San Cristóbal** church, built to his patron saint by Cristóbal Paullu Inca. The church's atrium has been restored and there is access to the Sacsayhuaman Archaeological Park. North of San Cristóbal, you can see the 11 doorway-sized niches of the great Inca wall of the **Palacio de Colcampata**, which was the residence of Manco Inca before he rebelled against the Spanish and fled to Vilcabamba. Cristo Blanco, arms outstretched and brilliantly illuminated at night, stands over the town and is clearly visible if you look north from the Plaza de Armas. He was given to the city as a mark of gratitude by Palestinian refugees in 1944. A quick glance in the local telephone directory reveals there is still a large Arab population in Cusco.

Sacsayhuaman

① *0700-1730. You can get in earlier if you wish and definitely try to get there before 1200 when the tour groups arrive. Free student guides are available, but you should give them a tip. There are lights to illuminate the site at night. The site is about a 30-min walk from the town centre. Walk up Pumacurco from Plaza de las Nazarenas. Taxi US$1.50.*

There are some magnificent Inca walls in the ruined ceremonial centre of Sacsayhuaman, on a hill in the northern outskirts. The Inca stonework is hugely impressive. The massive rocks weighing up to 130 tons are fitted together with absolute perfection. Three walls run parallel for over 360 m and there are 21 bastions.

Sacsayhuaman was thought for centuries to be a fortress, but the layout and architecture suggest a great sanctuary and temple to the Sun, rising opposite the place previously believed to be the Inca's throne – which was probably an altar, carved out of the solid rock. Broad steps lead to the altar from either side. Zigzags in the boulders round the 'throne' are apparently '*chicha* grooves', channels down which maize beer flowed during festivals. Up the hill is an ancient quarry, the Rodadero, now used by children as a rock slide. Near it are many seats cut perfectly into the smooth rock.

The hieratic, rather than the military, hypothesis was supported by the discovery in 1982 of the graves of priests, who would have been unlikely to be buried in a fortress. The precise functions of the site, however, will probably continue to be a matter of dispute as very few clues remain, due to its steady destruction.

The site survived the first years of the conquest. Pizarro's troops had entered Cusco unopposed in 1533 and lived safely at Sacsayhuaman, until the rebellion of Manco Inca, in 1536, caught them off guard. The bitter struggle which ensued became the decisive military action of the conquest, for Manco's failure to hold Sacsayhuaman cost him the war, and the empire. The destruction of the hilltop site began after the defeat of Manco's rebellion. The outer walls still stand, but the complex of towers and buildings was razed to the ground. From then, until the 1930s, Sacsayhuaman served as a kind of unofficial quarry of pre-cut stone for the inhabitants of Cusco (Peter Frost).

Other sites near Cusco

Along the road from Sacsayhuaman to Pisac, past a radio station, at 3,600 m, is the temple and amphitheatre of **Qenqo**. These are not exactly ruins, but are of the finest examples of Inca stone carving *in situ*, especially inside the large hollowed-out stone that houses an altar. The rock is criss-crossed by zigzag channels that give the place its name and which served to course *chicha*, or perhaps sacrificial blood, for purposes of divination. The open space that many refer to as the 'plaza' or 'amphitheatre' was used for ceremonies. The 19 trapezoidal niches, which are partially destroyed, held idols and mummies.

Known as an Inca fortress, **Puka Pukara**, whose name translates as 'Red Fort', was more likely to have been a *tambo*, a kind of post-house where travellers were lodged and goods and animals housed temporarily. It is worth seeing for the views alone.

A few hundred metres up the road is the spring shrine of **Tambo Machay**, still in excellent condition. There are many opinions as to what this place was used for. Some say it was a resting place for the Incas and others that it was used by Inca Yupanqui as a hunting place. There are three ceremonial water fountains built on different levels. It is possible that the site was a centre of a water cult. Water still flows by a hidden channel out of the masonry wall, straight into a little rock pool traditionally known as the Inca's bath.

It is possible to walk from Sacsayhuaman to Tambo Machay, via Qenqo, **Cusilluchayoc** (Templo de los Monos, or Monkey Temple), an area of rocks and galleries with the remains of a fountain, then on a section of the Incas' Cusco-Pisac road to **Laqo** (Templo de la Luna, or Temple of the Moon), with sculptures in caves and an observatory, Chilcapuquio and Puka Pukara.

Taking a guide to the sites mentioned above is a good idea and you should visit in the morning for the best photographs. Carry your multi-site ticket as there are roving ticket inspectors. You can visit the sites on foot. It's a pleasant walk through the countryside requiring half a day or more, though remember to take water and sun protection, and watch out for dogs. An alternative is to take the Pisac bus up to Tambo Machay (which costs US$0.35) and walk back. Another excellent way to see the ruins is on horseback, arranged at travel agencies. An organized tour (with guide) will go to all the sites for US$6 per person, not including entrance fees. A taxi will charge US$15-20 for three to four people. Some of these ruins are included in the many City Tours available. For details, see page 173.

● Sleeping

Tourists should not pay tax (IVA), but service may be extra to the bill. When there are fewer tourists hotels may drop their prices by as much as half. Always ask for discounts; the prices shown at reception are usually negotiable. Also, hotel prices, especially in the mid to upper categories, are often lower when booked through tour agencies. You should book more expensive hotels well in advance through a good travel agency, particularly for the week or so around Inti Raymi, when prices are much higher.Be wary

of unlicensed hotel agents for mid-priced hotels, they are often misleading about details; their local nickname is *jalagringos* (gringo pullers), or *piratas* (pirates). Taxis and tourist minibuses meet arriving trains and take you to the hotel of your choice for US$0.50, but be insistent. It is cold in Cusco and many hotels do not have heating. It is worth asking for an *estufa*, a heater, which some places will provide for an extra charge. When staying in the big, popular hotels, allow yourself plenty of time to check out if you have a plane or train to catch: front desks can be very busy. All the hotels listed below offer free luggage storage unless otherwise stated. Assume hotels have 24-hr hot water in pre-heated tanks unless otherwise stated. Cusco's low-power electric showers often do a poor job of heating the very cold water and their safety is sometimes questionable.

Plaza de Armas and around
p95, map p151

L Picoaga, Santa Teresa 344 (2 blocks from the Plaza de Armas),T084-227691, www.picoagahotel.com. Price includes buffet breakfast. Originally the home of the Marqués de Picoaga, this beautiful colonial building has large original bedrooms set around a shady courtyard and a modern section, with a/c, at the back. Cable TV, minibar and safe, pleasant staff. Recommended.

L Ruinas, Ruinas 472, T084-260644, www.hotelruinas.com. A comfortable hotel conveniently located close to the plaza, good facilities (TV, minibar, etc) and comfortable beds, a little expensive but helpful staff, price includes buffet breakfast.

AL Casa Andina Plaza, Portal Espinar 142, T084-231733, www.casa-andina.com. 1½ blocks from the plaza, this brand new hotel has 40 rooms with cable TV, bath, safe deposit box, heating, duvets on the beds and all the facilities common to this chain. Equally recommendable are the **Casa Andina Koricancha**, San Agustín 371, T084-252633, and the **Casa Andina Catedral**, Santa Catalina Angosta 149, T084-233661, both of which are in the same vein and price range.

AL Royal Inka I, Plaza Regocijo 299, T084-231067, royalin@ terra.com.pe. Price includes buffet breakfast. Bedrooms, with cable TV and heating, are set in a colonial house around a shady central patio. Tranquil atmosphere, bar, restaurant with set menu. Recommended.

AL Royal Inka II, close by, on Santa Teresa, same phone and website. More modern and expensive but the price includes buffet breakfast, saunas and jacuzzi (massage US$25). The colonial façade hides a modern building, the rooms of which open out onto a huge atrium dominated by an incong-

ruous, 3-storey high mural. All rooms have cable TV and heating. Free bus for guests to Pisac at 1000 daily, returning at 1800.

AL Sonesta Posada del Inca, Portal Espinar 108, T084-201107, www.sonesta.com. Price includes buffet breakfast. Warmly decorated rooms with heating and cable TV. Some rooms on third floor have view of the Plaza. Very helpful staff who speak English, restaurant serves Andean food, excellent service.

A Del Prado Inn, Suecia 310, T084-224442, admin@delpradoinn.com. New and very smart hotel just off the plaza. 24-hr room service available, and closed-circuit TV in the public areas for additional security. Suites with jacuzzi cost US$90.

A Emperador Plaza, Santa Catalina Ancha 377, T084-227412, emperador@terra.com.pe. Price includes buffet breakfast. A modern, light, airy hotel with friendly and helpful English-speaking staff. Cable TV, hairdryer, gas-heated showers and electric radiators.

B Hostal Corihuasi, C Suecia 561, T084-232233, www.corihuasi.com. Price includes continental breakfast and airport pick-up. A tough climb up from the northernmost corner of the Plaza de Armas, tranquil, popular with tour groups. Friendly, some rooms with good views, cable TV, solar heating. Recommended.

B Hostal Qosqo, Portal Mantas 115, near the Plaza de Armas, T084-252513. Bargain hard for a discount. Price includes continental breakfast, a heater and cable TV. The state of decor and quality of mattress varies from room to room but most stay here for its proximity to the plaza. Clean, friendly and helpful.

B Pensión Loreto, Pasaje Loreto 115, Plaza de Armas (it shares the same entrance as Norton's Rat pub), T084-226352, hloreto @terra.com.pe. Price includes continental breakfast and a heater for the spacious rooms with original Inca walls. Great location; they will serve you breakfast in bed. Laundry service, will help organize travel services including guides and taxis, free airport pick-up.

C Hostal Q'Awarina, at the top of Suecia 575, T084-228130. Price includes continental breakfast, heating US$2, TV extra. No laundry service. Rooms are good, ask for those with a view. Lovely living room with views across the city; the breakfast area upstairs is even better. Good value.

D Hostal Turístico Plateros, Plateros 348, T084-236878. Price includes continental breakfast. Clean, good value *hostal* in a great location, pleasant communal area with cable TV. The best rooms overlook the street.

D-E Hostal Royal Frankenstein, San Juan de Dios 260, 2 blocks from the Plaza de Armas, T084-236999, ludwig_roth@hotmail. com. This unforgettable place, with its ghoulish theme, has good services: fully equipped kitchen (just US$0.30 a day), cable TV in the living room, safe, laundry facilities, excellent mattresses but few rooms have outside windows. German owner. Recommended. Next door is the rather funky jazz café, **Tangible Myth**.

E Hostal Casa Grande, Santa Catalina Ancha 353, T084-264156. Price includes breakfast; heaters extra. Family-run *hostal* in a colonial building with a courtyard, very helpful, popular with backpackers. Laundry service, parking, kitchen.

E Munay Wasi, Huaynapata 253, not far from the Plaza de Armas, T084-223661. Price includes hot drinks and laundry facilities. Quiet, but run-down colonial house, with basic, clean rooms, friendly and helpful.

E Posada del Viajero, Santa Catalina Ancha 366, down lane next to Rosie O'Grady's, T084-261643. Select your room carefully and you could find a real bargain at this centrally located *hostal*. Some are drab with dodgy mattresses piled 3 high but the owners are making real efforts and others have newly

tiled bathrooms and comfy beds. Use of the kitchen costs US$0.60.

E-F Hostal Resbalosa, Resbalosa 494, T084-224839. Breakfast is US$1.45 extra; laundry costs US$0.75 per kg. Superb views of the Plaza de Armas from a sunny terrace. Owner Georgina is very hospitable. Best rooms have a view (US$1.45 extra), others may be pokey. The electric showers are reportedly cool, but most guests love this place; it's often full.

F El Procurador del Cusco, Coricalle 440, Prolongación Procuradores, at the end of Procuradores, T084-243559, hostal-procur ador-cusco@hotmail.com. (**G** per person without bathroom), price includes use of the basic kitchen (no fridge) and laundry area. Basic rooms and the beds somewhat hard, but upstairs is better. Staff are very friendly and helpful, good value. Recommended.

F Tumi 1, Siete Cuartones 245, 2 blocks from Plaza de Armas, T084-244413. Price includes use of the kitchen and laundry area; free book exchange, laundry service US$0.85. Colonial house, clean rooms around a sunny courtyard, all with shared bath. Facilities are basic and you have to pay for more than one shower a day, friendly, popular, good value; bargain for longer stays.

North and northeast of the Plaza de Armas *p152, map p148*
LL El Monasterio, Palacios 136, T084-241777, reservas@peruorientexpress. com.pe. This 5-star, beautifully restored Seminary of San Antonio Abad is central and quite simply the best hotel in town for

historical interest; it is worth a visit even if you cannot afford the price tag (see p153). Soft Gregorian chants follow you as you wander through the baroque chapel, tranquil courtyards and charming cloisters, admiring the excellent collection of religious paintings. Rooms have all facilities, including cable TV, some even offer an oxygen-enriched atmosphere to help clients acclimatize, for an additional fee of US$25. Staff, who all speak English, are very helpful and attentive. The price includes a great buffet breakfast (US$17 to non- residents) which will fill you up for the rest of the day. The restaurant serves lunch and dinner à la carte. Recommended.

LL Novotel, San Agustín 239, T084-228282, reservations@novotelcusco.com.pe. 4-star, is US$50 cheaper (US$180 as opposed to US$230) in modern section; price includes buffet breakfast. Converted from the home of *conquistador* Miguel Sánchez Ponce (it was remodelled after the 1650 earthquake with lovely stone archways and paintings of the saints on the grand stairway). Beautiful courtyard, roofed in glass, with sofas, coffee tables and pot plants around the central stone fountain. The modern 5-storey rear extension has excellent airy and bright rooms. Rooms in the colonial section are not much different but have high, beamed ceilings and huge beds. There are 2 restaurants and a French chef.

A Hostal Cusco Plaza 1, Plaza Nazarenas 181 (opposite **El Monasterio**), T084-246161. Price includes continental breakfast. Situated on a lovely small plaza in the town centre, clean rooms all with cable TV. Room 303 has the best view.

B Hostal Rumi Punku, Choquechaca 339, T084-221102, www.rumipunku.com. A genuine Inca doorway leads to a sunny, tranquil courtyard. 20 large, clean, comfortable rooms, helpful staff and safe. Highly recommended.

B Hotel El Arqueólogo, Pumacurco 408, T084-232569, www.hotelarqueologo.com. Price includes buffet breakfast. Services include oxygen, a library and hot drinks. A colonial building on Inca foundations, this has rustic but stylish decor. Lovely sunny garden with comfy chairs and a small restaurant that serves interesting Peruvian food and fondue. French and English

spoken. Recommended. Also has **Vida Tours**, at this address, T084-227750, www.vidatours.com. Traditional and adventure tourism.

C Hostal María Esther, Pumacurco 516, T084-224382. Price includes continental breakfast; heating extra. This very friendly, helpful place has a lovely garden, a lounge with sofas and a variety of rooms. There is also car parking. Recommended.

E Casa Elena, Choquechaca 162, T084-241202, www.geocities.com/casa_elena. French/Peruvian hostel, very comfortable and friendly, breakfast included. Highly recommended.

E per person **El Balcón Colonial**, Choquechaca 350, T084-238129, balcon colonial@hotmail.com. Continental breakfast extra, use of the kitchen US$1 per day and laundry US$0.70 per kg. Accommodation for 16 people in this family house. Basic rooms with foam mattresses but the hospitality is exceptional. Free airport pick-up.

G Hostal Pumacurco, Pumacurco 336, Interior 329, T084-243347 (3 mins from the Plaza de Armas). Some large rooms in the

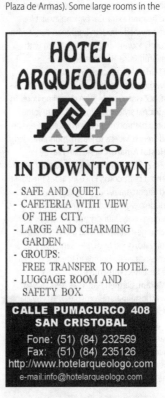

160

newly restored part of a colonial house. Clean, secure and laundry facilities. Owner Betty is very friendly and helpful.

San Blas p153, map p148

AL Los Apus Hotel y Mirador, Atocsaycuchi 515 y Choquechaca, T084-264243, www.losapushotel.com. Price includes buffet breakfast and airport pick-up; laundry US$1 per kg. Swiss-owned, very clean and smart with beamed bedrooms fitted with cable TV and real radiators!

B Hostal Casa de Campo, Tandapata 296-B (at the end of the street), T084-244404, info@hotelcasadecampo.com. Price (10% discount for Footprint owners) includes continental breakfast and free airport/rail/bus transfer with reservations. Bedrooms have fabulous views but it's quite a climb to get to them! Safe deposit box, laundry service, meals on request and a sun terrace. Dutch and English spoken; take a taxi there after dark.

B Pensión Alemana, Tandapata 260, T084-226861, pensioalemana@terra.com.pe. Price includes American breakfast; laundry and heating extra. Car parking available. Swiss-owned, modern European decor with a comfy lounge area, lovely garden with patio furniture. Recommended.

C El Grial, Atocsaycuchi 594, T084-223012, www.cusco-peru.de. With continental breakfast, hot water, cable TV. A charming hotel, in traditional style, spacious and clean, some shared bathrooms, books in English, German and French, videos to watch, tours arranged.

C Hostal Amaru, Cuesta San Blas 541, T084-225933, www.cusco.net/amaru (**D** without bathroom), Price includes breakfast and airport/train/bus pick-up. Services include oxygen, kitchen for use in the evenings only, laundry and free book exchange. Rooms around a pretty colonial courtyard, good beds, pleasant, relaxing, some Inca walls. Rooms in the first courtyard are best. Recommended.

C Marani, Carmen Alto 194, T084-249462, www.hostalmarani.com. Breakfasts available. Book exchange and information on Andean life and culture. Large rooms with heaps of character, set around a courtyard. The Hope Foundation (www.stichtinghope.org) operates here: Walter Meekes and his wife, Tineke, have built 20 schools in poor

mountain villages and *barrios*, established a programme to teach teachers and set up a 30-bed burns unit in Cusco general hospital. Good value, a great cause and highly recommended.

C Posada del Sol, Atocsaycuchi 296, T084-246394. Includes American breakfast, heater and airport pick-up. Cheerfully decorated, sun terrace with great views, fantastic showers. Use of kitchen, laundry service, food is available. Cannot be reached by taxi. Recommended.

C Hospedaje Turístico San Blas, Cuesta San Blas 526, T084-225781, sanblascusco@yahoo.com. Price includes continental breakfast; heaters are extra. Cable TV in the comfortable, covered courtyard. Well-decorated bedrooms, charming for a basic *hostal*.

D El Arcano, Carmen Alto 288, T084-232703. The old **Hostal Cristales** and **El Arcano** are now run by 1 person and share the same name. Breakfast and laundry available, cheaper rooms with shared bath. Lovely little communal area with comfortable seating and a small breakfast area with cable TV and a book exchange. Friendly owners will help arrange trips and own 2 lodges; one in the jungle and another in cloudforest. Highly recommended.

LOS APUS HOTEL & MIRADOR
Under Swiss Management

CUZCO · PERU

★ ★ ★

Quietly nestled in the foothills of the unspoiled historical site of San Blas, only a short walk from the Plaza de Armas, Velasco Astete International Airport and the San Pedro rail station to Machu Picchu.

All rooms with private bath and central heating. Two restaurants featuring regional, novoandina and international cuisine.

Tel: ++51/84/264243   Fax: ++5184/264211
info@losapushotel.com www.losapushotel.com

Winner of the XXIX INTERNATIONAL AWARD FOR TOURIST, HOTEL AND CATERING INDUSTRY. Madrid, Spain, January 2004

D Hostal Kuntur Wasi, Tandapata 352-A, T084-227570. **E** without bath, services include a safe, use of the kitchen (for US$0.60 a day) and laundry. Great views from the terrace where you can breakfast. Very welcoming, helpful owners, a very pleasant place to stay.

D Hostal El Mirador de la Ñusta, Tandapata 682, T084-248039, elmiradordelnusta@hot mail.com. Snug, tasteful and friendly family *hostal*, tucked in behind **The Muse** café, above the San Blas Plaza. Laundry service and a safe for valuables.

D Hostal Pakcha Real, Tandapata 300, T084-237484, pakcharealhostal@hotmail. com. Price includes breakfast and airport/ train/bus pick-up; heaters and use of kitchen extra. Family-run with the comforts of home. Laundry service, spotless rooms, friendly and relaxed.

D-E Hospedaje Jhuno, Carmen Alto 281, T084-233579. A small family run *hospedaje*, clean rooms, family lounge. Breakfast is not included but guests can use the tiny kitchen.

D-E Hospedaje Plaza de San Blas, Plazoleta San Blas 630, T084-235358, psanblas@ corihuasi.com. Colourful, welcoming and a great location. Price includes continental breakfast. The 4-bed family room has a balcony and overlooks the plazoleta.

E Hostal Familiar Mirador del Inka, Tandapata 160, off Plaza San Blas, T084-261384, miradordelinka@latin mail.com. This *hostal* looks very stylish with its Inca foundations and white colonial walls; completely redeveloped in 2003. Bedrooms with bath are spacious and some have great views. The owner's son Edwin runs trekking trips and has an agency on site.

E Hostal Sambleño, Carmen Alto 114, T084-262979. A lovely jumble of staircases over-looks a central courtyard. Rooms of varying quality, breakfast available, laundry service. Beds are comfortable, showers are electric.

F per person **Hospedaje Inka**, Suytuccato 848, T084-231995. Taxis leave you at Plaza San Blas, walk steeply uphill for 5-10 mins, or phone the *hostal*. Price includes bath and breakfast. Wonderful views, spacious rooms, very helpful owner, Américo.

F Hospedaje El Artesano de San Blas, Suytucato 790, T084-263968, manosand inas@yahoo.com. Many clean, bright and airy rooms, hot water fairly reliable, use of kitchen, helpful. As with the **Hospedaje Inka**, you need to walk up from San Blas.

F Hostal Familiar Carmen Alto, Carmen Alto 197, first on the right down steps (no sign), T084-224367. If there's no answer when ringing the bell, go to the shop next door, it's run by the same family. Basic rooms with great character (in one case, constructed around a huge tree) Tranquil, family run, use of kitchen and washing

Cusco **Cusco city** Listings

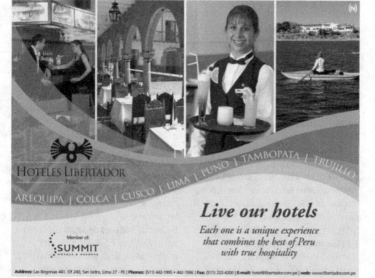

machine. Carmen will make you a very good breakfast for US$2. All rooms with shared bath, electric showers. Recommended.
G Hospedaje Familiar Inti Quilla, Atocsaycuchi 281, T084-252659. Breakfast not included and no facilities for making food. Colourful rooms around a little courtyard, quiet (on pedestrian street so taxis cannot drop you at the door). Good value.

East and southeast of the Plaza de Armas *p153, map 148*
LL Libertador, in the Casa de los Cuatro Bustos, at Plazoleta Santo Domingo 259, T084-231961, www.libertador.com.pe. This splendid 5-star, award-winning hotel is built on Inca ruins (the walls can be seen in the restaurant and bar) and is set around courtyards. It has 254 well-appointed rooms; the attention to detail is so great there are even Nazca Lines drawn in the sand of the ashtrays! Enjoy Andean music and dance over dinner in the excellent **Inti Raymi** restaurant. Recommended.

AL San Agustín Internacional, San Agustín y Maruri 390, T084-221169, www.hotelsan agustin.com.pe. (Also **AL San Agustín Plaza**, Av Sol 594, T084-238121, www.hotelsan agustin.com.pe). Price includes continental breakfast. There is a rustic Mexican feel to the lobby with its fireplace and water feature, while Andean music is piped to the communal areas. Heated bedrooms, the staff will organize tours.

AL Savoy Internacional, Av Sol 954, T084-224322, www.hotelsavoyplaza.com. Price includes American breakfast. This is one of the earliest modern hotels in the city and some of the features are dated. However, bedrooms are spacious, with heating, and some have good views. Bar, coffee shop, and the staff speak many languages. Warm, friendly atmosphere.

B Los Portales, Matará 322, T084-223500, reservas@portalescusco.com. Price includes continental breakfast and airport pick-up; ask for a heater at no extra charge. Safe deposit box, laundry (US $3 per kg), oxygen and a money exchange. Modern, friendly and helpful, children welcome. Recommended.

E-F Maison de la Jeunesse, (affiliated to Hostelling International), Av Sol, Cuadra 5, Pasaje Grace, Edificio San Jorge (down a

small side street opposite Qoricancha), T084-235617, elia25@msn.com. Price includes breakfast. Very friendly French/Peruvian-run hostel with a selection of dormitories and private rooms. TV and video room, cooking facilities and very hot water.
G Estrellita, Av Tullumayo 445, parte Alta, T084-234134. Price includes breakfast and tea and coffee all day. TV, video and old stereo in the tiny communal sitting area, basic kitchen for guests. Rooms are multiples with shared bath, plus 2 with private bath. Basic but excellent value. It is about a 15-min walk from the centre. When you arrive ring the bell several times and wait; you will be given your own keys when you register. Safe parking for cars and bikes. Recommended (related to **Explorers' House** in Lima).

West and northwest of the Plaza de Armas *p154, map 148*
AL Cusco Plaza 2, Saphi 486, T084-263000, F084-262001. New hotel, with same management as the Cusco Plaza (see above). The 24, nicely decorated rooms are set around 3 charming covered patios. Price includes American breakfast, and all rooms have cable TV and heating.

A Hostal El Balcón, Tambo de Montero 222, T084-236738, balcon1@terra.com.pe. Price includes breakfast. Lovingly restored 1630 colonial house with rooms set around a beautiful, homely atmosphere, well-maintained garden. Ask for a TV if you want one. Restaurant and kitchen for guests, laundry service. Recommended.

B Hostal Cahuide, Saphi 845, T084-222771, F248262. Price (negotiate for a discount, especially for longer stays) includes American breakfast. Cable TV in all rooms, ask for a heater. A modern hotel with 1970s furniture, plain white walls and comfortable beds. Helpful staff.

B Hostal San Isidro Labrador, Saphi 440, T084-226241, labrador@qnet.com.pe. Continental breakfast included in the price. Very pleasant 3-star hotel with elegant but simple decor, colonial arches and lovely patios. Plenty of hot water and heating. Recommended.

B-C Hostal Andenes de Saphi, Saphi 848, T084-227561, F235588. Price includes continental breakfast and all rooms have heaters. Very friendly little hostel with a cosmopolitan atmosphere. Each room is decorated in a different style; the 4-bed family room is very nice. Lovely entertainment/games room, and a small but pleasant garden.

C Niños Hotel, C Meloc 442, T084-231424, www.ninoshotel.com. Price does not include the excellent breakfast, which costs US$1.70-2.50. Services include the cafeteria and laundry service (US$1.15 per kg), Dutch, English, German and French spoken. Spotless, beautiful rooms in a 17th-century colonial house funding a fantastic charity established by Dutch couple, Titus and Jolande Bovenberg. Recently opened is the new **Niños 2**, on C Fierro, a little further from the centre, 20 nicely decorated, clean and airy rooms, surrounding the central courtyard.

D Hostal Familiar, Saphi 661, T084-239353. (**E** without bathroom), luggage deposit costs US$2.85 a day for a big pack. Popular *hostal* in a colonial house 3 blocks from the central plaza. Most beds are comfy, hot water all day. Recommended.

E Albergue Municipal, Kiskapata 240, near San Cristóbal, T084-252506, albergue@mun icusco.gob. Private rooms with double beds and dormitories in this very clean, helpful youth hostel. Nice communal area with cable TV and video. No rooms have bath. Great views, cafeteria and laundry facilities (laundry service US$0.75 per kg). Showers are electric, but there is no kitchen.

E Hostal Qorichaska, Nueva Alta 458, T084-228974, F084-227094. Price includes continental breakfast, use of the well-equipped kitchen and safe. Laundry service. Rooms in this colonial house are clean and sunny; ask for the older rooms which are bigger and have traditional balconies. Friendly and recommended.

E Suecia II, Tecseccocha 465 (no bell – knock!), T084-239757 (it is wise to book ahead). **F** without bath, breakfast US$1.40. Rooms are set around a glass-covered colonial courtyard and are warm. Beds have thick foam mattresses, but but no seats on the toilets, water not always hot or bathrooms clean, can be noisy and the luggage store is closed at night, otherwise OK.

E Hostal Rickch'airy, Tambo de Montero 219, T084-236606. (**F** without bath). Popular backpackers' haunt with views from the

garden. Full breakfast (US$2). Owner Leo has tourist information and will collect guests from the station. 15 new rooms with bath under construction (**C**).

F Chaska Wasi, Amargura 130 (there is no sign), T084-622831. Pay US$3 extra for cable TV and American breakfast. Use of basic kitchen (there is no fridge), laundry service. Family house with character, hard beds (singles only), good showers, excellent value for its location.

F Inka's Inn, Saphi 652, upstairs, T084-248572, tilovi@hotmail.com. Price includes American breakfast, with bath (but dubious hot water supply). Rooms are basic, a bit of a mixture and those in the front are noisy, but the location is good and the staff are very friendly. Clean and safe.

G Hostal Luzerna, Av Baja 205, near San Pedro train station (take a taxi at night), T084-232762. Price includes breakfast. A nice family run *hostal*, hot water, good beds, clean, safe to leave luggage. Recommended.

● Eating

Plaza de Armas and around
p95, map p151

♏♏♏ Inka Grill, Portal de Panes 115, T084-262992, 1000-2400 (Sun 1200-2400). According to many the best food in town is served here, specializing in Novo Andino cuisine (the use of native ingredients and 'rescued' recipes) and innovative dishes, also home-made pastas, wide vegetarian selection, live music, excellent coffee and home-made pastries 'to go'. A good place to spoil yourself, recommended. Being redesigned in late 2004.

♏♏♏ Pachacútec Grill and Bar, Portal de Panes 105. International cuisine including seafood and Italian specialities, also features folk music shows nightly. Excellent value quality *menú* for just US$2.50.

♏♏♏ Paititi, Portal Carrizos 270. Live music and good atmosphere in a setting with Inca masonry. Excellent pizzas but the service is variable depending on how busy they are.

♏♏♏ La Retama, Portal de Panes 123, 2nd floor. Excellent Novo-Andino food and service. Recommend the mouth-watering trout sashimi as a starter followed by steak. There is also a balcony, an enthusiastic music and dance group and art exhibitions.

¶¶¶ El Truco, *Plaza Regocijo 261*. Excellent local and international dishes, used a lot by tour groups, buffet lunch 1200-1500, nightly folk music at 2045, next door is **Taberna del Truco**, which is open 0900-0100.

¶¶¶ MAP Café, in the Museo de Arte Precolombino, Plaza de las Nazarenas 231. Under the same ownership as the Inka Grill, it is a café (1000-1830) and restaurant (1830-2000), serving the best Peruvian-Andean and international cuisine, also has an innovative chiuldren's menu.

¶¶¶ Tunupa, Portal Confiturías 233, 2nd floor (same entrance as Cross Keys). One of the finest restaurants on the plaza (often used by tour groups). Also has the longest (glassed-in) balcony but this is narrow and best for couples only. Food is international, traditional and Novo Andino; wine list, as everywhere in Cusco, is limited. Also an excellent buffet for US$15 including a *pisco sour* and a hot drink. In the evenings there is an excellent group playing 16th and 17th-century-style Cusqueñan music of their own composition accompanied by dancers. Recommended.

¶¶ Al Grano, Santa Catalina Ancha 398, T084-228032, 1000-2100, closed on Sun. Lunchtime menu US$2.15 is a good option if you are fed up with other menus. Evening serves 5 authentic Asian dishes for US$5.50, menu changes daily. Without doubt some of the best coffee in town, vegetarian choices and breakfasts, including a 'Full English'. Recommended.

¶¶ Kintaro, Heladeros 149. 1200-2200, closed Sun. Excellent home-made food, set menu (1200-1500) particularly good value at US$3, run by Japanese. Low-fat food is said to be good for high altitude.

¶¶ El Patio, Portal de Carnes 236, Plaza de Armas, left of the cathedral. Closed 1530-1830. In a colonial courtyard, this has a short menu with great pasta, Mediterranean dishes and salads as well as a good-value lunch. Ideal for a quick meal; get there early as the sun disappears around 1300/1330. Recommended.

¶¶ Pizzería Marengo, Plaza Regocijo 246, T084-252627. Excellent pizzas for US$5-6 per person. Ask for a table in the back room next to the cosy clay oven and watch your food being prepared. Also does deliveries.

¶¶ Varayoc, Espaderos 142, T084-232404.

Open daily 0800-2400. Swiss-owned restaurant including Peruvian ingredients (the only place in Cusco that serves cheese fondue). Also has a variety of pastas, good desserts, 'tea time' beverage and pastry for US$2.80 accompanied by Andean harp music. Pleasant, literary atmosphere.

¶ Auliya, C Garcilaso 265, 2nd floor. Beautifully renovated colonial house, excellent vegetarian food, also stocks a wide range of dried food for trekking.

¶ Babieca, Tecseccocha 418, T084-221122. Walk to the top of Procuradores, turn left and this place is on the corner opposite the **Sunset Video Bar**. Serves excellent pizzas with light, crispy bases and a varied selection of menus ranging from US$2-6. Warm decoration and efficient service.

¶ El Encuentro, Santa Catalina Ancha 384. One of the best-value eateries in Cusco, 3 courses of good healthy food and a drink will set you back US$1.

¶ Paccha, Portal de Panes 167. Good for breakfast, it also has a bookstore, posters for sale, English and French spoken.

¶ Víctor Victoria, Tigre 130. Israeli and local dishes, highly recommended for breakfast, good value.

¶ La Yunta, Portal de Carnes, Plaza de Armas. Good salads, pancakes and juices, also vegetarian, popular with tourists, same owners as **Instinct Travel Agency**.

Procuradores (Gringo Alley) and Plateros

These 2 streets lead off the northwest side of the Plaza de Armas. Procuradores, or Gringo Alley as the locals call it, is good for a value feed and takes the hungry backpacker from Mexico to Italy, to Spain and Turkey with its menus. None is dreadful, many are very good indeed, especially for the price; do not be too worried if a tout drags you into one (demand your free *pisco sour*) before you've reached the restaurant you have chosen from the list in Eating, below. Parallel with Gringo Alley but further southwest, Plateros also has good-value places to eat. It is also lined with a great many tour operators, so you can wander up and down checking what deals are on offer.

¶¶ Kusikuy, Plateros 348B, T084-262870. 0800-2300 Mon-Sat. Some say this serves the best *cuy* (guinea pig, US$10.90) in town and the owners say if you give them an hour's warning they will produce their absolute best. Many other typical Cusco dishes on the menu. Set lunch is unbeatable value at only US$2. Good service, live music, highly recommended.

Pucará, Plateros 309. 1230-2200, closed Sun. Peruvian and international food. Japanese owner does very good US$2 set lunch, pleasant atmosphere. Recommended.

Ama Lur, Plateros 325. This is the restaurant below **Amalu** where you go for breakfast. Clean, cheap, very good set menu for US$2 as well as tasty evening meals.

Chez Maggy, has 3 branches: La Antigua (the original) at Procuradores and, on the same street, **El Corsario** No 344 and **Clave de Do** No 374 (opens at 0700 for buffet breakfast). Hotel delivery T084-234861. All have good atmosphere, serving pizzas freshly baked in a wood-burning oven, pastas, Mexican food and soups. All are popular.

El Cuate, Procuradores 386. Mexican food, great value, big portions and simple salads. Recommended.

El Fogón, Plateros 365. Huge local *menú del día* for US$1.80, good solid food at reasonable prices. Very popular with locals and increasingly so with travellers.

Los Candiles, *Plateros 323*. Good set lunch for US$2.50, also serves typical food in the evenings, but not as cheap.

Mía Pizza, Procuradores 379. Good range of cheap menus, including a good curry.

Paloma Imbil, Procuradores 362. Has doner kebabs. The *rollo mixto* is US$3 and comes in delicious home-baked bread. For vegetarians the *rollo de falafel y queso* is a tasty option.

Cafés, delis, panaderías and heladerías

Amaru, Plateros 325, 2nd floor. Limitless coffee, tea, great bread and juices served, even on non-buffet breakfasts (US$1.15 for simple). Colonial balcony. Recommended.

Ayllu, Portal de Carnes 208, to the left of the cathedral. Probably one of the oldest cafés in Cusco and a great place to go. Fantastic breakfasts (have the special fruit salad, US$2.30), sandwiches, coffee and classical music as well as wonderful apple pastries. Very much a local venue with superb service.

Café Halliy, Plateros 363. Popular meeting place, especially for breakfast, good for comments on guides, has good snacks and *copa Halliy* (fruit, muesli, yoghurt, honey and chocolate cake, also good vegetarian menu and set lunch).

The Deli, Portal de Carnes 236, next to the Blueberry Lounge. This is closest you'll get in Peru to a European delicatessen, and very nice it is too! Great salad bar, good takeaway including sandwiches, pricey, but worth it.

Due Mondi, Santa Catalina Ancha (near Rosie O'Grady's). 1000-2100. At just US$0.30 per delicious Italian scoop, this is an absolute must. There's even *chicha* flavour!

La Tertulia, Procuradores 50, 2nd floor. Breakfast, served 0630-1400, includes muesli, bread, yoghurt, eggs, juice and coffee, eat as much as you like for US$3, superb value, book exchange, newspapers, classical music.

Trotamundos, Portal Comercio 177, 2nd floor. Open Mon-Sat 0800-2400. One of the most pleasant cafés in the plaza if a bit pricey. Has a balcony overlooking the plaza and a warm atmosphere especially at night with its open fire. Good coffees and cakes, safe salads, *brochetas*, sandwiches and pancakes as well as 4 computers with internet access.

Sunset Video Café, inside Hostal Royal Qosqo, turn left at the top of Gringo Alley. Shows 3 films a day: 1600, 1900, 2130. It has good sound and you can order popcorn and other snacks while you watch. US$0.70.

Yaku Mama, Procuradores 397. Good for breakfast; unlimited fruit and coffee.

North and northeast of the Plaza de Armas *p152, map p148*

Fallen Angel, Plazoleta Nazarenas 221, T084-258184, fallenangelincusco@hotmail. com. Under the same ownership as **Macondo** (see below), this is an art gallery like nowhere else ("completely OTT") that just happens to serve great food, in an original *conquistador* residence. The menu features steaks of a quality to equal any in Peru, and there are some innovative pasta dishes. Cocktails are excellent. Regular parties/fashion shows are always events to remember.

A Mi Manera, corner of Triunfo and Palacios. Great-tasting food and good value if you ask for a set menu (not often advertised).

¶ **Café Cultural Ritual**, Choquechaca 140 and also Plazoleta San Blas 614. Good value and tasty vegetarian *menú*, including some decent Indian dishes, for US$2.20.

Cafés, delis, panaderías and heladerías

Chocolate, Choquechaca 162, T974 9343 (mob). Good for coffee and cakes but the real highlights are the fresh gourmet chocolates (up to European standards).
Manzana Azul, Choquechaca 131a. Great cakes, especially of the chocolate variety, but the coffee is terrible.

San Blas *p153, map p148*

¶ **La Bodega**, Carmen Alto 146. Snug Dutch-and Peruvian-owned café/restaurant serving hot chocolate by candlelight in the afternoons, eveening meals - dishes come with side trip to salad bar, American breakfast and a US$1.50 lunch menu. Highly recommended.
¶¶ **Greens**, Tandapata 700, behind the church on Plazoleta San Blas, T084-243820, greens_cusco@hotmail.com. Modern international food in a trendy but warm and relaxed setting with sofas to kick back in while sipping wine and reading English magazines. Famous for huge Sun roasts (US$10, booking essential) as well as English breakfasts (0700-1500) and curries. Vegetarian options. Desserts and toasted sandwiches available 1500-1830; restaurant re-opens 1830, closes 2300. Games, book exchange and library.
¶¶ **Macondo**, Cuesta San Blas 571, T084-229415, macondo@ telser.com.pe. Bit pricier than others in this range but fantastic. A casual, cosy, arty and comfortable restaurant with sofas of iron bedsteads covered in dozens of cushions mixed with chairs, tables and candles. Walls are decorated with local art. Popular, gay-friendly and a steep 3-block walk from the central plaza. Dishes of local ingredients with an artistic twist.
¶¶ **Jack's Café**, on the corner of Choquechaca and San Blas. T084-806960. Opens at 0630. Excellent varied menu with generous portions, all in a light and relaxed atmosphere. Great American-style pancakes and freshly ground local coffee. Lunchtime can be very busy.
¶¶ **Pachapapa**, Plazoleta San Blas 120,

opposite church of San Blas, T084-241318. Open 1000-2200. A beautiful patio restaurant in a wonderful old colonial house, under same ownership as Inka Grill. Very good Cusqueña dishes, including *pachamanca* (previous reservation required for 6 people). At night diners can sit in their own, private colonial dining room. Recommended.
¶¶ **Witches Garden**, Carmen Bajo 169, just off Plazoleta San Blas, T084-9623866, witchesgardenrestaurant@hotmail.com. Good Novo Andino and international cuisine served in this warmly decorated little restaurant. There is a TV and video, with a selection of movies, available for patrons.
¶ **Granja Heidi**, Cuesta San Blas 525, T084-238383. US$2.50 gets you an excellent 3- or 4-course *menú del día* in a clean and relaxed environment. There are usually vegetarian options.
¶ **Gypsy Pub**, Carmen Alto 162-C. Comfortable bar/restaurant a little further down the street from **La Bodega**. Good *menú del día* for US$2 and the chicken is some of the best in Cusco.
¶ **Hatunrumiyoc**, on the corner of Hatunrumiyoc and Choquechaca. Good location on the 2nd floor with a nice balcony. Decent set menu at lunchtime for around US$2.50.
¶ **Inca Fe**, Choquechaca 131, opposite **Jack's Café**. Great food and value in a nice setting, staff speak English, helpful.

Cafés, delis, panaderías and heladerías

The Muse, Tandapata 682, Plazoleta San Blas. Funky little café with a cosy feel and great views over the plaza. Fresh coffee, good food, including vegetarian lasagne, chicken curry and carrot cake. There's often live music in the afternoons/evenings with no cover charge. English owner Clair is very helpful. **The Muse** will refill water bottles for a small charge in an attempt to minimize plastic waste in Cusco.
Panadería El Buen Pastor, Cuesta San Blas 579. Very good bread and pastries, the proceeds from which go to a charity for orphans and street children. Very popular with backpackers. Recommended.
Planet Cusco, Carmen Alto 162, T084-223010. Great buffet breakfast in a

warm, stylish atmosphere for only US$1.40, plus 10 mins free internet.

East and southeast of the Plaza de Armas *p153, map p148*

¶¶¶ **Parrilla Andina**, Maruri. Good-value meat-fest. Mixed grill will feed 2 people for around US$15. Restaurant is part of the former palace of the Inca, Túpac Yupanqui.

¶¶ **Casa Noble**, Av Sol 616, T084-222994. Andean food and other dishes, well-prepared and served by excellent staff. Hospitable owner speaks many languages, delightful atmosphere.

¶¶ **Inkanato**, Plazoleta Santo Domingo 279, interior 2A, T084-222926. Staff dressed in Inca and Amazonian outfits should not scare you off this interesting restaurant. Kitsch it may be but you can watch the staff preparing the food in the open-plan kitchen that stretches into the dining area.

¶¶ **Los Toldos**, Almagro 171 y San Andrés 219. If you're feeling peckish, on a budget and fancy being served by waiters in a bow tie, try their great chicken *brocheta*. Comes with fries, a trip to the salad bar and is enough for 2 people at just US$2.30. Also *trattoria* with home-made pasta and pizza, delivery T084-229829.

¶ **Chifa Sipan**, *Quera 251* (better than their other branch for tourists in Plateros). Owner Carlos may not sound Chinese but he is and joins in the cooking at this excellent restaurant. There is no great ambience but it's busy at lunchtimes with locals which speaks volumes. Skip to the back of the menu for their better deals.

South and southwest of the Plaza de Armas *p154, map 148*

For cheap restaurants, try Calles Ayacucho, Belén and Matará. There are vegetarian places such as **Dharma** (Belén) and **Vrinda** (Matará) and the **Dimart** supermarket restaurant (Matará 271) open on Sun night.

¶ **Túpac Amaru market**, to eat really cheaply, and if your stomach is acclimatized to South American food, make your main meal lunch and escape the Plaza de Armas. Head for the market 5 blocks southwest at Túpac Amaru and eat at one of the many stalls. Food will cost no more than US$0.70 and 3-fruit juices are just US$0.45! Otherwise, look for the set *menús*, usually served

between 1200-1500, although they are no good for vegetarians. Between 1200 and 1400 on Puente Rosario, just off Av Sol, pick up a piece of deep-fried potato or deep-fried, battered yucca from one of the street stalls for just US$0.15.

Cafés, delis, panaderías and heladerías

Café Manu, Av Pardo 1046. Good coffee and good food too in a jungle decor. It would be a sin to miss one of their liqueur coffees.
Moni, San Agustín 311, T084-231029, www. moni-cusco.com. Peruvian/English-owned, good fresh food and breakfast, British music, magazines, bright, clean and comfy.

⊙ Bars and clubs

Bars

Amaru Quechua Café Pub, Plateros 325, 2nd floor, T084-246976. Bar with pizzería, also serves breakfast for US$2.50, games, happy hour 1030-1130, 2000-2200.
Blueberry Lounge, Portal de Carnes 235, T084-742472. Dark, moody and sophisticated, this is a slice of London's Soho on the Plaza de Armas. There's a good menu, featuring many Asian dishes.
Cross Keys Pub, Portal Confiturías 233 (upstairs). 1100-0130. Run by Barry Walker of **Manu Expeditions**, a Mancunian and ornithologist, darts, cable sports, pool, bar meals, happy hours 1830-1930 and 2130-2230, plus daily half price specials Sun-Wed, great *pisco sours*, very popular, loud and raucous, great atmosphere.
Km 0 (Arte y Tapas), Tandapata 100, San Blas. Lovely Mediterranean-themed bar tucked in behind San Blas. Good snacks and tapas (of course), affordable, and with live music every night (around 2200 – lots of acoustic guitar, etc).
Los Perros Bar, Tecseccocha 436, above Gringo Alley (Procuradores). Completely different vibe and a great place to chill out on comfy couches listening to excellent music. There's a book exchange, English and other magazines and board games. Opens 1100 for coffee and pastries; kitchen opens at 1300. Occasionally hosts live music and special events.
Mandela's Bar, Palacios 121, 3rd floor, T084-222424, www.mandelasbar.com.

The festival of Inti Raymi

The sun was the principal object of Inca worship and at their winter solstice, in June, the Incas honoured the solar deity with a great celebration known as Inti Raymi, the sun festival. The Spanish suppressed the Inca religion, and the last royal Inti Raymi was celebrated in 1535.

However, in 1944 a group of Cusco intellectuals, inspired by the contemporary 'indigenist' movement, revived the old ceremony in the form of a pageant, putting it together from chronicles and historical documents. The event caught the public imagination, and it has been celebrated every year since then on 24 Jun, now a Cusco public holiday. Hundreds of local men and women play the parts of Inca priests, nobles, chosen women, soldiers (played by the local army garrison), runners, and the like. The coveted part of the Inca emperor Pachacuti is won by audition, and the event is organized by the municipal authorities.

It begins around 1000 at the Qoricancha – the former sun temple of Cusco – and winds its way up the main avenue into the Plaza de Armas, accompanied by songs, ringing declarations and the occasional drink of chicha. At the main plaza, Cusco's presiding mayor is whisked back to Inca times, to receive Pachacuti's blessing and a stern lecture on good government. Climbing through Plaza Nazarenas and up Pumacurcu, the procession reaches the ruins of Sacsayhuamán at about 1400, where scores of thousands of people are gathered on the ancient stones.

Before Pachacuti arrives the Sinchi (Pachauti's chief general) ushers in contingents from the four Suyus (regions) of the Inca empire. Much of the ceremony is based around alternating action between these four groups of players. A Chaski (messenger) enters to announce the imminent arrival of the Inca and his Coya (queen). Men sweep the ground before him, and women scatter flowers. The Inka takes the stage alone, and has a dialogue with the sun. Then he receives reports from the governors of the four Suyus. This is followed by a drink of the sacred chicha, the re-lighting of the sacred fire of the empire, the sacrifice (faked) of a llama, and the reading of auguries in its entrails. Finally the ritual eating of sankhu (corn paste mixed with the victim's blood) ends the ceremonies. The Inca gives a last message to his assembled children, and departs. The music and dancing continues until nightfall.

Cutting-edge bar/restaurant with an African theme. Good atmosphere and lots of space to spread out and relax. Serves breakfast, lunch and drinks in the evening, also Sun barbecues and special events through the year. Great 360° panorama from the rooftop.
Norton Rat's Tavern, Loreto 115, 2nd floor, on the plaza but has a side entrance off a road to the left of La Compañía (same entrance as **Hostal Loreto**), T084-246204, nortonrats@yahoo.com. Pleasant pub with a pool table, dart board, cable TV and lots of pictures of motorbikes! Owner Jeffrey Powers loves the machines and can provide information for bikers. There's a

balcony which offers great views of the Plaza de Armas. Also has a juice bar serving Amazonian specials. Happy hour 1900-2100 every night with other daily specials.
Paddy Flaherty's, C Triunfo 124 on the corner of the plaza, 1300-0100. An Irish theme pub, deservedly popular. Now under new management with improved seating and great food – the jacket potatoes, shepherd's pie and baguettes are all highly recommended.
Rosie O'Grady's, at Santa Catalina Ancha 360, T084-247935. Open 1100 till late (food served till midnight, happy hours 1300-1400,

1800-1900, 2300-2330). Has good music, tasty food. English and Russian spoken.

Clubs

Before your evening meal don't turn down flyers being handed out around the Plaza de Armas. Then, over dinner, you should work out your free drink circuit – for each coupon not only gives you free entry, it is worth a *cuba libre*. On the back of this tour you will be able to check out which club is the 'in' place to be that week – they are constantly changing. If you fancy learning a few Latin dance steps before hitting the dancefloor, many of the clubs offer free lessons. Ask at the door for details or look out for flyers.

Excess, on Suecia, next door to **Magtas Bar** (see below). An old Cusco staple. Movies are shown late afternoon and early evening, but after midnight this place really gets going with an eclectic range of music, from 60's and 70's rock and pop to techno and trance. This place seems to give out more free drinks than most, so it's a good option for kicking off a big night on the town!

El Garabato Video Music Club, Espaderos 132, 3rd floor. Daily 1600-0300. Dance area, lounge for chilling, bar with saddles for stools, tastefully decorated in a colonial setting, with live shows 2300-0300 (all sorts of styles) and a large screen showing music videos. Recommended.

Kamikaze, Plaza Regocijo 274, T084-233865. Peña at 2200, good old traditional rock music, candle-lit cavern atmosphere, entry US$2.50 but usually you don't have to pay.

Magtas Bar, Suecia 302, corner of the Plaza. New in 2003, it seems to be aimed at the Peruvian market with lots of salsa and Latin beats – even so, the odd pop-classic slips in.

Mama, Portal Belén 115, 2nd floor. The mother of all clubs in Cusco, **Mama Africa**, has become 2 separate entities: **Mama América** is decorated in a jungle theme, with a dancefloor and a large video screen, although people dance anywhere they can. The music is middle of the road, from local music through 70's classics to the latest releases. **Mama Africa** now resides in the Portal de Harinas, 2nd floor. It claims to have cooler music and be more of a serious clubber's spot. It also serves good food from a varied menu, happy hour till 2300, good value and friendly.

Spoon, Plateros 334, 2nd floor, spoonclub@ peru.com. 2000-0500. This joint tends to play more hard-core dance, trance and techno tunes than other nightspots, but it still verges into hip-hop and funk on occasion. Happy hour from 2300-2400.

Tangible Myth, San Juan de Dios 260 (on the 2nd floor, next to Hostal Frankenstein), T084-260519. Live jazz, sometimes edging into funk and Latin rhythms, Mon to Sat, usually warming up at around 2100. This is a great place to enjoy a relaxed night out.

Ukuku's, Plateros 316. US$1.35 entry or free with a pass. This is somewhat different to the other clubs as every night there is a live band that might play anything from rock to salsa. The DJ then plays a mixture of Peruvian and international music but the emphasis is on local. It has a good mix of Cusqueños and tourists. Happy hour 0730-0930.

😊 Entertainment

Centro Qosqo de Arte Nativo, Av Sol 604, T084-227901. There's a regular nightly folklore show here 1900-2030, entrance on the BTU visitors' ticket.

Teatro Inti Raymi, Saphi 605. Music nightly at 1845, US$4.50 entry and well worth it.

Teatro Municipal, C Mesón de la Estrella 149 (T084-227321 for information 0900-1300 and 1500-1900). This is a venue for plays, dancing and shows, mostly on Thu-Sun. Ask for their programmes. They also run classes in music and dancing from Jan-Mar which are great value.

✡ Festivals and events

On **20 Jan** is a procession of saints in the **San Sebastián** district of Cusco. **Carnival** in Cusco is a messy affair with flour, water, cacti, bad fruit and animal manure thrown about in the streets. Be prepared. **Easter Mon** sees the procession of El Señor de los Temblores (Lord of the Earthquakes), starting at 1600 outside the cathedral. A large crucifix is paraded through the streets, returning to the Plaza de Armas around 2000 to bless the tens of thousands of people who have assembled there. On **2-3 May** the **Vigil of the Cross**, which takes place at all mountaintops with crosses on them, is a boisterous affair.

In **Jun** is **Corpus Christi**, on the Thu after Trinity Sunday, when all the statues of the Virgin and of Saints from Cusco's churches are paraded through the streets to the cathedral. This is a colourful event. The Plaza de Armas is surrounded by tables with women selling *cuy* (guinea pig) and a mixed grill called *chiriuchu* (*cuy*, chicken, tortillas, fish eggs, water-weeds, maize, cheese and sausage) and lots of Cusqueña beer. In **early Jun**, 2 weeks before Inti Raymi (see below) is the highly recommended **Cusqueño Beer Festival**, held near the rail station, which boasts a great variety of Latin American music. The whole event is well-organized and great fun.

Also in **Jun** is **Qoyllur Rit'i** (Snow Star Festival), held at a 4,700-m glacier north of Ocongate (Ausangate), 150 km southeast of Cusco. It has its final day 58 days after Easter Sun. To get there involves a 2-hr walk up from the nearest road at Mawayani, beyond Ocongate, then it's a further exhausting climb up to the glacier. It's a good idea to take a tent, food and plenty of warm clothing. Many trucks leave Cusco, from Limacpampa, in the days prior to the full moon in mid-Jun; prices from US$2 upwards. This is a very rough and dusty overnight journey lasting 14 hrs, requiring warm clothing and coca leaves to fend off cold and exhaustion. Several agencies offer tours, see p173.

On **24 Jun**, **Inti Raymi**, the Inca festival of the winter solstice (see p168), where locals outnumber tourists, is enacted at the fortress of Sacsayhuaman. The spectacle starts at 1000 at the Qoricancha (crowds line the streets and jostle for space to watch), then proceeds to the Plaza de Armas. From there performers and spectators go to Sacsay huaman for the main event, which starts at 1300. It lasts 2½ hrs, and is in Quechua. Locals make a great day of it, watching the ritual from the hillsides and cooking potatoes in pits in the ground. Tickets for the stands can be bought in advance from the **Emufec** office, Santa Catalina Ancha 325 (opposite the Complejo Policial), and cost US$35. Standing places on the ruins are free but get there at about 1030 as even reserved seats fill up quickly, and defend your space. Travel agents can arrange the whole day for you, with meeting points, transport, reserved seats and packed lunch. Don't believe anyone who tries to persuade you to buy a ticket for the right to film or take photos. On the night before **Inti Raymi**, the Plaza de Armas is crowded with processions and food stalls. Try to arrive in Cusco 15 days before Inti Raymi. The atmosphere in the town during the build up is fantastic and something is always going on (festivals, parades, etc).

On the **last Sun in Aug** is the Huarachicoy Festival at Sacsayhuaman, a spectacular re-enactment of the Inca manhood rite, performed in dazzling costumes by boys of a local school. On **8 Sep**, the Day of the Virgin, there is a colourful procession of masked dancers from the church of Almudena, at the southwest edge of Cusco, near Belén, to the Plaza de San Francisco. There is also a fair at Almudena, and a bull fight the following day.

On **8 Dec** is Cusco Day, when churches and museums close at 1200. On **24 Dec** is **Santuranticuy**, 'the buying of saints'. This is a huge celebration of Christmas shopping with a big crafts market in the Plaza de Armas, which is very noisy until the early hours of the 25th.

O Shopping

Bicycle repair
Atoq, Saphi 704, T993 9725 (mob), atoqis@hotmail.com. Run by Juan Carlos Salazar Triveño, high-end bike hire, repairs, spare parts, information and guided tours, English spoken.

Bookshops
Centro de Estudios Regionales Andinos Bartolomé de las Casas, Heladeros 129A. Mon-Sat 1100-1400, 1600-1900. Good books on Peruvian history, archaeology, etc. The main branch, with the best selection, is at Limacpampa Grande 571, Plaza Limacpampa. **Jerusalem**, Heladeros 143, T084-235408. English books, guidebooks, music, postcards, book exchange.
SBS (Special Book Services), Av Sol 781-A, opposite the post office, T084-248106. Sells Footprint's *South American Handbook*, *Peru* and *Cusco and Inca Trail*.

Camping equipment
There are several places on Plateros which rent out equipment but check it carefully as

it is common for parts to be missing. An example of prices per day: tent US$3-5, sleeping bag US$2 (down), US$1.50 (synthetic), stove US$1. A deposit of US$100 is asked, plus credit card, passport or plane ticket. Wherever you hire equipment, check the stoves carefully. White gas (*bencina*) costs US$1.50 per litre and can be bought at hardware stores, but check the purity. Stove spirit (*alcohol para quemar*) is available at pharmacies. Blue gas canisters, costing US$5, can be found at some hardware stores and at shops which rent gear. You can also rent equipment through travel agencies.

Soqllaq'asa Camping Service, Plateros 365 No 2F, T084-252560. Owned by English-speaking Sra Luzmila Bellota Miranda, recommended for equipment hire, from down sleeping bags (US$2 per day) to gas stoves (US$1 per day) and **ThermaRest** mats (US$1 per day); pots, pans, plates, cups and cutlery are all provided free by the friendly staff. They also buy and sell camping gear and make alpaca jackets, open Mon-Sat 0900-1300, 1600-2030, Sun 1800-2030.

Handicrafts

Cusco has some of the best craft shopping in all Peru. In the Plaza San Blas and the surrounding area, authentic Cusco crafts still survive and woodworkers can be seen in almost any street. A market is held on Sat. In its drive to 'clean up' Cusco, the authorites have moved the colourful artisans' stalls from the pavements of Plaza Regocijo to the main market at the bottom of Av Sol. There are, however, small markets of 10 or so permament stalls dotted around the city which offer goods made from alpaca as well as modern materials. For example, at **Feria Artesanal Tesores del Inka**, Plateros 334 (open 0900-2300), the first stall in the doorway will tailor- make reversible fleeces in 2 colours for US$10. Cusco is also the weaving centre of Peru and excellent textiles can be found at good value; but watch out for sharp practices when buying gold and silver objects and jewellery. Note that much of the wood used for picture frames, etc, is *cedro*, a rare timber not extracted by sustainable means.

Alpaca 111, Plaza Regocijo 202, T084-243233. High-quality alpaca clothing, with shops also in hotels **Monasterio, Libertador**

and **Machu Picchu Sanctuary Lodge** and at the airport.

Alpaca 3, Ruinas 472. Quality alpaca items.

Away, Procuradores 361, T084-229465. Sells blankets, leather goods and handmade shoes, prices from US$15-40 for a pair, allow 2 days delivery for your own design.

Cuzmar II, Portal Mantas 118T. For good quality alpaca items (English spoken).

Agua y Tierra, Plazoleta Nazarenas 167, and also at Cuesta San Blas 595, T084-226951. Excellent quality crafts from lowland rainforest communities, largely the Shipibo and Ashaninka tribes from the Selva Central whose work is considered to be among the finest in the Amazon Basin.

Andean Spirit, Hatun Rumiyoc 487-B, T084-232962. Potter Lucho Soler claims to use traditional Inca methods in his work. Whether this is true or not the ceramics on display are excellent.

Carlos Chaquiras, Triunfo 375 y Portal Comercio 107, T084-227470, www.carlos chaquiras.com. 1000-1930. Very upmarket jewellery, with lots of Inca figures, among other designs, enhanced with semi-precious stones and shells.

La Casa de la Llama, Palacio 121, www. llamactiva.com. A smart establishment with a variety of excellent quality, well-designed llama wool sweaters, scarves and llama-leather bags.

The Center for Traditional Textiles of Cusco, Av Sol 603-A, T084-228117, www.incas.org. A non-profit organization that promotes the weaving traditions of the area. Tours of workshops in Chinchero and beyond can de arranged, also weaving classes. In the Cusco outlet you can watch weavers at work. Excellent quality textiles at prices reflecting the fact that over 50% goes direct to the weaver. Recommended.

Josefina Olivera, Portal Comercio 173, Plaza de Armas. She sells old ponchos and antique *mantas* (shawls), without the usual haggling. Her prices are high, but it is worth it to save pieces being cut up to make other items, open daily 1100-2100.

Mon Repos, Portal de Panes 139, Plaza de Armas, T084-251600. High-quality alpaca clothing, expensive, but nicely presented and with a wide selection.

Ilaria, Portal Carrizos 258, T084-246253, and in Hotels Monasterio, Libertador and at the airport. Branches of the recommended jewellery and silver stores from Lima. **Joyería H Ormachea**, Plateros 372, T084-237061. Handmade gold and silver. **La Mamita**, Portal de Carnes 244, Plaza de Armas, sells the ceramics of Seminario-Behar, (see p189), plus cotton, basketry, jewellery, etc. **La Pérez**, Urb Mateo Pumacahua 598, Huanchac, T084-232186. A big cooperative with a good selection. They will arrange a free pick-up from your hotel. **Maky Artesanías**, Carmen Alto 101, T084-653643. A great place to buy individually designed ceramics. Ask for discounts if buying several pieces. **Pedazo de Arte**, Plateros 334B. A tasteful collection of Andean handicrafts, many designed by Japanese owner Miki Suzuki. **Primitiva**, Hatun Rumiyoc 495, San Blas, www.coscio.com. Excellent Peruvian contemporary art gallery, largely featuring the work of Federico Coscio. **Spondylus**, Cuesta San Blas 505 y Plazoleta San Blas 617, T084-226929, spondylus cusco@mixmail.com. Interesting jewellery in gold and silver, also using semi-precious stones and shells. They also sell T-shirts featuring Inca and pre-Inca designs. **Taki Museo de Música de los Andes**, Hatunrumiyoq 487-5. Shop and workshop selling and displaying musical instruments, knowledgeable owner, who is an ethnomusicologist. Recommended.

Leading artisans who welcome visitors include the following: **Hilario Mendivil**, Plazoleta San Blas 634 and 619, who makes biblical figures from plaster, wheatflour and potatoes. **Edilberta Mérida**, Carmen Alto 133, who makes earthenware figures showing the physical and mental anguish of the indigenous peasant. **Antonio Olave Palomino**, Plazoleta San Blas 651, makes reproductions of pre-Columbian ceramics and colonial sculptures. **Maximiliano Palomino de la Sierra**, Triunfo 393, produces festive dolls and traditional wood-carvings. **Santiago Rojas**, Suytuccato 751, above San Blas, makes statuettes. **Coordinadora Sur Andina de Artesanía**, C del Medio 130, off Plaza de Armas, has a good assortment of crafts and is a non-profit making organization. **Mercado Artesanal**, Av Sol, block 4, is good for cheap crafts. **Museo Inca Art Gallery**, Huancaro M-B - L8, T084-231232 (PO Box 690), telephone between 0900 and 2100. Run by Amílcar Salomón Zorrilla, a good place for contemporary art. **Nemesio Villasante**, Av 24 de Junio 415, T084-222915. For Paucartambo masks.

Markets

San Jerónimo, just out of town, is the new location of the wholesale Sat morning fruit and vegetable market, but food just as good and not much more expensive (and washed) can be bought at the markets in town: **Huanchac**, Av Garcilaso (not to be confused with C Garcilaso), or **Santa Ana**, opposite Estación San Pedro, which sells a variety of goods. The best value is at closing time or in the rain. Take care after dark. Sacks to cover rucksacks are available in the market for US$0.75. Both Huanchac and Santa Ana open every day from 0700.

Just down from **Santiago Church** (an unsafe area at night because of drunks high on chemically produced alcohol) is a sprawling affair of stall upon stall laid out on the pavements. Everything from stolen car jacks to useless junk is for sale. It's a fascinating sight but be sensible and leave valuables in the hotel safe.

The second less legitimate market – but equally well tolerated by Cusqueño authorities – is **El Molino**, under the Puente Grau, for contraband goods brought in from abroad without duty or tax being paid. Everything from computers to hi-fis, personal stereos to trekking boots, cheap camera film to wine can be bought here (take a taxi for US$0.60). It is clean and safe (but take the usual common sense precautions about valuables) and is open daily 0600-2030.

Supermarkets

La Canasta, Av La Cultura 2000 block. Very well stocked, takes credit cards, ATM outside. **D'Dinos Market**, Av La Cultura 2003, T084-252656. Open 24-hrs, well supplied, takes credit cards. **Dimart**, Matará 271, and Av La Cultura 742. Daily 0700-2200, credit cards accepted. El Pepito, Plaza San Francisco, Mon-Sat 0900-2000, closed lunchtime. Sells a wide variety of imported goods and also has a delicatessen, stocks multi-packs of food (eg chocolate bars) much cheaper than other shops, a good bargain for trekking supplies.

▲ Activities and tours

There are a million and one tour operators in Cusco, most of whom are packed into the Plaza de Armas. The sheer number and variety of tours on offer is bewildering and prices for the same tour can vary dramatically. You should only deal directly with the agencies and seek advice from visitors returning from trips for the latest information. Agencies listed below are included under the field in which they are best known and for which they receive consistent recommendations. Note, though, that only a restricted number of agencies are licensed to operate Inca Trail trips (INRENA, Av José Gabriel Cosio 308, Urb Magisterial, 1 etapa, T084-229297, will verify operating permits - the website www.inrena.gob.pe doesn't give a list). Other agencies will sell Inca Trail trips, but pass clients on to the operating agency. This can cause confusion and booking problems at busy times. Many agencies, and the alternatives they offer, can be found in the trip reports in the **South America Explorers'** clubhouse at Choque-chaca 188 (for members only). Beware also of tours which stop for long lunches at pricey hotels. Check if there are cancellation fees. Students will normally receive a discount on production of an ISIC card.

Ballooning and paragliding

The Sacred Valley offers exciting but challenging paragliding so if wind conditions are bad, flights may be delayed till the following day. Magnificent scenery, soaring close to snow-capped mountains makes this an awesome experience. 45 km from Cusco is Cerro Sacro (3,797 m) on the Pampa de Chincheros with 550 m clearance at take-off. It is the launch site for cross-country flights over the Sacred Valley, Sacsayhuaman and Cusco. Particularly good for parapenting is the Mirador de Urubamba, 38 km from Cusco, at 3,650 m, with 800 m clearance and views over Pisac.
Globos de los Andes, Arequipa 271, T084-232352, T969 3812 (mob), www.globosperu.com. Hot-air ballooning in the Sacred Valley and expeditions with balloons and 4WD lasting several days.
Richard Pethigal, T084-993 7333 (mob), cloudwalker@another.com. Richard offers a condor's-eye view of the Sacred Valley. From May-Sep he runs half-day tandem paraglider flights from Cusco. He is a very experienced pilot and uses high-quality equipment. He is licensed and charges US$60.

Cultural tours

Another Planet, Triunfo 120, T084-229379, www.anotherplanetperu.net. Run by Lesley Myburgh, who operates all kinds of adventure tours and conventional tours in and around Cusco, but specializes in jungle trips anywhere in Peru. Lesley is an expert in San Pedro cactus preparation and she arranges San Pedro journeys for healing at physical, emotional and spiritual levels in beautiful remote areas. The journeys are thoroughly organized and a safe, beautiful, unforgettable experience.
Inca Planet, www.incaplanetcusco.com, at the same address and in same family, is a tour operator.
Apu Expediciones, T084-271215, T995 7483 (mob), www.geocities.com/apuexpeditions. Deals mostly through internet. Cultural, adventure (including Inca Trail), educational/academic programmes, nature tours and jungle packages to Manu and Tambopata, bilingual personnel, very knowledgeable.
Casa de la serenidad, T084-222851, www.shamanspirit.net. A shamanic therapy centre run by a Swiss-American healer and Reiki Master who uses medicinal 'power' plants. It also has bed and breakfast and has received very good reports.
K'uichy Light International, Av Sol 814, of 219, T084-264107, T962 1722 (mob), kuichy@amauta.rcp.net.pe. Ruben E Palomino specializes in spiritual tours, good value.
Milla Tourism, Av Pardo 689 y Portal Comercio 195 on the plaza, T084-231710, www.millaturismo.com. Mon-Fri 0800-1300, 1500-1900, Sat 0800-1300. Mystical tours to Cusco's Inca ceremonial sites such as Pumamarca and The Temple of the Moon. Also private tours arranged to Moray agricultural terracing and Maras salt mines in Sacred Valley. Guide speaks only basic English. They also arrange cultural and environmental lectures and courses.
Mystic Inca Trail, Unidad Vecinal de Santiago, bloque 9, dpto 301, T084-221358, ivanndp@terra.com.pe. Specialize in tours of

sacred Inca sites and study of Andean spirituality. This takes 10 days but it is possible to have shorter 'experiences'.
Personal Travel Service, Portal de Panes 123, oficina 109, T084-225518, ititoss@terra.com.pe. Mainly deals with group bookings and package holidays. They will organize a personalized itinerary for individuals and groups including inter-national and national flights. They specialize in cultural tours in the Urubamba Valley.

Inca Trail

Unless stated othrwise the companies listed are licensed to operate the Trail (2004).
Amazonas Explorer, Av Collasuyo 910, Miravalle, PO Box 722, Cusco, T084-252846, T084-976 5448 (mob), www.amazonas-explorer.com. T01473-891743. Experts in rafting, hiking, biking and multi-activity tours; used by BBC. English owner Paul Cripps has great experience, but takes most bookings from overseas. However, he may be able to arrange a trip for travellers in Cusco.
Andean Adventures, T084-263498, www.andeanadventuresperu.com. An experienced outfit offering cultural trips and ecotourism. Tailor made tours of the region as well as treks to Machu Picchu.
Andean Life, Plateros 372, T084-221491, www.andeanlife.com. Offer a number of variations on the Inca Trail, as well as Salkantay and Ausangate, day trips in and around Cusco and jungle trips.
Andes Nature Tours, Garcilaso 210, Casa del Abuelo, oficina 217, T084-245961, ant@terra.com.pe. Owner Aurelio speaks excellent English and has 25 years' experience in Cusco and will tailor treks 'anywhere'. Specializes in natural history, trekking, botany and birdwatching.
Andina Travel, Plazoleta Santa Catalina 219, T084-251892, www.andinatravel.com. Agency specializing in trekking and biking. One of the company's specialities is the Lares Valley programme, which works together with some of the valley's traditional weaving communities. Recommended.
Apumayo, C Garcilaso 265 interior 3, T084-246018 (Lima: T01-444 2320), www.apumayo.com. Mon-Sat 0900-1300, 1600-2000. Rafting on the Urubamba and the Apurímac. Also mountain biking and treks. This company also offers tours for disabled people, including rafting.
Big Foot, Triunfo 392 (oficina 213), T084-238568, www.bigfootcusco.com. Conventional Inca Trail trips, but also specialists in tailor-made hiking trips, especially in the remote corners of the Vilcabamba and Vilcanota mountains.
Carla's Travel, Plateros 320, T084-228454, T993 0855 (mob), carlastravel@telser.com. Cheap and cheerful – this is about as economical as they come, so have realistic expectations. Will also arrange treks to Ausangate.
Ch'aska, Plateros 325, p 2, T084-240424, www.chaskatours.com. A Dutch-Peruvian owned company offering cultural, adventure, nature and esoteric tours. Specialize in the Inca Trail, but also llama treks to Lares, and other major treks (their Choquequirao trip is recommended). They can tailor tours throughout Peru.

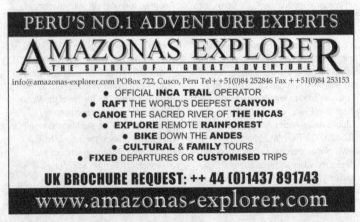

Destinos Turísticos, Portal de Panes 123, oficina 101-102, Plaza de Armas, T084-228168, www.destinosturisticosperu.com. The owner speaks Spanish, English, Dutch and Portuguese and specializes in package tours from economic to 5-star budgets. Individuals are welcome to come in for advice on booking jungle trips to renting mountain bikes. Ask in advance if you require guides with specific languages. Very informative and helpful.

Ecotrek Peru, Totorapaccha 769, San Blas, T084-247286, T976 2162 (mob), www.ecotrekperu.com. (The office is above San Blas, to the left of the plaza, on a Royal Inca trail.) Scot and long-time Cusco resident Fiona Cameron runs this environmentally friendly tour agency; she is often involved in river clean-ups in the area. Tour specialities currently focus on adventurous mountain biking trips in remote highland areas and jungle expeditions to the Pongo de Mainique and beyond (not Inca Trail).

Enigma, C Garcilaso 210, of 103, T084-222155, www.enigmaperu.com. Run by Spaniard Silvia Rico Coll. Has an excellent reputation for well-organized and innovative trekking expeditions in the region. In addition to the regular Inca Trail, she offers some new and interesting routes in the Ausangate area, Lares Valley and some longer routes. Silvia also runs cultural tours such as visits to traditional weaving communities and Ayahuasca Therapy.

Eric Adventures, Plateros 324, T084-228475, www.ericadventures.com. Specialize in adventure activities, rafting, mountain biking, also rent motorcross bikes. They clearly explain what equipment is included in their prices and what you will need to bring. Prices are higher if you book by email, you can get huge discounts if you book in the office. A popular company.

Exotic Adventures, Plateros 325, 2nd floor, T084-243826, www.exotic-adventures.com. One of the better budget operators. They offer a 9-day Huancacalle to Cachora trek, via Choquequirao and the pass of Choque-tacarpo at 4,600 m – a magnificent trek.

Explorandes, Av Garcilaso 316-A (not to be confused with C Garcilaso in the centre), T084-245700, www.explorandes.com. Experienced high-end adventure company. Their main office is in Lima, but trips can also be arranged from Cusco. Award-winning environmental practices.

HikingPeru, Portal de Panes 109, of 6, T084-263278 965 1414 (mob), www.hikingperu.com. It no longer operates classic Inca Trail treks, preferring instead to concentrate on alternative day walks and more remote, less beaten paths, eg Espíritu Pampa, Ausangate, Lares Valley.

Inca Explorers, Suecia 339, T084-241070, www.incaexplorers.com. Specialist trekking agency with a good reputation for small group expeditions executed in socially and environmentally responsible manner.

Instinct, Procuradores 50, T084-233451, www.instinct-travel.com (in the UK, **Land of the Inkas**, 29 Rotherfield Rd, Carshalton, Surrey, SM5 2DN, T07775-602416). Tailor-made trips, working a lot through the internet, plenty of involvement with community projects and opening up new routes. Mountain biking in the Sacred Valley; they also hire mountain bikes; also some rafting. Juan and Benjamín Muñiz speak good English.

Liz's Explorer, Medio 114B, T084-246619, www.lizexplorer.com. Inca Trail and a variety of trips available. Liz gives a clearly laid out list of what is and what is not included. If you need a guide who speaks a language other than English let her know in advance. Majority of reports are good.

Machete Tours, Tecseccocha 161, T084-224829, T969 2369 (mob), info@machetetours.com. Many innovative trekking trips, eg a complete 8-day traverse of the Cordillera Vilcabamba from the Apurímac Canyon and Choquequirao across the range to Machu Picchu itself. They also offer expeditions to Espíritu Pampa, Ausangate and, of course, the Inca Trail. They have recently opened a new rainforest lodge on the remote Río Blanco, south of the Manu Biosphere Reserve. Not all of the guides speak English so check this before trip details are confirmed.

Manu Expeditions, Av Pardo 895, PO Box 606, T084-226671, www.ManuExpeditions. com. As well as Manu trips (see p545), also runs tailor-made bird trips in cloud and rainforest around Cusco and Peru, and has horse riding and a 9-day/8-night trip to Machu Picchu along a different route from the Inca Trail, rejoining at Sun Gate. Barry runs horse supported treks to Choquequirao, starting from Huancacalle. Highly recommended.

Naty's Travel Agency, Triunfo 338-42, T084-239437, www.natystravel.com. Principally Inca Trail trips, but will organize all other trips including Puerto Maldonaldo and special fiestas. They also sell air tickets. Guides speak English.

Peru Treks and Adventures, Garcilaso 265 oficina 14 (2nd floor), T084-805863, www.perutreks.com. Trekking agency set up by Englishman Mike Weston and his partner Koqui González. They pride themselves on good treatment of porters and support staff (and tourists!). Treks offered include Salkantay, the Lares Valley and Vilcabamba Vieja (not Incal Trail). Mike also runs the **Andean Travel Web**, www.andeantravel web.com, with a focus on sustainable tourism in the region.

Peruvian Andean Treks, Av Pardo 705, T084-225701, www.andeantreks.com. Open Mon-Fri 0900-1300, 1500-1800, Sat 0900-1300. Manager Tom Hendrickson has 5-day/4-night Inca Trail using high-quality equipment and satellite phones. His 7-day/6-night Vilcanota Llama Trek to Ausangate (the mountain visible from Cusco) includes a collapsible pressure chamber for altitude sickness.

Q'ente, Garcilaso 210, int 210b, T084-222535, www.qente.com. Their Inca Trail service is recommended. They will organize private treks to Salkantay, Ausangate, Choquequirao, Vilcabamba and Q'eros. Also horse riding to local ruins. Very good, especially with children.

SAS Travel, Portal de Panes 143, T084-237292 (staff in a 2nd office at Medio 137, mainly deal with jungle information and only speak Spanish), www.sastravel.com. Inca Trail price includes the bus down from Machu Picchu to Aguas Calientes and lunch on the last day. SAS have their own hostel in Aguas Calientes – if clients wish to stay in Aguas after the trail and return the next morning this can be arranged at no extra cost. Group sizes are between 8 and 16 people. To go in a smaller group, costs rise considerably. Before setting off they ensure you are told everything that is included and give advice on what personal items should be taken. Also Manu, mountain bike, horse riding and rafting trips can be organized. All guides speak English (some better than others). Responsible, good equipment and food.

Sky Travel, Santa Catalina Ancha 366, interior 3-C (down alleyway next to Rosie O'Grady's pub), T084-261818, F084-261414. English spoken. General tours around city and Sacred Valley. Prides itself on leaving 30 mins before other groups, thus reaching sights and the lunch spot (!) before anyone else. Also Inca Trail (the group is asked what it would like on the menu 2 days before departure), Vilcabamba and Ausangate.

Trekperu, Ricaldo Palma N-9, Santa Mónica, T084-252899, www.trekperu.com. Experienced trek operator as well as other adventure sports and mountain biking. Offers 'culturally sensitive' tours. Biking Adventure includes support vehicle and good camping gear. Need sleeping bag.

United Mice, Plateros 351y Triunfo 392, T084-221139, www.unitedmice.com. For the Inca Trail, with good English-speaking guides (Salustio speaks Italian and Portuguese), city tours in Spanish and English, Sacred Valley Tours and Choquequirao.

Wayki Trek, Procuradores 44, T084-224092, waykitrek@hotmail.com. Budget travel agency, recommended for their Inca Trail service. Owner Leo grew up in the countryside near Ollantaytambo and knows the area very well. They run treks to several almost unknown Inca sites and many interesting variations on the 'classic' Inca Trail. They also run treks to Ausangate, Salkantay and Choquequirao.

Manu Biosphere Reserve tours

There are many operators in Cusco offering trips to Manu. To name a few, **Amazon Trails Peru**, **Expediciones Vilca**, **InkaNatura Travel**, **Manu Ecological Adventures**, **Manu Expeditions**, **Manu Nature Tours**, For full details of these operators and the tours on offer, see p558.

Mountain biking

From a half-day downhill exploring the nearby ruins to the ultimate 550-km Andes to Amazon challenge, Cusco offers a multitude of rides to suit all abilities. Here is a selection; all ideally require a guide as its very easy to get lost in the Andes.

Cusco Ruins: Cheat by taking a taxi to Puka Pukara and enjoying a tarmac descent (if un-guided) via Tambo Machay, Qenqo and Sacsayhuaman (don't forget your combined entrance ticket). Alternatively, with a guide, explore some of Cusco's less-visited ruins on the mass of old Inca tracks available only to those in the know.

Chinchero-Moray-Maras-Las Salinas-Urubamba: One of the finest one-day trips in Peru, best done with a guide. Largely downhill on a mixture of dirt road and single track, to the circular ruins of Moray and into the spectacular salt pans of Maras on an awesome mule track (watch out for mules!).

Huchuy Qosqo: For experts only, various routes, hard to find, are followed by what must be one of the hairiest single tracks in the world, along the top of and down into the Sacred Valley of the Incas.

Lares Valley: This offers some incredible down and uphill options on 2-3 day circuits including a relaxing soak in the beautiful Lares hotsprings.

Abra Málaga: From 4,200m, an 80-km descent to the jungle, or, alternatively a radical Inca Trail back to Ollantaytambo, both brilliant rides.

Tres Cruces to Manu: From Pisac to Manu is a 250-km, beautiful dirt road ride offering big climbs and an even bigger (2-day) descent. A side trip to Tres Cruces to see the sunrise is a must if time permits. Remember that the road to Manu only operates downhill every other day, so be sure to check before you set out.

Cusco-Puerto Maldonado: Possibly the greatest Trans-Andean Challenge on a bike: 550 km of hard work up to 4,700m and down to 230m on one of the roughest roads there is (with the odd full-on single track thrown in). Be prepared to get wet as there are a lot of river crossings, sometimes up to waist deep. Either a nine-day epic, or cheat on the hills and enjoy some of the biggest downhills out (3-4 days).

Private guides

As most of the sights do not have any information or signs in English, a good guide can really improve your visit. Either arrange this before you set out or grab one of those hanging around the sights' entrances (this is much easier to do in the low season). A tip is expected at the end of the tour. All of those listed are bilingual. Set prices: City tour US$15-20 per day; Urubamba/Sacred Valley US$25-30, Machu Picchu and other ruins US$40-50 per day.

Boris Cárdenas, T084-243306, boriscar@ terra.com.pe. Esoteric and cultural tours.

José Cuba and Alejandra Cuba, Urb Santa Rosa R Gibaja 182, Urb Santa Rosa R Gibaja 182, T084-226179, T968 5187 (mob), ale17ch1@yahoo.com. Both speak English, Alejandra speaks German and French, very good tours.

Victoria Morales Condori, T084-224877, kuntur01@yahoo.com.mx.

Percy Salas Alfaro, c/o Munditur, T084-240287, smunditur@hotmail.com. Serious, friendly, English-speaking.

Roger Valencia Espinoza, José Gabriel Cosio 307, T084-251278, vroger@qenqo. rcp.net.pe. Offers adventure trips.

The Cusco region is probably the 'rafting capital' of Peru, with more whitewater runs on offer than anywhere else in Peru. When looking for an operator please consider more than just the price of your tour. Competition between companies in Cusco is intense and price wars can lead to compromises in safety as corners are cut or less experienced (and therefore cheaper) guides are hired. Consider the quality of safety equipment (lifejackets, etc) and the number and experience of rescue kayakers and support staff. On a large and potentially dangerous river like the Apurímac (where fatalities have occurred), this can make all the difference.

The Urubamba: perhaps the most popular day run in the whole country, but sadly one heavily affected in parts by pollution both from Cusco and from the towns of the Sacred Valley. Clean-up campaigns are organized periodically, but they just touch the surface of the problem.

Huambutio-Pisac (all year availability, Grade 2): a scenic half-day float with a few rapids to get the adrenaline flowing right through the heart of the Sacred Valley. Fits in perfectly with a day trip to Pisac Market. A sedate introduction to rafting for all ages.

Ollantaytambo-Chilca (all year availability, Grade 3 to 4+ depending on season): a fun half-day introduction to the sport with a few challenging rapids and beautiful scenery near Ollantaytambo. This trip also fits in perfectly with the start of the Inca Trail. Try to go early in the morning as a strong wind picks up in the late morning.

Huaran Canyon (all year, Grade3+ to 5+ depending on season): a short section of fun whitewater that is occasionally rafted. Not for beginners in the rainy season.

Santa María to Quillabamba (dry season, Grade 3-4): a rarely-rafted two-day, high jungle trip. A long way to go for some fairly good whitewater but mediocre jungle.

Chuquicahuana (rainy season, Grade 4 to 5+, dry season, Grade 2-4): in the rainy season, this is a technically demanding one-day trip for genuine adrenaline junkies. In the dry season this section makes a good alternative to the now polluted sections further downstream and provides several hours of fun, with 3 km of rapids (technical), all in a pretty canyon. Strict safety procedures are needed all year round.

Cusipata (rainy season, Grade 3-4, dry season Grade 2-3): often used as a warm up section in high water before attempting Chuquicahuana. Fun rapids and a beautiful mini-canyon, which, in low water, is ideal for the fun sport of inflatable canoes (duckies). Again the water purity is much better than the lower sections.

Pinipampa (all year grade 1-2): a fun and beautiful section, rarely paddled but relatively clean - no major rapids but a fun canoeing or ducky trip for beginners.

Rafting operators

Mayuc Expediciones, Portal Confiturías 211, Plaza de Armas, T084-232666, www.mayuc. com. Rafting on the Urubamba and Apurímac rivers. They also have a permanent lodge, Casa Cusi, on the upper Urubamba, which forms the basis of 2-day, Class III-IV trips in the area. Also trekking and combinations of horse-trekking and walking can be organized.

Southern Rivers Expeditions, Plateros 319, T084-232061, www.southernrivers.net. Apurímac, Urubamba and occasional Tambopata river rafting. Peruvian owner Willie Villafuerte Solís has huge experience leading rafting trips around the world and possesses many safety and rescue qualifications. He leads many trips personally.

Swissraft-Peru, Plateros 361, T084-246414, www.swissraft-peru.com. Good reputation for professionally run tours on the Apurímac and Urubamba rivers, with the focus above all on safety. Equipment is new and of good quality.

Shamans and drug experiences

San Pedro and Ayahuasca have been used since before Inca times, mostly as a sacred healing experience. The plants are prepared with special treatments for curative purposes; they have never been considered a drug. If you choose to experience these incredible healing/teaching plants, only do so under the guidance of a reputable agency or shaman and always have a friend with you who is not partaking. If the medicine is not prepared correctly, it can be highly toxic and, in rare cases, severely dangerous. Never buy from someone who is not recommended, never buy off the streets and never try to prepare the plants yourself. We suggest the following, whom we know to be legitimate: **Another Planet**, Triunfo 120, T084-229379, www.anotherplanetperu.net. Run by Lesley Myburgh (who also runs **Casa de La Gringa**, C Pensamiento E-3, Urb Miravalle, 5 mins by taxi from plaza, sleeping in **D** range), who operates all kinds of adventure tours and conventional tours in and around Cusco, but specializes in jungle trips anywhere in Peru. The journeys are thoroughly organized and a safe, beautiful, unforgettable experience. **Casa de la serenidad**, T084-222851, www.shamanspirit.net. A shamanic therapy centre run by a Swiss-American healer and Reiki Master who uses medicinal 'power' plants. It also has bed and breakfast and has received very good reports.

Tour operators
Cóndor Travel, C Saphi 848-A, T084-225961, www.condortravel.com.pe (for flights diviajes@condortravel.com.pe). A high-quality, exclusive agency that will organize trips throughout Peru and the rest of the world. They have a specialized section for adventure travel (including the Inca Trail) and are representatives of **American Airlines**, **Servivensa**, **Avensa**, **Continental** and most other international airlines with ticket sales, connections, etc. They have many programmes to complement business trips and conferences.
Discount Designer Tours, Rieles 875 (C Hospital), T084-241298. Sr Wilver Gamarra Salas is very helpful and offers good local tours: professional, attention to detail.
Domiruth Travel Services, Jr Rio de Janeiro 216-218, Miraflores, T01-610 6022, www.domiruth.com. pe. Tours throughout Peru, from the mystical to adventure travel.
Gatur Cusco, Puluchapata 140 (a small street off Av Sol 3rd block), T084-223496, gatur@terra.com.pe. Esoteric, ecotourism, and general tours. Owner Dr José (Pepe) Altamirano is knowledgeable in Andean folk

traditions. Excellent conventional tours, bilingual guides and transportation. Guides speak English, French, Spanish and German. They can also book internal flights.
Kinjyo Travel Service, Av Sol 761, T084-231121, travel_express@msn.com. An agency that also deals with group bookings from overseas but they will arrange personalized itineraries for groups. They will book all international/national flights.
Lima Tours, Av Machu Picchu D-24, Urb Mañuel Prado, T084-228431, www.lima tours.com.pe. City and Sacred Valley tours, including lunch.
Servicios Aéreos AQP SA, T084-243229, 24 hrs T084-620585, aqpsa-cusco@mail.inter place.com.pe. Offers a wide variety of tours within the country, agents for **American**, **Continental**, **LAB** and other airlines; head office in Lima, Los Castaños 347, San Isidro, T01-2223312.

Transport

Air
Airport information T084-222611/601. You can book a hotel at the airport through a travel agency, but this is not really necessary. Many representatives of hotels and travel agencies operate at the airport, offering transport to the hotel with which they are associated. Take your time to choose your hotel, at the price you can afford. There is a post office, phone booths, restaurant and cafeteria at the airport. There is also a Tourist Protection Bureau desk, which can be very helpful if your flight has not been reconfirmed (not an uncommon problem). Do not forget to pay the airport tax at the appropriate desk before departure.
Airline offices **American Airlines**, Saphi 848, T084-226605 (toll free T0800-40350), reconfirm 72 hrs in advance, represented by **Cóndor Travel**. **LAB**, Santa Catalina Angosta 160, T084-222990. **Lan**, Av Sol 627-B, T084-225555. **Taca**, Av Sol 226, T084-249921, good service. **Tans**, San Agustín 315-317, T084-242725.

Bus
Local **Combis** run from 0500 to 2200 or 2300, US$0.15. Combis run to all parts of the city, including the bus and train stations and the airport, but are not allowed within 2

blocks of the Plaza de Armas. Stops are signed and the driver's assistant calls out the names of stops. By law all passengers are insured. After 2200 combis may not run their full route; demand to be taken to your stop, or better still, use a taxi late at night.

El Tranvía de Cusco is actually a motor coach which runs on the route of the original Cusco tramway system. The route starts in the Plaza de Armas (except on Sun morning) and ends at the Sacsayhuaman Archaeological Park. There is a 10-min stop at the mirador by the Cristo Blanco before descending to the Plaza de Armas. Departures 1000, 1150 and 1500, 1 hr 20 mins, with explanations of the city's history, architecture, customs, etc; US$2, US$1.40 for students with ID. For group reservations, T084-740640.

Long distance The bus terminal, Terminal Terrestre, is on Av Vallejo Santoni, block 2 (Prolongación Pachacútec). *Colectivo* from centre US$0.15, taxi US$0.60. Platform tax US$0.30.

All direct buses to **Lima** (20-24 hrs) now go via **Abancay**, 195 km, 5 hrs (longer in the rainy season), and **Nasca**, on the Panamerican Highway. This route is paved, but floods in the wet season can damage sections of the highway. If prone to carsickness, be prepared on the road to Abancay, there are many, many curves, but the scenery is magnificent (it also happens to be a great route for cycling). At Abancay, the road forks, the other branch going to **Andahuaylas**, a further 138 km, 10-11 hrs from Cusco, and **Ayacucho** in the Central Highlands, another 261 km, 20 hrs from Cusco. On both routes at night, take a blanket or sleeping bag to ward off the cold. All buses leave daily from the Terminal Terrestre.

Molina, who also have an office on Av Pachacútec, just past the railway station, has buses on both routes. They run 3 services a day to **Lima** via **Abancay** and **Nasca**, and 1, at 1900, to **Abancay** and **Andahuaylas**; Wari leaves at 0800, 1400, 1600 and 2000 to **Abancay**, **Nasca** and **Lima**. Cruz del Sur's cheaper *Ideal* service leaves for **Lima** via Abancay at 0730 and 1400, while their more comfortable *Imperial* service departs at 1500 and 1600. **San Jerónimo** and **Los Chankas** have buses to **Abancay**, **Andahuaylas** and **Ayacucho**, San Jerónimo at 1830. Turismo

Ampay goes to Abancay at 0630, 1300 and 2000, **Turismo Abancay** at 0630, 1300 and 2000, and **Expreso Huamanga** at 1600. **Bredde** has 5 buses a day to Abancay. Fares to **Abancay** US$3.40, **Andahuaylas** US$6, **Ayacucho** US$12, **Nasca** US$17-20, **Lima** US$20 (Cruz del Sur, *Ideal* class) to US$32 (**Cruz del Sur**, *Imperial* class). In Cusco you may be told that there are no buses in the day from Abancay to Andahuaylas; this is not so – **Señor de Huanca** does so. If you leave Cusco before 0730, with luck you'll make the onward connection at 1300, which is worth it for the scenery.

To **Lake Titicaca and Bolivia**: To **Juliaca**, 344 km, 5-6 hrs, US$8.60. The road is fully paved, but after heavy rain buses may not run. To **Puno**, 44 km from Juliaca, there is a good service with Ormeñoat 0900, US$10, 6 hrs. This service continues to **La Paz**, Bolivia. First Class, Av Sol 930, have a service at 0800, calling at Andahuayllas church, Raqchi and Pucará en route (lunch, but not entrance tickets, is included), US$25. Travel agencies sell this ticket. Other services are run by **Tour Perú** and **Libertad** (at night), US$8.60, 6½-8 hrs. **Tour Perú** also offers a direct service to **La Paz**, US$15.

To **Arequipa**, 521 km, **Cruz del Sur** use the direct paved route via Juliaca and have 3 *Ideal* services leaving daily, 10½ hrs, US$7, and 1 *Imperial* service at 1930, 10 hrs, US$10. Ormeño's fare is US$16. Other buses join the new Juliaca-Arequipa road at Imata, 10-12 hrs, US$7.75 (eg **Carhuamayo**, 3 a day).

Car
Avis, Av El Sol 808 and at the airport, T084-248800, avis-cusco@terra.com.pe.
Touring y Automóvil Club del Perú, Av Sol 349, T084-224561, cusco@touringperu.com.pe. A good source of information on motoring, car hire and mechanics (membership is US$45 per year).

Taxi
Local Taxis have fixed prices: in the centre US$0.60 (a little more after dark); and to the suburbs US$0.85-1.55 (touts at the airport and train station will always ask much higher fares). In town it is safest to take taxis which are registered; these have a sign with the company's name on the roof, not just a sticker in the window. Taxis on call are

reliable but more expensive, in the centre US$1.25 (**Ocarina** T084-247080, **Aló Cusco** T084-222222).

Long distance Taxi trips to **Sacsayhuaman** cost US$10; to the ruins of **Tambo Machay** US$15-20 (3-4 people); a whole-day trip costs US$40-70. For US$50 a taxi can be hired for a whole day (ideally Sun) to take you to **Chinchero**, **Maras**, **Urubamba**, **Ollantaytambo**, **Calca**, **Lamay**, **Coya**, **Pisac**, **Tambo Machay**, **Qenqo** and **Sacsayhuaman**.

Train
All details of the train services out of Cusco can be found on www.perurail.com. The train to **Juliaca** and **Puno** leaves at 0800, on Mon, Wed and Sat, arriving in Puno at 1800 (sit on the left for the best views). The train makes a stop to view the scenery at La Raya. Trains return from Puno on Mon, Wed and Sat at 0800, arriving in Cusco at 1645. Fares: tourist/backpacker class, US$16.66, 1st class US$119.

Tickets can be bought up to 5 days in advance. The ticket office at Wanchac station is open Mon-Fri 0800-1700, Sat 0900-1200. Tickets sell out quickly and there are queues from 0400 before holidays in the dry season. In the low season tickets to Puno can be bought on the day of departure. You can buy tickets through a travel agent, but check the date and seat number. Meals are served on the train. Always check whether the train is running, especially inthe rainy season, when services might be cancelled.

○ Directory

Banks All the banks along Av Sol have ATMs from which you can withdraw dollars or soles at any hour. Whether you use the counter or an ATM, choose your time carefully as there can be long queues at both. Most banks are closed between 1300 and 1600. **BCP**, Av Sol 189. Gives cash advances on Visa and changes TCs to soles with no commission, 3% to dollars. It has an ATM for Visa. It also handles Amex. **Interbank**, Av Sol y Puluchapata. Charges no commission on TCs and has a Visa/Plus and Mastercard/Cirrus ATM which gives dollars as well as soles. Next door is **Banco Continental**, also has a Visa ATM and

charges US$5 commission on TCs. **BSCH**, Av Sol 459. Changes Amex TCs at reasonable rates. Has an ATM for Visa. **Banco Latino**, Almagro 125 y Av Sol 395. Has ATMs for MasterCard. **Banco Wiese**, Maruri between Pampa del Castillo and Pomeritos. Gives cash advances on Mastercard, in dollars. Emergency number for lost or stolen Visa cards, 0800-1330.

As well as the ATMs in banks (most of which have 24-hr police protection), there are ATMs on the Plaza de Armas at the entrance to Inka Grill, Portal de Panes, Supermercado Gato's, Portal Belén, and the entrance to Cross Keys and Tunupa, Portal de Confiturías. There are other ATMs on Av La Cultura, beside Supermercado Dimart and beside Supermercado La Canasta. **Western Union** at Santa Catalina Ancha 165, T084-233727. Money transfers in 10 mins; also at **DHL**, see below.

Many travel agencies and casas de cambio change dollars. Some of them change TCs as well, but charge 4-5% commission. There are many *cambios* on the west side of the Plaza de Armas (eg Portal Comercio Nos 107 and 148) and on the west side of Av Sol, most change TCs (best rates in the *cambios* at the top of Av Sol). **LAC Dólar**, Av Sol 150, T084-257969, Mon-Sat 0900-2000, with delivery service to central hotels, cash and TCs, is recommended. The street changers hang around Av Sol, blocks 2-3, every day and are a pleasure to do business with. Some of them will also change TCs. In banks and on the street check the notes.

Clinics and doctors Clínica **Panamericana**, Av Infancia 508, Wanchac, T084-270000, T965 1552 (mob). 24-hr emergency and medical attention. **Clínica Pardo**, Av de la Cultura 710, T084-240387, T993 0063 (mob), www.clinicapardocusco. com. 24-hr emergency and hospitalization/ medical attention, international department, trained bilingual personnel, handles complete medical assistance coverage with international insurance companies, free ambulance service, visit to hotel, discount in pharmacy, dental service, X-rays, laboratory, full medical specialization. The most highly recommmed clinic in Cusco. Director is Dr Alcides Vargas. **Clínica Paredes**, C Lechugal 405, T084-225265. Offers a wide range of medical attention. Director is Dr Milagros Paredes, whose speciality is gynaecology. Recommended. **Hospital Regional**, Av de la Cultura, T084-227661, emergencies T084-223691. **Dr Ilya Gomon**, Av de la Cultura, Edif Santa Fe, oficina 207, T084-965 1906 (mob). Canadian chiropractor, good, reasonable prices, available for hotel or home visits. **Dr Gilbert Espejo** and **Dr Boris Espejo Muñoz**, both in the Centro Comercial Cusco, oficina 7, T084-228074 and T084-231918 respectively. If you need a yellow fever vaccination (for the jungle lowlands, or for travel to Bolivia or Brazil where it is required), it is available at the paediatric department of the **Hospital Antonio Lorena** from 0830 on Mon, Wed and Fri; they are free and include the international vaccination certificate.

Dentists Dr Eduardo Franco, Av de la Cultura, Edif Santa Fe, oficina 310, T084-242207, T965 0179 (mob). 24-hr.

Embassies and consulates Belgium, Av Sol 954, T084-221098, F084-221100. Mon-Fri 0900-1300, 1500-1700. **France**, Jorge Escobar, C Micaela Bastidas 101, 4th floor, T084-233610. **Germany**, Sra Maria-Sophia Júrgens de Hermoza, San Agustín 307, T084-235459, Casilla Postal 1128, Correo Central. Mon-Fri, 1000-1200, appointments may be made by phone, it also has a book exchange. **Ireland**, Charlie Donovan, Santa Catalina Ancha 360 (Rosie O'Grady's), T084-243514. **Italy**, Sr Fedos Rubatto, Av Garcilaso 700, T084-224398. Mon-Fri 0900-1200, 1500-1700. **Netherlands**, Marcela Alarco Zegaria, Av Pardo 854, T084-264103, 965 0204 (mob). **Spain**, Sra Juana María Lambarri, T965 0106 (mob). **UK**, Barry Walker, Av Pardo 895, T084-239974, bwalker@amauta.rcp.net.pe. **US Agent**, Dra Olga Villagarcía, Apdo 949, Cusco, T084-222183, F084-233541, or at the Binational Center (ICPNA), Av Tullumayo 125, Wanchac.

Internet You can't walk for 2 mins in Cusco without running into an internet café, and new places are opening all the time. Most have similar rates, around US$0.60 per hr, although if you look hard enough you can find cheaper places. The main difference between cafés is the speed of internet connection and the facilities on offer. The better places have scanners, webcams and CD burners, among other gadgets, and staff in these establishments can be very knowledgeable.

Language classes Academia **Latinoamericana de Español**, Av El Sol 580, T084-243364, www.latinoschools.com. Professionally run with experienced staff. Many activities per week, including dance lessons and excursions to sites of historical and cultural interest. Private classes US$170 for 20 hrs, groups, with a maximum of 4 students US$125, again for 20 hrs. **Acupari**, San Agustín 307, T084-242970. The German-Peruvian Cultural Association, Spanish classes are run here. **Amauta**, Suecia 480, 2nd floor, T084-262345, PO Box 1164, www.amautaspanish.com. Spanish classes, individual or in small groups, also Quechua classes and workshops in Peruvian cuisine, dance and music, US$9.50 per hr individual, but cheaper and possibly better value for group tuition (2-6 people), US$88 for 20 hrs. They have pleasant accommodation on site (but you can stay elsewhere if you wish), as well as a free internet café for students, and can arrange excursions and can help find voluntary work. They also have a school in Urubamba and can arrange courses in the Manu rainforest, in conjunction with Pantiacolla Tours. **Amigos Spanish School**, Zaguán del Cielo B-23, T084-242292, www.spanishcusco.com. Profits from this school support a foundation for disadvantaged children. Private lessons for US$8 per hr, US$100 for 20 hrs of classes in a group. Homestays available, many recommendations. **La Casona de la Esquina**, Purgatorio 395, corner with Huaynapata, T084-235830, www.spanishlessons.com.pe. US$5 per hr for one-to-one classes. Recommended. **Cusco Spanish School**, Garcilaso 265, oficina 6 (2nd floor), T084-226928, www.cuscospanish school. com. US$7.75 for private classes, cheaper in groups. School offers homestays, optional activities including dance and music classes, cookery courses, ceramics, Quechua, hiking and volunteer programmes. They also offer courses on an hacienda at Cusipata in the Vilcanota Valley, east of Cusco. **Excel**, Cruz Verde 336, T084-232272 , www.Excel-spanishlanguageprograms-peru.org. Very professional, US$7 per hr for private one-to-one lessons. US$200 for 20 hrs with 2 people, or US$80 per person in groups of 3 or more. The school can arrange accommodation with local families. **San Blas Spanish School**, Tandapata 688, T084-247898, www.spanish schoolperu.com. Private classes US$7 per hr, groups, with 4 clients maximum, US$80 for 20 hrs tuition. **The Spanish Centre**, T084-993 0177, www.studyspanishincusco.com. New in 2004, classes given by a team of local and non-Peruvian teachers, headed by Stephen Light (originally of the UK), discounts for SAE and ISIC card holders, special offers, homestays, can arrange cultural activities and trekking and provides travel advice.

Laundry There are several cheap laundries on Procuradores, and also on Suecia and Tecseccocha. **Dana's Laundry**, Nueva Baja y Unión. US$2.10 per kg, takes about 6 hrs. **Lavandería Louis**, Choquechaca 264, San Blas. US$0.85 per kg,

fresh, clean, good value. **Splendid Laundry Service**, Carmen Alto 195. Very good, US$0.75 per kg, laundry sometimes available after only 3-4 hrs. **Lavandería T'aqsana Wasi**, Santa Catalina Ancha 345. Same-day service, they also iron clothes, US$2 per kg, good service, speak English, German, Italian and French, Mon-Fri 0900-2030, Sat 0900-1900. **Lavandería**, Saphi 578. 0800-2000 Mon-Sat, 0800-1300 Sun. Good, fast service, US$1 per kg. String markers will be attached to clothes if they have no label.

Post **Central office**, Av Sol at the bottom end of block 5, T084-225232. Mon-Sat 0730-2000, 0800-1400 Sun and holidays. Poste restante is free and helpful. Sending packages from Cusco is not cheap. **DHL**, Av Sol 627, T084-244167. For sending packages or money overseas.

Telephone **Telefónica**, Av del Sol 386, T084-241111. For telephone and fax, Mon-Sat 0700-2300, 0700-1200 Sun and holidays. International calls can be made by payphone or go through the operator – a long wait is possible and a deposit is required. To send a fax costs (per page): US$4.75 to Europe and Israel; US$2.80 to North America. To receive a fax costs US$0.70 per page.

Useful addresses **Immigration** Av Sol, block 6, close to post office, T084-222740. Mon-Fri 0800-1300. Reported as not very helpful. **Perú Verde** Ricaldo Palma J-1, Santa Mónica, T084-243408, acss@telser.com.pe. For information and free video shows about Manu National Park and Tambopata National Reserve. They are friendly and have information on programmes and research in the jungle area of Madre de Dios.

The Urubamba Valley

The Río Urubamba cuts its way through fields and rocky gorges beneath the high peaks of the Cordillera. Brown hills, covered in wheat fields, separate Cusco from this beautiful high valley, which stretches from Sicuani (on the railway to Puno) to the gorge of Torontoi, 600 m lower, to the northwest of Cusco. That the river was of great significance to the Incas can be seen in the number of strategic sites they built above it, Pisac, Ollantaytambo and Machu Picchu among them. Upstream from Pisac the river is usually called the Vilcanota, downstream it is the Urubamba. ➤➤ *For Sleeping, Eating and other listings, see pages 192-198.*

A market for beads

A major feature of Pisac's popular market is the huge and varied collection of multi-coloured beads on sale. Though commonly called 'Inca beads', this is something of a misnomer. For although the Incas were highly talented potters and decorated their ware with detailed geometric motifs, they are not known to have made ceramic beads.

These attractive items have become popular relatively recently.

They used to be rolled individually by hand and were very time-consuming to produce. Now, in a major concession to consumerism, they are machine-made and produced in quantity, then hand-painted and glazed. Today, the clay beads are produced in countless, often family-run, workshops in Cusco and Pisac. Some are made into earrings, necklaces and bracelets, but many thousands are sold loose.

Ins and outs

Getting there The road from Cusco which runs past Sacsayhuaman and on to Tambo Machay, see page 155, climbs up to a pass, then continues over the pampa before descending into the densely populated Urubamba Valley. This road then crosses the Río Urubamba by a bridge at Pisac and follows the north bank to the end of the paved road at Ollantaytambo. It passes through Calca, Yucay and Urubamba, which can also be reached from Cusco by the beautiful, direct road through Chinchero, see page 190. ▸▸ *See under Cusco Tour operators page 173 and Transport page 197.*

Getting around Paved roads, plentiful transport and a good selection of hotels and eating places make this a straighforward place to explore. You can choose either a quick visit from the city or, better still, linger for a few days. Don't hurry; most organized tours are too fast. Explore it on foot, by bike or on horseback. Using public transport and staying overnight in Urubamba, Ollantaytambo or Pisac allows much more time to see the ruins and markets.

Best time to to visit April to May or October to November. The high season is from June to September, but the rainy season, from December to March, is cheaper and pleasant enough.

Pisac

Only 30 km north of Cusco is the little village of Pisac, which is well worth a visit for its superb Inca ruins, perched precariously on the mountain, above the town. They are considered to be amongst the very finest Inca ruins in the valley. Strangely, however, most visitors don't come to Pisac for the ruins. Instead, they come in droves for its Sunday morning market. Pisac is usually visited as part of a tour from Cusco but this often allows only 1½ hours here, not enough time to take in the ruins and splendid scenery.

Pisac market

The market contains sections for the tourist and for the local community. Traditionally, Sunday is the day when the people of the highlands come down to sell their produce (potatoes, corn, beans, vegetables, weavings, pottery, etc). These are traded for essentials such as salt, sugar, rice, noodles, fruit, medicines, plastic goods and tools. The market comes to life after the arrival of tourist buses around

1000, and is usually over by 1500. However, there is also an important ceremony every Sunday, in which the *Varayocs* (village mayors) from the surrounding and highland villages participate in a Quechua Catholic mass in **Pisac church**. It is a good example of the merging of, and respect for, different religious cultures. This aspect of the traditional Pisac Sunday market is still celebrated at 1100 sharp. Pisac has other, somewhat less crowded, less expensive markets on Tuesday and Thursday morning; it's best to get there before 0900.

On the plaza, which has several large *pisonay* trees, are the church and a small interesting **Museo Folklórico**. The town, with its narrow streets, is worth strolling around, and while you're doing so, look for the fine façade at Grau 485. There are many souvenir shops on Bolognesi.

Inca ruins

ⓘ *0700-1730. If you go early (before 1000) you'll have the ruins to yourself. Entry is by BTU multi-site ticket. Guides charge US$5, but the wardens on site are very helpful and don't charge anything to give out information.*

The ruins of Inca Pisac stand on a spur between the Río Urubamba to the south and the smaller Chongo to the east. It provides an ideal vantage point over the flat plain of the Urubamba, the terraces below and the terraced hillsides. This is one of the largest Inca ruins in the vicinity of Cusco and it clearly had defensive, religious and agricultural functions, as well as being an Inca country estate. To appreciate the site fully, allow five or six hours if going on foot. Even if going by car, do not rush as there is a lot to see and a lot of walking to do.

The walk up to the ruins begins from the plaza, passing the Centro de Salud and a control post. The path goes through working terraces, giving the ruins a context. The first group of buildings is **Pisaqa**, with a fine curving wall. Climb up to the central part of the ruins, the **Intihuatana** group of temples and rock outcrops in the most magnificent Inca masonry. Here are the **Reloj Solar** (Hitching Post of the Sun) – now closed because thieves stole a piece from it – palaces of the moon and stars, solstice markers, baths and water channels. From Intihuatana, a path leads around the hillside through a tunnel to **Q'Allaqasa** (military area). Across the valley at this point, a large area of Inca tombs in holes in the hillside can be seen. The end of the site is **Kanchiracay**, where the agricultural workers were housed. At dusk you will hear, if not see, the *pisaca* (partridges), after which the place is named, and you may see deer too.

Road transport approaches from the Kanchiracay end. The drive up from town takes about 20 minutes. Walking up, although tiring, is recommended for the views and location. It's at least one hour uphill all the way. The descent takes 30 minutes. Horses are available for US$3 per person. Combis charge US$0.60 per person and taxis US$3 one way up to the ruins from near the bridge. Then you can walk back down (if you want the taxi to take you back down negotiate a fare). Overnight parking is allowed in the car park.

Pisac to Urubamba

Near **Lamay**, the second village on the road from Pisac towards Urubamba, are warm springs, which are highly regarded locally for their medicinal properties. **Calca**, 18 km beyond Pisac at 2,900 m, is a busy hub in the valley, with a plaza which is divided into two parts. Look out for the *api* sellers with their bicycles loaded with a steaming kettle and assortment of bottles, glasses and tubs. There are mineral baths at **Machacancha**, 8 km east of Calca. These springs are indoors, pleasantly warm and will open at night for groups. They are half an hour by taxi from town. About 3 km beyond Machacancha are the Inca ruins of **Arquasmarca**.

Huchuy Cusco

The ruins of a small Inca town, **Huchuy Cusco**, are reached across the Río Urubamba and after a stiff three- to four-hour climb. Huchuy Cusco (also spelt Qosqo), which in Quechua means 'Little Cusco', was originally called Kakya Qawani, 'from where the lightning can be seen'. It is dramatically located on a flat esplanade almost 600 m above the villages of Lamay and Calca in the Sacred Valley. The views are magnificent. The ruins themselves consist of extensive agricultural terraces with high retaining walls and several buildings made from finely wrought stonework and adobe mud bricks.

The easiest route to the site follows the steep trail behind the village of Lamay, which is reached by crossing the bridge over the river. There is also a clearly marked trail from the village of Calca. Another longer route leads to Huchuy Cusco from Tambo Machay near Cusco, a magnificent one- or two-day trek along the route once taken by the Inca from his capital to his country estate at Huchuy Cusco; some sections of the original Inca highway remain intact.

Valle de Lares

In this four to five day hike you walk through the beautiful landscape of the Lares Valley, with its magnificent mountains, lakes and llamas and meet local people and stay in small villages. You start near an old hacienda in Huarán (2,830 m), cross two passes over 4,000 m and end at the hot springs near Lares. From this village, transport runs back to Calca. Alternatively, you can add an extra day and continue to

Urubamba

Sleeping
Capulí **1**
Hospedaje Perla de
  Vilcanota **3**
Hostal Urubamba **4**

Incaland **5**
K'uychi Rumi **8**
Las Chullpas **10**
Las Tres Marías **2**
Macha Wasi **6**

Perol Chico **9**
San Agustín
  Urubamba **11**
Sol y Luna **7**

0 metres 100
0 yards 100

Ollantaytambo. Several agencies in Cusco offer trekking and biking tours to the region and some offer this trek as an alternative Inca Trail. The 1:100,000 **Instituto Geográfico Nacional** map should be useful here. Treks usually include transport by bus, guide, cook, porters or horses to carry food and equipment, food from lunch on the first day to lunch on the fourth day and camping equipment.

Yucay
A few kilometres east of Urubamba, Yucay has two large, grassy plazas divided by the restored colonial church of **Santiago Apóstol**, with its oil paintings and fine altars. On the opposite side from Plaza Manco II is the **adobe palace** built for Sayri Túpac (Manco's son) when he emerged from Vilcabamba in 1558.

Urubamba, Chinchero and Moray

Urubamba → *Colour map 2, B2. Altitude: 2,863 m.*

Like many places along the valley, Urubamba has a fine setting, with views of the Chicón snow-capped peaks and glaciers, and enjoys a mild climate. The main plaza, with a fountain capped by a maize cob, is surrounded by buildings painted blue. Calle Berriózabal, on the west edge of town, is lined with pisonay trees. The large market square is one block west of the main plaza. The main road skirts the town and the bridge for the road to Chinchero is just to the east of town.

Seminario-Behar Ceramic Studio ① *C Berriózabal 111, a right turning off the main road to Ollantaytambo, T084-201002, kupa@terra.com.pe, open every day, just ring the bell,* founded in 1980, is located in the beautiful grounds of the former **Hostal Urpihuasi**. Pablo Seminario has investigated the techniques and designs of pre-Columbian Peruvian cultures and has created a style with strong links to the past. Each piece is handmade and painted, using ancient glazes and minerals, and is then fired in reproduction pre-Columbian kilns. The resulting pieces are very attractive. Reservations to visit the studio and a personal appointment with the artists (Pablo and Marilú) are welcomed.

Around Urubamba
Five kilometres west of Urubamba is the village of **Tarabamba**, where a bridge crosses the Río Urubamba. If you turn right after the bridge you'll come to **Pichingoto**, a tumbled-down village built under an overhanging cliff. Also, just over the bridge and before the town to the left of a small, walled cemetery is a salt stream. Follow the footpath beside the stream and you'll come to **Salinas**, a small village below which are a mass of terraced

9 de Noviembre
3

Av La Convención

To Yucay & Cusco via Calca

To Cusco via Chinchero

Coliseo
Municipal
ATM
6

Eating ●
La Casa de la Abuela **5**
Pintacha **3**
Pizzonay **4**
Quinta los Geranios **6**

Cusco The Urubamba Valley

Inca *salineras* (salt pans), which are still in production after thousands of years. It's a particularly spectacular sight as there are several hundred of them. These are now a fixture on the tourist circuit and can become congested with buses. The walk to the salt pans takes about 30 minutes. Take water as it can be very hot and dry here.

Chinchero → *Colour map 2, B3. Altitude: 3,762 m.*
ⓘ *0700-1730. Can be visited on the BTU combined entrance ticket (see page 147).*
Chinchero is northwest from Cusco, just off a direct road to Urubamba. The streets of the village wind up from the lower sections, where transport stops, to the plaza which is reached through an archway. The great square appears to be stepped, with a magnificent Inca wall separating the two levels. Let into the wall is a row of trapezoidal niches, each much taller than a man. From the lower section, which is paved, another arch leads to an upper terrace, upon which the Spaniards built an attractive church. The ceiling, beams and walls are covered in beautiful floral and religious designs. The altar, too, is fine. The church is open on Sunday for mass and at festivals. Opposite the church is a small local museum. Excavations have revealed many Inca walls and terraces.

The local produce **market** on Sunday morning is fascinating and very colourful, and best before the tour groups arrive. It's on your left as you come into town. There's also a small handicraft market, also on Sunday, up by the church. Chinchero attracts few tourists, except on Sunday. The town celebrates the **Day of the Virgin**, on 8 September.

Chinchero to Huayllabamba hike
There is a scenic path from Chinchero to Huayllabamba, the village on the left bank of the Río Urubamba between Yucay and Calca (see page 187). The hike is quite beautiful, with fine views of the peaks of the Urubamba Range, and takes about three to four hours. Follow the old Chinchero-Urubamba dirt road, to the left of the new paved road. Ask the locals when you are not sure. It runs over the pampa, with a good view of Chinchero, then drops down to the Urubamba Valley. The end of the hike is about 10 km before the town of Urubamba. You can either proceed to Urubamba or back to Cusco. An alternative hike from Chinchero follows the spectacular Maras-Moray-Pichingoto salt mines route.

Moray
This remote but beautiful site (US$1.45) lies 9 km to the west of the little town of **Maras** and is well worth a visit. There are three 'colosseums', used by the Incas, according to some theories, as a sort of open-air crop nursery, known locally as the laboratory of the Incas. The great depressions do not contain ruined buildings, but are lined with fine terracing. Each level is said to have its own microclimate. It is a very atmospheric place, which, some claim, has mystical power. The scenery around here is absolutely stunning, especially in the late afternoon whenthe light is wonderful. For photography, thgouh, it's best to arrive in the morning. The road eventually arrives at the guardian's hut, but there is little indication of the scale of the colosseums until you reach the rim.

The most interesting way to get to Moray is from Urubamba via the Pichingoto Bridge over the Río Urubamba. The climb up from the bridge is fairly steep but easy, with great views of Nevado Chicón. The path passes by the spectacular salt pans. Moray is about 1½ hours further on. There is public transport from Chinchero to Maras and regular pick-up trucks which carry people and produce in and out. Transport stops running between 1700 and 1800; it costs between US$0.60-1. If you cannot get transport to Maras, take any combi going between Urubamba and Chinchero, get out at the junction for Maras and walk from there. It's 4 km to Maras; once through the village, bear left a little, and ask directions to Moray, a further 9 km. Hitching back to Urubamba is quite easy, but there are no hotels at all in the area, so take care not to be stranded. The **Hotel Incaland** in Urubamba can arrange horses and guide and a pick-up truck for the return, all for US$30-40 per person (see page 193). Another option is to hire a taxi with driver to take you to Moray.

Ollantaytambo → *Colour map 2, A2. Altitude: 2,800 m.*

The attractive little town of Ollantaytambo, at the foot of some spectacular Inca ruins and terraces, is built directly on top of the original Inca town, or Llacta. The Inca canchas (blocks of houses) are almost entirely intact and can be clearly seen. It's an impressive sight and one that shouldn't be missed, even though many people only visit the ruins above the town.

Ins and outs

Ollantaytambo can be reached by bus from Cusco, Urubamba and Chinchera. The best way of getting to Machu Picchu is by train. You won't be allowed on the station unless you have previously bought a ticket for the train. The gates are locked and only those with tickets can enter. ▶▶ *See also Transport page 197.*

The fortress

① *0700-1730. Admission is by combined entrance ticket (see page 147), which can be bought at the site. Otherwise it's US$6.50.Guides at the entrance charge US$2.*

> ♪ *If possible arrive very early, 0700, before the tourists. Avoid Sun afternoons, when tour groups from Pisac descend in their hundreds.*

When Manco Inca decided to rebel against the Spaniards in 1536, he fell back to Ollantaytambo from Calca to stage one of the greatest acts of resistance to the *conquistadores*. Hernando Pizarro led his troops to the foot of the Inca's stronghold and, on seeing how well-manned and fortified the place was, described it as "a thing of horror". Under fierce fire, Pizarro's men failed to capture Manco and retreated to Cusco, but Manco could not press home any advantage. In 1537, feeling vulnerable to further attacks, he left Ollantaytambo for Vilcabamba.

When you visit Ollantaytambo you will be confronted by a series of 16 massive, stepped terraces of the very finest stonework after crossing the great high-walled trapezoidal esplanade known as *Mañariki*. Beyond these imposing terraces lies the so-called Temple of Ten Niches, a funeral chamber once dedicated to the worship of Pachacútec's royal household. Immediately above this are six monolithic upright blocks of rose-coloured rhyolite, the remains of what is popularly called The Temple of the Sun. The dark grey stone is embellished today with bright orange lichen.

You can either descend by the route you came up, or follow the terracing round to the left (as you face the town) and work your way down to the Valley of the Patacancha. Here are more Inca ruins in the small area between the town and the temple fortress, behind the church. Most impressive is the **Baño de la Ñusta** (Bath of the Princess), a grey granite rock, about waist high, beneath which is the bath itself. The front of the boulder, over which the water falls, was delicately finished with a three-stepped pyramid, making a relief arch over the pool.

The town

If you are visiting Ollantaytambo, begin your tour at **El Museo Catcco** (Centro Andino de Tecnología Tradicional y Cultural de las Comunidades de Ollantaytambo) ① *Casa Horno, Patacalle, 1 block from the plaza, To84-204024, www.cbc.org.pe/rao, 0900-1800, US$1.45 (donations welcome)*, which houses a fine ethnographical collection and its Information Center gives tips on day-hikes, things to see and places to dine and stay. Local guides are available for tours of the town and surrounding areas. Outside the museum, Catcco runs non-profit cultural programmes, temporary exhibitions, concerts and lectures. Also on site is a ceramics workshop, a textile revitalization programme and an educational theatre project. Ceramics and textiles are sold in the museum shop. The museum has internet access. Note the canal down the middle of the street outside the museum.

A two-dimensional '**pyramid**' has been identified on the west side of the main ruins of Ollantaytambo. Its discoverers, Fernando and Edgar Elorietta, claim it is the real Pacaritambo, from where the four original Inca brothers emerged to found their empire (this alternative Inca creation myth, The Inn of Origin, tells of four brothers and four sisters emerging from a cave in a cliff). Whether this is the case or not, it is still a first-class piece of engineering with great terraced fields and a fine 750-m wall creating the optical illusion of a pyramid. The wall is aligned with the rays of the winter solstice, on 21 June. People gather at mid-winter dawn to watch this event. The mysterious 'pyramid', which covers 50-60 ha, can be seen properly from the other side of the river. This is a pleasant, easy one-hour walk, west from the Puente Inca, just outside the town. You'll also be rewarded with great views of the Sacred Valley and the river, with the snowy peaks of the Verónica massif as a backdrop.

Entering Ollantaytambo from Urubamba, the road is built along the long wall of 100 niches. Note the inclination of the wall towards the road. Since it was the Incas' practice to build with the walls leaning towards the interiors of the buildings, it has been deduced that the road, much narrower then, was built inside a succession of buildings. The road leads into the main plaza, where public transport congregates in the centre. The original Inca town is behind the north side of the plaza. The road from the northwest corner of the plaza looks up to the Inca temple, but to get there you have to cross the bridge over the river and go down to the colonial church with its *recinto* (enclosure). Beyond is a grand plaza (and car park) with entrances to the archaeological site.

Around Ollantaytambo

The stone quarries of **Cachiccata** are some 9 km from Ollantaytambo. Standing to the left of the six monolithic blocks of the Temple of the Sun, you can see them, looking west-south-west across the valley. The stones that the Inca masons chose here had to be quarried, hewn into a rough shape, and hauled across the valley floor and up to the temple by means of a ramp, which can still be seen. Between the ruins and the quarries more that 50 enormous stones that never reached their destination lie abandoned. They are know as the *las piedras cansadas*, or 'the tired stones'. It takes about a day to walk to the Inca quarries on the opposite of the river and return to Ollantaytambo.

At **Pinkuylluna Hill**, on the western edge of Ollantaytambo, is an impressive collection of storehouses, or qolqas, sometimes referred to as prisons. It's a relatively straightforward climb up the mountain, although there are some difficult stretches. Allow two to three hours going up. The path is difficult to make out, so it's best not to go on your own.

◉ Sleeping

Pisac *p186*

AL Royal Inca Pisac, Carretera Ruinas Km 1.5, T084-203064, royalin@terra.com.pe. In the same chain as the **Royal Incas I** and **II** in Cusco, this hotel can be reached by the hotels' own bus service. It is a short distance out of town, on the road that goes up to the ruins, a taxi ride after dark. Price includes taxes and breakfast. Camping is available for US$5 per person. A guide for the ruins can be provided. The rooms are comfortable, in a number of blocks in the grounds of a converted hacienda; they are pleasantly furnished, with all conveniences. There is a pool, sauna and jacuzzi (US$7), tennis court, horse riding and bicycle rental. The restaurant is good and there is a bar. The hotel is popular with day-trippers from

Cusco. In the public area a rescued owl sits on a perch, casting an eye over the guests. A small deer wanders around the property, but there is also a puma in a cage. Staff are very helpful and accommodating.

E per person **Ulrika's Hostal and Café**, at the corner of Pardo, on the plaza in front of the church and marketplace, Casilla Postal 1179, Cusco, T084-203062, hotelpisaq@ terra.com.pe. There are 2 double rooms with bath in our **D** range. All others share bathrooms, which are spotless. Breakfast is US$2.50 extra (a bit more if you have eggs). Excellent brownies are on sale and pizza is served on Sun. There is hot water 24 hrs, pleasant decor, and a sauna. Friendly and knowledgeable staff who speak English, German and French. Recommended.

F Residencial Beho, Intihuatana 642, 50 m up the hill from the plaza, T/F084-203001. Ask for a room in the main building. They serve a good breakfast for US$1. The *hostal* has a shop selling local handicrafts including masks. The owner's son will act as a guide to the ruins at the weekend.

G Hospedaje Familiar Kinsa Ccocha, on the plaza. The rooms are basic and none has bath. Price per person; you pay less if you don't use hot water.

G Parador, on the plaza, T084-203061. Price per person. All rooms share bathrooms, which have hot water. Breakfast is not included, but the restaurant serves other meals.

Pisac to Urubamba *p187*
L-AL Sonesta Posadas del Inca, Plaza Manco II de Yucay 123, Yucay, T084-201107, posada@sonestaperu.com. The price includes taxes and buffet breakfast. A converted 300-year-old monastery is now a hotel which is like a little village with plazas, lovely gardens, a chapel, and many different types of room (one even has its own ghost – ask for room 111 if you want to be spooked). As well as rooms in the old part, there are recent additions, which are comfortable and well appointed. The restaurant serves an excellent buffet lunch. There is a conference centre. Highly recommended.

AL Sonesta Posada del Inca Yucay II, Plaza Manco II 104, Yucay, T084-201107. In the same chain, and just a short way from Posadas del Inca. Also called **Posada del Inca Libertador**, or **Casona**, this colonial house was where Simón Bolívar stayed during his liberation campaign in 1824. The price includes taxes and breakfast. The 39 rooms have heating and, outside, there are 2 patios and gardens. There is a restaurant and pizzería. Various activities can be arranged: canoeing, horse riding, mountain biking and guided treks and tours.

B-C Hostal Y'Llary, also on the plaza, Yucay, T084-201112. The price includes bathroom and breakfast.

F Hostal Jerseyhuasi, Lamay, beside the springs. A nice little place, price includes breakfast, with generous portions of good food at other meals, clean and comfortable rooms. They also have camping possibilities.

Urubamba *p189, map p188*
L Sol y Luna, west of town, T084-201620, www.hotelsolyluna.com. Attractive bungalows set off the main road in lovely gardens, pool, excellent buffet in restaurant, French-Swiss owned. Has **Viento Sur** adventure travel agency, for horse riding, mountain biking, trekking and paragliding, www.aventurasvientosur.com.

L-AL K'uychi Rumi, Km 73.5 on the road to Ollantaytambo, 3 km from town, T084-201169, www.urubamba.com. 6 cottages for rent with 2 bedrooms, fully equipped, fireplace, terrace and balcony, surrounded by gardens. Price is for 1-2 people, each house can accommodate 6.

AL Incaland Hotel and Conference Center, Av Ferrocarril s/n, 5 mins' walk from the centre, T084-201126, www.incalandperu.com. Special rates are also available. 65 comfortable, spacious bungalows set in extensive gardens, English-owned, good restaurant serving buffet meals, bar, disco, 2 pools, also horse riding (eg to Moray), mountain biking, kayaking and rafting. The staff are helpful and service is good.

AL-A San Agustín Urubamba, Km 71, T084-201443/44 (or book at San Agustín Internacional in Cusco, p162), 20 mins' walk from town, towards Yucay. Comfortable, small pool, restaurant serving a buffet on

Tue, Thu and Sun for US$3.50.

B Perol Chico, Km 77 on the road to Ollantaytambo, office Grau 203, Casilla postal 59, Correo Central, Urubamba, T084-201694, stables T084-624475, www.perolchico.com. Dutch/Peruvian-owned, private bungalows with fireplace and kitchen on a ranch, specializes in horse riding (see below). Recommended.

C Las Tres Marías, Zavala 307, T084-201004, (Cusco T084-225252). New, beautiful gardens, hot water, welcoming. Recommended.

D per person **Las Chullpas**, 3 km west of town in the Pumahuanca Valley, T084-976 1193, www.laschullpas.com. Very peaceful, includes excellent breakfast, vegetarian meals, English and German spoken, Spanish classes, natural medicine, treks, horse riding, mountain biking, camping US$3 with hot shower. Mototaxi from town US$0.85, taxi (ask for Querocancha) US$2.

D Macha Wasi, Jr Nicolás Barre, T084-201612, www.unsaac.edu.pe/machawasi.

Canadian-owned guesthouse with comfortable rooms and a dormitory, delicious breakfast extra, safe, lovely garden, laundry. Spanish courses and treks can be arranged. Recommended.

F Capulí, Grau 222. With bath, hot water and TV. Price per person, or **G** per bed with shared bath.

F Hostal Urubamba, Bolognesi 605. Basic but pleasant, rooms with bath and cold water, or **G** without bath.

G Hospedaje Perla de Vilcanota, 9 de Noviembre, T084-201135. Price is per bed, without bath, but shared bathrooms have hot water; some rooms are even cheaper.

Chinchero *p190*

F Hotel Restaurant Antabaraj, just beyond ticket control, T084-306002 (Patricia Cagigao), antabaraj@hotmail.com. Basic rooms, take sleeping bag, kitchen facilities, good views, food at reasonable prices.

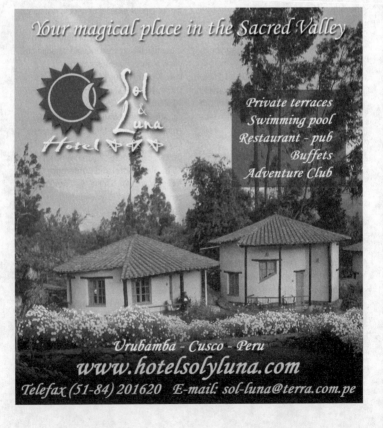
Cusco The Urubamba Valley Listings

Ollantaytambo p191

AL Ñustayoc Mountain Lodge and Resort, about 5 km west of Ollantaytambo, just before Chillca and the start of the Inca Trail, T084-204098, www.nustayoclodge. com. Large and somewhat rambling lodge in a wonderful location with great views of the snowy Verónica massif and other peaks. Lovely flower-filled garden and grounds. Nicely decorated, spacious rooms, all with private bath. Price includes continental breakfast served in the large restaurant area.

AL Pakaritampu, C Ferrocarril s/n, T084-204020, www.pakaritampu.com. The price includes breakfast and taxes. This modern, 3-star hotel has 20 rooms with bath and views. There is a TV room, restaurant and bar, internet service for guests, laundry, safe and room service. Adventure sports such as rafting, climbing, trekking, mountain biking and horse riding can be arranged. Meals are extra: buffet US$13, dinner US$12-15. Excellent quality and service.

C Hostal Munay Tika, on the road to the station, T084-204111, munaytika@latin mail.com. Price includes breakfast and bath. Dinner is served by arrangement. To use the sauna costs US$5 with prior notice. Also has a nice garden. New and good.

C-D Albergue Kapuly, at the end of the station road, T084-204017. Prices are lower in the off season. A quiet place with spacious rooms, some with and some without bath. The garden is nice and the price includes a good continental breakfast. Recommended.

D El Albergue Ollantaytambo, within the railway station gates, T084-204014, www. rumbosperu.com/elalbergue/. Owned by North American Wendy Weeks, the *albergue* has 8 rooms with shared bathrooms. Price (per person) includes breakfast; box lunch costs US$4, full dinner US$7 on request. The rooms are full of character and are set in buildings around a courtyard and lovely gardens. Great showers (24 hrs a day) and a eucalyptus steam sauna (US$5). The whole place is charming, very relaxing and homely. See the office-cum-shop-cum-exhibition where interesting handicrafts can be bought. Also for sale is Wendy's digestif, Compuesto Matacuy. It's very convenient for the Machu Picchu train and good place for

information. Private transport can be arranged to the salt mines, Moray, Abra Málaga for birdwatching and taxi transfers to the airport. Highly recommended.

E Hostal Chaskawasi, Chaupicalle (also C Taypi) north of the plaza, T084-208085, anna_machupicchu@hotmail.com. New *hostal* snuggled away in the small alleys behind the plaza. Owner Anna is very friendly.

E Hostal La Ñusta, C Ocobamba, T084-204035. Ask about accommodation in the shop/restaurant of the same name on the plaza or in the **Pizzería Gran Tunupa**. This is a decent although uninspiring budget option. Proprietor Rubén Ponce loves to share his knowledge of the ruins with guests. You get a good view of the ruins from the balcony. See below for the restaurant.

E Hostal Ollanta, on the south side of the plaza, T084-204116. Basic and clean, but with a great location. All rooms with shared bath.

E Las Orquídeas, near the start of the road to the station, T084-204032. A good choice. The price for this *hostal* includes breakfast, and meals are available, but may be used by tour groups.

F Hostal Chuza, just below the main plaza in town, T084-204113. Very clean and friendly with safe motorcycle parking. They have a TV in the front room for guests and one of the rooms features a wonderful view of the ruins with the Nevado de Verónica framed perfectly behind – a wonderful sight to wake up to in the morning. Recommended.

F Hostal Miranda, between the main plaza and the ruins, T084-204091. A basic *hostal* with shower included. It's very friendly, clean and the flower-filled garden is pleasant.

G Hostal Tambo, just walk up the street called Lari that heads north from the plaza. After 20 m or so you'll see an unmarked blue door on the left-hand side... bang on the door! If this doesn't work keep walking, turn left down the first small alley and bang on that blue door instead! Once past this unassuming exterior you emerge into a mini Garden of Eden, full of fruit trees, flowers, dogs, cats and domesticated parrots in the trees. There's no hot water and only 3 basic rooms (price per person), but the family is very friendly and the Señora is a character.

Eating

Pisac *p186*

Valle Sagrado, just out of town along from the bridge going towards Urubamba. Meals are not cheap, but the helpings are huge and good value. Recommended, especially for the fish.

Bakery, Av Mcal Castilla 372, sells excellent cheese and onion *empanadas* for US$0.25, suitable for vegetarians, and good whole-meal bread. The oven is tremendous.

Doña Clorinda, on the plaza opposite the church, doesn't look very inviting but cooks tasty food, including vegetarian options. A very friendly place.

Urubamba *p189, map p188*

La Casa de la Abuela, Bolívar 272, 2 blocks up from the Plaza de Armas, T084-622975. Excellent restaurant with rooms grouped around a small courtyard. The trout is fantastic and food is served with baskets of roasted potatoes and salad. Recommended.

El Fogón, Parque Pintacha, T084-201534. Traditional Peruvian food, large servings, nice atmosphere. Recommended.

Quinta los Geranios, on the main road before the bridge, T084-201043. Regional dishes, excellent lunch with more than enough food, average price US$13.

El Maizal, on the road before the bridge, T084-201454. Country-style restaurant with a good reputation, buffet service with a variety of typical Novo Andino dishes, plus international choices, beautiful gardens with native flowers and fruit trees. Recommended (they also have a hotel of the same name).

Pintacha, Bolognesi 523. Pub/café serving sandwiches, burgers, coffees, teas and drinks. Has games and book exchange, cosy, open till late.

Pizzonay, Av Mcal Castilla, 2nd block. Pizzas, excellent spinach ravioli (not so good lasagne). Mulled wine served in a small restaurant with nice decor. Clean, good value. Recommended.

Around Urubamba *p189*

Tunupa, on left side of the road on the riverbank, in a new, colonial-style hacienda (same ownership as Tunupa in Cusco), zappa

@terra.com.pe. Excellent food served indoors or outdoors, bar, lounge, library, chapel, gardens, stables and an alpaca-jewellery shop. Outstanding exhibition of pre-Columbian objects and colonial paintings. **Seminario**'s ceramics feature in the decor. People on valley tours (Tue, Thu, Sun) are served a varied buffet including Novo Andino cuisine; buffet lunch US$15, 1200-1500. Lunch and dinner (1800-2030) is available daily.

Ollantaytambo *p191*

Fortaleza, 2 branches, one on Plaza Ruinas, the other on the north side of the main plaza. Basic but good food, breakfasts, pizza and pasta – all the gringo restaurant favourites are on offer, as well as some more local dishes.

Gran Tunupa, corner of C ocobamba and Bentinerio, right-hand side between the plaza and the bridge. Nice view and reasonable food but the pizzas suffer from the usual Peruvian lack of tomato sauce.

Il Cappuccino, just before the bridge on the right-hand side. Offers the best cappuccino in town, great coffee generally, also café latte and expresso. Good continental and American breakfasts. Slightly more sophisticated ambience and service in comparison with many other establishments in town. Also run **Kusicoyllor**, Plaza Ruinas.

Mayupata, Jr Convención s/n, across the bridge on the way to the ruins, on the left, T084-204083 (Cusco). Serving international choices and a selection of Peruvian dishes, desserts, sandwiches and coffee. It opens at 0600 for breakfast, and serves lunch and dinner. The bar has a fireplace; river view, relaxing atmosphere.

Alcázar Café, C del Medio s/n, 50 m from the plaza, T084-204034, alcazar@ollantay tambo.org. Vegetarian restaurant, also offering fish and meat dishes, pasta specialities. Offers excursions to traditional Andean communities.

Bahía, on the east side of the plaza. Very friendly, vegetarian dishes served on request.

Bars and clubs

Urubamba *p189, map p188*

Tequila, Av Mcal Castilla 3rd block. The door is always closed so you must ring the bell. Disco, drinks, good coffee, open till late.

⊛ Festivals and events

Pisac *p186*
A local fiesta is held on **15 Jul**.

Pisac to Urubamba *p187*
The Fiesta de la Virgen Asunta is held in **Coya** on **15-16 Aug**. **Lamay** hosts a festival on **15 Aug**.

Urubamba *p189, map p188*
May and **Jun** are the harvest months, with many processions following mysterious ancient schedules. Urubamba's main festival, El Señor de Torrechayoc, takes place during the first week of **Jun**.

Ollantaytambo *p191*
On **6 Jan** there is the Bajada de Reyes Magos (the Magi), with traditional dancing, a bull fight, local food and a fair. **End May-early Jun**: Pentecostes, 50 days after Easter, is the Fiesta del Señor de Choquekillca, patron saint of Ollantaytambo. There are several days of dancing, weddings, processions, masses, feasting and drinking (the last opportunity to see traditional Cusqueño dancing). On **29 Jun**, following *Inti Raymi* in Cusco, there is a colourful festival, the Ollanta-Raymi, at which the Quechua drama, *Ollantay*, is re-enacted. **29 Oct** is the Aniversario de Ollantaytambo, a festival with dancing in traditional costume and many local delicacies for sale.

▲ Activities and tours

Urubamba *p189, map p188*
Horse riding
Perol Chico, T084-695188, see Sleeping p194. Owned and operated by Eddy van Brunschot (Dutch/Peruvian), 1- to 12-day trips out of Urubamba, good horses, riding is Peruvian Paso style; 1-day trip to Moray and the salt pans costs US$60 (6 hrs). Recommended. Also contact through SAS Travel in Cusco, p177.

⊕ Transport

To organize your own Sacred Valley transport, try one of these taxi drivers, recommended by **South America**

Explorers: Manuel Calanche, T084-227368, T969 5402 (mob); Carlos Hinojosa, T084-251160; Ferdinand Pinares, Yuracpunco 155; Tahuantinsuyo, T084-225914, T968 1519 (mob), speaks English, French and Spanish; Eduardo, T084-231809, speaks English.
Also recommended are: Angel Marcavillaca Palomino, Av Regional 877, T084-251822, amarcavillaca@yahoo.com, helpful, patient, reasonable prices; Movilidad Inmediata, T962 3821 (mob), runs local tours with an English-speaking guide. Angel Salazar, Marcavalle I-4 Huanchac, T084-224679 (to leave *messages*), is English-speaking and arranges good tours, very knowledgeable and enthusiastic; Milton Velásquez, T084- 222638, T968 0730 (mob), is also an anthropologist and tour guide and speaks English.

Pisac *p186*
Bus
From C Puputi on the outskirts of Cusco, near the Clorindo Matto de Turner school and Av de la Cultura. 32 km, 1 hr, US$0.85. *Colectivos*, minibuses and buses leave when full, between 0600 and 1600; also trucks and pick-ups. Buses returning from Pisac are often full. The last one back leaves around 2000. Taxis charge about US$20 for the round trip. To **Pisac**, **Calca** (18 km beyond Pisac) and **Urubamba**, buses leave from Av Tullumayo 800 block, Wanchac, US$1.

Urubamba *p189, map p188*
Bus
The bus and combi terminal is just west of town on the main road. To **Calca**, **Pisac** (US$0.80, 1 hr) and **Cusco** (2 hrs, US$1), from 0530 onwards. Also buses to Cusco via **Chinchero**, same fare.
Colectivos to **Cusco** can be caught outside the terminal and on the main road, US$1.15. Combis run to **Ollantaytambo**, 45 mins, US$0.30. Hotels such as the Incaland and Posadas del Inca, **Yucay**, run a twice-daily shuttle between Cusco airport and Urubamba for US$10. There are also buses from here to Quillabamba.

Train
See p215 for the Sacred Valley Railway from Urubamba to **Aguas Calientes**.

Chinchero *p190*

Combis and *colectivos* for Chinchero leave from 300 block of Av Grau, **Cusco**, 1 block before crossing the bridge. 23 km, 45 mins, US$0.45; and for **Urubamba** a further 25 km, 45 mins, US$0.45 (or US$1 Cusco-Urubamba direct, US$1.15 for a seat in a *colectivo*). To **Ollantaytambo**, 0745 and 1945 direct, or catch a bus to Urubamba from Av Grau.

Ollantaytambo *p191*

Bus There is a direct bus service from Ollantaytambo to **Cusco** at 0715 and 1945; the fare is US$2.85. The station is 10-15 mins walk from the plaza (turn left at the sign that says 'Centro de Salud' between the Plaza de Armas and the ruins). There are *colectivos* at the plaza for the station when trains are due. Also, a bus leaves the station at 0900 for **Urubamba** (US$0.30) and **Chinchero** (US$1).

Train See p215.

❻ Directory

Pisac *p186*

Banks If you need to change money, there is a shop on M Castilla, heading away from the plaza, near where the road bends; it will change TCs.

Internet and telephone On the same side of the plaza as the museum are the municipal building with a computer centre (internet for US$0.75 per hr, closed Sun morning) and a public phone booth.

Pisac to Urubamba *p187*

Internet In **Calca**, the municapial library has internet connection.

Urubamba *p189, map p188*

Banks Banco de la Nación, M Castilla at the start of the 2nd block. ATM on the main road not far from the bridge.

Internet Connections, corner of Av M Castilla and Av La Convención.

Post Serpost, post office, Plaza de Armas.

Telephone There are several phone booths around the centre. The one outside Hostal Urubamba makes international calls.

Ollantaytambo *p191*

Internet Internet Ollanta, just before the Plaza Ruinas on the left-hand side, opposite the Santiago Apóstol church. 3 machines, US$2 per hr, US$0.90 for 15 mins.

Machu Picchu and the Inca Trail

There is a tremendous feeling of awe on first witnessing this incredible sight. The ancient citadel, 42 km from Ollantaytambo by rail, straddles the saddle of a high mountain with steep terraced slopes falling away to the fast-flowing Río Urubamba snaking its hairpin course far below in the valley floor. Towering overhead is Huayna Picchu, and green jungle peaks provide the backdrop for the whole majestic scene.

If you take the Inca Trail to Machu Picchu, following in the footsteps of its creators, you are making a true pilgrimage and the sweat and struggle is all worth it when you set your eyes on this mystical site at sunrise from the Inca sun gate above the ruins. That way you see Machu Picchu in its proper context. Afterwards you recover in Aguas Calientes and soothe those aching limbs in the hot springs. The introduction of new regulations for walking the Inca Trail in 2001 opened up additional options for trekking to Machu Picchu, some shorter, some longer than the old route. So if you fancy widening the perspective of how the Incas walked to their sacred city, ask your chosen tour operator to show you the alternatives. ❯❯ For Sleeping, Eating and other listings, see pages 210-217.

Ins and outs

Getting there There are two ways to get to Machu Picchu. The easy way is by train from Cusco, Ollantaytambo or Urubamba, with a bus ride for the final climb from the timetables). The most rewarding way is to hike the Inca Trail, which is described in its own section (see page 202).

Tourist information Permission to enter the ruins before 0630 to watch the sunrise over the Andes, which is a spectacular experience, can be obtained from the **Instituto Nacional de Cultura** (INC) in Cusco, but it is often possible if you talk to the guards at the gate. The ruins are also quieter after 1530, but don't forget that the last bus down from the ruins leaves at 1730. The walk up takes 1½-two hours, following the Inca path. Walking down to Aguas Calientes, if staying the night there, takes between 30 minutes and one hour. In the dry season sandflies can be a problem, so take insect repellent and wear long clothing. It is possible that rules will change again in 2005; the INC website

> ‼ You are not allowed to walk back along the Inca Trail though you can pay US$4.50 at Intipunku to be allowed to walk back as far as Wiñay-Wayna.

publishes the regulations and lists of licensed tour operators and guides: www.inc-cusco.gob.pe. The agency officially responsible for the site is **Unidad Gestión de Machu Picchu** ① *C Garcilaso 223, Cusco, T084-242103.* It is an excellent source of information on Machu Picchu and this is the place to which any complaints or observations should be directed.

Machu Picchu ruins → *Colour map 2, grid A2. Altitude: 2,380 m.*

① *The site is open from 0700 to 1730. Entrance fee is US$20. It is possible to pay in dollars, but only clean, undamaged notes will be accepted. You cannot take backpacks into Machu Picchu; leave them at the entrance for US$0.50. Guides are available at the site, they are often very knowledgeable and worthwhile, and charge US$15 for 2½ hrs. See also Advice and information, above.*

For centuries Machu Picchu was buried in jungle, until Hiram Bingham stumbled upon it in July 1911. It was then explored by an archaeological expedition sent by Yale University. Machu Picchu was a stunning find. The only major Inca site to escape 400 years of looting and destruction, it was remarkably well preserved. And it was no ordinary Inca settlement. It sat in an inaccessible location above the Urubamba Gorge, and contained so many fine buildings that people have puzzled over its meaning ever since.

Once you have passed through the ticket gate you follow a path to a small complex of buildings which now acts as the main entrance to the ruins. It is set at the eastern end of the extensive terracing which must have supplied the crops for the city. Above this point, turning back on yourself, is the final stretch of the Inca Trail leading down from **Intipunku** (Sun Gate), see page 205. From a promontory here, on which stands the building called the **Watchman's Hut**, you get the perfect view of the city (the one you've seen on all the postcards), laid out before you with Huayna Picchu rising above the furthest extremity. Go round the promontory and head south for the **Intipata** (Inca bridge), see page 201. The main path into the ruins comes to a dry moat that cuts right across the site. At the moat you can either climb the long staircase which goes to the upper reaches of the city, or you can enter the city by the baths and Temple of the Sun.

The more strenuous way into the city is by the former route, which takes you past quarries, on your left as you look down to the Urubamba on the west flank of the mountain. To your right are roofless buildings where you can see in close up the general construction methods used in the city. Proceeding along this level, above the main plazas, you reach the **Temple of the Three Windows** and the **Principal Temple**, which has a smaller building called the **Sacristy**. The two main buildings are three-sided and were clearly of great importance, given the fine stonework involved.

The wall with the three windows is built onto a single rock, one of the many instances in the city where the architects did not merely put their construction on a convenient piece of land. They used and fashioned its features to suit their concept of how the city should be tied to the mountain, its forces and the alignment of its stones to the surrounding peaks. In the Principal Temple, a diamond-shaped stone in the floor is said to depict the constellation of the Southern Cross.

Machu Picchu

To Huayna Picchu

Ticket Gate

Inca Trail

To Train Station

To Intipata (Inca Bridge)

To Intipunku (Sun Gate)

N

| 0 metres | 50 |
| 0 yards | 50 |

Main entrance **1**
Agricultural sector **2**
Dry moat **3**

Ceremonial baths **4**
Principal bath **5**
Temple of the Sun **6**
Two fountains **7**
Royal sector **8**
Watchman's hut **9**
Funerary rock **10**
Main plaza **11**

Temple of the 3
  Windows **12**
Principal temple **13**
"Sacristy" **14**
Intihuatana **15**
Sacred rock **16**
Living quarters &
  workshops **17**

Mortar buildings **18**
Prison Group or Condor
  Temple **19**
Intimachay **20**

Sleeping
Machu Picchu
  Sanctuary Lodge **1**

Continue on the path behind the Sacristy to reach the **Intihuatana**, the 'hitching-post of the sun'. The name comes from the theory that such carved rocks (*gnomons*), found at all major Inca sites, were the point to which the sun was symbolically 'tied' at the winter solstice, before being freed to rise again on its annual ascent towards the summer solstice. The steps, angles and planes of this sculpted block appear to indicate a purpose beyond simple decoration and researchers, have sought the trajectory of each alignment. Whatever the motivation behind this magnificent carving, it is undoubtedly one of the highlights of Machu Picchu.

Climb down from the Intihuatana's mound to the **Main Plaza**. Beyond its northern end is a small plaza with open-sided buildings on two sides and on the third, the **Sacred Rock**. The outline of this gigantic, flat stone echoes that of the mountains behind it. From here you can proceed to the entrance to the trail to Huayna Picchu (see below). Returning to the Main Plaza and heading southeast you pass, on your left, several groups of closely packed buildings which have been taken to be **Living Quarters and Workshops**, **Mortar Buildings** (look for the house with two discs let into the floor) and the **Prison Group**, one of whose constructions is known as the **Condor Temple**. Also in this area is a cave called **Intimachay**.

A short distance from the Condor Temple is the lower end of a series of **Ceremonial Baths** or fountains. They were probably used for ritual bathing and the water still flows down them today. The uppermost, **Principal Bath**, is the most elaborate. Next to it is the **Temple of the Sun**, or Torreón. This singular building has one straight wall from which another wall curves around and back to meet the straight one, but for the doorway. From above it looks like an incomplete letter P. It is another example of the architecture being at one with its environment as the interior is taken up by the partly worked summit of the outcrop onto which the building is placed. All indications are that this temple was used for astronomical purposes. Underneath the Torreón a cave-like opening has been formed by an oblique gash in the rock. Fine masonry has been added to the opposing wall, making a second side of a triangle, which contrasts with the rough edge of the split rock. But the blocks of masonry appear to have been slotted behind another sculpted piece of natural stone, which has been cut into a four-stepped buttress. Immediately behind this is a two-stepped buttress. This strange combination of the natural and the man-made has been called the Tomb or Palace of the Princess. Across the stairway from the complex which includes the Torreón is the group of buildings known as the **Royal Sector**.

The famous Inca bridge – **Intipata** – is about 45 minutes along a well-marked trail south of the Royal Sector. The bridge, which is actually a couple of logs, is spectacularly sited, carved into a vertiginous cliff-face. The walk is well worth it for the fine views, but the bridge itself is closed to visitors. Not only is it in a poor state of repair, but the path beyond has collapsed.

Huayna Picchu

ⓘ *Access 0700-1300, with the latest return time being 1500.*

Synonymous with the ruins themselves is Huayna Picchu, the verdant mountain overlooking the site. There are also ruins on the mountain itself, and steps to the top for a superlative view of the whole magnificent scene, but this is not for those with vertigo. The climb takes up to 90 minutes but the steps are dangerous after bad weather and you shouldn't leave the path. You must register at a hut at the beginning of the trail. The other trail to Huayna Picchu, down near the Urubamba, is via the Temple of the Moon, in two caves, one above the other, with superb Inca niches inside, sadly blemished by graffiti. To reach the **Temple of the Moon** from the path to Huayna Picchu, take the marked trail to the left; it is in good shape. It descends further than you think it should. After the Temple you may proceed to Huayna Picchu, but this path is overgrown, slippery when wet and has a crooked ladder on an exposed part about 10 minutes before the top (not for the faint-hearted). It is safer to return to the main trail to Huayna Picchu, but this adds about 30 minutes to the climb. The round trip takes about four hours.

The Inca Trail

The wonder of Machu Picchu has been well documented over the years. Equally impressive is the centuries-old Inca Trail that winds its way from the Sacred Valley near Ollantaytambo, taking three to four days. What makes this hike so special is the stunning combination of Inca ruins, unforgettable views, magnificent mountains, exotic vegetation and extraordinary ecological variety. The government acknowledged all this in 1981 by including the trail in a 325 sq-km national park, the Machu Picchu Historical Sanctuary. Machu Picchu itself cannot be understood without the Inca Trail. Its principal sites are ceremonial in character, apparently in ascending hierarchical order. This Inca province was a unique area of elite access. The trail is essentially a work of spiritual art, like a Gothic cathedral, and walking it was formerly an act of devotion.

Ins and outs

Entrance tickets and tours An entrance ticket for the trail or its variations must be bought at the **Instituto Nacional de Cultura (INC)** office in Cusco; no tickets are sold at the entrance gates. Furthermore, tickets are only sold on presentation of a letter from a licensed tour operator on behalf of the visitor. There is a 50 per cent discount for students, but note that officials are very strict, only an ISIC card will be accepted as proof of status. Tickets are checked at Km 82, Huayllabamba and Wiñay-Wayna.

On all hiking trails (Km 82 or Km 88 to Machu Picchu, Salkantay to Machu Picchu, and Km 82 or Km 88 to Machu Picchu via Km 104) adults must pay US$50, students and children under 15 US$25. On the Camino Real de los Inkas from Km 104 to Wiñay-Wayna and Machu Picchu the fee is US$25 per adult, US$15 for students and children (or US$20 and US$10 respectively if you don't camp at Wiñay-Wayna) and Salkantay to Huayllabamba and Km 82, US$30.

Inca Trail

Aguas Calientes

Huayna Picchu (2,743m)
Machu Picchu
Puente Ruinas Station
Intipunku
Inca Bridge
Intipata
Km104
Choquesuysuy (2,699m)
Wiñay Wayna
Phuyupatamarca (3,650m)
Inca Steps
(3,700m)
Río Urubamba
Río Pacamayo
Runkuracay Pacamayo
Tunnel
Runkuracay Pass (3,850m)
Warmiwañusqa (Dead Woman) Pass (4,200m)
Ch'akicocha
Sayacmarca (3,600m)

0 km 1
0 miles 1

Sleeping
Youth Hostel 1

.... Inca trail original pathway
.... Inca trail deteriorated pathway

Travel agencies in Cusco arrange transport to the start, equipment, food, etc, for an all-in price. Prices vary from about US$200 to US$300 per person for a four day, three night trek. If the price is under US$180, you should be concerned as the company will be cutting corners and may not be paying the environment the respect the new rules were designed to instil. All are subject to strict rules first introduced in 2001 and must be licensed. Tour operators taking clients on any of the Inca Trails leading to the Machu Picchu Historical Sanctuary have to pay an annual fee. Groups of up to seven independent travellers who do not wish to use a tour operator will be allowed to hike the trails if they contact an independent, licensed guide to accompany them, as long as they do not contact any other persons such as porters or cooks. There is a maximum of 500 visitors per day allowed on the trail. Operators pay US$10 for each porter and other trail staff; porters are not permitted to carry more than 25 kg. Littering is banned, as is carrying plastic water bottles (canteens only may be carried). Pets and pack animals are prohibited, but llamas are allowed as far as the first pass. Groups have to use approved campsites only. There is a quota for agencies and groups to use the Trail, but modifications to the procedures in 2004 encouraged some agencies to make block bookings way in advance of departure dates. This made it much harder for other agencies to guarantee their clients places on the Trail. Consequently, current advice is to book your preferred dates as early as possible, even up to a year in advance, then confirm nearer the time. There were many instances of disappointed trekkers whose bookings did not materialise: don't wait till the last minute and always check your operators cancellation charges.

> ❗ *Camping is not allowed at Intipunku, nor anywhere else at the site; guards may confiscate your tent. There is a free campsite down beside the rail tracks at Puente Ruinas station.*

You can save a bit of money by arranging your own transport back to Ollantaytambo in advance, either for the last day of your tour, or by staying an extra night in Aguas Calientes and taking the early morning train, then take a bus back to Cusco. If you take your own tent and sleeping gear, some agencies give a discount. Make sure your return train ticket to Cusco has your name on it for the tourist train, otherwise you have to pay for any changes.

Advice and information Although security has improved in recent years, it's still best to leave all your valuables in Cusco and keep everything inside your tent, even your shoes. Avoid the July-August high season and the rainy season from November to April (note that this can change, so check in advance). In the wet it is cloudy and the paths are very muddy and difficult. Also watch out for coral snakes in this area (black, red, yellow bands). Please remove all your rubbish, including toilet paper, or use the pits provided. Do not light open fires as they can get out of control. **The Trail is closed each February for cleaning and repair.** The **Annual Inca Trail Clean-up** takes place usually in September. Many agencies and organizations are involved and volunteers should contact **South American Explorers** in Cusco (see page 147) for full details of ways to help.

Equipment It is cold at night and weather conditions change rapidly, so it is important to take strong footwear, rain gear and warm clothing (this includes long johns if you want to sleep rather than freeze at night): dress in layers. Also take food, water, water purification tablets, insect repellent, sunscreen, a hat and sunglasses, a supply of plastic bags, coverings, a good sleeping bag, a torch and a stove for preparing hot food and drink to ward off the cold at night. It is worth paying extra to hire a down sleeping bag if you haven't brought your own. A paraffin (kerosene) stove is preferable, as fuel can be bought in small quantities in markets.

A tent is essential, but if you're hiring one in Cusco, check carefully for leaks. Caves marked on some maps are little better than overhangs and are not sufficient shelter to sleep in. You could also take a first-aid kit; if you don't need it the porters probably will given their rather basic footwear.

All the necessary equipment can be rented in Cusco, see page 174. Good maps of the trail and area can be bought from **South American Explorers** in Lima or Cusco, see pages 90 and 147. If you have any doubts about carrying your own pack, porters/guides are available through Cusco agencies. Carry a day-pack, water and snacks in case you walk faster or slower than the porters and you have to wait for them to catch you up or you have to catch them up. Take around US$30 extra per person for tips and a drink at the end of the trail.

Those concerned about the working conditions of the porters on the trail should contact **Porteadores Inka Ñan** ① *Dept 4, Choquechaca 188, Cusco, T084-246829, associated with the International Porter Protection Group, www.peruweb.org/porters, Monday-Friday 0930-1730.*

The trek

Day 1 The trek to the sacred site begins either at Km 82, **Piscacucho**, or at Km 88, **Qorihuayrachina**, at 2,600 m. In order to reach Km 82 hikers are transported by their tour operator (see above) in a minibus on the road that goes to Quillabamba. From Piri onward the road follows the riverbank and ends at Km 82. Where there used to be an *oroya* (cable crossing), there is now a bridge. You can depart as early as you like and arrive at Km 82 faster than going by train. The Inca Trail equipment, food, fuel and field personnel reach Km 82 (depending on the tour operator's logistics) for the Inrena staff to weigh each bundle before the group arrives. When several groups are leaving on the same day, it is more convenient to arrive early. Km 88 can only be reached by train, subject to schedule and baggage limitations. The train goes slower than a bus, but you start your walk nearer to Llaqtapata and Huayllabamba. (See below for details of variations in starting points for the Inca Trail.)

The first ruin is **Llaqtapata**, near Km 88, the utilitarian centre of a large settlement of farming terraces which probably supplied the other Inca Trail sites. From here, it is a relatively easy three-hour walk to the village of **Huayllabamba**. Note that the route from Km 82 goes via **Cusichaca**, the valley in which Ann Kendall worked, rather than Llaqtapata.

A series of gentle climbs and descents leads along the Río Cusichaca, the ideal introduction to the trail. The village is a popular camping spot for tour groups, so it's a better idea to continue for about an hour up to the next site, **Llulluchayoc** – 'three white stones' – which is a patch of green beside a fast-flowing stream. It's a steep climb but you're pretty much guaranteed a decent pitch for the night. If you're feeling really energetic, you can go on to the next camping spot, a perfectly flat meadow, called **Llulluchapampa**. This means a punishing 1½-hour ascent through cloudforest, but it does leave you with a much easier second day. There's also the advantage of relative isolation and a magnificent view back down the valley.

Day 2 For most people the second day is by far the toughest. It's a steep climb to the meadow, followed by an exhausting 2½-hour haul up to the first pass – aptly named

Warmiwañusqa (Dead Woman) – at 4,200 m. The feeling of relief on reaching the top is immense and there's the added, sadistic pleasure of watching your fellow sufferers struggling in your wake. After a well-earned break it's a sharp descent on a treacherous path down to the Pacamayo Valley, where there are a few flat camping spots near a stream if you're too weary to continue.

Day 2/3 If you're feeling energetic, you can proceed to the second pass. Halfway up comes the ruin of **Runkuracay**, which was probably an Inca *tambo* (post-house). Camping is no longer permitted here. A steep climb up an Inca staircase leads to the next pass, at 3,850 m, with spectacular views of Pumasillo (6,246 m) and the Vilcabamba Range. The rail descends to **Sayacmarca** (Inaccessible town), a spectacular site over the Aobamba Valley, where it's possible to camp. Just below Sayacmarca lies **Conchamarca** (Shell town), a small group of buildings standing on rounded terraces.

Day 3 A blissfully gentle two-hour climb on a stone highway, leads through an Inca tunnel and along the enchanted fringes of the cloudforest, to the third pass. This is the most rewarding part of the trail, with spectacular views of the entire Vilcabamba Range, and it's worth taking the time to dwell on the wonders of nature. Then it's down to the extensive ruins of **Phuyupatamarca** (Cloud-level town), at 3,650 m, where Inca observation platforms offer awesome views of nearby Salkantay (6,270 m) and surrounding peaks. There is a 'tourist bathroom' here, where water can be collected, but purify it before drinking.

From here an Inca stairway of white granite plunges more than 1,000 m to the spectacularly sited and impressive ruins of **Wiñay-Wayna** (Forever Young), offering views of newly uncovered agricultural terraces at **Intipata** (Sun place). A trail, not easily visible, goes from Wiñay-Wayna to the newly discovered terracing. There is a youth hostel at Wiñay-Wayna (see Sleeping, below) and there are spaces for a few tents, but they get snapped up quickly. After Wiñay-Wayna there is no water, and no place to camp, until Machu Picchu. A gate by Wiñay-Wayna is locked between 1530 and 0500, preventing access to the path to Machu Picchu at night.

Day 4 From Wiñay-Wayna it is a gentle hour's walk through another type of forest, with larger trees and giant ferns, to a steep Inca staircase which leads up to **Intipunku** (Sun gate), where you look down, at last, upon Machu Picchu, basking in all her reflective glory. Your aching muscles will be quickly forgotten and even the presence of the functional hotel building cannot detract from one of the most magical sights in all the Americas.

Alternative Inca routes
The Inca Trail from Km 104 A short Inca Trail, the **Camino Real de los Inkas**, is used by those who don't want to endure the full hike. It starts at Km 104, where a footbridge gives access to the ruins of Chachabamba and the trail ascends to the main trail at Wiñay-Wayna. Half way up is a good view of the ruins of Choquesuysuy. The first part is a steady, continuous three-hour ascent (take water) and the trail is narrow and exposed in parts. About 15 minutes before Wiñay-Wayna is a waterfall where fresh water can be obtained (best to purify it before drinking).
Salkantay to Machu Picchu This route takes three nights. A trek from **Salkantay** joins the Inca Trail at Huayllabamba, then proceeds as before on the main trail through Wiñay- Wayna to Machu Picchu. There is no checkpoint at Salkantay for verifying that the relevant fees have been paid, but you will get checked at Huayllabamba. To get to Salkantay, you have to start the trek in **Mollepata**, northwest of Cusco in the Apurímac Valley. Buses of the **Ampay** company run from Arcopata on the Chinchero road, or you can take private transport to Mollepata (three hours from

Cusco). It is down an unpaved road which turns off the main road after Limatambo. From Mollepata it's an all-day trek to **Salkantay Pampa**, also called Soraypampa. Camp below Salkantay (6,271 m). From Salkantay Pampa a very demanding ascent leads to the **Incachiriaska Pass** (4,900 m). Descend to camp at Sisaypampa. From there, trek to **Pampacahuana**, an outstanding and seldom-visited Inca ruin. The remains of an Inca road then go down to the singular Inca ruins of **Paucarcancha**. This entire section is done with mules and/or horses. There is an obligatory change from animals to porters before you reach Huayllabamba.

An alternative from Salkantay is to go to Huayllabamba, then down to Km 88, from where you can take the train to Aguas Calientes, or back to Cusco. ① *There is an entrance fee of US$15 for this hike, but it does not include the entrance to Machu Picchu. If you combine this route with the short Inca Trail from Km 104, you have to pay the US$ 25 trail fee (see above for full details on prices).*

Paucarcancha to Machu Picchu A four-night trek from Paucarcancha to Huayllabamba, then on the traditional Trail to Machu Picchu. Paucarcancha is an abandoned set of ruins on the descent from Pampacahuana, before the village of Huayllabamba on the main Inca Trail. Paucarcancha is also shown as Incarakay on some maps. Nearby there are some hot springs. Paucarcancha is an important camping site on the trek from Salkantay, or from Ancascocha Lake pass on the route from the Sillque Valley. As an alternative to the Inca Trail, there is a trek from Paucarcancha to the Palcaycasa Pass between the Salkantay and Palcay snow peaks. From the pass you can walk on a wide, well-preserved Inca trail to Aobamba or the hydroelectric station.

Other routes

There are other routes which approach the Inca Trails to Machu Picchu, such as Km 77, Chillca, up the Sillque ravine in the Qente Valley, which is commonly called the Lago Ancascocha route. There is another access through the Millpo Valley in the Salkantay area. From the Vilcabamba mountain range, you can reach Machu Picchu by hiking down from Huancacalle to Chaulla by road, getting to Santa Teresa and walking to the hydroelectric (Aobamba) train station. Then it's an hour's train ride on the local train to Aguas Calientes (tourists are allowed to ride the local train for this short section). A three-night trek goes from Km 82 to Km 88, then along the Río Urubamba to Pacaymayo Bajo and Km 104, from where you take the trail described above to Wiñay-Wayna and Machu Picchu. Also, good hiking trails from Aguas Calientes have been opened along the left bank of the Urubamba river, for day hikes crossing the bridge of the hydroelectric plant to Choquesuysuy.

Aguas Calientes → *Phone code: 084. Colour map 2, A2.*

Only 1½ km back along the railway from Puente Ruinas, this is a popular resting place for those recovering from the rigours of the Inca Trail. It is called Aguas Calientes (or just Aguas) after the hot springs above the town. It is also called the town of Machu Picchu. Most activity is centred around the old railway station, on the plaza, or on Avenida Pachacútec, which leads from the plaza to the thermal baths.

The **baths** ① *0500-2030. US$1.50*, consist of a rather smelly communal pool, 10 minutes' walk from the town. You can rent towels and bathing costumes for US$0.65 at several places on the road to the baths. There are basic toilets and changing facilities and showers. Take soap and shampoo and keep an eye on your valuables.

Beyond Machu Picchu

The lower reaches of the Río Urubamba beyond Machu Picchu are the gateway to regions which are very different from the highlands of Cusco, yet intimately linked to it by history. The most important town is Quillabamba, from where you can set out to the mysterious last stronghold of the Incas, Vilcabamba, or to the Pongo de Mainique, frequently described as one of the most beautiful places on earth.

207

Cusco Machu Picchu & the Inca Trail

Aguas Calientes

Not to scale

Sleeping
Gringo Bill's
  (Hostal Q'oñi Unu) **3** B3
Hatuchay Tower **4** A2
Hospedaje Inca Tambo **1** B3
Hospedaje Las
  Bromelias **5** B3
Hospedaje Quilla **6** D3

Hostal Continental **7** A3
Hostal Don Guiller &
  Pizzería El Candamo **8** C2
Hostal Ima Sumac **9** D3
Hostal Los
  Caminantes **10** A3
Hostal Pachakúteq **11** D3
Hostal Samana Wasi **12** D2
Hostal Wiracocha
  Inn **13** D2
Jardín Real **18** D2
La Cabaña **14** D3
Las Orquídeas **19** D2
Machu Picchu Inn **15** C2

Machu Picchu
  Pueblo **16** C1
Presidente & Hostal
  Machu Picchu **17** A2
Rupa Wasi **3** B3

Eating
Aiko **1** A2
Café Inkaterra **19** C1
Clave de Sol **2** D2
Govinda **3** D3
Illary **4** B2
Inca Wasi **5** C2
Indio Feliz **6** C2

Inka Machu Picchu **7** C2
Inka's Pizza Pub **8** B2
La Chosa Pizzería **10** A2
Las Qenas **11** A2
Machu Picchu **12** C2
Pizzería Samana
  Wasi 1 **13** A2
Pizzería Samana
  Wasi 2 **14** B2
Pueblo Viejo **18** C2
Toto's House **15** B1

Bars & clubs
Waisicha Pub **17** C3

The last Incas of Vilcabamba

After Pizarro killed Atahualpa in 1532 the Inca empire disintegrated rapidly, and it is often thought that native resistance ended there. But in fact it continued for 40 more years, beginning with Manco, a teenage half-brother of Atahualpa.

In 1536, Manco escaped from the Spanish and returned to lead a massive army against them. He besieged Cusco and Lima simultaneously, and came close to dislodging the Spaniards from Peru. Spanish reinforcements arrived and Manco fled to Vilcabamba, a mountainous forest region west of Cusco that was remote, but still fairly close to the Inca capital, which he always dreamed of recapturing.

The Spanish chased Manco deep into Vilcabamba but he managed to elude them and continued his guerrilla war, raiding Spanish commerce on the Lima highway, and keeping alive the Inca flame. Then, in 1544, Spanish outlaws to whom he had given refuge murdered him, ending the most active period of Inca resistance.

The Inca line passed to his sons. The first, a child too young to rule named Sayri Túpac, eventually yielded to Spanish enticements and emerged from Vilcabamba, taking up residence in Yucay, near Urubamba in 1558. He died mysteriously –

possibly poisoned – three years later.

His brother Titu Cusi, who was still in Vilcabamba, now took up the Inca mantle. Astute and determined, he resumed raiding and fomenting rebellion against the Spanish. But in 1570, Titu Cusi fell ill and died suddenly. A Spanish priest was accused of murdering him. Anti-Spanish resentment erupted, and the priest and a Spanish viceregal envoy were killed. The Spanish Viceroy reacted immediately, and the Spanish invaded Vilcabamba for the third and last time in 1572.

A third brother, Túpac Amaru was now in charge. He lacked his brother's experience and acuity, and his destiny was to be the sacrificial last Inca. The Spanish overran the Inca's jungle capital, and dragged him back to Cusco in chains. There, Túpac Amaru, the last Inca, was publicly executed in Cusco's main plaza.

The location of the neo-Inca capital of Vilcabamba was forgotten over the centuries, and the search for it provoked Hiram Bingham's expeditions, and his discovery of Machu Picchu. Bingham did also discover Vilcabama the Old, without realizing it, but the true location at Espíritu Pampa was only pinpointed by Gene Savoy in the 1960s, and was not confirmed irrefutably until the work of Vincent Lee in the 1980s.

Ins and outs

As no trains run beyond Aguas Calientes, the only route to Quillabamba is by road from Cusco via Ollantaytambo. Beyond here, there are buses to Ivochote, for boats down river, and Huancacalle for the hike to Vilcabamba. After leaving Ollantaytambo, the road passes through Peña, a place of great beauty. Once out of Peña, the road climbs on endless zigzags, offering breathtaking views, to reach the Abra Málaga Pass, just below the beautiful glaciated peak of Verónica. At Chaullay, the road meets the old railway to Quillabamba, Machu Picchu and Cusco and continues up the east bank of the river.

Quillabamba and around → *Colour map 2, A2.*

La Ciudad de Eterno Verano (The City of Eternal Summer), as it is known, was once a prosperous town from the sale of coffee. It has now become the overnighting spot for people going to Vilcabamba, Espíritu Pampa and the Pongo de Mainique. This delightful market town now survives on the export of fruit, coffee, honey and other produce to Cusco. The tourist season is from June to July, when Peruvian holidaymakers descend on the place. Although Quillabamba has plenty to offer, it's normally overlooked because of the incredibly bumpy, but beautiful ride to get there.

For the weary traveller one of the biggest attractions, about 1½ km from Quillabamba, is **Sambaray** ⓘ *US$0.20, transport by combi costs US$0.20, taxi US$0.60*, a recreation area with an outdoor swimming pool, restaurant, volleyball and football field. As Sambaray is situated on the Río Alto Urubamba, you can also swim in the river, or, if you're feeling brave, tube down it. Ask locals for the best place to start, as the river can be quite rapid.

Siete Tinajas (Seven Small Baths) is a beautiful waterfall some 45 minutes by combi from town (take the bus from Paradero El Grifo, US$1). It is well worth the trip for the photos, although be careful when climbing to the top, as it can be very slippery. Another waterfall is **Mandor**, also around an hour from Quillabamba. You may go by taxi or walk, although it is advisable to take a guide. Ask at your hotel as there will always be someone willing to take you.

Pongo de Mainique and beyond

Before the Río Urubamba enters the vast plain of the Amazon Basin it carves its way through one last wall of foothills and the result is spectacular. The Pongo de Mainique is a sheer rainforest canyon, hundreds of metres deep with the Urubamba surging through its centre and many small waterfalls tumbling in on either side. The Machiguenga people who live in the area believe this to be a portal to the afterlife. They are, however, very private people and do not take kindly to uninvited strangers; if you wish to visit them on their reserve take someone who has contact with them.

To get to the Pongo de Mainique, take a bus from Quillabamba's northern bus 'terminal' (a dusty outdoor affair with many food stalls and the occasional ticket booth) to **Ivochote**, via a new road into the jungle. The road can be in terrible condition in places. En route you'll pass **Kiteni**, a rapidly expanding jungle town. Ivochote is the end of the road, literally, but it develops a party atmosphere on Saturdays, market day in the jungle. Due to the Camisea Natural Gas Project downriver boat traffic is fairly intense. *Lanchas* (boats) head downstream early in the morning on most days during the dry season. In the wet season (roughly December to April) the river may be too dangerous to navigate, especially the rapids in the Pongo itself. Depending on your bargaining ability, passage downriver to the Pongo or to the **Casa de los Ugarte** (see Sleeping page 210) will set you back between US$6 and US$8.50, providing the captain has trading business downstream. Hiring a boat independently will cost a lot more. To return upstream prices are roughly one third higher, owing to the increased amount of gasoline required to motor against the current.

Two to three hours downstream from the **Casa de los Ugarte**, on the right-hand bank of the river, you pass the Machiguenga community of **Timpia**, home of a high-level ecotourism project and comfortable lodge, run in co-operation with InkaNatura Travel, see page 558.

Beyond the Pongo a day's boat travel will bring you to **Malvinas**, centre of the hugely controversial Camisea Natural Gas Project, and on to **Camisea** itself. If you wish to stay here, you must ask the Presidente of the community first. Another day downriver and you'll reach **Sepahua**, a largely indigenous village on the edge of the Alto Purus region. It has a few *hostales* and you can buy pretty much anything. Those with time and an adventurous spirit can continue downriver to **Pucallpa** via Atalaya (several *hostales*, market and a tourist office on the plaza which will help with day trips). To go all the way to Iquitos means, overall, a journey of 2,500 km by boat, an incredible opportunity to see the Peruvian jungle.

At **Chaullay**, the historic **Choquechaca Bridge**, built on Inca foundations, allows drivers to cross the river to Huancacalle, a two-street village (no restaurants, but a few shops) between four and seven hours from Quillabamba. Huancacalle is the best base for exploring the nearby Inca ruins of Vitcos and the starting point for the trek to Espíritu Pampa. At **Vitcos** is the palace of the last four Inca rulers from 1536 to 1572, and **Yurac Rumi**, the sacred White Rock of the Incas (also referred to as **Chuquipalta**). The White Rock, once the most sacred site in South America, is very large (8 m high and 20 m wide), with intricate and elaborate carvings. Lichens now cover its whiteness.

You can also hike up to **Vilcabamba La Nueva** from Huancacalle. It's a three-hour walk through beautiful countryside with Inca ruins dotted around. There is a missionary building run by Italians, with electricity and running water, where you may be able to spend the night.

Huancacalle to Espíritu Pampa → *Colour map 2, grid A1.*

In 1536, three years after the fall of the Inca Empire to the Spanish conquistadores, Manco Inca led a rebellion against the conquerors. Retiring from Cusco when Spanish reinforcements arrived, Manco and his followers fell back to the remote triangle of Vilcabamba, where they maintained the Inca traditions, religion and government outside the reach of the Spanish authorities. Centuries after the eventual Spanish crushing of Inca resistance, it was difficult to locate and identify Manco's capital of Vilcabamba. See the box, page 208.

The trek to Espíritu Pampa from Huancacalle takes three days, but would be a more comfortable undertaking in four. Espíritu Pampa itself is quite a large site, and further groups of buildings may still be awaiting discovery in the densely forested

Vilcabamba

mountains surrounding the valley. Give yourself at least a day at the site to soak up
the atmosphere before continuing a further six hours to Chanquiri, the starting point
for transport to Kiteni and Quillabamba. The best time of year is from May to
November, possibly December. Outside this period it is very dangerous as the trails
are very narrow and can be thick with mud and very slippery. Insect repellent is
essential; there are millions of mosquitoes. Also take pain-killers and other basic
medicines; these will be much appreciated by the local people should you need to
take advantage of their hospitality.

An excellent guide is Jesús Castillo Alveres who can be contacted through the
Hospedaje Sixpac Manco in Huancacalle (see page 214). Many members of the
Cobos family (see page 214) also guide. A good rate of pay for guides/mule drivers
is US$5 per day, plus US$5 per mule or horse used. Before you leave be very clear
about your exact itinerary and expectations; some guides have been known to leave
clients in Espíritu Pampa, half a day's hike from the roadhead in Chanquiri. Always
provide sufficient food and a waterproof tent by way of accommodation for your
guide on the trail. If you enjoy your trip give your guide a tip; it will be appreciated.
Remember, arrieros (mule drivers) based in Huancacalle have to walk all the way
back along the route, a journey of at least 2½ days, and for this they don't charge.
Always take all plastic and non-biodegradable rubbish back to Cusco for more
efficient disposal. All supplies must be brought from Huancacalle as even basic
supplies are scarce on the trail.

⊜ Sleeping

Machu Picchu ruins *p199, map p200*
LL **Machu Picchu Sanctuary Lodge**, under
the same management as the **Hotel
Monasterio** in Cusco, T084-211167,
www.monasterio.orient-express.com. This
hotel, at the entrance to the ruins, was
completely refurbished in 2001 and has
included some environmentally friendly
features. They will accept American Express
TCs at the official rate. The rooms are
comfortable, the service is good and the staff
helpful. Electricity and water are available
24 hrs a day. Food in the restaurant is well
cooked and presented; the restaurant is for
residents only in the evening, but the buffet
lunch is open to all. The hotel is usually fully
booked well in advance; if struggling for a
booking try Sun night as other tourists find
Pisac Market a greater attraction.

The Inca Trail *p205*
G **Youth Hostel**, at Winay-Wayna, price per
person, with bunk beds, showers and a small
restaurant. It is often fully booked. You can
sleep on the floor of the restaurant more
cheaply, but it is open for diners until 2300.
There are also spaces for a few tents, but

they get snapped up quickly too. The
hostel's door is closed at 1730.

Aguas Calientes *p206, map p207*
Many hotels in Aguas Calientes seem to have
increased their prices sharply in recent years,
perhaps in response to the rising costs of
train services and excursions on the Inca
Trail. You should bargain hard for good
value accommodation.
LL **Hatuchay Tower**, Carretera Puente
Ruinas block 4, T084-211201 (reservations in
Lima T01-447 8170), www.hatuchaytower.
com.pe. Smart on the inside but in need of
exterior renovation. Buffet breakfast and all
taxes are included in the price, but the hot
water system seems to be unreliable. There
are standard rooms and luxury suites. It is
below the old station.
LL **Machu Picchu Pueblo Hotel**, Km 110.
Reservations: Jr Andalucia 174, San Isidro,
Lima, T01-6100404; in Cusco at Plaza las
Nazarenas 211, T084-245314,
www.inkaterra.com. Beautiful colonial-style
bungalows have been built in a village
compound surrounded by cloudforest 5
mins' walk along the railway from the town.

 *For an explanation of sleeping and eating price codes used in this guide, see inside the
front cover. Other relevant information is found in Essentials, pages 61-66.*

The hotel has lovely gardens in which there are many species of birds, butterflies and orchids. There is a pool, an expensive restaurant, but also a **campsite** with hot showers at good rates. It offers tours to Machu Picchu, several guided walks on the property and to local beauty spots. The buffet breakfasts for US$12 are great. It also has the **Café Amazónico** by the railway line. The hotel is involved in a project to rehabilitate spectacled bears, and re-release them back into the wild. Recommended, but there are a lot of steps between the public areas and rooms.

AL Machu Picchu Inn, Av Pachacútec 101, T084-211057, mapiinn@peruhotel.com.pe. The price includes bathroom and breakfast. A modern hotel, with a functional atmosphere.

A Presidente, at the old station, T084-211034 (Cusco T084-244598), presidente@terra.com.pe. Next to **Hostal Machu Picchu**, see below, this is the more upmarket half of the establishment. Rooms without river view are cheaper, but the price includes breakfast and taxes. There seems to be only minimal difference between this and **Machu Picchu**, which represents much better value for money.

B Gringo Bill's (Hostal Q'oñi Unu), Colla Raymi 104, T084-211046, gringobills@yahoo.com. Price includes bathroom and continental breakfast. An Aguas Calientes institution, it's friendly, relaxed, with a lot of coming-and-going, hot water, good beds, luggage store, laundry and money exchange. Good but expensive meals are served in **Villa Margarita** restaurant; breakfast starts at 0530 and they offer a US$4 packed lunch to take up to the ruins.

B La Cabaña, Av Pachacútec M20-3, T084-211048. Price includes bathroom and continental breakfast. Rooms have hot water. There is a café, laundry service and a DVD player and TV (with a good selection of movies) for clients in the lounge. The staff are helpful and can provide information on interesting local walks. The hotel is popular with groups.

C Hostal Ima Sumac, Av Pachacútec 173, T084-211021. 5 mins before the baths, so quite a climb up from the station. Some of the rooms smell a little damp, but are generally of a reasonable standard; they exchange money.

C Hostal Machu Picchu, at the old station, T084-211212. Price includes breakfast and taxes. A clean, functional establishment, which is quiet and friendly (especially Wilber, the owner's son). There is hot water, a nice balcony over the Urubamba, a grocery store and travel information is available. Recommended.

C Rupa Wasi, C Huanacaure 180, T084-211101, www.rupawasi.org. Rustic and charming 'eco-lodge', located up a small alley off Collasuyo. The lodge and its owners have a very laid-back, comfortable style, and there are great views from the balconies of the first floor rooms. This lodge is slowly adding to its environmentally friendly credentials with purified water available (so you don't have to buy more plastic) and an organic garden and rainwater collector in the pipeline. Great breakfasts for US$3.

C-D Jardín Real, C Wiracocha 7, T084-211234, jardinrealhotel@hotmail.com. A clean, modern hotel with good hot water. At the unofficial price this hotel represents great value, so bargain hard. Same owner as **Pizzería Los Jardines** on Pachacútec.

D Hostal Continental, near the old train station, T084-211065. Very clean rooms with good beds, hot showers. This *hostal* was closed for renovation at the time of writing.

D Hostal Don Guiller, Av Pachacútec 136, T084-211145. Price includes breakfast. Rooms have bath and hot water. In the same building is the **Pizzería El Candamo**.

D Las Orquídeas, Urb Las Orquideas A-8, T084-211171. From Av Pachacútec, cross the bridge over the river to the football pitch and follow the small dirt path on the right. Rooms have bath and hot water and are clean. This is a quiet, pleasant place away from the main part of town.

D Hostal Pachakúteq, up the hill beyond Hostal La Cabaña, T084-211061. Rooms with bathroom and 24-hr hot water. Good breakfast is included, quiet, family-run. Recommended.

D Hospedaje Quilla, Av Pachacútec, T084-211009, between Wiracocha and Túpac Inka Yupanki. Price includes breakfast, bath and hot water. They rent bathing gear for the hot springs if you arrive without your costume and towel.

D Hostal Wiracocha Inn, C Wiracocha, T084-211088. Rooms with bath and hot water. Breakfast included. There is a small garden at this very friendly and helpful *hostal*. It's popular particularly with European groups.

D-E Hospedaje Inca Tambo, C Huana-caure s/n, T084-211135, hostalinkatambo@ latin mail.com. Basic but clean, situated just below **Rupa Wasi** (above); negotiate.

D-E Hospedaje Las Bromelias, Colla Raymi, T084-211145. Just off the plaza before **Gringo Bill's**, this is a small place which has rooms with bath and hot water. Accommodation is cheaper without bath.

E Hostal Los Caminantes, Av Imperio de los Incas 140, by the railway just beyond the old station, T084-211007. Price per person for a room with bathroom. Hot water but breakfast extra. Basic but friendly and clean.

F Hostal Samana Wasi, C Túpac Inka Yupanki, T084-211170, quillavane@hotmail. com. Price includes bath and 24-hr hot water. There are cheaper rooms without bath at this friendly, pleasant place.

Camping
The only official campsite is in a field by the river, just below Puente Ruinas station. Do not leave your tent and belongings unattended.

Quillabamba *p208*
D Hostal Quillabamba, Prolongación y M Grau, just behind the main market, T084-281369, hostalquillabamba@latinmail.com. Highly kitsch design, one of the largest hostels in Quillabamba, all rooms have private bath, TV (local channels only) and telephone, swimming pool (which

occasionally has water in it), restaurant, parking. Less appealing is the small zoo. They also have a cockfighting school for the championship, which is held every year in late Jul.

E Hostal Alto Urubamba, Jr 2 de Mayo 333, T084-281131, altourub@ec-red.com. Rooms with shared bath cheaper. Spotlessly clean, pleasant hotel, 1 block from the Plaza de Armas. Staff are friendly and knowledgeable. Small local restaurant attached and there are great views over the town from the roof. Highly recommended.

E Hostal Don Carlos, Jr Libertad 566, T084-281371. Clean and simple, all rooms have private shower with generally hot water. There is a bar and restaurant.

Pongo de Mainique and beyond *p209*
F Hostal Pongo de Mainique, Ivochote, just behind **F Señor de Huanca**, Ivochote, on the right once over the footbridge. The former is the nicer of the 2 *hostales*, although both are basic.

G Hostal La Casa de los Ugarte, just beyond the Pongo, on the left bank of the river (if heading downstream). The small hacienda of Ida and Abel Ugarte. They are very helpful and will let you camp on their land for a small fee. They have a modest general store and basic supplies, fruit and very fresh eggs are available. The forest behind the hacienda is rich in wildlife and the family may be able to arrange expeditions in the jungle, given time to make the arrangements.

G Hostal Vanessa, Sepahua. On the main street close to the port, very pleasant.

F-G Sixpac Manco, managed by the Cobos family, this hostel is fairly comfortable and has good beds.

Villagers will accept travellers in their very basic homes (take a sleeping bag).

🍴 Eating

Aguas Calientes *p206, map p207*

Pizza seems to be the most common dish in town, but many of the pizzerías serve other types of food as well. The old station and Av Pachútec are lined with eating places. At the station (where staff will try to entice you into their restaurant), are, among others: **Aiko**, which is recommended; **La Chosa Pizzería**, with pleasant atmosphere, good value; **Las Quenas**, which is a café and a baggage store (US$0.30 per locker); and 2 branches of **Pizzería Samana Wasi**. See also under Sleeping, above.

‖‖‖ Café Inkaterra, on the railway, just below the **Machu Picchu Pueblo Hotel**. US$15 for a great lunch buffet with scenic views of the river.

‖‖‖ Indio Feliz, C Lloque Yupanqui, T084-211090. Great French cuisine, excellent value and service, set 3-course meal for US$10, good *pisco sours*. Highly recommended.

‖‖‖ Inka's Pizza Pub, on the plaza. Good pizzas, changes money and accepts TCs. Next door is **Illary**, which is popular.

‖‖‖ Pueblo Viejo, Av Pachacútec, near the plaza. Good food in a spacious but warm environment. Price includes salad bar.

‖‖ Toto's House, Av Imperio de los Incas, on the railway line. Same owners as **Pueblo Viejo**. Good value and quality *menú*.

‖ Clave de Sol, Av Pachacútec 156. Same owner as **Chez Maggy** in Cusco, serving Italian food for about US$4, changes money, also has a vegetarian menu, open 1200-1500, 1800-whenever.

‖ Govinda, Av Pachacútec y Túpac Inka Yupanki. Vegetarian restaurant with a cheap set lunch. Recommended.

‖ Inca Wasi, Av Pachacútec. A very good place to eat.

‖ Inka Machu Picchu, Av Pachacútec 122. Another good place on the avenue. The menu includes vegetarian options.

‖ Inti Killa, Av Imperio de los Incas 47. Good-value *menú* with excellent food and plenty of it. Credit cards accepted.

‖ Machu Picchu, Av Pachacútec. Good food in a friendly atmosphere.

Quillabamba *p208*

Quillabamba's a great place for freshly squeezed fruit juices – head for the 2nd floor in the main market. **Gabbi's Juice Stall**, on the far right-hand side, is especially good.

‖ El Gordito, on Espinar. A good place for chicken.

‖ Pub Don Sebas, Jr Espinar 235 on Plaza de Armas. Good, great sandwiches, run by Karen Molero who is very friendly and always ready for a chat.

‖ Pizzería Venecia, Jr Libertad 461, on the Plaza de Armas, T084-281582. Decent pizza, delivery available.

♥ Bars and clubs

Aguas Calientes *p206, map 207*
Waisicha Pub, C Lloque Yupanqui. For good music and atmosphere.

▲ Activities and tours

Rikuni Tours, at the old station, Av Imperio de los Incas 123, Aguas Calientes, T084-211036, rikuni@chaski.unsaac.edu.pe. Nydia is very helpful. They change money, have a postal service and sell postcards, maps and books (expensive).
Tambo Tours, 20919 Coral Bridge Lane, Suite 225-A, Spring, TX, 77388, USA, T 1-888-2-GO-PERU (246-7378) T001-281 528 9448, www.2GOPERU. com. Long-established adventure and tour specialist with offices in Peru and USA .

Customized trips to the Amazon and archaeological sites of Peru, including Machu Picchu. Daily departures for groups and individuals
Ecotrek Peru, Pongo de Mainique, see p175, run tours in the region.

⊙ Transport

Machu Picchu ruins *p199, map p200*
Bus
From **Aguas Calientes** for Machu Picchu every 30 mins from 0630 to 1300, US$9 return, valid for 48 hrs. Buses run down from the ruins from 1200 to 1730. It is also possible to take a bus down between 0700 and 0900. The ticket office is opposite the bus stop. Tickets can also be bought in advance at **Consetur**, Santa Catalina Ancha, Cusco, which saves queuing when you arrive in Aguas Calientes.

PerúRail trains to Machu Picchu run from San Pedro station in **Cusco**. They pass through Poroy and Ollantaytambo to Aguas Calientes (the official name of this station is Machu Picchu). The station for the tourist trains at Aguas Calientes is on the outskirts of town, 200 m from the **Pueblo Hotel** and 50 m from where buses leave for Machu Picchu ruins. The ticket office is open 0630-1730; there is a guard on the gate. A paved road in poor condition runs from Aguas Calientes to the start of the road up to the ruins.

There are 2 classes of tourist train: Vistadome and Backpacker. From **Cusco** the Vistadome costs US$101.15 return and the Backpacker costs US$65.45 return (a 1-way ticket is available for US$29.75, but only 48 hrs before departure). The **Vistadome** leaves Cusco daily at 0600, stopping at Ollantaytambo at 0805 and Machu Picchu at 0940. It returns from Machu Picchu at 1530, passing Ollantaytambo at 1700, reaching Cusco at 1920. The Backpacker leaves Cusco at 0615, passing Ollantaytambo at 0835 and Machu Picchu at 1010. It returns at 1555, passing Ollantaytambo at 1740, getting to Cusco at 2020.

The **Sacred Valley Railway Vistadome** service runs from **Urubamba** to Machu Picchu and costs US$69 return. It leaves Urubamba at 0600, reaching Machu Picchu at 0820, returning at 1645, reaching Urubamba at 1910. Price includes breakfast on the way out and a soft drink on the way back.

There are further **Vistadomes** and **Backpackers** from **Ollantaytambo** to Machu Picchu, at US$69 and US$51.17 return, respectively. Ilantaytambo **Vistadome** leaves at 1030 and 1455, journey time 1 hr 20 mins, returning from Machu Picchu at 1320 and 1645. The Ollantaytambo **Backpacker** leaves at 0925, arriving at 1100, returning from Machu Picchu at 1700, reaching Ollantaytambo at 1840. Seats can be reserved even if you're not returning the same day. The **Vistadome** tickets include food in the price. These trains have toilets, video, snacks and drinks for sale. Tickets should be bought at Wanchac station in Cusco, Av Pachacútec. **Sacred Valley Railway** office, Av El Sol 803, Cusco, T084-249076, or Casa Estación, Av Ferrocarril s/n, Urubamba, T084-201126/27, www.sacredvalleyrailway.com.

Several Urubamba and Yucay hotels offer free transport to and from the Urubamba station. Tickets can be bought through **PerúRail**'s website, www.perurail.com Services other than those listed above are entirely at the discretion of **PerúRail**. The timetable and prices are subject to change.

PerúRail also has the **Hiram Bingham** service from Cusco to Machu Picchu, a super-luxury train with dining car and bar. It leaves Poroy 0900 with brunch on board, arriving Machu Picchu 1230. It leaves Machu Picchu 1830, cocktails, dinner and live entertainment on board, arriving Poroy at 2200 with bus service back to Cusco hotels. The cost, including all meals, buses and entry to the ruins, US$476.

At the other extreme, there is a cheap way to travel by train to Machu Picchu, but you have to check on this train's existence at the time of travel. **Backpacker** coaches are added to the local train which leaves Ollantaytambo at 1945, arriving Aguas Calientes 2120. It returns from Aguas at

0545, arriving Ollantaytambo at 0740. Tickets cost US$11.90 one way (possibly rising to US$12.50 in 2004), they can only be bought 1-2 days before departure and they sell out fast. Tourists are not allowed to travel in the carriages for local people. If you use this service you have to stay 2 nights in Aguas Calientes if you want to see Machu Picchu. Timetables are not published for this train and the inclusion of **Backpacker** coaches is not guaranteed.

Quillabamba *p208*

Most buses leave **Cusco** for Quilla- bamba from the Terminal Terrestre de Santiago between 1800 and 2000. Journey time is about 8 hrs, although expect 14 hrs or more in the rainy season, because of land- slides. 4 bus companies on this route are: **Valle de los Incas**, T084-244787, **Ben Hur**, T084-229193, **Ampay**, T084-245734, and **Selva Sur**, T084-247975. **Selva Sur** has 2 buses on the route, one of which is quite comfortable, with good reclining seats, perhaps the best bus for the journey. Buy tickets in advance, US$3-4. The bus station in Quillabamba is on Av 28 de Julio and buses depart for Cusco daily, with buses leaving in the morning around 0700 and evening. There are extra services at weekends.

Pongo de Mainique and beyond *p209*
Boat

For boats beyond Ivochote, you may have to wait a few days for a boat downstream, but try to get as far as Bajo Pongo or **Timpia**, 4 hrs, US$10. It's a furthr 4 hrs, US$10 to **Camisea**. After **Sepahua** boats are larger, boats more frequent and distances greater. To **Atalaya** you can take an express, 10 hrs, US$15, or a delivery boat, up to 2 days. From here boats go to **Pucallpa**, but you may have to wait a week, 36 hrs, US$15. They stop at all main towns, food is usually available, but take your own snacks, fruit and drinks. Hammocks can be bought in

Sepahua or Atalaya. There are two flights a week from Atalaya to Pucallpa.

Bus

From **Quillabamba** buses take 10 hrs to reach **Ivochote** and cost around US$4. Ask locals for their opinions on the best companies for this route. Buses (combis) leave Quillabamba for **Huancacalle** daily from Jr San Martín, near Plaza Grau, at 0900 and 1200, US$2.50. The journey takes 4-7 hrs. On Fri they go all the way to Vilcabamba.

Espíritu Pampa *p210*

From **Chanquiri**, at the end of the Espíritu Pampa trail, trucks and buses leave for **Kiteni** and **Quillabamba** on Wed and Sun, 8-12 hrs, US$2.50.

● Directory

Aguas Calientes *p206, map p207*
Banks There are no banks in Aguas Calientes. Those businesses that change money will not do so at rates as favourable as you will find in Cusco. **Qosqo Service**, corner of Av Pachacútec and Mayta Cápac, has *cambio*, postal service and guiding service. **Internet** Yanantin Masintin, Av Imperio de los Incas 119, US$3 per hr, is part of the Rikuni group, as is **Tea House**, which is opposite. Both serve coffees, teas, snacks, etc. The town has electricity 24 hrs.
Post Serpost (post office), just off the plaza, between the Centro Cultural Machu Picchu and Galería de Arte Tunupa, and on the railway line. **Telephone** Oficina on C Collasuyo, and there are plenty of phone booths around town. There are lots of places to choose from for exchange, shop around.

Quillabamba *p208*
Banks BCP, Jr Libertad, is good for TCs. Banco Continental, Av F Bolognesi, accepts Visa and Cirrus. **Internet** Ciber Master, Jr Espinar, on the plaza.

East of Cusco

Along or near the main road from Cusco to Lake Titicaca and Peru's major southern city, Arequipa, are a number of archaeological sites, some fascinating colonial churches, beautiful lakes and the majestic Ausangate massif, where you can do some serious

high-altitude trekking. Off this route is also the gateway to Peru's southeastern jungle in the Department of Madre de Dios. ▸▸ *For Sleeing, Eating and other listings, see pages 220-222.*

Ins and outs

A paved road runs southeast from Cusco to Sicuani, at the southeastern edge of the Department of Cusco. It continues to Puno, on the shores of Lake Titicaca, then on to the border with Bolivia. Combis run every 15-20 minutes between Cusco and Sicuani, and more frequently to the villages and towns in between.

To Huambutío and Paucartambo

Tipón ruins, between Saylla and Oropesa, are extensive and include baths, terraces, irrigation systems and a temple complex, accessible from a path leading from just above the last terrace, all in a fine setting. From Tipón village it's an hour's climb to the ruins; or take a taxi. At the Tipón ruins, if you head to the left at the back, there is a trail round to where you will see more small ruins. From there you will find an amazing Inca road with a deep irrigation channel, which can be followed to Cerro Pachatusan. Oropesa is known as the national capital of bread - try the delicious circular loaves.

At **Huambutío**, north of Huacarpay, the road divides: northwest to Pisac (see page 186) and north to Paucartambo, on the eastern slope of the Andes. The road from Huambutío northwest to Pisac (about 20 km) is unpaved and poor. This is an access road for the first river-rafting section on the Río Urubamba, which also connects with another rafting route from Piñipampa. In the rainy season, and for less experienced rafters, the Huambutío (Piñipampa) to Pisac river section is safer to run. The rapids are Class II to III. The rafting trip is 30-35 km long with spectacular views of the Urubamba valley that are not seen in a conventional valley tour. This part of the river offers views of the **Sanctuary of El Señor de Huanca**, an image painted on a rock around which the sanctuary (church) has been built. The rock and surroundings date back to pre-Inca times as a *huaca*, or sacred place. The month of pilgrimage to El Señor de Huanca is September, with the 14th being the main day.

Paucartambo

This once remote town, 80 km east of Cusco, is on the road to Pilcopata, Atalaya and Shintuya. This is now the overland route used by tour companies from Cusco into Manu National Park. Consequently, it has become a popular tourist destination. It has a famous 17th-century stone bridge, built on the orders of King Carlos III of Spain. From Paucartambo, in the dry season, you can go 44 km to **Tres Cruces**, along the Pilcopata road, turning left after 25 km. Tres Cruces gives a wonderful view of the sunrise in June and July: peculiar climactic conditions make it appear as if three suns are rising. Tour operators in Cusco, see page 173, can arrange transport and lodging.

Piquillacta Archaeological Park

ⓘ *0700-1730, entry by BTU tourist ticket, see page 147. Buses to Urcos from Av Huáscar in Cusco drop you at the entrance on the north side, though this is not the official entry.*

The Piquillacta Archaeological Park is 30 km southeast of Cusco, with an area of 3,421 ha. Its nucleus is the remains of a lake, the Laguna de Huacarpay, around it are many pre-Columbian archaeological remains, the principal of which are Piquillacta and Rumicolca. The lake is a fvourite birdwatching destintion and it's good to hike or cycle round it. The Huari ruins of Piquillacta (which translates as the City of Fleas) are large, with some reconstruction in progress. It was an administrative centre at the southern end of the Huari Empire. The whole site is surrounded by a wall, there are many enclosed compounds with buildings of over one storey and it appears that the walls

 Roughly translated from Quechua, Apurímac means 'the river that speaks'. The roaring rapids along its course give ample justification for this title.

were plastered and finished with a layer of lime. The huge gateway of **Rumicolca** is on the right of the main road to Sicuani, shortly after the turn-off to Piquillacta. You can walk around it for free. This was a Huari aqueduct, built across this narrow stretch of the valley, which the Incas clad in fine stonework to create this gateway. If you look at the top you can see the original walls, four tiers high.

Andahuaylillas

Continuing southeast towards Urcos you reach Andahuaylillas, 32 km from Cusco, with a fascinating 17th-century church. This is a simple structure, but it has been referred to as the Andean Sistine Chapel because of its beautiful frescoes, and internal architecture. Go in, wait for your eyes to adjust to the darkness, to see on the right of the splendid door the path to heaven, which is narrow and thorny, and on the left the way to hell, which is wide and littered with flowers. Above is the high choir, built in local wood, where there are two organs. The carved ceiling is painted, too. The main altar is gilded in 24-carat gold leaf and has symbols from both the Quechua and Christian religions. Ask for Sr Eulogio; he is a good guide, but speaks Spanish only.

Huaro and Urcos

At the quiet village of Huaro, the church on the ugly plaza is stunning inside. The walls are plastered with frescoes used to evangelize the illiterate. Grinning skeletons compete with dragons and devils ushering the living into the afterlife and punishing them thereafter. They are now mostly in a sad state of repair.

Beyond Huaro is **Urcos**. There are lodgings here, but they're basic to say the least. A spectacular road from Urcos crosses the Eastern Cordillera to Puerto Maldonado in the jungle (see page 549). Some 47 km after passing the snow-line Hualla-Hualla pass, at 4,820 m, the super-hot thermal baths of **Marcapata** ① *US$0.10*, 173 km from Urcos, provide a relaxing break. Some 82 km from Urcos, on the road to Puerto Maldonado, at the base of **Nevado Ausangate** (6,384 m), is the town of **Ocongate**, which has two hotels on the Plaza de Armas.

Ausangate and Tinqui → *Colour map 2, B4.*

Beyond Ocongate is Tinqui, the starting point for hikes around Ausangate (6,372 m), the highest mountain in southeastern Peru, in the Cordillera Vilcanota. On the flanks of the Nevado Ausangate is **Q'Olloriti**, where a church has been built close to the snout of a glacier. This place has become a place of pilgrimage (see page 170).

The hike around the mountain of Ausangate takes five to six days. It is spectacular, but quite hard, with three passes over 5,000 m, so you need to be acclimatized. Alternatively, a shorter and easier return trek can be made from Ausangate down the beautiful **Pitumarca Valley** to the town of the same name and the Sacred Valley. It is recommended to take a guide or *arriero*. *Arrieros* and muleteers have formed a union and as such they are much more organized than in recent years. An *arriero* charges US$7 per day, US$6 per day for each mule, more for a saddle horse. A chief *arriero* takes along one to two assistants (US$5 per day per assistant). *Arrieros* expect foodstuffs (noodles, sugar, rice, coca leaves), plus cigarettes, alcohol, and kerosene to be provided for a well-planned expedition. *Arrieros* and mules can be hired in Tinqui. A recommended *arriero* is Enrique Mandura, who also rents out equipment. **South American Explorers** (who can supply all the latest advice) recommend Theo. Make sure you sign a contract with full details. Buy all food supplies in Cusco. Maps are available at the **Instituto Geográfico Militar** in Lima or **South American Explorers**. Some tour companies in Cusco have details about the hike (see page 173).

Acomayo and the Inca bridge

Between Cusipata and **Checacupe** a road branches west up what soon becomes a dirt road. At the first fork, just before a beautiful mountain lake, Lago Pomancanchi, turn right to travel past a small community and on to Acomayo, a pretty village which has a chapel with mural paintings of the 14 Incas. From Acomayo, you can walk to the canyons of the upper Apurímac, vast beyond imagination, and to Inca ruins in astonishing locations.

If you turn left at Lago Pomancanchi the road passes three more beautiful lakes. Stop awhile by the fourth. Set against the pale green grass banks, serene waters reflect the red soil of the hills behind. The only sound is the occasional splash and hoot of a white-beaked Andean coot. The air is thin, clear and crisp.

The road continues to Yanaoca, where you'll find basic accommodation and restaurants. From here it is possible to continue on to Sicuani, but a side trip to **Qeswachaka** and the grass Inca bridge 30 km away is well worth the effort. Turn right just before you leave the village to join a road which, at times, is very rough. The way is marked with kilometre signs and you must turn right just after Km 22 where another road begins, marked with a Km 0. You will find steps down to the bridge shortly before Km 31, two bends from the bright orange road bridge. The footbridge has been rebuilt every year for the past 400 years during a three-day festival. This starts on June 10 and is celebrated by the three communities who use the bridge. It is built entirely of *pajabrava* grass, woven and spliced to make six sturdy cables which are strung across the 15-m chasm. The work lasts five months, after which the fibres deteriorate and you should not attempt to cross.

Raqchi → *Colour map 2, B4.*

ⓘ *Entrance to the site is US$1.75. There is a basic shop at the site.*

About 120 km southeast of Cusco, in a fertile tributary valley of the Vilcanota, is the colonial village of **San Pedro de Cacha**, which stands within one of the most important archaeological sites in Peru, Raqchi. A few hundred metres beyond the village are the principal remains, the once great **Temple of Viracocha**, the pan-Andean creator of all living creatures. This is one of the only remaining examples of a two-storey building of Inca architecture. It was 90 m long and 15 m high and was probably the largest roofed building ever built by the Incas. Above walls of finely dressed masonry 3-4 m high rise the remains of another 5-6 m high wall of adobe brickwork of

❧ *The school next door greatly appreciates donations of books and materials.*

which only isolated sections remain. Similarly, of the 22 outer columns, which supported great sloping roofs, just one or two remain complete, the others being in various states of preservation. There are numerous other constructions, including *acllahuasi* (houses of chosen women), granaries, reservoirs, baths and fountains. The burial site includes round *chullpa* tombs of the sort found around Lake Titicaca. Much of it was damaged and demolished in search of treasure during or after the Spanish conquest.

Sicuani → *Phone code: 084. Colour map 2, B4. Altitude: 3,690 m.*

Sicuani is an important agricultural centre and an excellent place for items of llama and alpaca wool and skins. They are sold at the railway station and at the excellent Sunday morning market. Around the plaza are several shops selling local hats.

⬤ Sleeping

Andahuaylillas *p219*

E La Casa del Sol, close to the central plaza on Garcilaso. Relaxing, clean and bright *hostal*. Well-decorated rooms set around a courtyard, this is excellent value. Owned by Dr Gladys Oblitas, the *hostal* funds her project to provide medical services to poor

campesinos. While staying you can take a course or take part in workshops on natural and alternative medicine.

Ausangate and Tinqui *p219*

G Ausangate, Tinqui, very basic but warm, friendly atmosphere. Sr Crispin (or Cayetano),

the owner, is knowledgeable and can arrange guides, mules, etc. He and his brothers can be contacted in Cusco on F084-227768. All have been recommended as reliable sources of trekking and climbing information, for arranging trips and for being very safety conscious.
G Hostal Tinqui Guide, on the right-hand side as you enter the village, friendly, meals available, owner arranges guides and horses.

Acomayo and the Inca bridge *p219*
There are many places to camp wild by the lakes. Take warm clothing for night time and plenty of water. At **Qeswachaca** there's good camping downstream, but take water.

Sicuani *p220*
E Hotel Obada, Jr Tacna 104, T084-351214. At the new' end of the bridge, close to the centre of town. Has seen better days. There are large, clean rooms with hot showers.
E Royal Inti, Av Centenario 116, T084-352730, on the west side of the old pedestrian bridge across the river, is modern, clean and friendly.
E Samariy, Av Centenario 138 (next to Royal Inti), T084-352518. Offers good value rooms with bathrooms.
G per person **José's Hostal**, Av Arequipa 143, T084-351254. Rooms with bath, clean and good.

🍴 Eating

Sicuani *p220*
† El Fogón, C Zevallos, the main drag down from the plaza, smart, painted pink, on the left heading down. Serves up good chicken and chips for US$1.70.
† Mijuna Wasi, Jr Tacna 146 . Closed Sun. One of several *picanterías* which prepares typical dishes such as *adobo* served with huge glasses of *chicha* in a delapidated but atmospheric courtyard. Recommended.
† Pizzería Bon Vino, 2 de Mayo 129, 2nd floor, off the east side of the plaza, is good for an Italian meal.

🍸 Bars and clubs

Sicuani *p220*
Piano Bar, just off the first block of 2 de Mayo, is the best nightspot in town.

⚙ Festivals and events

Paucartambo *p218*
On **15-17 Jul**, the Fiesta of the Virgen del Carmen is a major attraction and well worth seeing. Masked dancers enact rituals and folk tales in the streets.

Acomayo and the Inca bridge *p219*
Jun 10 a 3-day festival is celebrated for the rebuilding of the grass Inca footbridge at **Qeswachaka**.

Raqchi *p220*
The **Wiracocha** festivities in San Pedro and neighbouring San Pablo start on **24 Jun**. Dancers come to Raqchi from all over Peru and through music and dance they illustrate everything from the ploughing of fields to bull fights. This leads into the feast of **San Pedro and San Pablo** on **29 Jun**.

🚌 Transport

Paucartambo *p218*
Private car hire for a round trip from Cusco on 15-17 Jul costs US$30. Tour operators in Cusco can arrange this. A minibus leaves for Paucartambo from Av Huáscar in Cusco, every other day, US$4.50, 3-4 hrs; alternate days Paucartambo-Cusco. Trucks and a private bus leave from the Coliseo, behind Hospital Segura in Cusco; 5 hrs, US$2.50.

Andahuaylillas *p219*
To Andahuaylillas take a taxi, or the **Oropesa** bus from Av Huáscar in Cusco, via Tipón, Piquillacta and Rumicolca.

Huaro and Urcos *p219*
Transportes Vilcanota depart from the terminal on Av de la Cultura, Cusco, at the Paradero Hospital Regional (on a side street), and run to **San Jerónimo**, **Saylla**, **Huasao**, **Tipón, Oropesa, Piquillacta/ Huacarpay, Andahuaylillas** and on to **Urcos**. These buses run from 0500 to 2100, fare US$ 0.72 to Urcos.

Ausangate and Tinqui *p219*
Buses leave for **Tinqui** from Cusco Mon-Sat at 1000 (6-7 hrs, US$3.50) from C Tomasatito Condemayta, near the Coliseo Cerrado.

Acomayo and the Inca bridge *p219*
To get to **Acomayo**, take a Cusco-Sicuani bus or truck (US$1, 1½ hrs), then a truck or bus to Acomayo (3 hrs, same price). Alternatively, get off at Checacupe and take a truck on to Acomayo. To visit the 4 beautiful mountain lakes and Inca bridge, it would be worth- while renting a 4WD for 2 days. Giving locals a lift is both fun and helpful – they will make sure you take the right road. Alternatively, hire a vehicle with a driver. It is just as feasible by combi, if you have more time. The bridge can also be reached from **Combapata** on the main Cusco-Sicuani road. Combis and *colectivos* leave for the 30-km trip when full from the plaza for **Yanaoca** (US$0.50). Then hitchhike to **Quehue** (no accommodation), a 1½-hr walk from Qeswachaka, or to **Qeswachaka** itself, on the road to Livitaca. Be prepared for long waits on this road. On Wed and Sat there are direct buses to **Livitaca** from Cusco with the **Warari** and **Olivares** companies

which pass the site, returning on Mon and Thu.

Raqchi *p220*
There are frequent buses and trucks to and from Cusco, or you can take the train.

Sicuani *p220*
Combis run every 15-20 mins between Cusco and Sicuani (137 km, US$1.25). It is 250 km to **Puno**. 38 km beyond the town is La Raya pass (4,321 m), the highest on this route, which marks the divide between Cusco Department and the altiplano which stretches to Lake Titicaca. It is impossible to buy unleaded petrol in this town.

⊙ Directory

Sicuani *p220*
Banks Banco de la Nación has a branch on the plaza as does BCP, but the one cash machine takes only local cards.

West of Cusco

West of Cusco is the road to Abancay (195 km from Cusco), where the principal overland route to Lima, via Nasca heads west nd another road continues in the highlands to Ayacucho. There are enough Inca sites on or near this road in the Department of Cusco to remind us that the empire's influence spread to all four cardinal points. Add to this some magnificent scenery, especially in the canyon of the Río Apurímac, and you have the makings of some fascinating excursions away from the centre. One, to the ruins of Choquequirao, is a tough but rewarding trip: getting there requires an expedition of four days or more. ▸▸ For Sleeping, Eating and other listings, see page 224.

Anta to Curahuasi → *Colour map 2, grid B2.*
The Cusco-Machu Picchu train follows the road west from the city through the Anta canyon for 10 km, and then, at a sharp angle, the Urubamba Canyon, and descends along the river valley, flanked by high cliffs and peaks. In the town of **Anta**, felt trilby hats are on sale.

Some 76 km from Cusco, beyond Anta on the Abancay road, and 2 km before Limatambo, are the ruins of **Tarahuasi**. A few hundred metres from the road there is a very well-preserved Inca temple platform, with 28 tall niches, and a long stretch of fine polygonal masonry. The ruins are impressive, enhanced by the orange lichen which give the walls a beautiful honey colour. Near here the *conquistadores* on their push towards the Inca capital of Cusco suffered what could have been a major setback. Were it not for the arrival of Spanish reinforcements, an Inca army at Vilcaconga almost routed the expeditionary army.

One hundred kilometres from Cusco along the Abancay road is the exciting descent into the **Apurímac Canyon**, near the former Inca suspension bridge that inspired Thornton Wilder's *The Bridge of San Luis Rey* (see Books page 612). The bridge itself was made of rope and was where the royal Inca road crossed the river.

When the *conquistadores* reached this point on the march to Cusco, they found the bridge destroyed. But luck was again on their side since, it being the dry season, the normally fierce Apurímac was low enough for the men and horses to ford. In colonial times the bridge was rebuilt several times, but it no longer exists.

Choquequirao → *Colour map 2, grid B2.*

Choquequirao is another 'lost city of the Incas', built on a ridge spur almost 1,600 m above the Apurímac. Its Inca name is unknown, but research has shown that it was built during the reign of Inca Pachacútec. Although only 30 per cent has been uncovered, it is believed to be a larger site than Machu Picchu, but with fewer buildings. The stonework is different from the classic Inca construction and masonry, simply because the preferred granite and andesite are not found in this region. A number of high-profile explorers and archaeologists, including Hiram Bingham, researched the site, but its importance has only recently been recognized. And now tourists are venturing in there, too. With new regulations being applied to cut congestion on the Inca Trail, Choquequirao is destined to replace the traditional hike as the serious trekker's alternative.

The main features of Choquequirao include the **Lower Plaza**, considered by most experts to be the focal point of the city. Three of the main buildings were two-storey structures. The **Upper Plaza**, reached by a huge set of steps or terraces, has what are possibly ritual baths. A beautiful set of slightly curved agricultural terraces run for over 300 m east-northeast of the Lower Plaza. The **Usnu** is a levelled hilltop platform, ringed with stones and giving awesome 360-degree views. Perhaps it was a ceremonial site, or was used for solar and astronomical observations. The Ridge Group, still shrouded in vegetation, is large collection of buildings some 50-100 m below the Usnu. Unrestored, with some significant hall-like structures, this whole area makes for great exploring. The Outlier Building, isolated and surrounded on three sides by sheer drops of over 1½ km into the Apurímac Canyon, possesses some of the finest stonework within Choquequirao. The Outlier's separation from other structures must also be significant, but exactly why, like so many other questions regarding the Incas and their society, remains a mystery. **Capuliyoc**, nearly 500 m below the Lower Plaza, is a great set of agricultural terraces, visible on the approach from the far side of the valley. These terraces enabled the Incas to cultivate plants from a significantly warmer climate in close geographical proximity to their ridge-top home.

There are three ways to reach Choquequirao. None is a gentle stroll. The shortest way is from **Cachora**, a village in a magnificent location on the south side of the Apurímac, reached by a side road from the Cusco-Abancay highway, near Saywite (see page 498, in Central Highlands). It is four hours by bus from Cusco to the turn-off, then a two-hour descent from the road to Cachora (from 3,695 m to 2,875 m). Buses run from Abancay to Cachora. Accommodation, guides (Celestino Peña is the official guide) and mules are available in Cachora.

From Cachora take the road heading down, out of the village, through lush cultivated countryside and meadows. There are many trails close to the village; if uncertain of the trail, ask. After 15 minutes' a sign for Choquequirao points to a left-hand path, initially following the course of a small stream. Follow the trail and cross a footbridge to the other side of a large stream. From here the trail becomes more obvious, with few trails diverging from the main route. After 9 km, 2-2½ hours from the start of the trek, is the wonderful mirador (viewpoint) of **Capuliyoc**, at 2,800 m, with fantastic vistas of the Apurímac Canyon and the snowy Vilcabamba range across the river (this also makes a gret day-hike from Cachora). With a pair of binoculars it's just possible to recognize Choquequirao, etched into the forested hills to the west. Condors are sometimes seen in this area. Beyond Capuliyoc the trail begins to descend towards the river. Further down the valley lies **Cocamasana**, a rest spot with a rough covered roof. From this point the river is clearly visible. At

Km 16 is **Chiquisca** (1,930 m), a lovely wooded spot; if you don't want to continue any further on the first day, this is a good campsite, but ask permission of the local family. Another one-hour descent leads to the suspension bridge crossing the Río Apurímac. On the other side the path ascends very steeply for 1½ hours. **Santa Rosa**, a good area for camping, again near the property of a local family, is just after the Km 21 sign. Clean water is available. If this area is occupied, another larger site is available 10 minutes further up the hill. Ask residents for directions. From Santa Rosa continue uphill on a steep zigzag for two hours to the mirador of Marampata, from where the trail flattens out towards Choquequirao. After 1½ hours on this flatter trail you enter some beautiful stretches of cloudforest, before a final short climb and arrival at Choquequirao itself. If coming from Santa Rosa you should have the afternoon free to explore the complex, but you could easily allow an extra day here. To return to Cachora, simply retrace the route, possibly camping at Chiquisca, which would nicely break the two-day return trek.

The second and third routes take a minimum of eight days and require thorough preparation. Both cross the watershed of the Cordillera Vilcabamba between the Urubamba and Apurímac rivers. The second hike uses the same route from Cachora as the first trek, then continues from Choquequirao to the Yanama river valley before continuing to Santa Teresa or Machu Picchu itself. The third route splits from the second in the Yanama Valley and goes to Huancacalle (see page 210), via the pass of Choquetacarpo, 4,600 m high. From Huancacalle it's possible to continue on to Espíritu Pampa on the edge of the rainforest. Either route can be undertaken in reverse. Both pass the mines of La Victoria and both involve an incredible number of strenuous ascents and descents. En route you are rewarded with fabulous views of the Sacsarayoc massif (also called Pumasillo), Salkantay, other snow peaks, and the deep canyons of the Río Blanco and the Apurímac. You will also see condors and meet very friendly people, but the highlight is Choquequirao itself.

ⓩ Sleeping

Anta to Curahuasi p222
G Hostal Central, Jirón Jaquijahuanca 714, Anta, a basic, friendly, place with motorbike parking; beware of water shortages.
G Hostal Rivera, near the river, at Limatambo, an old stone house built round a courtyard, clean, quiet and full of character.
G Hostal San Cristóbal, Curahuasi, clean, nice decor, pleasant courtyard, shared bath, cold shower (new bathroom block being built).
Camping in Curahuasi is possible on the football pitch, but ask the police for permission.

Choquequirao p223
G per person **La Casona de Ocampo**, San Martín 122, Cachora, T084-237514, lacasonadeocampo@yahoo.es. With hoth sjower all day, free camping, owner Carlos Robles is very friendly and knowledgeable,

rents camping equipment, organizes treks to Choquequirao and beyond.

ⓩ Eating

Anta to Curahuasi p222
⑨ **Tres de Mayo**, Anta, is very good and popular, with top service.
⑨ **Restaurant**, Limatambo, hidden from the road by trees, is a good option.
⑨ **La Amistad**, Curahuasi, is the best restaurant in town, is popular, with good food and moderate prices, but has poor service.

ⓩ Transport

Choquequirao p223
From Cachora to **Abancay**, buses at 0630 and 1100, 2 hrs, US$1.50; also *colectivo* taxis.

Lake Titicaca

Footprint features

Introduction

Straddling Peru's southern border with landlocked Bolivia are the deep, sapphire-blue waters of mystical Lake Titicaca, everyone's favourite school geography statistic. This gigantic inland sea covers up to 8,500 square km and is the highest navigable lake in the world, at 3,856 m above sea level. Its shores and islands are home to the Aymara and Quechua, who are among Peru's oldest peoples, predating the Incas by a 1,000 years. Here you can wander through old traditional villages where Spanish is a second language and where ancient myths and beliefs still hold true.

The main town on the lake is Puno, where chilled travellers gather to stock up on warm woollies to keep the cold at bay. The high-altitude town is the departure point for the islands of Taquile and Amanataní, as well as the floating reed islands of Los Uros. But while the latter may not be to everyone's taste, having acquired a reputation for tourism overkill, a trip to Taquile and Amantaní gains a real insight into traditional Andean life, especially during one of the the festivals. Taquile is also a good place to find those essential souvenirs.

Apart from the obvious attraction of the lake's islands, Puno is also well placed to visit the remarkable funeral towers of Sillustani. Even if you're feeling a bit ruined-out by this stage in your Peruvian odyssey, Sillustani is well worth the effort. There's also the beautiful train ride from Puno to Cusco, and the opportunity to reach the parts of Peru that other travellers rarely get to, by exploring the remote eastern shore of the lake, an area that is only just beginning to welcome curious visitors.

★ Don't miss...

1 **The Yavari** This museum ship, moored near one of Puno's upmarket hotels, is a reminder of how shipping once was on Titicaca, page 229.

2 **Sillustani** Wonder at the unique architectural quality of the funerary towers, emphasized all the more by the barrenness of the surroundings, page 230.

3 **Llachón** Community tourism has made a great start at this charming village on a peninsula, which still gives access to some of the lake's better-known attractions, page 231.

4 **Fiesta de la Virgen de la Candelaria** Of the umpteen festivals around the lake, this is deservedly the most famous and one of the best ways to immerse yourself in the extensive folklore of the region, page 239.

5 **Suasi** Watch the sun set from the summit of this island hideaway, whose only building is a hotel, page 246.

6 **Juli and Pomata** These two towns on the eastern shore have some of the most beautiful churches of the region. They make a good day out from Puno, page 248.

Puno and the islands → Colour map 6, grid B2.

On the northwest shore of Lake Titicaca, at 3,855 m, Puno is a major folklore centre and a great place to buy handicrafts, particularly those amazingly tactile alpaca jumpers and hats. It also boasts a rich tradition of music and dance and is a good place to enjoy a number of Andean festivals, some wild, some solemn. Puno is capital of its Department and while it isn't the most attractive of cities, it has a certain vitality, helped by the fact there is a large student population.» For Sleeping, Eating and other listings, see pages 235-242.

Ins and outs

Getting there The railway station for trains from Cusco is quite central and within walking distance of the centre, but if you've got heavy bags, it's a good idea to hire a three-wheel cycle cart, trici-taxi, which costs about US$0.35 per km per person. The new bus station and the depots for local buses are further away, southeast of the centre, but trici-taxis and conventional taxis serve this area.

Getting around The centre of town is easy to walk around, but as said above, a trici-taxi can make life a lot easier, even if this is not your first stop at high altitude. *Colectivos* (buses) in town charge US$0.20.

Best time to visit Being so high up, Puno gets bitterly cold at night, especially in June-August, when the temperature at night can plummet to -25°C. Days are bright

Puno

Sleeping 🛏
Albergue Juvenil
  Virgen de
  Copacabana **1** *B1*
Balsa Inn **2** *C2*
Casa Andina Plaza **5** *B2*
Casa Andina Tikarani **27** *B2*
Colón Inn **3** *Puno centre*
Eco Inn **29** *A4*
El Buho **4** *Puno centre*
Ferrocarril **16** *B3*
Hospedaje Residencial
  Margarita **6** *B2*

Hostal Arequipa **7** *B2*
Hostal Europa **8** *Puno centre*
Hostal Hacienda **9**
  Puno centre
Hostal Italia **10** *B2*
Hostal Los Pinos **11** *B2*
Hostal Monterrey **12**
  Puno centre
Hostal Nesther **13**
  Puno centre
Hostal Q'oñiwasi &
  Hostal Ilampu **14** *B3*

Hostal Rubi
  'Los Portales' **15** *C3*
Libertador Isla
  Esteves **30** *A4*
Los Uros & Hostal
  Imperial **19** *B3*
Manco Cápac Inn **20**
  Puno centre
Ollanta Inn **17** *B3*
Plaza Mayor **21** *Puno centre*
Posada Don Giorgio **22** *B2*
Pukara **23** *Puno centre*
Qelqatani **18** *Puno centre*

San Carlos **24** *Puno centre*
Santa Rosa **25** *B3*
Sillustani **26** *Puno centre*
Sonesta Posada
  del Inca **31** *A4*
Tambo Real **32** *B2*
Vylena **28** *C2*

Eating 🍴
Apu Salkantay, Lago
  de Flores &
  Pub Ekeko's **1** *Puno centre*

and the midday sun is hot, but you can never be quite sure what weather is going to come off the lake. The first two weeks in February, when the Fiesta de la Candelaria takes place, and 4-5 November, the pageant of the emergence of the founding Incas, are good times to visit, but crowded, too.

Tourist information i perú ① *Lima y Deústua, T051-365088, near Plaza de Armas, Mon-Sun 0830-1930.* They are friendly and helpful with general information and they provide all maps and information free. www.punored.com is useful.

Puno

Puno sits on a bay at the northwest end of the lake. The Bahía de Puno is only 3 m deep and a channel is dredged to the exit into the open water of Titicaca. The port and lakeside quarters are several blocks from the centre, whose focus is the Plaza de Armas. The impressive baroque exterior of the **Cathedral** ① *0800-1200, 1500-1700,* completed in 1657, belies an austere interior. Just across the street from the Cathedral is the famous **Balcony of the Conde de Lemos**, on the corner of Deústua and Conde de Lemos, where Peru's Viceroy stayed. Also here is the **Museo Municipal Carlos Dreyer** ① *Conde de Lemos 289, Mon-Fri 0730-1330, US$1.* The museum combines municipal collections with the private collection of pre-Columbian artefacts bequeathed to the city by their owner, Sr Carlos Dreyer. In the same block is the **Casa del Corregidor** ① *Deústua 576, T051-351921, www.casadelcorregidor.com.pe, open weekdays 1000-2200, closed Mon and for lunch on Sat.* One of Puno's oldest buildings has been converted into Puno's most important cultural centre, check website for exhibitons. It also has a great café (see cafés).

A short walk up Independencia leads to the **Arco Deústua**, a monument honouring those killed in the battles of Junín and Ayacucho. Nearby, is a mirador giving fine views over the town, the port and the lake beyond. The walk from Jr Cornejo following the Stations of the Cross up a nearby hill, with fine views of Lake Titicaca, has been recommended, but be careful and don't go alone. The same applies to any of the hills around Puno: Huajsapata is best known for music and folklore gatherings; Azoguine and Cancharani are higher, with good views and sacred associations. To get to Azoguine you have to go through Barrio Las Cruces, which is very dangerous.

On the way from the centre to the port is the **Museo Naval** ① *Av el Puerto y Av Sol, Mon-Fri 0900-1700, Sat-Sun 0900-1300.* Here you can find a small exhibit on navigating on Lake Titicaca.

The **Yavari** ① *0800-1700, then illuminated till 2230 for 'Happy Hour' managed by hotel staff, entry free in daytime, but donations welcome,* is the

Puno centre

Lake Titicaca Puno & the islands

Cafetería Mercedes **3** *Puno centre*
Casa del Corregidor **4** *C2*
Chifa Fon Seng **5** *Puno centre*
Don Piero **6** *Puno centre*
El Dorado **7** *Puno centre*
El Milagro **8** *Puno centre*
Fontana **9** *Puno centre*
Govinda **13** *Puno centre*
IncAbar **10** *Puno centre*
Keros **11** *Puno centre*
La Cayma **15** *Puno centre*
La Plaza **12** *C2*
Pizzería El Buho **14** *Puno centre*
Remembranzas **2** *Puno centre*
Ricos Pan **16** *Puno centre*
Vida Natural **17** *Puno centre*

Bars & clubs ◐
The Rocks **20** *B3*

oldest ship on Lake Titicaca. It was restored in the port of Puno and turned into a museum, before being moved to its present location in 2002. The iron-hulled ship, now painted in her original livery of black, white and red, was built in England in 1862 and, together with her twin, the Yapura (now the Peruvian Navy's Hospital ship and called the BAP Puno), was shipped in kit form to Arica. From Arica, the two ships went by rail to Tacna from where the 2,766 pieces were carried by mule to Lake Titicaca. The journey took six years. The Yavari was eventually launched on Christmas Day 1870 and on 14 June 1871 sailed on her maiden voyage. From after the War of the Pacific until the nationalization of the Railways and Lake Fleet in 1975, the Yavari was operated as a passenger/cargo vessel by the London-based Peruvian Corporation. The ship was bought in 1987 and is being restored by an Anglo-Peruvian Association. Visitors are very welcome on board the Yavari and will be shown over the ship and its exhibition of archival documentation and memorabilia on the Lake Fleet by the Captain, Carlos Saavedra, or a volunteer. The Yavari is berthed near the entrance to the **Sonesta Posada del Inca Hotel** (see below). You have to go through the hotel to get to the ship. To get there you can go by taxi, bus, or trici-taxi, but the most charming way is by boat from the port, about US$2 return, including wait. **Project addresses** ① *61 Mexfield Rd, London, SW15 2RG, England, T44-20 8874 0583, info@yavari.org; in Lima: Giselle Guldentops, T01-9998 5071, yavari.gulden@dwp. net; in Puno: Asociación Yavari, c/o Capitán Carlos Saavedra, T051-369329, carlosalberto@yavari.org*. For general information, volunteering, donations, etc, visit www.yavari.org.

In the harbour, moored at the jetty near which boats to the islands collect, is Hull (UK) – built **MS Ollanta**, which sailed the lake from 1926 to the 1970s. PerúRail has restored the vessel with a view eventually to starting cruises.

Around Puno

Sillustani → *Colour map 6, grid B2.*

① *US$2.25. Take an organized tour, which lasts about 3 to 4 hrs and leaves at 1430, US$6.30. Tours usually stop at a Colla house on the way to see local products, alpacas and guinea pigs. Alternatively, take a Juliaca bus to the Sillustani turnoff (US$0.35); from here a 15-km paved road runs across the altiplano to the ruins. Moto-taxis and some combis run to Atuncolla (4 km away with a lovely colonial church), US$0.40, or US$0.85 to Sillustani (out of season you may have to walk the 4 km from Atuncolla). Go early to avoid tour groups at the site. A taxi from Puno costs about US$12, including wait. Camping possible outside the museum (tip the guardian).*

A highly recommended trip is to the chullpas (pre-Columbian funeral towers) of Sillustani in a beautiful setting on a peninsula in **Lago Umayo** (3,890 m), 32 km from Puno on an excellent road. According to expert John Hemming, these are burial towers of the Aymara-speaking Colla tribe and most of them date from the period of Inca occupation in the 15th century. As Hemming also states: "The engineering involved in their construction is more complex than anything the Incas built – it is defeating archaeologists' attempts to rebuild the tallest 'lizard' chullpa. Two are unfinished: one with a ramp still in place to raise blocks; the other with cut stones ready to go onto a very ambitious corbelled false dome. A series of stone circles to the east of the site are now thought to be the bases of domed thatch or peat living huts, rather than having any religious meaning. The quarry near the towers is also worth seeing." Other Inca remains can be seen in the shape of square buildings, a temple of the Sun and a temple of the Moon. Underground burials at the site predating the Colla have been found from the Pukara and Tiahuanaco periods.

There is a museum and handicraft sellers in traditional costume wait at the exit. Guides are also available here. Photographers will find the afternoon light best,

Sacred lake

Lake Titicaca has played a dominant role in Andean beliefs for over two millenia. This, the highest navigable body of water in the world, is the most sacred lake in the Andes.

From the lake's profound, icy depths emerged the Inca creator deity, Viracocha. Legend has it that the sun god had his children, Manco Cápac and his sister, Mama Ocllo, spring from the its waters to found Cusco and the Inca dynasty.

The name Titicaca derives from the word 'titi', an Aymara mountain cat and the Quechua word 'caca' meaning rock. The rock refers to the Sacred Rock on the Isla del Sol (on the Bolivian side) which was worshipped by the pre-Incan people on the island. The mountain cat inhabited the shores of the lake and is said to have visited the Isla del Sol occasionally.

The link between the rock and the cat comes from the legend that the ancient indigenous people saw the eyes of a mountain cat gleaming in the Sacred Rock and so named it Titicaca, or Rock of the Mountain Cat. It was this that gave rise to the idea of the sun having its home there.

The titi has characteristics – such as its aquatic ability and the brilliance of its eyes – that conceptually link it with a myth-ological flying feline called ccoa. The role of the ccoa was (and in some parts still is) important throughout the Andes. It is believed to have thrown lightning from its eyes, urinated rain (hence the expression), spit hail and roared thunder. It was generally associated with the gods that coolled the weather.

Among indigenous people today the ccoa is believed to be one of the mountain god's servants and lives in the mountains. It is closely involved in their daily life and is considered the most feared of the spirits as it uses lightning and hail.

though this is when the wind is at its strongest and can kick up a mini-sandstorm. It's also best not to wear contact lenses. The scenery is barren, but nonetheless impressive. On the lake before the ruins there are flamingos and ducks. Take warm clothing, water and sun protection.

Llachón
The pretty farming village of Llachón, sitting at the eastern end of the Península de Capachica, has recently become a focus of community-based tourism. The sandy beaches, pre-Inca terracing and trees and flowers dotted around, make it a charming place to visit. You'll be welcomed with a necklace of cantuta flowers and then invited to share in local activities; 70 per cent of all produce served is from the residents' farms. The peninsula is also good for hiking and mountain-biking and sailing boats can be hired. After all that activity, take in the sunset from the Auki Carus hill; reckoned to be better even than from Taquile. Neither Taquile nor Amantaní are far away. The population of 1,300 enjoy electricity and share the one village phone. Twelve families offer accommodation on a rotational basis, see page 237. Llachón is great place to start a visit to Lake Titicaca, especially if you are flying in. It is closer to come here directly from Juliaca and you can go from Llachón to the islands or to Puno by boat.

Other sights
Another place where chullpas can be seen is **Cutimbo**, 34 km south of Puno in the district of Pichacani, between Puno and Laraqueri on the old road toMoquegua. Here the funeral towers are round and square and stand on a table-top mountain. There are

rock paintings on the mountain side. A road goes part of the way up. A taxi there costs US$19, including wait, three hours.

Some 8 km from Puno, just off the Puno-Juliaca road, is **Fundo Chincheros** ① *T051-351921, www.casadelcorregidor.com.pe, or go to La Casa del Corregidor, Jr Deústua 576, for more information, US$5 includes guided tour; US$10 for half-day stays including lunch (available for groups of 5 or more),* an old hacienda recently opened to the public. The colonial house with it's own chapel is in the middle of fields. Llamas, alpacas and vicuñas are on site as well as horses for riding. The wild flowers, cactus and views make this a worth while trip.

The islands

Los Uros → *Colour map 6, grid B2.*

Of the estimated 32 floating islands, only some 15 are regularly visited by tourists, and today we can talk about two kinds of Uros people; those close to the city of Puno and easily accessible to tourism, and those on islands which remain relatively isolated. The Uros' islanders fish, hunt birds and live off the lake plants, most important of which are the totora reeds they use for their boats, houses and the very foundations of their islands. (See the box, Like the fish and birds of the water.) Their diet is very rich in fats. This, plus the high red corpuscle content, leads to the saying that they have black blood. On those more far-flung islands, reached via narrow channels through the reed beds, the Uros do not like to be photographed and continue to lead relatively traditional lives outside the monetary economy. They hunt and fish and still depend on trade with the mainland for other essentials.

> ● There is no drinking water on the floating islands and you need to be careful where you walk, as the surface can be unsteady underfoot.

Visitors to the floating islands encounter more women than men. These women wait every day for the tour boats to sell their handicrafts. The few men one does see might be building or repairing boats or fixing their nets. The rest are to be found out on the lake, hunting and fishing. The Uros cannot live from tourism alone, and the extra income they glean from tourists merely supplements their more traditional activities.

Many tourists find that, though the people are friendly, they are very poor and a few subject visitors to a hard-sell approach for handicrafts. The islands visited by tour boats are little more than 'floating souvenir stalls'. All the same, this form of tourism on the Uros Islands is now well-established and, whether it has done irreparable harm or will ultimately prove beneficial, it takes place in superb surroundings.

Taquile

Isla Taquile, some 45 km from Puno, has numerous pre-Inca and Inca ruins, and Inca terracing. At the highest point is a ruin from which to view the sunset (the path is signed). The island is quiet and hospitable, but at the height of the season and at Sunday lunchtime it gets busy and touristy.

The island is only about 1 km wide and 6-7 km long. On the north side of the island is the warmest part of Lake Titicaca. Ask for the (unmarked) **museum of traditional costumes** and also where you can see and photograph local weaving. It is on the plaza and is free. There is a co-operative shop on the plaza that sells exceptional woollen goods which are not cheap, but of very fine quality. They are cheaper in the market at Puno. You need to spend a night on Taquile fully to appreciate its beauty and, therefore, it may be better to travel independently and go at your own pace.

Every Sunday, the island's four *suyos* (districts) coordinate their activities with a reunion in the main plaza after Quechua mass. Numerous **festivals** take place on the island. These include: **Semana Santa**, a festival from 2 to 7 June, the **Fiesta de**

⋮ A lasting tradition

One of the most enduring textile traditions in Peru is found among the people of Taquile. Each family possesses at least four different types of costume: for work; leisure; weddings and festivals.

For weddings, which all take place on 3 May, when the planet Venus – Hatun Chaska – is visible, the bridegroom wears a red poncho provided by the best man. As a single man he wore a half red, half white cap, but to signify his married status he wears a long red hat and a wide red wedding belt, or *chumpi*. His bag for coca leaves, *ch'uspa*, is also filled.

The bride wears a wide red hat (*montera*) and her hands are covered with a ritual cloth (*katana-oncoma*). A *quincha*, a small white cloth symbolizing purity, is hidden in her skirt. With her red wedding blouse, or gonna, she wears a gathered skirt or pollera, made from 20 different layers of brightly coloured cloth. She also wears a belt (*faja*) and black cloak known as a chukoo.

The wool used for weaving is usually spun by the women, but on Taquile men spin wool, as well as knitting their conical hats (*chullos*). In fact, only the men on Taquile know how to knit. By the age of 10, a boy can knit his own Chullo Santa María, which is white-tipped to show single status. When he marries, or moves in with a woman, he adopts the red-tipped chullo, which is exclusive to the island. Today, much of the wool for knitting is bought ready-spun from factories in Arequipa.

Santiago, held over two weeks in mid-July, and on 1 and 2 August, the principal festival days, with many dances in between. Weddings take place each May and August. The priest comes from Puno and there is a week-long party. The book, *Encuentro con los hijos del sol/Encounter with the Children of the Sun/Rencontre avec les fils du soleil*, by Christian Nonis of the Colón Inn, has been recommended.

The influx of tourists unfortunately prompts persistent requests by children for sweets or to have their photo taken. They whisper, quite politely, *caramelo* (sweet) or *foto* (photo). This irritates many travellers. When you arrive, boys tie friendship bracelets to your wrist, or give you *muña* (a herb used for infusions) for a sol. Above all, stay good-humoured. Buy their handicrafts instead of handing out sweets indiscriminately. Recordings of traditional music have been made and are on sale as an additional source of income for the islanders. Gifts of fruit, sugar, salt, spices, torches/flashlights (there is no electricity), moisturizer or sun block (the children suffer sore cheeks) are appreciated.

You are advised to take with you some food, particularly fruit, bread and vegetables, water, plenty of small-value notes, candles and a torch/flashlight. Take precautions against sunburn and seasickness. If staying the night, take warm clothes, a sleeping bag and a hot water bottle. The same applies to Amantaní. Tourism to both islands is community-based: the less you pay, the smaller the amount that goes to the islanders. Bear this in mind when you shop around for a good value tour (there is not much variation at the lower end of the price range).

There are two main entry points. The Puerto Principal at the south end has a very steep climb up many steps; the northern entry is longer but more gradual (remember you are at 3,800 m). Visitors pay US$1 to land. Plentiful accommodation can be found in private houses and, on arrival, you are greeted by a jefe de alojamiento, who oversees where you are going to stay. There used to be a system of assigning accommodation to visitors by rota, but this has fallen into disuse. You can either say where you are going, if you (or your guide) know where you want to stay, or the jefe

Lake Titicaca Puno & the islands

Like the fish and birds of the water

Titicaca's waters nourished great civilizations like the Tiahuanaco and Pukará and drew the Incas south in search of new lands and the origin of their own creation legend. But very little is known about a third people who made Titicaca their home. They were the Uros, the people of the floating islands. The ephemeral nature of their totora reed constructions and the watery world they inhabit make archaeological study impossible, and only their myths remain to teach us something of their history.

In their oral histories, the Uros say that their forefathers came from the south. We cannot know with any certainty when the Uros first arrived at Lake Titicaca, but it is thought that a great drought around 1200 AD provoked a series of massive migrations of entire peoples across the altiplano. In a scenario similar to the one predicted for many parts of the world in the 21st century, conflicts arose as competition increased for water and fertile land.

The Uros found the fertile shores of the great lake occupied by other, much larger ethnic groups. According to Uro tradition, facing inevitable defeat by their more established rivals, the Uros escaped to the reed beds. It is said that they hid in the water among the reeds. Tired and cold, they cut the totora and, by binding the reeds together, made a number of rafts on which they slept.

Legend has it that when the Inca Pachacútec arrived to conquer the lake region he asked the Uros who they were. These people who had hunted and fished in the same way for generations replied as they always had, saying: "We are the founders of the world, the first inhabitants of the planet. Our blood is black and we cannot drown. We are like the fish and birds of the water".

With the arrival of the Spanish in the 16th century, the Uros isolated themselves even more from the mainland. Persecuted by the invaders, the Uros began to meld themselves more than ever to their lake environment and their only outside contact was with other ethnic groups onshore, with whom they exchanged fish and birds for agricultural products.

Recalling their childhood, some old Uros islanders still remember when the first tourists arrived. Fearing that the Spanish had returned, their grandparents told them to run and hide.

Times have changed on some of the floating islands. There the Uros smile, pose for photographs, and then ask for a tip. After generations of intermarriage with their Aymara neighbours, what was once one of South America's most ancient tribal groups is in fact now ethnically extinct. The last Uro died in 1959, and the Uros' language died with her.

can find you a room. Guides have been instrumental in this change as large groups wish to stay close together, rather than be separated. See Sleeping.

Amantaní → *Colour map 6, grid B2.*

Another island well worth visiting is Amantaní. It is very beautiful and peaceful, and many say is less spoiled, more genuine and friendlier than Taquile. There are six villages and ruins on both of the island's peaks, Pacha Tata and Pacha Mama, from which there are excellent views. There are also temples and on the shore there is a throne carved out of stone, the Inkatiana. It is rather eroded from flooding. It's a 30

On both hills, a fiesta is celebrated on 15 January (or thereabouts). The festivities in January have been reported as spectacular, very colourful, musical and hard-drinking. There is also a festival on the first Sunday in March with brass bands and colourful dancers. Another fiesta is the Aniversario del Consejo (of the local council), which might not be as boring as it sounds. Islanders arrange dances for tour groups (independent travellers can join in), visitors dress up in local clothes and join the dances. Small shops sell water and snacks, but more expensive than Puno.

The residents make beautiful textiles and sell them at the **Artesanía Cooperativa**, at the east end of El Pueblo. They also make basketwork and stoneware. The people are Quechua speakers, but understand Spanish.

Anapia and Yuspique

In the Peruvian part of the Lago Menor are the islands of Anapia, a friendly, Aymara-speaking community, and Yuspique, on which are ruins and vicuñas. The community has organized committees for tourism, motor boats, sailing boats and accommodation with families (All Ways Travel arranges tours, See Activities and tours). This is part of PromPerú's Al Tur 'Turismo Vivencial' scheme. Visitors are involved with community projects during their visit and there is always a celebration at the end of the stay. It's highly worthwhile. On the island ask for José Flores, who is very knowledgeable about Anapia's history, flora and fauna. He sometimes acts as a guide. See Transport, below, on how to get to the islands in the lake.

◉ Sleeping

Puno *p228, map p228*
Puno sometimes suffers from power and water shortages. Check if breakfast is included in the price. Note also that some hotels are full of dubious street tour sellers. Others are linked to tour operators which may or may not belong to them, so are not above pressurized tour selling (see Tour operators, page 240).
L Libertador Isla Esteves, on an island linked by a causeway 5 km northeast of Puno (taxi US$3, or red *colectivo* No 16, or white Nos 24 and 33), T051-367780, www.libert ador.com.pe. Built on a Tiahuanaco-period site, the hotel is spacious with good views. Bar, good restaurant, disco, good service, electricity and hot water all day, parking.
L Sonesta Posada del Inka, Av Sesquicentenario 610, Huaje, 5 km from Puno on the lakeshore (take same transport as for Isla Esteves), T051-364111, www.sonesta.com/peru_puno/. 62 large rooms with heating, in similar vein to other hotels in this group but with local touches, such as the textile decorations and the Andean menu in the Inkafé restaurant. Has facilities for the disabled, fine views, attractive, good service, folklore shows.

AL Casa Andina Plaza, Jr Grau 270, T051-367520, www.casa-andina.com. Price includes breakfast and 10% service. One of this chain's modern hotels, a block from the plaza, rooms with bath, TV and heating, non-smoking rooms, clean, safe and central. Business centre with internet for guests, parking.
AL Casa Andina Tikarani, Independencia 143, T051-365803, www.casa-andina.com. Similar in most respects to the Casa Andina Plaza, fully renewed premises.
AL Eco Inn, Av Chulluni 195, Huaje (same transport as the above), T365525, F365526, www.ecoinnpuno.com. Price includes taxes and buffet breakfast. Comfortable, brightly decorated rooms with bath, safe, luggage store, internet,parking, nice view of the lake from the front. Has alpacas in the grounds.
AL-A Plaza Mayor, Deústua 342, T051-366089, www.plazamayorhostal.com. Price includes buffet breakfast. Comfortable, well-appointed and decorated, very close to the plaza. The rooms have good big beds, hot water and TV. There is a laundry, safe and a restaurant serving local and European food. Recommended.

A Colón Inn, Tacna 290, T051-351432, www.titicaca-peru.com. Price includes tax and buffet breakfast. Colonial style, good rooms with hot shower, good service, safe, internet for guests, restaurant Sol Naciente and pizzería Europa, the Belgian manager Christian Nonis is well known, especially for his work on behalf of the people on Taquile island. Recommended.

A El Buho, Lambayeque 142, T/F051-366122, www.peruhotelsguide.com/hotel buho. Breakfast included. Hot water, nicely decorated rooms with heaters, TV, restaurant, safe, special discount to Footprint Handbook owners, travel agency for excursions and flight reconfirmations. Recommended.

A Hostal Hacienda, Jr Deústua 297, T/F051-356109, haciendahostal@hotmail.com. Price includes breakfast. Refurbished colonial house, comfortable rooms with bath and hot water, TV, café. Rooms facing the front have private balconies. Recommended.

A Qelqatani, Tarapacá 355, T051-366172, www.qelqatani.com. A relatively new hotel in colonial style, central, very clean, a good option in this price range.

A Sillustani, Jr Lambayeque 195, T051-351881, www.sillustani.com. Price includes breakfast and taxes. Hot water, cable TV, safety deposit, heaters, internet, very good.

A Tambo Real, Jr Santiago Giraldo 362, T051-992 3136, www.tamborealtitikaka.com. New in 2003, a few blocks from the Plaza de Armas, clean, bright rooms, price includes breakfast, family-owned, professional and helpful staff.

B Balsa Inn, Cajamarca 555, T051-363144, www.balsainn.com. With breakfast (no other meals except for groups by arrangement). See the Nativity collection on display; comfortable lobby. Rooms are comfy, too, with big bathrooms, hot water, TV, safe, heating. Very helpful.

B Ferrocarril, Av La Torre 185, T051-351752, www.hotelferrocarril.com. This place is a 100 years old, by the train stations, price includes breakfast, central heating throughout the hotel is a big plus, parking space also available.

B Hostal Italia, Teodoro Valcarcel 122, T051-352521, www.hotelitaliaperu.com. 2 blocks from the station. With continental breakfast, cheaper in low season. Good, safe, hot water, good food, small rooms, staff helpful. Recommended.

B Hostal Pukara, Jr Libertad 328, T/F051-368448, pukara@terra.com.pe. Includes good American breakfast. Popular, with bath, hot water and heating. English spoken, central, quiet, free coca tea in evening. Recommended.

C Posada Don Giorgio, Tarapacá 238, T051-363648, dongiorgio@titicacalake.com. Breakfast included. Large, comfortable, pleasantly decorated rooms with bath, hot water, TV, parking US$1.50 extra.

C Hostal Imperial, Teodoro Valcarcel 145, T051-352386, imperial_hostal_puno@yahoo.com. **D-E** (low season), breakfast extra, US$1.85 (poor value). With bath, hot water, helpful, stores luggage, comfortable, safe, ask fore extra blanket if cold.

C Hostal Monterrey, Lima 441, T051-351691, monterreytours@hotmail.com. Price includes breakfast and cable TV. **E** without bath, better rooms with good showers, hot water, restaurant, laundry, secure for luggage, motorcycle parking US$0.50.

C-D Hostal Rubi 'Los Portales', Jr Cajamarca 152-154, T/F051-353384, www.mancocapa cinn.com. Breakfast US$2 extra, hot water, safe, TV, good, tours arranged.

D Hospedaje Residencial Margarita, Jr Tarapacá 130, T051-352820, hostalmargarita @hotmail.com. Large building, family atmosphere, hot water most of the day, stores luggage, tours can be arranged. Recommended.

D Los Uros, Teodoro Valcarcel 135, T051-352141, huros@speedy.com.pe. Cheaper without bath. Hot water, plenty of blankets, breakfast is available (at extra cost), quiet at the back, good value. They make a small charge to leave luggage, laundry, often full, changes TCs a reasonable rate. Recommended.

D Manco Cápac Inn, Av Tacna 227, T051-352985, www.mancocapacinn. With bath and hot water, luggage store, safe, average breakfast extra, as are heating and cable TV.

For an explanation of sleeping and eating price codes used in this guide, see inside the front cover. Other relevant information is found in Essentials, pages 61-66.

D San Carlos, Ugarte 161, T051-351862, hostalsancarlos@hotmail.com. One of several hospedajes near the station and market, with bath, hot water, TV and phone.

D Vylena, Jr Ayacucho 503, T/F051-351292, hostalvylena@hotmail.com Breakfast extra, with bath and hot water, quiet, safe, cheaper in low season.

D-E Hostal Arequipa, Arequipa 153, T051-352071, hotelarequipa@speedy.com. pe. With bath, hot water, will change TCs at good rates, stores luggage, secure, arranges tours to the islands, also has parking space.

D-E Hostal Los Pinos, Tarapacá 182, T/F051-367398, hostalpinos@hotmail.com. Cheaper without bath. Family run, electric showers, good breakfast, clean, safe, luggage store, laundry facilities, helpful, cheap tours organized. Recommended.

D-E Hostal Nesther, Deústua 268, T051-363308. Also has triples, with bath, hot water, clean. Recommended.

D-E Hostal Q'oñiwasi, Av La Torre 119, opposite the rail station, T051-365784, qoniwasi@mundomail.net. **E** without bath and in low season. Heating is extra, but hot water available all day, laundry facilities and service, luggage store, breakfast extra from 0600-0900, lunch on request, safe, very helpful. Recommended.

D-E Ollanta Inn, Jr Ilo E-1, 2da cuadra Jr Los Incas, T051-366743. New, just behind station, hot water 24 hrs a day, pleasant, clean, helpful owner fan heater and TV extra, breakfast is also extra but is good.

E Hospedaje Santa Rosa, Los Incas 208, T051-356733. Near the station and market, cheaper without bath, with hot water, helpful, but not very clean.

E Hostal Europa, Alfonso Ugarte 112, near the train station, T051-353026, hostaleuropa @hotmail.com. Very popular, cheaper with-out bath, luggage may be stored, but don't leave your valuables in the room, hot water sometimes, garage space for motorcycles.

E Hostal Illampu, Av La Torre 137-interior 9, T051-353284, illampu97@hotmail.com. With bath and warm water, breakfast and TV extra. Has a café, laundry, safe, exchanges money, arranges excursions (ask for Santiago).

Youth hostel

F-G pp Albergue Juvenil Virgen de Copacabana, Ilave 228, T051-T363766, hostelling_virgen_copacabana@yahoo.com. Huge rooms, well-furnished, "awesome bathroom" with hot water, good location, quiet, helpful owners, will wash your clothes for a reasonable fee, full breakfast for US$1.30, a real bargain. Entrance is down a passageway.

Around Puno *p230*

E Valentín Quispe is the organizer of tourism in Llachón. He offers lodging and meals (breakfast US$1.20, other meals US$2). To contact Don Valentín, T051-360226/7, llachon@yahoo.com or visit www.titicaca-peru.com/capachicae.htm. Another family is that of Tomás Cahui Coila, Centro Turístico Santa María Llachón, T051-992 3595 (mob); Tomás can arrange boat transport to Amantaní. There is a campsite towards the end of the peninsula. See Transport, below.

The Islands *p232*

Taquile The average rate for a bed is **G** , plus US$1.50 for breakfast. Other meals cost extra. Several families now have sizeable alojamientos (eg **Pedro Huille**, on the track up from the north entry, with showers, proper loos, no sign).

Instead of staying in the busy part around the main square, the Huayllano community is hosting visitors. This is on the south side of the island. Contact **Alipio Huata Cruz**, T051-952 4650 (mob, you can leave a voicemail that he will retrieve from Puno as there is no reception on the island) or you can arrange a visit with **Allways Travel**.

Amantaní Ask your boat owner where you can stay; families living close to the port tend to receive tour company business and more tourists. Accommodation is in our **F** range. This includes three meals of remarkable similarity. It's very good value for visitors, but the prices have been forced down to unrealistically low levels, from which the islanders benefit hardly at all.
Some contacts for accommodation are:
Hospedaje Jorge Wasi, basic, but nice family, great view of lake from room; j.mamani.cari@eudoramail.com; and
Familia Victoriano Calsin Quispe, Casilla 312, Isla Amantaní, T051-360220 (Irma) or 363320 (Puno contact).

Pot luck

One of the most intriguing items for sale in Andean markets is Ekeko, the god of good fortune and plenty and one of the most enduring and endearing of the Aymara gods and folk legends.

He is a cheery, avuncular little chap, with a happy face to make children laugh, a pot belly, because of his predilection for food, and short legs so he can't run away.

His image, usually in plaster of Paris, is laden with sacks of grain, sweets, household tools, baskets, utensils, suitcases, confetti and streamers, rice, noodles and other essentials. Dangling from his lower lip is the ubiquitous lit cigarette. Believers say that these little statues only bring luck if they are received as gifts, and not purchased.

Eating

Puno *p228, map p228*

Very cheap places on Jr Deústua serve lunch or dinner. There are many places on Lima, too many to list here, which cater for the tourist market, they usually have good atmosphere and very good food.

IncAbar, Lima 356-A. Open for breakfast, lunch and dinner, interesting dishes in creative sauces, fish, pastas, curries, café and couch bar, nice decor.

Internacional, Moquegua 201. Very popular, excellent trout, good pizzas, service variable.

La Plaza, Puno 425, Plaza de Armas. Good food, including fish.

Apu Salkantay, Lima 357 and in 400 block. Wide menu of meats, fish (more expensive), pastas, sandwiches, pizza, coffee, popular.

Don Piero, Lima 360. Huge meals, live music, try their 'pollo coca-cola' (chicken in a sweet and sour sauce), slow service, popular, tax extra.

El Dorado, Lima 371. Good for local fish, large portions.

Fontana, Lima 339. Pizzería and trattoria, good food.

Keros, Lambayeque 131. Bar/restaurant with very good food, mostly Peruvian, good service, pleasant surroundings, good drinks.

La Casona, Lima 521. Good for typical food, also Italian and pizzas.

La Caywa Andean Cuisine Bar, Jr. Arequipa 410. T051-351490. Open 1000-2200. Typical and international. New, recommended.

Lago de Flores, Lima 357. Local dishes and pizza, very good food, open fire in the shape of a pizza oven keeps diners warm.

Pizzería El Buho, Lima 349 and at Jr Libertad 386. Excellent pizza, lively atmosphere, open 1800 onwards, pizzas US$2.35-3.

Adventista, Jr Deza 349. Good, closed after lunch.

Chifa Fon Seng, Arequipa 552. Good food, service and value, Chinese, popular.

Chifa Nan Hua, Arequipa 167, one block from Plaza de Armas. Tasty, big portions of Chinese food.

El Milagro, Arequipa 336. Natural food shop, closed Sat.

Govinda, Deústua 312. Cheap vegetarian lunch menus, closes at 2000.

Remembranzas, Jr Moquegua 200. Pizzas as well as local food, new in 2004. Open 0630-2200.

Vida Natural, Libertad 449. Open for breakfast, salads, fruits, yoghurts.

Cafés

Cafetería Mercedes, Jr Arequipa 351. Good menú US$1.50, also breads, cakes, snacks, juices and tea.

Casa del Corregidor, Deústua 576, aptdo 2, T051-355694. In restored 17th century building, sandwiches, good snacks, coffee, good music, great atmosphere, nice surroundings with patio.

Panadería Una, Lima 317 and Arequipa 144. For croissants, fresh bread and cakes.

Ricos Pan, Jr Lima 424. Café and bakery, great cakes, excellent coffees, juices and pastries, good breakfasts and other dishes, reasonable prices, great place to relax, open 0600-2300, closed Sun. Branches of their panadería at Av Titicaca 155 and Moquegua 330.

The Islands *p232*
On **Taquile** there are many small restaurants around the plaza and on the track to the Puerto Principal (eg Gerardo Hualta's **La Flor de Cantuta**, on the steps; **El Inca** on the main plaza). Meals are generally fish (the island has a trout farm), rice and chips, tortilla and fiambre – a local stew. Meat is rarely available and drinks often run out. Breakfast consists of pancakes and bread. Shops on the plaza sell film, postcards, water, chocolate bars and dry goods.
On **Amantaní**, there is one restaurant, **Samariy**.

🍸 Bars and clubs

Puno *p228, map p228*
Dómino, Libertad 443. "Megadisco", happy hour 2000-2130 Mon-Thu, good.
Peña Hostería, Lima 501. Good music, also restaurant with good value set menu. Recommended.
Pub Ekeko's, Jr Lima 355, p 2. Live music every night, happy hour 2000-2200.
The Rocks, Valcarcel 181, T051-337441. New in 2004, live music starts at 2000 on Fri and Sat.

🎪 Festivals and events

Puno *p228, map p228*
The very colourful **Fiesta de la Virgen de la Candelaria** takes place during the first 2 weeks in **Feb**. Bands and dancers from all the local towns compete in this Diablada, or Devil Dance, with the climax coming on Sun. The festival is famous for its elaborate and grotesque masks, which depict characters in local legends as well as caricatures of former landowners and mine bosses. The festivities are better at night on the streets than the official functions in the stadium. Check in advance on the actual date because Candelaria may be moved if pre-Lenten carnival coincides with it. This festival is great fun and shouldn't be missed if you're in the vicinity around this time.

Other festivals include a candlelight procession through darkened streets, which takes place on **Good Friday**, with bands, dignatories and statues of Jesus. On **3 May** is **Invención de la Cruz**, an exhibition of local art. On **29 Jun** is the colourful festival of **San Pedro**, with a procession at Zepita (see p249). Another takes place on **20 Jul**. In fact, it is difficult to find a month in Puno without some sort of celebration.

Finally, remember, remember **5 Nov**, when there's an impressive pageant dedicated to the founding of Puno and the emergence of Manco Cápac and Mama Ocllo from the waters of Lake Titicaca. The royal couple sail from a point on the lake (it varies annually) and arrive at the port between 0900 and 1000. The procession from the lake moves up Av Titicaca to the stadium where a ceremony takes place with dancers from local towns and villages. If you buy an entrance ticket, US$0.60, you can watch from the top tier as the float carrying the Incas, followed by the local dancing groups, enters the stadium. Many of the groups continue dancing outside. This is not the best time to visit Taquile and Amantaní since many of their inhabitants are at the festival. This date coincides with the anniversary of the founding of Puno, celebrated with parades at night and a full military parade on the Sun.

🛍 Shopping

Puno *p228, map p228*
The markets between Av Los Incas and Arbulu (Ccori Wasi) and on the railway between Av Libertad and Av El Puerto are two of the best places in Peru (or Bolivia) for **llama and alpaca wool** articles, but bargain for a good price when buying in quantity (and you will!), especially in the afternoon. In the covered part of the market (bounded by Arbulu, Arequipa, Oquendo and Tacna) mostly **foodstuffs** are sold (good cheeses), but there are also model **reed boats**, attractive **carved stone amulets** and Ekekos (**household goods**). This central market covers a large area and on Sat it expands down to the stadium (mostly fruit and vegetables) and along Av Bolívar (potatoes and grains). You will be hassled on the street and outside restaurants to buy woollen goods, so take care.

Alpaca 111, Lima 343, T051-366050, www. alpaca111.com. A very good quality alpaca shop at the high end of the price range.
Alpaca's, Lima 394. T051-363551, alpacas @terra.com.pe. Another expensive, high quality alpaca store.
Cooperación Artesanal Ichuña, Jr Libertad 113, www.ichunia.org. The outlet for a cooperative of about 100 women from Ichuña, 90km southwest of Puno, selling hand-woven textiles made of alpaca wool.

▲ Activities and tours

Puno *p228, map p228*
Agencies organize trips to the Uros floating islands and the islands of Taquile and Amantaní, as well as to Sillustani, and other places. Make sure that you settle all details before embarking on the tour. Alternatively, you can easily go down to the lake and make your own arrangements with the boatmen. Watch out for the many unofficial street tour sellers – or *jalagringos* – who offer hotels and tours at different rates, depending on how wealthy you look. Once you realize they have charged more than the going rate, they'll be gone. They are everywhere: train station, bus offices, airport and hotels. Ask to see their guide's ID card. Only use agencies with named premises and compare prices.

Tour operators
Most agencies will go and buy train tickets for you, at varying rates of commission, similarly for bus tickets. The following have been recommended as reliable and helpful and offer good value.
Allways Travel, Tacna 234, T/F051-355552, www.titicacaperu.com. Very helpful, kind and attentive to visitors' needs. Reliable, staff speak German, French, English and Italian. They offer a unique cultural tour to the islands of Anapia and Yuspique in Lake Wiñaymarka, beyond the straits of Tiquina, 'The Treasuer of Wiñaymarka', departures Thu and Sun. You can contribute to owner Víctor Lazo's educational project by donating children's books for schools. They also have a speed boat for 40 passengers. Also doing an alternative visit to Taquile where you go to the south of the island to visit the Huayllano community, this is a lot less touristy then the regular Taquile visit.

Arcobaleno, Jr Lambayeque 175, T/F051-351052, www.titicacalake.com. Local tours, Western Union representative and agent for **Crillon Tours** of La Paz, Bolivia.
Edgar Adventures, Jr Lima 328, T/F051-353444 , www.titicacalake.com. Run by Edgar Apaza F and Norka Flórez L who speak English, German and French, very helpful.
Ecoturismo Aventura, Jr Lima 458, T051-355785. Very helpful.
Kontiki Tours, Jr Melgar 188. T051-353473, www.kntikiperu.com. Receptive tour agency specializing in special interest excursions. Recommended.
Nayra Travel, Jr Lima 419, of 105. T051-364774, www.nayratravel.com. Small but very helpful staff, offering local tours.
Pirámide Tours, Jr Rosendo Huirse 130, T051-366107, www.titikakalake.com. Out of the ordinary and classic tours, flexible, personalized service, modern fast launches, very helpful, but works only via internet and overseas clients.
Turpuno, Lima 208, stand 8-II, upstairs in Gallery, T051-352001, www.turpuno.com. Open 0700-1230, 1430-1800. Very good service for local tours, transfers and ticketing, DHL and Western Union agent.

⊖ Transport

Puno *p228, map p228*
Air
The nearest airport is at Juliaca. Airline offices: **Lan**, Tacna y Libertad, T051-367227.

Boat
Boats to the islands leave from the terminal in the harbour; trici-taxi from centre, US$1.

Bus
All long-distance buses, except some Cusco services and buses to La Paz (see below), leave from the new Terminal Terrestre, which is between Av Simón Bolívar and the lake, southeast of the centre. It has a tourist office, snack bars and toilets. Platform tax US$0.30. Bus prices to Cusco and La Paz have seasonal variations.

Daily buses to **Arequipa**, 5-6 hrs via **Juliaca**, 297 km by paved road, most buses take this route, US$8.60. Or 11 hrs via **Desaguadero** and **Moquegua**, US$10-15, sit on left for views of the lake and altiplano

(Cruz del Sur - office also at Lima 442, **Best Way**, **Destinos**, **Julsa** - office also at Melgar 232, T051-369447, **Señor de Milagros**, or **Sur Oriente**, T051-368133, most have a morning and evening bus – better quality buses go at night). To **Moquegua**, US$8.60, and **Tacna**, US$10. To **Lima**, 1,011 km, 22 hrs, US$18-43, all buses go through **Arequipa**, sometimes with a change of bus.

Small buses and *colectivos* for **Juliaca**, **Ilave** and towns on the lake shore between Puno and Desaguadero, including **Yunguyo**, leave from Av Bolívar between Jrs Carabaya and Palma. To **Juliaca**, 44 km, 45 mins, US$0.85. For **Yunguyo** and the **Bolivian border**, see p249.

To **Cusco**, 388 km, 5 hrs. If you wish to travel by bus and cannot get on a direct bus, it is no problem to take separate buses to Juliaca, then to Sicuani, then to Cusco, but obviously this takes longer. Do not take night buses to Cusco: in 2003-2004 many robberies have been reported. **Tour Perú**, at Terminal and Tacna 282, T051-352991, tourperu@mixmail.com, 0830, 2000, US$8.60 (less in low season); **Libertad**, at Terminal, T051-363694, 4 a day, **Cisnes**, at Terminal, T368674, 2 a day, **Pony Express** (this company had a lot of accidents in 2003-2004) and others. **First Class**, Jr Tacna 280, T051-365192, firstclass@terra.com.pe, and **Inka Express**, Jr Tacna 314-B, T051-365654, both at 0830 arriving 1800, US$25, daily. This service, while higher in price than the turismo train or other buses, leaves a little later and is comfortable, with a good lunch stop and visits to Pukará, La Raya, Raqchi and Andahuaylillas en route. This option is recommended and has become very popular so book in advance, especially in high season.

Train
The railway runs from Puno to **Juliaca** (44 km), where it divides, to **Cusco** (381 km) and **Arequipa** (279 km; no passenger service, 2004). To **Cusco** on Mon, Wed, Thu and Sat at 0800, arriving in Juliaca at 0910 and in Cusco at about 1800 (try to sit on the right hand side for the views). The train stops at **La Raya**. In the high season (Jun especially), tickets sell well in advance. In the wet season services may be cancelled for short periods. Always check, www.perurail.com.

Puno-Cusco return fares, turismo/backpacker, US$16.66; first class, US$119 including meal. The ticket office is open from 0630-1030, 1600-1900 Mon-Sat, and on Sun in the afternoons only. Tickets can be bought in advance, or 1 hr before departure if there are any left. The station is well-guarded by police and sealed off to those without tickets.

Around Puno *p230*
Public boats leave Puno for Llachón at 0830, usually daily, 3 hrs to Llachón. Private boat services take 1½ hrs: contact Pirámide or Kolla Tours in Puno. There is no direct road transport on the unpaved road to the peninsula that branches east from the main road half way between Puno and Juliaca. Take a *colectivo* from Bellavista market in Puno to the village of Capachica, then another *colectivo* to Llachón. Tour operators in Puno arrange visits, about US$25 per person staying overnight, in groups of 10-15.

The Islands *p232*
Motorboats charge US$3 per person to take tourists to the **Uros** islands for a 2-hr excursion. Boats leave from the harbour in Puno about every 30 mins from about 0630 till 1000, or whenever there are 10 or more people to fill the boat. The earlier you go the better, to beat the crowds of tourists. Almost any agency going to the other islands in the lake will stop first at Los Uros. Just to Los Uros, agencies charge US$6.

Boats leave Puno harbour for **Taquile** daily at 0700-0800. The journey takes 3 hrs. Boats return at 1430, arriving in Puno at 1730. It costs US$7 one way. This doesn't leave enough time to appreciate the island fully in one day. Organized tours can be arranged for about US$10-16 per person, but only give you about 2 hrs on the island. Make sure you and the boatman know exactly what you are paying for.

Boats for **Amantaní** from the harbour in Puno leave at 0700-0800 daily, and return at 0800, arriving in Puno around 1200. The trip costs US$5.80 one way. The journey takes 4-5 hrs - take water. A one-day trip is not possible as the boats do not always return on the same day. Several tour operators in Puno offer two to three day excursions to Amantaní, Taquile and a visit to the floating islands. These cost from US$12 per person upwards, including meals, depending on the season and size of group. This gives you one night on Amantaní and three or four hours on Taquile. There is little difference in price visiting the islands independently or on a tour, but going independently means that the islanders get all the proceeds, with no commission paid to Puno tour companies, you can stay as many nights as you wish and you will be able to explore the islands at your own pace. When not taking a tour, do not buy your boat ticket from anyone other than the boat operator at the harbour, do not believe anyone who says you can only visit the islands on a tour and do not be pressurized by touts. If you wish to visit both Taquile and Amantaní, it is better to go to Amantaní first. From there boats go to Taquile at around 0800, costing US$2.50 per person. There is no regular service – boats leave if there are enough passengers. You would then take the 1430 boat from Taquile to Puno.

To visit **Anapia** independently, take a *colectivo* from Yunguyo to Tinicachi and alight at Punta Hermosa, just after Unacachi. Boats to Anapia leave Punta Hermosa on Sun and Thu at 1300 (they leave Anapia for Yunguyo market on the same days at 0630). It's 2 hrs each way by boat.

❶ Directory

Puno *p228, map p228*
Banks BCP, Lima 510. Changes TCs before 1300 without commission, cash advance on Visa and Visa ATM. **Banco Continental**, Lima 444-411, Visa ATM. **Banco Wiese Sudameris**, Lima with Deústua, Mastercard ATM. **Interbank**, Lima 444, changes TCs

morning and afternoon, 0.5% commission, Visa ATM. For cash go to the cambios, the travel agencies or the better hotels. Best rates with money changers on Jr Lima, many on 400 block, and on Tacna near the market, eg Arbulu y Tacna. Check your Peruvian soles carefully. Exchange rates from soles to bolivianos and vice versa are sometimes better in Puno than in Yunguyo; check with other travellers. **Consulates Bolivia**, Jr Arequipa 136, T051-351251. Issues a visa on the spot, US$10, open 0830-1400 Mon-Fri. **Internet** There are offices everywhere in the centre, upstairs and down. Average price is US$0.60/hr; many have overnights. Good ones include **Chasquinet**, Jr Libertad 239, 0730-2230. **Chozanet**, Jr Lima 339, 0800-2300. **Kupidos**, Jr Libertad 233, 0730-2230. **Laundry Don Marcelo**, head office at Ayacucho 651, T352444, has agencies in several places in the centre, including on Lima 427, and will collect and deliver laundry. US$1.50 per kg, good service. **Lavandería América**, Moquegua 175, T051-351642. Also had a good service, US$1.50. **Post** Jr Moquegua 267. **Telephone Telefónica** at Puno y Moquegua for local and international calls. Another phone office is at Lima 489. **Useful addresses Immigration**, Ayacucho 240, T051-352801. For renewing entry stamps, etc. The process is very slow and you must fill in 2 application forms at a bank, but there's nothing else to pay. **Indecopi**, Lima y Fermín Arbulú, p 2, T/F051-366138, odipun@indecopi.gob.pe. The office of the tourist protection bureau. **Ministry of Tourism**, Jr Deústua 351, T051-352811. Helpful with complaints.

Juliaca and the eastern shore

The opposite shores of Lake Titicaca are quite different. Between Puno and Desaguadero at the lake's southeastern tip, the plain is intensively worked. The tin roofs of the communities glint everywhere in the sun. Heading north from Puno, the road crosses a range of hills to another coastal plain, which leads to Juliaca. North of Puno is the first sector (29,150 ha) of the Reserva Nacional del Titicaca. The smaller, Ramis sector (7,030 ha) is northeast of Juliaca, at the outflow of the Río Ramis which floods in the wet season. The reserve protects extensive totora reed beds in which thousands of birds live. On the flat, windy altiplano between Juliaca and Huancané (see below) you will see small, square houses with conical roofs, all made of blocks of earth, putukus de champa. After Huancané, the lakeshore becomes mountainous, with cliffs, bays and fabulous vistas over the water. ➤➤ *For Sleeping, Eating and other listings, see pages 246-248.*

Ins and outs

Heading north and west, Juliaca is a major transport hub for paved roads to Cusco and Arequipa and also has the only airport in the region. Transport along the north shore is less frequent, but that should not discourage you from travelling here. The road from Puno towards Bolivia runs along the western shore of the lake, so the villages described below are easily reached by frequent public transport.

Juliaca → *Colour map 6, grid B2. Population: 134,700. Altitude: 3,825 m.*

As the commercial focus of an area bounded by Puno, Arequipa and the jungle, Juliaca has grown very fast into a chaotic place with a large impermanent population, lots of contraband and counterfeiting and more tricitaxis than cars. Monday, market day, is the most disorganized of all. Other than waiting for a plane or a train, there is not much reason to stop here. If you do have to hang around, it's freezing cold at night. So make sure you're wrapped up well in your recently purchased alpaca clothing.

Sleeping
Hostal Don Carlos **1**
Hostal Ferrocarril **2**
Hostal Luquini **3**

Hostal Sakura **4**
Karlo's Hostal & Che
Karlín Restaurant **5**

Royal Inn & La Fonda
del Royal Restaurant **6**
Suites Don Carlos **8**
Yarur **7**

Eating
Ricos Pan & Trujillo 2 **2**
Trujillo 1 **3**

You can buy wool and alpaca goods at the large Sunday **market** in the huge Plaza Melgar, several blocks from the centre. On the same plaza is an interesting colonial **church**. Another good place to find cheap alpaca sweaters is the **Galería Artesanal Las Calceteras**, on Plaza Bolognesi. **Túpac Amaru market**, on Moquegua, seven blocks east of the railway line, is a cheap black market. The **Plaza de Armas** is mostly lined with modern buildings. On it stands the grey-stone cathedral, sombre inside and lit by candles and the yellow light through the windows. If you're unlucky enough to fall ill here, there's a first class hospital run by the Seventh Day Adventists.

Around Juliaca

A highly recommended trip is 34 km northwest of Juliaca to the unspoiled little colonial town of **Lampa**, known as the 'Pink City', with a splendid church, La Inmaculada, containing a copy of Michelangelo's 'Pietà' (the story goes that when the original in Rome was damaged, they came to Lampa to see how the repairs should be done). Also of interest is the **Kampac Museo** ① *Ugarte 462*, a museum with sculptures and ceramics from the Lampa and Juli areas. There is a tourist office with friendly guides for free. Nearby are three Inca fortresses. It also has a good Sunday market. Buses leave daily from 2 de Mayo (take a tricycle to get there), one hour, US$0.70.

The town of **Pucará** lies 63 km to the north, with pre-Inca ruins and its pottery. There are some restaurants along the main road. The sheep farm of San Antonio, between Ayaviri and Chiquibambilla, owned by the Prime family, who are descendants of British emigrants, can be visited.

Some 71 km northeast of Juliaca is the old town of **Azángaro** with a famous church, La Asunción, which is filled with *retablos* and paintings of the Cusco school. There are good thermal springs at the village of **Putina**, 84 km northeast of Juliaca, 5 ½ hours by bus or truck, US$2.50.

Some tours from Cusco to Lake Titicaca have the Isla de Suasi (see below) as their initial destination. The route taken goes through Pucará, Azángaro and Muñani and two nights are spent at **Mallkini** ① *Juan de la Torre 101, San Lorenzo, Arequipa, (head office) T054-202525, www.mallkini.com.pe*. This is an alpaca farm at over 4,000 m, owned by the Michell family, the largest alpaca textile group in Peru. If you wish to see an altiplano farm, this is a first-class set-up, rustic, guests are well-looked after and can take part in various activities such as riding, trekking with llamas and off-roading. You can also go independently and take advantage of Mallkini's packages; the ranch has six rooms and camping facilities.

Juliaca to Cusco

The road Puno-Juliaca-Cusco is now fully paved and in good condition. Bus services are consequently an acceptable alternative to the train, which runs at an average altitude of 3,500 m. There is much to see on the way, but neither the daytime buses nor the trains make frequent stops. You would have to be using your own transport, or taking buses from town to town to sample what the places en route have to offer. The road climbs steadily after Juliaca, passing Pucará (see above) then running through the villages of Ayaviri and Santa Rosa (where knitted alpaca ponchos and pullovers and miniature llamas are sold, rooms are available). It then rises further, up to the pass at La Raya. **Ayaviri** is a lively town with a daily market. In the pleasant plaza are two puya raimondi plants.

The road and railway cross the altiplano, climbing to **La Raya**, the highest pass on the line; 210 km from Puno, at 4,321 m. Up on the heights breathing may be a little difficult, but the descent along the Río Vilcanota is rapid. To the right of **Aguas Calientes**, 9 km from La Raya, are steaming pools of hot water. The temperature of the springs is 40°C, and they show beautiful deposits of red ferro-oxide. Several communal bathing pools and a block of changing rooms have been opened. Entrance US$0.15. At **Maranganí**, the river is wider and the fields greener, with groves of

Mother Earth

Pachamama, or Mother Earth, occupies a very privileged place in Aymara culture because she is the generative source of life. The Aymara believe that man was created from the land, and thus he is fraternally tied to all the living beings that share the earth. According to them, the earth is our mother, and it is on the basis of this understanding that all of human society is organized, always maintaining the cosmic norms and laws.

Women's and men's relationship with nature is what the Aymara call ecology, harmony and equilibrium. The Aymara furthermore believe that private land ownership is a social sin because the land is for everyone. It is meant to be shared and not only used for the benefit of a few.

Vicenta Mamani Bernabé of the Andean Regional Superior Institute of Theological Studies states: "Land is life because it produces all that we need to live. Water emanates from the land as if from the veins of a human body, there is also the natural wealth of minerals, and pasture grows from it to feed the animals. Therefore, for the Aymaras, the Pachamama is sacred and since we are her children, we are also sacred. No one can replace the earth, she is not meant to be exploited, or to be converted into merchandise. Our duty is to respect and care for the earth. This is what white people today are just beginning to realize, and it is called ecology. Respect for the Pachamama is respect for ourselves as she is life. Today, she is threatened with death and must be liberated for the sake of her children's liberation."

eucalyptus trees. At Km 147, next to a colonial house, is the Maranganí Fábrica Tejidos (T084-352215), a textile manufacturer using alpaca wool. Although little more than 10 years old, some of the machines are much older than that and all use punch cards (no computerization here). The textiles are exported all over the world. The administrator, Sr Walter Chung Valdez, is happy to show interested travellers around.

The Vilcanota plunges into a gorge, but the train winds above it and round the side of the mountain. At **Huambutío** the railway turns left to follow the Río Huatanay on the final stretch to Cusco. The Vilcanota here widens into the great Urubamba canyon, flanked on both sides by high cliffs, on its way to join the Ucayali, a tributary of the Amazon. For more information about places between La Raya and Cusco, see page 217.

Along the east side of Lake Titicaca

The crossing from Peru to Bolivia via Huancané and Moho is the most remote, but nevertheless a highly recommended route between the two countries. Moho is the last town of any size in Peru. As the road leaves Juliaca, it crosses a single track-bridge, which can get congested if opposing drivers do not give way. To Huancané the road is paved across the altiplano. The road then deteriorates, badly in places. There are two possibitle way of getting to Moho (40 km): inland, over the hills, the route the buses take as it is shorter; or clinging to the lakeshore, with lots of bends, but beautiful views. Moho is known as the 'Garden of the Altiplano'. Maximizing the climatic benefits of the lake, they grow roses and many other flowers. The plaza has rosebushes, topiary hedges and a colourful fountain. The large, green Consejo Municipal is totally out of keeping with the rest of the plaza, but it is supposed to have a hotel when finished. Buses for Juliaca collect on the plaza.

Beyond Moho, some walking may be involved as there is little traffic onwards to **Puerto Acosta**, the first town on the Bolivian side. Make sure you get an exit stamp in

Puno, post-dated by a couple of days. From Moho, hitchhike to **Tilali**, the last village in Peru (three hours on foot, basic accommodation). Night buses serve Tilali direct from Juliaca (6 hours, only for certain on Mon, Tue, Fri and Sun), but you miss the scenery. From Tilali it is 15 minutes' walk to the Peruvian customs post, the border a further 30 minutes (38 km from Moho) and **Puerto Acosta** is a further 10 km (possible on foot, two hours, or bike, not by car – the road is bad). From there take a bus for 2½ hours to Chaguaya, where there is a control post and immigration next door. Leave the bus to get a Bolivian entry stamp; the officials help you get transport to continue your journey. The road is good (paved from Escoma), several buses daily to La Paz.

The only tourist project on the north shore is on the **Isla de Suasi**. A fine, get-away-from-it-all hotel is the only house on this tiny, tranquil island. The microclimate allows for beautiful terraced gardens, which are at their best January-March. The non-native eucalyptus trees are being replaced by native varieties. You can take a community rowing boat around the island to see birds (US$1.50) and the island has four vicuñas, a small herd of alpacas and one vizcacha. The sunsets from the highest point are out of this world. See Sleeping and Transport, below.

Rinconada

At 5,200 m, Rinconada is a cold, isolated town near Ananea and Culijón mountain. Its population of about 25,000 is involved entirely in gold mining and the mines are all under a glacier. A glacier lake below the town is marred by the rock and sand dug out of the mines. You can see all the processes in extracting, refining and selling the gold (which can be found pretty cheaply in the local shops). There is no infrastructure for tourists: there are four or five basic *hostales*, countless basic restaurants serving good food and, apart from gold, shops sell mainly mining equipment. Wrap up warm as it is cold by day and bitter at night (it is hard to sleep in the thin air).

● Sleeping

Juliaca *p243, map p243*
There are water problems in town, especially in the dry season.
AL Suites Don Carlos, Jr M Prado 335, on the outskirts of town, T051-321571, www.hotelesdoncarlos.com. 45 rooms, including a presidential suite. Prices include taxes, good facilities, quite central, continental breakfast US$6.50, lunch/dinner US$13.
B Hostal Don Carlos, Jr 9 de Diciembre 114, Plaza Bolognesi, T051-323600, www.hotel esdoncarlos.com. Breakfast and taxes included. Owned by the same group, comfortable, modern facilities, hot water, TV, heater, good service, restaurant and room service. Recommended.
B Royal Inn, San Román 158, T051-321561, www.royalinnhoteles.com. Decent accommodation with hot water, TV, safe, laundry, good restaurant La Fonda del Royal. Recommended.
D Karlo's Hostal, Unión 317, T051-321817, lanzap@hotmail.com. Comfortable, firm beds, hot water, TV, laundry, restaurant.
D Hostal Luquini, San Brasesco 409,

T051-321510. **E** without bath, breakfast included. Comfortable, hot water, restaurant for all meals, menú US$1.50. Recommended.
E Hostal Sakura, San Román 133, T051-322072. Rooms with bath and hot water, TV extra. Also has rooms without bath, **F** . Breakfast is extra.
E Yarur, Jr M Núñez 414, T051-321501. **F** without bath, hot water all day, safe, no breakfast.
F-G Hostal Ferrocarril, San Martín 249. Shared and private rooms, shared bath, basic.

Around Juliaca *p244*
F Hostal La Casona, on the main plaza in **Lampa**, T051-360228, mariaelenafd@ hotmail.com. Recently opened, refurbished old house, clean. Recommended.

Juliaca to Cusco *p244*
G Paraíso, Jr Leoncio Prado 254 (about 3 blocks from the plaza), T051-863024. Hot showers, clean, friendly.
G Hostal Ayaviri, Grau 180. Basic and unfriendly.

Along the east side of Lake Titicaca p245

AL Albergue Rural Isla de Suasi, T051-962 2709, a Casa Andina Private Collection hotel, www.casa-andina.com. Facilities are spacious, comfortable and solar-powered. Rooms have bath and hot water and hot water bottles are put between your sheets at bedtime. Price includes breakfast but other meals are extra, US$10-15; good food, lots of vegetables, all locally-produced. Internet access, kayaks and spa. Recommended.

F-G Hostal Moheño, in Moho, across from the church, blue house, basic but clean

🍴 Eating

Juliaca p243, map p243

🍴-🍴 **Trujillo**, San Román 163. Extensive menu, daily specials, US$3-5.50 for mains.

🍴 **La Fonda del Royal**, Hotel Royal Inn, San Román158. US$3-5 for very good, varied food.

🍴 **Ricos Pan**, San Román, next door to Trujillo 2. A good bakery with a café.

🍴 **Trujillo 2**, San Román 175. Same owners as Trujillo at No 163. Serves chicken and snacks.

Juliaca to Cusco p244

🍴 **Restaurante La Mundial**, Jr Tacna 465, T051-863375. Serves cheap local food, including lamb, a speciality, friendly place.

🚌 Transport

Juliaca p243, map p243

Air

There are daily flights to/from Lima (2¼ hrs) with **Tans**, and **Lan**, all via **Arequipa** (30 mins). Lan also flies to Cusco. Minibuses 1-B, 6 and 14 to airport from 2 de Mayo at either Núñez or San Román, US$0.15; from airport to town they take you to your hotel. Taxi from Plaza Bolognesi, US$1.75. Tourist buses run direct from Puno to the airport and vice versa; US$3.50 pp, 1 hr. You can book ahead with **Rossy Tours** T051-366709. Rosa has mini-buses and will drop you off/pick you up at your hotel for US$3.50. Also taxis, US$11.75. If taking a public *colectivo* from Puno to Juliaca for a flight, allow plenty of time, as the drivers travel around town looking for more passengers.

Airline offices Lan, San Román 125, T051-322228 (airport 324441). Tans, San Román 152, T051-321272.

Bus

The new Terminal Terrestre is at Jr Mantaro y San Agustín: go down San Martín 10 blocks and cross Av Circunvalación. Lots of companies serve **Desaguadero**, **Moquegua**, **Arequipa** (US$8.60), **Lima** (US$17-43) and **Cusco** (US$8.60). Cruz del Sur, T051-322011; Julsa, T051-331952; Ormeño, T051-321181. To **Cusco**, 344 km, 5-6 hrs, with **Tour Perú** (tourperu@mixmail.com), day and night buses, prices as from Puno (see p241 for warning about night buses to Cusco). First Class (www.firstclassperu.com) and Inka Express (inkaex@yahoo.com) have pullman tourist buses which stop for sightseeing and lunch, with guide, see under Puno. The road is paved and in good condition. Buses from Puno will stop in Juliaca on the way to Cusco. To **Puno**, 44 km, 1 hr, US$0.85; small buses leave from Piérola y 18 de Noviembre, 2 companies, Pegaso Express and Los Angeles. Combis to Puno leave from another Terminal Terrestre on Plaza Bolognesi, also US$0.85. To **Huancané** (on the north side of Lake Titicaca), 51 km, 40 mins and **Moho**, a further 31 km, Santa Cruz and Joyas del Sur companies, Moquegua 1019, at the corner with Ballón near the Túpac Amaru market, US$1.75, 3 hrs to Moho. It is a bumpy ride on a poor road, but the views are wonderful. See below on how to get to the Bolivian border.

Train

The station at Juliaca is the junction for services between **Arequipa** (no passenger services in 2004), **Puno** and **Cusco**. See under Puno (p241) and Cusco (page 183) for more information. Fares to Cusco are the same as for Puno. The ticket office, whose entrance is on Plaza Bolognesi, opens 0700-1100, 1400-1800, except Tue 1400-1800, Thu 0600-1000, 1400-1800, Sat 0700-1100, Sun 0600-1000.

Along the east side of Lake Titicaca p245

From Juliaca there are several daily buses to **Huancané** and **Moho**, see above. Private boats from Puno to the **Isla de Suasi** are expensive and take 4-6 hrs (2½ hours by fast boat, US$450 up to 15 passengers), but you can call at the islands or Llachón en route. A car for four people will cost US$75. Otherwise take public transport from Juliaca to Moho to Moho and on to Cambría, near Conima, walk down to the shore and take a rowing boat to Suasi, 10 mins, US$1.50 per person.

Rinconada
Buses leave Juliaca at 0600-0700, taking 5-6 hrs, and the road is deteriorates after Huancané Buses return from Rinconada at 0500-0700, taking about 30 mins less on the downhill journey; US$3.50 one way. In 2001 a border crossing to Bolivia was opened, but no details are available. To be sure of hassle-free departure or entry, use one of the regular border points given above.

❶ Directory

Juliaca *p243, map p243*
Banks Interbank, M Núñez 231. With Red Activa 24 ATM for Visa/Plus, Mastercard/Cirrus and Amex. **BCP**, M Núñez entre Chávez y 9 de Diciembre, changes cash and TCs but has no ATM. **Internet** There are many places in the centre, all charging US$0.60 per hr (some charge less in the morning). **Click**, San Román 338; **Planet Ch@t**, Pje C Arestegui 111, also has café; **Vi@net**, Jauregui 117; and others.

The western shore and into Bolivia

Anybody interested in religious architecture should go from Puno to visit the villages along the western shore of Lake Titicaca. They are all on the main road to Bolivia; only Zepita is beyond the turn-off to Yunguyo, see page 249. ⏵ *For Sleeping, Eating and other listings, see pages 250-252.*

Chucuito
An Inca sundial can be seen near the village of Chucuito (19 km), which has an interesting church, La Asunción, and houses with carved stone doorways. Visits to Chucuito usually include the Templo de la Fertilidad, **Inca Uyo**, which boasts many phalli and other fertility symbols. The authenticity and original location of these objects is the subject of debate. The locals tend to expect a tip for every and any thing. Nearby, are cave paintings at **Chichiflope**.

Ilave
On the road to Juli is Ilave, where the old road for Tacna branches off. It is typical of a gaunt altiplano town, with a good Sunday market where you can buy woven goods. This town received a lot of press in 2004 when the local population lynched the corrupt mayor and besieged the police station. This also blocked all land transport to and from Bolivia.

Juli
The main road then by-passes the little town of Juli, 83 km southeast, which has some fine examples of religious architecture in its four churches. **San Pedro** on the plaza, designated as the Cathedral, has been extensively restored. It contains a series of paintings of saints, with the Via Crucis scenes in the same frame, and gilt side altars above which some of the arches have baroque designs. No opening hours are displayed. **San Juan Letrán** ① *mornings only, US$1.15*, has two sets of 17th-century paintings of the lives of St John the Baptist and of St Teresa, contained in sumptuous gilded frames. San Juan is a museum. It also has intricate mestizo carving in pink stone. A long flight of shallow steps leads past the Centro Comunal and schools to **Santa Cruz**. The church is partly roofless, with scaffolding and a shelter protecting what remains of the tower. It is completely closed to visitors, but there is a view of the lake from the

great nave is empty, but its walls are lined with colonial paintings with no labels. The
original painting on the walls of the transept is fading. Its fine bell tower was damaged
by earthquake or lightning. Outside is an archway and atrium which date from the
early 17th century. Needlework, other weavings, handicrafts and antiques are offered
for sale in town. Near Juli is a small colony of flamingoes. Many other birds can be
seen from the road.

Pomata

A further 20 km along the lake is Pomata (US$0.45 from Juli), whose **church of Santiago
Apóstol** ① *0700-1200, 1330-1600, free, but give a donation and a tip to the guardian*, is
built of red sandstone (1532, started by the Jesuits, finished by the Dominicans). If the
colectivo does not enter town, get out by the barracks – cuartel – and walk up. It stands
on a promontory above the main road and has wonderful carvings in Andean mestizo
baroque of vases full of tropical plants, flowers and animals in the window frames,
lintels and cornices. The windows and font are of alabaster. The beautiful interior
contains statues, painted columns, a Spanish tiled floor, paintings of the Cusqueña
school and a cupola decorated with figures whose florid, stylized bodies have linked
arms. Beneath the Altar of El Señor del Sepulcro is an altarpiece covered in all the tools
used in the construction. At **Zepita**, near Desaguadero, the 18th-century Dominican
church is also worth a visit.

Border with Bolivia

There are two principal routes across the border, both of which are fairly
straightforward. The one listed first is by far the more popular of the two. There is a
third and rarely travelled route (see under Juliaca, above), and, finally, it is possible to
cross the border by hydrofoil or catamaran as part of a tour. Peruvian time is one hour
behind Bolivian time.

Puno to Copacabana via Yunguyo The road is paved from Puno to Yunguyo (the
border) and the scenery is interesting. The views are also good on the Bolivian side.
The Peruvian immigration office is five minutes' drive from Yunguyo and 100 m from
the Bolivian post. It is open 24 hours a day (but Bolivian immigration is only open
0830-1930). When leaving you must get an exit stamp before crossing the border and
a tourist visa on the other side. 90 days is normally given when entering Peru (30 days
for Bolivia). Be aware of corruption at customs and look out for official or unofficial
people trying to charge you a fee on either side of the border (say that you know it is
illegal and ask why only gringos are approached to pay the 'embarkation tax').

The Bolivian border town of **Copacabana** is famous for its Dark Virgin of the Lake, La
Virgen de Candelaria. From the town, excursions can be made to Isla del Sol and Isla de
la Luna on Lake Titicaca. There is a wide variety of hotels, restaurants and other
services. All road transport from Copacabana to La Paz has to take the ferry across the
Straits of Tiquina.

Puno to La Paz via Desaguadero When leaving Peru for Bolivia, this is the most
direct road route, which continues 41 km beyond the turn-off to Yunguyo, all paved for
the 150 km to the border. Desaguadero is a scruffy, unscrupulous place, with poor
restaurants and dubious accommodation. There is no need to stopover in
Desaguadero as all roads to it are paved and if you leave La Paz, Moquegua or Puno
early enough you should be at your destination before nightfall.

Peruvian immigration is beside the bridge. It is open 0830-1230 and 1400-2000.
Bolivian immigration is open the same hours, except closes at 2100. Both offices are
usually closed for dinner around 1830-1900. 30 days is normally given on entering
Bolivia, ask for more if you need it, or get an extension in La Paz. Into Bolivia, the road to

Guaqui (22 km) and on to La Paz is paved. This particular border crossing allows you to stop at the archaeological site of Tiahuanaco en route. It is possible to do a round trip to the site from Puno in about 12-13 hours. Take an early *colectivo* to Desaguadero, cross the border and take another *colectivo* towards La Paz. Pay the full fare, but ask to be let out at the junction for Tiahuanaco; walk or hitch the 1½ km to the ruins (entry US$2.10).

● Sleeping

Chucuito *p248*
A Taypikala Hotel & Spa, 18 km south of Puno on the road to Desaguadero, T051-369689, www.taypikala.com. Built in "inka" style with lots of indoor plants, new age feel, lovely gardens, most rooms have a view of the lake. Good restaurant, bar, spa, store, disco, meditation room, popular with tour groups.
E per person**Albergue Juvenil Las Cabañas**, T051-351276, www.chucuito.com. Great wee cottages, meals, will collect you from Puno if you phone in advance. A very good choice.

Juli *p248*
G per person **Hostal San Pedro**, main plaza. Basic, cold water, shared bath, restaurant.

Border with Bolivia *p249*
D-E Hostal Corona, Av Panamericana 248, Desaguadero, T851120. The best hotel of a poor lot, **F** without bath, TV, hot water, parking, luggage store, no meals.
F San Carlos, Desaguadero. Without bath, extra for hot shower, basic, tiny rooms. There is also accommodation on the Bolivian side. Most places have rooms for sleeping and lock-ups in which to put all the goods you are going to sell on in Peru or Bolivia.
G per person **Hostal Isabel**, San Francisco 110, Plaza de Armas, Yunguyo, T051-856019. Shared bathroom, hot water, good value, will change money and arrange transport.

● Eating

Border with Bolivia *p249*
There are several restaurants in Desaguadero, mostly *pollerías*. On the Peruvian side **Panamericano**, **Así Es Mi Tierra** and **Perú Criollo** advertise a bit more variety.

● Transport

Ilave *p248*
Many buses and *colectivos* go to Ilave from Puno, US$1.40.

Juli *p248*
Colectivos from Puno to Juli cost US$1. They stop in the main plaza before going to the *paradero* outside market, at Ilave 349, from where they return to Puno.

Border with Bolivia *p249*
Puno to La Paz via Yunguyo and Copacabana In Puno 3 companies sell bus tickets for the direct route from Puno to La Paz, taking 6-8 hrs (the fare does not include

the Tiquina ferry crossing, US$0.25):
Colectur, Tacna 221, T051-352302, 0730,
US$6.50, combines with **Galería** in Bolivia;
Panamericano, Tacna 245, T051-354001,
0730, US$7.35, combines with **Diana Tours**;
Tour Perú (see p240), 0800, US$8.75,
combines with **Combi Tour** (fares rise at
holiday times). They stop at the borders and
one hour for lunch in Copacabana, arriving in
La Paz at about 1700. Passengers change
buses at Copacabana and it seems that the
Bolivian bus may not be of the company
indicated and may not be of the same
standard as the Peruvian bus. This can cause
discomfort and delays. You only need to
change money into Bolivianos for lunch on
this route. Bus fare Puno-Copacabana
US$4.40-5.80. There are local buses and
colectivos all day between Puno and Yunguyo,
3 hrs, US$1.20; they leave from Av Bolívar in
Puno. From Yunguyo to the border (Kasani),
colectivos charge US$0.25 per person. From
the border it is a 20-min drive to Copacabana.
Colectivos and minibuses leave from just
outside Bolivian immigration, US$0.50 per
person. A taxi from Yunguyo to Copacabana
costs about US$1.50 per person. Entering
Peru, don't take a taxi Yunguyo-Puno without
checking its reliability first, the driver may pick
up an accomplice to rob passengers.

Puno to La Paz via Desaguadero
Tricitaxis carry people and their baggage
around for US$0.30, but they'll probably ask
for more at some point in the ride. *Colectivos*
and buses run every 30 mins between **Puno**
and Desaguadero; 2¼ hrs, US$1.50. The last
bus from the border to Puno leaves at 1930.
There are minibuses to **La Paz** (105 km from
Desaguadero), 1½ hrs, US$1.50. The last one
leaves at 1700, though buses may leave later if
there are enough passengers. See p313 for
the road from **Moquegua**. Mily Tours, Av
Pan-americana 321, run *colectivos* to
Moquegua, US$10, 3½ hrs. Several bus
companies do the route for US$6, 4 hrs
(Ormeño US$11.75), continuing to **Arequipa**.

To La Paz by hydrofoil or catamaran
There are luxury services from Puno to La Paz
by **Crillon Tours** hydrofoil and **Transturin**'s
catamarans. **Crillon Tours** services can be
booked at their office at **Arcobaleno Tours**
(see p240), or all Puno travel agents have
details, or their head office at Av Camacho
1223, PO Box 4785, La Paz, T591 2-233 7533,

www.titicaca.com. The Puno office will take
care of all documentation for crossing the
border into Bolivia. The main itinerary is:
Puno-Copacabana by bus or hydrofoil;
Copacabana-Isla del Sol-Huatajata (Bolivia) by
hydrofoil; Huatajata-La Paz by bus; 13 hrs.
Visits to Pomata, Juli and reed-boat builders
are included. They run a tour which can start
at Juliaca airport (for new arrivals in the
region), thence to Copacabana, then to Isla
del Sol, back to Puno by hydrofoil, continuing
to Cusco and Machu Picchu. Visits to their
establishments can be incorporated into
Crillon's tours covering many options. **Crillon**
also has a sustainable tourism project with
Urus-Iruitos people from the Río Desaguadero
area which will be of great interest to anyone
who has visited the Urus of the bay of Puno.
    Similar services, by more leisurely
catamaran, are run by **Transturin**, whose dock
is at Chúa, Bolivia. Bookings can be made
through **Transturin**'s offices in La Paz, C
Alfredo Ascarrunz 2518, Sopocachi, Casilla
5311, T591 2-242 2222, www.travelbolivia.
com (this office offers economical, last-
minute bookings, 24 and 48 hrs in advance),
and Av Libertad 176, Puno, T051-352771. The
main route is Puno to Copacabana by bus,
Copacabana to the Isla del Sol (including a
land tour) and on to Chúa by catamaran, then
bus to La Paz. The trip can be done in one day,
or with a night on board the catamaran,
moored at the Isla del Sol. It is also possible to
go Puno (depart 0630)-Isla del Sol-Puno
(arrive 1930). Extensions from Cusco to Puno
by train are available. Transturin also run
buses between Puno and La Paz, with no
change of bus at the border.

⊕ Directory

Border with Bolivia *p249*
Banks Good rates are available for dollars or
bolivianos at the two casas de cambio in the
main plaza in Yunguyo, cash only. Travellers'
cheques can be exchanged but rates poor. It
is better to change money (even bolivianos)
on the Peruvian side in Desaguadero.
Consulates Bolivian Consulate, Jr Grau
339, T051-856032, near the main plaza in
Yunguyo. Mon-Fri 0830-1500, for those who
need a visa. Some nationalities have to pay,
the fee varies per nationality.

Arequipa

Footprint features

Introduction

The distinctive volcanic sillar used in the building of the city of Arequipa, has given it its nickname of the 'White City'. Spanish churches, mansions and the 19th-centruy Plaza de Armas all shine with this stonework. In contrast, the city's most famous colonial jewel, the Santa Catalina convent, is painted in bright colours, a gorgeous little city within a city. This is only one attraction in a region of volcanoes, deep canyons and terraced valleys. The perfect cone of El Misti and its companions Chachani and Pichu-Pichu overlook Arequipa itself. Active Sabancaya and frequent earth tremors are reminders that this is a very unstable region.

Two famous canyons are within relatively easy reach. To arrive at these great gorges, you must take rough roads at high altitudes. Cotahuasi Canyon is the deepest in the world at 3,354 m, but it has not yet achieved the same popularity as its neighbour, Colca. And it was only recently that the ancient peoples here, the Cabana and Collagua, had their villages and farms exposed to the gaze of tourism. There is excellent trekking and riding on the terraces of Colca, accommodation is improving all the time and the calendar is full of festivals. Above all, Colca also happens to be the best place in the whole world to get close-up view of the majestic condor rising on the morning thermals. On the altiplanos of this region there are herds of alpaca and vicuña and, at the World Heritage site of Toro Muerto, the largest field of petroglyphs in the world.

There's an individual feeling to this southwestern corner of Peru which, in part, stems from the stubborn pride of its people who have continuously attempted to gain more independence from Lima. Fellow Peruvians will jokingly refer to this region as the 'Independent Republic of Arequipa'.

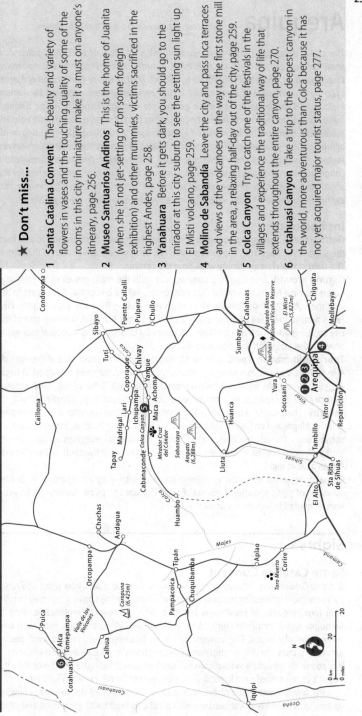

★ Don't miss...

1 Santa Catalina Convent The beauty and variety of flowers in vases and the touching quality of some of the rooms in this city in miniature make it a must on anyone's itinerary, page 256.

2 Museo Santuarios Andinos This is the home of Juanita (when she is not jet-setting off on some foreign exhibition) and other mummies, victims sacrificed in the highest Andes, page 258.

3 Yanahuara Before it gets dark, you should go to the mirador at this city suburb to see the setting sun light up El Misti volcano, page 259.

4 Molino de Sabandía Leave the city and pass Inca terraces and views of the volcanoes on the way to the first stone mill in the area, a relaxing half-day out of the city, page 259.

5 Colca Canyon Try to catch one of the festivals in the villages and experience the traditional way of life that extends throughout the entire canyon, page 270.

6 Cotahuasi Canyon Take a trip to the deepest canyon in the world, more adventurous than Colca because it has not yet acquired major tourist status, page 277.

Arequipa → Phone code: 054. Colour map 5, grid C6. Altitude: 2,380 m.

The city of Arequipa stands in a beautiful valley at the foot of El Misti volcano, a snow-capped, perfect cone, 5,822 m high, guarded on either side by the mountains Chachani (6,057 m), and Pichu-Pichu (5,669 m). The city was re-founded on 15 August 1540 by an emissary of Pizarro, but it had previously been occupied by Aymara Indians and the Incas. It has since grown into a magnificent city – fine Spanish buildings and many old and interesting churches built of sillar, a pearly white volcanic material were almost exclusively used in the construction of Arequipa – exuding an air of intellectual rigour and political passion. Among its famous sons and daughters are former President Fernando Belaúnde Terry and novelist and failed presidential candidate, Mario Vargas Llosa. Now, Arequipa is the main commercial centre for the south and its fiercely proud people resent the general tendency to believe that everything is run from Lima. ▶▶ *For Sleeping, Eating and other listings, see pages 260-270.*

Ins and outs

Getting there Rodríguez Ballón airport is 7 km from town. For transport to and from the airport, see page 268. The bus terminal is a 10-15 minute drive south of the centre. The train station is a 15-minute walk from the centre.

Getting around Arequipa is a compact city with the main places of interest and hotels within a few blocks of the Plaza de Armas. Take a bus or taxi if you want to the visit the suburbs. Taxis (can be shared) charge US$4-5 from the airport to the city. Fares around town are US$0.70-0.85, including to bus terminal. A cheap tour of the city can be made in a Vallecito bus - 1½ hours for US$0.30. It is a circular tour going down Calles Jerusalén and San Juan de Dios.

Tourist information i perú ① *in the Municipalidad on the south side of the Plaza de Armas, T054-221228, iperuarequipa@ptomperu.gob.pe, 0830-1930.* Airport ① *T054-444564, 0630-1730.* **Indecopi** (tourist protection bureau) ① *Moral 316, T054-212054, mcornejo@indecopi.gob.pe and Quezada 104, Yanahuara, T054-270181.*

Security Theft can be a problem in the market area, especially after dark, in the park at Selva Alegre and on Calles San Juan de Dios and Alvarez Thomas, but the police are conspicuous, friendly, courteous and efficient. Beware taxi muggings at night, drivers work with accomplices to rob passengers. It's best to avoid the south of the Plaza de Armas area at night.

Climate Arequipa enjoys a wonderful climate, with a mean temperature before sundown of 23°C, and after sundown of 14°C. The sun shines on 360 days of the year. Annual rainfall is less than 150 mm.

Sights

Santa Catalina Convent

① *Santa Catalina 301, T054-229798, www.santacatalina.org.pe, 0900-1600, US$7.25.*
By far the most interesting place to visit is the Santa Catalina Convent, opened in 1970 after four centuries of mysterious isolation. This is the most remarkable sight in Arequipa and a complete contrast to what you would expect from nuns who had taken vows of poverty. The convent has been beautifully refurbished, with period furniture, pictures of the Arequipa and Cusco schools and fully equipped kitchens. It is a complete miniature walled colonial town of over 2 ha in the middle of the city. About 450 nuns lived here in total seclusion, except for their women servants.

The few remaining nuns have retreated to one section of the convent, allowing visitors to see a maze of cobbled streets and plazas bright with geraniums and other

flowers, cloisters and buttressed houses. These have been finely restored and 257
painted in traditional white, orange, deep red and blue. The tour offered at the
entrance is worthwhile and lasts 1½ hours; there's no set price and many of the
guides speak English or German (a tip of US$2.85 is expected). There is a good café,
which sells cakes made by the nuns and a special blend of tea.

Around the centre

The elegant **Plaza de Armas**, beautifully laid-out with palm trees, gardens and
fountain, is faced on three sides by arcaded colonial buildings (rebuilt after an

Arequipa

Sleeping
Casa Andina 9
Casa de mi Abuela 2
Colonial House Inn II 1
Del Parque 13
El Conquistador 3
El Indio Dormido 22

Hostal Bolívar 4
Hostal Casa Grande 5
Hostal El Cóndor 6
Hostal Núñez 7
Hostal Rivero 17
Hostal Tumi de Oro 8
La Estación 21

La Hostería 10
Las Torres
de Ugarte 11
Libertador 12
Miamaka 14
Piccola Daniela 15
Queen's Villa 16

Tambo Viejo 18
Tierrasur 19
Tourist House 20

Eating
La Quinta 1
Nómadas 2

Related map
A Arequipa centre,
page 261.

earthquake in 1863) with many restaurants, and on the fourth by the **cathedral**. Behind the cathedral there is a very attractive alley, Pasaje Catedral, with a good selection of handicraft shops and places for tourists to eat.

The massive **cathedral** on the Plaza de Armas was founded in 1612 and largely rebuilt in the 19th century. It is remarkable for having its façade along the whole length of the church and takes up one full side of the plaza. Inside is a fine Belgian organ and elaborately carved wooden pulpit. Despite the care taken in building techniques, the June 2001 earthquake caused one of the cathedral's twin towers famously to collapse. Repairs were completed in 2003. The entrance to the Cathedral is on the plaza.

A visit to the church and cloister of **La Compañía** at General Morán y Alvarez Thomas, is recommended. The main façade (1698) and side portal (1654) are striking examples of the florid Andean mestizo style. There are two adjoining cloisters now

‡ *Churches are usually open 0700-0900 and 1800-2000.*

given over to attractive shops. Also of note is the **Capilla Real** (Royal Chapel) ① *Mon-Fri 0900-1130, 1500-1730, US$0.50*, to the left of the sanctuary, and its San Ignacio chapel with a beautiful polychrome cupola. The stark cloister is impressive.

Also worth seeing is the church of **San Agustín**, at San Agustín y Sucre, under restoration until 2005, and **La Casona Chávez de la Rosa**, at San Agustín 104, part of the Universidad San Agustín, which holds art and photography exhibitions.

Museo Santuarios Andinos ① *La Merced 110, T054-200345, www.ucsm.edu.pe/santury   Mon-Sat 0900-1800, Sun 0900-1700, US$5, includes a 20-min video of the discovery in English followed by an hour-long guided tour in English, French, German, Italian or Spanish (tip the guide), discount with student card*. Firmly established as one of the major sites in Arequipa, this museum contains the frozen mummies recently found on Ampato volcano. The mummy known as 'Juanita' is particularly fascinating (see page 272). From January to April, Juanita is often jetting round the world, and is replaced by other child sacrifices unearthed in the mountains. **Museo de Arte Textil** ① *Patio del Ekeko, Mercaderes 141, Mon-Sat 1000-2030, Sun 1000-1530*, has an interesting collection of textiles and shows short documentaries about Arequipa. The 16th-century church of **San Francisco** also has a convent and library and opposite is the interesting **Museo Histórico Municipal** ① *Plaza San Francisco 407, Mon-Fri 0900-1700, US$0.50*, with much war memorabilia.

Arequipa is said to have the best-preserved colonial architecture in Peru, apart from Cusco. Several fine seignorial houses with large carved tympanums over the entrances can be seen in the city centre. Thanks to their being one-storey structures, they have mostly withstood the earthquakes which regularly pound this city. They are distinguished by their small patios with no galleries, flat roofs and small windows, disguised by superimposed lintels or heavy grilles.

One of the best examples is the 18th-century **Casa Tristán del Pozo**, better known as the **Gibbs-Ricketts house** ① *San Francisco 108, Mon-Sat 0915-1245, 1500-2000*, with its fine portal and puma-head waterspouts. It is now the main office of Banco Continental.

Other good examples are the **Casa del Moral**, or Williams house ① *C Moral 318 y Bolívar, Mon-Sat 0900-1700, Sun 0900-1300, US$1.80 or US$1 for students*, with a museum, in the Banco Industrial. **Casa de la Moneda** ① *Ugarte y Villalba*, is behind Santa Catalina convent. **Casa Goyeneche** ① *La Merced 201 y Palacio Viejo*, is now an office of the Banco Central de la Reserva. Ask to see the courtyard and fine period rooms. In the next block south is the early 17th-century church of **La Merced** ① *La Merced 303*.

● *Because of the ever-present danger of earthquakes, churches in the city were built low.*
● *As recently as 2001 the city lost one tower of its cathedral in an earthquake.*

The church of **Santo Domingo**, at Santo Domingo y Piérola, dates from the 17th century. In its fine door, an Indian face can be seen amid the flowers and grapes. The central **San Camilo market**, between Perú, San Camilo, Piérola and Alto de la Luna, is worth visiting, as is the **Siglo XX market**, to the east of the rail station.

La Recoleta
① *Mon-Sat 0900-1900, US$1.*
La Recoleta, a Franciscan monastery built in 1647, stands on the other side of the river, on Recoleta. It contains several cloisters, a religious art museum, a pre-Columbian museum, an Amazon museum, a library with many rarities, and is well worth visiting.

San Lázaro
The oldest district in the city is San Lázaro, a collection of tiny climbing streets and houses quite close to the Hotel Libertador, where you can find the ancient **Capilla de San Lázaro**. At **Selva Alegre** there is a shady park in front of the **Hotel Libertador**, which is within easy walking distance of all the famous churches and main plaza (see Security, above). To the east of San Lázaro, the **archaeological museum** ① *Av Independencia between La Salle and Santa Rosa, apply to Dr E Linares, the Director, T054-229719, Mon-Fri 0800-1300, US$1,* is at the Universidad de San Agustín. It has a good collection of ceramics and mummies.

Excursions

Northwest
Some 2 km northwest of the city is the district is **Yanahuara**, where there is a 1750 mestizo-style church (opens 1500), with a magnificent churrigueresque façade, all in sillar. The church stands on a plaza, at the end of which is a mirador, through whose arches there is a fine view of El Misti with the city at its feet. There's live music at Peña El Moro, on Parque Principal. A score of *picanterías* specialize in piquant foods such as *rocoto relleno* (hot stuffed peppers), *cuy chactado* (seared guinea-pig), *papas con ocopa* (boiled potatoes with a hot spicy yellow sauce) and *adobo* (pork stew). To get there cross the Puente Grau and turn right up Avenida Bolognesi.

In the hillside suburb of **Cayma**, 3 km northwest of the city, is a delightful 18th-century church ① *open until 1700,* and many old buildings associated with Bolívar and Garcilaso de la Vega. Many local buses go to Cayma.

Beyond the airport, at **Las Canteras de Sillar**, you can see the quarries where the sillar blocks are cut for buildings in the city. They are worth a brief visit if passing, but not a special detour.

Southeast
Tingo has a very small lake and three swimming pools. You should visit on Sunday for local food such as anticuchos and buñuelos. Take bus 7, US$0.20. Three kilometres past Tingo, beside the Sabandía river on the Huasacache road, is **La Mansión del Fundador** ① *0900-1700, US$2.50,* with cafetería and bar. Originally owned by the founder of Arequipa, Don Garcí Manuel de Carbajal, in 1540, it has been open to the public since 1897 and restored as a museum with original furnishings and paintings. Nearby is the **Mirador Sachaca** ① *US$0.35, take a bus marked 'Sachaca' from C La Merced.* It has fine panoramic views, best between 0630 and 0730 before the smog obscures the view. In the district of Sachaca, 4 km from the centre, is the **Palacio Goyeneche**.

Molino de Sabandía ① *US$1.50, ring the bell for admission,* is 8 km from Arequipa. A round trip by taxi costs US$4. This was the first stone mill in the area, built

66 99 In August, when El Misti has its full covering of snow , they say it is wearing its poncho...

in 1621. It has been fully restored and the guardian diverts water to run the grinding stones when visitors arrive. The well-kept grounds have old willow trees and the surrounding countryside is pleasant; a worthwhile trip. Adjoining Sabandía is **Yumina**, with many Inca terraces which are still in use and between Sabandía and Arequipa is Paucarpata, with an old church and views of terraces, El Misti and Chachani. The **thermal baths of Jesús** ① *0500-1230*, are 30 minutes by car, on the slopes of Pichu-Pichu.

Yura → *Colour map 5, grid C6.*

Yura, is a pleasant town, 29 km from Arequipa in a small, interesting valley on the west slopes of Chachani. It is popular with Arequipeños for its **thermal baths** ① *Tue-Sat, until 1500, US$2.* To reach the baths, walk down to the river from the main road by the **Yura Tourist Hotel**, which also serves meals. The first set of baths contains four small pools which are not suitable for swimming. Follow the river to the next one, which is bigger. Note that the water is not very hot. To return to Arequipa, catch a *colectivo* on the main road by the hotel. A bus leaves every 3 hours from Calle San Juan de Dios in Arequipa, US$0.40.

El Misti → *Colour map 5, grid C6.*

At 5,822 m, El Misti volcano offers a relatively straightforward opportunity to scale a high peak. Start from the hydroelectric plant, after first registering with the police there, then you need one day to the Monte Blanco shelter, at 4,800 m. Start early for the four to six hours to the top, to get there by 1100 before the mists obscure the view. If you start back at 1200 you will reach the hydroelectric plant by 1800. Take a jeep at 3,300 m to the end of the rough road, then four to five hours hike to the campground at 4,600 m. Only space for three tents (two to three person tents).

Alternatively, buses leave Arequipa for Baños Jesús, then on to Chiguata, from where you can walk to the base of El Misti. Guides may be available at Cachamarca. Be sure to take plenty of food, water and protection against the weather; it takes two days to reach the crater. Remember that the summit is at a very high altitude and that this, combined with climbing on scree, makes it hard going for the untrained. Recent reports of hold-ups of climbers make it inadvisable for you to go alone. Join a group or take a guide. Further information is available from travel agencies and Miguel and Carlos Zárate, see Climbing page 267 for details.

● Sleeping

Arequipa *p256, map p257*

LL-L Libertador, Plaza Simón Bolívar, Selva Alegre, T054-215110, www.libertador. com.pe. Safe, large comfortable rooms, good service, swimming pool (cold), gardens, good meals, pub-style bar, cocktail lounge, squash court. Recommended.

AL Sonesta Posada del Inca, Portal de Flores 116, T054-215530, www.sonesta.com. On the Plaza de Armas, all the services

associated with this chain, Inkafé café and bar with good views, restaurant, tiny outdoor pool, business centre with internet.

AL-A Casa Andina, C Jerusalén 603, T054-202070, www.casa-andina.com. Part of the attractive Casa Andina chain, with breakfast, comfortable and colourful, central, modern, good restaurant, safe, cable TV, phones, friendly staff, car parking.

A El Conquistador, Mercaderes 409,

T054-212916, F218987. Clean, safe, lovely colonial atmosphere, owner speaks English, thin walls.

Arequipa centre

A Hostal Casa Grande, Luna Pizarro 202, Vallecito, T054-214000, F214021. Includes taxes, small, cosy, well-furnished, quiet, friendly, good services and restaurant. Recommended.

A La Plazuela, on Plaza Juan Manuel Polar 105, Vallecito (5 mins' walk from the centre), T054-222624, F234625. A lovely old house next to a small park some distance from centre, nicely furnished, hot water, cable TV, laundry service, cafeteria, restaurant, owners speak English.

A La Posada del Monasterio, Santa Catalina 300, T/F054-283076, www.posada delmonasterio.com.pe. Colonial building opposite Santa Catalina, breakfast included, furnished with antiques, garden, pleasant atmosphere.

A Maison Plaza, Portal San Agustín 143, T054-218929, arequipa@planet.com.pe. With breakfast, bathroom and TV, comfortable, clean, friendly, good value, older and newer rooms.

B Casa de Mi Abuela, Jerusalén 606, T054-241206, www.lacasdemiabuela.com. Very clean, friendly, safe, hot water, laundry, cable TV, swimming pool, rooms at the back are quieter and overlook the garden (but the room at the very back beyond the garden is dark and has no hot water), **D** without bathroom, self-catering if desired, English spoken, internet access US$3 per hr, tours and transport organized in own agency (Giardino, T054-221345, www.giardinotours.com), which has good information (expensive), small library of European books, breakfast or evening snacks on patio or in beautiful garden, parking, **A-B** for apartment for 4, lots of tour groups. Recommended.

B Hostal de la Fuente, Urb Campiña Paisajista D-14A, San Lázaro, T054-203996, delafuente_hostal@hotmail.com. In a residential district 4 blocks from the Plaza de Armas, comfortable rooms, with bath, 24-hrs hot water, cable TV, internet, laundry, café, bar, safe boxes.

B Hostal Solar, Ayacucho 108, T/F054-241793, solar@star.com.pe. Nice colonial building, TV, bath, hot water, includes good breakfast served in nice patio, sun lounge on roof, very secure, quiet.

B Queen's Villa, Luna Pizarro 512, Vallecito, T054-235233, jrowlands@terra.com.pe. With bath, hot water, breakfast, safe, parking, laundry.

B Tierrasur, Consuelo 210, T054-227132, www.tierrasur.com. Modern 3-star, convenient for centre, clean, comfortable, safe, very helpful staff, English spoken, gym. Recommended.

C Casa de Melgar, Melgar 108, T/F054-222459, www.lared.net.pe/lacasademelgar/. Excellent rooms, all different, delightful 18th-century building, with bathroom, hot water all day (solar panel), safe, clean, friendly, nice courtyard, good breakfast in café open in the morning and 1730-2100, book exchange, luggage store. Can arrange good taxi tours with driver, Angel. Recommended.

C Hostal Bolívar, Bolívar 202, T054-200280, www.hostalbolivar.com. Colonial-style, cable TV, internet and fax service, breakfast served in patio. Recommended.

C La Casa de Margott, Jerusalén 304, T054-229517, lacasademargotthostal@hotmail.com. Bright with a massive palm tree in patio, spotless, small bar/café, new, cable TV, phone, security box, bathroom. Recommended.

C La Casa de Tintin, Urbanización San Isidro F1, Vallecito, T054-284700, www.lacasadetintin.com. New B & B place 15 mins' walk, 5 mins by taxi from the Plaza de Armas, Belgian/Peruvian owned, with bath, hot water 24 hrs, cable TV, garden, terrace, sauna, laundry service, restaurant, café and bar and internet, mountain bike rental, very pleasant, clean. Breakfast included in the price. Recommended.

C La Hostería, Bolívar 405, T/F054-289269, lahosteria@terra.com.pe. Small, friendly, comfortable and attractive. Recommended.

C Los Balcones de Moral y Santa Catalina, Moral 217, T054-201291, losbalcones@hotmail.com. Convenient, 1 block from Plaza de Armas and close to Santa Catalina, large rooms, comfortable beds, with bath, hot water, laundry, café, tourist information.

C Miamaka, San Juan de Dios 402, T054-241496, hotel_miamaka@terra.com.pe. Excellent service and well-decorated, cable TV, helpful, English spoken. Recommended, but not the safest area.

C-D La Posada del Fraile, Santa Catalina 103, T054-282006, posadadelfraile@hotmail.com. Cheaper without breakfast, with bath, clean, safe, well-furnished, very central, new.

C-F Tambo Viejo, Av Malecón Socabaya 107, IV Centenario, 5 blocks south of the plaza near the rail station, T054-288195, www.tamboviejo.com. Family home, quiet, very friendly, English and Dutch spoken, walled garden, hot water, expensive laundry service, cable TV, safe deposit, coffee shop, bar book exchange (2 for 1), money changed, tourist information for guests, use of kitchen, internet, phone for international calls, bike rental, popular with young travellers, luggage store extra, tours arranged. For a small fee, you can use the facilities if passing through. When arriving by bus or train, do not believe taxi drivers who say the hotel is closed or full; ring the door bell and check for yourself. Better still, telephone the hostel and they will pick you up free of charge form 0500-2100. In high season and rooms with garden view are **C**, **D-E** with shared bath, **F** pp in dormitory.

D del Parque, Deán Valdivia 238A, T054-285936. In an old colonial house with big rooms, nice roof terrace, breakfast available, arranges tours to Colca, luggage store, laundry, pick-up service from bus terminal.

D Hospedaje El Caminante Class, Santa Catalina 207-A, 2nd floor, T054-203444. With bathroom, cheaper without, hot water, TV, clean, laundry service and facilities, sun terrace, very helpful owners. Recommended.

D Hostal Le Foyer, Ugarte 114 y San Francisco, T054-286473, hostallefoyer@yahoo.com. Comfortable, very hot water 24 hrs, laundry, luggage store, safe, helpful. Recommended.

D Hostal Núñez, Jerusalén 528, T054-233268, hostal_nunez@terra.com.pe. With bathroom, cheaper without, hot water, TV, laundry, safe, small rooms, breakfast on roof terrace overlooking the city.

D per person Hostal Regis, Ugarte 202, T054-226111. Colonial house, French-style interior, clean, hot water all day, **E** without bath, cooking and laundry facilities (good laundry service), sun terrace with good views, safe deposit, luggage store, video rental, book exchange, very helpful, tours

● *For an explanation of sleeping and eating price codes used in this guide, see inside the* ● *front cover. Other relevant information is found in Essentials, pages 61-66.*

arranged. Recommended.

D Hostal Tumi de Oro, San Agustín 311A, 2 blocks from the Plaza de Armas, T/F054-281319. With bathroom, French and English spoken, hot water, roof terrace, book exchange, tea/coffee facilities, safe. Recommended.

D La Estación, Loreto 419, Umacollo, T273852, www.backpackerperu.com. Unusual dormitory accommodation in two train carriages, includes breakfast, hot water, restaurant next door, friendly, clean and fresh. 10 mins' walk from Plaza, ask directions for 'el Ovalo del Vallecito', English spoken.

D La Posada del Cacique, Puente Grau 219, T202170, posadadelcacique@yahoo.es. Old house with tall ceilings, teeny patio, sun terrace, friendly, good hot water, English spoken, family atmosphere, **E** without bath, also dorm accommodation, safe storage facilities, breakfast available, laundry service, will pick up from terminal. Recommended.

D La Posada del Viajero, Jerusalén 404, T054-220677. Attractively furnished, airy, clean, hot water, very helpful.

D Las Torres de Ugarte, Ugarte 401-A, T/F054-283532, hostaltorresdeugarte@star.com.pe. Next to Santa Catalina convent, hot water all day, cable TV, roof terrace, laundry service, parking, safe, luggage store, helpful staff, discount for longer stays, price includes breakfast served in a sunny room. Recommended.

D Lluvia de Oro, Jerusalén 308, T054-214252, lluvia_de_oro@hotmail.com. Cheaper without bath, English-speaking, breakfast US$2, good views, laundry service, friendly. Recommended.

D Posada de Sancho, Santa Catalina 213 A and 223 A, near the convent, T/F054-287797, posadasancho@terra.com.pe. Hot showers, cheaper without bath, clean, safe, nice patio and terrace with a view of El Misti, good breakfast extra, very friendly owners, English, French and German spoken, information on travel and Spanish classes, offer cheap tours.

E Casa Itzhak, Av Parra 97, T054-204596. With and without bath, includes breakfast, cable TV, laundry service, restaurant, free transport to bus station, very helpful.

E Colonial House Inn, Puente Grau 114, T/F054-223533, colonialhouseinn@hotmail.com. Hot water, quieter rooms at the back, laundry facilities and service, kitchen facilities, roof terrace, good choice of breakfasts, owners speak English. Same owners run **Colonial House Inn II**, Rivero 504, which is more modern and nicer.

E Hostal La Reyna, Zela 209, T054-286578. With or without bath, two more expensive rooms at the top of the house (very good), hot water 24 hrs, clean, can be noisy because of location, the daughter speaks English, laundry, breakfast for US$1.15, pizza available at any hour, rooftop seating, can arrange Spanish classes, will store luggage and arrange trips to the Colca Canyon and volcanoes (a bit chaotic, but recommendable nonetheless). Do not believe taxi drivers who say the hotel is closed or full; ring the door bell and check for yourself.

E Hostal Rivero, Rivero 420, T054-229266, www.ciudadblanca.net/hostalrivero Cheaper with shared bath, hot water, cable TV extra, medical assistance, laundry facilities, very helpful, good value.

Arequipa Arequipa Listings

E Hostal Santa Catalina, Santa Catalina 500, T054-233705. Clean, hot water, TV, friendly, upper rooms quiet but elsewhere noisy, safe, luggage stored.

E Piccola Daniela, Bolivar 400, T054-405727, piccoladanielaaqp@hotmail.com. Includes breakfast, **F** without bath, good value, cable TV, hot water, tiny patio, no English.

E The Tourist House, Alvarez Tomás 435, T054-211752. In an unsafe area, hot showers, clean, safe hotel, friendly, kitchen, TV lounge, offers tours.

E-F Hostal El Cóndor, San Juan de Dios 525, T054-206166. Most rooms with bath, hot showers, cable TV, free luggage store, no breakfast, very friendly, tours arranged.

F per person **El Indio Dormido**, Av Andrés Avelino Cáceres B-9, T054-427401, the_sleeping_indian@ yahoo.com Close to bus terminal, free transport to centre, some rooms with bath, comfortable beds, **E**, TV, clean, very helpful.

F Fiorella, Octavio Muñoz Nájar 262, T054-226078. Family stay, cheap, a bit out of town, phone to ask if she has a room available.

F La Casita de Ugarte, Ugarte 212, T054-204363. English/Peruvian run, large basic rooms in a colonial building, new, good value.

F La Fiorentina, Puente Grau 110, T054-202571.**G** without bath, hot water, comfortable, ask for a good room, family atmosphere, tours arranged, laundry facilities, use of kitchen extra.

Youth hostels

D Hotel Premier, Av Quiroz 100, T/F054 227821, www.hostalpremier.com. HI-affiliated, **E** per person for HI members or in dormitory. Cultural, archaeological and adventure trips offered too.

F Youth Hostel Arequipa, Zela 313, T054-669253. Dormitory accommodation, kitchen, cosy lounge, cable TV, laundry facilities, very helpful, luggage stored.

Hostal Las Mercedes, Av La Marina 1001, T/F054-213601. US$6 for 2 including use of toilet and shower. Overnight vehicle parking.

● Eating

Arequipa *p256, map p257*
Several restaurants overlook the Plaza de Armas; their staff may pounce on you good-

naturedly as you pass. For typical Arequipeño food, head to Av Arancota, in the Tingo District, by the Río Chili. **La Cecilia** is highly recommended. Typical Arequipeño food is also available at the San Camilo market. A good local speciality is Mejía cheese. You should also try the queso helado, which is frozen fresh milk mixed with sugar and a sprinkling of cinnamon. The local chocolate is excellent: **La Ibérica**, in Patio del Ekeko, Mercaderes 141, is top quality, but expensive. The toffee and the fruit drinks called papayada and tumbada are also local specialities in the market and restaurants. Try **Casa Tropical**, on the first block of Rivero for a huge selection.

₩₩₩ El Gaucho Grill, underneath Sonesta hotel on Plaza de Armas. Huge portions, good value in this price category.

₩₩₩ La Quinta, Jerusalén 522. Excellent food, large portions but limited menu, quiet garden.

₩₩₩ La Rueda, Mercaderes 206. Excellent *parrilladas*.

₩₩₩ Picantería La Cantarilla, Tahuaycani 106-108, Sachaca, T054-251515, southwest of the centre. Good Arequipeña and Peruvian dishes, including ostrich.

₩₩₩ Tradición Arequipeña, Av Dolores 111, Paucarpata, T054-246467. Restaurant serving excellent food, popular with tourists and locals alike, also dance hall. There are many other restaurants and discos on this avenue, some distance from the centre.

₩₩ Ary Quepay, Jerusalén 502. Excellent local meat and vegetarian dishes, 1000-2400.

₩₩ Café-Restaurante Bóveda San Agustín, Portal San Agustín 127-129. Attractive, good value breakfasts and lunches, evening specials, opens at 0700.

₩₩ El Camaroncito, San Francisco y Ugarte. Recommended for seafood, with a good fixed-price lunchtime menu.

₩₩ El Turko II, San Francisco 315. Turkish, local and international. Recommended.

₩₩ Gianni, San Francisco 304. Good value for pasta and pizza.

₩₩ La Casita de José Antonio, Plaza San Francisco 401 y Zela. Cevichería, fish and seafood, lunchtime only.

₩₩ Mixto's, Pasaje La Catedral 113. With balcony, international food, fish specials.

₩₩ Nómadas, Melgar 306. Swiss and South American owned, breakfasts, wide menu including vegetarian, sandwiches.

♥♥ Pizzería Los Leños, Jerusalén 407. Excellent, good atmosphere, evenings only, popular, especially with tourists.

♥♥ Pizzería San Antonio, Jerusalén y Santa Marta. Popular.

♥♥ Sonccollay, Portal de San Agustín 149. Serving 'Inca and Pre-Inca' dishes, this restaurant gives a new twist to 'traditional' food. Stone-cooked alpaca steaks and meats are a speciality. Hosted by an entertaining owner, plenty of home-made *chicha*.

♥♥ Zig Zag, Zela 210. In a colonial house, European (including Swiss) and local dishes, excellent meats include ostrich and alpaca, top class. They also have a creperie in the Alianza Francesa (see Cultural centres).

♥♥ Zig Zag Crêperie, Santa Catalina 208. Excellent crepes, good value set lunch, also snacks, cocktails, coffee.

♥♥-♥ Ganesh, Santa Catalina 111, upstairs. Asian food and a limited number of vegetarian options, good service, relaxed and trendy atmosphere, bar. Recommended.

♥ Café El Buho, in Casona Chávez de la Rosa (UNSA), San Agustín. Evenings only. Recommended.

♥ Casa Vegetariana, Moral 205. Vegetarian and Asian, typical local food, western dishes.

♥ Colibri Café, San Francisco 225. Excellent value set lunches and dinners, open plan, attractive, good coffee.

♥ D'la Casa, San Francisco y Ugarte. Good stop-gap sandwiches and burgers.

♥ El Turko, San Francisco 216. Kebabs, coffee, breakfasts, good sandwiches, 0700-2200.

♥ Govinda, Santa Catalina 120, T285540. Set vegetarian meal for US$1.25, themed each day, eg, Hindu, Italian, Arequipeño (mixed reports), good yoghurt and muesli. Mon-Sat 0700-2100.

♥ Lakshmivan, Jerusalén 402. Vegetarian, set lunch for US$1.25, pleasant courtyard, good value and healthy, but slow service.

♥ Mandala, Jerusalén 207, mandala26@ correoweb.com. Good value vegetarian, breakfast, 3 set menus for lunch, buffet, dinner, friendly staff. Recommended.

♥ Sunlight, Moral 205. Good range of cheap Asian meals and snacks.

Cafés

Café Capriccio, Mercaderes 121. Not that cheap, but excellent coffee, cakes etc.

Café Manolo, Mercaderes 107 and 113. Great cakes and coffee, also cheap lunches, pastas, sandwiches and juices.

Café Valenzuela, Moran 114. Fantastic coffee, locals' favourite.

El Café, San Francisco 125. Popular meeting place.

La Canasta, Jerusalén 115. Bakes excellent baguettes twice daily, also serves breakfast and delicious apple and brazil nut pastries.

Gopal Nature Centre, Melgar 101. Excellent breakfasts and huge fruit salads.

Pushkin, Ugarte 121B. Good for set breakfasts, crêpes, burgers, very friendly, pleasant.

❶ Bars and clubs

Arequipa *p256, map p257*
There are many good dancing spots on Av Ejército in Yanahuara, but most night-owls head to Av Dolores, a short taxi ride away (US$1), which can get rowdy. Try **Salsodromo** for salsa, or **Cajuma** and **Siomama**.

Ad Libitum, Jerusalén y Ugarte. Friendly, unpretentious local bar, open late.

Blue Margarita, Melgar 119. Large club with several areas, good mix of music.

Déjà Vu, San Francisco 319-B. Café/restaurant and bar, good food, relaxing terrace, DJ evenings and live music, shows movies, 2000-2400. Recommended.

Farren's, Pasaje La Catedral. Friendly Irish bar with local and imported (expensive) beer.

Forum, San Francisco 317. Rock café, live music Thu-Sat 1800-0400, disco, pool tables, US$5 cover if band is playing, includes 1 drink, drinks US$1.50.

Kibosch, Zela 205, go late for pop, rock, salsa.

La Casa de Klaus, Zela 207. German bar and restaurant, foreign beers, expensive, popular.

La Quinta, Jerusalén 522. For *peña* folklore music, weekends mainly, US$1.50 cover.

Las Quenas, Santa Catalina 302. For *peña* music, Mon-Fri 2100.

Le Café Art Montreal, Santa Catalina 300B-1. Atmospheric Canadian-run jazz/blues restaurant/bar with live music Wed and Sat.

Siwara, Santa Catalina 210. Trendy hangout, lively in the evenings, good food, and some live music.

Zero, San Francisco 317 upstairs. Lively rock bar, good at weekends.

⚙ Festivals and events

Arequipa *p256, map p257*

In **Jan** is El Día del Reyes in the district of Tiabaya, traditionally celebrated by shaking the fruit from pear trees. On **10 Jan Sor Ana de Los Angeles y Monteagudo** is a festival for the patron saint of Santa Catalina monastery. On **2-3 Feb** the **Fiesta de la Virgen de la Candelaria** is celebrated in the churches of Cayma, Characato, Chiguata and Chapi with masses, processions of the Virgin through the streets, and fireworks. On **3 Mar** the **Fiesta de La Amargura** is a movable feast in Paucarpata, during which the Passion Play is enacted in the main plaza. **Domingo de Cuaresma**, in the district of Tiabaya, is also dedicated to Jesus Christ. Residents gather in the plaza and carry the cross from there up to a nearby hilltop, crossing the Río Chili. The **Semana Santa** celebrations in Arequipa are carried out Sevillano style, with the townsfolk turned out in traditional mourning dress. There are huge processions every night, culminating in the burning of an effigy of Judas on **Easter Sunday** in the main plazas of Cayma and Yanahuara, and the reading of his 'will', containing criticisms of the city authorities. Afterwards, people retire to the *picanterías* to partake of a little Adobo a la Antaño with some pan de tres puntas. On **1 May** the **Fiesta de la Virgen de Chapi** is a great pilgrimage to the sanctuary of Chapi and one of the most important religious ceremonies in the region. **May** is known as the 'Month of the Crosses', with ceremonies on hilltops throughout the city. On **15 May** the popular fiesta of **San Isidro Labrador** takes place in Sachaca, Chuquibamba and other towns and villages in the valley, and lasts for 7 days. On **13 Jun** a remembrance of **San Antonio de Padua**, patron of hopeless cases, is held in the churches of Tingo Grande and San Francisco, among others. On **29 Jun**, in Yanahuara, the **Fiesta de San Juan**, the local patron saint, is held with mass and fireworks. On **6-31 Aug** is the **Fiesta Artesanal del Fundo del Fierro**, a sale and exhibition of artesanía from all parts of Peru, taking place near Plaza San Francisco. At the same time, **6-17 Aug** is the celebration of the **city's anniversary**; various events are held, including music, dancing and exhibitions. On the eve of the actual day, the 15th, there is a splendid firework display in the Plaza de Armas and a decorated float parade. There is also a mass ascent of El Misti from the Plaza de Armas. It is virtually impossible to find a hotel room during the celebrations. On **30 Aug El Día de Santa Rosa** is celebrated in the churches of Tomilla, Cayma and Huancarqui in the Majes Valley. In Arequipa **Nov** is also the month of the traditional guaguas, which are bizcochos (sponge cakes) filled with manjar (caramel made from boiling milk and sugar).

⊜ Shopping

Arequipa *p256, map p257*
Bookshops
For international magazines, look along San Francisco, between Mercaderes and San José. **Compra y Venta de Libros y Revistas**, on C Puente Grau. Old books and magazines are bought and sold here. **Librería El Lector**, San Francisco 221. Wide selection, including of Peruvian authors, book exchange in various languages. **Librerías San Francisco** has branches at Portal de Flores 138, San Francisco 102-106 and 133-135. Books on Arequipa and Peru, some in English.

Leather
Arequipa is noted for its leather work. The main street of saddlers and leather workers is Puente Bolognesi. The handicraft shop in the old prison opposite San Francisco is particularly good for bags.

Markets
There are markets which are good for general handicrafts. The covered market opposite the Teatro Municipal on Mercaderes is recommended for knitted goods, bags, etc. Also worth a try is the market around Valdivia and Nicolas de Piérola. The large **Fundo del Fierro** handicraft market behind the old prison on Plaza San Francisco is also worth a visit. Shop 14 sells alpaca-wool handicrafts from Callalli in the Colca Canyon.
Casa Secchi, Av Víctor Andrés Belaunde 124, in Umacollo (near the aeroplane statue). This shop sells good arts, crafts and clothing.
Sombrería El Triunfino, N de Piérola 329-331. For a good selection of hats, but they are expensive.

Photography
Foto Esparza, Mercaderes 321-A-6132-2, T054-992783 (home 054-253125). Cameras mended. **Foto Mundo Color**, San Francisco 218-A. Will develop good quality prints in 1 hr, US$3.50 for 24. **Palacio Viejo 105**. The shop here stocks some Fuji slide film and can order from Lima for next day delivery.

Textiles
Arequipa is an excellent place to buy top quality alpaca knitwear. **Alpaca 21**, Jerusalén 115, of 125, T054-213425. Recommended. **Colca Trading Company**, Santa Catalina 300B, T054-242088 (Lima 01-254 1885), colcatradingperu@yahoo.com. Sells a wide variety of naturally-coloured cotton and alpaca clothing for adults and children. **Incalpaca**, parent company of Alpaca 111, at Av Juan Bustamante s/n, Tahuaycani, T054-251025, in outskirts (large store with some good bargains and a small zoo of camelids), also in Claustros del Compañía, local 18, T205931, www.incalpaca.com. **Lanificio**, La Pampilla sin número, T054-225305, is a factory selling high-quality alpaca cloth at better prices than Lima. **Patio del Ekeko**, Mercaderes 141, T054-215861, www.patiodelekeko.com, is a shopping and entertainment and cultural centre. Shops include Alpaca 111 for alpaca and vicuña (recommended for high-quality alpaca and wool products), Ilaria for fine jewellery and silverware, La Ibérica for chocolates and Artesanías del Ekeko. There is also the **Café del Ekeko**, which has internet (a bit more expensive than elsewhere, but a good place), as well as sandwiches, desserts, coffee and a bar (Centro del Pisco), and Museo de Arte Textil (see Sights p256).

▲ Activities and tours

Arequipa *p256, map p257*
Birdwatching
From here, it is possible to see many of the specialities which inhabit the arid scrub and Polylepis woodland of the Andean west slope. The best road to bird is the one to Laguna Salinas. This large salt lake regularly holds three species of Flamingo; Chilean, Andean and Puna. It is also a good place to see Andean Avocet and Puna Plover. In the dry season, you may have to hike out towards the middle of the lake, but do not forget your sunglasses as the glare from the salt is fierce. Between Arequipa and Laguna Salinas, birding the Polylepis-clad slopes and arid scrub can produce various earthcreepers and canasteros not found elsewhere, and this is one of only two places for Tamarugo Conebill.

Climbing and trekking
Colca Trek, Jerusalén 401 B, T054-206217, www.trekinperu.com. Run by the knowledgeable and English-speaking Vlado Soto. The company is recommended for climbing, trekking and mountain biking in the Colca Canyon. Vlado is one of the best guides for the Cotahuasi Canyon. He also rents equipment and has topographical maps. **Naturaleza Activa**, Santa Catalina 211, T054-204182, naturactiva@yahoo.com. Experienced guides, knowledgeable, climbing and trekking. **Volcanyon Travel**, C Villalba 414, T054-205078, mario-ortiz@terra.com.pe. Trekking and some mountain bike tours in the Colca Canyon, also volcano climbing. **Zárate Expeditions**, Santa Catalina 204, of 3, T054-202461/263107. Run by Carlos Zárate of the Mountaineering Club of Peru. Specialist mountaineering and exploring, with information and advice and some equipment rental. Carlos also runs trips to the source of the Amazon. His brother, Miguel, runs another tour operator which has had many problems.

Climbing guides
Julver Castro, who has an agency called Mountrekk, T054-601833, julver_mountrekk@hotmail.com. Recommended, experienced. **Jorg Krosel**, T054-997971, joergkrosel@hotmail.com.

Rafting
The **Río Cotahuasi** (May-Jun, Grade 4-5): this is a total expedition, including a long drive in past Corupuna mountain, a two-day trek around the spectacular Sipia Falls (where the river drops 150 m into an impenetrable gorge), followed by six days of non-stop technical whitewater. The scenery is out of this world, including pre-Inca Huari culture terracing and ruins all in an incredibly deep desert canyon. Probably the best whitewater river on offer in Peru, only a

handful of operators offer this trip and only one or two depart each year. Book early only with companies who have the experience. The **Río Colca** (Jun, Grade 4-5): possibly even harder than the Cotahuasi, this rarely run expedition river has had its fair share of casualties in the past. Be prepared for rocks falling off the cliffs almost continuously, sandflies, storms and out of this world whitewater. Recent seismic activity around Arequipa has caused major changes to several rapids; definitely book with the local experts. The **Río Majes** (all year, Grade 2-3): where the Colca emerges from its gorge it becomes the Río Majes and some day trips can be organized from Arequipa. Good fresh water shrimp make up for the pretty average whitewater. The **Río Chili** (year round, Grade 2-4): just outside Arequipa but highly water dependent and relying on dam releases to make it worthwhile. A fun half-day out if need a break from the heat.

Cusipata, Jerusalén 408, T054-203966, www.cusipata.com. Recommended as the best local operator, run 6-day trips on the Río Colca. May-Dec, Río Chili 1-day kayak courses, also trekking and mountain bike tours.

Tour operators

These agencies have been recommended as helpful and reliable. Most run tours to the Colca Canyon (see p270). Many agencies on Jerusalén, Santa Catalina and around Plaza de Armas sell air, train and bus tickets and offer tours of Colca, Cotahuasi, Toro Muerto, Campiña and city. Prices vary greatly so shop around. As a general rule, you get what you pay for, so check carefully what is included in the cheapest of tours. Always settle the details before starting the tour and check that there are enough people for the tour to run. Many tourists prefer to contract tours through their hotel. If a travel agency puts you in touch with a guide, make sure he or she is official. It is not advisable to book tours to Machu Picchu here. Make these arrangements in Cusco.

Castle Travel, Santo Domingo 302, castle@castletravel.com.pe. Arrange all kinds of local tours, friendly.

Illary Tours, Santa Catalina 205, T054-220844. English-speaking guides. Daily 0800-1300, 1500-1930.

Santa Catalina Tours, Santa Catalina 219-223, T054-216994. Offer unique tours of Collagua communities in the Colca Canyon. Daily 0800-1900. Recommended.

Pablo Tour, Jerusalén 400-A, www.pablo tour.com. Father-and-son agency that owns several *hostales* in Cabaconde; they know the area well.

Servitours, La Merced 123, of 204, T054-201636, servitours@hotmail.com. Run by Alejandro Paiva, usual tours but also climbing, Cotahuasi, and birdwatching in the Valle de Majes.

Transcontinential Arequipa, Puente Bolognesi 132, oficina 5, T054- 213843, transcontinental-aqp@terra.com.pe.Cultural and wildlife tours in the Colca Canyon.

General guides

Gerardo J Pinto Abraca, geratour@yahoo. com For general tours, speaks good English, helpful, lots of information.

Holley's Unusual Excursions, T/F054-258459 (home) any day 1700-0700, or all day Sat and Sun, or Mon-Fri 0800-1600 T054-222525 and leave a message, angocho@terra.com.pe. Expat Anthony Holley runs trips in his Land Rover to El Misti, Toro Muerto, the desert and coast.

Richard Saraya Chambi, PP JJ San José, Manzana T, Cote 6, Comité 10, Distrito de Tiabaya, T054-488063, sacgra@yahoo.com. Reliable, trustworthy, helpful, for tours to Colca, El Misti, etc.

⊙ Transport

Arequipa p256, map p257
Air

Airport information T054-443464. At the airport are two desks offering hotel reservations and free transport to town, a travel agency (Domiruth) and Avis car rental. To and from **Lima**, several flights daily with **Lan** and **Tans**. These airlines also serve **Juliaca**. Also daily flights to Cusco with **Lan**.

A reliable means of transport to and from the airport to the hotel of your choice is with **King Tours**, T054-243357/283037, US$1.30 per person. You need to give 24 hrs notice for the return pick-up from your hotel. The journey takes 30-40 mins depending on the traffic. Transport to the airport may be arranged when buying a ticket at a travel agency, for US$1 per person, but it's not always reliable. Local buses and combis go to about 500 m from the airport, look for ones marked 'Río Seco', 'Cono-Norte' or 'Zamacola'.

Airline offices Lan, Santa Catalina 118-C, T054-201100. **Servicios Aéreos AQP**, Santa Catalina 210, T054-281800, www.saaqp. com.pe. For private hire and tourist flights to the Colca Canyon and around the country. Most tour agencies sell air tickets. Prices are quoted in dollars but payment is in soles so check exchange rate carefully.

Bus

All buses leave from one of the two terminals at Av Andrés A Cáceres s/n, Parque Industrial, opposite Inca Tops factory, south of the centre; 15 mins by *colectivo* US$0.20, or taxi US$1.75. The older terminal is called Terminal Terrestre, which contains a tourist office, shops and places to eat. The newer terminal is Terrapuerto, the other side of the carpark, also with a tourist office (which makes hotel reservations with free transfer to affiliated hotels and its own *hostal*, T054-421375). A terminal tax of US$0.30 must be paid on entry to the platform. Check which terminal your bus will leave from as it may not depart from the terminal where you bought your ticket. All the bus companies have their offices in the Terminal Terrestre and several also have offices in Terrapuerto. Some companies also have offices around C San Juan de Dios (5-6 blocks from the Plaza de Armas), where tickets can be bought in advance, saving a trip to the terminal. Addresses are given below. Some tour operators also make bus reservations for a small fee. Theft is a serious problem in the bus station area. Take a taxi to and from the bus station and do not wander around with your belongings. No one is allowed to enter the terminal 2100-0500, so new arrivals cannot be met by hoteliers between those hours; best not to arrive at night.

To Lima, 1,011 km, 16-18 hrs, 'normal' service US$8.70, 'imperial' US$17.40 (video, toilet, meals, comfortable seats, blankets), 'crucero' US$23-29 several daily; **Enlaces** (T054-430333, office only in Terrapuerto), **Flores** (T054-238741), **Ormeño** (T054-424187, or booth in Carsa shop at San Juan de Dios 657, only open Mon-Fri for about 2 hrs a day) and **Cruz del Sur**

(T054-217728, or Av Salaverry 121, T054-213905) are recommended (prices quoted are of Cruz del Sur). The road is paved but drifting sand and breakdowns may prolong the trip. Buses will stop at the major cities en route, but not always Pisco. The desert scenery is spectacular.

To Nasca, 566 km, 9 hrs, US$7.25-10 (US$30 on Ormeño Royal service), several buses daily, mostly at night and most buses continue to Lima. Beware, some bus companies to Nasca charge the Lima fare. **To Moquegua**, 213 km, 3 hrs, US$3-5.85, several buses and *colectivos* daily. **To Tacna**, 320 km, 6-7 hrs, US$3.85-4.40, several buses daily, most with **Flores**.

To Cusco, all buses now go via Juliaca or Puno, US$12-15, 10 hrs. Most companies use double-decker buses (bath, TV, hostess, etc), eg Enlaces, Cruz del Sur, Cial and Ormeño, running one morning and, some companies, one afternoon bus. There is a new, quick paved road to **Juliaca**, via Yura and Santa Lucía, cutting the Arequipa-Juliaca journey time to 5 hrs, US$5.80, and **Puno**, 6 hrs, US$6. Most buses and *colectivos* continue to Puno. Sur Oriente and Julsa recommended. Another paved route runs Arequipa-Moquegua-Desaguadero- Puno-Juliaca: 12 hrs to **Puno** and 13 hrs to **Juliaca**, US$6-10.

Car and taxi
Car hire Avis, Palacio Viejo 214, T054-282519, or at the airport T054-443576. Transjesa, Urb Guardia Civil III Etapa E-6, Paucarpata, T054-460403, www.planet.com/ transjesa. Also at the airport. Good value and new vehicles. Genesis, Jerusalén y Puente Grau, T054-202033. Rents 4x4s in good condition, can also arrange drivers. Owner of **Hostal Reyna**, see Sleeping above, can also arrange cars, vans and 4x4s with drivers. Recommened. **Radio taxis**: Nova Taxi, T054-252511; Taxi 21, T054-212121; **Telemóvil**, T054-221515; **Taxitur**, T054-422323; **Henry Málaga**, T054-655095, Spanish only.

Train
The railway system goes from Arequipa to Juliaca, where it divides, one line going north to Cusco, the other south to Puno. With the opening of the new Arequipa-Juliaca highway, the decreased demand for rail

travel led to the suspension of regular passenger services on this route. PerúRail, Av Tacna y Arica 200, T054-215350, www.perurail.com, runs trains for private charter of for groups of over 40, and may reopen the route in the future.

⊙ Directory

Arequipa *p256, map p257*

Banks Interbank, Mercaderes 217. Mastercard representative and ATM, US$5 commission on TCs. BCP, San Juan de Dios 125, also at Santo Domingo y Jerusalén. Accepts Visa Card (has ATM) and gives good rates, no commission. Recommended. BBV Continental, San Francisco 108. Visa ATM, US$12 commission on TCs. BSCH, C Jerusalén. Changes Visa and Citicorp TCs, low rates, accepts Mastercard, has Visa ATM. Banco Wiese, Mercaderes 410. Change money at cambios on Jerusalén and San Juan de Dios, and several travel agencies. Sergio A del Carpio D, Jerusalén 126, T054-242987, good rates for dollars. Via Tours, Santo Domingo 114, good rates. Casa de Cambio, San Juan de Dios 109, T054-282528, good rates. It is almost impossible to change TCs on Sat afternoon or Sun; try to find a sympathetic street changer. Better rates for cash dollars in banks and casas de cambio. **Hospitals and clinics** Regional Honorio Delgado, Av A Carrión s/n, T054-238465/233812/231818 (inoculations). Central del Sur, Filtro y Peral s/n, T054-214430 in emergency. Clínica Arequipa SA, esquina Puente Grau y Av Bolognesi, T054-253424/416. Fast and efficient with English-speaking doctors and all hospital facilities, consultation costs

US$18, plus US$4 for sample analysis and around US$7 for a course of antibiotics. **Paz Holandesa**, Av Jorge Chávez 527, T/F054-206720, www.pazholandesa.com. Dutch foundation dedicated to helping impoverished, which also has a travel clinic for tourists. Dutch and English spoken, 24-hr service. Highly recommended (see their website if you are interested in volunteering). **Internet** C@tedr@l, Pasaje Catedral 101, T054-220622, internetcatedral@ hotmail.com. 0800-2400, fast machines, international calls. Chips Internet, San Francisco 202-A, chips@chips.com.pe. La Red Café Internet, Jerusalén 306, café@LaRed.net.pe. 0830-2200, US$0.45 per hr. Tr@vel Net, Jerusalén 218, US$0.75 per hr and international phone calls. Net Central, Alvarez Thomas 219, netcentral@netcentral. lared.net.pe 0900-2300, fast machines. Cybercafé.com, Santa Catalina 115-B, at Easy Market. US$0.75 per hr. Another at Puente Bolognesi 108. 0700-2300. See also Patio del Ekeko in Shopping, above. **Laundry** Magic Laundry, Jerusalén 404B and La Merced 125. Coin-operated, open daily. Don Marcelo, T054-421411 (morning), T054-229245 (afternoon). Delivery service. **Pharmacy** Farmacia Libertad, Piérola 108. Owner speaks English. **Post** Central office is at Moral 118, opposite Hotel Crismar. Letters can only be posted at the post office during opening hrs. Mon-Sat, 0800-2000, Sun 0800-1400. DHL, Santa Catalina 115, T054-234288, for sending documents and money. Also Western Union representative. World Courier, T054-241925, F218139. **Telephone** Alvarez Thomas y Palacio Viejo. **Useful addresses** Ambulance: San Miguel, T054-283330 (24 hrs).

Colca Canyon → *Colour map 5, grid B6.*

Twice as deep as the Grand Canyon and once thought to be the deepest canyon in the world (until the nearby Cotahuasi Canyon was found to be all of 163 m deeper), the Colca Canyon is an area of astounding beauty. Giant amphitheatres of pre-Inca terracing become narrow, precipitous gorges, and in the background looms the grey, smoking mass of Sabancaya, one of the most active volcanoes in the Americas, and its more docile neighbour, Ampato (6,288 m). Unspoiled Andean villages lie on both sides of the canyon, inhabited by the Cabana and Collagua peoples. The Río Colca snakes its way through the length of this massive gorge, 3,500 m above sea level at Chivay (the canyon's main town) falling to 2,200 m at Cabanaconde, at the far end of

the canyon. Now, the Colca Canyon is best known for its associations with some rather 271
large birds. Would-be David Attenboroughs flock here for a close encounter with the
giant Andean condor at the aptly-named Cruz del Cóndor. ▶▶ *For Sleeping, Eating and other*
listings, see pages 275-277.

Ins and outs

Getting there Most buses follow the new road via Yura following the railway, which
is being developed as a new route to Cusco from Arequipa. This is longer, but quicker,
than the old route through Cayma. It is a rough route and cold in the morning,
reaching 4,825 m at the Pata Pampa pass, but the views are worth it. In the rainy
season it is better to travel by day as the road can get icy and slippery at night. Buses
all leave from the main terminal in Arequipa but you can get your ticket the previous
day at the bus company offices in Calle San Juan de Dios.

Getting around Combis and *colectivos* run from Chivay to the villages in the
canyon. And, naturally, there all the trekking possibilities to consider.

Best time to visit From January to April is the rainy season, but this makes the area
green, with lots of flowers. This is not the best time to see condors. May to December
is the dry, cold season when there is more chance of seeing the birds.

Arequipa to Chivay → *Colour map 5, grid B/C6.*

A poor, very bumpy dirt road runs north from Arequipa, over the altiplano, to Chivay,
the first village on the edge of the Canyon. The road affords fine views of the
volcanoes Misti, Chachani, Ampato and the active Sabancaya. Despite being the
main road from Arequipa to Chivay, this is not suitable for ordinary cars: four-wheel
drive is best. Cyclists should use the new road via Yura; it is in better condition and
there is less of a climb at the start. Paving is under way on the road to Chivay.

About an hour out of Arequipa, on the road to Chivay, is the **Aguada Blanca
National Vicuña Reserve** If you're lucky, you can see herds of these rare and timid
camelids near the road. If taking a bus to the reserve to vicuña-watch, there should be
enough traffic on the road to be able to hitch a ride back to Arequipa in the evening.

Chivay is the main linking point between the two sides of the canyon. A road
heads northeast to **Tuti**, where there is a small handicrafts shop, and **Sibayo**, with a
pensión and grocery store. A long circuit back to Arequipa heads south from Sibayo,
passing through **Puente Callalli** (where Arequipa buses can sometimes be caught for
Cusco), **Chullo** and **Sumbay**. This is a little-travelled road, but the views of fine
landscapes with vicuña, llamas, alpacas and Andean duck are superb.

Another road from Sibayo goes northwest, following the northern side of the
Colca mountain range to **Cailloma**, **Orcopampa** and **Andagua** (see page 281). Water
from the Colca river has been diverted through a series of tunnels and canals to the
desert between Repartición and Camaná, to irrigate the Majes pampa.

Crossing the river at Chivay going west to follow the canyon on the far side, you
pass the villages of **Coporaque**, **Ichupampa** (a footbridge crosses the river between
the two villages and foot and road bridges connect the road between Coporaque and
Ichupampa with Yanque), **Lari**, **Madrigal** (a footbridge connects to Maca) and **Tapay**
(connected by a footbridge to Cabanaconde).

Chivay and around → *Colour map 5, grid B6. Altitude 3,600 m.*

Chivay is the gateway to the canyon and the overnight stopping point for two-day
tours run by agencies in Arequipa. The hot springs of **La Calera** ① *US$3*, are 4 km
away. To get there take one of the regular *colectivos* (US$0.25) from beside the market
or it's a pleasant hour-long walk. There are several large hot pools and showers but
only one pool is open to tourists; good facilities, beautiful setting. The hot springs are
highly recommended after a hard day's trekking. From La Calera you can trek through
the Canocota canyon to Canocota (four to five hours), or take a *colectivo* to Canocota

Appeasing the gods

To the Incas, Nevado Ampato, in the Colca region, was a sacred god who brought life-giving water and good harvests and, as a god claimed the highest tribute, the sacrifice of one of their own.

In September 1995, anthropologist, Johan Reinhard, of Chicago's Field Museum of Natural History, accompanied by Peruvian climber, Miguel Zárate, whose brother, Carlos is a well-known Arequipa mountain guide, were climbing Ampato when they made a startling discovery, at about 6,000 m. They found the perfectly preserved mummified body of an Inca girl. Wrapped tightly in textiles, this girl in her early teens must have been ritually sacrificed and buried on the summit.

Mummies of Inca human sacrifices have been found before on Andean summits, but the girl from Ampato, nicknamed Juanita, is the first frozen Inca female to be unearthed and her body may be the best preserved of any found in the Americas from pre-Columbian times. The discovery is considered of worldwide importance, as the body is so well-preserved. The intact body tissues and organs of naturally mummified, frozen bodies are a storehouse of biological information. Studies will reveal how she died, where she came from, who her living relatives are and even yield valuable insights about the Inca diet.

Juanita's clothes are no less remarkable. The richly patterned, dazzling textiles will serve as the model for future depictions of the way noble Inca women dressed. Her lliclla – a bright red and white shawl beneath the outer wrappings – has been declared "the finest Inca woman's textile in the world".

Ampato, with its icy summit, may seem an unlikely Inca ceremonial site. However, the mountain was described as one of the principal deities in the Colca Canyon region. The Incas appeased the mountain gods, who were said to supply water to their villages and fields, with children as sacrifices. The Cabana and Collagua people even bound their children's heads to make them look like the mountains from which they believed they were descended.

A subsequent ascent of Ampato revealed a further two mummies at the summit. One is a young girl and the other, though badly charred by lightning, is believed to be a boy. If so, it may mean that these children were ritually sacrificed together in a symbolic marriage.

Nowadays, villages in the Colca continue to make offerings to the mountain gods for water and good harvests, but thankfully the gods have modified their tastes, now preferring chicha to children.

and hike to La Calera, a beautiful trip, but ask directions. A reconstructed chullpa on the hilltop across Puente Inca gives good views over the town. There is a very helpful **tourist office** in the Municipalidad on the west side of the plaza which gives away a useful map of the valley. The tourist police, also on the plaza, can give advice about locally trained guides.

From Chivay you can hike to **Coporaque** (1¾ hrs) and **Ichupampa** (a further 1½ hrs), cross the river by the footbridge and climb up to **Yanque** (one hour), from where it's an 8-km hike back to Chivay. It's better to follow the road, which seems longer, or you'll end up lost in a maze of terraced fields. Half an hour above Coporaque there are interesting **cliff tombs** and just beyond the village the Huari ruins of **Ullu Ullu**. The foot and road bridges to Yanque (see below) are between Coporaque and Ichupampa. If you feel too tired to walk back to Chivay, catch a *colectivo* from the plaza in Yanque for US$0.25. It takes two days to walk from Chivay to Cabanaconde (70 km), you can camp along the route. You will have to walk all day in the sun – there is no shade. You'll need plenty of drinking water and sun block. Better to trek other parts of the canyon.

To visit the source of the Amazon and the Río Carhuasanta (at about 5,000 m), take a *colectivo* from Chivay to Tuti (50 minutes, US$0.60). In Tuti ask for the guide Emeterio uicano, T054-280365, who is very experienced and will take you there and back in three days. You will need a tent, sleeping bag, all food, etc. The scenery is astonishing. See also Colca Trek or **Zárate Expeditions** under Climbing page 267.

Chivay to Cabanaconde

From Chivay, the main road goes west along the Colca Canyon. The first village, after 8 km, is **Yanque**. There's an interesting church and a bridge to the villages on the other side of the canyon. Beside the renovated Inca bridge on the Yanque to Ichupampa road, a 20-minute walk from Yanque plaza, is a large, warm thermal swimming pool ① *US$0.75*. The next village after Yanque is **Achoma**, 30 minutes from Chivay along the Cabanaconde road. There is an old settlement where you can camp. The road continues to **Maca**, which barely survived an earthquake in November 1991. New housing has been built. Then comes the tiny village of **Pinchollo**, with a basic *hostal* on the plaza (a room full of beds and one shared bathroom). There are no restaurants but you can eat at the comedor popular. You can walk from here to the Sabancaya geyser in approximately seven hours. Boys offer to guide you there. For information, ask for Eduardo, who acts as a guide. He lives next to the plaza.

Cruz del Cóndor

① *Fee of US$4 is charged (may rise to US$10), not included in agency prices.*
From Pinchollo the road winds its way on to the Mirador, or Cruz del Cóndor at the deepest point of the canyon. The view from here is wonderful but people don't come for the view. This is where the immense Andean vulture, the condor, can be seen rising on the morning thermals. The reason this particular spot is so unique is that the condors swoop by in startling close up, so close, in fact, that you feel you can reach out and touch them. It is a breathtaking and very humbling experience. The best time to arrive in the morning is a matter of some dispute, though the consensus is around 0900. Arrive by 0800 for a good spot, any earlier and you may be faced with a long, chilly wait (this may be unavoidable by public transport – buses from Chivay stop here very briefly). The condors fly off to look for carrion on the higher slopes of the surrounding peaks at 0900-1000. The condors can also be seen returning from a hard day's food searching at around 1600-1800. Just below the Mirador is a rocky outcrop, which allows a more peaceful viewing but take great care on the loose scree (or you'll end up on the menu). Binoculars are recommended. Snacks and drinks are available. Camping here is officially forbidden, but if you ask the tourist police in Chivay they may help. To get to the Mirador from Cabanaconde, take one of the return buses which set off at around 0730, and ask to be dropped off at the Mirador, just in time for the morning performance. Or you can walk along the road, which takes about three hours. Horses can be hired to save you the walk; arrange the night before in Cabanaconde. To walk from the Mirador to Cabanaconde, follow the road until Cabanaconde is in sight, then turn off the road 50 m after a small reservoir down a walled track. After about 1 km turn left on to an old Inca road and continue down to rejoin the road into Cabanaconde.

Unfortunately, the peace of the Cruz del Cóndor has been disrupted by road-building projects, ironically to clear parking space for tourist buses. The bulldozers have disrupted the family of condors that live below in the canyon. For now, it's not

● *The name Colca derives from the Inca practice of storing harvested crops in sealed vaults*
● *which they called colcas, carved into the canyon walls.*

known what consequences this will have on future condor populations, but the fear is that they won't have laid eggs in 2004 because of the disturbances. Road building projects are also underway on the other side of the valley. The projects have been carried out without an environmental impact assessment and have been decried by locals and tour operators alike.

Cabanaconde → *Colour map 5, grid B5.*

From the Mirador it is a 20-minute bus ride to this friendly village at 3,287 m, the last in the Colca Canyon. The indigenous people of this part of the canyon are Cabanas and the women wear round, embroidered hats. The plaza is brimming with life. Women squat on their haunches, selling bruised fruit and a few knobbly root crops.

> ⁑ *Local women are very camera-shy. If you really must intrude, then at least ask permission first.*

Their distinctive flower-patterned hats, voluminous skirts and intricately embroidered blouses bring a splash of colour to the uniform brown adobe buildings. Children tend sheep, goats and llamas; old men lead burdened mules while pigs laze in the sun and chickens peck at the ground. At dusk large groups of animals wander back into the village to the corrals adjoining most houses. The views into the canyon are excellent and condors can be seen from the hill just west of the village, a 15-minute walk from the plaza, which also gives views of the amazing terraces, arguably the most attractive in the valley, to the south of the village. The hill is surrounded by a 2 km long Huari wall, 6 m high and 4 m wide in places. It also encompasses the village football field where it is possible to see condors overflying a late afternoon game. Cabanaconde suffered badly during the earthquake in April 1998. Many buildings collapsed and many people were injured.

There's a tourist information office attended by friendly locals willing to give plenty of advice, if not maps. It's a good place to find trekking guides and muleteers.

Trekking from Cabanaconde

There are many hiking possibilities in the area. Make sure to take enough water as it gets very hot and there is not a lot of water available. Moreover, sun protection is a must. Some treks are impossible if it rains heavily in the wet season, but most of the time the rainy season is dry. Check beforehand. Ask locals for directions as there are hundreds of confusing paths going into the canyon. Buy food for longer hikes in Arequipa. Topographical maps are available at the Instituto Geográfico Militar in Lima, from Colca Trek or Pablo Tour in Arequipa, and good information can be obtained from South American Explorers.

Two hours below Cabanaconde is **Sangalle**, an 'oasis' of palm trees and swimming areas and two campsites with basic bungalows and toilets, US$1.50-4 (three-4½ hours back up, ask for the best route in both directions, horses can be hired to carry your bag up, US$5.85), recommended. A popular hike involves walking east on the Chivay road to the Mirador de Tapay (before Cruz del Cóndor), then descending to the river on a steep track (four hours, take care). At the village of San Juan you can stay and eat at Hostal Roy, see Sleeping below. From there you go to the oasis, spend the night and return to Cabanconde on the third day.

Tapay is another two hours above the 'oasis', on a good trail with great views. It's possible to stay overnight in Tapay, or camp at the houses just before the bridge. There is running water in a supply channel in the morning and evening; ask the locals. A two-day trek from Cabanaconde climbs up to the **Lago Mucara**, reflecting the white peaks of the Ampato volcano.

A longer hike from Cabanaconde goes to **Chachas** and takes four or five days. Follow a small path to the west, descending slowly into the canyon (three hours); ask locals for directions to **Choco**. Then cross the Río Colca by the Puente Colgado (an Inca bridge) and go up to Choco, 2,473 m (five to six hours). From Choco climb high above the village to the pass at 4,500 m and then down to Chachas, at 3,100 m

This is a superb walk through untouched areas and villages. You need all camping
equipment, food and plenty of water, as there is hardly any on this trek.

⊛ Sleeping

Chivay and around *p271*
Ask if your hotel can provide heating. Many
of the better hotels are used by tour groups.
There are several other hotels and family
homes where you can stay; ask around.
AL Colca Lodge, between Coporaque and
Ichupampa, T054-202587 (Arequipa), www.
colca-lodge.com). Very pleasant and relaxing, safe, heating, restaurant with good
buffet, TV with pirated DVDs. Beautiful hot
springs by the river, trekking, cycling, riding,
rafting, spend at least a day there to make
the most of what's on offer. Recommended.
AL Estancio Pozo del Cielo, over the Puente
Inca from Chivay amid pre-Inca terraces,
T054-531144, www.pozodelcielo.com.pe.
Very confortable, friendly, warm rooms,
good views, good service and restaurant.
Recommended.
AL Parador del Colca, T054-288440,
res-mirapark@peruorientexpress.com.pe.
3½ km from Yanque, 10 km from Chivay,
owned by Orient Express. Built of local
materials, with solar power, on an old estate,
the hotel offers lots of activities; comfortable
cabin-like suites, typical food and home-
grown vegetables, meals extra, due for
expansion 2004-2005. Recommended.
A Casa Andina, Huayna Cápac s/n, T054-
531020, www.casa-andina.com. Attractive
cabins with hot showers and a cosy bar/
dining area, another member of this
recommended hotel chain, heating,
internet, parking.
B Colca Inn, Salaverry 307, T054-531111,
www.hotelcolcainn.com. A good mid-range
option, modern, spick and span, with a
decent restaurant.
C Hostal Posada Chivay, Salaverry 325,
T054-531032, posadachivay@hotmail.com.
Central, friendly, good rooms, some
problems with hot water, breakfast included.
C Tradición Colca, on main road, Yanque.
Contact Carelia and Emmanuel Derouet,
Jerusalén 300C, T205336, www.tradicion
colca.com   Price is per unit, **D** in low season
and includes breakfast, with gardens,

restaurant, bar, games room, also have
backpackers' rooms; they also have a travel
agency. Recommended.
C Wasi Kolping, 10 blocks south of the
town, opposite the Plaza de Toros, T054-
521076. Comfortable cabins with hot
shower, very clean and quiet, good views.
D El Posada del Inca, Salaverry 330,
T054-521032. Modern, with hot showers,
carpeted rooms, safe, hot water bottles,
clean and friendly. Recommended.
E Hostal Anita, on the north side of the
plaza, T054-531114. Clean, with bathroom,
rooms look onto a small garden, friendly.
Recommended.
E La Casa de la Bella Flor, Cusco 303,
T054-280454. Charming small lodge run by
Sra Hilde Checca, flower-filled garden,
tasteful rooms, good meals (also open to
non-residents), Hilde's uncle, Gregorio,
guides visitors to pre-Columbian sites.
F La Casa de Lucila, M Grau 131, T054-
607086, with bath, comfortable, coffee,
guides available.
F Hospedaje Jessy, Zarumilla 218, 1 block
from market. Simple, clean, excellent
showers, **G** without bath, helpful, parking.
F Hospedaje Restaurant Los Portales,
Sucre, T054-521101. Good accommodation,
breakfast US$0.75, same price for dinner
in restaurant.
G per person **Rumi Wasi**, C Sucre, 6 blocks
from plaza (3 mins'walk), T054-531114. Good
rooms, breakfast included, hot water, bike
hire, helpful.

Camping
Next to Pozo del Cielo, the place is called
both **Colca Camping** and **Star Rain**.
F Hostal El Tambo. Quiet rooms around
a garden.

Cabanaconde *p274*
B Kuntur Wassi, on the hill above the plaza,
T054-252989, kunturwassi@terra.com.pe.
New, attractive and original, restaurant/bar,
great views, helpful. Recommended.

C Posada del Conde, C San Pedro, T054-440197, pdelconde@yahoo.com. Cheaper in low season, with hot shower, excellent value but can be a bit noisy, very good restaurant. Booking advisable.

F Hostal San Pedro, 2 blocks from the plaza. Bright rooms, no shower.

G Hostal Valle del Fuego, 1 and 2 blocks from the plaza, T054-280367, www.pablo tour.com. Good but basic, has 2 places (**F** in newer annex), both with restaurants serving good meals for around US$3, breakfast over-priced. The owner and his son, both Pablo Junco, is a wealth of information. They usually meet the incoming buses. Otherwise turn left facing the church on the plaza and the first place is 1 block along on the right.

G Virgen del Carmen, 5 blocks up from the plaza. Clean, hot showers, friendly, may even offer you a welcoming glass of *chicha*. Recommended.

● Eating

Chivay and around *p271*

There are several good, attractively decorated restaurants in Chivay, both cosy and friendly. They serve good value set meals for around US$3 with a choice of dishes. Not all restaurants are open at night.

♥♥ Casa Blanca, on the main plaza, good, main dishes US$2.50-7.50, reasonable food, also has *peña* show with set meal.

♥♥ Fonda del Cazador, on the north side of the plaza, serves delicious alpaca steaks.

♥♥ Lobos Pizzería, on the plaza. Has good pizzas and fast food, internet access, pool, and a happy hour bar.

♥♥ Los Sismos, by the petrol station. Alsoserves great alpaca steaks, often has live folklore shows.

♥♥ Witete, Siglo XX 328. Good international food and some local dishes.

♥ Farren's, bar run by a Peruvian and an Irishman, handmade Guinness sign outside, warm, friendly, good selection of drinks, sandwiches and music, also bikes for hire.

♥ La Pascana, near the Plaza de Armas. For cheap local food. Also has good lodging in our **D** range.

Cabanaconde *p274*

There are several basic restaurants around the plaza (all **♥**), including **Rancho del Colca**, which is mainly vegetarian, and **Don Piero**, signposted just off main plaza, excellent choice and good information.

● Festivals and events

This is a region of wild and frequent festivals. El Día de San Sebastián is celebrated over five days from **20 Jan** in Pinchollo. On **2-3 Feb** Virgen de la Candelaria is celebrated in the towns of Chivay and Cabanaconde, with dancing in the plaza, and over 5 days in Maca and Tapay. Semana Santa is celebrated with particular gusto in the villages of the Colca Canyon.

27 Apr is the celebration of the apostle Santiago. During **Apr** and **May** many festivals are held in the Colca canyon: **La Cruz de Piedra** is celebrated over 5 days in **May** in the main plaza in Tuti, near Chivay. On **13 Jun** San Antonio is celebrated in the villages of Maca, Callalli and Yanque. On **14 Jun**, in Sibayo and Ichupampa, the **Fiesta de San Juan** is held over 5 days. On **21 Jun** is the anniversary of the district of Chivay in Cailloma.

On **14-17 Jul** the Fiesta de la Virgen del Carmen is held in Cabanaconde and Pampacolca, when folk dancing takes place in the streets. Of particular interest is the dance of Los Turcos, which represents the indigenous peoples' struggle against the conquistadors. This fiesta is also held in the churches of Yura, Carmen Alto, Congata, Tingo Grande and the Convent of Santa Teresa in Arequipa city. On **25 Jul** in Coporaque and Madrigal, in the Colca canyon, is the **Fiesta de Santiago Apostol**. From **26 Jul to 2 Aug** various religious ceremonies, accompanied by dancing, are held in honour of the **Virgen Santa Ana** in Maca.

On **15 Aug** in Chivay is the fiesta of the **Virgen de la Asunta**, the town's patron saint, which lasts 8 days. In **Sep** in Tisco, the **Virgen de la Natividad** is held over 5 days. On **8 Dec**, Inmaculada Concepción is held in Chivay and Yanque, when groups of musicians and dancers present the traditional dance, the Witite, lasting 5 days. On **25 Dec** once again in Yanque, just in case you haven't had enough, the **Witite** is held over 6 days.

▲ Activities and tours

Chivay and around *p271*

Travel agencies in Arequipa arrange a 'one-day' tour to the **Cruz del Cóndor** for US$18-20. They leave Arequipa at 0400, arriving at the Cruz del Cóndor at 0800-0900, followed by an expensive lunch stop at Chivay and back to Arequipa by 2100. For many, especially for those with altitude problems, this is too much to fit into one day (the only advantage is that you don't have to sleep at high altitude). It's also more dangerous since drivers get tired on the way back. Two day tours start at US$20-30 per person with an overnight stop in Chivay; more expensive tours range from US$45 to US$90 with accommodation at the top of the range. You should allow at least 2-3 days, more if planning to do some trekking, when visiting the Colca Canyon. Travel agents frequently work together in a 'pooling' system to fill buses (even the more expensive agencies may not have their own transport) and there are lots of touts. This can mean that a busload of tourists will come from different agencies, all paying different prices, but all expecting the same level of service. On occasion the company providing the transport may not have the same high standards as the operator through whom the tour was booked. **Colca Adventures**, 22 de Agosto 101, T054-531137, rcordova@terra.com.pe, offer bike hire and and rafting tours. Good machines and equipment, very helpful. The owner is Oscar Vela and the guide is Miguel Rumaldo Mamani Huanca.

Cabanaconde *p274*

Henry López Junco, is a guide in Cabana-conde, T054-280367. US$7.15 per day for 2 people.

☺ Transport

Chivay and around *p271*

Cristo Rey, **La Reyna** (recommended) and **Andalucia** have 7 departures daily from Arequipa to **Chivay**, continuing to **Cabanaconde**; a further 75 km, 2 hrs, US$1. La Reyna has the quickest service, about 6 hrs, US$3.85, others US$3. Buy a ticket in advance to ensure a seat (many agencies can buy them for you for a fee). Buses return to Arequipa from the market. For **Cabanaconde** and **Cruz del Cóndor** catch the 0500 bus from Chivay which stops briefly at the Mirador at 0700 (if this doesn't seem likely, ask), US$0.75. Combis run infrequently in each direction, fewer on Sun. You could also try hitching a lift with a tour bus. Combis and *colectivos* leave from the new terminal, three blocks from the main plaza in Chivay to any village in the area. Ask the drivers. **Combis** leave from the terminal for **Achoma** (every ½ hr), **Maca** (every hr), **Ichupampa** (every hr) and **Puente Callalli** (every hr). It is difficult to go to Cusco from Chivay: you can take a *colectivo* to Puente Callalli, but the police there are unwilling to let passengers wait for a passing Cusco-bound bus, which may not stop anyway. Best to go back to Arequipa.

Cabanaconde *p274*

See under Chivay for buses on the Arequipa-Chivay-Cabanaconde route. The buses leave Cabanaconde for **Arequipa** at between 0730 and 1500.

❶ Directory

Chivay and around *p271*

Banks Travellers' cheques and credit cards are seldom accepted so take plenty of cash in soles, not dollars.

Cotahuasi Canyon → *Colour map 5, grid B5.*

A road heads northwest off the Panamericana between Camaná and Repartición towards Corire, Aplao, and the Cotahuasi Canyon. It passes the Toro Muerto petroglyphs and traverses the western slopes of Nevado Coropuna, Peru's third highest peak at 6,425 m, before winding down into Cotahuasi. Considered one of the most beautiful canyons in the world, as well as the deepest (about 1,850 m deeper than the Grand Canyon in the USA), Cotahuasi has several traditional communities where ancient customs persist. The river, cutting its way through steep walls, is the focus of some tremendous scenery and top-quality rafting or kayaking. Once part of an Inca route from coast to Cusco, it is now a great place for hiking, with no end of ruins, hot springs, cascades and rivers to explore.▸▸ *For Sleeping, Eating and other listings, see pages 281-282.*

Ins and outs

The only way into the canyon is by road and there area bus services from Arequipa. Tour operators run to Toro Muerto and can arrange trips to Cotahuasi. Accommodation and services are basic. A website with pictures and some information on Cotahuasi is www.lared.net.pe/cotahuasi. The most knowledgeable contact for trekking and exploring is Vlado Soto of **Colca Trek**, see page 267.

Background

The canyon, in the northwest of the Department of Arequipa, has been cut by the Río Cotahuasi, whose waters are formed by the Río Huayllapaña flowing from the north, above Pampamarca, and the Río Huarcaya from the west, above Tomepampa. The river cuts its way westwards and then southwards through the deepest parts of the canyon, below Quechualla. It flows into the Pacific as the Río Ocuña, having joined with the Río Marán along the way.

At its deepest, at Ninochaca (just below the village of Quechualla), the canyon is 3,354 m deep, 163 m deeper than the Colca Canyon and the deepest in the world. From this point the only way down the canyon is by kayak and it is through kayakers' reports since 1994 that the area has come to the notice of tourists. It was declared a Zona de Reserva Turística in 1988 and there is pressure to make parts of it into a national park. The vertiginous gradient of the canyon walls and the aridity of its climate allow little agriculture but there are several charming citrus-growing villages downstream, among them **Chaupa**, **Velinga** and **Quechualla**.

In Inca times the road linking Puerto Inca on the Pacific coast and Cusco ran along much of the canyon's course. It was used for taking fish to the ancient Inca capital. Parts of the road are still intact and there are numerous remains of *andenes*, or terraces, which supported settlement along the route. There are also Huari and other pre-Inca ruins.

It is possible to raft or kayak from a point on the Upper Cotahuasi, just past the town, almost to the Pacific (boats are usually taken out of the water at the village of Iquipi), a descent of 2,300 m. The season is May-June; rapids class four to five; some portaging is unavoidable. See Rafting page 267.

Toro Muerto

The world's largest field of petroglyphs at Toro Muerto is near **Corire**. There are several restaurants around the plaza in Corire and a BCP. You can make a return day trip from Arequipa, if you leave really early, but it's better to allow two days, or combine it with a trip to the Cotahuasi Canyon.

To reach the petroglyphs, there's a turn-off on the right heading back out of Corire. It's about a one hour walk. Alternatively, ask to be let off the bus at the big sign to 'Toro Muerto' beside a small church. A track leads through the fields; at the end, turn right. Ask directions en route. Just before the site is a tiny settlement of very basic wattle and daub huts. From here follow the most worn track which veers right between the hills. There are two signposts on the track leading up from here into the desert valley.

The higher you go, the more interesting the petroglyphs, though many have been ruined by graffiti. The designs range from simple llamas to elaborate human figures and animals. The sheer scale of the site is awe-inspiring (it's on the UNESCO World Heritage list) and the view back down the arid desert valley against the backdrop of

‚ Ancient apparel

Four-thousand years before the Spanish conquistadors set foot on Peruvian soil, the indigenous peoples excelled at the textile arts. This age-old weaving tradition would not have been possible, however, without the necessary raw materials.

While cotton was cultivated for this purpose on the arid coast, up on the high Andean plain there was a ready supply of weaving fibre in the shape of the native camelids – llamas, alpacas, vicuñas and guanacos – which are distant cousins to the camel. The alpacas and llamas are thought to have been domesticated as early as 4,000 BC.

The fibres and skins of the wild camelids – guanacos and vicuñas – were used prior to domestication of their cousins. In fact, guanaco skins were used as clothing by the early hunters who roamed the bleak, high Andean plateau, or altiplano, before 4,000 BC. By 1,500-1,000 BC there is evidence of domesticated camelids on the coast while llamas

were being used for ritual burial offerings, indicating their increasing prestige. Thus, the import- ance of camelids to Andean man, both in practical and ideological terms, was probably a long-established tradition by this time.

Because camelid fibre is so easy to spin and dye, the ancient weavers developed extraordinarily fine spinning techniques. The pre-Columbian peoples prized the silky soft fibre of the alpaca, in particular. Living at altitudes of 4,000 m, where temperatures can drop to -15°C, these animals have adapted to the extreme conditions and developed a coat that not only has thermal properties but is also soft and resistant.

It is these qualities that have led to worldwide demand. Production of alpaca fibre, however, remains low owing to the fact that more than 75% of Peru's alpacas are in the hands of small breeders and peasant communities who still herd and manage their animals in much the same way as their ancestors.

the distant lush, green irrigated fields is wonderful. Allow several hours to appreciate the place fully and take plenty of water and protection against the fierce sun, including sunglasses (go early). Also take insect repellent if crossing the fields on foot. A guide is recommended if short of time because they guide you to some of the more interesting carvings.

Cotahuasi → *Population: 3,200. Altitude: 2,600 m.*

Cotahuasi town nestles in a sheltered hanging valley beneath Cerro Huinao, several kilometres away from the erosive action of the Río Cotahuasi. Though above the citrus zone itself, it has fertile, irrigated environs. The name Cotahuasi derives from the Quechua words 'Cota' (union) and 'Huasi' (house), literally translating as united house or close-knit community.

It is a peaceful, colonial town of narrow streets and whitewashed houses with gently subsiding balconies. The main street, Jirón Arequipa becomes a part of the plaza on busy Sunday mornings. The only traffic seen is the occasional glimpse of the mayor's car, the odd tractor and the infrequent comings and goings of the two buses and occasional combi (see below). From Cotahuasi, routes split in a 'Y': southwest to the Cataratas de Sipia, Quechualla and beyond along the Río Cotahuasi; north to Pampamarca up the Río Huayllapaña, and northeast to Tomepampa, Alca, Puica and its environs. Here, you can purchase expensive petrol/gasoline.

Arequipa Cotahuasi Canyon

Pampamarca, two bumpy hours by combi north of Cotahuasi, is a quaint, small village well-known for rugmaking. It is set on a plateau at 3,200 m. From here, you can trek up to the **Bosque de Piedras** (three hours), to the hot springs of **Josla** (3½ km), or down to the 50-m waterfall of **Uskuni** (under an hour). There's a mirador with beautiful views of the waterfall and the valley (15 minutes). Ask at the Municipio for directions. Some local women can prepare food given warning. Ask for Señora Julia to the right of the Municipio. There are a few rudimentary shops.

Following the Río Cotahuasi to the northeast up the valley, you come to the villages of **Tomepampa** (10 km), the hotsprings of **Luicho** (18 km) and **Alca** (20 km), all connected by buses and combis from Cotahuasi. Tomepampa is a neat little hamlet at 2,700 m, with painted houses and a handsome chapel. A days' walk beyond Tomepampa is the spectacular rock forest of **Santo Santo**. The recently rehabilitated and attractive hotsprings of **Luicho**① *24 hrs, US1.50*, are a short walk from the road, across a bridge. The small village of Alca has one *hostal* (see Sleeping, below), Buses leave for Arequipa around 1400, combis when full. Above Alca are the small ruins of Kallak, Tiknay and a 'stone library' of rock formations. Head out of Alca by climbing the stone stairs for the village of Cahuana.

Puica is the last village of any significance in the valley, hanging on a hillside at nearly 3,700 m and connected to Alca by combi (three hours, US$1.50). Though facilities are basic, it's an ideal springboard for nearby attractions: for Churca and a vast prairie of Puya Raimondi cacti; the Ocoruro geysers; the ruins of Maucallacta; and the Laguna de Igma. Horses can be hired for US$3 a day, and locals can act as guides. Puica's fiesta is on the 28 July.

About 4 km out of Cotahuasi on the road to Tomepampa, a bridge crosses over to **Taurisma**, from where it's a two-hour walk northeast to the village and pre-Inca ruins of **Huaynacotas**. The village of **Toro**, from where there are fantastic views of the Solimana glacier, the thermals springs of Sirhua and Siringay and some nearby ruins, can be reached in combis from Cotahuasi which go back up the main road, and then fork west (around two hours).

Trekking in the Cotahuasi Canyon

One of the main treks in the region follows the Inca trade road from **Cotahuasi to Quechualla**. The path starts next to the football pitch beside the airstrip. It heads downhill to **Piro**, which is almost a satellite of Cotahuasi and the gateway to the canyon (the path heads round to the right of the village, just above it). The path then crosses the river twice as it follows its course to **Sipia** (three hours), near which are the tremendously powerful, 150 m high **Cataratas de Sipia**. Climb to the bluff just beyond the mouth of the black hole and you'll have a superb view downriver. Take extreme care near the falls if it is windy. Water is a problem further down the canyon, if continuing, fill up your water bottles near the falls. You can get to within an hour's walk of the Cataratas by combi from Cotahuasi; they leave 0600 and 1930, return 0900 and 1400. It's best to visit at midday. A road is being built from this point to the falls, and may be complete by the time you read this.

The next three hour stretch to **Chaupo** is not for those of a nervous disposition as the path is barely etched into the canyon wall, 400 m above the river in places. The towering cliffs are magnificent reds and browns and dissected by near vertical water channels. You can stay at Chaupo, which lies on the pampa, 100 m above the river. Water is available, but ask permission.

Next is **Velinga**, a village which was almost wiped out by Chagas disease. Now only six families remain. Take the path down to the river before the village and cross over the bridge to the right bank. Half a km further on you may need to wade for about 15 m at the foot of a cliff to regain the path. Stay on the same side of the river. If it rains, Quechualla can be cut off for days as sections where the river has to be waded become too deep and treacherous (eg just past Velinga). Before Quechualla are the extensive ruins of **Huña**. They are dilapidated but the remains of terraces and houses give a good idea of the importance of this route in precolumbian times. There is an almost intact 100 m stretch of Inca road above a bend in the river on the approach to Quechualla. It can be a bit scary in parts but the alternative is to wade waist deep through the river.

Quechualla is a charming village and administrative capital of the district. It sits up on a cliff above the river. The church and school overlook the wooden bridge and the short climb up to the citrus groves. Trellised vines provide some welcome shade in the street. Though the village is populated by only eight families, you may be able to sleep in the schoolhouse. Ask Señor Carmelo Velásquez Gálvez for permission. Below the village, on the opposite side of the river are the ruined terraces of **Maucullachta**. A 16-km hike continues to the ruins of **Marpa**, which are in better condition than Maucullachta. The canyon walls, however, are too steep to continue along the river. You need to climb 8 km, on a path at right angles to the river, to Huachuy, then descend a further 8 km to the ruins near the river. There is no water en route; allow four more days.

Towards the Valley of the Volcanoes

A road goes to the east from Aplao on the Cotahuasi road to **Andagua**, a village lying at the head of the valley of the volcanoes. There are several hotels in Andagua (Casa Grande is recommended) and on the plaza Restaurant Sarita will cook good, cheap meals for you. No petrol/gasoline is available here. **Transportes Reyna**'s Arequipa-Andagua bus goes on to **Orcopampa**, from which the thermal springs of Huancarama can be visited.

From Andagua there is a road to **Chachas**, a picturesque little village on the edge of a lake. There is a daily minibus service between Chachas and Andagua at 1300. A truck leaves for Andagua around 1000, usually on Saturday, Tuesday and Thursday (ask the locals, they know when it's leaving). A woman in the village will let you sleep in a spare room next to her house. She also provides an evening meal. The cost is not fixed and is left up to you – around US$2 per person should be okay.

The area is heavily cultivated and there are perfect views of the valley of the volcanoes from the top of the hill above Chachas. It is possible to hike from Chachas to Choco and on to Cabanaconde via the Río Colca in four or five days (see page 274).

If you have a four-wheel drive vehicle, this is a superb area for driving some rough roads through stunning scenery, for instance a circuit Arequipa-Aplao-Andagua-Orcopampa-Cailloma-Chivay-Arequipa.

● Sleeping

Toro Muerto *p278*
E Hostal Willys, Av Progreso before the Plaza de Armas, Corire, T054-472046. It is clean and helpful.
E El Mirador, Lima 304, Chuquibamba, T054-489279. New, good showers, clean, friendly owner, good views, use of kitchen.
F Hostal Rodríguez, on main plaza in Chuquibamba, T054-489206. Primitive.

Cotahuasi *p279*
E Hostal Alcalá II, Arequipa 116, T054-581090. Run by same family as **Hostal Alcalá** in Alca, new, very good, 24-hr hot

showers, excellent beds, doubles and triples, friendly, a bit small. Recommended.
F Alojamiento Chávez, Jr Cabildo 125, T0554-581029. Has basic rooms around a pleasant, flower-filled courtyard, friendly, Sr José Chávez is helpful on places to visit.
F Hostal Fany Luz, Independencia 117, T054-581002. Opposite **Hostal Villa**, basic but amenable, with shared hot showers, double room available with cold water only.
F Hostal Villa, Independencia 118, just off the plaza, T054-581018. Basic, shared bathroom is miles from the rooms.

Around Cotahuasi *p280*

E-F **Hostal Alcalá**, Alca, T054-280224.
One of the best *hostales* in the valley. 2 bedrooms with private showers, others shared,
very clean, plenty of hot water, restaurant,
good food. Prices vary, sometimes wildly,
according to season and demand.
F **Hospedaje Primavera**, C Unión,
Tomepampa, T054-280356. On the main
street, accommodation with the local school
teacher, Señora Irma Sanabria, with hot
water and pretty rooms.
F **Hostal Uskuni**, the only *hostal* in Pampamarca, off the main square, T054-812189,
uskuni@aedes.com.pe. Run by the Vargas
family, very basic, cold water, friendly.
G **Wasi Punko**. Simple accommodation
near the turn off for the Luicho baths.
The Municipio in **Puica** has decrepit rooms
for guests and can give information,
T054-280458. Better accommodation is
with the Señora who runs the shop opposite
the Municipio, 3 rooms, shared cold water
baths, nice views.

❶ Eating

Toro Muerto *p278*
Recommended restaurants in Corire include
El Fogón and **La Sirena**, both on Av
Progreso. Try the local speciality of
camarones from the Río Majes.

Cotahuasi *p279*
Three small restaurants/bars on Jr Arequipa
offer basic fare, best is **BuenSabor**, opposite
Hostal Alcalá II. There are many well-stocked
tiendas, particularly with fruit, vegetables
and local wine.
⛏ **El Pionero**, Jr Centenario. Clean, good
menú.
⛏ **Las Quenas** and **Las Delicias**, both on
main square, have decent menus.

❷ Transport

Toro Muerto *p278*
Empresa Del Carpio buses to **Corire** leave
from Arequipa main terminal hourly from
0500 onwards, 3-4 hrs, US$3. Ask to be let
out at the beginning of the track to Toro
Muerto. You can also hire a taxi from the
plaza in Corire to the petroglyphs, US$6-10,
including a 2-hr wait.

Cotahuasi *p279*
Three bus companies leave daily from
Arequipa bus terminal, 11-12 hrs, US$9,
Alex, Reyna is a bit more: **Alex** at 1530, **Reyna**
at 1600; return from the plaza in Cotahuasi at
the same times. Both continue on to Alca. All
companies stop for refreshments in
Chuquibamba, about halfway.

**Towards the Valley of the
Volcanoes** *p281*
Transportes Trébol, T054-821319, and
Reyna, T054-430612, run daily buses to
Andagua via Aplao and Corire, both leaving
Arequipa around 0600, 10 hrs, US$7,
returning early afternoon. Both buses arrive
in Arequipa in the very early morning, but
you can sleep on the bus until daybreak.

❸ Directory

Cotahuasi *p279*
There is no place to change money. The **PNP**
are on the plaza; it is advisable to register
with them on arrival and before leaving.
Some survey maps are available in the
Municipalidad and PNP, ask for Richard
Posso, T054-581012. They may let you make
photocopies at the shop on the corner of the
plaza and Arequipa. Sr Chávez has
photocopies of the sheets covering
Cotahuasi and surroundings.

South Coast

: Footprint features

Introduction

The Pan-American Highway runs all the way south from
Lima to the Chilean border and the desert coast has some
distinctive attractions, the most famous, and perhaps the
strangest, are the enigmatic Nasca Lines, whose origin and
function continue to puzzle scientists. More designs on the
desert, plus tomb finds at neighbouring Palpa are casting new
light on the mystery. Paracas peninsula is one of the world's
great marine bird reserves and was home to one of Peru's
most important ancient civilizations. As you bob in a boat to
the Ballestas Islands to watch the seabirds, look for the giant
Candelbra, drawn on the cliffs by unknown hands.

Further south, the Ica Valley, with its wonderful climate, is
home to that equally wonderful grape brandy known as *pisco*.
South of Nasca, on a small bay, is Puerto Inca, the seaport and
fishing harbour for Cusco in pre-colonial times. The road from
here through the canyons to the sierra was a major Inca artery.
That route may have fallen into disuse, but new roads are
making it much easier to climb up from the coast with its
ramshackle fishing villages and brief flashes of green irrigated
valleys. One is the newly paved highway from Nasca to
Abancay which passes the Pampas Galeras vicuña reserve.
Further south the stunning road from the port of Ilo to Lake
Titicaca can be picked up in the oasis town of Moquegua.

South Coast

★ Don't miss...

1 **Cañete Valley** For some real off-the-beaten track adventure follow the Río Cañete towards the sierra to tiny villages, secret valleys and some of the most breathtaking scenery in Peru, page 287.

2 **Ballestas Islands** Visit the 'guano' producers of the Paracas National Reserve. Cormorants, boobies, pelicans and terns as well as penguins and sealions inhabit the rocks and arches of the islands, page 291.

3 **Bodegas** Sample table wines, sweet wines and, above all, *pisco* at one of the wineries in the river valleys south of Lima. The owners are usually pretty generous with their measures, pages 286 and 298.

4 **Nasca Lines** From a small plane, take a gods' eye view of the lines etched in the desert, one of the great archaeological enigmas, page 303.

5 **Puerto Inca** On the barren Pacific coast are the ruins of Cusco's port, from where runners carried fresh fish to the Inca's table, page 312.

Lima to Pisco

South to Lunahuaná → *Colour map 5, grid A1/2.*

The first 60 km south from Lima are dotted with a series of seaside resort towns and clubs that come alive in the summer months of December to March. The first popular beach is **El Silencio**, at Km 34, which is good for a day trip from Lima. The beach is lined with cebicherías, all offering fresh seafood, but go early to get an umbrella and lounge chair (you will be expected to buy food or drinks if using these facilities). The next notable beach is **Punta Hermosa** at Km 39, which is a popular summer retreat for Limeños. There are many summer houses here and some nice hostels for those looking to soak up some sun or to surf. Fresh seafood restaurants line the boardwalk of Punta Hermosa. The next beach from Punta Hermosa is **Punta Negra**, Km 47, a popular spot for surfers, well-known for having the most consistent surfing break south of Lima. San Bartolo is 49 km south from Lima. It is very busy from New Year's Eve to March, but at other times is quiet and relaxing. There are plenty of cheap places to eat. A further 2 km is Santa María.

Next comes the charming fishing village of **Pucusana**, 60 km south from Lima. There are excellent views from the cliffs above the village. You can hire a boat for an hour, but fix the price beforehand and stick to it. Don't sail in the direction of the smelly factory, but to the rocks where you can see seabirds close at hand. There is a compulsory police checkpoint before the turning to Pucusana. The Hotel Bahía has good seafood.

The small beach resort of **Chilca**, 14 km south of Pucusana, is 30 minutes by *colectivo* from the market place. There isn't much to see, but a long, deserted beach does present camping possibilities. You can walk along the beach from Chilca to Salinas (5 km), which has mineral baths. There are a few restaurants and pensiones. In summer (December-February), these places fill up with holidaymakers from Lima.

✷ *Most beaches have very strong currents and can be dangerous if swimming. If you're unsure, ask the locals.*

Chepeconde beach is reached by a dirt road from Km 120 of the Panamericana. It has fine sand and rocky outcrops which divide it into three sections. The northernmost is the safest and most visited. It's very popular with Peruvian campers in summer. If driving south from Lima, you can make a detour to visit the ruins of **Pachacámac** on the way, see page 113.

About 150 km south of Lima, on the Río Cañete, the prosperous market centre of **San Vicente de Cañete** is set amid desert scenery. It is commonly called **Cañete**. All the main services are within a couple of blocks of the plaza. The town hosts a festival during the last week in August, a good opportunity to hear black coastal music and see dance troupes such as Perú Negro.

A paved road runs inland, mostly beside the Río Cañete, through **Imperial**, which has a market on Saturday, Sunday and Monday (good for every type of household item), and Nuevo Imperial to the Quebrada de Lunahuaná. After the town of Lunahuaná (40 km from Cañete), the road continues unpaved to Huancayo up in the sierra, see page 484.

Lunahuaná → *Phone code: 01. Colour map 5, grid A2.*

Lunahuaná consists of the town of the same name and several districts (*anexos*) strung along the valley. They are totally dependent on the Río Cañete, for irrigation and for its chief tourist attraction of rafting and kayaking. Beyond the reach of the water, the surrounding countryside is completely barren, but not without its own appeal. In early morning and at dusk the hills are painted in infinite shades of grey, pink and brown, framed by the clear blue sky, fertile green valley and rushing water.

Eight kilometres before Lunahuaná is **Incawasi**, the ruins of an Inca city. A new road cuts right through the middle of the site, which dominates the valley and quebradas that run down into it. Incawasi is said to have been a replica of Cusco, with its divided trapezoidal plaza. The site was built outside the fertile zone of the valley and its rough walls blend in perfectly with the barren hills. **Paullo** is the first of the anexos reached after Incawasi. Here stand the ruins of the first church of Lunahuaná. In summer, when the river is high, rafting trips start from just below the plaza. In the low river season a temporary footbridge crosses the river to **Lúcumo**. Two kilometres further on is **San Jerónimo**, the area's white-water rafting centre; there are several agencies to choose from (see below). Other adventure tourism activities include paragliding and there is an artificial wall for climbing. At San Jerónimo, a poor but dramatic dirt road runs 40 km up to the small Andean village of **Viñac** (3,190m).

Lunahuaná town has an 18th-century church on the plaza. Opposite the west door, at the top of the plaza, are the Banco de la Nación and Municipalidad. There are several restaurants in town and in the surrounding anexos, some offering rafting.

Beyond Lunahuaná are Condoray and **Uchupampa**. Past Uchupampa the road paving ends before the road crosses the Río Cañete to **Catapalla**. A little further on is a puente *colgante* (suspension bridge). Across the road bridge turn right to the village or left to the pre-Inca remains of **Cantagallo**. The site is not signposted; ask directions. Miguel Casas Sánchez in Catapalla can guide to these ruins.

It is interesting to visit the **bodegas** (wine cellars) in the valley and try the wine. The best-known is **Los Reyes** ① *T01-284 1206*, in Condoray, where you can try their *pisco*, wine, manzanilla and *arope* (a grape juice concentrate). A good time to visit is during February and March when you can see the traditional methods of treading the grapes by foot to the beat of the drum. Other *bodegas* in the area include: **El Olimpo** ① *T01-460 7698*, in Uchupampa, beside the Hotel Embassy; **Viña Santa María** ① *T01-437 8892*, in Condoray, beside Hostal Río Alto. Also in Condoray are **Del Valle**, by La Laguna restaurant, and **Viñas del Sur** ① *T01-437 3187*. In Catapalla are *bodegas* **Reina de Lunahuaná**, a five-minute walk from the suspension bridge. It is the most rustic and authentic *bodega* in the valley and it produces an excellent *pisco*. They have a free tour and restaurant, open at weekends. Recommended.

Cañete Valley

Beyond Lunahuaná the road ascending the Cañete Valley leaves the narrow flood-plain and runs through a series of *retama* lined gorges. The market town of **Yauyos**, with basic accommodation, is 5 km off this road. At Alís a road branches off east to Huancayo. Shortly afterwards the small attractive village of **Huancaya** is reached and the valley is transformed into one of the most beautiful and amazing upper valleys of all the coastal river valleys of Peru, on a par with the Colca valley. Above Huancaya the high Andean terrain lies within the **Nor-Yauyos National Reserve** and the river descends through a seemingly endless series of incredibly attractive, absolutely clear, turquoise pools and lakes, interrupted by cascades and white-water rapids. In some pools huge clumps of tortora reed sway gently and in all there are prolific numbers of trout and abundant birdlife. Large parts of the valley are inaccessible in this section but marvellous day walks can be made upriver from Huancaya and 30 km further on at **Vilca**. At both there are also attractive old colonial bridges across the river.

Culturally, the valley is fascinating for its dying indigenous languages (plus one, Jaqaru, that still might just survive), and perhaps the best pre-Columbian terracing anywhere in Peru. **Tupe** is home to the Jaqaru people, distant cousins to the Aymara of Bolivia and the southern Peru. Astonishingly, the Jaqaru have managed to keep alive their traditions and language (which may hold many keys to help unravel the ultimate origins of the Aymara languages). Tupe's older women still wear their traditional red and black dress, though a modern tartan-style variant is taking over among most younger women. Dark red headscarves also abound, and for festivals they still wear *tupus* (traditional dress pins), identical to those depicted on colonial drawings of Inca women's dress. The main annual festival is for the Virgen de la Candelaria, the central day being 2 February. The village is overlooked by the almost sheer rock-face of Tupinachaka, complete with ancient rock-paintings.

Laraos is also a linguistic final refuge. A very few aged speakers of the local form of Quechua are to be found in a beautiful, old village of steep-streets. A few houses have the same structure as the reconstructed Inca houses in Machu Picchu, with steeply sloping thatched roofs much longer and lower on one side than on the other. The valley's sides here are lined with *andenes* covering about 300 m of altitude in a sweeping curve of several kilometres. Good times to visit are for the fiestas at Carnival (beware the water-bombs and flour or talc attacks!), the irrigation channel cleaning in May, or the town fiesta in August. There are scenic hikes further up the valley beyond the seasonal lake below the village.

Further upstream from **Llapay** (the turn-off for Laraos), the Cañete Valley narrows to an exceptionally tight canyon, with a hairy road squeezed between nothing but rock and rushing water for the steep climb to the mine workings near the 4,600-m pass. Beyond, the road drops to Huancayo.

Chincha Alta → *Colour map 5, grid A2. Population: 110,016.*

Some 35 km north of Pisco, near Chincha Baja, is **Tambo de Mora**, the old port, with nearby archaeological sites at Huaca de Tambo de Mora, La Centinela, Chinchaycama and Huaca Alvarado. **Chincha** itself is a fast-growing town where the negro/criollo

Pisco

Sleeping
El Condado 2
Embassy 3
Embassy Suites 4
Hostal Belén 5
Hostal Candelabro 6
Hostal La Portada 14
Hostal Los Inkas Inn 12

Hostal Pisco 7
Hostal Pisco Playa 8
Hostal San Isidro 13
Hostal Villa Manuelita 11
Las Olas 1
Posada Hispana 9
Regidor 10

Eating
As de Oro 3
Don Manuel 1
El Bossa Nova 5
El Dorado 2
La Casona 4
Panadería San Francisco 6

0 metres 50
0 yards 50

culture is still alive (for more details, see pages 583, 63 and 592) and is a good place to sample locally produce wine and *pisco*. One of the best *bodegas* is the 100-year-old **Naldo Navarro**, Pasaje Santa Rosa, Sunampe, 100 m west of the Panamericana (free guided tours, including tasting). Other *bodegas* have guided tours. The third Saturday in September is national *pisco* day.

Pisco → *Phone code: 056. Colour map 5, grid B2. Population: 82,250.*

Despite being christened as San Clemente de Macera by the Spanish in 1640, the town had already been unofficially named after the famous local brandy and always would be known as Pisco. Now the largest port between Callao and Matarani, 237 km south of Lima, it serves a large agricultural hinterland. The town is small and compact. All you want to do and see is contained within a 300-m radius of the Plaza de Armas.

The town was originally divided into two: Pisco Pueblo with its colonial-style homes, patios and gardens; and Pisco Puerto, which, apart from fisheries, has been replaced as a port by the deep-water Puerto General San Martín, beyond Paracas. The two have now expanded into one fairly unattractive town. If the wind is in the wrong direction, the smell of fish can be pretty bad.

In **Pisco Pueblo**, half a block west of the quiet Plaza de Armas, with its equestrian statue of San Martín, is the **Club Social Pisco** ① *Av San Martín 132*, the HQ of San Martín after he had landed at Paracas Bay. There is an old Jesuit church on San Francisco, one block from the plaza, separated from the Municipalidad by a narrow park. The newer **Cathedral** is on the main plaza. Avenida San Martín runs from the Plaza de Armas to the sea.

If staying on or near the Pisco Playa, it is not recommended to walk at night. Take taxi or mototaxi, as there are many reports of tourists being robbed while walking to the beach. It is best not to carry important items such as plane tickets, passports, flashy toys, etc, while out at night.

Paracas Peninsula and Ballestas Islands

→ *Phone code: 056. Colour map 5, grid B2.*

Fifteen kilometres down the coast from Pisco Puerto is the bay of Paracas sheltered by the Paracas Peninsula. It is named after the Paracas winds – sandstorms that can last for three days, especially in August. The whole peninsula, a large area of coast to the south and the Ballestas Islands are all part of a national reserve, created in 1975, which covers a total of 335,000 ha, on land and sea. It is one of the most important marine reserves in the world, with the highest concentration of marine birds. The region also is economically important, being a major producer of guano.

> The wind gets up every afternoon, peaking at around 1500.

Paracas National Reserve

① *US$1.50 per person.*

The wildlife on view also includes a wide variety of sea mammals and rare and exotic birds. Condors can even be seen in February and March from the rough road between Paracas and Laguna Grande. These massive vultures feed on the ready supply of sea lion carcasses. Rather more delicate are the flamingos which feed in Paracas bay, a short walk from the museum (see below). Boat trips do not go to see the flamingos and that from January to March the birds head for the sierra.

● *It is said that the graceful red and white flamingos of the Paracas Peninsula inspired*
● *General San Martín to design Peru's red and white flag of independence.*

South Coast Lima to Pisco

Textiles and trepanation

The Paracas Necropolis culture inhabited this region between 1300 BC and AD 200 and is renowned for its finely woven textiles, in particular their *mantos* (large decorated cloth) embroidered with anthropomorphic, zoomorphic and geometric designs. These *mantos* were used to wrap mummified bodies in their funerary bundles, the discovery of which gave anthropologists and archaeologists vital clues into this civilization. The bodies were often found to have trepanned skulls. Trepanation was a form of brain surgery performed by the Paracas people in which metal plates were inserted to replace broken sections of skull – a common injury among warring factions at that time. The Paracas culture also practised the intentional deformation of infants' skulls for aesthetic reasons.

Julio Tello site museum ① *0900-1700, US$2*, is at the entrance to the reserve with a shop which sells guide books, film and drinks, and a visitors' centre, information in Spanish only. The exhibits are from the burial sites discovered by the Peruvian archaeologist, Julio C Tello, under the Paracas desert in 1925. The best examples of textiles and funerary bundles can be found in the Museo de la Nación and archaeological museum, Pueblo Libre, in Lima.

The tiny fishing village of **Lagunilla** is 5 km from the museum across the neck of the peninsula. It has beaches which are free from sting rays, but not very clean, and eating places which tend to be overpriced (**Rancho de la Tía Fela** is recommended). A network of good dirt roads, reasonably well-signed, crosses the peninsula. Details of walking routes are available from the Park Office or ask for 'Hoja 28-K' map at Instituto Geográfico Nacional in Lima. It is not safe to walk if alone and that it is easy to get lost in the hot, wide desert area.

Paracas Peninsula

Islas Chincha
Isla Blanca
Islas Ballestas
Punta Pejerrey
El Candelabro
Puerto San Martín
Pisco
San Andrés
El Chaco Boats to Islas Ballestas
To Pan-American Highway
Paracas
Isla San Gallán
Reserva Nacional Paracas
Julio Tello Site Museum & Reserve Entrance
Punta El Arquillo
Mirador de los Lobos
Lagunillas
La Catedral
To Pan-American Highway
Isla Zarate
Pacific Ocean
Laguna Grande

0 km 5
0 miles 5

Sleeping 🛏
Paracas 1

Other sites on the peninsula include **Mirador de los Lobos** at Punta El Arquillo, 6 km from Lagunilla, which looks down on a raucous mob of sea lions. La Catedral is a rock formation in the cliffs, 6 km from Lagunilla in the opposite direction. Some guides may tell you that this was the site for the filming of Planet of the Apes.

Nearby, is a monument which marks the spot where San Martín landed in Peru, on 8 September 1820, after liberating Argentina. Soon after, a shipload of British troops, led by Lord Cochrane, arrived to help the General plan his strategy to break the Spanish stranglehold in the region.

About 14 km from the entrance to the Reserve is the pre-Columbian **Candelabro** (or Candelabra) traced in the hillside. At least 50 m long, it is best seen from the sea (see below). Approaching it by land is not a good idea as disturbance of the sand around it is beginning to destroy the monument. Some idiots have

An economic mess

The islands lying off the coast of Peru are the breeding grounds for millions of sea birds, whose droppings have accumulated over the centuries. These piles of mineral-rich excrement were turned into piles of cash during the last century.

Though the ancient Peruvians knew of the benefits of guano – the name given to the natural fertilizer – and used it on their crops, it wasn't until 1840 that the vast deposits of the stuff were exploited for commercial purposes. It was at this time that Peru first began to trade abroad, particularly with France and England. Almost simultaneously, guano began to replace rare metals as the country's main export.

However, with the economy heavily based on the sales of bird droppings, Peru was caught in a vicious circle of borrowing money on future sales, then having to repay loans at vastly inflated rates. This unhealthy state of affairs was exacerbated in 1864 when Spain, in a petulant show of aggression towards her ex-colony, decided to occupy the guano islands of Chincha, to the south of Lima, thereby leaving the Peruvian government really up to its neck in it.

The main producers of guano are the Guanay Cormorant and the Peruvian Booby. They gather in colonies on the islands, attracted by the huge shoals of anchovy which feed on the plankton in the cold water of the Humboldt current.

even driven over it. There are differing theories as to its exact purpose. Some believe it to be linked to the Nasca Lines (see page 303), 200 km to the south, others that it is related to the Southern Cross constellation and was used to help guide ancient sailors. Still others contend that it represents the cactus used by the ancient high priests for its hallucinogenic powers. A few cruel cynics have even suggested – God forfend – that it was the work of some opportunistic local guides.

Ballestas Islands

The Ballestas islands, dubbed the poor man's Galápagos by many, are nonetheless spectacular in their own right and well worth visiting. They are eroded into numerous arches and caves, hence their name – *ballesta* means bow, as in archery. These arches provide shelter for thousands of seabirds, some of which are very rare, and countless sea lions. A former guano factory can be seen on one of the islands and several others have installations. The book *Las Aves del Departamento de Lima* by Maria Koepcke is useful. Boat trips leave from the jetty at El Chaco, the beach and fishing port by Paracas village.

Boat trips to the islands usually start at 0730, returning at 1100 to avoid rougher seas in the afternoon. Tours may be cancelled if the sea is too rough. Few tours include Isla San Gallán, where there are thousands of sea lions. All boats are speedboats with life jackets, but some are very crowded. Wear warm clothing, but also take protection against the sun and wear sunglasses. You will see, close up, sea lions, guano birds, pelicans, penguins and, if you're lucky, dolphins swimming in the bay. The boats pass Puerto San Martín and the Candelabra en route to the islands.

Inland from Pisco

From the Pan-American Highway near Pisco, a paved road runs 317 km up to Ayacucho in the sierra, with a branch to Huancavelica. At Huaytará, four hours by bus from Pisco, the whole side of the church is a perfectly preserved Inca wall with niches and trapezoidal doorways. 20 minutes from town are the ruins of Incahuasi with thermal baths. On 24 June is the **Fiesta of San Juan Bautista**. At Castrovirreyna the road reaches 4,600 m. The scenery on this journey is superb.

Tambo Colorado ① *US$1.50*, one of the best-preserved Inca ruins in coastal Peru, is 48 km from Pisco. It includes buildings where the Inca and his retinue would have stayed. Many of the walls retain their original colours. On the other side of the road is the public plaza and the garrison and messengers' quarters. The caretaker will act as a guide, and he has a small collection of items found on the site.

● Sleeping

South to Lunahuaná *p286*
Many hotels advertise that they have swimming pools. If they do indeed have them, they are unlikely to be full other during the summer, Dec to Mar or Apr.
B Hostal 110, next door to Posada del Mirador, on Malecón San Martín, San Bartolo. Rents apartments and rooms with great views, some with chimney, all with fridge, pool, very comfortable.
C Posada del Mirador, Malecón San Martín 105, San Bartolo, T4307822. Price is for a bungalow, with full board it rises to **A**. Handbook users are welcome
C-D Casa Resort Peñascal, Av Las Palmeras 258, San Bartolo, T01-430 7436, www.surfpenascal.com. Relaxing, surf specials, with breakfast, hot water, laundry, balconies overlook the surf, a good place to chill for a couple of days.
D Casa Barco, Av Punta Hermosa 340, **Punta Hermosa**, T01-230 7081, www.casabarco.com. This is a funky little hostel with a pool, decorated with great art work, very clean and offers rooms with views and cable TV. Casa Barco is a short walk from where buses drop passengers off at the beginning of Punta Hermosa.
D Hostal Colibrí, Urb Los Libertadores, Mz A, Lote 9, San Vicente de Cañete, T01-581 1309. A clean hotel with basic rooms, which include TV.
D Hostal Edwar's, Benavides 150, San Vicente de Cañete, T01-581 3632. Clean, friendly, rooms with TV and bath, quieter rooms at the back.
D Hostal Rec, Urb Los Libertadores, Mz A, Lote 7, San Vicente de Cañete, T01-581 2623. This is a comfortable hotel with wooden floors and cable TV.
D La Rotunda, Av Bolognesi 592, Punta Hermosa, T01-440 2529. This is a quaint little

hostel above a restaurant of the same name. Large rooms, great views, right above the boardwalk, cable TV.
D-E El Mirador - Centro Turístico Belvedere, Pucusana, T01-430 9228. On a steep hill overlooking town, comfortable, charming owner, good but pricey restaurant.
D-E La Isla, Punta Hermosa, T01-230 7146. Also right on the boardwalk, not as charming as the others, but cheaper if staying in a dorm. Breakfast is included.
E Hostal Hamacas, Punta Negra, T01-231 5498, surfresortperu@terra.com.pe. Right on the beach, but the lodgings are basic.
E Hostal San Francisco, Santa Rosa 739, 2 blocks north of the plaza, San Vicente de Cañete, T01-581 2409. With bathroom, clean, friendly, quiet. Recommended.

Lunahuaná *p286*
A El Refugio, in Viñac, T01-421 6952 in Lima, ventasyreservas@refugiosdelperu.com. A beautiful lodge with fantastic views down the Viñac valley, excellent full board, log fires, jacuzzi. Trekking, horse riding and mountain biking available. A great place to escape from Lima for a couple of days.
A Embassy Río, same phone at **Embassy Jardín**, riverside location, is (**AL** in low season).
A Regina, in Condoray, T/F01-472 2370. Price is **C** in low season. Hot water, TV, swimming pool, cafetería, attractive, with good views over the valley.
B Embassy Jardín, in Uchupampa, T01-472 3525. Price is **C** in low season. With all facilities, restaurants, disco, gardens, rafting, large property, good, popular with families.
B Río Alto, T01-284 1125, just outside Lunahuaná, www.rioaltohotel.com. Rooms or bungalows for 7, pool, with bathroom, hot water, restaurant, disco, rafting, very nice.

D El Refugio, Jr Bolognesi 179, Lunahauná, T01-284 1020. A nice, serviceable *hostal* near the plaza, with TV, clean.
E Hostal, Casuarinas, Grau 295, Lunahuaná, T01-284 1045. Near the plaza, a clean, basic *hostal*, with TV, bath and hot water.
E Hostal, Lunahuaná, in Lunahuaná itself, T01-284 1089. At the southern entrance to the village, friendly, clean, hot water and private bath, good value. Recommended.

Cañete Valley p287
F The Torres family, Huancaya, T01-534 5860 (Lima). Accommodation and meals, basic but clean and friendly.
G Hospedaje, Vilca, is basic.
G per person. There is a municipal hotel in Laraos, basic but good, pay a little bit extra for a hot shower, and a restaurant.
In Tupe formal accommodation and 'restaurants' hardly exist, but there is a very basic municipal *hostal*, and you should always be able to find someone willing to put you up and cook you a basic meal. Alternatively there are flat grazing areas with streams both immediately below and above the village where a tent could be pitched.

Chincha Alta p288
A Hacienda San José, is a 17th-century sugar and cotton estate ranch-house, 9 km south of town in El Carmen district, turn off at Km 203, T056-221458, hsanjose@terra.com.pe (or book in Lima at Juan Fanning 328, of 202, Miraflores, T01-444 5242). The price is for full board (cheaper Mon-Thu), beautiful buildings but overpriced, with pool, garden, small church, colonial crafts, underground from the basement runs a labyrinth of tunnels believed to link up with Tambo de Mora in order to facilitate the contraband trade in black slaves from Africa. The catacombs, where many of those slaves are interred, can be visited, US$3 per person. Criollo shows and buffet lunches are extra. Take taxi for US$4 or 20-min *colectivo* for US$.30. It is very busy at weekends.
C El Valle, Panamericana, in Chincha itself, T056-262556. A central hotel with the excellent Palacio de los Mariscos restaurant.
E Hostal La Rueda, Santo Domingo 228,

near the plaza. The *hostal* is rustic, breakfast is extra, hot showers, small pool, lounge.
E-F Sotelo, Benavides 260, T056-261681. A basic hotel; rooms without bath are cheaper.

Pisco p289, map p288
The town is full at weekends with visitors from Lima. Mosquitoes are a problem at night in the summer.
B Hostal Villa Manuelita, San Fransisco 227, T056-535218, hostalvillamanuelita@hotmail.com. Very charming, elegantly decorated colonial mansion converted into hotel with cafeteria and restaurant. All rooms with private bath, cable TV, fan. Helpful staff, tranquil patios and warm atmosphere. Recommended.
B Las Olas, Av Miguel Grau 156, Pisco Playa, T056-532315, www.lasolasperu.com. This hotel on the beach of Pisco is clean, would be a great choice for lounging by the swimming pool. Modern, some rooms with ocean view, 10 minutes from Pisco, games room, buffet breakfast. IYH card discount. Recommended.
C Hostal Candelabro, Callao y Pedemonte, T056-532620. TV, fridge, fax service, hot water, café, bar on roof, laundry, safe, clean.
C Regidor, Arequipa 201, T/F056-535220, regidor@mail.cosapidata.com.pe. With bath, TV, fan, jacuzzi, café and restaurant, sauna, very good, price negotiable at quiet times.
D Embassy, Jr Comercio just off the Plaza de Armas, T056-535215. With bathroom, clean, noisy, nice bar on roof, has disco, trips to Ballestas Islands, under the same ownership as Embassy Suites on Bolognesi and the Embassy Beach.
D Posada Hispana Hotel, Bolognesi 236, T056-536363, www.posadahispana.com. Rooms each with loft and bathroom, also rooms with shared bath (**G** per person), hot water, TV, can accommodate groups, comfortable, clean, breakfast extra, information service, email, laundry facilities, luggage store, English, French, Italian and Catalan spoken. Recommended.
D Hostal San Isidro, San Clemente 103, T/F056-536471, www.hostalsanisidro.com. With bath, **E** without, hot water, safe, clean and welcoming, very nice pool and cafeteria,

For an explanation of sleeping and eating price codes used in this guide, see inside the front cover. Other relevant information is found in Essentials, pages 61-66.

free laundry facilities, use of kitchen, but no fridge, games room, English spoken, parking. Arranges dune buggy tours. Recommended.

E El Condado, Arequipa 136, Plazuela Belén, T056-533623, hostalcondado@hotmail.com. Hot water, cable TV, laundry, breakfast available, tours to Ballestas arranged.

E Hostal Belén, Arequipa 128, Plazuela ' Belén, T056-533046. Near three other hotels on the same plaza, all with the same feel: basic and a bit outdated, with hot water. The rooms in the new Belén annex are much better and the hotel is safe and clean, can book tours.

E Hostal La Portada, Alipio Ponce 250, T056-532098, hostallaportada@terra.com. Clean, free coffee, hot water, bath, cable TV, laundry service, friendly staff. Recommended.

E Hostal Los Inkas Inn, Prol Barrio Nuevo Mz M Lt 14, Urb San Isidro, T056-536634, los_inkas_inn@hotmail.com. 5 blocks from the Plaza de Armas, some may think it's too far to stay, but this *hostal* is comfortable and straightforward. The pool may not always be full but there is internet, cafetería, sauna, laundry services and garage. There are single and double/matrimonial rooms with bath and cable TV, and **E** dorms with shared bathrooms. Tours can be arranged.

E Hostal Pisco, Plaza de Armas, T056-536669, hotelpisco@terra.com. Lower prices Nov-Mar. With bathroom, **F** without, hot water, garden, breakfast US$1.75, safety deposit, internet, good tour company adjoining hotel, parking for motorcycles.

F per person **Hostal Pisco Playa** (Youth Hostel), Jr José Balta 639, Pisco Playa, T056-532492. Quite nice, clean, kitchen, washing facilities, breakfast US$1.50.

Paracas Peninsula and Ballestas Islands *p289, map p290*

A Paracas, T056-545100, hparacas@terra.com.pe. Bungalows on the beach, good food, not cheap, good buffet lunch on Sun US$25, fine grounds facing the bay, TCs can be changed here at good rates. It is a good centre for excursions to the Peninsula and flights over Nasca, it has tennis courts and an open-air swimming pool (US$2 for non-residents), it also houses the Masson ceramics collection, which is worth seeing. Dune-buggy trips of 2 hrs can be arranged at

the hotel for US$25 per person; you decide how many stomach-churning descents you want to do, or how much gentle viewing, good fun. Next door is the **Hostería Paracas**, Av Paracas 169, reasonably priced, comfortable.

C El Chorito, across the plaza from El Amigo, T056-545045. Nice rooms, ask for a room with a view, connected to El Chorito Restaurant, very good.

C El Mirador, at the turn-off to El Chaco, T056-545086, reserves@elmiradorhotel.com. Reservations in Lima, T01-545086. Hot water, good service, boat trips arranged, meals available, sometimes full board only.

D Alojamiento El Amigo, on the plaza. 5 rooms, nice terrace and good view from first floor, with bathroom.

? Eating

South to Lunahuaná *p286*

There are several good Chinese restaurants near the plaza in San Vicente de Cañete.

¶ Cevichería Muelle 56, Bolognesi 156, San Vicente de Cañete. A recommended restaurant serving seafood specialities.

¶ El Piloto, on the Panamerican Highway just before entering Cañete. This is a great restaurant serving fresh seafood and other Peruvian dishes, guaranteed to satisfy.

¶ Magdalena, Bolognesi 135, San Vicente de Cañete. Serves a good menú, including dishes such as pork cooked in wine and butter beans.

¶ Marinas Chicken on 2 de Mayo, 2 blocks from the plaza, San Vicente de Cañete. A welcoming restaurant with great chicken and other Peruvian food.

Cafés

Panadería Valentino, San Vicente de Cañete. For delicious baked empanadas and other sweet treats.

Lunahuaná *p286*

¶¶-¶ El Pueblo, Grau 406, Lunahuaná. Specializes in *camerones*. The *chupe de camerones* is recommended.

¶¶-¶ Pizzería de Camerones, Condoray. As the name suggests, serves huge pizzas covered in shrimp, open at weekends only.

¶¶-¶ Refugio de Santiago, Paullo. Excellent restaurant with a fine view, herb garden and

Pisco: a history in the making

A visit to Peru would not be complete without savouring a *pisco sour*. Peruvians are mighty proud of their national tipple, which has turned out to be one of the few positive results of conquest.

Peru was the first conquered territory in Spanish America to produce wines and brandies. The cultivation of grapes began with the import of vinestalks from the Canary Islands which were planted on the outskirts of Lima. The crop later reached as far as Cusco and Ayacucho in the Andes, but it was in Ica that the enterprise really took off, owing mainly to the region's exceptional climate.

A hundred years after the conquest, the wine and *pisco* trade had grown considerably. Ica sent its wine to Huamanga, Cusco, Lima and Callao. And from Pisco ships left for other important ports in Central America, as well as Valparaíso and Buenos Aires.

Pisco trade surged in spite of royal bans to halt the vineyard explosion that endangered the Spanish wine industry. In 1629, the prohibition included the transport of Peruvian wines aboard Atlantic-bound ships. But despite the restrictions, the industry continued to expand during most of the 18th century.

Though a few firms utilize modern procedures to manufacture and market larger quantities, *pisco* is still mostly made by small, independent producers using mainly traditional techniques. The traditional method of crushing the grapes by foot can still be found and the fermented grape juice is emptied into traditional Peruvian stills, called *falcas*, which are crucial to the process of true *pisco* production. Also more conventional wineries still rely on wood from the carob tree. This slow-burning fuel is said to provide a constant source of heat that makes for a finer flavour, rather like food cooked over a charcoal fire.

Another important factor in *pisco* production is the type of grape. The unscented *quebranta grape*, brought to the Americas by the Spaniards, lends its unique characteristics to the making of the renowned "pure pisco". There are also fragrant *piscos* from Moscatel and Albilla varieties, "creole *piscos*" made with prime fragrant grapes and green *piscos* made with partially fermented grape juice.

The Ica valley still ranks as Peru's foremost producer of *pisco*, followed by the nearby valleys of Pisco, Chincha and Lunahuaná and Moquegua further south. Other production centres include Vitor in Arequipa, Locumba in Tacna and Surco in Lima.

South Coast Lima to Pisco Listings

orchard. Try the *criollo* buffet, open at weekends only.

Cremoladas Josefina, Jita. Delicious, refreshing *cremoladas* of crushed ice (boiled water used) mixed with fruit pulp; grape and lúcuma varieties are especially good.

Pisco *p289, map p288*
There are restaurants on the pedestrianized block of Comercio and there are restaurants springing up along San Martín as well. Seafood restaurants can be found along the shore between Pisco and San Andrés, and in San Andrés itself (buses from Plaza Belén, near Hostal Perú).

As de Oro, San Martín 472, T056-532010. Good food at decent prices, closed Mon. Doubles as a disco and karaoke bar on Sat.

El Bossa Nova, Av San Martín 176, p 2, T056-807388. This new café/bar is a stylish place for an espresso or your favorite *trago*. Good night and day.

La Casona Restaurant and Churrascaría, San Martín. New restaurant specializing in grilled meats, large portions, good value.

¶ **Don Manuel**, Comercio 187. US$2-4 for a main dish.

¶ **El Dorado**, main plaza opposite Cathedral. Good value local dishes, popular.

Cafés
Panadería/Café San Fransisco, next to Zarcillos Tours on the main Plaza. Has great *empanadas* and baked goods, with a restaurant next door, cheap.

❂ Festivals and events

Lunahuaná *p286*
Fiesta de la Vendimia, a grape harvest festival, is held in first weekend in **Mar**. At the end of **Sep**/beginning **Oct** is the lively **Fiesta del Níspero** (medlar fruit harvesting festival).

Chincha Alta *p288*
Among other things (olives, for one) Chincha is famous for its many festivals. On **6 Jan** is the **Celebración del Nacimiento de la Beata Melchorita Saravia**. The **Verano Negro**, or Black Summer, is at the end of **Feb**. During this time the black culture of the area, repressed for so many centuries, is freely expressed in the dancing competitions, though black participation in the festival is still somewhat limited. In the second week of **Mar** is the **Festival de la Vendimia**. In **mid-Jul** is the **Virgen del Carmen festival** and the tourist week takes place during the end of **Oct**/beginning of **Nov**. Also in **Nov**, the **Festival de Danzas Negras** is held in the black community of El Carmen, 10 km south. Not enough? Well, on 4 **Dec** there's the **Peregrinación a la Ermita de la Beata Melchorita**.

Pisco *p289, map p288*
San Pedro is at the end of **Jun**. The second week of **Sep** is designated tourist week, and on **21 Nov** is the grandly titled **Peregrinación a la Hermita de la Beata de Humay.**

▲▲ Activities and tours

South to Lunahuaná *p286*
Peru Adventure Lodge, Manzana Ñ, Lote1, Urb La Planicie, Punta Hermosa, T01-230 8351, www.peruadventure.com. Offers accommodation, surfing, spearfishing, fossil hunting and more.

Surf Perú Surfcamp, Lote 27 y 28, Urb La Planicie, Punta Hermosa, T01-230 7421, www.peru-surf.com. Opposite Pico Alto, surfing, classes and equipment rental, bungalows and bunk rooms, hot water, all meals available, airport transfers, internet, living room with cable TV.

Lunahuaná *p286*
Several places in San Jerónimo and Paullo offer rafting and kayaking. From Nov-Apr the river is high (highest from Dec) and during those months the white-water rafting is at levels four to five. May-Oct is the low water season when only boat trips are possible (levels 1-2). Excellent kayaking is 2½ hrs upriver. Rafting costs US$15 per person for 1½ hrs. Annual championships and a festival of adventure sports are held every Feb.

Paracas Peninsula and Ballestas Islands *p289, map p290*
Tours to the islands cost US$9-10 per person, and to the peninsula US$20 per person, but are a lot cheaper out of season. Beware scams, only book tours in company offices not in hotels, nor on the street. The main hotels in Pisco and Paracas will also arrange tours, eg Hotel Paracas, US$18 in their own speed boat, 0900-1700. Operators usually go to Ballestas in the morning and the Paracas Reserve in the afternoon.
Amigos Adventure Travel Agency, Jr Progreso 167, p 2,T056-311984, amigos_adventures@hotmail.com. Island tours, Reserve tours, sandboarding, English, Italian, French, Dutch and Hebrew spoken. Recommended.
Ballestas Travel Service, San Francisco 249, T056-535564. Recommended.
Blue Sea Tours, C Chosica 320, San Andrés, Pisco; also at El Chaco. Guides Jorge Espejo and Hubert Van Lomoen (speaks Dutch) are frequently recommended and there is no time limit on tours.
The Zarcillo Connection, San Francisco 111, T056-536543, www.zarcilloconnections.net or www.zarcillotravel.com. For Paracas National Reserve, Tambo Colorado, trekking and tours to Ica, Chincha and the Nasca Lines and surrounding sites. Recommended.

⊕ Transport

South to Lunahuaná *p286*

At **San Vicente de Cañete**, the main bus stop is on the highway; wait for the service you want going north or south and hope there are free seats. From **Lima**, every 8 mins with Soyuz/PerúBus (2 de Mayo block 7 y Panamericana), 2 hrs, US$2.45. To **Pisco**, 2 hrs, US$1.50. To **Lunahuaná**: from Cañete take a taxi (US$1.20 fromthe Panamericana, US$0.90 from centre), or a *colectivo* from 2 de Mayo block 1 (US$0.75) to Imperial and then a *colectivo* from Av La Mar, 30 mins, US$0.90, or combi, 45 mins, US$0.75. For Condoray or Uchupampa, take a taxi, US$1-2. Imperial to **Viñac**, Turismo Viñac, Av La Mar, Mon, Wed, Sat, 5 hrs, US$3.50.

Cañete Valley *p287*

There is little regular traffic to **Huancaya** and **Vilca**. Occasional vehicles travel two rough roads, passing through Huancaya, across to Huancayo/Jauja. Other options include taking a bus to Yauyos or Alís and looking for onward traffic from there.

Direct buses from Lima for the Cañete valley leave daily around 1500 with **San Juan de Yauyos**, whose terminal is in the dodgy Grau area. The buses go to various destinations in the valley on different days of the week. Most pass by Catahuasi, the stop for **Tupe**, and on Thu go direct to **Laraos**. Otherwise go to Cañete and change there for the once daily **ETAS/Angoma** to **Huancayo** US$7.55. ETAS/Angoma in Huancayo at Loreto y Junín, tickets are best bought the day before, the office is usually open until about 1930. The bus leaves at 0600 and the scenery is great almost all the way (best views on the right). It passes through Llapay, US$4.55 any time from 1130 in the dry season to 1500 in the wet season (intermittent transport or hike an hour or more uphill to Laraos). If you do break your journey at Laraos, you may be lucky and get a direct Lima bus from Laraos itself (usually Thu, about 1000). On other days your best bet is to hitch or hike back down to Llapay for the **ETAS** bus as it passes through on its way to Yauyos (2 hrs from Llapay), Chavín (3 hrs), Catahuasi (3½ hrs, the stop for the footpath to Tupe) and Cañete, arriving from 1930 onwards. There may also be a few

Pisco *p289, map p288*

All the bus terminals are in the centre near the Plaza de Armas. However, if arriving by bus, make sure it is going into town and will not leave you at the Repartición right on the Panamericana, which is 5 km from the centre, a 10-min taxi (US$1) or mototaxi ride (US$0.50), and not a particularly safe area after dark. Transport from the Repartición stops at Hostal Comercio by Plaza Belén. If staying by the beach, it will cost US$0.50 to get to the Plaza de Armas, but drivers try to charge US$1.50.

Bus To **Lima**, 242 km, 3-4 hrs, US$4 with Ormeño (San Francisco, 1 block from the plaza), **San Martín** (San Martín 199), and Soyuz, Callao on the Plaza (US$0.30 taxi ride to Panamericana to catch the bus). Buses leave almost hourly 0715-1800. Also *colectivos*. For buses from Lima, see p134. To **Ayacucho**, 317 km, 8-10 hrs, US$7.55-15.15, several buses daily (Molina recommended), leave from San Clemente 10 km north on Panamericana Sur, take a *colectivo* (20 mins), book in advance to ensure seat and take warm clothing as it gets cold at night. The road is completely paved. To **Huancavelica**, 269 km, 12-14 hrs, US$7, with Oropesa (Conde de la Monclova 637) coming from Ica. There is regular transport to **Ica**, US$0.90 by bus, 45 mins, 70 km; with Ormeño and Saky (Pedemonte y Arequipa). To **Nasca**, 210 km, US$5, 3 hrs by bus, via Ica, at 0830 with **Oropesa** and 3 daily with Ormeño.
To **Arequipa**, US$12, 10-12 hrs, 2 daily.

Paracas Peninsula and Ballestas Islands *p289, map p290*

The reserve can be reached by the coast road from San Andrés, passing the fishing port and a large proportion of Peru's fishmeal industry. Alternatively, go down the Pan-American Highway to 14½ km past the Pisco turning and take the road to Paracas across the desert. After 11 km turn left along the coast road and 1 km further on fork right to Paracas village. Return to the main road for the entrance to the reserve, where you can ask for a map. By private transport it takes about 50 mins to get to Lagunilla from the park entrance, 45 mins to La Mina and an hour to Mirador de los Lobos. Make sure your car is in good condition, never leave it unattended and travel in a group as robbery has been a problem in the past.

A taxi from Pisco to Paracas costs about US$2.50-3. Combis to/from El Chaco beach (marked 'Chaco-Paracas-Museo') leave when full, US$0.50, 25 mins. The last one returns at around 2200. There is no public transport on the peninsula.

Inland from Pisco p291

There's a bus from Pisco to **Tambo Colorado** which leaves at 0800 from near the Plaza (ask for directions); US$1.60, 3 hrs. Also *colectivos*, US$1.20 per person. Get off 20 mins after the stop at Humay. The road passes right through the site. Return by bus to Pisco in the afternoon. For transport back to Pisco wait at the caretaker's house. A taxi

from Pisco is US$25. Tours from Pisco agencies cost US$10-15 with guide, minimum 2 people.

A bus from Pisco to **Huaytará** is US$2.25 (rising to US$5.50 for the San Juan Bautista festival!). A **Molina** bus from Lima takes 6 hrs.

❶ Directory

Pisco *p289, map p288*
Banks ATMs at banks on Plaza de Armas, mostly Visa. **BCP** on the Plaza de Armas. Gives good rates for Amex TCs and cash, Visa ATM. Also on Plaza is **Interbank**, for Mastercard. Doctor **Dr Carlos Alfonso Bonilla Flores**, at C San Francisco 219. Doesn't speak English but is very helpful and will make hotel visits. **Internet** At **Bill Gates** computer school, C San Francisco next to the church. **Telephone** On the Plaza de Armas between Av San Martín y Callao.

Ica and around

➜ Phone code: 056. Colour map 5, grid B2. Population: 161,406. Altitude: 410 m.

Ica is Peru's main wine centre. The city is on the Río Ica, which is almost permanently dry and rubbish-strewn. As well as wine, the city is also famous for its tejas, a local sweet of manjarblanco. Most travellers spend little time in Ica itself, preferring to stay at the oasis at Huacachina. Here you will find a lake surrounded by towering sand dunes, which are great for racing up and down on dune buggies and learning the skills of sandboarding. Increasingly popular are trips into the desert to experience the mysteries of this barren landscape. ➻ *For Sleeping, Eating and other listings, see pages 300-302.*

Ins and outs

Getting there Buses from Lima travel along the Av Municipalidad nearly into the centre of town. Most hotels though are on the far side of the Plaza de Armas. Most bus offices are on Lambayeque blocks 1 and 2 and Salaverry block 3.

Getting around Ica is much more spread out than Pisco. You will need a taxi to get around especially if you intend to visit the *bodegas*.

Tourist information Some information is available at travel agencies. Also try Touring y Automóvil Club del Perú ① *Fermín Tangüis 102, Urb San Miguel, T056-219393, ica@touringperu.com.pe.*

Ica

The waters of the Choclacocha and Orococha lakes from the eastern side of the Andes are tunnelled into the Ica valley and irrigate 30,000 ha of land. The lakes are at 4,570 m and the tunnel is over 9 km long. **San Jerónimo church** at Cajamarca 262 has a fine mural behind the altar.

Museo Regional ① *southwest of the centre, Mon-Sat 0800-1900, Sat-Sun and holidays 0900-1800, US$2, students US$0.65, take bus 17 from the Plaza de Armas (US$0.50),* houses mummies, ceramics, textiles and trepanned skulls from the

Paracas, Nasca and Inca cultures. There's a good, well-displayed collection of Inca counting strings (*quipus*) and clothes made of feathers. It also has good and informative displays with maps of all sites in the Department. Behind the building there is a scale model of the Nasca lines with an observation tower. It's a useful orientation before visiting the lines. The kiosk outside sells copies of motifs from the ceramics and textiles.

> ‼ *Look after your bags etc when transferring between buses to or from Nasca, Pisco or Lima. Watch out for bogus hotel or tour agents.*

Bodega El Carmen is on the right-hand side when arriving from Lima. This *pisco* distillery has an ancient grape press made from a huge tree trunk and is worth a visit.

Around Ica

Ten kilometres outside Ica, in the district of Subtanjalla, is José Carrasco González **Bodega El Catador** ① *T056-403295, 1000-1800, good tours in Spanish, take a combi from the second block of Moquegua, 20 mins, US$0.40, taxi, 10 mins, US$1.50*. It has a shop selling home-made wines and *pisco*, and traditional handicrafts associated with winemaking. There is also a restaurant-bar serving lunch and, in the evening, with dancing and music. The best time to visit is during harvest – late February to early April – when wine and *pisco* tasting is usually possible. Try Cachina, a very young white wine 'with a strong yeasty taste', which is drunk about two weeks after the grape harvest.

Near **Bodega El Catador** is **Bodega Alvarez**. The owner, Umberto Alvarez, is very hospitable and won the gold medal for the best *pisco* in Peru in 1995. Ask about their **pisco de mosto verde** and the rarer, more expensive, *pisco de limón*, which will set you back US$40 per bottle.

In **Ocucaje**, 30 km south of Ica, a very good, strong moscatel is made by Señor Luis Chipana and sold in unlabelled bottles. He is always short of bottles so it's best to take your own. A visit is recommended, but you'll need good Spanish. Señor

Ica

Sleeping
Arameli 10
Confort 7
Hostal Cristian 1
Hostal Paraíso 4
Hostal Siesta I & II 2
Hostal Tres
Copas de Oro 6
Sol de Ica 8
Sol y Luna 3

Eating
Café Mogambo 1
El Otro Peñoncito 2
Las Brujas de Cachiche 3
Pastelería Velazco 4
Pizzería Venecia 5
Tejas Helena 6

South Coast Ica & around

Chipana lives on the main plaza of Ocucaje beside his *bodega*. Ask for him in the bar on the plaza. The town is a popular excursion from Ica for tours of the Ocucaje winery which makes wines and *pisco*. There is a hotel at the winery, which also has a collection of fossilized whale and other sea creatures' bones in the garden. The winery's restaurant has a limited menu but serves good food.

Five kilometres from Ica, round a palm-fringed lake and amid impressive sand dunes, is the attractive oasis and summer resort of **Huacachina**. Its green sulphur waters are said to possess curative properties and attract thousands of visitors. Paddleboats can be rented for US$3 for 30 minutes of boating around the lake. Sandboarding on the dunes has become a major pastime here, attracting fans from Europe and elsewhere. Board hire is US$1.50 per hour. Dune buggies also do white-knuckle, rollercoaster tours for US$12, or you can hire a buggy and scare yourself for US$6 per person for three to four hours. In the town is the **Biblioteca de Abraham Valdelomar** ① *Mon-Sat 0900-1300, 1500-1800, take a taxi from Ica for US$1*, which is open to the public.

● Sleeping

Ica *p298, map p299*
Hotels are fully booked during the harvest festival and prices rise greatly.
AL Las Dunas, Av La Angostura 400, T056-256224, www.lasdunashotel.com. Lima office: Malecón Armendáriz 193, Miraflores, Lima, T01-241 8000. Prices don't include 19% tax (which tourists do not have to pay) and service, about 20% cheaper on weekdays, located in a complete resort with restaurant, swimming pool, water slide, horse riding and other activities, it has its own airstrip for flights over the Nasca Lines, 50 mins. Highly recommended.
C Sol de Ica, Lima 265, 1 block from Plaza de Armas, T056-236168, www.hotelsoldeica. com. Clean rooms, reasonably comfortable, breakfast extra, swimming pool, tour agency.
C-D Hostal Siesta I, Independencia 160, T056-233249. With bathroom, hot water, friendly owner, but very noisy. Also **Siesta II**, T056-234633, which is similar.
E Arameli, Tacna 239 T056-239107. One block from the Plaza de Armas, this clean hotel has cable TV and is a nice place to stay.
E Hostal Cristian, Ayacucho 352, T056-218048. Large, clean, friendly.
E Confort, La Mar 257, 4 blocks from the plaza, T056-233072. Clean but very basic, with damp beds and poor mattresses, dangerous electric showers, motorcycle parking is about the only thing to recommend this place.
E Princess, Urb Santa María D-103, T/F056-215421, www.geocities.com/hotel_ princess. A mototaxi ride from the main plaza, with hot water, TV, pool, tourist information, helpful, peaceful neighbourhood, clean, very good. Recommended.
E Sol y Luna, at Loreto y Salaverry, close to the bus stations. Friendly, clean, rooms with bath and cable TV.
E Hostal Tres Copas de Oro, Independencia y Castrovirreyna. Basic, in a noisy district.
F Hostal Paraíso, Bolívar 418, T056-227582. Clean, quiet, basic.

Around Ica *p299*
It's less stressful to stay in Huacachina than in Ica. The following are situated there.
A Hotel Mossone, at the eastern end of the lake, T056-213660, reserva@derrama.org.pe. An elegant hacienda-like hotel to relax at, full board available, with bath, pool (US$4 including snacks, US$15 including meals, for non-residents), bicycles and sandboards for guests' use. End the day with a Perú libre in the majestic bar/restaurant with a fantastic view over the lake.
B Hostería Suiza, Malecón 264, T056-238762, hostesuiza@terra.com.pe. Nice airy house with a huge terrace overlooking the lake, lovely grounds, quiet, friendly, clean, includes breakfast. Recommended.
E Casita de Arena, T056-215274, casadearena@hotmail.com. Basic rooms, **G** without bath, bar, small pool, laundry facilities, board hire, popular with backpackers, check your change carefully.
E Hostal Rocha, T056-222256. Rooms with bath (**F** without), hot water, family run, kitchen and laundry facilities, board hire,

small pool and nice grounds, popular with backpackers, but a bit run-down.

F Hostal del Barco, Balneario de Huacachina 180. A very relaxed place with hammocks on the front terrace, basic rooms, bar, use of kitchen, can arrange tours.

F Hostal Salvatierra, T056-232352. Though not on the waterfront, this is a charming *hostal*, a grand old place being renovated. It has a great pool, relaxing courtyard, all rooms with private bathroom, rents sandboards at a good price. Good value.

G Hostal Titanic, T056-229003. Small rooms, drab, pool, café, laundry, board hire, cheap.

🍴 Eating

Ica *p298, map p299*
There's a good restaurant at the Ormeño bus terminal.

¶¶¶ **Las Dunas Resort Hotel**, La Angostura 400, T056-256224. The resort has great buffet lunches and a nice restaurant, pricey but worth it.

¶¶-¶ **El Otro Peñoncito**, Bolívar 255. Set lunch (US$6) in a pleasant atmosphere, friendly, clean, good toilets.

¶¶-¶ **Chifa Karaoke Central**, Urb Los Viñedos de Santa María E-25, T056-221294. Excellent Chinese food.

¶¶-¶ **Las Brujas de Cachiche**, Cajamarca 118. Serves local dishes such as *chicharrones con pallares* (butter beans).

¶¶-¶ **Pizzería Venecia**, Lima 252. Best pizzas in town!

Cafés
Café Mogambo, Tacna 125. A good place for breakfast.

Olé, Loreto 223. Next to one of the oldest buildings in Ica, this is a pleasant place for a snack or drink.

Pastelería Velazco, on Plaza de Armas. Clean, good service, great caffeinated drinks. Recommended.

Tejas Helena, Cajamarca 137. This is the place for the best *tejas*.

Tejas Ruthy, Cajamarca 122. Also sells good *tejas* and they are a bit cheaper.

Around Ica *p299*
¶¶-¶ **La Sirena**, Huacachina. This is the best place to eat. The big corvina fish steaks are excellent, also serves good sandwiches.

¶¶-¶ **Morrón**, beside the lake, Huacachina. Also good, but it's closed in the evening.

🎉 Festivals and events

Ica *p298, map p299*
The wine harvest festival (**Festival Internacional de la Vendimia**) is held in early **Mar** as is the **Concurso Nacional de Marinera**. In the first week of **May** is **Fiesta de la Cruz**. Also in **May**, the third Sun, is **Día Internacional del Pisco** (you don't need to be told what happens – use your imagination). In the third week of **Jun** is **Ica Week** and the last week of **Sep** is **Tourist Week**. In the first 2 weeks of **Oct** the image of **El Señor de Luren**, in a fine church in Parque Luren, draws pilgrims from all Peru, when there are all-night processions.

🏃 Activities and tours

Ica *p298, map p299*
Ica Desert Trip, icadeserttrip@yahoo.es
Robert Penny Cabrera (speaks Spanish and English) and Marc Romain (speaks, Spanish, French and English) offer 1-, 2- and 3-day trips off-road into the desert, archaeology, geology, etc. US$50 per person per day (maximum 4 people), contact by email in advance, frequently recommended.

La Ruta del Pisco, Av Larco 345, M26, Miraflores, Lima, T01-445 3900, www.laruta delpisco.com. 3-day, 2-night tours from Lima including transport, accommodation and visits to *bodegas*, from US$69.99-99.99; additional options to Nasca or Paracas also available.

Around Ica *p299*
Many *hostales* in Huacachina help their guests arrange tours.

Desert Adventures, T01-981 69352, desertadventures@hotmail.com.. Frequently recommended for sandboarding and trips into the desert, French, English and Spanish.

🚌 Transport

Ica *p298, map p299*
Most bus offices are on Lambayeque blocks 1 and 2 and Salaverry block 3.
To **Pisco** (70 km), 45 mins, US$0.90 with **Saky** buses from opposite the Ormeño

terminal, leaving every half hour. **Ormeño** is at Lambayeque 180. To **Lima** (302 km), 4 hrs, US$5-10, several daily including **Soyuz** (Av Manzanilla 130 – every 8 mins 0600-2200) and **Flores** (see also Lima p134). To **Nasca** (140 km), 2 hrs, minimum US$1.50; several buses and *colectivos* daily, including **Ormeño**, **Flores**, 4 daily, and **Cueva** (José Elias y Huánuco), hourly on the hour 0600-2200. To **Arequipa** the route goes via Nasca, US$15-25, see also under Nasca; most

reliable buses with Ormeño, Cruz del Sur and Flores.

❶ Directory

Ica *p298, map p299*
Banks Avoid changing TCs if possible as commission is high. If you need to, though, **BCP** is reasonable. **Post** At Callao y Moquegua. **Telephone** At Av San Martín y Huánuco.

Nasca and around

→ *Phone code: 056. Colour map 5, grid B3. Population: over 50,000. Altitude: 598 m.*

Set in a green valley surrounded by mountains, Nasca would be just like any other anonymous desert oasis (the sun blazes for much of the year by day and the nights are crisp) were it not for the 'discovery' of a series of strange lines etched on the plains to the north. Tourists in their thousands now flock to the town to fly over the famous Nasca Lines, whose precise purpose still remains a mystery. Overlooking the town is Cerro Blanco (2,078 m), the highest sand dune in the world, which is popular for sandboarding and paragliding. ►► *For Sleeping, Eating and other listings, see pages 307-311.*

Ins and outs

Getting there There is no central bus station in Nasca, but offices are at the western end of town, close to the Panamericana Sur after it has crossed the Río Tierras Blancas. Do not pay attention to people selling tours or offering hotels on the street, especially near bus stations. Head straight to a hotel and find an official agency to handle your flights and tours. For more information, see Activities and tours, page 309.
Getting around Most of the hotels are spread out along Jr Lima and around the Plaza de Armas and are within easy walking distance of the bus stations.

Nasca

Nasca was badly damaged by an earthquake in 1996. Among the buildings destroyed was the municipality's museum on the main plaza. There are no plans to rebuild it. Instead, visit the large **Museo Antonini** ① *Av de la Cultura 600, at the eastern end of Jr Lima, ring the bell to get in, T056-523444, cahuachi@terra.com.pe, 0900-1900, US$3, including a local guide, US$1.50 extra to use a camera*, which was opened in 1999. A video is shown in the Conference Room. It is a 10-minute walk from the plaza, or a short taxi ride. It houses the discoveries of Professor Orefici and his team from the huge pre-Inca city at Cahuachi (see below), which, Orefici believes, holds the key to the Nasca Lines. Many tombs survived the huaqueros and there are displays of ceramics, textiles, amazing *antaras* (panpipes) and photos of the excavations and the Lines. Recommended.

The **Maria Reiche Planetarium** ① *Hotel Nasca Lines, T056-522293, shows are at around 1900 and 2100 nightly, US$6 (half price for students)*, was opened in May 2000 in honour of Maria Reiche (see below). It is run by Edgardo Azabache, who speaks English, Italian and French, and Enrique Levano, who speaks English and Italian. Both give stimulating lectures every night about the Nasca Lines, based on

" " The lines were not designed to be seen physically from above, but from the mind's eye of the flying shaman...

Reiche's theories, which cover archaeology and astronomy. The show lasts about 45 minutes (commentary in English), after which visitors are able to look at the moon, planets and stars through sophisticated telescopes.

Nasca Lines → *Colour map 5, grid B3.*

Cut into the stony desert are large numbers of lines, not only parallels and geometrical figures, but also designs such as a killer whale, a monkey, birds (one with a wing span of over 100 m), a spider and a tree. The lines, which can best be appreciated from the air, were etched on the Pampa sands by the Nasca people. It's estimated that they were begun around 400 BC and continued to be made for perhaps another thousand years. The famous lines are above the Ingenio valley on the Pampa de San José, about 22 km north of Nasca, and across the Ingenio river, on the plain around Palpa. The Pan-American Highway passes close to, even through, the Lines.

The mystery of the Lines

Since the Nasca Lines were first spotted from the air 70 years ago, their meaning, function and origin have tormented scientists around the world. Dr Paul Kosok, a North American scientist, gave the first scientific explanation in 1941, when he observed a line pointing towards the place where the sun would have risen on the

Nasca

(map of Nasca showing streets including Av César Vallejo, Juan Matta, Av Los Incas, San Martín, 28 de Julio, Bolívar, Progreso, Morasesk, Jr Fermín de Castilla, Jr Grau, Arica, María Reiche, Mejía, Tarapacá, Jr Callao, Municipalidad, Plaza de Armas, Jr Bolognesi, Jr Lima, Plaza Bolognesi, Tacna, Río Tierras Blancas. To Ica, To Museo Antonini, Coliseo, Panamericana Sur, Cruz del Sur, Civa, Ormeño, Flores, Air Nasca Travel, María Reiche Planetarium. To 13 14 15 16, Airport, Puquio & Cusco)

0 metres 200
0 yards 200

N

Sleeping 🛏
Alegría 1
Casa Andina 17
De La Borda 13

Estrella del Sur 2
Hostal Alegría 3
Hostal Internacional 7
Hostal Las Líneas 4
Hostal Restaurant Vía
  Morburg 12
Maison Suisse 14
Mirador 8
Nasca & Ormeño
  Royal Class Buses 9
Nasca Lines 10

Nido del Cóndor 15
Paredones Inn 18
Posada Guadalupe 6
Rancho Park 16
Sol de Nasca 11

Eating 🍴
Chifa Guang Zhou 2
Concordia 3
El Portón 1
El Puquio 4

Fuente de Soda
  Jumbory 5
Kañada 6
La Carreta 14
La Choza 11
La Púa 7
La Taberna 8
Los Angeles 9
Panadería 12
Plaza Mayor 13
Rico Pollo 10

Guardian of the lines

The greatest contribution to our awareness of the lines is that of Maria Reiche, who lived and worked on the Pampa for over 50 years. The young German mathematician arrived in Peru in the early 1930s and would dedicate the rest of her life to removing centuries of windswept debris and painstaking survey work. She even used to sleep on the Pampa.

Maria Reiche's years of meticulous measurement and study of the lines led her to the conclusion that they represented a huge astronomical calendar. She also used her mathematical knowledge to determine how the many drawings and symbols could have been created with such precise symmetry. She suggested that those responsible for the lines used long cords attached to stakes in the ground. The figures were drawn by means of a series of circular arcs of different radius. Reiche also contended that they used a standard unit of measurement of 1.30 m, or the distance between the fingertips of a person's extended arms.

As well as the anthropomorphic and zoomorphic drawings, there are a great many geometric figures. Reiche believed these to be a symbolic form of writing associated with the movements of the stars. In this way, the lines could have been used as a kind of calendar that not only recorded celestial events but also had a practical day-to-day function such as indicating the times for harvest, fishing and festivals.

Whatever the real purpose of the Nasca lines, one fact remains indisputable: that their status as one of the country's major tourist attractions is largely due to the selfless work of Maria Reiche, the unofficial guardian of the lines. Maria Reiche died in June 1998.

midwinter solstice in ancient Nasca times. So impressed was he, that he described the Nasca pampa as "the biggest astronomy book in the world".

By the 1950s Maria Reiche (see box), inspired by Kosok, was mapping the area and discovered giant animals too vast to be appreciated from the ground. Her many years of research led her to the conclusion that they were a huge astronomical calendar.

There are those who disagree with the German mathematician's hypothesis. The International Explorers Society, for example, was convinced that the desert artists would not have drawn something they themselves could not see. They set out to prove that the ancient Peruvians could fly, based on the fact that the lines are best seen from the air, and that there are pieces of ancient local pottery and tapestry showing balloonists as well as local legends of flying men. In 1975, they made a hot-air balloon of cloth and reed, called it Condor I and attempted to fly it for 15 minutes over the pampa. Unfortunately for them, the flight lasted only 60 seconds, thereby leaving the issue unresolved.

Some of the competing theories as to the function of the Nasca lines are rather far-fetched. Erich Von Daniken, in his book Chariots of the Gods, posited that the pampa was an extraterrestrial landing strip. This idea, however, only succeeded in drawing to the site thousands of visitors who tore across the lines on motorbikes, four-wheel drives, horses and whatever else they could get their hands on, leaving an indelible mark. It is now an offence to walk or drive on the pampa, punishable by heavy fine or imprisonment.

Other theories are that the Nasca designs were part of a giant running track (George A Von Breunig – 1980; also proposed by the English astronomer Alan Sawyer). Another suggestion is that they represent weaving patterns and yarns (Henri

Stirlin), or that the plain is a map demonstrating the Tiahuanaco Empire (Zsoltan Zelko). Dr Johan Reinhard brings together ethnographic, historical and archaeological data, including the current use of straight lines in Chile and Bolivia, to suggest that the Lines conform to fertility practices throughout the Andes.

Recent research

The BBC series *Ancient Voices* pointed to yet another theory. The clues to the function of the lines are found in the highly advanced pottery and textiles of the ancient Nascans, which relate directly to the subject matter of the lines. Some pots and tapestries show a flying being emitting discharge from its nose and mouth. This is believed to portray the flight of the shaman. The shaman consumes certain psycho-active drugs that convince him he can fly and so enter the real world of spirits in order to rid sick people of evil spirits.

In this way, the lines were not designed to be seen physically from above, but from the mind's eye of the flying shaman. This also explains the presence of incongruous creatures such as a monkey or killer whale. They were chosen because they possess the qualities admired and needed by the shaman in his spirit journeys.

But this does not explain the spectacular geometric figures. These straight lines are a feature of ancient Peruvian ritual behaviour, much like ley lines in Europe. They represent invisible paths of perceived energy. The Pampa's most remarkable features are the trapezoids, which are thought to have been ritual spaces where offerings were made to the gods, in the hope of favours in return.

Scientists have discovered evidence of a terrible 40-year drought around AD 550 or 600. This coincides not only with the abandonment of the nearby Cahuachi temples but also with a period of increased bloody warfare and increased line-making in the desert sands. This would seem to indicate that the Nascans grew increasingly desperate in the face of continued drought, abandoned traditional religious practices, and instead made more and more sacrificial offerings to the gods.

The results of six years' work by Peruvian archaeologist Johny Isla and Markus Reindel of the Swiss-Liechtenstein Foundation threw new light on the Lines in 2002. It ties together some of the earlier ideas and discredits both the astronomical calendar and extraterrestrial theories. Working at La Muña and Los Molinos, Palpa (see below) and with photogrammetry (mapping using aerial photographs), they have deduced that the lines on both the Palpa and Nasca plains are offerings dedicated to the worship of water and fertility. These two elements were paramount to the coastal people in this arid environment and they expressed their adoration not only in the desert, but also on their ceramics and on the engraved stones of the Paracas culture. Isla and Reindel believe that the Palpa lines predate those at Nasca and that the lines and drawings themselves are scaled up versions of the Paracas drawings, made at a time when the Nasca people were becoming independent of Paracas. In addition, objects in the shape of drops of water, whales and chilis, found in grave sites, are repeated in the desert. This new research proposes the theory that the Nasca culture succumbed not to drought, but to heavy rainfall, probably during an El Niño event.

In 1976 Maria Reiche had a 12-metre platform called the Mirador put up at her own expense, from which three of the huge designs can be seen – the Hands, the Lizard and the Tree. This is included on some arranged tours, enquire with your agency to be sure. If you get a taxi to the Mirador, make sure it will wait for you and take you back. Taxis will charge US$4-6 per hour. Reiche's book, *Mystery on the Desert*, is on sale for US$10 (proceeds to conservation work) in Nasca. In January 1994 Maria Reiche opened a small **museum** ⓘ *US$1, 5 km from town at the Km 416 marker, take micro from in front of* Ormeño *terminal, US$0.70, frequent*. Viktoria Nikitzhi, a colleague of Maria Reiche, gives one-hour lectures about the Nasca Lines at **Dr Maria Reiche Center** ⓘ *Av de los Espinales 300, 1 block from Ormeño bus stop, T056-969 9419, viktorianikitzki@hotmail.com*. She also organizes tours in June and December to see the sun at the solstice striking the Lines (phone in advance to confirm times) and has many original documents and objects. See www.magicperu.com/Maria Reiche/. See also the Planetarium, page 302.

Around Nasca

The Nasca area is dotted with over 100 cemeteries and the dry, humidity-free climate has preserved perfectly invaluable tapestries, cloth and mummies.

Cemeteries and ruins

Some 30 km south of Nasca – on the Panamericana Sur, heading south from Nasca – **Chauchilla** is on the left, unsigned, 12 km from the highway. At this cemetery site, grave robbing *huaqueros* ransacked the tombs and left remains all over the place. Bones, skulls, mummies and pottery shards litter the desert. A tour is worthwhile and takes about two hours. It should cost about US$10 per person, plus the cost of entrance to the cemetery, with a minimum of two people. The area has been cordoned off and has clean bathrooms.

There are other cemeteries in the vicinity. Some, like **Poroma**, have been so desecrated that there is nothing left to see. A good cemetery, with mummies still to be seen, is in the valley of **Jumana**, one hour west of Nasca in the river bed. Cemetery tours usually include a visit to a gold shop. Gold mining is one of the main local industries and a tour includes a visit to a small family processing shop where the techniques used are still very old-fashioned.

Some tours also include a visit to a local potter's studio. That of Señor Andrés Calle Benavides,-who makes Nasca reproductions, is particularly recommended. He is very friendly and takes time to explain the techniques he uses although his small gallery is a bit on the expensive side. Anyone interested in pre-Columbian ceramics is welcome to make an appointment to visit him independently. He is very knowledgeable on the coastal desert cultures.

The **Paredones ruins**, also called Cacsamarca, are Inca on a pre-Inca base. By taxi it is about US$10 round-trip, or go with a tour for US$10 per person, two people minimum. They are not well-preserved. The underground aqueducts, or *puquios*, built 300 BC-AD 700, still provide water for the local people. They are beautifully built and even have S-bends to slow down the flow of water, and they're very cool. 33 aqueducts irrigate 20 ha each and, to this day, local farmers have the job of cleaning the section for which their group has been responsible for as long as they can remember.

Cantalloc is a 30-minute to an hour walk through Buena Fe, to see markings in the valley floor. These consist of a triangle pointing to a hill and a *tela* (cloth) with a spiral depicting the threads. Climb the mountain to see better examples. There are also aqueducts here. This is best done with a guide, or by car. Take a taxi from Nasca and have the taxi wait there for you as it will be difficult to find transportation back to Nasca, cost US$7. Arranged tours cost US$10 per person, minimum two people.

Cahuachi, to the west of the Nasca Lines, comprises several pyramids and a site called **El Estaquería**. The latter is thought to have been a series of astronomical sighting posts, but more recent research suggests the wooden pillars were used to dry dead bodies and therefore it may have been a place of mummification. Tours of the ruins of Cahuachi costs US$10 per person, minimum two people. Some tours include a visit to the Museo Antonini, see above.

Palpa and around → *Population: 15,000.*

Known as the 'Capital de la Naranja' (the Orange Capital), Palpa is a hospitable town 43 km northwest of Nasca, 97 km south of Ica. The Plaza de Armas, on which the Municipalidad and church stand, is bordered by arches. Some colonial-style buildings survive. The climate is hot and dry (average annual temperature 21.4°C) and the main crops, besides oranges, are other fruits (eg plums, bananas) and cotton. There is also fishing for shrimp in the river. The **Fiesta de la Ciruela y Vendimia** (plum harvest) is in March/April. The town's tourist week is in the last week of July. The main fiesta is on 15 August.

There are several archaeological sites, of different periods, not far from the town. The **Ciudad Perdida de Hualluri**, on the west side of the Panamericana Sur, 16 km from Palpa, 5 km from the Highway (Distrito Santa Cruz), is a ruined pre-Inca city. At the entrance to the site is a huarango tree which is over 1,000 years old. In Sector Sacramento, 2 km from the Highway, is the **Puente Colgante del Inca**, built during the reign of Pachacútec. At **Chichictara** is a vast area of petroglyphs thought to date from the Formative Period, 3,000 to 500 BC (Chavín and Paracas cultures).

On the desert near Palpa there are drawings similar to those found at Nasca: a sun dial, the Reloj Solar, measuring 150 m across, a whale (35 m), a pelican (45 m), the so-called Familia Real, a man, woman and child (30 m tall) and another 1,000 or so lines and figures. Two Nasca culture centres have been excavated at **La Muña** and **Los Molinos**. Ceramics, necklaces, spondylus sea shells and gold objects have been found, despite earlier sacking by grave robbers. Los Molinos is a monumental complex where more burials have been uncovered. See under the **Nasca Lines**, above, for the relationship of these markings on the desert with those at Nasca.

Seek information from the Consejo Municipal. There are no travel agencies in town. Otherwise ask for information and guides in Nasca.

Sacaco
One-hundred kilometres south of Nasca is Sacaco, which has a museum built over the fossilized remains of a whale excavated in the desert. The keeper lives in a house nearby and is helpful. Take a bus from Nasca, C Bolognesi, in the morning (check times in advance) towards Puerto de Lomas. Ask the driver where to get off and be ready for a 2-km-walk in the sun. Return to the Pan-American Highway no later than 1800 for a bus back. Do not go two to three days after a new moon as a vicious wind blows at this time.

Puerto de Lomas
Lying 7 km off the Pan-American Highway, on the coast 98 km from Nasca, is Puerto de Lomas, a fishing village with safe beaches which are popular in February and March. It is 1½ hours by bus from Nasca, US$1.75 (one hour by car). There are several fish restaurants.

Nasca to Cusco

The highway from Nasca to Cusco is paved and safe. Two hours out of Nasca is the **Reserva Nacional Pampas Galeras** at 4,100 m, which has a vicuña reserve. There is an interesting Museo del Sitio, also a military base and park guard here. It's best to go early as entry is free. At Km 155 is **Puquio**, then it's another 185 km to **Chalhuanca**. There are wonderful views on this stretch, with lots of small villages, valleys and alpacas. From Chalhuanca to Abancay the road is paved. Fuel is available in Puquio and Chalhuanca. For the route from Abancay to Cusco, see page 497.

Sleeping

Nasca *p302, map p303*
Those arriving by bus should beware being told that the hotel of their choice is closed, or full. Go to the hotel and find out for sure.

L-A Maison Suisse, opposite the airport, T/F056-522434, maisonsuisse@infonegocio. net.pe. Nice, comfortable, safe car park, expensive restaurant, pool, suites with

jacuzzi, accepts Amex, shows video of Nasca Lines. Also has camping facilities. Ask for packages including flights over Nasca Lines.
AL Casa Andina, Jr Bolognesi 367, T056-523563, www.casa-andina.com. One of this new chain of hotels, which all offer standardized services in distinctive style. Bright, modern decor, clean, a/c, pool, friendly staff, TV, internet, restaurant open all day.
AL Nasca Lines, Jr Bolognesi, T056-522293, reservanasca@derramajae.org.pe. Large remodelled hotel with a/c, comfortable, rooms with private patio, hot water, peaceful, price includes American breakfast, restaurant, good but expensive meals, safe car park, pool (US$4.50 for non-guests, or free if having lunch), they can arrange package tours which include 2-3 nights at the hotel plus a flight over the lines and a desert trip: enquire about the price. Recommended.
B De La Borda, a charming old hacienda at Majoro about 5 km from town past the airstrip, T056-522750. Beautiful gardens, pool, restaurant, quiet, unpredictable service, serene surroundings.
B Nido del Cóndor, opposite the airport, Panamericana Sur Km 447, T056-522424, contanas@terra.com.pe. Large rooms, hot water, good restaurant, bar, shop, videos, swimming pool, camping US$3, parking, English, Italian German spoken, free pick-up from town, reservation advised.
C-E per person Alegría, Jr Lima 166, T056-522702, www.nazcaperu.com. Continental breakfast and tax included. Rooms with bathroom, carpet and a/c, rooms with shared bath **G** per person, hot water, cafeteria, pool, garden, English, Hebrew, Italian and German spoken, laundry facilities, safe luggage deposit, book exchange, email facilities for US$2 per hr, netphone also US$2, free video on the lines at 2100, very popular. Recommended. Efraín Alegría also runs a tour agency and guests are encouraged to buy tours (see Activities and tours), flights and bus tickets arranged. Don't listen to anyone who says that Alegría is closed, or full, and no longer runs tours; if you phone or email the hotel they will pick you up at the bus station free of charge day or night (Alegría gives 1 hr free internet use to those who email in advance).
C Paredones Inn, Jr Arica 115, T056-522181, paredoneshotel@terra.com. One block from the Plaza de Armas, nice, ample rooms with cable TV, clean bathrooms, modern, great views from rooftop terrace, laundry service, bar, suites with jacuzzi, helpful staff. Good.
D Hostal Internacional, Av Maria Reiche 112, T056-522744, hostalinternacional @hotmail.com. With bathroom, hot water, garage, café and very nice bungalows.
D Hostal Las Líneas, Jr Arica 299, T056-522488. Cheaper without bath, clean, spacious, restaurant. Recommended, but ask for a room away from the street.
D Mirador, Tacna 436, T056-523121. On main plaza, comfortable rooms with shower, cheaper with shared bath, hot water, good breakfast, TV downstairs, modern, clean. Recommended.
E Estrella del Sur, Callao 568, T056-522106. Small, friendly, clean rooms with shower, cable TV, price includes breakfast.
E Hostal Alegría, Av Los Incas 117, opposite Ormeño bus terminal, T056-522497. More basic than Alegría (above) with which it is unrelated, **F** without bathroom, hot water, clean, hammocks, nice gardens, camping permitted, restaurant.
E Hostal Restaurant Via Morburg, JM Mejía 108, 3 blocks from Plaza de Armas, T/F056-522566, hotelviamorburg@hotmail. com. Rooms are a bit small, with bathroom, hot water, family feel, small swimming pool, TV room, excellent and cheap restaurant on top floor, very helpful staff, luggage store. Recommended.
E Nasca, C Lima 438, T/F056-522085. **G** without bathroom, hot water, noisy, clean, nice lawn area, clothes washing facilities, luggage store, hard sell on tours and flights, bargain hard for better price, mixed reports, safe motorcycle parking.
E Posada Guadalupe, San Martín 225, T056-522249. Family-run, basic accommodation, **G** without bath, hot water, good breakfast, relaxing (touts who try to sell tours are nothing to do with hotel).
E Rancho Park, on Panamericana 1 km from town towards the airport, T056-521153.

 For an explanation of sleeping and eating price codes used in this guide, see inside the front cover. Other relevant information is found in Essentials, pages 61-66.

Hotel on farmland with two swimming pools (one for children), entry to pools US$1, popular at weekends, good restaurant.
E Sol de Nasca, Callao 586, T056-522730. Rooms with and without hot showers, TV, also has a restaurant, pleasant, don't leave valuables in luggage store; tours booked here are expensive.

Palpa and around *p306*
F San Francisco, 2 blocks from the plaza in Palpa. Other hotels include the **Palpa**. There are also several *pensiones*, including **El Sol**, which is not recommended.

Puerto de Lomas *p307*
C Hostal Capricho de Verano, T056-210282. Beautifully situated on the cliffs, bungalows with bathroom, clean, very friendly, special rates for young travellers. Recommended.

Nasca to Cusco *p307*
F Hostal Central, Av Castilla 625, Puquio. With shared bath, hot water and restaurant (motorcycle parking available).
F Hostal Victoria, Jr Arequipa 305, Chalhuanca, T083-321301. Shared bath, clean and comfortable. One other *hostal* on the main road between the plaza and the Wari bus stop, cheaper, very basic, dirty, parking.

❼ Eating

Nasca *p302, map p303*
There are many restaurants near the Plaza de Armas and along Bolognesi as well.
††-† Chifa Nam Kug, on Bolognesi near Plaza Bolognesi. Recommended for Peruvian/Chinese food, also a good value set lunch.
††-† Concordia, Lima 594. Good, also rents bikes at US$1 an hr.
††-† El Portón, Moresky 120, in front of **Hotel Nasca Lines**. A popular stopover with tours, and well worth the visit. Specializes in Peruvian food, has a great indoor/outdoor setting with wood decor. Can cater to large groups with advanced notice.
††-† El Puquio, Bolognesi 50 m from plaza. Good food, especially pastas, pleasant atmsophere, good for drinks, popular.
††-† La Carreta, Bolognesi, next door to **Los Angeles**. New, look for Nuevo Andino dishes using traditional Andean ingredients, rustic, lively atmosphere, stage for live music. Good.

†† † La Choza, Bolognesi 290. Nice atmosphere with woven chairs and thatched roof, all types of food, live music at night.
†† † La Taberna, Jr Lima 321, T056-521411. Excellent food, live music, popular with gringos, it's worth a look just for the graffiti on the walls.
†† † Plaza Mayor, on the Plaza. This new restaurant specializes in barbecue of all types, roasted chicken, steaks, anticuchos and great salads. Large portions, nice staff. Highly recommended.
† Chifa Guang Zhou, Bolognesi 297, T056-522036. Very good Peruvian/Chinese food.
† Kañada, Lima 160, nazcanada@yahoo.com. Cheap menú, excellent *pisco sours*, nice wines, popular, display of local artists' work, email service, English spoken, owner Juan Carlos Fraola is very helpful.
† La Púa, Jr Lima, next to **La Taberna**. Great espresso, also serves pizzas, pastas and sandwiches, good, also offers courtesy *pisco sour*.
† Los Angeles, Bolognesi 266. Good, cheap, try *sopa criolla*, and chocolate cake.
† Rico Pollo opposite **Hotel Alegría**. Good local restaurant with great chicken dishes, cheap.

Cafés
The Grumpys, Bolognesi 282. Despite its name, really friendly, salads, fish and chicken dishes, cocktails.
Fuente de Soda Jumbory, near the cinema. Good *almuerzo*.
Panadería, Bolognesi 387.

❀ Festivals and events

Nasca *p302, map p303*
Virgen de la Guadelupe festival is held on Aug 29-Sep 10.

❍ Shopping

Nasca *p302, map p303*
There is a market at Lima y Grau, and the Mercado Central is between Arica and Tacna.

▲ Activities and tours

Nasca Lines *p303*
All guides must be approved by the Ministry of Tourism and should have an official identity card. As more and more touts

(*jaladores*) operate at popular hotels and the bus terminals, they are using false ID cards and fake hotel and tour brochures. They are all rip-off merchants who overcharge and mislead those who arrive by bus. Only conduct business with agencies at their office, or phone or email the company you want to deal with in advance. Some hotels are not above pressurising guests to buy tours at inflated prices. Do not take just any taxi on the plaza for a tour as they are unreliable and can lead to robbery. It is not dangerous to visit the sites if you go with a trustworthy person. Taxi drivers usually act as guides, but most speak only Spanish. Taxis will charge from US $4-6 per hr to wait for you at the sites and bring you back to the city.

Aerial tours

Small planes take 3-5 passengers. Flights last 30-35 mins and are controlled by air traffic personnel at the airport. A taxi to the airport costs US$1.35; bus, US$0.10. Reservations should be made at the airport for flights with companies listed below. These companies are well-established and recommended. There are others. The price for a flight is US$40 per person (special deals are sometimes available, eg *hostal*; touts charge US$50; shorter flights on sale for US$25). You also have to pay US$2 airport tax. It is best to organize a flight direct with the airlines at the airport. Flights are bumpy – many people are airsick. May be best avoid food and drink. Best times to fly are 0800-1000 and 1500-1630 when there is less turbulence and better light (assuming there is no fog, in which case chaos may ensue).

Aerocóndor, Panamericana Sur Km 447, T056-522404, or their office in **Hotel Las Dunas** in Ica, T056-256230, www.aero condor.com.pe. The outfit offers flights over the lines from Lima in a 1-day tour (lunch in Nasca) for US$260 per person; or flights from Ica for US$130 per person.

Aero Ica, in Jr Lima and at the airport, Lima T01-446 3026, aeroica@terra.com.pe. Also offers flights from Lima and a night in Maison Suisse plus flight for US$65, but book 48 hrs in advance. Make sure you clarify everything before getting on the plane and ask for a receipt.

Alas Peruanas, T056-522444, www.alasperuanas.com. Their flights can

also be booked at **Hotel Alegría** (experienced pilots fluent in English). Often include other features in their 35-min flight over the Lines, such as the spiral ventilation holes of the aqueducts. They also offer 1-hr flights over the Palpa and Llipata areas (US$60 per person, minimum 3). They can also organize flights from Pisco (US$130) and Ica (US$120). All flights include the BBC film.

Taxi tours

Taxi-guides to the Mirador, 0800-1200, cost US$4-6 per person, or you can hitch, but there is not always much traffic. Travellers suggest the view from the hill 500 m back to Nasca is better. Go early as the site gets very hot. Better still, take a taxi and arrive at 0745 before the buses.

Tour operators

Air Nasca Travel, Jr Lima 185, T056-521027, guide Susi recommended. Very helpful and friendly staff, very competitive prices. Can do all types of tours around Nasca, Ica, Paracas and Pisco. Recommended.

Alegría Tours, Lima 168, T056-522444, (24 hrs), www.nazcaperu.com. Run by Efraín Alegría, offer inclusive tours (see Sleeping) which have been repeatedly recommended. Guides with radio contact and maps can be provided for hikes to nearby sites. They have guides who speak English, German, French and Italian, with tours to Palpa, Puerto Inca, Sacaco and the San Fernando Reserve to see the marine wildlife, to Chauchilla, Cantalloc, etc. Tours go as far as Ica, Paracas and the Ballestas Islands. In the high Andes they have birdwatching, visits to Pampas Galeras vicuña reserve, visits to the village of Andamarca and downhill mountain biking trips. Also sandboarding on Cerro Blanco. Alegría run a bus from Nasca to Pisco every day at 1000 (returns at 1000 from Pisco's Plaza de Armas), via Ica, Huacachina and *bodegas*. Ask Efraín Alegría to arrange a taxi for you to one of the sites outside Nasca (eg US$50 to Sacaco, 30 mins at site).

Jesús Erazo Buitrón, Juan Matta 1110, T056-523005. Very knowledgeable, he speaks a little English but his Spanish is easy to follow. Recdommended.

Fernández family, who run the **Hotel Nasca**, also run local tours. Ask for the hotel owners and speak to them direct. Ask them to arrange taxis for you, prices as above. **Nanasca Tours**, Jr Lima 160, T/F056-522917, nanascatours@yahoo.com. Very helpful. **Nasca Trails**, Bolognesi 550, T056-522858, nascatrails@terra.com.pe. Juan Tohalino Vera speaks English, French, German and Italian. **Félix Quispe Sarmiento**, El Nativo de Nazca, Fedeyogin5@hotmail.com. He has his own museum, Hantun Nazca, Panamericana Sur 447 and works with the Instituto Nacional de Cultura, tours off the beaten track, can arrange flights, knowledgeable, ask for him at Kañada restaurant. Recommended.

⊙ Transport

Nasca *p302, map p303*
Bus To **Lima** (446 km), 6 hrs, several buses and *colectivos* daily. Recommended companies include: **Ormeño**,T056-522058, Royal Class at 0530 and 1330 US$20, from Hotel Nasca Lines, Jr Bolognesi, normal service from Av Los Incas, 6 a day, US$5.50; **Civa**, Av Guardia Civil, T056-523019, normal service at 2300, US$6. **Cruz del Sur**, Av Guardia Civil 290, T056-523713. Four buses daily, US$6. Ormeño's Royal Class arrives in Santa Catalina, a much safer area of Lima.

Ormeño to **Ica**, 2 hrs, US$1.50, 4 a day, and to **Pisco** (210 km), 3 hrs, US$5, also 3 a day. Royal Class to **Paracas**, 2¾ hrs, and Pisco, both at 1330, US$12. **Flores** also goes to **Ica** 4 times daily for under US$2. Note that buses to Pisco don't go into the centre, but stop 5 km outside town; change to a *colectivo*.
To **Arequipa**, 565 km, 9 hrs: **Ormeño** 1530, 2000, 2400, from Av Los Incas, US$20, with

Royal Class at 2100, US$15, 8 hrs. **Cruz del Sur** has 4 buses daily between 1900 and 2400, with prices ranging between US$10 and US$27. **Civa**, 1100, US$20, 8 hrs. **Flores** has 9 buses daily, US$15, but trip takes 15-16 hrs. Delays are possible out of Nasca because of drifting sand across the road or mudslides in the rainy season. Travel in daylight.
Buses to **Cusco**, 659 km, 14 hrs, via **Chalhuanca** and **Abancay**. On the **Lima-Nasca-Abancay-Cusco** route **Expreso Wari** have 6 services a day, normal US$17, and Imperial at US$20 (bus may run if not enough passengers). Their offices are at the exit from Nasca on the road to Puquío. Also buses to Cusco with **Ormeño**, US$27, **Cruz del Sur**, 2000, 2015, US$22, and **Flores**, one a day to Cusco, 18 hrs, US$20.

⊙ Directory

Nasca *p302, map p303*
Banks **BCP**, Lima y Grau. Changes cash and Visa TCs at decent rates, also cash advance on Visa, Visa ATM. Some street changers will change TCs, but at 8% commission.
Hospital C Callao entre Morsesky y Castillo. Open 24 hours. **Internet** Many places on Jr Bolognesi. **Lucy@com**, Bolognesi 298. US$0.75 per hr. **Migsu Net**, Arica 295, p 2. Daily 0800-2400, good, US$1 per hr. Facilities at Hotel Alegría and Casa Andina.
Post Fermín de Castillo 379, T056-522016. Also at Hotel Alegría. **Police** Av Los Incas, T056-522105, T105 for emergencies.
Telephone **Telefónica** for international calls with coins on Plaza Bolognesi. Also on Plaza de Armas and at Lima 359.

Nasca to Chile

South of Nasca

From Nasca to the Chilean border the coastal desert continues, broken by the occasional irrigation scheme. In places the dunes are otherwordly. There are a few ports, old ones such as Puerto Inca, which served Imperial Cusco, and new ones like Matarani. If you head south on the Panamericana, instead of turning off at the junction to Arequipa and the Sierra, you reach the fruitful valley of Moquegua. the town has many historical associations and is the start of a great road up to Lake Titicaca. On the border with Chile is the city of Tacna, seemingly a long way from anywhere else in Peru.

From Puerto de Lomas (see under Nasca and around above) the Panamericana heads south through **Yauca** to **Chala**. The Yauca Valley is almost entirely devoted to olive trees, so have a few soles ready to buy some when the bus stops.

Chala and Puerto Inca → *Phone code: 054.*

Chala, 173 km from Nasca, is a friendly fishing village with nice beaches but it is only safe to swim near the harbour. The town has expanded greatly in recent years on the back of gold-mining in the nearby hills. It now consists of 'old' Chala and Chala Norte, spread out along 3 km of the Panamericana. Good fresh fish is available in the morning and it may be possible to go fishing with the local fishermen. There are dozens of restaurants, most catering for passing buses. Try *chicharrones de pulpo* (octopus) and *lenguado* (fried fish).

Ten kilometres north of Chala are the large pre-Columbian ruins of Puerto Inca on the coast in a beautiful bay. On their discovery in the 1950s, the ruins were misunderstood and thus neglected. It is now recognized that this was the port for Cusco. The site is in excellent condition. The drying and store houses can be seen as holes in the ground (be careful where you walk). On the right side of the bay is a cemetery, on the hill is a temple of reincarnation, and the Inca road from the coast to Cusco is clearly visible. The road was 240 km long, with a staging post every 7 km so that, with a change of runner at every post, fish for the Inca's table and messages could be sent in 24 hours.

In the two small bays the water is always calm and clear and the fishing and diving are excellent. There is a good two-hour walk from Puerto Inca to Chala. Take one of the paths going up behind the ruins on the south side of the bay and swing slightly inland to cross a deep quebrada. The path then continues through spectacular rock formations with dramatic views of the coast towards the road.

Camaná heading inland

South of Chala the Pan-American Highway passes **Atico**, where there is a basic *hostal*, and **Ocaña** before reaching Camaná. On June 2001, southern Peru was devastated by an earthquake measuring 7.9 on the Richter scale, whose epicentre was in the Pacific Ocean. A tidal wave three- storeys high hit, devastating resorts and agricultural land and causing severe damage. Consequently we do not include a section, Camaná and around. The Pan-American Highway swings inland from Camaná to **El Alto** where a road branches left off the Pan-American Highway and leads to **Corire**, Aplao and the valley of the Río Majes (see page 278). The Pan-American then runs along the top of a plateau with strange ash-grey sand dunes. These are unique in appearance and formation. All are crescent shaped and of varying sizes, from 6 to 30 m across and from 2 to 5 m high, with the points of the crescent on the leeward side. The sand is slowly blown up the convex side, drifts down into the concave side, and the dunes move about 15 m a year. If plans to extend the Majes project are completed, the irrigation of a further 60,000 ha of land will destroy a large portion of these unique sand dunes.

Mollendo → *Phone code: 054. Colour map 6, grid C1. Population: 30,000.*

Since Matarani, 14½ km to the northwest, has replaced it as a port, Mollendo depends partly upon the summer attraction of its beaches, despite the presence of a smelly oil refinery. Hotels can be full during the high season, which starts on 6 January, the first day of summer and anniversary of the district, and lasts to April. Out of season, Mollendo has the appearance of an abandoned wild west town, with its ramshackle wooden houses, some painted in gaudy colours. It still houses the port workers and has the main customs agencies for the harbour.

Three sandy beaches stretch down the coast. The small beach nearest town is the safest for swimming. The swimming pool on the beach is open January-March. Out of season the beaches are littered with rubbish. On the coast, a few kilometres southeast by road (US$0.40 by *colectivo*), is the summer resort of **Mejía**. The small national reserve at the lagoons ⓘ *US$1.50*, has 72 resident species of birds and 62 visiting species. Arrive early in the morning to see the birdlife at its best. The road into Mollendo goes down the fertile **Valle de Tambo**, which is full of rice paddies, sugar cane and fields of peppers and onions. Tambo is famous for its *alfajores de Tambo*, small round pastries filled with cane syrup or manjar blanco. The very best are made in **La Curva**, 10 km from Mollendo. Ask in the Palacio de Municipalidad for directions.

Moquegua → *Phone code: 053. Colour map 6, grid C2. Population: 110,000. Altitude: 1,412 m.*

Moquegua is a peaceful town in the narrow valley of the Moquegua River and enjoys a sub-tropical climate. The town was formerly known as Santa Catalina de Guadalcazar, but thankfully reverted to its original name, which means 'silent place' in Quechua. This could be due to the rather taciturn nature of its inhabitants. The Inca Emperor, Mayta Capac, sent his captains to carry out a pacifying occupation of the fertile valleys around Moquegua. They founded two settlements, Moquegua and Cuchuna, which is thought to be the site of present-day Torata. Today, most of the valley below the city grows grapes and the upper part grows avocados (*paltas*), wheat, maize, potatoes, some cotton, and fruits. Northeast from Moquegua is Cuajone, one of the most important copper mines in Peru.

Ins and outs

Getting there There is no bus station. All bus companies are on Av Ejército, 2 blocks north of the market at Jr Grau, except Ormeño, Av La Paz casi Balta. The road into town runs along Av La Paz. It joins the main street (Av Balta) at the large roundabout.

Getting around A compact town, the main street is Av Balta running two blocks north of Plaza de Armas. On Saturday nights Jr Moquegua west from the plaza to Jr Piura, becomes the centre of activity. Taxi in town US$0.60, US$0.85 outside the city.

Moquegua

Sleeping		Eating	
Arequipa 2	Hostal Carrera 5	Any's 1	Moraly 8
Hostal Adrianela 1	Hostal Piura 6	Bar Bandido 2	Panificadora Obrero 9
Hospedaje Cornejo 3	Limoneros 7	D'Onofrio 5	Tung Fong 4
Hospedaje Torata 4	Los Angeles 8	La Oficina 6	

0 metres 50
0 yards 50

South Coast Nasca to Chile

Moquegua is not a pretty sight from the Pan-American Highway, but the old centre, a few blocks above Avenida Balta, is well worth a look for its quiet, winding, cobbled streets and historic buildings. The **Plaza de Armas**, with its mix of ruined and well-maintained churches, colonial and republican façades and fine trees, is one of the most interesting small-town plazas in the country. The fountain is said to have been designed by Eiffel, though there is some debate on the matter. **Museo Contisuyo** ① *Plaza de Armas, T053-761844, http://bruceowen.com/contisuyo/ MuseoE.html, Mon-Sun 1000-1300, 1500-1730, except Tue 1000-1200, 1630-2000, US$0.45*, is within the ruins of the Iglesia Matriz, which was rebuilt after many earthquakes over the centuries, but finally left as a ruin in 1868. It covers the cultures which thrived in the Moquegua and Ilo valleys, including the Huari, Tiahuanaco, Chiribaya and Estuquiña, who were conquered by the Incas. Artefacts from the area are well-displayed and all the exhibits are clearly explained in Spanish and English.

The decadent statuary of the fountain in front of the Santo Domingo church (three twin-tailed mermaids with linked hands and bare breasts) is seen by some as a challenge to the traditional Catholic religious iconography within the church. Inside **Santo Domingo** itself is the body of the city's saint, Santa Fortunata, who lies in a glass-sided casket. She died in the 17th century, but her hair and nails are reputed to continue to grow miraculously. The old market beside Santo Domingo has a fine entrance but not much inside. The roofs of many of the old houses are built with sugar-cane thatch and clay and are of an unusual design, with semi-rounded gables, a little reminiscent of the 18th-century Dutch gables. This type of construction is called *mojinete* and is also found in the Valle de Tambo. The houses' sculpted door surrounds are particularly notable. See also the balconies, for example on 700 block of Moquegua.

There are several interesting colonial houses which make a good, short walking tour. **Casa de Regidor Perpetuo de La Ciudad** or **Casa Conde de Alastaya** ① *Jr Moquegua 404-414*, is an 18th-century house (just the portal remains after the 2001 earthquake). **Casa de Fernández Cornejo y Córdova** ① *Jr Ayacucho 540*, beside the post office on the plaza, has a fine 18th-century wooden balcony. Also on the south side of the Plaza is the office of the INC (corner of Ancash) and a museum of regional ethnography is being established. **Casa de Samuel Ordóñez** ① *Jr Lima 849*, stands empty. **Casa de Díaz Fernández Dávila** ① *Jr Ayacucho 828*, has a collapsed interior but baroque elements can be seen in the ornate portal.

Also worth seeing are: **Casa de Don Pacífico Barrios** ① *Jr Moquegua 820-848*, and opposite, the façade at No 831; **Casa de Diez Canseco** ① *esquina Tarapacá y Ayacucho*; and **Casa de la Serpiente** ① *Tarapacá 390*, the former offices of Essalud (the health service). Some of these houses are private, but the owners may allow entry. On Jr Lima, between Callao and Tacna, are the ruins of the convent of San Francisco. There is little to see and nothing inside except an open-air church with an awning roof.

Outside town in the direction of the airport are some interesting *bodegas*. Moquegua is famous for its *pisco*. Biondi is the best known brand. Another is **Bodega Villegas** ① *at the corner of Jr Ayacucho and Puno*. You can also find wine from Omate in town, eg **Bodegas Quinistaquillas**.

Around Moquegua

Samegua

Samegua, 4½ km from Moquegua, is known as 'avocado town', with many restaurants. To get there take a micro from Avenida Balta, between Tacna and Ancash. It takes 10 minutes.

Torata

Twenty-four kilometres northeast from Moquegua is Torata, a quiet, small town with a nice, shaded plaza. Above the town, on a hill above the right of the two crosses which overlook the town, are the Huari ruins of **Torata Alta**, a 30-minute walk away. The ruins are in a poor state but you can still get a good idea of their extent and the shape and size of the houses from the low surviving walls. The site enjoys good views over to Cerro Baúl. To get there take a micro or *colectivo* from Avenida Balta, between Jr Arequipa y Tacna, US$1.70, 30 minutes.

Cerro Baúl

A highly recommended trip is to Cerro Baúl, 2,590 m. This can be combined with the ruins at Torata to make a full day's excursion. The mountain is like a tepuy, with sheer sides and flat top, hence its name, which means trunk. There are excellent views for miles around from the summit. In the 7th century AD it was a Huari citadel and at the end nearest the path are extensive Huari ruins. The mountain became famous in legend as the place of refuge for the Cochunas, who resisted the peaceful invasion of the Incas. Eventually the Cochunas were starved off the mountain, but the refuge had lasted for a considerable time as their children regularly made nocturnal food raids into the Inca camps below. Covering the entire flat summit, which is 1½ km long and 200 m wide, are hundreds of modern arrangements of stones and miniature fields and houses, a mixture of pagan and Christian, which, together with looting, is destroying the place.

To get here, take a micro for Torata, or for Cuajone, and get off at the crossroads for Torata, at the top of the pass beneath the northern end of the mountain. The path leads up the gradual slope from the road. There is a steep section for the last 200 m, on which cement steps have been built. It takes an hour or so from the road to the top. The path leads to a Christian shrine (two crosses). Take water and sun protection.

Omate → *Population: 3,000. Altitude: 2,160 m.*

Omate is a small town, 146 km to the north of Moquegua on an unpaved road, and 129 km to the south of Arequipa (five hours). The town is important for its famed **Semana Santa processions**. It is also known for growing grapes, damascos and other fruits, and for its shrimp farms. Nearby are the thermal baths at **Ulucán**.

Moquegua to Desaguadero

The Carretera Binacional, from Ilo on the coast to La Paz, has a breathtaking stretch from Moquegua to Desaguadero at the southeastern end of Lake Titicaca. It skirts Cerro Baúl and climbs through zones of ancient terraces at Camata to its highest point at 4,755 m. At 4,610 m is lonely Restaurant Humajalso. On the altiplano there are herds of llamas and alpacas, watery *bofedales*, lakes with waterfowl, strange mountain formations and snow-covered peaks. At Mazo Cruz there is a PNP checkpoint where all documents and bags are checked. Approaching Desaguadero the Cordillera Real of Bolivia comes into view. The road is fully paved and should be taken in daylight.

Tacna → *Phone code: 052. Colour map 6, grid C2. Population: 174,366. Altitude: 550 m.*

Tacna was in Chilean hands from 1880 to 1929, when its people voted by plebiscite to return to Peru. It is an important commercial centre and the local authorities have been struggling to gain free-trade status from the government. There are good schools, housing estates, a stadium to seat 10,000 people, an airport, many military posts and one of the best hospitals in Peru. Chileans cross the border for cheap medical and dental treatment. Around the city the desert is gradually being irrigated. The local economy includes olive groves, vineyards and fishing. The waters of Laguna

Aricota, 80 km north, are now being tapped for further irrigation and hydroelectric power for industry.

With the peak of Tacora in the distance, Tacna is 156 km south of Moquegua by the Pan-American Highway, 36 km from the Chilean frontier, and 56 km from the international port of Arica, to which there is a railway. It is 1,292 km from Lima by road. As this is the nearest town to Chile, transport links are good with the rest of the country.

Ins and outs

Getting there The airport is some way out of town to the southwest; taxis run to the border but it's cheaper to go to town and take a *colectivo* from the international bus station. The two bus stations, one for international, one for domestic services, are on Hipólito Unánue, 1 km from the plaza (*colectivo* US$0.25, taxi US$0.60 minimum).
Getting around The town is quite spread out although there are several hotels around the Plaza de Armas. You will need to catch a bus or taxi to see much.
Tourist information Dirección Regional de Indistria y Turismo ① *Gral Blondell 50, by the Centro Cultural Miculla, corner of Francisco Lazo, T052-722784.*

Sights

The cathedral, designed by Eiffel, faces the Plaza de Armas, which contains huge bronze statues of Admiral Grau and Colonel Bolognesi. They stand at either end of the Arca de los Héroes, the triumphal arch which is the symbol of the city. The bronze fountain in the plaza is said to be a duplicate of the one in the Place de la Concorde (Paris) and was also designed by Eiffel. **Parque de la Locomotora**, near the city centre, has a British-built locomotive, which was used in the War of the Pacific. There is a very

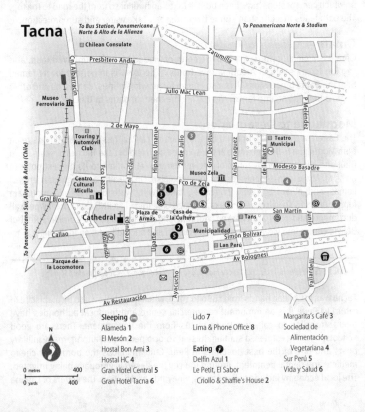

good railway museum ① *Coronel Albarracín, 0700-1700, US$0.30; knock at the gate under the clock tower on Jr 2 de Mayo for entry*, at the station. The house of Francisco Zela, who gave the Cry of Independence on 20 July 1811 is a museum, **Museo de Zela** ① *Zela 542, Mon-Sat 0830-1230, 1530-1900*. At Bolognesi 721 is **Feria La Caplina**, a shopping mall-cum-market selling jewellery, a few musical instruments, but mostly clothes. The main market is at Bolognesi y Pallardelli.

Some 8 km above the city, just off the Panamericana Norte, is the **Campo de la Alianza**, scene of a battle between Peru and Chile in 1880.

Border with Chile

There is a checkpoint before the border, which is open 0900-2200. Peruvian immigration is closed on public holidays. You need to obtain a Peruvian exit stamp and a Chilean entrance stamp; formalities are straightforward (see below). If you need a Chilean visa, you have to get it in Tacna (address below). For those leaving Peru by car buy *relaciones de pasajeros* (official forms, US$0.45) from the kiosk at the border or from a bookshop; you will need four copies. Next, return your tourist card, visit the PNP office, return the vehicle permit and finally depart through the checkpoints.

> ⁑ *Peruvian time is one hour earlier than Chilean time Mar-Oct; two hours earlier Sep/Oct-Feb/Mar (varies annually). No fruit or vegetables are allowed into Chile or Tacna.*

Arica, Chile's most northerly city with a population of 174,064, is 20 km south of the border. It has road links with La Paz, Bolivia, and with the rest of Chile. It is a good starting place for visits to Andean national parks, such as Lauca and has a wide selection of hotels and restaurants. There is a tourist office, **Sernatur** ① *San Marcos 101, T058-252054*, a kiosk next to the Casa de la Cultura.

South Coast Nasca to Chile Listings

● Sleeping

Chala *p312*
All the better hotels are in old Chala.
C Turistas, T054-551111. With bathroom, **D** without bathroom, large rooms, good beds, friendly, hot water, restaurant, great sea view.
F Hostal Evertyth, next door to Grau, T054-551095. Clean, comfortable and friendly with rooms facing the ocean.
F Hostal Grau, T054-551009. Rooms ocean facing, kitchen, cheap meals on request.

Puerto Inca *p312*
C Puerto Inka, at Km 603 on the Panamericana Sur (for reservations T054-551055, Chala). A great place to relax, with bungalows on a superb beach, boats and diving equipment for hire, disco, hammocks outside, highly recommended but used by tour groups and busy in the summer months. Also camping for US$2 per person.

Mollendo *p312*
C Hostal Cabaña, Comercio 240. A wooden building with huge balconies with bath, **F** per person with shared bath. Good.

D Hostal Willy, Deán Valdivia 437-443. Hot water, modern, spacious, noisy disco nearby. Recommended.
F Hostal California, Blondel 541, T054-535160. Best rooms at top, restaurant.

Moquegua *p313, map p313*
D Hostal Adrianella, Miguel Grau 239, T/F053-763469. Modern, hot water, TV, safe, helpful, group discounts available, close to market and buses. Recommended.
D Limoneros, Jr Lima 441, T053-761649. With bathroom, hot water, **E** without bath, car park, discount for groups of more than 10, pool (usually empty), old house with basic rooms, nice garden.
D Los Angeles, Jr Torata 100-A, T053-762629. Cheaper without bath, hot water, TV, large comfortable rooms, market right outside, close to buses. Recommended.
E Arequipa, Jr Arequipa 360, T053-761338. Clean, hot water sometimes.
E Hostal Carrera, Jr Lima 320, T053-762113. With bath and hot water (**F** shared bath, cold water), laundry facilities on roof. Good.

E Hostal Piura, Piura 225, T053-763974. With bath, hot water, TV, friendly.
F per person **Hospedaje Cornejo**, Tarapacá 281-A, T053-761034. Shared bath, hot water.
F per person **Hospedaje Torata**, Arequipa 3443, T053-761697. With bath, warm water.

Tacna *p315, map p316*

Accommodation is hard to find in the centre, especially at Christmas-time, when Chileans go on shopping sprees. Everything closes 1300-1600. Beware of pickpockets in the market area.
A Gran Hotel Tacna, Av Bolognesi 300, T052-724193, reserva@derrama.org.pe. Gardens, 2 swimming pools, safe car park, good breakfast for US$3-4, menú US$6, English spoken.
C Gran Hotel Central, San Martín 561, T052-712281. With breakfast, central, secure, English spoken. Recommended.
C El Mesón, Unánue 175, T052-725841, mesonhotel@terra.com.pe. With breakfast, TV, central, modern, comfortable, safe, internet service. Recommended.
D-E Lima, San Martín 442, on Plaza de Armas, T052-711912, american_tours@ hotmail.com. With breakfast, TV, hot water, bar, good restaurant, stores luggage.
E Alameda, Bolognesi 780, T052-744978. **F** without bath or TV, good food. Recommended.
E Hostal Bon Ami, 2 de Mayo 445, T052-711873. **F** without bath, hot water, secure.
E Hostal HC, Zela 734, T052-742042. Hot water, TV, discounts available, cafetería next door, laundry service, videos. Recommended.
E Lido, San Martín 876-A, near Plaza de Armas, T052-741598. With hot showers, no breakfast. Recommended.

❶ Eating

Mollendo *p312*

Several restaurants including **Cevichería Tío**, Comercio 208, excellent, cheap set meals. Others can be found on Comercio (eg **Tambo, Hong Kong Express**).

Moquegua *p313, map p313*

The best-known local dish is *cuy chactado*, pan-fried guinea pig. Two of the most famous places to try it are **Samagua** and **Los Angeles**, both a few kilometres out of town

(taxi US$0.50, or combi, 10 mins), with several restaurants in each town. **Damascos**, a type of small, yellow plum, can be found both stewed and *remojado*, steeped in *pisco* (delicious). *Chicha de jora* and *chicha de maíz morado* (from malted purple maize) can be found in the market; the latter is served with most menús at lunchtime. Local spirits and other liqueurs can be bought at **La Tranquita**, Piura 148 (no sign). All foodstuffs can be bought at the market (bounded by Grau, Torata, Av Balta and Libertad) and the streets around.
₸ El Bosque, Av 25 de Noviembre s/n, beyond La Villa bridge., T053-762245. Typical dishes including cuy, lomito saltado, fish, meat dishes and chifa. Recommended.
₸-₸ Bar Bandido, Jr Moquegua 333. European-style bar serving spirits, pizzas, wood oven, opens 1930, rock music, videos.
₸ Any's, Tacna, just off Plaza. Lunch menús US$1.15 and US$1.45, other dishes more expensive, *peña*.
₸ Moraly, Lima y Libertad. Good sized portions, moderate prices, best in town, menú del día US$1.75, good lunches, open for breakfast.
₸ Tung Fong, Ancash y Moquegua on Plaza. One of several *chifas*, serving Peruvian-Chinese fare.

Cafés

La Oficina, Ayacucho 685. Lunches, juices, snacks, opens early for breakfast. Recommended.
D'Onofrio ice cream on the Plaza.
Panificadora Obrero,Piura 270. For breads.

Tacna *p315, map p316*

₸-₸ Delfín Azul, Zela 375. Good, especially for seafood.
₸-₸ Sur Perú, Bolívar 380. A recommended eating place.
₸ El Sabor Criollo, Ayacucho No 86-C. One of three popular lunchtime eateries, all in a row.
₸ Le Petit, Ayacucho No 88-A. Lunch menú US$2.
₸ Shaffie's House, Ayacucho 84-B. Also popular for lunch.
₸ Sociedad de Alimentación Vegetariana, Zela 495, T711037. Vegetarian restaurant, open Mon-Fri and Sun with reservation.
₸ Vida y Salud, Bolívar 335. Swiss-Peruvian owned and run vegetarian restaurant,

German, French and English spoken, yoghurts and juices, natural products for sale, also serves meat, good, 0730-2030.

Cafés
La Espiga, San Martín 431. Good bakery and pastry shop.
Margarita's Café, Unánue 145, T711481. Excellent French pastry and desserts, nice inviting ambience, cheap. 1600-2130. Recommended.

🎵 Bars and clubs

Mollendo *p312*
El Observatorio, Comercio y Deán Valdivia. A massive, booming, semi-open-air disco, "has to be seen to be believed", no cover charge.

⊛ Festivals and events

Moquegua *p313, map p313*
On **14 Oct** is **Santa Fortunata**. The main celebration is **Día de Santa Catalina** on **25 Nov**, which is the anniversary of the founding of the colonial city.

▲ Activities and tours

Moquegua *p313, map p313*
Ledelca Tours, Ayacucho 625, T053-763890, opposite Santo Domingo. For local tours, eg to *bodegas* to taste *pisco*, city tours and archaeological sites.

⊖ Transport

Chala *p312*
Colectivos leave daily from **Nasca** in the morning, US$3.50 per person, 2 hrs. Buses stop in **Chala Norte**, a 10-min walk north of the hotels. If heading south, the night buses from **Lima** arrive at 0600-0700, and there are others in the early evening. Buses heading north come through nearer 0500, or in the early afternoon.

Puerto Inca *p312*
A Chala *colectivo* can be picked up just north of the town. A taxi from Chala costs US$5, or take a Yauca *colectivo* to Km 603 (US$0.50 per person) and walk down the track to the bay (3 km).

Bus To **Arequipa**, 129 km, buses and *colectivos* daily, 2 hrs, US$3, many companies on Comercio opposite the church. To **Moquegua**, 156 km, 2 hrs, US$2-3, several buses and *colectivos* daily. To **Tacna**, 315 km, direct transport does not go daily, best to take a *colectivo* early in the morning to El Fiscal (restaurant), US$0.40, about 100 km before Moquegua, where you can connect with Arequipa-Tacna buses.

Moquegua *p313, map p313*
All bus companies are on Av Ejército, 2 blocks north of the market at Jr Grau, except Ormeño, Av La Paz casi Balta. From **Lima**, US$23.50-11.75, 5 companies with executive and regular services. To **Tacna**, 159 km, 2 hrs, US$2, several buses and *colectivos* daily. To **Arequipa**, 3 hrs, US$3-5.85, several buses daily. To **Desaguadero**, 4 hrs, US$6 (11.75 Ormeño), and Puno, 5-6 hrs, US$7.35, several companies on the new road (see above). **Mily Tours**, Ev Ejército, T053-764000, run *colectivos* to Desaguadero, 3½ hrs, US$10. Ormeño continues to **La Paz**, US$30, and to **Cusco**, US$23.50, as does **Cruz del Sur**, US$17.65.

Tacna *p315, map p316*
Air To **Lima**, 1½ hrs; daily flights with Lan. A taxi to town and the bus terminal costs US$3. It is possible to take a taxi from the airport to Arica, US$30 (can be shared), but the cheapest way is to take a taxi to the bus station, then take a *colectivo*. **Airline offices** Lan, Apurímac y Bolívar, T052-743252. Tans, San Martín 611, T052-747002.
Bus The two bus stations, one for international, one for domestic services, are on Hipólito Unánue, 1 km from the plaza (*colectivo* US$0.25, taxi US$0.60 minimum). Both are well-organized, local tax US$0.30, baggage store, easy to make connections to the border, Arequipa or Lima. Tickets can be purchased several days before departure and buses fill up quickly. Beware of touts selling bus tickets at inflated prices. To **Moquegua**, 159 km, 2 hrs, US$2, several buses and *colectivos* daily (*colectivos* also leave from the town exit, uphill from the terminal, eg **El Buen Samaritano**, 5 passengers, US$3, less than 2 hrs). There are no direct buses to **Mollendo**, so catch one of the frequent

buses to El Fiscal (US$4, 4 hrs, see above), then a *colectivo* to Mollendo.

To **Arequipa**, 6 hrs, US$3.85-4.40, several buses daily, most with **Flores**, T052-725376.

To **Nasca**, 793 km, 12 hrs, US$9, several buses daily, en route for Lima. Several companies daily to **Lima**, 1,239 km, 21-26 hrs, US$9-27, eg **Flores, Cruz del Sur** and **Ormeño**, recommended.

To **Puno**, 395 km, go to Moquegua or Arequipa and change there.

At Tomasiri, 35 km north of Tacna, passengers' passports and luggage are checked, whether you have been out of the country or not. There is also a police control 10 km after the Camiara bridge (near a military base), just before the Tacna/Moquegua departmental border (also called Camiara, 59 km from Tacna, 61 km from Moquegua).

To **La Paz**, the best route is via Moquegua and Desaguadero. The most direct service is **Ormeño's** Royal service, 1930, US$35, but you have to change buses in Moquegua. **Samericano** *colectivos* go direct to Desaguadero, otherwise take transport from Moquegua (see above).

To **Santiago**, **Pullman Bus Internacional**, 6 a day, 28 hrs, US$25, semi cama with meals, to **Antofagasta**, 14 hrs, US$15. **Tramaca** also runs to Santiago.

Border with Chile *p317*

Some 56 km, 1-2 hrs, depending on waiting time at the border.

Bus To **Arica** buses charge US$1.50 and *colectivo* taxis US$3 per person. All leave from the international terminal in Tacna throughout the day. *Colectivos* (old Fords and Chevrolets which carry 5 passengers) only leave when full. As you approach the terminal you will be grabbed by a driver or his agent and told that the car is "just about to leave". This is hard to verify as you may not see the *colectivo* until you have filled in the paperwork. Once you have chosen a driver/agent, you will be rushed to his company's office where your passport will be taken from you and the details filled out on a Chilean entry form. You can change your remaining soles at the bus terminal while this is being done. It is 30 mins to the Peruvian border post at Santa Rosa, where all

exit formalities are carried out. The driver will hustle you through all the procedures. A short distance beyond is the Chilean post at Chacalluta, where again the driver will show you what to do. All formalities take about 30 mins. It's a further 15 mins to Arica's bus terminal. A Chilean driver is more likely to take you to any address in Arica.

❻ Directory

Moquegua *p313, map p313*

Banks **BCP**, esquina Moquegua y Tarapacá. The only bank that changes TCs, will also advance money on Visa. 0915-1315, 1630-1830, Telebanco 24 Horas ATM (Visa). **Internet** Several places on Jr Moquegua 400 block, just off Plaza de Armas, US$0.70 per hr. Also **Viv@net** on Plaza de Armas. **Post** On the Plaza de Armas in a colonial house. **Telephone** There is a public phone office at Jr Moquegua 617.

Tacna *p315, map p316*

Banks BCP, San Martín 574, no commission for TCs (Amex, Citicorp) into soles. Similarly at **Banco Wiese**, San Martín 476. **Interbank**, San Martín 646, has ATM for Visa/Plus, Mastercard/Cirrus and Amex. **Cambios Tacna** and **MoneyGram**, San Martín 612, T052-743607. Street changers stand outside the Municipalidad. **Consulates** Chile, Presbítero Andía block 1, T052-723063. Mon-Fri 0800-1300, closed holidays. **Internet** Several on San Martín and around the Plaza. **F@stnet.com**, 2 de Mayo 380. 0800-2400. Also international phone calls, cheaper than others. Average price US$0.45/hr, US$0.60 overnight. **Laundry** Lavamatic, Av Bolognesi 954, reliable and cheap. **Post** Av Bolognesi y Ayacucho. Mon-Sat 0800-2000. **Telephone** Public locutorio on Plaza de Armas, in same building as Hostal Lima. **Useful addresses** **Touring y Automóvil Club del Perú**, Av 2 de Mayo 67, T052-744237, tacna@touringperu.com.pe.

Border with Chile *p317*

Banks Money changers in Tacna are given above. They can also be found at counters in Tacna's international bus terminal; rates are similar in town.

Cordilleras Blanca & Huayhuash

⁞ Footprint features

Introduction

The Cordillera Blanca is a region of jewelled lakes and sparkling white mountain peaks which attracts mountaineers, hikers, cyclists and rafters in their thousands. Here stand the highest mountains in South America, with some 20 snow-crested peaks of over 6,000 m including Huascarán, the highest mountain in Peru at 6,768 m. From the region's main centre, Huaraz, several of these giants can be seen. This area contains the largest concentration of glaciers found in the world's tropical zone: a source of both beauty and danger. The turquoise-coloured lakes (*cochas*) which form in the terminal moraines are the jewels of the Andes and you should hike up to at least one during your stay. Laguna Churup is a day's walk from Huaraz, Lago Parón is close to Caraz, while the beautiful twin lakes of Llanganuco are within easy reach of Yungay and are on the route of the long-distance Santa Cruz trek. The tranquility of these glacial lakes masks a frightening history. They have caused much death and destruction when dykes have broken, sending tons of water hurtling down the canyons wiping out everything in their path. The levels of some have been artificially lowered for flood control and to feed the huge Cañón del Pato dam. Earthquakes, too, have scarred the high valleys and the mass grave which was once the old town of Yungay is a very humbling place.

Southeast of Huaraz, the Cordillera Huayhuash is an area that more than equals the Cordillera Blanca in beauty and majesty. It is rapidly gaining a reputation among long-distance trekkers and climbers.

Even the archaeologist is catered for here in the shape of the ruins of Chavín de Huantar. This fortress-temple belonged to one of the earliest and most influential cultures in pre-Inca Peru and it has some fine carvings and stonework.

★ Don't miss...

1 **Río Santa** For whitewater virgins, take a rafting trip, available all year round and with some stunning background scenery, page 338.

2 **Yungay** Besides its typical market on a Thursday, Yungay's *campo santo* is a poignant memorial to the devastating power of the mountains, page 343.

3 **Llanganuco lakes** Take a moment to study the bark of the quenoal trees (polylepis), like shreds of the finest paper, against the blue of the icy waters, page 344.

4 **Llanganuco to Santa Cruz trek** To visit the Cordillera Blanca without doing just one of the fantastic treks on offer is really missing the point of coming here at all, page 346.

5 **Puya Raimondi** There are many plants in the mountains, but keep an eye out for these remarkable bromeliads with their century-long lifespan, page 355.

6 **Chavín de Huantar** Don't leave without visiting the 2,500 year-old fortress temple; either take a tour, or hike three days from Olleros, page 356.

Cordilleras Blanca & Huayhuash

Huascarán National Park

Established in July 1975, the park includes the entire Cordillera Blanca above 4,000 m. It covers a total area of 3,400 sq km and is 180 km from north to south and 20 km from east to west. It is a UNESCO World Biosphere Reserve and part of the World Heritage Trust. The park's objectives are to protect the unique flora, fauna, geology, archaeological sites and extraordinary scenic beauty of the Cordillera. Please make every attempt to help by taking all your rubbish away with you when camping; there have been more than enough complaints that campsites are dirty and toilet pits foul. The park office is at Jr Federico Sal y Rosas 555, by Plazuela Belén, T043-722086. Open Monday-Friday 0830-1300, 1430-1700. It is principally administrative. Fees for visiting the national park are collected at rangers posts at Llanganuco (see page) and Huascarán (see page 346 for the Llanganuco to Santa Cruz trek), and at Collón on the way up the Quebrada Ishinca. It costs US$1.25 for a day visit. For visits of up to seven days (ie for trekking and climbing trips) a permit costing US$20 must be bought. If you stay longer than seven days, you will need another permit.

Ins and outs → Colour map 3, grid B3.

Getting there
There are three main routes to reach the Cordillera Blanca. Probably the easiest is the paved road which branches east off the Pan-American Highway north of Pativilca, 187 km from Lima, see page 372. A second route is via the Callán pass from Casma to Huaraz, see page 373, a rough but beautiful trip through the heart of the Cordillera Negra. The third alternative is from Chimbote to Caraz via the Cañón del Pato, see page 376, also a very scenic journey, with magnificent views of this spectacular canyon.

Getting around
In the Cordillera Blanca minibuses run between most of the towns on a regular basis, while more remote places have less frequent services. Sveral roads are being improved to cope with mining traffic. Of course, on some routes, you can always walk!

Best time to visit
The dry season (May-September) is the best time to visit the region, and the only time for climbing most summits. Trekking is also possible at other times of the year, but conditions are less amenable and the views are less rewarding. Christmas to New Year is a popular time for foreigners seeking an exotic location to spend the holidays.

Background

The snow-capped Cordillera Blanca runs north to south for almost 200 km. Alongside it to the west lies its alter ego, the bare and dry Cordillera Negra, which rises to 4,600 m. The valley of the Río Santa, known as the Callejón de Huaylas, separates the two ranges. The Santa rises in Laguna Conococha, at the south end of the two mountain chains and flows due north between them, before turning west to enter the spectacular Cañón del Pato and making its way to the Pacific.

To the east of the Cordillera Blanca lies another set of valleys, the Callejón de Conchucos, containing the archaeological treasures of Chavín de Huantar, see page lovely little villages of narrow cobblestone streets and odd-angled house roofs and inhabitants who grow potatoes and barley at the higher altitudes and maize, alfalfa, fruits and flowers lower down.

These valleys also provide road access to the region's wonders. Many excellent trekking routes and approaches to climbers' base camps cross from one callejón to the other, over the high passes of the Cordillera Blanca. Further south lie the Cordilleras Huayhuash and Raura, offering more spectacular climbing and hiking in a less-visited area, see page 363.

Communities are close to each other in the Callejón de Huaylas, so there is little sense of isolation until you are right up in the mountains, or in the remoter areas beyond this valley. Huaraz is undoubtedly at the heart of things, catering for the adventure sports market, with all the requisite services and facilities. Only an hour away, Caraz has the same mix of engineers (for the hydroelectric scheme) and tourism, but on a much smaller scale. Above all, though, the waters coming off the mountains make this a fertile area and it is agriculture which dictates the pace of life.

Trekking and climbing

The Cordillera Blanca offers the most popular – and some of the best – trekking and climbing in Peru, with a network of trails used by the local people and some less well-defined mountaineers' routes. There are numerous possibilities for day-hikes, trekking and climbing. Of these only a very few routes are currently used by most visitors, and so they have accumulated rubbish and other signs of impact. While these favourite treks (notably Santa Cruz-Llanganuco and the Alpamayo circuit) are undeniably interesting, you should consider the various excellent alternatives if you want to enjoy a less crowded experience and help conserve the area's great natural beauty.

Trekking options

The many other options include: **Laguna Parón**, with its impressive cirque of surrounding summits (access from Caraz, see page 344); **Hualcayán to Pomabamba**, traversing the northern end of the Cordillera Blanca with fine views of Alpamayo and many other peaks (access from Caraz); Laguna 69 at the end of Llanganuco valley (access from Yungay); the **Ulta Valley** and **Laguna Auquiscocha**, between the massifs of Huascarán, Ulta and Hualcán (access from Carhuaz, see page 341); to name but a few. There remains a good deal to be discovered in the area and your creativity in choosing a route is certain to be rewarded.

There are two traditional trekking routes in the **Huayhuash**: a complete loop around the range; and a half-circuit, starting from the trail head at Cuartel Huain and ending in Cajatambo. These are but two of very many excellent options however, and hikers are urged to be creative in choosing their routes and camp sites, both to enjoy more pristine surroundings and to allow over-used areas to recover.

Advice to climbers

The height of the mountains in the Cordillera Blanca and nearby ranges and their location in the tropics create conditions different from the Alps or even the Himalayas. Fierce sun makes the mountain snow porous and the glaciers move more rapidly. Deglaciation is rapidly changing the face of the Cordillera. Older maps do not provide a reliable indication of the extent of glaciers and snow fields, so local experience is important. Climbers should not think that their experience on other ranges would be sufficient for the Cordillera Blanca and first-timers here should take a guide for safety.

⁝ Mining in the mountains

The department of Ancash contains important mineral deposits including copper, zinc, silver, gold and perhaps uranium (the latter is not discussed openly). 12,000 different sites have been prospected in the Cordillera Negra alone. An open pit mine and smelter, 12 km north of Huaraz has brought major changes to the Callejón de Huaylas. The US/Canadian consortium operating the mine promised to minimize environmental impact, yet there are conflicting claims as to the extent of environmental damage. There has, however, been undeniable impact on some of the finest natural areas of the Peruvian Andes. Mining companies have built their own neighbourhoods and camps, while many new roads continue to be made by and for the mines.

Similar developments are taking place east of San Marcos, near Chavín in the Callejón de Conchucos, where a huge underground mine and concentrator at Antamina has come on stream. Hundreds of kilometres of good roads, thousands of jobs for Peruvians and a resident ex-pat community near Huaraz have undoubtedly had a significant effect on the local economy.

In the Cordillera Huayhuash, a Japanese corporation has a major mining project in the vicinity of Pocpa and Laguna Jahuacocha, the jewel of the entire region. Other mines are under consideration and some local residents have proposed the creation of a Huayhuash National Park to protect the region's unique natural beauty, as well as its economically important tourist potential.

The British Embassy advises climbers to take at least six days for acclimatization, to move in groups of four or more, reporting to a reliable fellow climber, an agency, your hotel or embassy before departing, giving the date at which a search should begin, and leaving the telephone number of your Embassy with money.

The Policía Nacional de Perú ① *To43-793327/333/291, usam@pnp.gob.pe*, has a 35-member rescue team in Yungay, with 24-hour phone service and vhf/uhf radio dispatch. They have two helicopters and trained search-and- rescue dogs. At present, they will rescue anyone – climbers, trekkers, tourists – without asking for cash up front. PNP rescues are currently free for uninsured climbers. They will bill insured climbers, but do not ask for any cash up front. Since this policy may change, and because they will only take the injured person as far as Huaraz hospital (from where additional costly medical evacuation may be required), it remains imperative that all climbers carry adequate insurance (it cannot be purchased locally).

Be well-prepared before setting out on a climb. Wait or cancel your trip when weather conditions are bad. Every year climbers are killed through failing to take weather conditions seriously. Climb only when and where you have sufficient experience.

Advice to hikers and trekkers

Most circuits can be hiked in five days. Although the trails are easily followed, they are rugged and the passes very high – between 4,000 and nearly 5,000 m – so you should be fit and properly acclimatized to the altitude, and carry all necessary equipment. In the Cordillera Huayhuash you must be entirely self-sufficient. Evacuation in the event of illness or accident may require several days. Essential items are a tent, warm sleeping bag, stove, and protection against wind and rain (climatic conditions are quite unreliable here and you cannot rule out rain and hail storms even in the dry season). Trekking demands less stamina since equipment can be carried by donkeys. Nobody

should trek entirely on their own. Something as minor as a sprained ankle can become 327
a disaster if there is no one to assist you or go for help.

Safety and conduct

In 2004, there were two hold-ups of trekking parties in the Cordillera Huayhuash carried out by large armed groups. A trekker was killed in one of these incidents. In 2003 there were three holdups in Huayhuash. The Cordillera Blanca was generally safer, but muggings did take place on the way to Laguna Churup, to the Mirador Rataquena above Huaraz, the Mirador above Monterrey, and at Wilkawain. At the close of this edition, local authorities and trekking operators were looking for ways to improve public safety. Before heading out on any route, trekkers and climbers should always enquire locally about public safety.

The eastern side of the Huayhuash/Raura range, in the Department of Huánuco, has a reputation for more aggressive behaviour, be especially cautious in this area.

On all treks in this area, respect the locals' property, leave no rubbish behind, do not give sweets or money to children who beg (a serious problem on popular routes) and remember your cooking utensils, tent, etc, would be very expensive for a campesino, so be sensitive and responsible. Do not leave your gear unattended at any time and stow everything in your tent overnight. Some camping areas in the Huayhuash have recently (2004) begun charging a small fee for trekkers. Insist on an official receipt.

You will encounter many cattle and dogs guarding them. It's best to give both a wide berth. Carrying a walking stick or crouching to pick up a stone will usually discourage the canines. Throwing stones has been known to provoke an attack.

Rubbish is an important problem at the usual camp sites and you should personally pack out everything you bring in; you cannot trust muleteers in this regard. Much of the area is above tree-line, the remainder has been badly deforested. Make sure you have a reliable stove and enough fuel for cooking and resist the temptation to use what little firewood remains. Improper disposal of human waste is also a problem. Use great care in this fragile environment.

Hiring guides and muleteers

The Dirección de Turismo issues qualified guides and arrieros (muleteers) with a photo ID. Always check for this when making arrangements; note down the name and card number in case you should have any complaints. Prices for specific services are set so enquire before hiring someone. You should also make your priorities clear to the muleteer in advance of the trek (pace, choice of route, camp sites, etc) or else you will be led around with the line, 'all the gringos do this'. Prices in 2004 for both Cordilleras Blanco and Huayhuash: arriero, US$10 per day; donkey or mule, US$5 per day; trekking guides US$35-50 per day (more for foreign guides); climbing guides US$70-120 per day (more for foreign guides), depending on the difficulty of the peak; cooks, US$20-30 per day. You are required to provide or pay for food and shelter for all porters, guides, cooks and arrieros. Some guides speak English and are friendly but lack technical expertise; others have expertise but lack communicative ability. You may have to choose between the former and the latter. Avoid 'private' guides who seek you out on the street.

For the Cordillera Huayhuash treks, it is sometimes a problem in the high climbing/trekking season to hire mules straightaway. This is because all the ones at the northern end are kept at Llamac and Pocpa and it may take a day to bring the mules to your starting point. The muleteers are a mixed bunch, ranging from excellent to irresponsible. Get a recommendation from someone who has recently returned from a trek, otherwise call ahead to Hostal San Miguel or ask at **Restaurant Yerupajá** or **Panadería Santa Rosa** (see Chiquián Listings, below).

Tour operators in Huaraz offer 11-day treks in the Huayhuash for US$350 including guide/cook, food, equipment, mules and driver, and public transport. Tours without guide cost US$160 per person: you have to cook your own food and feed the mule driver, do your own setting up of tents, etc.

Mountain shelters

Refugios have been built at Pisco (4,700 m), Huascarán (4,800 m) and Ishinka (4,300 m and 4,700 m). Operated by Organización Mato Grosso, Huaraz, T043-793061. US$30 per person including breakfast and supper. Only open high season.

Provisions

Huaraz is the region's supply centre, all but the most specialized items may be obtained here (see page 337). If you require freeze-dried meals however, these should be brought from abroad. In the Huayhuash, Chiquián's shops are usually well stocked with basic supplies, including locally produced butter and cheese, although prices may be a bit higher here. Almost nothing is available in the hamlets along the route, but fresh trout may be purchased by some of the lakes and a very few items (mostly beer, soft drinks and potatoes) might be purchased in Llamac, Pocpa, Carhuacocha, Huayllapa and Pacllón. Take coins and small notes as there is seldom any change. Bring a fishing line and lure to supplement your diet.

Guides and agencies

Casa de Guías, Plaza Ginebra 28-g in Huaraz, T043-721811, casa_de_guias@hotmail.com, Mon-Sat 0900-1300, 1600-1800, Sun 0900-1300. This is the climbers' and hikers' meeting place. It is useful with information, books, maps, arrangements for guides, arrieros, mules, etc. There is a notice board, postcards and posters for sale. The Casa de Guías has a full list of all members of the **Asociación de Guías de Montaña del Perú** (AGMP) throughout the country. A great site for trekking is www.huaylas.com.

Mountain guides

Those listed below are not necessarily members of AGMP but are recommended.
Ted Alexander, Skyline Adventures, T043-727097, www.sladventureschool.com. American, Outward Bound instructor, very knowledgeable, lots of information.
Koky Castañeda, T043-721694 (La Casa de Zarela) or through Café Andino. Speaks English and French, AGMP certified.
Sr Delao Callupe is a guide for the Huayhuash. Ask for him in Chiquián.
Aritza Monasterio, through Casa de Guías. Speaks English, Spanish and Euskerra.
Augusto Ortega, Jr San Martín 1004, T043-724888, is the only Peruvian to have climbed Everest.
Filiberto Rurush Paucar, Sucre 1240,

T043-722264 (Lodging Casa Sucre), speaks English, Spanish and Quechua.
Hugo Sifuentes Maguiña and his brother **César** (speaks English and a little French) at **Siex** (Sifuentes Expeditions), Av Centenario 687, T043-726529, www.siex.org.

Trekking guides

Irma Angeles, T043-722205 (Sol Andino travel agency), speaks some English, knows the Huayhuash well.
Christopher Benway, La Cima Logistics, T043-721203, cafeandino@hotmail.com. American, leads treks in the Huayhuash.
Vladimiro and Máximo Hinostrosa, at Mountain Shop Chacraraju, T043-969 2395, trekking guides with knowledge of the entire region.
Tjen Verheye, Jr Carlos Valenzuela 911, T043-722569, is Belgian and speaks Dutch, French, German, and reasonable English, runs trekking and conventional tours and is knowledgeable about the Chavín culture.
Genaro Yanac Olivera, T043-722825, speaks good English and some German, also a climbing guide. See also under Tour operators in Huaraz for organized trips.

Climbing courses

Ask tour agencies, independent guides and **Casa de Guías** about rock climbing courses at Monterrey (behind Hotel Baños Termales Monterrey, see p330), Chancos, Recuay and

Huanchac (30 mins' walk from Huaraz), and about ice climbing on Vallanaraju and Pastoruri (for example).

Equipment and maps

Hiring camping gear

Check all camping and climbing equipment very carefully before taking it. Gear is of variable quality, mostly second hand left behind by others. Also note that some items may not be available, so it's best to bring your own. All prices are standard, but not cheap, throughout town. All require payment in advance, passport or air ticket as deposit and will only give 50% of your money back if you return gear early.

Many trekking agencies sell camping gaz cartridges. White gas (called *bencina*) is available from *ferreterías*, but shop around to avoid overcharging. It should cost about US$1 per litre. For trekking provisions see Shopping, p337. The following agencies are recommended for hiring gear.

Andean Kingdom; Anden Sport Tours; Monttrek; Kallpa (see p338 for their addresses). **Skyline** (see above) and **Montañero**, Parque Ginebra 30-B, T043-726386, andeway@terra.com.pe. **MountClimb**, Jr Mcal Cáceres 421,

T043-726060, mount climb@yahoo.com. **Casa de Guías**, see above, rents equipment and sells dried food.
Lobo, Luzuriaga 557, T043-724646.

Maps

A good tourist map of the Callejón de Huaylas and Cordillera Huayhuash, by Felipe Díaz, is available in many shops in the region and at Casa de Guías in Huaraz; it's not accurate enough for hiking the less-travelled trails.
Alpenvereinskarte Cordillera Blanca Nord 0/3a at 1:100,000 is easily the best map; it is available in Huaraz for US$12 (also in Lima – stocks locally are small, best to get it before you arrive).
Cordillera Huayhuash map, 1:80,000, (The Alpine Mapping Guild's, 2nd edition, 2004) is also recommended (available from **Café Andino**, US$15).
Instituto Geográfico Nacional has mapped the area with its 1:100,000 topographical series. These are more useful to the mountaineer than hiker, however, since the trails marked are confusing and inaccurate.
South American Explorers publishes a good map with additional notes on the popular Llanganuco to Santa Cruz loop. For guide books, see Books p604.

Huaraz → *Phone code 043. Colour map 3, grid B3. Population: 80,000. Altitude: 3,091 m.*

The main town in the valley, Huaraz is expanding rapidly as a major tourist centre but it is also a busy commercial hub, especially on market days (Monday and Thursday). The region is both a prime destination for hikers and international climbers, as well as a vacation haven for Peruvian urbanites seeking clean mountain air and a glimpse of the glaciers. School groups flock to the city from mid-September to mid-December (the 'época de promociones colegiales'). The city was half destroyed in the earthquake of May 1970 so don't expect red-tiled roofs or overhanging eaves. However, the Plaza de Armas has been rebuilt, with a towering, white statue of Christ and a new Cathedral is still being built. What the reconstructed city lacks in colonial charm, it makes up by its spectacular setting between the mountains of the Cordilleras Blanca and Negra. The peaks of Huamashraju, Churup, Rima Rima and Vallunaraju loom so close as to seem almost a part of the architecture while, in the distance, the giants Huascarán and Huandoy can be seen.➤➤ *For Sleeping, Eating and other listings, see pages 333-340.*

Ins and outs

Getting there The bus offices are in the centre of town and are conveniently close to many of the hotels and hostels.
Getting around Small enough to get around by foot providing sensible precautions are taken especially at night (see below).

Tourist information iPerú ⓘ *Luzuriaga on Plaza de Armas, T043-728812, iperu huaraz@promperu.gob.pe, Mon-Fri 0800-1300, 1700-2000, Sat-Sun 0800-1300.* **Policía de Turismo** ⓘ *on second floor of same building, T043-721341, ext 315, Mon-Fri 0900-1300, 1600-1900, Sat 0900-1300,* is the place to report all crimes and mistreatment by tour operators, hotels, etc. Huaraz has its share of crime, especially since the arrival of mining in the area (see box page 326) and during the high tourist season. On no account should women go to surrounding districts and sites alone. See the safety note, page 327.

Sights

Museo Arqueológico de Ancash ⓘ *in the Instituto Nacional de Cultura, on Plaza de Armas, 0800-2000. US$1.45,* contains stone monoliths and huacos from the Recuay and other cultures. The exhibits are well labelled and laid out. The **Sala de Cultura SUNARP** ⓘ *Av Centenario 530, Independencia, T043-721301, Mon-Fri 1700-2000, Sat 0900-1300, free,* often has interesting art and photography exhibitions by local artists.

The main thoroughfare, Avenida Luzuriaga, is bursting at the seams with travel agencies, climbing equipment hire shops, restaurants, cafés and bars. Within a block or two you can find a less frantic ambience, but a good alternative for those seeking peace and quiet is the La Soledad neighbourhood, 6 blocks uphill from the Plaza de Armas on Av Sucre. Here, along Sucre as well as Jr Amadeo Figueroa, every second house seems to rent rooms, most without signs. We list but a few, below. There are several decent neighbourhood eateries nearby, many shops, internet facilities, etc.

Excursions

Willkawain

ⓘ *Entrance to the site is US$1.50. Take a combi from 13 de Diciembre y Comercio, US$0.55 direct to Willkawain. If walking up, go past the Hotel Huascarán. After crossing a small bridge take a second right (well-signposted), from where it's about a 2-hr uphill walk. Ask frequently as there are many criss-crossing paths. Beware of dogs en route (and begging children). Alternatively, the purple city bus (line 2B) will take you to Marian, a 15-min walk from the ruins.*
The Willkawain archaeological site lies about 8 km to the northeast of Huaraz. The ruins date from AD 700-1000, which was the second and imperial phase of the Huari empire. During this period, the Huari influence spread north from the city of the same name near Ayacucho. The Huari empire was remarkable for the strong Tiahuanaco influence in its architecture and ceramics. The Huari introduced a new concept in urban life, the great walled urban centre. The site consists of one large three-storey structure with intact stone slab roofs and several small structures. The windowless inner chambers can be explored as electric light has been installed; all the rooms are accessible. A few, however, have been opened up to reveal a sophisticated ventilation system and skilful stone craftsmanship. About 500 m past Willkawain is Ichiwillkawain with several similar but smaller structures.

Even if you're not an archaeology buff, the trip is worth it for a fascinating insight into rural life in the valley. Take a *colectivo* up to the ruins and walking back down to Huaraz is thoroughly recommended (about a two-hour walk). A good grasp of Spanish will greatly enhance the pleasure of this experience as the locals are very welcoming.

Monterrey → *Colour map 3, grid B3. Altitude: 2,780 m.*
North of Huaraz, 6 km along the road to Caraz, are the thermal baths at Monterrey. It's a good place for a day trip to soak in the **thermal baths** and an alternative place to

Huaraz

*Related map
A Huaraz centre, page 332.*

```
0 metres    100
0 yards     100
```

Sleeping
Albergue Churup **1** *C3*
Alojamiento El Jacal **2** *C3*
Alojamiento Marilia **3** *C3*
Alojamiento Nemy's **4** *C3*
Alojamiento Norma **5** *D2*
Alojamiento Soledad **6** *C3*
Andino Club **8** *D3*
Angeles Inn & Sol Andino **9** *D2*
Backpackers **10** *B1*
Casa de Jaimes **11** *C1*
Casa Jansy's **12** *C2*
Edward's Inn **30** *B1*
El Tumi I **15** *D1*
Hostal Colomba **18** *A2*
Hostal Continental **19** *C1*
Hostal Galaxia **20** *C1*
Hostal la Montañesa **34** *A1*
Hostal Los Andes **21** *B1*
Hostal Mi Casa **22** *C1*
Hostal Quintana **23** *C1*
Hostal Yanett **24** *A2*
Jo's Place **32** *A1*
La Cabaña **25** *C3*
La Casa de Zarela **26** *C3*
La Estancia **33** *A2*
Lodging Casa Sucre **13** *C3*
Olaza Guesthouse **27** *C3*
San Sebastián **29** *B3*

Eating
Café El Centro **1** *C1*
Huaraz Querido **4** *D2*
Panadería La Alameda **2** *B1*
Pizza Bruno **8** *D1*
Sucre **5** *C3*

Bars & clubs
Extreme **3** *D1*

Transport
Chavín Express **1** *C1*
Combis to Caraz **2** *A1, A2*
Combis to Llupa (for
  Laguna Churup) **3** *B2*
Combis to Wilcawain **4** *A2*
Terminal Terrestre
  Transportistas Zona Sur **8** *C1*
Trans Huandoy **12** *A2*
Trans Rodríguez **9** *C1*
Trans Sandoval **10** *C1*
Virgen de Guadalupe **11** *B2*

stay for those seeking peace and quiet. The baths are run by the **Hotel Baños Termales Monterrey** and, owing to the high iron content, the water is dark brown but not dirty. There are 2 pools: the lower pool is US$0.85; the upper pool, which is nicer is US$1.35. There are also individual and family tubs which cost US$1.35 per person for 20 minutes. The upper pool is closed on Monday for cleaning. It gets crowded at weekends and holidays. City buses along Avenida Luzuriaga go as far as Monterrey costings US$0.22, until 1900. A taxi costs US$2-3.

Laguna Churup
① *US$20 payable to local cooperative, only for groups with pack animals.*
To the east of Huaraz, off the road between Unchus and Pitec is a trail to Laguna Churup, which makes a good one-day excursion from Huaraz. Take a *colectivo* from

Huaraz centre

Sleeping 🛏
Alpes Andes &
  Casa de Guías **15** C2
El Pacífico **1** C1
Familia Meza &
  Café Andino **2** B2
Hostal Copa **3** C3
Hostal Estoico **4** C1
Hostal Gyula **5** D2
Hostal Los Portales **7** A3
Hostal Montañero
  & Tour agency **8** C2
Hostal Raymondi **9** A2
Hostal Tany **10** B2
Imperio **6** B1
Oscar's Hostal **11** B2
Residencial
  Cataluña **12** A1
Schatzi **14** A3

Eating 🍴
Bistro de los Andes **2** C3
Chifa Jim Hua **3** C1
Créperie Patrick **4** A1
Fuente de Salud **6** B1
La Placita:
  Rinconcito Minero,
  El Querubín &
  Vagamundo **7** C2
Las Puyas **8** C1
Las Tulpas y
  Chimichurri **1** C2
Monte Rosa **10** B2
Monttrek Pizza Pub &
  Trekking agency **21** C1
Pachamama **20** D1
Pepe's Place **11** A1
Piccolo **12** C1
Pizza B&B **13** B2
Pizzería Landauro **14** D2
Sabor Salud **15** D1
Siam de Los Andes **16** C3

Bars & clubs 🍸
Amadeus **17** D2
Monttrek Disco **18** D2
Taberna Tambo **21** B2
Makondo's **19** B3

Caraz y Comercio early in the morning for the 40-minute ride along the Río Quilcay to Llupa (US$0.60), then hike one hour to Pitec and, from the National Park entrance, a further three hours up to the lake, which is surrounded by high mountains. The last part involves scrambling over rocks (dangerous when raining). It's about three hours back to Llupa, where *colectivos* run until about 1800.

From Pitec there are **three-day hikes** up the Quebrada Quillcayhuanca to Cayesh or to Lagunas Tullpacocha and Cuchilacocha. From the latter you can cross a pass to the Cojup Valley (see page 341 below) and descend to Llupa (a further two days). You have to pay a national park entrance fee in Pitec to do these treks.

Punta Callan walk

ⓘ *A taxi to Punta Callan will cost about US$25 and take about one hour, or take a Casma bus and get off at the pass.*

This is an excellent day walk from Huaraz, with superb views of almost the whole of the Cordillera Blanca and some nice rural scenery. It is best to leave Huaraz early in the morning, ideally about 0800, for the best light on the mountains. From the pass at 4,200 m walk northwards (the right hand side of the road) to a small hill of 4,600 m for the best views. Then head directly back down to Huaraz, which you'll see in the valley below you. Follow various trails and farm tracks, with several routes being possible. It takes about four hours walking to reach the first places where you'll get return minibus transport. Add another hour or so if you want to, or have to walk all the way back to Huaraz.

● Sleeping

Huaraz *p329, maps p331 and p332*
Hotels are plentiful (there are many more than those listed below) but fill up rapidly during the high season (May-Sep), especially during public holidays and special events (such as the Semana de Andinismo in Jun) when prices rise. Lodging in private homes is common during these periods. Avoid touts at bus stations offering accommodation and tours.
AL Andino Club, Pedro Cochachín 357, some way southeast from the centre (take a taxi after dark), T043-721949, www.hotelandino.com The best in town, expensive Swiss restaurant, free internet for guests, safe parking, Swiss run, friendly, 2nd floor rooms with balconies and views of Huascarán are more expensive. Recommended.
B Baños Termales Monterrey, Av Monterrey, at the top of the hill in Monterrey, T/F043-721717. Slightly run down but classic old spa, price includes breakfast and use of pools, restaurant, bar, good location for walking, there is a rock face behind the hotel which is used for climbing practice.
B El Patio, Av Monterrey, 250 m downhill from the Monterrey baths, T043-724965. Includes breakfast, meals on request, bar,

friendly, colonial-style. Recommended.
B Hostal Los Portales, Raymondi 903, T/F043-728184. With bathroom, hot water, parking, a pleasant place to stay.
B San Sebastián, Jr Italia 1124, T043-726960, www.hotelhuaraz.com. 2-star (price rises to **A** in high season), very helpful, breakfast included, good views. Recommended.
B-C Hostal Montañero, Plaza Ginebra 30-B, T/F043-726386, www.trekkingperu.com. Price includes breakfast. Hot water, very clean, modern, comfortable, friendly, climbing equipment rental and sales.
C Edward's Inn, Bolognesi 121, T/F043-722692. Cheaper without bathroom, clean, not always hot water, laundry, friendly, breakfast extra and other meals available, insist on proper rates in low season, popular, Edward speaks English and knows a lot about trekking and rents gear (not all guides share Edward's experience). Highly recommended.
C El Tumi I, San Martín 1121, T/F043-721784, hottumi@terra.com.pe. Good restaurant (serves huge steaks), fairly good, advance reservations advised.
C Hostal Colomba, Francisco de Zela 278, on Centenario across the river, T043-721501, colomba@terra.com.pe. Lovely old hacienda,

bungalow, family-run (German), garden, friendly, safe car parking.

D Albergue Churup, Jr Figueroa 1257, T043-722584, www.churup.com. Price includes breakfast and bath, **F** in dormitory without breakfast, hot water, nice garden and fire in sitting room, internet access, cafeteria, use of kitchen, lots of information and travel agency, luggage store, laundry, book exchange, English spoken, Spanish classes, extremely helpful, motorcycle parking. Recommended.

D Alojamiento Soledad, Jr Amadeo Figueroa 1267, T043-721196, ajsoled@terra.com.pe. Prive includes breakfast and bath, **E** without, some hard beds, hot water, kitchen, use of internet, family-run and very friendly, secure, trekking information. Recommended.

D El Pacífico, Luzuriaga 630, T043-721683, F724416. With bathroom, not always hot water, friendly, helpful good restaurant.

D Hostal Raymondi, Raymondi 820, T043-722720 (in Lima T01-427 9016). With bathroom, cheaper without, hot water only in the mornings in the ground floor shower, comfortable, charges for left luggage, café serves good breakfast from 0600.

D La Casa de Zarela, J Arguedas 1263, T043-721694, www.lacasadezarela.com. With bath, hot water, breakfast available, use of kitchen, laundry facilities, popular with climbers and trekkers, owner Zarela, who speaks English, organizes groups and is very knowledgeable, stores luggage, has a nice terrace.

D Residencial Cataluña, Av Raymondi 622, T043-722761. With bathroom, hot water, TV, **E** for more basic rooms, restaurant open only in the high season, clean, safe, noisy.

D Schatzi, Bolívar 419, near Raimondi, T043-723074. Clean, nice courtyard, with bath, hot water, breakfast extra.

D-E The Way Inn, Jr Buenaventura Mendoza 821, near Parque Fap, T043-728714, thewayinn@hotmail.com. No fixed fee for staying, people are asked to pay what they think it`s worth. Run by Alex and Bruni, all mattresses are orthopaedic, fully-functioning kitchen (including oven and fridge), huge video library, laundry facilities, camping equipment for hire, free information on treks, places to eat, hanging out/etc, a health food bar, sauna and steam facilities as well as

exercise equipment to help with the acclimatization.

E Alojamiento Marilia, Sucre 1123, T043-728160, alojamaril@latinmail.com. Good views, modern, clean rooms with bath, **F** without bath, also dormitory accommodation, hot water, breakfast available, kitchen facilities, luggage store, knowledgeable, friendly owners.

E Alojamiento Nemy's, Jr Figueroa 1135, T043-722949. Secure, hot shower, breakfast US$2.40, good for climbers, luggage store. Recommended.

E Familia Meza, Lúcar y Torre 538, T043-726367, familiameza_lodging@hot mail.com. Shared bath, hot water, use of kitchen and laundry facilities, terrace with view, popular with trekkers, mountaineers and bikers.

E Hostal Copa, Jr Bolívar 615, T043-722071, F722619. Cheaper without bathroom, hot water, laundry facilities, clean, owner's son Walter Melgarejo is a well-known guide, popular with trekkers, restaurant, travel agency with local tours.

E Hostal Estoico, San Martín 635, T043-722371. Cheaper without bathroom, friendly, clean, safe, hot water, laundry facilities, good value. Recommended.

E Hostal Galaxia, Jr de la Cruz Romero 638, T043-722230. Cheaper without bathroom, hot water, laundry facilities, basic, friendly. Recommended.

E Hostal Gyula, Parque Ginebra 632, opposite the Casa de Guías, T043-721567, hotelperu@infoweb.com.pe. With bathroom, hot water, very friendly and helpful, has information on local tours, stores luggage. Noisy at weekends.

E Hostal Los Andes, Tarapacá 316, T043-724700. Cheaper without bathroom, warm water, clean, laundry facilities, noisy, not very comfortable but friendly.

E Hostal Quintana, Mcal Cáceres 411, T043-726060. Cheaper without bathroom, hot shower, laundry facilities, clean, basic, stores luggage, breakfast extra, friendly, popular with trekkers, climbing gear for rent. Recommended.

E Hostal Tany, Lúcar y Torre 468A, T043-722534. With bathroom, cheaper without, hot water at night, spotlessly clean, money exchange, tours, café/restaurant.

E Hostal Yanett, Av Centenario 164, at the

north end of town across the river, T043-727150. Friendly, hot water, clean, large rooms, restaurant for breakfast, has parking. Recommended.

E Imperio, José de la Mar 528 y San Martín. With private electric shower, clean, good beds, ask for hot water.

E Jo's Place, Jr Daniel Villayzan 276, T043-725505. Safe, hot water, kitchen facilities, nice mountain views, garden, terrace, warm atmosphere, English owner. Highly recommended.

E La Cabaña, Jr Sucre 1224, T723428, www.huaraz.com/lacabana. Shared and double rooms, hot showers, laundry, kitchen, computer, DVD, very friendly, popular (especially with Israelis), safe for parking, bikes and luggage, English and French spoken.

E Lodging Caroline, Urb Avitentel Mz D – Lt 1, T043-722588. Price includes breakfast, free pick-up from bus station (phone in advance), hot water, kitchen facilities, tourist information and guides, laundry, very helpful. Frequently recommended.

E Lodging Casa Sucre, Sucre 1240, T043-722264, F721111. Private house, with bath, kitchen, laundry facilities, friendly, clean, hot water, English and French spoken, good value. Mountaineering guide, Filiberto Rurush, can be contacted here.

E Oscar's Hostal, La Mar 624, T/F043-722720, marciocoronel@hotmail.com. With bathroom, hot water, cheap breakfast next door, good beds, helpful, cheaper in low season. Recommended.

E-F Casa Jansy's, Jr Sucre 948. Hot water, meals, laundry, owner Jesús Rivera Lúcar is a mountain guide. Recommended.

F Alojamiento El Jacal, Jr Sucre 1044, blue house with no sign. Cheaper without shower, hot water, very nice family, good value.

F Alojamiento Norma, Pasaje Valenzuela 837, near Plaza Belén, T043-721831. Includes breakfast, cheaper without bathroom, hot water. Recommended.

F Casa de Jaimes, Alberto Gridilla 267, T043-722281, 2 blocks from the main plaza. Price for room with bath, cheaper without, clothes-washing facilities and cheap laundry

service, has maps and books of the region, equipment rental, use of kitchen, popular with Israelis. Noisy but recommended.

F Hostal Continental, 28 de Julio 586 near Plaza de Armas, T043-724171. With bath, clean, hot water, friendly, cafeteria serving good breakfasts. Recommended but avoid the rooms overlooking the street as there are 2 noisy *peñas* nearby.

F per person Hostal Mi Casa, Tarapacá 773 (Av 27 de Noviembre), T043-723375, bmark@ddm.com.pe Includes breakfast, cheaper in low season, hot water, English spoken, very friendly and pleasant, owner Sr Ames is an expert on glaciers, his son is a climbing and rafting guide.

F La Estancia, Jr Huaylas 162, Centenario, T043-723183. With shared shower only, luggage store, safe motorcycle parking, good value.

F per person, Olaza Guest house, J Arguedas 1242, T043-722529, www.andean explorer.com/olaza. Safe, comfortable, luggage stored, terrace with views, discount for bikers.

F-G Angeles Inn, Av Gamarra 815, T043-722205, solandperu@yahoo.com. No sign, look for Sol Andino travel agency in same building (www.solandino.com) New, kitchen and laundry facilities, small garden, hot water, owners Max and Saul Angeles are official guides, helpful with trekking and climbing, rent equipment.

G per person Backpackers, Av Raimondi 510, T043-721773, http://huaraz.com/backpackers. Price does not include breakfast. Spacious, hot showers, good views, friendly, a real bargain.

G per person Casa de Familia Gómez Díaz, Jr Eulogio del Río 1983, T043-723224. Hot water, quiet, family atmosphere, good beds.

G per person Lodging House Ezama, Mariano Melgar 623, Independencia, T043-723490, 15 mins' walk from Plaza de Armas (US$0.50 by taxi). Light, spacious rooms, hot water, safe, helpful.

Youth hostels

F per person Alojamiento Alpes Andes, at Casa de Guías, Plaza Ginebra 28-g, T043-721811, casa_de_guias@hotmail.com.

Member of the Peruvian Youth Hostel Association, 1 dormitory with 14 beds and another with 6 beds, hot water, with very good restaurant (open 0700-1100, 1700-2300), laundry, free luggage store, the owner Sr López speaks English, French and German and is very helpful, he is the mountain guides administrator.

F **Albergue El Tambo**, Confraternidad Internacional Interior 122-B, T043-725144, marielafm@yahoo.com. Shared bath, free coffee and tea, laundry service, use of kitchen, book exchange, luggage store, safe, helpful.

F per person **Hostal la Montañesa**, Av Leguía 290, Centenario, T711217. Member of the Peruvian Youth Hostel Association.

● Eating

Huaraz *p329, maps p331 and p332*
For local dishes, such as pachamanca, go to C José Olaya at the weekend, where stalls are set up. There are several country style restaurants in Monterrey which are popular with locals and busy at weekends, serving trout, pachamanca and other regional specialities. There are several cheaper restaurants and stands along Av Monterrey.

₩₩₩ **Bistro de los Andes**, J de Morales 823, T/F043-726249. Great food, owner speaks English, French and German. Recommended.

₩₩₩ **Pizza Bruno**, Luzuriaga 834. 1600-2300. Excellent pizzas, crêpes and pastries, good service. French owner Bruno Reviron also has a 4WD with driver for hire.

₩₩₩ **Huaraz Querido**, Bolívar 981. Excellent *cevichería*.

₩₩₩ **Monte Rosa**, J de la Mar 661. 1000-2300. Pizzería, also fondue and other Swiss specialities. Swiss owner is Victorinox representative, offering knives for sale and repair service, also Suunto (altimeters, GPS), sells mountaineering gear and excellent postcards, rents skiis and snowboards and has climbing and trekking books to read.

₩₩₩ **Crêperie Patrick**, Luzuriaga 422. Excellent crepes, fish, quiche, spaghetti and good wine.

₩₩₩-₩₩ **Siam de Los Andes**, Gamarra corner J de Morales. Authentic Thai cuisine, has an excellent buffet dinner with 2 starters and a main course. There is a nice fireplace, too. Recommended.

₩₩ **Alpes Andes**, Plaza Ginebra in Casa de Guías. Muesli, yoghurt etc in the morning, pastas and pizzas in the evening.

₩₩ **El Cortijo**, Monterrey, along the Huaraz-Caraz road at Km 6.5. Serves very good food, eg chicken and barley stew, and *anticuchos*.

₩₩ **El Rinconcito Minero**, J de Morales 757. Breakfast, lunch (including vegetarian), coffee and snacks, popular for good food and service, also has a video bar.

₩₩ **Fuente de Salud**, J de la Mar 562. Vegetarian, also meat and pasta dishes, good soups, breakfast, recommended.

₩₩ **Monttrek Pizza Pub**, Luzuriaga 646 (upstairs from the agency). Good pizzas and pastas, indoor climbing wall, shows videos.

₩₩ **Pachamama**, San Martín 687. Bar, café and restaurant, concerts, art gallery, garden, nice place to relax, good toilets, pool table and table-tennis, information on treks, Swiss-owned. Recommended.

₩₩ **Pepe's Place**, Raymondi 624, good pizza, chicken, meat, warm atmosphere, run by Pepe from Residencial Cataluña.

₩₩ **Piccolo**, J de Morales 632. Pizzería, very popular with gringos.

₩₩ **Pizza B&B**, La Mar beside laundry of same name. Pizza is excellent, as is their dessert specialty *tarte flambée*, wood oven, pleasant décor and atmosphere, attentive service. Recommended.

₩₩ **Pizzería Landauro**, Sucre, on corner of Plaza de Armas. Very good for pizzas, nice atmosphere.

₩₩ **Sabor Salud**, Luzuriaga 672, upstairs. Restaurant and pizzería specializing in vegetarian and Italian food.

₩₩-₩ **Chifa Jim Hua**, Luzuriaga 645, upstairs. Large, tasty portions, menú US$1.15 and a wide variety of other Peruvian-Chinese dishes. Mon-Sat 0900-1500, 1800-2400, Sun 1800-2200.

₩₩-₩ **Encuentro**, Parque Ginebra, off Luzuriaga cuadra 6. Opens 0700 for breakfast, serves good lunches and dinners, very busy, try the fillet mignon. Recommended.

₩ **El Querubín**, J de Morales 767. Clean, friendly, good breakfast and set meals (high season only), also vegetarian, snacks and à la carte, very good, decorated with nice regional paintings. Recommended.

₩ **Las Puyas**, Morales 535. Popular with gringos, serves an excellent *sopa criolla* and

very good trout, also serves breakfast.
🍴 **Sucre**, Sucre 1284 in La Soledad neighboourhood. Good simple *menú* for quality, variety and value.
🍴 **Vegetarian Food**, Sucre y Av Bolívar. Excellent vegetarian, 3-course meal US$1.

Cafés

Café Andino, Lúcar y Torre 538, T043-721203, cafeandino@hotmail.com. American run café and book exchange, extensive lending library in many languages, a nice place to relax and write postcards, great atmosphere, good meeting place, occasional movies, new Huayhuash maps for sale, owner guides treks in Cordillera Huayhuash, lots of advice offered. Recommended.
Café El Centro, 28 de Julio 592. Good breakfast for US$1.30-2, great chocolate cake and apple pie.
Comedor 14, San Martín 525. Good value breakfasts, sandwiches, teas, etc.
Las Tulpas y Chimichurri, J de Morales 660, between Luzuriaga y Bolívar. Open 0730-2300, for good breakfast, free internet for customers.
Panadería Ancash, Raymondi cuadra 7. Different types of bread, including integral, cakes, ice cream.
Panadería La Alameda, Juan de La Cruz Romero 523 near market. Excellent bread and sweets.
Panadería Robles, Bolívar 479. Sells good bread that keeps well on treks.
Samuels, José de la Mar y Luzuriaga. Great ice cream.

🍸 Bars and clubs

Huaraz *p329, maps p331 and p332*
Amadeus, Parque Ginebra, bar-disco.
Extreme, Jr Gabino Uribe near Luzuriaga. Upstairs bar popular with gringos. 1900-0200.
La Cascada, Luzuriaga 1276, disco tavern.
Makondo's, José de la Mar opposite Cruz del Sur bus station. Disco, bar and nightclub, safe, popular.
Monttrek Disco, Sucre just off Plaza de Armas, in a converted cinema, reasonable prices.
Taberna Tambo, José de la Mar 776, folk music daily, disco. 1000-1600, 2000-0200,

knock on door to get in.
Vagamundo, J de Morales 753. Popular bar with snacks and football tables.

🎭 Entertainment

Huaraz *p329, maps p331 and p332*
Cinema
Huaraz Satyricon, Luzuriaga 1036 (may move in 2005, check in www.huaraz.com). American-run café and movie theatre, classic films, big screen, comfortable sofas, big chocolate chip cookies, US$1.20.

🎉 Festivals and events

Huaraz *p329, maps p331 and p332*
Semana Santa, or Holy Week, is widely celebrated and always colourful and lively. The town's Patron saints' day is **El Señor de la Soledad**, during the week starting **3 May**, with parades, dancing, music, fireworks and much drinking.
Semana del Andinismo is an international climbing and skiing week, held in **Jun**.
San Juan and **San Pedro** are celebrated throughout the region during the last week of **Jun**. On the eve of San Juan fires are lit throughout the valley to burn the chaff from the harvest. The following day the entire valley is thick with smoke.

🛍 Shopping

Huaraz *p329, maps p331 and p332*
Food and drink
The central market offers a wide variety of canned and dry goods, including nuts and dried fruit, as well as fresh fruit and vegetables. Be sure to check expiry dates.
Militos, Sucre 775. A well-stocked supermarket.
Ortiz, Luzuriaga 401 corner Raymondi. Another well-stocked supermarket with a good selection of items, but expensive.
Rosa Rosita, Jr San Martín, ½ block from Morales. Local cheese and manjarblanco are sold here.

Handicrafts
Local sweaters, hats, gloves, ceramics, and wall hangings can be bought from stalls on Pasaje Mcal Cáceres just off Luzuriaga, in the stalls off Luzuriaga between Morales and

Sucre, also on Bolívar cuadra 6 and elsewhere.

Andean Expressions, Jr J Arguedas 1246, near La Soledad church, T043-722951, olaza@qnet.com.pe 0800-2200, run by Lucho, Mauro and Beto Olaza, and recommended for hand-printed T-shirts and sweatshirts with unusual motifs.

La Perla, Sr Enrique Salazar Salas, Jr San Martín 574. Handmade boots, cowboy-style can be made to fit in 3 days for about US$80.

Shumaq Maki, Lucar y Torre next to Café Andino. Good quality crafts.

Photography

Foto Galería Andes, at Pasaje Cayetano Requena, near the market. Good for camera repairs and sells professional photos of the Cordillera Blanca.

▲▲ Activities and tours

Huaraz p329, maps p331 and p332
Huaraz is overflowing with agencies and quality varies. Try to get a recommendation from someone who has recently returned from a tour, climb or trek. All agencies run conventional tours to Llanganuco, Pastoruri (both US$8.50 per person) and Chavín (8-10 hrs, US$6-10 per person), entry tickets not included. Many hire equipment (see Trekking and climbing in the Cordillera Blanca, p325) and also climbing and trekking tours and ski instruction.

Rafting on the Río Santa is also available (US$15 for half a day), year round, Grade 2-3, not particularly special whitewater, but in pretty surroundings. Most agencies provide transport, food, mules and guides. Prices are generally 20% lower during the low season, which is from Oct-Apr. **Note** Tour agencies shouldn't recommend Pastoruri as a first trip. It's best to go to Llanganuco first to acclimatize.

Horseriding

Sr Robinson Ayala Gride, T043-723813. Contact him well in advance for half-day trips (enquire at El Cortijo restaurant – see p336). He is a master paso rider.

Posada de Yungar, at Yungar (about 20 km on the Carhuaz road), T043-721267, 967 9836 (mob). Swiss run. Ask for José Flores or Gustavo Soto. US$4.50 per hr on nice horses;

good 4-hr trip in the Cordillera Negra with fabulous views.

Mountain biking

The Callejón de Huaylas offers superb variety for mountain bikers, from one-day routes to popular attractions to longer trails through agricultural land, over bridges and into traditional villages. More demanding are the routes over the Cordillera Negra to the Pacific coast and, toughest of the lot, the energy-sapping, highly exhilarating climbs over 5,000-m passes beneath the snow peaks of the Cordillera Blanca. A typical circuit is Huaraz-Recuay-Chavín-Huari-San Luis-Chacas-Punta Olímpica which lasts two days; or returning through Quebrada Llanganuco, lasting six days. Camping gear is needed. Local agencies can supply bikes, guides and full back-up, including driving you up some of the steepest bits if your leg muscles can't cope. See also Trekking below.

Mountain Bike Adventures, Lúcar y Torre 530, T043-724259, julio.olaza@terra.com.pe, or www.chakinaniperu.com   Contact Julio Olaza. US$20 for 5 hrs, various routes (see p71). Julio speaks excellent English and also runs a book exchange, sells topo maps and climbing books.

Parapenting and hang gliding

Launch sites near Huaraz are the Puca Ventana near the Mirador, or from Churup-Pitec.

River rafting and canoeing

Ario Ferri, T043-961 3058 (mob, between 1800-2000), www.yurakyaku.com, or contact through Café Andino. Multilingual rafting guide and certified kayak instructor.

Trekking and climbing

Trekking tours cost US$40-70 per person per day, climbing US$90-140 per person per day. There is a great deal of variability in pricing.

Andean Kingdom, Luzuriaga 522. Free information, maps, climbing wall, rock and ice climbing, treks, equipment rental, very helpful, English and some Hebrew spoken, can be very busy.

Anden Sport Tours, Luzuriaga 571, T043-721612. Have a basic practice wall behind the office. They also organize mountain bike tours, ski instruction and river rafting.

Andeno Viaggio, Av Luzuriaga 627, T043-728047, www.andenoviaggio.com. Offers the usual range of day tours (Llanganuco, Pastoruri, Chavin) plus trekking and climbing, reputable.

Baloo Tours, Bolívar 471, T043-723928. Organizes tours and rents gear.

Cordillera Blanca Adventures, run by the Mejía Romero family, T043-724352. Experienced, quality climbing and trekking trips, good guides and equipment.

Explorandes, Av Centenario 489, T043-721960, postmast@exploran.com.pe.

Galaxia Expeditions, Jr Mariscal Cáceres 428, T043-725691, galaxia_expeditions @hotmail.com. Reputable agency with the usual range of tours, equipment rental, etc.

Hirishanka Sport, Sucre 802, T043-722562. Climbing, trekking, horse riding, 4-wheel drive hire, they also rent rooms, **E** per person, with bath, hot water, breakfast.

Kallpa, José de la Mar y Luzuriaga, T043-727868, www.peruviantrek.com. Organizes treks, rents gear, arranges arrieros and mules, very helpful.

Montañero, Parque Ginebra 30-B, T043-726386, www.trekkingperu.com. Run by veteran mountain guide Selio Villón, German, French and English spoken.

Monttrek, Luzuriaga 646, upstairs, T043-721124, F726976. Good trekking and climbing information, advice and maps, run ice and rock climbing courses (at Monterrey), tours to Laguna Churup and the 'spectacular' Luna Llena tour; they also hire out mountain bikes, run ski instruction and trips, and river rafting. Next door in the Pizzería is a climbing wall, good maps, videos and slide shows. For new routes and maps contact Porfirio Cacha Macedo, 'Pocho', at Monttrek or at Jr Corongo 307, T723930.

Tour operators
It is difficult and pricey to purchase airline tickets in Huaraz. Best to do so in Lima.
Chavín Tours, Luzuriaga 502, T043-721578, F724801. All local tours, long-standing agency.
Pablo Tours, Luzuriaga 501, T043-721142. All local tours, also with many years of operation.

Huaraz *p329, maps p331 and p332*
Bus
Many bus companies have offices selling tickets in the centre, but buses leave from the edge of the centre.

Several buses and frequent minivans run daily, 0500-2000, between Huaraz and **Caraz**, 1 hr, US$1. They stop at all the places in between. They depart from the parking area under the bridge on Fitzcarrald and from the open space beside the bridge on the other side of the river (beware of thieves here). To **Chavín**, 110 km, 4 hrs (sit on left side for best views), US$3: **Chavín Express**, Mcal Cáceres 338, T043-724652, daily at 0730, 0830, 1100 and 1400, Sun 1500; **Trans Sandóval**, 27 de Noviembre 582, T043-726930, 0800 and 1300; **Trans Río Mosna**, Tarapacá 576, T043-726632, 0700 and 1300. All 3 companies have buses that go on to Huari, 6 hrs, US$5, and Llame- llín, 8 hrs, US$7. To **Chacas** (US$3.75) and **San Luis** (US$5.75), at 0700 with **Virgen de Guadalupe**, Caraz 607, also to La Unión, US$4.35 at 0700. **Renzo**, Raymondi 821, T043-724915, runs to Chacas and San Luis (0615 Mon-Sat, 0645 Sun), **Yanama, Pisco- bamba** and **Pomabamba** (0630, best). **Los Andes**, same office as Yungay Express, T043-727362, goes daily at 0630 to Yungay, US$0.75, Lagunas de Llanganuco, US$3.45, Yanama, US$3.45, Piscobamba, US$5.20 and Pomabamba, US$6 (8 hrs). Also with **Copa**, J de Morales y Lúcar y Torre, daily at 0630 and 1430. To **Pomabamba** via **Yungay**, Lakes **Llanganuco** and **Yanama**, Transvir, Caraz y Comercio, and **La Perla de Alta Mayo**, 0630, 8 hrs, US$6. Transvir to **Pombamba** and **Sihuas** at 1400 daily. To **Sihuas** with **Chavín Express**, Tue and Fri, 0800, and **Perú Andino**, 1 a week, 8 hrs, US$7. *Colectivos* to **Recuay**, US$0.45, **Ticapampa** and **Catac**, US$0.55, leave daily at 0500-2100, from Gridilla, just off Tarapacá (Terminal Terrestre Transportistas Zona Sur). To **Chiquián** for the Cordillera Huayhuash, see p365. To **Huallanca**, the route is along a paved road through Conococha, Chiquián, Aquia to Huansala, then good dirt road to Huallanca and La Unión. Departs Huaraz 0800, 1300, 1500, 6 hrs, with **Trans El Rápido**, Bolognesi 216, T043-722887. There are regular *colectivos* from Huallanca to La Unión from the corner of Comercio y 28 de Julio, 1 hr, US$0.75.

To/from **Lima**: 420 km, 7-8 hrs, US$6-14. The road is in good condition. There is a large selection of buses to Lima, both ordinary service and luxury coaches, with departures throughout the day. Many of the companies have their offices along Av Raymondi and on Jr Lúcar y Torre. Some recommended companies are: **Cruz del Sur**, Bolívar y José de la Mar, T043-723969, with terminal at Prolongación Raymondi 242; **Transportes Rodríguez**, Tarapacá 622, T043-721353; **Civa**, Morales opposite Lúcar y Torre; **Móvil Tours**, Bolívar 452, T043-722555; **Empresa 14**, Fitzcarrald 216, T043-721282, terminal at Bolívar 407.

To **Casma** via the Callán pass and Pariacoto (150 km) 7 hrs, US$6, the lower section of the road is very poor, landslides and closures are common (sit on the left for best views, as long as you don't mind precipices): **Transportes Huandoy**, Fitzcarrald 261, T043-727507 (terminal at Caraz 820), daily at 0800, 1000 and 1300. **Yungay Express**, Raymondi 744, T043-724377, 3 a day. They continue to **Chimbote**, 185 km. To Chimbote via Caraz and the Cañon del Pato (sit on the right for the most exciting views; see p376) **Yungay Express**, daily at 0700, US$7, 10 hrs. Other companies go to **Chimbote via Pativilca**; US$6, 7 hrs (to **Pativilca**, 160 km, 4 hrs, US$3.50). Most continue to **Trujillo**, all buses go at night, 8-9 hrs, US$10: **Chinchaysuyo** (J de Morales 650, T043-726417), **Línea** (Simón Bolívar 450, T043-726666), **Empresa 14** and, **Móvil Tours**, addresses above.

Taxi

The standard fare for a taxi in town is about US$0.60, US$0.70 at night. The fare to Monterrey or Huanchac is US$1.45. Radio taxis T043-721482 or T043-722512.

⊕ Directory

Huaraz *p329, maps p331 and p332*
Banks BCP, on the Plaza de Armas. Closed 1300-1630, changes cash, 3.25% commission on TCs into soles, good rates, 5% commission charged on TCs into dollars, cash advance on Visa, very long queues, two ATMs (Visa). **Interbank**, on Plaza de Armas. Cash and TCs (no commission into soles), Mastercard ATM. **Banco Wiese**, Sucre 766. Changes cash and cheques. **Casa de Cambio Oh Na Nay**, across the street from Interbank. Gives good rates for cash dollars, but poor rates for other currencies. There are several other casas de cambio and many street changers (be careful) on Luzuriaga. **Internet** There are internet places everywhere, US$0.30 per hour on average. **Sayuri**, Jr Bolívar 683. As well as internet, has digital photo services (including scanning, burning to CD, printing) and international phone calls. **Laundry B & B**, La Mar 674. US$1.20 per kg, special machine for down garments and sleeping bags, French run. Recommended. **Huaraz**, on the plaza on Mcal Cáceres, next to Galaxia Mountain Shop. **Lavandería Liz**, Bolívar 711. US$2 per kg. Also at the Casa de Guías (see p328) and **Laundry Express** at JM Expediciones, on the lane between Luzuriaga and Plaza Ginebra. **Takshar**, Jr Bolívar 617. Next day service, US$1 per kg. **Post Serpost** is on Luzuriaga opposite the Plaza de Armas. 0800-2000 daily. **Telephone Telefónica**, Sucre y Bolívar, corner of Plaza de Armas. National and international phone and fax. 0700-2300 daily. There are many other private calling centres along Luzuriaga. Many coin phones.

North from Huaraz

The road north out of Huaraz goes through the beautiful Callejón de Huaylas, giving access to some wonderful treks which go up into, or over the mountains of the Cordillera Blanca. Caraz, the focus of the northern end of the valley, is less hectic than Huaraz, but just as good a place to stay. It is definitely worth spending some time in this area. ➤ For Sleeping, Eating and other listings, see pages 348-353.

There are frequent small buses running up and down the Callejón from Huaraz and in between the towns en route. ▶▶ *For further details, see Transport page 352.*

Huaraz to Carhuaz → *Colour map 3, grid B2/3.*

The main road north from Huaraz through the **Callejón de Huaylas** goes to **Taricá** (not to be confused with Tarica at the north end of the Cordillera Blanca), where there is a home pottery industry. Good value purchases can be made from Francisco Zargosa Cordero.

A good place for acclimatization and trekking at high altitude is the **Ishinca** hut at 4,350 m in the Quebrada Ishinca. To get there, take a bus towards Paltay (before Taricá) and then take a *colectivo* to Collón, or taxi from Huaraz US$20. From Collón it's a nice four-hour walk to the hut; donkeys can be arranged in Collón, ask for Lorenzo. To sleep at the hut costs US$10, breakfast and dinner are US$10 each; you can also camp here. It's very popular with climbers. The easiest nearby climbs are Urus, 5,420 m, and Ishinca, 5,530 m. It is also possible to make a circuit to Huaraz via Quebrada Cojup in three days, going over 5,000 m. This is a good trek with great views.

❧ The road through the Callejón de Huaylas was being renumbered in 2004. All the references to Km XX along this road will change from the 200-300 range to approx 600-700 range.

The next town is **Marcará**, 26 km from Huaraz (one hour, US$0.45). There are a couple of hotels, basic restaurants and shops. Pick-ups and *colectivos* go east from Marcará along a branch road 3 km to **Chancos**, a little settlement with hot baths. There is an uninviting lukewarm pool (US$0.45), as well as some none too clean private tubs (US$0.90) and very popular natural steam baths in caves (US$1.35 per person). The caves are interesting and worth a try, with locked changing rooms (cave 5 is the smallest and hottest). Buy eucalyptus leaves and other aromatic herbs from the local children to add some fragrance to your steam bath.

Just before Chancos hot springs on the left side of the road is a very good 10-m climbing wall (free), with bolts and anchor chains in place. There is accommodation in the shape of two very basic *alojamientos* and there are also several basic restaurants and food stalls.

From Chancos the road and transport continue to **Vicos**, 3 km further up the Huandoy valley. Vicos is 7 km from Marcará (US$0.30). Vicos is in superb surroundings with views of Nevados Tocllaraju and Ranrapalca. To hike from Chancos to Vicos takes about two hours up the valley through farmland. A trail leads from Vicos to Laguna Lejíacocha, taking four hours.

There are archaeological sites at **Copa**, **Kekepampa** and **Joncopampa**. The last named is considered to be second only to Chavín in the region. From Vicos, cross the river on a footbridge, and it's about one hour further to Joncopampa.

From Vicos, you can walk through the Quebrada Honda, over the Portachuelo de Honda pass at 4,750 m, to **Chacas**, an excellent, not difficult hike, which takes about four days.

Carhuaz → *Colour map 3, grid B2.*

Carhuaz, a friendly, quiet mountain town with a pleasant plaza with tall palm trees and lovely rose bushes is 7 km further on from Marcará. There is very good trekking in the neighbourhood (outlined below). Market days are Wednesday and Sunday. The latter is much larger, and campesinos bring their produce to town. Good peaches are grown locally, among other crops. The locals are renowned for their lively celebrations, hence the town's nickname, Carhuaz alegría.

Treks from Carhuaz

Trek 1 to Yanama The trek up to the **Ulta valley** over the Punta Yanayacu pass to Yanama is little used but offers impressive views of Huascarán and other peaks. It takes three days. If you catch a truck up the valley to where the road begins to zig-zag up to the pass, it will shorten the trek by one day. If not, start hiking from Shilla, 13 km east of Carhuaz, or Huaypan. There are combis to Shilla when full (early morning) from Jr 9 de Diciembre y La Merced, one block northeast of the Plaza, US$0.30. A taxi to Shilla costs US$3 (sharing possible). Transport Shilla-Carhuaz is scarce. Combis go to Huaypan on Wednesday and Sunday only, US$0.50, one hour.

Trek 2 to hot springs Seven kilometres east of Carhuaz, near the village of Hualcán, are the Baños de Pariacaca, which were badly damaged by a landslide in 1993. The hot springs can be seen bubbling between the rocks by the river's edge and there are some small rock pools in which the enthusiastic can bathe. From the plaza in Carhuaz follow Comercio to the top of the hill, turn right as far as cinco esquinas (five corners), turn left and follow the road uphill. When you reach the bridge, cross it left to Hualcán and ask directions from there. There is transport to Hualcán leaving from the plaza in Carhuaz on Wednesday and Sunday.

Trek 3 to Laguna 513 Half an hour beyond Baños de Pariacaca (see Trek 2 above) is the village of **Pariacaca** (no facilities) from where a trail continues into the mountains. In three hours you can reach **Laguna Rajupaquinan** and, 45 minutes beyond, the imaginatively named **Laguna 513**, with beautiful views of the surrounding peaks. If you continue, you will see the Auquiscocha lakes which you can reach in another three hours. Laguna 513 can also be reached directly from Hualcán in about four hours, along the north side of the river. This latter trail has fewer rocks to negotiate. Make sure to take adequate gear and a map if you plan to go beyond Pariacaca.

Yungay

Sleeping
Complejo Túristico Huascarán **8**
Hostal Gledel **2**
Hostal Las Rosas **3**
Hostal Mery **4**
Hostal Sol de Oro **5**
Hostal Yungay **7**

Eating
Alpamayo **1**
Café Pilar **2**

Mancos → *Colour map 3, grid B2.*

From Carhuaz it is a further 14 km to Mancos, at the foot of Huascarán. There's a nice dormitory at **La Casita de mi Abuela**, Barrio Huascarán, Pukio, Jr Comercio 110, and La Plazza, on the Plaza de Armas, can provide meals. There are also some basic shops and restaurants.

Climbers of Huascarán can go to **Musho** to reach the base camp. You can do a strenuous 30-km, one-day walk which gives great views of Huascarán. From Mancos follow the road east and take the branch for Tumpa, about 13 km away. Ask directions as the road branches several times. Continue north to Musho for about 1 km. You can descend via Arhuay to Ranrahica, which is between Mancos and Yungay on the main road. There are daily *colectivos* from Mancos to Musho. Transport to Ranrahica and Arhuay is on Wednesday and Sunday only.

Cueva Guitarreros is a cave in the Cordillera Negra which contains rock paintings dating back some 12,000 years. Access is either through Mancos, from where it is about 30 minutes walking along an overgrown trail (with many spines!), or through Tingua and Shupluy further south, from where it takes about one hour.

The **Chirpas thermal springs**, which have a high lithium (used in the treatment of manic depression) content, are near the caves. There are good views of Huascarán from around this area.

Yungay and around → *Colour map 3 grid A2. Altitude 2,500 m.*

Yungay is 8 km north of Mancos on the main road. The original town of Yungay was completely buried during the 1970 earthquake by a massive mudslide caused when a piece of Huascarán's glacier was pried loose by the quake and came hurtling towards the town. It was a hideous tragedy in which 20,000 people lost their lives. The earthquake and its aftermath are remembered by many residents of the Callejón de Huaylas and the scars remain part of the local psyche.

The original site of Yungay, known as **Yungay Viejo** ① *officially open 0800- 1800*, has been consecrated as a *camposanto* (cemetery). If you enter through the main entrance, which has a café, toilets and shops, off the Huaraz-Yungay road, there is a fee of US$0.75. It is a haunting place, with flower beds and paths covering the 8-12 m of soil under which the old town lies. Of the four palm trees from the old Plaza de Armas that protrude through the landslide, only one remains alive. Five pine trees and a monument mark the site where five policemen died. Nearby, on top of a hill, is the old cemetery with a large statue of Christ, where a handful of residents managed to escape the disaster. Many of the town's children also escaped as they were in the stadium watching the circus. There are a few monuments marking the site of former homes.

The **new settlement** is on a hillside just north of the old town, and is growing gradually. It has a pleasant modern plaza, which was being rebuilt in 2004, and a concrete market, busiest on Wednesday and Sunday, which is good for stocking up on supplies for hiking. The predominant colour in the town is celeste (sky blue). One part of town is called the Barrio Ruso, where typical, Russian wooden houses, erected temporarily in the 1970s as a gift from the USSR, are still in use. The tourist office ① *on the corner of the Plaza de Armas (Monday-Friday 0800-1300, 1400-1800*.

A day walk from Yungay to **Mirador de Atma** gives beautiful views of Huascarán, Huandoy and the Santa valley. From town, follow a dirt road east for 3 km (about one hour). You can return via the Quebrada Ancash road which runs further north, between the Río Ancash and Cerro Pan de Azúcar. This will bring you to the Yungay-Caraz road about 1 km north of Yungay. It is about a three hours round trip.

Matacoto, 6 km from Yungay, a village in the Cordillera Negra at 3,000 m, with excellent views of Huascarán, Huandoy and other major peaks. The turn-off is at Huarazcucho (Km 251), 3 km south of new Yungay. It is another 3 km from here, across the bridge over the Río Santa to Matacoto. Matacoto can also be reached in three hours from Mancos. There is no tourism infrastructure in the town. *Colectivos* go daily 0700-1300, US$0.30, taxis charge US$2.

Laguna 69 can also be done as a day trip from Yungay. Take a combi from Yungay going past the Llanganuco lakes. After about 90 minutes get off the bus at Campsite 3 on the above route and start the wlk at the campsite along clear footpaths. Keep to the right of the river along the valley bottom. You will see the gentle zigzags going up to the right to a col with a small lake. Pass this and you come to a large plateau: keep to the right-hand side. There is a signpost inthe middle pointing right to a glacier and straight ahead to Laguna 69, heading to a large wall of rock. The path zigzags steeply up to the left of this rock face to the lake, near glaciers and the snow line. It takes three to four hours up to about 4,600 m and two hours down, with superb views of waterfalls, glaciers and Huascarán. Ask the combi to return for you at about 1630, the latest time to get back to Yungay for a combi back to Huaraz. There will be no transport to Yungay after 1630.

> ‼ This trek can also be done as a day trip from Huaraz by taking the 0700 combi to Yungay.

Lagunas de Llanganuco

The Lagunas de Llanganuco (see trek on page 346) are two lakes nestling 1,000 m below the snowline beneath Huascarán and Huandoy. The first you come to is Laguna Chinancocha (3,850 m), the second Laguna Orconcocha (3,863 m). The story goes that in times gone by, when the water levels were higher, each evening the day's snow melt and rainfall would raise Orconcocha sufficiently for it to flow into Chinancocha. By dawn they had separated. Hence the lakes' other names, Laguna Macho (male – Orconcocha) and Laguna Hembra (female – Chinancocha). A nature trail, Sendero María Josefa (sign on the road), takes 1½ hours to walk to the western end of Chinancocha where there is a control post, descriptive trail and boat trips on the lake (a popular area for day-trippers). Walk along the road beside the lake to its far end for peace and quiet among the quenoal trees. These trees (polylepis, or paper bark) are the symbol of the Huascarán national park; they provide shelter for 75 per cent of the birdlife found in the park.

Caraz and around → *Altitude: 2,290 m. Colour map 3, grid A2.*

The pleasant town of Caraz is a good centre for walking and the access point for many excellent treks and climbs. It is increasingly popular with visitors as a more tranquil alternative to Huaraz. In July and August the town has splendid views of Huandoy, Huascarán from its lovely plaza filled with rose bushes, palms and jacarandas. In other months, the mountains are often shrouded in cloud. Caraz has a milder climate than Huaraz and is more suited to day trips. The sweet-toothed will enjoy the excellent locally produced *manjar blanco*, a sort of toffee, from which the town derives its nickname, Caraz dulzura. Market days are Wednesday and Sunday. The **tourist office** ① *on Plaza de Armas, in the municipality, T043-791029, Mon-Fri 0745-1300, 1430-1700*, has limited information.

The ruins of **Tunshukaiko** are 1 km from the Plaza de Armas, in the suburb of Cruz Viva, to the north before the turn-off for Parón. This is a poor area so be discreet with cameras etc. There are seven platforms from the Huaraz culture, dating from around 2000-1800 BC, between the Galgada and Chavín periods. Recent excavations have uncovered some structures 300 m in diameter, 25 m high. They are on a promontory with a panoramic view of the farms, fields, eucalyptus and other trees between the Cordilleras Blanca and Negra. To get there, from the plaza in Caraz follow San Martín

● *According to legend, the rise and fall of the waters in Lagunas de Llanganuco is also*
● *related to the tears of Huáscar and Huandy, the prince and princess of enemy tribes whose forbidden love was discovered, causing them to be turned into the mountains Huascarán and Huandoy.*

uphill, turn left on 28 de Julio, continue about 400 m past the bridge over the Río Llullán. Look for a wide track between houses on your left (it's about 300 m before the turn-off for Lago Parón); ask the way.

Five kilometres north of Cashapampa (see page 347), or a one- to two-hour hike, are the hot-baths of **Huancarhuaz**. These have been improved, with an outdoor pool, US$0.30, and individual baths, US$0.60. *Colectivos* from Jr Ramón de Castilla y Jorge Chávez in Caraz go to Cashapampa and continue to Huancarhuaz.

The road out of the Callejón de Huaylas heads north from Caraz, en route to Chimbote. After some 30 km the road enters the very narrow and spectacular **Cañon del Pato**. You pass under tremendous walls of bare rock and through 45 tunnels, but the flow of the river has been greatly reduced by the hydroelectric scheme, which takes the water into the mountain at the Bocatoma.

For a half-day trip from Caraz, take a microbus from near the market towards Yuramarca, see Transport page 339. Sit in the front or on the right for great views. Get off at Huallanca and get on the next bus going back, sitting in the front or on the left. Ask the driver to drop you off at the yellow footbridge where the canyon is narrowest (ask for Cañón del Pato). Walk back north through one small tunnel. In the second tunnel, take the first side tunnel to the right that leads to a very precarious footpath that goes along the edge of the canyon at its narrowest point. Walking back south you come to a dam and the hydroelectric plant with water pouring over the dam wall. Pick up another bus going back to Caraz. Take great care on the path in the canyon and in the tunnels as they are narrow and have no places to retreat if a large vehicle comes through. Take a torch. The trip is best at midday when the sun shines directly into the gorge.

Caraz

0 metres 50
0 yards 50

Sleeping
Alojamiento Caballero 1
Caraz Dulzura 12
Chamanna 17
Chavín 3
Cordillera Blanca 2
Familia Aguilar 4
Hostal La Casona 5

La Alameda 13
La Perla de los Andes 6
La Perla de los Andes Annex 7
Los Pinos 9
O'Pal Inn 14
Ramírez 10
Regina & Huandoy 11
Tunshukaiko 15
Villa Huandy 16

Eating
El Mirador 4
El Turista 5

Esmeralda 6
Heladería Caraz Dulzura 2
Jeny 7
La Olla de Barro 10
La Punta Grande 9
Oasis 3
Panificadora La Alameda 8

Bars & clubs
El Tabasco Taberna 11
Taberna Disco Huandy 12

Transport
Chinchaysuyo & Región Norte 3
Combis to Huallanca 2
Coop Ancash 5
El Huaralino 6
Expreso Ancash 1
Móvil 7
Transportes Rodríguez 8
Yungay Express 10

Treks from Caraz

Pueblo Libre

A good day hike with nice views of the Cordillera Blanca is to Pueblo Libre. Follow Jr D Villar east across the Río Santa bridge and turn south to Tunaspampa, an interesting desert area with cacti and hummingbirds. Continue through the villages of Shingal, Tocash and Rinconada on to Pueblo Libre. It is about a four hour round trip, or you can take a *colectivo* back to Caraz.

❖ For people who don't want to walk, some of these treks can also be done by motorized transport. Pony's Expeditions (see page 351) has a bulletin board where people who want to share transport leave their name and groups are formed.

A longer walk – six to seven hours – is on **Cerro San Juan**, with views of Huandoy and Huascarán. It follows the foothills of the Cordillera Blanca, south from Caraz. Leave town on Bolognesi up to 28 de Julio, turn right, go past the 2 de Mayo (Markham) High School and climb Cerro San Juan; about 45 minutes. Continue south to the main local summit in an area known as Ticrapa (two hours). Head down to Pata-Pata, from where a track goes down beside the Río Ancash to Puente Ancash on the Caraz-Yungay road (two to three hours), where you can take transport back to Caraz. The hike can be done the other way by getting out of a combi from Huaraz or Caraz at Puente Ancash. The tourist office and **Pony's Expeditions** have a map of this trek.

Laguna Parón

From Caraz a narrow, rough road goes east 32 km to Laguna Parón, in a cirque surrounded by several, massive snow-capped peaks, including Huandoy, Pirámide Garcilazo and Caraz. The water level has been lowered to protect Caraz, and the water from the lake is used for the Cañon del Pato hydroelectric scheme. The gorge leading to it is spectacular.

It is a long days' trek from Caraz for acclimatized hikers (25 km) up to the lake at 4,150 m, or a four- to five-hour walk from the village of Parón, which can be reached by combi. Where possible follow the walking trail which is much shorter than the road. By climbing up the slippery moraine to the south of the lake towards Huandoy, you get a fine view of Artesonraju. Camping is possible next to the **Duke Energy** refuge.

A trail follows the north shore of the lake to a base camp on the north side of the inflow, about two hours past the refuge. Beyond this point, the trail divides, one branch goes towards Pirámide Garcilazo (5,885 m) and Pisco (5,752 m), another to Laguna Artesoncocha at the base of an enormous glacier, and a third towards Artesonraju (6,025 m).

There are camping possibilities along these trails. Try to find shelter in the quenoal stands or behind a ridge, as the wind can be very strong and the nights are cold. The views are magnificent as you are always surrounded by many beautiful peaks. When you ford a river, remember that the flow increases in the afternoon with the meltdown, so make sure you can get back to your camp early. On the route to Artesonraju there is a morraine camp, just before reaching the glacier. You will need a map if you are going past Laguna Parón. A taxi from Caraz costs US$25 for four, with two hours wait.

Santa Cruz Valley

This loop is one of the finest and most heavily used walks in the Cordillera Blanca. It usually takes three to five days depending on your starting point. It is considered easier in the opposite direction (Santa Cruz to Llanganuco), requiring four to five days, depending where you finish. **Please take all your rubbish with you**.

Day 1 To **Llamacorral** (3,850 m): taking a combi to Cashapampa covers the first 600m and one hour, 20 minutes of the trip (see Caraz Buses in the Callejón de Huaylas, page 352). Here *arrieros* and their mules can be hired. From here it's a 10-km, 900-m climb to the Llamacorral campsite (four hours).

Day 2 To **Taullipampa** (4,250 m) is an easy day, perfect for acclimatizing (a total of 12 km, climbing about 400 m). The trail leads to the Ichiccocha and Jatuncocha lakes, both providing shelter for many water birds and exotic plants. Beyond the lakes there is a *quisuar* forest, providing perfect shade for lunch. A side trip to the north (left) of the main valley takes a series of switchbacks to the famous Alpamayo Base Camp. After 45 minutes and climbing some 200 m, the circle of glaciers and snow peaks comes into full view. Go no further unless you plan to camp here. If returning to the main trail, look on the left of the trail (east) for a tiny path that will take you to **Taullipampa**, the next campsite. It's only 3 km to the camp, which is one of the most beautiful in the whole region, surrounded by snow peaks, a silent river and incredible plants.

Day 3 Punta Unión-Huaripampa (3,750 m): make an early start for the **Punta Unión Pass**, the highest point on the trail, at 4,750 m. The trail makes a series of switchbacks, but at a gently pace you will reach this point in two-three hours, about 4 km. From the campsite it seems to be just a notch on the rock ridge right of Taulliraju (5,850 m). Once there, the view is a 360° panorama of the snow peaks. The descent starts steeply, then traverses the granite slabs close to the ridge, before another series of switchbacks drive to the far left of the valley to descend on the lake below, another nice spot for lunch. Now the trail becomes slippery, crossing grass-like meadows towards Quebrada Huaripampa. After about two hours, granite tower on your left will tell to look for the bridge to cross the river. Now, with the river on your right, you will soon reach the Quebrada Paría. This is a good campsite, with great views of Paría mountain. It's usually crowded in July-August, so for more privacy, continue 2 km down the valley to camp at **Quenoapampa**. This is a spot at the end of the *quenoal* forest. For most travellers, the next campsite, some 3 km away, known as **Cachina Pampa** (3,750 m), is a better option as it makes a shorter fourth day to catch the early buses back to Yungay. Total distance from the pass is 9 km, some three to four hours, descending 1000 m.

Day 4 For those who have only four days, the exit is at **Vaquería**, a group of houses at the side of the Yanama to Yungay road. Descend for 4 km in about one hour to the bridge on your right, climb to the left until you meet the fork to Colcabamba, take the right path steeply upwards and after 1½ hours you will meet the road.

If making a five-day trek, at Vaquería, continue along the road for some 4 km to a green meadow, a toilet block (or what is left of it) and a huge rock forming a sort of cave (**Pampa Machay**, 4,000 m). This is a good campsite. If you have energy enough, and want to gain on the next day, continue by taking the first short cut on the right. Walk uphill across the trail through bushes to the **Paccha Pampa** campsite, named after the waterfalls by the campsite.

Day 5 Portachuelo-Llanganuco lakes, 3,850 m: A final climb reaches the pass at 4,767 m, in about two hours. You can see, on a clear day, more snow peaks than on any of the previous days, including the twin-peaks Huascarán, four summits of Huandoy, two of Pisco, two of Chacraraju, three of Yanapaccha and the giant Chopicalqui. The trail to the lakes starts on the south (left) of the pass, then after 5 km you reach the area of Cebollapampa, a popular campsite for climbers going to Cerro Pisco. At this point, cars are available to take you back to Yungay. If you wish, pause on the way down at the Llanganuco lakes.

This offers a beautiful, but difficult six- to eight-day trek from Hualcayán to Pomabamba, which is for the experienced only. It involves five-six passes between 4,600 and 4,850 m, and high camps so you must be self sufficient. From Hualcayán you head up to the Cullicocha lake, passing the first pass at Los Cedros (4,850 m - a horrible climb). From here there is a second pass and the Mayobamba valley to negotiate before climbing to the third pass at 4,500 m. Then into the Tayapampa valley, on to the village of Huillca, up the fourth pass at 4,280 m and down to Collota, Yanacollpa and Pomabamba. The way down to Pomabamba can be routed via the Yaino ruins. Please carry out all your rubbish.

Cordillera Negra

For hikes in the Cordillera Negra, a truck leaves from Caraz market at 1000 to Huata at 2,700 m, where there is a religious sanctuary and a dirty hotel (F). From here you can climb to the Quebrada de Cochacocha (3,500 m) at the top of which is the Inca ruin of Cantu (excellent views), and on to the Inca lookout, Torreón Andino (5,006 m).

Take water, food and tent with you. Allow three days for the hike, as there are lagoons near the peak. Some 6 km down a track off the Caraz-Huata road are the Inca ruins of Chonta. Seek advice from Professor Bernardino Aguilar Prieto in Caraz, San Martín 1143, T043-791161. Also refer to his Torreón Andino Information book before climbing it.

A large stand of **Puya Raimondi** can be seen in the Cordillera Negra west of Caraz. Beyond Pueblo Libre (see above), the road which continues via Pamparomas and Moro joins the coastal highway between Casma and Chimbote. After 45 km (two hours) are the Puya Raymondi plants at a place called Winchos, with views of 120 km of the Cordillera Blanca and to the Pacific. 'Wincho' is the local name for the giant hummingbird, Patagona gigas, 18-cm wingspan. The flowers are usually in bloom in May or October.

There are two possible routes going to Winchos and Pamparomas: Caraz-Huata-El Cruce (2-km walk to the puyas)-Pamparomas, or Caraz-Pueblo Libre-Huashtacruz-El Paso (15 minutes' walk to the puyas)-El Cruce-Pamparomas. Which route is taken by public transport depends on where the passengers need to go. This complicates the return to Caraz as you cannot be sure there will be transport going by the pass (El Paso), the closest place to the puyas. You have to walk 2 km to El Cruce to be sure to catch the returning transport between 1230-1300. This will not give you too much time at the puyas. Alternatives which are becoming increasingly popular: to rent a bicycle, go by public transport, ride back in about three hours. Or form a group and hire a car which will wait for you. See note above about bulletin board at **Pony's**.

● Sleeping

Huaraz to Carhuaz *p341*
There are interesting homestay opportunities in Vicos, contact **The Mountain Institute** in Huaraz, Ricardo Palma 100, Pedregal Alto, T043-723446, www.mountain.org.

Carhuaz *p341*
B El Abuelo, Jr 9 de Diciembre y Tumbes, T043-794149, www.elabuelohostal.com. Modern, 3-star, comfortable, cafeteria, parking, ask at Heladería El Abuelo on main plaza.
C per person **Casa de Pocha**, 1½ km out of

town towards Hualcán, at foot of Nevado Hualcán, ask directions in town, T043-961 3058 (mob, 1800-2000), lacasadepocha@ hotmail.com. Advance bookings required. Nice country setting, price includes breakfast and dinner, entirely solar and wind energy powered, hot water, sauna and pool, home-produced food (vegetarian available), horses for hire, camping possible, Spanish, Portuguese, English, French and Italian spoken. Recommended.
C COMTUCAR, 200 m south of town on main road to Huaraz, T043-794051,

www.qnet.com.pe/carhuaz. Includes
breakfast, restaurant, pool, sauna, gardens.
E Four family run *hospedajes* have been built
as part of a community development
project. All have private bath and hot water.
The better two are: **Hospedaje Robri**, Jr
Comercio 935, T043-794505. New in 2003,
modern. **Alojamiento Las Torresitas**, Jr
Amazonas 603, T043-794213.
F Hostal La Merced, Ucayali 724,
T043-794241 (in Lima T01-442 3201). 'Like
going back to the 1950s', clean, friendly, hot
water (usually), some rooms with private
bathroom, luggage store.

Yungay and around *p343, map p342*
E per person **COMTURY**, Complejo Turístico
Yungay, Prolongación 2 de Mayo 1019, 2½
km south of the new town, 700 m east of the
main road in Aura, the only neighbourhood
of old Yungay that survived, T043-969 1698
(mob). Nice bungalows with space for up to
10, in a pleasant country setting, hot water,
fireplace, friendly, restaurant with regional
specialities, camping possible.
E Hostal Gledel, Av Arias Grazziani, north
past the plaza, T043-793048. Owned by Sra
Gamboa, who is hospitable and a good cook,
very clean but tiny rooms, shared bathroom,
hot water, no towels or soap, meals prepared
on request, nice courtyard.
E Hostal Las Rosas, T043-793073. Clean and
friendly, with hot water.
E Hostal Yungay, Jr Santo Domingo on the
plaza, T043-793053. A clean, basic *hostal*,
with private bath, electric shower and
small rooms.
E Hostal Sol de Oro, Santo Domingo 07,
T043-793116. Private bath, hot water,
comfortable and good value. The best
in town.
E Pan de Azúcar, Jr La Merced 32, on a back
street behind the hospital, T043-793057,
pandeazucar@yahoo.com. Includes
breakfast, shared bath, small and quiet,
garden, new in 2003, good.
F Complejo Turístico Huascarán, Leoncio
Prado s/n, T043-793023, www.huascaran
peru.com. With private bath, hot water and
parking, modern but uninspiring.
F Hostal Mery, 28 de julio s/n, T043-313007.

Simple but OK, hot water, the rooms at the
front can be noisy.

Caraz and around *p344, map p345*
A-B O'Pal Inn, 3 km south of Caraz,
T/F043-791015, www.opalsierraresort.com.
This scenic hotel is outside town, set back
from road. Bungalows and rooms, which
have private bath, in a country setting,
swimming pool. Recommended.
C Chamanna, Av Nuev Victoria 185, 25 mins
walk from centre, T043-978 1094 (mob),
www.chamanna.com. Clean cabañas in
beautiful garden, hot water, secure, excellent
French and international cuisine in expensive
restaurant, German run. Recommended.
C-E Los Pinos, Parque San Martín 103, 5
blocks from plaza, T043-791130, lospinos
@apuaventura.com. Rooms with and without private bath, hot water, comfortable and
airy, garden open to all travellers, camping
US$2.50, use of internet US$0.50 per hr, use
of kitchen US$3, laundry service, clean, safe,
book exchange, information and travel
agency Apu-Aventura (see below). Breakfast
and dinner are available, bar with movies
every night. Recommended.
D Caraz Dulzura, Sáenz Peña 212, about 10
blocks from the town centre, T043-791523,
hostalcarazdulzura@hotmail.com. Modern
building in an old street, 6 double rooms, hot
water, with bathroom and TV, very
comfortable, great service, very helpful
owner (Carlos), clean and airy rooms,
breakfast included, very good food available.
Highly recommended.
D La Alameda, Av Noé Bazán Peralta 262,
T043-791177, jtorres@viabcp.com.pe.
Comfortable rooms, also has simple rooms in
E range, hot water, breakfast, parking,
gardens. Recommended.
D La Perla de los Andes, Plaza de Armas
179, T/F043-792007. Comfortable rooms
with bath, hot water, TV, helpful, good
restaurant. Has a large new, cheaper annex 1
block up San Martín. Recommended.
D Tunshukaiko, Jr Melgar 114, T043-792212.
Private bath, hot water, balconies, nice
garden, sitting room with fireplace.
D Villa Huandy, by Puente Llullan just
before Tunshukaiko ruins, T043-791104,

ocanadav@qnet.com.pe. Modern and spacious, balconies, swimming pool, parking, restauarnt, far from centre.

E Chavín, San Martín 1135 just off the plaza, T043-791171, hostalcahvin66@hotmail.com. With bathroom, warm water, good service but a bit grubby and some rooms dark, breakfast extra, guiding service, tourist information (adventure and conventional), owner can arrange transport to Lago Parón.

E Cordillera Blanca, Grau 903, T043-791938. Modern concrete building opposite market, new in 2003, rooms with private bath, hot water and TV.

E Huandoy, Los Olivos s/n, T043-791441. Private bath and hot water, new in 2003, modern, good value.

E Regina, Los Olivos s/n y Gálvez, at the south end of town, 1 block west of road to Yungay, T043-791520. Modern, with bathroom, hot water, clean, quiet, good value.

F Alojamiento Caballero, D Villar 485, T043-791637, or ask at **Pony's Expeditions** on the plaza. Shared bathroom, hot water, washing facilities, stores luggage, basic, family run.

F Familia Aguilar, San Martín 1143, next to Chavín, T043-791161. Basic, one room with bath, otherwise shared bathroom, owner is Prof Bernardino Aguilar Prieto.

F Hostal La Casona, Raymondi 319, 1 block east from the plaza, T043-791334. **F** without bathroom, hot water, clean, lovely little patio, basic but good.

F per person Ramírez, D Villar 407, T043-588254. Basic, clean, shared bathroom, limited hot water.

🍴 Eating

Carhuaz *p341*

🍴 El Abuelo, on the Plaza de Armas. Restaurant serving international and local fare. Produce is from their own garden, including all natural ice cream.

🍴 La Bicharra, just north of Carhuaz on main road, T043-9780893 (mob). Innovative North African/Peruvian cooking, lunch only, busy at weekends, call ahead to check if they are open on weekdays.

🍴 La Cabaña, at Acopampa, 3 km south of town. Specialities are regional dishes, including *cuy*.

Yungay and around *p343, map p342*

🍴 Alpamayo, Av Arias Grazziani s/n, at the northern entrance to town. Best in town serving excellent value local dishes such as trout, cuy, tamales and pachamanca at weekends. Open lunch only.

🍴 Café Pilar, on the main plaza. Good for juices, cakes and snacks.

Caraz and around *p344, map p345*

🍴🍴 La Punta Grande, D Villar 595, 10 mins' walk from centre. Best place for local dishes, good, open for lunch only till 1700.

🍴 Heladería Caraz Dulzura, D Villar on the plaza, next to Perla de los Andes. Excellent home made ice cream, good value meals, pastries.

🍴 El Mirador, Sucre 1202 on the plaza. Nice view from terrace, set lunch and BBQ chicken at night.

🍴 Esmeralda, Av Alfonso Ugarte 404. Good set meal, breakfast, friendly, recommended.

🍴 Jeny, Daniel Villar on the plaza between cathedral and phone office. Good food at reasonable prices, also *pollería*.

🍴 La Olla de Barro, Sucre 1004. Good set menu.

🍴 Oasis, Raymondi, just off the plaza. Meals for about US$1-1.50, also has rooms (**E**).

Cafés

Café de Rat, Sucre 1266, above **Pony's Expeditions**. Serves breakfast, vegetarian dishes, pizzas, drinks and snacks, darts, travel books, nice atmosphere, recommended.

El Turista, San Martín 1117. Open in morning and evening only. Small, popular for breakfast, ham omelettes and ham sandwiches are specialities.

Panificadora La Alameda, D Villar y San Martín. Very good bread and pastries, ice cream, popular with locals. Also

Establo La Alameda, D Villar 420. Excellent *manjar blanco* (they let you try it first), cakes and sweets. Good manjar blanco is also sold by the Lúcar family, Villa Luisa brand, in a house next to the phone office on Raymondi.

🍸 Bars and clubs

Caraz and around *p344, map p345*

Taberna Disco Huandy, Mcal Cáceres 119. Reasonable prices, good atmosphere, young crowd, Latin music. Fri-Sat.

El Tabasco Taberna,3 blocks from the plaza. Disco, latin and other music

❀ Festivals and events

Carhuaz *p341*
The local fiesta in honour of the Vírgen de las Mercedes is celebrated from **14 to 24 Sep** and rated as the best in the region.

Yungay and around *p343, map p342*
Oct 28 is the anniversary of the founding of the town, celebrated with parades, fireworks and dances.

Caraz and around *p344, map p345*
Virgen de Chiquinquirá is held on **20 Jan**. **Holy Week** features processions and streets carpeted with flower petals.
Semana Turística takes place during the last week in **Jul**, with sports festivals, canoeing, parasailing and folkloric events.

◐ Shopping

Caraz and around *p344*
Shop for camping supplies, such as fresh food, in the market. Some dried camping food is available from **Pony's Expeditions**, who also sell camping gas.

▲ Activities and tours

Yungay and around *p343, map p342*
Cycle World, Arias Graziani 3ra cuadra, near bridge at south end of Yungay, T043-303109. Bike rentals at US$10/day including helmet

and gloves. For US$3 a combi will take you and your rented bike to Llanganuco. The ride down is beautiful and exhilarating, but cold. Recommended.

Caraz and around *p344, map p345*
Horse riding
La Almeda bakery, at 4 km south of Caraz, 5 mins by combi towards Yungay, T043-791935. Offers a variety of horse riding routes through flower fields, across the Río Santa and up in to the Cordillera Negra to give fine views of the peaks are possible, US$5 per hr, with guide. Horses for both experienced and inexperienced riders are available.

Mountain biking
Llanganuco is a popular one-day ride from Caraz, like Lago Parón, the Cañón del Pato and the Puya Raimondii plants at Winchus. The Santa Cruz Valley forms part of another long circuit.

Parasailing
Parasailing is practiced 9 km on the road to Huaraz but you must supply all your own equipment. A good launch site is Cayasbamba, near Caraz, at 3,000 m.

Tour operators
Apu-Aventura, D Villar 215, T043-792159, www.apuaventura.com. Offer all sorts of adventure sports and equipment rental.
Pony's Expeditions, Sucre 1266, near the Plaza de Armas, T/F043-791642, www. ponyexpeditions.com. Mon-Sat 0800-2200,

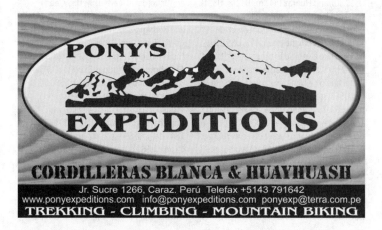

English, French and Quechua spoken, reliable information about the area. Owners Alberto and Aidé Cafferata are very knowledgeable about treks and climbs. They arrange local and trekking tours and transport for day excursions, maps and books for sale, also equipment for hire, mountain bike rental (US$15 for a full day). Highly recommended.
Mariano Araya, ask at the municipality. He is a trekking guide who is also keen on photography and archaeology.

⊖ Transport

Carhuaz *p341*
All transport leaves from the main plaza. To **Huaraz**, *colectivos* and buses leave 0500-2000, US$0.75, 40 mins. To **Caraz**, 0500-2000, US$0.75, 1 hr. There are buses from Huaraz going up the **Ulta valley** to **Chacas** (see p339 and 358), 87 km, 4-5 hrs, US$4.50 (buses pass through Carhuaz about 40 mins after leaving Huaraz). The road works its way up the Ulta valley to the pass at Punta Olímpica from where there are excellent views. The dirt road is not in a very good condition owing to landslides every year (in the wet season it can be closed). The trucks continue to **San Luis** (see p358), a further 10 km, 1½ hr. Each Thu, a bus (**Trans Huandoy**) does the trip from Carhuaz to **Chacas** and returns; US$6 one way, 5 hrs.

Yungay and around *p343, map p342*
Most transport leaves from Jr 28 de Julio. Buses, *colectivos* run all day to **Caraz** (12 km, US$0.30), and **Huaraz** (54 km, 1½ hrs, US$1). To lakes **Llanganuco**, combis leave when full, especially 0700-0900, from Av 28 de Julio 1 block from the plaza, 1 hr, US$1.50, US$9 to hire a vehicle to drop you off, US$12 with 2 hrs wait. To **Yanama**, via the Portachuelo de Llanganuco Pass, 4,767 m, 3 hrs, US$3; stopping at María Huayta, after 2 hrs, US$2. To **Pomabamba**, via Piscobamba, **Trans Los Andes**, daily at 0700-07300, the only company with a ticket office in Yungay; **Transvir** and **La Perla de Altamayo** buses coming from Huaraz, 0730, stop if they have room, 6-7 hrs, US$6. After passing the Llanganuco lakes and crossing the Portachuelo the buses descend to Puente Llacma, where it is possible to pick up buses

and combis heading south to San Luis, Chacas and Huari.

Caraz and around *p344, map p345*
Local From Caraz to **Huaraz**, frequent combis leave daily, 0400-2000, 1 ¼ hrs, US$1.10, the road is in good condition. They are supposed to leave from a terminal on the way out of town, but if there is no police control they pick up passengers by the market and along Jr José Gálvez. By combi to **Yungay**, 12 km, 15 mins, US$0.30. To the village of **Parón** (for trekking in Laguna Parón area) combis leave from the corner Santa Cruz and Grau by the market, from Mon to Sat 0400 and 1300, and Sun 0300 and 1300, 1 hr, US$1.20. They return from Parón at 0600 and 1400. To **Cashapampa** (Quebrada Santa Cruz) buses from Ramón Castilla y Jorge Chávez, hourly from 0830 to 1530, 2 hrs, US$1.50. To **Huallanca** (Caraz) and Yuramarca for the Cañon del Pato (see above), combis and cars leave from Córdova y La Mar, 0700-1730, US$1.50. Combis to **Hualcayán** for the Alpamayo Valley trek from Ramón Castilla y Jorge Chávez, about 1030-1100, US$2.45, 2 hrs. To **Huata** for the Cordillera Negra, combis and cars from Caraz market at 0700, 1000, 1200, 1 hr. For the **Puya Raimondi at Winchos**, take a combi from Grau y Ugarte between 0800-0900, or a bus from Ramón Castilla y Jorge Chávez, also 0800-0900, to **Pamparomas**, 2 ½ hrs, US$2 (see p348), or hire a combi for US$42.50 for 8 people, plus US$7.20 for a guide.
Long distance From Caraz to **Lima**, 470 km; several buses (5 companies, on D Villar and Jr Córdova) leave daily, US$7, eg **El Huaralino**, **Expreso Ancash**, T791509, **Móvil**, and **Rodríguez**, T791184, 10-11 hrs. All buses go via Huaraz and Pativilca. Most buses on the Lima-Huaraz route continue to Caraz. To **Chimbote**, with **Yungay Express** (D Villar 318), via Cañón del Pato, 0830, US$6.60, 8 hrs. Sit on the right for best views. To **Trujillo**, via Huaraz and Pativilca, with **Chinchaysuyo** (Córdova 830, T791930), at 1845 daily, US$9.10, 11-12 hrs, stops in Casma (US$7.60) and Chimbote (US$7.60).

⊕ Directory

Caraz and around *p344, map p345*
Banks BCP, D Villar 217. Cash and TCs at

good rates, no commission. Mon-Fri 0915-1315, 1630-1830, Sat 0930-1230. **Pony's Expeditions** (see above) cash only, good rates. Also change cash. **Importaciones América**, Sucre 721, T043-791479. Good rates and service, open weekends and evenings. **Internet** Many places around the plaza and throughout town, US$0.30.

Post At San Martín 909. **Telephone** National and international phone and fax service at Raymondi y Sucre. Also several others, eg at Sucre y Santa Cruz, and on Plaza de Armas next to Jeny. No collect calls can be made except from private lines. Very few of the coin boxes take phone cards.

East of the Cordillera Blanca

A trip to Chavín de Huantar is a must if you are in the area, as it is one of the most important archaeological sites in the country. At the height of its power, Chavín's influence was felt over a vast area. Along the east side of the Cordillera Blanca, which is known as the Callejón de Conchucos, runs a good, but narrow, dirt road, subject to rapid deterioration when it rains. The region has seen fewer foreign tourists than the Callejón de Huaylas, so some discretion, as well as responsible behaviour, is called for. ▸▸ *For Sleeping, Eating and other listings, see pages 360-363.*

Ins and outs

Many people only go as far as Chavín de Huantar, taking a tour with a Huaraz company. If you decide to go north from Chavín all, or part way up the eastern side of the Cordillera Blanca, public transport is less frequent and less reliable here than in the Callejón de Huaylas, with some towns getting only two buses per week, direct from Lima. Private vehicles, usually large trucks, are few and far between. There are some buses running across the passes back to the Callejón de Huaylas. For further details, see Transport page 361.

Huaraz to Chavín

South of Huaraz on the main road (27 km, 30 minutes) is **Recuay**, one of the few provincial capitals which survived the 1970 earthquake and conserves its colonial features. There is a sizeable cave with stalagmites and stalactites on the main road, entry free. On 11-16 September is the **Festividad Señor de Burgos de Recuay**.

The road passes the turn-off for **Olleros** at 3,450 m, the starting point for the spectacular three-day hike to Chavín, along a pre-Columbian trail (see below). Some basic meals and food supplies are available here.

An alternative trek from Olleros is to **Quebrada Rurec** via **Huaripampa**, a small village with a few *bodegas* which will sell or prepare food. Public transport is available to Huaripampa. There are granite walls of up to 600 m at Rurec, the highest in the Cordillera Blanca, which are recommended for rock climbing. The trek itself is also worthwhile.

Olleros to Chavín trek

The route follows an impressive pre-Inca road with several unexplored ruins along the way. This lovely and relatively easy three to four day trek has become less popular with agencies and groups, perhaps because of persistent begging on the Chavín side. Hence there is an opportunity for independent trekkers to fill the gap, and try to remedy the social situation. Never give money, medicines or sweets, which will do more harm than good. Consider sharing other food if you feel it is appropriate, otherwise offer only a polite smile. There are also dogs along the route, generally raucous but innofensive. The trek begins at the village of Canrey Chico. Combis leave from Parque PIP or Avenida Tarapacá in Huaraz, starting early morning, but no reliable schedule,

❖ *The following numbers correspond to the numbers on the map.*

US$1.50. Better to take a taxi from Huaraz to Canrey Chico, 30 minutes, US$4. The route follows the south (right) shores of the Río Negro, Quebrada Uquián, Quebrada Shongo, and Quebrada Huachecsa all the way to the Chavín archaeologic site.

1 When you reach Canrey Chico, turn right to keep on the road which follows the Río Negro. Keep the river on the left. The track is perfectly clear and there is a large Parque Nacional Huascarán sign.

2 At this point a track branches off to the left into the Quebrada Rurec (see above); continue straight ahead. A small sign marks the intersection.

3 The valley becomes flatter here and the river more sinuous. By some stone corrals, you see a lateral morraine on your right, evidence of old glacial activity. To avoid the boggy valley floor, you can climb along the crest of the morraine.

4 The morraine leads to more corrals and straw-thatched stone huts. Here you begin to see the large flat top of the valley.

5 Sacrapampa, marked with a large sign, is a convenient spot to camp before starting the climb to the pass. At the top of the valley, it divides into four valleys. The path swings right to avoid the marsh then heads up the second valley on the left, often with a ridge between the path and the river, to the highest point. It is quite easy to lose the track here, but keep heading in the direction of the pass and you'll pick it up eventually. It's a slow, gradual climb to the pass.

6 There are stone cairns and several small ponds at **Punta Yanashallash** pass (4,700 m), and great views of the surrounding summits. The trail then follows the ancient road over impressive zigzags making light work of what would otherwise be a difficult 400-m descent.

7 Shongo (also called Shongopampa), marked with a large sign, is a good camping spot; the last before entering populated areas where begging is a problem.

8 At Lluchucaca (bare cliff) the trail crosses a narrow ledge. This is safe in dry weather but can be avoided by descending to the river. Fifteen minutes ahead is a wooden bridge over Quebrada Shongo. Cross here to the north side if you wish to make a side-trip to Jato and explore the valleys up from there. Otherwise, stay on the south side of Quebrada Shongo and follow the trail through the hamlet of **Chichucancha**.

9 Head down into the Quebrada Huachecsa till you reach Punta Huancayo where you can see the ruins of **Chavín de Huantar**.

10 Go through the village of Nueva Florida to reach the road. The town of Chavín is on the left and the archaeological ruins are straight ahead (see below).

Olleros to Chavín trek

© Trekking & Backpacking Club Lima

A blooming century

The giant Puya Raimondi, named after Antonio Raimondi, the Italian scholar who discovered it, is a rare species, considered to be one of the oldest plants in the world.

Often mistakenly referred to as a cactus, it is actually the largest member of the Bromeliad family and is found in only a few isolated areas of the Andes. One of these areas is the Huascarán National Park, particularly the Ingenio and Queshque gorges, the high plateaus of Cajamarquilla, along the route leading to Pastoruri in the Pachacoto gorge and by the road from Caraz to Pamparomas.

At its base, the Puya forms a rosette of long, spiked, waxy leaves, 2 m in diameter. The distinctive phallic spike of the plant can reach a height of 12 m during the flowering process. This takes its entire lifespan – an incredible 100 years – after which time the plant withers and dies.

As the final flowering begins, usually during May for mature plants, the spike is covered in flowers. As many as 20,000 blooms can decorate a single plant. During this season, groups of Puya Raimondi will bloom together, creating a spectacular picture against the dramatic backdrop of the Cordillera Blanca.

Recuay to Chavín → *Colour map 3, grid B3.*

The main road continues 11 km south from Recuay to **Catac**, where a road branches east for Chavín (paved to the Cahuish Tunnel, 38 10 km, then 36 km being paved – due for completion end-2005). From Catac to Chavín is a magnificent, scenic journey, if frightening at times. Beyond Laguna Querococha, there are good views of the Yanamarey peaks and, at the top of the route, the road is cut through a huge rock face, entering the Cahuish tunnel at 4,550 m. On the other side it descends the Tambillo Valley, then the Río Mosna gorge before Chavín.

Several kilometres south of Catac on the main road is **Pachacoto** from where a road goes to **Huallanca** (Huánuco) on the other side of the Cordillera Blanca (133 km, 4½ hours), not to be confused with the town of the same name by the Cañón del Pato. Buses to Huallanca no longer take this route but go on the paved road via Chiquián. See under Huaraz, Transport, for buses to Huallanca; and under the Cordillera Huayhuash for Chiquián.

In this southern part of the Cordillera there are few high, snow-covered peaks, but the glacier of **Pastoruri** is used as the only skiing area in Peru. It is nothing compared to other skiing areas in South America, there aren't even ski lifts, but it is a place to get in a little practice. Pastoruri receives many large groups, and rubbish is a serious problem here. The glacier is receding rapidly and a famous ice cave has melted away to almost nothing.

A good place to see the impressive **Puya Raimondi plants** is the Pumapampa Valley. Take the 14-km gravel road from Pachacoto to park entrance (4,200 m), then 2 km to plants. Daily tours from Huaraz (0900-1800) run to the Pastoruri valley, which is now a reserve with basic tourist facilities, to see the Puya Raimondi plants, lakes and the glacier, a steep one-hour walk up from the car park. Take extra clothing. You can hike up the trail from Pachacoto to the park entrance – 2½ hours – where there is a park office. You can spend the night here. Walking up the road from this point, you will see the gigantic plants. Another good spot, and less visited, is the **Queshque Gorge**. Follow the Río Queshque from Catac; it's easy to find.

Chavín de Huantar → *Colour map 3, grid B3.*

① *0800-1700, US$3, US$5 for a group with Spanish-speaking guide.*

The famous ruins of Chavín de Huantar lie just to the south of the town of Chavín. This fortress temple, built about 800 BC, is the only large structure remaining of the Chavín culture which, in its heyday, is thought to have held influence in a region between Cajamarca and Chiclayo in the north to Ayacucho and Ica in the south. In 1985, UNESCO designated Chavín a World Heritage Trust site.

‡ *From Chavín you can return to Huaraz by road, via Huari, San Luis, Yanama and Yungay (see page 343), but travel along this route can be very slow as the bus service is infrequent.*

The site is in good condition despite the effects of time and nature. The easternmost building was damaged in 1993 when the Río Mosna burst its banks, while in 1945 a major landslide along the Río Huachecsa completely covered the site with mud. It took many years to remove the rubble and some structures remain hidden. Investigations are going on which suggest an extensive tunnel system beyond the boundaries of the current site, which has yet to be excavated. This may lead to the Huaraz road, which cuts across this area, being moved to the other side of the valley some time in the future.

The main attractions are the marvellous carved stone heads and designs in relief of symbolic figures and the many tunnels and culverts which form an extensive labyrinth throughout the interior of the structures. The carvings are in excellent condition, though many of the best sculptures are in Huaraz and Lima. The famous Lanzón dagger-shaped stone monolith of 800 BC is found inside one of the temple tunnels. Excavations in 2001 uncovered a collection of 20 *pututos* (wind instruments) dating from the site's origins.

Chavín

To San Marcos & Huari

Municipalidad
Plaza de Armas
Chavín Express
Inca Roca
Tupac Yupanqui
Mayta Capac
Librería Aquariu's
Julio Tello
17 de Enero
Wiracocha
Combis to San Marcos & Huari
Pol

Río Huachecsa

To Olleros

Chavín Ruins
To Thermal Baths (2 km) & Huaraz

Sleeping
Chavín 1
Hostal Chavín 3
Inca 4
La Casona 5
R'ickay 7

Eating
Chavín Turístico 1
La Ramada 2
La Portada 3

N
Not to scale

In order to protect the site some areas are closed to visitors. All galleries open to the public have electric lights. The guard is also a guide and gives excellent explanations of the ruins. There is a small museum at the entrance, with carvings and some Chavín pottery.

Day tours from Huaraz are a long day out, but when the road is fully paved (see above), this will change. In high season, the site is busy with tourists all day through. You will receive an information leaflet in Spanish at the entrance. The guard also sells other reference material including Chavín de Huantar by Willhelm and Nancy Hoogendoorn, an English/Spanish guide to the ruins which includes a description of each building and an historical overview.

Chavín → *Colour map 3, grid B3. Altitude: 3,160 m.*

The town of Chavín is the commercial centre for the nearby potato and corn growing area. Carved stone replicas are produced for the tourist trade. Chavín

The stone gods of Chavín

Archaeologists have learnt very little about the Chavín culture, whose architecture and sculpture had a strong impact on the artistic and cultural development of a large part of the coast and central highlands of Peru. Based on physical evidence from the study of this 17-acre site, the temple of Chavín de Huantar is thought to have been a major ceremonial centre.

What first strikes visitors upon arrival at Chavín is the quality of the stonework found in the temple walls and plaza stairways. The sculptures have three functions: architectural, ornamental and the third is purely cultist and includes the Lanzón, the Tello obelisk and the Raimondi stela. The latter two currently grace the Museum of Anthropology and Archaeology in Lima.

At 5 m high, the Lanzón is the crowning glory of the Chavín religion and stands at the heart of the underground complex. Its Spanish name comes from the lance, or dagger-like shape of the monolith which appears to be stuck in the ground. Carved into the top of the head are thin, grooved channels and some speculate that animals, or even humans, may have been sacrificed to this god. Others suggest that the Lanzón was merely the dominant figure for worship.

Named after the Peruvian scientist, Julius C Tello, the Tello obelisk belongs to the earliest period of occupation of Chavín (ca 100 BC). It represents a complex deity – perhaps a caiman-alligator – connected with the earth, water and all the living elements of nature. Carved on the body are people, birds, serpents and felines which the divine beast has consumed.

The Raimondi stela was named after the Italian naturalist, who also gave his name to the famous plant, not to mention a fair percentage of the streets in the region. It shows a feline anthropomorphic divinity standing with open arms and holding some sort of staff in each hand.

Together, the figures carved on the stones at Chavín indicate that the resident cult was based principally on the feline, or jaguar, and secondarily on serpents and birds.

has a pleasant plaza with palm and pine trees. There are several good, simple hotels and restaurants, the shops are well stocked with basic supplies and there is a small market. There is nowhere to change money in town. The local *fiesta* takes place on July 13-20. Gasoline is available at the north end of town. Once the road from Huaraz is fully paved (see above), the trip will take about two hours, short enough for a day-trip. Sadly, perhaps because it has been flooded by tour groups, Chavín has become increasingly uncomfortable for gringos, with overcharging, begging and hostile stares.

There are hot sulphur baths, **Baños Termales de Chavín**, about 2 km south of Chavín (US$0.30), at Km 68 in the village of **Quercos**. They consist of one small pool and four individual baths in a pleasant setting by the Río Mosna. Tip the boy who cleans the bath for you (he doesn't get paid). Camping is possible here.

Callejón de Conchucos

The road north from Chavín descends into the dry Mosna river canyon. This is the start of the route to Pomabamba and beyond. If you plan to travel in this area, allow plenty of time, especially in the rainy season.

San Marcos → *Altitude 2,960 m.*

After 8 km is San Marcos, a small, friendly town with a nice plaza and a fancy modern church. It is known as 'City of the Magnolias', but there are few in evidence around the town. Gasoline is available 24 hours.

Combis run from San Marcos to the large, Canadian-run mine, high on the puna, at **Antamina**, two hours. Unfortunately, the impressive mine road from Antamina, via Huallanca (Huánuco), to Conococha is privately owned and it is not possible to travel direct from Chavín to Huallanca without returning to Huaraz at present.

Twenty kilometres beyond San Marcos, at the junction of the Huari and Mosna rivers, is the village of **Pomachaca** (Las Tunas), where a road branches northeast to **Llamellín**. The main road continues north and climbs, criss-crossing the Huari river amid dry hills, to reach Huari 12 km further on.

Huari → *Colour map 3, grid B2. Altitude 3,150 m.*

The town, perched on a hillside at 3,150 m, has steep streets with good views of the mountains. The Plaza de Armas and cathedral are modern, having been rebuilt after the 1970 earthquake. It has a small fruit and vegetable market, which is quite busy on Sunday, and well-stocked shops. The water supply can be intermittent. The local *fiesta* of **Nuestra Señora del Rosario** is held during the first two weeks of October.

Huari to Chacas trek

There is a spectacular two to three days walk from Huari to Chacas via Laguna Purhuay. The route is clearly shown on the IGM map, sheet 19. The walking is very easy, over a 4,500-m pass and through the beautiful Purhuay Valley, at 3,500 m, with its own microclimate and where the animals, insects and flowers are more like those found in a tropical jungle. At the northern end of Purhuay, a 'quenoal' forest. There's plenty of running water and lots of good places for camping. A day walk to Laguna Purhuay is recommended for those who don't want the longer walk to Chacas, and fantastic for ecologists and photographers.

To get to Laguna Purhuay, climb the stairs at the end of Jr Luzuriaga, in Huari, to the main road, turn right, or north, and walk for about 3 km to the village of Acopalca, which has a fish farm where you can buy trout. Turn left after crossing the bridge in town (ask directions). It is a 1½-walk up to the lake. The path to Chacas forks left just before the lake. Another good trail crosses the outflow and climbs above the eastern shore to a good lookout, then divides: the left fork descends to the inflow, which is a narrow gorge called La Cola (the tail); the right fork climbs to the village of Cachitzin (no facilities). There are no good trails along the shore of the lake.

Chacas to Pomabamba

Chacas → *Colour map 3, grid A3. Altitude 3,360 m.*

Ten kilometres south of San Luis, off the main road, is Chacas, with its fine church. The local fiesta patronal is in mid-August, with bullfights, a famous carrera de cintas and fireworks. Seek out the Taller Don Bosco, a woodcarving workshop run by an Italian priest. There are a few basic shops, restaurants, a small market and two or three basic *hostals*, including **Hostal de Pilar**.

It is a two-day hike from Chacas to **Marcará** (see page 341) via the Quebradas Juytush and Honda (lots of condors to be seen). The **Quebrada Honda** is known as the Paraíso de las Cascadas because it contains at least seven waterfalls.

San Luis → *Colour map 3, grid A3. Altitude 3,130 m.*

From Huari the road climbs to the Huachacocha pass at 4,350 m and descends to San Luis at 3,130 m. There is basic and cheap accommodation at **Hostal Rotta**, also a few basic restaurants, shops and a market. Buses run to Chavín on Wednesday and Sunday, five hours, US$6. To Huaraz via Yanama and the pass at 4,730 m under Huascarán takes eight hours, but public transport is scarce on this route (Virgen de Guadalupe and Renzo buses go to Huaraz via Chacas). You may have to hire a minibus to take you to Puente Llacma, 28 km north, the junction of the roads for Yanama and Pomabamba (US$15 for the vehicle). From there you can hitchhike to Yanama and Yungay. Trucks also provide transport in this area.

A large sanctuary to **Nuestro Señor de Pumayukay**, built by Italian priests, is a 15-minute ride from San Luis towards Pomabamba and then a turn-off to the east.

Yanama → *Colour map 3, grid A3.*

The road which branches left at Puente Llacma goes to Yanama, 45 km from San Luis, at 3,400 m. It has one marked hotel outside and one unmarked hotel on the plaza; ask at the pharmacy. Food is available, but no electricity in the village, which is beautifully surrounded by snow-capped peaks. A day's hike to the ruins above the town affords superb views.

Piscobamba → *Colour map 3, grid A3. Altitude 3,290 m.*

The main road through the Callejón de Conchucos continues north from San Luis for 62 km to Piscobamba (the pampa of the birds, from the quechua 'Pishco Pampa'). It has a pleasant plaza. There are spectacular views across the heavily wooded valley to the Cordillera Blanca, from the Alpamayo massif to the north to beyond Huascarán to the south. Hostales San Pedro and Yomara are both basic. There are also a few shops and small restaurants. Twenty-two kilometres beyond Piscobamba is Pomabamba.

Pomabamba → *Colour map 3, grid A3. Altitude 2,950 m.*

Known as 'City of the Cedars', though only two very old specimens remain in the centre of the plaza, surrounded by roses and jacarandas, Pomabamba (the pampa of the pumas, quechua 'Puma Pampa') is worth a visit on several counts. The plaza was being rebuilt in late 2004. There are very hot natural springs across the river, a five-minute walk down a steep path from the main plaza. There are three different bathing establishments, all with private baths, US$0.30 per person, no time limit. Ask for the baths to be cleaned before you use them. There is a small museum and tourist office at Huaraz 515, variable opening hours. The main festival is 24 June.

Treks from Pomabamba

Several good walks into the Cordillera Blanca start from near Pomabamba. You can go via Palo Seco or Laurel to the Lagunas Safuna, from where you can go on, if you're fit enough, to **Nevado Alpamayo**, dubbed 'the most beautiful mountain in the world'. The glacier of Alpamayo is an incredible sight. From there, continue down to Santa Cruz and Caraz for several days' hard walking in total.

For the less energetic, a good day trip can be made to the quite large and extensive, though sadly dilapidated, Huari ruins of **Yaino**, on top of a very steep mountain and visible from the main plaza of Pomabamba. The walls are beautifully built and there are two very large buildings, a square one and a circular one. The site commands excellent views of the many peaks of the Cordillera. To get there take a combi to Huaychó, one hour, US$1. Take the path to Garhuay, smaller Huari ruins, two hours, and continue upwards to Yaino, two hours. An alternative return route is to walk down to Huayllan, on the Pomabamba/Huaychó road, and catch a combi (30 minutes). Take food and lots of water; you can get very dehydrated climbing and perspiring in the thin dry air. It's also very cold high up if the sun goes in, so go with warm, waterproof clothes.

Another good day walk leaves Pomabamba to the Inca Road: climb from the **Curayacu** fountain to the hamlet of Cushurú and then up along the ridge on your right. You can follow the road south and return to Pomabamba via Pajash. There are several unexplored ruins along the Inca Road. To the north is Mesa Rumi, two hours, a remarkably precise and unique metre-square block of Inca stone with ceremonial holes in its upper surface.

A shorter walk (three to four hours) begins from the bridge over the river and runs up a side valley, past a trout farm, to the beautiful **Jancapampa** valley below the Alpamayo massif. Camping is possible there.

Sihuas and beyond → *Colour map 3, grid A2. Altitude 2,730 m.*

From Pomabamba a dusty road runs up the wooded valley crossing the puna at Palo Seco, 23 km. The road then descends steeply into the desert-like Sihuas valley, passing through the village of Sicsibamba. The valley is crossed half an hour below Sihuas.

The small town of Sihuas itself is divided into three sections spreading over a kilometre up the valley. The lowest district is the oldest with a fine colonial interior to the church. All the bus company offices, hotels and restaurants are in the middle district. The town is a major connection point between the Callejón de Conchucos, Callejón de Huaylas, the upper Marañón and the coast. Other than as a stopover while travelling between these areas there is little to do in the immediate surrounding area. The town suffers from water shortages.

From Sihuas it is now possible to travel, via Huancaspata, Tayabamba, Retamas and Chahual, to Huamachuco along a road which is very poor in places and involves crossing the river Marañón twice. The building of a new bridge over the river means that it is now possible to travel from Cusco to Quito through the Andes, without going down to the Pacific Lowlands, entirely by public transport. This journey is best undertaken in this direction though the road may be almost impassable in the wet season. A detour up the Marañón Valley leads to Huacrachuco, where there are several basic *hostals*. The significant Inca ruins of Mamahuagay are nearby and a five-day walk down to Uchiza in the Huallaga valley can be made.

● Sleeping

Huaraz to Chavín *p353*

C **Altas Montañas**, at edge of Olleros, T043-722569, altasmont@yahoo.es. Small 3-star lodge, Belgian-run, with hot showers, good breakfast included, dinner available, bar, birdwatching, guided treks, information, laundry, recommended for start or end of trek, phone 24 hours in advance, preferably at 2000, to arrange free pick-up from Huaraz.

Chavín *p356, map p356*

D **La Casona**, Wiracocha 130, Plaza de Armas, T043-754048, lacasonachavin@ peru.com. In an old house with attractive courtyard, private bathroom, cheaper with

shared bath, insufficient hot water, friendly, one room with a double bed, motorcycle parking.
D **R'ickay**, on 17 de Enero 172N (north), T043-754068, www.sorem.com.pe/rickay. Set around two patios, modern, pricey, all rooms with private bathroom and TV, hot water, restaurant (see below).
E **Hostal Chavín**, Jr San Martín 141-151, half a block from the plaza, T/F043-754055. Set around a pleasant courtyard, F without bath, hot water, provides breakfast for groups, best of the more basic hotels, same owner as Hotel Chavín, friendly and helpful.
E **Hotel Chavín**, Roca 151 y Tello,

T043-754055. Temporarily closed to tourists in 2004, should reopen in 2005 when the road is complete. Modern, clean, hot water, all rooms with bath and TV.
E Inca, Wiracocha 160, T043-754021. Also all but closed to tourists while the road project is under way. In a renovated house, garden, friendly.

Camping
Possible for vehicles inside park gates at Chavín de Huantar, with permission from the guard.

San Marcos p358
F La Rinconada, La Merced 325. Best of the several basic *hostales*.

Huari p358
F El Dorado, Bolívar 341. Basic, comfortable, sunny patio, shared bathroom, hot water.
F Añaños, Alvarez 437, next to the market. Very basic but clean.

Pomabamba p359
E Albergue Turístico Vía, Jr Primavera 323, T043-741052, verladicho@hotmail.com. Family run, breakfast available, shared bath, cold water, friendly and helpful. New rooms with private bath under construction in 2004. Also private bath-house at thermal baths.
F Anny, Jr Moquegua y Jorge Gálvez, barrio El Convento, T043-751125. Some rooms with private bath, cold water.
F Hostal Estrada Vidal, Huaraz 209, T043-804615. Run by friendly Sra Estrada Vidal, rustic, rooms around a pleasant courtyard, clean, cold water, good value. Recommended.
F Hostal Pomabamba, Jr Huamachuco 338 on Plaza de Armas, T043-751276. With private bath, G without, cold water, basic but OK.

Sihuas and beyond p360
E Hostal Liliana, Jr Ramón Castilla y Ricardo Palma, T043-741125. In a newer building, large rooms some with bath, **F** without bath, basic but OK.
F Hostal Don César, Av 28 de Julio 309, T043-741044. With shared bath, neither clean nor friendly, very basic.

● Eating

Chavín p356, map p356
It is possible to eat very well in the better restaurants where specialities include rabbit stew, trout ceviche and llunca, a solid, wheat-based soup.
♈ R'ickay, see Sleeping, above. Pasta and pizza dishes in the evenings.
♈♈ Chavín Turístico,17 de Enero. Overpriced and mediocre menú, but good à la carte, delicious apple pie, clean, nice courtyard. Beware overcharging.
♈♈ La Portada, 17 de Enero. In an old house with tables set around a garden.
♈ La Ramada, 17 de Enero. Regional dishes, also trout and set lunch.

San Marcos p358
♈ Las Magnolias and **Crillón Chico**, in the main plaza, are the best of several basic restaurants.

Huari p358
♈ Centro Virgen del Rosario, San Martín by Parque Vigíl. Serves coffee, sweets and snacks, very clean and friendly, open evenings and Sun, run by an Italian nun and her students.
♈ Los Angeles, Ancash 669, off the main plaza. Mainly chicken, popular.
♈ Rinconcito Huaracino, Bolívar 530. Good menú, open till 2100.

Pomabamba p359
There is a limited choice of places to eat and most close by 2100.
♈ Davis-David, Huaraz 269. Offers the best menú and can prepare soups to order.
♈ Las Piedras, Jr Arica 350. Menú and à la carte including trout.
♈ Los Cedros, Huaraz 531. Good for breakfast.

Sihuas and beyond p360
♈ Chosas Nauticas is a basic comedor, also good for breakfast. There are other similar places in town.

● Transport

Chavín p356, map p356
Bus It is much easier to get to Chavín (even walking!) than to leave the place by

bus. All buses to **Huaraz** originate in Huari or beyond. They pass through Chavín at irregular hours and may not have seats available. Buying a ticket at an agency in Chavín does not guarantee you will get a seat or even a bus. In Oct 2004, the ride to Huaraz, 110 km, took 2 1/2 hrs, US$3. For buses from **Huaraz**, see under Huaraz. **Chavín Express** passes through around 1200, 1600 and 1700 daily; **Río Mosna** around 0430, 1600, 1800, 2000, and 2200 daily. All schedules are subject to change during road construction, expected to continue to late 2005.

To **Lima**: 438 km, 12 hrs, US$9, with **Trans El Solitario** and **Perú Andino** daily. Most companies use older, uncomfortable buses and many locals prefer to travel first to Huaraz and then take one of the more reputable companies from there.

To other destinations in the Callejón de Conchucos it is necessary either to use buses coming from Huaraz or Lima, or to hop on and off combis which run between each town. Combis to **San Marcos**, every 20 mins from the Plaza de Armas, 25 mins, US$0.50; to **Huari**, 2 hrs , US$1.50. There are buses during the day from Lima and Huaraz which go on to Huari, with some going on to **San Luis**, a further 61 km, 3 hrs; **Piscobamba**, a further 62 km, 3 hrs; and **Pomabamba**, a further 22 km, 1 hr; such as **El Solitario** which passes through Chavín at 1800. Other buses from Huaraz and Lima terminate in Llamellín, 120 km, 4 hrs, US$3.

Huari *p358*
Bus Bus companies have their offices around Parque Vigil. To **Huaraz**, 5-6 hrs, US$3.75; departures through the day. To **San Luis**, buses leave on Tue and Sat: with **El Solitario** at 0600, **Perú Andino** at 0830. Buses heading north pass through Huari between 2200 and 2400, but not every day. To **Lima**, 13 hrs, US$10: with **Turismo Huari** on Sun, Wed and Fri at 0630, **Perú Andino** on Sun and Wed at 0800. On the other days, except Thu, buses bound for Lima originating further north pass Huari between 1000 and 1200.

Yanama *p359*
There are several combis a day, especially in the early morning and late afternoon,

between Yungay and Yanama over the 4,767 m Portachuelo de Llanganuco (3 hrs, US$4), continuing to Pomabamba. Yanama to Yungay combis can be caught at Vaquería more or less between 0800-1400, US$3, 3 hrs.

Piscobamba *p359*
Combis to **Pomabamba** from the Plaza de Armas, hourly 0700-1800, 1 hr, US$1.20. There are no combis from Piscobamba to San Luis.

Pomabamba *p359*
All transport leaves from the Plaza de Aramas. To **Piscobamba**, combis depart hourly, 1 hr, US$1.20. To **Sihuas**, combis at 0200 and 1600 daily but best to reserve your seat by arriving at least an hr before, 4 hrs, US$3. To **Huaraz** (7 hrs, US$6) via **Yungay** (6 hrs, US$6) with **Renzo** at 1330 and 1945 daily, **Los Andes** at 1945 daily. To **Lima** (18 hrs, US$11): via **San Luis** (4 hrs, US$3), **Huari** (6 hrs, US$4.50) and **Chavín** (9 hrs, US$6) with **El Solitario**, Sun, Mon and Thu at 0800; via **Yungay** and **Huaraz** with **La Perla del Alto Mayo**, Wed, Thu, Sat, Sun, 16 hrs, US$11.

Sihuas and beyond *p360*
To **Pomabamba**, combis at around 0700 and 1100 daily, 4 hrs, US$3; no office, be out on the street early to get a seat. To **Huaraz**, via Huallanca, with **Transvir**, daily at 0830, 8 hrs, US$7; **Trans Chavín Express**, Wed and Sat, and **Perú Andino** on Tue, 1100, 8 hrs, US$7. To **Tayabamba**, for theMarañón route north to Huamachuco and Cajamarca: **Andía** passes through from Lima on Mon, Wed and Sat at 0100-0200, **La Perla del Alto Mayo** passes through from Lima on Wed and Sat 0000-0200; also twice a week with **Garrincha** and once a week with **San Antonio de Padua**; all 7-8 hrs, US$6, the beginning of a long wild ride. To **Huacrachuco**, Trans Andina, daily at 1000. To **Chimbote**, La Perla de Alta Mayo on Tue, Thu and Sun, 10 hrs, US$9. To **Lima** (17 hrs, US$9) via Chimbote, Andía daily around 0200-0500; confirm all times locally. To **Trujillo** via Chimbote, **Garrincha** on Mon and Thu, 2200, 12 hrs, US$10.

● Directory

0630-2200. **Telephone** Pay phones all over town.

Chavín p356, map p356
Internet At **Librería Aquariu's**, 17 de Enero y Túpac Yupanqui, US$1 per hr.
Post At 17 de Enero 365N (north).

Huari p358
Post Luzuriaga 324 by Parque Vigíl.
Telephone Libertad 940. 0700-2200 daily.

Cordilleras Huayhuash and Raura → Colour map 3, grid B3/4.

Lying south of the Cordillera Blanca, the Cordillera Huayhuash has been dubbed the 'Himalayas of America' and is perhaps the most spectacular in Peru for its massive ice faces which seem to rise sheer out of the contrasting green of the Puna. Azure trout-filled lakes are interwoven with deep quebradas and high pastures around the hem of the range. You may see tropical parakeets in the bottom of the gorges and condors circling the peaks.

Although the area may well have been inhabited for thousands of years, the Huayhuash only became known to the outside world following a plane crash on the southeast face of Jirishanca in 1954. Since then the number of visitors has grown steadily, with a hiatus during the era of insurgency in the 1980s. The mountain range's renown has increased with story of Joe Simpson and Simon Yates' near-tragic climbing expedition in 1985, recounted in Simpson's book and the subsequent film, Touching the Void. Although less touristy than the Cordillera Blanca, it nonetheless receives significant numbers of trekkers and climbers every year. ➤➤ *For Sleeping, Eating and other listings, see pages 365-366.*

Ins and outs

Trekking in the Cordillera Huayhuash is generally considered difficult, and certainly requires stamina (10 to 12 days for the complete loop, see page 363) but the trails are good and most gradients are relatively gentle. There are up to eight passes over 4,600 m, depending on the route.

Both the Huayhuash and Raura ranges are approached from **Chiquián** in the north, **Oyón**, with links to Cerro de Pasco to the southeast, **Churín** in the south or **Cajatambo** to the southwest. The area is remote and the local villagers are generally herdsmen, tending flocks of cattle, sheep and alpacas.

Huayhuash Circuit

The trail head is at **Cuartel Huain** (1 - figures indicate usual camping sites on the map), between Matacancha and the **Punta Cacanan** pass (the continental divide at 4,700 m). This northernmost point on the trek gives access to the village of **Janca**, **Laguna Mitucocha** (2) and the eastern flank of the Cordillera.

A very steep short cut on scree is through the gap in the northern spur of the range above Matacancha and Janca village on the other side. This could save two or three hours.

The eastern side of the Cordillera is a chain of passes, lakes and stunning views of **Jirishanca Chico**, **Yerupajá Chico**, **Yerupajá** (Peru's second highest peak at 6,634 m) and **Siulá Grande**. From Janca, a small side valley leads off **Quebrada Mitucocha** to **Punta Carhuac** (4,650 m) and beyond to **Laguna Carhuacocha**, with magnificent camping (3) and views. Following on from there are **Punta Carnicero** (4,600 m, a section of Inca road and petroglyphs are found nearby), the twin lakes of **Azulcocha** and **Atoqshaico** (just beyond the pass) and **Huayhuash village** (4 - one house). This is the regular route, but a new route is also open, following round Laguna Carhaucocha, passing Laguna Siulá and emerging on the regular route just before Huayhuash village. This trail has gained popularity thanks to Touching the Void, the book by Joe Simpson; there are no maps and it is advisable for experienced trekkers only. A guide is recommended. The weather can change very suddenly.

The next pass, **Portachuelo Huayhuash** (4,750 m, the continental divide) overlooks the superb southward line of pyramidal peaks and rounded ice caps of the **Cordillera Raura**. A path leads from **Laguna Viconga** below (5 - near the dam), over a pass and hugs the western flank of the Raura all the way to **Oyón**. Transportes Javier run a daily bus from Raura to Cerro de Pasco, seven hours, US$5.50, to which there are also daily buses from Oyón.

Four hours away from Oyón is **Churín**, which boasts the 'best thermal baths in Peru'. There is also a small thermal pool 1 km past the outflow of Viconga, along the trail to Cajatambo. Note that water is released from the Viconga dam daily 0500-1100, and you cannot ford the outflow during this time.

If you are bailing out at **Cajatambo** (6), it is downhill all the way from Laguna Viconga, apart from a short sting in the tail at the end. Those continuing the circuit must cross the **Punto Cuyoc** (5,000 m), sometimes snowbound, with outstanding 360° views. The highpoint of the circuit in every sense of the word.

There follows a long, gentle descent into the **Quebrada Huanacpatay** (6 on the full circuit) and an optional one day side trip up the valley of the **Río Huayllapa** to **Laguna Jurau** and **Laguna Sarapococha**, both beautiful lakes.

The route continues downhill to the village of **Huayllapa** (with shop and basic lodging and meals), just before town it turns north to begin climbing to the **Tapush Pass** (4,800 m) below the summit of **Diablo Mudo** (also known as **Suerococha**), via **Huatac** (7).

Cordilleras Huayhuash & Raura

After the pass you reach **Cashpapampa** (8), from where you head east to the
Yaucha Pass (4,800 m, outstanding views), then north, by way of the **Quebrada Huacrish**, to **Laguna Jahuacocha**, which lies beneath **Yerupajá** and Nevados **Jirishanca** and **Rondoy**. The lake offers the most idyllic campsite (9) in the Cordillera. It can also be reached from Llamac over the Punta Llamac pass at 4,300 m, southeast of that town. First head southwest along a path just beneath the cemetery and zig-zag up above the town. Llamac is also used as a starting point for the trek. You can camp on the football pitch (US$1.50 per night). Drinking water is available from the water source which is 200 m on the trail north to Pocpa – ask locals.

A 4,800-m pass, Sambunya, beneath Rondoy, leads to the descent to the town of Rondoy (10), Matacancha and the trail head.

Chiquián → *Phone code: 043. Altitude: 3,400 m.*

Chiquián is a little town of narrow streets and overhanging eaves. An interesting feature is a public television mounted in a box on a pedestal which sits proudly in the Plaza de Armas, around which folks gather every evening. There is a Semana Turística during the first week of July and the local fiesta is celebrated on 30 August in honour of Santa Rosa.

Cajatambo → *Phone code: 043. Altitude: 3,380 m.*

The southern approach to the Cordillera Huayhuash is a small, developing market town, with a beautiful 18th-century church and a lovely plaza. Note that the road out of Cajatambo is not for the fainthearted. For the first three to four hours it is no more than a bus-width, clinging to the cliff edge.

Sleeping

Chiquián *p365*
E Gran Hotel Huayhuash, Figueredo esquina 28 de Julio, T043-747049. Private bathroom, hot water, TV, restaurant, laundry, parking, modern, great views.
E Hostal San Miguel, Jr Comercio 233, T043-747001. Nice courtyard and garden, clean, many rooms, popular.
G per person **Los Nogales de Chiquián**, Jr Comercio 1301, T043-747121 (in Lima T01-460 8037), hotel_nogales_chiquian@ yahoo.com.pe. With bath, cheaper without, hot water, cable TV, cafetería, parking. Recommended.

Cajatambo *p365*
F Hostal Miranda, Jr Tacna 141. Homely, friendly, small rooms, cold shower, basic. Recommended.
G Hostal Cajatambo, on the plaza. Basic, cheap, not for the squeamish as the courtyard is a chicken slaughterhouse.
G Hostal Tambomachay, Jr Bolognesi 110, T043-242046. Nice courtyard and restaurant.
G Hostal Trinidad, Jr Raimondi 141. A basic place to stay.

Eating

Chiquián *p365*
El Refugio de Bolognesi, Tarapacá 471. Offers basic set meals.
Panificadora Santa Rosa, Comercio 900, on the plaza. For good bread and sweets, has coin-operated phones and fax.
Yerupajá, Jr Tarapacá 351. For basic set meals and information.

Cajatambo *p365*
Restaurant Andreita, Av Grau 440.

Transport

Chiquián *p365*
Coming from Huaraz, the road is now paved beyond Chiquián to Huansala, on the road to Huallanca (Huánuco). Four bus companies run from **Huaraz to Chiquián**, 120 km, 3½ hrs: El Rápido, at Bolognesi 216, T043-722887, at 1345, **Virgen del Carmen**, around the corner from Huascarán on Raymondi; **Chiquián Tours**, on Tarapacá behind the market; and **El Amigo del Milenio**, opposite the Frigorífico de Huaraz on Bolognesi. From Chiquián to Huaraz: all

buses leave the plaza at 0500 daily, and **El Rápido**, Jr Figueredo 216, T747049, at 0500 and 1330. The companies have pretty good buses, US$1.75 (except El Rápido, US$3.65). Also *colectivo* Chiquián-Huaraz 1500, 3 hrs, US$2.45 pp. From **Chiquián to Llamac**, 0900 and 1700, return 0800, 1200, 1½ hrs, US$2, book as early as possible. Llamac to Huaraz, with a change in Chiquián, 1130, arrive 1630. There is also a connection from Chiquián to Huallanca (Huánuco) with buses coming up from Lima in the early morning and combis during the day, which leave when full, 3 hrs, US$2.50. From Huallanca there are regular combis on to La Unión, 1 hr, US$0.75, and from there transport to Huánuco.

Cajatambo *p365*
Buses to **Lima** leave daily at 0600, US$8.80, with **Empresa Andina** (office on plaza next to Hostal Cajatambo) and **Tour Bello**, one block off the plaza. The only way back to Huaraz is via Pativilca on the coast, a long detour. Buses from Cajatambo arrive in Pativilca around midday; wait for Lima-Huaraz buses to pass between 1330 and 1400 and arrive in Huaraz about 1700. **Turismo Cajatambo**, Jr Grau 120 (in Lima, Av Carlos Zavala 124 corner of Miguel Aljovin 449, T01-426 7238, in Barranca, Prologación Sáenz Peña 139).

🎙 Footprint features

Introduction

Peru's north coast could well be described as the Egypt of South America. This is a region of numerous monumental ruins, built by the many highly skilled pre-Inca cultures that once thrived here. The recent, ground-breaking discovery at Caral is now open to visitors. Not far from Trujillo, Chan Chán was the capital of the Chimú Kingdom; its crumbling remains still represent the largest adobe city in the world. The Huaca de la Luna of the Moche empire is revealing fabulous, multicoloured friezes of gods from the first millennium AD. Further north, near Chiclayo, the adobe brick pyramids of Túcume, Sipán and Sicán rise massively from the coastal plains. The wealth from some of their tombs is now displayed in new, state-of-the-art museums.

But it's not all pyramids and royal tombs. The elegant city of Trujillo is one of the finest examples of colonial architecture in the country. There are charming towns such as Huanchaco, with its bizarre-looking reed fishing rafts, and Chulucanas, with its famous pottery. Lambayeque Department has umpteen festivals; you can visit witchdoctors or simply buy their potions; up and down the coast the seafood is wonderful and the hospitality unrivalled. In addition, the northern seaboard enjoys a rain-free climate all year, and sports Peru's finest beaches for bathing and surfing. Around Tumbes, the most northerly provincial capital, three reserves protect mangroves, equatorial dry scrub and rainforest, each of which contains endangered species, ranging from crocodiles to eagles.

★ Don't miss...

1 **Caral** A city, 4,600 years old, whose peace-loving inhabitants seem to have upset all previous theories of urban archaeology, page 372.
2 **Trujillo** See the Sunday morning flag-raising ceremony in the Plaza Mayor, surrounded by colonial buildings, page 380.
3 **Huanchaco** Ride the waves on the totora-reed boats-cum-surfboards, known as 'little horses', page 393.
4 **El Brujo** Bones and pottery shards crunch under your feet as you explore this mysterious archaeological complex, page 394.
5 **Lambayeque** The Brüning and Royal Tombs of Sipán museums, two ultra-modern settings for some of Peru's richest historical finds, page 400.
6 **Chiclayo's Mercado Modelo** Buy your fish, your soap powder and your cat's claw all under one roof – for all your shamanic shopping needs, page 410.

North Coast

Lima to Chimbote

Between Lima and Pativilca there is a narrow belt of coastal land deposited at the mouths of the rivers and, from Pativilca to the mouth of the Río Santa, north of Chimbote, the Andes come down to the sea. The Pan-American Highway parallels the coast all the way to the far north, and feeder roads branch from it up the various valleys. ▸▸ For Sleeping, Eating and other listings, see pages 377-380.

Pasamayo sand dune

Just north of Ancón, see page 113, the Pasamayo sand dune, stretching for 20 km, comes right down to the seashore. The old road which snakes above the sea is spectacular, but is now closed except to commercial traffic and buses. The new toll road (US$0.85), which goes right over the top, is safe and gives spectacular views over the nearby coast and valleys.

Chancay Valley → *Colour map 3, grid C3.*

Though the Chancay Culture once extended across many valleys to the north of Lima and much evidence of ceramic artefacts can be seen in museums, there are no significant remains in the valley. There are, however, two curiosities to distract the traveller. As the old coastal descends in to the valley a complex of strange, decorated, conical structures made of adobe comes in to view (Km 63). **Eco Truly Park** ① *Eco Truly Tours, Javier Prado Este 185, Lima, T01-421 0016, www.ecotrulypark.org, complex tour, 1 hr, US$2.50*, is run by the Hare Krishna movement and consists of a temple complex, vegetarian restaurant, organic farm and rustic accommodation for visitors in the trulys (conical constructions, F). Mediation, Tai Chi and other courses are run regularly. **Chancay 'castle'** ① *entrance and tour US$1.50*, built by a bohemian descendant of the last Viceroy in the 1920s, is located on the cliff tops in Chancay town. Once visited by the elite of Lima, it is now a decaying recreational centre with restaurants, bars, pools and a museum containing many Chancay culture artefacts.

Just inland from the coastal town of Chancay is **Huaral**, which gives access to the Chancay Valley, up which are the extraordinary, little-visited ruins of **Chiprac**, **Rupac** and **Añay**. Chiprac is a 2½-hour climb from **Huascoy** (see below). The Salvador family has accommodation and Carlos is a recommended guide for the ruins, though a guide is not strictly necessary. It is a good day's walk there and back with time to take photographs and eat. Huascoy celebrates the **Fiesta de San Cristóbal** in the week before Independence (28 July), with a procession, masses, dancing, fireworks and football matches. **Rupac** is best reached from La Florida. Its ruins are the best preserved of the group, though less extensive than Chiprac. All the ruins have complete roofs, which is unique in Peru. For **Añay**, go to Huaral as for the other ruins, then get transport to Huayopampa (basic accommodation) or La Perla from where the ruins can easily be reached. Get a guide to take you there from either village.

Loma de Lachay National Reserve

① *0900-1800, US$1.50, Lima-Huacho buses drop off/pick up from Km 83.*
One kilometre north of the southern turn-off to Sayán is a sandy track signposted to the **Loma de Lachay** (5,070 ha). It is 4 km, one-hour walk up to the guard post.

This small reserve is a typical example of 'loma' habitat, and it holds several important species. Loma vegetation is formed during the winter months, when fog caused by the Humboldt Current drives inland, rises and condenses, and forms a dew on the surrounding landscape. This dew is sufficient to sustain the seasonal loma or 'fog vegetation' that is the home of birds such as the endemic Raimondi's Yellow-finch and Thick-billed miner. Within just 5 km the landscape changes from barren desert to a green carpet, resonating with the sound of birdcalls. In September and October the plants are in bloom and very beautiful. There is a visitors' centre, trails and picnic areas. Camping is permitted at the visitors' centre in the heart of the Reserve, 2 km beyond the guard post, US$3 for up to three days, bring all food and water, especially in the dry season (January-March). The reserve is very popular with Lima residents at the weekend.

Huacho → Colour map 3, grid B3. Population: 35,900.

At Km 101 is Huacho, where you can turn off the Pan-American and head west to Puerto Huacho, which is the outlet for cotton and sugar grown in the rich Huaura valley. There are cotton-seed oil and other factories. The port and sea are sometimes alive with huge jellyfish. There are several basic hotels at Huacho. A turn-off at Km 135 leads to **El Paraíso**, where endless, empty beaches and calm, clear waters attract campers in summer. There is good fishing and windsurfing. Birdwatchers should go to the nearby lagoon, formed by run-off from an irrigation project, where over 100 species have been recorded.

Huacho to Churín

The journey inland from Huacho, up the Huaura Valley, is spectacular. **Sayán**, 30 km inland, is an attractive agricultural town at the base of the Andean foothills. It would be a nicer place to stay en route to Churín than the coastal towns, if there were more choice in the way of hotels. Combis go every half hour to Huacho from Avenida Balta. Buses from Lima for Churín stop at the bridge.

Churín → Colour map 3, grid B3. Population: 2,000. Altitude: 2,080 m.

Beyond Sayán the road follows the Huaura Valley which narrows almost to a gorge before climbing steeply to Churín, one of Peru's best-known spas, with hot, sulphurous springs which are used to cure a number of ailments. The climate is dry, temperatures ranging from 10°C to 32°C. The area is famous for cheese, yoghurt and other natural products. Churín is very popular with Limeños. Accommodation and buses are fully booked at holiday times.

A highly recommended excursion can be made up a side valley, 5 km below Churín, to **Huancahuasi**. The new Huancahuasi baths include a pool that ex-President Fujimori swam in (hot, US$0.70 per person), while on the opposite side of the river the new **Picoy** baths include excellent private pools carved out of the rock (hot, US$0.30 per person). Snacks such as pachamanca are available at riverside stalls. The trip also includes a stop-off at Picoy, which has a remarkable colonial church with a highly carved façade, and at **Chiuchin. Chiuchin baths** ① *US$30 per person for pool; US$0.50 per person for private baths*, are now rather neglected and run down. Combis leave from beside the church in Churín for the two-hour trip 0800-0900, returning 1500-1700. A round trip costs US$3.

Huacho to Barranca

The town of **Huaura**, on the north bank of the Río Huaura river, has grown little over the last 200 years but remains hugely significant in the annals of Peruvian independence. It was here that General San Martín first proclaimed the country's independence from Spain, 8 months prior to the official declaration of independence in Lima. The house with the balcony from which he made the proclamation is now a small museum ① *0900-1700, US$0.75*. Stand on the balcony yourself and re-enact the declaration.

The road passes from the wide valley of Mazo through the irrigated valley of San Felipe. There is more desert and then the cotton-fields of San Nicolás lead to **Supe** at Km 187, a small busy port shipping fishmeal, cotton, sugar and minerals. At **El Aspero**, near Supe, is one of the earliest prehistoric sites in Peru, see page 564.

At **Barranca** (Km 195), 1 km below the town, lies the long, sandy Chorrillos beach, which is windy but popular with surfers. Banco de la Nación accepts TCs, poor rates.

Caral

ⓘ *All visitors must report to the tourist post in the car park. US$3, US$1 with a student card, plus US$6 per group for a guide (Spanish only) if required. Further details can be obtained from Proyecto Especial Caral, Unión 1040, Lima 1, T01-332 5380, www.caralperu.gob.pe. Camping is permitted at the house of the archaeologists working on the site for a small fee. Bring all food.*

A few kilometres before Barranca, a turning to the right (east) leads to Caral, a city 20 km from the coast whose date (about 2,600 BC) and monumental construction are overturning many of the accepted theories of Peruvian archaeology. It appears to be easily the oldest city-state in South America. Tours operate from Lima, see page 379. See also Transport page 379.

The dry, desert site lies on the southern fringes of the Supe valley, along whose flanks there are many more unexcavated ruins. Caral covers 66 ha and contains eight significant pyramidal structures. To date seven have been excavated by archaeologists from the University of San Marcos, Lima. One remains unexcavated, a rounded mound of stone and sand showing no discernible sign of its likely inner contents. The seven pyramids investigated reveal a stone and mortar construction with a yellow and white wash the most common finish, small areas of which remain visible. Archaeologists are undertaking careful renovation upon the existing foundations to re-establish the pyramidal tiers. It is possible to walk around and, in some cases, up on to the pyramids. A viewpoint provides a panorama across the whole site. **Pirámide de Anfiteatro** (the amphitheatre pyramid, 11m high): on the north side of the small pyramid there is a large amphitheatre from which a series of ceremonial rooms rise. **Pirámide de la Huanca** (12 m high): constructed in three tiers with a 23-step staircase leading up to the ceremonial platform. It takes its name from the large stone obelisk (*huanca*) in the centre of the plaza, which it overlooks. The residence of the elite, a complex of well built adobe rooms, abuts the pyramid. **Pirámide de la Galería** (the gallery pyramid, 17 m high): a nearly seven-metre wide stairway leads up to a room sunk into the ceremonial platform lined with huarango wood and containing eight huge whalebone vertebrate seats. **Pirámide Menor** (7.5 m) is the smallest of the pyramids. **Pirámide Mayor** (great pyramid, 153.5 by 110 by 28 m): the largest pyramid with a sunken circular plaza on its south side. Two *lanzones* (obelisk sized stones) frame the two entrances to the plaza and a further *lanzón* sits atop the pyramid which is reached by an impressive 9-metre wide stairway from the plaza. **Pirámide de la Cantera** (the quarry pyramid, 13.5 m high): the only pyramid partly straddling a rock outcrop, much of which was used in its construction. A 4.2-metre wide stairway with 32 steps ascends to the summit, on which is a round, walk-in altar with an outer wall 8 metres in diameter and an inner wall 3.7 metres in diameter, inside which there was a central fireplace. In addition, there is a long building containing eighteen internal niches along each facing wall. **El Templo de Altar Circular** (temple of the circular altar, 4 m high) consists of at least 13 rooms in at least two groupings. Inside one square room there is a 2.7-metre diameter walk-in altar with a central fireplace. Some later adobe ruins of the Chancay era fringe the site. Detailed, illustrated, bilingual (Spanish/English) information panels are located around the site. The site is well organized, criss-crossed by marked paths which must be adhered to. Allow at least two hours to fully visit the site.

Pativilca to Huaraz

The straggling town of Pativilca (Km 203), has a small museum and a good, cheap restaurant, Cornejo. Just beyond town, a good paved road turns east for Huaraz in the Cordillera Blanca, see page 329.

The road at first climbs gradually from the coast. At Km 48, just west of the town of **Chasquitambo** (**Restaurante Delicias**) it reaches Rumi Siki (Rump Rock), with unusual rock formations, including the one that gives the site its name. Beyond this point, the grade is steeper and at Km 120 the chilly pass at 4,080 m is reached. Shortly after, **Laguna Conococha** comes into view, where the Río Santa rises. Delicious trout is available in Conococha village. A dirt road branches off from Conococha to **Chiquián** (see page 365) and the Cordilleras Huayhuash and Raura to the southeast. After crossing a high plateau the main road descends gradually for 47 km until **Catac** (see page 355), where another road branches east to Chavín and on to the Callejón de Conchucos (see page 357). Huaraz is 36 km further on and the road then continues north through the Callejón de Huaylas.

Four kilometres beyond the turn-off to Huaraz, beside the highway, are the well preserved ruins of the Chimú temple of **Paramonga** ⓘ *US$1.20, no buses run to the ruins, only to the port (about 15 mins from Barranca), a taxi from Paramonga and return after waiting costs US$4.50, otherwise take a Barranca-Paramonga port bus, then it's a 3-km walk.* Set on high ground with a view of the ocean, the fortress-like mound is reinforced by eight quadrangular walls rising in tiers to the top of the hill. It is well worth visiting. The town of Paramonga is a small port, 3 km off the Pan-American Highway, 4 km from the ruins and 205 km from Lima.

Between Pativilca and Chimbote the mountains come down to the sea. The road passes by a few very small protected harbours in tiny rock-encircled bays – **Puerto Huarmey**, **Puerto Casma** and **Vesique**. Between Paramonga and Huarmey there are restaurants at Km 223 and 248.

Casma to Huaraz via Pariacoto → *Colour map 3, grid B2.*

Casma, largely destroyed by the 1970 earthquake, has since been rebuilt, partly with Chilean help. It has a pleasant Plaza de Armas, several parks and two markets including a good food market. Sechín ruins are only 5 km away and it is a much nicer place to stay than Chimbote. The weather is usually sunny, hence its title Ciudad del Sol Eterno (City of Eternal Sun).

From Casma a road runs inland over the **Callán pass** (4,224 m) 150 km to Huaraz. It's a difficult but beautiful trip, and worth taking in daylight. Few buses take this route, so check before leaving (see Casma Transport, below).

From Casma the first 30 km are paved, then a good dirt road follows for 30 km to **Pariacoto**. From here to the pass the road is rough, with landslides in the rainy

Casma

Sleeping 🛏
Hostal El Farol 1
Hostal Gregori 2
Hostal Celene 3
Las Dunas 4
Monte Carlo 5

Eating 🍴
Café Lucy 3
Tío Sam 4
Venecia 5

season, but once the Cordillera Negra has been crossed, the wide, gravel road is better with spectacular views of the Cordillera Blanca. To catch the best views, before the Cordillera Blanca becomes covered in cloud (usually in the afternoon), take the earliest bus possible. Sit on the righthand side of the bus.

Sechín → *Colour map 3, grid B2.*

① *www.xanga.com/sechin, 0800-1800, US$1.50, children half price; the ticket is also valid for the museum and Pañamarca (see page 376). Frequent colectivos leave from in front of the market in Casma for US$0.30 per person, but leave early in the morning; or take a moto-taxi for US$1 per person.*

This is one of the most important ruins on the Peruvian coast. It consists of a large square temple completely faced with carved stone monoliths – probably over 500 of them – representing two lines of warriors marching towards the principal entrance from opposite sides. Between each warrior are carvings of men being eviscerated, heads with blood gushing from eyes or mouths, dismembered legs, arms, torsos, ears, eyes and vertebrae.

The mural is thought to narrate the results of a battle, with the fates of the conquerors and the conquered graphically depicted. The style is unique in Peru for its naturalistic vigour. The importance of the site lies in the fact that it is one of the oldest centres in the country to demonstrate the development of warlike activity and the extent to which extreme violence was a part of life.

Within the stone temple is an earlier, pre-ceramic mud temple with painted walls. The complex as a whole forms a temple-palace associated with the development of the local pre-Chavín Sechín culture, dating from about 1600 BC. Three sides of the large stone temple have been excavated and restored. You cannot see the adobe buildings inside the stone walls, which belong to an earlier period. They were later covered up and used as a base for a second storey which, unfortunately, has been completely destroyed.

Some experts think the temple and surroundings were buried on purpose. Others believe it was engulfed by natural disaster. The latter theory is supported by finds of human skeletons. Tombs have been found in front and at the same level as the temple. A wall of a large adobe building under excavation can be seen and runs round the sides and back of the temple.

There is an attractive, shady picnic garden. Photography is best around midday. **Max Uhle Museum** by the ruins has an interesting display of Sechín artefacts and a replica of the façade of the inner adobe temple. If you need a guide ask in advance for Wilder León or Carlos Cuy, who speaks English and French. Outside the museum is a map showing the location of the different archaeological sites in the Casma area.

Two kilometres further along is **Sechín Alto**, two pyramids of the late Chavín period, but these have not yet been extensively excavated. Follow the track to the west (left) at the Km 4 post past the first, smaller pyramid and the farm house. The second pyramid is huge, measuring 300 x 250 x 25 m, covering 50 ha, and once consisted of three levels. Though most of the stone façade has turned to rubble, small sections of the exterior wall and huge entrance stones on the north side are visible. Recent investigations have uncovered some storage chambers and adobe platforms built from unusual conical adobes atop the pyramid.

Among numerous other sites in the area, there are two of particular interest, but a mototaxi is needed to visit them. At Km 15 on the Pariacoto road there are several lines and figures etched in the desert surface, as at Nasca. Though nowhere near as impressive as the Nasca Lines, the figure of a 'warrior' is clearly visible from a nearby hill-top. The lines are up to 25 m long, 20 cms wide and have been dated to 1,000BC. Archaeologists are uncertain as to their purpose.

Chanquillo, located off the Panamericana at Km 361, is a 2,300-year old fortress on a hill-top. It consists of three concentric stone walls with rectangular and circular

buildings inside the interior wall. Some of the original algarrob tree supports remain.
If driving there off the Panamericana, four-wheel-drive is recommended, otherwise
ask for directions from other roads.

Playa Tortugas

Located 2 km east of the Pan-American Highway at Km 391, 18 km north of Casma,
Playa Tortugas is a fishing village on a nice bay with calm water and a rocky beach.
Colectivos leave Casma when full from Plaza Poncianos between the Plaza de Armas
and the market, 0500-2000, US$0.75, 15 minutes. From the north end of the bay the
road continues to **Playa Huayuna**, a windy, closed bay with a sandy beach and a
scallop farm. From the south end of Tortugas a road goes to **Rincón de Piños**, a beach
with wild surf. To the south of Casma, at Km 345, are the sandy beaches of **La Gramita**
and **Las Aldas**.

Chimbote → *Phone code: 043. Colour map 3, grid A2. Population: 296,600.*

Not only is Chimbote Peru's largest fishing port, it is also the
smelliest city in the country, with the powerful stench of the
fishmeal plant permeating every nook and cranny, and one of
the least desirable places, with an palpable sense of danger
lurking around every corner. There are no tourist attractions as
such, in fact the best thing about the place is the road out, but
the city has become increasingly important as an access to the
Cordillera Blanca. It will come as no surprise that this was the
spot where cholera first appeared in South America.

> ‡ *Chimbote is not a safe
> city by day or night. Many
> travellers are attacked and
> robbed here. Take exten-
> sive precautions. Although
> it is small enough to walk
> around, don't; take a taxi
> instead, except for going
> out to eat near your hotel.
> On no account walk from
> the bus station to town.*

The city was damaged by the 1970 earthquake. Today, it has a spacious **Plaza de
Armas**, the cathedral and several public buildings have since been rebuilt, and the
modern Municipal building has a small **art gallery** ① *0900-2000*, downstairs.

North Coast Lima to Chimbote

Chimbote

To Trujillo, Caraz & Northern Peru

Jr Ladislao Espinar
Jr Carlos de los Mares
Jr Leoncio Prado
Jr Manuel Villavicencio
Jr Elías Aguirre
Jr Manuel Ruíz
Av José Gálvez
Jr José Balta
Municipalidad
Plaza de Armas
Av VR Haya de la Torre (J Pardo)
Jr Enrique Palacios
Los Casmeños
Jr Tumbes
Chimbote Tours
To New Bus Terminal, Casma & Lima
Jr Francisco Bolognesi
Plaza Grau
Malecón Grau

Pacific Ocean

N

0 metres 50
0 yards 50

Sleeping		Eating
Cantón & Chifa Cantón **1**	Hostal Antonio's **6**	Residencial El Parque **3**	Aquarius **1**
D'Carlo **2**	Hostal Karol Inn &	San Felipe **10**	Recutecu **2**
Felic **4**	Chifa Jin Lon **8**	Tany **11**	
Gran Hotel Chimú **5**	Hostal Persia **9**		
	Ivansino Inn **12**		

Bathing is forbidden on the bay, though there is a public swimming pool at Vivero Forestal. Flocks of brown pelicans and masked boobies can be seen from the beach. At weekends two-hour boat trips go around the bay to visit the cliffs and islands to see the marine birdlife and rock formations. Take suntan lotion.

The Nepeña Valley

About 25 km south of Chimbote, at Km 405 on the Pan-American Highway, a paved road leads east to the Nepeña Valley, where several pre-Columbian ruins including Cerro Blanco, Pañamarca and Paredones can be found. The valley is dominated by the vast San Jacinto sugar plantation. The village of Capellanía is 11 km from the crossroads. Just beyond are the ruins of **Pañamarca**. The site includes a two-storey stone structure, built on a hill, dating from the formative period (2000 BC-AD 100) and many adobe structures from the Moche period, including three pyramids. Remains of polychromatic murals and animal sculptures can also be seen. Twenty kilometres from Pañamarca, via the villages of San Jacinto and Moro, is the site of **Paredones**, a large stone structure, with 4-m high granite walls and a very impressive gateway known as 'Portada de Paredones' or 'Puerta del Sol'. It is believed to have been a Chavín palace.

Chimbote to Huaraz

The route from Chimbote to Huaraz passes through the **Santa Valley** and the spectacular Cañon del Pato, one of the most thrilling bus trips in all of Peru. Just north of the smelly port, a road branches northeast off the Pan-American Highway and, joining another road from the town of Santa, goes up the Santa valley following the route, including tunnels, of the old Santa Corporation Railway. This used to run as far as **Huallanca** (Ancash – not to be confused with the town of the same name southeast of Huaraz), 140 km up the valley, but the track was largely destroyed by the 1970 earthquake. At Chuquicara, three hours from Chimbote, some 60 km before Huallanca, is **Restaurante Rosales**, a good place to stop for a meal (US$1-1.30 – you can sleep here, too, but it's very rough). The road goes between barren hills and passes poor mining camps. The geology is fantastic, with ravines, whorls, faults and strata at all angles to each other. The colours are also amazing, with rock in various shades. The next village is **Yuramarca** where there is lodging, places to eat, fuel and a police station.

At Huallanca is an impressive hydroelectric plant, built into a mountain, which cannot be visited. There is accommodation at the **Hotel Huascarán**, which is good and friendly; also **Koki's Hostal** and **Fantasy's Pollería**. Fuel is available. Everything closes early.

At the top of the valley by the hydroelectric centre, the road turns right to go through the **Cañon del Pato**. After this point the road is paved for all but a few kilometres around Cooperativa Chiquinquirá. Soon you reach the Callejón de Huaylas and the road south to Caraz and Huaraz (see page 345).

An alternative road for cyclists (and vehicles with a permit) is the private road known as the 'Brasileños', used by the Brazilian company Odebrecht which has built a water channel for the Chavimochic irrigation scheme from the Río Santa to the coast. Permits from the company HQ in San José de Virú; they cost US$6.50. The turn-off is 35 km north of the Santa turning, 15 km south of the bridge in Chao, at Km 482 on the Pan-American Highway. It is a good all-weather road to Tanguche, 22 km from the turn-off, where it continues up the north bank of the Río Santa, crosses a bridge 28 km from Tanguche, to meet up with the public road (which is in worse condition).

North of Chimbote

The highway crosses the valleys of Chao and Virú, and after 137 km reach the first great city of Northern Peru, Trujillo. The Virú valley contains the largest single sand dune in South America, known as Pur Pur. Between Virú and Trujillo the desert is being turned 'green' with asparagus and other crops, thanks to the huge Chavimochic project. It is hard to believe that the irrigated land was once as lifeless as the desert that surrounds it. For different reasons, both Virú and Chavimochic are proposing to promote their tourist potential, the former for its little known archaeological sites and adventure sports, the latter for its economic and social developments. There is basic lodging available and places to eat in both Chao and Virú.

● Sleeping

Huacho p371
D Centenario, Av 28 de Julio 836, T01-232 3731, www.goto/hotelcen. Modern, clean, hot water, with outdoor pool, café, internet, negotiate price for best value. Good choice.
E Hostal Carolina, Av 28 de Julio 590, T/F01-232 4952. The best of the cheaper *hostales* in this area.

Churín p371
All hotels are within a couple of blocks of each other. Prices double at holiday periods.
C Las Termas, Av Larco Herrera 411, T01-237 3094. Has rooms with a pool in the town centre and others up at the La Meseta baths, gardens, restaurant and bar.
E Hostal La Cabaña, Av Larco Herrera 368, T01-237 3023. Clean, rooms with bath, hot water and TV, with attractive courtyard, use of kitchen.

Huacho to Barranca p371
There are many hotels on the main street in Barranca, and plenty of bars and restaurants.
D Chavín, Gálvez 222, Barranca, T01-235 2358. With bathroom, warm water, clean, good value and recommended, though the front rooms are noisy, it also has a restaurant on the 1st floor for lunch and dinner (try *arroz con conchas*), breakfast bar and café opens onto the street by the main entrance.
F Jefferson, Lima 946, Barranca, T01-235 2184. Clean, friendly.

Pativilca to Huaraz p372
C-D La Posada de Huarmey, Panamericana 293, Huarmey, T043-600330. Small, with bath, TV, hot water, clean, good service, restaurant, noisy from road traffic.

Casma to Huaraz via Pariacoto
p373, map p373
Most of the following hotels in Casma are on the Panamericana so rooms at the back will be quieter. The Panamericana is divided into

3 sections: Av Luis Ormeño, Av Tarapacá and Av Nepeña, which leads to the Plaza.
C Hostal El Farol, Túpac Amaru 450, Casma, T043-711064, hostalfaro@yahoo.com. Ask for the cheaper rate in the low season, with bathroom, breakfast extra, hot water, swimming pool, good restaurant, pleasant garden setting surrounded by a wall, parking, good local information.
E Gregori, Luis Ormeño 530, Casma, T043-711073. Cheaper without bathroom, clean, friendly, café downstairs.
E Monte Carlo, Nepeña 370, Casma, T043-711421. Clean, friendly, TV, internet, laundry, good value.
E Hostal Celene Ormeño 595, Casma, T043-711065. Large rooms in a clean and friendly *hostal*.
F Hostal Eddier, on the plaza in Pariacoto. Basic but nice.
F Las Dunas, Ormeño 505, Casma, T/F043-711057. A converted, upgraded and enlarged family home, friendly.
G Alojamiento Sáenz Peña, Gonzalo Salazar, cuadra 5, Pariacoto. Basic.

Playa Tortugas p375
C Las Terrazas, www.lasterrazas.com, open Nov-Apr.
C Hotel Farol Beach Inn, sister to the one in Casma, open all year.

Chimbote p375, map p375
There are plenty of hotels in Chimbote so it is often possible to negotiate a lower rate. The main street, Av Victor Raul Haya de la Torre, is commonly known as José Pardo.
A Cantón, Bolognesi 498, T043-344388. The most modern, luxury hotel in the city, has a good but pricey chifa restaurant.
B Gran Hotel Chimú, José Gálvez 109, T/F043-321741. Price includes breakfast, minibar, safe parking.
B Ivansino Inn, Haya de la Torre 738, T043-321811, ivansino@hotmail.com.

Includes breakfast, comfortable, clean, modern, cable TV, minibar.

C D'Carlo, Villavicencio 376, on the plaza, T/F043-321047. Spacious, friendly, TV, mini-bar, restaurant.

C San Felipe, Haya de la Torre 514, T043-323401. With bathroom, hot water, clean, friendly, comfortable, restaurant.

D Hostal Antonio's, Bolognesi 745, T/F043-32 5783. Clean, hot water, minibar.

D Felic, Haya de la Torre 552, T043-325901.

E without bathroom, clean, quiet. Recommended.

D Hostal Karol Inn, Manuel Ruiz 277, T/F043-321216. Clean, with bathroom, hot water, a good place to stay, family run, laundry service, cafeteria.

D Residencial El Parque, E Palacios 309, on the main plaza, T043-323963. A converted old home, with bathroom, hot water, clean, nice, secure, friendly, no breakfast.

E Hostal El Ensueño, Sáenz Peña 268, 2 blocks from Plaza Central, T043-328662. **F** without bath, very good, safe, welcoming.

E Tany, Palacios 553, T/F043-323411. Clean, friendly, TV, includes breakfast, good value.

F Hostal Persia, L Prado 623, T/F043-342540. Clean, friendly, TV, cheap, but nearer market.

North of Chimbote *p376*

G per person **La Posada**, Carretera Virú con Panamericana. Simple, with cold water; cheap, good restaurant downstairs.

🍴 Eating

Huacho *p371*

Y D'Coco, Túpac Amaru 156. Serves very good soups and steaks. Try the delicious local speciality *salchicha huachana*, scrambled egg and sausage meat.

Huacho to Churín *p371*

Y Jalisco, Balta 342, Sayán. The best place to eat, sometimes has local river shrimp and wine on the menu.

Churín *p371*

Churín is full of restaurants and cafés offering healthy portions and a wide range of *dulces* (desserts). Local delicacies include honey, alfajores, flavoured *manjar blanca*, cheeses and calabaza (a delicious pudding made from squash).

Huacho to Barranca *p371*

YY-Y Tacu Tato, on Chorrillos beach. Has won national prizes for its *tacu tacu*, a Peruvian seafood paella.

Y Cevichería Fujino, Arica 210, Barranca. Good for fish. Try the *tamales*.

Casma to Huaraz via Pariacoto
p373, map p373

In Casma, there are several cheap restaurants on Huarmey. The famous locally made ice cream, Caribe, includes some delicious flavours such as *lúcuma* and *maracuyá*. Available at the *panadería* at Ormeño 545.

Y Tío Sam, Huarmey 138, Casma. Decorated with photos of Sechín, this restaurant specializes in excellent fresh fish dishes, such as *lenguado sudado*.

Y Venecia, Huarmey 204, Casma. Serves local dishes such as goat stew, popular with locals.

Cafés

Café Lucy, Mejía 150, Casma. Opens early for breakfast, which includes fried fish and soups.

Playa Tortugas *p375*

YY-Y Costa Azul, on the seafront as you enter the settlement. One of the best seafood restaurants for fried fish or ceviche.

Chimbote *p375, map p375*

There are several cheap restaurants on Haya de la Torre by the plaza. **Delca**, Haya de la Torre 568, excellent bakery.

Y Aquarius, Haya de la Torre 360. A vegetarian restaurant in the centre.

Y Chifa Jin Lon, adjoining **Hostal Karol Inn**. Well-prepared Chinese food, popular and convenient.

Y Las Flores, Jr Enrique Palacios, 2 blocks west of the plaza. Open 24 hrs, serves good food for breakfast.

Y Recutecu, L Prado 556. Good set lunch with a wide choice.

⛰ Activities and tours

Caral *p372*

For tours from Lima: **Expedition de la Vega, Aventuras de oro**, Malecón Miramar 207, Punta Hermosa, Lima 24, T01-230 7246, www.aventuras-de-oro.com. Fenny is the contact here; she is Dutch, married to a Peruvian.

Tur Al Full Day Tours, Av Larco 101, local 215, Miraflores, T01-242 2970, www.tural.websevicios.net (US$59).

Casma to Huaraz via Pariacoto
p373, map p373
Sechín Tours, in Hostal Monte Carlo, Casma, T043-711421. Organizes tours in the local area. The guide, Renato, only speaks Spanish but has knowledge of local ruins and can be contacted on T043-712528, renatotours@yahoo.com. US$3 per hr, including mototaxi.

◉ Transport

Chancay Valley *p370*
Take a bus to Huaral from Plaza de Acho, by the bullring, in Lima (beware of thieves). Then take the Juan Batista bus, on Tue and Fri, to Huascoy, US$2, 2 km beyond San Juan, which is up beyond Acos, at 3,500 m.

Huacho *p371*
Litsa runs every 30 mins Lima-Huacho, from 0445 to 2045, 2½ hrs, US$2. Also Comité 18, daily *colectivos*, US$2.50. Buses north usually arrive full. They can be caught at the roundabout on the Pan-American. There are regular combis to Sayán. There is a toll post at El Paraíso Huacho, US$0.75 for cars.

Churín *p371*
Trans Estrella Polar, Espadín and Beteta each have several buses a day to Lima, 4-5 hrs, US$5. Some buses from Lima continue to Oyón, 1 hr. From Oyón it is possible to continue over the sierras to Cerro de Pasco on a very rough high altitude road, Trans Javier, 0800, 5 hrs, US$3.50.

Huacho to Barranca *p371*
From Lima to Barranca takes 3½ hrs, US$3. Several bus companies serve the Lima-Barranca route such as Trans América and Trans Paramonga. To continue to Huaraz or northern coastal cities, take a *colectivo* to the service station (El Grifo) at the northern end of Pativilca, where buses from Lima with space stop. There are also *colectivos* to Huarmey, 1¼ hrs, US$2, from where it is also possible to continue northward.

Caral *p372*
Caral is best visited from Barranca or Supe. *Colectivos* leave from Av Lima, 2 blocks from the market, in Barranca for the village of Caral from 0700, 1½ hrs, US$1.50. The ruins are 25 km along a rough road which runs up the Supe valley following the route of an old railway for much of the way. A path leads from the road across the valley to the ruins, though the river may be impassable when the rains fall in the Andes (Dec-Mar), 30 mins. The *colectivos* can also be picked up in Supe or at the signposted turn-off to the ruins on the Panamericana at Km 185, if they have room (there is some confusion with the km posts along this section of the Panamericana). Alternatively, a taxi in Barranca or Supe may be prepared to take you, US$20, including a 2-hr wait while you visit the ruins. Caral can also be approached from the south along a rough road, 28 km, passing through the Granja Toshi chicken farm. There is no regular transport but it may be possible to hire one of the taxis waiting at the Km 160 turn-off on the Panamericana, 2 hrs, US$20, including a 2-hr wait. This route is unsigned but may be the only way to reach the ruins in the rainy season.

Casma to Huaraz via Pariacoto
p373, map p373
There are half hourly buses from Lima to Chimbote which can drop you off in Casma, 370 km, 6 hrs, US$5. If going to Lima many of the buses from Trujillo and Chimbote stop briefly opposite the petrol station, block 1 of Ormeño or, if they have small offices, along blocks 1-5 of Av Ormeño. To Chimbote, 55 km, it is easiest to take a Los Casmeños *colectivo*, huge old Dodge cars, which depart when full from in front of the petrol station, block 1 of Ormeño, or from plaza Poncianos, 45 mins, US$1.20. To Trujillo it is best to go first to Chimbote bus station and then take an América Express bus (see Chimbote p370). To Huaraz (150km), via Pariacoto, buses come from Chimbote, 6-7 hrs, US$4.25 (for a description of the route see above). Transportes Huandoy, Ormeño 166, T043-712336, departs at 0700, 1100 and 1400, while Yungay Express, Ormeño 158, departs

● *For an explanation of sleeping and eating price codes used in this guide, see inside the*
● *front cover. Other relevant information is found in Essentials, pages 61-66.*

at 0600, 0800 and 1400. Most Huaraz buses go via Pativilca, which is further but the road is better, 6 hrs, US$5, **Móvil Tours** and **Trans Chinchaysuyo**, all run at night.

Chimbote *p375, map p375*
Air

The airport is at the south end of town, but there are no scheduled flights.

Bus

The bus station is 4 km south of the city centre on Av Meiggs. Some buses to/from places north of Chimbote will drop people off in the centre if they only have hand luggage, but not in a safe area. Likewise *colectivo* taxis from Casma, drop passengers near the market; ask to be let out at the bus terminal. Always go to the terminal and, under no circumstances, walk from there to the centre: a *colectivo* costs US$0.30, taxi US$1. There are no hotels near the terminal, but some bus companies have ticket offices in the centre. If arriving from Caraz via the Cañón del Pato there is usually time to make a connection to Casma or Trujillo/Huanchaco and avoid overnighting in Chimbote. If travelling to Caraz, however, overnighting in Chimbote is almost unavoidable. Casma is near enough to stay in but you will need to buy your Caraz ticket the day before; the bus station is on the Casma side of Chimbote.

From **Lima** to Chimbote, 420 km, 6 hrs, US$7-9. Buses depart every 30 mins, **Trans Isla Blanca** has the most frequent service, **Línea** (T043-322416), **ECS** (T043-318132) and **Oltursa** (T043-328275). To **Trujillo**, 130 km, 2 hrs, US$1.20, **América Express** have buses every 20 mins until 2100, after which you must hope for Lima buses passing through with space. To **Huaraz** most companies, with the best buses, go the 'long way round', ie down the Panamericana to Pativilca, then up the paved highway, 7 hrs, US$8.45. The best companies are **Móvil Tours**, T043-353616,

and **Chinchaysuyo**; both start in Trujillo, their buses continue on to **Caraz**. To **Huaraz** via Pariacoto, 7 hrs, US$5.50, **Trans Huandoy** (Etseturh), T043-354024, at 0600, 1000 and 1300, 7 hrs, US$5.50, and **Yungay Express** at 0500, 0700 and 1300. See above for a description of this route. To **Caraz** via Cañón del Pato, 7-8 hrs, US$7, **Yungay Express** at 0830 (for a description of this route see above). To guarantee a seat on this bus if coming from Trujillo or Casma, T043-321235 the evening before and they will meet your incoming bus and transfer you. To **Sihuas**, 10 hrs, US$7, **Trans Andino** is the only company with a daytime bus at 0800 on Wed, Fri and Sun.

Taxi
Radio taxis from T043-334433.

🅓 Directory

Casma to Huaraz via Pariacoto
p373, map p373
Banks Good rates for cash and TCs, no commission, at **BCP**, Bolívar 111, Casma. Dollars can be changed in Casma at Ormeño 529 and Nepeña 384. **Internet** Café on west side of Plaza, Casma. 0900-2100. **Post** Fernando Loparte, ½ block from Plaza de Armas, Casma.

Chimbote *p375, map p375*
Banks **BCP** and **Interbank**, both on Bolognesi and M Ruiz. For TCs and cash. **Casa Arroyo**, M Ruiz 292. For cash only. There are other casas and street changers along M Ruiz between Bolognesi and VR Haya de la Torre. **Internet** At Palacios 518, Aguirre 278 and J.Pardo 660. **Post Serpost**, Jr Tumbes behind market. Also at Palacios 441. **Telephone Telefónica** main office, Tumbes 356. National and international fax and phone. Also at Haya de la Torre 420 and M Ruiz 253.

Trujillo → *Phone code: 044. Colour map 3, grid A1. Population: 850,000.*

Trujillo, capital of the Department of La Libertad, disputes the title of second city of Peru with Arequipa. Founded by Diego de Almagro in 1534 as an express assignment ordered by Francisco Pizarro, the city was named after the latter's native town in Spain. There is enough here to hold the attention for several days. The area abounds

in pre-Columbian sites, there are beaches and good surfing within easy reach and the 381
city itself still has many old churches and graceful colonial homes, built during the
reigns of the viceroys. ▸▸ For Sleeping, Eating and other listings, see pages 384-390.

Ins and outs

Getting there The airport is to the west of town. You will enter town along Avenida
Mansiche. There is no central bus terminal and none of the bus stations is in the centre.
They are spread out on three sides the city, beyond the inner ring road, Avenida España.
Plenty of taxis and *colectivos* can be found at the terminals to get you to your hotel
(insist on being taken to the hotel of your choice). ▸▸ *See Transport page 388 for more details.*

Getting around With its compact colonial centre and mild,
spring-like climate, Trujillo is best explored on foot. However,
should you need a taxi, there are plenty of them. Always use
official taxis, which are mainly yellow. The major sites outside
the city, Chan Chán, the Moche pyramids and Huanchaco beach
are easily reached by public transport or taxi/*colectivo*, but care
is needed when walking around. Beware of overcharging, check
fares with locals. A taxi can be hired from in front of the Hotel

‡ *The very centre of Trujillo
has confusing double
street names: the smaller
printed name is that
generally shown on maps,
in guide books and in
general use.*

Libertador for US$7 an hour about the same rate as a tour with an independent guide
or travel agent for one to two people. A number of recommended guides run expert
tours to these and other places.

Tourist information i perú ① *Municipalidad, Pizarro 402, p 2, Plaza Mayor, T044-
294561, iperutrujillo@prompertu.gob.pe, Mon-Sat 0800-1900, Sun 0800- 1400.* As
well as the obvious places (bus terminals, markets, ATMs), take care anywhere beyond
the inner ring road, Avenida España, and in the Sánchez Carrión district (southwest of
Avenida España around Avenida Los Incas) at night. Tourists may be approached by
vendors selling *huacos* and necklaces from the Chimú period. The export of these items
is strictly illegal if they are genuine, but they almost certainly aren't.

Sights

Plaza Mayor

The focal point is the pleasant and spacious Plaza Mayor (used more commonly than
Plaza de Armas here). The prominent sculpture represents agriculture, commerce,
education, art, slavery, action and liberation, crowned by a young man holding a torch
depicting liberty. Fronting it is the **Cathedral**, dating from 1666, with its museum of
religious paintings and sculptures next door. Also on the plaza are the Hotel Libertador,
the colonial style Sociedad de Beneficencia Pública de Trujillo and the Municipalidad.

The **Universidad de La Libertad**, second only to that of San Marcos at Lima, was
founded in 1824. Two beautiful colonial mansions on the plaza have been taken over.
The Banco Central de Reserva is in the Colonial-style **Casa Urquiaga (or Calonge)**,
① *Pizarro 446, Mon-Fri, 0900-1500, Sat-Sun 1000-1330*, free guided tour lasts 30
minutes, take passport. It contains valuable pre-Columbian ceramics. The other is
Casa Bracamonte (or Lizarzaburu), at Independencia 441, with occasional exhibits.
Opposite the Cathedral on Independencia, is the **Caja Rural** (officially known as Casa
Garci Olguín), recently restored but boasting the oldest façade in the city, baroque
and rococo features and Moorish-style murals. The buildings that surround the Plaza,
and many others in the vicinity, are painted in bright pastel colours. Street lamps are
on brackets, adding to the charm of the centre.

North and east of the Plaza Mayor

In **San Francisco** ① *on the corner of Gamarra and Independencia*, is the pulpit which
survived the earthquake of Saint Valentine's Day in 1619. It has three golden altars

North Coast Trujillo

To Emtrafesa Buses

To Arco Iris,
Pampas, Chicama,
Chicayo &
Cajamarca

To Esmeralda, Chan Chán, Airport & Huanchaco

Old City Wall
Santa Rosa
Coliseo
Gran Chimú
Estadio
Mansiche
Museo Cassinelli
Manuel Vera
Colón
Museo del
Juguete
Santa Clara
EC Office
Merpisa
Supermarket
Palacio
Iturregui
San
Francisco
Casa Ganoza
Chopitea
Santa Ana
Guía Tours
Casa de la
Emancipación
Línea Bus Office
Caja
Rural
INC
Cathedral
Librería
Peruana
Trujillo Tours
Casa
Bracamonte
La Merced
Casa de los
Condes de
Aranda
Cabinas Públicas
Universidad
de la Libertad
Museo de Zoología
de Juan Ormea
Casa del Mariscal
de Orbegoso
Plaza
Mayor
Casa
Urquiaga
Central Market
San Agustín
La Compañía
Municipalidad
Delta Net
Club
Libertad
University
Santo
Domingo
LAN
Casa del
Mayorazgo
de Facalá
Belén
Chacón
Tours

Avenidas/streets labels:
Av Miraflores, De la Torre, Av N de Piérola, Av Mansiche, Jorge Cháves, Gral Pedro Muñiz, Raimondi, Av España, Daniel Carrión, Jesús de Nazareth, Juan Pablo I, San Martín, Zepita, Salaverry, Independencia, Francisco Pizarro, Alfonso Ugarte, Av España, Av Larco, Diego de Almagro, Bolognesi, Orbegoso, Nicaragua

N
0 metres 100
0 yards 100

Sleeping
Almagro 18 *E4*
Chan Chán Inn 2 *A5*
Clara Bravo & Michael
White 9 *F6*
Colonial 3 *C4*
Continental 4 *D4*
El Gran Marqués 19 *F2*

El Peregrino 5 *B4*
Gran Bolívar 6 *B5*
Hospedaje El Conde
de Arce 16 *C3*
Hostal Americano 7 *C4*
Hostería El Sol 20 *A1*
La Alameda del
Peregrino 10 *B4*
Libertador 11 *D3*
Los Conquistadores 12 *E3*
Malibu Hostal 8 *F2*
Primavera 13 *A1*
Residencial Vanini 1 *F1*
Saint Germain 14 *C4*

San Martín 15 *B3*
Turismo 17 *D5*

Eating
ABC 1 *C3*
Café Amaretto 3 *C3*
Cafetería Buenos
Aires 2 *D3*
El Chileno 7 *E4*
El Mochica 9 *E3*
El Sol 8 *C4*
Isla Bonita 4 *C3*
Juguería San
Agustín 10 *D4*

Milenium 12 *C3*
Panadería José
Antonio 13 *D4*
Panadería Sandoval 14 *E5*
PASE 15 *C3*
Pizzería Pizzanino 16 *E1*
Rincón de Vallejo 18 *C3*
Romano, Asturias,
Demarco & Oviedo 19 *C4*
Romano-Rincón
Criollo 20 *F3*
Sal y Pimienta 21 *B3*

To 1, 3, 19 & Móvil Tours

To Huamachuco
& Otuzco

To Ovalo Grau, Southern Bus Terminal,
Línea, Chimbote & Lima

Plaza de Toros

Unión Market

El Carmen
San Lorenzo

Museo de Arqueología

Dirección Regional de Turismo

Mercado Mayorista

⑤ ⑥

Bars & clubs 🍸
Canana **5** *B3*
Taverna Chelsea **22** *B5*

Buses 🚌
Cruz del Sur **3** *A5*
Buses to
  Huaca del Sol y
  de la Luna **4** *D6*
Combi 'B' & 'H' to
  Huanchaco,
  Chan Chán & Huaca La
  Esmeralda **5** *B1, B3 & B5*
Chinchaysuyo **6** *B2*

CIAL **7** *A5*
ITTSA **8** *B2 & C2*
Turismo Díaz **9** *B1*
Oltursa & Flores **10** *A5*
Ormeño **11** *A5*
Línea North
  Terminal & El Dorado
  old terminal **12** *C2*

and others inside. **Casa Ganoza Chopitea** ① *Independencia 630 opposite San Francisco church*, is architecturally the most representative house in the city and considered the most outstanding of the viceroyalty. It combines Baroque and Rococo styles. Continuing up Independencia you come to the **Museo del Juguete** ① *Independencia 705 y Junín, Mon-Sat 1000-1800, US$0.85, children US$0.30*, the toy museum. It contains examples from prehistoric times to 1950, collected by painter Gerardo Chávez. Downstairs is the **Espacio Cultural Angelmira** ① *0900-2300*, with a café bar; in a restored *casona*, worth a visit. Turn off Independencia to **Santa Clara**, on the fourth block of Junín (open Sunday only). The next cross street is Pizarro. Turn left to **Plazuela El Recreo** at the north end of Pizarro. It was known as El Estanque during the colonial period as it housed a pool from which the city's water was distributed. A marble fountain by Eiffel now stands in the square, transferred from the Plaza de Armas, fronted by restaurants.

If you head back to the Plaza de Armas, you pass the spacious 18th-century **Palacio Iturregui**, now occu- pied by the **Club Central** ① *Jr Pizarro 688, Mon-Sat 1100-1800*. To enter the patio is free, but to see more of the palace and the ceramics collection costs US$1.45. This exclusive social centre of Trujillo houses a private collection of ceramics. **Casa de la Emancipación** ① *Jr Pizarro 610, Banco Continental, 0900-1300 and 1700-2000*, is where independence from Spain was planned and was the first seat of government and congress in Peru. The first room on the right as you go in displays plans and the history of the building. There are exhibits on the life of the poet César Vallejo and Bishop Martínez Compagñon (1737-1797), whose tours took him all round northern Peru. There are watercolours of life in the 18th century. Before you arrive back at the Plaza you come to the 17th-century church of **La Merced** ① *Pizarro 550, US$2*, with picturesque moulded figures below the dome, has been restored. It has a mock rococo organ above the

North Coast Trujillo

choir stalls and *retablos* from the 17th century which, unusually, are painted on the walls, from the time before free-standing altars were used.

If you leave the Plaza on Orbegoso, the **Casa del Mariscal de Orbegoso** ① *Orbegoso 553, open during banking hours from 0930, free*, is at the first junction. It was named after the ex-President, General Luis José de Orbegoso, is the Museo de la República, owned by Banco de Crédito. It holds temporary exhibitions and cultural events most Thursday evenings. Opposite is **San Agustín** ① *Bolívar at the 6th block of Mcal Orbegoso*. Turn up Bolívar and go one block right for the **Museo de Arqueología** ① *Casa Risco, Junín 682 y Ayacucho, T044-249322, Tue-Fri 0900- 1300, 1500-1900, Sat and Sun 0930-1600. US$1.40*. Guided tours in Spanish available. It houses a large collection of thematic exhibits from prehispanic cultures of the area. Further up Bolívar is the church and monastery of **El Carmen** ① *Colón y Bolívar, church and pinacoteca open Mon-Sat 0900-1300, US$0.85*. The church is open for mass at 0700-0730 Sunday. Described as the 'most valuable jewel of colonial art in Trujillo', El Carmen has five gilt altars, balconies and religious paintings. Next door is the Pinacoteca Carmelita, with more paintings. It includes a room on picture restoration.

South and west of the Plaza Mayor

Museo de Zoología de Juan Ormea ① *Jr San Martín 368, Mon-Fri 0700-1900, US$0.60*, has interesting displays of Peruvian animals. **La Compañía**, the former Jesuit church near Plaza de Armas, is now an auditorium for cultural events. Other churches in this area are **Santo Domingo** ① *on the 4th block of Bolognesi*, and **Belén** ① *on the 6th block of Almagro*. The **Casa del Mayorazgo de Facalá** ① *Pizarro 314*, which is now the Banco Wiese, was owned by Don Pedro de Tinoco whose wife embroidered the first Peruvian flag to be hoisted following Trujillo's independence from Spanish rule in 1820.

Northwest of the Plaza Mayor

Heading northwest from Plaza, you pass **Santa Ana** ① *on the 2nd block of Mcal Orbegoso*, one of the three 'iglesias menores'. The others were San Lorenzo and Santa Rosa. The street becomes Avenida Mansiche which leads to the routes out of town. The basement of the **Cassinelli** garage ① *on the fork of the Pan-American and Huanchaco roads, 0915-1230, 1515-1830, US$1.50*, contains a superb private collection of Mochica and Chimú pottery and is highly recommended. The caretaker sometimes gives a thorough explanation including demonstrations of the whistling huacos and is knowledgeable on any subject you care to discuss (in Spanish).

Las Delicias

Las Delicias is a clean beach with good surf, about 25 minutes by *colectivo* (US$0.30) and 15 minutes by taxi from Trujillo. *Colectivos* leave from Las Incas y Atahualpa.

● Sleeping

L Libertador, Independencia 485 on Plaza de Armas, T044-232741, trujillo@libertador. com.pe. Price includes tax, pool (can be used by non-guests if they buy a drink), cafeteria and restaurant, continental breakfast US$5, excellent buffet lunch on Sun. Recommended.

AL El Gran Marqués, Díaz de Cienfuegos 145-147, Urb La Merced, T/F044-249366, www.elgranmarques.com. Price includes tax and breakfast, modern, free internet connection in rooms, pool, sauna, jacuzzi,

restaurant. Recommended.

AL Los Conquistadores, Diego de Almagro 586, T044-203350, losconquistadores@ viabcp.com. Price includes tax and American breakfast, bar, restaurant, garage and internet connection, very comfortable.

A-B Gran Bolívar, Bolívar 957, T044-222090, www.granbolivarhotel.com. Price includes breakfast, airport transfer and welcome drink, in converted 18th-century house, internet, café, bar, gym and parking.

B La Alameda del Peregrino, Jr Pizarro 879, T044-470512, www.perunorte.com/alameda peregrino. Includes breakfast, cable TV, internet service, restaurant, bar, café, safe, money exchange. Recommended. Also **B El Peregrino**, Independencia 978, T044-203990, www.elperegrinohotel.com. which is convenient for the Lima buses.

B Malibu Hostal, Av Larco 1471, T044-284811, http://hostalmalibu.com. A business hotel near the Ovalo Larco, with all services, comfortable rooms, bar-restaurant, airport transfer.

B Saint Germain, Junín 585, T044-208102, www.perunorte.com/saintgermain. Price includes breakfast. With bath, hot water, TV, internet, laundry, safe, parking.

C Continental, Gamarra 663, T044-241607, F249881. Opposite the market, includes good buffet breakfast, clean, good, safe, the staff are very helpful.

C-D Colonial, Independencia 618, T044-258261, hostcolonialtruji@hotmail. com. Price includes basic breakfast. Clean, attractive, friendly, rooms are a bit small, hot showers, good restaurant, especially for the set lunch. Recommended.

D Almagro, Jr Almagro 748, T044-223845. New hotel with cable TV, hot water, cafetería (breakfast extra), good.

D Residencial Vanini, Av Larco 237, T044-200878. Outside Av España in location, a good option but not in the centre, 9 rooms.

D San Martín, San Martín 749, T/F044-252311, www.publinet.com.pe/hotelsan martin. Good value, with bath and TV, small restaurant, good for breakfast, clean but noisy from neighbouring establishments. Recommended.

D Turismo, Gamarra 747, T044-244181. Price includes continental breakfast. Central hotel with good services, cable TV, restaurant, parking and travel agency.

E Hostal Americano, Pizarro 764, T044-241361. A vast, rambling old building, which is getting rundown, rooms without bathrooms are noisy and very basic, most rooms don't have window (Nos 134 and 137, and those either side of 303, have windows, balconies and good views), cold water only, friendly staff, but mixed reports.

E Hostería El Sol, Brillantes 224, Urb Santa Inés, T044-231933, near bus terminals on Av Nicolás de Piérola. With hot shower, restaurant, all meals available for US$2.60.

E per person Hostal Wyllie's, Raimondi 318, T044-205671. Hot water, good service, negotiate price.

E Primavera, Av N de Piérola 872, Urb Primavera, T044-231915, F257399. With bathroom, hot water, restaurant, bar, pool.

F per person Chan Chán Inn, Av Ejército 307, T/F044-294281, mocheperu @hotmail.com. Close to several bus terminals so very noisy from 0500 till late at night, price includes breakfast (cheaper without), popular with backpackers, luggage store, café, laundry, internet, money exchange and information.

F per person Clara Bravo and Michael White, Cahuide 495, T044-243347, www. xanga.com/TrujilloPeru. With bath, groups can be accommodated, good meals on request, very helpful and friendly, loads of information available, meeting place and lots going on, many languages spoken (see Activities and tours p387). Recommended. Restaurants and fast internet nearby.

F per person Hospedaje El Conde de Arce, Independencia 577, T044-943236. Small, central, rooms with bath, cheaper rates available, convenient. Recommended.

● Eating

It's difficult to find a meal before 0800. A speciality is *shambar*, a thick minestrone made with gammon. There are five cheap seafood restaurants at Plazuela El Recreo, at the end of Pizarro. For really cheap meals try the central market at Grau y Ayacucho.

Ψ Demarco, Pizarro 725. Good food and excellent desserts at this place in a cluster of restaurants in the centre.

Ψ El Mochica, Bolívar 462. Typical restaurant with a good reputation, the food is good and, on special occasions, has live music. There is another branch on the road to Las Delicias beach and another in Huanchaco.

Ψ Romano, Pizarro 747. International food, good menús, breakfasts, coffee and cakes, but slow service.

¶¶ **Romano-Rincón Criollo**, Estados Unidos 162, Urb El Recreo, a 10-min walk from the centre, T044-244207. Specializes in northern Peruvian cuisine and has a good value lunch menú for US$2 in smart surroundings.

¶¶ **Pizzería Pizzanino**, Av Juan Pablo II 183, Urb San Andrés, opposite the University, T044-263105. Recommended for pizzas, also pasta, meats and desserts, open in evenings.

¶¶-¶ **Isla Bonita**, Orbegoso 341, T044-204272. Mon-Sat 0800-2300. Run by a Peruvian-Swiss couple, offering a wide variety of dishes, including Swiss and other European fare. They also do breakfast, lunch menú and have a bar, German, Italian and French spoken. Recommended.

¶ **ABC**, Orbegoso 290 y San Martín. Good for chicken.

¶ **Asturias**, Pizarro 741. Nice café with excellent meals, good juices and snacks.

¶ **Café Oviedo**, Pizarro 737. With vegetarian options, good salads, helpful.

¶ **El Sol**, Pizarro 660. The original and best vegetarian, cheap set meals, also serves other dishes.

¶ **Juguería San Agustín**, Bolívar 526. Good juices, good menú, popular, excellent value.

¶ **La Selecta**, Pizarro 870. Set lunch for US$1.75, good value, also *heladería*.

¶ **Milenium**, Gamarra 316. A cheap vegetarian place.

¶ **PASE**, Gamarra 353, T/F044-234715. Hotel and restaurant school, good menú US$1.70 and US$2.25, served Mon-Sat 1300-1600, also open Thu-Sat 1900-2300, but small portions.

¶ **Rincón de Vallejo**, Orbegoso 303. Good menú, typical dishes, very crowded at peak times.

¶ **Sal y Pimienta**, Colón 201. Very popular for lunch, US$1 and US$1.85, close to buses for Huanchaco and Chan Chán.

Cafés

Café Amaretto, Gamarra 368. Good selection of coffees, sweets, snacks and drinks.

Cafetería Buenos Aires, Pizarro 332, near Banco Wiese. Substantial breakfasts, very busy at peak times.

El Chileno, Ayacucho 408. Café and ice cream parlour, popular.

Kasumy, Pizarro 857. Good value food and beer, beware overcharging.

Fitopán, Bolívar 406. Good selection of breads, also has a small cafeteria for lunch, very popular.

Panadería José Antonio, Ayacucho 561-65, in the Mercado Central. Another good bakery.

Panadería Sandoval, Orbegoso 822. Good bread selection.

◑ Bars and clubs

Canana, San Martín 788, T044-232503. Bars and restaurant, disco, live music at weekends (US$1.50-3 depending on the show), video screens (also has travel agency). Recommended, but take care on leaving.

Las Tinajas, Pizarro 389, Plaza Mayor. A pub-disco with live rock music and *peña* on Sat.

Luna Rota, América Sur 2119, at the end of Huayna Capac. Very popular with locals.

Nuestro Bar, Bolognesi 502. A nice bar.

Taverna Chelsea, Estete 675, T044-257032. Bar, restaurant, live Salsa at weekends (US$4 entry), exclusive and lively. Recommended.

◉ Festivals and events

The two most important festivals are the **National Marinera Contest** and the **Festival Internacional de La Primavera**. The former is held at the end of **Jan** for 2 weeks and consists of hundreds of couples competing in six categories, from children to seniors (see p594). This event is organized by the Club Libertad and has taken place since 1960. **Festival de la Primavera** is held in the last week in **Sep**. Organized by the Club de Leones, it is a celebration of the arrival of Spring and has grown over the years to become one of Peru's most important tourist events. The final parade (*corso*) has plenty to enjoy, with many local dancers, dog owners' clubs, schools parades, and so on. Those who are strongly opposed to beauty pageants may want to give it a miss as there are floats with beauty queens from South and North America participating (but it's all very decorous). Other days feature cultural events (some philanthropic/charitable), and, above all, Trujillo's famous Caballos de Paso, a fine breed of horses with a tripping gait that has made them renowned worldwide. These horses, a Spanish legacy, have been immortalized in Peruvian waltzes. Riders still compete in their own form of the Marinera dance and buyers from around the world congregate to see them shown at the Spring Festival (see www.rcp.net.pe/rcp/caballos). Other major festivals include the **Feria de San José** held in Las Delicias on **19-22 Mar**. **Festival de la Música** takes place on **18 Jun**.

O Shopping

Trujillo is renowned for its leather and shoe industry. Prices for shoes are very attractive, but sizes over European 42 are hard to find. Try on both sides of block 18 of Av España, or Alameda del Calzado, Av España, block 20.

Bookshops
Librería Adriatica, Jr Junín 565, T044-291569, libreria@adriaticaperu.com. A very good bookshop, stocks Footprint. **Librería Peruana**, Pizarro 505, just off the Plaza Mayor. Has the best selection in town, ask for Sra Inés Guerra de Guijón.

Camera repairs
Fotolab, Av España 2755, T044-295590. Hugo Guevara repairs all makes, film developing. **Fotovisión Para Tí**, Pizarro 523, also repairs cameras.

Handicrafts
APIAT, Av España near Zela, open daily 0900-2300, Sun 0900-1400. The largest crafts market in Trujillo, selling ceramics, woodcarvings, totora boats, etc, and kiosks selling shoes and leather goods at competitive prices. **Artesanía del Norte**, Independencia 616. A branch of the shop which can be found in Huanchaco. **Liga de Artesanos**, Colón 423. **Los Tallanes**, San Martín 455. For souvenirs, artworks and antiques.

Markets
Mercado Central, Gamarra, Ayacucho and Pasaje San Agustín. **Mercado Mayorista** between Sinchi Roca and Av Los Incas (not a safe zone).

▲ Activities and tours

Caballos de paso
La Asociación de Criadores de Caballos de Paso Peruanos has an enclosure with plots

for each member's house and stables on the Vía de Evitamiento, just north of its junction with Av Larco. Owners may be prepared to show visitors around.
El Palmar, stables, on the Vía de Evitamiento near **Hotel El Golf**, charges US$12 per person to see and maybe ride the horses at its stables. Book the day before at the office on Pizarro, on the Plaza Mayor.
For group visits to **Manucci** stables, just south of the Huaca del Sol, and **Vásquez Nacarino** at Paijan, contact Clara Bravo and Michael White, see below.

Cycling
Bicycle Tours, Bolognesi 350, T044-993 9064 (mob), peruguide@hotmail.com.

Swimming
Academia Berendson, Bolognesi 231, heated pool. There's an outdoor swimming pool next to Mansiche stadium, where buses leave for Chan Chán and Huanchaco. Open 0900-1300 and 1600-1800, entry US$0.50.

Tour operators
Prices vary and competition is fierce so shop around for the best deal. Average tour costs are: to Chan Chán, El Dragón and Huanchaco, 3 hrs for US$8.50 per person, not including entrances. To Huacas del Sol and de la Luna, 2 hrs for US$7 per person. To El Brujo, US$17 per person. City tours cost US$5.65 per person (minimum of 2 people; discounts for 4 or more). Few agencies run tours on Sun and often only at fixed times on other days. Check exactly which sites are included in the tour, if transport, entry and guide are included and whether guides speak anything other than Spanish.
Chacón Tours, Av España 106-112, T044-255212. Open Sat afternoon and Sun morning. Recommended.
Guía Tours, Independencia 580, T044-234856, guiatour@amauta.rcp.net.pe. Also Western Union agent. Recommended.
Tesores del Perú, Pizarro 575, of 03, T044-582381, oscarcampos10@hotmail.com. Oscar Campos Santa María organizes custom-made tours at affordable prices to archaeological sites, as far as Lambayeque.
Trujillo Tours, San Martín y Almagro 301, T044-257518, ttours@pol.com.pe. Work with Lima Tours.

Many hotels work on a commission basis with taxi drivers and travel agencies. If you decide on a guide, make your own direct approach. The tourist police (see Information, above) has a list of official guides; average cost is US$7 per hr. **Clara Bravo**, Cahuide 495, T044-243347, www.xanga.com/TrujilloPeru. An experienced tourist guide with her own transport, who speaks Spanish, German and understands Italian. She takes tourists on extended circuits of the region and is good for information (archaeological tour US$16 for 6 hrs, city tour US$7 per person, US$53 per car to El Brujo, with extension to Sipán, Brüning Museum and Túcume possible). Clara works with English chartered accountant **Michael White** (same address, microbewhite @yahoo.com) who speaks German, French and Italian and provides transport. He is very knowledgeable about tourist sites. They run tours any day of the week; 24-hr attention. They can also arrange tours to see and possibly ride caballos de paso.

Laura Durán, T044-281590, lauraduran@ yahoo.com. Speaks English, German and some Hebrew, lots of information, very accommodating.

Zaby Miranda Acosta, Camelias 315, Huanchaco, T044-461246, Zaby_miranda@ hotmail.com. Works at the tourist office, speaks German, Italian, US$10 per day.

José Ocas Cuenca, Túpac Amaru 596, Villa del Mar, T044-583556, jocas_cuenca@hot mail.com. Speaks English, German and French, very knowledgeable, plays an ancient flute.

Jannet Rojas Sánchez, T044-401184, jannarojas@hotmail.com. Speaks English, enthusiastic, works independently and for **Guía Tours**.

José Soto Ríos, Atahualpa 514, dpto 3, T044-251489. He speaks English and French.

Pedro Puerta T044-960 9603 (mob), works with Guía Tours and independently.

Celio Eduardo Roldán, celioroldan@hot mail.com. Helpful and informative taxi driver. Other experienced guides are **Oscar and Gustavo Prada Marga**, Miguel Grau 169, Villa del Mar, or at Chan Chán.

⊖ Transport

Air

There are daily flights to and from **Lima** with **Aero Cóndor** and **Lan**. To **Cajamarca** daily with **Aero Cóndor**. Taxi to airport costs US$4; or take a bus or *colectivo* to Huanchaco, get out at airport turn-off then walk 2 km (US$0.25). **Airline offices** Aero Cóndor, T044- 255212. **Lan**, Pizarro 340-42, T044-221469.

Bus

Local Buses and combis, on all routes, cost US$0.15-0.30; *colectivos* (cars carrying six passengers), US$0.25, tend to run on main avenues starting from Av España. **Long distance** Concentrations of companies are around Avs Ejército/ Amazonas/Túpac Amaru; on Av Nicolás de Piérola, blocks 10-13 for northbound buses; and on Av La Marina, between Ovalos Grau and La Marina, for southbound buses. The better bus companies maintain their own terminals. To and from **Lima**, 561 km on a good road, 8 hrs in the better class buses, average fare US$14.30-18.50 in luxury classes, 10 hrs in the cheaper buses, US$7.15-11.50. There are many bus companies doing this route, among those recommended are: Ormeño, Av Ejército 233, T044-259782, 3 levels of service, 5 daily; Cruz del Sur, Amazonas 437 near Av Ejército, T044-261801; Turismo Días, Nicolás de Piérola 1079 on Panamericana Norte, T044-201237, leaves at 2230; Línea, Av América Sur 2855, T044-297000, ticket office at San Martín y Orbegoso, T245181, 3 levels of service, also to Chimbote and Chiclayo hourly, Huaraz 2100, 9 hrs, US$8.65, Cajamarca 5 a day, US$4.25-10, and Chiclayo, US$3.35 (from Carrión by Av Mansiche, T044-235847, on the hr), and Piura, 2300, US$7. Also Flores (Av Ejército 350, T044-208250), Ittsa (Av Mansiche 145, T044-251415; No 431 for northern destinations, T044-222541), Móvil Tours (Av América Sur 3959 – Ovalo Larco, T044-286538). Oltursa, Av Ejército 342, T044-263055, offers a bus cama service to Lima, with full reclining seats, a/c, heating, meals and drinks, depart at 2200, with connection at Lima for Arequipa. Small Pakatnamú buses leave when full, 0400-2100, from Av N de Piérola 1092, T044-206564, to Pacasmayo, 102 km, 1¼ hrs, US$2. To Chiclayo, another 118 km, 3 hrs from Trujillo, US$2.85, several companies. Among the best are Emtrafesa, Av Túpac Amaru 285, T044-471521, on the ½-hr every hr; to Piura, 278 km beyond Chiclayo, 6 hrs, US$7 (Ittsa's 1330 bus is a good choice); and Tumbes, a further 282 km, US$7.15, 8 hrs. Other companies include: Transportes El Dorado, Av América Norte opposite Díaz (old terminal next to Línea on Mansiche), T044-291778, leave at 1245, 2220 to Piura and Sullana, US$4.30/5.75; and Olano, Civa, Ormeño, US$8.60; Ormeño also has US$14.35 (2215) and US$8.65 (1915) services to Tumbes. Móvil's Lima-Chiclayo-Chachapoyas services pass through Trujillo at 1600 and 0130 (US$11.50). Direct buses to Huaraz, 319 km, via Chimbote and Casma (169 km), with Móvil and Línea (see above), 8 hrs, US$8.60 special. Also Chinchaysuyo, Av Mansiche 391, at 2030; US$7.15, 10 hrs. There are several buses and colectivos to Chimbote, with América Express from Lloque 162, 135 km, 2 hrs, US$1.20,

departures every 30 mins from 0530 (ticket sales from 0500); then change at Chimbote (see above - leave Trujillo before 0600 to make a connection with the 0830 Cañón del Pato service (see under Chimbote Transport); Línea's 0600 bus also makes the connection). Ask Clara Bravo and Michael White (see Guides p388) about transport to Caraz avoiding Chimbote (a very worthwhile trip via the Brasileños road and Cañon del Pato). To Cajamarca, 300 km, 7-8 hrs, US$5.75-8: with Línea (see above), best at 1030; Emtrafesa, see above, at 1000, 2230, and Tur Díaz 6 a day. To Huamachuco, 170 km, 6 hrs, US$5.50, Trans Agreda, JB Farfán 647, 0800, 1300; Trans Gran Turismo, Prol Vallejo 1368, T044-425391, 4 a day; Trans Horna, América Sur 1363, T044-257605, 4 a day; Turismo Negreiros, Prol Vallejo block 13, 0900, 1300, recommended. To Tarapoto, via Moyobamba, Turismo Tarapoto, Av N de Piérola 1221, T044-221493, at 2230, US$14.30, and Ejetur Av N de Piérola 1238, T044-222228, at 1100 and 1315, US$15, also to Yurimaguas at 0900, US$20, and to Jaén at 1600, US$7.50. To Tayabamba (see p438) via Sihuas with Trans Garrincha, Prol Santa 1919, T044- 214025, 1800 Sun and Wed, US$25, 18 hrs on a very rough road. From the Santa Cruz terminal at Av Santa Cruz y Av América Sur, microbuses, combis and colectivos depart for Puerto Malabrigo/ Puerto Chicama, Cartavio, Casagrande, Paiján, Ascope, Chao and Virú.

Taxi
Taxis charge US$0.55 within Av España and US$0.70 within the Av América ring road (drivers may ask for more at night). To Chan Chán US$3 per car, to the airport is US$4; to Huanchaco, US$3-5.

O Directory

Banks Note that banks, except Interbank, close 1300-1615. There is little difference between the rates for cash dollars given by banks and street changers, casas de cambio and travel agencies. BCP, Gamarra 562. No commission on cash into soles, but US$12 fee on TCs or changing into dollars, cash advance on Visa card, ATM (Visa). Interbank, Pizarro y Gamarra. Good rates for cash, no commission on Amex TCs into soles, Visa cash advance, quick service, also has Visa and Mastercard ATM. Mon-Fri 0915-1815, Sat 0900-1230. **Banco Wiese Sudameris**, Pizarro 314. Good rates for Amex TCs, 2% commission into soles or dollars, ATM for Mastercard/Cirrus. **BBV Continental**, Pizarro 620. Amex TCs and Visa card accepted, US$10 commission up to US$500. **Western Union**, Almagro 579, España y Huayna Cápac. **Cultural centres Alianza Francesa**, San Martín 858-62, T044-204504. **Instituto de Cultura Peruano Norteamericano**, Av Venezuela 125, Urb El Recreo, T044-261944. **Consulates UK**, Honorary Consul, Mr Winston Barber, Jesús de Nazareth 312, T044-235548, winston barber@terra.com.pe, Mon-Fri 0900-1700. **Doctors** Dr César Aníbal Calderón Alfaro, T044-255591, 948 2466 (mob). Understands English. **Hospitals Hospital Belén** Bolívar 350, T044-245281, emergency entrance from Bolognesi. **Clínica Peruano Americana**, Av Mansiche 702, T044-231261. English spoken, good. **Clínica Sánchez Ferrer**, Los Laureles 436, Urb California, T044-284889.

Immigration Av Larco 1220, Urb Los Pinos. Entrance is at the back of the building on Los Torcazos. Mon-Fri 0815-1230, 1500-1630. Gives 30-day visa extensions, US$20 (proof of funds and onward ticket required), plus US$0.80 for *formulario* in Banco de la Nación (fixers on the street will charge more). **Internet** There are offices all over the centre, mostly on Pizarro, blocks 1

and 6, and Av España, blocks 1 and 8. **Laundry American dry cleaners**, Bolognesi 782, US$1.45 wash only, ironing extra. 24-hr service. **Aquarelas**, Bolívar 355, laundry and dry cleaner. **Lavandería y Tintorería Luxor**, Grau 637. 0800-2000, cheap, charges per item, next day service. **Pharmacies** Several pharmacy chains in the centre (on Pizarro and Gamarra) and others on either side of Belén hospital on Bolognesi. **Farmacia La Libertad**, Bolívar 498. Old-fashioned, but good stock at competitive prices. **Post** Independencia 286 y Bolognesi. 0800-2000, Sun 0930-1300, stamps only on special request. **DHL**, Almagro 579. **Telephone Telefónica**, headquarters at Bolívar 658. Private call centre at Pizarro 561, Ayacucho 625, Gamarra 450, others on 5th block of Orbegoso and Av España 1530. **Tourist police** Independencia 630, Casa Ganoza Chopitea, T044-291705, policia_turismo_tru @hotmail.com. Open Mon-Sat 0800-2000. They provide useful information. **Useful addresses Touring and Auto- mobile Club**, Av Argentina 258, Urb El Recreo, T044-290736, trujillo@touring peru.com.pe. **Gobierno Regional deLa Libertad**, Los Brillantes 6550, Urb Santa Inés, T044-231791. For information on rural tourism in the department. **Instituto Nacional de Cultura**, Independencia 572. **The Indecopi** tourist complaints office, Junín 454, T044-242422, ldiaz@indecopi.gob.pe.

Around Trujillo

Perhaps Trujillo's greatest attractions are the impressive Pre-Inca ruins which surround it: the Moche pyramids of Huaca del Sol and de la Luna, Chan Chán and the more distant El Brujo. All can be reached by public transport, but if that sounds complicated, there are many tours available. You need at least an hour to gain a full explanation of Chan Chán and Huaca La Luna, but many tours only allow 20 minutes each. If you are all ruined-out, just a few minutes up the coast from Trujillo is the seaside town of Huanchaco, long a favourite of travellers for surfing, watching the fishermen on their reed boats and just hanging out. ▸▸ *For Sleeping, Eating and other listings, see pages 396-399.*

Huacas del Sol and de la Luna

ⓘ *0830-1600, US$3, with a professional or student guide, some of whom speak European languages (students half price, children US$0.30). A booklet in English or Spanish is sold for US$2.85.*

A few kilometres south of Trujillo are the huge Moche pyramids, the Huaca del Sol and Huaca de la Luna. The Huaca del Sol was once, before the Spanish diverted the nearby river and washed a third of it away in a search for treasure, the largest man-made structure in the western hemisphere, reaching a height of 45 m. It consisted of seven levels, with possibly six remodellings over the first six centuries AD. Built from 143 million adobe bricks, it was the political centre of the site. The ceremonial platforms have been further eroded by the weather and visitors, but climbing on them is prohibited. Today, about two-thirds of the pyramid have been lost.

The Huaca de la Luna, 500 m away, was a 'religious pyramid'. It received relatively little attention compared to its larger neighbour until more than 6,000 sq m of remarkable mural paintings and reliefs were uncovered throughout 1990s. In fact, this is the only site where the fascinating brightly coloured moulded decorations found on the interior walls of huacas can be easily viewed. The yellow, white, red and black paint has faded little over the centuries and many metres of the intricate geometric patterns and fearsome feline deities depicted are virtually complete. It has now been established that the pyramid once consisted of six levels, each pertaining to a different ruler-priest. When each priest died he was buried within the huaca and a new level was built covering up entirely the previous level. The number of levels suggests that there were six ruler-priests over a period of approximately 200 years. It is now possible to view impressive brightly coloured moulded friezes of the upper four levels on the northern exterior wall of the huaca. The highest mural is a 'serpent' which runs the length of the wall, beneath it there are repeated motifs of 'felines' holding decapitated heads of warriors, then repeated motifs of 'fishermen' holding fish against a bright blue background and, finally, huge 'spider/crab' motifs, discovered in mid-2002. Archaeologists planned to uncover the final two levels in 2004. Combined with intricate, brightly painted two-dimensional motifs in the sacrificial area atop the huaca, Huaca de la Luna is now a truly significant site well worth visiting.

Between the two huacas lie the remains of a once sizeable settlement, now mainly lost beneath the sands, though some excavations are taking place.

The visitors' centre has and café showing videos and a souvenir shop selling attractive ceramics, T-shirts, woven bags, wooden boxes, etc. In an outside patio craftsmen reproduce ceramics in designs from northern Peru. Also good toilets.

Chan Chán → Colour map 3, grid A1.

ⓘ A ticket which covers the entrance fees for Chan Chán, the site museum, as well as Huaca El Dragón and Huaca La Esmeralda (for 2 days) costs US$2.85 (half price for students with an official ISIC card – tickets can be bought at any of the sites, except

Around Trujillo

Masters of sculpture

One of the most remarkable pre-Inca civilizations was that of the Moche people, who evolved during the first century AD and lasted until around AD 750. Though these early Peruvians had no written language, they left a vivid artistic record of their life and culture in beautifully modelled and painted ceramics.

Compared with the empires of their successors, the Chimú and Inca, the realm of the Moche was very small, covering less than 250 miles of coast from the valleys of Lambayeque to Nepeña, south of present-day Chimbote. Though a seemingly inhospitable stretch of coast, the Moche harnessed rivers spilling from the Andean cordillera, channelling them into a network of irrigation canals that watered the arid coastal valleys. The resultant lush fields produced plentiful crops, which, along with the sea's bountiful harvest of fish and seafood, gave the Moche a rich and varied diet. With the leisure allowed by such abundant food, Moche craftsmen invented new techniques to produce their artistic masterpieces. It is these ancient pottery vessels that have made the greatest contribution to our understanding of this great civilization.

These masters of sculpture used clay to bring to life animals, plants and anthropomorphic deities and demons. They recreated hunting and fishing scenes, combat rituals, elaborate ceremonies and sexual intercourse (sometimes with contraception). They depicted the power of their rulers as well as the plight of their sick and invalid.

The violence and death of war is a common theme in their work; prisoners of war are apparently brought before congregations where their throats are cut and their blood offered to those present. Decapitation and dismemberment are also shown.

Moche potters were amazingly skilled at reproducing facial features, specializing in the subtle nuances of individual personality. In addition to these three-dimensional sculptures, the Moche potter was skilled at decorating vessels with low-relief designs. Among the most popular scenes are skeletal death figures holding hands while dancing in long processions to the accompaniment of musicians. The potters also developed a technique of painting scenes on ceramic vessels. Over a period of several centuries the painters became increasingly skillful at depicting complex and lively scenes with multiple figures. Because of their complexity and detail, these scenes are of vital importance in reconstructing Moche life.

The early introduction of moulds and stamps brought efficiency to the production of Moche ceramics. By pressing moist clay into the halves of a mould, it was possible to produce an object much more rapidly than by hand. Similarly, the use of stamps facilitated the decoration of ceramic vessels with elaborate low-relief designs. Mould-making technology thus resulted in many duplications of individual pieces. Since there were almost no unique ceramic objects, elaborate ceramics became more widely available and less effective as a sign of power, wealth and social status of the élite.

Although among the most sophisticated potters in Spanish America, the Moche did not use ceramics for ordinary tableware. Neither do their ceramics show many everyday activities, such as farming, cooking and pottery making. This is because Moche art expresses the religious and supernatural aspects of their culture and nothing of everyday life is illustrated for its own sake. See also under History, on page 567.

Esmeralda). A guide at the site costs US$5.80 per hour. The price is the same for a small group. A map and leaflet in English is on sale for US$0.75. It is relatively safe to walk on the dirt track from turn-off to the site (20 mins) but preferably go in a group. If alone, contact the Tourist Police in Trujillo to arrange for a policeman to accompany you (should be no charge). On no account walk the 4 km to, or on Buenos Aires beach, near Chan Chán as there is serious danger of robbery, and of being attacked by dogs.

This crumbling imperial city of the Chimú is the largest adobe city in the world and lies about 5 km from Trujillo. Heavy rain and flooding in 1925 and 1983 damaged much of the ruins and although they are still standing, eight palaces are closed to visitors. Thankfully, UNESCO donated US$100,000 and protection work ensured that the 1998 El Niño had little effect. Conservation work has uncovered more friezes since then.

The ruins consist of nine great compounds built by Chimú kings. The 9-m high perimeter walls surrounded sacred enclosures with usually only one narrow entrance. Inside, rows of storerooms contained the agricultural wealth of the kingdom, which stretched 1,000 km along the coast from near Guayaquil, in Ecuador, to beyond Paramonga.

Most of the compounds contain a huge walk-in well which tapped the ground water, raised to a high level by irrigation higher up the valley. Each compound also included a platform mound which was the burial place of the king, with his women and his treasure, presumably maintained as a memorial. The Incas almost certainly copied this system and transported it to Cusco where the last Incas continued building huge enclosures. The Chimú surrendered to the Incas around 1471 after 11 years of siege and threats to cut the irrigation canals.

> ♪ *Sometimes a singer waits in the Plaza Principal of the Ciudadela to show the perfect acoustics of the square (she expects a tip).*

The dilapidated city walls enclose an area of 28 sq km containing the remains of palaces, temples, workshops, streets, houses, gardens and a canal. Canals up to 74 km long kept the city supplied with water. What is left of the adobe walls bears well-preserved moulded decorations showing small figures of fish, birds and various geometric motifs. Painted designs have been found on pottery unearthed from the debris of a city ravaged by floods, earthquakes, and *huaqueros*.

The **Ciudadela of Tschudi** has been restored. It is a 20-minute walk from the main road. It is open 0900 to 1630 (but it may be covered up if rain is expected); arrive well before 1600 as you will not be allowed in much after that. Besides, you need more than 30 minutes to see the site. The **site museum** on the main road, 100 m before the turn-off, has a son-et-lumière display of the growth of Chan Chán as well as objects found in the area. It also has a good table showing Peruvian archaeology in the context of world history.

Huacas El Dragón and La Esmeralda

The partly restored temple, **Huaca El Dragón** ⓘ *0900-1630*, dating from Huari to Chimú times (AD 1000-1470), is also known as **Huaca Arco Iris** (rainbow), after the shape of friezes which decorate it. It is on the west side of the Pan-American Highway in the district of La Esperanza. Take a combi from Avenida España y Manuel Vera marked 'Arco Iris/La Esperanza', or, more safely, from Huayna Cápac y Avenida Los Incas; a taxi costs US$2.

The poorly preserved **Huaca La Esmeralda** is at Mansiche, between Trujillo and Chan Chán, behind the church (not a safe area). Buses to Chan Chán and Huanchaco pass the church at Mansiche.

Huanchaco → *Phone code: 044. Colour map 3, grid A1.*

A popular alternative to staying in Trujillo is the fishing and surfing town of Huanchaco, which is full of hotels, guesthouses and restaurants. It has great beaches to the south; to the north are marshes good for birdwatching. The town is famous for its narrow pointed fishing rafts, known as *caballitos* (little horses), made of totora

⁝ Absolute power

Chimú was a despotic state which based its power on wars of conquest. Rigid social stratification existed and power rested in the hands of the great lords. These lords were followed in the social scale by a group of urban courtiers who enjoyed a certain amount of economic power. At the bottom were the peasants and prisoners for sacrifice. The Chimú

economy was based on agriculture supplemented by fishing, hunting and craft production. They were renowned metalsmiths, who, like the Moche, alloyed and plated copper with gold and silver. The burial mounds of the Chimú nobles at Chan Chán were despoiled of all their gold and silver statuettes and ornaments by the Spaniards.

reeds and depicted on Salinar, Gallinazo, Virú, Moche, Lambayeque and Chimú pottery. These are still a familiar sight in places along the northern Peruvian coast. Unlike those used on Lake Titicaca, they are flat, not hollow, and ride the breakers rather like surfboards. You can see the reeds growing in sunken pits at the north end of the beach. Fishermen offer trips on their caballitos for US$1.50, be prepared to get

⁑The strength of the sun is deceptive. A cool breeze off the sea reduces the temperature, but you can still be badly sunburned.

wet; groups should contact Luis Gordillo, El Mambo, T044-461092. Fishermen will give demonstrations for US$2.85; groups should give more. You can see fishermen returning to shore in their reed rafts about 0800 and 1600 when they stack the boats upright to dry in the fierce sun.

The town, now developed with beach houses, is overlooked by a huge **church**, one of the oldest in Peru, from the belfry of which are extensive views. The pier also gives good views. Drivers should note that the municipality charges US$0.55 per vehicle to enter town in summer.

Chicama Valley
North of Trujillo is the sugar estate of **Hacienda Cartavio**, in the Chicama Valley (43 km). The plant includes a distillery and rum factory. Visits are possible by appointment only. One of the biggest sugar estates in the world, also in the Chicama Valley, is the **Casa Grande cooperative**. It covers over 6,000 ha and employs 4,000 members. Visits (guided) are only possible before 1200; many buses and combis go there from the Santa Cruz terminal in Trujillo, US$0.75.

El Brujo
Sixty kilometres north of Trujillo, is considered one of the most important archaeological sites on the entire north coast. The complex, covering 2 sq km, consists of Huacas Prieta, Cortada and Cao Viejo. This complex is collectively known as El Brujo and was a ceremonial centre for perhaps 10 cultures, including the Moche.

Huaca Cortada (or El Brujo) has a wall decorated with high-relief, stylized figures. **Huaca Prieta** is, in effect, a giant rubbish tip dating back 5,000 years, which once housed the very first settlers to this area. **Huaca Cao Viejo** ① *US$1.40*, has extensive friezes, polychrome reliefs up to 90 m long, 4 m high and on five different levels, representing warriors, prisoners, sacrificer gods, combat and more complex scenes, with a total of seven colours in reliefs. In front of Cao Viejo are the remains of one of the oldest Spanish churches in the region. It was common practice for the Spaniards to build their churches near these ancient sites in order to counteract their religious importance. The excavations at the site will last many years, but part is already open to the public. On view, but extensively sheltered by awnings to prevent further fading of the colours, is the sacrificer god, warriors and prisoners and what

Huanchaco

Pacific Ocean

North Coast Around Trujillo

Sleeping
Caballito de Totora 6 *D1*
Casa Gaviotas 1 *D2*
Casa Hospedaje
   Los Ficus 13 *D2*
Cherry's 16 *D2*
El Malecón 3 *E1*
Golden Club 4 *D1*

Hospedaje El
   Boquerón 20 *A2*
Hospedaje Okey 17 *C2*
Hostal Bracamonte 5 *E2*
Hostal Huanchaco 7 *C2*
Hostal Los Esteros 8 *B2*
Hostal Solange 9 *D2*
Hostal Sol y Mar 10 *D2*
Huanchaco's
   Garden 11 *A2*
Huanchacho
   Internacional 14 *E2*
La Casa Suiza 2 *D2*

Las Brisas 12 *A2*
Las Palmeras 18 *A2*
Naylamp 19 *A2*
Plazza's 15 *D2*

Eating
Big Ben 1 *A2*
Casa Tere 2 *C2*
Chelita 3 *D3*
Club Colonial 4 *C2*
El Anzuelo 6 *B2*
El Caribe 17 *B2*
El Mococho 7 *B2*

El Suco 15 *A2*
El Tramboyo 8 *C2*
El Tribu 9 *C2*
Estrella Marina 10 *B2*
La Barca 11 *C2*
La Esquina 12 *C2*
Lucho del Mar 13 *B2*
Mamma Mia &
   El Mochica 14 *B2*
Piccolo 16 *D3*
Sabes? 18 *A2*

Seventy kilometres north of Trujillo, Puerto Malabrigo (Chicama) is a real surfers' hang-out, as it's the best surf beach in Peru, claiming that it has the longest left-hand point-break in the world. There are several basic places to stay and eat. Combis and *colectivos* go there from the Santa Cruz terminal in Trujillo. Pacasmayo, port for the next oasis north, is 102 km north of Trujillo, and is the main road connection from the coast to Cajamarca. The paved 180 km road to Cajamarca branches off the Pan-American Highway soon after it crosses the Río Jequetepeque.

A few kilometres northwest on the other side of Río Jequetepeque are the ruins of Pacatnamú, comparable in size to Chan Chán. It consists of pyramids, cemetery and living quarters of nobles and fishermen, possibly initiated in the Chavín period. There is evidence also of Moche and Chimú occupation. No explanations at the site. To get there, take a taxi bus to Guadalupe, 10 km from the ruins, and a taxi is possible from there for US$20. Micros run in summer.

Where the Pan-American Highway crosses the Jequetepeque are the well-signed ruins of Farfán, separate from those of Pacatnamú, but probably of the same period. It has yielded important Inca burials in recent years. For web information, search `Carol Mackey+Farfan' for various sites and articles.

● Sleeping

Huanchaco *p393, map p395*

B Las Palmeras, Av Larco 1150, sector Los Tumbos, T044-461199, www.lasplameras dehuanchaco.com. One of the best hotels in town, rooms with terrace, bath, TV, hot water, small dining room, pool and gardens.

C Caballito de Totora, Av La Rivera 219, T/F044-651828, totora@terra.com.pe. Includes taxes, **D** in low season, surfers' room **F**, pool, friendly, English spoken, nice garden, clean, restaurant with good food and coffee, parking, good value. Recommended. Owners Elvira and Walter are very friendly and knowledgeable.

C Hostal Bracamonte, Los Olivos 503, T044-461162, www.hostalbracamonte.com. Comfortable, good, chalets with private bathroom **B**, you can camp on the grass (US$4.25), pool, secure, good restaurant, English spoken. Highly recommended.

C Hostal Huanchaco, Larco 287 on the plaza, T044-461272, huanchaco_hostal@ terra.com.pe. With bath and breakfast, TV, hot water, clean and friendly, pool, car park, expensive cafeteria with home-made cakes and other good meals, video, pool table, back door is ½ block from beach. Recommended.

C Huanchaco Internacional, Autopista a Huanchaco Km 13.5 (Playa Azul), T044-461754, huanchacoint@pmail.net. Some distance from town, **B** in bungalows, also has bunk rooms, breakfast included,

comfortable, clean, hot water, TV, internet, pool (open to non-residents in summer), airport pick-up, restaurant.

C-D El Malecón, Av La Rivera 225, T044-461275. Overlooking the sea, some rooms with terrace, clean, hot water, TV, café, friendly staff.

D Hostal Los Esteros, Av Larco 618, T044-461300, los steros@trujillobusiness.com. Bathroom, hot water, cable TV, restaurant, friendly, safe car and motorcycle parking, can arrange surfing and caballitos de totora trips.

D Hostal Sol y Mar, Los Pinos 570, T044-461120. With pool, restaurant, friendly owner, garden. Recommended.

D Las Brisas, Raymondi 146, T044-461186, lasbrisas@hotmail.com. 20 rooms with bathroom, hot water, cafeteria, cable TV, comfy.

D Plazza's, Los Ficus 207, T044-461757, plazzashotel@terra.com.pe. A new hotel with cable TV in rooms, bath and hot water, no café though.

E Naylamp, Prolongación Víctor Larco 3, northern end of the seafront in El Boquerón, T044-461022, naylamp@terra.com.pe. Rooms set around a courtyard, dorms too. **F** per person, hammocks, nice garden, kitchen, very clean, with bath, hot water 24 hrs, camping US$1.45 with own tent, US$2.30 to hire tent, laundry facilities, safe, good views of the sunset from the campsite and terrace restaurant, Italian food, good breakfasts. Recommended.

F per person **Casa Gaviotas**, Los Pinos 535, T044-461858. Small, comfortable, snacks, restaurant and cocktails, run by a responsible and honest old couple.

F **Casa Hospedaje Los Ficus**, Los Ficus 516, T044-461719, www.huanchaco.net/ losficus. Cheaper with shared bath. Family run, hot water, use of kitchen, breakfast, laundry. Recommended.

F per person **Cherry's**, Los Pinos 448, T044-461837, juancarlos160@yahoo.es. Owner Juan Carlos speaks English, cheaper without bath, hot water, use of kitchen, it has a shop, bar, internet with good machines, even a small swimming pool.

F per person **Golden Club**, Av La Rivera 217, T044-461306. 8 rooms, gym, pool, restaurant, use of kitchen, popular with surfers, very laid back atmosphere, excellent value, rooms on 1st floor cheaper. Recommended.

F **Hospedaje Okey**, Sra Fanny Valente, Atahualpa 147, T044-461457. 4 rooms with bath, 6 without, hot water all day.

F **Hostal Solange**, Los Ficus 484, 1 block from the beach, T044-461410, hsolange@yahoo.es. With bathroom, hot water, good food, laundry facilities, limited use of kitchen. Highly recommended.

F per person **Huanchaco's Garden**, Av Circunvalación Mz U, Lote 3, El Boquerón, T044-461194, huanchacogarden@yahoo.es. Family-run, bungalows, also camping, hot water, use of kitchen, friendly and helpful, garden with small pool, parking, laundry. Frequently recommended.

G per person **La Casa Suiza**, Los Pinos 451, T044-461285, www.huanchaco.net/casa suiza. 3 blocks from the beach, run by Heidi and Oscar Stacher, speak German and English, cheaper with shared bathroom, 4 rooms with bath, others share bathroom, hot water, nice roof balcony, excellent breakfast for US$1.50, friendly, family home (no drugs), surf boards to rent, book exchange, internet access. Highly recommended.

G per person **Hospedaje El Boquerón**, R Palma 330, T044-461968, maznaran@ hotmail.com. One block from beach, a modern house with shared bathrooms, hot water, fully equipped kitchen, laundry facilities and service, Speedy internet, clean, friendly landlady speaks French.

G per person **Sra Mabel Díaz de Aguilar**,

Túpac Amaru 248, T044-461232, mabel _minerva@hotmail.com. Near the football ground. Shared bath, hot water, Sra Mabel speaks English, very friendly.

North of Chicama *p396*
F **Panamericano**, Leoncio Prado 18, Pacasmayo, T044-522521. With private cold shower, small, basic, friendly, safe, reasonable restaurant downstairs.
F **San Francisco**, Leoncio Prado 21, Pacas-mayo, T044-522021. Basic, but cleaner than the Panamericano which is opposite, OK.

● Eating

Huanchaco *p393, map p395*
There are about 30 restaurants on the beachfront. Many close in the low season.
♥♥♥ **Big Ben**, Víctor Larco 836, near A Sánchez, T461869. Seafood and international menu, most expensive but very good.
♥♥♥ **El Mochica**, Av Larco, next to Mamma Mia. Same owners and quality as this restaurant in Trujillo, very nice dining area and panorama.
♥♥♥ **El Mococho**, Bolognesi 535. Said to be one of the best seafood restaurants, expensive, caters for groups.
♥♥♥-♥♥ **Club Colonial**, Grau 272 on the plaza. Reputedly the best restaurant, though expensive, serving fish, chicken or meat, has atmosphere of a traditional colonial dining club, but with private zoo.
♥♥ **El Anzuelo**, next to Estrella Marina. Good *ceviche*, offers 'taster' dishes at lower prices.
♥♥ **El Caribe**, just around the corner from Pisagua at Atahualpa 291. Another good seafood and fish place.
♥♥ **El Tramboyo**, on the little plaza opposite the pier. Good, helpful and friendly.
♥♥ **El Tribu**, Pasaje M Seoane 140, Plaza de Armas. Atmospheric bar in an old house, live music on Fri, opens 1900.
♥♥ **Estrella Marina**, Av Víctor Larco, next door to Lucho del Mar. Great value for fish.
♥♥ **La Barca**, Unión 320 (and Raimondi 111). Very good seafood, well-run, popular, but loud music or TV usually playing.
♥♥ **La Esquina**, Unión 299, T044-461081. Recommended for local food (also has accommodation **G** per person).
♥♥ **Lucho del Mar**, Av Víctor Larco. On seafront road, serves excellent sea food.

🍴 **Mamma Mia**, on the seafront. Good value Italian food and delicious home-made ice cream, English spoken by owner Fernando, good lodging (**F** per person, shared showers) available next door, rents surfboards.

🍴 **Sabes?**, V Larco 920, T044-461555, ysabes@yahoo.com. Pub with food, internet café, popular, American run.

🍴-🍴 **Otra Cosa**, Av Larco 921, www.otracosa.info. New vegetarian restaurant, European run, also has a volunteering agency, massage, tourist information and surfing services.

🍴 **Casa Tere**, Víctor Larco 280, Plaza de Armas. For best pizzas in town, also pastas, burgers and breakfasts.

🍴 **Chelita**, Los Abetos 198. Good value menú, fish dishes are best, very popular.

🍴 **Piccolo**, Los Abetos 142, 5 blocks from the plaza. Cheap, friendly, live folk music weekend evenings, excellent, surf and art shop.

🍴 **El Suco**, at the north end of the beach. Good seafood, including ceviche, cheaper than those in the centre.

❀ Festivals and events

Huanchaco *p393, map p395*
In the first week of **May** is the **Festival del Mar**, a celebration of the disembarkation of Taycanamo, the leader of the Chimú period. A procession is made in Totora boats.
30 Jun, **San Pedro**, patron saint of fishermen: his statue is taken out to sea on a huge totora-reed boat. Also the annual **Olímpiadas Playeras** and **El Festival Internacional de la Primavera** (see Trujillo). There are also surf competitions. **Carnival** and **New Year** especially are also popular.

🛍 Shopping

Huanchaco *p393, map p395*
A small market selling a wide range of artesanía is on the seafront beside the pier.
Artesanías del Norte, Los Olivos 504, T044-461220, marycortijo@usa.net. Sells mostly items of her own design, using prehispanic methods and motifs, primarily ceramics, but also cotton and alpaca goods and hand-painted products in wood. Food in the shops is a bit more expensive than Trujillo. There is a small fresh food market on Pilcomayo, ½ block from Deán Saavedra.

⛰ Activities and tours

Huanchaco *p393, map p395*
La Marea, Pilcomayo 173, near the market. For rental and instruction; **Picolo**, Los Abetos 142. Instruction, rent wet suits and boards, owner is a local champion; **The Wave**, Av Larco 525, next to Mamma Mia. Staff speak English; **Un Lugar**, Pilcomayo 176, T044-992 1371. Ask for English-speaking Juan Carlos.

🚌 Transport

Huacas del Sol and de la Luna *p390*
A taxi to the site costs US$3 (there are plenty at the site for the return). *Colectivos* (blue and yellow) every 15 mins from Suárez y Los Incas, US$0.30, run to the visitors' centre. It's safer to catch the bus from Huayna Cápac, southeast of Av Los Incas, and safer still at the Ovalo Grau. On the return you can get out at Huayna Cápac y Los Incas. If you want a walk take any Moche *colectivo* or bus and ask to get off at the track to the Huacas. It's about an hour's interesting walk through farmland beside irrigation canals, but don't walk after dusk.

Chan Chán *p391*
Buses and combis leave from Zela, on the corner of Los Incas, near the market (No 114A) inTrujillo, but it's safer to catch bus at north corner of Huayna Cápac y Avenida Los Incas or from the corner of España and Manuel Vera (114B); US$0.35, 20 mins; US$0.25 to Chan Chán entrance. A taxi is US$3 from Trujillo, US$0.85 from museum to ruins, US$2.85 to Huanchaco from ruins.

Huanchaco *p393, map p395*
Combis between Trujillo and Huanchaco are routes A, B and Crun 0500-2100 every 5-10 mins. A and B do an anti-clockwise circuit of Huanchaco and enter Trujillo by the roundabout on Av Mansiche, 3 blocks northwest of Av España in front of the Cassinelli museum, then A goes round the west side of Trujillo onto Av 28 de Julio, while B goes round the east side on Av Manuel Vera, España as far as Bolívar. At night they go only to España y Grau. Fare is US$0.30 for the 20-min journey. Slower 'micros', B and H, follow similar routes to América; leaving Trujillo B goes north of the centre on España, H goes south

(convenient stops are shown on the Trujillo map), in daylight only. There are also *colectivos* and taxis, minimum fare US$3, more likely US$4-5.

El Brujo *p394*
The complex can be reached by taking one of the regular buses from Trujillo to Chocope, US$0.55, and then a *colectivo* (every 30 mins) to Magdalena de Cao, US$0.45, then a taxi to the site, including wait, US$4.50, or a 5-km walk to the site.

The Pacasmayo-Cajamarca bus US$4.30, 5 hrs; to Chiclayo US$1.70, 2 hrs.

⊙ Directory

Huanchaco *p393, map p395*
Internet Beach Internet, Jr Los Pinos 533. 1300-1800. Both on Plaza de Armas: **JEC Café Internet**, 1400-2400, US$0.70 per hr, **www@ chat**, from 1730 Mon-Fri, 1100 Sat-Sun.
Post Manco Cápac 306. 1300-1800.

Chiclayo and around
→ *Phone code: 074. Colour map 1, grid C2. Population: 411,536.*

Chiclayo, founded in the 1560s as a rural Indian village by Spanish priests, has long since outgrown other towns of the Lambayeque Department. Sandwiched between the Pacific Ocean and the Andes, Lambayeque is one of Peru's principal agricultural regions, and its chief producer of rice and sugar cane. It is also the outlet for produce from the northern jungle, which comes by road over the comparatively low Porculla Pass. Chiclayo is the major commercial hub of the zone, but also boasts distinctive cuisine and musical tradition (Marinera, Tondero and Afro-indian rhythms), a famous witch doctors' market and an unparalleled archaeological and ethnographic heritage. Chiclayo is dubbed 'The Capital of Friendship', and while that tag could equally apply to most of the north coast of Peru, there is an earthiness and vivacity about its citizens that definitely sets it apart. ▶▶ *For Sleeping, Eating and other listings, see pages 408-413.*

Ins and outs
Getting there José Abelardo Quiñones González airport is 1 km from the town centre; taxi from centre costs US$2. There is no terminal terrestre; most buses stop outside their offices, many on or around Bolognesi, which is south of the centre. Confusingly many of the buses leaving for the surrounding area are to the north of the centre.
Getting around Calle Balta is the main street but the markets and most of the hotels and restaurants are spread out over about five blocks from the Plaza de Armas. Mototaxis are cheap. They cost US$0.50 anywhere in city, but are not allowed in the very centre. The surrounding area is well-served by public transport.
Tourist information Centro de Información Turística CIT ① *Sáenz Peña 838, T074-238112.* There are tourist kiosks on the Plaza and outside **El Rancho restaurant**.

Chiclayo

On the Plaza de Armas is the 19th-century neoclassical **cathedral**, designed by the English architect Andrew Townsend, whose descendants can still be identified among the town's principals. The **Palacio Municipal** is at the junction of Avenida Balta, the main street and the Plaza. The private **Club de la Unión** is on the Plaza at the corner of Calle San José. Where Avenida Balta meets Bolognesi, a Paseo de Las Musas has been built, with pleasant gardens, statues of the Greek Muses and imitation Greek columns. A similar Paseo de Los Héroes is at the opposite end of town. Another newish plaza is Parque Leonardo Ortiz, with a statue of Ñaylamp, buildings in the Lambayeque style and fountains.

Around Chiclayo

Lambayeque

Twelve kilometres northwest from Chiclayo is the quiet town of Lambayeque. Its narrow streets are lined by colonial and republican houses, many retaining their distinctive wooden balconies and wrought iron grill-work over the windows. For some fine examples, head along Calle 8 de Octubre: at No 410 is the opulent **Casona Iturregui Aguilarte** and, at No 328, **Casona Cuneo** is the only decorated façade in the

Chiclayo

0 metres 100
0 yards 100

N

Las Musas **23** C2
Lido **12** B2
Mochicas **13** C2
Paracas **14** A3
Paraíso **15** A3
Pirámide Real **22** C3
Royal **16** B3
Santa Rosa **9** B2
Sol Radiante **18** C2

Sleeping
Adriático **7** B3
América **1** B2
Aristi **2** C1
Costa del Sol **21** C3
El Sol **3** B1
Europa **4** B2
Garza **5** C3
Gran Chiclayo **6** B1
Hospedaje San
  Eduardo **20** C3
Hostal San José **8** A2
Hostal Santa Victoria **19** C2
Hostal Sicán **17** C2
Inca **10** B2
Kalu **11** A3

Eating
Boulevar **1** B2
Café Astoria **3** C2
D'Onofrio **4** C3
El Huaralino **18** C1
Govinda **6** B3
Hebrón **7** C3
Kaprichos **8** A3

La Fiesta **17** B1
La Panadería **9** B2
La Parra **10** C3
La Plazuela **11** B1
Las Américas **12** B3
Mi Tía **13** B2
Roma **15** C3
Romana **16** C3
Tradiciones **19** C3

Transport
Brüning Express to
  Lambayeque **1** B1
Buses to Chonoyape **2** B3
Civa **3** C3
Colectivos to
  Lambayeque **4** A2
Colectivos to

Monsefú **5** A3
Colectivos to Puerto
  Etén **6** A3
Combis to Pimentel **7**
  A2, B1
Cruz de Chalpón &
  Paredes Estrella **8** C3
Cruz del Sur **9** C3
Emtrafesa **10** C3
Flores/Cial **11** C3
Línea **12** C2
Oltursa **13** B1
Tepsa **14** C2
Transportes
  Chiclayo **15** B1

Legend of Ñaylamp

Like much else along this stretch of the Peruvian coast, the exact origin of the people's forebears is something of a mystery. The Spaniard, Cabello de Balboa, in 1578, is said to be the first outsider to hear of a local folk legend referring to a person named Ñaylamp who arrived on the coast of Lambayeque along with his court, his servants and his many concubines in numerous balsa rafts.

He then built residential buildings near the coast and a temple called Chota, or Chotuna, where he placed an idol called Yampallec, from which Lambayeque is supposed to derive its name. (At Cerro Cerrillos (Reque), 15 km west of Chiclayo, a new museum of the Lambeyeque culture is to built - opening 2006 - at the site of Chota.)

The name Ñaylamp came to occupy an important place in the religious imagery of later civilizations through the designs of tumis, or ceremonial knives, funerary masks and countless other objects. In the ancient Muchik language spoken by the Moche, ñam means bird and lá means water, and the figures on Moche ceramics, jewellery and temple walls often have bird-like features and eyes shaped like wings. On his death, the people were told that Ñaylamp had grown wings and flown away.

Ñaylamp had many children but only three are known of: Cium, Nor and Cala, who founded the present site of Túcume. This dynasty is said to have ended with the death of the last governor, Fempellec, as a result of his illicit relationship with a demon in the shape of a beautiful woman. With catastrophic consequences, she tricked him into moving Yampallec away from Chota.

town. Opposite is **Casona Descalzi**, perhaps the best preserved of all Lambayeque's colonial houses. Calle 2 de Mayo is also a good source of colonial and republican architecture, especially **Casa de la Logia o Montjoy**, whose 64-m long balcony is said to be the longest in the colonial Americas.

Also of interest is the 16th-century **Complejo Religioso Monumental de San Pedro** and the baroque church of the same name which stands on the Plaza de Armas 27 de Diciembre. The French neo-baroque **Palacio Municipal** is also on the plaza.

The reason most people come to visit is to see the two museums: the longer established and highly recommended **Brüning Archaeological Museum**, located in an impressive modern building, and the new **Museo de las Tumbas Reales de Sipán**. The **Brüning** ① *0900-1700, US$2, a guided tour costs an extra US$2.85*, most exhibits labelled in English, specializes in Mochica, Lambayeque/Sicán and Chimú cultures, and has a fine collection of Lambayeque gold. A board outside shows Peruvian cultures in relation to each other.

Three blocks east is the **Museo de las Tumbas Reales de Sipán** ① *Tue-Sat 0900-1700, US$3, a guide is advisable as no explanations are in English, http://. sipan.perucultural.org.pe*, shaped like a pyramid. The magnificent treasure from the tomb of 'The Old Lord of Sipán', found at Sipán in 1987, and a replica of the Lord of Sipán's tomb are displayed here (see Archaeological sites page 403). A ramp from the main entrance takes visitors to the third floor, from where you descend, mirroring the sequence of the archaeologists' discoveries. This museum is frequently recommended.

Mórrope

At Mórrope, on the Pan-American Highway north of Chiclayo (20 km beyond Lambayeque), craftsmen still produce pottery for the towns of northern Peru using

402 prehispanic techniques. Using a *paletín* (paddle) the potter manipulates the coil of clay into shape. Sometimes the *paletín* has a pattern on it, which is transferred onto the clay. Step inside the 16th-century **Capilla de la Ramada Las Animas** on the plaza and you'll know how Jonah felt inside the whale. The pillars and rafters were hewed from the local algarrob tree, giving the church interior the appearance of the skeleton of some enormous beast. Poor restoration work converted the crown and keys of Saint Peter into a skull and crossbones.

Monsefú, Pimentel, Santa Rosa and Puerto Etén

The traditional town of **Monsefú**, 16 km to the southwest, is worth a visit. The town's **music** is nationally famous, and there are many popular orchestras. It is also known for **handicrafts** and has a good **market** on Avenida Venezuela, four blocks from the plaza. Handicraft stalls open when potential customers arrive. See also Local festivals under Chiclayo. **Feria de Monsefú**, at the end of September, has market stalls around the plaza selling *artesanía*, bread, plastic toys and ceramics. The town market covers one block, entered off the plaza (with your back to the church, on the left side). At the entrance are bread sellers with huge baskets of breads and buns.

There are three ports serving the Chiclayo area, all beyond Monsefú. **Pimentel**, 8 km from Chiclayo by a new highway, is the closest beach resort to the city. It gets very crowded on Sundays. The surfing between Pimentel and the Bayovar Peninsula is excellent, reached from Chiclayo (14½ km) by road branching off from the Pan-American Highway. Sea-going reed boats (*caballitos de totora*) are used by

Chiclayo area

Old Lord of Sipán

The excavations at Sipán by the archaeologist Walter Alva have already revealed a huge amount of riches in the shape of 'El Señor de Sipán'. This well-documented discovery was followed by an equally astounding find dating from AD 100. The tomb of the 'Old Lord of Sipán', as it has come to be known, predates the original Lord of Sipán by some 200 years, and could well be an ancestor of his.

Some of the finest examples of Moche craftsmanship have been found in the tomb of the Old Lord. One object in particular is remarkable; a crab deity with a human head and legs and the carapace, legs and claws of a crab. The gilded piece is over half a metre tall – unprecedented for a Moche figurine. This crab-like figure has been called Ulluchu Man, because the banner on which it was mounted yielded some of the first samples yet found of this ancient fruit.

The ulluchu fruit usually appears in scenes relating to war and the ritual offering of a prisoner's blood. One theory is that the ulluchu is part of the papaya family and has anticoagulant properties which are useful to prevent clotting before a man's blood is offered.

fishermen and can be seen returning in the late afternoon. The old, decaying pier, ⓘ *US$0.25*, from which huge quantities of cotton and sugar were once exported, can be visited to watch the fishermen unloading their catches. There is a **Casa/Museo** dedicated to **José Quiñones**, hero of the 1942 war with Ecuador, at Quiñones 448.

A more traditional fishing village is nearby **Santa Rosa**, where fishermen use two groups of boats caballitos and bolicheros – pastel-painted craft which line the shore after the day's fishing. Take a combi between the two towns – on no account walk. The most southerly is **Puerto Etén**, a quaint port 24 km by road from Chiclayo. Its old railway station has been declared a national heritage site. In the adjacent roadstead, **Villa de Etén**, panama hats are the local industry.

Zaña and Chepén

The ruined Spanish town of **Zaña** (also spelt Saña), lies 51 km south of Chiclayo. Zaña was destroyed by floods in 1726, and sacked by English pirates on more than one occasion. The ruins of five colonial churches and the convents of San Agustín, La Merced and San Francisco bear witness to the former splendour of this town which, at one time, was destined to become the country's capital. Further south, on the Pan-American Highway to Trujillo, lies **Chepén**. The town itself is not particularly fascinating but **Cerro Chepén**, towering over it, is the site of an ancient fortress from the Middle Horizon (late Moche/Huari). The fortress contains the ruins of what may be a palace, surrounded by other buildings. The as yet unexcavated site could have been the main station in a chain of lookout posts along the north coast. Take any Trujillo bus, US$1.10.

Sipán → *Colour map 2, grid C2.*

ⓘ *Site is open 0800-1600 and the museum 0800-1700. Entrance for the tombs and museum is US$2, students half price. A guide at the site costs US$2.85 (may not speak English). Small boys offer to guide you (other kids hang around the handicraft stalls and pester for a tip for doing nothing). Allow about 3-4 hrs. Take mosquito repellent.*

At this imposing twin pyramid complex 35 km southeast of Chiclayo, excavations since 1987 in one of the three crumbling pyramids have brought to light a cache of funerary objects considered to rank among the finest examples of pre-Columbian art.

The Peruvian archaeologist Walter Alva, leader of the dig, continues to probe the immense mound that has revealed no less than 12 royal tombs filled with 1,800-year-old offerings worked in precious metals, stone, pottery and textiles of the Moche culture (circa AD 1-750). In the most extravagant Moche tomb discovered, **El Señor de Sipán**, a priest was found clad in gold (ear ornaments, breast plate, etc), with turquoise and other valuables. A site museum was opened in 1992 featuring photos and maps of excavations, technical displays and replicas of some finds.

In another tomb were found the remnants of what is thought to have been a priest, sacrificed llama and a dog, together with copper decorations. In 1989 another richly- appointed, unlooted tomb contained even older metal and ceramic artefacts associated with what was probably a high-ranking shaman or spiritual leader, called '**The Old Lord of Sipán**'.

Three tombs are on display, containing replicas of the original finds. Replicas of the Old Lord and the Priest are awaited. You can wander around the previously excavated areas of the Huajada Rajada to get an idea of the construction of the burial mound and adjacent pyramids. For a good view, climb the large pyramid across from the excavated Huaca Rajada. There is a path, but it looks as though it should be closed off to prevent erosion of the pyramid.

Around Sipán

Twenty-five kilometres from Sipán is **Pampagrande**, a Mochica settlement dating from circa AD 550. This was the largest Moche complex 1,400 years ago, at which time as many as 10,000 people may have lived here. Pampagrande was a ceremonial centre, possibly including ritual offering of human blood as represented in the Sipán exhibits. These were presided over by a lord who also directed production and distribution, including precious materials to the artisans. Some experts believe that a prolonged drought around AD 562-594 displaced large groups of Moche people living to the south who moved to Pampagrande, which become the centre of a state holding sway over the Lambayeque and Jequetepeque valleys.

The reason for the downfall of this once-powerful city remains in dispute. The structures associated with the rich and powerful ruling class appear to have been selectively burned and then abandoned leading some to conclude that a peasant revolution may have been the cause. Others (eg Moseley) believe that an earthquake, El Niño events and drought combined to lead to the demise of the Moche.

A minor road runs to Chongoyape, a pleasant old town 70 km to the east (3 km before the city, turn left/west to the Chavín petroglyphs of Cerro Mulato). Nearby are the vast Taymi and Pampagrande pre-Columbian and modern irrigation systems (the modern are also called Taymi). Also near Chongoyape are the aqueduct of Racarrumi, the hill fort of Mal Paso and the ruins of Majín (12-14 pyramids). In the district of Chongoyape is the **Chaparrí Private Conservation Area** ① *Comunidad Campesina Muchik Santa Catalina de Chongoyape, www.chaparri.org*. Visits by prior arrangement only via visit@chaparri.org. This community-owned project (the first of its kind in Peru) covers over 36,000 ha, extending from 1540 to 1,350 m above sea level. The variety of habitats, including dry desert forest, harbours many bird and mammal species, some of which are extremely rare. Notable birds are the white-winged guan and the Peruvian plantcutter, while there are also spectacled bears, Sechuran fox, puma and other cats. Small numbers of visitors are accommodated in a secluded lodge beside a river.

Túcume → *Colour map 1, grid C2.*
① *0800-1700, museum 0800-1600, US$2, guides charge US$2.85.*

About 35 km north of Chiclayo, beside the old Panamericana to Piura, lie the ruins of this vast city built over a thousand years ago. This mysterious and evocative site is worth visiting around sundown, not only to avoid the fierce sun, but to add to the eerie

A tale of demons and fish

Just one of the many legends that abound in this part of Northern Peru pertains to the hill which dominates the pyramids at Túcume and the precise origin of its name. The hill is known locally as 'El Purgatorio' (purgatory), or more commonly, Cerro La Raya.

The former name derives from the conquering Spaniards' attempts to convert the indigenous people to the Christian faith. The Spanish invaders encountered fierce local resistance to their new religion and came up with the idea of convincing the people of Túcume that the hill was, in fact, purgatory. They told the locals that there lived on the hill a demon who would punish anyone not accepting the Roman Catholic faith.

In order to lend some credence to this tale, a group of Spaniards set out one dark, moonless night and built a huge bonfire at the foot of 'El Purgatorio', giving it the appearance of an erupting volcano and frightening the townsfolk half to death. Thus they came to accept the Spaniards' assertion that any unbelievers or sinners would be thrown alive into the flames of this diabolical fire.

As if that wasn't enough to terrify the local populace, the Spanish also concocted the fiendish tale of 'El Carretón', or waggon. This was an enormous waggon pulled by four great horses which supposedly would speed forth from the bowels of 'El Purgatorio' on the darkest of nights. Driven by a dandily-dressed demon boss, and carrying his equally dandy demon buddies, this hellish vehicle careered round the town of Túcume making a fearsome racket. Any poor unbelievers or sinners unfortunate enough to be found wandering the streets would immediately be carted off and thrown into the flames of purgatory.

The alternative name of Cerro La Raya refers to the local legend of a Manta Ray that lived in a nearby lake. The local children constantly tormented the fish by throwing stones at it, so, to escape this torment, the poor creature decided to move to the hill and become part of it. The lake then disappeared and ever since, the hill has been enchanted.

thrill that it induces. It may be difficult to persuade anyone to accompany you, though, as local people are very superstitious.

A short climb to the two miradores on **Cerro La Raya**, or **El Purgatorio**, as it is also known, offers an unparalleled panoramic vista of 26 major pyramids, platform mounds, walled citadels and residential compounds flanking a ceremonial centre and ancient cemeteries. The entire complex covers well over 200 ha and measures 1.7 km from east to west and 2 km from north to south. One of the pyramids, Huaca Larga, where excavations were undertaken from 1987-1892, is the longest adobe structure in the world, measuring 700 m long, 280 m wide and over 30 m high.

There is no evidence of occupation of Túcume previous to the Sicán, or Lambayeque people (see below) who developed the site between AD 1050/1100 and 1375 until the Chimú came, saw and conquered the region, establishing a short reign until the arrival of the Incas around 1470. The Incas built on top of the existing structure of **Huaca Larga** using stone from Cerro La Raya. Among the tombs excavated so far is one dating from the Inca period. It is thought to be that of a warrior, judging by the many battle scars. The body is heavily adorned and was interred along with two male compatriots and no less than 19 females aged between 10 and 30. Beside the Huaca Larga is the shrine known as the Templo de la Piedra Sagrada (Temple of the Sacred Stone), which was clearly very holy to the Lambayeque, Chimú and Incas.

Among the other pyramids which make up this huge complex are: **Huaca El Mirador, Huaca Las Estacas, Huaca Pintada** and **Huaca de las Balsas,** which is thought to have housed people of elevated status such as priests.

Excavations at the site, led by the late Norwegian explorer-archaeologist, Thor Heyerdahl of Kon-Tiki fame, challenge many conventional views of ancient Peruvian culture. Some suspect that it will prove to be a civilization centre greater than Chan Chán. There is also evidence, including art and remains of navigation gear, that the people of Túcume were intrepid seafarers. A five-year excavation project was undertaken by Thor Heyerdahl, since when there has been no further excavation work for lack of funds.

The **site museum**, with three halls, is built from adobe and mezquite logs in prehispanic style. The collections show architectural reconstructions, photographs and drawings, highlighting the finds, which include weaving paraphernalia, a ceremonial oar and a fabulous bas relief and mural depicting maritime scenes suggesting former sea trade and interregional contact. Traditional dishes and drinks are available at the site.

The town of Túcume is a 15-minute walk from the site, or a US$0.85 mototaxi ride. On the plaza is the interesting **San Pedro Church**, a mixture of baroque, churrigueresque and neo-classical styles. There are no hotels in town. The surrounding countryside is pleasant for walks and swimming in the river. The present site of the town is not the original one but dates from 1720. Local legend has it that the town was moved following an apparition of the Virgin. The icon of the Virgin mysteriously disappeared but was later seen on top of Cerro Cueto, having her long hair combed by a native girl while gazing over pasture lands below. This was taken as a sign to relocate the church and the rest of the town with it. See Festivals and events page 410.

Ferreñafe and Sicán → *Colour map 1, grid C2.*

The colonial town of **Ferreñafe**, 18 km northeast of Chiclayo, is worth a visit, especially for the **Museo Nacional Sicán** ① *T074-286469, Tue-Sat 0900-1700, US$2 plus US$4 per guide (Spanish only).* This excellent new museum is designed to house objects of the Sicán (Lambayeque) culture from near Batán Grande (fascinating exhibits, knowledgeable staff, but little English spoken). There is a helpful Mincetur tourist office ① *T074-282843, citesipan@mincetur.gob.pe,* on the Plaza de Armas

The entrance to **El Santuario Histórico Bosque de Pómac**, which includes the ruins of **Sicán**, lies 16 km beyond Ferreñafe along the road to Batán Grande. Visiting the sanctuary is not easy because of the very arid conditions, lack of marked trails and distances involved which mean that walking around the site is only for the intrepid and well prepared: it is 10 km to the nearest huaca (pyramid). At the visitors' centre ① *T074-963 2390, bosquepomac@ecoportal.zzn.com, 0700-1600,* a guide (Spanish only) can be hired with transport, US$3 with motorbike and US$7 with mototaxi, which includes the entrance fee. This covers a two-hour tour of the area which includes a mirador (viewpoint) over the forest, some of the most ancient algarrob trees and at least two *huacas*. Food and drinks are available at the centre and camping is permitted. Sicán has revealed several sumptuous tombs dating to the middle Sicán period, AD 900-1100. The ruins comprise some 34 adobe pyramids, arranged around a huge plaza, measuring 500 by 250 m. They range in size with the largest reaching 40 m in height and approximately100 m square. The site as a whole covers 45 square km. A visit to the mirador affords a beautiful view across the emerald green tops of the algarrob forest with the enormous pyramids dramatically breaking through. The two main tombs discovered were located either side of the entrance

● *In the ancient Muchik language, Sicán means 'house or temple of the moon' and Poma, as*
● *it was also known, was the centre of the mid-Sicán culture which shares many stylistic*
similarities with the later Chimú culture.

ramp leading up the south face of **Huaca de Loro**. In one tomb 20 bodies were excavated and nearly a tonne of metal and other objects unearthed. There is nothing to see on the ground now both sites are completely overgrown with scrub. Here some of the best examples of pre-Columbian gold artefacts were found, notably the oldest *tumi* (ceremonial knife) unearthed in Peru. *Tumis* so commonly found in other cultures are all later which suggests that they were copied from Sicán. A Sicán tumi can be identified from the particularly feline, slanted form of the eyes, reflecting the iconografic representation of their principal diety. Many gold objects have been removed to private collections and museums, such as the Gold Museum in Lima, but many are in the new Museo Nacional Sicán in Ferreñafe. The *huacas* were badly eroded by the rains of the 1998 El Niño and are now semi-protected by flimsy corrugated-iron 'roofs'.

Professor Izumi Shimada has worked here for more than 15 years researching a culture which has, to a large extent, been forgotten. It is now seems that the origins of the Sicán culture lie with the Mochica (Muchik), though there are clear influences of other contemporary cultures: Wari and Pachacámac. Recent research suggests that when the Mochica religio-political centre based around Huaca Fortaleza, at Pampagrande, collapsed in AD 700-750 the population was displaced. It moved 30 km north to Poma on the banks of the river La Leche, which was not then a dry river. The resulting culture extended across the Motupe valley to the north, La Leche valley, and Zaña and Lambeyeque valleys to the south. It is known today as the Sicán culture (although some refer to it as Lambayeque), which reached its height in AD 900-1100. The city was probably moved to a new site at Túcume, 6 km west, following 30 years of severe drought and then a devastating El Niño related flood in AD 1050-1100. These events appear to have provoked a rebellion in which many of the remaining temples atop the pyramids were burnt and destroyed. At the new Túcume site the Sicán culture continued to flourish for another 300 years until conquest by the Chimú.

Historical Sanctuary Bosque de Pómac, established in 2001, covers 5,887 ha of algarrob forest either side of the river La Leche which remains dry most years. It is the largest intact algarrob forest in the world, containing trees up to 1,000 years old. Despite the dry, scrubby terrain the tree tops shimmer emerald green and there is prolific birdlife (47 species) as well as numerous reptiles and mammals, including an endangered species of wild cat.

Laquipampa Reserved Zone, covering 14,000 ha, and habitat of the rare and endangered white-winged turkey, is situated in a green and fertile high Andean valley. It lies two hours beyond Sicán; take a passing bus for Incahuasi. For further information see zr_laquipampa@inrena.gob.pe.

North to Piura

Sixty kilometres north of Chiclayo, beside the old Panamericana, is the site of **Apurlec**. It comprises a stone wall surrounding a hill and pyramids dating from the Tiahuanaco period, as well as irrigation canals and reservoirs. The system was enlarged during Moche, Chimú and Inca occupation of the site. The ruins are overgrown, but climb the Cerro Viejo to get an idea of its size. To get there from Chiclayo, take a bus from Pedro Ruíz block 5. The bus continues to Motupe (10 km).

Further north on the old Pan-American Highway, 885 km from Lima, is the peaceful town of **Olmos**. During the last week of June the **Festival de Limón** is celebrated here. At Olmos, a road runs east over the Porculla Pass for Jaén and Bagua, see page 471. The old Pan-American Highway continues from Olmos to Cruz de Caña and on to Piura.

At Lambayeque the new Pan-American Highway, which is in good condition, branches off the old road and drives 190 km straight across the Sechura Desert to Piura. There is also a coast road, narrow and scenic, between Lambayeque and Piura, via Bayovar and the town of **Sechura**. The fine 17th-century cathedral has a lovely west front which has been under renovation for a long time and is normally closed to the public. There is a restaurant at the junction to Bayovar, where you can sleep.

Sechura Desert → *Colour map 1, grid B2.*

A large area of shifting sands separates the cities of Chiclayo and Piura. Water for irrigation comes from the Chira and Piura rivers, and from the Olmos and Tinajones irrigation projects which bring water from the Amazon watershed by means of tunnels (one over 16 km long) through the Andes to the Pacific coast.

The northern river – the Chira – has usually a superabundance of water. Along its irrigated banks large crops of Tangüis cotton are grown. A dam has been built at Poechos on the Chira to divert water to the Piura valley. In its upper course the Piura – whose flow is far less dependable – is mostly used to grow subsistence food crops, but around Piura, when there is enough water, the hardy long-staple Pima cotton is planted.

In the 1870s, the government of Manuel Pardo decreed that all native cotton, including kapok, should be destroyed because it was believed that it gave parasites to the favoured, imported varieties. This was not the case and the value of Peruvian cotton is now recognized. It grows on a tall bush, unlike the short, Egyptian variety, and comes in seven colours, each of which was given a name by the Moche.

Solo cyclists should not cross the Sechura Desert as muggings have occurred. Take the safer, inland route. There are several restaurants between Km 845 and 848, and another midway between Mórrope and Piura, but there are no hotels. Do not camp out if possible, though heading south, strong headwinds may make camping unavoidable.

● Sleeping

Chiclayo *p399, map p400*
There are several cheap hotels on Av Balta, near the bus offices, which range from basic to hygienically challenged. Most have only cold water. There are other cheap hotels near the Mercado Modelo, especially on Arica.
AL Gran Hotel Chiclayo, Villareal 115, T074-234911, granhotel1@terra.com.pe. Refurbished to a high standard, price includes taxes and breakfast, pool, jacuzzi, entertainments, restaurant, safe car park, changes dollars, casino. Recommended.
AL-A Garza, Bolognesi 756, T074-228172, www.chiclayo.net/garzahotel. Excellent bar and restaurant, a/c, pool, car park, tourist office in lobby provides maps, information in English, vehicle hire. Highly recommended, but it is close to the bus stations so there is activity at all hours.
A Costa del Sol, Balta 399, T074-227272, www.costadelsolperu.com. New, smart, direct dial telephones, TV, minibar, non-smoking rooms, small pool, sauna, jacuzzi. Páprika restaurant, good value Sunday buffets US$7.50, vegetarian options.
A Las Musas, Los Faiques 101, by Parque Las Musas, T074-239885, reservaslasmusas@

hotmail.com. Quiet area, large rooms, bathtubs, TV, minibar, affable service, internet available, tours arranged. Recommended.
B Inca, Av L González 622, T074-235931, pewww.incahotel.com. Recently refurbished, with TV and a/c, **A** with jacuzzi, restaurant, garage, comfortable and helpful.
C América, Av L González 943, T074-229305, americahotel@latinmail.com. Comfortable, friendly, breakfast included, restaurant, good value (except for the expensive laundry). Recommended.
C Aristi, Francisco Cabrera 102, T074-28673. With TV, fan, parking costs US$1 per day extra, clean, comfortable, reasonable value.
C Hostal Santa Victoria, La Florida 586, Urb Santa Victoria, T074-225074. Hot water, restaurant, free parking, dollars exchanged, quiet, 15-20 mins' walk from the centre.
C-D El Sol, Elías Aguirre 119, T074-232120, hotelvicus@hotmail.com. Price includes taxes, with bathroom, hot water, restaurant, pool, TV lounge, clean, parking, good value.
D Europa, Elías Aguirre 466, T074-237919, hoteleuropachiclayo@terra.com.pe. With bath (**F** without, single rooms can be small), hot water, restaurant, good value.

D Kalu, Pedro Ruíz 1038, T/F074-229293, HOTELKALU@terra.com.pe. Near the Mercado Modelo. Comfortable, with bath and TV, laundry, safe, good.

D Mochicas, Torres Paz 429, T074-237217, mochcas1@hotmail.com. Fan, TV, helpful, good service.

D Paracas, Pedro Ruíz 1046, T074-221611. Near the Mercado Modelo. With bathroom, TV, good value. Recommended.

D Paraíso, Pedro Ruíz 1064, T/F074-222070, hotelparaiso@ terra.com.pe. Also near the Mercado Modelo, also comfortable and well-appointed, but can be noisy. Recommended.

D Pirámide Real, MM Izaga 726, T074-224036. Compact but spotless, good value, very central.

D Santa Rosa, L González 927, T074-224411. With bathroom, clean, laundry service, international phone service, breakfast downstairs in snack bar. Good value.

E Hospedaje San Eduardo, 7 de Enero 235, Urb San Eduardo, T074-209423. A 10-min walk from the centre; no sign other than a little notice in the window. Family run, large rooms, quiet, safe, cable TV, hot water.

E Hostal Sicán, Izaga 356, T074-237618. With breakfast, bath, hot water, cable TV, clean, comfortable but some rooms are gloomy, welcoming and trustworthy. Recommended.

E Lido, Elías Aguirre 412A, T074-237642. With bathroom, fairly clean, safe, rooms near reception are noisy.

E Sol Radiante, Izaga 392, T074-237858, robertoiza@mixmail.com. With bath and TV, cold water, comfortable, pleasant, but noisy at the front.

F Royal, San José 787, on the Plaza, T074-233421. With bathroom, a big, rambling old building, a bit seedy and rundown, the rooms on the street have a balcony but are noisy.

F-G per person **Adriático**, Av Balta 1009. The best of a bad bunch on Av Balta, fairly clean but basic, cold water.

F-G Hostal San José, on Juan Cuglievan 1370, 1 block from the Mercado Modelo, T074-273394. Basic, clean, acceptable, cold water.

Around Chiclayo p400

E Hostal Karla, Av Huamachuco 758, Lambayeque, T074-282930. Opposite the museum.

E Jopami, Grau 143, Lambayeque, T074-282367.

E Lambayeque, Tarapacá 261, Lambayeque, T074-283474.

F Hotel Puente Azul, outside Chepén on the Panamericana. Pleasant, clean, with bath and cold water. The restaurant is open in the afternoon only, not for dinner.

F per person **La Posada Norteña**, Panamericana Norte Km 780, Lambayeque, T074-282602. With bath, quiet, safe, clean, cold water, more expensive with TV.

🍴 Eating

Chiclayo p399, map p400

Local specialities include *ceviche* and *chingurito* (a *ceviche* of strips of dried guitar fish, which is chewy but good). For delicious and cheap *ceviche*, go to the Nativo stall in the Mercado Central, a local favourite. *Cabrito* is a spiced stew of kid goat. *Arroz con pato* is a paella-like duck casserole. *Humitas* are *tamale*-like fritters of green corn. King Kong is a baked pastry layered with candied fruit and milk caramel, appealing to those with a very sweet tooth (of whom there would appear to be a great many as there are countless shops selling the stuff; San Roque is the best brand). *Chicha* is the fermented maize drink with delicious fruit variations.

¶¶¶ El Huaralino, La Libertad 155, Santa Victoria. Serves a wide variety of international and creole dishes.

¶¶¶ La Fiesta, Av Salaverry 1820 in 3 de Octubre suburb, T074-201970. Local specialities, first class.

¶¶ Hebrón, Balta 605. For more upmarket than average chicken, but also local food and parrilla. Also does an excellent breakfast and a good buffet at weekends.

¶¶ Kaprichos, Pedro Ruíz 1059, T232721. Chinese, delicious, huge portions.

¶¶ Las Américas, Aguirre 824. Open 0700-0200, good service. Recommended.

¶¶ Roma, Izaga 706. Wide choice of dishes; also has a bar.

For an explanation of sleeping and eating price codes used in this guide, see inside the front cover. Other relevant information is found in Essentials, pages 61-66.

¶¶ Romana, Balta 512,T223598. First-class food, usually good breakfast, popular with locals.

¶¶ Tradiciones, 7 de Enero Sur 105, T074-221192. Open 0900-1700 daily. Good variety of local dishes, including ceviche, and drinks, nice atmosphere and garden, good service.

¶ Café Astoria, Bolognesi 627. Open 0800-1200, 1530-2100 for breakfast, and a good value menú.

¶ Boulevar, Colón entre Izaga y Aguirre. Good, friendly, menú and à la carte.

¶ Govinda, Balta 1029. Good vegetarian, open daily 0800-2000.

¶ La Parra, Izaga 752. Chinese and creole, parrillada, very good, large portions.

¶ La Plazuela, San José 299, Plaza Elías Aguirre. Good food, seats outside.

¶ Mi Tía, Aguirre 650, just off the plaza. Huge portions, great value menú, very popular at lunchtime. Recommended.

Cafés

D'Onofrio, Balta y Torres Paz. For great ice cream.

Greycy, Elias Aguirre y Lapoint. Also serves good ice cream.

La Panadería, Lapoint 847. Good choice of breads, including integral, also snacks and soft drinks.

Around Chiclayo *p400*

¶ El Cántaro, on the 1st block of 2 de Mayo, Lambayeque. Serves excellent traditional local dishes cooked by Juanita.

¶ El Flamenco, Atahualpa 159, opposite Museo Brüning, Lambayeque. Excellent restaurant with set menu.

¶ La Cabaña, on the 4th block of Calle Libertad, Lambayeque. Good for ceviche.

¶ La Huaca, on the 3rd block of Calle Junín, Lambayeque. Also good for ceviche.

❊ Festivals and events

This is an area rich in traditional customs and beliefs.

Around Chiclayo *p400*

Among the many festivals held in and around the city is **Reyes Magos** in Mórrope, Illimo and other towns on **6 Jan**. This is a recreation of a medieval pageant in which pre-Columbian deities become the Wise

Men. On **4 Feb** are the **Túcume devil dances**. On **14 Mar** in Monsefú is **Festividad Señor Cautivo**. During **Holy Week** are traditional Easter celebrations and processions in many villages. **Fiesta de la Cruz** is held in Pimentel from **1 May**, and in the last week of **Jun** is **Festividad de San Pedro** in Morrope. In the first week of **Jun** is the Divine Child of the Miracle, in Villa de Etén. Also in Monsefú, on **27-31 Jul**, is **Fexticum**, with traditional foods, drink, handicrafts, music and dance. On **5 Aug** is the pilgrimage from the mountain shrine of Chalpón to Motupe, 90 km north of Chiclayo. The cross is brought down from a cave and carried in procession through the village. On **24 Sep** is **Virgen de las Mercedes** in Incahuasi, 12 hrs by truck east of Chiclayo. Indians still sing in the ancient Mochica language in this post-harvest festival. At **Christmas** and **New Year**, processions and children dancers (pastorcitos and seranitas) can be seen in many villages, eg Ferreñafe, Mochumi, Mórrope.

Túcume celebrates the **Fiesta de la Purísima Concepción**, the town's Patron Saint, 8 days prior to Carnival in **Feb**, and also in **Sep**. This is the most important festival, with music, dancing, fireworks, cockfights, sports events and, of course, much eating and drinking. During the Dance of the Devils (which is common in northern Peru), the participants wear horned masks, forked tails and long capes and are said to represent the diabolical drunken Spanish priests from colonial times. It also features a song and dance dedicated to the native girl who was seen combing the Virgin's hair.

◎ Shopping

Chiclayo *p399, map p400*

Markets

Mercado Modelo, five blocks north of the main plaza on Balta. This is one of northern Peru's liveliest and largest daily markets. Don't miss the colourful fruits, handicrafts stalls (see Monsefú) and the well-organized section of ritual paraphernalia used by traditional curers and diviners (curanderos), which is just off Calle Arica on the south side. **Mercado de Brujos** (witch doctors' market) is considered by James Vreeland, a North American anthropologist, to be one of the most comprehensive in South America. It is filled with herbal medicines, folk charms, curing potions, and exotic objects used by *curanderos* and *brujos* to cure all manner of real and imagined illnesses. The stallholders are generally very friendly and will explain the uses of such items as monkey claws, dried foetuses and dragon's blood! **Casa La Cabalonga**, stand 43, near the corner of Arica and Héroes Cíviles, has been recommended as particularly helpful and informative. As in all markets, take good care of your belongings.

There is a **Mercado Central** in the city centre, smaller than the **Mercado Modelo**. **Paseo de Artesanías**, 18 de Abril at the end of Colón. Stalls sell woodwork, basketwork and other handicrafts in a quiet, peaceful, custom-built open-air arcade.

Photography
J&M Color, Av Balta 801, T074-224096. Repairs all kinds of photographic and electrical equipment.

▲▲ Activities and tours

Chiclayo *p399, map p400*
Expect to pay US$18-25 per person for a 3-hr tour to Sipán, and US$25-35 per person for Túcume and the Brüning Museum (5 hrs). Brüning Museum, Sipán and Túcume, however, can easily be done by public transport. Sicán, which has less frequent public transport, is US$45-55 per person for a full-day tour including Ferreñafe and Pómac. To Zaña and the coastal towns is US$35-55 per person. These prices are based on 2

people; there are discounts for larger groups. **411**
Indiana Tours, Colón 556, T074-222991, www.indianatoursperu.com. Daily tours to Sipán (US$15), Thor Heyerdahl's Kon Tiki museum, archaeological excavations in Túcume, Brüning Museum in Lambayeque, Sicán and a variety of other daily and extended excursions with 4WD vehicles, as well as reservations for national flights and hotels. English and Italian spoken and handbook users welcome. Recommended.
Peruvian Treasures Explorer, Balta 398, T074-233435. Archeological tours, helpful.
Tambo Tours, USA and Peru, www.2GOPE RU.com, www.tambotours.com. Adventure and general tour operator.

⊖ Transport

Chiclayo *p399, map p400*
Air
Daily flights to and from **Lima** and **Piura** with Lan.

Bus
To **Lima**, 770 km, US$12 and US$22 for bus cama: **Civa**, Av Bolognesi 714, T074-223434; **Cruz del Sur**, Bolognesi 888, T074-225508 (*bus cama*; has the only daytime service at 0800, US$22); **Ormeño**, Haya de la Torre 242 (two blocks south of Bolognesi), T074-234206, *especial* and *bus cama* (US$20); **Las Dunas**, Bolognesi block 1, luxury service with a/c, toilet, meals, leaves at 2000; **Línea**, Bolognesi 638, T074-222221, *especial* and *bus cama* service (recommended); **Móvil**, Bolognesi 195, T074-271940 (goes as far as Tarapoto); **Oltursa**, ticket office at Balta e Izaga,

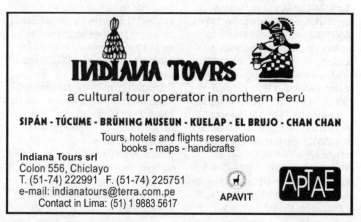

T074-237789, terminal at Vicente de la Vega 101, T074-225611, full range of services; **Transportes Chiclayo**, Av L Ortiz 010, T074-237984, www.transportes chiclayo.com. Most companies leave from 1900 onwards. To **Trujillo**, 209 km, with **Línea**, as above, and **Emtrafesa**, Av Balta 110, T074-234291, almost hourly from 0530-2015, US$3.35. To **Piura**, US$3.65, **Línea** and **Trans Chiclayo** leave hourly throughout the day; also **Emtrafesa** and buses from the Cial/Flores terminal on Bolognesi 751, eg Flores, T074-239579, and **Turismo Tarapoto**, T074-492274. To **Sullana**, US$4.35. To **Tumbes**, US$5.75, 9-10 hrs; with Cial, or Transportes Chiclayo (see above); **Oltursa** has an overnight service which leaves at 2015 and arrives at 0530 (this is a good bus to take for crossing to Ecuador the next day), seats can be reserved, unlike other companies which tend to arrive full from Lima late at night.

Many buses go on to the **Ecuadorean border** at **Aguas Verdes**, while Ormeño goes direct to Guayaquil (daily 0200) and Quito (Tue 0100). It's possible to get a substantial discount on the fare to the border: go to the Salida on Elías Aguirre, mototaxi drivers know where it is, be there by 1900. All buses stop here after leaving their terminals to try and fill empty seats. Bear in mind that the cheapest buses may not be the most secure. Direct bus to **Cajamarca**, 260 km, 6 hrs; with **Línea** (Bolognesi 638), 1315, US$5.65, 2200, US$8.45, bus cama 2245 US$7.60; many others from Tepsa terminal, Bolognesi y Colón, eg **El Cumbe**, T074-272245, 4 a day, **Días**, T074-224448, 3 a day, **Mendoza**, 2 a day, all US$4.55. To **Chachapoyas**, 230 km, US$6-10.60: with **Civa** at 1730 daily, 10-11 hrs; **Móvil** at 1900; **Turismo Kuelap**, in Tepsa station, 1830 daily. To **Jaén**, US$4.35-6.15: **Línea** at 1300 and 2300, 8 hrs; **Señor de Huamantanga**, in Tepsa station, T074-274869, 1145 and 2230 daily; **Turismo Jaén**, in Tepsa station, 7 a day. To **Tarapoto**, 18 hrs, US$11.50, with **Ejetur**, Bolognesi 536, T074-209829; also **Turismo Tarapoto**, Bolognesi 751, T074-492274, and **Sol Peruano**, in Tepsa station, T074-204880. To **Huancabamba**, with **Etipthsa**, on Mon and Fri from the Tepsa terminal, T074-229217; at 1700, 12 hrs, US$8.65.

Around Chiclayo *p400*

For **Lambayeque**, *colectivos* from Chiclayo; US$0.45, 25 mins. They leave from Pedro Ruíz at the junction with Av Ugarte. Also **Brüning Express** combis from Vicente de la Vega between Angamos and Av L Ortiz, every 15 mins, US$0.20.

From **Monsefú** combis to Chiclayo cost US$0.45; from Chiclayo they leave from Amazonas y 7 de Enero, beyond the Mercado Modelo. *Colectivos* to Monsefú leave from 7 de Enero y Arica.

The ports of **Pimentel**, **Santa Rosa** and **Puerto Etén** can all be visited on a pleasant half day trip from Chiclayo. Combis leave from Vicente de la Vega 200 to Pimentel; others leave from González y L Prado. Both take 20 mins, US$0.25. *Colectivos* to Etén leave from 7 de Enero y Arica.

Buses to **Sipán** leave from Terminal Este Sur-Nor Este on C Nicolás de Piérola, east of the city (take a taxi there, US$1; it can be a dangerous area), US$0.45, 1 hr. *Colectivos* leave from 5-6 blocks east of Mercado Modelo, take care here, too. The way to the village is well-signed through fields of sugar cane. Once you get to the village, the signs end: turn left, then right and go through the village to get to the site.

Buses from Chiclayo to **Chongoyape** leave from the corner of Leoncio Prado and Sáenz Peña; US$1, 1½ hrs.

For **Túcume** combis go from Chiclayo, Angamos y Manuel Pardo, US$0.70, 45 mins. A combi from Túcume to the village of **Come** passes the ruins hourly. You cannot miss the town of Túcume with its huge sign. Soon after the sign take a right turn on the paved road which leads to the museum and site. Don't be fooled by the pyramid close to the sign; it's part of the group, but some distance from the entrance. A combi from Túcume to **Lambayeque** is US$0.35 and takes 25 mins.

Colectivos from Chiclayo to **Ferreñafe** leave every few minutes from 8 de Octubre y Sáenz Peña, 15 mins, U$0.30, but only run to Ferreñafe town centre so take a mototaxi on to the museum, 5 mins, US$0.50. Alternatively, combis for Batán Grande depart from the Terminal Nor-Este, in Av N de Piérola in Chiclayo, and pass the museum every 15-20 mins, 20 mins, US$0.50.

Directory

Chiclayo *p399, map p400*

Beware of counterfeit bills, especially among street changers on the 6th block of Balta, on Plaza de Armas and 7th block of MM Izaga. **Banks** BCP, Balta 630, no commission on Amex TCs for US$100 or more (US$12 commission if less), cash on Visa, also Telebanco 24 Horas ATM for Visa. Opposite, at Balta 625, is **Banco Wiese Sudameris**, changes Amex TCs, cash advance on Visa card, ATM for Visa/Plus. **Banco Santander**, Izaga y Balta, changes Amex TCs. **Interbank**, on the Plaza de Armas, no commission on TCs, OK rate, good rates for cash, Visa cash advance, Mastercard and Visa ATM. You may have to wait for a while in the banks. It's much quicker and easier to use the ATMs. Banking hrs 0915-1315, 1630-1830, Sat 0930-1230. **Western Union** is at Tumi Tours, Elías Aguirre 560, also DHL, also both at Cruz del Sur. **Cultural centres** Alianza Francesa, Cuglievan 644, T074-236013. **Instituto de Cultura Peruano-Norteamericana**, Av MM Izaga 807, T074-231241. **Instituto Nacional de la Cultura**, Av L González 375, T074- 237261. Has occasional poetry readings, information on local archaeological sites, lectures, etc. It sells a combined entrance ticket for US$4.35

to Sipán, the Brüning Museum, San Pedro church and Casa Montjoy in Lambayeque, Túcume, Sicán, Zaña and other sites. **Instituto Peruano Británico**, Av 7 de Enero 256. T074-227521. **Internet** Lots of places, particularly on San José and Elías Aguirre, average price US$0.60 per hr. **Africa Café**, San José 473, T074- 229431, with café downstairs. Another at San José 389. **Internet 20**, San José y Luis González. On MM Izaga: **Ciber Net** opposite Hostal Sicán, fast connection. **Ciber Café Internet**, No 716. **Post** On the first block of Aguirre, 6 blocks from the plaza. **Telephone** Telefónica, headquarters at Aguirre 919; bank of phone booths on 7th block of 7 de Enero behind Cathedral for international and collect calls. Phone card sellers hang around here. **Tourist police** Av Sáenz Peña 830, T074- 236700, ext 311, 24 hrs a day, are very help- ful and may store luggage and take you to the sites themselves. **Useful addresses** Ambulance: Max Salud, 7 de Enero 185, T074-234032, maxsalud@tele matic.edu.com. **Touring y Automóvil Club del Perú**, San José 728, T074-231821, chiclayo@touringperu.com.pe. Also has a travel agency selling air tickets. **Indecopi**, Av Balta 506, T074-209021, ctejada@indecopi. gob.pe, Mon-Fri 0800- 1300, 1630-1930, for complaints and tourist protection.

Piura and around → *Phone code: 073. Colour map 1, grid B1.*

Population: 324,500.

A proud and historic city, 264 km from Chiclayo, Piura was founded as San Miguel at Tangarará in 1532, three years before Lima, by the conquistadores left behind by Pizarro. It was relocated, first as Pirwa, then with its current name, in 1534. There are two well-kept parks, Cortés and Pizarro (with a statue of the conquistador, also called Plaza de las Tres Culturas), and public gardens. Old buildings are kept in repair and new buildings blend with the Spanish style of the old city. Close to the city are interesting towns on the coast and others specializing in handicrafts. Further afield is the culturally fascinating area of Las Guaringas shamanic practices and the more prosaic route to Ecuador through Sullana. ▸▸ *For Sleeping, Eating and other listings, see pages 418-422.*

Ins and outs

Getting there A taxi to the airport costs US$1.85 by day, more by night. Most bus companies are on Avenida Sánchez Cerro, blocks 11, 12 and 13 in the northwest of the town. There are some hotels in this area, but for central ones take a taxi.

Getting around From the Plaza de Armas, some of the hotels and bus companies are too far to walk, but many of the sights and places to stay can be reached on foot.

North Coast Piura & around

Three bridges cross the Río Piura to Castilla, the oldest from C Huancavelica (Puente San Miguel), from C Sánchez Cerro, and the newest from Avenida Panamericana Norte, west of town. A fourth bridge was lost in El Niño of 1997-1998. Taxis in town charge US$1, mototaxis US$0.50. Transport to nearby towns is easy to find, likewise buses going to Sullana and on to Ecuador. For Las Guaringas, expect a long journey.

Tourist information Information at the tourist office on the Plaza de Armas ① *next to Municipio, Mon-Fri 0900-1300, 1600-2000, Sat 0900-1300.*

Best time to visit The winter climate, May to September, is very pleasant although nights can be cold and the wind piercing, while December to March is very hot. It is extremely difficult to find a room in the last week of July because of Independence festivities. The city suffers from water shortages.

Piura

Sights

Standing on the **Plaza de Armas** is the **cathedral**, with gold covered altar and paintings by Ignacio Merino. A few blocks away at Lima y Callao is the **San Francisco** church, where the city's independence from Spain was declared on 4 January 1821, nearly eight months before Lima. The church was being completely rebuilt in 2002.

The church of **María Auxiliadora** stands on a small plaza on Libertad, near Avenida Sánchez Cerro. Across the plaza is the **Museo de Arte Religioso**. **San Sebastián**, on Tacna y Moquegua, is also worth seeing. The birthplace of Admiral Miguel Grau, hero of the War of the Pacific with Chile, is **Casa Museo Grau** ① *Jr Tacna 662, opposite the Centro Cívico, 0800-1300, 1600-1900, free.* It has been opened as a museum and contains a model of the Huáscar, the largest Peruvian warship in the War of the Pacific, which was built in Britain. It also contains interesting old photographs.

Interesting local craftwork is sold at the **Mercado Modelo**. **Museo Municipal Vicús**, with archaeological and art sections, is open on Sullana, near Huánuco, and though small it is very interesting.

Excursions

Catacaos is a small town famous for its *chicha* (maize beer) – though be careful as the quality is not always reliable – and *picanterías*, which are local restaurants, some with music. The village is also noted for its artesanía such as tooled leather, gold and silver filigree jewellery, wooden articles and straw hats, though prices are relatively high and streets are lined with shops, including some jewellers more suited to a shopping mall. Inside the large church are vivid murals and, in 2000, a miracle was said to have occurred when an image of Christ appeared in the paintwork on an exterior wall. The village is also renowned for its celebrations in **Holy Week**, Good Friday especially (when all of Piura seems to be there). There is a procession at 1800 and the town centre is closed to traffic. Two kilometres south of Catacaos is the Narihualá archaeological site. It includes a large adobe pyramid, 40 m high, from the Tallán culture which populated the Chira and Piura valleys before it was conquered by the Chimús.

The port for the area is **Paita**, 50 km from Piura. It exports cotton, cotton seed, wool and flax. Built on a small beach, flanked on three sides by a towering, sandy bluff, it is connected with Piura and Sullana by paved highways. It is a very old fishing port. Several colonial buildings survive, but they are in poor condition. Bolívar's mistress, Manuela Sáenz, lived the last 24 years of her life in Paita, after being exiled from Quito. She supported herself until her death in 1856 by weaving and embroidering and making candy after refusing the fortune left her by her husband. The house can be visited if you ask the people living in it, but there's not much to see. It is on the main road into town, after the market, just before and overlooking a petrol station. Fishing and fishmeal are prosperous industries.

On a bluff looming over Paita is a small colonial **fortress** built to repel pirates.
Paita was a port of call for Spanish shipping en route from Lima to Panama and
Mexico. It was a frequent target for attack, from Drake (1579) to Anson (1741).

Twenty-five kilometres up the coast is **Colán**, reached by driving down a large,
sandy bluff (turn off at Km 989). Near the base is a striking and lonely colonial church,
with breath-taking architecture and beautiful paintings in good condition. It is
claimed by some to be the oldest church in Peru, if not South America. The key-holder
can be found by asking in the adjoining village of San Lucas de Colán. The seafront
houses in the holiday resort stand on wooden stilts and are surrounded by palms. The
seawater is clear and warm (but beware stingrays – drag your feet when entering the
water) and sunsets are spectacular and the town has excellent seafood restaurants.
By public transport, go to Paita and change buses there.

Piura

North Coast Piura & around

Sleeping
Algarrobo Inn 1
California 2
Continental 3
Costa del Sol 4

El Almirante 5
El Sol 6
Esmeralda 7
Hospedaje Aruba 8
Hostal Los Jardines 10
Hostal Moon Night 11
La Capullana 13
Los Portales 14
Oriental 15
Pacífico 9
Perú 16
San Jorge 17

San Miguel 18
Vicus 19

Eating
Alex Chopp's 1
Brosti Chopp 2
Café R&B Zelada
  & Bloom Moon 4
Carburmer & Picantería
  Los Santitos 5
Chef R 6
D'Pauli 3

El Chalán de
  la Avenida 8
El Chalán del Norte 7
Frutilandia 9
Ganímedes 10
Grand Prix 11
Italia 12
Las Tradiciones
  Peruanas &
  Piura Tours 13
Romano &
  La Cabaña 14

Fifty kilometres northeast of Piura and 10 km off the old Pan-American Highway is the small town of **Chulucanas**, centre of the lemon and orange growing area. An ancient pottery technique has been discovered and revived here since the 1960s. The local potters formerly produced only large, utilitarian terracotta pots, until the 1960s when graverobbers brought to light examples of pottery from the Vicus and Tallane cultures dating from the second half of the first millennium BC. A group of Quechua pottery specialists researched and experimented with forms and techniques based on the pre-Columbian finds. These produce a very subtle and unusual effect. At first, the potters imitated the forms of the Vicus pieces but gradually they began to develop their own stylized figures. The most popular form is now the Chichera, a fat lady who makes and sells *chicha*. The most highly prized pieces are signed and sold in galleries and shops in Lima and abroad. Excellent ceramics can also be bought in the town, at a shop on the plaza and three others are within one block.

Huancabamba and Las Guaringas → *Colour map 1, grid B2.*

From Chulucanas the paved road heads southeast. A turn-off east to Morropán leads to a dirt road to **Canchaque**, a delightfully situated small centre for coffee, sugar-cane and fruit production (basic lodging). The difficult and tiring road, impossible for ordinary vehicles in the wet season, continues over a pass in the Andes of more than 3,000 m for 69 km to Huancabamba. This very pretty town in a wonderful setting hosts a tourist week in early July and the Virgen del Carmen festival in mid-July. It has three claims to fame. First, the predominance of European features, due to the fact that it was an important Spanish settlement in colonial times. Second, it is called 'the walking town', la ciudad que camina, as it is built on irregularly slipping causing much subsidence. Evidence for this includes the fall of the bridge over the Río Huancabamba.

Sullana

Sleeping	Hostal Príncipe 6	Due Torri 7
El Churre 1	Hostal Turicarami 5	Monterrico 10
Hospedaje Hugo 2		
Hospedaje San Miguel 3	**Eating**	
Hostal La Siesta 7	Café Café 1	
Hostal Lion's Palace 4	Chifa El Dorado 3	

0 metres 100
0 yards 100

The third, and by far the most remarkable claim to fame, is that Huancabamba is the base for reaching **Las Guaringas**, a series of lakes at about 4,000 m. Around here live the most famous witch doctors of Peru, to whom sick people flock from all over the country and abroad. The shamanic ceremony is definitely off the gringo trail and is an unforgettable trip. To take part in the ceremony, arrive in town and prepare to be approached almost immediately by a shaman's 'agent'. As dodgy as this sounds, this person can help you by doing all preparations. Go to the tourist centre in the plaza beforehand and double check if the agent's witch doctor is trustworthy. You'll then hop in a van, travel to the doctor's house, agree on a price and commence the ceremony immediately. It is an outdoor affair involving light hallucinogenic San Pedro cactus juice that is quite vile. The ceremony lasts all night and participants dance, reveal and predict the future. The entire ceremony is very mellow and most witch doctors have the disposition of concerned uncles. A spartan meal is provided so bring snacks. The next day involves a three-hour horseback ride to a high mountain lagoon where near-skinny dipping and more ceremonies take place. You're back in Huancabamba (tired and cold) by late afternoon.

Horses to the lakes can be hired for US$5. There are also trips to the village of **San Antonio** below Lago Carmen, and the village of **Salalá** below Lago Shumbe. Ignacio León, who owns a *bodega* opposite **El Dorado** (see Sleeping, below) runs an early pick-up service to the outlying villages and takes trips at negotiable prices.

Sullana to Ecuador

Sullana → *Colour map 1, grid B1. Population: 147,361.*

Sullana, 39 km north of Piura, is built on a bluff over the fertile Chira valley and is a busy, modern place. Avenida José de Lama, once a dusty, linear market, has a green, shady park with benches along the centre. Many of the bus companies have their offices along this avenue. San Martín is the main commercial street. Parks and monuments were added in 1994-1995, which have greatly improved the city's appearance. At the entrance, on the Pan-American Highway is an interesting mosaic statue of an iguana. There are lookouts over the Chira Valley at Plaza Bolognesi and by the arches near the Plaza de Armas. The local fiesta and agricultural fair is Reyes, held on 5-29 January. Although the city is safer than it once was, you should still take great care by the market. Do not arrive in the town after dark.

To Ecuador via Ayabaca → *Colour map 1, grid B2. Altitude: 2,850 m.*

Some 182 km northeast of Sullana in the highlands is the pleasant town of Ayabaca. This is the access point for the **Aypate** archaeological site and the **Samanga** hieroglyphics. It is also the home of **El Señor Cautivo de Ayabaca** (the captured Christ on his way to crucifixion). Many devotees make pilgrimages to his shrine, the most famous in northern Peru, especially on 12 October. Some leave from Piura, taking months over the journey. There are several *hostales* in town. From Ayabaca the road goes via the town of Samanguilla to the frontier bridge near the village of Espíndola . Over the bridge it's 4 km to the Ecuadorean village of Jimbura, from where you can get a pick-up to Amaluza (45 minutes). There are three basic hotels in Amaluza and buses run from here to Quito.

Border at La Tina-Macará

At Sullana the Pan-American Highway forks. To the east it crosses the Peru-Ecuador border at La Tina and continues via Macará to Loja and Cuenca. The road is scenic and paved to the border, 128 km. Macará is a dusty town in a rice-growing area. There are plenty of hotels and a few restaurants in town.

The border crossing is problem-free, open 24 hours and officials are helpful. Go to Peruvian immigration at the end of the bridge, get a stamp, walk across and then go to Ecuadorean immigration. There are no customs searches (vehicles, including *colectivos*, are subject to full searches, though). There are banks at each side for changing cash only, open during the week; rates are a little better in Macará.

> ● *The more frequently used route to the border is the coastal road which goes from Sullana north-west towards the Talara oilfields and then follows the coastline to Máncora and Tumbes, see page 422.*

Border at Alamor → *Colour map 1, grid B2.*

Colectivos run from Sullana for three dusty, bumpy hours to Alamor, a rather remote, but official border crossing west of La Tina (US$3, or US$18 for whole car). A rowing boat crosses the Río Lalamor to Lalamor in Ecuador (US$0.20), or you can wade across. Peruvian immigration is a short walk from the ferry and there are money changers offering regular rates. On the Ecuadorean side immigration is by the church, a long walk from the crossing (ask directions). Officials on both sides have to leave their post once a fortnight to register their documents. If you are unlucky enough to arrive on one of these days, you can't cross because you cannot get the right stamps. From Lalamor trucks run to the riverside town of Zapotillo (21 km, dirt, 40 minutes, US$1), also on the border, but not an official crossing. A paved road goes to Macará.

● Sleeping

Piura *p414, map p415*

AL Costa del Sol, Loreto 649, Piura, T/F073-302864, www.costadelsolperu.com. Luxury, pool, casino, internet facilities, restaurant.

AL Los Portales, Libertad 875, Plaza de Armas, Piura, T073-323072, www.acceso. peru. com/countryclub. Price includes breakfast, tax and welcome cocktail. This ex-government hotel, in the Country Club group, has been attractively refurbished and is the city's social centre, elegant, a/c, hot water, pleasant terrace and patio, nice pool.

B Bocatoma Resort, Av Costanera Norte, Colán, T074-970100, www.bocatoma.com. Prices rise in high season and there are a variety of cabins and offers. Cabins on a spit of land between the occean and lagoons, with restaurant, pool and sports facilities.

B Hotel Sol de Colán, on the promenade, Colán, T073-321784. With pool, bar, games room, restaurant and bungalow accommodation with en-suite facilities.

C Esmeralda, Loreto 235, Piura, T/F073-327109, www.hotelesmeralda. com.pe. With bathroom, hot water, fan (**B** with a/c), clean, comfortable, good, restaurant.

C San Miguel, Lima 1007, Plaza Pizarro, Piura, T073-305122. Modern, comfortable, with bath, TV, café.

C Vicus, Av Guardia Civil B-3, in Castilla 2 blocks across the river on the Sánchez Cerro bridge, Piura, T073-343186. With bathroom,

hot water, fan, clean, quiet, parking.

D Algarrobo Inn, Av Los Cocos 389, Piura, T073-307450, algarrobo@compunet.com.pe. With bath, hot water, TV, safe, everything works OK but it is rundown, good breakfast, very friendly. Handy for buses.

D El Almirante, Ica 860, Piura, T/F073-335239. With bathroom, fan, clean, modern, owner is knowledgeable about the Ayabaca area (see p417).

D El Sol, Sánchez Cerro 411, Piura, T073-324461. With bathroom, hot water, small pool, snack bar, parking, accepts dollars cash or TCs but won't change them. Recommended.

D Frente al Mar, Colán, T073-615465. Owner Alfred Leigh is of English descent, 4 rooms, damp, sea terrace, friendly. Its seafood restaurant is quite cheap and will cook vegetarian pasta if you wish.

D Perú, Arequipa 476, Piura, T073-333421. With bathroom and fan, clean, safe, friendly, laundry service, cold water, modern small rooms, all meals in restaurant extra.

D San Jorge, Jr Loreto 960, Piura, T073-327514. With bathroom and fan, cheaper without cable TV, hot water, clean but a little overpriced.

E La Capullana, Junín 925, Piura, T073-321239. With bath, some cheaper single rooms, welcoming.

E Continental, Jr Junín 924, Piura, T073-334531. Some rooms with bathroom, clean, comfortable, no breakfast.

E **El Faro**, Junín 322, Paita, T073-611076. Small and clean.

F **El Mundo**, on 300 block of Bolívar, Paita. Not bad but short-stay.

E **Hostal Los Jardines**, Av Los Cocos 436, Piura, T073-326590. With bath, hot water, TV, laundry, parking, good value.

E **Hostal Moon Night**, Junín 899, Piura, T073-336174. Comfortable, modern, spacious, with bath, F without bath or TV, clean, good value.

E **Las Brisas**, Av Ugarte, Paita. The best, with bathroom but little cold water, safe.

E **Miramar**, Malecón J Chávez 418, opposite Credicoop Paita, Paita, T073-611083. A filthy old wooden mansion on seafront.

E **Pacífico**, Apurímac 717, Piura, T073-303061. With bath and fan, simple and clean, good value.

F **Hospedaje Aruba**, Junín 851, Piura, T073-303067. Small rooms but clean and comfortable, shared bath, fan on request, very friendly. Recommended.

F per person **California**, Jr Junín 835, upstairs, Piura, T073-328789. Shared bath, own water-tank, mosquito netting on windows, roof terrace, clean, brightly decorated, the owner is very friendly. Recommended (some rooms rented by the hour, though).

F **Oriental**, Callao 446, Piura, T073-304011. Cheaper without bathroom and fan, clean, good value but very noisy, TV in reception.

Huancabamba amd Las Guaringas *p416*

F **Hotel El Dorado**, on the main plaza, Huancabamba. Good, clean, informative owner, with restaurant.

G **Hotel San José**, Salalá. Very basic, take your own food.

Sullana to Ecuador *p417*

At the border of La Tina-Macará, there is one hospedaje and several eating places on the road down to the bridge. At Suyo (a pretty place), 1½ hrs from Sullana , there are 2 *hospedajes*.

A **Hostal La Siesta**, Av Panamericana 400, Sullana, T/F073-502264, at the entrance to town. Hot water, fan, cable TV, B with cold water, pool, restaurant, laundry.

D **El Churre**, Tarapacá 501, Sullana,

T/F073-507006. With bath, TV, laundry, café. **419** Recommended.

D **Hostal Turicarami**, San Martín 814, Sullana, T073-502899. With bathroom, fan, some rooms have hot water, clean, E without bathroom or fan.

D **Los Charanes**, Quito y Roldós, Zapotillo, T073-265 9242. The best of th town's three hotels. There are also eating places.

E **Hostal Lion's Palace**, Grau 1030, Sullana, T073-502587. With bathroom, fan, patio, pleasant, quiet, no breakfast.

E **Hospedaje San Miguel**, C J Farfán 204, Sullana, T073-502789. F without bathroom, all rooms open off a central passageway, basic, helpful, good showers, staff will spray rooms against mosquitoes, cafeteria.

F **Hospedaje Hugo**, San Martín 1022, Sullana, T073-504016. Basic, small rooms.

F **Hostal Príncipe**, Espinar 588, Sullana. Clean and friendly.

F **Huambo Real**, T07-265 3184, Amaluza. The best of the three hotels in town.

Eating

Piura *p414, map p415*

Piura's special dishes include *Majado de Yuca* (manioc root with pork); *Seco de Chavelo* (beef and plantain stew); and *Carne Seca* (sun-dried meat). Its best-known sweet is the delicious *natilla*, made mostly of goats' milk and molasses. Its local drink is *pipa fría*, chilled coconut juice drunk from the nut with a straw.

₩₩₩ **Carburmer**, Libertad 1014, Piura. Very good lunches and dinners, also pizza.

₩₩₩ **Picantería Los Santitos**, in the same precinct as Carburmer. Lunch only, wide range of traditional dishes in a renovated colonial house.

₩₩ **La Cabaña**, Ayacucho 598, esquina Cusco, Piura. Pizzas and other good Italian food.

₩ **Alex Chopp's**, Huancavelica 538, Piura. A la carte dishes, seafood, fish, chicken and meats, beer, popular at lunchtime.

₩₩ **Brosti Chopp**, Arequipa 780, Piura. Similar to Alex Chopp's, but with lunch menú for US$1.45.

₩₩ **Grand Prix**, Loreto 395, Piura. Good food, reasonable prices.

₩₩ **La Carreta**, Huancavelica 726, Piura. One of the most popular places for roast chicken.

Chef R, Sánchez Cerro 210, near the bridge, Piura. Seafood restaurant.

Las Tradiciones Peruanas, Ayacucho 579, Piura. Regional specialities, also an art gallery.

Romano, Ayacucho 580, Piura. Popular with locals, extensive menu, excellent set meal for US$1.55. Highly recommended.

La Chayo, San Francisco 439, Catacaos. Recommended for its local dishes and *chicha*. There are several other places to eat on and close to Calle San Francisco.

Chifa Hong Kong, Junín 358, Paita. Considered by locals to offer really authentic Chinese food.

Club Liberal building, 2nd floor, Jorge Chávez 161, Paita. This serves good fish, seafood and crêpes, and is good value.

Ganímedes, Lima 440, Piura. A good vegetarian restaurant, very popular set lunch, à la carte is slow but well worth it, try the excellent yoghurt and fruit.

Cafés

Chalán del Norte, Tacna 520, Plaza de Armas, Grau 173 and 450 (Chalán de la Avenida), Piura. Several branches of this popular chain, for good sweets, cakes and ice cream.

D'Pauli, Lima 541, Piura. Also for sweets, cakes and ice cream, good.

Frutilandia, Jr Tacna 376, Piura. Good menú, good for breakfast, juices, ices and desserts.

Italia, Grau 172, Piura. For breakfasts, snacks, desserts and juices.

Huancabamba amd Las Guaringas *p416*

Local specialities include rompope, a rich and strong drink made of egg, spices and *cañazo* (sugar-cane spirit), roast *cuy* (guinea-pig) and local cheeses.

Sullana to Ecuador *p417*

Café Café, Tarapacá 484, Sullana. Sandwiches, tamales, lunch menú US$1, juices and drinks.

Chifa El Dorado, on the Plaza, Sullana. One of the more authentic of several *chifas*.

Due Torri, E Palacios 122, Sullana. Italian and regional, popular with locals.

Monterrico, Plaza de Armas, Sullana. Set menu for US$1, popular.

◑ Bars and clubs

Piura *p414, map p415*
Many of the nightspots are concentrated on Ayacucho, and some of them are also restaurants. **Bloom Moon**, Ayacucho 522. **Café R & B Zelada**, Ayacucho 562.

❀ Festivals and events

Piura *p414, map p415*
26-28 Jul Festival Internacional de Tunas. **27 Aug** to **2 Sep** Semana Turística de Piura, tourism week. **7 Oct** Festival Nacional de Marinera y Tondero, celebrating local dances.

◎ Shopping

Piura *p414, map p415*
There are delicatessens around Plaza de Armas. The market on **Sánchez Cerro** is good for fruit. Excellent ceramics can be bought at two shops on Libertad and from **Milagros García de Linares**, who lives in Urbanización Santa Inés, T073-327322.

▲ Activities and tours

Piura *p414, map p415*
Piura Tours, C Ayacucho 585, T073-328873, piuratours@mail.udep.edu.pe. The manager Mario speaks very good English.

◉ Transport

Piura *p414, map p415*
Air
There are daily flights to and from **Lima** and **Chiclayo** with Lan.

Bus
Most companies are on Av Sánchez Cerro, blocks 11, 12 and 13. To **Lima**, 1,038 km, 14-16 hrs, from US$7 (eg **Tepsa**), on the Panamericana Norte. Most buses stop at the major cities on route; **Flores**, Av Libertad 1210, T073-306664; **Ittsa**, Sánchez Cerro 1142, T073-333982 (US$17.15 on top floor, US$21.50 on lower floor); **Línea**, Sánchez Cerro 1215, T073-327821; **Tepsa**, Loreto 1198, T073-323721. To **Chiclayo**, 190 km, 3 hrs, US$3.65, several buses daily. To **Trujillo**, 7 hrs, 487 km, US$7, several daily. To travel by day

change in Chiclayo. To **Talara**, US$2, 2 hrs, with **Eppo**, T073-331160. To **Máncora**, US$3.15, 3 hrs, with **Eppo**. To **Tumbes**, 282 km, 4½ hrs, US$4.80, several buses daily, eg **Cruz del Sur** (La Libertad 1176, T073-337094, also to Lima), **Cial** (Bolognesi 817, T073-304250) and **Emtrafesa** (Los Naranjos 235, T073-337093, also to Chiclayo and Trujillo); also *colectivos*, US$5.75. Go to Tumbes and travel on from there for the **Aguas Verdes crossing to Ecuador**. To **Paita**, Trans Dora, Sánchez Cerro 1391, every 20 mins, 1 hr, US$0.75; also from Paita terminal on Av Gullman, just off Sánchez Cerro. All services drop off and collect passengers in the market area in Paita. To **Catacaos**, *colectivos* leave Piura from the far side of Puente San Miguel, US$0.20, 15-20 mins; also combis from the bus terminal, block 12 Av Sánchez Cerro, US$0.25. For **Chulucanas** combis from Piura charge US$1.50.

Taxis
Radio Taxis, T073-324509 or 324630.

Huancabamba amd Las Guaringas *p416*
To get to **Huancabamba**, take a bus from Piura to Canchaque and Huancabamba, which leaves daily at 0900 and 1000 (at least 10 hrs, US$9), from Av Ramón Castilla 196. Buy your ticket early on the day before travelling. It returns from Huancabamba at 0700 and 1000. A truck costs US$11.50. If driving, take the Pan-American Highway south of Piura for 66 km where there is a signpost to Huancabamba. Buses to **Las Guaringas** lakes leave at 0400 from the main plaza in Huancabamba.

Sullana to Ecuador *p417*
There are frequent buses from Piura to **Sullana**, 38 km, 30 mins (US$0.45), **Eppo**, **Sullana Express** and **Turismo del Norte**, all on 1100 block of Sánchez Cerro; also *colectivos* (US$1). To **La Tina** on the Ecuadorean frontier, is a further 128 km, 1¾ hrs, US$2.85. It's best to take an early bus to Sullana (start at 0430, leave when full), then a *colectivo* (see under Sullana). **Coop Loja**, Av Prol Sánchez Cerro 2-28 y Av Vice, T073-309407, office opens 0700 (mototaxi US$0.70 from centre, taxi US$2), direct buses to **Loja**, 4 a day, 8 hrs, US$8. The route is

Sullana-La Tina-Macará (US$3.40)-Loja. There is also a connecting *colectivo* to Vilcabamba from Loja. Coop Loja also have a direct bus to **Machala** via Aguas Verdes at 2245, US$6.20. Try not to arrive in Sullana or Piura after dark, it's unsafe.

In **Sullana**, several bus companies, including **Ormeño** use a new Terminal Terrestre. There are several daily buses to and from **Tumbes**, 244 km, 4-5 hrs US$5. If you have time, it is worth continuing to Piura rather than staying in Sullana. To **Chiclayo** and **Trujillo** see under Piura. To **Lima**, 1,076 km, 14-16 hrs, US$9-18, several buses daily, most coming from Tumbes or Talara. A luxury overnight bus via Trujillo with **Ittsa** (T073-501710) is US$18; also with **Cruz del Sur** and **Ormeño**, who also have buses to **Loja**, US$7.60, and **Guayaquil**. To **Paita** *colectivos* leave from the market, 2 blocks from Av Lama, US$1, 1 hr. To **Talara**, **Eppo** and **Emtrafesa**, C Comercio, 1 block from Av Lama, each leave hourly. **Eppo** are faster but more expensive, 1 hr, US$1.25. To **Máncora**, **Eppo**, 5 a day, 2½ hrs, US$3, or travel to Talara and then on from there via Los Organos. Mototaxis in Sullana charge US$0.30 around town. **Radio Taxis**, T073-502210/504354.

From **Sullana to the border** combis leave from Terminal Terrestre La Capullana, off Av Buenos Aires, several blocks beyond the canal, to the international bridge . They leave when full, US$2.85 per person, 1¾ hrs. It's best to take a taxi or mototaxi to and from the terminal. From the border to Macará is 4 km: walk over the bridge and take one of the pick-ups which run from the border (10 mins, US$0.30, or US$1.25 for whole car). Frequent buses leave the Ecuadorean side for Loja (5-6 hrs, US$5), so if you are not taking the through bus (see under Piura), you can go from Sullana to Loja in a day. From the border to Sullana, cars may leave before they are full, but won't charge extra.

For **Ayabaca**, buses leave from Piura in the morning, starting at 0800, from the Mercado Modelo; 6 hrs, US$7. From Ayabaca to **Espíndola** takes 2½ hrs, US$3 by public transport. From **Amaluza** a daily bus runs to Quito, taking about 24 hrs.

From **Zapotillo**, buses go to **Loja**, 7 hrs, and **Quito**.

❶ Directory

Piura *p414, map p415*

Banks **BCP**, Grau y Tacna. Cash and Visa and Amex TCs (US$12 commission), cheques changed in the mornings only, has ATM. **Banco Continental**, Plaza de Armas. Changes Amex TCs with US$10 commission. **Interbank**, Grau 170, changes Visa TCs, ATM for Visa, Mastercard and AmEx. Casas de cambio are at Arequipa 722, and Ica 429 and 460. Street changers can be found on Grau outside BCP. **Consulates** **Honorary British Consul**, c/o American Airlines, Huancavelica 223, T073-305990. **Honorary German Consul**, Jutta Moritz de Irazola, Las Amapolas K6, Urb Miraflores, Casilla 76, T073-332920. **Internet** Arequipa 728 and others in the centre. 10 machines in the Biblioteca Municipal, Urb Grau, US$0.60 per hr. **Laundry** **Lavandería Liz-to**, Tacna 785. Charges by weight. **Post** On the corner of Libertad and Ayacucho on Plaza de Armas is not too helpful. Perhaps it's better going to Hotel Los Portales. **Telephone** Loreto 259,

national and international phone and fax. Also at Ovalo Grau 483. **Useful addresses** **Dirección Regional de Turismo**, Av Fortunato Chirichigno, Urb San Eduardo, T073-327351, at the north end of town; **Indecopi** is also here, T073-304045, helpful when there are problems. **Touring y Automóvil Club del Perú**, Sánchez Cerro 1237, T073-325641, has little information.

Sullana to Ecuador *p417*

The following facilities are in Sullana.
Banks **BCP**, San Martín 685. Changes cash and TCs. There are casas de cambio and street changers on San Martín by Tarapacá. **Immigration** Grau 939. **Internet** San Martín 798 and 847 (World Net, US$0.60 per hr), and at Av José de Lama 125 and corner with Tarapacá. **Post** Farfán 326. **Telephone** Telephone and fax at Miró Quesada 213. **Travel agents** Pesa Tours, Espinar 301 y Tarapacá, T/F073-502237. For airline tickets (flights from Piura) and information. **Pola Tours** on the main plaza. Tans agency.

Coastal route to Ecuador

Although it leads to the tiresome border crossing of Aguas Verdes/Huaquillas, this road passes some of Peru's best and most popular beaches and to the area around Tumbes. The region also has national parks protecting habitats not found anywhere else in the country. ➤ *For Sleeping, Eating and other listings, see pages 427-432.*

Talara and around → *Phone code: 073. Colour map 1, grid B1.*

Talara is the main centre of the coastal oil area, with a state-owned 60,000 barrel-a-day oil refinery and a fertilizer plant. Set in a desert oasis 5 km west of the Panamericana, the city is a triumph over formidable natural difficulties, with water piped 40 km from the Río Chira. A couple of kilometres from the town is La Peña beach, which is unspoilt. Other attractions in the area can be reached via paved highways which connect the town with the Negritos, Lagunitos, La Brea and other oilfields.

Of historical interest are the old tarpits at **La Brea**, 21 km inland from Punta Pariñas, south of Talara, and near the foot of the Amotape mountains. Here the Spaniards boiled the tar to get pitch for caulking their ships. Surfers will love the empty swell north and south of town, especially near Negritos where a gentle beach break and rolling thunder are separated by Punta Balcones, the western-most point of South America. The impressive sea lion colony and the occasional dolphin make this an interesting spot.

Some 31 km north of Talara, is the small port of **Cabo Blanco**, famous for its excellent sea-fishing and surfing. The scenery has, unfortunately, been spoilt by numerous oil installations. The turn-off from the Pan-American Highway is at the town

Camping is permitted free of charge at Cabo Blanco, on the beach or by the **Fishing Club** overlooking the sea, at least in the off-season, June-December. The film of Ernest Hemingway's *The Old Man and the Sea* was shot here, see page 426. Marlin grew scarce in the late 1960s owing to commercial fishing and to climatic and maritime factors but in the last few years the Marlin have returned. The old **Fishing Club** in Cabo Blanco, built in the 1950s, has been remodelled in the shape of the **Fishing Club Lodge Hotel**, which has a restaurant, pool, and offers watersports (it's likely to be full in the New Year period). A launch also provides all the necessary facilities for deep-sea fishing. Now, would-be Ernest Hemingways can return to Cabo Blanco in search of their dream catch.

Los Organos is a small town and fishing port with a fine long sandy beach and easy surfing at its southern end, it provides a quieter and cheaper alternative to Máncora. For those looking to relax, it's especially suitable at peak periods.

Máncora and around → *Colour map 1, grid B1.*

A small resort stretching along 3 km of the Highway, Máncora is parallel to a long, attractive, sandy beach with safe bathing. It is a popular stop-off for travellers on the Peru-Ecuador route, even more so with young Limeños who arrive at weekends and holiday times. Consequently it has a very lively feel with numerous bars and music playing all night. The water here is warm enough for bathing and the town has some of the friendliest local surfers on the planet. Surfing is best November to March (boards and suits can be hired from several places along the southern blocks of Avenida Piura, US$1.50 each per hour). This stretch of coast is famous for its excellent *mero* (grouper).

The Pan-American Highway runs through the centre of town and is the main street, called Avenida Piura. Most of the tourist facilities are south of the town centre and artesanía stalls line the avenue between the centre and south end. At peak times youngsters spill out from the conentration of bars bringing traffic to a complete standstill. At the north end of town the beach is inaccessible and dirty, and this is not a safe area. South of Máncora along the coastal road (old Pan-American Highway) are some excellent beaches which are being developed, for example **Las Pocitas**, a resort ideal for families, or just for relaxing.

Fresh water is piped into the area, producing the incongruous but welcome sight of green lawns and lush gardens between the sea and desert cliffs. There is a line of rocks parallel to the beach, which form interesting bathing pools at low tide, though these can be dangerous at high tide.

At **Las Arenas** resort, 4 km south of Máncora, the beach is completely unspoiled, with armies of small crabs and abundant bird life, including frigates and masked and brown pelicans.

East of Máncora are hot mud baths (*baños del barro*), which are nice after a day in the surf. There is no infrastructure, but the landscape, desert foothills and shrub lands, is beautiful. The access is north of town, at Km 1,168, from where you head for Quebrada Fernández. Beyond is **El Angolo game reserve**, which extends as far south as the Río Chira. Take a mototaxi from Máncora, 20 minutes, and pay US$5.75 for the return journey and an hour's wait while you bathe.

North of Máncora

At Km 1,182 is an enormous customs house for checking southbound traffic. 22 km north of Máncora, at Km 1,187 (El Arco – or arch), is the turn-off for **Punta Sal Grande**, a posh resort town at the southern end of beautiful Playa Punta Sal, a 10 km long sandy beach, with calm surf. It's a favourite of well-to-do Lima businessmen and politicians, but in the low season is almost deserted and hotel rates are significantly lower. The beach offers kilometres of golden sand, relatively warm turquoise water, interesting sea-life in the rock pools and huge schools of whales passing on the distant horizon at dusk. A pleasant walk can be made along the beach to **Punta Sal Chica**, allow at least 3 hours for the round trip and carry water with you.

The fishing village of **Cancas** has a few shops, restaurants and a gas station. From Punta Mero (Km 1,204) north, the beach is used by larveros, extracting shrimp larvae from the ocean for use in the shrimp industry, and is no longer considered safe for camping. Several new resorts are being built between Punta Mero and Tumbes.

Zorritos, 27 km south of Tumbes (US$0.55 by combi), is an important fishing centre, with a good beach. Several new hotels and resorts have been built. At **Caleta La Cruz** is the only part of the Peruvian coast where the sea is warm all year. There are two good beaches near Tumbes, one is at Caleta La Cruz 16 km southwest, where Pizarro landed in 1532. The original Cruz de Conquista was taken to Lima. Regular *colectivos* run back and forth from Tumbes, US$0.30 each way.

Tumbes → *Phone code: 072. Colour map 1, grid A1. Population: 34,000.*

Tumbes, about 141 km north of Talara, and 265 km north of Piura, is the most northerly of Peru's provincial capitals. It is not the most beautiful, but it does have some interesting historic wooden buildings in the centre. Tumbes is also a garrison town, so watch where you point your camera. Mosquito repellent is a must for the Tumbes area.

Ins and outs
Getting there A taxi to the airport costs US$4, 20 minutes. Combis charge US$1.50. Taxis meet flights to take passengers to the border for US$7-9. There are no combis from the airport to the border. Beware of overcharging. All bus companies have offices on Avenida Tumbes.

Getting around Everything is fairly conveniently located close to the Plaza de Armas, although transport to the Ecuadorean border is a little bit farther out. Hotels are mostly central to the north of the river either side of Av Tumbes and Bolívar.

Tourist information Centro Cívico ① *Bolognesi 194, 2nd level, on the plaza, T072-524940, tumbes@mincetur.gob.pe, 0800-1300, 1400-1800*. Helpful, provides map and leaflets.

Sights
The long promenade, the Malecón Benavides, beside the high banks of the Río Tumbes, gives good views of the river. It is decorated with arches and a monstrous statue called El Beso (the Kiss), has several cafés, but is rather dilapidated. Old houses are best seen on **Calle Grau**, particularly at the junction with C Los Andes, and a colonial public library with a small museum stands in the **Plaza de Armas**. The **cathedral**, dating in its present incarnation from 1903, was restored in 1985. There are two pedestrian malls, arranged with benches and plants, Paseo de Los Libertadores on Bolívar and Paseo de la Concordia on San Martín, both leading north from the Plaza de Armas. In the main Plaza and the Paseo de la Concordia there are several ornate, brightly-coloured mosaic statues giving the city a slightly more exotic, tropical feel than anywhere else on the Peruvian coast.

The Río Tumbes forms a significant boundary between the dry, scrubby desert vegetation to the south and the more lush green landscape north of the river. The river was only bridged in 1930 and the long-term isolation of Tumbes from the rest of Peru is still reflected in the people and their approach to life today.

Around Tumbes

The remains of the Cabeza de Vaca cult centre of the Tumpis Indians can be found at **Corrales,** 5 km south of Tumbes, but were heavily damaged by the 1983 and 1997/98 rains. The Incas built their fort of San Pedro on the site of the Tumpis settlement. The fort was visited by Pizarro on his way from the coast along the Inca coastal highway up to Cajamarca.

Three protected areas consisting of three distinct environments form the UNESCO Biosphere Reserve of northwest Peru. It is an area rich in wildlife and flora, but little visited by travellers passing by en route between Peru and Ecuador. In a single day it is possible to visit all three areas and sample the rainforest, dry scrub and mangrove swamps.

Santuario Nacional los Manglares de Tumbes

This national reserve was created to protect the mangrove ecosystem in the northernmost part of the Peruvian coast. It extends between the border with Ecuador in the north and Puerto Pizarro (see below) in the south. 4,750 ha remain, of which 2,988 ha are protected. There are 5 species of mangrove, the main one being the red mangrove on whose roots the conchas negras live. At least 200 bird species have been recorded, eight of which are endemic, including the mangrove eagle. The mangroves are under threat from fresh water brought down by the rivers during El Niño and the expanding shrimp farming industry, though at 3,000 ha it's small

Tumbes

To Airport & Aguas Verdes (Ecuador Border)

Río Tumbes

To Sullana, Piura & Lima

Sleeping	Florián 6	Roma 15	Classic 2
Amazonas & Chicho 1	Franco 7	Sudamericano 16	Latino & Los Gustitos 3
César 2	Hostal Tumbes 9	Toloa 1 17	Sí Señor 4
Costa del Sol 3	Italia 10	Toloa 2 18	
El Estoril 4	Judgem 11		
Elica 5	Kikos 12	**Eating**	**Bars & clubs**
	Lourdes 14	Chifa Wakay 1	Pub Discoteca Keops 5

North Coast Coastal route to Ecuador
The old man and the marlin

Though Ernest Hemingway's famous novel, The Old Man and the Sea, was set in a Cuban fishing village, the people of Cabo Blanco, on the north coast of Peru, claim that the great writer was inspired by their own fishing waters.

The protagonist of the book, the old fisherman, Santiago, was perhaps the product of Hemingway's own obsession with the idea of catching a marlin weighing more than 1,500 pounds. One of the very few places where such a feat is possible is off the coast of Cabo Blanco. Here, in the 1950s, the marlin were abundant and reached extraordinary sizes. Indeed, during that decade Cabo Blanco became a sort of world sport fishing capital and fishermen the world over congregated there to chase the great black marlin, the largest and the most difficult to catch owing to its tremendous strength.

So it was that when Hollywood producers decided to make a film based on Hemingway's novel they realized that the only place they could find a suitably large fish was in the waters off Cabo Blanco. In April 1955, the shooting team arrived with the writer, who was there to help them locate the fish that would appear in the movie.

Hemingway wasn't too interested in the movie, he was along for the fishing and quickly struck up a rapport with the down-to-earth local fisherfolk. In one particularly poignant anecdote they made him a gift of a bottle of *pisco*, a popular grape brandy, with a note saying "As long as the grapevines cry, I will drink their tears". The following morning, before going out to fish, the writer met those who had given him the *pisco*, smiled and said to them in Spanish, "I have drunk the tears".

Hemingway did not realize his dream of the 1,500 pound marlin during almost two months on the Peruvian coast, though he did manage to catch one weighing a little over 900 pounds. It was one of the largest black marlin he had ever caught and probably the last one of that size he would catch during the few remaining years of his life.

compared to that of Ecuador. The mangrove swamps are full of pelicans; best to visit them at high tide. A few tame birds beg for fish on the beaches.

Puerto Pizarro

Puerto Pizarro, a small, rubbish-strewn fishing port 13 km northeast of Tumbes, is another access point for the mangroves. Worth visiting from here is the research station where the **Río Tumbes crocodile**, a UN Red-data species, is protected. The crocodile is found at the river's mouth, threatened by shrimp farming, and in the Río Tumbes' upper reaches, threatened by gold-mining. Boats from Comité de Transporte Acuático, Malecón Turístico, T072-543019 go to: **Isla de Amor** (bars, restaurants, camping, windsurfing, hammocks for rent, overnighting 'homeless lovers', US$4.30); **Isla Hueso de Ballena** (open ocean and quiet bay, swimming, no services, US$5.75); **crocodile farm** (US$7.15), **Isla de los Pájaros** (best to see birds 1700-1800, US$8.55); full tour including mangroves, two hours, US$12.85 (price per boat, maximum eight people). **Festival of San Pedro y San Pablo** takes place on 29-30 June.

Parque Nacional Cerros de Amotape

The Parque Nacional Cerros de Amotape was created to protect an area representative of the equatorial forest. It extends southeast from the south bank of the Tumbes river, towards the El Angolo game preserve northeast of Máncora. It area of dry forest on the Pacific coast. Some of the endemic species are the Tumbes crocodile, the river otter and white-winged turkeys. Other species to be seen are black parrot, puma, deer, tigrillo and white-backed squirrels. Permission to enter is needed from Inrena, which Pronaturaleza can arrange. There is no entrance fee. All water must be carried which is why most visitors choose to visit by tour.

Amazonas Explorer, see page 173, organizes commercial descents of the Río Tumbes once a year around Christmas time, to take advantage of the best weather. It involves the chance to see the rare wildlife, with four-wheel drive, trekking and rafting through a spectacular canyon in the heart of Amotape. The expedition ends just a few hours from the beach at Máncora.

Zona Reservada de Tumbes

The Zona Reservada de Tumbes, formerly Bosque Nacional de Tumbes (75,000 ha), lies to the northeast of Tumbes, between the Ecuadorean border and Cerros de Amotape National Park. It was created to protect dry equatorial forest and tropical rainforest. The wildlife includes monkeys, otters, wild boars, small cats and crocodiles. Access from Tumbes is via Cabuyal, Pampas de Hospital and El Caucho to the Quebrada Faical research station or via Zarumilla and Matapalo. The best accessible forest is around El Narango, which lies beyond the research station.

Border at Aguas Verdes (Ecuador)

The main Peruvian immigration and customs complex is outside Zarumilla, about 4 km before the international bridge. The frontier is open 24 hrs a day and passports can be stamped on either side of the border at any time.

Police officers on either side of the international bridge sometimes ask for bribes. Try to avoid them if possible but if approached be courteous but firm. Porters on either side of the border charge exorbitant prices, but don't be bullied. Taxi drivers can also try to rip passengers off. If you wish to photograph the border, ask the Ecuadorean immigration officers first. There are virtually no customs formalities at the border for passengers crossing on foot, but spot-checks sometimes take place.

Having obtained your exit stamp, proceed across the bridge into Huaquillas. Passports are stamped 3 km north of town along the road to Machala. There's no urban transport; inter-city buses charge US$0.20 from Huaquillas; taxis US$1.50. When driving into Peru vehicle fumigation is not required, but there is one outfit who will attempt to fumigate your vehicle with water and charge US$10. Beware of officials claiming that you need a carnet to obtain your 90-day transit permit. This is not so; cite Decreto Supremo 015-87-ICTI/TUR (but check that rules have not changed). There are frequent road tolls between Tumbes and Lima, approximately US$0.75 each.

Huaquillas is a small city with a reasonable selection of hotels and other services. Transport links to other parts of Ecuador (Machala – 80 km, one hour, Quito, Guayaquil, Cuenca, Loja) are good. Transit Police, Customs and the Military have checkpoints on the road north so keep your passport to hand.

● Sleeping

Talara and around *p422*
All hotels in Talara have problems with the water supply.
A Gran Pacífico, Av Aviación y Arica, T/F073-385450. The most luxurious in town, suites, hot water, pool, restaurant, bar, parking, pay in dollars.
D Residencial Grau, Av Grau 77,

T073-382841, near the main plaza. Clean, friendly, possible to park one motor bike, owner changes dollars.
D Hostal La Perla, Los Organos, southern end of the beach (mototaxi US$0.50, 5 mins), T073-857389, www.elaperla.com.pe. With pool and restaurant, clean and friendly, good value. Recommended.

E **Hostal Anymarke**, Av Túpac Amaru 709, Los Orgnanos. In the town centre, slightly less well kept than Roland Kent.

E **Hostal Roland Kent**, Av Túpac Amaru 769, Los Organos, T/F073-857163, rolandkent peru@yahoo.com. Yes, it's named after the owner and his favourite brand of cigarettes! Clean, friendly, TV, good value, with the best restaurant in town.

E **Hostal Talara**, Av del Ejército 217, T073-382186. Clean and comfortable.

Máncora and around *p423*

All places to stay are to be found along the Panamericana between the main plaza at the north end of Máncora town and the bridge at the south end. The better hotels are at the southern end of Máncora. Prices can increase by up to 100% in high season (Dec-Mar).

L **Las Arenas**, 3½ km south of Máncora, T073-858240, hotellasarenasdemancora@ terra.com. Full board, 8 luxury bungalows, pool, lush gardens, trampoline, playground, kayaks, free transport from Tumbes airport.

B **Puerto Palos**, along the old Pan-American Highway south of town (10 mins by moto-taxi, US$1.45), T073-858199, www.puerto palos.com. Excellent, small, nice pool overlooking the ocean. Restaurant is good but expensive. Recommended.

B-C **Las Olas** on the beach in block 1 of Piura, T073-858109. Offers smart, cabin-style rooms with bath, hammocks and gardens, half and full-board rates available. **El Mar** in the same area has the same prices and facilties.

C **Punta Ballenas**, south of Cabo Blanco bridge at the south entrance to town, T073-858136. B in high season, lovely setting on beach, garden with small pool, price includes breakfast, expensive restaurant. Recommended.

D **Hosal Casa Azul del Turista**, Av Piura 224, T073- 858126. New, clean, friendly, family run, with bath and TV, and roof terraces giving sea views. Recommended (but not at weekends or holiday times due to its prox-imity to the Sol y Mar disco – see below).

D **Sausalito**, Piura block 4, T073-858058. Comfortable, quieter rooms at back, some

rooms without windows, breakfast included.

E **Sol y Mar**, Piura block 2, on beach, T073-858106 (ask for Coqui Quiroga). With bath, fan and mosquito repellent extra, basic, restaurant, shop, internet café (very slow connection), occasionally host parties, noisy disco till 0600 at weekends and holidays blights even its neighbours.

E-F **Hospedaje Crillon**, Paita 168, 1 block back from Panamericana in centre, T073-858001, basic rooms with 4 or more beds, shared bath, plenty of water, recommended.

North of Máncora *p423*

A **Caballito de Mar**, Playa Punta Sal, 500 m along at the southern end of the bay, T072-540058, caballito@amauta.rcp.net.pe.

A per person **Punta Sal Club Hotel**, at the north end of the beach at Punta Sal Chica, access road at Km 1,193, T072-608878. 18 bungalows, 12 rooms, solar heated water, relaxing, private beach, watersports, pool, horse riding, deep-sea fishing, transport to Tumbes airport US$10 per person. Recommended. B without full board (AL/A in high season). With bathroom, nice location overlooking the ocean, all rooms have ocean view, comfortable, friendly, pool, excellent restaurant. Recommended.

B **Hotel Punta Camarón**, at Km 1,235, T072-608007. With secluded private beach, swimming pool, restaurant. Recommended.

C per person **Hospedaje El Bucanero**, at the entrance to Playa Punta Sal, set back from the beach, T072-540118, htlelbucaneropta sal@hotmail.com. With a variety of rooms, pool, restaurant, bar, gardens and billiards, popular with travellers, great view.

C **Hotel Playa Florida**, at Km 1,222, T/F072-320251. Pleasant bungalows on the ocean (look for the red roofs), food available.

C **Los Delfines**, T072-320251, near the beach at the entrance to Playa Punta Sal. Shared bathroom, clean, nice rooms, restaurant open in high season, meals on request in low season, vegetarian available, Canadian-run, very friendly, full board AL, more during high season for full board, A for a room only in high season.

C per person **Sunset Punta Sal**, 500 m south

along the beach, T072-807702, puntasunset @hotmail.com. **B** in high season, full board, wonderful place overlooking the sea, small, with pool, restaurant, popular with travellers. **D Huá**, on the beach at the entrance to Playa Punta Sal, T072-540023, www.huapuntasal. com. **B** in the high season. A rustic old wooden building, rooms with bath, pleasant terrace overlooking ocean, discount for IYHF card holders, camping permitted on the beach beside the hotel, meals available. **D** per person **Las Terrazas**, opposite Sunset Punta Sal, T072-964 0353, lasterrazaspunta sal@yahoo.com. One of the more basic and cheaper hotels in Punta Sal, friendly, restaurant has sea view, some rooms better than others, not all with own bath. **E** per person **Casa Grillo Centro Ecoturistico Naturista**, Los Pinos 563, between Bocapán and Los Pinos, 30 km from Tumbes, T/F072-544222, casagrillo@yahoo. es. To get there take a *colectivo* from Tumbes market to Los Pinos, or get off bus on Pan-American Highway at Km 1,236.5. Youth Hostel with excellent restaurant including vegetarian meals, very friendly, great place to relax, 6 rustic-style rooms for up to 4 people, shared bath, hot water, laundry, also surfing, scuba diving, fishing, cycling, trekking, horse riding (US$4 per hr), camping available. Recommended.

Tumbes *p424, map p425*
The water supply is poor. There are many cheap hotels by the market. At holiday times it can be very difficult to find a vacant room.
A Costa del Sol, San Martín 275, Plazuela Bolognesi, T072-523991, ventastumbes@ costadelsolperu.com. Clean, hot water, minibar, fan, front rooms noisy, restaurant has good food and service (US$5.75-7), parking extra, has nice garden with swimming pool, racquetball court, provides some tourist information.
D César, Huáscar 311, T/F072-522883. With bathroom, fan, TV.
D Chicho, Tumbes 327, T/F072-523696. With bathroom, fan, mosquito net, TV, clean, quieter rooms at the back.
D Florián, Piura 414 near El Dorado bus company, T072-522464, F524725. Clean, private bath, fan.
D Kikos, Bolívar 462, T072-524482. With bathroom, basic.

D Lourdes, Mayor Bodero 118, T072-522966. With bathroom, fan, clean, friendly, roof restaurant, slow service. Recommended.
D Roma, Bolognesi 425 Plaza de Armas, T072-524137, F525879. With bathroom, fan, pleasant, convenient.
E Amazonas, Av Tumbes 317, T072-525266. With bathroom, fan, clean, friendly, water supply in the mornings is unreliable, noisy.
E El Estoril, Huáscar 317, 2 blocks from the main plaza, T072-521360. With bathroom, good, clean, friendly, discount for long stay.
E Elica, Tacna 319, T072-523870. With bathroom, clean, fan, quiet, góod.
E Franco, San Martín 107, Paseo de la Concordia, T072-525295. With bathroom, fan, upper rooms are quieter and pleasanter.
E Hostal Tumbes, Grau 614, T072-522203. With bathroom, cold water, fan, friendly, clean, good value. Recommended.
E Italia, Grau 733, T072-523396. Cold showers, friendly, also good value.
E Judgem, Bolívar 344, T072-523530. With bathroom, basic, OK.
E Toloa 1, Av Tumbes 436, T072-523771. With bathroom, fan, clean, safe, helpful.
E Toloa 2, Bolívar 458, T072-524135. With bathroom, fan, OK.
F Sudamericano, San Martín 130, Paseo de la Concordia. Shared bathroom, basic but good value.

Around Tumbes *p425*
E per person **Hospedaje Bayside**, by the Malecón, Puerto Pizarro, T072-543045. Bungalows with bath, pool, food available.
E Hostal Francis, Av República del Perú 220, Aguas Verdes, T072-561177. An OK option if you are stuck overnight in the border area. There are also 4 hotels in Zarumilla, at Km 1,290 on the Pan-American Highway, 5 km south of Aguas Verdes. There is a signpost on the highway and the main plaza is only a few blocks away from the turn-off: **E Imperio**, on the plaza, is small, modern, basic, very clean, very friendly. Cold water turned off at night, mosquito nets. Recommended.

❶ Eating

Talara and around *p422*
The better restaurants in Talara can be found in the main hotels. There are many cheap

North Coast Coastal route to Ecuador Listings

restaurants on the main plaza. Overlooking the beach in Los Organos are several restaurants. **Bambu** is clean and prepares an excellent *ceviche* with fish freshly caught by the fishing boats bobbing in the bay.

Máncora and around *p423*
There are many small restaurants and surprisingly trendy bars lining the Panamericana. Among the good ones are **La Espada** and **Don Pedro**, on the highway, both offer excellent value lobster dishes. ₩-₩ **Chan Chan**, also on the Panamericana. Good Italian restaurant with resonable prices; the pizzas are better than the pasta. ₩ **Stephanie's**, café adjoining **Sol y Mar** overlooking beach. Serves *fuentes*, huge plates big enough for two. ₩ **Café La Bajadita** is the best place in the evening to hang out, eat chocolate cake or manjarblanco and listen to rock and reggae

North of Máncora *p423*
Good restaurants in Zorritos include **El Brujo**; **Sunset Beach**, Km 1,245, T072-542243, good for seafood; **Zuco Zuco**, for pizza.

Tumbes *p424, map p425*
There are inexpensive restaurants on the Plaza de Armas, Paseo de la Concordia and near the markets.
₩-₩ **Chifa Wakay**, Huáscar 413. Smart Chinese, good, recommended.
₩-₩ **Classic**, Tumbes 185. Popular and recommended for local food.
₩-₩ **Latino**, Bolívar 163, on Plaza de Armas. Good set meals and à la carte, also *peña* most evenings.
₩-₩ **Los Gustitos**, Bolívar 148. Excellent *menús* and à la carte.
₩ **Pizzería Studio** on the plaza. Good pizza and desserts.

Cafés
Heladería La Suprema, Paseo Libertadores 298. Good ice cream, sweets and cold drinks.
Sí Señor, Bolívar 119, on plaza. Good snacks.

○ Bar and clubs

Tumbes *p424, map p425*
Pub Discoteca Keops, Bolívar 121 on the plaza. Sometimes has live groups at weekends.

○ Shopping

Tumbes *p424, map p425*
Anilu, on Bolívar. A well-stocked supermarket.

▲ Activities and tours

Tumbes *p424, map p425*
Most companies offer day tours of the local area for US$20 per person, minimum 2, and US$35-50 per person to the hinterland.
Preference Tours, Grau 427, T072-525518. Knowledgeable and friendly.
Rosillo Tours, Tumbes 293, T/F072-523892. Information, tickets, Western Union agents.

○ Transport

Talara and around *p422*
Bus See under Sullana. To and from **Tumbes**, 171 km, 3 hrs, US$3.50, several daily. Most come from Piura and most stop at major towns going north. To **Piura**, 111 km, 2 hrs, US$1.75. To **El Alto** (Cabo Blanco), 32 km, 30 mins, US$0.75. To **Máncora** take a combi from beside the Tepsa terminal to Los Organos (an oil workers town on the Panamericana with a windy beach and good seafood restaurants on the plaza), US$1, 1 hr; change combis there and continue to Máncora, 28 km, 20 mins, US$0.50. **Los Organis to/from Piura**, Eppo 3 hrs, US$3.50, and **Dorado**, 2½ hrs, US$4. *Colectivos* leave when full for **Máncora**, 15 mins, US$0.40, and **Tumbes**, 2½ hrs, US$1.80. All transport leaves from the Panamericana in the town centre.

Máncora and around *p423*
To **Sullana and Piura** with EPPO, Grau 470, 1 block north of plaza, and **Dorado** both offer hourly service, just over 3 hrs, US$4, and just under 3 hrs, US$5, respectively. Other buses stop en route from Tumbes in the main plaza. To **Tumbes** (and points in between), combis tour the length of Av Piura all day as far as the bridge until sufficiently full to depart, US$1.50, 2 hrs.

North of Máncora *p423*
A taxi from Máncora is the quickest and easiest way to get to Punta Sal Grande, 20 mins, US$9. Mototaxis are also prepared to make the trip, 40 mins, US$6. Alternatively,

take a combi from Máncora heading for Tumbes which can drop you at El Arco, 15 mins, US$0.50, as can buses from Tumbes or the south. A mototaxi to/from El Arco and the hotels costs US$1.50, up to 10 mins, or you can walk it in half an hour. However, if popping in to Máncora for anything while staying at Punta Sal it is best not to use passing buses for the short journey as they can be held up at the Customs checkpoint; use combis instead.

Tumbes *p424, map p425*

Air Daily flights to and from **Lima**; at the time of going to prress, after the grounding of Nuevo Continente, it was not known who would be offering this service.

Bus Daily buses to and from **Lima**, 1,320 km, 18-20hrs, US$12 (normal service), US$25 (Cruz del Sur), US$34 (Cruz del Sur VIP service). Most bus companies have offices on Av Tumbes: **Civa**, No 518, T072-525120; **Cruz del Sur**, Tumbes Norte 319, T072-896163; **Ormeño**, Av Tumbes s/n, T072-522228; **Trans Chiclayo**, 466, T072-525260. Cheaper buses usually leave 1600-2100, and more expensive ones 1200-1400. Except for luxury service, most buses to Lima stop at major cities en route. Tickets to anywhere between Tumbes and Lima sell quickly, so if arriving from Ecuador you may have to stay overnight. Piura is a good place for connections in the daytime. To **Talara**, 171 km, US$3.50, 3 hrs. To **Sullana**, 244 km, 3-4 hrs, US$4.50, several buses daily. To Piura, 4-5 hrs, 282 km, US$4.50; with **Trans Chiclayo, Cruz del Sur, El Dorado** (Piura 459, T072-523480, also to Máncora and Trujillo) 8 a day. **Comité Tumbes/Piura** *colectivos* (Tumbes 308, T072-525977) costs US$5.75, fast cars, leave when full, 3½ hrs. To **Chiclayo**, 552 km, 6 hrs, US$5.75, several each day with **Cruz del Sur, El Dorado**. To **Trujillo**, 769 km, 10-11 hrs, US$7.15-14.35, **Ormeño, Cruz del Sur, El Dorado** and **Emtrafesa**, Tumbes 596, T072-522894. To **Chimbote**, 889 km, 13-14 hrs, US$10. For transport to the border, see p427 .

Around Tumbes *p425*

The best access to **Santuario Nacional los Manglares de Tumbes** is via the Pan-American Highway north as far as Zarumilla. Combis leave every few minutes from Tumbes, US$0.50, 30 mins. Then hire a motorbike in Zarumilla to go to CEDECOM (Centro de Conservación para el Desarrollo de los Manglares), 7 km, US$1.50 each way but you must arrange for the bike to return to collect you. The standard tour price is US$12 for a boat that takes up to 6 passengers, 2½ hrs, and includes the mangrove walkway and a trip up several creeks by boat, subject to tide levels. Book with Pronaturaleza, in Tumbes, who can also arrange a sanctuary visitors permit from Inrena. There is no entry fee.

For **Puerto Pizarro**, take *colectivo* No 6 from the small plaza on C Piura in Tumbes; US$0.50, 20 mins.

Access to **Parque Nacional Cerros de Amotape** is via the road which goes south- east from the Pan-American Highway at Bocapán (Km 1,233) to Casitas and Huásimo, it takes about 2 hrs by car from Tumbes, and is best done in the dry season (Jul-Nov). Also access via Quebrada Fernández from Máncora and via Querecotilo and Los Encuentros from Sullana.

From Tumbes to border *colectivos* leave from block 3 of Av Tumbes. US$1 per person or US$6 to hire a car, but over-charging of gringos is very common, especially from the border to Tumbes. Make sure the driver takes you all the way to the border and not just as far as the complex 4 km south of the bridge. Combis leave from the market area along Mcal Castilla across the Calle Alipio Rosales, US$0.50 (luggage on the roof). Run down city buses ply the same route as combis, US$0.40, but are slower. All vehicles only leave when full, 30-45 mins to Aguas Verdes on the Peruvian side of the international bridge. They pass the turn-off for the airport from which it is a 500-m walk to the terminal. *Colectivos* to the airport charge US$1.50 per person, but often ask for much more. From the border to Zarumilla by moto-taxi costs US$0.50 per person. *Colectivos* can cross the bridge, taxis cannot (so don't hire a Peruvian taxi to take you into Ecuador).There is an **Aero Continente** office in Aguas Verdes, good for booking flights from Tumbes or Piura.

❶ Directory

Máncora and around *p423*

Banks Tienda Marlón, Piura 613. Changes US$ cash at poor rates. **Internet** Several internet cafés on the highway. **Telephone** Piura 509, opposite the church. National and international calls, also collect.

Tumbes *p424, map p425*

Banks BCP, Paseo de los Libertadores 261, for cash only, poor rates. **Banco Continental**, Bolívar 121, changes cash and Amex TCs only, US$5 commission. **Cambios Internacionales**, Av Bolívar 161, Plaza de Armas. Cash only, good rates. Money changers on the street (on Bolívar, left of the Cathedral), some of whom are unscrupulous, give a much better rate than the banks or cambios, but don't accept the first offer you are given. Street changers don't change cheques. All banks close for lunch. Rates offered at the airport are bad. If you are travelling on to Ecuador, it is better to change your Soles at the border as the rate is higher. **Consulates** Ecuadorean Consulate, Bolívar 155, Plaza de Armas, T072-523022, 0900-1300 and 1400-1630. Mon-Fri. **Internet** Widely available in many cheap cafés and major hotels. Around the Plaza de Armas, **El Mundo** and **Planet.com** are open late, and there is a good place between Latino and Los Gustitos.

Laundry Lavandería Flash at Piura 1000. Pay by weight. **Post** San Martín 208, on Paseo de la Concordia. **Telephone** San Martín 210, on Paseo de la Concordia.

Useful adresses Pronaturaleza, Av Tarapacá 4-16, Urb Fonavi, T072-523412. **Touring y Automóvil Club**, Huáscar 330, T072-523475, tumbes@touringperu.com.pe.

Around Tumbes *p425*

Banks Money can be changed on either side of the border, but note that, since 2000, Ecuador has been using the dollar as currency. Beware of sharp practices by money changers using fixed calculators and passing false bills (examine ALL notes). Do not change money on the minibus in Aguas Verdes, very poor rates.

Northern Highlands

● Footprint features

Introduction

This vast area stretches from the western foothills of the Andes across the mountains and down to the fringes of the Amazon jungle. It contains Peru's most spectacular pre-Columbian ruins, some of them built on a massive scale unequalled anywhere in the Americas. A good road rises from the coast to the city of Cajamarca, where the Inca Atahualpa was captured by the Spanish. Only one Inca building remains, the so-called Ransom Chamber, but the city has a pleasant colonial centre with comfortable hotels and good restaurants. Change is coming fast as a huge gold mine is bringing new investment, but also conflict, to the area. Close by are the hot springs where Atahualpa used to bathe, still very much in use today, and a number of pre-Inca sites. Beyond Cajamarca, a tortuous road winds its way east to the functional town of Chachapoyas. This is a friendly place, opening its doors to visitors as it lies at the centre of a region full of fantastic archaeological treasures whose mysteries are just being uncovered. There are fortresses, mysterious cities and strange burial sites replete with mummies and giant sarcophagi.

From Chachapoyas there are three options: carry on eastwards on one of Peru's most beautiful roads to the tropical lowland town of Tarapoto passing waterfalls and high moors before dropping down to the jungle zone; return to the coast at Chiclayo; or you can head north to Ecuador on a new route via Jaén and San Ignacio for the crossing to Zumba and Vilcabamba. With new roads and bridges in operation, a great adventure is opening up. It's possible now to travel from Ecuador, through Chachapoyas and Cajamarca on to the Cordillera Blanca, even to Cusco, without touching the coast, and all by public transport. It may be a slow route, but it will take some beating. All these possibilities are getting easier as the area becomes the focus of tourism development to rival the Lima-Cusco-Arequipa axis.

★ Don't miss...

1 **Marca Huamachuco** For an out-of-the-way archaeological experience, go to this archaeological site, in its strategic location overlooking all the surrounding valleys, page 437.

2 **Los Baños del Inca** Fancy an invigorating swim? More like a quick dip, as the waters are so potent you are advised not to say in for long, page 445.

3 **Heladería Holanda** If you are in need of refreshment, try one of the exotic fruit-flavoured ice creams on the plaza in Cajamarca, page 449.

4 **Kuélap** Hike up to the vast fortress of the Chachapoyans. Seeing it in sunshine gives the clearest view, but on a misty day the Cloud People's citadel is truly atmospheric, page 456.

5 **Tarapoto** From the high passes, follow the waters as they rush down to the gateway to the jungle, page 473.

Northern Highlands

The coast to Cajamarca

Cajamarca can be reached from the coast, directly northeast from Trujillo on a rough road (see below), or via a much faster road, from the port of Pacasmayo, midway between Trujillo and Chiclayo. The paved 180 km road branches off the Pan-American Highway soon after it crosses the Río Jequetepeque at Madre de Dios. The old road northeast to Cajamarca from Trujillo is lonely – especially for cyclists – but is being improved. It takes a couple of days by bus via Huamachuco and Cajabamba, as opposed to seven hours on the paved road from either Trujillo or Chiclayo.The old road is more interesting, passing through sierra towns and over the bare puna before dropping into the Huamachuco Valley, where the archaeological site of Marca Huamachuco is one of the main attractions. ›› *For Sleeping, Eating and other listings, see pages 439-441.*

Chilete and Kuntur Wasi

Some 103 km east of Pacasmayo is the mining town of **Chilete**. Some 21 km from Chilete, on the road north to San Pablo, are the pyramid and stone monoliths of **Kuntur Wasi**. If you are rushing along the paved road, do try to pause here, it is a very fine pre-Inca site. Devoted to a feline cult, it is undergoing new development under a Japanese archaeological team. It now has an excellent on-site museum, making a visit worthwhile. There are a couple of hotels at Chilete but rooms are hard to find on Tuesday because of the Wednesday market. Further along the road to Cajamarca is Yonán, where there are petroglyphs.

Trujillo to Huamachuco

After **Simbal** (just off the road itself) the road is paved to Otusco, arguably the most accessible sierra town, in terms of proximity to the coast, anywhere in Peru. Being 1½ hours from Trujillo, it makes a pleasant half-day excursion. 'La Ciudad de la Fe', as it is known, is an attractive Andean town at 2,200 m with some narrow cobbled streets. The modern church houses the important **Virgen de la Puerta**, which attracts devotees from all over Peru, especially during the big **festival** on 15 December. Adjoining it, in the old colonial church, is an amazing **museum** ① *0830-1230, 1400-1600, US$0.25*, filled with public gifts for the Virgen, including endless cabinets filled with elaborately embroidered capes, cheap jewellery and even shoes.

The route passes the mining town of **Shorey**, 5 km beyond which, at **Quiruvilca**, there is one hotel. The pollution in these mining towns is shocking. About 8 km east of Quiruvilca, Alto Chicama (the second largest open cast gold mine in Peru) is about to enter production. When this happens, there will be great changes in the Trujillo-Huamachuco area. In Shorey a road branches off to **Santiago de Chuco**, birthplace of the poet César Vallejo (see Literature, page 597), where there is the annual festival of Santiago El Mayor in the second half of July. The main procession is on 25 July, when the image is carried through the streets. Two hours beyond Santiago de Chuco is **Cachicadan**, where there are good hot baths.

Huamachuco → *Phone code: 044. Colour map 3, grid A2. Altitude: 3,180 m.*

The road runs on to this colonial town, which was formerly on the Royal Inca Road coming from Cajabamba. The main reason for visiting Huamachuco is to see the spectacular, but little known ruins of **Marca Huamachuco**, which are located on the summit (3,600 m) of one of the mountains northwest of town. The town also has the largest main plaza in Peru, with fine topiary, and a controversial modern **cathedral**, likened by some to an aeroplane hangar, sitting on top of the remains of an Inca palace. There is a colourful **Sunday market** and **Museo Municipal Wamachuko**

① *Sucre 195, Mon-Fri 0900-1300, 1500-1900, plus holiday weekends, free*, displays artefacts found at Cerro Amaru and Marca Huamachuco, plus a model and aerial photos of the latter.

Marca Huamachuco

① *No entry fee. A minimum of 2 hrs is needed, 4 hrs to really explore. Carry all food and drink with you. Access is along a poor vehicle road, off the road to Sanagorán. There is an archway at the turnoff, about 5 km from Huamachuco. In dry weather, 4WDs can make it to the top. There is a mule trail that starts just after you pass under the archway, to the right of the road. It is much faster to walk on it than along the winding vehicle road. A mototaxi to the turnoff costs US$2. There are also combis to Sanagorán in the morning.*

The Marca Huamachuco ruins surely rank in the top 10 archaeological sites in Peru. It is an extensive site, 3 km long, dating back to at least 300 BC though many structures were added later. Its most impressive features are: El Castillo, a remarkable circular structure with walls up to 8 m high located at the highest point of the site. This and other structures are the oldest-known buildings in Peru to extend to more than two storeys and may have reached five storeys. The outer defensive wall, which is accessible where it bisects the hill halfway along, also reaches up to 8 m in height. It consists of two parallel walls with gallery rooms in between. El Convento complex consists of five circular structures of varying sizes located towards the northern end of the hill. These are later constructions dating back to AD 600-800. The largest one has been partially reconstructed by the Instituto Nacional de Cultura (INC) and provides an interesting insight into how they must once have appeared, with two or three parallel outer walls, gallery rooms between them and several other internal structures. It has been suggested that these buildings housed the privileged members of an elite class. (The guardian should be tipped, US$1.)

Some 3 km before the ruins you will pass the remarkable **Cerro Amaru** on the left. It would seem that the whole of this relatively small hilltop was adapted to store water by placing an impermeable layer of clay around it. Wells (Los Chiles) on the summit, which can still be viewed, then provided access to the water within. Almost certainly the hill acquired major religio-cultural significance within the Huari-Tiahuanaco empire and became a place of pilgrimage and sacrifice in times of drought.

It seems likely that Marca Huamachuco existed for many centuries as the centre of an autonomous religious cult, separate from the activities of the Chachapoyans to the north and east. The site was certainly used as much as a ceremonial centre as it was for defensive purposes. Latest theories suggest that the Huari-Tiahuanaco culture (AD 600-1100) may have developed from the north out of places such as Marca Huamachuco and Yaino and then spread south, rather than the other way round. Apparently, the chronology of sites fits much better on this basis, but, if correct, this would require a complete reassessment of the Huari-Tiahuanuco culture.

Around Huamachuco

Wiracochapampa is an extensive Huari site, 3 km away, a 45-minute walk, to the north of the town. Much of the site is overgrown and poorly conserved, but walls up to 3 m high can still be found. It is believed that the complex was never completed, possibly because the principal builder was taken south to construct Piquillacta, near Cusco, with which it has many similarities.

Also worth seeing is **Laguna Sausacocha** (3,150 m), a beautiful spot surrounded by low hills, along the road to Cajabamba. Here are Hospedaje Piscis and several simple comedores. It is possible to go rowing on the lake.

The Yanasara **thermal baths** are a 30-minute walk from the village of El Pallar set in a beautiful valley at 2,300 m. The hot, clean baths consist of a pool and four individual baths, all US$0.30 per person.

A pleasant two-hour walk can be made up the Río Grande valley to the hacienda of **Cochabamba**, once the Andean retreat of the owners of the Laredo sugar plantation, near Trujillo.

South from Huamachucoca → *Colour map 3, grid A2.*

It is now possible to travel, via Retamas and Tayabamba (see below), to Sihuas (see page 360) and the Cordillera Blanca along a road which is very poor in places and involves crossing the Río Marañón twice. The building of a new bridge over the river means that it is feasible to go from Cusco to Quito entirely by public transport without going down to the Pacific coast, though few travellers have made this journey. The route from Cajamarca to Huaraz via Huamachuco and the upper Marañón Valley is considerably longer, more difficult and more expensive than going via Trujillo and Chimbote on the coast. The rewards, however, are incomparable views and a glimpse of everyday life in some of the country's most tranquil highland villages as well as its most grimiest mining camps. For those with plenty of time, the route also provides access to the wilds of Río Abiseo National Park. Along the way, narrow vertiginous roads repeatedly traverse altitudes ranging from 4,200 m to 1,450 m, with tremendous changes in temperatures between the puna and Marañón valley, and vertical drops of 1,000 m from hair-pin bends. Note that the road may be almost impassable in the wet season.

From Huamachuco, follow the main road to Cajabamba as far as Sausacocha, where a turnoff goes down to Yanasara (see above). The Río Grande is then crossed before climbing to Chugay (3,400 m, Hospedaje Pérez and basic comedores) and on to a pass at 3,900 m. From here the road plummets 2,450 m to **Chahual** (1,450 m), a small hot settlement where a bridge spans the Río Marañón. The hillsides are covered in cactuses, mango and avocado trees.

At Chahual, right after the bridge, the road forks: left to Pataz, and right to climb 1,000 m to the **Balcón del Diablo**, overlooking **Laguna Pías**. The town of Pías, down by the lake and reached via a turnoff from the main road, has an office for **Parque Nacional Río Abiseo** and a landing strip (only charter flights to Lima for mining companies were operating in 2004, but spare seats may be available). **Pataz** is a small gold-mining town, about 100 km from Huamachuco. From here you can reach the World Heritage Site of **Pajatén**, with its circular pre-Inca ruins (it requires a 10-day trip with mules from Los Alisos, near Pataz). The ruins lie within the Río Abiseo National Park, and in the past both INRENA and INC permits have been needed to visit. These are usually only issued to archaeologists and researchers, though day passes to enter the Park can also be obtained (check with both Institutes before going). Pataz is one hour by road from Chahual but there is no regular transport. Your best chance of finding a *camioneta* going up is early in the morning.

The road continues to **Retamas** (2,700 m), a rough-and-tumble mining town. To avoid sleeping in Retamas, take a shared taxi to **Llacuabamba** (15 minutes, US$0.60), which is more tranquil. La Huanqueña serves an adequate menú. You must return to Retamas for onward transport. Near Retamas is **Parcoy**, the original settlement in the area with a colonial church. After Retamas are more hectic and scarred mining communities, Marsa and Buldibuyo, bordering the Río Abiseo National Park. The road then drops down to **Tayabamba** (3,300 m). This small, chilly Andean town is surrounded by scenic countryside. It has a large church and a rotating bronze angel in the neat plaza. The interesting annual fiesta is held in honour of Santo Toribio, 24-31 April.

North from Huamachuco

From Huamachuco the gravel road runs on 55 km past Laguna Sausacocha through some small highland villages where roof tiles are baked in round ovens, to **Cajabamba**, which sits on a balcony overlooking the sugar producing Condebamba valley. The climate is mild for its altitude because of influence from this large warm valley. Founded in 1572, this is an especially friendly town with an attractive Plaza de Armas. The annual festival is **Virgen del Rosario,** starting the first weekend of October and featuring the Danza de los diablos. The surrounding countryside offers good walking amid lakes, waterfalls and Inca Road remnants, well worth taking a few days to explore. An excellent source of information is Sr Miguel Rodríguez ① *Bolgnesi 849 Yachayhuasi, T044-851329, ccyachayhusic@hotmail.com.* He has a small private museum (donations appreciated), sells local crafts and can arrange for guides to nearby attractions.

The road continues from Cajabamba unpaved, but in good condition, through **San Marcos** (2,400 m) to Cajamarca. There is a short section of asphalt road to the south of San Marcos, which is important for its Sunday cattle market. Both it and Cajabamba are on the Inca Road. From San Marcos to Cajamarca (124 km) the road is paved and excellent; three hours by bus, US$2.50.

● Sleeping

Chilete and Kuntur Wasi *p436*
G **Hotels Amazonas**, Chilete, dirty with bathroom.
G **San Pedro**, Chilete, also dirty with bathroom.

Trujillo to Huamachuco *p436*
E **Hostal Silita Star**, in Cachidan. Attractive and rustic with hot water, TV and restaurant. Recommended.
E **Los Portales**, Santa Rosa 680, Otusco. Hot water, with bath, TV, clean, good value.
F **Progreso**, Progreso 653, Otusco. Best of the basic *hostales*, shared bathroom, some rooms without windows. All hotels are full in mid-Dec.

Huamachuco *p436*
B-D **Hostal Real**, Bolívar 250, T044-441402, hostalreal@hotmail.com. New, clean, with bath, TV, sauna, internet, many of the fittings are of wood. Recommended.
C-D **Hostal Santa Fe**, San Martín 297, T044-441019, santa_fe@hotmail.com. New, clean, TV, hot water. Recommended.
D **Hostal Colonial**, Castilla 537, T044-441334, colonialgrill@yahoo.com. An attractive old colonial house, with bath, hot water, TV. Its restaurant is clean and good value. Recommended.
D-E **Hostal Noche Buena**, San Román 401 on the main plaza. Clean, with hot showers (supposedly) and TV, also has cheaper dormitory.
E **Huamachuco**, Castilla 354, on the plaza, T044-441393. Clean, with hot showers (F without), friendly, good value, has parking.

Around Huamachuco *p437*
E **Hotel Yanasara**, Yanasara, T044-441245. A large new hotel set among meadows and a 5-min walk from the thermal baths, with restaurant and a pool, booking may be required in peak periods. Camping is also permitted within the grounds.Chahual

South from Huamachuco *p438*
E **Hostal Morillo**, Llacuabamba. With private bath, hot water, parking, basic, some short stay but OK for where it is.
E **Hostal Caballero**, Bolognesi 649, Tayabamba, T044-330024. With private bath, hot water, basic but OK, suffers from water shortages.
F **Hostal El Triunfo**, Salaverry 227, Tayabamba. Near bus agencies. With private bath and electric shower, cheaper without, new in 2004, small rooms, basic and friendly, suffers from water shortages.
F **Hostal El Triunfo**, Salaverry 227, Tayabamba. Near bus agencies. With private bath and electric shower, cheaper without, new in 2004, small rooms, basic and friendly, suffers from water shortages.
F **Hostal Imperial Class**, Retamas. Shared bath, basic, caters to short stay couples.
G **Hostal Oasis**, Chahual, is clean and friendly and has a restaurant. There are a couple of simple comedores by the bridge.
G **Hostal Paraíso**, Huancaspata. Possibly best in town, but rustic, rooms around a courtyard, shared bath, hot water.
G **Hostal Roldán**, Huancaspata. Also rustic with rooms around a courtyard, cold water and shared bath.

North from Huamachuco *p438*

E **Hostal La Casona**, Jr Alfonso Ugarte 586, Plaza de Armas, Cajabamba, T076-848385. Small rooms, electric shower, clean and friendly, with restaurant.

E **Jhoel**, Jr Grau 633, Cajabamba, T076-851653. Private bath with electric shower, patio, clean and pleasant, good value.

F **Hostal Flores**, Leoncio Prado 137, on the Plaza de Armas, Cajabamba, T076-851086. With electric shower, **G** without bath, friendly and clean but rooms are gloomy, nice patio; no breakfast.

D **Sol Naciente**, Jr Inclán 485, 1 block from Plaza de Armas, San Marcos, T076-858191. With private bath and hot water, cheaper without.

🍴 Eating

Trujillo to Huamachuco *p436*

††-† **Otuzco**, Tacna 608, Otusco. Also good for guinea pig and turkey dishes.

†† -† **Zagitario**, Tacna 769, Otusco. The best place in town for the delicious local speciality of jamón con yuca.

Huamachuco *p436*

† **El Túnel**, on the Trujillo road at the entrance to town. With tables outside, good for typical dishes and a game of 'sapo'.

† **La Casona**, Sánchez Carrión 294. Open daily 0700-0900, 1200-1430, 1900-2030. Serves good value and quality set meals and local dishes, popular.

Café Doña Emilia, Sánchez Carrión esq San Ramón, on Plaza de Armas. For pastries and coffee.

Café Venecia, Castilla 687. Serves excellent, coffee, cakes and pies.

South of Huamachuco

† **Juan Baptista**, Bolognesi 461, Tayabamba. The only proper restaurant in town but has a limited menu. Closes at 2100, like most places in town. There's also an unnamed comedor at Bolognesi y Sucre. Good home cooking.

† **Cosas Dulces**, next to church on the Plaza de Armas, for sweets and hot drinks.

† **Restaurant Kananga**, in Huancaspata, apparently named after a Japanese cartoon character, is the best place to eat and serves an excellent *caldo*.

North from Huamachuco *p438*

† **Cafetería La Otuscana**, Grau 929. Good bakery, sweets and sandwiches, 0730-2200 daily.

† **Don Lucho**, Jr Leoncio Prado 227, Cajabamba. Good local trout and other à la carte dishes.

† **Fuente de soda Grau**, Grau 832. Serving big fresh fruit salads and cakes.

† **La Casona**, in hotel of same name. Menú and à la carte, opens early, good meals.

🍸 Bars and clubs

Huamachuco *p436*

Bar Michi Wasi, San Román 461, on the plaza. An attractive, atmospheric bar and a good place to meet locals who know the area. Recommended.

🎉 Festivals and events

Huamachuco *p436*

On the second Sun in **Aug** is **Waman Raymi**, a major festival held in the ruins of Wiracochapampa (see above), a northern version of Inti Raymi in Cusco. Another colourful festival is **Los Wamachucos**, held **10 Aug** in the neighbourhood above the centre. A week of festivities begins on **15 Aug** to mark the **founding of Huamacucho** and features spectacular fireworks and the remarkable Turcos – aggressive male dancers from a nearby village who wear at least 10 layered skirts when dancing. Huamachuco (founded in 1553) has made an effort to rescue its pre-hispanic and pre-Inca traditions. Celebrations include many native themes and dances.

🚌 Transport

Trujillo to Huamachuco *p436*

From **Otusco to Trujillo**, colectivos leave when full from the south side of town, 1½ hrs, US$1.20. Línea operates several buses during the day, US$1.40. Buses to **Santiago de Chuco from Trujillo**: Horna, Av América del Sur 1368, and **Agreda**, J B Farfán 647, 8 hrs, US$6, only at night; they continue to **Cachicadan**. Combis also depart frequently, when full, from Santiago de Chuco to Cachicadan, US$1.50, 1½ hrs.

Air
Charter flights only.

Bus
From **Trujillo**, 170 km, improved road, 6 hrs:
Agreda (J B Farfán 647, Trujillo; Balta 865,
Huamachuco) at 0800, 1300 and 1800. **Gran
Turismo** 4 a day from Trujillo (Prol Vallejo
1368, T044-425391, in Huamachuco Balta
798). **Turismo Negreiros** (Prol Vallejo block
13, Trujillo; Balta y Suárez, Huamachuco) at
0900 and 1300 in each direction.
Recommended. **Trans Horna**, América Sur
1363, T044-257605 (Trujillo), San Martín 875,
T044-441070 (Huamachuco), 4 a day
including bus cama service. Recommended.
Días also has several daily departures. To
Cajabamba, **Trans Los Andes**, Psje Hospital
109, have 4 combis a day, 3 hrs, US$3. **Horna**
also has daily departues at 0430 and 1600,
2½ hrs, US$1.50. From Huamachuco to
Retamas, **Trans Garrincha** (Garcilazo de la
Vega s/n esquina Román, T044-441594) Sun,
Wed, Fri at 0600, 12 hrs, US$7.50. The bus
passes through Trujillo but seats may
sometimes be booked in Huamachuco.
Enquire in advance. Combis leave from near
the hospital daily 0200-0600, depending on
demand, 10 hrs, US$10. They are less
comfortable than the bus but faster, and
have an easier time negotiating the narrow
winding road.

Around Huamachuco *p437*
Combis and shared taxis go directly from
Huamachuco to Yanasara (1½ hrs, US$1.20),
from which the baths are a 15-min walk.

South from Huamachuco *p438*
For **Chahual**, there is a small airport 5 km
down the valley. **Air Líder** have flights to

Lima, Mon-Sat, US$90, one hour. Buses also
arrive in Chahual after 8 hrs from
Huamachuco, US$7.

From **Retamas**, Garrincha travel to
Huamachuco Mon 0800, Thu 2000, Sat
0400, 12 hrs, US$7.50, continuing to **Trujillo**
19 hrs, US$13.50. You can also take combis
to **Huamachuco** starting 1800 daily, 10 hrs,
US$10. Combis and shared taxis to **Taya-
bamba**, 6 a day 0500-1700, 3 hrs, US$4.50;
Tayabamba-Retamas 6 a day 0700-1630.

Most transport in **Tayabamba** leaves
from Salaverry corner Cahuide (behind the
church), where their agencies are located,
except as noted below. To **Sihuas** for the
Cordillera Blanca: **La Perla de Alto Mayo**,
Grau y Sucre, Mon, Wed, Sat at 1930; **Andía**,
Mon, Wed, Sat at 1900; **Garrincha**, Mon and
Thu at 0800; **San Antonio de Padua**, Fri at
1900; all 7-8 hrs, US$6. Most buses continue
to **Chimbote** (17 hrs, US$13.50) and some to
Trujillo (20 hrs, US$15) or **Lima** (24 hrs,
US$16.50).

North from Huamachuco *p438*
From **Cajabamba** to **Huamachuco**: Trans
Los Andes, Grau 1170, buses leave from
police station below the market, at 0400,
0830, 1230, 1600; **Horna**, Av L Martínez 405,
at 0430 and 0900, 2½ hrs, US$1.50. From
Cajabamba to **Cajamarca**, companies
include **Rojas** and **Perú Bus**, several daily, 4
hrs, US$3. Some continue to **Trujillo**, 10 hrs,
US$7.50, and to **Lima**, 18 hrs, US$13.70.

❶ Directory

Huamachuco *p436*
Banks **Caja Norperuano**, Sánchez Carrión
on Plaza de Armas, has good rates; cash only.
Obtain soles elsewhere if relying on ATMs or
TCs. **Internet** Best access is in **Hostal Real.**

Cajamarca and around

→ *Phone code: 076. Colour map 1, grid C3. Population: 117,500. Altitude: 2,750 m.*

*Cajamarca is a beautiful colonial town and the most important in the northern
highlands. It sits at the edge of a green valley which is ideal for dairy farming. Around
the Plaza de Armas are many fine old houses, which are being converted into tasteful
hotels, restaurants and galleries to cater for engineers and incomers from the
adjacent Yanacocha mining project. The airport has been expanded to cater for the*

mining personnel, but tourism has yet to catch on to this facility. The mine, now that it is fully operational and looking to expand, has provoked opposition from farmers and created worries over pollution, intruding on the provincial calm of a city once closely tied to its pastoral surroundings. It remains, though, a great place to buy handicrafts, but lest you forget where the money now lies, you can find soapstone carvings of miners with power drills alongside more traditional figures. Outside town are several good haciendas which offer bed, board and rural pursuits, while at the Baños del Inca, just up the road, you can unwind as the steam from the thermal waters meets the cool mountain air. ▸▸ *For Sleeping, Eating and other listings, see pages 446-451.*

Ins and outs

Getting there The airport is 3 km from town; taxi US$1.50, mototaxi US$0.75. It is to the northeast: take the Cerrillo road. The bus offices are to the southeast of the centre, on the Baños del Inca road past La Recoleta church; a 20-minute walk from the Plaza de Armas.

Getting around All the main sights are clustered around the Plaza de Armas. With its many old colonial buildings it is an interesting town to wander around although the climb up Santa Apolonia hill is quite demanding. The district around Plaza Francia (Amazonas y José Gálvez), the market area and east of Amazonas are not safe at night because of prostitution and drugs. Buses in town charge US$0.15. Taxis US$0.60 within city limits. Mototaxis US$0.30. Combis run to the main places outside town, like Baños del Inca. Others, like Cumbemayo, are best reached on a tour, while still others make good day walks.

Best time to visit Cajamarca has a pleasant climate the year round, with warm days and chilly nights. The wettest months are Dec-Mar. Depending on your point of view, Carnival (February or March) is the time to be there, or the time to avoid – it is a riotous, messy affair. Hotels are also booked up at this time. More sedate festivals are Holy Week, especially Palm Sunday at nearby Porcón, and Corpus Christi in May. During October and November there are numerous school trips to this area, so most of the budget hotels are full at this time.

Tourist information **Dirección Regional de Turismo** and **Instituto Nacional de Cultura** ① *in the Conjunto Monumental de Belén, Belén 631, T076-822997, cajamarca@mitinci.gob.pe, Mon-Fri 0730-1300, 1415-1900; www.inccajamarca. org.* **Cámara Regional de Turismo (Caretur)** ① *José Gálvez 771, T076-831579, careturcajamarca@regionalcaj.zzn.com.* The University tourist school's office ① *Del Batán 289, T076-821546, Mon-Fri 0830-1300, 1500-2200,* voluntary donation requested.

Background

Before Cajamarca became an Inca religious centre and favoured haunt of the nobility in 1456, it had been at the heart of a culture known as Caxamarca, which flourished from AD 500 to 1000. The violent events of 1532-1533 are today belied by the city's provincial calm. It was named provincial capital in 1855 and Patrimonio Histórico y Cultural de las Américas by the Organization of American States in 1986. It is now seeking UNESCO World Heritage status. In addition to its historical associations, Cajamarca is best known for its dairy industry, textiles and intricately worked mirrors (see Shopping below). Change is coming, though, in the form of the Circuito Turístico Nororiental, which is opening up the Chiclayo-Cajamarca-Chachapoyas tourist route, and in the effect on the town from the Yanacocha gold mine. This has brought many foreign mining engineers and economic benefits, but also serious debates over ecological impact, compensation to *campesinos* and threats to the city's drinking water supply. The mine's public relations office is at Avendia Evitamiento B-17,

Cajamarca

Plaza de Armas

The main Plaza de Armas, where Atahualpa was executed, has a 350-year-old
fountain, topiary and gardens. The impressive **Cathedral**, opened in 1776, is still
missing its belfry, but the façade has beautiful baroque carving in stone. Many
belfries were left half-finished in protest against a Spanish tax levied on the
completion of a church. The altar is covered in original gold leaf.

On the opposite side of the plaza is the 17th-century **San Francisco Church**, older
than the Cathedral and with more interior stone carving and elaborate altars. A side
chapel has an ornate ceiling. **Museo de Arte Colonial** ① *Mon-Sat 1430-1800.
US$0.85, entrance is unmarked on far left corner of church*. Tickets are sold from an
unmarked office on right of courtyard as you walk towards the church. Attached to
San Francisco, the museum is filled with colonial paintings and icons. The guided tour
of the museum includes entry to the church's spooky catacombs.

Complejo Belén

① *0900-1300, 1500-1730, 0900-1230 Sat-Sun. US$1.20, valid for more than one day.
A ticket is also valid for the Cuarto de Rescate. A guide for all the sites costs US$2.85
(US$5.75-8.50 for guides in other languages).*
This group of buildings comprises the tourist office and Institute of Culture, a
beautifully ornate church, considered the city's finest, and two museums. The arches,
pillars and walls of the nave of Belén church are covered in lozenges (rombos), a
design picked out in the gold tracery of the altar. See the inside of the dome, where
eight giant cherubs support an intricate flowering centrepiece. The carved pulpit has
a spiral staircase and the doors are intricately worked in wood. In the same courtyard
is the **Museo Médico Belén**, which has a collection of medical instruments (closed
late 2004). Across the street is a maternity hospital from the colonial era, now the
Archaeological and Ethnological Museum (Junín y Belén). It has a wide range of
ceramics from all regions and civilizations of Peru.

Cuarto de Rescate

① *Entrance is at Amalia Puga 750, Mon-Sat 0900-1250, 1500-1750, Sun 0900-1250.*
The Cuarto de Rescateshown to tourists is not the actual ransom chamber but in fact
the room where Atahualpa was held prisoner. A red line on the wall is said to indicate
where Atahualpa reached up and drew a mark, agreeing to have his subjects fill the
room to the line with gold treasures. The chamber is roped off and can only be viewed
from the outside. Pollution and weather have had a detrimental effect on the stone.

Other sights

Also worth seeing are **La Recoleta church** ① *Maestro y Avenida Los Héroes*, and **San
Pedro** ① *Gálvez y Junín*. The city has many old colonial houses with garden patios,
and 104 elaborately carved doorways: see the **Bishop's Palace** across the street from
the Cathedral; the **palace of the Condes de Uceda** ① *Jr Apurímac 719*, now occupied
by BCP bank; and the **Casa Silva Santiesteban** ① *Junín y 2 de Mayo*.

Museo Arqueológico Horacio H Urteaga ① *Del Batán 289, Mon-Fri 0700-1445,
free, donations accepted*, of the Universidad Nacional de Cajamarca, has objects of
the pre-Inca Cajamarca and other cultures The university maintains an experimental
arboretum and agricultural station, the **Museo Silvo-agropecuario** ① *Km 2.5 on the
road to Baños del Inca*, with a lovely mural at the entrance.

Northern Highlands Cajamarca & around

You can also visit the plaza where Atahualpa was ambushed and the stone altar set high on **Santa Apolonia hill** ① *US$0.30, take bus marked Santa Apolonia/Fonavi, or micro 'A' or combis on Sabogal or Tarapacá.* Here the Inca is said to have reviewed his subjects. There is a road to the top or, if you are fit, you can walk up from Calle 2 de Mayo, using the stairway. The view from the top, over red-tiled roofs and green fields, is worth the effort, especially very early in the morning for the beautiful sunrises.

Cajamarca

Plaza de Armas detail

Sleeping
Casa Blanca 2
Casa Pensión Karimbó 3
Clarín 20
Colonial Inn 21
Continental 4
El Cabildo 5
El Cumbe Inn 6
El Ingenio 22
Hospedaje Los Jazmines 15
Hostal Atahualpa 9
Hostal Becerra 1
Hostal Cajamarca 10

Hostal Dos de Mayo 11
Hostal El Portal del
  Marqués 7
Hostal Los Pinos 17
Hostal Portada del Sol 19
La Hispana 12
Los Balcones de la
  Recoleta 14

Eating
Casa Club 22
Casa Luna 2
Cascanuez Café Bar 3

Christian 4
Donde Octavio 20
Don Paco 11
El Batán Gran
  Bufet de Arte 5
El Cajamarqués 6
El Capulí 21
El Pez Loco 7
El Zarco 8
El Zarco Campestre 23
Heladería Holanda 9
Las Tullpas 1
Om-Gri 12

Pizzería El Marengo 13
Pizzería Vaca Loca 19
Querubino 14
Rosana D'Avila 16
Salas 17
Sanguchón.com 18

Bars & clubs
La Noche 10
Rodeo Vídeo 15

Around Cajamarca → *Colour map 1, grid C3.*

Los Baños del Inca

ⓘ *0500-1900, closed Mon and Fri, entry US$0.60. The main baths are divided into 3 categories, from simplest to best: units A, B, C (US$1); Turistas (US$1.20); and Imperial (US$1.50); all with private tubs and no pool. Sauna US$3, massage US$3 (take your own towel; soaps are sold outside). Only spend 20-30 mins maximum in the water; obey instructions; many of the facilities allow bathers in shifts, divided by time and/or sex. Combis marked Baños del Inca cost US$0.30, 15 mins. Taxis US$1.40.*

Six kilometres away are the sulphurous thermal springs known as Los Baños del Inca, where there are baths whose water temperature is 78ºC. Atahualpa tried the effect of these waters on a festering war wound and his bath is still there. The best time to bathe is first thing in the morning. The complex is regularly renewed, with gardens and two types of accommodation, detailed in Sleeping below. The area formerly known as La Isla is being converted into a Complejo Recreativo beside the river, with one small and two larger hot pools, a water-slide, playground, and showers. The Piscina Municipal (same hours and price as above) is a large pool with tepid water, best for swimming laps. The construction of luxury homes for upper echelon mining personnel has given Baños del Inca an increasingly suburban feel, complete with commuter traffic.

Cumbe Mayo

ⓘ *A guided tour costs US$6 per person and runs from 0900-1300, and a taxi US$15 (no buses). It may be possible to go with the milk truck leaving at 0400 from C Revilla 170; ask Sr Segundo Malca, Jr Pisagua 482. There's a small charge, dress warmly. To walk up takes 3-4 hrs (take a guide or tour, best time May-Sep). See below for details.*

Cumbe Mayo (3,600m), a pampa on a mountain range, is 20 km southwest of Cajamarca. It is famous for its extraordinary, well-engineered pre-Inca channels, running for 9 km across the mountain tops. It is said to be the oldest man-made construction in South America. The sheer scale of the scene is impressive and the huge rock formations of Los Frailones ('big monks') and others with fanciful names are strange indeed. It is worth taking a guided tour since the area has a lot of

Around Cajamarca

petroglyphs, altars and sacrificial stones from pre-Inca cultures. On the way to Cumbe Mayo is the Layzón ceremonial centre from 500-200 BC (7 km).

The trail to the site starts from the hill of Santa Apolonia (Silla del Inca), and goes to Cumbe Mayo, straight through the village and up the hill. At the top of the mountain, leave the trail and take the road to the right to the canal. The walk is not difficult and you do not need hiking boots. Take a good torch/flashlight. The locals use the trail to bring their goods to market.

Other sights near Cajamarca

Llacanora is a typical Andean village in beautiful scenery (13 km southeast). Nearby is **La Collpa**, a hacienda which is now a cooperative farm of the Ministry of Agriculture which breeds bulls and has a lake and gardens. The cows are handmilked at 1400, not a particularly inspiring spectacle in itself, but the difference here is that the cows are called by name and respond accordingly.

Ventanillas de Otusco ① *0800-1800, US$1*, part of an old pre-Inca cemetery, has a gallery of secondary burial niches. A one-day round trip can be made: take a bus from Del Batán to Ventanillas de Otusco (30 minutes) or a *colectivo* leaving hourly from Revilla 170, US$0.15, then walk to Baños del Inca (1½ hours, 6 km). You can either follow the east shore of the Río Chonta, or take a higher route with better views through the village of Puylucana. Ask for directions often and take a stick to fend off dogs. From Baños del Inca walk to Llacanora (one hour, 7 km), passing the caves and rock art at Callacpuma, and then a further hour to La Collpa.

Another typical Andean village from which you can walk to Baños del Inca is **Pariamarca**. Take a micro from Ovalo Bolognesi heading towards the coast. Ask to be let out at the turn-off to Pariamarca and walk from there.

A road goes to **Ventanillas de Combayo**, some 20 km past the burial niches of Otusco. These are more numerous and more spectacular, being located in a rather isolated, mountainous area, and are distributed over the face of a steep 200-m high hillside. There are occasional combis on weekdays, but more transport to the site on Sun when a market is held nearby, one hour.

Porcón, at 3,400 m, is a rural cooperative, with its evangelical faith expressed on billboards, is a popular excursion, 30 km northwest of Cajamarca. It is tightly organized and has a bakery, cheese and yoghurt-making, zoo and vicuñas. Its carpentry utilizes wood from extensive pine plantations. A good guide helps to explain everything. If not taking a tour, contact **Cooperativa Agraria Atahualpa Jerusalén** ① *Chanchamayo 1355, Fonavi 1, T/F076-825631, granjaporcon@yahoo.com.*

● Sleeping

Cajamarca *p443, map p444*

L Posada del Puruay, 5 km north of the city, T076-827928, postmast@p-puruay.com.pe. A 17th-century hacienda which has been converted into a 'hotel museum' with all rooms appointed to a high standard and containing beautiful pieces of colonial furniture. All rooms en suite. Recommended.

A El Ingenio, Av Vía de Evitamiento 1611-1709, T/F076-827121. With bathroom, solar-powered hot water, spacious, very relaxed, fax service, helpful. Highly recommended.

A-B Continental, Jr Amazonas 760, T076-822758, www.hotelescontinental peru.com. Price includes breakfast. Often full as mining personnel have preference. Very clean, hot water, modern, good restaurant (popular for lunch, specializes in cuy frito).

B Clarín, Amazonas 1025, T076-831275, Hotel_clarin@hotmail.com. A modern hotel with pleasant decoration, rooms with bath, good beds, laptop connection, 5th floor terrace with view, car park, restaurant, *panadería* next door.

B El Cumbe Inn, Pasaje Atahualpa 345, T076-826858, elcumbeinn@terra.com. Includes breakfast, ask for discount in low season. Comfortable, bright rooms, with bath, hot water, personal service, two patios, small gym, well-kept, will arrange taxis. Recommended.

B Hostal El Portal del Marqués, Del Comercio 644, T/F076-828464, portalmarques@terra.com.pe. Price includes breakfast. Located in an attractive converted colonial house, all rooms carpeted, en suite, with TV, laundry, safe, parking, tourist restaurant De Caña y Barro. Recommended.

B La Hispana, Jr La Mar 542, T076-824225. New in 2003, small, quiet, modern and very comfortable. Recommended.

C Casa Blanca, Dos de Mayo 446 on Plaza de Armas, T/F076-822141. Price includes breakfast. Room service, clean, safe, nice old building with garden, good restaurant.

C El Cabildo, Junín 1062, T/F076-827025, cabildoh@latinmail.com. Includes breakfast. In a historic monument with patio and modern fountain, full of character, elegant, local decorations, comfortable, breakfast served, gym, massage if booked in advance. Recommended.

C Hostal Cajamarca, in a colonial house at Dos de Mayo 311, T076-822532, F821432. Sizeable rooms, clean, hot water, food excellent in Los Faroles restaurant (T825113) which also has good local music and disco/pub, **Cajamarca Tours** next door. Recommended.

C Los Balcones de la Recoleta, Amalia Puga 1050, T076-823302, hslosbalcones@ speedy.com.pe. A beautifully restored 19th-century house, with a pleasant courtyard full of flowers; some rooms with period furniture but all are en suite, breakfast extra, internet access in rooms, use of kitchen, helpful staff, some English spoken. Recommended.

C Hostal Los Pinos, Jr La Mar 521, T/F076-825992, pinoshostal@yahoo.com. Price includes small breakfast. Lovely colonial house with a new extension, comfortable and secure, helpful staff, expensive laundry, lunch menú available for US$3.

C Hostal Portada del Sol, Pisagua 731, T076-823395, PortadadelSol@terra.com.pe. Good rooms, tastefully decorated, with bath, hot water, comfortable beds, internet access. Also has **Portada del Sol Hacienda** at Km 6 on road to Cumbe Mayo (**C**). Good choice.

D Colonial Inn, Av Los Héroes 350, T076-825300, F827249. Hot water, cheaper with shared bath, English spoken, 24-hr attention, meals extra, convenient for buses.

D Hostal Becerra, Del Batán 195, T076-827867. With bath, hot water and TV, modern, pleasant, clean and friendly, but front rooms can be noisy, they'll let you leave your luggage until late buses depart.

D Hospedaje Los Jazmines, Amazonas 775, T076-821812, assado@hotmail.com. In a converted colonial house with a pleasant courtyard and café, 3 rooms with bath, 2 without, all funds go to handicapped children, some staff are handicapped, guests can visit the project's school and help. Owner Christa Stark from Germany also has Fundo Ecológico El Porongo on road to Baños del Inca, bunk beds, **G** per person. Recommended.

E Hostal Atahualpa, Pasaje Atahualpa 686, T076-827840. Hot water 0600-1100, a bit rundown but clean, meals extra, restaurant open 0800-2200.

E Hostal Dos de Mayo, Dos de Mayo 585, T076-822527. With bath, hot water, basic, quite dark, friendly and helpful, good value menú in the restaurant.

E Hostal San Carlos, Av Atahualpa 324, T076-822600, and **E Hostal Pepe**, opposite at No 343, T076-821887, are the most convenient for bus offices on Atahualpa. Both are cheaper without bath, hot water, no breakfast, noisy from all-night traffic.

F per person **Casa pensión Karimbó**, Dos de Mayo 700, T076-829888. Full board, shared rooms, some with bath.

Around Cajamarca *p445*

L-AL Laguna Seca, Av Manco Cápac 1098, Los Baños del Inca, T076-894600, www.lagunaseca.com.pe. In pleasant surroundings with thermal streams (atmospheric misty mornings), private hot thermal baths in rooms, swimming pool with thermal water, good restaurant, bar, health spa with a variety of treatments (US$10-48), disco, horses for hire. Recommended.

B Hostal Fundo Campero San Antonio, is 2 km off the Baños road (turn off at Km 5 from Cajamarca), T/F076-838237, http://hsanantonio.cjb.net. An old hacienda, wonderfully restored, with open fireplaces and gardens, 15 mins walk along the river to Baños del Inca. All rooms en suite. The price includes breakfast and a ride on the hotel's caballos de paso. Restaurant serves the hotel's own dairy produce, fruit and vegetables, catch your own trout for supper; try the licor de sauco (elderberry). Recommended.

B-D Los Baños del Inca, address above, T076-838385. Various levels of accommodation:**B** bungalows for 2 to 4 with thermal water, TV, fridge; **D** per person Albergue Juvenil, not IYFH, rooms with 3 bunk beds, private bath, caters to groups, basic and overpriced. Camping possible.

C La Hispana, Jr Manco Cápac 1031, Los Baños del Inca, T076-838489. Includes breakfast. New in 2004, with restaurant, swimming pool, gym, sauna, pool table, free internet, very comfortable. Recommended.

F La Notte, Manco Cápac 450 (no sign, yet), Los Baños del Inca. New in 2004, parking, nice patio, two thermal baths, sauna, large bare rooms, some with electric shower, others with private thermal bath, basic and friendly, good value.

⊘ Eating

Cajamarca *p443, map p444*

There are cheap eating places on Del Comercio and 2 de Mayo y Sabogal.

ŤŤŤ El Batán Gran Bufet de Arte, Del Batán 369, T076-826025, elbatanrestaurant@ yahoo.mx. International dishes and nouvelle cuisine, good wine list and wide choice of drinks, local dishes on non-tourist menu, some of the staff speak English, live music at the weekend, art gallery on the 2nd floor.

ŤŤŤ Querubino, Amalia Puga 589. Mediterranean-style decoration with American and French influence in the cooking, specializes in fish, but lots of choice, breakfasts, cocktails, coffees, expensive wines.

ŤŤ Casa Club, Amalia Puga 458-A, T076-830198. Open 0800-2300. Menú and extensive selection à la carte, family atmosphere, slow but attentive service. Recommended.

ŤŤ Don Paco, Amalia Puga 390, T076-848009. Opposite Sn Francisco. Typical, including

novo andino, and international dishes, tasty food, desserts and drinks.

ŤŤ El Cajamarqués, Amazonas 770, T076-822128. Has good value menúes available after 1300, elegant colonial building with garden full of exotic birds, nice place for families.

ŤŤ El Pez Loco, San Martín 333. Recommended for fish, also on road to Baños del Inca.

ŤŤ Las Tullpas, 2 de Mayo 930. Open 0730-2300. Local and international dishes, à la carte and menú ejecutivo.

ŤŤ Om-Gri, San Martín 360, near the Plaza de Armas. Good Italian dishes, small, friendly, French spoken, opens at 1300 (1830 Sun).

ŤŤ Pizzería El Marengo, Junín 1201. Good pizzas and warm atmosphere, T076-828045 for delivery.

ŤŤ Salas, Amalia Puga 637, on the main plaza. A Cajamarca tradition, open 0700-2200. Fast service, excellent local food (try their cuy frito), best tamales in town; also has a branch in Baños del Inca (1100-1600, Fri-Sun and holidays). Both serve the same food at same prices, own production. Recommended.

ŤŤ-Ť El Zarco, Jr Del Batán 170, T076-823421. Open Sun-Fri 0700-2300. Very popular with local residents, also has short chifa menu, good vegetarian dishes, excellent fish, popular for breakfast.

ŤŤ-Ť El Zarco Campestre, off road to airport, open daily. Both **El Zarco's** use own produce, recommended for pork.

Ť Christian, Del Comercio 719. Snacks, juices, set lunch for US$1.10.

Ť Donde Octavio, Jr Del Batán 190-196 corner Amazonas. Recommended for tamales and humitas.

Ť Pizzería Vaca Loca, San Martín 330. Popular, the name doesn't seem to put the locals off.

Ť Rosana D'Avila's restaurant, Del Batán 368. Good value, tasty buffet, set lunches, open for dinner too. For early breakfasts go to the market.

Cafés

Casa Luna, 2 de Mayo 334. Café with couches, also has a bar, live music Fri night, closed Sun.

Cascanuez Café Bar, Amalia Puga 554, near the Cathedral. Great cakes, extensive menu including *humitas*, breakfasts, ice creams and coffees.

El Capulí, Jr Junín, in the Complejo Belén. Open 0900-1300, 1500-2000 (2400 Fri-Sat). Coffee, drinks, sandwiches and snacks. Lovely atmosphere for a quiet coffee, reading your Handbook and planning your next activity.

Heladería Holanda, Amalia Puga 657 on the Plaza de Armas, T076-830113. Dutch-owned, easily the best ice-creams in Cajamarca, 50 flavours (but not all on at the same time), try *poro poro*, *lúcuma* or *sauco*, also serves coffee. Also has a branch in Baños del Inca.

Sanguchón.com, Junín 1137. Best burgers in town, sandwiches, also popular bar.

Around Cajamarca *p445*
There are several cheap restaurants at or near the thermal complex at Los Baños del Inca, as well as the **Salas restaurant** (see above). Many people, after a bathe, go to the **Bodega Baños del Inca** (at the bus stop, opposite **Heladería Holanda**) for a good selection of cakes at great prices.

🎵 Bars and clubs

Cajamarca *p443, map p444*
El Brujo, Apurímac 519. Disco bar, popular with younger set.
La Noche, San Martín y Junín. Popular nightspot for young crowd.
Rodeo Video, San Martín 352. Pub/disco.

✺ Festivals and events

Cajamarca *p443, map p444*
Cajamarca is known as the Carnival capital of Peru. It hosts a messy, raucous **carnival week** in **Feb** with many processions and dances. But note that the level of water, motor oil and paint-throwing would put Laurel and Hardy to shame. This is not for the faint-hearted. You have been warned!
Corpus Christi is held in **May** or **Jun** and is a solemn religious affair. On **24 Jun** is **San Juan** in Cajamarca, Chota, Llacanora, San Juan and Cutervo. On the **first Sun in Oct** is the **Festival Folklórico** in Cajamarca. Also in **Oct**, in the second week, is the city's '**Tourist Week**'.

An agricultural fair, **Feria Fongal**, is held in **Jul** at Baños del Inca. It coincides with **Fiestas Patrias** and besides agricultural displays, has artesanía and caballos de paso.
Domingo de Ramos (Palm Sunday) processions in Porcón are worth seeing.

🛍 Shopping

Cajamarca *p443, map p444*
Food and drink
The area is renowned for its dairy produce. Many shops sell cheese, butter, honey, etc. Look out for queso ahumado, smoked cheese, sold at shops at 2 de Mayo y Amazonas. The Asociación de Productores Lácteos sticker assures quality. Eucalyptus honey is sold in the market on C Amazonas and is said to be a cure for rheumatism.
El Porcón, see Eating, Chanchamayo 1355 (hard to find, take a mototaxi). It sells excellent queso suizo.
El Tambo, 2 de Mayo 576. Has a good selection of cheeses.
La Collpa, see p446, has a shop at Romero 124, sells some of the best cheese and butter. Try the *queso mantecoso*, which is full-cream cheese, or sweet *manjar blanco*.
Los Alpes, Junín 965. Recommended for quality and variety, Swiss run, pricey but excellent.

Handicrafts
Cajamarca is famous for its gilded mirrors. The Cajamarquiña frames are not carved but decorated with patterns transferred onto pieces of glass using the silkscreen process. This tradition lapsed during the post-colonial period and present production goes back less than 20 years.
Cajamarca is also an excellent place to buy handicrafts. They're cheap and the quality is good. Specialities include cotton and wool saddlebags (*alforjas*), found at the San Antonio market, at the north end of Jr Apurímac. Handwoven woollen items can be made to order. Other items include painted ceramic masks and soapstone figures (including miners with power drills). The market on Amazonas is good for artesanía. There are stalls in the street on block 7 of Belén every day. There are several shops on 300 block of Dos de Mayo. All offer

a good range of local crafts.

Textiles y Artesanías Paredes, 2 de Mayo 264, up the steps. Has a different selection from what you find in the streets.

▲▲ Activites and tours

Cajamarca *p443, map p444*

Several travel agencies around the Plaza de Armas offer trips to local sites and further afield (eg Kuntur Wasi, Kuélap), trekking on Inca and other trails, riding caballos de paso and handicraft tours. Average prices of local tours: Cumbe Mayo, US$6, Ventanillas de Otusco US$4.50, Porcón US$6. Recommended are:

Atahualpa Inca Tours, La Mar 435, T076-827014 (in Hostal El Mirador), www.nunura.com/elmirador.

Cajamarca Tours, Dos de Mayo 323, T/F076-822813 (also DHL, Western Union and flight reconfirmations).

Cajamarca Travel, 2 de Mayo 570, T076-830074, cajamarcatravel@hotmail.com.

Clarín Tours, Del Batán 161, T/F076-826829, clarintours@yahoo.com.

Cumbemayo Tours, Amalia Puga 635 on the plaza, T076-822938, cumbemayotours@ usa.net. Guides in English and French.

Inca Baths Tours, Amalia Puga 667, T076-824310, incablaz@hotmail.com.

Variservice, Silva Santisteban 134, T076-822228, variservice@infonegocio. net.pe. Helpful office where flights can be bought or reconfirmed (domestic and international).

⊙ Transport

Cajamarca *p443, map p444*

Air

To/from **Lima** (US$92) daily with **Aero Cóndor**, **Atsa**, daily except Sun, **LC Busre**, Sun-Fri, and **Nuevo Contininte**, Thu-Sun.

Aero Cóndor, 2 de Mayo 323, at Cajamarca Tours, T076-825674. Atsa, 2 de Mayo 570, at Cajamarca Travel, T076-828642. LC Busre, Comercio 1024, T076-821098.

Bus

To **Lima**, 856 km, 12-14 hrs, económico US$10-11.45, to US$14.30-20 on **Civa's** double-deckers, to US$20-26 for **Cruz del Sur's** luxury service (includes taxi to your lodging in Lima), several buses daily (see below). The road is paved. To **Pacasmayo**, 189 km, 5-6 hrs, US$7, several buses and hourly *colectivos*. To **Trujillo**, 296 km, 6½ hrs, US$4.30-10, regular buses daily 0945-2230 most continue to Lima. To **Chiclayo**, 260 km, 6 hrs, US$4.55- 7.60, several buses daily; you have to change buses to go on to Piura and Tumbes. To **Celendín**, 112 km, 4 hrs, US$3, **Atahualpa** at 0700 and 1300, **Royal Palace's** 0900 and 1300 (poor minibuses). Also combis from Av Atahualpa cuadra 3, leave when full 0400-1800, 3½ hrs, US$3. The route follows a fairly good dirt road through beautiful countryside. To carry on from Celendín to **Chachapoyas**, at 1100 Thu and Sun only. **Perú Bus, Rojas** and others go to **Cajabamba**, 75 km, US$3, 4 hrs, several daily. These buses, and Royl Palace's, also go to **Bambamarca, Chota and Cutervo.**

Bus companies: **Atahualpa**, Atahualpa 299, T076-823060 (Lima, Celendín, Cajabamba, Bambamarca, Chota). **Civa**, Ayacucho 753, T076-821460 (Lima). **Cruz del Sur**, Atahualpa 600, T076-821737 (Lima). **El Cumbe**, Sucre 594, T076-823088 (to Chiclayo). **Emtrafesa**, Atahualpa 447, T829663 (to Trujillo); **Línea**, Atahualpa 318, T076-823956 (Lima, Trujillo, Chiclayo). **Rojas**, Atahualpa 405, T076-820548 (to Cajabamba, buses not coming from Lima). **Royal Palace's**, Atahualpa 339, T076-825855 (Lima, Trujillo, Celendín, Bambamarca, Chota). **Turismo Días**, Sucre 422, T076-828289 (to Lima, Chimbote, Trujillo, Chiclayo).

Taxi
Radio taxi: **El Sol**, T076-828897,.24 hrs.

⊙ Directory

Cajamarca *p443, map p444*

Banks BCP, Apurímac 719. Open 1000-1800. Changes Amex TCs without commission, cash advance on Visa, Mastercard and Amex, 0.5% commission, Visa and Mastercard ATM. **Banco Continental**, Tarapacá 721. Changes Amex and Visa TCs, commission US$12, takes Visa credit cards. **Banco Wiese**, Amazonas 650. Accepts Amex TCs, US$3 commission, cash advance and ATM for Visa and Mastercard. **Interbank**, 2 de Mayo 546, on Plaza. Closed 1400-1600. Accepts Vias TCs without commission if paid in soles, US$5 for dollars, Visa ATM. There is a **Telebanco 24 Horas** ATM (Visa) at the gas station next to Cial buses on Av Atahualpa. Dollars can be changed in most banks and travel agencies on east side of Plaza, but euros are hard to change. Casa de cambio in **Casa del Artefacto** musical and electrical store at Amazonas 537. Good rates, cash only. Casas de cambio also at Jr del Comercio y Apurímac and at Amalia Puga 673. **Street changers** on Jr Del Batán by the Plaza de Armas and at Del Batán y Amazonas. **Hospitals Clínica Limatambo**, Puno 265, T076-824241. Private, recommended. Doctor Gurmandi speaks English. **Clínica San Francisco**, Av Grau 851, T076-822050.

Private, recommended. Hospital at Av Mario Urteaga. **Internet** There are internet cabins everywhere; rates are US$0.35 per hr. **Laundry Lavandería Dandy**, Jr Amalia Puga 545. Pay by weight. **Lava Express**, Jr Belén 678. Good service, US$1.50 per kg. **Post Serpost**, Jr Amalia Puga 778. 0800-2045. **Telephone** Public phone offices cn be found all over the centre. **Useful addresses Cenfotur**, José Gálvez 767, T076-829714, cenfocaj@enfoturcaja marca.org.pe. The organization overseeing the Circuito Turístico Nororiental. **Indecopi**, Amalia Puga 516, T076-823315, caraujo@ indecopi.gob.pe. The place to go if you have a complaint about tourist services.

Chachapoyas Region

The Chachapoyas Region contains so many archaeological riches that you need at least a week to begin to appreciate the remarkable legacy of the Chachapoyans, also known as 'The Cloud People'. Great pre-Inca cities, immense fortresses such as Kuélap and ancient effigies which gaze over a dramatic landscape reward the visitor to a region which is due to become a major tourist destination as soon as regular air service begins. There are many cities and burial sites scattered around the cloud-covered mountain slopes, often in inaccessible places. To reach them is an adventure in itself. » *For Sleeping, Eating and other listings, see pages 464-470.*

Ins and outs

Getting there The city of Chachapoyas is the best base for visiting this region. As there are no scheduled flights, it has to be reached overland from Chiclayo, Cajamarca or Tarapoto. Civa and Móvil Tours offer reasonably comfortable bus services from Lima, travelling Chiclayo-Chachapoyas by day. Bus schedules starting from Chiclayo all involve an overnight journey, missing the fine scenery along the way. An alternative is to go by bus from Chiclayo to Jaén, continuing the next day to Chachapoyas, via Bagua Grande and Pedro Ruíz, using combis. From Cajamarca, you can go first to Celendín (see page 453) and then on to Chachapoyas, crossing the Marañón at Balsas between descents and climbs of thousands of vertical metres. The journey is an entirely unforgettable experience in its own right, but half of it is done at night. Also beautiful is the route from Tarapoto via Moyobamba and Pedro Ruíz, especially since the highway has been paved for the most part. It is possible to do this journey in one day, leaving Tarapoto at 0800 or 0900, but the last part will be done in darkness. Break the journey in Moyobamba or Pedro Ruíz and take combis on some stretches.

Best time to visit The dry season is infinitely preferable (normally May-September, but the seasons are less stable than in the past; in the last few years it has been sunny and dry well into December). During the rains, roads may become impassable due to landslides and access to the more remote areas may be impossible, or involve weeks of delay. Likewise, trekking in the area can be very pleasant in the dry season, but may involve too much wading through waist-deep mud on some routes during the rainy season. Other places are still accessible in the wet, but rubber boots are essential. Good hiking gear is always a must; also a sleeping bag, tent and canned goods.

Tourist information iperú ⓘ *Jr Ortiz 588, Plaza de Armas, Chachapoyas, T041-777292, iperuchachapoyas@promperu.gob.pe, Mon-Sat 0800-1300, 1500-1900.* **Dirección Regional de Turismo** ⓘ *Jr Triunfo 1051, T041-778355.* Websites: www.regionamazonas.gob pe and www.chachapoyas.com.pe.

Background

Theories about the Chachapoyan Empire show that their cities, highways, terracing, irrigation, massive stonework and metalcraft were all fully developed. The culture began about AD 800 and covered an area bounded by the rivers Marañón and Huallaga, as far as Pataz in the south and Bagua in the north. Socially the

Chachapoyas

To Capilla de la Virgen Asunta (500m)
To Airport
To Pozo de Yanayacu (500m)

Jr Santa Ana
Quebrada Santa Lucía

Jr L'Ibertad
Santo Domingo

To Miraflor Guayamil (300m)

Distribuidora Comercial Universal & Cambio
Banco de Crédito
INC
Iperú
Palacio Municipal
Plaza de Armas
Banco de la Nación

Jr Salamanca

Cathedral

Jr Ayacucho
Jr Recreo

Jr Amazonas

Jr Ortiz Arrieta
Jr Junin
Jr Grau
Jr 2 de Mayo

Cyber Club

Jr Triunfo

Jr Piura
Jr La Merced
Jr Unión

To Pampas de Higos Urco

Jr Bolivia

Señor de Burgos

To Chiclayo, Calendin & Kuélap

N
0 metres 200
0 yards 200

Sleeping
Belén 1 *B1*
Casa Vieja 2 *B1*
Casona Monsante 12 *B2*
El Dorado 3 *A1*
El Tejado & Restaurant 4 *B2*
Gran Vilaya & Café de Guías 5 *B2*

Hostal El Danubio 7 *C3*
Hostal Johumaji 8 *B2*
Hostal Kuélap 9 *B1*
Laguna de los Cóndores 10 *A2*
Puma Urcu & Café Café 13 *B2*
Revash 11 *B2*

Eating
Chacha 1 *B2*
Chifa Chuy Xien 10 *B2*
El Edén 3 *A2*
Kuélap 4 *B2*

La Estancia 5 *B2*
La Tushpa 2 *B1*
Las Rocas 6 *B2*
Mari Pizza 11 *B3*
Mass Burger 7 *B1*
Matalache 8 *B2*
Panadería San José 9 *B2*
Pizzería 505 12 *B2*

Transport
Bus to Leymebamba 1 *A2*
Cars to Pedro Ruíz & Bagua Grande 2 *A2*

Colectivos to Huancas 4 *A2*
Combis to Huancas 5 *A2*
Combis to Leymebamba, Comité Interprovincial Santo Tomás & Trans Rollers Combis 6 *A2*
Combis to Pedro Ruíz 7 *A2*
San Juan de Luya Combis 8 *A2*
Trans Zelada 9 *A2*
Turismo Kuélap 10 *A1*
Virgen del Carmen 11 *A2*

Chachapoya were organized into chiefdoms, which formed war-alliances in the case of external aggression. Archaeologists claim that this region overwhelms even Machu-Picchu and its neighbouring Inca sites in grandeur and mystery. By some counts, its 'lost' and uncharted cities, such as Pueblo Alto, near the village of Pueblo Nuevo (25 km from Kuélap) and Saposoa in the northeast of San Martín department, exceed three dozen. By far the majority of these cities, fortresses and villages were never discovered by the Spanish. In fact many had already returned to the jungle by the time they arrived in 1532.

This region is called La Ceja de la Selva (the eyebrow of the jungle), whose beautiful scenery includes a good deal of virgin cloud-forest (although other sections are sadly deforested), as well as endless deep dry canyons traversed by hair-raisingly dangerous roads. The temperature is always in the 20s (70s Farenheit) during the day, but the nights are cool at around 3,000 m. Many ruins are overgrown with ferns, bromeliads and orchids and easily missed.

The central geographic feature of the department, and its boundary with neighbouring Cajamarca, is the great Río Marañón, one of the major tributaries of the Amazon. Running roughly parallel to the mighty Marañón, one range to the east, is the gentler valley of the Utcubamba, home to much of the area's ancient and present population. Over yet another cordillera to the east, lie the isolated subtropical valleys of the province of Rodríguez de Mendoza, the origin of whose inhabitants, has been the source of much debate (see page 463).

The German ethnologist, Doctor Peter Lerche ① *F041-778438*, is the resident expert regarding Chachapoyan cultures and trekking. He is very knowledgeable, speaks English, sometimes guides groups and may be contacted for information on anthropology and history. In an article in National Geographic, September 2000, "Quest for the Lost Tombs of the Peruvian Cloud People", Doctor Lerche writes about the discovery of a Chachapoya tomb named the 'White House' and gives a good general introduction to the history and archaeology of the region (he has also provided information for this section).

Charles Motley ① *Grau 534, Chachapoyas, T041-778078, www.kuelap.org*, is directing a long-term project with volunteers called **Los Tambos Chachapoyanos (LTC)**. LTC have lodges at Choctámal and Levanto. LTC also have an English-speaking Peruvian guide and an American on the staff who can sometimes guide.

Cajamarca to Chachapoyas

East from Cajamarca, the first town of note is **Celendín**, whose residents are known as Shilicos. It is a clean and tranquil place, with warm friendly people but a decidedly chilly climate. The plaza and cathedral are both appealing. There is also an interesting local market on Sunday. Walk up the hill to the chapel of San Isidro Labrador for views of town and surroundings. Note the huge hats worn by the townsfolk. These are woven from fine straw and can be bought, along with other straw handicrafts, at **Artesanías San José de Pilco**, 2 de Mayo 319.

The rough narrow road from Celendín to Chachapoyas (226 km) follows a winding course, crossing the wide and deep canyon of the Río Marañón at Balsas (Altitude: 950 m). It then climbs steeply, over countless hair-raising hairpin bends, with superb views of the mountains and the valleys below, to reach the Barro Negro pass at 3,680 m, before descending to Leymebamba in the upper Utcubamba valley (see page 458). The journey takes 12-14 hours in the dry season. It can be much longer and more dangerous when it rains. Take warm clothing, food and water. Paving of the road to Chachapoyas will shorten the journey time. The route is generally safe but vehicle robberies are not unknown.

Chachapoyas and around

→ *Phone code: 041. Colour map 1, grid C4. Population: 25,000. Altitude: 2,335 m.*

Chachapoyas, or 'Chacha', as it is known among locals, is the capital of the Department of Amazonas. It was founded on 5 September 1538, but retains only some of its colonial character, in the form of large old homes with their typical patios and wooden balconies. The city's importance as a crossroads between the coast and jungle began to decline in the late 1940s, with the building of the road through Pedro Ruíz. However, archaeological and ecological tourism have grown gradually since the 1990s and there are hopes that these will bring increasing economic benefits to the region.

Chachapoyas

The modern cathedral faces a spacious plaza which fills with locals for the evening paseo. Other interesting churches are the **Capilla de la Virgen Asunta**, the city's patroness, at Asunción y Puno, and **Señor de Burgos**, at Amazonas y Santa Lucía. The **Instituto Nacional de Cultura (INC)** has a small **museum** ① *Ayacucho y Grau, Plaza de Armas.* It contains a few mummies and artefacts.

The **Mirador Guayamil** offers fine views of the city, especially at early dusk. Nearby is the **Pozo de Yanayacu**, also known as the *fuente del amor*, at the west end of Avenida Salamanca. Legend has it that those who visit this well will fall in love and remain in Chachapoyas. A decisive battle for independence from Spain took place at the **Pampas de Higos Urco**, at the east end of town, a 20-minute walk, with great views of lush Andes to the east.

Huancas

Huancas, a picturesque village, stands on a hilltop north of Chacha. It's a two-hour walk starting on the airport road. The town is developing a reputation as an artisans' centre and local pottery can be bought. Walk uphill from Huancas for a magnificent view into the deep **canyon** of the Río Sonche. There is good walking in the area, which also has Inca and pre-Inca ruins.

Levanto → *Colour map 1, grid C4.*

The Spaniards built this, their first capital of the area, in 1538, directly on top of the previous Chachapoyan structures. Although the capital was moved to Chachapoyas a few years later, Levanto still retained its importance, at least for a while, as it had been one of the seven great cities of the Chachapoyans as described by Cieza de León and Garcilaso de la Vega. Nowadays Levanto is a small, unspoilt colonial village set on flat ground overlooking the massive canyon of the Utcubamba River. Kuélap can, on a clear day, be seen on the other side of the rift. The town is a good centre for exploring the many ruins around. *Colectivos* for Huancas leave from Jr Ortiz Arrieta y Salamanca; 20 minutes, US$0.45. A large prison complex has been built nearby and all *colectivos* go there on the way to the village.

The Kuélap east-west Highway starts at Levanto and links with the Inca military highway at Jalca Grande (see page 457). Levanto was about mid-way on the north-south route from Colombia to the Huari, then Inca hub, at Huánuco. This stone road crosses the modern vehicle road at La Molina, about 5 km from Chachapoyas. A 10-km walk on this ancient road from Levanto is worthwhile.

Yalape

About five minutes' drive, or a pleasant 30-minute walk, from Levanto on the road to Chachapoyas are the partly cleared ruins of Yalape. The local people are helpful and will guide you to the ruins which can be easily seen from the road (look for the three, linked curving walls above the road, opposite a solitary modern building). Yalape seems to have been a massive residential complex extending over many hectares. The majority of the walls visible from the road are of white limestone and there are well-preserved examples of typical Chachapoyan architecture and masonry with elaborate friezes. It is easy to climb up to the ruins, but many of the structures are overgrown.

Near Yalape is the site of **San Pedro de Wushpu**: coming from Chachapoyas, at the point where the road drops over the crest, is a fork in the road. Take the left branch (right goes to Levanto). The ruins are similar to Yalape but easier to get to; ask at the first house on the left on the side road.

Sites around Chachapoyas

Archaeological sites ∴

Balsas 1
Cerro Olán 2
Colcamar 3
Complejo Inca de
  Cochabamba 4
Jalca Grande, Ollape,
  Moyuk Viejo 5
Kuélap 6
Laguna de los
  Cóndores 7
Lónguita, María,
  Choctamal, Huiquilla 8

Luya, Lamud, Trita, Chipuric,
  Karajía, San Antonio,
  Pueblo de Los Muertos 9
Magdalena 10
Milpuc, Omia 11
Molinopampa 12
Purunllacta
  (Monte Peruvia) 13
Rumichaco/Monja 14
Santo Tomás, Revash 15
Soloco, Daguas, Cheto 16
Yalape 17

Morgan Davis has reconstructed an Inca building at **Colla Cruz**, about 20 minutes' walk from Levanto. On a classic Inca stone terrace, a regional-style round building has been constructed, with a three-storey high thatched roof. This garrison guarded the road which ran past Colcamar, over the Cordillera Oriental on a 1½-km-staircase, through Gran Vilaya, to Cajamarca's central north-south road and on to the coastal highway.

Kuélap and Tingo

The undisputed highlight among the archaeological riches around Chachapoyas is Kuélap (3,000 m), a spectacular pre-Inca walled city which was rediscovered in 1843 by Juan Crisótomo Nieto. Even the most exaggerated descriptions fail to do justice to the sheer scale of this site great fortress. Tingo is the village from which to reach it.

Kuélap → *Colour map 1, grid C4.*

ⓘ *0800-1700, US$3, 50 per cent discount for students with identification. A small Centro de Interpretaciones is open 0800-1630; it has a good model of the site. There is a toilet block. The ruins are locked. The guardian, Gabriel Portocarrero, has the keys and accompanies visitors. He's very informative and friendly. Guides are available; pay them what you think appropriate. There is a drinks and snacks stall.*

Kuélap was built over a period of 200 years, from AD 900-1100 and contained three times more stone than the Great Pyramid at Giza in Egypt. The site lies sprawled along the summit of a mountain crest, more than a kilometre in length. It is divided into three parts: at the northwest end is a small outpost; at the southeast end of the ridge is a spread out village in total ruin; and the cigar-shaped fortress lies between the two, 585 m long by 110 m wide at its widest. The walls are as formidable as those of any pre-Columbian city. They vary in height between 8 and 17 m and were constructed in 40 courses of stone block, each one weighing between 100 and 200 kg. It has been estimated that 100,000 such blocks went into the completion of this massive structure.

The majority of the main walls on all four levels are original. Also original is the inverted, cone-shaped structure, long assumed to be a dungeon, although recent studies claim it to be a giant solar calendar, known as *el tintero* (the inkwell). There are a number of defensive walls and passageways as well as very many houses. Some reconstruction has taken place, mostly of small houses and walls, but only one building has been completely restored. The remainder have been left in their cloud forest setting, the trees covered in bromeliads and moss, the flowers visited

Kuélap

Sleeping ⊕
Albergue León 1
El Bebedero 2

INC Hostel 3
Tambos Chachapoyanos
Choctámal Lodge 4

66 99 Kuélap was built over a period of 200 years, from AD 900-1100 and contained three times more stone than the Great Pyramid at Giza in Egypt...

by hummingbirds. Although there are no carvings, some structures are adorned with simple geometric friezes which represent the eyes of animals and birds. An interesting feature is that almost all the buildings (about 420 in number) are circular.Recent archaeological findings indicate that the buildings were public spaces and served as kitchens, toilets and storage areas, rather than warriors' barracks as was first thought. It is estimated that up to 3,500 people lived in Kuélap at its zenith. The fortress was built, some believe, as the first large Chachapoya city in the region. Defence was vital for the developing culture against the constant raids from the Huari armies. With the Huari defeated, the Chachapoya moved out of Kuélap and into lower, less fortified altitudes where the farming was better. Kuélap was never mentioned in Inca chronicles, meaning that by the time of the Inca invasion in the 1470s, it was of little significance to the Chachas.The five rectangular structures indicate that the Incas occupied the fortress.

Public transport is not plentiful in this region. Most journeys are done by *colectivos* and combis, starting their routes in Chachapoyas. To reach the more remote archaeological sites you will have to do some walking, in one or two cases for several days. Tours can also be arranged.

Tingo → *Colour map 1, grid C4. Altitude: 1,800 m.*

Tingo is about 37 km south of Chachapoyas. Much of the village was washed away in the floods of 1993. In the hills above Tingo, 3½ km away, is Tingo Nuevo, with its plaza of flowers and topiary in front of the church. There is no running water or electricity. Market day is Sunday.

Sites between Tingo and Leymebamba

South of Tingo and Kuélap there are many sights of interest on either bank of the Río Utcubamba. To visit the sites south of Chacha, you have to descend to the road in the Río Utcubamba valley, cross the bridge to the west bank and head to Tingo. At Shipamarca there is a Sunday feria of handicrafts. Before Tingo is a sign to Kuélap, but this is a poor road. It's better to continue to Tingo itself where the new road to Kuélap starts beside the river. Between these two roads, look for the ruins of Macros above the east bank of the river.

Jalca Grande

The town of Jalca Grande (or La Jalca as it is known locally), at 2,600 m, lies between Montevideo and Tingo, up on the east side of the main valley. There is a market on Saturday. In the town itself, one block west of the Plaza de Armas, is the **Choza Redonda**, the remains of a Chachapoyan roundhouse which was inhabited until 1964. Half an hour west of the town are the ruins of **Ollape**, a series of platforms with intricate fretwork designs and wide balconies. A much larger site, though more primitive, is **Moyuk Viejo**, a 2½-hours' walk to the north.

A strenuous but rewarding three to four day trek can be made from La Jalca to Huambo or Limabamba (see page 463), over the cordillera and through cloud forests to the subtropical valleys. Part of the route follows an ancient road and there are undeveloped ruins along the way. Trekking experience and self-sufficiency are indispensable.

Ubilón

Jalca Grande can also be reached from Ubilón, on the main road north to Tingo. Lots of transport passes Ubilón, but there is only one daily bus direct to the village. It's a strenuous three-hour walk uphill to La Jalca. There is not much in Ubilón itself, save for a few shops selling next to nothing. Cheap, basic accommodation is available at **Bodega Irmita**.

Revash

Further south are the towns of **Yerbabuena** and **Puente Santo Tomás**, which is at the turn-off for the vivid burial chullpas of **Revash**, belonging to the Revash culture (around AD 1250). In Yerbabuena the Sunday market is the largest in the area, with animals, local produce, including cheeses, farming implements, etc on sale or for barter. There is one unnamed basic hospedaje, G, with running water but no electricity. There is also **Restaurant Karina**, which is cheap.

The ruins of **Revash** are roughly three hours' walk from Puente Santo Tomás. Follow the dirt road towards **Santo Tomás**, then cross the wooden bridge on the right and take the dirt track towards the mountains; it is a steep climb up. Eventually small adobe houses can be seen in the cliff face, covered by an overhang. The houses are buff coloured with red roofs and resemble tiny Swiss cottages with crosses in the form of bricked-up windows. They are, in fact, small tombs. There are lots of human bones lying around and cave paintings. The tombs have long since been looted. To get close, climb up a small goat track and walk along a ledge. Please do not climb on the houses as they are incredibly fragile. Examine the cliff face to the left of the houses and you'll notice several more tombs, peeking out from the limestone face. It is about an hour's walk back downhill from Santo Tomás to Puente Santo Tomás, from where there is transport north towards Chachapoyas.

Rumichaco/Monja

Beyond Puente Santo Tomás there is a turn-off which heads east beyond **Duraznopampa** to the small town of **Montevideo**. An hour's walk southeast of Montevideo is the ruined complex of **Rumichaco/Monja**, spread along a ridge above the town. The upper Rumichaco sector consists of massive undecorated platforms while the lower Monja sector is better preserved with some intricate fretwork on the platforms. Local guides can be hired; ask for Tito Rojas Calla in Montevideo. There are no hotels in the town but ask the owner of the only restaurant if you can sleep there.

Cerro Olán

Another Chachapoyan site is Cerro Olán, reached by *colectivo* to **San Pedro de Utac**, a small village beyond Montevideo, then a 30 minutes' walk. From the plaza a clear trail rises directly into the hills east of town to the ruins, which can be seen from the village. Here are the remains of towers which some archaeologists claim had roofs like mediaeval European castles. According to Morgan Davis this was essentially a military installation and once a small city of considerable luxury, similar in construction to La Congona (see page 459) but on a grander scale. Ask the alcalde for accommodation. The road south from Chachapoyas crosses the Utcubamba River then passes through **Palmira** and heads to Leymebamba.

Leymebamba→ *Colour map 1, grid C4.*

This pleasant town derives its name from a visit in around 1475, by the Inca Túpac Yupanqui, who stayed to celebrate the **Fiesta de Inti-Raymi**. From that moment, the

town came to be known as the Field of the Festival of The Sun, or **Raymi-Pampa**, 459
which in turn became Leymebamba. The city was moved from its original location,
3 km south, following an epidemic of yellow fever in the 1600s. The local fiesta is held
in honour of the Virgen del Carmen on the week preceeding 16 July.

The town's market is very limited; try the one at Yerbabuena on Sunday morning
(see above). The young Spanish priest, Padre Diego, is very helpful, especially to
Europeans. He is involved in the new museum project (see below). In addition to
those at hotels (see Listings), there are a couple of phone lines in town, T041-770209
and T041-770264, which are shared. Water is sporadic and should be boiled to within
an inch of its life. The Centro de Salud is helpful and will even visit your hotel if you're
too ill to move. The Comité Turístico on the plaza is the place to go for all information
on how to reach sites, including Laguna de los Cóndores (see below), for guides
and horse hire.

Laguna de los Cóndores
In 1996 a spectacular site consisting of six burial chullpas, containing 219 mummies
and vast quantities of ceramics, textiles, woodwork, quipus and everyday utensils
from the late Inca period, was discovered at Laguna de los Cóndores, a beautiful lake
in a jungle setting, south of Leymebamba.

In order to protect this major discovery from huaqueros, who had already done
considerable damage, all the material was moved to a spectacular new **museum**
① *Mon-Sat 0900-1200, 1400-1700, entry fee US$4.35*, but anything over that amount
is most welcome. From the town it's a 30-40 mins' walk, take the footpath and ask
directions constantly, the road is much longer. It was opened in 2001, with Austrian
financial assistance, at San Miguel (3 km south), the site of the original Leymebamba
town. Over 5,000 artefacts are on display, the great majority of them saved from the
Laguna de los Cóndores site. The museum and its materials were entirely made by
hand, a true artisan construction. There is a café, a great place to admire the
architecture and lush surroundings. For further information contact Dr Sonia Guillén,
Director, Centro Mallqui Bioanthropology Foundation ① *Av A Márquez 2014, Jesús
María, Lima 11, T01-261 0095, mallqui@amauta.rcp.net.pe*.

The **trip to Laguna de los Cóndores from Leymebamba** takes 10-12 hours on foot
and horseback, nine hours return (three days in all). It is not for the fainthearted, but
is generally agreed to be one of the trips of a lifetime. The route climbs to 3,700 m
before descending to the laguna where there is a basic lodge, US$5. Bring all food
and cook it there or pay the family to prepare it. Make sure your horse is in good
condition as the track is often knee deep in mud. Also take food and warm clothes. It
is best done during the dry season (May to September); hire a local guide and horses.
Three-day tours cost about US$70 per person. Unfortunately, the impressive funerary
site overlooking the river has been stripped of artefacts and even some of its colourful
plaster. Please do not climb on the houses or remove anything from the site.

La Congona
There are many ruins around Leymebamba, many of which are covered in vegetation.
The most spectacular is the Chachapoyan site of La Congona.

The site is a brisk three hours' walk along a clear trail which starts at the lower
end of 16 de Julio. The path climbs steeply from the town, then levels off before
descending to a large flat pasture. Turn left at the end of the pasture and follow the
white sand, then bear right where the trail divides, to reach the middle of three peaks,
identified by a white limestone cliff. The ruins are clustered in a small area,
impossible to see until you are right among them. The views are stupendous and the
ruins worth the effort. This is the best preserved of three sites, with 30 decorated
round stone houses and a watch tower. It is supposed to be the only site displaying
all three Chacha friezes – zigzag, rhomboid and Greek stepped.

There are two other sites, **El Molinete** and **Pumahuanyuna**, nearby. All three can be visited in a day but a guide is essential to explain the area and show the way to the ruins as it is easy to get lost.

Northwest of Chachapoyas

There are more extraordinary archaeological remains, including strange sarcophagi in cliffs, with rewarding trekking possibilities in this area.

Luya, Karajía, Lamud and Pueblo de los Muertos

The village of **Luya** is on a turn-off from the road north to Pedro Ruíz (see below). Three kilometres or 1½ hours' walk from Luya is **Chipuric**, a residential complex belonging to the Chachapoyas culture. The site consists of burial tombs set in a cliff face on a high ledge with circular stone buildings on the hill above. The tombs, which are 1 m high and look like beehives, have all been looted. Continue along the dirt road from Luya until it forks; take the higher road with the irrigation canal. At **Pueblo Molino** (a small cluster of houses and one shop), the cliff face and the burial tombs are visible. On the lower road which passes below the cliff on the other side of the river, is Chipuric town. The cliff is steep but it's possible to climb up to the tombs with some difficulty and quite a few scratches from the thorn bushes. There are great views from the top, though.

Gran Vilaya Region

Archaeological sites

Cerro Negro,
  Paxamarca, Tulalon **1**
Kuélap **2**
Machu Llacta **3**

Pueblo Alto **4**
San Pablo **5**
San Pedro **6**
Vista Hermosa **7**

0 km 5
0 miles 5

Karajía, also known as Solmol, is 2½ hours' walk from Luya but more accessible from **Trita**. A short walk from Trita, in the valley behind the village, are the remarkable, 2½-m high sarcophagi, which date from AD 1200, set into an impressive cliff face. Just below these inscrutable figures are plenty of human bones, if you look carefully. Study the cliff face for a dozen more, smaller sarcophagi. The main figures have been looted long ago by tourism-minded grave robbers who broke in via holes in the back, thus preserving the striking effigies. Ask for directions in Luya. Expect to pay around US$3.50-5 a day with a local guide. In dry weather a short way to get there is from Luya or Cohechán (see below) to Cruzpata (*colectivos* run from Luya to Cruzpata). At other times the road can be very muddy.

A good way to get to know the local people and to appreciate fully the magnificent scenery of this region is a three to four day trek starting from Luya. Walk 2-2½ hours to **Shipata** and from there to Karajía (30-40 minutes). Ask around for directions. You cannot get to the sarcophagi, but can view them from the other side of the valley (the same view point as from Trita), with binoculars preferably. At Shipata you can stay with Sra Rosa Zota, who will cook you dinner and breakfast. A better option, however, is to continue 1-1½ hours to **Cohechán**. To get there from Karajía, you have to go back to Shipata. Continue from Cohechán to **Belén** (four to five hours) and **Vista Hermosa,** thence to Yumal and Choctámal (see under Gran Vilaya).

Ten minutes north of Luya, 37 km northwest of Chachapoyas, is Lamud, a convenient base for several interesting archaeological sites. The local fiesta of **Señor de Gualamita** on 14 September is well-attended.

At **San Antonio**, half an hour from Lamud, is a sandstone cliff face with several groups of burial tombs high on a ledge. They are difficult to see unless you know what you're looking for (there are sarcophogi and other tombs, but you need binoculars to see them). The ruins, set on the hill above, are a residential complex, thought to form part of a group of people belonging to the Chipuric. The main nucleus is almost completely ruined, but the ruins are unusual in that the stucco is still in place. A guide is not necessary, but ask for directions. On the bottom of the hill, where the road ends, a colonial-era tunnel and water-wheel can be explored.

Ten kilometres from Lamud are the mind-boggling ruins of **Pueblo de los Muertos**, circular stone houses overlooking the valley a thousand m below. A road goes to within 40 minutes of the site and then you have a steep, 40-minute walk on loose rock. The view is spectacular and the ruins are difficult to find as they are overgrown. Since being brought to public attention by Gene Savoy in the mid-1960s, the site has been largely destroyed by local grave robbers. Despite this, it is unmatched for location and scenery in the area. Ask directions before setting out.

Gran Vilaya → *Colour map 1, grid C4.*

The name Gran Vilaya was created by US explorer, Gene Savoy, one of the candidates for the original 'Indiana Jones', who discovered this extensive set of ruined complexes in 1985.There are about 30 sites spread over this vast area, 15 of which are considered significant. Among the sites are Pueblo Alto, Pueblo Nuevo, Paxamarca and Machu Llacta.

To get to this area, head north from Tingo or south from Chachapoyas as far as the Huinchuco bridge across the Río Utcubamba. On the west bank of the river a road leads to the left, if heading north, to the town of Colcamar, which is the starting point for exploring this area. A road from Choctámal to the Yumal pass into the Gran Vilaya region facilitates access but also places the area's cloud forests at considerable risk of destruction.

The whole area stretches west from the Río Utcubamba to the Río Marañon. Moist air pushing up from the Amazon Basin creates a unique biosphere of clouds and mist in which bromeliads and orchids thrive. Being near to the equator and over 3,000 m above sea level, the daytime temperature is a constant 22º C. While the Marañón

The Valley of the Whites

The tiny villages in the Guayabamba valley could be any other sleepy, sub-tropical settlements. A collection of wooden houses on a fertile plain where oranges, bananas, guava and yucca grow, where colourful butterflies and mesmerizing birdsong fill the warm, humid air. But the people of this remote region are very different from your average jungle dweller. They are blond-haired, blue-eyed and fair-skinned and could easily have just stepped off the 1700 flight from Stockholm.

The population of the Guayabamba valley themselves don't know where they came from and opinions among experts vary. Some posit the theory that they originate from warring conquistador factions in the early 16th century. This view hasn't satisfied those who point to the rarity of this phenomenon. It's true that the Spanish chronicler Garcilaso de la Vega described the fair-skinned people resisting the Incas before the conquest, but evidence tends to show that it is unlikely that the people of Guayamba have anything to do with the Chachapoyas cloud people.

Dr Jacques de Mahieu of Buenos Aires believes the latter to be descendants of the Vikings, who came to Peru in the 11th century. He supports such a theory with evidence on Easter Island, west of Chile, of drawings showing Viking longships, as well as linguistic parallels between the Quechua language and Scandinavian tongues.

The romantic theories are countered by research showing that the pre-conquest peoples did not speak Quechua in this region and that the Spanish chroniclers have been misunderstood: the phrase "the Chachapoyas were of fair complexion" has been taken to mean, wrongly, that they were blond. Perhaps the mystery will be solved by investigation into the DNA of the mummies found at Laguna de Cóndores and Scandinavian bog people and other European mummies. Moreover, in Guayamba DNA samples can be traced back to one Spanish family who lived in the region for a long time and there is evidence that the people of Chirimoto were originally Italian and Spanish settlers in the 1820s.

Whatever the explanation, the incongruous presence of these fair-skinned people in such a remote part of the country will continue to attract the attention of ethnologists.

valley is a desert, the peaks are always misted from June to September and drenched in rain the rest of the year. This creates a huge variety of mini-ecological zones, each with its own flora and fauna, depending on altitude and which flank of the mountain they are on.

The Inca Roads in this region make for incredible trekking. Three villages are possible starting points, Cohechán, Inguilpata or Colcamar. Trails all lead to Belén, a gigantic silted-in glacial tarn with a spectacular panorama of the river meandering below. This is above the nightly freeze line and the only large flat spot in the zone. From here you cross the spine of the Andes on a 1.6-km Inca stairway, dropping into Gran Vilaya. You pass many ruins near Vista Hermosa (3½-4 hrs from Belén). You can lodge with Sr Cruz. The Kuélap East-West ancient road takes you over the Abra Yumal pass with a climb of 1,600-1,700 m ('a killer'), from where the trail thankfully descends to Choctámal. The Choctámal Lodge is therefore a good finishing (or starting) point for treks in the Gran Vilaya. It is recommended to take a letter of introduction from the Instituto Nacional de Cultura in Chachapoyas, or ask Los Tambos Chachapoyanos for assistance in finding a guide (essential), accommodation, meals and perhaps horses. Also ask local alcaldes for help. Padre Juan Castelli, an English priest who has been living in the area for many years, is very knowledgeable.

East and north of Chachapoyas

Purunllacta and the route to the Valley of the Whites

Forty kilometres east from Chachapoyas, on the road to Mendoza, are the pre-Inca ruins of Monte Peruvia (known locally as **Purunllacta**). They consist of hundreds of white stone houses with staircases, temples and palaces. The ruins have been cleared by local farmers and some houses have been destroyed. A guide is useful as there are few locals of whom to ask directions. The area is currently undergoing initial excavation by archaeologist Jorge Ruiz (ask for him in the Café de Guías in Chachapoyas). He believes that the entire structure is one of the largest in the Chachapoyas realm.

If you're stuck in **Pipus**, ask to sleep at restaurant Huaracina or at the police station next door. There are no hotels in **Cheto** but a house high up on the hill above the town with a balcony has cheap bed and board. The same family also has a house on the plaza. There are two small shops selling very little and a small house with one room serves basic but good meals.

The road east from Chachapoyas continues through Pipus to **Molinopampa**, two hours' drive from Chachapoyas, it then carries on, passing a forest of palms, to Mendoza, capital and supply centre of the subtropical province of the same name (Rodríguez de Mendoza), which reportedly produces the best coffee in Peru. Organically grown coffee from the area is exported directly to Europe. There are several simple restaurants on Rodríguez de Mendoza.

Mendoza is also the starting point for an ethnologically interesting area in the Guayabamba Valley where there is a high incidence of fair-skinned people. There are roads and public transport to the small towns of Huambo, Santa Rosa, Totora, Limabamba, Chirimoto Viejo and Milpuc; and horse trails to other remote villages. Visitors going beyond Mendoza should be self sufficient.

North of Chachapoyas

The road north from Chachapoyas, paved for 13 km, heads through the beautiful Utcubamba River canyon with steep mountains on either side. In places the road is cut into the canyon wall. In the rainy season landslides may occur, especially near **Pedro Ruíz**, the town at the crossroads where you can either head west to Chiclayo on the coast or east to Tarapoto, Yurimaguas and the jungle. This is a small but important junction at the confluence of the Río Ingenio and the Utucubamba.

There are many interesting options for walking in the surrounding hills, covered with patches of cloud-forest and a good deal of undeveloped archaeology. **Catarata Chinata** is a lovely 150-m waterfall which can be reached by walking along the trail to the village of San Carlos, about two hours uphill. Continue uphill past San Carlos then turn left along a smaller track to the waterfall, a further two hours. Ask the locals for directions. It's a very nice full-day hike through sections of cloud-forest.

Pomacochas lake, at 2,150 m above sea level, is near the town of Florida. The blue-green water is surrounded by totora reeds. Take a combi to Florida or Balsapata along the road to Rioja (one hour, US$1.75); there are good views of the lake from the road. Where the buses stop in Florida, women sell cheese and bread spread with dulce/manjar. There are a couple of hotels in the town and it is a popular day excursion from Chachapoyas.

Near Florida is the **Río Chido** trail, a famous birdwatching site with some rare species, including the marvellous spatule tail hummingbird. Access is five minutes before the high point on the road to Florida, at San Ignacio. A highly recommended guide is young Dilberto Faustino, who is very enthusiastic and knowledgeable.

● Sleeping

Cajamarca to Chachapoyas *p453*

E Imperial, Jr 2 de Mayo 568, Celendín. Quite a good option.

E Loyer's, José Gálvez 410, Celendín, T076-855210. With bathroom, cheaper without, patio, nice.

E-F Celendín, Jr Unión 305, Plaza de Armas, Celendín, T076-855041, F855239. Colonial, with bathroom, very limited hot water, patio, poor rooms with old mattresses, overpriced and noisy, restaurant.

F Amazonas, Dos de Mayo 316, Celendín. With bathroom, cheaper without, cold water, basic, helpful.

F José Gálvez, Dos de Mayo 344, Celendín. With bathroom, cheaper without, cold water, basic, friendly.

F Maxmar, Dos de Mayo 349, Celendín. With bathroom, cheaper without, hot shower extra, basic, clean, parking, good value, owner Francisco is very helpful.

F Raymi Wasi, Jr José Gálvez, Celendín, beside La Reserve (same owner), T076-855374. With bath, hot water, TV, large rooms, has patio, quiet, clean, parking, good value.

Chachapoyas and around *p454*

C Gran Vilaya, Ayacucho 755, T041-777664, vilaya@wayna.rcp.net.pe. The best in town, comfortable rooms with firm beds, parking, English spoken, all services. Gumercindo 'Gumer' Zegarra, the proprietor, is knowledgeable about happenings in and around Chachapoyas.

C-D Casona Monsante, Jr Amazonas 746, T041-777702, www.casonamonsante.com. Rooms have cable TV, there is a cafeteria, breakfast costs US$1.50.

D Casa Vieja, Chincha Alta 569, T041-777353, www.casaviejaperu.com. In a converted old house, very nicely decorated, all rooms different, family atmosphere, hot water, cable TV, living room and comedor with open fire, continental breakfast, internet and library. Repeatedly recommended.

D El Tejado, Grau 534, Plaza de Armas. On first floor, same entrance as restaurant, good, laundry.

D Revash, Grau 517, Plaza de Armas, T041-777391, www.chachapoyasperu. com.pe. With private bathroom, plenty of hot water, clean, patio, friendly, helpful, laundry, good local information, restaurant, sells local items. Recommended. The proprietor, Carlos Burga, can organize tours.

D Puma Urcu, Jr Amazonas 833, T041-777871, hotelpumaurcu@peru.com. Carpeted rooms, hot water, cable TV, **Café Café** next door, both hotel and café receive good reports.

E Belén, Jr Ortiz Arrieta 540, T041-777830, www.hostalbelen.com.pe. On the plaza next to the bank. With bath, hot water, nicely furnished.

E El Dorado, Ayacucho 1062, T041-777047. With bathroom, hot water, clean, helpful.

F Hostal El Danubio, Tres Esquinas 193 y Junín 584, Plazuela Belén, some distance from centre, T041-777337. With private bathroom, hot water, cheaper with shared bath and cold water, clean, friendly, meals can be ordered in advance.

F Hostal Johumaji, Ayacucho 711, T041-777279, olvacha@ddm.com.pe With bathroom, hot water, TV, cheaper without TV, meals extra.

E Hostal Kuélap, Amazonas 1057, T041-777136, kuelaphotel@hotmial.com. With private bathroom, hot water and TV, cheaper without TV, cheaper still with shared bathroom and cold water, parking. Recommended.

G Laguna de los Cóndores, Salamanca 941, T041-777492. Very basic, shared bathroom, cold water.

Tambos Chachapoyanos' Levanto, *hostal*, two circular buildings with tall thatched roofs, stand behind Levanto's church; they can accommodate 12 people and have bathroom, basic but with hot shower, lounge with fireplace and kitchen. Beds and

Northern Highlands Chachapoyas Region

bedding are provided in the mayor's office and village meeting hall for small groups of travellers.

Kuélap and Tingo p456, map p456

F pp Albergue León, Jr Saenz Peña s/n, Tingo, no sign, walk 50 m from the police checkpoint to the corner and turn left, it's the third house on the left (righthand door), T041-999 9390. Basic, shared bathroom, cold water, friendly, run by Lucho León, who is very knowledgeable.

When walking up to Kuélap from Tingo, the last house to the right of the track (**El Bebedero**, just above a small spring) offers accommodation: bed, breakfast and evening meal for US$6; good meals, friendly and helpful. A bit further, on the left, 100 m below the ruins, is the **Instituto Nacional de Cultura (INC)** hostel. It's a clean dormitory with room for about 12 people, in a lovely setting, US$1.75 per person, no running water (please conserve the rainwater in the buckets); simple meals may be available from the caretaker for US$1. There is free camping outside the hostel.

Choctámal village has no hotels, but accommodation may be available in local homes. 3 km outside Choctámal the **Tambos Chachapoyanos** project, known locally as 'el hotel', operates a lodge with space for 35 people in 7 rooms with private bath, US$5 per person if you have a sleeping bag, US$7 per person if you want sheets and towels. It's in a lovely setting with great views, but cold at night. The facilities are not always open. Check beforehand at the address given above, or ask in Choctámal for whoever has the key. In María, eight small hospedajes all charge US$3 per night, comfortable, friendly, big meals.

Sites between Tingo and Leymebamba p457

D Hostal La Casona, Jr Amazonas 221, Leymebamba, T041-770261. With bath, hot water, breakfast available on request.
E Hostal La Petaca, Jr Amazonas 461, Leymebamba, opposite the church, T041-770288. With bath, hot water, new in 2004.
E Laguna de los Cóndores, Jr Amazonas,

Leymebamba, half a block from the plaza, T041-770271, www.chachapoyasperu.com.pe/hostallagunadeloscondores.htm. Cheaper without bath, warm water, a good choice.

There is a *hostal* in La Jalca, one block from the plaza, passing the church, where the phone is, very basic. You may be able to find a room through the Alcaldía. Don't expect too much privacy, however, as it is used until 2200, after which time there is no electricity. So bring a torch (and a pack of cards; there isn't much in the way of nightlife, other than drinking).

F Didogre, 16 de Julio 320, Leymebamba. Basic, cold water, shared bathroom, friendly.
F Escobedo, 16 de Julio 518, Leymebamba. Cold water, very basic, doors locked at 2130.

Northwest of Chachapoyas p460

D Hostal Kuélap, Garcilaso de la Vega 452, Lamud, on the plaza. Clean, basic, friendly, hot water, **E** with cold water and shared bathroom.
G Hostal Jucusbamba, in Luya. Basic accommodation.

East and north of Chachapoyas p463

E per person Casablanca, Pedro Ruíz, on the main road, close to the Chachapoyas turning. Private bathroom, comfortable, the best in town.
E Amazonense, Pedro Ruíz, near Policía Nacional on the main road. Cheaper with shared bathroom, basic, clean, friendly, helpful. Recommended.
F Altiplano, Rodríguez de Mendoza 321, Mendoza. With bathroom, cheaper without, cold water, very basic.
F Grandez, Pje Hilario López 110, Mendoza. With bathroom, cheaper without, cold water, very basic.
F Marginal, Pedro Ruíz. Shared bathroom, basic.

❶ Eating

Cajamarca to Chachapoyas p453

⊪⊩ La Reserve, José Gálvez 313, Celendín. Good quality and value. Recommended.
⊩ Bella Aurora, Grau 485, Celendín. Good.

There is some very tasty local cuisine in this area. Try the tropical fruits, the local sausage (chorizo) and fried green bananas (tocacho).

♥ **Jalisco**, Jr Unión, Plaza de Armas, Celendín. Good value breakfasts and other meals, but beware overcharging.

♥ **Santa Isabel**, Jr José Gálvez 512, Celendín. Clean, OK.

Chachapoyas and around *p454*
♥♥ ♥ **El Tejado**, upstairs at Grau 534, Plaza de Armas, T041-777654. Good quality, slightly upscale, nice view and atmosphere. Recommended.

♥ **Chacha**, Grau 541, Plaza de Armas. Especially popular with locals, clean, serves good, huge portions, friendly. Recommended.

♥ **Chifa Chuy Xien**, Jr Amazonas 848, opposite Hotel Puma Urcu. Authentic Chinesse cooking, daily specials and à la carte.

♥ **El Edén**, Grau y Ayacucho. Very good vegetarian, large helpings, open by 0830, closed Sat afternoon/evening.

♥ **La Estancia**, Amazonas 861. Grill and video pub.

♥ **La Tushpa**, Jr Ortiz Arrieta y El Triunfo 1½ blocks from the Plaza. The best in town, international food, wine list, but slow service.

♥ **Las Rocas**, Ayacucho 932 on Plaza. Popular, good local dishes, open Sun evening.

♥ **Kuélap**, Ayacucho 832. Good, friendly. Recommended.

♥ **Mari Pizza**, Jr Recreo y Jr Libertad. Serves a good pizza.

♥ **Matalache**, corner of Amazonas and Grau. Good and very popular, Serves huge portions. After a hard trek, try the massive bistek a lo pobre (tenderised steak) piled high with fried plantains, fries and egg. Recommended.

♥ **Panadería San José**, Ayacucho 816. Does good breakfasts, open Sun evening when many other places are shut.

♥ **Pizzería 505**, Jr 2 de Mayo y Ayacucho. Another good pizza place (pizza familiar US$7.60).

Cafés
Café de Guías, in Hotel Gran Vilaya, serves snacks, meals and organic coffee from the area, also has lots of local information, good. It is run by Tom Gierasimczuk, a Canadian guide, journalist and part-owner of Vilaya Tours.
Dulcería Santa Elena, Amazonas 800. Try

here for sweets.
Mass Burger, Ortiz Arrieta, Plaza de Armas. Excellent juices, cakes, fruit salads.
Patisserie, Jr 2 de Mayo 558. Good pastries. There are two small bar-*bodegas* in Levanto selling drinks, but little food: **Laurita** on the plaza, and **Alexsandra**, just before the plaza on the road in.

Kuélap and Tingo *p456, map p456*
Kuélap, at the junction of the main road with the road on the south bank of the Río Tingo. Clean and OK. Two other eating places.

Sites between Tingo and Leymebamba *p457*
♥ **Cely Pizza's**, Jr La Verdad, Leymebamba, 2 blocks from Plaza de Armas, opposite the health centre. Good value, 2-course set meals for US$2.50, pizzas take 20 mins unless you book in advance, will cook vegetarian meals at 24 hrs notice, great for breakfast, very clean, has fridge for cold beer, friendly. Recommended.
♥ **El Caribe** on the plaza, Leymebamba. Basic meals.
♥ **El Sabor Tropical**, 16 de Julio, Leymebamba. Good chicken and chips, friendly.

Northwest of Chachapoyas *p460*
♥ **María**, Lamud, a few doors down from Hostal Kuélap. Cheap, friendly and obliging, steak and chips is recommended, ask for pension which is 3 meals for US$1.80, excellent value, popular.

East and north of Chachapoyas *p463*
♥ **Shilico**, Pedro Ruíz, is recommended.

⊕ **Festivals and events**

Cajamarca to Chachapoyas *p453*
Celendín hosts its **Virgen del Carmen** festival on **16 July**. Bullfights with matadores from Spain and cock fighting are all part of the well-attended celebrations.

Chachapoyas and around *p454*
Among the town's festivals are Semana Turística de Amazonas, held in the first week of **Jun**. Virgen Asunta takes place in the second week of **Aug**.

● Shopping

Chachapoyas and around *p454*
Comercial Tito, Libertad 860. A good place for supplies. **Rojasa**, Amazonas 821. Another good place for supplies.

▲ Activities and tours

Chachapoyas and around *p454*
Tours in the surrounding area include: city tour, Levanto, Yalape (0800-1530, US$8.65), Kuélap (see p456), Karajía, La Jalca, Leymebamba (all full day, US$12-20, depending on distance and number of passengers, including guide and food), Revash (by vehicle to Santo Tomás, then 2-hr hike), Gran Vilaya or Laguna de los Cóndores (4-5 days each, depending on size of group), Mendoza (groups of 6 to 8). **Chachapoyas Tours SAC**, Grau 534, Plaza Armas, p 2 (Hotel El Tejado), T041-778078 www.kuelapperu.com, or in the USA T(1-800)743-0945/(407)851-2289. Reliable, English-speaking guide, good service. Recommended. **Vilaya Tours**, c/o Gran Hotel Vilaya, Jr Grau 624, T041-777506, www.vilayatours.com. Or internationally T(1-416) 535-1163. All-inclusive area treks throughout northern Peru catering to international clientele. Excellent guides: Robert Dover is a British, contact him through **Vilaya Tours** , or the **Café de Guías** (see Eating, above). Also Luis, who speaks good English. They have a regular newsletter and also work in conjunction with community projects. Recommended.

Kuélap and Tingo *p456, map p456*
Oscar Arce Cáceres based at 'El Chillo' near the Río Utcubamba, 4½ km outside Tingo. He owns a farm and knows the area very well. He is a very reliable guide but only speaks Spanish. He also has accommodation with bath, provides good meals and stores luggage. The trek into this area, like the walk up to Kuélap, starts from Tingo – the way is all mule track. The walk from El Chillo to Kuélap is shorter than from Tingo. The return to El Chillo can be made via the village of Nogalcucho (ask for directions). El Chillo is one of the places where the marvellous spatule tail hummingbird, unique to the Río Utcubamba, may be seen.

Leo Cobina, G Prada y Dos de Mayo, Leymebamba, recommended guide.
Lázaro Mostanza Lozano, San Martín y Dos de Mayo, or through Hotel Laguna de los Cóndores.

Northwest of Chachapoyas *p460*
Angel Mestanza Bobadilla, Garcilaso de la Vega 458, Lamud, near the hotel on the plaza, T041-780213/780223, amesbo@latinmail.com. He is a photographer and is recommended. His prices are reasonable. One trip is to local caves (be prepared to get muddy, take a torch); also to waterfalls.

East and north of Chachapoyas *p463*
Augustus Grandez Loja, Mendoza, is a local guide and hunter and can take travellers around the little known environs of Mendoza. He can provide horses for longer treks. Ask for him in town.

● Transport

Cajamarca to Chachapoyas *p453*
From Celendín To **Cajamarca**, 107 km, 4-5 hrs (or 3½-4 hrs in a combi) : with **Atahualpa**, 2 de Mayo 707, Plaza de Armas, T076-855256, at 0700 and 1300 daily, US$2.85; **Royal Palace's**, Jr Unión 333, Plaza de Armas, at 0645 and 1300 daily, poor minibuses, US$3. To **Chachapoyas** via Balsas and Leymebamba, 12-14 hrs (may be much longer in the rainy season, take warm clothing, food and water): **Virgen del Carmen**, Cáceres 117, on Sun and Thu at 1100, US$7.20. Other local transport leaves from the market area.

Chachapoyas and around *p454*
Bus
To **Chiclayo** with **Civa** (Salamanca y Ortiz Arrieta, T041-778048), at 1600 daily, 10 hrs (may be longer in the rainy season), US$9-10.60; to **Lima** 0800, 22 hrs, US$21-24; **Turismo Kuélap** (Ortiz Arrieta 412, T041-778128), at 1500 daily, except Mon and Fri at 1700, US$7; **Móvil Tours**, Jr Libertad 464, T041-778545, also have buses to Chiclayo and Lima, 0800, 20 hrs. To **Celendín**, from which there are connections on to Cajamarca: with **Virgen del Carmen** (Av Salamanca y 2 de Mayo, in El Aguila), on

Tue and Fri at 0600 , 14-15 hrs (may be much longer in the rainy season, an unforgettable journey, take warm clothing, food and water), US$7.20. To **Pedro Ruíz**, for connections to Chiclayo or Tarapoto, combis (US$2, 0600-2000) and cars/*colectivos* – more common (US$3, US$5.20 to Bagua Grande) leave from either side of the corner of Grau and the small street between Salamanca and Libertad, 3 hrs. To **Mendoza** (86 km), **Trans Zelada** buses leave from Ortiz Arrieta 310 (also to Chiclayo, Trujillo and Lima); combis (1000 and 1400, 4½ hrs, US$3.45) and cars (leave when full, 3 hrs, US$5.20) leave from **Comité Interprovincial Santo Tomás**, Grau, by the cul-de-sac between Salamanca and Libertad.

For **Kuélap**: if intending to walk up to the fortress, combis leave daily to **Tingo** between 0900 and 1600 Comité Interprovincial Santo Tomás, 2 hrs, US$1.45; alternatively, **Transportes Rollers**, Grau 300 y Salamanca, have combis to **Choctámal** at 0300 (`dirección Yumal') and 0400 ('dirección María') daily, 3½ hrs, US$2, and to **Lónguita** and **María** at 0400, US$3, ask the María combi if it will take you to Quisongo, the last village before the Kuélap carpark, US$3.65. To **Leymebamba**, bus leaves from Grau y Salamanca (vehicle parks on west side, if no one around knock on door opposite), at 1200 daily, 0300 Sun, 3½ hrs, US$3.65. Cars for Leymebamba leave from next to Rollers regulalrly, not so many on Sun, 2½-3½ hrs. To **Jalca Grande**, Comité Interprovincial Santo Tomás, departures about 1300 onwards (few if any on Sat), US$1.75 (return in morning). To **Lamud**, from Comité Interprovincial Santo Tomás between 0600 and 1600, 1½ hrs, US$1.80, or from **San Juan de Luya**, Ortiz Arrieta 364, also to Luya, throughout the day till 1800, US$1.45. Taxis may be hired from the Plaza for any local destination, eg US$35 per vehicle to Kuélap, US$14.50 to Levanto, return.

Car

If driving your own vehicle, Chacha is the last petrol for a long way (84 octane only), though small amounts can be bought in Leymebamba. Note also that there are two roads out of Chachapoyas, one for heavy vehicles, one for light vehicles.

Levanto is 2 hrs by truck or a 6-hr walk from Chachapoyas by a very rough road (barely passable in the rainy season). Trucks leave from the market in Chachapoyas most days at 0600, US$0.90, and there are trucks and combis (2 hrs, US$1) from outside **Bodega El Amigo** on Jr Hermosura at 1400. The nicest way to get there is by the Inca Road, 4-5 hrs. Take the heavy transit road out of Chachapoyas for 40 minutes, then take the stone path on the left. It is in pretty good shape, with one 15-m long stone stairway in excellent condition. Ask in Chachapoyas market if anyone returning to Levanto will guide you for a small fee. A taxi from Chachapoyas to Levanto and back, including driver waiting while you look around, is US$14.50.

Kuélap and Tingo *p456, map p456*

For transport from Chachapoyas to **Tingo**, see above. There are several combis (from 0500) daily to Chachapoyas. Tingo to Leymebamba takes 2 hrs, US$1.75. There are 4 options to get to **Kuélap**:

1) Take a tour from Chachapoyas with one of the agencies listed above. Most hotels will organize tours to Kuélap and other archaeological sites when there are sufficient people. Expect to pay around US$12-18 per person for a full-day trip to Kuélap, including guide and lunch. When booking a tour, request a guide who speaks English, if you so wish. Tours leave at 0800 and, after a spectacular, if not disconcerting, 3-hr drive, you arrive at Kuélap. The tours usually allow a sufficient 3-4 hrs for exploration before returning to Chachapoyas, with a possible stop along the way for a late lunch.

2) Hire your own vehicle with driver in Chachapoyas. Check at Salamanca on the corner with Grau. Also Sr Victor Torres, T041-777688.

3) A less expensive option and, in many ways, the recommended one since it allows you to see Kuélap wrapped in early-morning mist, is to take the local combi to Choctámal, María or Quisongo (see Chachapoyas Transport, above). Please be ready to go. This is a public bus and locals have better things to do than wait for a tardy gringo. You can spend the night in Choctámal village or at María (see Sleeping above). The next day, it is a relatively gentle 19 km, 4-5 hr, walk

along the vehicle road to Kuélap. It's best to visit the site at your leisure and spend the night here (see sleeping above), then walk down the steep path (3-4 hrs) to Tingo the next day.

4) Take a combi from Chachapoyas to Tingo, see above. Either spend the night in Tingo and start climbing at dawn the next day, or hike straight up and spend the night in María. The strenuous 3½-4 hr hike (with a 1,200 m vertical gain) to Kuélap begins on the right hand side of the bridge, past the police station. At first the track follows the west bank of the Utcubamba, before turning right and climbing steeply into the mountains. The route is intermittently marked with red arrows painted on the rocks. It can get very hot and there is no water whatsoever until the top, but the trail may be muddy in the rainy season. Take water, food, adequate clothing and footwear, etc. You reach the small village of Kuélap first, the walls of the fortress become visible only at the very end of the climb. To walk down takes about 3 hrs.

Sites between Tingo and Leymebamba p457
Jalca Grande: Comité Interprovincial Santo Tomás combis from Chachapoyas (see above) depart from about 1300 daily (except Sat); 3½ hrs, US$1.85. They return from La Jalca to Chachapoyas at 0500 daily.
Leymebamba: buses from Chachapoyas to **Celendín** (see p467) pass through Leymebamba about 4 hrs after departure and make a lunch stop here. There's no guarantee of a seat, but you might have a better chance if you purchase your ticket in advance in Chachapoyas, advising that you will get on in Leymebamba. Combis run direct to Celendín on Sun and Tue, 1100. Combis to **Chachapoyas** leave the plaza regularly. The road between Chachapoyas and Leymebamba takes 2½-3½ hrs by car, but both car and bus take longer in the rainy season.

Northwest of Chachapoyas p460
Buses and combis from Chachapoyas to **Luya** and **Lamud** are detailed above under Chachapoyas, Transport. The road is unpaved but in reasonable condition.

East and north of Chachapoyas p463
There is no direct transport from Chachapoyas to **Cheto** for Purunllacta. Take a combi at 0930 and 1500 from Jr Salamanca, fourth block down from the market, to Pipus, which stands at the turn-off to Cheto; 1½ hrs, US$1.35. You may have a long wait in Pipus for transport to Cheto; a camioneta leaves early in the morning, US$0.90. Or it's a 2-hr walk on a rough road.

Mendoza: to **Chachapoyas**, from Jr Toribio Rodríguez de Mendoza, **Civa** 3 a week, and **Kuélap** twice a week, 5 hrs, US$3.50; **Trans Zelada** buses run to Chachapoyas, Chiclayo, Trujillo and Lima; combis (4½ hrs, US$3.45) leave twice daily, and cars (3 hrs, US$5.20) leave at 0500 or when full. To **Limabamba**, three daily between 1300 and 1500, 2 hrs, US$1.20. To and from **Pedro Ruíz** there are many buses on the **Chiclayo**, **Tarapoto** (8-9 hrs) and **Chachapoyas** routes. All pass through town, mostly at night from 2000-2400. There is no way to reserve a seat and buses are usually full. **Móvil**, Av Marginal 123, T041-780238, for buses to Lima and Tarapoto. Combis (US$1.75) and cars (US$2.30) go to **Bagua Grande**, 1½ hrs. Cars (US$3) and combis (US$2) also go to Chachapoyas, 3 hrs, and to Nuevo Cajamarca, US$3.45 (combi), 4½ hrs. Combis to Moyobamba, US$5.75, 4 hrs. One side of the junction for Chachapoyas, by the bridge, is the **Trans Kuélap** office. Opposite the turning, in **Restaurante Gissela** (breakfasts and lunches) is the **Civa** office. Cars to Bagua Grande stop outside the restaurant. For cars and combis to Chachapoyas, from the junction walk down the main road towards Bagua and turn left a short way down a side street.

ⓘ Directory

Cajamarca to Chachapoyas p453
Banks There are no banks or casas de cambio in Celendín, but try the local shops. **Post** Jr Unión 415, Celendín. **Phone** José Gálvez 600 y Pardo, Plaza de Armas, Celendín.

Chachapoyas and around p454
Banks **BCP**, Ortiz Arrieta 576, Plaza de Armas. Gives cash on Visa card, changes cash

and TCs, ATM (Visa/Plus). **Hostal Revash** changes cash only, as do **Distribuidora Comercial Universal**, Ayacucho 940, Plaza de Armas, and the Librería at Amazonas 864. **Internet Cyber Club**, Triunfo 761, T041-778419. 2 terminals, closed Sun. **Lili@n's Explorer**, Jr 2 de Mayo 445, T041-778420, US$0.85 per hr. Also at Ortiz Arrieta 520, Plaza de Armas, formerly Amazon Tours (they can still organize tours). **Laundry Lavandería Speed Clean**,

Ayacucho 964 on Plaza, T041-777665. **Post** Grau on Plaza de Armas. **Telephone** Ayacucho 926, Plaza de Armas. Also at Grau 608.

East and north of Chachapoyas p463 **Banks Banco de la Nación** in Pedro Ruíz, changes cash only. **Post and telephone** On Rodríguez de Mendoza in Mendoza. Telephone on the main road in Pedro Ruíz between Casablanca and Policía Nacional.

To Ecuador and to the Amazon

The road from Pedro Ruíz, see page 463, goes west for 65 km to Bagua Grande, at first through a narrow gorge, the ridges covered with lush cloud-forest, then along the broad and fertile lower Utcubamba valley. It then crosses the Marañón at Corral Quemado. From the confluence of the Marañón with the Río Chamaya, the road follows the latter, past bare cliffs covered by dry scrub, towering over the deep river canyons. ▸▸ *For Sleeping, Eating and other listings, see pages 474-478.*

To Ecuador

With the opening of a bridge at Balsas on the Peru-Ecuador border, this route is becoming a worthwhile, if tiring route between the two countries for those who do not want to leave the highlands.

The Baguas and Chamaya

This is the first town of note heading west from Pedro Ruíz is **Bagua Grande**. It's a hot and dusty place, sprawled along its main street, Avenida Chachapoyas, where all the hotels and restaurants are located. Bagua Grande is not very safe. If arriving late, ask to sleep on the bus until daybreak. Police may ask to see travellers' documents here. The town celebrates the **Fiesta de Santiago** over the last week in July and in September holds its tourist week festivities. Cash can be acquired at BCP.

Near Bagua Grande, along a side road is **Bagua Chica** (colour map 1, grid B2), also referred to as just Bagua, a garrison. Pay careful attention to the names when arranging transport, so you are not taken to the wrong Bagua. Between Bagua Grande and the turning for Bagua Chica is a toll post, US$0.75 for cars. By the 24 de Julio bridge over the Río Marañón is a forestry control post. From Bagua Grande the main road continues northwest, then forks: southwest to **Chamaya** (50 km from Bagua Grande, one basic hostel, **El Volante**), for Jaén and the coast, and northeast to Sameriza, the first port on the Marañón. From Chamaya it's 15 minutes to Jaén, the best place to break the journey from Chachapoyas or the jungle to Ecuador or Chiclayo and vice-versa.

Jaén and around → *Phone code: 076. Colour map 1, grid B3. Population: around 25,000 Altitude: 740 m.*

Although it was founded in 1536, Jaén retains little of its colonial character. Rather, it is the modern and prosperous centre of a rich agricultural region producing rice, coffee, and cocoa. From 1563 to 1789 it was governed by the Real Audiencia de Quito and it is close to territory that used to be disputed by the two countries, hence its former

designation 'Corazón de la Peruanidad'. The local festival of **Señor de Huamantanga**
on 14 September is widely attended. It is a friendly place, but Jaén is currently
developing the dubious reputation as the centre for Peruvian opium poppy production.

A colourful modern **cathedral** dominates the large plaza around which most
services of interest to the visitor are clustered. A **museum** at the Instituto 4 de Junio,
Hermógenes Mejía s/n, displays pre-Columbian artifacts from the Pakamuros culture.

There is no organized tourism around Jaén. To bathe in the **Marañón**, take a
combi from the corner of Cajamarca and Eloy Ureta to Bellavista (40 minutes,
US$0.50). From here it is a 45-minute walk beside rice paddies to the river, ask for
directions. Swimming is possible but mind the strong current. Many locals go there
on Sundays. A motorboat across the Marañón costs US$0.45 one way.

Jaén to the border→ *Colour map 1, grid B3.*
A road runs north from Jaén to **San Ignacio** (107 km), near the frontier with Ecuador. It
passes the valley of the Chinchipe, renowned for its lost Inca gold. San Ignacio has a
fiesta on 31 August. From San Ignacio *colectivo* taxis run to Namballe (one new,
concrete hotel, G pp) and on to the border at La Balsa. This new, official border post
has a vehicle bridge. To leave Peru, go first to the PNP police office, then knock loudly
on the door of the new immigration building to summon the officer. It may be possible
to change money in the immigration posts. Allow one hour of formalities. Once
through Ecuadorean immigration, you can take a chiva to Zumba, and then a bus to
Vilcabamba (six hours) and Loja, a further 1½ hours, eight a day, US$4. To get to
Vilcabamba in one day, you need to leave Jaén by 0700, a gruelling journey. It may be
necessary to stay the night in Zumba.

To the coast
Heading west from Chamaya (see above), the highway reaches the Abra de Porculla
(at 2,150 m, the lowest pass through the Peruvian Andes) in 60 km, before
descending to join the old Pan-American Highway at Olmos (see page 407). From here
you can go southwest to Chiclayo, or northwest to Piura. The road from Pedro Ruíz
west to Olmos is paved, but prone to landslides in the rainy season.

Northeast to Sameriza → *Colour map 1, grid B4.*
The road from Buagua Grande to **Sameriza** first passes through **Aramango** and
Chiriaco and continues to another fork, northeast to **Oracuza** and **Santa María de
Nieve**, and east to Sameriza and **Puerto Delfus**, both on the Río Marañón.

Santa María de Nieve is a welcoming place, typical of a small riverside town with
a mixed community. It has a zoo, good swimming in the river, fishing and trips to
indigenous villages and downriver to the Pongo de Manseriche.

Travelling beyond Bagua Chica, even though some birdwatching groups do go
here, is not recommended unless you have permission from the Aguaruna Indian
communities and take local guides who know each community that you will pass
through. The road is in very bad condition and it is not advisable to stop en route. The
Aguaruna have shown some hostility towards foreigners as a result of oil exploration
on their lands and the local political situation is very sensitive. There have also been
robberies and sexual assaults on desolate parts of road.

East to the Amazon

The eastern branch of the road at Pedro Ruíz runs all the way to Yurimaguas. The road
has been paved as far as Tarapoto. All sections are still prone to landslides in the wet
season. This is a very beautiful journey where the high Andes tumble into the Amazon
Basin before your eyes.

Nuevo Cajamarca → *Colour map 1, grid B4.*

After Florida, the road winds down then up through Buenos Aires to a cultivated zone around the villages of La Esperanza, El Progreso and Oso Perdido. A further descent through forested mountains leads to the new town of Nuevo Cajamarca (with a few thousand inhabitants), 152 km east of Pedro Ruíz. There is a large market for local produce. There is accommodation on the main road.

Rioja → *Colour map 1, grid B5.*

Just beyond Nuevo Cajamarca is Rioja. There are a number of caves (Diamante, Cascayunga) and river sources (Tioyacu, Negro) nearby and the chief local tourist attractions are complejos and recreos turísticos with accommodation, local foods and swimming pools. The best is the Yacumama Lodge, where the owner gives guests tours of his property and can arrange local excursions.

Moyobamba → *Phone code 042. Colour map 1, grid B5. Population: 14,000. Altitude: 915 m.*

Moyobamba, a pleasant town in an attractive valley, was founded in 1540 as the original capital of Maynas. It then became capital of Loreto before the establishment of the department of San Martín, of which it became capital in 1906. This area has to cope with lots of rain in the wet season and in some years the whole area is flooded. In the last week of June the town celebrates its annual tourist week festival, in the last week of July is the **Fiesta de Santiago** and in November (a different week each year) is the **Semana de la Orquídea**. The valley, including both Moyobamba and Rioja, is renowned for its orchids.

Puerto Tahuishco is the town's harbour on the Río Mayo, where locals sell their produce at weekends. From **Morro de Calzada**, there is a good view of the area. Take a truck to Calzada (30 minutes), then walk up for 20 minutes. There are Baños Termales at **San Mateo**, 5 km from Moyobamba, which are hot and worth a worth a visit on weekends when the entire town seems to be there, and sulphur baths at **Oromina**, 6 km from town.

The more adventurous can hike to the **Gera waterfalls**, 21 km from Moyobamba in the jungle. Take a micro to Jepelacio. From there, take a good path through a well-populated valley, crossing two bridges on the way, then head along the river

Moyobamba

To Puerto Tahuishco

Alonso de Alvarado

Instituto Nacional de Cultura & Museum

Serafín Filomeno

Court House

Plaza de Armas

School

Banco de la Nación

Manuel del Aguila

To Av Grau, Terminal Terrestre & main road to Rioja & Tarapoto

Callao

Transportes y Turismo Selva

N

0 metres 100
0 yards 100

Sleeping
Atlanta 1
Cobos 2
Country Club 3
Marcoantonio 4
Royal 5

Eating
Chifa Kikeku 1
Edén 2

La Olla de Barro 3
Panadería América 4
Panadería Las Orquídeas 5
Rocky's 6

through dense jungle. There are three more river crossings but no bridges, so access **473** may be tricky, even dangerous when the rivers are high.

The tourist office, Mincetur ⓘ *Jr San Martín 301, T042-562043, dritincism@ terra.com.pe*, is on the plaza. Information on excursions and hikes is available from the Instituto Nacional de Cultura ⓘ *Jr Benavides 352*, which also has a small departmental museum.

Tarapoto → *Phone code: 042. Colour map 1, grid C5.*

Rioja, Moyobamba and Tarapoto are growing centres of population, with much forest clearance beside the Carretera Marginal de la Selva. The 109 km from Moyobamba to Tarapoto has been greatly improved and is almost entirely paved. It is heavily used by trucks, with fuel and meals available. You can stop at Tabalosas to buy fresh fruit from women at the roadside. Tarapoto is a busy town, founded in 1782, with a good local market 1½ blocks from the Plaza Mayor on Avenida Raimondi. It is a very friendly place, eager to embrace tourism and agricultural development now that the threat of terrorism and drug-trafficking has receded from the area. It competes with Iquitos for the record number of motorcycle taxis per square metre of road. There are three parts to the town: Tarapoto itself, Morales to the west and La Banda de Shilcayo to the east.

Museo Regional de la Universidad Nacional de San Martín ⓘ *Maynas, half a block from the Plaza, behind the church, Mon-Fri 0800-1200, 1230-2000, US$0.35*, contains a little of everything, paleontology, geology, ethnography, stuffed animals, and so on, but it's rather faded and dusty. In the second week of July is the town's rowdy **tourist week festival**, but between May and September, it seems like every weekend celebrates something. It doesn't take much for the Tarapoteños to party. Some tourist information can be found at the Casa del Turista, Moyobamba on the Plaza Mayor, which is mostly a handicrafts shop, and at the Cámara de Comercio, Moyobamba y Manco Cápac.

Tarapoto

Sleeping
Alojamiento Santa
  Juanita **10**
Alojamiento Tarapoto **1**
Edinson **2**
El Mirador **3**

July **4**
La Posada **5**
Lily **6**
Los Angeles **7**
Nilas **8**
San Antonio **9**

Eating
Chifa Lug Ming **1**
Las Terrazas **2**
Pizza Selecta **3**
Real & El Camarón **4**

0 metres 100
0 yards 100

To Airport

There are petroglyphs at **Demor** and **Pólish** east of the city, 4 and 5 km respectively. **Laguna Azul** (or Laguna Sauce as it is also known) is a big lake 52 km south of Tarapoto, with cabañas for rent on the shore. They cost US$80 per night for four beds and a shower. They are very basic and no fresh water or food is available. You can go river rafting on the Río Mayo for US$10 per person.

Twenty-two kilometres from Tarapoto, on the road to Moyobamba, a road leads off to **Lamas** where there is a small but highly recommended **museum**① *US$0.60*, custodian will show you round in garbled Spanish, with exhibits on local Indian community, the Lamistas. Turn right out of the museum and walk a couple of blocks uphill, then down into the part of town where the Lamistas live. There's a market in the morning. From Lamas you can visit the waterfalls at **Chapawanqui** (taxi US$7, 15 minutes) and many others.

About 14 km from Tarapoto on the spectacular road to Yurimaguas are the 50-m falls of **Ahuashiyacu**① *can be visited by tour from Tarapoto (US$14.50 by mototaxi), entry US$0.30 (toilets US$0.15)*. A walkway leads up to a pool at the foot of one of lower parts of the falls. You can swim here, but wait until after the sun has warmed the water; before 0900 it's freezing. This is a popular place at lunchtimes and weekends. The entire falls can be seen from the recreo turístico El Paraíso Verde, with a restaurant serving typical food, drinks, toilets, swimming pool (US$0.60), also popular. About 300 m beyond Ahuashiyacu is El Mono y La Gata restaurant, beyond which is El Pozo, a manmade pool for swimming and washing. Carry on along the road to Yurimaguas for 22 km and you come to the **Baños Termales de San José y Cascada de Carpishoyacu**.

Tarapoto to Yurimaguas

The journey from Tarapoto to Tingo María (see page 457) is not advisable. In the rainy season the roads are impossible and it is a drugs-growing area. From Tarapoto it is 129 km to Yurimaguas on the Río Huallaga (see page 525). The spectacular road can be very bad in the wet season, taking six to eight hours for trucks (schedules above). Once the plains are reached, the road improves and there is more habitation. It is not advisable to take the road to Yurimaguas very early in the morning or in the evening as hold-ups may occur. **Shapaja** is the port for Tarapoto, 14 km from town, served by *colectivos*. At Shapaja cargo boats can be caught to Yurimaguas. There's plenty of birdlife and river traffic to be seen. From Yurimaguas on the Río Huallaga, launches go to Iquitos.

● Sleeping

Jaén and around *p470*

C **El Bosque**, Mesones Muro 632, Jaén, T/F076-731184. With fridge, pool, parking, gardens, best in town.

C **Hostal Bolívar**, Bolívar 1310, Plaza de Armas, Jaén, T/F076-734077, . Refurbished, clean, with fan, TV, no breakfast.

C **Prim's**, Diego Palomino 1353, Jaén, T076-731039, hotel prims@terra.com.pe. Good service, comfortable, hot water, friendly, full internet and computer service for guests and non-guests, US$1.50 per hr,

small pool. Recommended.

D **Hostal Cancún**, Diego Palomino 1413, Jaén, T076-733511. Clean and pleasant, with bath, hot water, fan, restaurant, pool. Recommended.

D **Hostal Diana Gris**, Urreta 1136, Jaén, T076-732127. Family run and friendly, with bath, TV, fan, laundry service, café.

E **Hostal César**, Mesones Muro 168, Jaén, T076-731277, F731491. Fan, phone, TV (cheaper without), parking, restaurant, nice.

E **Santa Elena**, San Martín 1528, Jaén,

T076-732713. With bath, basic.
F San Martín, San Martín 1642, Jaén. With bathroom, hot water, basic, negligent staff.

Jaén to the border *p471*
D La Posada, in San Ignacio. Clean, but no hot water, noisy, OK but overpriced.
F Hostal La Choza, Av 12 de Febrero, Zumba. With restaurant, shared bath, cold water. There are other *hostales* and two restaurants serve set meals.

Northeast to Sameriza *p471*
F The Torres family, in Santa María de Nieve ask to be taken to Inigo's house then contact the Torres who have rooms, serve meals, do laundry and offer guiding service. The house, with garden and hammocks on the balcony, has great views of the river. Contact luidelrio@hotmail.com.

Rioja *p472*
Hostal San Martín, Grau 540; **San Ramón**, Jr Faustino Maldonado 840; and **Carranza**, Jr Huallanga. All basic.

Moyobamba *p472, map p472*
A Puerto Mirador, Jr Sucre, 1 km from the centre, T/F042-562050 (in Lima T01-442 3090, F442 4180, Av R Rivera Navarrete 889, of 208, San Isidro). Includes breakfast, nice location, pool, good restaurant.
C Marcoantonio, Jr Pedro Canga 488, T/F042-562045. Smartest in town centre, with bath and hot water, TV, restaurant.
E Hostal Atlanta, Alonso de Alvarado 865, T042-562063. With bathroom, hot water, TV, fan, clean, good but noisy, no breakfast.
E Hostal Country Club, Manuel del Aguila 667, T042-562110. With bath, hot water, clean, comfortable, friendly, nice garden. Recommended.
E Hostal Royal, Alonso de Alvarado 784, T042-562662, F562564. With bath, hot water, TV (cheaper without), laundry, cafeteria.
G pp Hostal Cobos, Jr Pedro Canga 404, T042-562153. With bathroom, cold water, simple but good, friendly.

Tarapoto *p473, map p473*
A Nilas, Jr Moyobamba 173, T042-527331, nilas-tpto@terra.com.pe Modern, the best in the centre, with bath, hot water, a/c, TV, fridge, internet access, pool, jacuzzi, gym,

airport transfer, very well-appointed, also has conference facilities.
A Río Shilcayo, Pasaje Las Flores 224, 1 km east of town in La Banda de Shilcayo, T042-522225, (in Lima T01-447 9359). With bathroom, excellent meals, non-residents can use the swimming pool for a fee.
B Lily, Jiménez Pimentel 405-407, T042-523154, F522394. With bath, hot water, a/c, TV, price includes breakfast and tax, laundry, sauna, restaurant.
C La Posada Inn, San Martín 146, T042-522234, laposada@ terra.com. pe Another good central hotel, comfortable, with bath, hot water, fridge, TV, some rooms with a/c, nice atmosphere, breakfast and lunch, small library of books in Spanish on the region.
D El Mirador, Jr San Pablo de la Cruz 517, T042-522177. 5 blocks uphill from the plaza, with bath, cold water, fan, TV, very welcoming, clean, laundry facilities, breakfast (US$2) and hammocks on roof top terrace with good views, also offers tours. Recommended.
E Alojamiento Tarapoto, Jr Grau 236, T042-522150, alojatarapoto@mixmail.com With bath, cold water, TV, fan, clean, nice rooms, no breakfast.
E Edinson, Av Raimondi y Maynas, 10 m from Plaza Mayor, T042-523997, T/F524010. With bathroom, a/c, cheaper without, cold water, breakfast, clean and comfortable, also has karaoke bars and disco.
E July, Jr Alegría Arias de Morey 205, T042-522087. With bath, cold water, TV, fridge, no breakfast.
F Hostal San Antonio, Jr Jiménez Pimentel 126, T042-522226. With private bathroom and TV, fan, courtyard, no breakfast. Noisy but recommended.
F Los Angeles, Jr Moyobamba, near the Plaza, T042-525797. Good value, **G** without bath, laundry facilities, restaurant.
F Misti 1, Leoncio Prado 341, 3 blocks from the Plaza. Rooms with bath, cold shower, quiet, with small garden, snacks and fruit juices on offer for US$1, very helpful (Misti 2 on the Plaza is not as good and is noisy, but they'll tell you how to get to No 1).
G pp Alojamiento Santa Juanita, Av Salaverry 602, Morales (20 mins from centre). Good beds, fan, spotless, family run, owner speaks English, safe.

🍴 Eating

Jaén and around *p470*
There are many eating plces around the plaza.
🍴 **La Cueva**, Pardo Miguel 304. Recommended.

Jaén to the border *p471*
In San Ignacio, there are a couple of restaurants on the main street, eg El Olivar, US$1 for set meal, and one internet café.

Rioja *p472*
🍴 **Restaurante Los Olivos**, recommended.

Moyobamba *p472, map p472*
🍴🍴 **La Olla de Barro**, Pedro Canga y S Filomeno. Typical food, expensive compared with other places in town but still good value. It opens for breakfast.
🍴 **Chifa Kikeku**, Pedro Canga 451. Chinese-Peruvian food.
🍴 **Edén**, 3rd block of Callao. Vegetarian.
🍴 **Rocky's**, Pedro Canga 402. Typical food, good but cheaper than La Olla de Barro. Open for breakfast.

Tarapoto *p473, map p473*
Regional specialities, which can also be found in Moyobamba, include *cecina* (dried pork), *chorizo* (sausage – good and tasty), both usually served with *tocacho* (see under Iquitos, Eating), also *juanes*, *inchicapi* and *ensalada de chonta* as in Iquitos. Interesting juices are *cocona*, made with cloves and cinnamon, and *aguajina*, from the aguaje fruit (deep purple skin, orange inside, sold on street corners). Regional fruits include grapes and pineapples, and many more besides.
🍴🍴 **Real** and **El Camarón**, both in the same building on Moyobamba on the Plaza. These are the best restaurants in town and are more expensive than elsewhere.
🍴 **Las Terrazas**, Ramírez Hurtado, on the Plaza. Serves typical food and is recommended.
🍴 **Pizza Selecta**, J Vargas 185. For pizza, lasagne and chicken.

Around Tarapoto *p474*
🍴 **Rolly's**, San Martín 925, just off the plaza in Lamas. Serves good food.

🍸 Bars and clubs

Tarapoto *p473, map p473*
There are many bars and pubs around the centre. The adventurous can try any of Tarapoto's many local inebriators, made from sugarcane liquor and a host of fruit juices. For local discos, check out the neighbourhood of Morales, about 10 mins west of town on the highway. Popular local discos include **El Papillon** and **Las Pumas**. They sometimes charge a US$1.50 cover at weekends.

▲ Activities and tours

Moyobamba *p472, map p472*
Ecotours Moyobamba, Callao 878, T042-563363, www.altomayo.com. Tours throughout the region.

Tarapoto *p473, map p473*
Quiquiriqui Tours, Jiménez Pimentel 314, T042-527863, F524016. Sells flight tickets, **Turismo Tarapoto** bus tickets (see Transport, below) and tours.

🚌 Transport

The Baguas and Chamaya *p470*
Many buses pass through **Bagua Grande** en route from Chiclayo to Tarapoto and Chachapoyas and vice-versa, mostly at night. Cars (US$2) and combis (US$1) to **Jaén** leave from the west end of Av Chachapoyas, 1 hour. From the east end of Av Chachapoyas, cars (US$2.30) and combis (US$1.75) leave to **Pedro Ruíz**, 1½ hrs. Taking a mototaxi (US$0.30) between the two stops is a good alternative to walking in the heat.
   Marañón or Cenepa buses Chiclayo-Bagua Chica, 6 hrs, US$4.50, at 1030, 2100 or 2130.
   From Bagua Chica, take a car or combi to **Imaza** (also called Imacita), 6 hrs, US$8.60. From Imaza boats go to **Santa María de Nieve**, 4 hrs, US$13 (**Civan** or **Riomar** companies, none after 1500).

Jaén and around *p470*
To **Chiclayo** with Civa, Mariscal Ureta 1300 y V Pinillos (terminal at Bolívar 936), at 1030 and 2130 daily, 8 hrs, US$3.75. To **Lima**

(US$17) on Mon, Wed and Fri, 1500, US$13-14.50. Many others to Chiclayo including Ejetur, Mesones Muro 410, at 2030, US$4.35, continuing to Trujillo, US$7.20; several from a terminal in the middle of the 4th block of Mesones Muro (eg Transcade, El Cumbe – also to Cajamarca), and Línea, Mesones Muro 475, T076-733746, 1300 and 2300, US$4.35. To Moyobamba via Pedro Ruiz (the crossroads for Chachapoyas, 4 hrs), Nuevo Cajamarca and Rioja: Turismo Jaén, R Castilla 421, T076-731615, US$7.20. Continuing to Tarapoto: Ejetur, address above, US$3.75 to Pedro Ruíz, US$5.75 to Nuevo Cajamarca, US$7.20 to Rioja and Moyobamba, US$10 to Tarapoto and US$14.40 to Yurimaguas; Jaén Express and Guadalupe, Mesones Muro first block, and Transportes Mejía and Jaén Express, from terminal on fourth block of Mesones Muro, all have the same prices to Moyobamba and Tarapoto. (Jaén Express also has an office at Túpac Amaru 109.) Cars (US$2) run in the early morning and when full from San Agustín, Av Mesones Muro y Los Laureles to Bagua Grande (1 hr), where connections can be made for Pedro Ruíz. Combis do the same route (US$1.30) from Servicentro San Martín de Porras, Mesones Muro 4th block.

Jaén to the border p471
Combis run from the paradero at the northern exit of Jaén for the 2½-hr journey on a good, unmade road to San Ignacio (US$3, from 0330 till the afternoon). San Ignacio to Namballe, US$2.30 by colectivo, then a further 2 hrs, US$3 to the border at La Balsa. Chiva from La Balsa to Zumba, 3 a day, including 1200, 2½ hrs on a bad road, US$1.50.

Nuevo Cajamarca p472
There are frequent colectivos to Rioja (US$1.15, 45 mins) and to Pedro Ruíz (they usually continue to Bagua Grande).

Rioja p472
There are regular combis to Moyobamba (US$0.85, 45 mins).

Moyobamba p472, map p472
Be careful travelling at night in this region; buses tend to travel in convoy.
Bus Buses leave from the Terminal

Terrestre, about a dozen blocks from the centre on Av Grau, which leads out of town to the main highway (mototaxi to the centre US$0.30). Several companies to Tarapoto (eg Turismo Tarapoto, T563307, Paredes Estrella, Sol Peruano, Guadalupe), US$2.85, 3¼ hrs. Buses heading west, en route from Tarapoto to Pedro Ruíz, Chiclayo and Lima, arrive at about 1400 or later, except Mejía, which has a departure to Pedro Ruíz and Chiclayo at 1100. Combis leave from Transportes y Turismo Selva terminal, Jr Callao between Benavides and Varacadillo. To Tarapoto US$2.85, Yurimaguas US$6.35, Rioja US$0.85, Pedro Ruiz US$5.75; departures between 0530 and 1900, leave when full. Cars to Tarapoto (3 hrs, US$6) and Rioja (30 mins, US$1.30) leave when full from Jr Pedro Canga.

Tarapoto p473, map p473
Air
Flights to Lima with Lan, daily, and Tans, Plaza Mayor 491 (T042-525339), daily except Tue and Fri, Lan and Tans also fly to Iquitos. Book flights in advance, particularly in the rainy season. A taxi to the airport is US$1.75, mototaxi US$1.45. There's no bus service, but it's no problem to walk.

Bus
Buses to destinations to the west all leave from Av Salaverry, Morales, about 10 mins by mototaxi from the Plaza, except Turismo Ejecutivo/Ejetur, whose office is on Cabo A Leveau in the centre. The following companies have buses to Moyobamba, 116 km, US$2.85, 3¼ hrs, Pedro Ruíz, US$7.20 (US$8.65 Turismo Tarapoto and Paredes Estrella), 9 hrs, Chiclayo, 690 km, 22 hrs, US$11.50, Trujillo, 25 hrs, and Lima, US$20: Móvil, Av Salaverry 858; Paredes Estrella (T042-523681) at 0800 and 1400, Turismo Tarapoto (T042-523259), at 1230 and 1300, Turismo Ejecutivo, Trans Guadalupe at 0900 and 1300, Sol Peruano at 1100, Expreso Huamanga at 1230 and 1400 and Guadalupe Express at 0900 and 1300. Combis to Moyobamba leave from Turismo La Selva, Av Salaverry, closer to the centre than the bus offices. Cars also run to Moyobamba, US$5.75. To Yurimaguas, US$3.45, 5-6 hrs, several bus companies (same price by combi); pick-ups, daily,

Northern Highlands To Ecuador & to the Amazon Listings

charge US$5.75 in the front, US$2.85 in the back; cars charge US$7.20 (see next page for road conditions). Buses to Yurimaguas leave from the eastern side of Tarapoto.

Truck/pick-up leaves for Yurimaguas (usually 0800-0900, and in the afternoon) from Jorge Chávez 175, down Av Raimondi 2 blocks, then left along Av Pedro de Urzua.

From Tarapoto to **Laguna Azul**, a *colectivo* takes 2½ hrs and costs US$3.45.

To **Lamas**, *colectivo* from Tarapoto, 30 mins, US$0.85, from Paradero Lamas on road to Moyobamba (take mototaxi from centre, US$0.45). There are infrequent combis.

O Directory

Jaén and around *p470*
Banks **BCP**, Bolívar y V Pinillos. Cash only; ATM (Visa/Plus). **Banco Continental**, Ramón Castilla y San Martín. Cash, US$5 commission for TCs. **Cambios Coronel**, V Pinillos 360 (Coronel 2 across the street at 339). Cash only, good rates. **Ceymar** and **John Lennon**, V Pinillos on plaza, next to public phones. Cash only. **Internet Foto center Erick**, Pardo Miguel 425. US$1.15 per hr. **Post** Pardo Miguel y Bolívar. **Telephone** V Pinillos, on the plaza.

Moyobamba *p472, map p472*
Banks **BCP**, Alonso de Alvarado 903 y San Martín. ATM (Visa/Plus). **BBV Continental**, San Martín 494.

Tarapoto *p473, map p473*
Banks **BCP**, Maynas 134. Changes TCs, ATM for Plus/Visa. **BBV Continental**, Ramírez Hurtado, Plaza Mayor, with Visa/Plus ATM. **Interbank**, Grau 119, near the Plaza. No commission on changing TCs for soles, handles Mastercard. Street changers near the corner of Maynas and Jiménez Pimentel, on the Plaza Mayor. **Internet** 4 places close to each other: at San Martín y Arias de Morey, Arias de Morey 109 (**C@binas Internet**) and 136 (**Club Internet**) and San Martín 129 (also **C@binas Internet**).

Central Highlands

Footprint features

Introduction

Stretching from the southern end of the Cordillera Blanca right up to Cusco department, this area of stunning mountain scenery and timeless Andean towns and villages is a must for those who appreciate traditional, good-quality textiles and ceramics. The main highlights include the cities of Huancayo, Ayacucho and the surrounding villages – the main production centres of handicrafts. The people of Ayacucho, shrugging off the area's reputation as former home of the Maoist terrorist movement, Shining Path (see page 577), are relieved to see tourists return to their towns and cities and Ayacucho also hosts one of the largest and most impressive Holy Week celebrations in Latin America. The Central Railway from Lima to Huancayo has started up passenger services, so one of the outstanding train rides in South America can be experienced once more.

More than just fabulous landscapes, this area also hides important pre-Inca sites, such as Kotosh, near Huánuco, and Huari, outside Ayacucho, two early examples of Andean urban civilizations. Stretches of the Royal Inca Road run from the temple fortress of Huánuco Viejo and up the Yanahuanca Valley, reminders of this great imperial causeway. The Spaniards, too, left their mark, with fine churches and mansions in Ayacucho. ˙

★ Don't miss...

1 Mantaro Valley Go shopping in this souvenir-hunter's paradise. Each village specializes in its very own variety of artesania, page 486.

2 Train from Lima to Huancayo Time your arrival (or departure) with the occasional running of one of the the engineering marvels of South America, page 484.

3 Ayacucho Don't miss the fine array of colonial churches, spectacular processions with carpets of flowers decorating the streets and the artists' quarter of Santa Ana, page 493.

4 Quinua Above this charming town with its handicraft shops is a telling, 44-m high obelisk commemorating South America's struggle for independence, page 496.

5 Puerto Bermúdez Here the Selva Central begins, approachable by car from Lima, but far enough away for real jungle experience, page 508.

6 Capaq Ñan (Royal Inca Road) Hike the route which will lead you back to times before the Spaniards arrived. One fine section goes to the temple-fortress of Huánuco Viejo near La Unión, page 517.

Central Highlands

Lima to Jauja

The Central Highway between Lima and Huancayo more or less parallels the course of the railway. The roads from Lima to Huancayo and Pisco to Ayacucho are paved, but all the other roads in this region are in poor condition, especially when wet. At La Oroya, see page 482, the central highway divides. Its southern branch follows the valley of the Río Mantaro, to Huancayo, and on to Huancavelica or Ayacucho. ➤ *For Sleeping, Eating and other listings, see pages 483-484.*

Chosica, San Pedro de Casta and Marcahuasi → *Colour map 3, grid C4.*

Chosica, 40 km from Lima, is the real starting place for the mountains. Around 40 km beyond Chosica, up the picturesque Santa Eulalia valley, is the village of San Pedro de Casta, which has some interesting sights nearby. **Marcahuasi** ① *US$3 (US$0.90 for students)*, is a table mountain (*meseta*) about 3 sq km, at 4,200 m. There are three lakes, a 40-m high 'monumento a la humanidad', and other mysterious lines, gigantic figures, sculptures, astrological signs and megaliths which display non-American symbolism. The trail starts behind the village of San Pedro, and bends to the left. About halfway you have to choose between the longer trail (the easier of the two) and the shorter tail, which is better for views of the valley below. It's a minimum of three hours to the *meseta*. Guides cost about US$3 a day, and are advisable in misty weather. Mules for carrying bags cost US$4 to hire, a horse costs US$4.45 (standard prices from the tourist office). The tourist information at the municipality on the plaza, T01-571 2087 will advise on routes and lodging; buy a map of the plateau here for US$1.50, otherwise you will not find the monuments. If you speak good Spanish, ask in town for Manuel Olivares, who knows a lot about the plateau. He also sells maps for US$0.20. Tours can be arranged with travel agencies in Lima.

Chosica to La Oroya → *Colour map 3, grid C4.*

Beyond Chosica each successive valley looks greener and lusher, with a greater variety of trees and flowers. The road climbs to the Ticlio Pass, before the descent to **Morococha** (Km 169, altitude 4,600 m) and **La Oroya**. A large metal flag of Peru can be seen at the top of Mount Meiggs, through which runs Galera Tunnel, 1,175 m long, in which the main line of the Central Railway reaches its greatest altitude, 4,782 m (see box). **Ticlio**, at Km 132, the highest passenger station in the world, is at 4,758 m. It lies at the mouth of the tunnel, on one side of a crater. La Oroya (3,755 m), the main smelting centre for the region's mining industry, can seem a dreary place with its slag heaps, but is nevertheless full of vitality. It stands at the fork of the Yauli and Mantaro rivers, 196 km from Lima by a road. For places to the east and north of La Oroya, see pages 505 and 513 respectively.

Jauja and around → *Colour map 3, grid C5. Altitude: 3,330 m.*

Some 80 km southeast of La Oroya is Jauja, a friendly, unspoilt town, in the middle of a good area for walking. There is a good **archaeological museum** ① *free, but donations welcome*, with artefacts from the Huari culture. On a hill above Jauja is a fine line of Inca storehouses, and on hills nearby, the ruins of hundreds of circular stone buildings from the Huanca culture. There are also ruins near the **Laguna de Paca** ① *3½ km away, colectivos leave regularly from Av Pizarro, 10 mins, US$0.30.* The western side of the lake is lined with restaurants which are good for lunches. Try the delicious *ceviche de trucha* and, at weekends, pachamanca. It is possible to walk around the lake in about three hours. Many of the restaurants have launches which offer half-hour boat trips at weekends, US$0.75 per person.

From Concepción, 18 km to the south of Jauja, a branch road leads for 6 km to the **Convent of Santa Rosa de Ocopa** ⓘ *0900-1200 and 1500-1800, and closed Tue, tours start on the hour and last 45 mins, US$1.10, colectivos run from the market in Concepción, 15 mins, US$0.25*. This Franciscan monastery, set in beautiful surroundings, was established in 1725 for training missionaries for the jungle. It contains a fine library with over 20,000 volumes and a biological museum with animals and insects from the jungle. The convent also contains a large collection of paintings, including copies by the priests of many works by masters such as Murillo and Ribera. On the walls are paintings by the contemporary painter, Josue Sánchez, of Huancayo.

● Sleeping

Chosica, San Pedro de Casta and Marcahuasi *p482*
E Marcahuasi, just off the plaza. The best hotel in San Pedro (**F** per person without bath), clean, has a restaurant.

Chosica to La Oroya *p482*
F Hostal Inti, Arequipa 117, La Oroya, T064-391098. Shared bathroom, warm water, clean but basic.
F Hostal Chavín, Tarma 281, La Oroya. Shared bathroom, cheap restaurant.

Jauja and around *p482*
E per person **Hostal Manco Cápac**, Jr Manco Cápac 575, T064-361620, niegemannilse@hotmail.com. Central, with good rooms and a beautiful patio, pleasant, relaxing, good breakfast and coffee, German run. Best to make a reservation at weekends and holiday periods. Recommended.
E Hostal María Nieves, Jr Gálvez 491, 1 block from the Plaza de Armas, T064-362543. Clean, safe, helpful, friendly, price includes large breakfast, hot water all day. Good choice.
F Hostal Los Algarrobos, Huancayo 264, T064-362633. Shared bathroom, hot water in the morning, very clean, good value.

● Eating

Chosica to La Oroya *p482*
♥♥ **El Tambo**, 2 km outside La Oroya on the road to Lima. Good trout and frogs. The Chanchamayo bus stops here en route Lima-Tarma.
♥ **La Caracocha**, Lima 168, La Oroya. Cheap, good menu.

Jauja and around *p482*
♥ **Centro Naturista**, Huarancayo 138. Serves fruit salad, yoghurt, granola, etc.

♥ **El Paraíso**, Ayacucho 915. Just off the plaza, this is a good place for chicken and Andean dishes.
♥ **Ganso de Oro**, R Palma 249. Good restaurant in hotel of same name, US$2-4 per meal, the best in town.
♥ **La Rotunda**, Tarapacá 415. Tables in a pleasant courtyard or dining rooms, good lunch menu and pizzas in the evening.
♥ **Marychris**, Jr Bolívar 1166, T362386. For lunch only, menú US$1.55, excellent food.

● Transport

Chosica, San Pedro de Casta and Marcahuasi *p482*
Colectivo minibuses for **Chosica** leave from Av Grau, Lima, when full, between 0600 and 2100, and cost US$0.60. *Colectivo* taxis leave from the **Sheraton Hotel**, behind the Centro Cívico on Av Garcilaso de la Vega, charging US$1.50 for a seat or US$6 for the whole car. A regular taxi will charge US$6-10 Lima-Chosica. Most buses on the Lima-**La Oroya** route are full; *colectivo* taxi to **La Oroya** US$3.60, 3 hrs, very scenic, passing the highest railway in the world (see above). For **San Pedro de Casta**, buses leave **Chosica** from Parque Echenique, opposite the market, at 0900 and 1500, 4 hrs, US$2; return 0700 and 1400. The road is in a reasonable condition until the Callahuanca hydroelectric station.

Chosica to La Oroya *p482*
For buses to the Central Highlands see p134. To **Lima** from La Oroya takes 4½ hrs and costs US$5.20. To **Jauja** (80 km), takes 1½ hrs and costs US$1. To **Tarma**, 1½ hrs, US$1.35. To **Cerro de Pasco**, 131 km, 3 hrs, US$2.20. To **Huánuco**, 236 km, 6 hrs, US$4.35. *Colectivos* also run on all routes (see under Lima). They

are quicker but only leave when full and prices are double that of the bus fares.

Jauja and around *p482*

Bus To **Lima** Cruz del Sur, Pizarro 220, direct, 5 hrs, US$8. To **Huancayo**, 44 km, 1 hr, US$1.25, continuous combis and *colectivos* leave from Av Pizarro y Junín.

To **Cerro de Pasco**, Oriental leave from 28 de Julio 156, and **Turismo Central** from 28 de Julio 150, 5 hrs, US$3.55. **Oriental** and Turismo Central also go to **Huánuco**, 7 hrs, US$5.35. To **Tarma**, Trans Muruhuay, hourly, 0600-1900, 2 hrs, US$2. Also ET San Juan, both from Jr Tarma; the latter continues to

Chanchamayo, 4 hrs, US$4.50. To **Satipo**, with **Turismo Central**, 12 hrs, US$6.25.

❶ Directory

Jauja and around *p482*
Banks No TCs are accepted at the **BCP**, Junín 790. **Banco de la Nación**, Bolívar 821. **Dollar Exchange Huarancayo**, on Jr Huarancayo, gives a much better rate than BCP. **Internet** All along Junín blocks 9 to 12. **Post** Jr Bolívar. **Telephone** Telefónica at Bolognesi 546. Also at Ricardo Palma, opposite the Hotel Ganso de Oro, gives better service and prices.

Huancayo and Huancavelica

The large, sprawling departmental capital of Huancayo is a functional kind of place. As the main commercial centre for inland Peru it has had to eschew the tourist trappings in favour of the no-nonsense comings and goings of everyday trade. Huancavelica, capital of the next department south, is a friendly and attractive town, surrounded by huge, rocky mountains. It's not really geared up for tourism, either, but more because of remoteness than the pressures of commerce. ➤➤ *For Sleeping, Eating and other listings, see pages 487-492.*

Ins and outs
Neither city is on an air route, but both are served, if a bit haphazardly, by train. Bus services to Huancayo are good, but Huancavelica is not so well served. Mechanical problems aside, the Huancayo-Huancavelica train service should run daily. As elsewhere in the Andes, buses and *colectivos* serve the entire region. **Ministry of Tourism** ① *C Real 481, to the right of the Casa de Artesano, T064-214192, junin@ mitinci.gob.pe, Mon-Fri 0900-1400, 1600-2000,* has information about the area and is helpful. Beware of theft if arriving early in the morning.

Huancayo and around → *Colour map 3, grid C5. Altitude: 3,271 m.*
Huancayo's attractions are outwith its boundaries. It lies in the beautiful Mantaro Valley, surrounded by villages that produce their own original crafts and celebrate festivals all year round, see page 489. The city has its own important festivals, however, when people flock from far and wide with an incredible range of food, crafts and music. At this height, nights are chilly and altitude can be a problem for those arriving straight from the coast.

The Plaza de Armas is called **Plaza Constitución**. The main sights, though, as well as the Sunday market, are quite a way from the centre. The **Sunday market** gets going after 0900 (giving a little taste of Huancayo at festival time) every week even though it has been described as expensive and offering little choice. It is better to go to the villages for local handicrafts. The stalls on Jirón Huancavelica, 3 km long, still sell

● *The Lima-Huancayo railway, was the project of the great American railway engineer,*
● *Henry Meiggs (whom died before it was finished) and built by the Pole Ernesto Malinowski.*
Along the whole of its length (335 km to Huancayo) it traverses 66 tunnels, 59 bridges, and
22 zig-zags where the steep mountainside permits no other way of negotiating it.

typical clothes, fruit, vegetables, hardware, handicrafts and, especially, traditional
medicines and goods for witchcraft. There is also an impressive daily market behind
the railway station.

Parque de Identidad Wanka ① *Jr San Jorge in the Barrio San Carlos, northeast of
the city (35 mins' walk from Plaza), free but contributions are appreciated*, is a
fascinating mixture of surrealistic construction, interwoven with indigenous plants
and trees and the cultural history of the Mantaro Valley. It can get crowded at

Huancayo

Museo, Colegio Salesiano 🏛

To Jauja, La Oroya, Tarma & Lima

Sleeping 🛏
Casa Alojamiento de Aldo
  y Soledad Bonilla 1 *C2*
Casa Hospedaje 2 *B2*
Central 3 *B2*
Confort 4 *A2*
El Dorado 5 *C2*
El Marqués 6 *B2*
Hostal Baldeón 7 *B3*
Hostal Huaracaya 8 *A3*
Hostal Plaza 9 *A2*

Hostal Santo
  Domingo 10 *B1*
Kiya 11 *B2*
Percy's 12 *D2*
Peru Andino Lodging
  & Excursions 18 *A3*
Presidente 13 *C2*
Pussy Cat 14 *B3*
Roger 15 *B2*
Santa Felicita 16 *B2*
Turismo 17 *B2*

Eating 🍴
Berisso 2 *B2*
Café El Parque 1 *B2*
Chez Viena 3 *B3*
Chifa El Centro 4 *B2*
El Paraíso 7 *C2*
El Pino 8 *B2*
La Cabaña 5 *B3*
Pizzería Antojitos 11 *B2*

0 metres 200
0 yards 200

weekends. Opposite are the Misti Wasi and Pacaywasi restaurants serving traditional meals; there are about six others.

Mantaro Valley → *Colour map 3, grid C5.*

The main attraction in the area is the Mantaro Valley, which is rich in culture, music, local food, dances and handicrafts and plays host to numerous festivals. To the west of the Río Mantaro, 19 km from Huancayo, is **Viques**, which is known for the production of belts and blankets. Sra María Magdalena Huzco, Calle San Martín, two blocks from the Plaza Principal, offers **weaving lessons**, US$34 for 15 hours, plus the cost of materials. Other weavers may also give lessons. It's a worthwhile experience, not just for learning how to weave, but also for an insight into the life of this part of Peru. **Huayucachi**, 7 km away, organizes festivals with dancing and impressive costumes in January and February and also makes embroidery.

The ruins of **Warivilca** ① *15 km from Huancayo, 1000-1200, 1500-1700, US$0.15, to get here take one of the micros for Chilca, which leave from Calle Real*, feature the remains of a pre-Inca temple of the Huanca culture. There is a museum in the plaza (open in the morning only), with deformed skulls, and modelled and painted pottery of successive Huanca and Inca occupations of the shrine. The ruins and museum are under the supervision of a local archaeologist and are slowly being restored.

The villages of **Cochas Chico** and **Cochas Grande**, 11 km away on the east side of the river, are both well worth visiting. Micros leave from Plaza Hunamarco or by the market near the railway line, US$0.25. This is where the famous mate burilado, or gourd carving, is done (see page 592). You can buy them cheaply direct from the manufacturers, but ask around. You can also enjoy beautiful views of the Valle de Mantaro and Huancayo.

In the village of **Hualhuas**, 12 km from Huancayo, you can find fine alpaca weavings, which you can watch being made. The weavers take special orders; small items can be finished in a day. Negotiate a price. One particularly recommended place to buy them is Tahuantisuyo, run by Familia Faustino Maldonado y Agripina, on a side road on the way to the San Jerónimo junction. The town of **San Jerónimo** is renowned for the making of silver filigree jewellery, on sale at the Wednesday market. A major fiesta is held in the town on the third Saturday in August, when one of the two plazas is converted into a temporary bullring.

Huancavelica and around → *Colour map 3, grid C5. Altitude: 3,660 m.*

Founded in the 16th century by the Spanish to exploit rich deposits of mercury and silver, Huancavelica has very few mines open now. It is predominantly an indigenous

Huancavelica

Sleeping
Camacho 1
Presidente 3

Santo Domingo 4
Savoy 5
Virrey 6

Eating
Cami 1
Mochica Sachún 2

town, and people still wear traditional costume. The **Ministerio de Industria y Comercio, Turismo y Artesanías** ① *Arica 202, T067-672509, earhvca@terra.com.pe,* is very helpful. Don't wander around the surrounding hills alone.

The **cathedral** on the Plaza de Armas has an altar considered to be one of the finest examples of colonial art in Peru. Bisecting the town is the Río Huancavelica. South of the river is the main commercial centre. North of the river, on the hillside, are the **thermal baths** ① *0600-1500, US$0.15 for private rooms (water is not very hot), US$0.10 for the hot public pool.* There are also hot showers, but take a lock for the doors. The **handicraft sellers** congregate in front of the

❖ *If you wish to visit the mines, remember that the miners consider it a bad omen if a woman enters.*

Municipalidad on M Muñoz and the Biblioteco on the Plaza de Armas (V Toledo). The **food market** at Muñoz y Barranca is being demolished so food is sold along Barranca, blocks 2-3 (not much variety).

Between Huancayo and Huancavelica, Izcuchaca is the site of a bridge over the Río Mantaro. On the edge of town is a fascinating pottery workshop whose machinery is driven by a water turbine. There is also a small shop. The town celebrates the **Fiesta de la Virgen de Cocharcas** on 5-10 October. It's a nice hike to the chapel on a hill overlooking the valley (one to 1½ hours each way).

Huancavelica to Ayacucho → *Colour map 3, grid C5/6.*

The direct route from Huancavelica to Ayacucho (247 km) goes via **Santa Inés** (4,650m), 78 km. Out of Huancavelica the road climbs steeply with switchbacks between herds of llamas and alpacas grazing on rocky perches. Around Pucapampa (Km 43) is one of the highest habitable altiplanos (4,500m), where the rare and highly prized ash-grey alpaca can be seen. Snow-covered mountains are passed as the road climbs to 4,853m at the Abra Chonta pass, 23 km before Santa Inés. By taking the turnoff to Huachocolpa at Abra Chonta and continuing for 3 km you'll reach the highest drivable pass in the world, at 5,059m. Some 52 km beyond Santa Inés at the Abra de Apacheta (4,750m), 98 km from Ayacucho, the rocks are all the colours of the rainbow, and running through this fabulous scenery is a violet river. These incredible colours are all caused by oxides. The journey is a cold one but spectacular (and the road is good) as it is the highest continuous road in the world, rarely dropping below 4,000m for 150 km.

● Sleeping

Huancayo and around *p484, map p485*
The places listed below are situated in Huancayo. Prices may rise in Holy Week.

B Turismo, Ancash 729, T064-231072, hotelhyo@correo.dnet.com.pe. In an old building. Rooms with bathroom, some rooms are small, quiet. Restaurant serves good meals for US$3.50.

B Presidente, C Real 1138, T064-231736, same email address as Turismo. With bathroom, clean, friendly, helpful, safe, breakfast only. Recommended.

C El Marqués, Puno 294, T064-219026, F219202. Rooms with bathroom and TV, free internet access, good value.

C Kiya, Giráldez 107, Plaza Constitución, T064-214955, F214957. With bath, hot water, restaurant does not serve breakfast, avoid noisy rooms on Av Real.

C Santa Felicita, Giráldez 145, Plaza Constitución, T064-235285. With bathroom, hot water, good.

D per person **Casa Alojamiento de Aldo y Soledad Bonilla**, Huánuco 332, no sign, half a block from Mcal Cáceres bus station, T064-232103. Prices are for full board, beautiful colonial house, some hot water, owners speak English, laundry, secure, relaxing, nice courtyard, they can arrange local tours, book ahead to guarantee a reservation.

D El Dorado, Piura 452, T064-223947. With bathroom, hot water, friendly, clean, some rooms with TV are in the **C** category.

D Hostal Plaza, Ancash 171, T064-214507. Clean, hot water, ask for a room at the front.

D Roger, Ancash 460, T064-233488. With bathroom, hot water, basic, clean.

488

D **Hospedaje César Ada**, Pasaje Santa
Teresa 294, El Tambo-3 Esquinas, Vilcacoto, 5
km from centre, T064-253646 for pick-up,
wadaycesar@hotmail.com. Quiet, shared
bath, garden, meals available, use of kitchen,
breakfast included.

E **Confort**, Ancash 231, 1 block from the
main plaza, T064-233601. Rooms with hot
water are nicer, but more expensive than
those with cold water, all rooms are good
value, very clean, ask for a room not facing
the street for peace and quiet, safe for
bicycles, car parking costs US$1.

E **Hostal Huaracaya**, Amazonas 323. Hot
water and TV, good value.

E **Percy's**, Real 1399, T064-231208. Shared
bathroom, hot water in morning, TV, basic
but clean and good value.

E **Pussy Cat**, Giráldez 359, T064-231565. Not
what the name might suggest, F with shared
bathroom, hot water, safe, friendly, luggage
stored, comfortable beds.

F per person **Peru Andino Lodging and
Excursions**, Pasaje San Antonio 113-115, San
Carlos, on Av Centenario go 3 blocks from 2
de Mayo to San José, then 3 blocks north
(left), 10-15 mins' walk from the centre,
T064-223956; if taking a taxi, stress that it's
Pasaje San Antonio), www.geocities.com/
peruandino_1. Price includes breakfast, clean
rooms with hot showers, several with private
bathroom, safe area, cosy atmosphere, run by
Sra Juana, her daughter speaks some English,
friendly, they also organize trekking and
mountain bike tours, Spanish classes, cooking
and laundry facilities. Highly recommended.

F **Hostal Santo Domingo**, Ica 655,
T064-235461. Set around two pleasant
patios, clean, basic, good value.

G per person **Hostal Baldeón**, Amazonas
543, T064-231634. Friendly, kitchen and
laundry facilities, nice patio, good hot
shower on request, basic rooms with poor
beds, security-conscious.

G per person **Casa hospedaje**, Huamanmarca 125, T064-219980. Central, small,
comfortable, hot water, shared showers,
family run, nice atmosphere.

G **Central**, Loreto 452, T064-211948.
Large place, basic, shared bath, hot water
in the morn.

Mantaro Valley p486
D **Hostal La Llamita**, Jr Huancayo 445,

Hualhuas. New, 30 rooms with bath, hot
water, also dormitories (F per person with
shared bath and cold water), friendly owner,
swimming pool, laundry and restaurant. It
also has a handicraft shop.

Huancavelica and around
p486, map p486
The options listed here are in Huancavelica.
C **Presidente**, Plaza de Armas, T067-952760.
Lovely colonial building, cheaper without
bathroom, price includes breakfast and bath,
very clean but not a warm building, hot
water a 'hit and miss' affair, overpriced.
E **San José**, Jr Huancayo, at top of Barranca
(past Santo Domingo), T067-752958. With
bath, hot water 1700-1900, G without bath,
clean, comfortable beds, helpful.
F **Camacho**, Jr Carabaya 481. Best of the
cheap hotels, G without bath, hot shower in
morning and early evening, clean and well
maintained, excellent value.
F **Santo Domingo**, Av Barranca 366,
T067-953086. Cheap, very basic, with shared
bathroom and cold water.
F **Savoy**, Av Muñoz 294 (no sign, difficult to
find). Also cheap, very basic, with shared
bathroom and cold water.
F **Virrey**, Av Barranca 317. Basic, cold water.

Huancavelica to Ayacucho p487
G **Hostal Recreo Sol y Sombra**, Quichuas.
Charming, small courtyard, helpful, basic.

❶ Eating

Huancayo and around p484, map p485
♥♥ **La Cabaña**, Av Giraldez 652. Pizzas,
ice-cream, calentitos, and other dishes, roast
New Zealand lamb, folk music at weekends
(see Incas del Perú under Tour operators,
below).
♥♥ **Pizzería Antojitos**, Puno 599. Attractive,
atmospheric pizzeria with live music some
nights.
♥ **Chifa El Centro**, Giráldez 245. Chinese
food, good service, excellent value and
atmosphere (waterfall and rainforest).
♥ **El Pino**, Real 539. Serves typical food for
about US$2-3 a dish, and fixed price menú.

Cafés
Berisso, Giráldez 258. Good for cakes and
quiche, friendly.

Café El Parque, Giráldez y Ancash, on the main plaza. Smart place to take coffee and cake.

Chez Viena, Puno 125. Another posh place for coffee and cakes.

El Paraíso, Arequipa 929, very good vegetarian food, good value and service.

Panadería Koky, Ancash y Puno. Good for breakfasts and pastries during the day, pricey.

Huancavelica and around
p486, map p486

There are lots of cheap, basic restaurants on C Muñoz and Jr Virrey Toledo. All serve typical food, mostly with a set menú for around US\$1.50. There area also chifas on Toledo.

♥♥ Mochica Sachún, Av Virrey Toledo 303. Great menú for US\$1.50, otherwise expensive, popular.

♥♥ La Casona, Jr Virrey Toledo 230. Good value menú and peña.

♥ Cami, Barranca y Toledo. No sign, small, lively, good set menus and juices.

❶ Bars and clubs

Huancayo and around *p484, map p485*
Café Billar, Paseo de Breña 133. 0900-2400, serves beer and snacks, pool tables.
El Cereco, Puno just below Plaza, near Fuente de Soda El Inca, good for late-night drinks, sandwiches, music videos, popular. All the *peñas* have folklore shows with dancing, open normally Fri, Sat and Sun from 1300 to 2200. Entrance fee is about US\$2 per person, eg Ollantaytambo, Puno, block 2.
Taki Wasi, Huancavelica y 13 de Noviembre. Most discos open around 2000 and close at 0200. Some charge an entrance fee of US\$3-4.

⊛ Festivals and events

Huancayo and around *p484, map p485*
Festividad del Tayta Niño is held on **19-31 of Jan**. Festividad de la Virgen de Cocharcas is held on **8 Sep** (see also Mantaro Valley below). Festividad de San Jerónimo de Tunan takes place on **30 Sep**. In **Oct**: San Francisco de Asís, San Lucas is the culmination of month-long celebrations for El Señor de los Milagros. The Semana Turística de Huancayo begins on **16 Nov**.

There are so many festivals in the Mantaro Valley that it is impossible to list them all. Practically every day of the year there is a celebration of some sort in one of the villages. We list a selection below.
La Huaconada de Mito takes place in Mito on **1-3 Jan**. Festividad del Tayta Niño on **19-31 Jan** in Huayucachi. As in the rest of the country, there are carnival celebrations for the whole of **Feb**, with highlights on **2**, Virgen de la Candelaria, and **17-19** Concurso de Carnaval.
Semana Santa is impressive throughout the valley, especially the **Good Friday** processions. Fiesta de la Cruz also takes place throughout the valley on **1 May**, as does Fiesta de Santiago on **24-30 Jul**. On **8 Sep** is La Virgen de Cocharcas, held in Concepción, Jauja and more famously in Sapallanga, 8 km south from Huancayo. Held on different dates in **Sep** is the Semana Turística del Valle del Mantaro.

Huancavelica and around
p486, map p486

The whole area is rich in culture with many festivals and dances.
Fiesta de los Reyes Magos y los Pastores, **4-8 Jan**. Fiesta del Niño Perdido is held on **2nd Sun in Jan**. Pukllaylay Carnavales, celebration of the first fruits from the ground (harvest), **20 Jan-mid Mar**. Semana Santa, Holy Week. Toro Pukllay festival **last week of May, first week of Jun**. Fiesta de Santiago is held in **May and Aug** in all communities. Los Laygas **22-28 Dec**.

⬤ Shopping

Huancayo and around *p484, map p485*
All handicrafts are made outside Huancayo in the many villages of the Mantaro Valley (see below), or in Huancavelica. The villages are worth a visit to learn how the items are made. Casa de Artesano, on the corner of Real and Paseo La Breña, at Plaza Constitución, has a wide selection of good quality crafts. There is a large handicrafts market between Ancash and Real, block 7, offering a wide selection of local handicrafts. Two supermarkets on Real between Breña and Lima. Watch out for pickpockets in the market.

▲▲ Activities and tours

Huancayo and around *p484, map p485*
Tour operators
Incas del Perú information office next to La Cabaña restaurant (Av Giráldez 652) offers artesan and archaeological day tours, walking tours and mountain biking trips, US$35, which can include visits to Huamancaca prison. Inmates' handicrafts are sold, they cook meals and will discuss politics (many are ex-Sendero Luminoso). Incas del Perú also have maps and a book exchange, bicycle hire (US$15 per day), www.incasdelperu.com.
Peruvian Tours, Puno 488, on the main plaza, T064-213069. A reputable organizer of local tours.
Turismo Huancayo, C Real 517 oficina 6, T064-233351. Organizes local tours and is recommended.
Wanka Tours, Real 550, T064-231743. Another reputable organizer of tours to a variety of places in the Mantaro Valley.

Guides
Marco Jurado Ames, andinismo_peru@yahoo.es. Organizes long-distance treks on the `hidden paths of Peru'. Many of these include Huancayo, such as a two-week trip from Lima to Machu Picchu via Huancayo, the Amazon lowlands and Vilcabamba.

⊖ Transport

Huancayo and around *p484, map p485*
Bus
Most of the bus offices of the better companies running to Lima are 2-3 blocks north of the main plaza, while those of the cheaper companies are located to the north of the Río Shullcas, a 10-15 min walk from the centre. The offices of bus companies operating to destinations to the south of Huancayo, such as Huancavelica and Ayacucho, are 4-5 blocks south of the main plaza. A new bus terminal for all buses, to all destinations, is planned 3 km north of the centre.

There are regular buses to **Lima**, 6-7 hrs on a good paved road, costing US$10. Travelling by day is recommended for the fantastic views and, of course, for safety. If you must travel by night, take warm clothing. Recommended companies are **Ormeño**, Av Mcal Castilla 1379, El Tambo; **Cruz del Sur**, Ayacucho 281, T064-235650; and **Transportes Rogger**, Lima 561, T064-212687, cama and semi-cama at 1300 and 2330, comercial at 2230.

To **Ayacucho**, 319 km, 9-10 hrs, US$6.65-7.55. **Molina**, C Angaráes 334, T064-224501, 3 a day, recommended. The road is in poor condition and is very difficult in the wet. Take warm clothing. After Izcuchaca, on the railway to Huancavelica, there is a good road to the Quichuas hydroelectric scheme, but thereafter it is narrow with hair-raising bends and spectacular bridges. The scenery is staggering.

To **Huancavelica**, 147 km, 5 hrs, US$2.85. Many buses leave daily, including **Transportes Yuri**, Ancash 1220, 3 a day. The road is in poor condition but being improved, and takes longer when wet. The scenery is spectacular.

To **Cerro de Pasco**, 255 km, 5 hrs, US$4, several departures. Alternatively, take a bus to La Oroya, about every 20 mins, from Av Real about 10 blocks north of the main plaza. From La Oroya there are regular buses and *colectivos* to Cerro. The road to La Oroya and on to Cerro is in good condition.

To **Huánuco**, 7 hrs, **Turismo Central** have a direct bus at 2115, US$6, good service. To **Chanchamayo**: Empresa San Juan, Ferrocarril 161 and Plaza Amazonas, and **Trans Muruhuay** each have an hourly service via Jauja to **Tarma**, 3 hrs, US$2.50, some of which continue on to **La Merced**, 5 hrs, US$4. The only company with a direct day service to **Satipo** is Selva Tours, Giráldez block 3, at 0800, US$6, 229 km, 12 hrs, on a very difficult road, which is impossible in the wet. Some trucks and a few buses travel to **Cañete**, 289 km, 10 hrs, US$4. It is a poor road, with beautiful mountain landscapes before dropping to the valley of Cañete.

To **Jauja**, 44 km, 1 hr. *Colectivos* and combis leave every few mins from Huamanmarca y Amazonas, and Plaza Amazonas, US$1.50. Ones via San Jerónimo and Concepción have 'Izquierda' on the front. Most buses to the **Mantaro Valley** leave from several places around the market area. Buses to **Hualhuas**,

Cajas and **Huamancaca** leave from block 3 of Pachitea. Buses to **Cochas** leave from Amazonas y Giráldez.

Car
If driving to Ayacucho and beyond, roads are "amazingly rough". Don't go alone. Count kilometres diligently to keep a record of where you are as road signs are poor.

Train
There are 2 unconnected railway stations. The Central station serves Lima, via La Oroya (298 km). Service on the **Lima-Huancayo** railway recommenced in 2002, with trains running several weekends a year, usually coinciding with public holidays. The fare is US$15 one way, US$25 return (the train returns a day or two later). Information on forthcoming departures can be obtained from Incas del Perú, see Activities and tours, above

From the small station in Chilca suburb (15 mins by taxi, US$1), trains run 128.7 km to **Huancavelica**, on a narrow gauge track (3 ft). There are 2 trains: the autovagón leaves at 1300 daily. It costs US$3.70 and has 1st class and Buffet carriages. The journey takes 7 hrs, and is a spectacular one with fine views, passing through typical mountain villages. There are 38 tunnels and the line reaches 3,676 m. Meals, drinks and snacks are served on the train, and at the village stations vendors sell food and crafts. The local train leaves at 0630 daily and takes 5 hrs. There are 1st, US$2.55, 2nd, US$2.20, and Buffet, US$3.70, classes. Tickets can only be bought on the day of travel; get in the queue at 0600 at the latest. Services are often suspended, especially when rainy; the trains frequently suffer technical problems.

Huancavelica and around
p486, map p486
Bus
All bus companies have their offices at and leave from the east end of town, around Parque M Castilla, on Muñoz, Iquitos, Tumbes and O'Donovan. To **Huancayo**, 147 km, 5 hrs, US$2.85, rough road. **Transportes Yuri** at 2200 and **Transportes Ticllas**, 6 a day. To go only as far as **Izcuchaca** costs US$1.45. To **Lima** there are two routes: one is via Huancayo, 445 km, 13 hrs minimum,

US$5.70. **Libertadores** buses to Huancayo at 1830 go on to Lima, also Ticllas at 1700. The other route is via **Pisco**, 269 km, 12 hrs, US$7 and **Ica**, US$8, at 1730 daily, with **Oropesa**, O'Donovon 599. Buy your ticket 1 day in advance. The road is poor until it joins the Ayacucho-Pisco road, where it improves. The views are spectacular, but most of the journey is done at night.

Train
Just a little beyond the bus stations and about 500m from the Plaza de Armas is the train station. See under Huancayo for services. The autovagón leaves for **Huancayo** daily at 0630, the local train leaves at 1300, daily. The 0630 **train** from **Huancavelica** arrives in Izcuchaca at 0800, then continues to **Huancayo**. The trip costs US$1.70. The train tends to be very crowded. The 1300 train passes at 1400-1430. Sit on the left for the best views. The trains from Huancayo pass at around 0900 and 1600. The direct Huancayo-Ayacucho **bus** passes through at 0800, alternatively take a truck, about 8 hrs to Ayacucho. A **taxi** Huancavelica-Izcuchaca will cost US$22 minimum.

Huancavelica to Ayacucho *p487*
There is no daily direct transport from Huancavelica to Ayacucho, other than 0430 on Sat with **San Juan Bautista**, Plaza Túpac Amaru 107 at Av Andrés Avelino Cáceres, T067-803062, US$5.70. Otherwise you have to go to **Rumichaca**, just beyond Santa Inés, 4 hrs, also San Juan Bautista bus at 0430, then change to Ayacucho, bus at 1500, 3 hrs, US$2, or take a truck (nothing in Rumichaca other than a couple of foodstalls and some dirty, hole-in-the-ground toilets). From Rumichaca it's a beautiful journey to Ayacucho on the paved road.
Alternatives are: go from Huancavelica to **Izcuchaca** and get on a Huancayo-Ayacucho bus there. Huancavelica-**Lircay**: **Transportes 5 de Mayo**, Av Sebastián Barranca y Torre Tagle, US$3, 2 hrs, leave when full. Then **5 de Mayo** from Lircay Terminal Terrestre hourly from 0430 to **Julcamarca** 2½ hrs, US$3. Julcamarca-Ayacucho by combi US$1.50, 3-3½ hrs.

● Directory

Huancayo and around *p484, map p485*
Banks BCP, Real 1039. Changes TCs with no commission, cash advance on Visa. **Banco Wiese**, Real casi Ica. ATM does not accept international cards, poor rates for TCs. **Interbank** and **Banco Continental** are on block 6 of Real. There are several casas de cambio on Ancash and on Av Lima between Ancash and Real. Street changers hang out in front of Hotel Kiya. **Internet** Numerous places round Plaza Constitución on Giráldez, Paseo La Breña, eg **Cyberwanka**, No 173, very good, and Real 1300 block. Average price under US$0.75 per hr. **Language classes** Katia Cerna is a recommended teacher, T064-225332, katiacerna@hotmail .com She can arrange home stays; her sister works in adventure tourism. **Incas del Perú** (see Tour operators) organize Spanish courses for beginners for US$100 per week, 3-hrs a day, including 5 nights'

accommodation at **La Casa de La Abuela** and all meals, also homestays, and classes in weaving, playing traditional music, Quechua and gourd carving. See also Peru Andino Lodging above. **Laundry** Good lavandería on Paseo La Breña behind Casa de Artesano. **Post** On Plaza Huamanmarca. **Useful addresses** Touring y Automóvil Club **del Perú**, Jr Lima 355, T064-231204, huancayo@touringperu.com.pe.

Huancavelica and around
p486, map p486
Banks BCP, Virrey Toledo 300 block, west of Plaza. There is a Multired ATM on M Muñoz in the arches of the Municipalidad. **Internet** Despite what they say, internet places open around 0900 till 2100-2200. There are places on V Toledo and M Muñoz. Also **Librería Municipal**, Plaza de Armas, US$0.60 per hr. **Post** On Ferrua Jos, at block 8 of M Muñoz. **Telephone** Carabaya y Virrey Toledo.

Ayacucho and its hinterland

→ *Colour map 5, grid A4. Altitude: 2,748 m.*

The city of Ayacucho is famous for its hugely impressive Semana Santa celebrations, its splendid market and, not least, a plethora of churches - 33 of them no less - giving the city its alternative name La Ciudad de las Iglesias. A week can easily be spent enjoying Ayacucho and its hinterland. The climate is lovely, with warm, sunny days and pleasant balmy evenings. It is a warm, hospitable, tranquil place, where the inhabitants are eager to promote tourism. It also boasts a large, active student population. ➤➤ *For Sleeping, Eating and other listings, see pages 499-505.*

Ins and outs
Getting there The airport is to the east of the city along Av Castilla. A taxi to the centre costs US$2; buses or *colectivos* leave for the Plaza Mayor. At the airport walk half a block down the street for a bus to the centre. Most of the bus offices are much nearer the centre of town, in the north and northeast.
Getting around This is a large city but the interesting churches and colonial houses are all fairly close to the Plaza Mayor. Barrio Santa Ana is further away to the south and you will probably want to take a taxi to get to it (US$1 - it's easy to walk back). Taxis are cheap and mototaxis are plentiful.
Tourist information iperú ① *Portal Municipal 48, on the Plaza, T066-818305, iperuayacucho@promperu.gob.pe. Daily 0830-1930, Sun 0830-1430. Very helpful.* Ask Smith Pariona Medina here for guides who work with the Asociación de Guías e Turismo - Ayacucho (Agotur-A). There is also helpful desk at the airport to meet incoming flights. **Dirección Regional de Industria y Turismo** ① *Asamblea 481, T066-812548/813162. Mon-Fri 0800-1300,* friendly and helpful.

Ayacucho

The city is built round the Plaza Mayor, the main plaza, in the centre of which is a statue of Independence hero Antonio José de Sucre. Facing onto the plaza are the Cathedral, Municipalidad, the Prefectura, the Supreme Court in fine colonial buildings, most within the Plaza's arcades.

Background

Ayacucho is the capital of its Department. The city was founded on 9 January 1539 by the invading Spaniards, who named it San Juan de la Frontera. This was changed to San Juan de la Victoria after the Battle of Chupas, when the king's forces finally defeated the rival Almagrist power. Despite these Spanish titles, the city always kept its original name of Huamanga. It became an important base for the army of the Liberator Simón Bolívar in his triumphant sweep south from the Battle of Junín. It was here, on the Pampa de Quinua, on 9 December 1824, that the decisive Battle of Ayacucho was fought, bringing Spanish rule in Peru to an end. Huamanga was, therefore, the first city on the continent to celebrate its liberty. In the midst of the massive festivities, the Liberator decreed that the city be named Ayacucho - meaning 'City of Blood'. For much of the 1980s and early 1990s, this title seemed appropriate as the Shining Path terrorized the local populace, severely punishing anyone they suspected of siding with the military. Now, though, peace has returned to this beautiful colonial Andean city.

Sights

The construction of Ayacucho's many colonial religious buildings is said to have been financed by wealthy Spanish mine-owners and governors. Unfortunately many have fallen into disrepair and are closed to the public. Those that are not shut tend only to open for Mass in the early morning and evening. The **Cathedral** ① *1700-1900, Sun 0900-1700*, was built in 1612. The two towers are in green stone, while the portal is pink. It has three strong, solid naves of simple architecture, in contrast to the elegant decoration of the interior, particularly the superb gold leaf altars. It also has a Museo de Arte Religioso, but it is closed indefinitely. The Cathedral is beautifully lit at night. Next to the Cathedral is the **Universidad Nacional de San Cristóbal de Huamanga**, UNSCH, in the Casona de Castilla y Zamora. It has a small courtyad in which grows fig tree, after which the university café, **La Higuera**, is named.

On the north side of the Plaza Mayor, on the corner of Portal de la Unión and Asamblea, are the **Casonas de los Marqueses de Mozobamba y del Pozo**, also called Velarde-Alvarez. On the same Portal is the house of **Canon Manuel Frías**, where the writer and caricaturist, Abraham Valdelomar (who also used the pseudonym El Conde de Lemos after 1915), tragically died. Leading north from the Plaza is Jr Asamblea, one of the busiest streets in the centre. It is due for pedestrianisation in 2005. It is full of eating places, internet cafés and discos. On a parallel street is one of the city's most notable churches is **Santo Domingo** (1548) ① *9 de Diciembre, block 2, open for Mass daily 0700-0800*. Its fine façade has triple Roman arches and Byzantine towers.

Jirón 28 de Julio is pedestrianised for two blocks. A stroll down here towards the prominent **Arco del Triunfo** (1910), which commemorates victory over the Spaniards, passes **La Compañía de Jesús** (1605) ① *28 de Julio, block 1, open only for Mass*. It has one of the most important façades of Viceregal architecture. It is of baroque style and guarded by two impressive 18th century towers. Its altar is covered in gold leaf and large paintings of saints adorn the nave. The church also has an adjacent chapel.

Go through the arch to the church of **San Francisco de Asís** ① *28 de Julio , block 3, open daily for morning mass and 1730-1830*. It dates from 1552 and has an elaborate gilt main altar and several others. It claims the largest bell in the city in its tower. Across

To Cabo Blanco & Los Manglares de Tumbes

To Museo Arqueológico Hipólito
Unanue, Cruz de la Paz, Pisco & Lima

Mercado
Artesanal y
Shosaku
Nagase

Quinua

Manco Capac

Garcilaso de la

9 de Diciembre

Libertad

Asamblea

Pasaje Cáceres

Los Andes

Miller

To Huancayo & Wari

Av Mariscal Cáceres

Santo
Domingo

Tres Máscaras

Bellido

Sol

Casonas de los
Marqueses de
Mozobamba y
del Pozo

Callao

Cusco

Prefectura

Plaza
Mayor

Municipalidad

Cathedral

University

Arequipa

Lima

Casas de
Cambio

La Compañía
de Jesús

Centro Turístico
Cultural San Cristóbal

28 de Julio

San Martín

La Merced

Casa
Jaúregui

Grau

Libertad

Nazareno

Carlos F Vivanco

Arco del
Triunfo

Av Ramón Castilla

Londres

To Airport, Ciudadela Warpa Picchu & Cusco

Santa
Clara

Mercardo
de Abastos
Carlos F
Vivanco

San Francisco
de Asís

2 de Ma

Huancasolar

Raymondi

S J de Dios

Mercado 12
de Abril

C Chorro

Museo Andrés A
Cáceres (Casona
Vivanco)

Río Alameda

N

0 metres 100
0 yards 100

To Barrio
Santa Ana

To Santa Teresa
& San Cristóbal

Central Highlands Ayacucho & its hinterland

Sleeping
Alameda Bolognesi 3
Ayacucho Hotel Plaza 1
Central 2
El Mesón & Las Orquídas 4
Florida 5
Grau 6
Hospedaje El Centro 8
Hostal 3 Máscaras 12
Hostal San Blas &
La Posada de Santa Inés 11
Hostal El Marqués
de Valdelirios 18
La Crillonesa 15

Marcos 7
San Francisco 17
Santa María 10
Santa Rosa 13
Sebastián 9

Eating
Bras Roja 8
Café Dorado 9
Cameycar & Chita
Hua Lina 1
La Casona 3
La Miel 10
La Pradera 2

Los Flores 11
Los Portales 6
Marcos 12
Mia Pizza 4
Nino 5
Panadería 13
Portal 1 18
Punta Caliente 14
Santa María 15
Sebastián 16
Tradición 7
Urpicha 17

Transport
Civa 5
Colectivos to Julcamarca 2
Combis for Huari, Qinua and
Huanta, & San Francisco 10
Combis to Vilcashuamán 11
Cruz del Sur 9
Libertadores 8
Molina 6
Ormeño 3
Punto Caliente
Reybus 4
Turismo Los Chankas 7
Wari 1

28 de Julio from San Fancisco is the **Mercado de Abastos Carlos F Vivanco**, the packed central market. As well as all the household items, meat and other local produce, look for the cheese sellers, the breads and the section dedicated to fruit juices.

Santa Clara de Asís ① *Jr Grau, block 3, open for Mass*, is renowned for its beautifully delicate coffered ceiling. It is open for the sale of sweets and cakes made by the nuns (go to the door at Nazarenas 184, it's usually open). On the 5th block of 28 de Julio is the late 16th-century **Casona Vivanco**, which houses the **Museo Andrés A Cáceres** ① *Jr 28 de Julio 508, T066-812360, Mon-Sat 0900-1300, 1400-1800. US$1.25*. The museum has a collection of baroque painting and colonial furniture, some republican and contemporary art, and exhibits on Mariscal Cáceres' battles in the War of the Pacific.

Further south still, on a pretty plazuela, is **Santa Teresa** (1683) ① *28 de Julio, block 6, open daily for Mass 1600*, with its monastery. It has magnificent gold-leafed altars heavily brocaded and carved in the churrigueresque style. **San Cristóbal** ① *Jr 28 de Julio, block 6, rarely open*, was the first church to be founded in the city (1540), and is one of the oldest in South America. With its single tower, it is tiny compared with Santa Teresa, which is opposite. The 16th-century church of **La Merced** ① *2 de Mayo, block, open for Mass*, is the second oldest in the city. The high choir is a good example of the simplicity of the churches of the early period of the Viceroyalty. In 1886 a flagstone was discovered with the sculpted image of a sleeping warrior, known popularly as the 'Chejo-Pacheco'. **Casa Jáuregui** ① *opposite the church of La Merced on 2 de Mayo, Mon-Fri 0800-1700*, also called **Ruiz de Ochoa**, was built in the second half of the 18th century and became the Jáuregui family home, until Peruvian banks restored it in 1974-97. Its oustanding feature is its doorway, which has a blue balcony supported by two fierce beasts with erect penises. The plain central patio is now surrounded by the classrooms of a school.

Suburbs

For a fascinating insight into Inca and pre-Inca art and culture, a visit to **Barrio Santa Ana** is a must. Here, about 200 families have workshops making *artesanías*: textiles, *retablos*, ceramics and work in stone. Their work is distributed through the galleries in the Barrio.

Galería de Arte Latina ① *Plazuela de Santa Ana 105, T066-528315, wari39@hot mail.com*, is recommended. The owner, Alejandro Gallardo Llacctahuamán, and his son, Alexander, are very friendly and have lots of information on weaving techniques and the preservation of their culture. They plan to open a textile museum soon and Alexander is working with local communities and orphans. Also **Wari Art Gallery** ① *Jr Mcal Cáceres 302, Santa Ana, T066-812529*. Run by Gregorio Sulca and his family, who will explain the Quechua legends, weaving and iconography. Next door is the Sulcas' Instituto de Cultura Quechua, which affords wonderful views of the city and surrounding hills from its roof. Both the Gallardos and the Sulcas are renowned internationally. A good grasp of Spanish is essential to appreciate the galleries fully.

Around Ayacucho

Vilcashuamán and Vischongo

The impressive Inca ruins of **Vilcashuamán** are four hours to the south of Ayacucho (120 km), beyond Cangallo. According to John Hemming Vilcashuamán was an important provincial capital, the crossroads where the road from Cusco to the Pacific met the empire's north-south highway. The tourist office on the Plaza in Ayacucho has a guide book, in Spanish, which can be consulted. Market day is Wednesday. For tours, see page 503 and transport, page 503. Near Vilcashuamán is the village of **Vischongo**. About an hour's walk uphill from the village are the Inca baths of **Intihuatana**, which are worth seeing as much for their superb location on a beautiful lake as for the ruins themselves. It is possible to see both ruins in a day, though it's more relaxing to spend the night in Vilcashuamán, or better still, camp at the lake near Vischongo. Tours to Vilcashuamán from Ayacucho include Vischongo and Intihuatana.

Huari

① *22 km from Ayacucho, 0800-1700, US$0.75.*

A good road going north from Ayacucho leads to Huari (frequently spelt Wari), dating from the 'Middle Horizon' (AD 600-1000), when the Huari culture spread across most of Peru. This was the first urban walled centre in the Andes and was used for political, administrative, ceremonial, residential and productive purposes. The huge irregular stone walls are up to 3-4 m high (but many are long and low) and rectangular houses and streets can be made out. There are large areas of flat stone which may have been for religious purposes and there are tomb complexes and subterranean canals and tunnels.

The most important activity here was artistic production. High temperature ovens were used to mass produce ceramics of many different colours. The Huari also worked with gold, silver, metal and alloys such as bronze, which was used for weapons and for decorative objects. The ruins now lie in an extensive tuna cactus forest. There is a small museum at the site, but very little direction and the few explanations are only in Spanish. Tombs of the Huari nobles are being excavated along the road from Ayacucho to Quinua.

Quinua

This village, 37 km northeast of Ayacucho, has a charming cobbled main plaza and many of the buildings have been restored. There is a small market on Sunday. Nearby, on the Pampa de Quinua, a huge obelisk commemorates the battle of Ayacucho. The obelisk is 44 m high, representing 44 years of struggle for independence. The village's handicrafts are recommended, especially ceramics. The pieces made in Quinua range from model churches and nativity figures to humorous groups of musicians and gossiping women. The rich red local clay is modelled mainly by hand and decorated with local mineral earth colours. Traditionally, the churches are set on the roofs of newly-occupied houses to ward off evil spirits. Virtually every roof in the village has a church on it – including the church itself. San Pedro Ceramics, at the foot of the hill leading to the monument, and Mamerto Sánchez, Jr Sucre, are good places to find typical local ceramics, but there are many others. By the *paradero* are several *recreos*, tourist restaurants serving typical food.

Huanta Valley → *Colour map 5, grid A4.*

The town of **Huanta**, one hour from Ayacucho on the road to Huancayo, overlooks the valley and has a pleasant plaza with palms and other trees. Huanta celebrates the **Fiesta de la Cruz** during the first week of May, with much music and dancing. Its Sunday market is large and interesting, while the permanent daily market covers quite an area. There are many places to eat around town and lots of internet places.

From Huanta, the lakes of **Qarqarcocha**, **San Antonio**, **Chakaccocha**, **Yanacocha** and **Pampacocha** can be visited. In the rainy season only the nearest lake, Chakaccocha, can be reached in a four-wheel drive. The **valley of Luricocha**, 5 km away, can also be visited. It has a lovely, warm climate. The *recreos* (tourist restaurants) at Luricocha are famous for their *platos típicos*. Take a combi from Parque Hospital in Huanta (US$0.15).

 It was in Huanta that the Pokras and Chancas warriors put up their last, brave fight against the Inca invasion.

The Huari influence

The city of Huari had a population of 50,000 and reached its apogee in AD 900. Its influence spread throughout much of Peru: north to Cajamarca; along the north coast to Lambayeque; south along the coast to Moquegua; and south across the sierra to Cusco. Before the Inca invasion the Huari formed a *chanca* – a confederation of ethnic groups – and populated the Pampas river and an area west of the Apurímac. This political agreement between the peoples of Ayacucho, Andahuaylas, Junín and Huancavelica was seen by the Incas in Cusco as a threat. The Incas fought back around 1440 with a bloody attack on the Huari on the Pampa de Ayacucho, and so began a period of Inca domination. The scene of this massacre is still known as *Rincón de los Muertos*.

The area is notable as the site of perhaps the oldest known culture in South America, 20,000 years old, evidence of which was found in the cave of **Pikimachay**. The cave is 24 km from Ayacucho, on the road to Huanta. It is a 30-minute walk from the road. The remains are now in Lima's museums. Another local attraction is the **Mirador de Huatuscalla**, 35 minutes from Huanta on a bad road. Some 800 m below is the meeting of the rivers Urbamba, Cachi and Mantaro, with a view of mountains behind. The only reasonable way to get there is with a travel agency from Ayacucho: tours to Huanta, Pikimachay and Huatuscalla cost US$10 per person, while taxis in Huanta ask US$22 to go to the Mirador.

North to the Río Apurímac → *Colour map 5, grid A4.*

A road runs northeast from Ayacucho to **San Francisco**, lying in the tropical lowland forests of the Apurímac Valley. There are many small restaurants on both sides of the bridge. Launches ply up and down the river and 15 minutes east is the village of Sampantuari, where the inhabitants still wear face paint, traditional clothing and live in bamboo huts (don't go to stare - they don't welcome outsiders).

Ayacucho to Cusco

Andahuaylas and around → *Colour map 5, grid A4.*

About 240 km from Ayacucho, in a fertile, temperate valley of lush meadows, cornfields and groves of eucalyptus, alder and willow, stands Andahuaylas (2,980 m). The town offers few exotic crafts, but it has a good market on Sunday and the surrounding scenery is beautiful. The church of San Pedro ① *1600-1670*, takes up the south side of the plaza, which has tulip and other trees, flowers and statues. On the north side is the Municipalidad, with a small **Museo Arqueológico**, which has a good collection of pre-Columbian objects, including mummies. For more information there is an Andahuaylas Archaeological Project. There is an office of the Dirección de Comercio y Turismo at Avenida Túpac Amaru 374, T083-721627. Every two months an Agenda (proyectoculturis@hotmail.com) is published, with local tourist news and a map. Ask for it in bus offices, hotels, etc.

A good nearby excursion is to the **Laguna de Pacucha**, beautifully set among the hills. On the shore is the town of Pacucha and various places to eat. Take a *colectivo* from Avenida Los Chankas y Avenida Andahuaylas, at the back of the market, US$0.75, about 40 minutes. A road follows the north shore of the lake and a turn-off climbs to **Sóndor** ① *US$0.60 (beware overcharging by the guardian)*, an Inca archaeological site at 3,300 m. Various buildings and small plazas lead up to a conical hill which has been set around with concentic stone walls or terracing. At the summit is a large rock said to be an *intihuatana* (hitching post of the sun). There are wonderful views back to Pachuca and over the surrounding valleys and mountains. Each 18-19 June Sóndor Raymi is celebrated. To get there you can take a taxi from Andahuaylas, US$10, a *colectivo* to Pahuca, then walk 8-10 km, or a *colectivo* to Argama (also behind Andahuaylas market), which passes the entrance. With any form of public transport you will have to walk back to Pacucha, unless very lucky.

Abancay and around → *Colour map 5, grid A5.*

Nestled between mountains in the upper reaches of a glacial valley at 2,378 m, this friendly town is first glimpsed when you are 62 km away (about two hours on the bus coming from Andahuaylas). The last few kilometres are on the paved highway from Nasca, a relief after the rough, tortuous descent from the high sierra. The town is a functional, commercial centre, growing in importance now that the paved road Lima-Nasca-Cusco passes through. It also hopes to benefit from the tourist trade to Choquequirao and much investment is taking place in hotels and generally improving the town.

Local tourism is in its infancy. **Hotel Turistas**, see Sleeping, runs half-day tours around town and to nearby sites such as the former haciendas of **Yaca** and **Illanya**. Near the former is a place where silk worms are bred. Also included is the colonial bridge at Pachachaca (which can be seen from an bus going to Cusco), the **Mirador at Taraccasa** for good views over the city and the thermal baths of Santo Tomás. **Santuario Nacional de Ampay**, north of town, has lagoons called Angasccocha (3,200m) and Uspaccocha (3,820m), a glacier on Ampay mountain at 5,235m and flora and fauna typical of these altitudes. By public transport, take a *colectivo* to Tamburco and ask the driver where to get off. To get to the glacier you need two days trekking, with overnight camping.

One hour out of Abancay, at a place called **Carbonera**, a road to the left goes to Huanipaca (40 minutes, US$15.15 in car, lodging available, and guides). It continues to Ccenhualla, from where Choquequirao is visible. You descend 1½ hours to Hacienda San Ignacio by the Río Apurímac, then climb four hours up to Choquequirao. Shortly after Carbonera is the turn to Cachora. See West from Cusco, page 222, for Cachora and the route to Choquequirao.

The **Saywite stone** ① *3 km from the main road at Km 49 from Abancay, well-signed, US$3*, at 3,500 m, is a large carved rock. It is a UNESCO World Heritage site. The principal monolith is said to represent the three regions of jungle, sierra and coast, with the associated animals and Inca sacred sites of each. The holes aroud the perimeter suggest that it was covered in gold. It is said to have been defaced when they took a cast of it, breaking off many of the animals' heads. It is all fenced in and clean (ask the guardian for a closer look). Six main areas fall away from the stone and its neighbouring group of buildings. There is a staircase beside an elegant watercourse of channels and pools, a group around a stone (split by lightning), called the Casa de Piedra, or Rumi Huasi, an *usnu* platform and another monolith, called the Intihuatana. About 20 minutes from Saywite is **Curahuasi** (126 km from Cusco), famous for its aromatic anise herb, which has several roadside restaurants and hospedajes. A good two-hour walk is up Cerro San Cristóbal to **Capitán Rumi**, a huge rock overlooking the Apurímac canyon. The views are staggering, particularly if Salkantay and its snowy neighbours are free of cloud. Ask for directions, especially at the start.

Not far from the new road bridge over the Apurímac are the thermal baths of **Cconoc** ① *US$1.80*. An unmade road twists down to the river's edge where several pools and spouts are fed by warm water coming out of the cliffs. They are fairly clean, but watch out for the biting midges.

Ayacucho *p493, map p494*

A Ayacucho Hotel Plaza, 9 de Diciembre 184, T066-812202, hplaza@derramajae.org.pe. Beautiful colonial building but the rooms don't match up to the palatial splendour of the reception. It's comfortable, has TV, and some rooms overlook the plaza.

B-C Santa María, Arequipa 328, T066-814988, santamariahotel@hotmail.com. A modern hotel with suites and huge rooms, some on two floors (the stairs are a bit flimsy), price includes breakfast. Bedrooms are comfortable, with a proper bath, large TV and good fixtures and furnishings. There is a restaurant/bar, a garage in the basement and a great view from the roof.

C Marcos, 9 de Diciembre 143, T066-816867, www.hostalmarcos.com. A comfortable, modern hotel in a cul-de-sac 1/2 block from the Plaza. It's quiet, clean and rooms have bath, hot water and TV. The price includes breakfast in the cafetería.

C Santa Rosa, Jr Lima 166, T066-812083. Lovely colonial courtyard in th Casona Gutiérrez (1630); the Monja Alferez lived here for a while. It also served as the press HQ during the terrorist years. There is a roof terrace. Rooms are very clean and warm, hot water all day, friendly, attntive staff, car parking, good restaurant (♚) with good value menu. Recommended.

D Hostal El Marqués de Valdelirios, Alameda Bolognesi 720, T066-818944. Go through the arch below Santa Teresa to the broad Alameda for this lovely colonial-style mansion, beautifully furnished, with blue flower pots, pick-up from the airport for US$3, reserve at least 24 hrs in advance. Price includes breakfast, hot water, bar. Recommended.

D Hostal Tres Máscaras, Jr 3 Máscaras 194, T066-812921, hoteltresmascaras@yahoo.com. New rooms with bath are better, but with less character, than the old ones, some of which have shared bathroom (**E**), in this nice colonial building, which has a deep red patio with plants and caged parrots. Clean, basic rooms, hot water, breakfast extra, car park.

D San Francisco, Jr Callao 290, T066-812353, hotelsanfrancisco@viabcp.com. Rather like an old museum with a nice patio, this is a friendly hotel and a popular choice. Breakfast

is extra (US$1 - none on Sun), hot water, TV, comfortable rooms and some suites. Recommended. Will book El Encanto de Oro in Andahuaylas.

D-E Florida, Jr Cusco 310, T066-812565, F816029. Small and pleasant: a leafy courtyard leads to a modern block with clean, quiet rooms with bath and TV, hot water from electric showers. There are caged birds in the patio.

E Central, Jr Arequipa 188, T066-812144. A colonial doorway leads to a patio with plants and a modern block of rooms at the back. Rooms without bath and TV are cheaper, clean, spacious, good value.

E El Mesón, Jr Arequipa 273, T066-812938. A nice, clean, friendly *hostal*, hot water on request, laundry service, not as close to disco as Las Orquídeas.

E Hospedaje El Centro, Av Cáceres 1048, T813556. Rooms without bath and TV are **F**, large rooms, hot water, very clean, good value, but on a busy avenue.

E Grau, Jr San Juan de Dios 192, T066-812695. On the third floor (the second is a separate *hospedaje*), by the markets. With bath (F without, but with TV), hot water in all bathrooms, clean, clothes washing facilities and laundry service, good value, safe, friendly, noisy, breakfast extra. Recommended.

F Hostal San Blas, Jr Chorro 167, T066-812712. Special tourist price represents good value, nice rooms with bath, hot water all day, clean, friendly, kitchen facilities and laundry service, cheap meals available, bicycles to lend, tourist information. Recommended.

F La Crillonesa, El Nazareno 165, T066-812350, hotecrillonesa@latinmail.com. A big blue and white building just up from Santa Clara and the market, with colourful, locally-made decorations and excellent services. The price, set specially for tourists, includes bath, hot water in the basins as well as the shower, 1-hour free internet, kitchen and laundry facilities, discount for longer stay, great views from roof terrace. English and Italian spoken, clean, friendly, lots of tourist information. Carlos will act as a local tour guide and knows everyone. Recommended.

F La Posada de Santa Inés, Jr Chorro 139, T066-819544, posada_staines@hotmail.com. Opposite Mercado 12 de Abril, with bath, hot water morning and evening, TV, terrace with small swimming pool (ask in advance for it to be cleaned), clean, very good value.

Andahuaylas and around *p497*

D El Encanto de Oro, Av Pedro Casafranca 424, T083-723066, www.encantodeoro. 4t.com. A large modern hotel, 1 block from the market, 2 from the Plaza, with spacious, comfortable rooms, well decorated and good facilities. Discount available making for excellent value, breakfast included, TV, hot water 24 hrs, laundry service, restaurant with mirador, internet across the street, organizes trips on request. Advisable to reserve 15 days in advance.

D Sol de Oro, Jr Juan A Trelles 164, T083-721152, soldeorohotel@hotmail.com. A tall blue building, with lift to upper floors, near the bus stations. Price includes breakfast, hot water 24 hrs, plain rooms, TV, clean, laundry service, garage and tourist information. **El Dorado Inn** restaurant alongside.

E El Encanto de Apurímac, Jr Juan Francisco Ramos 401, T083-723527. Close to Los Chankas and other bus stations, with bath, TV, hot water, clean, very friendly and helpful.

F La Pradera, Jr Ramos 409, T083-801942. Also convenient for buses, plain rooms but OK, with bath, cheaper without TV, hot water, no breakfast.

F Las Américas, Jr Ramos 410, T721646. Near the bus stations. A bit gloomy in the public areas, but rooms are fine if basic. Cheaper without bath, **G** per person with shared bath, hot water, clean, friendly. Recommended.

G Hostal Waliman, Av Andahuaylas 266. Cold water in the shared bathrooms, very basic but clean and helpful. Due to have a vegetarian restaurant in late 2004.

Abancay and around *p498*

B-D Turistas, Av Díaz Bárcenas 500, T083-321017, hotursa@terra.com.pe. With bathroom, breakfast included. The original building is in colonial style, but a new block

is being built (Sep 2004). The whole hotel is being refurbished, with new bedrooms, more restaurant space and gardens and a travel agency, Apu-Rimac Tours y Travel. Rooms are large and, in the old block, the better and more expensive ones are on the top floor, quiet, clean, good restaurant, internet (US$0.60 per hour), parking space.

C-D Imperial, Díaz Bárcenas 517, T083-321578. Rooms are around the central parking space in this hospitable, efficient and spotless hotel. Rooms have great beds,TV and hot water (also in the shared bathrooms). The price of rooms without bath does not include breakfast. Helpful and good value.

D-E Hostal El Dorado, Av Arenas 131, T083-322005. This is an excellent choice. You go down to a little garden with a lemon tree, around which are the clean, comfort-able rooms with an oriental feel. With bath, hot water, TV, breakfast extra.

D-E Kavaxio Palace, Díaz Bárcenas 1112, at El Olivo, T083-803050. New, rooms with bath have hot water, TV; hot water also in the shared bathrooms. Breakfast extra. Good service, welcoming.

E Arenas, Av Arenas 192, T083-322107. A brand new hotel is being built beside the old one, with plain but well-appointed rooms, good beds, big showers, hot water, TV, new restaurants, internet, parking, lift to top floor, which has good views. The old part has rooms without bath and cold water. Hospitable.

F Apurímac Tours, Jr Cusco 421, T083-321446. Another new building, with rooms upstairs, with bath and hot water. The comedor in the courtyard serves breakfast and lunch, pay extra for either.

🍴 Eating

Ayacucho *p493, map p494*
Those wishing to try *cuy* should do so in Ayacucho as it's a lot cheaper than Cusco. Try mondongo, a soup made from intestines, maize and mint. Many restaurants include this, and *puca picante*, beef in a thick spicy sauce, rather like Indian curry, on their Fri lunch menu. You can also find *mondongo* at

the central market. Cooked meals can be found in the Sección Comidas in the main building, or Pasajes 2 and 3 outside; make sure the food is piping hot. For a cheap, healthy breakfast try *maca*, a drink of maca (see p513), apple and quinoa. It is sold opposite Santa Clara between 0600 and 0800. There are countless small, unnamed eating places around the centre. Few vegetarian options in town, so buy food in the market and prepare it yourself in *hostales* such as La Crillonesa or San Blas.

₩ Las Flores, Jr José Olaya 106, Plaza Conchopata, T066-816349, east of city. Specializes in *cuy*, with *chicharrón*, *ccapchi* and beer, bougainvillea-filled patios, rustic. Similar restaurants on the plaza, boys guard cars, taxi US$1 from centre. Open 0900-1900.

₩ Los Portales, on plaza, Portal Unión. A popular restaurant in a courtyard, regional meals, nice tortillas and other dishes.

₩ Tradición, San Martín 406. Another popular place, specializing in local food, also has a good cheap *menú*.

₩ Urpicha, Jr Londres 272, T066-813905. Recommended for typical food, which is its only cuisine. The dish called *urpicha* includes something of everything.

₩ ₣ La Casona, Jr Bellido 463. Open 1200-2200. Dining under the arches and in dining room, regional specialities, try their *puca picante*, and a wide menu. Recommended for food, service and cleanliness.

₩ ₣ Los Manglares de Tumbes, Av 26 de Enero, Asoc UNSCH, mz B lote 2. Open 0900-1600/1700 daily, big, smart place, for ceviches and seafood, à la carte, very good.

₩ ₣ Nino, Jr 9 de Diciembre 205, on small plaza opposite Santo Domingo church, T066-814537. Open Sun evening, very nice dining rooms with pleasant décor, terrace and garden (look for the owls in the trees); chicken, pastas and pizzas, including take-away, friendly.

₣ Brasa Roja, Jr Cusco block 1. More upmarket chicken place with food cooked *a la leña*, salads, very good.

₣ Cabo Blanco, Av Maravillas 198, T066-818740, close to Shosaku Nagase market (see Shopping) .Ceviches, seafood and fish dishes, small place with friendly personal service.

₣ Café Dorado, Jr Asamblea 310. Excellent

value set menu and chicken dishes in a long, cavernous dining room, mirrors and wood oven.

₣ Chifa Hua Lin, Asamblea 257. Very popular Chinese, said to be the best in town.

₣ Mía Pizza, San Martín 420-424. Open 1800-2400, for pizzas, pastas and karaoke (also has a bar to get you in the mood for singing).

Cafés

Centro Turístico Cultural San Cristóbal, 28 de Julio 178, some expensive cafés (eg **Lalo's**, No 115, open 0900-2100, **New York**, No 114) as well as other restaurants; all have tables in the pleasant courtyard. **La Higuera**, in UNSCH, next to Cathedral on Plaza. Off pretty courtyard, open Mon-Sat 0700-2100, for breakfasts, lunch specials Mon-Fri.

La Miel, Portal Constitución 11-12, two locations. Good coffee, hot drinks, juices, shakes, cakes and snacks, also ice creams.

Portal 1, Portal Constitución 1. A good café on the corner of the plaza serving snacks, light meals and ice cream.

Huanta Valley *p496*

₣ La Casona, Gral Córdoba 162. A huge place on the plaza in Huanta serving traditional dishes, chicken and good value menú.

Andahuaylas and around *p497*

₣ La Casona, Jr R Castilla 259 and Av Perú 260. A more upmarket pair of chicken restaurants, also *parrilladas*.

₣ El Dragón, Jr Juan A Trellas 279. A recommended chifa serving huge portions, excellent value (same owner as Hotel El Encanto de Apurímac).

₣ Il Gatto, Jr G Cáceres 334. A warm pizzería, with wooden furniture, pizzas (generous toppings, not thin cust) cooked in a wood-burning oven, very friendly.

₣ Napolitano, Jr R Castilla 431. A small pizzería which also sells *macerados* (fuit steeped in *pisco*) and has a cambio.

₣ Nuevo Horizonte, Jr Constitución 426. Vegetarian and health food restaurant, clean, open for breakfast.

Abancay and around *p498*

₣ Focarela Pizza's, Díaz Bárcenas 521, T083-322036. Simple but pleasant décor, pizza from a wood-burning oven, fresh, generous toppings, popular (ask for vino de la casa!).

♥ Il Giardino, Díaz Bárcenas 500 block opposite Hotel Turistas. "Ckicken Palace" (sic) serving *pollo a la leña*, typical dishes, *parrilladas* and other specials in smart, clean atmosphere.

♥ Los Portales, Av Arenas at the plazuela opposite **Hotel El Dorado**. Good *chifa* with clean tables, big windows, friendly service (one staff member speaks English), lunches are excellent value and other dishes plentiful.

Cafés

Dulce & Salad, Arequipa y 2 de Mayo. A pleasant café and heladería, four type of breakfast, daily salad specials, sandwiches, hot and cold drinks, cakes and a bar.

La Delicia, Díaz Bárcenas 217. A small vegetarian place serving breakfast, lunch buffet, juices, yoghurts and other products.

Natur Center, Díaz Bárcenas 211. An equally small vegetarian café with breakfast, lunch menú, juices and treatments.

Panadería y baguetería Buen Gusto, Huancavelica 324. Good breads and cakes baked on the premises.

❶ Bars and clubs

Ayacucho *p493, map p494*
There are many discos on Jr Asamblea, but their names and locations change frequently, owing to non-compliance with safety laws.
Punto Caliente, Cáceres 1045. Pizzas, drinks and music videos, same owner as Mía Pizza.

Andahuaylas and around *p497*
El Garabato, on main plaza beside Municipalidad. Video and music club, with tables from tree trunks, animal skins on the wall, woollen seat covers, expensive drinks, popular. There are many others around the plaza.

Abancay and around *p498*
Av Arenas has many *peñas turísticas*, bars and clubs.

❀ Festivals and events

Ayacucho *p493, map p494*
This area is well-known for its festivals throughout the year. Almost every day there

is a celebration in one of the surrounding villages, even in Ayacucho itself. Check with the tourist office.

Bajada de Reyes, **6 Jan**, people pay to take gifts from an adorned Baby Jesus. Festival Internacional de la Tuna y Cochinilla is held in **Feb and Mar** (date varies, lasts for 15 days), for real 'dye' hards. **Carnival in Feb or Mar** has a respectable side and a riotous side, the *comparas urbanas* and the *comparsas rurales*; ask Carlos at Hotel La Crillonesa about taking part. Ayacucho is famous for its **Semana Santa** which begins on the **Fri before Holy Week**. There follows one of the world's finest Holy Week celebrations, with candle-lit nightly processions, floral 'paintings' on the streets, daily fairs (the biggest on Easter Sat), horse races and contests among peoples from all central Peru. All accommodation is fully booked for months in advance of Holy Week. Many people offer beds in their homes during the week. Look out for notices on the doors, especially on Jr Libertad. One of the main festivals in Barrio Santa Ana is **30 Aug**, with processions and bull running in the plaza.

❐ Shopping

Ayacucho *p493, map p494*
Ayacucho is a good place to buy local crafts including filigree silver, which often uses mudéjar patterns. Also look out for little painted altars which show the manger scene, carvings in local alabaster, harps, or the pre-Inca tradition of carving dried gourds. The most famous goods are carpets and *retablos*. In both weaving and *retablos*, scenes of recent political strife have been added to more traditional motifs. Even the newspaper stands on the Plaza, along with the Coca Cola emblems, are painted like *retablos*. For carpets, go to **Barrio Santa Ana**, see under Sights above. See also Arts and crafts p588).
Centro Turístico Cultural San Cristóbal, Jr 28 de Julio 178. New complex with a quiet courtyard, art galleries, shops and restaurants, etc.
Familia Pizarro, Jr San Cristóbal 215, Barrio Belén. Works in textiles, masks for Carnaval and piedra de huamanga (local alabaster) and produces good quality.

Shosaku Nagase, a large new Mercado Artesanal y Centro de Capacitación, on Jr Quinua. Some of the same goods can be found in the **Mercado Carlos Vivanco** (see Sights, above).

Taller y Galería de Arte Robert Torre, Mz 0, lote 5, Urb César Mujica Cacho-Yanamilla, T066-970 7511, rotma4@hotmail.com. Sculpture, painting, see Robert's work in progress, full explanations in Spanish, public art as well as his own styles (not artesanal), works for sale.

▲▲ Activities and tours

Ayacucho *p493, map p494*
Tours to Vilcashuamán with travel agencies include Intihuatana, full day US$13, but they only run with eight passengers. Alternatively stay overnight. Trips to Huari, Quinua village and the battlefield with travel agencies, US$7.55 per person, minimum 4 people.
Urpillay Tours, Portal Independencia 62, T066-815074, urpillaytours@terra.com. All local tours and flight tickets.
Wari Tours, Portal Independencia 70, T066-811415. Local tours. Also handles Ormeño bus tickets and Western Union.
Warpa Picchu, Portal Independencia 66, T066-815191, www.warpapicchu.com. All the regular tours, but with an ecotourism angle.
Willy Tours, Jr 9 de Diciembre 107, T066-814075. Personal guide, also handles flight and bus tickets.
Orlando Román, T066-960-1982, orlandoyabish@starmedia.com. English-speaking guide, also gives Spanish classes (at La Crillonesa if you wish), reliable.

Abancay and around *p498*
Local tour prices US$32-28 per person, depending on numbers.
Hotel Turistas, see Sleeping, runs 1 and 2-day tours to Santuario Nacional de Ampay: one-day, 7 hours, US$40 per person for 1-2 people (cheaper for more people).
Karlop Andean Trek, T083-961 4297, karlop_36@hotmail.com. Guides tours to local sites, camping equipment, horse riding.
Carlos Valer, guide in Abancay – ask for him at **Hotel Turistas**, very knowledgeable and kind.

⊖ Transport

Ayacucho *p493, map p494*
Air
To **Lima**, with **Aero Cóndor**, Tue, Thu, Sun, US$83, 45 mins, also to **Andahuaylas**, 30 mins, US$82, usually Tue, but may fly more often if demand is sufficient. LC Busre daily from **Lima** (US$70). **Airline offices** Aero Cóndor, 9 de Diciembre 123, T966-813060, open daily 0900-2100. LC Busre, Jr Lima 178, T816012, but most travel agents sell tickets.

Bus
To **Lima**, 9-10 hrs on a good new paved road, via **Ica** (7 hrs). For **Pisco**, 332 km, you have to take a Ica/Lima bus and get out at San Clemente, 10 mins from Pisco, and take a bus or combi (same fare to San Clemente as for Ica). Companies include: **Wari**, Pasaje Cáceres (opposite ReyBus), US$5.15 at 1800, and **ReyBus**, Pasaje Cáceres 166, US$5.80. More expensive are **Libertadores**, Tres Máscaras 493, T066-813614, **Molina**, Jr 9 de Diciembre 458, T066-812984, 6 a day US$7.55-15.15, bus-cama at 2200, US$18.20; **Ormeño**, Jr Libertad 257, T066-812495 (ticket office at Asamblea 354), US$7.55 at 0730 and US$12 at 2030 (with video, toilet, heating, a/c), good meal stops (US$6.65 to San Clemente for Pisco); also to Ica at 2100, 7 hrs, US$7.55; **Civa**, Av Mcal Cáceres 1242, T066-819948, US$10, and **Cruz del Sur**, Av Mcal Cáceres 1264, T066-812813, US$15.15.

To **Huancayo**, 319 km, 9-10 hrs, US$6.65-7.55. Daily with Molina, 3 a day. The road is paved as far as **Huanta**, thereafter it is rough, especially in the wet season, but the views are breathtaking.

For **Huancavelica**, take an Ormeño 0730 bus as far as **Rumichaca**, US$2, where combis wait at 1030 for **Huancavelica**, 4 hrs. Otherwise take a Huancayo bas as far as **Izcuchaca**, then take another bus, a longer route.

To **Andahuaylas**, 261 km, takes 10-11 hrs (more in the rainy season), the road is unpaved but in good condition when dry. Daytime buses stop for lunch at Chumbes (4½ hrs), which has a few eateries, a shop selling fruit, bread and refrescos, and some grim toilets. **Molina** passes through from

Lima en route to Cusco at 2200, check if there is a seat; **Wari** at 0400, **ReyBus** at 1830 (not Sun), and **Los Chankas**, Pasaje Cáceres 144, T066-812391, at 0630 (good) and 1900, all US$6. Only **Los Chankas'** 1900 service is direct to **Cusco**, US$12, but you still have to change buses in Andahuaylas. To get to **Abancay**, a further 138 km, 5 hrs, you must change buses and then go on to Cusco, a further 195 km, 5 hrs. It takes 24 hrs to Cusco. There are no direct buses. Road conditions are quite good, given the terrain crossed, but landslides a common occurrence in the wet season. The scenery, though, is stunning and makes up for it.

Vilcashuamán and Vischongo *p495*
Combis to **Vilcashuamán** run from Av Ramón Castilla, daily from 0400 to 1500, 4 hrs, US$3, leave when full. From Vilcashuamán to **Vischongo** costs US$0.45. Vischongo to Ayacucho takes a little under 4 hrs, and costs US$2.70.

Huari *p496*
Combis leave from Paradero to **Huari Quinua**, below the Ovalo de la Magdalena, at the corner of Jr Ciro Alegría and Jr Salvador Cavero. They leave when full from 0700 onwards. They go to **Huari**, 40 mins, US$0.75, then on to **Quinua**, a further 25 mins (US$0.50, US$1 from Ayacucho – ask the driver to go all the way to the Obelisco for an extra 50 cents, then walk back to the town).

Huanta Valley *p496*
Combis and cars to **Huanta** leave from the same place, US$1.35. The *paradero* in Huanta is at R Castlla y Amazonas. In Huanta, **Expreso Huamanga**, Amazonas 404, and **Molina**, G Santillana at Parque Alameda, have night buses to **Lima**, US$7.55. The latter and Turismo Central, G Santillana 464, run daily to **Huancayo**, US$6.60.

North to the Río Apurímac *p497*
Combis leave from the Paradero San Francisco in Ayacucho, also below the Ovalo de la Magdalena, at the corner of Jr Ciro Alegría and Jr Salvador Cavero. They run from 0500 till late morning, 7 hrs, US$5. The road, 143 km in all, is paved to Quinua, then goes through **Tambo**.

Andahuaylas and around *p497*
Air
Aero Cóndor to **Lima**, Tue, Thu, Sun, 1 hr 10, US$83. Office Jr R Castilla 429, T083-722877.

Bus
Daily buses to **Ayacucho**, a minimum of 10 hrs, US$6; **Wari**, Av José María Arguedas opposite El Piloto petrol station, at 0800; **Los Chankas**, Av José María Arguedas y Jr Trelles, T083-722441, 0600 and 1800 or 1840, one coming from Cusco. To **Abancay**, Señor de Huanca, Av Martinelli 170, T083-721218, at 0600, 1300 and 2000 daily, 5 hrs, US$3.40; **Los Chankas** at 0630, US$3.60. To **Cusco**, San Jerónimo, Av José María Arguedas 425, T083-801767, via Abancay, 1800 or 1830, also 1900 Sun, US$6, and **Los Chankas**. To **Lima**, buses go via Ayacucho or Pampachiri and Puquio: **Wari** take the latter route, 3 a day, US$15.15. **Molina**, Av José María Arguedas y Av Lázaro Castilla, over the bridge, takes both routes to Lima, 1000 via Ayacucho, 1045 and 1600 via Pampachiri, US$15.15. Also to Abancay and Cusco at 1900. On all night buses, take a blanket.

Abancay and around *p498*
All interprovincial buses leave from the new Terminal Terrestre, on Av Pachacútec, on the west side of town. It has a restaurant, internet and phones, a cambio, toilets and shops. Taxi to centre US$0.60, otherwise it's a steep 5 blocks up Av Juan Pablo Castro to Jr Lima, another block to Jr Arequipa and cheap hotels, and one more to hotels Turistas and Imperial. Several companies have offices on or near the El Olivo roundabout at Av Díaz Bárcenas y Gamarra. Several through buses stop for lunch on Prol Av Venezuela.There are bus services from Abancay to **Cusco, Andahuaylas**, and **Nasca** on the Panamericana Sur, 464 km, via Chalhuanca and Puquío, continuing to **Lima**. All buses on the Lima-Nasca-Cusco route pass through Abancay at about midnight. The journey Abancay-**Cusco** takes 4½ hrs and costs US$3.65. The scenery en route is dramatic, especially as it descends into the Apurímac valley and climbs out again. There is a checkpoint at the Apurímac border. The road is paved and in good condition. Coming from Cusco, after the pass it takes 1 hr to zig-zag down to Abancay.

Bus companies, all leave from Terminal Terrestre; office addresses are given: **Bredde**, Gamarra 423, T083-321643, and Av Arenas 210, 5 a day to Cusco, including 0600, 1300. **Cruz del Sur**, Díaz Bárcenas 1151, T083-323028, serving the whole country. **Los Chankas**, Díaz Bárcenas 1011, El Olivo, T083-321485, to Andahuaylas and Cusco. **Molina**, Gamarra 422, T083-322646. 3 a day to Lima US$13.65-16.65, 3 a day to Cusco, to Andahuaylas at 2330, US$4.25. **San Jerónimo**, to Cusco at 2130 and Andahuaylas at 2130. **Señor de Huanca** (Av Arenas 198, T083-322377), to Andahuaylas at 0600, 1300, 2000, US$3.40. **Wari**, Díaz Bárcenas 1147, also on Av Arenas 200 block, 6 a day to Lima, also to Andahuaylas. **Huamanga** and **Civa** also have office at El Olivo, Estados Unido B-50, by Las Vegas petrol station, for Lima. Several others to Lima and Cusco.

To **Cachora** (for Choquequirao): terminal is at Jr Prado Alto, between Huancavelica and Núñez (5 blocks uphill from Díaz Bárcenas; it's not the first Jr Prado you come to). At 0500 and 1400, 2 hrs, US$1.50. Cars from the Curahuasi terminal on Av Arenas, next to the Wari office, charge US$15.

⊙ Directory

Ayacucho p493, map p494
Banks BCP, Portal Unión 28. No commission on cheques, cash advance on Visa, AmEx and Visa ATM. **Interbank**, opposite **Hotel Ayacucho**, Jr 9 de Diciembre 183, has ATM for Visa, Mastercard/Cirrus and AmEx. 0915-1315, 1630-1830, Sat 0930-1230. Many street changers and **casas de cambio** can be found at Portal Constitución Nos 2, 3 and 5 on the plaza, they offer a good rate for cash, another on same side as BCP.
Chemists Farmacia del Pino, 28 de Julio 123. **Inka Farma**, 28 de Julio 250. **Internet** All over the centre. Connections and machines are good, average price is US$0.60 per hr, some charge US$0.90 at night. All 0800-2300 daily. **Internet El Hueco**, Portal Constitución 9, inside, downstairs. Open 0700-2400, has plug-in for laptops, printers, phone cabins, even a playpen. **Post** Asamblea 293 **Telephone** Telefónica office, Asamblea 293, is administrative but phones outside and girls selling phone cards on the street. Many phone offices in the centre.
Useful addresses Tourist Police at 2 de Mayo y Arequipa.

Andahuaylas and around p497
Banks BCP, Av Perú, 6th block east of the Plaza. Multi-Red ATM on north side of Plaza. **Cambio Machi**, Jr R Castilla 371, closes 1800. Another cambio in **Pizzería Napolitana**. **Internet** J F Ramos 317, US$0.45 per hr, also has phone cabins. **FutureNet**, Constitución 445, also has phones. Many others around town, all the same price.

Abancay and around p498
Banks BCP, Jr Arequipa 218, has ATM outside, Visa and AmEx. There are several **cambios** on Jr Arequipa, opposite the Mercado Central, including **Machi**, No 202 (also at Díaz Bárcenas 105) and **Oro Verde**. **Internet** The town is full of internet places. Some, like the one on Díaz Bárcenas opposite **Hotel Turistas**, and **Conacasa**, Díaz Bárcenas 107, have phone cabins. The one at Cusco 209 has a café serving almuerzos.

East of La Oroya and La Selva Central

A paved road heads north towards Cerro de Pasco and Huánuco. A turn-off 25 km north of La Oroya branches east and drops 600 m before it reaches Tarma, which is 30 km off the Carretera Central. Beyond Tarma the road continues its steep descent. In the 80 km between Tarma and La Merced the road, passing by great overhanging cliffs, drops 2,450 m and the vegetation changes dramatically from temperate to tropical. This is a really beautiful run, leading to Peru's central jungle area which, until recently, has received scant attention compared with the Iquitos and southeastern areas. All this is about to change. ▶▶ *For Sleeping, Eating and other listings, see pages 508-513.*

Ins and outs

The main city of this region, Tarma, is easily reached by road from Lima in 6 hrs, and from Huancayo in 3 hrs. From Tarma, roads descend the eastern flanks of the Andes to the Selva Central. Tourist information is available in Tarma ① *2 de Mayo 775 on the plaza, T064-321010, turistarma@hotmail.com, Mon-Fri 0800-1300, 1600-1800.* The office is very helpful and has good displays on the walls about the surrounding area.

Tarma and around → *Colour map 3, grid C4. Altitude: 3,050 m.*

Tarma, 'the Pearl of the Andes', was founded in 1538 and is one of the oldest towns in Peru. Though this little, flat-roofed place, with plenty of trees, is now growing with garish modern buildings, it still has a lot of charm. The **Semana Santa** celebrations are spectacular, with a very colourful Easter Sunday morning procession in the main plaza. With it's beautiful surrounding countryside, the town is also notable for its locally made fine **flower-carpets**, see Festivals below. In 1999 it recorded the largest flower carpet in the world.

The **Odria Museum** ① *2 de Mayo 755, Mon-Sat 0900-1300, 1530-2100, free,* celebrates the life of Tarma's most famous son, General Manuel Odria, who became president of Peru in the 1930s. The museum contains personal memorabilia. There is a large *Artesanía* market at Lima 548.

Some 8 km from Tarma, the small hillside town of **Acobamba** has some attractive old buildings. There are festivities during May, see Festivals below. Some 2 km up beyond the town is the futuristic **Santuario de Muruhuay**, with a venerated picture painted on the rock behind the altar. Its design was inspired by Le Corbusier's work. It also has fine tapices made in San Pedro de Cajas which depict the Crucifixion. The **Grutas de Huagapo**, also known as La gruta que llora (the cave that weeps), is 4 km

Tarma

Sleeping 🛏
Albania 1
Hacienda Santa María 10
Hostal El Caporal 11
Hostal Central 3
Hostal El Dorado 4
Hostal El Márquez 2
Hostal Internacional 5
Hostal Tuchu 6
La Colmena 7

Los Portales 8
Vargas 9

Eating 🍴
Café Picaflor 1
Chifa Roberto Siu 3
Comedor Vegetariano & Salud y Vida 6
El Sabor Criollo 2
Inti Killa 8

La Grima 4
La Pastora 9
La Tarmeñita 10
Lo Mejorcito de Tarma 5
Señorial 7

Bars & clubs 🍸
Danny Disco 11
La Calesa 12
La Esquina del Recuerdo 13

from the town of **Palcamayo**, which is 15 km northwest of Acobamba. The caves can be entered for about 100 m, at which point it is up to 30 m high and 20 m wide. Guides with torches and ropes can be hired near the entrance to reach 300 m. Beyond that wet suits and simple caving gear are needed. Even without a guide you can penetrate the cave for some way with a torch. The cave is the deepest in South America and investigations, which have penetrated up to 2,800 m, suggest that the system extends over 30 km underground. There is a small but impressive gorge, **Cañón de Ushtu**, 10 minutes walk down river from the cave.

Northwest beyond Palcamayo, the road climbs steeply for 14 km to **San Pedro de Cajas**, a large village which is famed for its coloured sheep-wool weavings. The principal shops are on the central plaza and the road to Palcamayo. This road joins the one from La Oroya to Cerro de Pasco below Junín. The town holds the **Festival de La Pukcha** (Hilado) on 28-30 June. There is accommodation in the village and a couple of restaurants.

Three kilometres beyond San Pedro on the road to La Oroya is a **vicuña reserve** and co-operative, which is the best place to see vicuña at close range. The animals are accustomed to people and roam near the road. Every August they are sheared and the money from the sale of the fleece goes to the reserve.

About 8 km on the road from Tarma to Huancayo, at **Tarmatambo**, is the start of a good section of Inca road which runs 3 km to Huasqui on the Tarma-La Oroya road. There are also ruins and caves and a spectacular view of terrace farming and Tarma itself. It's 20 minutes by car from Tarma. Some 30 km from Tarma on the Huancayo road is **El Santuario Rupestre Pintish Machay**, near Huairicolca. Here is the largest site of cave paintings in Peru, some 600 pictures dating back 4,000-10,000 years.

Chanchamayo → *Colour map 3, grid B5.*

Some 73 km east of Tarma are the towns of San Ramón and La Merced, collectively known as Chanchamayo. **San Ramón** is 11 km before La Merced on the banks of the Río Tarma. It is a busy, attractive town, in the lower foothills of the Andes where the temperature is noticeably higher than in Tarma. The surrounding hills are covered in coffee plantations. **La Merced** lies in the fertile Chanchamayo Valley, famous for its citrus and coffee production. Campa Indians can usually be found around the central plaza selling bows, arrows, necklaces and trinkets. La Merced has two central **markets**, the Mercado Nuevo and the Mercado Viejo. At the latter you can usually find Campa articles, exotic herbs and jungle medicines such as uña de gato and sangre de grado. The hill behind the town can be climbed up to **La Cruz** for a wonderful view of the entire Chanchamayo Valley, or you can hire a mototaxi for US$1. There is a restaurant and small recreation area. A one-hour walk through the Quebrada de los Italianos leads to **Colombo**, where a distillery produces aguardiente. There is a **festival** in the last week of September. At holiday times prices double as the area is full of Limeños seeking tropical warmth.

East of Chanchamayo

A 123-km paved road leads to Satipo. At Km 20 the confluence of the Chanchamayo and Paucartambo rivers forms the Río Perené. The road follows the river, winding through lush jungle and Asháninka villages, where Indian artifacts are often for sale. At Km 70, an expanse of palm-thatched huts signals the outskirts of Pichinaki. A few years ago this village represented the remotest of Peruvian outposts, but its fertile lands and warm climate were ideal for coffee, bananas and citrus. Tens of thousands of Andean campesinos flocked to the region in search of jobs and land. A paved road reached the town in 1999 and it is now the commercial hub of the region. Its long sandy beaches on the Río Perené make an ideal retreat from the encircling jungle and a jumping off point to visit the waterfalls, lakes and remote Indian villages in the area. During the dry season (April-August), the town's plaza and streets are covered with drying coffee beans. At **Playa Pescadora** (El Puerto Pichinaki) are most of the good restaurants, which serve the local delicacy, doncella fish (**El Bambú** is recommended).

Beyond Pichinaki the paved road pulls away from the Río Perené and goes to the jungle town of **Satipo**, the main centre of this region. It is a noisy, semi-modern town. 1 km from town is **Isla de Fantasía** and **El Lagarto**, with restaurant, nightclub and swimming in the river.

A dirt road continues east to **Mazamari** and **Puerto Ocopa** near the confluence of the Satipo and Perené rivers. Some 10 km along this road are the **Arcoiris waterfalls**. *Colectivos* Satipo-Puerto Ocopa take two hours, US$8.50 for four. From here you can take a boat down the Río Tambo to its confluence with the Urubamba at **Atalaya**

North of Chanchamayo

The road has been extended from San Luis de Shuaro over an intervening mountain range. A turn-off east leads to **Puerto Bermúdez** on the Río Neguachi. There is an eating house opposite the airstrip. This is a great base for exploring further into the Selva Central Peruana, with trips upriver to the Asháninka community. Boat passages are possible from passing traders.

Oxapampa → *Colour map 3, grid B4. Altitude: 1,794 m.*

Oxapampa is set on a fertile plain on the Río Huancabamba, a tributary of the Ucayali, 81 km from La Merced. A third of the inhabitants are descendants of a German-Austrian community of 70 families which settled in 1859 at **Pozuzo**, 80 km downstream, and spread later to Oxapampa. There is much livestock farming and coffee is planted on land cleared by the timber trade. On 5 August the town hosts a festival, the **Virgen de Las Nieves**. The tourist office ① *Bolívar 464, 2nd floor, T063-762375, Mon-Fri 0800-1230, 1400-1700*, sells maps and guidebooks.

North of Oxapampa

On the main road to Pozuzo, at the end of Oxapampa, go to Inrena for authorization to visit the **Yanachaga Chemillén National Park** (camping is possible for US$1.50). There is good bird watching very early in the morning. The staff are extremely helpful and will give you trekking information. Some 25 km from Oxapampa is **Huancabamba**, from where it is 55 km to Pozuzo. The whole road between La Merced and Pozuzo is very rough, depending on the season. There are no less than 30 rivers to be crossed. Downstream 40 km from Pozuzo is Nuevo Pozuzo. There is no transport, it's a two-day walk. There is an interesting museum opposite the church in the town centre ① *US$0.75*. The town celebrates the **Semana Turística de Pozuzo** during the last week in July.

● Sleeping

Tarma and around *p506, map p506*
Accommodation is hard to find at Easter but you can apply to the Municipalidad for rooms with local families. Also contact the tourist information office (address above).
A **Los Portales**, Av Castilla 512, T064-321411, F321410. Out of town, with bathroom, hot water, heating, quiet, secluded, price includes breakfast, very good restaurant, but expensive.
B **Hacienda La Florida**, 6 km from Tarma, T064-341041, www.haciendalaflorida.com. 18th-century working hacienda, 12 rooms,

some furnished with antiques, with bathroom, hot water, price includes breakfast but US$5 extra for lunch and dinner, owned by German-Peruvian couple Inge and Pepe who arrange excursions. Great for kids as you can milk cows before breakfast and ride tractors. Recommended. Also camping for US$3 and new backpacker rooms under construction.
B **Hacienda Santa María**, 2 km out of town at Sacsamarca 1249, T064-321232, www.haciendasantamaria.com. A beautiful (non-working) 17th-century hacienda, has

less land than **La Florida** but beautiful gardens and antique furniture, great fireplace. Includes breakfast and light evening meal. Excellent guides will arrange local day trips for you. Recommended.

C-D El Caporal, Lima 616, T064-323636, hostalelcaporal@yahoo.es. Includes breakfast, very clean, good location, rooms with large new bathrooms, hot water, cable TV. Recommended.

D Hostal Campestre Auberge Normandie, beside the Santuario de Muruhuay, Acobamba, T064-341028, www.normandie.com.pe. 16 cabins with bath and hot water, TV, bar, restaurant, parking, fine views over the valley.

D Hostal Internacional, Dos de Mayo 307, T064-321830. With bathroom and hot water, clean. The owner is a dentist, whose practice is next to the *hostal*.

E Albania, Amazonas 534, T064-321399. Clean, small rooms with bath and hot water.

E Hostal Central, Huánuco 614, T064-310149. Shared bathroom, hot water, friendly, laundry facilities, a bit rundown but popular with gringos, has an observatory which opens Fri at 2000.

E Hostal El Márquez, Huaraz 389, T064-321060. An old building with character, with bathroom but shared shower, hot water.

E Hostal Tuchu, Dos de Mayo 561, T064-323483. Large rooms with bath, hot water in the morning, but the beds are poor.

E La Colmena, Jauja 618, T064-321157. An old building with character, even if a bit rundown, with bath, clean, convenient for Lima and Huancayo buses.

E Vargas, Dos de Mayo 627, T064-321460. With bath, hot water in morning, clean, large rooms, cable TV.

F Hostal El Dorado, Huánuco 488, T064-321598. **G** without bath, hot water, rooms set round a patio, first floor rooms better, clean.

Chanchamayo *p507*

There are many places to stay just outside San Ramón, all just off the main road toward La Merced.

B Coco's, Km 102.5 on road to La Merced, T064-337874, cocosinn@hotmail.com. Price includes breakfast. Bungalows ideal for families or groups, great garden, swimming pool, friendly staff.

B El Refugio, Ejército 490, San Ramón, T/F064-331082, www.hotelelrefugio.com.pe. Bungalows set in a beautiful tropical garden, with pool, run down but friendly staff, price includes breakfast, good value.

B Río Grande Inn, Km 97, San Ramón, T064-332193, www.riograndebungalows. com. Price includes breakfast, bungalows, swimming pool, very good service, overlooking river.

C Residencial Rey, Junín 103, La Merced, T064-531185. Same owner as Reyna, which is slightly more expensive, private bathroom, cable TV, brightly lit.

C Reyna, Palca 259, La Merced, T064-531780. Clean rooms with private bath, cable TV and, like its partner, brightly lit.

C-D El Rancho, Playa Hermosa, San Ramón, T064-331076, www.geocities. com/elrancho peru. Bungalows, which are basic, large grounds, camping possible US$6 per tent.

D Conquistador, Progreso 298, San Ramón, T064-331771, conquistador@viabcp.com. Modern, hot water, TV, parking, has a good *chifa* downstairs.

D El Parral, Uriate 355-361, San Ramón, T064-331128. Modern, with hot water, TV, clean, good restaurant serving local specialities, especially meat.

D Los Portales, Jiménez 119, La Merced, T064-531283. Hot water, with bathroom, TV, comfortable, friendly.

D-E Primavera, Arequipa 175, La Merced, T064-531433. Friendly, rooms with TV, private bathroom, hot water. Recommended.

E Chanchamayo, Progreso 291, T064-809659, hotel-chanchamayo_7@ hotmail.com. With hot water, TV, rooms without bathroom half the price.

F Hospedaje Los Víctor, Jr Tarma 373, on Plaza de Armas, La Merced, T064-809550. With bath, cold water, good, clean and friendly.

F Santa Rosa, 2 de Mayo 447, La Merced, T064-531012. With private bath, clean, cheaper than many others.

● *For an explanation of sleeping and eating price codes used in this guide, see inside the*
● *front cover. Other relevant information is found in Essentials, pages 61-66.*

D **Hostal Majestic**, on the plaza, Jr
Fundadores 408, Satipo, T064-545015. With
bathroom, electricity 1900-2300 only, noisy.

North of Chanchamayo *p508*

E **Albergue Cultural Humboldt**, by the Río
Pacitea at La Rampa, 4 mins' walk from the
centre of Puerto Bermúdez, T063-720267,
www.geocities.com/puerto_bermudez.
US$4 extra for 3 meals a day. The owner,
Basque writer Jesús, has created a real haven
for backpackers, with maps, library and book
exchange. Recommended. Jesús will arrange
tours, from day trips to camping and trekking in the primary forest. He has a good
relationship with many Asháninka communities that you can visit. Ask him about
volunteering at a local Asháninka school.

E **Hostal Pinto**, Oxapampa s/n, T063-
720212. Basic but has rooms with
own bathroom.

Oxapampa *p508*

C **D'Palma Lodge**, Prolongación Thomas
Schauss, T063-762123, depalmalodge@
hotmail.com. Price includes breakfast.
Bungalows set in a spacious area, friendly.
Permits camping at US$3 per tent.

D **Albergue Turístico Bottger**, Jr Mcal
Castilla 6th block, T063-762456, bottger
_d@yahoo.com. Very popular, in a quiet
area, serves good meals.

D **Posada Edelweiss**, Carretera Central, Lote
58-Miraflores, T063-722567, www.romaperu.
com/posada. Buffet kreakfast and lunch
included, very nice owner. Recommended.

E **Don Calucho**, San Martín 411, T063-
762109. Rooms with private bath, quiet,
pleasant, a good option.

North of Oxapampa *p508*

E **Albergue Turístico Frau Maria Egg**,
Los Colonos, Pozuzo, T01-444 9927 (Lima),
fraumariaegg@pozuzo.com. Includes
breakfast, nice garden, swimming pool.
Recommended.

E **Hostal Tirol**, includes meals. Clean.
Recommended.

🍴 Eating

Tarma and around *p506, map p506*

There are several eating places on Lima,
including a vegetarian. The *manjarblanco* of
Tarma is famous, as well as *pachamanca*,
mondongo and *picante de cuyes*. In the
central market try *cachanga*, fried bread with
cinnamon. Good places to buy local produce
such as *manjar blanco* and honey are
El Tarmenito, Lima 149, or **La Pastora**,
Arequipa 656, open since 1902.

🍴 **Café Picaflor**, Lima 306. A small place
opposite the Cathedral, good for snacks.

🍴 **Chifa Roberto Siu**, Lima 557, T064-704025.
A good option for Chinese food, popular
with locals.

🍴 **Comedor Vegetariano**, Arequipa 695.
Open 0700-2100, vegetarian, small and
cheap, sells great bread.

🍴 **El Sabor Criollo**, Huaraz 296. A pleasant
local restaurant, try *aji de gallina*, cheap
and friendly.

🍴 **Lo Mejorcito de Tarma**, Arequipa 501,
T064-321766. Open 0700-2300, offers a
good set *menú* with choices at US$1.50,
good for local specialities, popular, also has
tourist information.

🍴 **Salud y Vida**, Arequipa 677. Open
0730-2000, a small vegetarian place,
good value.

🍴 **Señorial/Pollería Braserita**, Huánuco
138-140, T064-323334. Good menú,
extensive choice, excellent *sopa criolla*,
open late.

Chanchamayo *p507*

🍴🍴 **Boris**, Tarma 376 interior, Plaza de
Armas, La Merced. Great food, very extensive
menu, and very helpful and informative
owner, Boris Rojas.

🍴🍴 **Rincón Gaucho**, Junín 234, La Merced,
T064-337966. Best place for steak,
anticuchos and other meat dishes.

🍴🍴 **Shambari-Campa**, on the Plaza de
Armas, La Merced. It has an extensive menu,
an excellent set menú at US$3, and
hundreds of interesting old photos, some
dating back to the start of the century, of
the local area cover the walls. Highly
recommended.

🍴 **Café Prisci**, Progreso 256, San Ramón.
Good for snacks, including home made
lemon pie.

🍴 **Chifa Felipe Siu**, Progreso 440, San
Ramón. One of the most popular
restaurants in town, along with **Chifa
Conquistador**, see Sleeping.

¶ Chipipizzas, Junín 234, La Merced, T064-337966. Pizzas, burgers, pasta, sandwiches. Good service and clean.

Oxapampa *p508*
¶ La Casa de Baco, Carretera Central, Miraflores Oxapampa. Typical food, good for meats.
¶ Oasis, Jr Bolognesi 120, T063-762206. This is a highly recommended restaurant.
¶ Típico Oxapampino, Plaza de Armas. Very popular, good food, nice owner.

North of Oxapampa *p508*
¶ Guten Appetit, Av los Colonos, Pozuzo. A very popular restaurant in the town.
¶ Típico Pozucino, Av Los Colonos s/n, La Colonia-Pozuzo, T063-707001. Good, cheap food, try *albondigas de carne* or potato salad.

🍸 Bars and clubs

Tarma and around *p506, map p506*
Disco El Gato Pardo, Callao 227. A smart club for a small town playing the latest Latin hits.
La Calesa, Arequipa 433. An old, quiet pub-style bar.
La Esquina del Recuerdo, Huánuco 998. Good for drinks.

⚅ Festivals and events

Tarma and around *p506, map p506*
Apart from **Semana Santa**, Tarma hosts many other festivals. **Carnaval Tarmeño** is held on **20-25 Feb**. Also taking place during Semana Santa is the **Concurso de Alfombras de Flores** (flower carpet competition). Taking place throughout **May** is Festividad Señor de Muruhuay. On **23-24 Jun** is the Circuito Turístico de Ciclismo de Montaña in Huasihuasi. **Festival de la Papa** is held on **23-27 Jun** and, on 24 Jun, the **Tayta Inti ceremony** is held in Tarmatambo. **23-29 Jul** is the Semana Turística. Fiesta de la Siembra del Maíz is on **28-30 Sep**, in Tarma as well as Acobamba (see below). **Señor de Los Milagros** processions are held on 1,18, 28 and 29 Oct. Festival del Pan Tarmeño 'La Wawa' is held on **1-2 Nov** (the same time as All Saints).

▲▲ Activities and tours   511

Tarma and around *p506, map p506*
For the local guides association, taruma84@hotmail.com, or ask at the tourist office on the main plaza. Many tour operators come and go, especially during the holidays. They offer a variety of day trips to local sites, leaving around 0930 and returning at 1800, average cost US$7. The following seem to be the most permanent:
Centro Tours, 2 de Mayo 658, T064-704038, www.turismoperucentro.8m.com.
Mega Tours, Lima 419, T064-906042, mega_turismodeaventura@hotmail.com.

Chanchamayo *p507*
There are a number of informal tour operators on the main plaza in La Merced catering to Lima weekenders; they are often closed in low season. Check on safety record if going rapelling, or other adventure sports.
Impala Tours, Jr Tarma 290, La Merced, T064-532476, gadc28@yahoo.com, also Jr Progreso 290, San Ramón. Owner Gustavo de Madariaga is very helpful. They offer a number of day trips to surrounding area, costing around US$10 pp.
Luis Cornejo Silva, Pje San Pablo 151, La Merced, T064-962 8149 (mob), luchoteguia @hotmail.com. Very reliable and helpful local guide. Fee from US$15/day.

⊖ Transport

Tarma and around *p506, map p506*
Direct buses leave daily to **Lima**, 231 km, 6 hrs, US$5.50. Transportes Chanchamayo, Callao 1002, T064-321882, is recommended as the most reliable, even though some buses are not so new, 0900, 1400 en route from Chanchamayo; **Transportes Junín**, Amazonas 667, 3 a day, with brand new *bus cama* for night bus. Transportes La Merced, Vienrich 420, 3 a day. **Trans Muruhuay**, Huaraz y Amazonas (several daily) start their journey in Tarma. There is a good lunch stop at El Tambo before La Oroya, with superb fried trout. *Colectivos* to Lima leave from Castilla y Vienrich, wait till full, US$11 per person, 4 hrs. The road is paved throughout. To **Jauja** and **Huancayo**, Transportes San Juan, buses leave from the stadium every hr departing on the ½ hr, but their buses come

from Chanchamayo; and **Trans Muruhuay**, 0500-1800 (leave when full), to **Jauja** 2 hrs, US$2. All buses continue to **Huancayo**, 3 hrs, US$3. *Colectivos* (cars) depart when full from Callao y Jauja, 2 hrs, US$4, and 3 hrs, US$6, respectively. Buses to **La Oroya** leave regularly from opposite the petrol station on Av Castilla block 2, 1 hr, US$1.25, while *colectivos* leave from the petrol station itself, 45 mins, US$2. To **Chanchamayo**, Transportes San Juan from the stadium every hr on the half ½ hr, Trans Angelitos every hr on the hr, and Empresa Junín, 3 a day direct, 1½ hrs, US$1.50 to **San Ramón**, and 2 hrs, US$1.75 to La Merced. Also, Selva Tours *colectivos*, 1¼-1½ hrs, US$3 and US$3.50 respectively. *Colectivos* and **Canary Tours** buses run from the centre of Tarma to **Acobamba** and up to **Muruhuay** every 10 mins, US$0.35. *Colectivos* for San Pedro, which pass the cave, depart from 2 de Mayo y Puno in Tarma, 40 mins, US$1. Combis, 1 hr, US$0.50, and *colectivos*, 30 mins, US$0.75, go from Paucartambo y Otero, Tarma, to **Palcamayo**, a 30-min walk down river from the cave. There are regular combis from Junín, 1 hr, US$1, while from Tarma there are fairly regular *colectivos*, 1 hr, US$1.50; also buses and *colectivos* to La Oroya.

Chanchamayo *p507*
Air Flights leave from San Ramón. There is a small airstrip where **Aero Montaña**, T064-339191, rfmamsa@hotmail.com, has air taxis that can be chartered (viaje especial) to the jungle towns, with a maximum of 3 people, but you have to pay for the pilot's return to base. Flights cost US$250 per hr. **Puerto Bermúdez** takes 33 mins. You can also just go to the air base, across the river, on the east side of town.
Bus From **San Ramón** to **Lima**, Transportes La Merced, Paucartambo y Alvariño, 5 a day, 7 hrs, US$6. To **Huánuco** Transportes León de Huánuco, Paucartambo 380, at 2200, 6-7 hrs, US$7. To **Tarma** Transportes San Juan, Progreso 105, or Trans Angelitos, hourly, 2 hrs, US$1.50, or Selva Tours *colectivos*, 1 hr, US$3.

Between San Ramón and **La Merced** there is a continuous flow of combis and *colectivos*, 15 mins, US$0.20 and US$0.30 respectively (from San Ramón market and main plaza; from Arica y Junín in La Merced).

In **La Merced**, there is a large bus station on the east side of town, from which most buses arrive and depart. To **Satipo** Transportes Lobato at 1130 and 2330, 2½ hrs, US$3. Other buses coming through from Huancayo and Lima may also have room. To **Oxapampa** Empresa Santa Rosa, every ½ hr, 3 hrs, US$3. There are also regular *colectivos*, 2 hrs, US$5. To **Pozuzo** Empresa Santa Rosa at 0430 and 0830, 6 hrs, US$4.50. The condition of the road improves after Oxapampa. To **Puerto Bermúdez** Empresa Transdife, Villarrica and Servicio Especial all have 4x4 pick-ups or minibuses and go at 0330 and 0430 (or when full). You can buy your tickets in advance at the bus terminal. Cost is minibus US$8.80; standing in the back of pick-up US$7; seat in pick-up cabin, US$10. This is not a paved road and takes around 8 hrs in the dry season. To **Lima** Expreso Satipo, Transportes Lobato, Junín, La Merced and Chanchamayo (recommended) each have several buses during the day, 8 hrs, US$6.50. To **Tarma** Transportes San Juan, hourly, 2½ hrs, US$1.75, or Selva Tours *colectivos*, just over 1 hr, US$3.50.

East of Chanchamayo *p507*
Buses from **Satipo** to **Huancayo** and **Lima** go at night, a very cold journey, US$9.50, 12 hrs, with Apóstol San Pedro (more expensive but no better), Expreso Satipo and Lobato.

North of Chanchamayo *p508*
You can either go to **La Merced** (8 hrs) or **Pucallpa** (12 hrs) by public transport.

Oxapampa *p508*
Empresa Santa Rosa, corner of Kennedy and Loaechle, T063-762582, buses and *colectivos* run to **La Merced** regularly, US$2.50, 3 hrs. Combis to **Pozuzo**, 3-5 per day, US$3, 3-4 hrs.

North of Oxapampa *p508*
Buses leave from **Lima** to **Pozuzo** with La Victoria (28 de Julio 2405, Lima) on Mon, Thu and Sat at 0800, US$12, about 16 hrs.

● Directory

Tarma and around *p506, map p506*
Banks BCP, Lima 407. Changes Amex TCs,

ATM. **Banco del Trabajo**, Lima and Jauja, also has an ATM. Various casas de cambio will change dollars and euros. **Internet** Internet offices can be found all along Av Lima or Malecón José Gálvez just off Lima. **Telephone** Telefónica, Plaza de Armas.

Chanchamayo *p507*

Banks Banco de la Nación, Ancash y Lima. **BCP**, Junín y Tarma. **Internet** There are over a dozen internet cafés in La Merced. **SoftService**, Palca 279, and **Selva net**, Junín 210, are good. Next to El Parral on Uriate, San Ramón. **Post** Progreso 402, San Ramón.

North of La Oroya and the Huallaga Valley

A paved road runs 130 km north from La Oroya to Cerro de Pasco. It runs up the Mantaro valley through narrow canyons to the wet and mournful Junín pampa at over 4,250 m, one of the world's largest high-altitude plains. An obelisk marks the battlefield at Pampas de Junín where the Peruvians under Bolívar defeated the Spaniards in 1824. Blue peaks line the pampa in a distant wall. This windswept sheet of yellow grass is bitterly cold and the only signs of life are the young herders with their sheep and llamas. The road passes the eastern shores of the Lago de Junín, which is famous for its birdlife. From Junín to Cerro de Pasco the landscape is dominated by the cultivation of maca, through the Sierra Verde project – since it was declared that this tuber has strong nutritional value demand has soared. Maca juice, cake, bread, liquor, etc, is sold from roadside stalls all around the lake. It is even claimed to have aphrodisiac properties. The Central Highway from Cerro de Pasco continues northeast another 528 km to Pucallpa, the limit of navigation for large Amazon river boats. The western part of this road (Cerro de Pasco-Huánuco) is a good paved highway. The descent along the Río Huallaga is dramatic. The road drops 2,436 m in the 100 km from Cerro de Pasco to Huánuco, and most of it is in the first 32 km. From the bleak vistas of the high ranges the road plunges below the tree line into another world of tropical beauty. ▶▶ *For Sleeping, Eating and other listings, see pages 518-520.*

Ins and outs

There are good roads all the way down to Huánuco, with bus services from the capital. There is also a road connection from the Callejón de Huaylas to Huánuco, so if you wish you stay in the Sierra, you do not have to backtrack to the coast. In Junín, the regional department of tourism may be contacted, T063-200550/51, junin@mit inci.gob.pe. **Dircetur Pasco** ① *in the San Juan district of Cerro de Pasco, T063-722275, pasco@mincetur.gob.pe.* In Huánuco ① *Gen Prado 716, on the Plaza de Armas, T062-512980.* Regional tourism department, huanuco@mincetur.gob.pe. A website giving local information is www.webhuanuco.com.

Junín and Chacamarca → *Colour map 3, grid B4. Altitude 4,135 m.*

The town of Junín lies some distance south of Lago de Junín and has the somewhat desolate feel of a high puna town, bisected by the railway. Although small, it is typical of the lifestyle of the Peruvian Andes, with 16th-century architecture, strong local traditions and distinctive cuisine. It is a good starting point for seeing Andean wildlife and as such is becoming increasingly popular with birdwatchers and photographers. The town has two plazas, one old, one new, called La Libertad. In the latter is a small underground museum with memorabilia from the battle. There is a large handicrafts centre at the southern entrance to the town. The municipality is a few blocks from Plaza La Libertad and just behind is the Inrena, where you can buy tickets for the Sanctuary of Chacamarca and the National Reserve of Junín. Staff are very friendly.

Three kilometres south of Junín the **Chacamarca Historical Sanctuary** covers 2,500 ha and includes the site of one of the most important battles of independence, fought in 1824, with a large obelisk at its centre, an interesting underground museum and the remains of the pre-Inca citadel of Chacamarca. The wildlife of the high puna includes vicuña and foxes and there are springs at Yaropuquio. A taxi from the main street will cost you US$1.50-2.

Lago Junín National Reserve

ⓘ *US$5, ticket from Inrena in Junín.*

Peru's largest lake after Titicaca, 30 km by 14 km, it protects one of the best birdwatching sites in the central Andes, where all the highland waterbirds and raptors may be seen. The surrounding fields abound with sierra-finches and ground-tyrants. Giant coot and even flamingos may be seen and, if you are really lucky, you can spot the diademed sandpiper, and white-bellied cinclodes. Note that the *zambullidor de Junín*, Junin grebe, is in danger of extinction but can still be found here. About 131 different species of birds can be found on the lake, 20 percent of which depend entirely on the lake's specific conditions for survival. Birdwatchers should sail around the lake and local fishermen are usually around to take visitors out.

There are several ways to get to the lake. The easiest is from the village of Huayre, 5 km south of Carhuamayo on the east side, from which it is a 20-minute walk down to the lake. Carhuamayo is the best place to stay near the lake, 50 minutes north of Junín. Nearby are Lago Shalipaico, the Minahuaraco fortress and Chuyroc caves. Another good viewing point is close to the village of Ondores on the west side of the lake; no paved roads here. Nearby are the interesting caves of Pachamachay with prehistoric paintings and El Mirador de Canoc lookout point. Beyond Ondores is San Pedro de Pari. On the way you can stop to see some outstanding geological formations, ancient paintings on the rocks, the church of San Pedro and the Mirador de Comac Punta, with breathtaking views.

Cerro de Pasco → *Colour map 3, grid B4. Altitude: 4,330 m. 130 km from La Oroya by road.*

This long-established mining centre is is 8 km, 10 minutes, off the Carretera Central, between Lago Patarcocha and the huge abyss of the mine above which its buildings and streets cling precariously. Not surprisingly for a place that claims to be the highest city in the world, nights are bitterly cold. Cerro de Pasco is famous as the site of one of the battles of the War of Independence, on 6 December 1820, when local hero, Antonio Alvarez de Arenales, defeated Diego de O'Reilly's royalist troops. The actual battlefield is 1 km away, on Cerro Uliachin. Although Cerro de Pasco is not an attractive place, nevertheless the old corrugated iron buildings have a certain charm and it is very friendly. The deep canyon of Goyllarisquisga, the 'place where a star fell', 42 km north of Cerro de Pasco, is the highest coal mine in the world.

Huayllay

Forty kilometres southwest of Cerro de Pasco is Huayllay. Nearby is the **Santuario Nacional de Huayllay**, commonly called **Bosque de Piedras** ⓘ *US$1, payable only if the guides Ernesto and Christian are there.* It has unique weathered limestone formations in the shape of a tortoise, elephant, alpaca, etc. At the Sanctuary (4,100-4,600 m), four tourist circuits through the spectacular rock formations have been laid out. They pass archeological remains and rock paintings, springs and beautiful high Andean landscapes. This is another great place for birdwatching. Visits are recommended between April and August although nights become bitterly cold. Camping is permitted within the Sanctuary. The village of Huallay, is 20 minutes beyond the sanctuary entrance.

Also near Huallay are the ruins of an Inca community centre, **Bon Bón Marca**, which marks the course of a good section of Inca road, and the thermal springs of

Calera ① *10 mins beyond the sanctuary entrance, 0700-2200, US$0.75 per person.* The new individual baths, which can take up to four people, are the cleanest. Take a swimsuit; the baths are very hot and clean, ideal for a splash after a tiring day.

Yanahuanca Valley → *Colour map 3, grid B4.*

Some 65 km northwest of Cerro de Pasco is **Yanahuanca**, in the beautiful valley of the same name. Nearby are good **hot baths**. From the village you can reach one of the longest surviving stretches of Inca road. Two kilometres up the Yanahuanca Valley a lesser valley cuts northwards between the towering crags. The road, its paving uneven and disturbed by countless horse and donkey convoys, leads up the smaller valley, its course sometimes shared by a stream, to the village of **Huarautambo**, about 4 km away. This village is surrounded by many pre-Inca remains. For more than 150 km the Capaq Ñan (the **Royal Inca road**) is not only in almost continuous existence from the Yanahuanca Valley but is actually shown on the map issued by the Instituto Geográfico Militar. The clearest stretch ends at Huari in Ancash (see under La Unión page 517 below).

Huánuco → *Colour map 3, grid B4. Altitude: 1,894 m.*

Huánuco is an attractive Andean town with an interesting market on the Upper Huallaga. The city was founded in 1539, by Gómez de Alvarado, and is one of the

Huánuco

Sleeping	Imperial 6	La Casona 3
Caribe 1	Las Vegas 7	La Casona de Gladys 4
Cusco 2	Mariño 8	La Olla de Barro 5
El Roble 3	Quintito 9	La Tullpa 8
Gran Hotel Huánuco 4		Pizzería Don Sancho 6
Hostal Beijing 10	**Eating**	Vegetariano 7
Hostal Lima 11	Chifa Men Ji 1	
Hostal Miraflores 5	Govinda 2	

0 metres 100
0 yards 100

oldest in Peru and was originally known as 'Los Caballeros de León de Huánuco'. Its most famous son is Leoncio Prado, who refused to surrender to the Chileans at the Battle of Huamachuco in 1882 and is commemorated all over the city. There is a large main plaza fringed by enormous ficus trees, which are much more attractive than the modern cathedral. There is a natural history museum called **Museo** de **Ciencias** ① *Gen Prado 495, Mon-Fri 0900-1200, 1500-1800, Sat-Sun 1000-1200, US$0.50*. It claims to have 10,000 exhibits of fauna from Peru's three regions, plus a good collection of shells and minerals. Many of the displays have multiple language signs.

Tomaykichwa ① *0800-1800, US$0.25*, 25 km south of Huánuco, on the edge of the Huallaga valley, is a small attractive village set among the sugar cane plantations, which once supplied a substantial local aguardiente industry. It is famous as the birthplace of 'La Perricholi'. As an 18-year-old actress she rose to become the mistress of the 62-year old Viceroy de Amat and the centre of Lima society at the end of the 18th century. However, when he returned to Spain a few years later and remarried, she retreated to spend the rest of her days in a convent. Her small, recently restored, ancestral home can be visited in the village. It contains furniture and other artefacts from the 18th and 19th centuries and copies of documents relating to her life. To reach Tomaykichwa take the Ambo *colectivo* that passes by Santo Domingo church, 20 minutes, US$0.25.

West of Huánuco

Five kilometres from Huánuco on the road west to La Unión at an altitude of 1,912 m is **Kótosh** ① *US$0.75, including a guide (in Spanish) around a marked circuit which also passes through a small botanical garden of desert plants*. The Temple of Crossed Hands, the earliest evidence of a complex society and of pottery in Peru, dates from 2000 BC. Investigations suggest that the site was occupied for over 2,000 years. Six distinct phases of occupation have been identified the oldest of which dates back 4,000 years. It is said to be the 'oldest temple in the Americas'. There are three main temple buildings, some of which have been partly reconstructed, though the original 'crossed hands' sculpture is now in the Archaeology Museum in Lima. The site has a new access bridge, is in good condition and has a small museum which gives clear explanations of Kótosh. The site can only easily be reached by taxi, US$5 from the city centre, including a 30-minute wait.

Tantamayo and around → *Colour map 3, grid B3. Altitude: 3,600 m.*

Tantamayo 50 km beyond the turn off to La Unión is a farming village surrounded by pre-Columbian ruins from the **Yarowillca** culture. **Japallan** is perhaps the most scenically sited, guarding the entrance to the valley leading from the spectacular Marañón canyon. To get there, cross the river from Tantamayo and walk west to San Pedro de Pariarca. At the start of the village take the path to the right to Pariash (Upper Pariarca), and head for the ruins silhouetted on a ridge.

The ruins of **Selinin** are just above Pariash. The most elaborate ruins are **Piruru** and **Susupillu**. Piruru was occupied continuously for 1,700 years, from 3000 BC as a ceremonial, and later ceramics, centre. Both sites have high-rise stone dwellings. To reach Susupillu head northeast through the tiny village of La Florida. There are other ruins further afield.

All the above mentioned ruins are visible from Tantamayo and can be reached on foot in about three to four hours; guides are available to visit the sites. The walks to the ruins are arduous; take warm clothing, a hat and suntan lotion. The scenery is stunning. Pictures and information on the sites are available from Huánuco post office. In Tantamayo there are four basic hotels and one restaurant, Ortega, on the corner of the plaza. For details of transport, see under Huánuco page 519.

From Huánuco, a spectacular but very poor dirt road, impassable at times in the wet
season, leads all the way to La Unión, capital of Dos de Mayo district (137 km). From
Huánuco it climbs out of the Higueras Valley to **La Corona del Inca** (the 'Crown of the
Inca'), also known as Lacsahuarina, meaning 'Two Princesses' in Quechua. This
distinctive rock formation is at the pass before the descent into the upper canyon of
the Río Marañón. The route then follows the Marañón to its confluence with the Río
Vizcarra. La Unión is a very friendly, fast-developing town which straddles the Río
Vizcarra. Electricity can be a problem and it gets very cold at night. There are good **hot
baths** at Tauripampa, 5 km up the Vizcarra valley, US$0.50 per person. A good section
of the **Royal Inca Road**, just upriver from the baths on the north side of the valley, runs
on towards Huari.

Huánuco Viejo
① *US$1.50; a local farmer may be available to act as a guide (US$1).*
On the pampa above La Unión are the Inca ruins of Huánuco Viejo, a great
temple-fortress with residential quarters, 2½ hours' walk from the town. To get there,
take the very steep path starting behind the market and climb towards the cross,
which is at the edge of a plateau (this takes one hour). Continue straight through the
village on the wide path. Note that, though the locals are friendly, some of their dogs
are not always well disposed to strangers. The views of the pampa, surrounded on all
sides by mountains, are beautiful. Seemingly at the foot of a mountain, in front and to
your right, is a silvery metallic roof of a little chapel, behind which are the ruins, 4 km
from the plateau's edge.

Huánuco Viejo was a major Inca settlement on the royal highway from Cusco to
Quito. The site has examples of very fine Inca stonework comparable with anything to
be seen in Cusco. This includes an usnu, measuring 30 m by 50 m and 4 m high,
encased with superb stone blocks and carved monkeys adorning the entrance and at
one corner. An usnu was a ceremonial or judging platform, though its exact function is
still uncertain. The usnu is surrounded by a huge central plaza, 547 m by 370 m,
which, possibly, had to accommodate huge herds of animals. On the east side of the
plaza are two kallankas (barracks), 84 m and 75 m long, nearly 10 m wide and
two-storeys high, with thatched roofs. Running from the kallankas down to the royal
Inca quarters and Inca bath are a series of six fine stone gateways adorned with
beautifully carved pumas. A fine Inca road runs south from the site to the town of
Baños. Illa Tupac used the site as his stronghold from which he mounted resistance
against the Spanish from 1536 until at least 1542. The site was then largely forgotten
by the outside world and left untouched until the mid-20th century.

Allow at least one hour to visit the main part of the site and at least two hours for
the whole site, which covers over 2 sq km and contains the remains of over 3,500
structures. You should take warm clothing and be prepared for some violent
thunderstorms. A major festival, **Fiesta del Sol**, is held at the site on 27 July each year,
but lodgings in the town are almost impossible to find at this time.

La Unión to Huaraz → *Colour map 3, grid B3. It's best to travel this route by day.*
It is possible to get to the **Callejón de Huaylas** from here. Take a *colectivo* to **Huallanca**
and from there take El Rápido bus to Huaraz via **Chiquián** (see page 329). La
Unión-Huallanca is a good dirt road, following the attractive and, in places, very
narrow Vizcarra gorge for most of the journey. Thereafter paving starts in Huansala, all
the way to Huaraz. Often known as Huallanca (Huánuco) to distinguish it from the
settlement of the same name in the Cañon del Pato, this is an attractive, unspoilt
small town set between four hills in the Vizcarra valley. Large-scale mining projects in
the area are likely to bring rapid change to the town and are polluting the Río Vizcarra.

You can hike to the Cordillera Raura (see page 362) from **Laguna Lauricocha**. To reach the lake from La Unión take a camioneta to **Baños,** then take another camioneta from there to **Antacolpa.** It's half a day's walk to the lake from here. In 1959, caves were discovered by the lake with 9,500-year-old human remains and some paintings. This is where the Río Marañón rises, eventually becoming the Ucayali and then Amazon rivers, before spilling into the Atlantic Ocean, 5,800 km away to the east.

● Sleeping

Junín and Chacamarca *p513*
G **Hostal Leo**, on Plaza La Libertad. The best of several small, basic *hostales* on the plaza, very clean, hot water, nice rooms.
Gianmarco, Maravillas 454, and **Patricia**, Tarapacá 862, are the best of several basic *hostales* in Carhuamayo.

Cerro de Pasco *p514*
D **Señorial**, in the district of San Juan where there are also some other good *hostales*, 5 mins north of Cerro by taxi, T063-721026, hotelsenorial@hotmail.com. The most comfortable hotel in Cerro with hot water, TV, and a fine view back across the mine pit.
D **Wong**, Carrión 99, T063-721515. Modern, hot water 24 hrs, TV, clean, comfortable, attractive decorations.
E **Hostal Arenales**, Jr Arenales 162, near the bus station, T063-723088. Clean, modern, TV, friendly, hot water in the morning. Good.
E **Welcome**, Av La Plata 125, T063-721883, opposite the entrance to the bus station. Some rooms without window, hot water 24 hrs, clean, friendly.

Huánuco *p515, map p515*
B **Gran Hotel Huánuco**, Damaso Beraun 775, T062-514222, hotel.huanuco@terra.com.pe. Restaurant, pool, sauna, gym, parking. Recommended.
D **Hostal Caribe**, Huánuco 546, T062-513645. Large modern hotel with big rooms, bathroom, TV. **Hostal Mariño** is next door.
D **Hostal Quintito**, 2 de Mayo 987, T062-512691. Another large modern hotel.
E **Hostal Beijing**, Abtao 770, close to Plaza de Armas. A small place, but very clean, TV, hot water. Recommended.
E **Hostal Lima**, Av. 28 de Julio 922, on the Plaza de Armas. TV, hot water and private bathrooms, clean.
E **Las Vegas**, 28 de Julio 936, on Plaza de Armas, T/F062-512315. Small rooms, hot water, TV. Restaurant next door. Good.

E **Hostal Miraflores**, Valdizan 564. Hot water, clean, TV, quiet.
F **El Roble**, Constitución 629, T062-512515. Without bath, clean, good value.
F **Imperial**, Huánuco 581, T062-513203. With cold shower (intermittent water), reasonable value, clean and quiet.

La Unión *p517*
E-F **Hostal Gran Abilia Alvarado**, Comercio 1196, has a once-grand reception area and a nice garden, rooms are small but clean, some have private bathrooms. Breakfast extra before 0700; good restaurant. Helpful owners provide some information about visiting Huánuco Viejo.

La Unión to Huaraz *p517*
D **Hotel Milán**, 28 de Julio 107, Huallanca (Huánuco). Modern, TV and hot water in all rooms, best in town. The restaurant in Hotel Milán is good and serves trout caught in lakes high above the town.
F **Hostal Yesica**, L Prado 507, Huallanca (Huánuco). Hot water, shared bathroom, the best of the basic ones.

● Eating

Junín and Chacamarca *p513*
There are numerous restaurants along the main road in Carhuamayo. The best is **Savoy**. You can also find locals selling *pachamanca*, fried frogs' legs and maca products.
♥ **San Ignacio de Loyola**, on the corner of Plaza La Libertad. Perhaps the best place to try as most restaurants are unreliable.
♥ **El Escorpion**, reasonable.

Cerro de Pasco *p514*
Local specialities are trout, fried frog, *ferro-carril* (which is known elsewhere as *bistec a lo pobre*), and maca, the tuber, see p513.
♥ **Los Angeles**, Jr Libertad, near the market. Serves an excellent menú for US$1.50.

¶ **San Fernando** bakery in the plaza. First-rate hot chocolate, bread and pastries.
¶ **Tito's**, on the Plaza de Armas. The best place in Cerro for chicken.

Huánuco *p515, map p515*
¶¶ **La Casona**, Ayacucho 750, overlooking Plaza Santo Domingo. Specializes in *anticuchos* and steaks. Recommended.
¶ **Chifa Men Ji**, 28 de Julio, block 8. Good prices, nice Chinese food, clean.
¶ **Govinda**, 2 de Mayo 1044. Reckoned to be the best vegetarian in town.
¶ **La Olla de Barro**, Gral Prado 852, close to main plaza. Serves typical food, good value.
¶ **La Tullpa**, Gral Prado 819. Regional food. Recommended.
¶ **Pizzería Don Sancho**, Prado 645. For the best pizzas in town.

La Unión *p517*
¶ **Chifa Khon Wa**, 2 de Mayo 611. The best Chinese in town serving of authentic chifa.
¶ **Vizcarra**, beside the old bridge over the river. The best of the local restaurants.

La Unión to Huaraz
¶ **El Norteño**, Comercio 441, Huallanca (Huánuco). Apart from the Hotel Millán, this is a popular place to eat.

🕴 Bars and clubs

Huánuco *p515, map p515*
El Alambique, Damaso Beraun 635. Very nice place to drink cocktails and natural juices. Recommended.
Trapiche, Gral Prado 691. Café bar serving good regional drinks, nice music.
Cheers, 2 de Mayo 1201. Neon-bright and cheaply chic.

❋ Festivals and events

Cerro de Pasco *p514*
Festival de La Chonguinada Cerreña takes place during the first week in **May**. In **May or Jun** is Semana Turística de Huarica. On **5 Aug** is the Virgen de Las Nieves. In the last week of **Nov** is Semana Turística de Pasco.

Huánuco *p515, map p515*
On the **20-25 Jan** is the Carnaval Huanuqueño. On **21 Mar** is the Festival de

las Cataratas. In San Rafael, in the province of Ambo, is the festival of **El Señor de Chacos** on **1 May**. On **3 May** is La Cruz de Mayo, in Huánuco. On **16 Jul**, the Fiesta de la Virgen del Carmen. The Festival de la Perricholi is held during the last week of **Jul**. **12-18 Aug** is Tourist Week in Huánuco. **15 Aug** commemorates the founding of the city. **25-27 Sep** is the Festival del Cóndor Pasa. **28-29 Oct** is Fiesta del Rey y del Señor de Burgos, the patron of Huánuco. **25 Dec**, Fiesta de los Negritos.

⊖ Transport

Junín *p513*
To **Carhuamayo** taxi *colectivos* charge US$ 1.50 from Junín. From Carhuamayo to **Cerro de Pasco** is 40 min, *colectivos* charge US$1.50.
Taxi Junín-**Ondores** US$0.90-1.50 for a 30-min ride. To **San Pedro de Pari**, US$1.50.

Cerro de Pasco *p514*
All services use the large, enclosed bus station. To **Lima** there are several companies including **Carhuamayo** and **Transportes Apóstol San Pedro**, hourly 0800-1200, plus 4 departures 2030-2130, 8 hrs, US$4-5. If there are no convenient daytime buses, you could change buses in La Oroya. To **Carhuamayo, Junín** and **La Oroya**: buses leave when full, about every 20-30 mines, to Carhuamayo 1 hr, US$1; to Junín 1½ hrs, US$1; to La Oroya, 2½ hrs, US$2. *Colectivos* (cars) also depart with a similar frequency to all places, 1½ hrs, US$2.50, to La Oroya. To **Tarma** Empresa Junín at 0600 and 1500, 3 hrs, $2.50. *Colectivos* hourly, 1½ hrs, US$4. To **Huancayo**, various companies leave throughout the day, 5 hrs, US$4. To **Oyón** Transportes Javier, 1230, 5 hrs, US$3.50; and there is also a bus to the mine at Raura, 1100, 7 hrs, US$5. To **Yanahuanca** Transportes Javier, 0500, 1230, 1445, 3 hrs, US$2. To Huánuco buses and cars leave when full, about half hourly, 2½ hrs and 1½ hrs, US$2 and US$4 respectively.

Huayllay *p514*
Minibuses to Huayllay from Cerro de Pasco's terminal leave throughout the day, about 1 hr, US$1. They return until 1800-1900. Taxis run to the Calera thermal baths from Cerro throughout the day,

US$1.50, 45 mins, or pick-up a Huayllay combi, US$1.20, just over 1 hr.

Yanahuanca Valley *p515*
To Yanahuanca from Cerro de Pasco, US$2 by taxi, 45 mins.

Huánuco *p515, map p515*
Air
Airport T062-513066. From **Lima**, **Aerocóndor** (2 de Mayo 1253, T517090) Tue, Thu, Sat, 50 mins, US$70. There are connecting flights to **Tingo María**, **Tocache**, **Juanjui**, **Pucallpa**, **Saposoa** and other jungle towns. Check all flight details in advance. Flights may be cancelled in the rains or if not full.

Bus
Buses to **Lima**: US$9, 8 hrs. **León de Huánuco**, Malecón Alomía Robles 821, 1000, 2030, 2130. Also **Intertrans**, Crespo Castillo 690, 2100, **Bahía Continental**, Valdizan 718, 2100, 2200, recommended, **Etposa**, Valdizan block 7, and **Transportes El Rey**, 28 de Julio 1215 (28 de Julio 1192, La Victoria, Lima). The majority of buses of all companies leave in the evening, 2030-2200, most also offer a bus at 0900-1000. A *colectivo* to Lima, costing US$20, leaves at 0400, arriving at 1400; book the night before at Gen Prado 607, 1 block from the plaza. Recommended. Buses to **Cerro de Pasco**, take 3 hrs, US$2, *colectivos* take less than 2 hrs, US$4. All leave when full from the roundabout, Ovalo Carhuayna, on the north side of the city, 3 km from the centre. To **Huancayo**, 6 hrs, US$5: **Turismo Central**, Tarapacá 530, at 2130. Trans Rey at 2215 from depot on 28 de Julio, US$5.70, 7 hrs.
Colectivos run to **Tingo María**, from block 1 of Prado close to Puente Calicanto, 2½ hrs, US$5. Also **Etnasa**, 3-4 hrs, US2. For **Pucallpa**, take a *colectivo* to Tingo María, then a bus from there. This route has many checkpoints and robberies can occur. You are advised to travel by day and check on the current situation regarding safety.
To **La Unión** Transportes El Niño, Aguilar 530, is a *colectivo* service, departs when full, 5 hrs, US$7.15. This is a rough road operated by old buses of which **Transportes Santa Peregrina**, Tarapacá 448, and **Transportes Rosario**, Tarapacá 400 block, 0730, 6 hrs,

US$5.70, are the more reliable. To **Tantamayo** Turismo Bella, San Martín 571, at 0630 and 0730, operate old buses on this rough route, but are recommend by locals, 8 hrs, US$6. Also **Chasqui**, Mayro 572. To **Baños** Transportes Legionario, Independencia 656, run buses and truck-buses on alternate days, 0830, or Transportes Romancero, Tarapacá 500 block, 0900, 4 hrs, US$3.50.

La Unión *p517*
To **Huánuco**: Transportes El Niño *colectivo* service from Jr Comercio 12, T062-515952; **Transportes Santa Peregrina** and **Rosario** buses leave at 0630, prices and journey times above (there is an afternoon bus on Fri only). To **Tantamayo**: several combis and buses daily, 5-6 hrs, US$4. However, it may be easier to take a combi first to Tingo Chico at the Vizcarra/ Marañón confluence, 1 hr, US$0.75, and then wait for the more frequent bus services from Huánuco to Tantamayo.
To **Huallanca (Huánuco)**: combis leave from the market, about half hourly, when full and follow the attractive Vizcarra valley, 1 hr, US$0.75. Combis leave when full about half hourly, from the corner of Comercio y 28 de Julio in Huallanca for La Unión.

Huánuco Viejo *p517*
Combis run from La Unión, about hourly, to El Cruce from where it is a 30-min walk to the site. The last combi down leaves El Cruce at 1800.

❶ Directory

Cerro de Pasco *p514*
Banks BCP is on Jr Bolognesi. Money changers can be found on Jr Bolognesi between the market and the Cathedral.

Huánuco *p515, map p515*
Banks BCP, at Dos de Mayo 1005. **Casa de cambio** at Gral Prado 635. **Internet** Next to the Cathedral on the Plaza. Many on Jr 2 de Mayo, 3 blocks southwest of the Plaza. **Laundry** D Beraún 530. Reasonable prices. **Post** 2 de Mayo on the Plaza. 0800-2000 Mon-Sat, 0800-1400 Sun. **Telephone** Telefónica del Perú, 28 de Julio 1170.

Footprint features

Introduction

The immense Amazon Basin covers a staggering 4,000,000 square kilometres, an area roughly equivalent to three quarters the size of the United States. But despite the fact that 60 per cent of Peru is covered by this green carpet of jungle, less than 6 per cent of its population lives here, meaning that much of Peru's rainforest is still intact. The Peruvian jungles are home to a diversity of life unequalled anywhere on Earth. It is this great diversity which makes the Amazon Basin a paradise for nature lovers. The area is home to 10,000,000 living species, including 2,000 species of fish and 300 mammals. It also has over 10 per cent of the world's 8,600 bird species and, together with the adjacent Andean foothills, 4,000 butterfly species. This incredible biological diversity, however, brings with it an acute ecological fragility. Ecologists consider the Amazon rainforest to be the lungs of the earth – producing 20 per cent of the Earth's oxygen – and any fundamental change could have disastrous effects for our future on this planet.

The two major tourist areas in the Peruvian Amazon Basin are the northern and southern jungles. They share many charac-teristics, but the main difference is that the northern tourist area is based on the River Amazon itself; at its centre is Iquitos. Although it has lost its rubber-boom dynamism, the city is still at the heart of life on the river. There are jungle lodges upstream and down, none more than half a day away by fast boat. To get right into the wilds from here, head for Peru's largest national reserve, Pacaya-Samiria. In the south the Manu Biosphere Reserve and Tambopata National are also far removed from the modern world. Most of Manu, is in fact off limits to tourists, but where access is possible, there are unparalleled opportunities for wildlife spotting. Many lodges in the area are close to the river port of Puerto Maldonado and include local communities as part of the jungle experience.

★ Don't miss...

1 **Pacaya-Samiria** The wildlife of endless waterways and wetlands is the latest jungle hotspot for nature tourism, page 526.

2 **Iquitos** Amid the buzz of a thousand motorcycle taxis, look at the Iron House, or any other old mansion, and try to imagine the days of the rubber barons, when this city was closer to Paris than Lima, page 528.

3 **Canopy walkway** Watch the bird and animal life in the forest canopy at first, or last light from the highest possible level, page 536.

4 **Jungle lodges** Your days will be filled with brand new sights, smells, sounds and things to touch (with care!), thanks to the sharpness of your guide and boatman's eye, pages 533 and 552.

5 **Manu** Make an early start to visit a collpa (macaw lick) to see the multitude of macaws and parrots getting their essential minerals, page 545.

6 **Tambopata** Take your patience to an ox-bow lake and hope to see giant river otters, page 551.

Northern Jungle

From the heights of the Andes down to the Amazonian lowlands a road runs to the second city of this region of Peru, Pucallpa. It passes through the Huallaga Valley, not the safest part of the country owing to the narcotics trade, but if you stick to the main route you should be OK. From Pucallpa and Yurimaguas, further north, you can venture into the jungle and if you want to continue beyond, the only way is to spend several days in a boat, getting to know the rivers and their traffic.

Standing on the banks of the Amazon itself is the city of Iquitos, made famous during the rubber boom of the late 19th century and now the main tourist attraction in this part of the country, and still retains something of a frontier feel. For jungle visits there are many lodges to choose from and two fine protectd areas, Pacaya-Samiria and Allpahuayo-Mishana. ▸▸ *For Sleeping, Eating and other listings, see pages 533-543.*

Tingo María to Iquitos

The overland route from the Central Andes to Pucallpa runs from Huánuco east to Tingo María on a paved road, and gives the first views of the vast green carpet of jungle. Beyond Huánuco the road begins a sharp climb to the heights of Carpish (3,023 m). A descent of 58 km brings it to the Huallaga river again; it then continues along the river to Tingo María. Landslides along this section are frequent and construction work causes delays. This route is periodically disrupted by violence related to drug growing and trafficking. Robberies also occur and it is advisable to travel only by day. Seek local advice.

Tingo María → *Phone code: 062. Colour map 3, grid A4. Altitude: 655 m.*

Tingo María is on the middle Huallaga, in the Ceja de Montaña, or edge (literally, eyebrow) of the mountains. The meeting here of Sierra and Selva makes the landscape striking. Bananas, sugar cane, cocoa, rubber, tea and coffee are grown. The main crop of the area, though, is coca, grown on the *chacras* (smallholdings) in the countryside, and sold legitimately (and otherwise) in Tingo María. These crops are able to thrive in the tropical climate, with an annual rainfall of 2,642 mm. In the height of the rainy season the town can be isolated for days. The altitude, however, prevents the climate from being oppressive: the maximum temperature is 34ºC, minimum 18ºC, with a relative humidity of 77.5 per cent.

There are some worthwhile attractions around the town. On a rough road, 6½ km from Tingo, is a fascinating cave, the **Cueva de las Lechuzas** ① *US$0.90*. Take a motorcycle-taxi from town, US$1.75, then pay US$0.45 for the ferry to cross the Río Monzón just before the cave. Take a torch, and do not wear open shoes. The cave can be reached by boat when the river is high. There are many oilbirds in the cave and parakeets near the entrance. The cave is in the 18,000-ha **Parque Nacional de Tingo María**,① *US$1.75*, the second national park created in Peru. A mototaxi to the entrance costs US$0.60.

The small gorge known as **Cueva de las Pavas**, is 1 km from Tingo. Here is **El Velo de las Ninfas**, a magnificent waterfall set in beautiful jungle with lagoons where you can swim. Ten kilometres away, on the Huánuco road, are the **Cuevas de Tambillo**, with beautiful waterfalls and pools for swimming.

Closer to town, is a small university just beyond the **Hotel Madera Verde**, which has a little **museum-cum-zoo**. The entrance is free but a small tip would help. It has animals native to the area. The university also has botanical gardens in the town.

North to Yurimaguas → *Colour map 1, grid C5.*

The Río Huallaga winds northwards for 930 km from its source to the confluence with the Marañón. The Upper Huallaga flows fast and furiously, but by the time it becomes the Lower Huallaga it moves slowly through a flat landscape. The main port of the Lower Huallaga, Yurimaguas, is below the last rapids and only 150 m above the Atlantic Ocean, yet distant from that ocean by over a month's voyage. Between the Upper and Lower lies the Middle Huallaga: that third of the river which is downstream from Tingo María and upstream from Yurimaguas.

The valleys, ridges and plateaux have been compared with Kenya, but the area is so isolated that less than 100,000 people now live where a million might flourish. The southern part of the Middle Huallaga centres upon Tingo María. Down-river, beyond Bellavista, the orientation is towards **Yurimaguas**, which is connected by road with the Pacific coast, via Tarapoto and Moyobamba, see page 471.

Tingo María

Sleeping 🛏
Hostal Central **1**
Hostal Cusco **2**
Hostal Marco
Antonio **3**
Madera Verde **4**
Nueva York **5**
Viena **6**

Eating 🍴
El Antojito **4**
Girasol **1**
La Cabaña **3**
Marco Antonio **2**

At **Tulumayo**, soon after leaving Tingo María, a road runs north down the Huallaga past **La Morada**, successfully colonized by people from Lima's slums, to **Aucayacu**, which has a couple of poor hotels, and **Tocache**, which also has a couple of hotels, plus an airport. The road has been pushed north from Tocache to join another built south from Tarapoto and has now been joined at Tarapoto to the Olmos-Bagua-Yurimaguas Transandean Highway to the coast at Chiclayo. The road is paved to 20 km past Aucayacu, thereafter it is gravel.

Yurimaguas → *Colour map 1, grid B5.*
Population: 25,700.

Although Yurimaguas has great tourism potential, it still remains pretty much off the tourist trail. The town has a fine church of the Passionist Fathers, based on the Cathedral of Burgos, in Spain. A colourful market is held from 0600- 0800, full of fruit and animals. There are some interesting excursions in the area too, including to the gorge of **Shanusi** and the lakes of **Mushuyacu** and **Sanango**. Tours can also be made to meet people in the region, to the villages of **Balsapuerto** (70 km west) and **Puerto Libre**.

The Yurimaguas region was affected by guerrilla activity and anti-narcotics operations in the recent past. Seek the latest advice before going off the beaten track. Tourist information is available from the Consejo Regional building on the main plaza.

Lagunas → *Colour map 1, grid B6*
The river journey to Iquitos can be broken at Lagunas, 12 hours from Yurimaguas.

0 metres   100
0 yards   100

Map labels: To Pucallpa; Jr Chiclayo; Av Tito Jaime; Jr Pucallpa; Av Alameda Perú; To 4; Jr Lamas; Plaza de Armas; Río Huallaga; Av Antonio Raimondi; Jr José Pratto; Malecón Lima; Jr Monzón; Jr Cayumba; Colectivos to Huánuco & Pucallpa; Jr Callao; To Airport, Monzón & Cueva de Lechuzas; Av Enrique Pimentel; To 4 University & Huánuco

The Amazon Basin Northern Jungle

Androgynous Amazonians

The Amazon is the longest river in the world. It rises high up in the Andes as the Marañón, then joins the Ucuyali and winds it way east to disgorge itself finally into the Atlantic, over 6,000 km from its source. At its mouth, the Amazon is 300 km wide.

This mighty waterway was so named by the Spaniard Francisco de Orellana, during his epic voyage in 1542, owing to an encounter with a hostile, long-haired indigenous group which he took to be the fearsome women warriors of Greek legend.

You can ask the local people to take you on a canoe trip into the jungle where there's a good chance of seeing caiman (alligators), monkeys and a variety of birds, but only on trips of four days or so. There are also good jungle trips from Lagunas to the Pacaya-Samiria Reserve.

Pacaya-Samiria Reserve

① *Reserve office in Iquitos, Ricardo Palma 113, 4to piso, T065-232980, Mon-Fri 0800-1300, 1500-1800, has general information and an up to date list of tour operators. You must go here to obtain proof of payment for the park entry fee (US$33), payment itself must be made at Banco de la Nación.*

Pacaya-Samiria Reserve, at 2,080,000 ha, is the country's largest such protected area. It is bounded by the rivers Marañón and Ucuyali – and a tributary of it, the Canal de Puinahua – narrowing to their confluence near the town of **Nauta**. The reserve's waterways, lakes and swamps provide habitat for mammals such as the manatee, tapir, river dolphins and giant river otters, black caiman, boas and the charapa (yellow-headed river turtle), 193 species of fish and some 330 bird species. Many of the animals found here are in danger of extinction. Trips are mostly on the river, sleeping in hammocks, and include fishing. Iquitos operators enter through Nauta to Yarina where there is a shelter, also through Requena. Another entry point is the village of **Maipuco**, 18-20 hours from Yurimaguas.

To make the most of the park, stay for a minimum of five days.

The main part of the reserve is off-limits to tourists, who may only be taken to forest surrounding the reserve. Some guides, however, penetrate Pacaya-Samiria illegally: if caught, you may face stiff penalties for trespassing. You must make sure that your tour will not do anything that will endanger the wildlife in the reserve. Above all, do not join a tour that involves living off the land. When arranging a guide and boat from Lagunas, make sure you take enough fuel for the boat. Take bottled water, or purifier, and mosquito repellent.

Tingo María to Pucallpa → *Colour map 3, grid A4/5.*

From Tingo María to the end of the road at Pucallpa is 255 km, with a climb over the watershed – the Cordillera Azul – between the Huallaga and Ucuyali rivers. The road is in poor shape for most of the journey, but paving around Aguaytía and of the last stretch to Pucallpa is in progress. It is affected by mud and landslides in the rainy season. Apart from it being insecure, another reason not to travel this road at night is that you will miss the tremendous views as you go from the high jungle to the Amazon Basin. Sit on the right side of the bus to appreciate the landscape and the hairpin bends and sheer drops. When the road was being surveyed it was thought that the lowest pass over the Cordillera Azul was over 3,650 m high, but an old document

 Pucallpa is notable for defying the traditional rules of Spanish pronunciation – the double 'l' is pronounced as one.

stating that a Father Abad had found a pass through these mountains in 1757 was rediscovered, and the road now goes through the pass of Father Abad, a gigantic gap 4-km long and 2,000 m deep. At the top of the pass is a Peruvian Customs house; the jungle land to the east is a free zone. Concrete stairs and metal handrails have been built for viewing the waterfalls. Coming down from the pass the road bed is along the floor of a magnificent canyon, the **Boquerón Abad**. It is a beautiful trip through luxuriant jungle and ferns and sheer walls of bare rock punctuated by occasional waterfalls plunging into the roaring torrent below. East of the foot of the pass the road goes over the flat pampa, with few bends, to the village of **Aguaytía**. Here you'll find a narcotics police outpost, gasoline, accommodation, see Sleeping page 533, and two restaurants. Nearby is the 20-m high **Velo de la Novia** waterfall, in a beautiful setting. From Aguaytía the road continues for 161 km to Pucallpa – five hours by bus. There is a gas station three hours before Pucallpa.

Pucallpa → *Phone code: 061. Colour map 3, grid B5. Population: 400,000.*

The capital of the Department of Ucayali is a rapidly expanding jungle town on the Río Ucayali, navigable by vessels of 3,000 tons from Iquitos, 533 nautical miles away. The town's newer sections have paved streets, sewers and lights, but much of the frontier atmosphere still exists. The climate is tropical. The dry season is during June to October when it's hot and dusty. The rainy seasons are October to November and February to March and the town is muddy through to May.

There is narcotics activity in the area. The city itself is safe enough to visit, but don't travel at night. The tourist office is the **Dirección Regional de Turismo** ① *Jr 2 de*

Pucallpa

Sleeping ⬤
Barbtur 2
Hostal Arequipa 3
Hostal Komby 4
Hostal Sun 5
Mercedes 6
Sol del Oriente 7

Eating ⬤
El Alamo 1

Bars & clubs ⬤
Billy's Place 2

0 metres 100
0 yards 100

Mayo 111, T061-571303, ucayali@mincetur.gob.pe, Mon-Fri 0730-1300, 1330-1515. Information is also be available at **Consejo Transitorio de Administración Regional** (CTAR-Ucayali) ① *Raymondi 220, T061-575018, oppto-ucayali@pres.gob.pe.*

Museo Regional ① *Jr Inmaculada 999, 0800-1200 and 1600-1800, US$0.90,* has some good examples of Shibipo ceramics, as well as some delightful pickled snakes and other reptiles. You will probably want to take a taxi or mototaxi to visit it. **Usko Ayar Amazonian School of Painting**, in the house of artist Pablo Amaringo, a former *vegetalista* (healer), is at Jr LM Sánchez Cerro 465-467, Pucallpa, www.egallery.com/coll/amazon.php. The school provides art classes for local people and is financially dependent upon selling their art. The internationally renowned school welcomes overseas visitors for short or long stays to study painting and learn Spanish and/or teach English with Peruvian students. The painting is oriented around the Amazonian cultures, in particular the healing and hallucinogenic effects of ayahuasca. For more information see the book, *Wizard of the Upper Amazon.*

The floating ports of **La Hoyada** and **Puerto Italia** are about 5 km away and worth a visit to see the canoe traffic and open-air markets. Both are reached by dirt roads. When river levels are low, boats leave from a different port, **Pucallpillo**, five minutes from the centre. The economy of the area includes sawmills, plywood factories, a paper mill, oil refinery, fishing and boat building; timber is trucked out to the highlands and the coast. Large discoveries of oil and gas are being explored, and gold mining is underway nearby. **Ganso Azul oilfield** has a 75-km pipeline to the Pucallpa refinery.

Lake Yarinacocha

The main tourist attraction of the area, especially with Peruvians, is the picturesque Lake Yarinacocha, where you can see river dolphins. On the lake are the **Hospital Amazónico Albert Schweitzer**, which serves the local Indians, and **Summer School of Linguistics** for the study of Indian languages (callers by appointment only). A good place to swim is at **San José**; take the road out behind the power station round the lake beyond the Summer School of Linguistics. Certain sections of Lake Yarinacocha have been designated as a reserve. The beautifully located **Jardín Botánico Chullachaqui** can be reached by boat from Puerto Callao to Pueblo Nueva Luz de Fátima. It's a 45-minute trip, then an hour's walk to the garden, entry is free. For information about traditional medicine contact Mateo Arevalomayna ① *San Francisco de Yarinacocha, T061-573152,* or ask at Moroti-Shobo, president of the group Ametra, an organization which is working to re-establish the use of traditional remedies.

San Francisco and **Santa Clara** can be visited at the far end of the lake on its western arm. Both are Shibipo villages still practising traditional ceramic and textile crafts. A canal near Santa Clara links Lake Yarinacocha with the Río Ucayali. There are a few other villages nearby, such as **Nuevo Destino** and **Santa Marta**, which are within an hour's walk. The Shibipo people are very kind and friendly and a visit is recommended. To reach these villages take one of the motorized canoes, or peke-pekes, which leave from Puerto Callao when full, US$0.90.

You can take a *colectivo* from Pucallpa south to **Zungaro** (US$4.50), where a 30-minute boat ride can be taken to Puerto Inca on the Río Pachitea, about 120 km north by air from Puerto Bermúdez (see page 508), or by road on the Carretera Marginal. It is a gold-rush town, expanding quickly.

Iquitos → *Phone code: 065. Colour map 2, grid B4. Population: 600,000.*

Capital of the Department of Loreto and chief town of Peru's jungle region, Iquitos is some 800 km downstream from Pucallpa and 3,646 km from the mouth of the Amazon. It is an urban oasis, completely isolated except by air and river, and while retaining something of a frontier feel, it is a pleasant tropical city. It's active, friendly and generally safe. The central area is always busy with traders' shops up and down the streets leading north and south. It may seem, too, that Iquitos is attempting a new world record for the highest concentration of motorcycles in a built-up area. As a result of the motorcycle noise, the city suffers from collective hearing loss and televisions and music are played at top volume, making the din even worse.

Ins and outs

Getting there Francisco Secada Vigneta airport is in the southwest, T065-260147. There are several ports in Iquitos, but the main one for all long-haul service in large vessels is Masusa, 2 km north of the centre. The rise and fall of the river is such that the islands off Iquitos are constantly moving.

Getting around Iquitos is well spread out. Hotels are dotted about all over the place. The best way to get around is by motorcycle taxi.

Tourist information i perú ① *Napo 232 on Plaza de Armas, T065-236144, iperu iquitos@promperu.gob.pe, 0830-1930 daily; also at the airport 0800-1300 and 1600-2000 daily*. Both iperu offices are knowledgeable and helpful. If arriving by air, go first to this desk. They will give you a list of clean hotels, a map, tell you about the touts outside the airport etc. Municipal tourist office ① *Napo 236, T065-235621, www.munimaynas.com, Mon-Fri 0700-1445*, has local information. All three tourist offices speak some English. The local paper is *La Región*, www.diariolaregion.com.

Background

Founded in 1757 as the mission settlement of San Pablo de los Napeanos by the Jesuits, this became in 1864 the first port of note on the great river. Rapid growth followed the Rubber Boom of the late 19th century, though the city's new-found wealth was short lived. By the second decade of the twentieth century the rubber industry had left for the more competitive Oriental suppliers. Remnants of the boom period can still be seen in the fine houses decorated with Portuguese tiles lending an air of faded beauty to the river embankment. The main economic activities are logging, commerce and pertoleum. It is also the main starting point for tourists wishing to explore Peru's northern jungle.

Sights

The incongruous **Casa de Fierro** (Iron House) ① *Plaza de Armas at Próspero y Putumayo*, was designed by Eiffel for the Paris exhibition of 1889. It is said that the house was transported from Paris by a local rubber baron and is constructed entirely of iron trusses and sheets, bolted together and painted silver. It now houses a restaurant upstairs. Also on the plaza, is the **Casa de Fitzcarrald** or **de Barro** (Clay House) ① *Napo 200-12*. Built entirely of adobe, with wooden balconies, this warehouse predates the rubber boom, but the famous *cauchero*, Carlos Fermín Fitzcarrald, used it as his house and office in the early years of the 20th century. This is now a *Cuaracao* appliance store; descendants of Fitzcaraldo still live upstairs. Werner Herzog's film Fitzcarraldo is a cause célèbre in the town. Next door to the tourist office on the plaza is a **Museo Municipal** ① *Napo 224, T065-234272, Mon-Fri 0700-1445, free*, with stuffed animals and wood carvings of local native peoples.

Also worth seeing is the old **Hotel Palace** ① *on the corner of Malecón Tarapacá and Putumayo*, now the army barracks. Of special interest are the older buildings, faced with *azulejos* (glazed tiles). Many are along the Malecón. They date from the rubber boom of 1890-1912, when the rubber barons imported the tiles from Portugal and Italy and ironwork from England to embellish their homes. **Museo Amazónico** ① *on the corner of Malecón Tarapacá and C Morona, Mon-Fri 0830-1200, 1530-1800, free*, is housed in the renovated Prefetura palace. It has a lovely carved wooden ceiling. Amazon art and scuplutres of local native peoples are on display. The malecón has been refurbished and is a nice place for a stroll, with great views around sunset.

Belén, the picturesque, friendly waterfront district, is lively, but not safe at night. Most of its huts were built on rafts to cope with the river's 10-m change of level during the year: it begins to rise in January and is highest from May to July. Now, the cabins are built on wooden or concrete stilts (floating houses can still be seen below the north end of Malecón Maldonado). The main plaza has a bandstand designed by Alexandre Gustave Eiffel. In the high water season canoes can be hired on the waterfront to visit Belén for US$3 an hour. The market at the end of the Malecón is well worth visiting, though you should get there before 0900 to see it in full swing. On Pasaje Paquito, one of its side streets, vendors sell local medicinal herbs and potions.

Iquitos

Sleeping
Acosta 1
Amazonas 2
Anaconda 3
El Dorado 4

El Dorado Plaza 5
El Sitio 6
Europa 7
Hostal Alfert 22
Hostal Ambassador 10
Hostal Tacna 15
Internacional 16
Isabel 17
Jhuliana 18
Marañón 8

Posada de Lobo 9
Royal Inn 11
Victoria Regia 20

Eating
Ari's Burger, Heladería
 & Pollón 1
Chifa Long Fung 2
El Nuevo Mesón 3
Fitzcarrald 5

Huasaí 10
La Gran Maloca 6
La Vida es Salud 11
Montecarlo 8
Paulina 1
Yellow Rose of Texas 12

Bars & clubs
Arandú 13
Teatro Café Amauta 14

:: Rubber barons

The conquest and colonization of the vast Amazon basin was consolidated by the end of the 19th century with the invention of the process of vulcanizing rubber. Many and varied uses were found for this new product and demand was such that the jungle began to be populated by numerous European and North American immigrants who came to invest their money in rubber.

The rubber tree grew wild in the Amazon but the indigenous peoples were the only ones who knew the forests and could find this coveted tree. The exporting companies set up business in the rapidly expanding cities along the Amazon, such as Iquitos. They sent their 'slave-hunters' out into the surrounding jungle to find the native labour needed to collect the valuable rubber resin. These natives were completely enslaved, their living conditions were intolerable and they perished in their thousands, which led to the extinction of many indigenous groups.

One particularly notable figure from the rubber boom was Fitzcarrald, son of an immigrant Englishman who lived on the Peruvian coast. He was accused of spying during the 1879 war between Peru and Chile and fled to the Amazon where he lived for many years among the natives.

Thanks to Fitzcarrald, the isthmus between the basin of the Ucayali river and that of the Madre de Dios river was discovered. Before this, no natural form of communication was known between the two rivers. The first steamships to go up the Madre de Dios were carried by thousands of natives across the 8-km stretch of land which separated the two basins. Fitzcarrald died at the age of 36 , one of the region's richest men, when the ship on which he was travelling sank.

The Rubber Barons lived in the new Amazonian cities and travelled around in luxurious boats which plied the great river. Every imaginable luxury was imported for their use: latest Parisian fashions for the women; finest foreign liqueurs for the men; even the best musical shows were brought over from the Old World. But this period of economic boom came to a sudden end in 1912 when rubber grown in the French and British colonies in Asia and Africa began to compete on the world market.

Excursions

Allpahuayo-Mishana Reserve ⓘ *Instituto de Investigaciones de la Amazonía Peruana (IIAP), Av Quiñones on the way to the airport, T065-265515*. Some 22 km south of Iquitos by road or 2-3 hours by boat from Bellavista, this reserve protects the largest concentration of white sand jungle (*varillales*) in Peru. Part of the Napo eco- region, biodiversity here is among the highest in the Amazon basin. It has several endangered species including two primates, several endemic species; the area is rich in birds.

There is a beach at **Bellavista**, a suburb of Iquitos, which is safe for swimming and very popular at weekends in summer. Boats can be hired from here to see the meeting of the Nanay and Amazon rivers, and to visit beaches and villages en route. There are lots of food stalls selling typical local dishes. Take a bus from Jr Próspero to 'Bellavista Nanay'. It takes around 15 minutes and costs US$0.40.

Boats leave Iquitos for the village of **Indiana**. A road leads from Indiana to the village of Mazán through the secondary jungle. It's about a two-hour walk or a US$0.80 mototaxi ride. If the hotel in Indiana is full, ask at the mission or municipality for a tent for the night. From Indiana you can do several hikes of between two and four hours to little villages along the Napo River.

Some 4 km south of the city, **Lake Quistococha** is beautifully situated in lush jungle, with a fish hatchery at the lakeside. On the lake, **Parque Zoológico de Quistococha** ① *0900-1700, US$1.30*, gives an example of the local wildlife, though conditions are squalid (big cats in tiny cages, and so on). At the entrance are pictures and texts of local legends, which are interesting. The ticket office will supply a map of the lake and environs. There's a good two-hour walk through the surrounding jungle on a clearly marked trail. See particularly the paiche, a huge Amazonian fish whose steaks (*paiche a la loretana*) you can eat in Iquitos' restaurants. There are also bars and restaurants on the lakeside and a small beach. Boats are for hire on the lake and swimming is safe but the sandflies are vicious, so take insect repellent.

On the road to Quistococha is the turn-off to the village of **Santo Tomás**. Take a left turn just before the airport, and then another left 300 m further on. Then it's about another 4 km to the village. There are restaurants open on Sunday and dugout canoes can be hired daily. The village hosts a *fiesta* on 22-25 September. Trucks go there, taking passengers.

Pilpintuhuasi Butterfly Farm ① *near the village of Padre Cocha, T065-232665, www.amazonanimalorphanage.org, Tue-Sun 0900-1600, US$5*. As well as butterflies, it also has a small well-kept zoo, Austrian-Peruvian run. It is a 20-minute walk from Padre Cocha to the butterfly farm.

Iquitos to the Brazilian/Colombian border

→ *Colour map 2, grid B5/6.*

The village of **Pebas**, on the north bank, is three hours from Iquitos. **Pituayac**, a part of Pebas, is a military area. One of the greatest of Peru's abstract painters, Francisco Grippa, lives in Pebas. His house overlooks the river and you can stay there if you are interested in his work and art in general. Anyone in town will tell you where he lives. If you want to see his paintings, but don't want to stop in Pebas, there are several on display in the **Hotel El Dorado** in Iquitos.

San Pablo, a further three hours downstream, is a refuelling stop, where children swim next to the jetty. You can buy crackers and drinks during the five-minute halt; the boat will wait for you. After another hour you reach **Chimbote**, where there is a police and customs point. Your passport will be stamped and your bags checked. Food can be bought, but it's not that hygienic.

Caballococha, 45 minutes from Chimbote, is the kind of town you always imagined when reading the books of García Márquez: lost in the jungle and in time, hot, humid and nostalgic. It is built on a small arm of the river, surrounded by lush, green, tropical vegetation.

Between Caballococha and Santa Rosa, the journey is beautiful, taking about two hours. To your left are rolling green hills of Colombia's Amacayacu National Park. The Iquitos-Tabatinga *rápidos* usually take the narrow, southern arm of the river, which does not give views of Colombia, so ask before you buy your ticket which route it will take. Otherwise you must take a Leticia-Caballococha boat.

Santa Rosa is the small Peruvian military base across the river from **Leticia** (Colombia) and **Tabatinga** (Brazil), in the region known as the 'tri-border'. It is the only place with a good beach, so it gets busy at weekends. It only has one very basic *hostal* next to the jetty and the large, pleasant café on the waterfront only sells refrescos, no water of coffee. There are no money changers.

Crossing the border

The border is open 24 hours a day. When leaving Peru, check procedures in Iquitos first at Immigration (see below) or with the Capitanía at the port. Travelling by *rápido*, you get your exit stamp at the police station in Santa Rosa in front of the jetty. After across the river (five minutes).

If you go to Brazil or Colombia from Santa Rosa, you will need a Peruvian exit stamp, which means that you will need an entry and exit stamp from either Colombia or Brazil if you want to re-enter Peru. There is an immigration office in the port of Tabatinga. Your best bet is to take a taxi and ask the driver to take you to the Polícia Federal, whose office is on the main road, some 2 km from the port. The process is very straightforward; Brazilian immigration is friendly and there is always somebody who speaks English. If you intend to stay in the border region, choose Brazilian immigration formalities over Colombian, which take more time, with more questions asked. All immigration services are free of charge. Once you have a Brazilian or Colombian entry stamp, you can move freely between Leticia and Tabatinga as there is no border between the two (for example, if you have a Brazilian entry stamp, you can stay in any hotel in Leticia – no questions asked). Nobody will check your passport if you just walk or drive (if you take a boat – for which there is no need – between Tabatinga and Leticia, the Colombians may give you a hard time). US citizens have to have a Brazilian visa. Those who don't have one should enter via Colombia. If you go to any other destination in Brazil, you will have to get a Brazilian entry stamp. The same goes for Colombia. Peruvian immigration will give you a 30-day entry stamp in Santa Rosa. The officer is friendly and he will usually ask if you need more days.

● Sleeping

Tingo María *p524, map p525*
Hotels are often fully booked.
B Madera Verde, Av Universitaria s/n, a way out of Tingo María on the road to Huánuco, near the University, T/F062-561800, maverde@ terra.com.pe. Several chalets set in beautiful surroundings, with and without bathroom, restaurant, swimming pool.
D Hospedaje Agroturístico Villa Jennifer, Km 3.4 Carretera a Castillo Grande, 10 mins from Tingo María, T062-960 3509, www. villajennifer.es.vg. This Danish-Peruvian owned hotel offers breakfast in the price, weekend packages and tours to local sites, restaurant, laundry service. Rooms are surrounded by local flora, with lots of birdlife.
E Hostal Marco Antonio, Jr Monzón 364, T062-562201. Quiet, restaurant of the same name next door.
E Nueva York, Av Alameda Perú 553, T062-562406. With bath and TV, cheaper without, hot water, restaurant, laundry, good value.
F Hostal Central, Av Tito Jaime 440. Central, as the names suggests, OK.
F Viena, Jr Lamas. With bathroom, good value, clean.
G Hostal Cusco, Raimondi 671. Basic, but very cheap.

Yurimaguas *p525*
E Hostal Residencial El Naranjo, Arica 318, T065-351560, lillian@olva.com. pe. Best in town, excellent value, friendly, clean, with good restaurant. Recommended.
E Leo's Palace, Plaza de Armas 104-6. Good, friendly, reasonably priced, restaurant.

Lagunas *p525*
F Hostal La Sombra, Jr Vásquez 1121. Shared bathroom, basic, friendly, good food.

Pucallpa *p527, map p527*
AL Sol del Oriente, Av San Martín 552, T061-575154, www.dhperu.net/eng/ pucallpa.html. Price includes breakfast and taxes. With bathroom, pool and good restaurant. The hotel also has a mini zoo.
A Divina Montaña, 14 km outside Pucallpa on the road to Tingo María, T061-571276. Bungalows for rent, restaurant, swimming pool, sports facilities.
D Hostal Arequipa, Jr Progreso 573, T061-571348. With bathroom but no a/c, good, comfortable rooms with safe, cable TV, clean, restaurant, friendly staff.
D Mercedes, Raimondi 601, T061-575120. Good, but noisy with good bar and restaurant attached, swimming pool.
E Barbtur, Raimondi 670, T061-572532.

With bathroom, **F** without, friendly, clean, good beds.

E Hostal Komby, Ucayali 360, T061-571184. Comfortable, pool, excellent value.

E Hostal Sun, Ucayali 380, next to Komby. With bathroom, cheaper without, clean, good value.

Lake Yarinacocha *p528*

B La Cabaña Lodge, T061-616679. Prices include all meals and transport to and from Yarinacocha harbour, run by Ruth and Leroy from the USA, great food, jungle trips from US$50 per day including boat, guide and food.

B-C La Perla, next door to La Cabaña Lodge. Price (per person) includes all meals, German-Peruvian owned, English and German spoken, no electricity after 2100, good, jungle tours organized.

C Jana Shobo Amazonian Lodge, T061-596943, www.janashobo.tk. Owned by the Ugarte family, this small lodge is set in 10 ha of forest on the lakeshore. Price includes meals and airport transfer, packages and tours available. Camping possible,living room, reading room and kitchen.

D-E Los Delfines, T061-571129. Rooms with bathroom, fan, fridge, some with TV, clean.

F Casa Artesanal Shibipo, San Francisco. A good place to spend the night, in the house of Alberto Sánchez Ríos, which is very friendly and warmly recommended.

F El Pescador, Puerto Callao. The cheapest place in town, friendly, restaurant, 20 rooms and an extension.

G Don José's Alojamiento, Puerto Inca. Clean, safe, laundry, big rooms. Recommended.

Iquitos *p528, map p530*

Around Peruvian Independence Day (27 and 28 Jul) and Easter, Iquitos can get crowded and excursion facilities overloaded. Prices rise at this time. At all times, hotels are more expensive than the rest of the country, but discounts of 20% or more can be negotiated in the low season (Jan-Apr). Taxi drivers and touts at the airport are paid comission by some hotels, insist on being taken where you want to go.

L El Dorado Plaza, Napo 258 on main plaza, T065-222555, www.eldoradoplazahotel.com. 5 star, very good accommodation and restaurant, excellent service, friendly, bar, internet access, prices include service charge, breakfast, welcome drink and transfer to/from airport. The hotel offers special 3-day/2-night packages from Lima in conjunction with some of the Amazon lodges. Recommended.

A El Dorado, Napo 362, T065-232574, dorado@eldoradoplazahotel.com. Same ownership as El Dorado Plaza, pool (open to restaurant users), cable TV, bar and restaurant, prices include service and airport transfer. Highly recommended.

A Victoria Regia, Ricardo Palma 252, T065-231983, F232499. Regarded as the second best in the city. Price includes breakfast and airport transfer, a/c, fridge, cable TV, free map of city, safe deposit boxes in rooms, good restaurant and pool. Has own internet next door. Recommended.

B Acosta, Calvo de Araujo y Huallaga, T065-235974, www.hotelacosta.com. Price includes breakfast and airport transfer, a/c, fridge, cable TV, safety deposit boxes, good restaurant.

B Amazonas, Plaza de Armas, Arica 108, T065-242431. Modern, a/c, phone, fridge bar, TV.

B Europa, Prospero 494, T065-231123, rcpowerv@terra.com.pe. A/c, cable TV, phone and fridge in every room, pleasant café/bar, good views from 5th floor.

B Jhuliana, Putumayo 521, T/F065-233154. Includes tax and breakfast, friendly, nice pool, restaurant. Recommended.

B La Posada de Lobo, Pantoja 417 with Yavari, T065-236140, www.laposada delobo.com. A/c, hot water, TV, fridge, swimming pool, jacuzzi, gym, laundry, email service, price includes breakfast, relaxed atmosphere, pleasant and good value.

C Anaconda, Arica 427, T065-232519, anacondah@terra.com. Price includes breakfast, a/c, hot water, new in 2003.

C Hostal Ambassador, Pevas 260, T065-233110, www.paseosamazonicos.com. Includes breakfast, a/c, transport to and from airport, member of Peruvian Youth Hostel

● *For an explanation of sleeping and eating price codes used in this guide, see inside the*
● *front cover. Other relevant information is found in Essentials, pages 61-66.*

Association, cafeteria, owns **Sinchicuy Lodge**. Recommended.

C Internacional, Próspero 835, T/F065-234684. A/c, with bathroom, cable TV, fridge, phone, friendly, secure, medium-priced restaurant, good value. Recommended.

C Marañón, Nauta 285, T065-242673, wwww.hotelmaranon.cjb.net. Includes breakfast and airport transfers, small pool, a/c, frigobar, hot water, comfortable. Recommended.

C Royal Inn, Aguirre 793, T065-224244, royalinn_casinohotel@terra.com. Includes breakfast, a/c, frigobar, hot water, bidet, new in 2004, modern and comfortable.

D Hospedaje Yacuruna, Pevas 225, T065-223801, yacurunalodge@hotmail.com. A small place with private bath, cold water and fan.

E El Sitio, Ricardo Palma 545 (no sign), T065-234932. With bathroom, very clean, fan, good value. Highly recommended.

E Hospedaje Mi Selvita, Av Quiñonez Km 3.5, Pasaje Roma No 14, T065-260165, raxafe@operamail.com. A charming small *hostal* in lovely gardens, run by Aydee Ríos Cárdenas, who is a travel agent (she speaks some English). Near the airport, clean, simple rooms with cool shower, fan, TV, meals.

E Hostal Alfert, García Sanz 01, T065-234105. Hard beds, check fan before you need it, friendly, good views to the river, safe but in the market area, arranges jungle trips, but not an authorized operator.

F Hostal Tacna, Tacna 516, T065-230714. With fan, basic but clean, rooms at front with balcony are noisy, don't leave valuables.

F Isabel, Brasil 164, T065-234901. In 1910 building, with bathroom, basic, clean, but plug the holes in the walls, secure, often full.

Jungle lodges

Lodges close to Iquitos are less likely to have as great a variety of wildlife as those further away. See Activities and tours below for general hints on booking tours. Note especially the advice on checking credentials.

Amazon Lodge and Safaris, Av La Marina 592A, T065-251078, www.theamazon lodges.com. 48 km down-river from Iquitos. Friendly and comfortable; 3 days/2 nights, US$200 per person for 2-4 people, US$50 per person for additional nights.

Amazon Yarapa River Lodge, Av La Marina 124, T065-993 1172, www.yarapariverlodge. com. On the Río Yarapa, a tributary of the Amazon, in a pristine location, the lodge has a field laboratory in conjunction with Cornell University. It uses ecofriendly resources, local materials and works with nearby villages. Flexible and responsible.

Amazon Wilderness Expeditions, Jr Putumayo 163, altos 202, T065-234565. Good tours to Emerald Forest Camp, on Río Yanayacu, 185 km from Iquitos, US$65 per day. Comfortable, simple accommodation (no shower – wash in river), clean, good food. Ask for guide JuanCarlos Palomino Berndt, T065-993 5472 (mob).

Blue Morpho Tours, Moore 144, T065-961 9801 (mob), in USA T831-425 7437, www.bluemorphotours.com. A rustic camp on the Río Aucayacu, a tributary of the Ucayali 300 km south of Iquitos, shamanism tours, US run, US$80 per person per day, all inclusive except for bar and snacks.

Cumaceba Lodge and Expeditions, Putumayo 184 in the Iron House, T/F065-232229, www.cumaceba.com. Tours of 2-8 days to their lodges on the Amazon and Yarapa rivers, good birdwatching guides, 3 days/2 nights for US$120 per person. Very good all round.

Explorama Tours, by the riverside docks on Av La Marina 340, PO Box 446, T065-253301, www.explorama.com, are highly recommended as the most efficient and, with over 40 years in existence, certainly the biggest and most established. Their sites are: **Ceiba Tops**, 40 km (1½ hrs) from Iquitos, is a resort providing 'an adventure in luxury', 75 a/c rooms with electricity, hot showers, pool with hydromassage and beautiful gardens. The food is good and, as in all Explorama's properties, is served communally. There are attractive walks and other excursions, a recommended jungle experience for those who want their creature comforts, US$200 per person for 1 night/2 days, US$98 for each additional night (1-2 people).

Explorama Lodge at Yanamono, 80 km from Iquitos, 2½ hrs from Iquitos, has palm-thatched accommodation with separate bathroom and shower facilities connected by covered walkways, cold water, no electricity, good food and service.

US$285 for 3 days/2 nights and US$85 for each additional day (1-2 people).

Explornapo Lodge at Llachapa on the Sucusai creek (a tributary of the Napo), is in the same style as **Explorama Lodge**, but is further away from Iquitos, 160 km (4 hrs), and is set in 105,000 ha of primary rainforest, so is better for seeing wildlife, US$395 for 3 days/2 nights. Nearby is the impressive canopy walkway 35 m above the forest floor and 500 m long, 'a magnificent experience and not to be missed'. It is associated with the **Amazon Center for Tropical Studies** (ACTS), a scientific station, only 10 mins from the canopy walkway. **Explor Tambos**, 2 hrs from Explornapo, offer more primitive accommodation, 8 shelters for 16 campers, bathing in the river, offers the best chance to see rare fauna. Close to Explornapo is the ReNuPeRu medicinal plant garden, run by a curandero. Members of South American Explorers are offered 15% discount.

Heliconia Lodge, Ricardo Palma 242, T065-231959, www.amazonriverexpeditions. com. On the Río Amazonas, 1½ hrs from Iquitos, the lodge has hot water, electricity for 3 hrs a day, good guiding and staff; rustic yet comfortable, 3 days/2 nights US$180. Under same management as Zungarococha, see below, and in same group as Hotels Victoria Regia and Acosta, see above. They oraganize trips to Allpahuayo-Mishana, to Pacaya-Samiria with Amazon Tours and Cruises, see Activities and tours, below, and to the ACTS canopy walkway.

Loving Light, Putumayo 128, T065-243180, in USA 7016 248th Avenue NE, Redmond, WA98053, T425-836 9431, www.jungle lodge.com. Near San Juan village on the Yanayacu tributary which branches off the Amazon 3 hrs upriver from Iquitos. Prices for 3-day, 2-night packages for 2 people US$315 per person, including boat transfer, all meals, guides, transfers in Iquitos. Ayahuasca ceremony is US$25 extra.

Muyuna Amazon Lodge, Putumayo 163, T065-242858, 993 4424 (mob), www.muyu na.com. 120 km from Iquitos, also on the Yanayacu, before San Juan village. Packages from 1 to 5 nights available, 2 nights/3 days US$300, but users of this Handbook should make reservations in person for discounted price (similarly SAE members, 10%). Everything is included in the price. Good

guides, accommodation, food and service, very well organized and professional, flexible, radio contact, will collect passengers from airport if requested in advance. They offer a 7-day birdwatching trip, combining several areas including Allpahuayo-Mishana Reserve; also have a new underwater microphone for listening to dolphins. Highly recommended.

Paseos Amazónicos Ambassador, Pevas 246, T/F065-231618, operates the **Amazonas Sinchicuy Lodge**, US$70 per person per night. The lodge is 1½ hrs from Iquitos on the Sinchicuy river, 25 mins by boat from the Amazon river. The lodge consists of several wooden buildings with thatched roofs on stilts, cabins with bathroom, no electricity but paraffin lamps are provided, good food, and plenty activities, including visits to local villages. Recommended. They also organize visits to Lake Quistococha.

Tahuayo Lodge, Amazonia Expeditions, 10305 Riverburn Drive, Tampa, FL 33647, toll free T800-262 9669, www.perujungle.com. Near the Reserva Comunal de Tamshiyacu- Tahuayo on the Río Tahuayo, 145 km upriver from Iquitos, clean, comfortable cabins with cold shower, buffet meals, good food, laundry service, wide range of excursions, excellent staff. A 7-day programme costs US$1,295, all inclusive, extra days US$100. Recommended. The lodge is associated with the Rainforest Conservation Fund (www.rain forestconserva tion.org), which works in Tamshiyacu-Tahuayo, one of the richest areas for primate species in the world, but also amphibians (there is a poison dart frog management programme), birds, other animals and plants.

Zungarococha Amazon Lodge, Ricardo Palma 242, T/F065-231959 (see Heliconia, above). A recreation centre on the Río Nanay, 35 mins from Iquitos. Comfortable lakeside bungalows reached by road (12 km), swimming pool, watersports, mini-zoo, full day US$40, 1 night/2 days US$95.

Iquitos to the Brazilian/Colombian border *p532*

There are several very basic *hostales* in Caballococha, including **F Hostal Internacional** (shared facilities).

Eating

Tingo María *p524, map p525*

¶**El Antojito 2**, Jr Chiclayo 458. Good local food.

¶**Girasol**, Av Raimondi 253, T062-562065. Chicken, burgers, cakes, juices.

¶**La Cabaña**, Raimondi 600 block. A good restaurant with fairly clean rooms **F** rooms.

Pucallpa *p527, map p527*

¶¶¶**El Alamo**, Carretera Yarinacocha 2650, T061-571510. Here you can find good local food, such as *patarashca*, barbecued fish wrapped in bijao leaves, and *Zarapatera*, a spicy soup made with turtle meat served in its shell, Chonta salad, made with palm shoots, and *juanes*, rice with chicken or fish served during the **San Juan festival**.

Lake Yarinacocha *p528*

Around Lake Yarinacocha there are many restaurants and bars on the waterfront and near the plaza, and also stalls which barbecue fresh fish and local dishes.

¶¶**Grande Paraíso**, Lake Yarinacocha. Good view, also has a *peña* at night, popular with young people.

¶¶-¶**Estoraque**, on the shore of Lake Yarinacocha. Excellent food in a beautiful setting, extensive menu, friendly service, set menu starts at US$3.

¶¶-¶**Orlando's**, Jr Aguaytía, Lake Yarinacocha. Another recommended place to eat.

Iquitos *p528, map p530*

Try palm heart salad (*chonta*), or a la Loretana dish on menus; also try *inchicapi* (chicken, corn and peanut soup), *cecina* (fried dried pork), *tacacho* (fried green banana and pork, mashed into balls and eaten for breakfast or tea), *juanes* (chicken, rice, olive and egg, seasoned and wrapped in bijao leaves and sold in restaurants). Many jungle species such as deer and wild boar still figure prominently in Iquitos restaurants. Please be responsible. Try the local drink *chuchuhuasi*, made from the bark of a tree, which is supposed to have aphrodisiac properties but tastes like fortified cough tincture (for sale at Arica 1046), and *jugo de cocona*, and the alcoholic *cola de mono* and *siete raices* (aguardiente mixed with the bark of 7 trees and wild honey), sold at **Exquisita Amazónica**, Abtao 590. Camu-camu is an interesting but acquired taste, said to have one of the highest vitamin C concentrations in the world. Many private homes offer set lunch, look for the board outside.

¶¶¶¶**Fitzcarrald**, Malecón Maldonado 103 y Napo. Smart, best pizza in town, also good pastas and salads.

¶¶¶¶**La Gran Maloca**, Sargento Lores 170, opposite **Banco Continental**. A/c, high class.

¶¶¶¶**Montecarlo**, Napo 140. Next to the casino, "best food in town".

¶¶¶**Ari's Burger**, Plaza de Armas, Próspero 127. Fast food, good breakfasts, popular with tourists.

¶¶¶**El Nuevo Mesón**, Malecón Maldonado 153. Local specialities include wild boar, alligator, turtle, tapir and other endangered species, has lots of regular dishes, too.

¶¶¶**Long Fung**, San Martín at Plaza 28 de Julio. Good Chinese if a little expensive, a/c dining room, open 1200-1500 and 1900-0000 daily.

¶¶¶**Pollón**, on the Plaza next to **Ari's Burger**. For chicken and chips, open in the daytime.

¶¶¶**The Regal**, in the Casa de Hierro, Plaza de Armas, Próspero y Putumayo, 2nd floor. Nice location, good set lunch for US$2.30, other meals more expensive.

¶¶¶**Yellow Rose of Texas**, Putumayo 180. Run by the ex-director of the tourist office, Gerald W Mayeaux. Varied food, Texan atmosphere. Open 24 hrs so you can wait here if arriving late at night, good breakfasts, lots of information, also has a bar, Sky TV and Texan saddle seats.

¶**Huasaí**, Napo 326. Varied and innovative menú, popular and recommended, 0730-1600 daily.

¶**La Casa de Lidia**, Bolognesi 1181. For regional specialties, very popular with locals, Mon-Sat 1800-2300.

¶**La Vida es Salud**, Aguirre 759 on Plaza 28 de Julio. Vegetarian, simple little place, good value, open daily.

¶**Paulina**, Tacna 591. Good set lunch, popular with locals and tourists, very noisy.

Cafés

Heladería, Próspero 415. Excellent ice-cream, several local flavours including *aguaje*

and *camu-camu*. Highly recommended.
Juguería Paladar, Próspero 245.
Excellent juices.

Iquitos to the Brazilian/Colombian border *p532*
♥ **Restaurant El Sabroso**, next to the port, In Caballococha. This is the best place to eat here, good sandwiches for about US$1. There are several cheap *comedores* around the main plaza, which is also next to the port.

◑ Bars and clubs

Pucallpa *p527, map p527*
Billy's Place, on Arica, on the street east of Jr Mcal Cáceres, Pucallpa. A decent bar run by an American called Rick (Billy is his pet jaguar). He only sells beer, has TV and pinball. All the locals know it; the area is very dark late at night.

Iquitos *p528, map p530*
La Ribereña, Raymondi 453. With terraced seats on a nice plaza.
Noa Noa, Pevas y Fitzcarrald. Disco, popular with locals and tourists, varied music, open Tue-Sun.
Snack Bar Arandú, Malecón Maldonado. Good views of the Amazon river.
Teatro Café Amauta, Nauta 248. Live music, open 2200-2400, good atmosphere, popular, small exhibition hall.
Tuspa, Raimondi block 2. Light rock, lively, good place to listen to music.

✹ Festivals and events

Pucallpa *p527, map p527*
Fiesta de San Juan on **24 Jun**, and during **5-20 Oct** is Pucallpa's **Aniversario Political** and the **Ucayali regional fair**.

Iquitos *p528, map p530*
On **5 Jan** is the anniversary of the **founding of Iquitos**. During **Carnival** you can see the local dance La Pandilla. On **24 Jun** is the **Festival of San Juan**, patron saint of Loreto. **Tourist week**, with regional music, held in the Mercado Artesanal de San Juan, is celebrated around the same time. On **28-30 Aug** is **Santa Rosa de Lima**, celebrated in Rumococha. On **22-25 Sep** is **Santo Tomás**, in the village of the same name (also

see p532). On **8 Dec** is **La Purísima**, celebrated in Punchana, near the docks.

◎ Shopping

Pucallpa *p527, map p527*
Many Shibipo women carry and sell their products around Pucallpa and Yarinacocha. **Agustín Rivas**, at Jr Tarapacá 861, above a small restaurant whose entrance is at No 863 (ask for it), Pucallpa. For local wood carvings visit the workshop of this sculptor. His work is made from huge tree roots and when Sr Rivas is in town he is happy to chat over a cup of tea. His family runs the gallery when he is in Iquitos.
Artesanías La Selva, Jr Tarapacá 868, Pucallpa, has a reasonable selection of indigenous craftwork.

Iquitos *p528, map p530*
Good hammocks in the markets in Iquitos cost about US$5.75.
For arts and crafts: **Amazon Arts and Crafts**. Napo block 100. **Artesanías de la Selva**, R Palma 190. **Mercado Artesanal de Productores**, 4 km from the centre in the San Juan district, on the road to the airport (take a *colectivo*). Cheapest in town with more choice than elsewhere.
Mad Mick's Trading Post, next to the Iron House. Hires out rubber boots for those going to the jungle.

▲ Activities and tours

Tingo María *p524, map p525*
Tingo María Travel Tours, Av Raimondi 460, Tingo María, T064-562501. Local excursions.

Yurimaguas *p525*
To organize tours in Yurimaguas, go to the Municipalidad and ask for Jorge or Samuel (who speaks English).
Nilotour, Tte César López 717, niloelguia@hotmail.com. Two-day tours US$240 not including food. Recommended.

Pacaya-Samiria Reserve *p526*
For Pacaya-Samiria Reserve, there are 5 registered operators in Lagunas. Guides charge US$15 per day. Trips to Pacaya-Samiria can also be arranged in Iquitos. Expeditions must be booked in advance,

all equipment and food is provided.

Asiendes (Asociación Indígena en Defensa de la Ecología Samiria), asiendesperu@hot mail.com, or contact through **Yellow Rose of Texas** restaurant in Iquitos, see Eating above. A local association which runs trips into Pacaya-Samiria, promoting the jungle and benefiting the community, from 4 to 7 days, US$50 per day, all inclusive except boat passage from Iquitos and price of entry to the park. You stay at rangers' stations or can camp, very good experience, respectful of wildlife, knowledgeable and accommodating guides. Recommended.

Pucallpa p527, map p527

Jungle tours from Pucallpa are not very well-organized. You can negotiate a price for a group with the boatmen on the waterfront. Expect to pay around US$30 per day per person and use only accredited guides. Ask the tourist office (see p527) for advice about visiting the Río Piski area, which has authentic Shibipo culture. There is no passenger traffic, so the trip may be pricey.

Laser Viajes y Turismo, Raimondi 470, T061-571120. Recommended as helpful for planning a jungle trip.

Iquitos p528, map p530

See Sleeping above for jungle lodges and the trips that they offer. All agencies are under the control of the local Chamber of Tourism. They arrange one day or longer trips to places of interest with guides speaking some English. Package tours booked in Lima or abroad are much more expensive than those booked in Iquitos and personal approaches to lodge operators will often yield better prices than booking through an agency or the internet. Take your time before making a decision and don't be bullied by the hustlers at the airport (they get paid a hefty commission). You must make sure your tour operator or guide has a proper licence (the Municipalidad's *Iquitos Guía Turística*, 2004, gives a full list). Do not go with a company which does not have legal authorization; there are many unscrupulous people about. Find out all the details of the trip and food arrangements before paying (a minimum of US$45 per day). Speed boats for river trips can be hired

by the hour or day at the Embarcadero Turístico, at the intersection of Av de la Marina and Samánez Ocampo in Punchana. Prices vary greatly, usually US$10-20 per hr, and are negotiable. In fact, all prices are negotiable, except Muyuna, who do not take commissions.

Take a long-sleeved shirt, waterproof coat and shoes or light boots on jungle trips and a good torch, as well as espirales to ward off the mosquitoes at night – they can be bought from pharmacies in Iquitos. Premier is the most effective local insect repellent. The dry season is from Jul-Sep (Sep is the best month to see flowers and butterflies).

Amazon Tours and Cruises, Requena 336, T065-231611, www.amazontours.net. An American-owned company. Luxury cruises on the *Andrea* Iquitos-Leticía-Manaus-Iquitos, US$5,150 per person, 9 days, and to Belém, US$6,950, 15 days; the *Río Amazonas* sails Iquitos-Leticia-Iquitos, US$765; *Amazon Explorer* to Pcaya-Samiria, US$795; and nature cruises on the *Delfín* and *Arca*. They also organize rugged expeditions to various jungle *tambos* (thatched shelters). Conscientious and efficient.

Jungle Bike, Libertad 549, T065-266631, www.junglebike.net. For cycle tours through the jungle.

● Transport

Tingo María p524, map p525

There are no regular flights to/from Tingo María, only charters. Check with the tourist office for any departures.

Buses to **Huánuco**, 119 km, 3-4 hrs, US$2 with **Etnasa** (but this company is not recommended because of theft and drug-trafficking). Better to take one of the several micros daily, US$2 per seat, and *colectivos*, US$3.50, 2 hrs. Direct buses continue to Lima, 12 hrs, with **Trans Rey** (T01-431 9808 in Lima), US$15 bus cama, **León de Huánuco** and **Bahía** (T01-424 1539), US$11. From Lima to Tingo María, León de Huánuco buses leave at 1900, so if continuing to Pucallpa, there is time to grab breakfast on Raimondi and then take another León bus, or a *colectivo* onwards. To **Pucallpa**, 255 km, 12 hrs, US$4.30-8.50.

Ucayali Express *colectivos* leave from the corner of Raimondi and Callao. There are other *colectivos* and taxis, which all leave in the early morning in convoy. There is daily transport to **Juanjui**, 340 km, 15-20 hrs, US$9. This is not a recommended journey because of narco-terrorist activity. **Tarapoto** is a further 145 km; 4 hrs, US$2.

North to Yurimaguas *p524*
Colectivos run from Tingo María to **Tocache** US$13, 4½ hrs; or bus US$9.50, 6 hrs. **Tarapoto**-Tocache, US$7.50 by *colectivo*. *Colectivos* and taxis run from Tocache to **Yurimaguas**. A daily *camioneta* runs from Tarapoto to Yurimaguas, US$7-9, 6-8 hrs. The **Juanjui**-Tocache road has 5 bridges, but the last one across the Huallaga, just before Juanjui, was washed away in 1983 to be replaced by an efficient ferry; it costs US$9.20 per vehicle. Juanjui-Tarapoto by *colectivo* US$12.50.

For the river journey, start early if you do not wish to spend a night at the river village of **Sión**. There are no facilities, but the nights are not cold. The river runs through marvellous jungle with high cliffs. Boats sometimes run aground in the river near Sión. Take food and bottled water. Balsa wood rafts also ply this stretch of river.

Yurimaguas *p525*
To/from **Tarapoto** (a beautiful journey), several companies, 5-6 hrs, US$3.45, same price by combi; in a *camioneta* it costs US$5.75 up front, US$2.90 in the back. Cars charge US$7.20. Mopeds can be hired for US$2.35 per hr, with fuel.

By *lancha* to **Iquitos** takes 2 days and 2 nights, take a hammock, mosquito net, bottled water – or purification, fruit and drinks. There are police inspections at each end of the trip. Fares usually include meals, US$18 2nd class hammock, US$25 1st class hammock, US$35 for one bunk in a cabin. **Eduardo** is company is best. To buy a hammock costs US$5.75-8.50 in Yurimaguas, on C Jáuregui (make sure to buy string to tie it up with). Arriving bus passengers are surrounded by touts trying to sell boat tickets to Iquitos. It is not wise to go to the docks at night to find a boat. Check into a hotel and ask advice in town, then go to the docks next day. The trip is a great

experience, but you should take care of your belongings, especially at embarkation and disembarkation, and all travellers should be wary of unwanted attention from the crew.

Lagunas *p525*
The **Constante** sails from Yurimaguas to Lagunas 2-3 times a week (US$4.50). From there connections are difficult to **Iquitos**. Times of boats to Iquitos and **Pucallpa** are very vague; you should confirm departures the day before by radio. The boats pass by the villages of **Castilla** and **Nauta**, where the Huallaga joins the Ucayali and becomes the Amazon.

Pucallpa *p527*, *map p527*
The airport is to the northwest of the town. Bus from the airport to town, US$0.25; motos US$1; taxi US$2-3. Daily flights to/from **Lima** (1 hr), with **Tans**, whose flights continue to/proceed from **Iquitos**. Tans, Arica 500, T061-591852.

The ticket office of **Ucayali Express** as well as the depot for buses to Yarinacocha are in blocks south of the Plaza de Armas. There are regular bus services to **Lima**, 812 km, 18-20 hrs (longer in the rainy season, Nov-Mar), US$11. To **Tingo María**, 255 km, 7-9 hrs, US$4.30-8.50, combis leave at 0600, 0700 and 0800 with Ucayali Express (7 de Junio y San Martín). All buses have police guard and go in convoy. For road conditions see Ins and outs, above. Take blankets as the crossing of the Cordillera at night is bitterly cold.

By river to **Atalaya**, Mon, Tue, Wed, 3-4 days, US$17. To **Iquitos**, the trip takes 3-5 days, and costs US$20 per person for hammock space, or US$30 for a bed in a cabin. You can go to Puerto La Hoyada, 5 km northeast of the town, Puerto Italia and Pucallpillo to find boats going to Iquitos. A mototaxi to any of the ports costs US$0.75 from the Plaza de Armas, but strap all your bags on tight as things can fall off on the bumpy roads. Taxis charge US$3. Pucallpillo is the low water port, but there are times when all ports are in use. The large boats to Iquitos and beyond will all be docked at one of them, so you must ask around. The Capitanía on the waterfront may give you information about sailings, but this is seldom reliable. There are usually 2-3 boats in port at any given time. Quality varies, so talking to the staff can help you get a feel for the atmosphere aboard. Departure times are marked on chalk boards on the deck. Schedules seem to change almost hourly, which means that you need to keep a close eye on developments and for Peruvians in the know starting to embark.

Do not pay for your trip before you board the vessel, and only pay the captain. Some boat captains may allow you to live on board a couple of days before sailing. It's safer to club together and pay for a cabin in which to lock your belongings, even if you sleep outside in a hammock. There's a risk of illness as the river water is used for cooking and drinking. Bottled drinking water can be bought in Pucallpa, but not cheaply. You can buy crackers, toilet paper and some sweets on board at inflated prices; warm beer is reasonable at US$1.45 for a big bottle. Vegetarians must take their own supplies. Also take lots of insect repellent, long sleeves and long trousers for the night-time.

Boats going upstream on the Amazon and its tributaries stay closer to the bank than boats going down, which stay in mid-stream. Further down the Río Ucayali are **Contamaná**, with a frontier-town atmosphere, and **Requena**, from which launches sail to Iquitos, taking 12 hrs. Unlike most other villages, which are mestizo, **Roroboya**, about 12 hrs downstream from Pucallpa, is Shipibo Indian.

Travellers to Iquitos may need confirmation from the PNP that their documents are in order, this must then be signed by the Capitanía otherwise no passenger can be accepted on a trip leaving Pucallpa. No such clearance is necessary when returning to Pucallpa.

Lake Yarinacocha *p528*
Yarinacocha is 20 mins by *colectivo* or bus from the market in Pucallpa, US$0.30, or 15 mins by taxi, US$2.

Iquitos *p528, map p530*
Air
Iquitos flights are frequently delayed; be sure to reconfirm your flight in Iquitos, as they are often overbooked, especially over Christmas. Check times in advance as itineraries frequently change. A taxi to the airport costs US$2.85 per car (T065-241284). A motocarro

(motorcycle with 2 seats) is US$2. To take a city bus from the airport, walk out to the main road; most bus lines run through the centre of town, US$0.20. **Lan** has 2 direct flights daily to **Lima** (US$86). **Tans** also has 2 flights daily to **Lima** (US$86), one via **Tarapoto** or **Pucallpa** (US$77) and one direct. **Grupo 42** (military) has one flight a week, currently on Tue, in a Twin Otter to **San Lorenzo** (US$50), **Lagunas** (US$50, for Parque Nacional Pacaya Samiria), **Yurimaguas** (US$55), **Tarapoto** (US$60) and **Pucallpa** (US$60). Irregular flights with **Aviaselva** are sometimes available to **Leticia** (Colombia), ask around Iquitos travel agencies.

Airline offices Grupo 42, Sgto Lores 127, T065-233224, Mon-Fri 0800-1300 and 1400-1800. Lan, Napo 374, T065-232421, Mon-Sat 0900-1900, Sun and holidays 0900-1200. Tans, Arica 273, open 0830-1300, 1530-1900, Sun 0830-1300.

Bus
To get to **Lake Quistococha**, combis leave every hour until 1500 from Plaza 28 de Julio. The last one back leaves at 1700. Alternatively take a mototaxi there and back with a 1-hour wait, which costs US$6. Another option is to hire a motorbike and spend the day there.

Motorcycle hire
Park Motors, Tacna 579, T/F065-231688. The tourist office has details of other companies. Expect to pay US$2.50 per hr, US$25 for 24 hrs; remember that traffic in town is totally chaotic.

River
Both the quality of river boats and frequency of service are much better than they used to be. Large passenger and cargo vessels are called *lanchas*, smaller faster craft are called *rápidos* or *deslizadores* (speedboats). You can find information on boats and tickets at **Bellavista**, Malecón Tarapacá 596; or in the Puerto Masusa district of Puchana, at Av La Marina with Masusa (take a bus from the centre, 10 mins).
Local A *rápido* boat to **Indiana** costs US$3 from El Embarcadero Turístico, at the intersection of Av de la Marina and Samánez Ocampo in Punchana. To **Pilpintuhuasi Butterfly Farm** take a *colectivo* boat from

Bellavista to Padre Cocha (US$0.30, leave when full) or hire a boat for US$2.50; US$10 with 2 hr wait.

Long distance All *lanchas* leave from Masusa, 2 km north of the centre, a dangerous area at night. All sailings around 1800-2000, the first night's meal is not included. Always deal directly with boat owners or managers, avoid touts and middle-men. All fares are negotiable. You can buy either a ticket to sling your hammock on deck, or for a berth in a cabin sleeping four people. There are adequate washing and toilet facilities, but the food is rice, meat and beans (and whatever can be picked up en route) cooked in river water. There is a good cheap bar on board. If arriving in Iquitos on a regular, slow boat, take extreme care when disembarking. Things get very chaotic at this time and theft and pickpocketing is rife.

Lanchas serve all of the following destinations: **Pucallpa**, 3-5 days up river along the Amazon and Ucayali, hammock US$22, berth US$35. **Baylon I** is an OK vessel. To **Yurimaguas**, 3-4 days up river along the Amazon, Marañón and Huallaga, 2nd class hammock space US$18, 1st class hammock space US$25, berth US$35. **Eduardo** company is recommended, **Eduardo V** is their newest vessel. **Islandia** for **Leticia** (Colombia) and **Tabatinga** (Brazil), 2-3 days down river on the Amazon, hammock space US$15, berth US$22. **Gran Diego** is a nice vessel. Passengers disembark in Peru for immigration formalities (no exchange facilities), then take another US$1 boat to **Marco**, the port for **Tabatinga**. Most boats for **Manaus** depart from Marco.

If you plan to stop off along the way at small villages on the river in Peru (see Iquitos to the Brazilian/Colombian border), you can usually get a passing boat to make an unscheduled stop and pick you up. The best way to do this is to flag it down with a white sheet. This is what the villagers do if they want a passing boat to stop at their village. Note that this method doesn't work on the Brazilian part of the river, where boats don't make unscheduled stops. The only way to board a Brazilian boat between stops is to hire a canoe to take you out to meet it in mid-river then flag it down.

Pantoja (for Ecuador), 5-7 days up river on the Napo, hammock space US$30, no berths. The **Victor**, **Camila**, and **Siempre Adelante** (all small basic boats, contact T065-242082) each sail twice a month, but will not go all the way to Pantoja unless there is cargo. To make this long and arduous voyage a day shorter, you can take a small boat to **Indiana** (see Excursions, above) and cross to Mazán to catch the lancha on the Napo, but there may not be much space left onboard. Alternatively, you can take a *rápido* from Mazán to **Santa Clotilde** (less than half-way to Pantoja) and try to board the *lancha* when it calls there. The trip requires plenty of time and patience.

See **Amazon Tours and Cruises** in Activities and tours above for luxury cruises on the Amazon, to Leticia. Manaus and as far as Belém.

Rápidos for **Tabatinga** (Brazil) leave from El Embarcadero Turístico, at 0600 daily except Mon, 11 hrs journey, US$50. There are no boats direct to Manaus. Boats go to **Santa Rosa** on the border, opposite **Tabatinga**. They leave most days at 0600-0615; be at the port at 0445 for customs check. They go to Santa Rosa for immigration formalities then take passengers across to Tabatinga. Purchase tickets in advance from company offices: **Transtur**, Raymondi 384, T065-231278, transtur@terra.com.pe; **River Fox**, Raymondi 344, T065-243404. All include a small breakfast of a sandwich and coffee, a passable lunch and mineral water (ask for it). All carry life jackets and have clean bathrooms. Luggage limit is 15 kg. Most travel agencies sell tickets. Hotels have details of sailings; ask around which boats are reliable. *Rápidos* leave Tabatinga for Iquitos every morning at 0600: the same price and almost the same time, 11-12 hrs.

See p72 for general tips on river travel.

Iquitos to the Brazilian/Colombian border p532
Air
Grupo 42 (the Peruvian Air Force) flights between **Santa Rosa** and **Iquitos** were suspended in 2004. Ask in any travel agency in Iquitos about resumption of this service. In Tabatinga, **Blue Moon**,

T92-97-412 2227; andyturismo@yahoo.com.br.

There are flights 3 days from Tabatinga to Manaus with **Varig** and others with **Rico** (expensive so ask about discounts). **Aero República** flies 4 days a week from **Leticia** to **Bogotá**.

River
Details of ferry services from Iquitos to the border are given above. Slow boats between **Iquitos** and **Santa Rosa** stop in **Caballococha**. Rápidos between **Iquitos** and **Tabatinga** only make a brief stop, so to see the town, take a rápido boat from **Leticia** (Colombia), 2-3 hrs depending on the number of stops, then catch a flight out or a rápido the next day. Small boats between **Tabatinga** and **Santa Rosa**, or **Leticia** and Santa Rosa are readily available and charge US$1, 2 reais, 5 soles or 2000 pesos per passenger.

❶ Directory

Tingo María *p524, map p525*
Internet Several places in Tingo María on Raimondi and in the streets near the Plaza de Armas, fast and cheap but they keep strange hours and few open early in the morning. **Telephone** Catel, Av Raimondi 272, Tingo María, T062-562551. For all phone, fax and related services, internet also.

Pucallpa *p527, map p527*
Banks In Pucallpa it is easy to change dollars cash at the banks, travel agencies, the better hotels and bigger stores. There are also lots of street changers (watch them carefully). BCP, Raimondi y Tarapacá, is the only place to change TCs. Cash advances can be made on Visa at BCP and Interbank. **Police** Policia Nacional, Jr Independencia 3rd block, Pucallpa, T061-575211. **Post** Office Tarapacá y San Martín, Pucallpa.

Iquitos *p528, map p530*
Banks Don't change money on the streets. Visit the tourist office and obtain a list with the names of reliable money changers. BCP, Plaza de Armas. For Visa, also cash and TCs at good rates, has a Visa ATM around the corner on Próspero. BBV

Continental, Sgto Lores 171. For Visa, 1% commission on TCs. **Banco de la Nación**, Condamine 478. Good rates. **Banco Wiese Sudameris**, Próspero 282. **Banco del Trabajo**, Próspero 223. Has Unicard ATM for Visa/Plus and Mastercard/Cirrus. **Casa de cambio** at Tienda Wing Kong, Próspero 312, Mon-Sat 0800-1300 and 1500-2000, Sun 0900-1200. **Western Union**, Napo 359, T065-235182. **Embassies and consulates** Consulates: Britain, Casa de Hierro (Iron House), Putumayo 189, T065-222732, Mon-Fri 1100-1200. **Colombia**, Calvo de Araujo 431, T065-231461. There are no Brazilian or Ecuadorean consulates. If you need a visa for either of these countries and plan to travel there from Iquitos, you must get the visa beforehand at home or in Lima. **Hospitals** Clínica Loreto, Morona 471, T065-233752, 24-hr attention. Recommended, but only Spanish spoken. **Immigration** Mcal Cáceres 18th block, T065-235371. Quick service. **Internet** There are internet places everywhere, US$0.80 per hr. **Police** Tourist police, Sargento Lores 834, T065-242081. Helpful with complaints against tour operators. In emergency T065-241000 or 241001. **Post** On the corner of C Arica with Morona, near the Plaza de Armas, 0700-2000. **Telephone** Telefónica, Arica 276. **Useful addresses** Indecopi, C Huallaga 325, T065-243490, ameza@indecopi.gob.pe. For the tourism protection service.

Iquitos to the Brazilian/Colombian border *p532*
Banks There is no exchange office in Santa Rosa, but you can pay in reais. You can use Colombian pesos in Brazil and reais in Colombia. Peruvian soles are not accepted in Colombia, but sometimes you pay with soles in Brazil. There are no exchange facilities in Tabatinga port, but there are several casas de cambio in Leticia, the best place to change money, even for reais into soles. US dollars are accepted everywhere. **Internet** The only place with internet is Leticia. Connection is very slow. Try the internet in the librería, next to the church in the centre.

Southern Jungle

Both the Manu Biosphere Reserve and Tambopata National Park offer amazing wildlife spotting, large parts being remote and pristine, with such highlights as macaw clay licks and birdwatching on undisturbed lakes. The southern selva is found mostly within the Department of Madre de Dios, created in 1902 and contains the Manu National Biosphere Reserve (2.2 million ha), the Tambopata National Reserve (254,358 ha) and the Bahuaja-Sonene National Park (1.1 million ha) which is more than four times larger than the Tambopata National Reserve. ▸▸ *For Sleeping, Eating and other listings, see pages 552-562.*

Ins and outs

Getting there and around To visit Manu you must go as part of a tour leaving from Cusco, either by road or by air. The frontier town of Puerto Maldonado is the starting point for expeditions to the Tambopata National Reserve and is only a 30-minute flight from Cusco. ▸▸ *For further details see Tours and activities page 558 and Transport page 561.*

▸▸ *For further details see Tours and activities page 558 and Transport page 561.*

🔊 *A pair of binoculars is essential for wildlife viewing and insect repellent is a must.*

Best time to visit The climate is warm and humid, with a rainy season from November to March and a dry season from April to October. Cold fronts from the South Atlantic, called *friajes*, are characteristic of the dry season, when temperatures drop to 15-16°C during the day, and 13°C at night. Always bring a sweater at this time. The best time to visit is during the dry season when there are fewer mosquitoes and the rivers are low, exposing the beaches. This is also a good time to see birds nesting and to view the animals at close range, as they stay close to the rivers.

Background

The forest of this lowland region is technically called Sub-tropical Moist Forest, which means that it receives less rainfall than tropical forest and is dominated by the floodplains of its meandering rivers. One of most striking features is the former river channels that have become isolated as ox-bow lakes (*cochas*). These are home to black caiman and giant otter and a host of other living organisms. Other rare species living in the forest are jaguar, puma, ocelot and tapir. There are also capybara, thirteen species of primate and many hundreds of bird species. If you include the cloud forests and highlands of the Manu Biosphere reserve, the bird count almost totals 1,000.

The relative proximity to Cusco of Manu in particular has made it one of the prime nature watching destinations in South America. Despite its reputation, Manu is heavily protected, with visitor numbers limited and a large percentage of the park inaccessible to tourists. Nevertheless, there is no need to worry that this level of management is going to diminish your pleasure. There is more than enough in the way of birds, animals and plants to satisfy the most ardent wildlife enthusiast. Tambopata does have a town in the vicinity, Puerto Maldonado, and the area was under threat from exploitation and settlement. The suspension of oil exploration in 2000 led to a change of status for a large tract of this area, giving immediate protection to another of Peru's zones of record-breaking diversity.

In 2003 the new emerging threat to the forests of Madre de Dios was the planned construction of the Transoceánica, a road linking the Atlantic and Pacific Oceans via Puerto Maldonado and Brazil. The paving of this road system, creating a high speed link between the two countries, will certainly bring more uncontrolled colonization in the area, as seen so many times in the Brazilian Amazon, placing the forests of the Tambopata region under further pressure. Uncontrolled colonization along Bahuaja-Sonene's southern border, in the Tambopata headwaters area, is another cause of growing concern.

Manu Biosphere Reserve → *Colour map 4, grid C4.*

No other rainforest can compare with Manu for the diversity of its life forms and this is one of the world's great wilderness experiences. The reserve is one of the best bird-watching spots of the world (see below) as well as offering the best chance of seeing giant otters, jaguars, ocelots and several of the 13 species of primates which abound in this pristine tropical wilderness. The more remote areas of the reserve are home to uncontacted indigenous tribes and many other indigenous groups with very little knowledge of the outside world. Covering an area of 1,881,000 ha, Manu

Manu Biosphere Reserve

Sleeping
Amazonia Lodge 7
Erika Lodge 9
Manu Cloud Forest
  Lodge 8
Manu Lodge 1
Manu Wildlife Centre 2
Pantiacolla Lodge 6
Tambo Blanquillo 4
Yanayaco Lodge 5
Yine Lodge 3

Cultural Zone

Biosphere Reserve is also one of the largest conservation units on Earth, encompassing the complete drainage of the Manu river, with an altitudinal range from 200 m to 4,100 m above sea-level.

The park areas

The Biosphere Reserve formally comprised the **Manu National Park** (1,692,137 ha), where only government sponsored biologists and anthropologists may visit with permits from the Ministry of Agriculture in Lima, the **Manu Reserved Zone** (257,000 ha), set aside for applied scientific research and ecotourism, and the **Cultural Zone** (92,000 ha), containing acculturated native groups and colonists, where the locals still employ their traditional way of life. In 2003 the former Manu Reserved Zone was absorbed into the Manu National Park, increasing it's protected status. Ecotourism activities have been allowed to continue in specially designated tourism and recreational zones along the course of the Lower Manu River. These tourism and recreational areas are accessible by permit only. Entry is strictly controlled and visitors must visit the area under the auspices of an authorized operator with an authorized guide. Permits are limited and reservations should be made well in advance, though it is possible to book a place on a trip at the last minute in Cusco. In the former Reserved Zone there are two lodges, the rustic **Casa Machiguenga** run by the Machiguenga communities of Tayakome and Yomibato with the help of a German NGO, and the upmarket **Manu Lodge**. In the Cocha Salvador area, several companies have tented safari camp infrastructures, some with shower and dining facilities, but all visitors sleep in tents. Some companies have installed walk-in tents with cots and bedding.

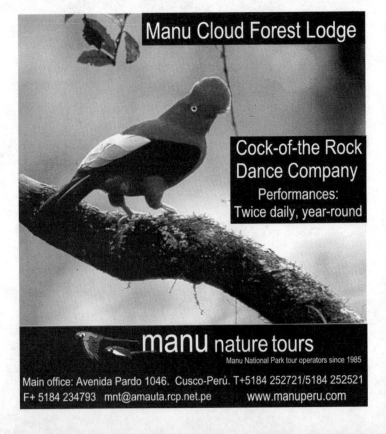

The Cultural and Multiple Use Zones are accessible to anyone and several lodges exist in the area. It is possible to visit these lodges under your own steam. Among the ethnic groups in the Multiple Use Zone (a system of buffer areas surrounding the core Manu area) are the Harakmbut, Machiguenga and Yine in the Amarakaeri Reserved Zone, on the east bank of the Alto Madre de Dios. They have set up their own ecotourism activities, which are entirely managed by indigenous people. Associated with Manu are other areas protected by conservation groups, or local people (for example the Blanquillo reserved zone and a new conservation concession in the adjacent Los Amigos river system) and some cloud forest parcels along the road. The **Nuhua-Kugapakori Reserved Zone** (443,887 ha), set aside for these two nomadic native groups, is the area between the headwaters of the Río Manu and headwaters of the Río Urubamba, to the north of the Alto Madre de Dios.

To Manu from Cusco → Colour map 5, grid A5/6.

The arduous trip over the Andes from Cusco to the end of the road at Shintuya takes a whole day by local truck (16-24 hours in the dry, 20-40 hours in the wet season). It is long and uncomfortable, but, throughout, the scenery is magnificent.

Leaving Cusco
From Cusco you climb up to the Huancarani pass before **Paucartambo** (3½ hours), before dropping down to this picturesque mountain village in the Mapacho Valley, for details of accommodation etc in Paucartambo, see page 221. The road then ascends to the Ajcanacu pass (cold at night), after which it goes down to the cloud forest and then the rainforest, reaching **Pilcopata** at 650 m (12 hours).

Atalaya
After Pilcopata, the route is hair-raising and breath-taking. Even in the dry season this part of the road is appalling and trucks often get stuck. Travelling towards Atalaya, the first village on the Alto Madre de Dios river and about an hour away from Picopata, you pass **Manu Cloudforest Lodge**, **Cock of the Rock Lodge** and the **San Pedro Biological Station** (see below). Atalaya consists of a few houses, and basic accommodation can be found here. Meals are available at the very friendly family of Rosa and Klaus, where you can also camp. Boats are available here to take you across the river to **Amazonia Lodge**, see page 552. The village is also the jumpoff point for river trips further into the Manu. The route continues to **Salvación**, where a Manu Park Office is situated. There are basic hostels and restaurants.

Shintuya → Colour map 5, grid A6.
The end of the road is Shintuya, the starting point for river transport. It is a commercial and social centre, as wood from the jungle is transported from here to Cusco. There are a few basic restaurants and you can camp (beware of thieves). The priest will let you stay in the dormitory rooms at the mission. Supplies are expensive. There are two Shintuyas: one is the port and mission and the other is the native village. You can find a boat in the native village or down on the beach (port); if waiting for a local trading boat to head down river you may be hanging around for some time, perhaps 1-2 days; ask for Diego Ruben Sonoco or Miguel Vise, they may be able to help. It is not possible to arrange trips to the tourist zones of the National Park from Shintuya, owing to park regulations. All arrangements (including permits) must be made in Cusco.

Boca Colorado
From Shintuya infrequent cargo boats sail to the gold mining centre of Boca Colorado on the Río Madre de Dios, via Boca Manu, and passing several ecotourism lodges

⁞ Top of the morning

At first sight, as the dawn comes up and the collpas's features emerge from the dark, it looks like nothing more than a long, brown, muddy cliff. But these mundane places are very special, for here macaws and parrots `lick' the clay in one of the world's great wildlife spectacles. It is believed that they do this because they need the soil's alkalis to neutralize the toxicity in fruit, especially at the end of the dry season (August-October). There is no guarantee that the birds will come, so you wait for the sun to warm the air and hope that being woken at some ungodly hour will be worth it.

A 25-minute boat ride from the Manu Wildlife Center is a floating hide (two canoes lashed together with a platform and leaves for walls) to view one important collpa. "The green parrots were already mustering as we arrived at the hide. The first shift comprised mealy and yellow-crowned parrots, which look like they have been lightly dusted with flour, and glossy blue-headed and orange-cheeked parrots. It was a riot of green, jabbering and bickering, fluttering like butterflies, then flying en masse when little more than a shadow alarmed them. After the parrots had had their fill, we spectators breakfasted on pancakes and maple syrup and waited for the macaws. Soon, in the trees, on the vines and on the lick itself, red and green macaws were putting on their

show. They hung and swivelled just like captive macaws, but with more joie-de-vivre. Individuals and pairs preened. As they spread their wings for balance while picking off lumps of the cliff, it was clear that whoever named the species was only telling half the story. Red and green, yes, but the blue in their feathers is electric." In order not to disturb the birds, you are not allowed to leave the hide before they have departed.

Another macaw clay lick is a short boat ride and walk from the Tambopata Research Center. Here you watch from the river bank, perched on small camping chairs. As at Manu, absolute silence must be maintained, but, in addition, no bright colours can be worn (those with red or yellow raincoats may get a little wet in the early morning showers). "On the first day, the blue-headed parrots were the first to 'dance'. Then chestnut-fronted, blue and yellow and scarlet macaws, mealy parrots and white-eyed parakeets also turned up, but not a bird settled on the cliff. They waited in the trees, but mostly flew overhead in huge, swirling, shrieking clouds of green. Next morning, more species came: yellow-headed macaws, yellow-crowned and orange-cheeked parrots in addition to those seen the day before. To us it seemed much the same sort of day, but to the birds conditions were much more favourable for a breakfast of clay as they all settled".

including **Pantiacolla Lodge** and **Manu Wildlife Centre**, see page 552. The trip takes around nine hours, and costs US$15. Basic accommodation can be found here and is not recommended for lone women travellers. To Boca Manu is three to four hours, US$12. From Colorado there are plenty of boats to **Laberinto** (six to seven hours, US$20). From here there are combis to **Puerto Maldonado**, see page 549, 1½ hours.

Boca Manu

Boca Manu is the connecting point between the rivers Alto Madre de Dios, Manu and Madre de Dios. It has a few houses, an airstrip and some well-stocked shops. It is also group. The entrance fee to the Reserved Zone is 150 soles per person (about US$40) and is included in package tour prices. The Park ranger station is located in **Limonal**, 20 minutes by boat from Boca Manu. You need to show your permit here and camping is allowed if you have a permit.

To the Reserved Zone

Upstream on the Río Manu you pass the **Manu Lodge** (see page 552), on the Cocha Juárez, three to four hours by boat. You can continue to Cocha Otorongo, 2½ hours and Cocha Salvador, 30 minutes, the biggest lake with plenty of wildlife where the **Casa Machiguenga Lodge** is located and several companies have safari camp concessions. From here it is one hour to **Pakitza**, the entrance to the National Park Zone. This is only for biologists and others with a special permit.

Between Boca Manu and Colorado is **Blanquillo**, a private reserve (10,000 ha). Bring a good tent with you and all food if you want to camp and do it yourself, or alternatively accommodation is available at the Tambo Blanquillo (full board or accommodation only). Wildlife is abundant, especially macaws and parrots at the macaw lick near Manu Wildlife Centre (see page 552). There are occasional boats to Blanquillo from Shintuya; US$10, six to eight hours.

The Amazon Basin Southern Jungle

Puerto Maldonado → *Phone code: 082. Colour map 6, grid A3. Altitude: 250 m.*

Puerto Maldonado is an important starting point for visiting the rainforest, or for departing to Brazil or Bolivia. Still, most visitors won't see much of the place because they are whisked through town on their way to a lodge on the Río Madre de Dios or the Río Tambopata. The city dwellers aren't too pleased about this and would like tourists to spend some time in town, which is a major timber, gold mining and tourism centre. It's a safe place, with *chicha* music blaring out from most street corners.

Ins and outs

The road from Cusco to Puerto Maldonado can only be described as a challenge (and is not recommended). It is expertly described in Matthew Parris' book *Inka-Cola*. The road passes through Ocongate and Marcapata before reaching Quincemil, 240 km from Urcos, a centre for alluvial gold-mining. Quincemil marks the half-way point and the start of the all-weather road. Gasoline is scarce here because most road vehicles continue on 70 km to Mazuko, where it's cheaper. The journey is very rough, but the changing scenery is magnificent. This road is rarely passable in the wet season. Take warm clothing for travelling through the sierra. For an alternative route, see page 547.

Sights

Overlooking the confluence of the rivers Tambopata and Madre de Dios, Puerto Maldonado is a major logging and brazil-nut processing centre. From the park at the end of Jr Arequipa, across from the Capitanía, you get a good view of the two rivers, the ferries across the Madre de Dios and the stacks of lumber at the dockside. The brazil-nut harvest is from December to February and the crop tends to be good on alternate years. Nuts are sold on the street, plain or coated in sugar or chocolate. **El Mirador** ① *at the junction of Av Fitzcarrald and Av Madre de Dios, 1000-1600, US$0.30*, is a 30-m high tower with three platforms giving fine views over the city and surrounding rainforest. There is also a toilet at the top – no curtains – from which there is an equally fine view over the city! **Museo Huamaambi** ① *26 de Diciembre 360, US$1*, contains photos and artefacts pertaining to the Harakmbut culture of central Madre de Dios. **Jippa Butterfly House** ① *adjoining the airport entrance (a 5-min walk from the terminal building), www.butterflyhouse.com.pe, US$3*, breeds butterflies as part of a sustainable development project and offers guided tours. Worth a visit if your arrive early for your flight or if it is delayed.

Excursions

The beautiful and tranquil **Lago Sandoval** ① *costs US$5, you must go with a guide (see page 558); this can be arranged by the boat driver*, is a one-hour boat ride along the Río Madre de Dios from Puerto Maldonado, and then a 5-km walk into the jungle. There is an interpretation centre at the start of the trail and a 35-m high observation tower overlooking the lake. It is possible to see giant river otters early in the morning and several species of monkeys, macaws and hoatzin. There are two jungle lodges at the lake, see Sleeping. At weekends, especially on Sundays, the lake gets quite busy.

Upstream from Lago Sandoval, towards Puerto Maldonado, is the wreck of the **Fitzcarrald**. The steamer (a replica of Fitzcarrald's boat) lies a few metres from the Madre de Dios in the bed of a small stream. The German director, Werner Herzog, was inspired to make his famous film of the same name by the story of Fitzcarrald's attempt to haul a boat from the Ucuyali to the Madre de Dios drainage basins (this happened in what is now the Manu National Park).

For those interested in seeing a gold rush town, a trip to **Laberinto** is suggested. There is one hotel and several poor restaurants. Boats leave from here to Manu, see

Puerto Maldonado

To Iberia & Brazil

Río Madre de Dios

Port

To Lago Sandoval & Bolivia

Jr Billinghurst

Capitanía

Tans

Bolivian Consul

Jr Loreto

Jr Puno

Av León Velarde

Municipalidad

Plaza de Armas

Jr Arequipa

Jr 26 de Diciembre

Artesanía Shabuya

Jr Carrión

Museo Huamaambi

Jr Cusco

Teatro Municipal

To 5

Jr Moquegua

Jr Ernesto Rivero

To El Brombus, Airport, Jippa Butterfly House & Cusco

Av 2 de Mayo

Lan Perú

Scooter Hire

Jr González Prada

Casas de Cambio

Jr J Troncoso

To Market, El Mirador, Bahuaja port & lodges on the Tambopata

To 9 & Tambopata Port

N

0 metres 100
0 yards 100

Sleeping
Cabañaquinta & Restaurant 1
Don Carlos 9
Hospedaje Español 4
Hospedaje La Bahía 10
Hostal El Astro 3
Hostal El Solar 2
Rey Port 5

Royal Inn 6
Wasai & Restaurant 7
Wilson 8

Eating
Café Cosa Nostra 1
Café Tu Dulce Espera 2
El Buen Parador 3
El Califa 5

El Hornito/Le Boulevard 4
La Estrella 6

Bars & clubs
Amnesia 7
Discoteca Anaconda 8
El Witite 9

The Amazon Basin Southern Jungle

page 561. At Km 13 on the Cusco road is a pleasant recreational centre with a restaurant and natural pools where it's possible to swim. It gets busy at weekends. It's US$2 each way by mototaxi from town. Trips can be made to **Lago Valencia**, 60 km away near the Bolivian border; four hours there, eight hours back. It is an ox-bow lake with lots of wildlife, and many excellent beaches and islands are located within an hour's boat ride.

Tambopata National Reserve (TNR)

From Puerto Maldonado you can visit the Tambopata National Reserve by travelling up the Tambopata river or down the Madre de Dios river. The area was first declared a reserve in 1990 and is a very reasonable alternative for those who do not have the time or money to visit Manu. It is a close rival in terms of seeing wildlife and boasts some superb ox-bow lakes. There are a number of lodges here which are excellent for lowland rainforest birding. Explorers' Inn is perhaps the most famous, but the Posada Amazonas/Tambopata Research Centre and Libertador Tambopata Lodge are also good. In an effort to ensure that more tourism income stays in the area, a few local families have established their own small-scale 'Casas de Hospedaje', which offer more basic facilities and make use of the nearby forest.

Ins and outs
The fee to enter the TNR is US$9 per person and US$20 per person to go beyond the Mlinowski/Tambopata confluence. If staying at a lodge, they will organize the payment of the fee, otherwise, you need to visit the INRENA office, Cusco 165, Monday to Saturday 0830-1300, 1530-1800. ►► For Transport details, see page 561.

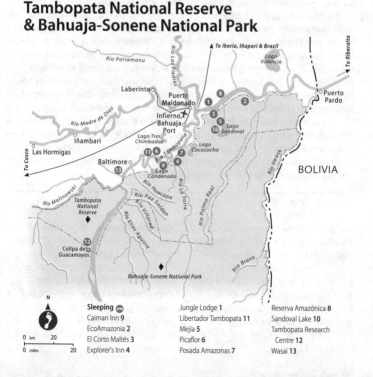

Tambopata National Reserve
& Bahuaja-Sonene National Park

Sleeping
Caiman Inn **9**
EcoAmazonia **2**
El Corto Maltés **3**
Explorer's Inn **4**

Jungle Lodge **1**
Libertador Tambopata **11**
Mejía **5**
Picaflor **6**
Posada Amazonas **7**

Reserva Amazónica **8**
Sandoval Lake **10**
Tambopata Research Centre **12**
Wasai **13**

The Amazon Basin Southern Jungle

The **Bahuaja-Sonene National Park** runs from the Río Heath, which forms the Bolivian border, across to the Río Tambopata, 50-80 km upstream from Puerto Maldonado. It was expanded to 1,091,416 ha in August 2000, with the Tambopata National Reserve (254,358 ha) created to form a buffer zone. The Park is closed to visitors though those visiting the collpa (macaw lick) on the Tambopata or river rafting down the Tambopata will travel through it. The little-visited Las Piedras river flows northwest from Puerto Maldonado. It is navigable for about 500 km, a journey that takes three weeks. In recent years loggers have been operating in its upper reaches, at times coming into conflict with uncontacted native peoples. However, there are still excellent reports of wildlife sightings all along its length.

To Iberia and Iñapari → *Colour map 4, grid C5.*

Daily public transport runs on the improved dirt road which begins across the Río Madre de Dios and runs to Iberia and Iñapari on the border with Brazil. Take one of the frequent ferries which crosses from Puerto Maldonado. In the wet season the road may only be passable with difficulty, especially between Iberia and Iñapari.

Check in advance that you do not need a consular visa for Brazil or Bolivia; they are not issued at the border.

In the dry, though, it is a fast road and dangerous for motorcyclists because of passing traffic. Along the road there remains no primary forest, only secondary growth and small *chacras* (farms). There are also picturesque *caseríos* (settlements) that serve as collecting and processing centres for the brazil nut. Approximately 70 per cent of the inhabitants in the Madre de Dios are involved in the collection of this prized nut.

Iberia, at Km 168, has accommodation. Just outside the town the local rubber tappers association has set up a Reserve and Information Centre. It has a swimming pool (US$0.50). **Iñapari**, at the end of the road, Km 235, has two accommodation, but **Assis Brasil** across the border is more attractive. In 2004 the foundations were laid for a bridge from Iñapari to Assis Brasil by presidents Toledo of Peru and Lula da Silva of Brazil. Peruvian immigration is in Iñapari. Exit stamps can be obtained between 0800-1830. Walk across the bridge over the Rio Acre to Assis Brasil, where there is no Policía Federal office. Travel on to Brasiléia to obtain your Brazil entry stamp at Policía Federal. You must have a yellow fever certificate to enter Brazil. Officials in Iñapari are reported to be obstructive to foreign travellers entering Peru, giving only 30 days entry.

There is a road from **Assis Brasil to Brasiléia** in Brazil (120 km, buses run in the dry season, 2½ hours, US$3.60; four-wheel drive vehicles in the wet season), from where a new bridge has been opened to Cobija in Bolivia. It can be cold travelling this road, so take a blanket or sleeping bag. There are no exchange facilities en route and poor exchange rates for Brazilian currency at Iñapari.

🛌 Sleeping

Manu Biosphere Reserve *p545, map p545*
Amazonia Lodge, in Cusco at Matará 334, T/F084-231370, amazonia1@correo.dnet. com.pe. On the Río Alto Madre de Dios just across the river from Atalaya, an old tea hacienda run by the Yabar family, famous for its bird diversity and fine hospitality, a great place to relax, contact Santiago in advance and he'll arrange a pick-up.

Casa Machiguenga, contact Manu Expeditions or the Apeco NGO, T084-225595. Near Cocha Salvador, upriver from Manu Lodge, Machiguenga-style cabins run by the local community of Tayakome with NGO help. **Cock of the Rock Lodge**, run by the Perú Verde group. On the same road at 1,500 m, next to a Cock of the Rock lek, double rooms with shared bath and 7 private cabins with en-suite bath.

Erika Lodge, contact **Aventuras Ecológicas Manu**, Plateros 356, Cusco; or Ernesto Yallico, Casilla 560, Cusco, T084-227765. On the Alto Madre de Dios, 25 mins from Atalaya. Like **Amazonia Lodge**, this is good place for birds. It offers basic facilities and is cheaper than the other, more luxurious lodges.

Manu Cloud Forest Lodge, owned by **Manu Nature Tours** (see Tours and activities below). Located at Unión at 1,800 m on the road from Paucartambo to Atalaya, 6 rooms with 4 beds.

Manu Lodge, run by **Manu Nature Tours** (see Tours and activities below) and only bookable as part of a full package deal with transport. Situated on the Manu river, 3 hrs upriver from Boca Manu towards Cocha Salvador, It's a fine location over-looking Cocha Juárez, an ox-box lake, which often plays host to a family of giant otters. The lodge has an extensive trail system, and stands of mauritia palms near the lake provide nesting sites for colonies of blue and yellow macaws.

Manu Wildlife Centre, book through **Manu Expeditions** or **InkaNatura**. 2 hrs down the Río Madre de Dios from Boca Manu, near the Blanquillo macaw lick and also counts on a Tapir lick and walk-up canopy tower. 22 double cabins, all with private bathroom and hot water. Also canopy towers for birdwatching.

Pantiacolla Lodge, book through **Pantia-colla Tours**. 30 mins down-river from Shin-tuya. Owned by the Moscoso family. This lodge is located underneath the Pantiacolla Mountains, which due to the large altitudinal range in a small area boasts great biological diversity, particularly with birds. Good trail system. Also managed by Pantiacolla is the new **Yine Lodge**, see Boca Manu above.

Yanayaco Lodge, book through **Expediciones Vilca** in Cusco. 1-hr upriver from Diamante village. A new lodge located close to a small parrot lick.

To Manu from Cusco *p547*
Tambo Amana, 30 mins from Shintuya on foot, tamboamana@yahoo.com. Run by the indigenous Chinipa family, this is a cultural as opposed to wildlife watching tour, learning about Harakmbut culture, plant uses, how to shoot bows and arrows etc. If you make your own way there, this is a very economical

jungle trip at US$190 for 5 days/4 nights for those prepared to rough it a bit. Jessica Bertram de Sasari helps the Chinipa family with marketing and is a good source of information. You can contact her at **Hospedaje Mario's**, C Choquechaca 469, Cusco, T084-225500, jessicabertrampe@yahoo.com. Perudiscovery sell the trip with a stay in the cloudforest and a mountain biking descent, www.perudiscovery.com. Culturas Perú focus more on trekking and cultural aspects, www.culturasperu.com. If contacting the family direct, you need to speak Spanish (or Harakmbut!).

C **Boca Manu Lodge**, book through **Emperadores Tours**, Procuradores 190, Cusco, T084-239987, www.emperadores. com.pe. Run by long-standing Manu resident Juan de Dios Carpio. Juan owns a general store in Boca, so if stranded in Boca Manu and your looking for reasonably priced place to stay this could be an option – just ask at the store.

F **Albergue Eco Turístico Villa Carmen**, Pilcopata, www.business.com.pe/villa-car men. A fairly pleasant place to stay.

F The unnamed place of Sra Rubella in Pilcopata, is very basic, but friendly.

G **The Mission**, Shintuya. The priest will let you stay in the dormitory rooms. There are a few basic restaurants and you can camp (beware of thieves). Supplies are expensive.

Yine Lodge, next to the airstrip, Boca Manu, is smart and new and run by **Pantiacolla Tours**, see below. This is a co-operative project between the company and the native Yine community of Diamante.

Puerto Maldonado *p549, map p549*
A **Wasai**, Billinghurst opposite the **Capitanía**, T082-572290, www.wasai.com. Price includes breakfast, a/c, TV, shower. In a beautiful location overlooking the Madre de Dios, with forest surrounding cabin-style rooms which are built on a slope down to the river, small pool with waterfall, good restaurant if slightly expensive. Recomm-ended, although service can be stretched if hotel is full. They run local tours and have a lodge on the Tambopata River (see p551).

C **Cabañaquinta**, Cusco 535, T082-571045, cabanaquinta@webcusco.zzn.com. With bathroom, fan, good restaurant, friendly, lovely garden, very comfortable but could be cleaner, airport transfer. Recommended.

C **Don Carlos**, Av León Velarde 1271, T082-571029. Nice view over the Río Tambopata, a/c, restaurant, TV, phone, good.

E **Amarumayo**, Libertad 433, 10 mins from centre, T082-573860, residenciamarumayo @hotmail.com. Price includes breakfast. Comfortable, with pool and garden, good restaurant. Recommended.

E **Royal Inn**, Av 2 de Mayo 333, T082-571048. Modern and clean, best of mid-range hotels, rooms at back are less noisy.

E **Hospedaje Español**, González Prada 670, T082-572381. Garden setting, clean, friendly.

E **Hostal El Solar**, González Prada 445, T082-571571. With bath (cheaper without), basic but clean, fan.

E **Hospedaje La Bahía**, 2 de Mayo 710, T082-572127. Cheaper without bath or TV, large rooms, clean. Best of cheaper options.

E **Rey Port**, Av León Velarde 457, T082-571177. With bathroom (cheaper without), clean, fan, good value.

E **Wilson**, Jr González Prada 355, T082-572838. With bathroom, basic.

F **Hostal El Astro**, Velarde 617, T082-572128. Clean, safe, family run.

F **Hotel Toni**, in Quincemil, on the road from Cusco to Puerto Maldonado. Friendly, clean, cold shower, good meals.

Tambopata National Reserve (TNR)
p551, map p551

Most of the lodges in the Tambopata area use the term 'ecotourism', or something similar, in their publicity material, but it is applied pretty loosely. **Posada Amazonas'** collaboration with the local community is

unique in the area, but fortunately no lodge offers trips where guests hunt for their meals. See p49 for points to note. Lodges on the Tambopata are reached by vehicle to Bahuaja port, 15 km up river from Puerto Maldonado by the community of Infierno, then by boat. Some of the lodges mentioned above also offer guiding and research placements to biology and environmental science graduates. For more details send an SAE to TReeS: UK- c/o J Forrest, PO Box 33153, London NW3 4DR. Long-term visitors should be aware that leishmaniasis exists in this area.

Río Madre de Dios

C **Casa de Hospedaje Mejía**, to book T082-571428, visit **Mejía Tours**, L Velarde 333, or just turn up. An attractive rustic lodge on Lago Sandoval, with 10 double rooms, full board can be arranged, canoes are available.

Eco Amazonia Lodge, book through their office in Lima: Av Larco 1083, of 408, Miraflores, T01-242 2708, www.ecoamaz onia.com.pe. On the Madre de Dios, 1 hr down-river from Puerto Maldonado. Accommodation for up to 80 in basic bungalows and dormitories, good for birdwatching with viewing platforms and tree canopy access, has its own Monkey Island with animals taken from the forest, US$150 for 3 days/2 nights.

El Corto Maltés, Billinghurst 229, Puerto Maldonado, T/F082-573831, cortomaltes @terra.com.pe. On the south side of the Madre de Dios river, halfway to Sandoval, the focus of most visits. Hot water, huge dining room, well run. Attracts French groups. **Jungle Lodge**, book through **Cusco-Maldonado Tour**, Pasaje de Harinas 177 T/F084-244054, Cusco. Bungalows 15 km out on the northern bank of the Río Madre de Dios. 2, 3 and 4-day jungle programmes available, from US$90 per person in low season, tours visit Lago Sandoval.

Reserva Amazónica Lodge, 45 mins by boat down the Río Madre de Dios. To book: **Inkaterra**, Andalucía 174, Lima 18, T01-610 0400, Cusco T084- 245314, Puerto Maldonado T082-572283, www.inkaterra.com. Caters mainly for large groups. Jungle tours available with multi-lingual guides, the lodge is surrounded by its own 10,000 ha but most tours are to Lago Sandoval, US$120 per person (double occupancy) for 2 days/1 night package, rising to US$370 for 5 days/4 nights, a naturalists programme is also provided, negotiable out of season. Has the largest number of ants recorded in a single location, 342. The lodge has a Monkey Island (Isla Rolín). A hotel in the jungle with 6 suites and 38 rustic bungalows with private bathrooms, solar power, good food.

Sandoval Lake Lodge, to book, **InkaNatura**, Manuel Bañon 461, San Isidro, Lima, T01-440 2022, www.inkanatura.com. Also have an office in Cusco. 1 km beyond Mejía on Lago Sandoval, usually accessed by canoe across the lake after a 3-km walk or rickshaw ride along the trail, this lodge can accommodate 50 people in 25 rooms, bar and dining area, electricity, hot water. There is a short system of trails nearby, guides are available in several languages. Prices start at US$140 per person (double occupancy) for 2 days/1 night, to US$250 double for 4 days/3 nights. They also have a small lodge on the Río Heath.

Río Tambopata

Albergue Inatowa, T082-572511, www.inotawaexpeditions.com. On the Tambopata, just downstream from **Explorer's Inn**, visits are made to the nearby Lago Tres Chimbadas. It is part of the scheme to show visitors the life of long-term colonists in the Tambopata area; facilities are quite basic, transport, food, mosquito net and Spanish-speaking guides.

Caiman Lodge, to book T082-571045, Puerto Maldonado, www.webcusco.com/ sachavacasinn. Two bungalows for up to 20 people, located between Explorer's Inn and Libertador Tambopata Lodge. Visits are made to Lago Sachavacayoc.

Casa de hospedaje Picaflor, Casilla 105, Puerto Maldonado, picaflor_rc@yahoo.com. A small (4 rooms), family run guest house with solar lighting, a good library, great cakes and fresh bread baked daily. It's located just downriver from **Libertador Tambopata Lodge**, guiding in English/Spanish, good trail system, visits also made to Lake Condenados. Suited to backpackers wanting a more intimate rainforest experience and birders, US$20pp per night plus TNR fee and transport. Special arrangements also for researchers and volunteers wanting to stay 4 or more weeks.

Explorer's Inn, book through **Peruvian Safaris**, Alcanfores 459, Miraflores, Lima, T01-447 8888, or Plateros 365, T084-235342 Cusco, www.peruviansafaris.com. The office in Puerto Maldonado is at Fitzcarrald 136, T/F082-572078. The lodge is located adjoining the TNR, in the part where most research work has been done, 58 km from Puerto Maldonado. It's a 2½-hr ride up the Río Tambopata (1½ hrs return, in the early morning, so take warm clothes and rain gear), one of the best places in Peru for seeing jungle birds (580 plus species have been recorded here), butterflies (1,230 plus species), also giant river otters, but you probably need more than a 2-day tour to benefit fully from the location. Offers tours through the adjoining community of La Torre to meet local people and find out about their farms (*chacras*) and handicrafts.

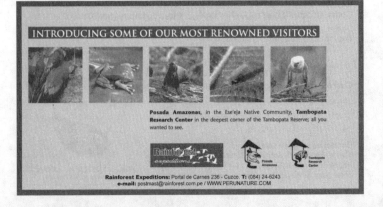

The guides are biologists and naturalists from around the world who undertake research in the reserve in return for acting as guides. They provide interesting wildlife-treks, including to the macaw lick (collpa). US$180 for 3 days/2 nights, US$165 in the low season.

Libertador Tambopata Lodge, on the Río Tambopata, make reservations at Suecia 343, Cusco, T084-245695, tplcus@terra.com.pe. Associated with the Libertador hotel chain, the lodge has rooms with solar-heated water, accommodates 60. Good guides, excellent food. Trips go to Lake Condenado, some to Lake Sachavacayoc, and to the Collpa de Chuncho, guiding mainly in English and Spanish, package US$210 per person for 3 days/2 nights, naturalists programme provided.

Posada Amazonas Lodge, on the Tambopata river, 2 hrs upriver from Puerto Maldonado. Book through **Rainforest Expeditions**, Aramburú 166, of 4B, Miraflores, Lima 18, T01-421 8347, or Portal de Carnes 236, Cusco, T084-246243, www.perunature. com. A unique collaboration between a tour agency the local native community of Infierno. 24 large attractive rooms with bathroom, cold showers, visits to Lake Tres Chimbadas, with good birdwatching opportunities including the Tambopata Collpa. Offers trips to a nearby indigenous primary health care project where a native healer gives guided tours of the medicinal plant garden. Tourist income has helped the centre become self-funding. Service and guiding is very good. Recommended. Prices start at US$190 for a 3 day/2 night package, or US$690 for 5 days/4 nights including the Tambopata Research Centre, the company's older, more intimate, but comfortable lodge. Rooms are smaller than **Posada Amazonas**, shared showers, cold water (the TRC has had to be renewed because of river encroach- ment, but it's as good as ever). The lodge is next to the famous Tambopata macaw clay lick. Tapir are often seen here on the bank opposite the collpa.

Wasai Lodge, on the Río Tambopata, 120 km (3½ hrs) upriver from Puerto Maldonado, T082-572290, 1½ hrs return, same owners as **Hotel Wasai** in town; www.wasai.com. Small lodge with 7 bungalows for 40 people, 20 km of trails around the lodge, guides in English and Spanish. The Collpa de Chuncho, one of the biggest macaw licks in the world, is only 1 hr upriver; 3 day/2 night trips US$275, 4 day/3 nights US$375, both including a visit to Lake Sandoval plus two nights in Puerto Maldonado. Just to spend a night in the jungle without guided tours costs US$50.

Río Las Piedras

Albergue Inatowa, T082-572511, www.ino tawaexpeditions.com. On the Tambopata, just downstream from **Explorer's Inn**, visits are made to the nearby Lago Tres Chimbadas. It is part of the scheme to show visitors the life of long-term colonists in the Tambopata area; basic facilities, transport, food, mosquito net and Spanish-speaking guides.
Las Piedras Biodiversity Station is, in effect, a casa de hospedaje, T/F082-573922, info@ tambopataexpeditions.com. A small lodge located 90 km up the Río Las Piedras, visitors camp en route to the lodge. With only 20 beds the lodge looks to offer a more personalized experience of the rainforest. Central dining-room, shared bath, no electricity, library, guiding in English/ Spanish. Owing to the remoteness of the lodge the minimum package is for 5 days/4 nights, US$410 pp based on a group of 4 people. Special rates offered for those wanting to stay longer than 2 weeks.

To Iberia and Iñapari *p552*

F **Hostal Aquino**, Iberia, Km 168. Best of the two hotels here. Basic, cold shower.
F **Hostal Milagros**, Iñapari, at the end of the road, Km 235. Of the two basic hotels here this is the best one. With restaurant.
F In Assis Brasil, across the border, has three hotels, and a good *churrascaria*.

🍴 Eating

Puerto Maldonado *p549, map p550*
The best restaurant in town is at the **Hotel Wasai**, the best lunchtime menu is at the **Cabañaquinta**.
††-† **El Califa**, Piura 266. Often has bushmeat, mashed banana and palm hearts on the menu. Recommended.
††-† **El Hornito/Chez Maggy**, on the plaza. Cosy atmosphere, good pizzas, but pasta dishes are not such good value.
† **El Buen Paladar**, González Prada 365. Good value lunch menu.
† **La Cosa Nostra**, Av León Velarde 515. The best place for snacks and cakes.
† **La Estrella**, Av León Velarde 474. The smartest and best of the *pollos a la brasa* places.

🍸 Bars and clubs

Puerto Maldonado *p549, map p550*
Bar Amnesia, on the south side of the plaza.
Discoteca Anaconda, east side of the plaza.
El Witite, Av León Velarde 153. A popular, good disco, latin music, open Fri and Sat.
Le Boulevard, behind **El Hornito**. Live music, popular. There is a billiard hall at **Puno 520**.

🏔 Activities and tours

Manu Biosphere Reserve *p545, map p545*
The tour operators listed below are situated in Cusco, the gateway to the reserve.
Amazon Trails Peru, Triunfo 342, T084-974 1735 (mob), www.amazontrailsperu.com. Small agency operated by Abraham Huaman León who has many years' experience guiding in the region. Mainly offers interesting itineraries in the buffer zones surrounding Manu, but trips to the former Reserved Zone (now part of the National Park) are possible.
Expediciones Vilca, Plateros 363, T084-251872, www.cbc.org.pe/manuvilca/. Manu jungle tours: 8-day/7-night, other lengths of stay are available. Will supply sleeping bags at no extra cost. Minimum 5 people, maximum 10 per guide. Arto Ovaska, author of *Manu, Nature's Paradise*, works as a guide for **Vilca** so if you want a Finnish guide – ask! This is the only economical tour which camps at the Otorongo camp, which is supposedly quieter than Salvador where many agencies camp. There are discounts for students. In the low season they will organize other tours. Very efficient, good service.

InkaNatura Travel, Plateros 361, 1st floor, T084-251173 (in Lima: Manuel Bañón 461, San Isidro, T01-440 2022), www.inkanatura. com. A non-profit organization with proceeds directed back into projects on sustainable tourism and conservation. Arranges trips to the Manu Reserved Zone, Manu Wildlife Centre, The Biotrip, 6-day/5-night, which takes you through the Andes to lowland jungle, **Sandoval Lake Lodge** in Tambopata, and also a tour into Machiguenga Indian territory, including the Pongo de Mainique. They have also opened the remote **Heath River Wildlife Center**, 1 hr up the Río Heath (4-5 hrs from Puerto Maldonado) on the Peru/Bolivia border, a cooperative project with traditional Ese'eja community of Sonene. They sell book called *Peru's Amazonian Eden-Manu*, US$80, proceeds go to the projects. The same title can be found in other bookshops at a much inflated price. 10% discount on all trips for Footprint Handbook readers.

Manu Ecological Adventures, Plateros 356, T084-261640, www.manuadventures.com. Manu jungle tours, either economical tour in and out overland, or in by land and out by plane, giving you longer in the jungle, both leave on Sun. Other lengths of stay are available leaving on Mon and Tue. Options include a mountain biking descent through the cloudforest and 3 hrs of white-water rafting on the way to **Erika Lodge** on the upper Río Madre de Dios. They operate with a minimum of 4 people and a maximum of 10 people per guide.

Manu Expeditions, Av Pardo 895, PO Box 606, T084-226671, www.ManuExpeditions. com. English spoken, Mon-Fri 0900-1300, 1500-1900; Sat 0900-1300. Run by ornithologist and British Consul Barry Walker of the **Cross Keys Pub**. 3 trips available to the reserve and Manu Wildlife Centre. Two of the trips visit a lodge run by Machiguenga people on the first Sun of every month and cost an extra US$150.

Manu Nature Tours, Av Pardo 1046, T084-252721, www.manuperu.com. Owned by Boris Gómez Luna. English spoken. This company aims more for the luxury end of the market and owns 2 comfortable lodges in the cloudforest and reserved zone. Tours are very much based around these sites, thus entailing less travel between different areas. **Manu Lodge** has an extensive trail system and also offers canopy climbing for an additional US$45 per person. In the cloudforest zone a novel 'Llama Taxi' service is offered, in conjunction with local community of Jajahuana.

Pantiacolla Tours, Plateros 360, T084-238323, www.pantiacolla.com. Manu jungle tours: 5- and 7-day trips include return flights, the 9-day trip is an overland return. Prices do not include park entrance fee. Guaranteed departure dates regardless of number, maximum 10 people with 1 guide. The trips involve a combination of camping, platform camping and lodges. All clients are given a booklet entitled, *Talking About Manu*, written by the Dutch owner, Marianne van Vlaardingen, who is a biologist. She is extremely friendly and helpful. Marianne and her Peruvian husband Gustavo have recently opened an ecotourism lodge in conjunction with the Yine native community of Diamante. Yine guides are used and community members

are being trained in the various aspects of running the project.

Tambopata National Reserve (TNR)
p551, map p551

Peruvian Safaris, Plateros 365, T084-235342, www.peruviansafaris.com. For reservations for the **Explorer's Inn** – excluding park entrance fees and flights.

Tambo Tours, 20919 Coral Bridge Lane, Suite 225-A, Spring, TX, 77388, USA, T001-281 528 9448, www.2GOPERU. com. Long-established adventure and tour specialist with offices in Peru and USA. Customized trips to the Amazon and Archaeological sites of Peru and Ecuador. Daily departures for groups and Individuals.

Puerto Maldonado *p549, map p550*

The usual price for trips to Lago Sandoval is US$25 per person per day (minimum of 2 people), and US$35 per person per day for longer trips lasting 2-4 days (minimum of 4-6 people). All guides should have a carnet issued by the Ministry of Tourism (DIRCETUR), which also verifies them as suitable guides for trips to other places and confirms their identity. Check that the carnet has not expired. Reputable guides are **Hernán Llave Cortez**, **Romel Nacimiento** and the **Mejía** brothers, all of whom can be contacted on arrival at the airport, if available. Boat hire can be arranged through the Capitanía del Puerto (Río Madre de Dios), T573003. **Perú Tours**, Av 2 de Mayo 400, T082-803064, perutoursytravel@hotmail.com. Organize local trips. **Transtours**, G Prada 341, T082-572606.

⊖ Transport

Manu Biosphere Reserve *p545, map p545*
Air
There is an airstrip at Boca Manu, but no regular flights from Cusco. These are arranged the day before, usually by Manu tour operators, if there are enough passengers. If you want to arrange a private flight this will set you back around US$750 one-way (this cost can be divided between the number of passengers). Contact **Transandes**, T084-224638, or **Aerocóndor**, T084-252774. Both airlines have offices in the Cusco airport terminal. Flights, which use small prop-engined aircraft, are sometimes delayed by bad weather.

Road
Trucks leave every Mon, Wed and Fri from the Coliseo Cerrado in Cusco at about 1000 (be there by 0800) to **Pilcopata** and **Shintuya** (passing Atalaya). The journey can take at least 24 hrs and is rough and uncomfortable. They return the following day, but there is no service on Sun. There is also a bus service, which leaves from the same place to Pilcopata, on Mon and Fri and returns on Tue and Sat. The journey takes 12 hrs in the dry season and costs US$8-10. From Pilcopata there are trucks to Atalaya (1 hr, US$8) and Shintuya (4 hrs, US$10). Trucks leave in the morning between 0600 and 0900. Make sure you go with a recommended truck driver. Only basic supplies are available after leaving Cusco, so take all your camping and food essentials, including insect repellent.

Transport can be disrupted in the wet season because the road is in poor condition (tour operators have latest details). Tour operators usually use their own vehicles for the overland trip from Cusco to Manu.

Puerto Maldonado *p549, map p550*
Air
To **Lima**, daily with **Tans** and **Lan**. Both fly via Cusco, but **Tans** also has a direct flight from Lima on Fri and Sun. Combis to the airport run along Av 2 de Mayo, 10-15 mins, US$0.60. A moto-taxi from town to the airport is US$2. If on the last flight of the day into Puerto Maldonado, usually Lan, don't hang around as most vehicles return to town quickly. A yellow fever vaccination is offered free , but check that a new needle is used.
Airline offices Lan, Av León Velarde y 2 de Mayo, T082-573677. **Tans**, Av León Velarde 160, T082-571429.

Bus
There is a daily bus from **Cusco** with **Transportes Huareño**, which takes 24-30 hours to Puerto Maldonado. It costs US$15. Another option is to go from Cusco to **Urcos**, 1 hr, US$2.25, then look for the **Transportes Juan Carlos** bus in Urcos' main plaza. This is a Volvo truck modified with seats and windows. In the dry season this takes 26 hrs to Puerto Maldonado, US$13; it leaves about 1500 daily. There are also daily buses from **Mazuko** to Puerto Maldonado with **Transportes Bolpebra** and **Transportes Señor de la Cumbre**, 8 hrs, US$5.

River
To **Boca Manu** and **Shintuya**, via **Colorado**. Take a combi to **Laberinto**, 1½ hrs, US$2.50, uncomfortable (return in the afternoon daily - see Puerto Maldonando excursions above) and take a cargo boat from there to Colorado; several daily, US$12. You can get a daily cargo boat from there to Boca Manu and Shintuya, 9-10 hrs, US$15. From Shintuya trucks go to Pilcopata and Cusco (see under Manu Biosphere Reserve).

To **Puerto Heath** (Bolivian border), it can take several days to find a boat going all the way to the Bolivian border. Motorized dugout canoes go to Puerto Pardo on the Peruvian side, 5 hrs, US$4.50 per person (no hotels or shops); wait here for a canoe to Puerto Heath.

It is fairly hard to get a boat from the border to Riberalta (a wait of up to 3 days is not uncommon), US$15-20. Alternatively, travel to the naval base at América, then fly.

Motorcycles/taxis
Scooters and mopeds can de hired from San Francisco, and others, on the corner of Puno and G Prada for US$1.15 per hour or US$10 per day. No deposit is required but your passport and driving licence need to be shown. Mototaxis around town charge US$0.50; riding pillion on a bike is US$0.20.

Tambopata National Reserve (TNR)
p551, map p551
A river taxi makes 2 journeys a week, Mon and Thu upriver, Tue and Fri down, up to 10 hrs, US$5 to travel as far as **Wasai Lodge**. It leaves Puerto Maldonado between 0600 and 0900.

To Iberia and Iñapari *p552*
The easiest way to reach the border with Brazil is to take one of the car *colectivos* (three companies) that leave for the border from Calle Piura, one block from the market in **Puerto Maldonado** between 0700-0800, 5-5½ hours, US$10.
To Bolivia take the boat to Puerto Heath (see p561) and get a tourist visa at the Bolivian consulate in Puerto Maldonado.

● Directory

Manu Biosphere Reserve *p545, map p545*
Conservation organizations Asociación Peruana para la Conservación de la Naturaleza (Apeco), Parque José Acosta 187, 2nd floor, Magdalena del Mar, Lima 17, T01-264 0094, www.apeco.org. **Manu National Park Office**, Av Micaela Bastidas 310, Cusco, T084-240898, pqnmanu@terra. com.pe. Casilla Postal 591. Open 0800-1400.

They issue a permit for the former Reserved Zone. **Perú Verde**, Ricaldo Palma J-1, Santa Mónica, Cusco, T084-243408, www.peru verde.org. A local NGO that can help with information and has free video shows about Manu National Park and Tambopata Reserve. They are friendly and helpful and also have information on programmes and research in the jungle area of Madre de Dios. **ProManu**, Urb Magisterial, 2da etapa G-3, Cusco, T084-252937, www.promanu.org. **Pronaturaleza**, Av Alberto de Campo 417, Lima 17, T01-264 2736, www.pronaturale za.org. Their office in Puerto Maldonado is at Jr Cajamarca cuadra 1 s/n, T082-571585.

Puerto Maldonado *p549, map p550*
Banks BCP, cash advances with Visa, no commission on TCs (Amex only). **Banco de la Nación**, cash on Mastercard, quite good rates for TCs. Both are on the south side of the Plaza. The best rates for cash are at the casas de cambio/gold shops on Puno 6th block, eg Cárdenas Hnos, Puno 605.
Embassies and consulates Bolivian Consulate: on the north side of the plaza. Peruvian immigration: is at 26 de Diciembre 356, 1 block from the plaza, get your exit stamp here. Immigration Ica y 28 de Julio. **Internet** All over town, along Av León Velarde and most main streets.
Language schools Tambopata Language Centre, T082-573935, www.tambopata-language. com. It is now possible to learn Spanish while living close to the rainforest and this is a cheaper option than studying in Cusco.
Post Serpost: at Av León Velarde 6th block. **Telephone** Telefónica, on west side of the Plaza, adjoining the Municipalidad. A phone office on the Plaza, next to **El Hornito**, sells all phone cards for national and international calls.

Background

⁝ Footprint features

History

Pre-Columbian history

Despite Peru's formidable geographical difficulties and frequent natural disasters, archaeologists have uncovered a pre-Columbian history of highly advanced societies that prevailed against these awesome odds. The coastal desert from Lambayeque department south to Paracas has revealed an 'American Egypt', although this has meant a bias towards the coastal region and a reliance on the contents of tombs for information. knowledge of these tombs often only comes to light following their looting by gangs of huaqueros (grave robbers), incited by demand from the international antiquities market.

The Incas told the Spaniards that before they established their Tawantinsuyo Empire, the land was overrun by primitives constantly at war with one another. There were, in fact, many other civilized cultures dating back as far as 2000 BC. The most accomplished of these were the Chavín and Sechín (circa 900-200 BC), the Paracas-Nasca (circa 200 BC-AD 500), the Huari-Tiahuanaco (circa 750 BC-AD 1000), and the Moche-Chimú (200 BC-AD 1400).

Early settlement
It is generally accepted that the earliest settlers in Peru were related to people who had crossed the Bering Straits from Asia and drifted through the Americas from about 20,000 BC. However, theories of early migrations from across the Pacific and Atlantic have been rife since Thor Heyerdahl's raft expeditions in 1947 and 1969-1970, see also under Túcume page 404.

The earliest evidence of human presence has been found at three sites: Pikimachay near Ayacucho, Pachamachay in Junín and the Guitarrero Cave in the Callejón de Huaylas. All have a radiocarbon date prior to 9000 BC. It had been thought that village settlement in Peru, on the central coast at Pampa, dated from 2500 BC. The theory was that, between these two dates, people lived nomadically in small groups, mainly hunting and gathering but also cultivating some plants seasonally. Domestication of llamas, alpacas and guinea pigs also began at this time, particularly important for the highland people around the Titicaca basin. Caral, however, has overturned many of the accepted tenets of Peruvian archaeology for this period. Caral is a city, 20 km from the coast in the Supe Valley whose date is about 2,600 BC. It is a monumental construction and appears to be easily the oldest city in South America, flourishing for some 500 years. The evidence points to complex urban society beginning much earlier than previously thought and the city seems to have had a primarily religious, rather than warlike purpose. If these deductions are correct, they also upset some long-held beliefs about city-building worldwide being principally bellicose rather than peaceful.

The abundant wealth of marine life produced by the Humboldt Current, especially along the north coast, boosted population growth and settlement in this area. Around 2000 BC climatic change dried up the lomas ('fog meadows'), and drove sea shoals to deeper water. People turned to farming and began to spread inland along river valleys.

Origins of Andean civilization
From the second millennium BC to around the first century BC is known as the Formative Period (also called Preceramic Period VI and Initial Period) when the first signs of the high culture of Andean society appeared. During this period

sophisticated irrigation and canal systems were developed, farming productivity increased and communities had more time to devote to building and producing ceramics and textiles. The development of pottery also led to trade and cultural links with other communities. Distribution of land and water to the farmers was probably organized by a corporate authority, and this may have led to the later 'Mit'a' labour system developed by the Incas.

Above all, this period is characterized by the construction of centres of urban concentration (Caral notwithstanding) that promoted labour specialization and the development of cultural expression. The earliest buildings built were huacas, adobe platform mounds, centres of cult or sacred power. Huaca Florida was the largest example of this period, near the Río Rimac, later replaced by Huaca Garagay as a major centre for the area. Similar centres spread along the north coast, such as El Aspero and Piedra Parada.

During this period, however, much more advanced architecture was being built at Kotosh, in the central Andes near Huánuco. Japanese archaeological excavations there in the 1960s revealed a temple with ornamental niches and friezes. Some of the earliest pottery was also found here, showing signs of influence from southern Ecuador and the tropical lowlands, adding weight to theories of Andean culture originating in the Amazon. Radiocarbon dates of some Kotosh remains are as early as 1850 BC.

Chavín and Sechín

For the next 1,000 years or so up to c 900 BC, communities grew and spread inland from the north coast and south along the northern highlands. Farmers still lived in simple adobe or rough stone houses but built increasingly large and complex ceremonial centres, such as at Las Haldas in the Casma Valley (dated at 1700 BC). As farming became more productive and pottery more advanced, commerce grew and states began to develop throughout central and North-central Peru, with the associated signs of social structure and hierarchies.

Around 900 BC a new era was marked by the rise of two important centres; **Chavín de Huantar** in the central Andes and **Sechín Alto**, inland from Casma on the north coast (some date the latter from 1600 BC).

Chavín takes its name from the site of Chavín de Huantar in the northern highlands. This was the first of several 'horizon styles' that were of the greatest importance in Peru and had very widespread influence. The other later ones, the Huari-Tiahuanaco and the Inca, were pan-Peruvian, affecting all parts of the country. The chief importance of Chavín de Huantar was not so much in its highly advanced architecture as in the influence of its cult coupled with the artistic style of its ceramics and other artefacts. The founders of Chavín may have originated in the tropical lowlands as some of its carved monoliths show representations of monkeys and felines.

Objects with Chavín traits have been found all along the coast from Piura to the Lurin valley south of Lima, and its cult ideology spread to temples around the same area. Richard L Burger of Yale University has argued that the extent of Chavín influence has been exaggerated. Many sites on the coast already had their own cult practices and the Chavín idols may have been simply added alongside. There is evidence of an El Niño flood that devastated the north coast around 500 BC. Local cults fell from grace as social order was disrupted and the Chavín cult was snatched up as a timely new alternative.

Chavín cult

The Chavín cult was paralleled by the great advances made at this time in textile production and in some of the earliest examples of metallurgy (whose origins have been attributed to some gold, silver and copper ornaments found in graves in Chongoyape, near Chiclayo, which show Chavín-style features). But earlier evidence has been discovered in the Andahuaylas region, dating from 1800-900 BC. The religious symbolism of gold and other precious metals and stones is thought to have been an inspiration behind some of the beautiful artefacts found in the central Andean area. The emergence of social hierarchies also created a demand for luxury goods as status symbols.

The cultural brilliance of Chavín de Huántar was complemented by its contemporary, **Sechín**. This huge granite-faced complex near Casma, 370 km north of Lima, was described by JC Tello as the biggest structure of its kind in the Andes. According to Michael Moseley of Harvard University, Chavín and Sechín may have combined forces, with Sechín as the military power that spread the cultural word of Chavín, but their influence did not reach far to the south where the Paracas and Tiahuanaco cultures held sway.

Upper Formative Period

The Chavín hegemony, which is also known as the Middle Formative Period (or Early Horizon), broke up around 300 BC. The 'unity' of this period was broken and the initial phase of the regional diversification of Andean cultures began. The process of domestication of plants and animals culminated in the Upper Formative Period. Agricultural technology progressed leading to an economic security that permitted a considerable growth in the centres of population. Among the many diverse stylistic/cultural groups of this period are: the Vicus on the north coast; Salinar in the Chicama valley; Paracas Necrópolis on the south coast; and Huarás in the Ancash highlands.

Paracas Necrópolis was the early phase of the Nasca culture and is renowned for the superb technical quality and stylistic variety in its weaving and pottery. The mantos (large, decorated cloth) rank amongst the world's best, and many of the finest examples can be seen in the museums of Lima. The extreme dryness of the desert here has preserved the textiles and ceramics in the mummies' tombs which have been excavated.

Paracas Necrópolis is, in fact, a cemetery located on the slopes of Cerro Colorado, in the Department of Ica, from which 429 funerary bundles were excavated (see page 290). Each bundle is a mummy wrapped in many fine and rough textiles. Paracas Necrópolis corresponds to the last of the 10 phases into which Paracas ceramics have been divided. The previous ones, known as Paracas Cavernas, relate to the Middle Formative Period and were influenced by the Chavín cult.

Nasca culture

The Regional Development Period up to about AD 500, was a time of great social and cultural development. Sizable towns of 5-10,000 inhabitants grew on the south coast, populated by artisans, merchants, government administrators and religious officials.

One of the most famous cultures of this period, or indeed of pre-Columbian history was the Nasca. The Nasca Lines are a feature of the region. Straight lines, abstract designs and outlines of animals are scratched in the desert surface forming a lighter contrast that can be seen clearly from the air. There are many theories of how and why the lines were made but no explanation has yet been able to establish their place in Peruvian history (see Nasca Lines, page 303). There are similarities between the style of some of the line patterns and that of the pottery and textiles of the same period. It is clear from the scale of the lines and quality of the work that, they were important to the Nasca culture.

In contrast to the quantity and quality of the Nasca artefacts found, relatively few major buildings belonging to this period have been uncovered in the southern desert. Dos Palmas is a complex of rooms and courtyards in the Pisco Valley, while Cahuachi in the Nasca Valley is a large area including adobe platforms, a pyramid and a 'wooden Stonehenge' cluster of preserved tree trunks. Most recently excavated are the architectural complex of Los Molinos, with large buildings, patios and passages, and the necropolis of La Muña, both near Palpa. As most of the archaeological evidence of the Nasca culture came from their desert cemeteries, little is known about the lives and social organization of the people. Alpaca hair found in Nasca textiles, however, indicates that there must have been strong trade links with highland people.

Moche culture

Nasca's contemporaries on the north coast were the militaristic Moche who, from about AD 100-800 built up an empire whose traces stretch from Piura in the north to Casma, beyond Chimbote, in the south. The Moche built their capital in the middle of the desert, outside present day Trujillo. It features the pyramid temples of the Huaca del Sol and Huaca de la Luna (see page 390). The Moche roads and system of way stations are thought to have been an early inspiration for the Inca network. The Moche increased the coastal population with intensive irrigation projects. Skillful engineering works were carried out, such as the La Cumbre canal, still in use today, and the Ascope aqueduct.

The Moche's greatest achievement, however, was its artistic genius. Exquisite ornaments in gold, silver and precious stones were made by its craftsmen. Moche pottery progressed through five stylistic periods, most notable for the stunningly lifelike portrait vases. A wide variety of ceremonial and everyday scenes were created in naturalistic ceramics, telling us more about Moche life than is known about other earlier cultures, and perhaps used by them as 'visual aids' to compensate for the lack of a written language (see also page 392).

A spectacular discovery of a Moche royal tomb at **Sipán** was made in February 1987 by Walter Alva, director of the Brüning Archaeological Museum, Lambayeque. Reports of the excavation in the National Geographic magazine (October 1988 and June 1990), talked of the richest unlooted tomb in the New World (see page 403). The find included semi-precious stones brought from Chile and Argentina, and seashells from Ecuador (the Moche were also great navigators).

The cause of the collapse of the Moche Empire around AD 600-700 is unknown, but it may have been started by a 30-year drought at the end of the sixth century, followed by one of the periodic El Niño flash floods (identified by meteorologists from ice thickness in the Andes) and finished by the encroaching forces of the Huari Empire. The decline of the Moche signalled a general tipping of the balance of power in Peru from the north coast to the southern sierra.

Huari-Tiahuanaco

The ascendant Huari-Tiahuanaco movement, from circa AD 600-1000, combined the religious cult of the Tiahuanaco site in the Titicaca basin, with the military dynamism of the Huari, based in the central highlands. The two cultures developed independently but, as had occurred with the Chavín-Sechín association, they are generally thought to have merged compatibly.

Up until their own demise around AD 1440, the Huari-Tiahuanaco had spread their empire and influence from Cajamarca and Lambayeque in the north and across much of southern Peru, northern Bolivia and Argentina. The Huari introduced a new concept in urban life, the great walled urban centre, the best example of which is their capital city, 22 km north of Ayacucho (see page 497). They also made considerable gains in art and technology, building roads, terraces and irrigation canals across the country.

The Huari-Tiahuanaco ran their empire with efficient labour and administrative systems that were later adopted and refined by the Incas. Labour tribute for state projects had been practised by the Moche and was further developed now. But the empire could not contain regional kingdoms who began to fight for land and power. As control broke down, rivalry and coalitions emerged, and the system collapsed.

Chimú culture

After the decline of the Huari Empire, the unity that had been imposed on the Andes was broken. A new stage of autonomous regional or local political organizations began. Among the cultures corresponding to this period were the Kuelap, centred in the Chachapoyas region (see page 451), and the Chimú.

The Chimú culture had two centres. To the north was Lambayeque, near Chiclayo, while to the south, in the Moche valley near present-day Trujillo, was the great adobe walled city of Chan Chán. Covering 20 sq km, this was the largest pre-Hispanic Peruvian city (see page 391).

Chimú has been classified as a despotic state that based its power on wars of conquest. Rigid social stratification existed and power rested in the hands of the great lord Siquic and the lord Alaec. These lords were followed in social scale by a group of urban couriers who enjoyed a certain degree of economic power. At the bottom were the peasants and slaves. In 1450, the Chimú kingdom was conquered by the Inca Túpac Yupanqui, the son and heir of the Inca ruler Pachacuti Inca Yupanqui.

Inca Dynasty

The origins of the Inca Dynasty are shrouded in mythology. The best known story reported by the Spanish chroniclers talks about Manco Cápac and his sister rising out of Lake Titicaca, created by the Sun as divine founders of a chosen race. This was in approximately AD 1200. Over the next 300 years the small tribe grew to supremacy as leaders of the largest empire ever known in the Americas, the four territories of Tawantinsuyo, united by Cusco as the umbilicus of the Universe. The four quarters of Tawantinsuyo, all radiating out from Cusco, were: 1 Chinchaysuyo, north and north-west; 2 Cuntisuyo, south and west; 3 Collasuyo, south and east; 4 Antisuyo, east.

At its peak, just before the Spanish Conquest, the Inca Empire stretched from the Río Maule in central Chile, north to the present Ecuador-Colombia border, containing most of Ecuador, Peru, western Bolivia, northern Chile and northwest Argentina. The area was roughly equivalent to France, Belgium, Holland, Luxembourg, Italy and Switzerland combined (980,000 sq km).

The first Inca ruler, Manco Cápac, moved to the fertile Cusco region, and established Cusco as his capital. Successive generations of rulers were fully occupied with local conquests of rivals, such as the Colla and Lupaca to the south, and the Chanca to the northwest. At the end of Inca Viracocha's reign the hated Chanca were finally defeated, largely thanks to the heroism of one of his sons, Pachacútec Inca Yupanqui, who was subsequently crowned as the new ruler.

From the start of Pachacútec's own reign in 1438, imperial expansion grew in earnest. With the help of his son and heir, Topa Inca, territory was conquered from the Titicaca basin south into Chile, and all the north and central coast down to the Lurin Valley. The Incas also subjugated the Chimú, their highly sophisticated rivals on the coast (see above). Typical of the Inca method of government, some of the Chimú skills were assimilated into their own political and administrative system, and some Chimú nobles were even given positions in Cusco.

Perhaps the pivotal event in Inca history came in 1527 with the death of the ruler, Huayna Capac. Civil war broke out in the confusion over his rightful successor. One of his legitimate sons, Huáscar, ruled the southern part of the empire from Cusco. Atahualpa, Huáscar's half-brother, governed Quito, the capital of Chinchaysuyo. In 1532, soon after Atahualpa had won the civil war, Francisco Pizarro arrived in Tumbes with 179 conquistadores, many on horseback. Atahualpa's army was marching south, probably for he first time, when he clashed with Piazarro at Cajamarca.

Francisco Pizarro's only chance against the formidable imperial army he encountered at Cajamarca was a bold stroke. He drew Atahualpa into an ambush, slaughtered his guards, promised him liberty if a certain room were filled with treasure, and finally killed him after receiving news that another Inca army was on its way to free him. Pushing on to Cusco, he was at first hailed as the executioner of a traitor: Atahualpa had ordered the death of Huáscar in 1533, while himself a captive of Pizarro, and his victorious generals were bringing the defeated Huáscar to see his half-brother. Panic followed when the conquistadores set about sacking the city, and they fought off with difficulty an attempt by Manco Inca to recapture Cusco in 1536.

Inca society

The Incas were a small aristocracy numbering only a few thousand, centred in the highland city of Cusco, at 3,400 m. They rose gradually as a small regional dynasty, similar to others in the Andes of that period, starting around AD 1200. Then in the mid-1400s, they began to expand explosively under Pachacútec, a sort of Andean Alexander the Great, and later his son, Topa. Under a hundred years later, they fell before the rapacious warriors of Spain. The Incas were not the first dynasty in Andean history to dominate their neighbours, but they did it more thoroughly and went further than anyone before them.

Empire building

Enough remains today of their astounding highways, cities and agricultural terracing for people to marvel and wonder how they accomplished so much in so short a time. They seem to have been amazingly energetic, industrious and efficient – and the reports of their Spanish conquerors confirm this hypothesis.

They must also have had the willing cooperation of most of their subject peoples, most of the time. In fact, the Incas were master diplomats and alliance-builders first, and military conquerors only second, if the first method of expansion failed. The Inca skill at generating wealth by means of highly efficient agriculture and distribution brought them enormous prestige and enabled them to 'out-gift' neighbouring chiefs in huge royal feasts involving ritual outpourings of generosity, often in the form of vast gifts of textiles, exotic products from distant regions, and perhaps wives to add blood ties to the alliance. The 'out-gifted' chief was required by the Andean laws of reciprocity to provide something in return, and this would usually be his loyalty, as well as a levy of manpower from his own chiefdom.

Thus, with each new alliance the Incas wielded greater labour forces and their mighty public works programmes surged ahead. These were administered through an institution known as mit'a, a form of taxation through labour. The state provided the materials, such as wool and cotton for making textiles, and the communities provided skills and labour.

Mit'a contingents worked royal mines, royal plantations for producing coca leaves, royal quarries and so on. The system strove to be equitable, and workers in such hardship posts as high altitude mines and lowland coca plantations were given correspondingly shorter terms of service.

Organization

Huge administrative centres were built in different parts of the empire, where people and supplies were gathered. Articles such as textiles and pottery were produced there in large workshops. Work in these places was carried out in a festive manner, with plentiful food, drink and music. Here was Andean reciprocity at work: the subject supplied his labour, and the ruler was expected to provide generously while he did so.

Aside from mit'a contributions there were also royal lands claimed by the Inca as his portion in every conquered province, and worked for his benefit by the local population. Thus, the contribution of each citizen to the state was quite large, but apparently, the imperial economy was productive enough to sustain this.

Another institution was the practice of moving populations around wholesale, inserting loyal groups into restive areas, and removing recalcitrant populations to loyal areas. These movements of mitmakuna, as they were called, were also used to introduce skilled farmers and engineers into areas where productivity needed to be raised.

Communications

The huge empire was held together by an extensive and highly efficient highway system. There were an estimated 30,000 km of major highway, most of it neatly paved and drained, stringing together the major Inca sites. Two parallel highways ran north to south, along the coastal desert strip and the mountains, and dozens of east-west roads crossing from the coast to the Amazon fringes. These roadways took the most direct routes, with wide stone stairways zig-zagging up the steepest mountain slopes and rope suspension bridges crossing the many narrow gorges of the Andes. The north-south roads formed a great axis which eventually came to be known as **Capaq Ñan** – "Royal, or Principal Road", in Quechua – which exceeded in grandeur not only the other roads, but also their utilitarian concept. They became the Incas' symbol of power over men and over the sacred forces of nature. So marvellous were these roads that the Spaniards who saw them at the height of their glory said that there was nothing comparable in all Christendom.

Every 12 km or so there was a tambo, or way station, where goods could be stored and travellers lodged. The tambos were also control points, where the Inca state's accountants tallied movements of goods and people. Even more numerous than tambos, were the huts of the chasquis, or relay runners, who continually sped royal and military messages along these highways.

The Inca state kept records and transmitted information in various ways. Accounting and statistical records were kept on skeins of knotted strings known as quipus. Numbers employed the decimal system, and colours indicated the categories being recorded. An entire class of people, known as quipucamayocs, existed whose job was to create and interpret these. Neither the Incas nor their Andean predecessors had a system of writing as we understand it, but there may have been a system of encoding language into quipus.

Archaeologists are studying this problem today. History and other forms of knowledge were transmitted via songs and poetry. Music and dancing, full of encoded information which could be read by the educated elite, were part of every major ceremony and public event information was also carried in textiles, which had for millennia been the most vital expression of Andean culture.

Textiles

Clothing carried insignia of status, ethnic origin, age and so on. Special garments were made and worn for various rites of passage. It has been calculated that, after agriculture, no activity was more important to Inca civilization than weaving. Vast stores of textiles were maintained to sustain the Inca system of ritual giving. Armies and mit'a workers were partly paid in textiles. The finest materials were reserved for the nobility, and the Inca emperor himself displayed his status by changing into new clothes every day and having the previous day's burned.

Most weaving was done by women, and the Incas kept large numbers of 'chosen women' in female-only houses all over the empire, partly for the purpose of supplying textiles to the elite and for the many deities, to whom they were frequently given as burned offerings. These women had other duties, such as making chicha – the Inca corn beer which was consumed and sacrificed in vast quantities on ceremonial occasions. They also became wives and concubines to the Inca elite and loyal nobilities. And some may have served as priestesses of the moon, in parallel to the male priesthood of the sun.

Religious worship

The Incas have always been portrayed as sun-worshippers, but it now seems that they were mountain-worshippers too. Recent research has shown that Machu Picchu was at least partly dedicated to the worship of the surrounding mountains, and Inca sacrificial victims have been excavated on frozen Andean peaks at 6,700 m. In fact, until technical climbing was invented, the Incas held the world altitude record for humans.

Human sacrifice was not common, but every other kind was, and ritual attended every event in the Inca calendar. The main temple of Cusco was dedicated to the numerous deities: the Sun, the Moon, Venus, the Pleiades, the Rainbow, Thunder and Lightning, and the countless religious icons of subject peoples which had been brought to Cusco, partly in homage, partly as hostage. Here, worship was continuous and the fabulous opulence included gold cladding on the walls, and a famous garden filled with life-size objects of gold and silver. Despite this pantheism, the Incas acknowledged an overall Creator God, whom they called Viracocha. A special temple was dedicated to him, at Raqchi, about 100 km southeast of Cusco. Part of it still stands today.

Military forces

The conquering Spaniards noted with admiration the Inca storehouse system, still well-stocked when they found it, despite several years of civil war among the Incas. Besides textiles, military equipment, and ritual objects, they found huge quantities of food. Like most Inca endeavours, the food stores served a multiple purpose: to supply feasts, to provide during lean times, to feed travelling work parties, and to supply armies on the march.

Inca armies were able to travel light and move fast because of this system. Every major Inca settlement also incorporated great halls where large numbers of people could be accommodated, or feasts and gatherings held, and large squares or esplanades for public assemblies.

Inca technology is usually deemed inferior to that of contemporary Europe. Their military technology certainly was. They had not invented iron-smelting, and basically fought with clubs, palmwood spears, slings, wooden shields, cotton armour and straw-stuffed helmets. They did not even make much use of the bow and arrow, a weapon they were well aware of. Military tactics, too, were primitive. The disciplined formations of the Inca armies quickly dissolved into melees of unbridled individualism once battle was joined.

This, presumably, was because warfare constituted a theatre of manly prowess, but was not the main priority of Inca life. Its form was ritualistic. Battles were suspended by both sides for religious observance. Negotiation, combined with displays of superior Inca strength, usually achieved victory, and total annihilation of the enemy was not on the agenda.

Architecture

Other technologies, however, were superior in every way to their 16th century counterparts: textiles; settlement planning; and agriculture in particular with its sophisticated irrigation and soil conservation systems, ecological sensitivity, specialized crop strains and high productivity under the harshest conditions. The Incas fell short of their Andean predecessors in the better-known arts of ancient America – ceramics, textiles and metalwork – but it could be argued that their supreme efforts were made in architecture, stoneworking, landscaping, roadbuilding, and the harmonious combination of these elements.

These are the outstanding survivals of Inca civilization, which still remain to fascinate the visitor: the huge, exotically close-fit blocks of stone, cut in graceful, almost sensual curves; the astoundingly craggy and inaccessible sites encircled by great sweeps of Andean scenery; the rhythmic layers of farm terracing that provided land and food to this still-enigmatic people. The finest examples of Inca architecture can be seen in the city of Cusco and throughout the Sacred Valley. As more evidence of Inca society is uncovered each year, our knowledge of these remarkable people can only improve: in 2002 alone two new cities in the Vilcabamba region have been revealed, as well as the huge cemetery at Purucucho (see Excursions from Lima section, page 113) and a mummy at Machu Picchu.

Ruling elite

The ruling elite lived privileged lives in their capital at Cusco. They reserved for themselves and privileged insiders certain luxuries, such as the chewing of coca, the wearing of fine vicuña wool, and the practice of polygamy. But they were an austere people, too. Everyone had work to do, and the nobility were constantly being posted to state business throughout the empire. Young nobles were expected to learn martial skills, besides being able to read the quipus, speak both Quechua and the southern language of Aymara, and know the epic poems.

The Inca elite belonged to royal clans known as panacas, which each had the unusual feature of being united around veneration of the mummy of their founding ancestor – a previous Inca emperor, unless they happened to belong to the panaca founded by the Inca emperor who was alive at the time. Each new emperor built his own palace in Cusco and amassed his own wealth rather than inheriting it from his forebears, which perhaps helps to account for the urge to unlimited expansion.

This urge ultimately led the Incas to overreach themselves. Techniques of diplomacy and incorporation no longer worked as they journeyed farther from the homeland and met ever-increasing resistance from people less familiar with their ways. During the reign of Wayna Cápac, the last emperor before the Spanish invasion, the Incas had to establish a northern capital at Quito in order to cope with permanent war on their northern frontier. Following Wayna Cápac's death came a devastating civil war between Cusco and Quito, and immediately thereafter came the Spanish invasion. Tawantisuyo, the empire of the four quarters, collapsed with dizzying suddenness.

Conquest and after

Peruvian history after the arrival of the Spaniards was not just a matter of conquistadores versus Incas. The vast majority of the huge empire remained unaware of the conquest for many years. The Chimú and the Chachapoyas cultures were powerful enemies of the Incas. The Chimú developed a highly sophisticated culture and a powerful empire stretching for 560 km along the coast from Tumbes south to present-day Lima. Their history was well-recorded by the Spanish chroniclers and continued through the conquest possibly up to about 1600. The Kuélap/ Chachapoyas people were not so much an empire as a loose-knit 'confederation of ethnic groups with no recognized capital' (Morgan Davis *Chachapoyas: The Cloud People*, Ontario, 1988). But the culture did develop into an advanced society with great skill in roads and monument building. Their fortress at Kuélap was known as the most impregnable in Tawantinsuyo. It remained intact against Inca attack and Manco Inca even tried, unsuccessfully, to gain refuge here against the Spaniards.

In 1535, wishing to secure his communications with Spain, Pizarro founded Lima, near the ocean, as his capital. The same year Diego de Almagro set out to conquer Chile. Unsuccessful, he returned to Peru, quarrelled with Pizarro, and in 1538 fought a pitched battle with Pizarro's men at the Salt Pits, near Cusco. He was defeated and put to death. Pizarro, who had not been at the battle, was assassinated in his palace in Lima by Almagro's son three years later.

For the next 27 years each succeeding representative of the Kingdom of Spain sought to subdue the Inca successor state of Vilcabamba, north of Cusco, and to unify the fierce Spanish factions. Francisco de Toledo (appointed 1568) solved both problems during his 14 years in office: Vilcabamba was crushed in 1572 and the last reigning Inca, Túpac Amaru, put to death.

For the next 200 years the Viceroys closely followed Toledo's system, if not his methods. The Major Government – the Viceroy, the Audiencia (High Court), and corregidores (administrators) – ruled through the Minor Government – Indian chiefs put in charge of large groups of natives – a rough approximation to the original Inca system.

Towards independence

The Indians rose in 1780, under the leadership of an Inca noble who called himself Túpac Amaru II. He and many of his lieutenants were captured and put to death under torture at Cusco. Another Indian leader in revolt suffered the same fate in 1814, but this last flare-up had the sympathy of many of the locally-born Spanish, who resented their status, inferior to the Spaniards born in Spain, the refusal to give them any but the lowest offices, the high taxation imposed by the home government, and the severe restrictions upon trade with any country but Spain.

Help came to them from the outside world. José de San Martín's Argentine troops, convoyed from Chile under the protection of Lord Cochrane's squadron, landed in southern Peru on 7 September 1820. San Martín proclaimed Peruvian independence at Lima on 28 July 1821, though most of the country was still in the hands of the Viceroy, José de La Serna. Bolívar, who had already freed Venezuela and Colombia, sent Antonio José de Sucre to Ecuador where, on 24 May 1822, he gained a victory over La Serna at Pichincha.

San Martín, after a meeting with Bolívar at Guayaquil, left for Argentina and a self-imposed exile in France, while Bolívar and Sucre completed the conquest of Peru by defeating La Serna at the battle of Junín (6 August 1824) and the decisive battle of Ayacucho (9 December 1824). For over a year there was a last stand in the Real Felipe fortress at Callao by the Spanish troops under General Rodil before they capitulated on 22 January 1826. Bolívar was invited to stay in Peru, but left for Colombia in 1826.

Post-independence Peru

Following independence Peru attempted a confederation with Bolivia in the 1830s but this proved temporary. Then, in 1879 came the disastrous War of the Pacific, in which Peru and Bolivia were defeated by Chile and Peru lost its southern territory.

Economic change

Peru's economic development since independence has been based upon the export of minerals and foodstuffs to Europe and the United States. Guano, a traditional fertilizer in Peru and derived from the manure of seabirds, was first shipped to Europe in 1841. In the three decades that followed it became an important fertilizer in Europe and by the early 1860s over 80 per cent of the Peruvian government's revenues were derived from its export. Much of this income, though, went to pay off interest on the spiralling national debt. By the 1870s the richer deposits were exhausted and cheaper alternatives to guano were being discovered. One of these was nitrates, discovered in the Atacama desert, but Peru's defeat by Chile in the War of the Pacific ensured that she would lose her share of this wealth.

After the decline of guano Peru developed several new exports. In the 1890s the demand in Europe and USA for Amazonian rubber for tyres and for use in electrical components led to a brief boom in both the Brazilian and Peruvian Amazon, the Peruvian industry being based on the Amazon port of Iquitos. This boom was

⁝ War of the Pacific

One of the major international wars in Latin America since independence, this conflict has its roots in a border dispute between Chile and Bolivia. The frontier between the two in the Atacama desert was ill-defined.

There had already been one conflict, in 1836-1839, when Chile defeated Peru and Bolivia, putting an end to a confederation of the two states. The discovery of nitrates in the Atacama only complicated relations, for in the Bolivian Atacama province of Antofagasta nitrates were exploited by Anglo-Chilean companies.

In 1878 the Bolivian government, short of revenue, attempted to tax the Chilean-owned Antofagasta Railroad and Nitrate Company. When the company refused to pay, the Bolivians seized the company's assets. The Chilean government claimed that the Bolivian action broke an 1874 agreement between the two states. When Peru announced that it would honour a secret alliance with Bolivia by supporting her, the Chilean president, Aníbal Pinto, declared war on both states.

Control of the sea was vital, and this was where Chile concentrated her efforts. Following a successful naval campaign, the Chileans invaded the southern Peruvian province of Tarapacá and then landed troops north of Tacna, seizing the town in May 1880 before capturing Arica, further south. The Chilean armies were hot stuff, and in January 1881 they seized control of Lima.

Despite these defeats and the loss of their capital, Peru did not sue for peace, although Bolivia had already signed a ceasefire, giving up her coastal province. Under the 1883 peace settlement Peru gave up Tapapacá to Chile. Although the provinces of Tacna and Arica were to be occupied by Chile for 10 years, it was not until 1929 that an agreement was reached under which Tacna was returned to Peru, while Chile kept Arica. Apart from souring relations between Chile and her two northern neighbours to this day, the War gave Chile a monopoly over the world's supply of nitrates and enabled her to dominate the southern Pacific coast.

Background History

short-lived as cheaper rubber was soon being produced from plantations in the East Indies. Peru's colonial mineral exports, gold and silver, were replaced by copper, although ownership was mainly under control of foreign companies, particularly the US-based Cerro de Pasco Copper Corporation and Northern Peru Mining. Oil became another important product, amounting to 30 per cent of Peruvian exports by 1930. Further exports came from sugar and cotton, which were produced on coastal plantations, see also page 581.

Social change

Independence from Spanish rule meant that power passed into the hands of the Creole elite with no immediate alternation of the colonial social system. The contribución de indíginas, the colonial tribute collected from the native peoples was not abolished until 1854, the same year as the ending of slavery.

Until the 1970s land relations in the sierra changed very little, as the older landholding families continued to exert their traditional influence over 'their' peones. The traditional elite, the so-called '44 families', were still very powerful, though increasingly divided between the coastal aristocracy with their interests in plantation agriculture and trade, and the serrano elite, more conservative and inward-looking.

The pattern of export growth did, however, have major effects on the social structure of the coast. The expansion of plantation agriculture and mining led to the growth of a new labour force; this was supplied partially by Chinese indentured labourers, about 100,000 of whom arrived between 1855 and 1875, partly by the migration of Indians from the sierra and partly by the descendants of black slaves.

Political developments

19th century
For much of the period since independence Peruvian political life has been dominated by the traditional elites. Political parties have been slow to develop and the roots of much of the political conflict and instability which have marked the country's history lie in personal ambitions and in regional and other rivalries within the elite.

The early years after independence were particularly chaotic as rival caudillos (political bosses) who had fought in the independence wars vied with each other for power. The increased wealth brought about by the guano boom led to greater stability, though political corruption became a serious problem under the presidency of José Rufino Echenique (1851-1854) who paid out large sums of the guano revenues as compensation to upper class families for their (alleged) losses in the Wars of Independence. Defeat by Chile in the War of the Pacific discredited civilian politicians even further and led to a period of military rule in the 1880s.

Early 20th century
Even though the voting system was changed in 1898, this did little to change the dominance of the elite. Voting was not secret so landowners herded their workers to the polls and watched to make sure they voted correctly. Yet voters were also lured by promises as well as threats. One of the more unusual presidents was Guillermo Billinghurst (1912-1914) who campaigned on the promise of a larger loaf of bread for five cents, thus gaining the nickname of "Big Bread Billinghurst". As president he proposed a publicly funded housing programme, supported the introduction of an eight hour day and was eventually overthrown by the military who, along with the elite, were alarmed at his growing popularity among the urban population.

The 1920s This decade was dominated by Augusto Leguía. After winning the 1919 elections Leguía claimed that Congress was plotting to prevent him from becoming president and induced the military to help him close Congress. Backed by the armed forces, Leguía introduced a new constitution which gave him greater powers and enabled him to be re-elected in 1924 and 1929. Claiming his goal was to prevent the rise of communism, he proposed to build a partnership between business and labour. A large programme of public works, particularly involving building roads, bridges and railways, was begun, the work being carried out by poor rural men who were forced into unpaid building work. The Leguía regime dealt harshly with critics: opposition newspapers were closed and opposition leaders arrested and deported. His overthrow in 1930 ended what Peruvians call the "Oncenio" or 11 year period.

The 1920s also saw the emergence of a political thinker who would have great influence in the future, not only in Peru but elsewhere in Latin America. Juan Carlos Mariátegui, a socialist writer and journalist, argued that the solution to Peru's problems lay in the reintegration of the Indians through land reform and the breaking up of the great landed estates. See also page 597.

The formation of APRA Another influential thinker of this period was Víctor Raúl Haya de la Torre, a student exiled by Leguía in 1924. He returned after the latter's fall to create the Alianza Popular Revolucionaria Americana, a political party which called for state control of the economy, nationalization of key industries and protection of the middle classes, which, Haya de la Torre argued, were threatened by foreign economic interests.

In 1932 APRA seized control of Trujillo; when the army arrived to deal with the rising, the rebels murdered about 50 hostages, including 10 army officers. In reprisal the army murdered about 1,000 local residents suspected of sympathizing with APRA. APRA eventually became the largest and easily the best-organized political party in Peru, but the distrust of the military and the upper class for Haya de la Torre ensured that he never became president.

A turning point in Peruvian history occurred in 1948 with the seizure of power by General Manuel Odría, backed by the coastal elite. Odría outlawed APRA and went on to win the 1950 election in which he was the only candidate. He pursued policies of encouraging export earnings and also tried to build up working class support by public works projects in Lima. Faced with a decline in export earnings and the fall in world market prices after 1953, plus increasing unemployment, Odría was forced to stand down in 1956.

In 1962 Haya de la Torre was at last permitted to run for the presidency. But although he won the largest percentage of votes he was prevented from taking office by the armed forces who seized power and organized fresh elections for 1963. In these the military obtained the desired result: Haya de la Torre came second to Fernando Belaúnde Terry. Belaúnde attempted to introduce reforms, particularly in the landholding structure of the sierra; when these reforms were weakened by landowner opposition in Congress, peasant groups began invading landholdings in protest.

At the same time, under the influence of the Cuban revolution, guerrilla groups began operating in the sierra. Military action to deal with this led to the deaths of an estimated 8,000 people. Meanwhile Belaúnde's attempts to solve a long-running dispute with the International Petroleum Company (a subsidiary of Standard Oil) resulted in him being attacked for selling out to the unpopular oil company and contributed to the armed forces' decision to seize power in 1968.

The 1968 coup

This was a major landmark in Peruvian history. Led by General Juan Velasco Alvarado, the Junta had no intention of handing power back to the civilians. A manifesto issued on the day of the coup attacked the 'unjust social and economic order' and argued for its replacement by a new economic system 'neither capitalist nor communist'. Partly as a result of their experiences in dealing with the guerrilla movement, the coup leaders concluded that agrarian reform was a priority.

Wide-ranging land reform was launched in 1969, during which large estates were taken over and reorganized into cooperatives. By the mid-1970s, 75 per cent of productive land was under cooperative management. The government also tried to improve the lives of shanty-town dwellers around Lima, as well as attempting to increase the influence of workers in industrial companies. At the same time efforts were made to reduce the influence of foreign companies. Soon after the coup, IPC was nationalized, to be followed by other transnationals including ITT, Chase Manhattan Bank and the two mining giants Cerro de Pasco and Marcona Mining. After a dispute with the US government, compensation was agreed.

Understandably, opposition to the Velasco government came from the business and landholding elite. The government's crack-down on expressions of dissent, the seizure of newspapers and taking over of TV and radio stations all offended sections of the urban middle class. Trade unions and peasant movements found that, although they agreed with many of the regime's policies, it refused to listen and expected their passive and unqualified support. As world sugar and copper prices

dropped, inflation rose and strikes increased. Velasco's problems were further
increased by opposition within the armed forces and by his own ill-health. In August
1975 he was replaced by General Francisco Morales Bermúdez, a more conservative
officer, who dismantled some of Velasco's policies and led the way to a restoration of
civilian rule.

Belaúnde returned to power in 1980 by winning the first elections after military
rule. His government was badly affected by the 1982 debt crisis and the 1981-1983
world recession, and inflation reached over 100 per cent a year in 1983-1984. His term
was also marked by the growth of the Maoist guerrilla movement Sendero Luminoso
(Shining Path) and the smaller, Marxist **Túpac Amaru** (MRTA) – see box page 579.

Initially conceived in the University of Ayacucho, Shining Path gained most
support for its goal of overthrowing the whole system of Lima-based government from
highland Indians and migrants to urban shanty towns. The activities of Sendero
Luminoso and Túpac Amaru (MRTA) were effectively curtailed after the arrest of both
their leaders in 1992. Víctor Polay of MRTA was arrested in June and Abimael Guzmán
of Sendero Luminoso was captured in September. Although Sendero did not
capitulate, many of its members in 1994-1995 took advantage of the Law of
Repentance, which guaranteed lighter sentences in return for surrender, and freedom
in exchange for valuable information. Meanwhile, Túpac Amaru was thought to have
ceased operations (see below).

In 1985 APRA, in opposition for over 50 years, finally came to power. With Haya de
la Torre dead, the APRA candidate Alan García Pérez won the elections and was
allowed to take office by the armed forces. García attempted to implement an
ambitious economic programme intended to solve many of Peru's deep-seated
economic and social problems. He cut taxes, reduced interest rates, froze prices and
devalued the currency. However, the economic boom which this produced in
1986-1987 stored up problems as increased incomes were spent on imports.
Moreover, the government's refusal to pay more than 10 per cent of its foreign debt
meant that it was unable to borrow. In 1988 inflation hit 3,000 per cent and
unemployment soared. By the time his term of office ended in 1990 Peru was
bankrupt and García and APRA were discredited.

Modern Peru

Peru under Fujimori

In presidential elections held over two rounds in 1990, **Alberto Fujimori** of the Cambio
90 movement defeated the novelist **Mario Vargas Llosa**, who belonged to the
Fredemo (Democratic Front) coalition. Fujimori, without an established political
network behind him, failed to win a majority in either the senate or the lower house.
Lack of congressional support was one of the reasons behind the dissolution of
congress and the suspension of the constitution on 5 April 1992. The president
declared that he needed a freer hand to introduce market reforms and combat
terrorism and drug trafficking, at the same time as rooting out corruption.

In elections to a new, 80-member Democratic Constituent Congress (CCD) in
November 1992, Fujimori's Cambio 90/Nueva Mayoría coalition won a majority of
seats. Though three major political parties, APRA, Acción Popular and the Movimiento
de Libertad, boycotted the elections, they satisfied many aid donor's requirements
for the resumption of financial assistance.

A new constitution drawn up by the CCD was approved by a narrow majority of the
electorate in October 1993. Among the new articles were the immediate re-election of

the president (previously prohibited for one presidential term), the establishment of a single-chamber congress, the designation of Peru as a market economy and the favouring of foreign investment. As expected, Fujimori stood for re-election on 9 April 1995 and the opposition chose as an independent to stand against him former UN General Secretary, Javier Pérez de Cuéllar. Fujimori was re-elected by a resounding margin, winning about 65 per cent of the votes cast. The coalition that supported him also won a majority in Congress.

The government's success in most economic areas did not appear to accelerate the distribution of foreign funds for social projects. Rising unemployment and the austerity imposed by economic policy continued to cause hardship for many, despite the government's stated aim of alleviating poverty.

Dramatic events on 17 December 1996 thrust several of these issues into sharper focus: 14 Túpac Amaru guerrillas infiltrated a reception at the Japanese Embassy in Lima, taking 490 hostages. Among the rebel's demands were the release of their imprisoned colleagues, better treatment for prisoners and new measures to raise living standards. Most of the hostages were released and negotiations were pursued during a stalemate that lasted until 22 April 1997. The president took sole responsibility for the successful, but risky assault which freed all the hostages (one died of heart failure) and killed all the terrorists. By not yielding to Túpac Amaru, Fujimori regained much popularity.

But this masked the fact that no concrete steps had been taken to ease social problems. It also deflected attention from Fujimori's plans to stand for a third term following his unpopular manipulation of the law to persuade Congress that the new constitution did not apply to his first period in office. His chances of winning looked remote as demands grew for a more open, democratic approach, though opposition to his standing for a third term of office remained fragmented. Ultimately, his chances hinged on the economy, which looked to be improving until the worst El Niño of the 20th century hit Peru in late 1997, causing chaos, many deaths and devasting damage.

Fujimori's unpopularity was further driven home by Shell-Mobil's withdrawal from the multi-million dollar Camisea natural gas project, which was supposed to pull Peru out of its energy deficit. In July 1998, a 1.4 million-name petition was presented to the National Electoral Authority, requesting a referendum on whether Fujimori should be allowed to stand for a third term. In spite of the amendment to the constitution following Fujimori's auto golpe in 1993, allowing presidents to run for only two successive terms, the president had, in 1996, pushed through congress a law of 'authentic interpretation' of the constitution, allowing him to run for election once more on the grounds that the new constitution did not apply to his first term. All the same, until the last month of campaigning for the 2000 presidential elections, Fujimori had a clear lead over his rivals, who insisted that he should not stand. Moreover, local and international observers voiced increasing concern over the state domination of the media. Meanwhile, the popularity of a fourth candidate, Alejandro Toledo, a former World Bank official of humble origins, surged to such an extent that he and Fujimori were neck and neck in the first poll. Toledo, a pro-marketeer given to left-wing rhetoric, and his supporters claimed that Fujimori's slim majority was the result of fraud, a view echoed in the pressure put on the president, by the US government among others, to allow a second ballot. The run-off election, on 28 May 2000, was also contentious since foreign observers, including the Organization of American States, said the electoral system was unprepared and flawed, proposing a postponement. The authorities refused to delay. Toledo boycotted the election and Fujimori was returned unopposed, but with scant approval. Having won, he proposed "to strengthen democracy".

This pledge proved to be utterly worthless following the airing of a secretly shot video on 14 September 2000 of Fujimori's close aide and head of the National

Revolutionary movements – until the final victory

Officially speaking, the Peruvian civil war ended in 1992. On 12 September of that year, leader of the Shining Path, Abimael Guzmán, stood after his arrest in front of the television cameras, reduced from "National Enemy Number One" to "Prisoner Number 1509". Nobody knows how many people died in the carnage that lasted for more than a decade, but the most conservative estimates speak of 35,000.

The Maoist Shining Path was officially fighting for the resurrection of the Inca state and against Western imperialism and white supremacy in this racially and economically divided society. However, its methods were brutal and counter-productive. They included intimidation and the killing of several progressive leaders and hundreds of members of other revolutionary movements (including the contemporaneous Movimiento Revolucionario Túpac Amaru - MRTA). The plan was to reduce Peru's economy to ashes by destroying its infrastructure, military and police posts, power plants, tourism and other 'strategic targets'.

Both the army and the Shining Path were responsible for the eradication of countless towns and villages in the jungle and Andes, mass executions and torture of civilians. Sandwiched between these opposing forces, villagers in the mountains were forced to migrate to the coast, settling in enormous shantytowns, doubling the population of Lima in little more than a decade. Both sides forcibly recruited children from poor neighbourhoods and both controlled the traffic in drugs (they took it in turns to "tax" the same airstrips used by Colombian drug cartels).

During his term of office ex-president Fujimori did remove terrorism from Peru, however questionable the methods now appear. Evidence has recently come to light that many war crimes initially blamed on the Shining Path were in fact committed by the armed forces, even though it suited the guerrillas to claim responsibility at the time. And investigations into the web of intrigue surrounding Fujimori's henchman, Vladimiro Montesinos, indicate some form of 'working relationship' with Sendero Luminoso. The Fujimori-Montesinos propaganda machine managed to discredit the entire Peruvian Left by comparing it to the Shining Path. Consequently, when the war ended, there was almost no legitimate opposition in the country from this end of the political spectrum.

Both Professor Guzmán (yes, he graduated from the Philosophy Department of the University of Arequipa and was a respected expert on the German philosopher Kant) and Víctor Polay (leader of the Marxist MRTA) are now locked away in underwater cells in the navy bunker on the island of San Lorenzo (Callao). They were condemned to life imprisonment by military tribunal. Nevertheless, many Peruvian and foreign analysts believe that both Shining Path and MRTA are recruiting again, albeit with softer methods, gaining support in the jungle, the Andes and in Lima. Unless the gap between the rich and poor can be narrowed, this period of relative peace in Peru may be at risk.

Intelligence Service (SIN), Vladimiro Montesinos, allegedly handing US$15,000 to a congressman, Alberto Kouri, to persuade him to switch allegiances to Fujimori's coalition. Fujimori's demise was swift. His initial reaction was to close down SIN and announce new elections, eventually set for 8 April 2001, at which he would not stand.

Montesinos was declared a wanted man and he fled to Panama, where he was denied asylum. He returned to Peru in October and Fujimori personally led the search parties to find his former ally. Peruvians watched in amazement as this game of cat-and-mouse was played out on their TV screens. While Montesinos himself successfully evaded capture, investigators began to uncover the extent of his empire, which held hundreds of senior figures in its web. His activities encompassed extortion, money-laundering, bribery, intimidation, alleged arms and drugs dealing and possible links with the CIA and death squads. Swiss bank accounts in his name were found to contain about US$70 million, while other millions were discovered in accounts in the Cayman Islands and elsewhere. In early 2001 he was eventually captured in Venezuela and returned to Peru where he is now being tried on a multitude of charges. About 2,700 'Vladivideos', films of Montesinos' dealings with public figures, continue to send shockwaves through society. Fujimori, on the other hand, is in exile in Japan from where, on 20 November 2000, he sent Congress an email announcing his resignation. Congress rejected this, firing him instead on charges of being "morally unfit" to govern. An interim president, Valentín Paniagua, was sworn in, with ex-UN Secretary General Javier Pérez de Cuéllar as Prime Minister, and the government set about uncovering the depth of corruption associated with Montesinos and Fujimori. Further doubt was cast over the entire Fujimori period by suggestions that he may not have been born in Peru, as claimed, but in Japan. His hosts certainly declared that, through his parents, he was a Japanese national and therefore exempt from extradition. If he was indeed Japanese by birth as well as ancestry, he should never have been entitled to stand for the highest office in Peru. Fujimori has not relinquished the hope of being cleared and having some part to play in Peruvian politics.

In the run-up to the 2001 elections, the front-runner was Alejandro Toledo, but with far from a clear majority. Ex-President Alan García emerged as Toledo's main opponent, forcing a second ballot on 3 June. This was won by Toledo with 52 per cent of the vote. He pledged to heal the wounds that had opened in Peru since his first electoral battle with the disgraced Fujimori, but the first half of his presidency was marked by slow progress on both the political and economic fronts. With the poverty levels still high and few jobs created, Toledo's popularity plummeted; voters regarded his desire to be democratic as indecisive. He did briefly recoup some approval points by admitting paternity of an illegitimate daughter, but corruption scandals involving several ministers and charges of voter fraud laid at his own door held his approval rating at a mere 10 per cent in 2004. A series of major confrontations occurred, such as riots in the south over the mishandling of the sale of electricity companies in 2002. A series of damaging strikes by farmers, teachers and government workers forced the president to declare a state of emergency in May 2003 to restore order and further violent protests, such as by teachers in Ayacucho, took place 2004. In April 2004, protestors at Ilave, in the Titicaca region, angry at the mayor's refusal to resign over corruption and his failure to deliver on election promises, lynched him to death.

All the while, the past continued to dog the present. In July 2002 Montesinos was convicted of usurping power and sentenced by the Peruvian anti-corruption court to nine years and four months in prison. In further trials he was sentenced to five and eight years on other counts, with yet more prosecutions in process. In 2004, prosecutors also sought to charge exiled Fujimori with ordering the deaths of 25 people in 1991 and 1992. This followed the Truth and Reconciliation Committee's report (2003) into the civil war of the 1980s-1990s, which stated that over 69,000 Peruvians had been killed. Fujimori also stood accused of diverting charitable donations from Japan into his own bank accounts. Meanwhile the spectre of Sendero Luminoso still hung over the country, with a leader of the group threatening the recommencement of activities in mid-2004 if the government did not grant amnesty to jailed leaders. In addition, members of both Sendero Luminoso and MRTA were arrested in May 2004 on suspicion of infiltrating educational establishments.

A way of life

Coca leaves have long been used by the people of the Andes as a tonic. As casual as a coffee-break and as sacred as Communion, coca chewing is an ancient ritual.

The coca leaves are chewed with a piece of *cal*, or lime, which activates with the saliva. Some cocaine is absorbed into the bloodstream through the mouth, providing a slight numbing of cheek and tongue and more is absorbed in the stomach and intestinal tract. The desired effect is to numb the senses, which helps stave off hunger pangs and exhaustion, and to help people live at high altitude with no ill-effects.

As well as being a prerequisite for manual workers, such as miners, coca is also taken in a social context. The native population used to deny this because, in the eyes of their Spanish bosses and clergy, an increase in labour productivity was the only permissible reason for tolerating consumption of 'the devil's leaf'. The only places where coca is not chewed is in church and in the marital bed. The masticated leaves are spat out at the bedside.

Coca is also used in various rites, such as in offerings to Pachamama, or Mother Earth, to feed her when she gets hungry. Various items such as flowers and sweets, along with the coca leaves, are put together in bundles called pagos and burned on the mountains at midnight. In Andean markets different pagos are sold for different purposes: to put into the foundation of a new house; for help in matters of health, business or love; or for magic, white or black. The leaves are also used for fortune-telling.

Background Modern Peru

Constitution and government

Under a new constitution (approved by plebiscite in October 1993), a single chamber, 80-seat congress replaced the previous, two-house legislature. Men and women over 18 are eligible to vote, and registration and voting is compulsory until the age of 60. Those who do not vote are fined. The President, to whom is entrusted the Executive Power, is elected for five years and may, under the constitution which came into force on 1 January 1994, be re-elected for a second term.

Peru is divided into 24 Departments (divided into 150 Provinces, subdivided into 1,321 Districts).

Economy

Structure of production

Agriculture, forestry and **fishing** account for about 15 per cent of gdp and employ about a third of the labour force. The coastal region is the most productive area of the country and has traditionally been the dominant economic region. Occupying 11 per cent of the total land area, most of the export crops are grown here: cotton, rice, sugar, artichokes, asparagus and fruit where the coastal desert is irrigated. Most food production is in the sierra, where revitalization of agriculture is a government priority, with the aim of returning to the self-sufficiency of Inca times. There have been improvements in living standards, but two-thirds of the inhabitants of the Sierra still live in poverty and prices for many crops remain very low. In 1983 and 1997-1998, fishing suffered a dramatic decline as the Niño current forced the main catch, anchovy, out of Peruvian waters. On both occasions Peru had been the world's leading exporter of fishmeal before El Niño struck.

The government estimates that the **illegal drugs** trade generates some US$600 million a year. Efforts are being made to curb the cultivation of coca for the production of cocaine. While Peru is now regarded as the second-largest grower of coca leaf in the world after Colombia, United Nations officials recorded a five per cent drop in coca production in 2003 to 44,200 ha.

Manufacturing contributes 22 per cent of gdp with food processing, fishmeal and transport equipment important sectors. Manufacturing is suffering from a lack of investment and therefore performance. This posed the threat of insufficient growth to boost employment and lower poverty.

Mining has traditionally been important in Peru since pre-Conquest times. The sector contracted sharply in the 1980s because of poor world prices, strikes and guerrilla activity in mining areas, but a new Mining Law in 1992 encouraged domestic and foreign investment and the sector has since boomed. Copper and iron deposits are found on the south coast, but the Sierra is the principal mining area for all minerals, including silver, gold, lead and zinc. The largest gold mine in Latin America, Yanacocha, is in Cajamarca, contributing the majority of Peru's annual production of 130 tonnes.

Oil production comes from the northeast jungle, although some is produced on and off the northwest coast. No major new reserves of oil have been found since 1976 and proven reserves have declined to 380 million barrels. However, the Camisea gas and condensates field in the southeast jungle is huge, with reserves in two deposits estimated at 11 trillion cu ft of natural gas and 600 million barrels of condensates, equivalent to more than six times current reserves of oil.

Since the early 1990s, when the threat of terrorism had receded, numbers of foreign **tourists** to Peru have grown steadily. The total number of visitors in 2003 was 933,000 with over one million expected in 2004. Most visitors come from the USA (21 per cent), followed by Chile (17 per cent), then the UK (five per cent) and France (four per cent). Average spending per head is US$83 per day.

Society

The most remarkable thing about Peru is its people. For most Peruvians life is a daily struggle to survive in the face of seemingly insurmountable problems. Most people do get by, through a combination of ingenuity, determination and sheer hard work. Many work full time and study at night school. Those without work (and employment opportunities are few and far between) invent their own jobs.

Peru may not be the poorest country in South America, but recent estimates put the number of poor at 49 per cent of the population, while almost a fifth of people live in extreme poverty. Over a third of homes have no electricity or running water and a third of children suffer from chronic malnutrition.

Health

There have been major improvements in health care in recent years, but almost a third of the population has no access to public health services. The infant mortality rate is high – 37 deaths per 1,000 births – and the figure rises steeply in some rural areas where 1 in 10 infants dies within a year of birth.

As only a small percentage of the population contributes to social security schemes, medical consultations are not necessarily free. People also have to pay for prescribed medicines, which are very expensive, and so rarely finish a course of treatment. As with other areas, there is a huge gulf between those who can afford to pay for health care and those who cannot. Lack of health education and limited primary health care also means that many women die in childbirth. Abortion is illegal in Peru, but those with cash can always find a private doctor. Those

without the means to pay for a doctor run the risk of death or infection from
botched abortions.

Education
Education is free and compulsory for both sexes between six and 14. There are public and private secondary schools and private elementary schools. There are 32 state and private universities, and two Catholic universities. But resources are extremely limited and teachers earn a pittance. Poorer schoolchildren don't have money to buy pencils and notebooks and textbooks are few and far between in state schools. Furthermore, many children have to work instead of attending school; a quarter of those who start primary school don't finish. This is also due to the fact that classes are taught in Spanish and those whose native tongue is Quechua, Aymara or one of the Amazonian languages find it difficult and give up.

Migration
The structure of Peruvian society, especially in the coastal cities, has been radically altered by internal migration. This movement began most significantly in the 1950s and 1960s as people from the Highlands sought urban jobs in place of work on the land. It was a time of great upheaval as the old system of labour on large estates was threatened by the peasant majority's growing awareness of the imbalances between the wealthy cities and impoverished sierra. The process culminated in the agrarian reforms of the government of General Juan Velasco (1968-1975). Highland-to-city migration was given renewed impetus during the war between the state and Sendero Luminoso in the 1980s. Many communities which were depopulated in that decade are now beginning to come alive again.

Culture

People

Peruvian society today is a melting pot of Native Andeans, Afro-Peruvians, Spanish, immigrant Chinese, Japanese, Italians, Germans and, to a lesser extent, indigenous Amazon tribes, who have lived together for so long that many Peruvians can claim to have mixed blood. The total population in 2004 was 27.6 million, with an annual average growth rate of 1.5 per cent (2000-2005, UN statistics). Forecast growth rate for 2000-2005 is 1.5 per cent. The urban population in 2002 represented 73 per cent of the total.

Criollos and mestizos
The first immigrants were the Spaniards who followed Pizarro's expeditionary force. Their effect, demographically, politically and culturally, has been enormous. They intermarried with the indigenous population and the children of mixed parentage were called mestizos. The Peruvian-born children of Spanish parents were known as criollos, though this word is now used to describe people who live on the coast, regardless of their ancestry, and coastal culture in general.

Afro-Peruvians
Peru's black community is based on the coast, mainly in Chincha, south of Lima, and also in some working-class districts of the capital. Their forefathers were originally imported into Peru in the 16th century as slaves to work on the sugar and cotton plantations on the coast. The black community represents between 2-5 per cent of the total population.

Asian immigrants

There are two main Asian communities in Peru, the Japanese and Chinese. Large numbers of poor Chinese labourers were brought to Peru in the mid-19th century to work in virtual slavery on the guano reserves on the Pacific coast and to build the railroads in the central Andes. The culinary influence of the Chinese can be seen in the many chifas found throughout the country.

The Japanese community, now numbering some 100,000, established itself in the first half of the 20th century. The normally reclusive community gained prominence when Alberto Fujimori, one of its members, became the first president of Japanese descent outside Japan anywhere in the world. During Fujimori's presidency, many other Japanese Peruvians took prominent positions in business, central and local government. The nickname 'chino' is applied to anyone of Oriental origin.

Europeans

Like most of Latin America, Peru received many emigrés from Europe seeking land and opportunities in the late 19th century. The country's wealth and political power remains concentrated in the hands of this small and exclusive class of whites, which also consists of the descendants of the first Spanish families. There still exists a deep divide between people of European descent and the old colonial snobbery persists.

Peru's indigenous people

Peru has a substantial indigenous population, only smaller as a percentage of the total than Bolivia and Guatemala of the Latin American republics. The literacy rate of the indigenous population is the lowest of any comparable group in South America and their diet is 50% below acceptable levels. The highland Indians bore the brunt of the conflict between Sendero Luminoso guerrillas and the security forces, which caused thousands of deaths and mass migration from the countryside to provincial cities or to Lima. Many indigenous groups are also under threat from colonization, development and road-building projects. Long after the end of Spanish rule, discrimination, dispossession and exploitation are still a fact of life for many native Peruvians.

Quechua

Predominantly an agricultural society, growing potatoes and corn as their basic diet, they are largely outside the money economy. Today, there remain two enduring legacies of Inca rule; their magnificent architecture and their language, Quechua, which, although predating the Incas themselves, has become synonymous with the descendants of their subjects. Quechua is one of the key channels of continuity with the captivating pre-European past and indigenous identity of the Andes. Sadly, that continuity still takes the form of a distinctly underprivileged status in relation to the dominant Spanish and it is only the remoteness of many Quechua speakers which has preserved the language in rural areas. This isolation has also helped preserve many of their ancient traditions and beliefs. Most speakers today are bilingual in Spanish and Quechua is still losing ground fast. It remains primarily a spoken, in-group language, strongly bound up with the distinct indigenous identity, but unlike the Aymara (see below), the seven million or so Quechua-speakers have generally been much less successful in asserting themselves. There is no real sense of unity between the disparate groups of speakers scattered through Ecuador, Peru and Bolivia. Some recent developments in these three countries have at last been more positive. The language is

 According to legend, the Incas were a small group who originally lived near Lake Titicaca.
● *They later moved to Cusco, from where they expanded to create their empire of Tawantinsuyo.*

The Afro-Peruvian experience since 1532

The first person of African descent to arrive in the Americas came in 1492 with Christopher Columbus. He was a mulatto from Spain, and a free man. During the next three centuries an estimated 15 million Africans arrived in the Americas as slaves. Francisco Pizarro brought the first black slaves to Peru. They were present at the capture of Atahualpa in Cajamarca in 1532 and saved the Spanish during Manco Inca's siege of Cusco in 1536, when they put out the flames on the thatched roof of the great hall of Sunturwasi, where the embattled conquistadores had taken refuge.

When Hernando de Soto returned to Spain in 1534 bearing Atahualpa's gold and silver ransom, he asked the crown for permission to take one hundred blacks back to Peru. By 1550, their number had risen to 3,000 – half of whom lived in Lima – and by 1640 to 30,000. In total, between 1532 and 1816, an estimated 100,000 African slaves were transported to the Viceroyalty of Peru.

Africans were brought to Peru to replace an indigenous labour force ravaged by the destruction of its sociopolitical infrastructure and struck down by European diseases. Some worked in the cities as servants, artisans or porters, others were sent to the mines of Huancavelica or Potosí and the majority toiled on the coast in sugar cane plantations, cotton fields and vineyards.

Indigenous and African workers transformed Peru into the richest of all the Spanish colonies of the 16th and 17th centuries. Many fortunes, including that amassed by the Jesuits, were made using black labour. The ownership of black slaves was a status symbol and became such a powerful measure of social mobility that even some blacks who had achieved their own freedom subsequently acquired slaves.

The location of Afro-Peruvian communities today reflects the colonial distribution of black labour. They are concentrated in the coastal areas where the great haciendas once dominated Peru's feudal economy; Chincha, Cañete and Ica south of the capital, the northern departments of Piura and Lambayeque and the main cities, particularly Lima. In these places, the vibrant new culture created as a survival mechanism by slaves from diverse African heritages lives on in local art, music, dance, religious expression, folklore and food (see pages 592 and 63).

In Hispanic America, the wars of independence spread the libertarian ideal of emancipation. Promised their freedom, hundreds of Afro-Peruvians joined the republican armies, only to find their situation little changed in 1821 under a fledgling government unwilling or too weak to challenge the landowning elite. Finally, in 1854, Generals Ramón Castilla and José Rufino Echenique found themselves engaged in civil war and in need of troops. To attract black recruits Echenique offered freedom to those who would join him and in reply Castilla announced the definitive abolition of slavery, paying off the landowners with huge compensation awards raised from guano exports.

The 25,000 black slaves freed in 1854 were received by society with contempt and they remained oppressed by labour laws which still favoured the landowners. Peru has changed since 1854, but racism lives on. Colour is still identified with inferiority, from unconscious everyday attitudes to the poverty and marginalization of black communities and their lack of representation in government. 150 years after the abolition of slavery, those who shared the hardships of the first conquistadores have still not shared in their glory or wealth.

now increasingly written and is being fitfully introduced in primary education, though the impact of Spanish, and polemics about standardisation, continue to have a very disruptive effect. At least some Quechua-speaking communities are gradually recovering a long-deserved semblance of pride in their native tongue and culture, such as the successful Otavalo traders in Ecuador, or the Jalq'a and Tarabuco peoples around Sucre in Bolivia thanks to their beautiful weaving traditions. See also Festivals, on page 595.

Aymara

High up in the Andes, in the southern part of Peru, lies a wide, barren and hostile plateau, the altiplano. Prior to Inca rule Tiahuanaco on Lake Titicaca was a highly organized centre for one the greatest cultures South America has ever witnessed: the Aymara people. Today, the shores of this lake and the plains that surround it remain the homeland of the Aymara. The majority live in Bolivia, the rest are scattered on the southwestern side of Peru and northern Chile. The climate is so harsh on the altiplano that, though they are extremely hard-working, their lives are very poor. They speak their own unwritten language, Aymara. More so than the scattered group of different peoples that speak Quechua, the Altiplano Aymara people form a compact group with a clear sense of their own distinct identity and in many respects have been able to preserve more of their indigenous traditions and belief system.

The Aymaras are a deeply religious people whose culture is permeated with the idea of the sacred. They believe that God, the Supreme Being, gives them security in their daily lives and this God of Life manifests him/herself through the deities, such as those of the mountains, the water, wind, sun, moon and *wa'qas* (sacred places).

As a sign of gratitude, the Aymara give wax'ta (offerings), wilancha (llama sacrifices) and ch'alla (sprinkling alcohol on the ground) to the achachilas (the protecting spirits of the family and community), the Pachamama (Mother Earth), Kuntur Mamani and Uywiri (protecting spirits of the home).

The remote mountains of the bleak altiplano are of particular importance for the Aymara. The most sacred places are these high mountains, far from human problems. It is here that the people have built their altars to offer worship, to communicate with their God and ask forgiveness. The community is also held important in the lives of the Aymara. The achachila is the great-great grandfather of the family as well as the protector of the community, and as such is God's representative on earth.

The offerings to the sacred mountains take place for the most part in August and are community celebrations. Many different rituals are celebrated: there are those within the family; in the mountains; for the planting and the harvest; rites to ask for rain or to ask for protection against hailstorms and frosts; and ceremonies for Mother Earth.

All such rituals are led by Aymara Yatiris, who are male or female priests. The Yatiri is a wise person – someone who knows – and the community's spiritual and moral guide. Through a method of divination that involves the reading of coca leaves, they guide individuals in their personal decision-making.

Amazonian peoples

Before the arrival of the Europeans, an estimated six million people inhabited the Amazon basin, comprising more than 2,000 tribes or ethnic-linguistic groups who managed to adapt to their surroundings through the domestication of a great variety of animals and plants, and to benefit from the numerous nutritional, curative, narcotic and hallucinogenic properties of thousands of wild plants.

It's not easy to determine the precise origin of these aboriginal people. What is known, however, is that since the beginning of colonial times this population slowly but constantly decreased, mainly because of the effect of western diseases such as influenza and measles. This demographic decline reached dramatic levels during the rubber boom of the late 19th and early 20th centuries, due to forced labour and slavery.

Andean mysticism

In the 1990s Andean shamanism and mysticism have attracted increasing attention, though they have always played an important part in the lives of indigenous people.

In highland cities, especially, it is common to engage a ritual specialist, called an altomisayoq, to perform a pago, or offering, when laying the foundations of a house or starting a business venture. Ritual objects for use in these ceremonies are sold at specialized stands in the local markets. Another type of ritualist, called a curandero, is summoned when someone is ill.

Some of these healers are experts in the use of dozens of medicinal plants, while others invoke spirit powers to expel illness. Sometimes eggs or guinea pigs are passed over the patient's body, and then cracked, or killed, in order to read the innards and diagnose the illness. Inevitably this field has its share of charlatans, but there are also curanderos who have many attested cures to their credit.

One thing shamans from all the Andean regions have in common is the use of a mesa – a layout of ceremonial power objects – which is thought to attract spirit power and channel it to the shaman. Another feature running through all strains of Andean mysticism, despite the usual presence of Christian elements, is a living connection, via innumerable practices and associations, to Peru's precolombian past.

Those ritualists who seek to communicate with 'the other side' in their ceremonies often use psychoactive plants. These vary according to the region. On the coast, curanderos often take an infusion of the San Pedro cactus, a form of mescaline. The highland shamans invariably chew coca leaf, a much milder psychoactive, but with broader uses. Coca is burned with every offering, and many ritualists cast the leaves to read the fortunes of their clients. These shamans usually invoke the power of the mountain deities in their ceremonies. In the rainforest regions shamans use the powerful psychedelic vine, ayahuasca (vine of the dead – so called because it is believed to transport the user to the spirit world), as they have for millenia.

Today, at the basin level, the population is calculated at no more than two million inhabitants making up 400 ethnic groups, of which approximately 200-250,000 live in the Peruvian jungle. Within the basin it is possible to distinguish at least three large conglomerates of aboriginal societies: the inhabitants of the varzea, or seasonally flooded lands alongside the large rivers (such as the Omagua, Cocama and Shipibo people); the people in the interfluvial zones or firm lands (such as the Amahuaca, Cashibo and Yaminahua) and those living in the Andean foothills (such as the Amuesha, Ashaninka and Machigvenga).

The Amazonian natives began to be decimated in the 16th century, and so were the first endangered species of the jungle. These communities still face threats to their traditional lifestyles, notably from timber companies, gold miners and multinational oil companies. There appears to be little effective control of deforestation and the intrusion of colonists who have taken over native lands to establish small farms. And though oil companies have reached compensation agreements with local communities, previous oil exploration has contaminated many jungle rivers, as well as exposing natives to risk from diseases against which they have no immunity.

Religion

The Inca religion (described on page 571) was displaced by Roman Catholicism from the 16th century onwards, the conversion of the inhabitants of the 'New World' to Christianity being one of the stated aims of the Spanish conquistadores. Today, official statistics state that 92.5 per cent of the population declares itself Catholic.

One of the first exponents of Liberation Theology, under which the Conference of Latin American Bishops in 1968 committed themselves to the 'option for the poor', was Gustavo Gutiérrez, from Huánuco. This doctrine caused much consternation to orthodox Catholics, particularly those members of the Latin American church who had traditionally aligned themselves with the oligarchy. Gutiérrez, however, traced the church's duty to the voiceless and the marginalized back to Fray Bartolomé de las Casas (see *The Peru Reader*, pages 293-96; reference under Books, page 604).

The Catholic Church faced a further challenge to its authority when President Fujimori won the battle over family planning and the need to slow down the rate of population growth. Its greatest threat, however, comes from the proliferation of evangelical Protestant groups throughout the country. Five and a half percent of the population now declare themselves Protestant and one million or more people belong to some 27 different non-Catholic denominations.

Although the vast majority of the population ostensibly belongs to the Roman Catholic religion, in reality religious life for many Peruvians is a mix of Catholic beliefs imported from Europe and indigenous traditions based on animism, the worship of deities from the natural world such as mountains, animals and plants. Some of these ancient indigenous traditions and beliefs are described throughout this section.

Arts and crafts

Peru has a rich variety of handicrafts. Its geographic division into four distinct regions – coast, mountains, valleys and Amazon basin – coupled with cultural differences, has resulted in numerous variations in technique and design. Each province, even each community, has developed its own style of weaving or carving.

The Incas inherited 3,000 years of skills and traditions: gold, metal and precious stonework from the Chimu; feather textiles from the Nasca; and the elaborate textiles of the Paracas. All of these played important roles in political, social and religious ceremonies. Though much of this artistic heritage was destroyed by the Spanish conquest, the traditions adapted and evolved in numerous ways, absorbing new methods, concepts and materials from Europe while maintaining ancient techniques and symbols.

Textiles and costumes

Woven cloth was the most highly prized possession and sought after trading commodity in the Andes in pre-Columbian times. It is, therefore, not surprising that ancient weaving traditions have survived.

In the ninth century BC camelid fibre was introduced into weaving on the south coast. This allowed the development of the textiles of the Paracas culture which consist of intricate patterns of animalistic, supernatural and human forms embroidered onto dark backgrounds. The culture of the Chancay valleys cultivated cotton for white and beige dyed patterned cloth in preference to the camelid fibres used by the Paracas and Nasca cultures.

The Incas inherited this rich weaving tradition. They forced the Aymaras to work in mitas or textile workshops. The ruins of some enormous mitas can be seen at the temple of Raqchi, south of Cusco (see page 220). Inca textiles are of high quality and

⁝ A belt for every occasion

The belt plays a particularly important role in the lives of the indigenous peoples. The Incas developed a range of belts, or *chumpis*, of ritual and spiritual significance which are still used today.

Chumpis are believed to have protective and purifying qualities. In the Cusco area, some communities place *chumpis* on sacred mountain tops, or *apus*, in order to communicate with the gods.

Traditionally women give birth lying on a *chumpi* and the baby is wrapped in a softer version, known as a *walt'ana*, which ensures he or she will grow up properly. From adolescence, women wear a *chumpi* under their skirt to encourage a lover or deter an unwanted suitor. It is even common practice for the bridegroom to lasso his bride with one. And the age-old tradition of burying the dead with the family *chumpi* is still occasionally observed.

very different from coastal textiles, being warp-faced, closely woven and without embroidery. The largest quantities of the finest textiles were made specifically to be burned as ritual offerings – a tradition which still survives. The Spanish, too, exploited this wealth and skill by using the mitas and exporting the cloth to Europe.

Prior to Inca rule Aymara men wore a tunic (*llahua*) and a mantle (*llacata*) and carried a bag for coca leaves (*huallquepo*). The women wore a wrapped dress (*urku*) and mantle (*iscayo*) and a belt (*huaka*); their coca bag was called an *istalla*. The *urku* was fastened at shoulder level with a pair of metal *tupu*, the traditional Andean dress-pins. Inca men had tunics (*unkus*) and a bag for coca leaves called a *ch'uspa*. The women wore a blouse (*huguna*), skirts (*aksu*) and belts (*chumpis*), and carried foodstuffs in large, rectangular cloths called llicllas, which were fastened at the chest with a single pin or a smaller clasp called a ttipqui. Women of the Sacred Valley now wear a layered, gathered skirt called a pollera and a montera, a large, round, red Spanish type of hat.

Textiles continue to play an important part in society. They are still used specifically for ritual ceremonies and some even held to possess magical powers. One of the most enduring of these traditions is found among the Aymara people of Taquile island on Lake Titicaca.

Textile materials and techniques

The Andean people used mainly alpaca or llama wool. The former can be spun into fine, shining yarn when woven and has a lustre similar to that of silk, though sheep's wool came to be widely used following the Spanish conquest. A commonly used technique is the drop spindle. A stick is weighted with a wooden wheel and the raw material is fed through one hand. A sudden twist and drop in the spindle spins the yarn. This very sensitive art can be seen practised by women while herding animals in the fields.

Spinning wheels were introduced by Europeans and are now prevalent owing to increased demand. In Ayacucho and San Pedro de Cajas, centres of the cottage textile industry, the wheel is the most common form of spinning. Pre-Columbian looms were often portable and those in use today are generally similar. A woman will herd her animals while making a piece of costume, perhaps on a backstrap loom, or waist loom, so-called because the weaver controls the tension on one side with her waist with the other side tied to an upright or tree. The pre-Columbian looms are usually used for personal costume while the treadle loom is used by men for more commercial pieces.

The skills of dyeing were still practised virtually unchanged even after the arrival of the Spanish. Nowadays, the word makhnu refers to any natural dye, but originally was the name for cochineal, an insect which lives on the leaves of the nopal cactus. These dyes were used widely by pre-Columbian weavers. Today, the biggest centre of production in South America is the valleys around Ayacucho. Vegetable dyes are also used, made from the leaves, fruit and seeds of shrubs and flowers and from lichen, tree bark and roots.

Symbolism
Symbolism plays an important role in weaving. Traditionally every piece of textile from a particular community had identical symbols and colours which were a source of identity as well as carrying specific symbols and telling a story. One example is on the island of Taquile where the Inti (sun) and Chaska (Venus) symbols are employed as well as motifs such as fish and birds, unique to the island.

Animal figures dominated the motifs of the Chavín culture and were commonly used in Paracas textiles. Specimens of cotton and wool embroidery found in Paracas graves often show a puma as a central motif. Today, this and other pre-Columbian motifs are found on many rugs and wall-hangings from the Ayacucho region. Other symbols include Spanish figures such as horses and scenes depicting the execution of Túpac Amaru.

Pottery
The most spectacular archaeological finds in South America have been made in Peru. The Nasca culture (100 BC-AD 900) excelled in polychrome painting of vessels with motifs of supernatural beings, often with strong feline characteristics, as well as birds, fish and animals. Many of the Nasca ceramic motifs are similar to those found in Paracas textiles.

Moche or Mochica vessels combined modelling and painting to depict details of Moche daily life. Human forms are modelled on stirrup spout vessels with such precision that they suggest personal portraits. The Moche also excelled in intricate linear painting often using brown on a cream base. See also page 290.

Inca ceramic decoration consists mainly of small-scale geometric and usually symmetrical designs. One distinctive form of vessel which continues to be made and used is the arybola. This pot is designed to carry liquid, especially *chicha*, and is secured with a rope on the bearer's back. It is believed that arybolas were used mainly by the governing Inca élite and became important status symbols. Today, Inca-style is very popular in Cusco and Pisac.

With the Spanish invasion many indigenous communities lost their artistic traditions, others remained relatively untouched, while others still combined Hispanic and indigenous traditions and techniques. The Spanish brought three innovations: the potter's wheel, which gave greater speed and uniformity; knowledge of the enclosed kiln; and the technique of lead glazes. The enclosed kiln made temperature regulation easier and allowed higher temperatures to be maintained, producing stronger pieces. Today, many communities continue to apply prehispanic techniques, while others use more modern processes.

Jewellery and metalwork
Some of the earliest goldwork originates from the Chavín culture – eg the Tumi knife found in Lambayeque. These first appeared in the Moche culture, when they were associated with human sacrifice. Five centuries later, the Incas used Tumis for surgical operations such as trepanning skulls. Today, they are a common motif.

The Incas associated gold with the Sun. However, very few examples remain as the Spanish melted down their amassed gold and silver objects. They then went on to send millions of Indians to their deaths in gold and silver mines.

From pagan ritual to folk art

Retablos – or St Mark's boxes, as they were originally known – were introduced to Latin America by the Spanish in the 16th century. These simple, portable altars containing religious images were intended to aid in the task of converting the native population to Catholicism. Early examples often contained images of St James, patron saint of the Spanish army.

The *retablos* were made from a variety of materials and two distinct styles evolved to suit different needs. Those of clay, leather and plaster were destined for the native rural population, while those for use by the colonial hierarchy were made of gold and silver, or the famous alabaster of Ayacucho, known as Huamanga stone.

Traditional *retablos* had 2 floors inside a box. On the top floor were the patron saints of animals: St Mark, patron saint of bulls; St Agnes, patron saint of goats; and St Anthony, patron saint of mules, among others. On the lower floor was a scene of a cattle thief being reprimanded by a landowner.

From the 17th century onwards, the native rural population used the *retablo* in ceremonies accompanying cattle branding. During August, a ritual believed to have its roots in pagan fertility festivals took place in which the *retablo* was placed on a table and surrounded by offerings of food and coca leaves. People danced round and sang in front of the box, asking for protection for their animals and celebrating their well-being.

In the 1940s the first *retablo* reached Lima, by which time the art of making them had virtually disappeared. However, with the new-found outside interest a revival began. The traditional elements began to be varied and the magical or ritualistic value was lost as they became a manifestation of folk art. The artist Joaquín López and his family created the early examples, but today they are made in many workshops.

The figures are made from a mixture of plaster and mashed potato, modelled or made in moulds, sealed with glue, then painted and positioned inside the brightly painted box. Some miniature versions are made in chiclet boxes or egg shells, while, at the other end of the scale, some have five floors and take months to complete.

Extracted from Arts and Crafts of South America, by Lucy Davies and Mo Fini,Tumi.

During the colonial period gold and silver pieces were made to decorate the altars of churches and houses of the élite. Metalworkers came from Spain and Italy to develop the industry. The Spanish preferred silver and strongly influenced the evolution of silverwork during the colonial period. A style known as Andean baroque developed around Cusco embracing both indigenous and European elements. Silver bowls in this style – cochas – are still used in Andean ceremonies.

False filigree This was practised by some pre-Hispanic cultures. The effect of filigree was obtained with the use of droplets or beads of gold. True filigree work developed in the colonial period. Today, there are a number of centres. Originally popular in Ayacucho, the tradition continues in the small community of San Jerónimo de Tunan, near Huancayo. Here, silversmiths produce intricate filigree earrings, spoons and jewellery boxes. Catacaos near Piura also has a long tradition of filigree work in silver and gold.

Seeds, flowers and feathers These continue to be used as jewellery by many Amazonian peoples. Prehispanic cultures also favoured particular natural materials; eg the sea shell spondylus was highly revered by the Chavín and Moche. It was found only along part of the Ecuadorean coast and must have been acquired through trade. The western fashion for natural or ethnic jewellery has encouraged production, using brightly-coloured feathers, fish bones, seeds or animal teeth.

Woodcarving

Wood is one of the most commonly used materials. Carved ceremonial objects include drums, carved sticks with healing properties, masks and the Incas' keros - wooden vessels for drinking *chicha*. Keros come in all shapes and sizes and were traditionally decorated with scenes of war, local dances, or harvesting coca leaves. The Chancay, who lived along the coast between 100 BC and AD 1200, used keros carved with sea birds and fish. Today, they are used in some Andean ceremonies, especially during Fiesta del Cruz, the Andean May festival.

Glass mirrors were introduced by the Spanish, although the Chimú and Lambayeque cultures used obsidian and silver plates, and Inca *chasquis* (messengers) used reflective stones to communicate between hilltop forts. Transporting mirrors was costly so they were produced in Lima and Quito. Cusco and Cajamarca then became centres of production.

In Cusco the frames were carved, covered in gold leaf and decorated with tiny pieces of cut mirror. Cajamarca artisans, meanwhile, incorporated painted glass into the frames.

Gourd-carving

Gourd-carving, or *máte burilado*, as it is known, is one of Peru's most popular and traditional handicrafts. It is thought even to predate pottery – engraved gourds found on the coast have been dated to some 4,500 years ago. During the Inca empire gourd-carving became a valued art form and workshops were set up and supported by the state. Gourds were used in rituals and ceremonies and to make poporos - containers for the lime used while chewing coca leaves. Today, gourd-carving is centred around the small communities of Cochas Grande and Chico, near Huancayo.

The information on arts and crafts in this Handbook has been adapted from *Arts and Crafts of South America*, by Lucy Davies and Mo Fini, published by Tumi, 1994. Tumi, the Latin American Craft Centre, specializes in Andean and Mexican products and produces cultural and educational videos for schools: at 8/9 New Bond Street Place, Bath BA1 1BH, T01225-480470, www.tumicrafts.com. Tumi (Music) Ltd specializes in different rhythms of Latin America.

Music and dance

The music of Peru can be described as the very heartbeat of the country. Peruvians see music as something in which to participate, and not as a spectacle. Just about everyone, it seems, can play a musical instrument or sing. Just as music is the heartbeat of the country, so dance conveys the rich and ancient heritage that typifies much of the national spirit. Peruvians are tireless dancers and dancing is the most popular form of entertainment. Unsuspecting travellers should note that once they make that first wavering step there will be no respite until they collapse from exhaustion.

Each region has its own distinctive music and dance that reflects its particular lifestyle, its mood and its physical surroundings. The music of the sierra, for example, is played in a minor key and tends to be sad and mournful, while the music of the lowlands is more up-tempo and generally happier. Peruvian

Highlands

When people talk of Peruvian music they are almost certainly referring to the music of the Quechua- and Aymara-speaking Indians of the highlands which provides the most distinctive Peruvian sound. The highlands themselves can be very roughly subdivided into some half dozen major musical regions, of which perhaps the most characteristic are Ancash and the north, the Mantaro Valley, Cusco, Puno and the Altiplano, Ayacucho and Parinacochas.

Musical instruments Before the arrival of the Spanish in Latin America, the only instruments were wind and percussion. Although it is a popular misconception that Andean music is based on the panpipes, guitar and charango, anyone who travels through the Andes will realize that these instruments only represent a small aspect of Andean music. The highland instrumentation varies from region to region, although the harp and violin are ubiquitous. In the Mantaro area the harp is backed by brass and wind instruments, notably the clarinet. In Cusco it is the charango and quena and on the Altiplano the sicu panpipes.

The Quena is a flute, usually made of reed, characterized by not having a mouthpiece to blow through. As with all Andean instruments, there is a family of quenas varying in length from around 15-50 cm. The sicu is the Aymara name for the zampoña, or panpipes. It is the most important prehispanic Andean instrument, formed by several reed tubes of different sizes held together by knotted string. Virtually the only instrument of European origin is the Charango. When stringed instruments were first introduced by the Spanish, the indigenous people liked them but wanted something that was their own and so the charango was born. Originally, they were made of clay, condor skeletons and armadillo or tortoise shells.

Highland dances The highlands are immensely rich in terms of music and dance, with over 200 dances recorded. Every village has its fiestas and every fiesta has its communal and religious dances.

Comparsas are organized groups of dancers who perform for spectators dances following a set pattern of movements to a particular musical accompaniment, wearing a specific costume. They have a long tradition, having mostly originated from certain contexts and circumstances and some of them still parody the ex-Spanish colonial masters.

One of the most notable is the comical Auqui Auqui (auqui is Aymara for old man). The dance satirizes the solemnity and pomposity of Spanish gentlemen from the colonial period. Because of their dignified dress and manners they could appear old, and a humped back is added to the dancers to emphasize age. These little old men have long pointed noses, flowing beards and carry crooked walking sticks. They dance stooped, regularly pausing to complain and rub aching backs, at times even stumbling and falling.

Many dances for couples and/or groups are danced spontaneously at fiestas throughout Peru. These include indigenous dances which have originated in a specific region and ballroom dances that reflect the Spanish influence.

One of the most popular of the indigenous dances is the **Huayno**, which originated on the Altiplano but is now danced throughout the country. It involves numerous couples, who whirl around or advance down the street arm-in-arm, in a Pandilla. During fiestas, and especially after a few drinks, this can develop into a kind of uncontrolled frenzy.

Two of the most spectacular dances to be seen are the **Baile de las Tijeras** ('scissor dance') from the Ayacucho/Huancavelica area, for men only and the pounding, stamping **Huaylas** for both sexes. Huaylas competitions are held annually in Lima and should not be missed. Also very popular among Indians and/or Mestizos are the Marinera, Carnaval, Pasacalle, Chuscada (from Ancash), Huaylas, Santiago and Chonguinada (all from the Mantaro) and Huayllacha (from Parinacochas).

Urban and other styles Owing to the overwhelming migration of peasants into the barrios of Lima, most types of Andean music and dance can be seen in the capital, notably on Sundays at the so-called 'Coliseos', which exist for that purpose. This flood of migration to the cities has also meant that the distinct styles of regional and ethnic groups have become blurred. One example is **Chicha music**, which comes from the pueblos jóvenes, and was once the favourite dance music of Peru's urban working class. Chicha is a hybrid of Huayno music and the Colombian Cumbia rhythm – a meeting of the highlands and the tropical coast.

Tecno-cumbia originated in the jungle region with groups such as Rossy War, from Puerto Maldonado, and Euforia, from Iquitos. It is a vibrant dance music which has gained much greater popularity across Peruvian society than *chicha* music ever managed. There are now also many exponents on the coast such as Agua Marina and Armonía 10. Many of the songs comment on political issues and Fujimori used to join Rossy War on stage.

For singing only, the mestizo Muliza, are popular in the Central Region, and the soulful lament of the Yaraví, originally Indian, but taken up and developed early in the 19th century by the hero of independence Mariano Melgar, from Arequipa, see page 597.

Coast

Música Criolla, the music from the coast, could not be more different from that of the Sierra. Here the roots are Spanish and African. The immensely popular **Valsesito** is a syncopated waltz that would certainly be looked at askance in Vienna and the **Polca** has also undergone an attractive sea change.

Reigning over all, though, is the **Marinera**, Peru's national dance, a splendidly rhythmic and graceful courting encounter and a close cousin of Chile's and Bolivia's Cueca and the Argentine Zamba, all of them descended from the Zamacueca. The Marinera has its 'Limeña' and 'Norteña' versions and a more syncopated relative, the Tondero, found in the northern coastal regions, is said to have been influenced by slaves brought from Madagascar.

All these dances are accompanied by guitars and frequently the cajón, a resonant wooden box on which the player sits, pounding it with his hands. Some of the great names of 'Música Criolla' are the singer/composers Chabuca Granda and Alicia Maguiña, the female singer Jesús Vásquez and the groups Los Morochucos and Hermanos Zañartu.

Afro-Peruvian Also on the coast is the music of the small but influential black community, the 'Música Negroide' or 'Afro-Peruano', which had virtually died out when it was resuscitated in the 1950s, but has since gone from strength to strength, thanks to Nicomedes and Victoria Santa Cruz who have been largely responsible for popularizing this black music and making it an essential ingredient in contemporary Peruvian popular music. It has all the qualities to be found in black music from the Caribbean – a powerful, charismatic beat, rhythmic and lively dancing, and strong percussion provided by the cajón and the quijada de burro, a donkey's jaw with the teeth loosened.

Its greatest star is the Afro-Peruvian diva Susana Baca. Her incredible, passionate voice inspired Talking Head's David Byrne to explore this genre further and release a compilation album in 1995, thus bringing Afro-Peruvian music to the attention of the world. Other notable exponents are the excellent Perú Negro, one of the best music and dance groups in Latin America, and the singer Eva Ayllón.

66 99 After several days of this, you will awake with a hangover the size of the Amazon rainforest and probably have no recollection of what you did with your backpack...

Some of the classic dances in the black repertoire are the Festejo, Son del Diablo, Toro Mata, Landó and Alcatraz. In the last named one of the partners dances behind the other with a candle, trying to set light to a piece of paper tucked into the rear of the other partner's waist.

Festivals

Fiestas (festivals) are a fundamental part of life for most Peruvians, taking place up and down the length and breadth of the country and with such frequency that it would be hard to miss one, even during the briefest of stays. This is fortunate, because arriving in any town or village during these inevitably frenetic celebrations is one of the great Peruvian experiences.

While Peru's festivals can't rival those of Brazil for fame or colour, the quantity of alcohol consumed and the partying run them pretty close. What this means is that, at some point, you will fall over, through inebriation or exhaustion, or both. After several days of this, you will awake with a hangover the size of the Amazon rainforest and probably have no recollection of what you did with your backpack.

Peruvian festivals also involve widespread balloons-filled-with-water fights, bags of flour and any other missile guaranteed to cause a mess. In the Amazon region various petroleum by-products are favoured ingredients, which can be bad news for smokers. Some travellers complain that they are being picked on, but to someone from the Altiplano, a 6-ft tall, blond-haired gringo makes an easier target. So, don't wear your best clothes, do arm yourself with plenty of water bombs, and get into the spirit and have some fun!

With over 3,000 fiestas, there are too many to mention them all. The main national ones are described in Holidays and festivals, on page 66, and details of local fiestas are given under the listings for each town.

Among the most notable celebrations are Carnival week in Cajamarca – a raucous and messy affair, even by Peruvian standards – and the fiesta of the Virgen de la Candelaria, which takes place in the first week in February along the shores of Lake Titicaca near the Bolivian border and features dance groups from all around the region. The most famous Holy Week is held in Ayacucho, when many thousands of fervent devotees participate in daily processions. On the coast, the Marinera festival in January and the Spring festival in September in Trujillo are opportunities to see the Marinera dancers, while in the black communities of Chincha, south of Lima, you can enjoy the best of Afro-Peruvian music and dance (see Music and dance above).

Meaning of fiestas

It is only when they don their extravagant costumes and masks and drink, eat and dance to excess that the Peruvian Indians show their true character. The rest of the time they hide behind a metaphorical mask of stony indifference as a form of protection against the alien reality in which they are forced to live. When they

Day of the Dead

One of the most important dates in the indigenous people's calendar is the 2 November, the 'Day of the Dead'. This tradition has been practised since time immemorial. In the Incaic calendar, November was the eighth month and meant Ayamarca, or land of the dead. This celebration, or 'All Saints' as it is also known, is just one example of religious adaptation in which the ancient beliefs of ethnic cultures are mixed with the rites of the Catholic Church.

According to Aymara belief, the spirit (*athun ajayu*) visits its relatives at this time of the year and is fed in order to continue its journey before its reincarnation. The relatives of the dead prepare for the arrival of the spirit days in advance. Among the many items necessary for these meticulous preparations are little bread dolls, each one of which has a particular significance. A ladder is needed for the spirit to descend from the other world to the terrestrial one. There are other figures which represent the grandparents, great grandparents and loved ones of the person who has 'passed into a better life'. Horse-shaped breads are prepared that will serve as a means of transport for the soul in order to avoid fatigue.

Inside the home, the relatives construct a tomb supported by boxes over which is laid a black cloth. Here they put the bread, along with sweets, flowers, onions and sugar cane. This latter item is an indispensable part of the table as it symbolizes the invigorating element which prevents the spirit from becoming tired on its journey towards the Earth. The union of the flowers with the onion is called *tojoro* and is a vital part of the preparations. It ensures that the dead one does not become disoriented and arrives in the correct house.

The tomb is also adorned with the dead relative's favourite food and drink, not forgetting the all-important glass of beer as, according to popular tradition, this is the first nourishment taken by the souls when they arrive at their houses. Once the spirit has arrived and feasted with its living relatives, the entire ceremony is then transported to the graveside in the local cemetery, where it is carried out again, beside the many other mourning families.

This meeting of the living and their dead relatives is re-enacted the following year, though less ostentatiously, and again for the final time in the third year, the year of the farewell. It does not continue after this; just as well as the costs can be crippling for the family concerned.

consume alcohol and coca and start dancing, the pride in their origins resurfaces. The incessant drinking and dancing allows them to forget the reality of poverty, unemployment and oppression and reaffirms their will to live as well as their unity with the world around them.

The object of the fiesta is a practical one, such as the success of the coming harvest or the fertility of animals. Thus the constant eating, drinking and dancing serves the purpose of giving thanks for the sun and rain that makes things grow and for the fertility of the soil and livestock, gifts from Pachamama, or Mother Earth, the most sacred of all gods. So, when you see the Aymara spill a little *chicha* (maize beer) every time they refill, it's not because they're sloppy but because they're offering a *ch'alla* (sacrifice) to Pachamama.

The participants in the dances that are the central part of the fiesta are dressed in garish, outlandish costumes and elaborate masks, each one depicting a character

the Inca Empire or even further back. Often the costumes caricature the Spanish. In
this way, the indigenous people mock those who erased their heritage.

Literature

Quechua

The fact that the Incas had no written texts in the conventional European sense and
that the Spaniards were keen to suppress their conquest's culture means that there is
little evidence today of what poetry and theatre as performed in pre-conquest times.
It is known that the Incas had two types of poet, the amautas, historians, poets and
teachers who composed works that celebrated the ruling class' gods, heroes and
events, and haravecs, who expressed popular sentiments. There is strong evidence
also that drama was important in Inca society.

Written Quechua even today is far less common than works in the oral tradition.
Although Spanish culture has had some influence on Quechua, the native stories,
lyrics and fables retain their own identity. Not until the 19th century did Peruvian
writers begin seriously to incorporate indigenous ideas into their art, but their
audience was limited. Nevertheless, the influence of Quechua on Peruvian literature
in Spanish continues to grow.

Colonial Period

In 16th-century Lima, headquarters of the Viceroyalty of Peru, the Spanish officials
concentrated their efforts on the religious education of the new territories and literary
output was limited to mainly histories and letters.

Chroniclers such as Pedro Cieza de León (*Crónica del Perú*, published from 1553)
and Agustín de Zárate (*Historia del descubrimiento y conquista del Perú*, 1555) were
written from the point of view that Spanish domination was right. Their most
renowned successors, though, took a different stance. Inca Garcilaso de la Vega was
a mestizo, whose *Comentarios reales que tratan del origen de los Incas* (1609) were at
pains to justify the achievements, religion and culture of the Inca Empire. He also
commented on Spanish society in the colony. A later work, Historia general del Perú
(1617) went further in condemning Viceroy Toledo's suppression of Inca culture.
Through his work, written in Spain, many aspects of Inca society, plus poems and
prayers have survived.

Writing at about the same time as Inca Garcilaso was Felipe Guaman Poma de
Ayala, whose *El primer nueva corónica y buen gobierno* (1613-15) is possibly one of
the most reproduced of Latin American texts (eg on T-shirts, CDs, posters and carrier
bags). Guaman Poma was a minor provincial Inca chief from Ayacucho province
whose writings and illustrations, addressed to King Felipe III of Spain, offer a view of a
stable pre-conquest Andean society (not uniquely Inca), in contrast with the
unsympathetic colonial society that usurped it.

In the years up to Independence, the growth of an intellectual elite in Lima
spawned more poetry than anything else. As criollo discontent grew, satire increased
both in poetry and in the sketches which accompanied dramas imported from Spain.
The poet Mariano Melgar (1791-1815) wrote in a variety of styles, including the yaraví,
the love-song derived from the pre-Columbian harawi (from haravek). Melgar died in
an uprising against the Spanish but played an important part in the Peruvian struggle
from freedom from the colonial imagination.

After Independence

After Independence, Peruvian writers imitated Spanish costumbrismo, sketches
of characters and life-styles from the new Republic. The first author to transcend

⁞ Mario Vargas Llosa

The best known of Peru's writers is Mario Vargas Llosa, born in 1936 in Arequipa and educated in Cochabamba (Bolivia), from where his family moved to Piura. After graduating from the Universidad de San Marcos, he won a scholarship to Paris in 1958 and, from 1959 to 1974, lived first in Paris then in London in voluntary exile. Much has been written about his personal life, and his political opinions have been well documented, but, as befits an author of the highest international standing and one of the leading figures in the so-called 'Boom' of Latin American writers in the 1960s, it is for his novels that Vargas Llosa the writer is best known.

The first three – *La ciudad y los perros* (1963), *La casa verde* (1966) and *Conversación en la Catedral* (1969) – with their techniques of flashback, multiple narrators and different interwoven stories, are an adventure for the reader. Meanwhile, the humorous books, like *Pantaleón y las visitadoras* and *La tía Julia y el escribidor* cannot be called lightweight. *La guerra del fin del mundo* marked a change to a more direct style and an intensification of Vargas Llosa's exploration of the role of fiction as a human necessity, extending also to political ideologies. *La fiesta del chivo* (2000) is another fictionalized account of historical events, this time the assassination of President Trujillo of the Dominican Republic in 1961 and the intrigue and fear surrounding his period in office. It is a gripping story, widely regarded as one of his best. His latest novel is *El paraíso en la otra esquina* (2003 – The Way to Paradise), which interweaves the lives of Paul Gauguin and his grandmother, Flora Tristan. Vargas Llosa has always maintained that in Peruvian society the writer is a privileged person who should be able to mix politics and literature as a normal part of life. This drive for authenticity led to his excursion into national politics. He stood as a presidential candidate in 1990, losing to Alberto Fujimori. He has since taken up Spanish citizenship and now has homes in Lima, Paris, Madrid and London.

this fashion was Ricardo Palma (1833-1919), whose inspiration, the tradición, fused costumbrismo and Peru's rich oral traditions. Palma's hugely popular *Tradiciones peruanas* is a collection of pieces which celebrate the people, history and customs of Peru through sayings, small incidents in mainly colonial history and gentle irony.

Much soul-searching was to follow Peru's defeat in the War of the Pacific. Manuel González Prada (1844-1918), for instance, wrote essays fiercely critical of the state of the nation: *Páginas libres* (1894), *Horas de lucha* (1908). José Carlos Mariátegui, the foremost Peruvian political thinker of the early 20th century, said that González Prada represented the first lucid instant of Peruvian consciousness. He also wrote poetry, some Romantic, some, like his *Baladas peruanas*, an evocation of indigenous and colonial history, very pro-Indian, very anti-White.

20th century

Mariátegui himself (1895-1930), after a visit to Europe in 1919, considered deeply the question of Peruvian identity. His opinion was that it could only be seen in a global context and that the answer lay in Marxism. With this perspective he wrote about politics, economics, literature and the Indian question (see *Siete ensayos de interpretación de la realidad peruana*, 1928).

Other writers had continued this theme. For instance Clorinda Matto de Turner (1854-1909) intended to express in *Aves sin nido* (1889) her "tender love for the indigenous people" and hoped to improve their lot. Regardless of the debate over whether the novel achieves these aims, she was the forerunner by several years of the 'indigenist' genre in Peru and the most popular of those who took up González Prada's cause.

Other prose writers continued in this vein at the beginning of the 20th century, but it was Ciro Alegría (1909-1967) who gave major, fictional impetus to the racial question. Like Mariátegui, Alegría was politically committed, but to the APRA party, rather than Marxism. Of his first three novels, *La serpiente de oro* (1935), *Los perros hambrientos* (1938) and *El mundo es ancho y ajeno* (1941), the latter is his most famous.

Contemporary with Alegría was José María Arguedas (1911-1969), whose novels, stories and politics were also deeply rooted in the ethnic question. Arguedas, though not Indian, had a largely Quechua upbringing and tried to reconcile this with the hispanic world in which he worked. This inner conflict was one of the main causes of his suicide. His books include *Agua* (short stories, 1935), *Yawar fiesta* (1941), *Los ríos profundos* (1958) and *Todas las sangres* (1964). They portray different aspects of the confrontation of Indian society with the changing outside world that impinges on it.

In the 1950s and 1960s, there was a move away from the predominantly rural and indigenist to an urban setting. At the forefront were, among others, Mario Vargas Llosa, Julio Ramón Ribeyro, Enrique Congrains Martín, Oswaldo Reynoso, Luis Loayza, Sebastián Salazar Bondy and Carlos E Zavaleta. Taking their cue from a phrase used by both poet César Mora and Salazar Bondy (in an essay of 1964), "Lima, la horrible", they explored all aspects of the city, including the influx of people from the Sierra. These writers incorporated new narrative techniques in the urban novel, which presented a world where popular culture and speech were rich sources of literary material, despite the difficulty in transcribing them.

Many writers, such as Vargas Llosa, broadened their horizons beyond the capital. His novels after La ciudad y los perros encompassed many different parts of the country. An additional factor was that several writers spent many years abroad, Vargas Llosa himself, for instance, and Ribeyro (1929-1994). The latter's short stories, though mostly set in Lima, embrace universal themes of delusion and frustration. The title story of *Los gallinazos sin pluma* (1955), a tale of squalor and greed amid the city's rubbish tips, has become a classic, even though it does not contain the irony, pathos and humour of many of his other stories or novels.

Other writers of this period include Manuel Scorza (1928-83), who wrote a series of five novels under the general title of *La guerra silenciosa* (including *Redoble por Rancas*, *El jinete insomne*, *La tumba del relámpago*) which follow the indigenist tradition of the Indians' struggle, and also emphasize the need to defend indigenous society with growing militancy if necessary.

Alfredo Bryce Echenique (born 1939) has enjoyed much popularity following the success of *Un mundo para Julius* (1970), a brilliant satire on the upper and middle classes of Lima. His other novels include *Tantas veces Pedro* (1977), *La última mudanza de Felipe Carrillo* (1988), *No me esperen en abril* (1995), *Dos señoras conversan* (1990), *La amigdalitis de Tarzan* (2000) and *El huerto de mi amada*, which won the Premio Planeta (Barcelona) in 2002. Other contemporary writers of note are: Jaime Bayly (born 1965), who is also a journalist and TV presenter. His novels include *Fue ayer y no me acuerdo*, *Los últimos días de la prensa*, *No se lo digas a nadie* and *La noche es virgen*. The last named is typical of his style, full of irony and slang, dealing with the lives the young and affluent in Lima, gay/bisexual, bored, dope-smoking rock-music fans. His most recent novel is *El huracán lleva tu nombre* (2004). A highly-rated short-story writer is Pilar Dughi (born 1956), for instance *Ave de la noche* (1996). See also Rodolfo Hinostroza (born 1941), novelist, playwright and poet, whose books include *Cuentos de Contranatura* (1972) and *Extremo occidente* (2002); Fernando Ampuero (born 1949), whose books include *Miraflores Melody* (1979), *Malos modales* (1994), *Bicho raro* (1996), *Cuentos escogidos* (1998) and *El enano, historia de una enemistad* (2001); Alonso Cueto (born 1954), *La batalla del pasado*, *El tigre blanco* and *El otro amor de Diana Abril*; Mario Bellatín (born 1960 in Mexico but educated in Peru), among whose works are the excellent short novels *Salón de belleza* (1994) and *Damas chinas* (1995); and Ivan Thays (born 1968), *Escena de caza* (1996) and *Viaje interior*, as well as short stories.

20th-century poetry

At the end of the 19th century, the term Modernism was introduced in Latin America by the Nicaraguan Rubén Darío, not to define a precise school of poetry, but to indicate a break with both Romanticism and Realism. In Peru one major exponent was José Santos Chocano (1875-1934), who labelled his poetry "mundonovismo" (New Worldism), claiming for himself the role of Poet of South America. He won international fame (see, for example, *Alma América*, 1906), but his star soon waned.

A much less assuming character was José María Eguren (1874-1942) who, feeling alienated from the society around him, sought spiritual reality in the natural world (*Simbólicas*, 1911; *La canción de las figuras*, 1916; *Poesías*, 1929). It has been said that with Eguren the flourishing of Peruvian 20th century poetry began.

Without doubt, the most important poet in Peru, if not Latin America, in the first half of the 20th century, was César Vallejo. Born in 1892 in Santiago de Chuco (Libertad), Vallejo left Peru in 1923 after being framed and briefly jailed in Trujillo for a political crime. In 1928 he was a founder of the Peruvian Socialist Party, then he joined the Communist Party in 1931 in Madrid. From 1936 to his death in Paris in 1938 he opposed the fascist takeover in Spain. His first volume was *Los heraldos negros* in which the dominating theme of all his work, a sense of confusion and inadequacy in the face of the unpredictability of life, first surfaces. *Trilce* (1922), his second work, is unlike anything before it in the Spanish language. The poems contain (among other things) made-up words, distortions of syntax, their own internal logic and rhythm, graphic devices and innovative uses of sounds, clichés and alliterations. *Poemas humanos* and *España, aparta de mí este cáliz* (written as a result of Vallejo's experiences in the Spanish Civil War) were both published posthumously, in 1939.

In the 1960s writers began to reflect the broadening horizons of that increasingly liberal decade, politically and socially, which followed the Cuban Revolution. One poet who embraced the revolutionary fervour was Javier Heraud (born Miraflores 1942). His early volumes, *El río* (1960) and *El viaje* (1961) are apparently simple in conception and expression, but display a transition from embarking on the adventure of life (the river) to autumnal imagery of solitude. In 1961 he went to the USSR, Asia, Paris and Madrid, then in 1962 to Cuba to study cinema. He returned to Peru in 1963 and joined the guerrilla Ejército de Liberación Nacional. On 15 May 1963 he was shot by government forces near Puerto Maldonado. Heraud's friend César Calvo, now living in Cuba, is a poet and essayist worth reading.

Other major poets born in the early 20th century are Emilio Adolfo Westphalen (1911) and Jorge Eduardo Eielson (see his book *Celebración*), who began to publish in the 1960s were Luis Hernández (1941-1977), Antonio Cisneros (born 1942) and Marco Martos (born 1942).

In the 1970s, during the social changes propelled by the Velasco regime (1968-1975), new voices arose, many from outside Lima, eg the Hora Zero group

(1970-1973 – Enrique Verástegui, Jorge Pimentel, Juan Ramírez Ruiz), whose energetic poetry employed slang, obscenities and other means to challenge preconceptions. Other poets of the 1970s and after José Watanabe (born 1946), a film-maker as well as poet, with *Album de familia* (1971) and *Historia natural* (1996); Giovanna Pollarolo (poet, short story writer and screenwriter, born 1952) whose collections include *Huerto de olivos*, 1982, *Entre mujeres solas*, 1996, *La ceremonia de adios*, 1997 and *Atado de nervios*, 1999, and Rocio Silva Santiesteban (born 1967) who has published short stories as well as the poetry collections *Asuntos circunstanciales* (1984), *Este oficio no me gusta* (1987) and *Mariposa negra* (1996). Younger poets of note are: Ericka Ghersi (born 1972), *Zenobia y el anciano* (1994), *Contra la ausencia* (2002), Renato Cisneros (born 1976), *Ritual de los prójimos* (1998) and *Maquina fantasma* (2002), Rosella di Paolo (born 1960), *Piel alzada* (1993), *Tablillas de San Lázaro* (2001) among other collections, and Marita Troiano, whose works include *Mortal in puribus* (1996) and *Secreto a veces* (2003).

Fine art and sculpture

The Catholic Church was the main patron of the arts during the colonial period. The innumerable churches and monasteries that sprang up in the newly conquered territories created a demand for paintings and sculptures, met initially by imports from Europe of both works of art and of skilled craftsmen, and later by home-grown products.

Colonial period

An essential requirement for the inauguration of any new church was an image for the altar and many churches in Lima preserve fine examples of sculptures imported from Seville during the 16th and 17th centuries. Not surprisingly, among the earliest of these are figures of the crucified Christ, such as those in the Cathedral and the church of La Merced by Juan Martínez Montañés, one of the foremost Spanish sculptors of the day, and that in San Pedro, by his pupil Juan de Mesa of 1625. Statues of the Virgin and Child were also imported to Lima from an early date, and examples from the mid-16th century survive in the Cathedral and in Santo Domingo by Roque de Balduque, also from Seville although Flemish by birth.

Sculptures were expensive and difficult to import, and as part of their policy of relative frugality the Franciscan monks tended to favour paintings. In Lima, the museum of San Francisco now houses an excellent collection of paintings imported from Europe, including a powerful series of saints by Zubarán, as well as other works from his studio, a series of paintings of the life of Christ from Ruben's workshop and works from the circles of Ribera and Murillo, see page 98.

The Jesuits commissioned the Sevillian artist Juan de Valdés Leal to paint a series of the life of St Ignatius Loyola (1660s) which still hangs in San Pedro. The Cathedral museum has a curious series from the Bassano workshop of Venice representing the labours of the monks and dating from the early 17th century. Another interesting artistic import from Europe that can still be seen in San Pedro (see Lima Churches) are the gloriously colourful painted tile decorations (*azulejos*) on the walls of Dominican monastery, produced to order by Sevillian workshops in 1586 and 1604.

Painters and sculptors soon made their way to Peru in search of lucrative commissions including several Italians who arrived during the later 16th century. The Jesuit Bernardo Bitti (1548-1610), for example, trained in Rome before working in Lima, Cusco, Juli and Arequipa, where examples of his elegantly Mannerist paintings are preserved in the Jesuit church of the Compañia, see Arequipa page 256.

Another Italian, Mateo Pérez de Alesio worked in the Sistine Chapel in Rome before settling in Peru. In Lima the Sevillian sculptor Pedro de Noguera (1592-1655) won the contract for the choirstalls of the Cathedral in 1623 and, together with other Spanish craftsmen, produced a set of cedar stalls decorated with vigorous figures of saints and Biblical characters, an outstanding work unmatched elsewhere in the Viceroyalty.

Native artists

European imports, however, could not keep up with demand and local workshops of creole, mestizo and Indian craftsmen flourished from the latter part of the 16th century. As the Viceregal capital and the point of arrival into Peru, the art of Lima was always strongly influenced by European, especially Spanish models, but the old Inca capital of Cusco became the centre of a regional school of painting which developed its own characteristics.

A series of paintings of the 1660s, now hanging in the Museo de Arte Religioso, see Cusco page 152, commemorate the colourful Corpus Christi procession of statues of the local patron saints through the streets of Cusco. These paintings document the appearance of the city and local populace, including Spanish and Inca nobility, priests and laity, rich and poor, Spaniard, Indian, African and mestizo. Many of the statues represented in this series are still venerated in the local parish churches. They are periodically painted and dressed in new robes, but underneath are the original sculptures, executed by native craftsmen. Some are of carved wood while others use the pre-conquest technique of maguey cactus covered in sized cloth.

A remarkable example of an Andean Indian who acquired European skills was Felipe Guaman Poma de Ayala whose 1,000 page letter to the King of Spain celebrating the Andean past and condemning the colonial present contained a visual history of colonial and precolonial life in the Andes, see also page 597.

One of the most successful native painters was Diego Quispe Tito (1611-1681) who claimed descent from the Inca nobility and whose large canvases, often based on Flemish engravings, demonstrate the wide range of European sources that were available to Andean artists in the 17th century. But the Cusco School is best known for the anonymous devotional works where the painted contours of the figures are overlaid with flat patterns in gold, creating highly decorative images with an underlying tension between the two- and three-dimensional aspects of the work. The taste for richly-decorated surfaces can also be seen in the 17th and 18th century frescoed interiors of many Andean churches, as in Chinchero, Andahuaylillas and Huaro, and in the ornate carving on altarpieces and pulpits throughout Peru.

Andean content creeps into colonial religious art in a number of ways, most simply by the inclusion of elements of indigenous flora and fauna, or, as in the case of the Corpus Christi paintings, by the use of a specific setting, with recognizable buildings and individuals.

Changes to traditional Christian iconography include the representation of one of the Magi as an Inca, as in the painting of the Adoration of the Magi in San Pedro in Juli (see Puno Excursions, page 230). Another example is that to commemorate his miraculous intervention in the conquest of Cusco in 1534, Santiago is often depicted triumphing over Indians instead of the more familiar Moors. Among the most remarkable 'inventions' of colonial art are the fantastically over-dressed archangels carrying muskets which were so popular in the 18th century. There is no direct European source for these archangels, but in the Andes they seem to have served as a painted guard of honour to the image of Christ or the Virgin on the high altar.

Independence and after

Political independence from Spain in 1824 had little immediate impact on the arts of Peru except to create a demand for portraits of the new national and continental heroes such as Simón Bolívar and San Martín, many of the best of them produced by

⁝ Viringo

If you go to a Peruvian museum at a coastal archaeological site, you will probably see an elegant dog, with a long, thin nose and arched neck prowling around the entrance. It may be a bit shy, and, if the weather is cold, it may be waring a little woollen jacket. This is because the dog has no hair.

The Peruvian Hairless, or viringo, is a rare breed today, but in Inca times was a companion animal whose main job was to warm his master's bed. The Chavín, Moche and Chimú cultures represented it on their ceramics, but its origins are unknown. The most likely theory is that it accompanied the first migrants to the Amercian continent from Asia. In its most common, hairless form, it has no fleas and no smell.

Breeders note that it needs protecting against the sun and the cold, but there is also a coated variety (called 'powder puff' in the dog world).

In recognition of the importance of this dog in its history, the Peruvian government decreed in Law number 27537 that every site museum on the coast must have at least one viringo on the premises.

Background Culture (side)

the mulatto artist José Gil de Castro (died Lima 1841). Later in the century another mulatto, Pancho Fierro (1810-1879) mocked the rigidity and pretentiousness of Lima society in lively satirical watercolours, while Francisco Laso (1823-1860), an active campaigner for political reform, made the Andean Indian into a respectable subject for oil paintings.

It was not until the latter part of the 19th century that events from colonial history became popular. The Museo de Arte in Lima (see Lima page 97) has examples of grandiose paintings by Ignacio Merino (1817-1876) glorifying Columbus, as well as the gigantic romanticized 'Funeral of Atahualpa' by Luis Montero (1826-1869). A curious late flowering of this celebration of colonial history is the chapel commemorating Francisco Pizarro in Lima cathedral which was redecorated in 1928 with garish mosaic pictures of the conqueror's exploits.

Impressionism arrived late and had a limited impact in Peru. Teofilo Castillo (1857-1922), instead of using the technique to capture contemporary reality, created frothy visions of an idealized colonial past. Typical of his work is the large 'Funeral Procession of Santa Rosa' of 1918, with everything bathed in clouds of incense and rose petals, which hangs in the Museo de Arte, in Lima. Daniel Hernández (1856-1932), founder of Peru's first Art School, used a similar style for his portraits of Lima notables past and present.

20th century to today

During the first half of the 20th century, Peruvian art was dominated by figurative styles and local subject matter. Political theories of the 1920s recognized the importance of Andean Indian culture to Peruvian identity and created a climate which encouraged a figurative indigenista school of painting, derived in part from the socialist realism of the Mexican muralists. The movement flourished after the founding of the Escuela de Bellas Artes in 1920. José Sabogal (1888-1956) is the best known exponent of the group which also included Mario Urteaga (1875-1957), Jorge Vinatea Reinoso (1900-1931), Enrique Camino Brent (1909-1960), Camilo Blas (1903-1984) and Alejandro González (1900-1984). Their work can be seen in the Museo de Arte and the Museo Banco Central de Reserva in Lima.

The Mexican muralist tradition persisted into the 1960s with Manuel Ugarte Eléspuru (1911) and Teodoro Núñez Ureta (1914), both of whom undertook large-scale commissions in public buildings in Lima. Examples of public sculpture in the indigenist mode can be seen in plazas and parks throughout Peru, but it was in photography that indigenism found its most powerful expression. From the beginning of the century photographic studios flourished even in smaller towns. Martín Chambi (1891-1973) is the best known of the early 20th century Peruvian photographers but there were many others, including Miguel Chani (1860-1951) who maintained the grandly named Fotografía Universal studios in Cusco, Puno and Arequipa.

From the middle of the century artists have experimented with a variety of predominantly abstract styles and the best-known contemporary Peruvian painter, Fernando de Szyszlo (1925) has created a visual language of his own, borrowing from Abstract Expressionism on the one hand and from pre-Columbian iconography on the other. His strong images, which suggest rather than represent mythical beings and cosmic forces, have influenced a whole generation of younger Peruvian artists. Look for his monument, Intihuatana 2000, near the sea in Miraflores.

Other leading figures whose work can be seen in public and commercial galleries in Lima include Venancio Shinki, Tilsa Tsuchiya, José Tola, Ricardo Weisse, Ramiro Llona and Leoncio Villanueva. Carlos Revilla, whose wife is his muse and principal subject of his painting, is clearly influenced by Hieronymous Bosch, while Bill Caro is an important exponent of hyperrealism. Víctor Delfín, a painter and sculptor (with beautiful work in iron) can be visited at his house in Barranco (Domeyko 366). His piece, The Kiss (El beso) is in the Parque del Amor in Lima. Pedro Azabache (from Trujillo) is a disciple of José Sabogal; his work is much broader in scope than the indigenism of his mentor. There are many other new artists whose work could be mentioned (Luz Letts, Eduardo Tokeshi, Carlos Enrique Polanco, Bruno Zepilli, Christian Bendayan – try to contact him in Iquitos, Flavia Gandolfo, Claudia Coca) and there are plenty of galleries in Lima with representative exhibitions. A new foundation is working towards opening a museum of contemporary art in Barranco, Lima, which is long overdue in a country where art is constantly changing. One striking modern piece outside Lima is the mosaic mural at the Ciudad Universitaria UNT in Trujillo, which, at several kilometres long, will be the longest work of art in the world when complete.

Land and environment

Geography

Peru is the third largest South American country, the size of France, Spain and the United Kingdom combined, and presents formidable difficulties to human habitation. Virtually all of the 2,250 km of its Pacific coast is desert. From the narrow coastal shelf the Andes rise steeply to a high plateau dominated by massive ranges of snow-capped peaks and gouged with deep canyons. The heavily forested and deeply ravined Andean slopes are more gradual to the east. Further east, towards Brazil and Colombia, begin the vast jungles of the Amazon basin.

Geology

The geological structure of Peru is dominated by the Nasca Plate beneath the Pacific Ocean, which stretches from Colombia in the north southwards to mid Chile. Along the coastline, this Plate meets and dives below the mass of the South American Plate which has been moving westwards for much of the Earth's geological history. Prior to the middle of the Tertiary Period, say 40 million years ago, marine sediments suggest that the Amazon basin drained west to the Pacific, but from that time to the

66 99 Peru has more tropical glaciers than any other country in South America, but in recent years scientists have recorded rapid shrinkage of snow and glaciers from Peruvian peaks. This loss is blamed on global warming...

present, tectonic forces have created the Andes range the length of the continent, forming the highest peaks outside the Himalayas. The process continues today as shown by the earthquakes and active volcanoes and, in spite of erosion, the mountains still grow higher.

Coast

The coastal region, a narrow ribbon of desert 2,250 km long, takes up 11% of the country and holds 44% of the population. It is the economic heart of Peru, consuming most of the imports and supplying half of the exports. When irrigated, the river valleys are extremely fertile, creating oases which grow cotton throughout the country, sugar-cane, rice and asparagus in the north, and grapes, fruit and olives in the south. At the same time, the coastal current teems with fish, and Peru has on occasion had the largest catch in the world.

Not far beyond the border with Ecuador in the north, there are mangrove swamps and tropical rainforest, but southwards this quickly changes to drier and eventually desert conditions. South of Piura is the desert of Sechura, followed by the dry barren land or shifting sands to Chimbote. However, several rivers draining the high mountains to the east more or less reach the sea and water the highly productive 'oases' of Piura, Trujillo, Cajamarca and Chimbote.

South of Chimbote, the Andes reach the sea, and apart from a thin strip of coastland north of Lima, the coastal mountains continue to the Chilean border at Arica. This area receives less rain than the Sahara, but because of the high Andes inland, over 50 Peruvian rivers reach the sea, or would do naturally for at least part of the year. As in the north, there are oases in the south, but mostly inland at the foot of the mountains where the river flow is greatest and high sunshine levels ensure good crop production.

The climate of this region depends almost entirely on the ocean currents along the Pacific coast. Two bodies of water drift northwards, the one closest to the shore, known as the Humboldt Current, is the colder, following the deep sea trench along the edge of the Pacific Plate. The basic wind systems here are the South-East Trades crossing the continent from the Atlantic, but the strong tropical sun over the land draws air into Peru from the Pacific. Being cool, this air does no more than condense into mist (known as the garúa) over the coastal mountains. This is sufficient to provide moisture for some unusual flora but virtually never produces rain, hence the desert conditions. The mixing of the two cold ocean currents, and the cloud cover which protects the water from the strongest sunlight, creates the unique conditions favourable to fish, notably sardines and anchovy, giving Peru an enormous economic resource. In turn, the fish support vast numbers of seabirds whose deposits of guano have been another very successful export for the country. This is the normal situation; every few years, however, it is disrupted by the phenomenon known as 'El Niño', see page 607.

The Highlands, or la sierra, extend inland from the coastal strip some 250 km in the north, increasing to 400 km in the south. The average altitude is about 3,000 m and 50% of Peruvians live there. Essentially it is a plateau dissected by dramatic canyons and dominated by some of the most spectacular mountain ranges in the world.

Mountains

The tallest peaks are in the Cordillera Blanca (Huascarán; 6,768 m) and the neighbouring Cordillera Huayhuash (Yerupajá; 6,634 m). Huascarán is often quoted as the second highest point in South America after Aconcagua, but this is not so; there are some five other peaks on or near the Argentina-Chile border over 6,770 m.

The snowline here, at nine degrees south, is between 4,500 m and 5,000 m, much lower than further south. For example, at 16° south, permanent snow starts at 6,000 m on Coropuna (6,425 m). Peru has more tropical glaciers than any other country in South America, but in recent years scientists have recorded rapid shrinkage of snow and glaciers from Peruvian peaks. This loss is blamed on global warming.

The reasons for this anomaly can be traced again to the Humboldt current. The Cordillera Blanca is less than 100 km from the coast, and the cool air drawn in depresses temperatures at high altitudes. Precipitation comes also from the east and falls as snow. Constant high winds and temperatures well below freezing at night create an unusual microclimate and with it spectacular mountain scenery, making it a mecca for snow and ice mountaineers. Dangers are heightened by the quite frequent earthquakes causing avalanches and landslides which have brought heavy loss of life to the valleys of the region. In 1970, 20,000 people lost their lives when Yungay, immediately west of Huascarán, was overwhelmed.

Canyons

Equally dramatic are the deep canyons taking water from the high mountains to the Pacific. The Colca Canyon, about 100 km north of Arequipa, has been measured at 3,200 m from the lower rim to the river, more than twice as deep as the Grand Canyon. At one point it is overlooked by the 5,227 m Señal Yajirhua peak, a stupendous 4,150 m above the water level. Deeper even than Colca is the Cotahuasi Canyon, also in Arequipa Department, whose deepest point is 3,354 m. Other canyons have been found in this remote area yet to be measured and documented.

In spite of these ups and downs which cause great communications difficulties, the presence of water and a more temperate climate on the plateau has attracted people throughout the ages. Present day important population centres in the Highlands include Cajamarca in the north, Huancayo in central Peru and Cusco in the south, all at around 3,000 m. Above this, at around 4,000 m, is the 'high steppe' or puna, with constant winds and wide day/night temperature fluctuations. Nevertheless, fruit and potatoes (which originally came from the puna of Peru and Bolivia) are grown at this altitude and the meagre grasslands are home to the ubiquitous llama.

Volcanoes

Although hot springs and evidence of ancient volcanic activity can be seen almost anywhere in Peru, the southern part of the sierra is the only area where there are active volcanoes. These represent the northernmost of a line of volcanoes which stretch 1,500 km south along the Chile-Bolivia border to Argentina. Sabancaya (5,977 m), just south of the Colca canyon, is currently active, often with a dark plume downwind from the summit. Beyond the Colca canyon is the Valle de los Volcanes, with 80 cinder cones rising 50-250 m above a desolate floor of lava and ash. There are other dormant or recently active volcanoes near the western side of Lake Titicaca – for example Ubinas – but the most notable is El Misti (5,822 m) which overlooks Arequipa. It is perfectly shaped, indicating its status as active in the recent geologic

When the winds blow

Anyone who tuned into a weather forecast during late 1997 now knows about the climatic effect called El Niño, which means "Christ child". El Niño was so named by Peruvian fishermen who noticed the warming of the waters of the eastern Pacific around Christmas time.

Every three to seven years, for some as yet unexplained reason, the trade winds that usually blow west from South America subside. So the warm waters of the Pacific – a giant pool the size of Canada – drift eastwards towards South America. The result is worldwide weather chaos.

In 1997 El Niño made its third visit of the decade – one that made everyone sit up and take notice. The eastern Pacific heated faster than at any time in recorded history to become the most devastating climatic event of the century, surpassing even the 1982-83 El Niño, which killed thousands and caused almost US$14 billion in damage.

The 1997 El Niño caused drought in Australia, New Zealand, Thailand, Malaysia and Papua New Guinea, the forest fires in Indonesia, famine in North Korea, hurricanes along the US Pacific coast and the failure of the fish harvest in Peru (causing the seabird population to fall dramatically). El Niño also sparked epidemics of cholera, encephalitis and bubonic plague.

Despite being implicated in all these weather crimes, scientists appear to know little about it, but monitoring and research continue around the globe. El Niño used to arrive every five to eight years, but this has been revised downwards to three to seven years. Nevertheless, the 1997-1998 event, the worst for 50 years, remains the most recent.

past. Some experts believe it is one of the most potentially dangerous volcanoes in South America. Certainly a major eruption would be a catastrophe for the nearby city.

Lake Titicaca

The southeastern border with Bolivia passes through Titicaca, with about half of the lake in each country. It is the largest lake in South America (ignoring Lake Maracaibo in Venezuela which is linked to the sea) and at 3,812 m, the highest navigable body of water in the world. It covers about 8,300 sq km, running 190 km northwest to southeast, and is 80 km across. It lies in a 60,000 sq km basin between the coastal and eastern Andes which spread out southwards to their widest point at latitude 18° south.

The average depth is over 100 m, with the deepest point recorded at 281 m. 25 rivers, most from Peru, flow into the lake and a small outlet leaves the lake at Desaguadero on the Bolivia-Peru border. This takes no more than 5% of the inflow, the rest is lost through evaporation and hence the waters of the lake are slightly brackish, producing the totora reeds used to make the mats and balsa boats for which the lake dwellers are famed.

The lake is the remnant of a vast area of water formed in the Ice Age known as Lake Ballivián. This extended at least 600 km to the south into Bolivia and included what is now Lake Poopó and the Salar de Uyuni. Now the lake level fluctuates seasonally, normally rising from December to March and receding for the rest of the year but extremes of 5 m between high and low levels have been recorded. This can cause problems and high levels in the late 1980s disrupted transport links near the shoreline. The night temperature can fall as low as -25°C but high daytime temperatures ensure that the surface average is about 14°C.

Eastern Andes and Amazon basin

Almost half of Peru is on the eastern side of the Andes and about 90% of the country's drainage is into the Amazon system. It is an area of heavy rainfall with cloudforest above 3,500 m and tropical rainforest lower down. There is little savanna, or natural grasslands, characteristic of other parts of the Amazon basin.

There is some dispute on the Amazon's source. Officially, the mighty river begins as the Marañón, whose longest tributary rises just east of the Cordillera Huayhuash. However, the longest journey for the proverbial raindrop, some 6,400 km, probably starts in southern Peru, where the headwaters of the Apurímac (Ucayali) flow from the snows on the northern side of the Nevado Mismi, near Cailloma.

With much more rainfall on the eastern side of the Andes, rivers are turbulent and erosion dramatic. Although vertical drops are not as great – there is a whole continent to cross to the Atlantic – valleys are deep, ridges narrow and jagged and there is forest below 3,000 m. At 1,500 m the Amazon jungle begins and water is the only means of surface transport available, apart from three roads which reach Borja (on the Marañón), Yurimaguas (on the Huallaga) and Pucallpa (on the Ucayali), all at about 300 m above the Atlantic which is still 4,000 km or so downstream. The vastness of the Amazon lowlands becomes apparent and it is here that Peru bulges 650 km northeast past Iquitos to the point where it meets Colombia and Brazil at Leticia. Oil and gas have recently been found in the Amazon, and new finds are made every year, which means that new pipelines and roads will eventually link more places to the Pacific coast.

Climate

Coast

On the coast summertime is from December-April, when temperatures range from 25° to 35°C and it is hot and dry. Wintertime is May-November, when the temperature drops a bit and it is cloudy.

The coastal climate is determined by the cold sea-water adjoining deserts. Prevailing inshore winds pick up so little moisture over the cold Humboldt current, which flows from Antarctica, that only from May to November does it condense. The resultant blanket of sea-mist (called garúa) extends from the south to about 200 km north of Lima. It is thickest to the south as far as Chincha and to the north as far as Huarmey, beyond which it thins and the sun can be expected to break through.

Sierra

From April-October is the dry season. It is hot and dry during the day, around 20°-25°C, and cold and dry at night, often below freezing. From November-April is the wet season, when it is dry and clear most mornings, with some rainfall in the afternoon. There is a small temperature drop (18°C) and not much difference at night (15°C).

Selva

April-October is the dry season, with temperatures up to 35°C. In the jungle areas of the south, a cold front can pass through at night. November-April is the wet season. It is humid and hot, with heavy rainfall at any time.

Flora and fauna

Peru is a country of great biological diversity. The fauna and flora are to a large extent determined by the influence of the Andes, the longest uninterrupted mountain chain in the world, and the mighty Amazon river, which has the largest volume of any river in the world. Of Earth's 32 known climate zones Peru has 28, and of the 104 recognized micro- climates Peru has 84. Throughout the country there are 53 protected natural areas.

Natural history

This diversity arises not only from the wide range of habitats available, but also from the history of the continent. South America has essentially been an island for some 70 million years joined only by a narrow isthmus to Central and North America. Land passage played a significant role in the gradual colonization of South America by species from the north. When the land-link closed these colonists evolved to a wide variety of forms free from the competitive pressures that prevailed elsewhere. When the land-bridge was re-established some four million years ago a new invasion of species took place from North America, adding to the diversity but also leading to numerous extinctions. Comparative stability has ensued since then and has guaranteed the survival of many primitive groups like the opossums.

Coast

The coastal region of Peru is extremely arid, partly as a result of the cold Humboldt current (see Climate above). The paucity of animal life in the area between the coast and the mountains is obviously due to this lack of rain, though in some areas intermittent lomas, which are areas of sparse scrubby vegetation caused by moisture in the sea mist. The plants which survive provide ideal living conditions for insects which attract insectivorous birds and humming birds to feed on their nectar. Cactuses are abundant in northern Peru and provide a wooded landscape of trees and shrubs including the huarango (*Prosopis juliflora*). Also common in the north is the algorrob tree – 250,000 ha were planted in 1997 to take advantage of the El Niño rains. Algorrob forests (*algorrobales*), scrub thicket (*matorrales*) and coastal wetlands each provide habitat for some 30 species of birds. Mammals include foxes, three species of deer and six species of dogs from pre-Columbian times.

Andes

From the desert rise the steep Andean slopes. In the deeply incised valleys Andean fox and deer may occasionally be spotted. Herds of llamas and alpacas graze the steep hillsides. Mountain caracara and Andean lapwing are frequently observed soaring, and there is always the possibility of spotting flocks of mitred parrots or even the biggest species of hummingbird in the world (Patagonia gigas).

The Andean zone has many lakes and rivers and countless swamps. Exclusive to this area short-winged grebe and the torrent duck which feeds in the fast flowing rivers, and giant and horned coots. Chilean flamingo frequent the shallow soda lakes.

The puna, a habitat characterized by tussock grass and pockets of stunted alpine flowers, gives way to relict elfin forest and tangled bamboo thicket in this inhospitable windswept and frost-prone region. Occasionally the dissected remains of a Puya plant can be found; the result of the nocturnal foraging of the rare spectacled bear. There are quite a number of endemic species of rodent including the viscacha, and it is the last stronghold of the chinchilla. Here pumas roam preying on the herbivores which frequent these mountain – pudu, a tiny Andean deer or guemal and the mountain tapir.

Tropical Andes

The elfin forest gradually grades into mist enshrouded cloud forest at about 3,500 m. In the tropical zones of the Andes, the humidity in the cloud forests stimulates the growth of a vast variety of plants particularly mosses and lichens. The cloud forests are found in a narrow strip that runs along the eastern slopes of the spine of the Andes. It is these dense, often impenetrable, forests clothing the steep slopes that are important in protecting the headwaters of all the streams and rivers that cascade from the Andes to form the mighty Amazon as it begins its long journey to the sea.

This is a verdant world of dripping epiphytic mosses, lichens, ferns and orchids which grow in profusion despite the plummeting overnight temperatures. The high humidity resulting from the 2 m of rain that can fall in a year is responsible for the maintenance of the forest and it accumulates in puddles and leaks from the ground in a constant trickle that combines to form a myriad of icy, crystal-clear tumbling streams that cascade over precipitous waterfalls.

In secluded areas orange Andean Cock-of-the-Rock give their spectacular display to females in the early morning mists. Woolly monkeys are also occasionally sighted as they descend the wooded slopes. Mixed flocks of colourful tanagers are commonly encountered as are the golden-headed quetzal and Amazon umbrella bird.

Amazon basin

At about 1,500 m there is a gradual transition to the vast lowland forests of the Amazon basin, which are warmer and more equable than the cloud forests clothing the mountains above. The daily temperature varies little during the year with a high of 23-32°C falling slightly to 20-26°C overnight. This lowland region receives some 2 m of rainfall per year most of it falling from November to April. The rest of the year is sufficiently dry, at least in the lowland areas to inhibit the growth of epiphytes and orchids which are so characteristic of the highland areas. For a week or two in the rainy season the rivers flood the forest. The zone immediately surrounding this seasonally flooded forest is referred to as terre firme forest.

The vast river basin of the Amazon is home to an immense variety of species. The environment has largely dictated the lifestyle. Life in or around rivers, lakes, swamps and forest depend on the ability to swim and climb and amphibious and tree-dwelling animals are common. Once the entire Amazon basin was a great inland sea and the river still contains mammals more typical of the coast, eg manatees and dolphins.

Here in the relatively constant climatic conditions animal and plant life has evolved to an amazing diversity over the millennia. It has been estimated that 3.9 sq km of forest can harbour some 1,200 vascular plants, 600 species of tree, and 120 woody plants. Here, in these relatively flat lands, a soaring canopy some 50 m overhead is the power-house of the forest. It is a habitat choked with strangling vines and philodendrons among which mixed troupes of squirrel monkeys and brown capuchins forage. In the high canopy small groups of spider monkeys perform their lazy aerial acrobatics, whilst lower down, cling to epiphyte-clad trunks and branches, groups of saddle-backed and emperor tamarins forage for blossom, fruit and the occasional insect prey.

The most accessible part of the jungle is on or near the many meandering rivers. At each bend of the river the forest is undermined by the currents during the seasonal floods at the rate of some 10-20 m per year leaving a sheer mud and clay bank, whilst on the opposite bend new land is laid down as broad beaches of fine sand and silt.

A succession of vegetation can be seen. The fast growing willow-like Tessaria first stabilizes the ground enabling the tall stands of caña brava Gynerium to become established. Within these dense almost impenetrable stands the seeds of rainforest trees germinate and over a few years thrust their way towards the light. The fastest growing is a species of Cercropia which forms a canopy 15-18 m over the caña but even this is relatively short-lived. The gap in the canopy is quickly filled by other species. Two types of mahogany outgrow the other trees forming a closed canopy at 40 m with a lush understory of shade tolerant Heliconia and ginger.

The debonair dolphin

Two species of dolphin live in the Amazon, the pink Inia geoffrensis and the grey Sotalia fluvialis.The pink dolphin is mainly solitary, but small groups are often found. Instead of a dorsal fin, it has a hump on its back and it also has a long bottle nose. Because of its surfacing habits, you are unlikely to see its nose as it normally only exposes its dorsal ridge. The grey dolphin swims in groups and is a more 'conventional' shape, with a dorsal fin and shorter snout. When surfacing it often jumps right out of the water. For centuries the dolphins have lived peacefully with man on the river and as a result many myths have grown up around them. Sadly, destruction of habitat and pollution have threatened this harmonious coexistence.

The best-known legend concerns the night-time exploits of the pink dolphin. Indigenous people of the Amazon have passed down stories from generation to generation about this strange animal, which they call the bufeo. They believe that the dolphins live in an underwater city in Lake Caballococha, downriver from Iquitos, near the Peru-Colombia border. By night, the bufeo can transform himself into a suave gentleman in a white linen suit and, in this guise, he preys on unsuspecting local women. Even today, unwanted pregnancies within Indian communities are sometimes blamed on this magical animal with an impressive line in seduction techniques. There are many other stories up and down the river and its tributaries. For some communities the dolphin is a semi-divine being, for others a untrustworthy witchdoctor. Its teeth, says Alex Shoumatoff in The Rivers Amazon, are claimed to cure children's diarrhea, its ear to grant a long-lasting erection and its "grated left eye is an aphrodisiac powder."

The pink river dolphins were, until recently, a forgotten species, considered extinct.

All that remained was the skeleton of one in Paris, brought back from South America as a gift to Napoleon, and a few vague scientific papers dating from the 19th century in the Natural History Museum in London. The bufeo was re-discovered by a British expedition in 1956. Then it was forgotten again until 1987, when Jacques Cousteau astounded TV viewers around the world with the first ever pictures of pink dolphins frolicking in the waters of the Amazon.

Now many Amazon lodges take travellers on dolphin-spotting expeditions. With some patience you can see one, or both types of dolphin in the flesh. The more curious pink ones circle quite close to the boat, while the grey will be further away, plunging into the river in unison – a fantastic sight. Back on land, though, women travellers should beware of a charming, smartly-dressed gentleman who doesn't raise his hat (it covers his blowhole).

Eventually even the long-lived trees die off to be replaced by others providing a forest of great diversity.

Jungle wildlife

The meandering course of the river provides many excellent opportunities to see herds of russet-brown capybara – a sheep-sized rodent – peccaries and brocket deer. Of considerable ecological interest are the presence of ox-bow lakes, or *cochas*, since these provide an abundance of wildlife which can easily be seen around the lake margins.

The best way to see the wildlife, however, is to get above the canopy. Ridges provide elevated view points from which you can enjoy excellent views. From here, it is possible to look across the lowland flood plain to the foothills of the Andes, some 200 km away. Flocks of parrots and macaws can be seen flying between fruiting trees and troupes of squirrel monkeys and brown capuchins come very close.

The lowland rainforest of Peru is particularly famous for its primates and giant otters. Giant otters were once widespread in Amazonia but came close to extinction in the 1960s owing to persecution by the fur trade. The giant otter population in Peru has since recovered and is now estimated to be at least several hundred. Jaguar and other predators are also much in evidence. Although rarely seen their paw marks are commonly found along the forest trails. Rare bird species are also much in evidence, including fasciated tiger-heron and primitive hoatzins.

The (very) early-morning is the best time to see peccaries, brocket deer and tapir at mineral licks (collpa). Macaw and parrot licks are found along the banks of the river. Here at dawn a dazzling display arrives and clambers around in the branches overhanging the clay-lick. At its peak there may be 600 birds of up to six species (including red and green macaws, and blue-headed parrots) clamouring to begin their descent to the riverbank where they jostle for access to the mineral rich clay. A necessary addition to their diet which may also neutralize the toxins present in the leaf and seed diet. Rare game birds such as razor billed curassows and piping guans may also be seen.

A list of over 600 species has been compiled. Noteworthy species are the black-faced cotinga, crested eagle, and the Harpy eagle, the world's most impressive raptor, easily capable of taking an adult monkey from the canopy. Mixed species flocks are commonly observed containing from 25 to 100+ birds of perhaps some 30 species including blue dacnis, blue-tailed emerald, bananaquit, thick-billed euphoria and the paradise tanager. Each species occupies a slightly different niche, and since there are few individuals of each species in the flock, competition is avoided. Mixed flocks foraging in the canopy are often led by a white-winged shrike, whereas flocks in the understorey are often led by the bluish-slate antshrike. For more information on the birds of Peru, see page 69.

Books

History and culture
Alden Mason, J *The Ancient Civilizations of Peru* (1991).
Cáceres Macedo, Justo *The Prehispanic Cultures of Peru* (1988).
Hemming, John *The Conquest of the Incas* (1970). The one, invaluable book on the period of the Conquest.
Kendall, Ann *Everyday Life of the Incas* (1978) Batsford.
Mosely, Michael E *The Incas and their Ancestors: The Archaeology of Peru*.
Portal Cabellos, *Manuel Oro y tragedia de los Incas*, excellent on the division of the empire, civil war and huaqueros.

Cusco and Machu Picchu
See Footprint's *Cusco and the Inca Trail Handbook*.
Bingham, Hiram *Lost City of the Incas* (2002), Weidenfeld & Nicolson. A new illustrated edition, with an introduction by Hugh Thomson.
Frost, Peter *Exploring Cusco*. On Cusco, the Sacred Valley, Inca Trail, Machu Picchu and other ruins.
Frost, Peter *The Machu Picchu Historical Sanctuary*, Nuevas Imagenes. A recommended book on Machu Picchu, with colour photographs.
Milligan, Max *In the Realm of the Incas* (2001) Harper Collins. A beautiful book with

photographs and text.

Morrison, Tony Qosqo. The Navel of the World (1997) Condor Books, describes Cusco's past and present with an extensive section of photographs of the city and its surroundings.

Reinhard, Johan The Sacred Center explains Machu Picchu in archaeological terms.

Thomson, Hugh The White Rock (2002), Phoenix, describes Thomson's own travels in the Inca heartland, as well as the journeys of earlier explorers and the history of the region.

Nasca

Hadingham, E Lines to the Mountain Gods: Nasca and the Mysteries of Peru (1987) Random House.

Morrison, Tony Pathways to the Gods: The Mystery of the Andes Lines (1978).

Michael Russell, obtainable in Lima; and The Mystery of the Nasca Lines (1987), nonesuch Expeditions, with an introduction by Marie Reiche.

Reinhard, Dr Johan The Nasca Lines – a new perspective on their origin and meaning, Editorial Los Pinos, Lima 18.

Woodman, Jim Nasca, the flight of Condor 1 (1980) Pocket Books, NY. An account of the balloon flight project over the lines.

Chachapoyas area

Muscutt, Keith Warriors of the Clouds: A Lost Civilization in the Upper Amazon of Peru (1998) New Mexico Press, an excellent coffee table book and Chachapoyas memoir; its related website (www.chachapoyas.com) is also worth consulting.

Bowen, Sally The Fujimori File. Peru and its President 1990-2000 (2000). A very readable account of the last decade of the 20th century; it ends at the election of that year so the final momentous events of Fujimori's term happened after publication. Bowen has also written, with **Jane Holligan**, The Imperfect Spy: the Many Lives of Vladimiro Montesinos (2003), Peisa.

Literature

The following novels are recommended

Matthiessen, Peter At Play in the Fields of the Lord (1965); **Shakespeare, Nicholas** The Vision of Elena Silves (1989); **Thubron, Colin** To the Last City (2002) Chatto & Windus;

Wilder, Thornton The Bridge of San Luis Rey (1941) Penguin. Good travel books are:

Murphy, Dervla Eight Feet in the Andes (1994); **Parris, Matthew** Inca-Kola (1990); Shah, Tahir Trail of Feathers (2001) Phoenix;

Wright, Ronald Cut Stones and Crossroads: a Journey in Peru (1984) Viking.

Climbing, trekking and cycling

Biggar, John The Andes. A Guide for Clilmbers (1999) Andes Publishing, contains a chapter on the peaks of Northern Peru.

Bartle, Jim Parque Nacional Huascarán, is a beautiful soft-cover photo collection with English and Spanish text.

Díaz, Felipe Callejón de Huaylas y Cordillera Blanca (Spanish, English and German editions), available locally.

Gómez, Antonio, and Tomé, Juan José La Cordillera Blanca de Los Andes (1998) Desnivel, Spanish only, principally a climbing guide, but contains some trekking and general information, also available locally. Juanjo Tomé has also written Escaladas en los Andes. Guía de la Cordillera Blanca (1999) Desnivel (Spanish only), a climbing guide.

Kolff, Helen and Kees Flores silvestres de la Cordillera Blanca/Wildflowers of the Cordillera Blanca (1997) El Instituto Montaña, is a bilingual guide, fully illustrated.

Sharman, David Climbs of the Cordillera Blanca of Peru (1995) Whizzo. Another climbing guide, available locally, from South American Explorers, as well as from Cordee in the UK and Alpenbooks in the USA.

Simpson, Joe Touching the Void (1997) Vintage. A nail-biting account of Simpson's almost fatal accident in the Cordillera Huayhuasah.

Capaq Ñan, the Royal Inca Road

Espinosa, Ricardo, La Gran Ruta Inca, The Great Inca Route (2002), Petróleos del Perú. A photographic and textual record of Espinosa's walk the length of the Camino Real de los Incas, from Quito to La Paz, including some of the Inca routes from the coast to the Sierra, in Spanish and English. He has also walked the length of Peru's coast, described in El Perú a toda Costa (1997) Editur. The same company has published Zarzar, Omar Por los Caminos del Perú en Bicicleta.

Muller, Karin Along the Inca Road. A

Woman's Journey into an Ancient Empire (2000), National Geographic.

Portway, Christopher *Journey Along the Andes* (1993) Impact Books. An account of the Andean Inca road.

Wildlife and environment

Frost, Peter et al (Edited by Jim Bartle), *Machu Picchu Historical Sanctuary*, with superb text and photos on all aspects of the Inca Trail and the endangered ecosystem of the sanctuary.

Clements, James F and Shany, Noam *A Field Guide to the Birds of Peru* (2001) Ibis.

Emmons, Louise H *Neotropical Rainforest Mammals*. A field guide.

Hilty, Steve, and Brown, William *A guide to the Birds of Colombia* (1986), covers the vast majority of the Amazonian species likely to be seen.

Koepcke, Maria *The Birds of the Department of Lima* (1983), is useful for the coast.

Krabbe, Nils and Fjeldsa, Jon *Birds of the High Andes* (1990) University of Copenhagen, which covers all Peruvian birds that occur above 3,000 m – a large proportion of the birds likely to be seen in the Andes.

MacQuarrie, Kim, and André and Cornelia

Bartschi, *Manu National Park*, is a large, expensive and excellent book, with beautiful photographs.

Parker, Ted, Parker, Susan, and Plenge, Manuel *An Annotated checklist of Peruvian Birds* (1982), is slightly outdated but still useful, it lists all Peruvian birds by habitat type.

Person, David L and Beletsky *Les Ecotraveller's Wildlife Guide: Peru* (2001) Academic Press, is recommended.

Ridgely, Robert, and Tudor, Guy *Birds of South America Volumes 1 & 2* (1989 and 1994) helps tremendously with the passerines, especially volume 2.

TreeS (see under Tambopata National Reserve for address) publish *The Ecology of Tropical Rainforests* (republished 2001), *Tambopata – A Bird Checklist, Tambopata – Mammal, Amphibian & Reptile Checklist* and *Reporte Tambopata*; they also produce tapes, Jungle Sounds and Birds of Southeast Peru.

Valqui, Thomas, *Where to Watch Birds in Peru* (2004), www.granperu.com/bird watchingbook/. Describes 151 sites, how to get there and what to expect once there.

Walker, Barry, and Jon Fjeldsa *Birds of Machu Picchu*.

615

Footnotes

Spanish words and phrases

No amount of dictionaries, phrase books or word lists will provide the same enjoyment as being able to communicate directly with the people of the country you are visiting. Learning Spanish is a useful part of the preparation for a trip to the Peru and you are encouraged to make an effort to grasp the basics before you go. As you travel you will pick up more of the language and the more you know, the more you will benefit from your stay. The following secion is designed to be a simple point of departure.

Whether you have been taught the 'Castillian' pronunciation (all z's, and c's followed by i or e, are pronounced as the th in think) or the 'American' pronunciation (they are pronounced as s), you will encounter little difficulty in understanding either: Spanish pronunciation varies geographically much less than English. There are, of course, regional accents and usages; but the basic language is essentially the same everywhere.

General pronunciation

The stress in a Spanish word conforms to one of three rules: **1** if the word ends in a vowel, or in **n** or **s**, the accent falls on the penultimate syllable *(ventana, ventanas)*; **2** if the word ends in a consonant other than **n** or **s**, the accent falls on the last syllable *(hablar)*; **3** if the word is to be stressed on a syllable contrary to either of the above rules, the acute accent on the relevant vowel indicates where the stress is to be placed *(pantalón, metáfora)*. Note that adverbs such as *cuando*, 'when', take an accent when used interrogatIvely; *¿cuándo?*, 'when?'

Vowels

a	not quite as short as in English 'cat'
e	as in English 'pay', but shorter in a syllable ending in a consonant
i	as in English 'seek'
o	as in English 'shop', but more like 'pope' when the vowel ends a syllable
u	as in English 'food', after 'q' and in 'gue', 'gui' **u** is unpronounced; in 'güe' and 'güi' it is pronounced
y	when a vowel, pronounced like 'I'; when a semiconsonant or consonant, it is pronounced like English 'yes'
ai, ay	as in English 'ride'
el, ey	as in English 'they'
oi, oy	as in English 'toy'

Consonants

Unless listed below consonants can be pronounced in Spanish as they are in English.

b, v	their sound is interchangeable and is a cross between the English **b** and **v**, except at the beginning of a word or after **m** or **n** when it is like English **b**
c	like English **k**, except before **e** or **i** when it is the **s** in English 'sip'
g	before **e** and **i** it is the same as **j**
h	when on its own, never pronounced
j	as the **ch** in the Scottish 'loch'
ll	as the **g** in English 'beige'; sometimes as the 'lli' in 'million'
ñ	as the 'ni' in English 'onion'
rr	trilled much more strongly than in English
x	depending on its location, pronounced as in English 'fox', or 'sip', or like 'gs'
z	as the **s** in English 'sip'

Pronouns

In the Americas, the plural, familar pronoun *vosotros* (with the verb endings - *áis*, - *éis*), though much used in Spain, is never heard. Two or more people, including small children, are always addressed as *Ustedes* (*Uds*).

Inappropriate use of the familiar forms (*tú, vos*) can sound imperious, condescending, infantile, or imply a presumption of intimacy that could annoy officials, one's elders, or, if coming from a man, women.

To avoid cultural complications if your Spanish is limited, stick to the polite forms: *Usted* (*Ud*) in the singular, *Ustedes* in the plural, and you will never give offense.

Remember also that a person who address you as *tú*, does not necessarily expect to be *tuteada* (so addressed) in return.

You should, however, violate this rule when dealing with a small child, who might be intimidated by *Usted*: he/she is, after all, normally so addressed only in admonitions such as *'¡No, Señor, Ud no tomará un helado antes del aimuerzo!'* 'No, Sir, you will not have ice cream before lunch!'

General hints

Note that in Peru, a common response to *¡Gracias!* is often *¡A sus ordenes!* ('Yours to command!') rather than the *'¡De nada!'* ('Tis nought!') taught in school.

Travellers whose names include *b*'s and *v*'s should learn to distinguish between them when spelling aloud as *be larga* and *ve corta* or *uve*. (Children often say *ve de vaca* and *be de burro* to distinguish between the two letters, pronounced interchangeably, either as *b* or *v*, in Spanish.)

Greetings, courtesies

excuse me/I beg your pardon	*permiso*
Go away!	*¡Váyase!*
good afternoon/evening/night	*buenas tardes/noches*
good morning	*buenos días*
goodbye	*adiós/chao*
hello	*hola*
How are you?	*¿cómo está?/¿cómo estás?*
I do not understand	*no entiendo*
leave me alone	*déjame en paz/no me moleste*
no	*no*
please	*por favor*
pleased to meet you	*mucho gusto/encantado/encantada*
see you later	*hasta luego*
thank you (very much)	*(muchas) gracias*
What is your name?	*¿Cómo se llama?*
yes	*sí*
I speak ...	*Hablo ...*
I speak Spanish	*Hablo español*
I don't speak Spanish	*No hablo español*
Do you speak English?	*¿Habla usted inglés?*
We speak German	*Hablamos alemán*
They speak French	*Hablan francés*
Please speak slowly	*hable despacio por favor*
I am very sorry	*lo siento mucho/disculpe*
I'm fine	*muy bien gracias*

I'm called_   *me llamo_*
What do you want?   *¿Qué quiere?*
I want   *quiero*
I don't want it   *No lo quiero*
long distance phone call   *la llamada a larga distancia*
good   *bueno*
bad   *malo*

Nationalities and languages

American *Americano/a*
Australian *Australiano/a*
Austrian *Austriaco/a*
British *Británico/a*
Canadian *Canadiense*
Danish *Danés/Danesa*
Dutch *Holandés/Holandesa*
English *Inglés/Inglesa*
French *Francés/Francesa*
German *Alemán/Alemana*
Irish *Irlandés/Irlandesa*

Italian *Italiano/a*
Mexican *Mexicano/a*
New Zealand *Neozelandés/Neozelandesa*
Norwegian *Noruego/a*
Portuguese *Portugués/Portuguesa*
Scottish *Escocés/Escocesa*
Spanish *Español/a*
Swedish *Sueco/a*
Swiss *Suizo/a*
Welsh *Galés/Galesa*

Basic questions

Have you got a room for two people?
  ¿Tiene habitación para dos personas?
How do I get to_? *¿Cómo llegar a_?*
How much does it cost? *¿Cuánto cuesta?*
How much is it? *¿Cuánto es?*
When does the bus leave?
  ¿A qué hora sale el bus?

-arrive? *-llega-*
When? *¿Cuándo?*
Where is_? *¿Dónde está_?*
Where is the nearest petrol station?
  ¿Dónde está el grifo más cerca?
Why? *¿Por qué?*

Basics

bank *el banco*
bathroom/toilet *el baño*
bill *la factura/la cuenta*
cash *el efectivo*
cheap *barato*
church/cathedral *La iglesia/catedral*
exchange house *la casa de cambio*
exchange rate *la tasa de cambio*
expensive *caro*

market *el mercado*
notes/coins *los billetes/las monedas*
police (policeman) *la policia (el policia)*
post office *el correo*
supermarket *el supermercado*
telephone office *el centro de llamadas*
ticket office *la boletería/la taquilla*
travellers' cheques *los travelers/los
            cheques de viajero*

Getting around

aeroplane/airplane *el avión*
airport *el aeropuerto*
bus station *la terminal (terrestre)*
bus stop *la parada*
bus *el bus/el autobus etc*
minibus *el combi*
motorcycle taxi *el mototaxi*
bus route *el corredor*
first/second class *primera/segunda clase*

on the left/right *a la izquierdo/derecha*
second street on the left
  la segunda calle a la izquierda
ticket *el boleto*
to walk *caminar*
Where can I buy tickets?
  ¿Dónde se puede comprar boletos?
Where can I park?
  ¿Dónde se puede parquear?

Orientation and motoring

arrival *la llegada*
avenue *la avenida*
block *la cuadra*
border *la frontera*
car used for public transport on a
  fixed route *colectivo*
corner *la esquina*
customs *la aduana*
departure *la salida*
east *el este, el oriente*
empty *vacío*
full *lleno*
highway, main road *carretera*
immigration *la inmigración*
insurance *el seguro*
the insured *el asegurado/la asegurada*
to insure yourself against *asegurarse contra*

luggage *el equipaje*
motorway, dual carriageway *autopista/carretera*
north *el norte*
oil *el aceite*
passport *el pasaporte*
petrol/gasoline *la gasolina*
puncture *el pinchazo*
south *el sur*
street *la calle*
that way *por allí/por allá*
this way *por aquí/por acá*
tourist card *la tarjeta de turista*
tyre *la llanta*
unleaded *sin plomo*
visa *el visado*
waiting room *la sala de espera*
west *el oeste/el poniente*

Accommodation

air conditioning *el aire acondicionado*
all-inclusive *todo incluído*
blankets *las mantas*
clean/dirty towels *las toallas limpias/sucias*
dining room *el comedor*
double bed *la cama matrimonial*
guest house *la casa de huéspedes*
hot/cold water *agua caliente/fría*
hotel *el hotel*
Is service included? *¿Está incluído el servicio?*
Is tax included? *¿Están incluidos los
  impuestos?*
noisy *ruidoso*

pillows *las almohadas*
power cut *apagón/corte*
restaurant *el restaurante*
room *el cuarto/la habitación*
sheets *las sábanas*
shower *la ducha*
single/double *sencillo/doble*
soap *el jabón*
to make up/clean *limpiar*
toilet *el sanitario*
toilet paper *el papel higiénico*
with private bathroom *con baño privado*
with two beds *con dos camas*

Health

aspirin *la aspirina*
blood *la sangre*
chemist/pharmacy *la farmacia*
condoms *los preservativos*
contact lenses *las lentes de contacto*
contraceptive (pill) *el anticonceptivo (la
píldora anticonceptiva)*

diarrhoea *la diarrea*
doctor *el médico*
fever/sweat *la fiebre/el sudor*
(for) pain *(para) dolor*
head *la cabeza*
period/towels *la regla/las toallas*
stomach *el estómago*

Time

At one o'clock *a la una*
At half past two/two thirty
  a las dos y media
At a quarter to three *a cuarto para las tres*
or *a las tres menos quince*
It's one o'clock *es la una*
It's seven o'clock *son las siete*

It's twenty past six/six twenty
  son las seis y veinte
It's five to nine *son cinco para las
  nueve/son las nueve menos cinco*
In ten minutes *en diez minutos*
five hours *cinco horas*
Does it take long? *¿Tarda mucho?*
We will be back at ... *Regresamos a las ...*
What time is it? *¿Qué hora es?*

Monday *lunes*
Tuesday *martes*
Wednesday *miércoles*
Thursday *jueves*
Friday *viernes*
Saturday *sábado*
Sunday *domingo*
January *enero*
February *febrero*
March *marzo*

April *abril*
May *mayo*
June *junio*
July *julio*
August *agosto*
September *septiembre*
October *octubre*
November *noviembre*
December *diciembre*

Numbers

one *uno/una*
two *dos*
three *tres*
four *cuatro*
five *cinco*
six *seis*
seven *siete*
eight *ocho*
nine *nueve*
ten *diez*
eleven *once*
twelve *doce*
thirteen *trece*
fourteen *catorce*
fifteen *quince*

sixteen *dieciséis*
seventeen *diecisiete*
eighteen *dieciocho*
nineteen *diecinueve*
twenty *veinte*
twenty one, two *veintiuno, veintidos etc*
thirty *treinta*
forty *cuarenta*
fifty *cincuenta*
sixty *sesenta*
seventy *setenta*
eighty *ochenta*
ninety *noventa*
hundred *cien or ciento*
thousand *mil*

Family

aunt *la tía*
brother *el hermano*
cousin *la/el prima/o*
daughter *la hija*
family *la familia*
father *el padre*
fiance/fiancee *el novio/la novia*
friend *el amigo/la amiga*
grandfather *el abuelo*

grandmother *la abuela*
husband *el esposo/marido*
married *casado/a*
mother *la madre*
single/unmarried *soltero/a*
sister *la hermana*
son *el hijo*
uncle *el tío*
wife *la esposa*

Key verbs

To go *ir*
I go *voy*
you go (familiar singular) *vas*
he, she, it goes, you (unfamiliar singular) go *va*
we go *vamos*
they, you (plural) go *van*
To have (possess) *tener*
I have *tengo*
You have *tienes*
He she, it have, you have *tiene*
We have *tenemos*
They, you have *tienen*
(Also used as 'To be', as in 'I am hungry' *tengo hambre*)

(NB *Haber* also means 'to have', but is used with other verbs, as in 'he has gone' *ha ido*)
I have gone *he ido*
You have said *has dicho*
He, she, it has, you have done *ha hecho*
We have eaten *hemos comido*
They, you have arrived *han llegado*
Hay means 'there is' and is used in questions such as ¿*Hay cuartos?* 'Are there any rooms?'; perhaps more common is *No hay* meaning 'there isn't any'

To be (in a permanent state) *ser*
I am (a teacher) *soy (profesor)*
You are *Eres*
He, she, it is, you are *es*
We are *somos*
They, you are *son*

To do/make *Hacer*
I do *hago*
You do *haces*
He, she, it does, you do *hace*
We do *hacemos*
They, you do *hacen*

To be (positional or temporary state) *estar*
I am (in London) *estoy (en Londres)*
You are *estás*
He, she, it is, you are (happy) *está (contenta)*
We are *estámos*
They, you are *están*

The above section was compiled on the basis of glossaries by André de Mendonça and David Gilmour of South American Experience, London, and the LatinAmerican Travel Advisor, No 9, March 1996

Food

avocado *la palta*
baked *al horno*
bakery *la panadería*
beans *los frijoles/las habichuelas*
beef *la carne de res*
beef steak or pork fillet *el bistec*
boiled rice *el arroz blanco*
bread *el pan*
breakfast *el desayuno*
butter *la mantequilla*
cassava, yucca *la yuca*
casserole *la cazuela*
chewing gum *el chicle*
chicken *el pollo*
chilli pepper or green pepper *el ají*
clear soup, stock *el caldo*
cooked *cocido*
dining room *el comedor*
egg *el huevo*
fish *el pescado*
fork *el tenedor*
fried *frito*
fritters *las frituras*
garlic *el ajo*
goat *el chivo*
grapefruit *el pomelo*
grill *la parrilla*
grilled/griddled *a la plancha*
guava *la guayaba*
ham *el jamón*
hamburger *la hamburgueso*
hot, spicy *picante*
ice cream *el helado*
jam *la mermelada*
knife *el cuchillo*
lime *el limón*
lobster *la langosta*

lunch *el almuerzo*
margarine, fat *la manteca*
meal, supper, dinner *la comida*
meat *la carne*
minced meat *el picadillo*
mixed salad *la ensalada mixta*
onion *la cebolla*
orange *la naranja*
pepper *el pimiento*
plantain, green banana *el plátano*
pasty, turnover *la empanada/el pastelito*
pork *el cerdo*
potato *la papa*
prawns *los camarones*
raw *crudo*
restaurant *el restaurante*
roast *el asado*
salad *la ensalada*
salt *el sal*
sandwich *el bocadillo*
sauce *la salsa*
sausage *la longaniza*
scrambled eggs *los huevos revueltos*
seafood *los mariscos*
small sandwich, filled roll *el bocadito*
soup *la sopa*
spoon *la cuchara*
squash *la calabaza*
squid *los calamares*
supper *la cena*
sweet *dulce*
sweet potato *la batata*
to eat *comer*
toasted *tostado*
turkey *el pavo*
vegetables *los legumbres/vegetales*
without meat *sin carne*
yam *el camote*

Drink

beer *la cerveza*
boiled *hervido*
bottled *en botella*
camomile tea *la manzanilla*
canned *en lata*
cocktail *el coctel*
coconut milk *la leche de coco*
coffee *el café*
coffee, small, strong *el cafecito*
coffee, white *el café con leche*
cold *frío*
condensed milk *la leche condensada*
cup *la taza*
drink *la bebida*
drunk *borracho*
fruit milk shake *el batido*
glass *el vaso*
glass of liqueur *la copa de licor*
hot *caliente*
ice *el hielo*

juice *el jugo*
lemonade *la limonada*
milk *la leche*
mint *la menta*
orange juice *el jugo de naranja*
pineapple milkshake *el batido de piña con leche*
rough rum, firewater *el aguardiente*
rum *el ron*
soft drink *el refresco*
soft fizzy drink *la gaseosa/cola*
sugar *el azúcar*
tea *el té*
to drink *beber/tomar*
water *el agua*
water, carbonated *el agua mineral con gas*
water, still mineral *el agua mineral natural/sin gas*
wine, red *el vino tinto*
wine, white *el vino blanco*

Glossary

Food has always played an important role in Peruvian culture. The country's range of climates has also made this South American nation internationally recognized for its diverse cuisine.

Ají (hot pepper)
Ají is found in many varieties and is used to add 'spice' to everything from soup to fish to vegetable dishes. It is a staple in Peruvian kitchens from the coast to the most remote jungle villages. These peppers can be extremely spicy, so the inexperienced palate should proceed with caution!

Papa (potato)
The potato is as Peruvian as the Inca himself. There are more than 2,000 varieties of tubers although only a fraction are edible. The International Potato Institute is located on the outskirts of metropolitan Lima so those with a potato fetish might wish to visit. The papa amarilla (yellow potato) is by far the best-tasting of the lot.

Causa
A casserole served cold with a base of yellow potato and mixed with hot peppers, onion, avocado, with either chicken, crab or meat. A fantastic starter.

Estofado
A mild chicken stew, with lots of potatoes and other vegetables, served with rice.

Lomo saltado
Strips of sirloin sautéed with tomato, onion, ají amarillo (a spicy orange pepper) and french fried potatoes served with rice.

Papa Ocopa
A typical dish from the Arequipa region. A spicy peanut sauce served over cold potatoes with a slice of hard boiled egg.

Papa a la Huancaína
A dish which originated in the central department of Huancayo. This creamy cheese sauce served over cold potatoes is a common starter for set menus everywhere.

Papa Rellena (stuffed potato)
First baked then fried, the potato is stuffed with meat, onions, olives, boiled egg and raisins. Camote (yams) can be substituted for potatoes.

Choclo (corn)
Another staple in the Peruvian diet. The large kernels are great with the fresh cheese produced all over the country.

Maíz morado (purple corn)
This type of corn is not edible for humans. It's boiled and the liquid is used to make chicha, a sweet and very traditional Peruvian refreshment.

Chicha de Jora
A strong fermented beverage mostly found in mountain communities. The people who make it use their saliva to aid in the fermenting process.

Ají de gallina

This spicy chicken dish is a favourite in Lima as was kindly supplied by Mónica Moreno and Leo Rovayo.

To garnish:
Potatoes, black olives, hard-boiled egg.

Ingredients
One 2 kg chicken
100 ml oil
250 g diced onions
1 large clove of garlic, crushed
6 green chillis liquidized
breadcrumbs from 4 slices of bread with their crusts removed
1 can of evaporated milk
100 g parmesan cheese
250 g of ground nuts
salt and pepper

Method
Boil the chicken in salted water until cooked. Drain off the stock, but do not discard it. Allow the bird to cool, then shred the meat. Heat the oil and fry the onion, garlic and chilli. Add the breadcrumbs and a little of the chicken stock. Cook for 10 minutes. Add the nuts, the parmesan cheese and the chicken. Before serving add the evaporated milk and combine well. Garnish the dish.

Granos (grains)
Kiwicha and Quinoa are very high sources of protein and staples of the Inca diet. Quinoa is wonderful in soups and Kiwicha is a common breakfast food for children throughout the country.

Arroz (rice)
Another major staple in Peruvian cooking.

Anticuchos (beef heart kebabs)
Beef heart barbecued and served with cold potato and a wonderful assortment of spicy sauces. A must for all meat lovers.

Cuy (guinea pig)
Prepared in a variety of ways, from stewed to fried.

Cau Cau
Tripe and potatoes.

Rocoto relleno (stuffed hot peppers)
Stuffed with meat and potatoes, then baked.

Pachamanca
Typical mountain cuisine, so popular it's now prepared everywhere. Beef, pork and chicken mixed with a variety of vegetables, and cooked together over heated stones in a hole in the ground.

Seco de cabrito
A favorite dish from the north coast. Roasted goat marinated with fermented chicha, served with beans and rice.

Ají de Gallina
A rich mix of creamed, spicy chicken over rice and boiled potatoes. A wonderfully tasty dish, see the recipe for details of how to make it.

Arroz con pato (duck with rice)
A dish originally from the north coast but found everywhere.

Ceviche
The national dish of Peru. Raw fish or seafood marinated in a mixture of lime juice, red onions and hot peppers served with a boiled yam (camote) and corn. With a coastline of more than 1,800 km, the fruits of the sea are almost limitless. Sea bass, flounder, salmon, red snapper, sole and shellfish are all in abundance. Ceviche is a dish served for lunch. Most *cevicherías* (ceviche restaurants) close around 1600.

Postres (desserts)
Arroz con leche
Rice pudding.

Manjar blanco
A caramel sweet made from boiled milk and sugar.

Picarones
Deep-fried donut batter bathed in a honey sauce.

Suspiro a la limeña
Manjar blanco with baked egg-white.

Turrón
This popular sweet, shortbread covered in molasses or honey, is sold everywhere during the October celebration of Señor de los Milagros (Lord of Miracles) in Lima.

Fruta (fruit)
There's a great selection of fruit in Peru. Aside from common fruits such as mandarins, oranges, peaches and bananas, there are exotic tropical fruits to choose from.

Chirimoya
Custard apple. In Quechua means 'the sweet of the gods'.

Lúcuma
Eggfruit.

Maracuyá
Passionfruit, often served as a juice.

Tuna
Prickly pear.

Bebidas (drinks)
The national beers are Cristal, Cusqueña, Bremen and Pilsen. There are also some dark beers.

Although not known as great wine producing country, there are a couple of good quality wines to choose from. Blanco en Blanco is a surprisingly pleasant white wine from the Tacama winery which also makes a great red wine called Reserva Especial.

Pisco, a strong brandy made from white grapes is produced in the departments of Ica, Moquegua and Tacna. Pisco Sour, the national drink is made with lime juice, egg white, sugar and a dash of cinnamon.

Index

Map index

Map symbols

Administration

- ◻ Capital city
- ◦ Other city/town
- International border
- Regional border
- Disputed border

Roads and travel

- ▬▬ National highway, motorway
- ▬ Main road
- ▬ Minor road
- ---- Track
- ······· Footpath
- ▬▬ Railway with station
- ✈ Airport
- 🚌 Bus station
- Ⓜ Metro station
- ---- Cable car
- ++++ Funicular
- ⚓ Ferry

Water features

- River, canal
- Lake, ocean
- Seasonal marshland
- Beach, sand bank
- Waterfall

Topographical features

- Contours (approx)
- Mountain
- Volcano
- Mountain pass
- Escarpment
- Gorge
- Glacier
- Salt flat
- Rocks

Cities and towns

- Main through route
- Main street
- Minor street

- Pedestrianized street
- Σ ⊂ Tunnel
- → One way street
- Steps
- ⇌ Bridge
- Fortified wall
- Park, garden, stadium
- Sleeping
- Eating
- Bars & clubs
- Entertainment
- Building
- Sight
- Cathedral, church
- Chinese temple
- Hindu temple
- Meru
- Mosque
- Stupa
- Synagogue
- Tourist office
- Museum
- Post office
- Police
- Bank
- Internet
- Telephone
- Market
- Hospital
- Parking
- Petrol
- Golf
- A Detail map
- A Related map

Other symbols

- Archaeological site
- National park, wildlife reserve
- Viewing point
- Campsite
- Refuge, lodge
- Castle
- Diving
- Deciduous/coniferous/palm trees
- Hide
- Vineyard
- Distillery
- Shipwreck
- Historic battlefield

Footnotes Map symbols

Advert index

Colour adverts

Acknowledgements

I should like to thank most warmly all those collaborators in the UK, Peru and Ecuador, who made the preparation of the fifth edition of Footprint Peru possible.

Robert and Daisy Kunstaetter updated the Cordillera Blanca, Cajamarca, parts of the North Coast, Iquitos and Chachapoyas. They would like to thank the following for their assistance: **Walter and Frederike Eberhart** (Cajamarca), **Miguel Rodríguez Sánchez** (Cajabamba), **Aristóteles Cruz Ledesma** (Huamachuco), **Alberto and Aidé Cafferata** (Caraz), **Manuel and María Quintana** (Huaraz), **Christopher and Isabel Benway** (Huaraz), **Philippe Bigourd** (Huaraz), **Carlos and Jesu Burga** (Chachapoyas), **Rob Dover** (Chachapoyas), **Felipe and Beatriz Díaz** (Carhuaz), **Percy Sánchez and Analía Sarfaty** (Iquitos), **Neycer Pizango** (Iquitos), **Craig Kolthoff** (Miami), **Isaac Mas Mariño** (Chachapoyas) and **Zarela** (Huaraz).

South American Explorers again provided great support, researching the Selva Central and parts of the Central Highlands, the Titicaca region, Pisco and Nasca. I am most grateful to **Leda Duif**, **Margaree Bigler**, **Tilak Valdivia** and **Miguel Espinoza** from the Lima club, and **Lucy Bertenshaw** from Cusco.

John Forrest and Julia Porturas sent updates from their latest travels on the North Coast, the Cañete Valley, parts of the Central Highlands and Tambopata. **Dominic Hamilton** updated the Arequipa, Colca and Cotahuasi canyons. In addition to help given to Robert and Daisy Kunstaetter, **Walter and Frederike Eberhart** sent masses of useful material on Trujillo and Cajamarca. **Clara Bravo and Michael White**'s contribution on Trujillo and the text in general was, as ever, most helpful.

For significant help with the text I should like to thank: **Fiona Cameron**, for the river route from Cusco to Iquitos; **Paul Heggarty**, for new information on Quechua and Aymara and the Cañete Valley; **Mariella Bernasconi**, for Cusco news; **Miguel Angel Moulet** (Librerías La Familia, Lima), contemporary literature; **Hilary Emberton**, **Florence Lawson** and **Ewout Heuker**, for new information on the Cordillera Blanca, especially trekking; **Dineke Veerman**, for Cusco updates; and **Daniel Buck**, for Colca background information.

Finally, it was great travelling with **Katie Box** and **Ross Mackenzie** in Peru in September 2004. For their help and hospitality we should like to thank **Cecilia Kamiche**, **Ricardo Espinosa**, **Mónica Moreno**, **Home Perú** (Rómulo, Chela, Giovanna and Janett), **Siduith Ferrer** and **Rick Vecchio** and **Leda Duif**, all of Lima; **Carlos Manco**, the staff at **Hotel Santa Rosa** and the **Gallardo family** in Ayacucho; **Tito Lozano**, **Carlos Valer** and **Don Félix** in Abancay; and **Nicholas Asheshov** and the staff at the **Incaland** in Urubamba, and **Yasmin Martin** and **Richard Webb** in Huayllabamba. I'm also most grateful to **John Lewis** for logistical support and **Sasha MacInnes** for her advice.

The health section was written by **Dr Charlie Easmon**, MBBS, MRCP, Msc Public Health, DTM&H, DoccMed, Director of Travel Screening Services'.

For all their assistance at Footprint, very many thanks go to **Stephanie Lambe**, **Alan Murphy**, **Sarah Sorensen**, **Jo Morgan** and all the other editorial and mapping staff who helped to put the book together. I'd also like to thank **Steve Frankham**, whose work in Cusco has contributed heavily to this edition.

Travellers' letters

Many thanks to the following travellers for sending in their comments:

Alex Adams (UK); Mary Day, Clif, Steven and Jonathan Allen (USA); Rene Alt; Roeland Ambting and Anke Wiegmans (The Netherlands); Ilan Aminia (Israel); Oded and Maya Anderman (Israel); Lauren Armistead (UK); Paul Armistead (UK); Eva Au (Australia); Matt B (Canada); Timothy Baird (USA); Simon Bartlett; Christine Bass (USA); Frank Beer; Noam Bibi; Tony Bellette and Ainsley Gallagher (Australia); Amos Belmaker (Israel); Ariel Ben Hur (Israel); Eva Bertsch (Switzerland); Christian Biendl (Germany); Willem Biesheuvel and Gretha Oost (The Netherlands); Itziar Bilbao (Spain); Clint and Carly Blackbourn (UK); Eitan Bluer; David Brandenberger (Switzerland); Caroline Brandtner (Australia); Margaret Brindley (Ireland); Larissa Broger; Naomi van den Brom (The Netherlands); Eric Bronder (The Netherlands); Dr Paterson Brown (Greece); P J Bruyniks and D Ireland; Claudia Canales (UK); Danielle Carpenter (UK); Imogen Casebourne; Tjitske Colenbrander (The Netherlands); Bill Conn; Eric Coronado (USA); Christian Coutures and Rossie Corrales Cosmelli; Curt Crandall (USA); Darren Cullen (Ireland); John Cussons (UK); Mark Dana (USA); Guy and Sheila Danhieux (France); Sue Dean; Carmen Doyle (Australia); Dominic Durand (Canada); David Eisenman (USA); Hilary Emberton; Johan Engdahl (Sweden); Erik and Olaf (Germany); Larry Fish (USA); Chrisitan Furrer (Switzerland); Alessandro Fuso (Switzerland); Karine Gaujon (France); Andrée-Anne Giasson (Canada); Michel Givon (France); Wendy Glen; Diane B Goodpasture (USA); Coronel Grace (Ecuador); Jenny Gray (UK); Davina Greeves (UK); Annelies Hamerlink (Belgium); Sofie van Hapert (The Netherlands); Richard Hartmann (Germany); Wouter van der Heijde (The Netherlands); Aaraon Heller (USA); Andrew Henderson; Lena Hermenjat (Switzerland); Ewout Heuker (The Netherlands); Ernst Heusch (Germany); Timo Hogenhout (The Netherlands); Saul Huarcayo Meza (Peru); Stefan Hueppi (Switzerland); Martina Hunkeler (Switzerland); Monica Hupperich; Georgina Hyslop (UK); Iddo; Stephen James (UK); Gudmund Tore Killi Jensen and Cathrine; Andrew Johnson (UK); Caimin Jones; Jordan Jones (USA); Sarah Jones (Australia); Mark Joris (France); Assaf Kadar (Israel); Ziv and Gali Katzir (Israel); Hilary King; Pirmin Kurzmeyer; Pat Laas (USA); Marion Labatut (France); Angela Lawson and Simon McIntyre (Scotland); Florence Lawson; Denis Le Jeune; Pieter Lekkerkerk; Michal Lenkiewicz (Israel); Achim Lieth (Germany); Nicholas Light (Switzerland); Claas Linnewedel (Germany); Tikva Looijen (The Netherlands); Anthony T Lunn; Mike McKinley; Anne McLauchlan (Belgium); Franz Magerl (Germany); Adi Mahler (Israel); Doris Manser (Switzerland); Brigitte Marti (Switzerland); Martin and Iris; Andrea Matthews (USA); Michelangelo Mazzeo (Italy); Christine Meier; Víctor Melgar (Peru); Marianela Melgrejo; Jarl Molvaer (Norway); Richard Moss; Maillekeul Newman (France); Laila and Michael Nygaard (Denmark); Maayan Ofir (Israel); Ea Øgendahl (Denmark); Renata C Ogassavara (Brazil); Mercedes Olavide; Oliver and Fabian (Peru); Nick O'Riordan and Caroline Brown; Juliane Palm; Jeremy Parker (USA); Geoff Pavey (USA); Pablo Peña; Anna Perkins; Gina Perry; Luke Peters (UK); James Petersen; Nadja Poschung (Switzerland); Carolyn Preece (UK); Charles Brian Pryke (Australia); Simon Pyne; Martin Rajah; Stuart Reed, Marnie Simpson, Lily Crowley and Bridget Heffernan (UK); Imke Reibedanz, Kyle Reid (UK); Rhi; Marie-Claude Ringuette and Sebastien Leblanc (Canada); Sarah Roberts (UK); Katia Robinson (Sweden); Udi Ron (Israel); Betty Rose (USA); Claude Roulin (Switzerland); Michael Ruess (Switzerland); Montse Sanchez; Teresa Saunders; Hugo Savard (Canada); Philipp Schaab (Germany); Kirsten Schadach (Germany);Caroline Scarles (UK); Falk Schleicher (Germany); Gabriel Schnaider (Israel); Michael Schoute (The Netherlands); Martin Schwarz and Kathrin

(Switzerland); Redmond Shannon (Ireland); Nadav Shoshan; Yuval Shtekelmacher (Israel); Debbie Simpson (UK); Glenn Simpson; Ann Smith; James Sturcke (UK); Jonathan Streit (Germany); Dror Suhami (Israel); Aline Tayar (UK); Muriele Tesauri and Calvin; Gry Thorsen (Denmark); Yaron Tidhar (Israel); Jens Tobiska (The Netherlands); Edward Tothill and Libby Nunn (UK); Philippe Tulula (USA); Patterson Molina Vale (Brazil); Dineke Veerman (The Netherlands); Jean-Marc Vierset and Nicolette Fockedey;   Doreen Wang; Philip Whitehead (Australia); Luane Wielichowski (USA); Manuel Weiss (Germany); Pierre Willems (Belgium); Thea Winnips (The Netherlands); Carmen Wuethrich and Rene Schuepbach (Switzerland); Vicky Yucra (Belgium); Sandra Ziegler and Javier (Switzerland).

Credits

Footprint credits

Editor: Stephanie Lambe
Map editor: Sarah Sorensen
Picture editor: Rob Lunn

Publisher: Patrick Dawson
Editorial: Alan Murphy, Sophie Blacksell, Sarah Thorowgood, Claire Boobbyer, Felicity Laughton, Laura Dixon, Nicola Jones
Cartography: Robert Lunn, Claire Benison, Kevin Feeney, Angus Dawson
Series development: Rachel Fielding
Design: Mytton Williams and Rosemary Dawson (brand)
Advertising: Debbie Wylde
Finance and administration: Sharon Hughes, Elizabeth Taylor

Photography credits

Front cover: Eye Ubiquitous
(Masked youngster at Inti Raymi)
Back cover: Alamy
(Ladies wrapped in brightly coloured shawls)
Inside colour section: Alamy

Print

Manufactured in Italy by LegoPrint
Pulp from sustainable forests

Footprint feedback

We try as hard as we can to make each Footprint guide as up to date as possible but, of course, things always change. If you want to let us know about your experiences – good, bad or ugly – then don't delay, go to **www.footprintbooks.com** and send in your comments.

Publishing information

Footprint Peru
5th edition
© Footprint Handbooks Ltd
January 2005

ISBN 1 904 777 19 8
CIP DATA: A catalogue record for this book is available from the British Library

® Footprint Handbooks and the Footprint mark are a registered trademark of Footprint Handbooks Ltd

Published by Footprint

6 Riverside Court
Lower Bristol Road
Bath BA2 3DZ, UK
T +44 (0)1225 469141
F +44 (0)1225 469461
discover@footprintbooks.com
www.footprintbooks.com

Distributed in the USA by

Publishers Group West

About the author

One of the first assignments **Ben Box** took as a freelance writer in 1980 was some sub-editing work on Footprint's *South American Handbook*. From this humble beginning came editorship of the title in 1989. Involvement in many of Footprint's other Latin American titles has meant that he has been able to travel extensively in the region for 25 years. Whilst not daring to express a preference for any country in particular, he finds Peru totally captivating and is eager for others to share the joys of exploring its grandeur and intricacies. Ben has a doctrate in Spanish and Portuguese Studies from the University of London and he lives with his family and various two- and four-legged friends in rural Suffolk (England).

Complete title listing

Footprint publishes travel guides to over 150 destinations worldwide. Each guide is packed with practical concise and colourful information for everybody from first-time traveller to travel aficionados. The list is growing fast and current titles are noted below.

Available from all good book shops and online

www.footprintbooks.com

(P) Denotes pocket guide

Latin America & Caribbean
Antigua & Leeward Islands (P)
Argentina
Barbados (P)
Bolivia
Brazil
Caribbean Islands
Central America & Mexico
Chile
Colombia
Costa Rica
Cuba
Cusco & the Inca Trail
Dominican Republic (P)
Ecuador & Galápagos
Guatemala
Havana (P)
Mexico
Nicaragua
Patagonia
Peru
Rio de Janeiro (P)
St Lucia (P)
South American Handbook
Venezuela

North America
Vancouver (P)
New York (P)
Western Canada

Africa
Cape Town (P)
East Africa
Egypt
Libya
Marrakech (P)
Morocco
Namibia
South Africa
Tunisia
Uganda

Middle East
Dubai (P)
Israel
Jordan
Syria & Lebanon

Asia
Bali
Bangkok & the Beaches

Australasia

Europe

Lifestyle guides

What the papers say...

"I carried the South American Handbook from Cape Horn to Cartagena and consulted it every night for two and a half months. I wouldn't do that for anything else except my hip flask."
Michael Palin, BBC Full Circle

"My favourite series is the Handbook series published by Footprint and I especially recommend the Mexico, Central and South America Handbooks."
Boston Globe

"If 'the essence of real travel' is what you have been secretly yearning for all these years, then Footprint are the guides for you."
Under 26 magazine

"Who should pack Footprint-readers who want to escape the crowd."
The Observer

"Footprint can be depended on for accurate travel information and for imparting a deep sense of respect for the lands and people they cover."
World News

"The guides for intelligent, independently-minded souls of any age or budget."
Indie Traveller

Mail order
Available worldwide in bookshops and on-line. Footprint travel guides can also be ordered directly from us in Bath, via our website www.footprintbooks.com or from the address on the imprint page of this book.

MIRAFLORES PARK
HOTEL

ORIENT-EXPRESS HOTELS
TRAINS & CRUISES

Av. Malecón de la Reserva 1035, Miraflores
Lima 18 - Perú ☎ (51-1) 242-3000 / 610-4000
Fax: (51-1) 242-3393
E-mail: res-mirapark@peruorientexpress.com.pe
www.mira-park.com   www.orient-express.com

El Parador del Colca

Reservas / Oficinas Lima
T 242 3425 **F** 242 3365
E res-mirapark@peruorientexpress.com.pe

MACHU PICCHU
SANCTUARY LODGE

ORIENT-EXPRESS HOTELS
TRAINS & CRUISES

Carretera Hiram Bingham s/n
Ciudadela Machu Picchu Urubamba - Cusco
☎ (084) 211167 / 211039 / 211038 / 211052
Fax (084) 211053
E-mail: res-mapi@peruorientexpress.com.pe
www.monasterio.orient-express.com

HOTEL
MONASTERIO

ORIENT-EXPRESS HOTELS
TRAINS & CRUISES

Calle Palacio 136, Plazoleta Nazarenas
Cusco - Perú ☎ (51 84) 241777
Fax: (51 84) 246983
E-mail: reservas@peruorientexpress.com.pe
www.monasterio.orient-express.com
The Leading Small Hotels of the World

ORIENT-EXPRESS HOTELS
TRAINS & CRUISES

www.orient-express.com

Map 1

Altitude in metres
4000
3000
2000
1000
500
200
0
Neighbouring Country

Paved road
Unpaved road
Railway
Departmental border
▲ Mountain

Pacific Ocean

Ⓐ

ECUADOR

Inset map locations:
① Tumbes
② Iquitos / Rio Amazonas
③ LIMA / Pacific Ocean
④
⑤
⑥

Piura
Moyobamba
Chiclayo
Cajamarca
Trujillo
Pucallpa
Huaraz
Huánuco
Cerro De Pasco
Huancayo
Puerto Maldonado
Huancavelica
Machu Picchu
Ayacucho
Cusco
Ica
Abancay
Lake Titicaca
Arequipa
Puno
Moquegua
Tacna

Aguas Verdes
Santuario Nacional los Manglares de Tumbes
Puerto Pizarro
Zarumilla
Tumbes
San Jacinto
Zorritos
Zona Reserva de Tumbes
Bocapán
Cancas
TUMBES
Cañaveral

Ⓑ

Los Organos
Máncora
Punta Sal
Parque Nacional Cerros de Amotape
Cabo Blanco
Atascadero
La Tina-Macará
Alamor
Suyo
Ayabaca
Lobitos
Paimas
Espíndola
Talara
Negritos
Las Lomas
Vichayal
Amotape
San Jacinto
Tambo Real
Frias
Namballe
San Ignacio
La Huaca
Sullana
Piura
Chulucanas
Sapalache
Colán
Paita
Morropón
Huancabamba
Tabaconas
Aramango
Piura
Canchaque
Catacaos
PIURA
Bagua Chica
La Unión
Vice
Bellavista
Jaén
Bagua Grande
Sechura
L. Ramón
Sechura Desert
Chamaya
Bayovar
Pomahuaca
Pucará
Lunya Grande
Reventazón
Cascajal
Olmos
Sto Tómas
CAJAMARCA
Motupe
Chochope
Incahuasi
Cutervo
LAMBAYEQUE
Apurlec
Batán Grande
Chota
Sicán
Jayanca
Chongoyape
Santa Cruz
Bambamarca
Túcume
Hualgayoc
Mórrope
Ferreñafe
Picsi
Sipán
Lambayeque
Chiclayo
Oyotún
San Miguel de Pallaques
Pimentel
Monsefú
Zaña
Sta Rosa
Zaña
Cajamarca
Puerto Etén
Cumbe Mayo
Mócupe
San Juán
Contumazá
Laguna
Tembladera
Chilete
Chepén
Reservoir
Cascas
Pueblo Nuevo
Ascope
LA LIBERTAD
Pacasmayo
San Pedro de Lloc
Otusco
Paiján
Chicama
Pto Chicama
I de Macabí
El Brujo

Ⓒ

N

0 km   30
0 miles   30

①   ②   ③

Map 2

ECUADOR

A

Güeppi

Pantoja

Campuya

Curaray

Copal Urco

Sta Clotilde

Vidal

Napó

Marsella

Soldado

Bartra

Map 1

San Jacinto

Andoas

B Tambo

Tigre

Intuto

Trompeteros

Pastaza

LORETO

San Fernando

Miraflores

Nauta

Concordia

Parinari

Bagazán

Marañón

Yanayacu

Requena

ca C

San Ramón

La Libertad

◆

*Reserva Nacional
Pacaya-Samiria*

Bretaña

Flor de Punga

Jeberos

Lagunas

Iberia

Tamanco

Nva Alejandr

Sta Cruz

Ucayali

Sta Isabel

Tapiche

1

2

3

COLOMBIA

N

0 km   30
0 miles   30

Flor de
Agosto

○ Puca Urco

Putumayo

Yaguas

Ipora

LORETO

Napo   Ampiyacu   Pebas
Francisco de Orellana

Mazán
○ Indiana   Amazonas

ta Maria de Nanay
quitos
ago Quistacocha

Caballaococha

San Pablo ○

Leticia

Ramón
Castilla

Amelia

Reserva
Comunal
Tamshiyacu
Tahuayo

Yavari Mirim

Yavari

BRAZIL

Map 4   4   5   6

Map 3

LAMBAYEQUE

Cajamarca · Mayo
San Miguel de Pallaques
Tembladera · Contumazá
San Juan · Llacanora · Bolívar
San Marcos
Campanilla

Pacasmayo
San Pedro de Lloc
Cascas · Ascope
Pto Chicama · Paiján
I de Macabí · Chocope
El Brujo
Santiago de Cao
Huanchaco · Chan Chán · Laredo
Trujillo · Huacas del Sol & de la Luna
Salaverry

SAN MARTIN
Puerto Pizarro
Tocache Nuevo

Cajabamba
Huamachuco
Patáz
Parque Nacional Río Abiseo
Chahual · Retamas
Parcoy · Marsa
Buldibuyo
Tayabamba
Huancaspata

Otusco
Quiruvilca · Shorey
Simbal
Mollepata
Santiago de Chuco

LA LIBERTAD

Pto Morin
El Carmelo
Virú
Pallasca
Cabana
Tauca
Sihuas
Huacrachuco
San Pe de Cho

Tanguche
Chuquicara
Corongo · Tarica · Pasacancha
Pomabamba
Piscobamba
Llamellín

Santa
Chimbote
Pamparomas
Tres Cruces
Alpamayo (5,947m)
Cashapampa · Yanama
Cañón del Pato
Huallanca
Caraz · Huascarán (6,768m)
Yungay · Chacas
San Luis
Chavín de Parfarca

Nepeña · Moro
Pueblo Libre
Mancos
Carhuaz · Chancos
Marcará · Anta
ANCASH
Samanco
Monterrey
Huari
Llata
Quivilla
Chaví

Playa Tortugas
Pariacoto
Huaraz
Olleros · Chavín
San Marcos
Chavín de Huantar
La Unión
Huán Vie
Casma · Sechín
Yaután
Recuay
Catac · Huanzala
Huallanca

Pacific Ocean

Culebras
La Merced
Aija
Huayán
Pachacoto
Carpa
Baños

Huarmey
Huayllapampa
Marca
Aquia
Chiquián
Conococha (4,100m)
Yerupa (6,634n
Cordi Huayhua

Pampa Mata Caballos
Chasqitambo
Cajatambo
Raura
Oyón
Chu

Paramongá
Pativilca · Cochas
Barranca
Supe
Pto Supe · Caral
Cochamarca
Huancahu

Véqueta
Huaura
Huacho
Sayán
Huaura
Chu

Paraíso
Reserva Nacional Loma de Lachay
Las Salinas
Huaral
Santa Ro de Quiv
Yangas
Chancay · Aucallama
Chillón

Ancón
Puente Piedra
Sta Rosa
Ventanilla
Comas
Callao · **LIMA**
Cienegu
Miraflores · Pachacá
Chorrillos
Pántanos de Villa
Sta María del M
Pucusa

N

0 km 30
0 miles 30

Map 4

Map 2

Map 1

LORETO

Orellana

A Conamaná

Cerro do Canchyauya

Pampas de Sacramento

Sierra Contamana

Abuja

L Yarinacocha Pucallpa

Masisea

L Chauya Cocha

San Alejandro

Honoria

Ganzo Azul

L Inuria

Tournavista

Pachitea

aytia

B

HUANUCO

Puerto Inca

UCAYALI

Map 3

Chorropampa

Puerto Victoria

Puerto Pachitea

Pozuzo

palcazú

Puerto Bermúdez

Curanja

PASCO

Huancabamba

Neguachi

Oxapampa

Atalaya

Ucayali

San Luis de Shuaro

C La Merced (Chanchamayo)

San Ramón

Pichanaki

Puerto Ocopa

Shepahua

camayo

Satipo

Mazamari

Tambo

CUSCO

Acobamba

JUNIN

Mariposa

arma

Huairicolca

Jauja Comas

apalpa Concepción 1

Camisea 3

Chupaca

2

N

| 0 km | 30 |
| 0 miles | 30 |

BRAZIL

Esperanza

Curanja

Iñapari

Iberia

San Lorenzo

Alerta

Las Piedras

MADRE DE DIOS

◆ Manu
National
Park

Madre de Dios

Map 5

Mavila

Planchón

Boca Manu

4   5   6

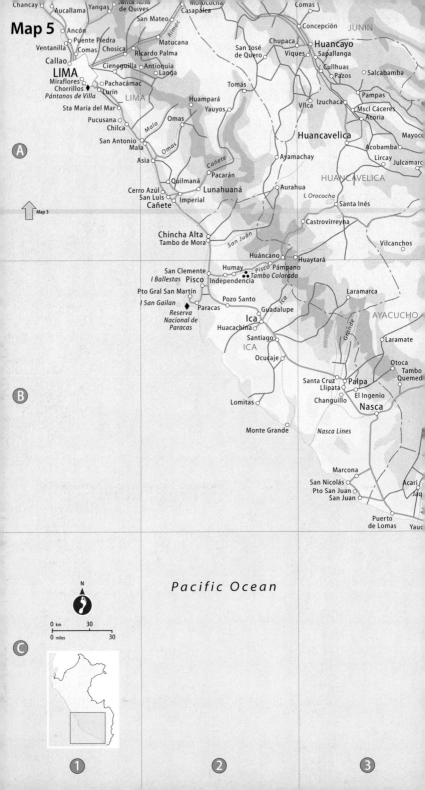

Map 5

JUNIN

Chancay
Aucallama
Yangas
Santa Rosa de Quives
Casapalca
Comas
Concepción
Ancón
San Mateo
Puente Piedra
Matucana
Chupaca
Huancayo
Ventanilla
Chosica
San José de Quero
Viques
Sapallanga
Comas
Ricardo Palma
Callao
Cieneguilla
Antioquia
Cullhuas
Salcabamba
LIMA
Pachacámac
Langa
Pazos
Miraflores
Chorrillos
Lurín
Tomás
Pampas
Pántanos de Villa
Vilca
Izuchaca
Mscl Cáceres
Sta María del Mar
LIMA
Huampará
Acoria
Pucusana
Omas
Yauyos
Mayocc
Chilca
Huancavelica
San Antonio
Mala
Mayocc

A

Asia
Omas
Ayamachay
HUANCAVELICA
Acobamba
Lircay
Julcamarc

Cañete
Pacarán
Aurahua
L Orococha
Quilmaná
Lunahuaná
Santa Inés
Cerro Azúl
Imperial
San Luis
Cañete
Castrovirreyna

Map 3

Chincha Alta
Tambo de Mora
San Juán
Vilcanchos

Huáncano
Huaytará

B

Humay
Pámpano
San Clemente
I Ballestas
Pisco
Independencia
Tambo Colorado
Pto Gral San Martín
Pozo Santo
Laramarca
I San Gailan
Paracas
Guadalupe
AYACUCHO
Reserva Nacional de Paracas
Ica
Huacachina
Santiago
Laramate
ICA
Ocucaje
Otoca
Tambo Quemed
Santa Cruz
Palpa
Llipata
El Ingenio
Lomitas
Changuillo
Nasca

Monte Grande
Nasca Lines

Marcona
San Nicolás
Acari
Pto San Juan
Jaq
San Juan

Puerto de Lomas
Yauc

Pacific Ocean

N

0 km   30
0 miles   30

C

1   **2**   **3**